NINTH EDITION

W9-BZP-548

FIELDS OF READING

Motives for Writing

Nancy R. Comley
Queens College, CUNY

David Hamilton
University of Iowa

Carl H. Klaus
University of Iowa

Robert Scholes
Brown University

Nancy Sommers
Harvard University

Jason Tougaw
Queens College, CUNY

BEDFORD/ST. MARTIN'S Boston ◆ New York

For Tom Broadbent, in memoriam, founding editor of *Fields of Reading* and raconteur extraordinaire.

For Bedford/St. Martin's

Developmental Editor: Joelle Hann
Production Editor: Ryan Sullivan
Production Supervisor: Andy Ensor
Marketing Manager: Molly Parke
Art Director: Lucy Krikorian
Text Design: Linda Robertson
Copy Editor: Jamie Nan Thaman
Photo Research: Linda Finigan
Cover Design: Donna Lee Dennison
Cover Art: Paul Powis, Pink Hill. Courtesy of the Bridgeman Art Library.
Composition: Macmillan Publishing Solutions
Printing and Binding: Haddon Craftsmen, Inc., an RR Donnelley & Sons Company

President: Joan E. Feinberg
Editorial Director: Denise B. Wydra
Editor in Chief: Karen S. Henry
Director of Development: Erica T. Appel
Director of Marketing: Karen R. Soeltz
Director of Editing, Design, and Production: Marcia Cohen
Assistant Director of Editing, Design, and Production: Elise S. Kaiser
Managing Editor: Shuli Traub

Library of Congress Control Number: 12009935038

For information, write: Bedford/St. Martin's, 75 Arlington Street, Boston, MA 02116   (617-399-4000)

ISBN-10: 0-312-55374-9
ISBN-13: 978-0-312-55374-6

Acknowledgments
Acknowledgments and copyrights appear at the back of the book on pages 829–33, which constitute an extension of the copyright page.

It is a violation of the law to reproduce these selections by any means whatsoever without the written permission of the copyright holder.

Preface

For the ninth edition, we have reimagined *Fields of Reading: Motives for Writing* as a lively new text while maintaining the book's original — and well-received — premise: that good readings representing major divisions of the curriculum and major rhetorical modes will lead to good writing and to great classroom discussions. Recognizing the needs of today's students (and instructors), this new edition strives to go even further by reflecting three additional premises. First, that students learn to write more effectively when their writing is a clear contribution to cultural conversations whose stakes they understand. Second, that students learn through continuous writing, both informal and formal, in a variety of styles and modes. And finally, that we are living through a cultural moment in which new media are transforming the relationship among reading, writing, and thinking — a transformation our students are poised to understand and benefit from as they move through college and into their careers and lives beyond. We believe this new edition of *Fields of Reading* is an excellent cornerstone for today's classroom because it bridges innovation and tradition, reflecting emerging approaches to literacy and education in relation to enduring ideas about the written word.

As with the eight previous editions, the title *Fields of Reading: Motives for Writing* represents our goal of introducing students to the writing and thinking they will do in college — writing and thinking motivated by genuine intellectual questions and problems. We emphasize, as before, readings in the arts and humanities, social sciences, and sciences (the major divisions of the curriculum) and *Fields*'s four major rhetorical modes: reflecting (considers past experience), reporting (conveys information), explaining (makes sense of knowledge), and arguing (debates controversial ideas and issues). However, for this edition, we have expanded our goal substantially by placing a much greater emphasis on conversations among writers, both explicit and implicit. We introduce many more pairings of key readings in each academic area that focus on related questions, issues, or themes. We have also assembled an entirely new section comprising four casebooks of six readings each that represent in-depth conversations about topics significant to the lives of twenty-first-century students — and society at large. We arranged the sixty-nine readings so as to invite students into such conversations, highlighting the particular and unique perspectives offered by writers working from various professional backgrounds, disciplinary methods, and writing traditions.

In the spirit of fostering engaged reading and writing, we have also reconceptualized the question sets that follow each reading to reflect more active — and interactive — classroom pedagogy. By engaging students directly with formal and informal writing assignments, we hope to encourage them to build new and flexible thinking and writing skills. Likewise, the accompanying Instructor's Manual — completely rewritten to answer the new question sets — is designed to help instructors stimulate active learning in the classroom. Throughout, it offers support for teaching rhetorical technique and writing craft, so that instructors can better help students to take advantage of online (and other) resources and become reflective and critical users of those resources.

Features of the Ninth Edition

Sixty-nine exceptional readings from key voices across the curriculum. Selected for their superior writing, the pieces represent a wide range of genres and intellectual interests, from writers as diverse as brain scientist Dr. Jill Bolte Taylor, public intellectual Andrew Sullivan, graphic novelist Marjane Satrapi, and polemicist George Orwell. Four documented essays provide models of researched writing and academic citations.

***Fields*'s four major rhetorical classifications help students understand the purposes of writing.**   Because it is important for students to know how to adapt their writing to a particular situation, all selections are categorized as one of four modes: *reflecting*, *reporting*, *explaining*, or *arguing*. These modes are clearly marked in both the table of contents and at the top of each selection for easy reference. An alternative, thematic table of contents guides instructors who may also wish to organize by theme.

Helpful apparatus.   Headnotes before each reading provide students with key biographical and rhetorical context for readings, introducing students to the writer's professional distinctions and main concerns. The introduction — completely rewritten for the ninth edition — also offers a helpful overview of the writing process.

New to This Edition

Thirty-five exceptional new essays offer up-to-the-moment coverage of issues that engage students in cross-curricular conversations.

- **Fresh pieces include:** Clive Thompson on Internet socializing, Olivia Judson on genetic programming, Michael Pollan on the politics of food, and Barack Obama on race relations.
- **Tried-and-true pieces include:** Gloria Anzaldúa on Chicano language, Mike Rose on education, and John Berger on ways of seeing.

Organized to emphasize conversations between writers and cross-curricular explorations, this new structure reflects the kinds of thinking and teaching students and instructors do today.

- **Nine new pairs** (three in each discipline) — for example, "On Bilingualism," "On the Reality of War," and "On Sexual Reproduction" — create exciting conversations between writers in the disciplines on college-level issues. Students can analyze the subject of the essays while comparing and contrasting the form of each approach.
- **Four new casebooks** (six readings each): "Virtual Experience: Life Online"; "The Classroom: Ideals, Obstacles, Solutions"; "The Visual World: Sight and Insight"; and "Gray Matter: The Brain and the Self." Presenting divergent perspectives on a common theme, these cross-disciplinary casebooks are perfect for longer individual projects or class projects that involve research, analysis, and argument.

Completely reconceptualized apparatus helps students and instructors to engage in the dynamic thinking and writing work of the writing class.

- **All new questions following each essay** emphasize activities that engage students in explorative reading, writing, and collaboration. Students are also prompted to master basic comprehension, rhetorical structures, and academic essay writing.
- **A new introduction** orients students to *Fields*'s unique approach, covers essential aspects of the writing process, and includes a separate explication — with examples — of the book's major rhetorical purposes: *reflecting*, *reporting*, *explaining*, and *arguing*.

A new, robust research appendix provides extensive, practical help for students learning to create a research question, find and evaluate sources, sketch an essay draft, and cite sources correctly. The appendix includes a fully annotated, multisource student research paper.

Print and New Media Resources

Fields of Reading Instructor's Edition. ISBN-10: 0-312-59019-9; ISBN-13: 978-0-312-59019-2. The Instructor's Edition includes a full copy of the text, plus the Instructor's Manual bound into the middle of the book.

Fields of Reading Instructor's Manual (downloadable from bedfordstmartins .com/fields/catalog). ISBN-10: 0-312-59018-0; ISBN-13: 978-0-312-59018-5. This manual, completely rewritten for the ninth edition, contains an introduction that outlines four approaches to teaching, as well as comprehensive answers to the new questions that appear at the end of every selection. Also included are suggestions for interactive classroom activities and further topics for classroom discussion. Invaluable for new and experienced instructors alike.

Re:Writing at bedfordstmartins.com/rewriting is an online collection of free and easy-to-access resources for the writing class such as model documents, grammar exercises, and documentation guidelines, as well as tutorials on such topics as avoiding plagiarism, doing research, and creating bibliographies. Through the *Re:Writing* site, students and instructors also get access to *TopLinks*, additional topics related to themes introduced in *Fields of Reading*. *TopLinks* is helpful for students — in individual or class projects — doing further research.

Acknowledgments

For their detailed responses to the eighth edition of *Fields of Reading* and their suggestions for improving the book, we are grateful to the following reviewers: Jane E. Addison, University of South Carolina Upstate; Sarah Baker, Sonoma State University; Cynthia Bates, University of California, Davis; Angela Adamides Bodino, Raritan Valley Community College; Barbara Bretcko, Raritan Valley Community College; Peter Caster, University of South Carolina Upstate; Bonnie Colemire, St. Charles Community College; La Forrest Cope, York College/CUNY; Brian J. Daffron, Comanche Nation College; Heidi Estrem, Boise State University; Shirley Frank, York College/CUNY; Karen Gardiner, University of Alabama; Jenny M. Grosvenor, University of Vermont and Johnson State College; John Hodgson, Cameron University; Sandra Hurst, Cameron University; Jessica Fordham Kidd, University of Alabama; Janet Lawless, Macomb Community College; Dana Teen Lomax, University of San Francisco; Alicia M. Middendorf, Southwestern Illinois College; Theresa Mlinarcik, Macomb Community College; Eleanor Montero, Daytona Beach College; Gary Alan Negin, California State University, San Bernardino; Judith Wrase Nygard, Mercer County Community College; John W. Osman, Southwestern Illinois College; Pamela

Ralston, Tacoma Community College; Heather Rodgers, St. Charles Community College; Kate Schwadron, St. Charles Community College; Candace Taylor, University of California, Davis; Jennifer Valley, California State University, San Bernardino; Deborah Vause, York College of Pennsylvania; and Leanne Warshauer, Suffolk County Community College.

Finally, we would like to thank our editor, Joelle Hann, who guided us through this revision of *Fields of Reading*. We'd also like to thank other staff members of Bedford/St. Martin's for their help and encouragement with this edition and along the way, in particular, Thomas Broadbent, who originally signed us up with St. Martin's Press, College Division, and Nancy Perry, now Editorial Director of Custom Publications, who first worked with *Fields* and has remained a friend of the project. We are grateful to Joan Feinberg, President, Bedford/St. Martin's; Denise Wydra, Editorial Director; Karen Henry, Editor in Chief; and Erica Appel, Director of Development in New York. John Sullivan and Steve Scipione, executive editors in Boston, provided excellent counsel along the way; Molly Parke, Marketing Manager, offered astute advice about the vagaries of the textbook market; and Nina Gantcheva and Andrew Flynn, editorial assistants, provided invaluable assistance with tasks big and small. Ryan Sullivan, Project Editor, kept production on time and on track, with the assistance of copy editor Jamie Nan Thaman and proofreaders Virginia Rubens and Carolyn Hassett. Linda Winters, the text permissions researcher, and Linda Finigan, the art permissions researcher, secured invaluable rights. We were very fortunate to have the editorial services of Elizabeth Bachner, who helped us — with intelligence and alacrity — with the enormous task of rewriting the book's entire apparatus, as well as the Instructor's Manual.

Finally, we appreciate the writers and artists who let us publish their work and put them into conversation with each other for the purpose of further engagement and further study across disciplines, modes, and generations.

Contents

ARTS AND HUMANITIES

Paired Readings: On Descriptive Writing

SOCIAL SCIENCES AND PUBLIC AFFAIRS

Sciences

CASEBOOKS

Gray Matter: The Brain and the Self

Thematic Contents

CONTEMPORARY ISSUES AND EXPERIENCES

CULTURES IN CONTACT AND COLLISION

EDUCATION

ETHICS, VALUES, AND BELIEFS

FAMILY

GENDER AND WOMEN'S EXPERIENCES

HEALTH, DISEASE, AND MEDICINE

HISTORY AND INTERPRETING THE PAST

HUMAN PORTRAITS

IDENTITY

INTERPRETING THE BODY

LIFE AND DEATH

OBSERVING AND UNDERSTANDING THE WORLD

RACE

VIOLENCE AND WAR

Introduction

Fields of Reading is an introduction to the basic work of college — the reading, discussion, thinking, and writing that stimulate and challenge the minds of students and faculty alike. The writing included here explores timely questions within three broad areas of academic study: Arts and Humanities, Social Sciences and Public Affairs, and Sciences. For readers in all disciplines — and for readers beyond this anthology — it seems that the more we learn about social life, identity, and the nature of the universe, the more unanswered questions emerge: What will climate change mean for the future of the planet? How will a globalized economy affect the daily lives of people from various cultures? Might the election of the United States' first biracial president transform race relations? Is brain science on the verge of solving the mysteries of the self? How does language shape knowledge or identity? What is writing good for? What role will the Internet play in addressing questions like these? How will it change who we are and how we learn?

The readings within are intended to provoke you to think and write about these kinds of questions — questions that will inevitably arise throughout your college course work. Thus we begin with a few observations about the relationship of reading and writing, and the importance of each in various academic fields.

From Reading to Writing: Conversations across the Disciplines

Take, as an example, a single writer in this reader: Barack Obama, the forty-fourth president of the United States. His speech, "A More Perfect Union" (p. 303), embodies a conversation involving a multitude of other texts and writers, some of which are also collected here. Obama's title is a deliberate reference to the preamble of the United States Constitution: "We the people, in order to form a more perfect union . . ." In fact, the speech

1

begins by quoting the preamble. In less direct ways, however, it's also a response to the work of other writers, including Thomas Jefferson's "The Declaration of Independence" (p. 243) and Martin Luther King Jr.'s "Letter from Birmingham Jail" (p. 288). Obama's influential speech on the future of race relations was shaped culturally, historically, and rhetorically by the words and deeds of Jefferson and King. Jefferson, a slave owner, was one of the central thinkers to craft the language on which the nation was founded. King's heroic efforts to argue — and fight — for civil rights in the 1960s made it possible, forty years later, for the nation to elect its first biracial president.

Obama wrote his speech in response to a controversy. His former pastor, Reverend Jeremiah Wright, had made inflammatory statements about the legacy of slavery and the state of race relations in contemporary American culture. Many in the press and in politics questioned Obama's judgment — and his patriotism — as a result of Wright's words. Rather than defend himself personally, Obama took the opportunity to assess and explain the complex state of race relations today, in the wake of both slavery and the civil rights movement. The speech was widely applauded as a brilliant *rhetorical* move, becoming a defining moment in his campaign — and, ultimately, in American politics and culture. Its success was due, in large part, to the ingenious way that Obama responded to — and reframed — the words and ideas of Wright, Jefferson, and King.

At the same time — and in a larger sense — it would be impossible to know the true number of texts that gave essence to Obama's speech. We know that Obama is an avid reader; the words he ultimately delivered were his, but they were surely informed by his lifetime of reading, in more ways than he could even know himself. In this sense, the speech is a moment in a conversation at least two hundred years old (if not older).

Every piece of writing, including your own, is part of a conversation like this. For example, Oliver Sacks's "The Man Who Mistook His Wife for a Hat" (p. 680), which tells the story of a man whose visual experience is profoundly altered by brain damage, can be understood as an implicit response to Plato's classic "The Cave" (p. 665), in which the philosopher suggests that the visual experience of human beings represents a mere shadow of reality. Plato's text might also be understood in dialogue with any number of other texts, including physician Lewis Thomas's "The Corner of the Eye" (p. 339) or Lucy Grealy's "Mirrors" (p. 33). All these texts are about how we know what we think we know, based on firsthand observation. Thomas's essay is philosophical and scientific, whereas Grealy's is personal and political. While each of these texts is very different in terms of focus, style, and rhetoric, they can be understood as pieces of an ongoing conversation — one that shapes and documents the world we inhabit.

Conversations among texts take many forms and can address almost any topic, often involving writers from very different eras or cultures.

George Orwell entered into a centuries-old conversation on language with his essay "Politics and the English Language" (p. 97). Its concern for the degradation of language as propaganda — social, political, and commercial — bears witness to increasingly insidious ways of promoting doubtful versions of the truth. James Baldwin (p. 109) and Gloria Anzaldúa (p. 131) do not address Orwell's particular concerns, but their reflections on black English and the "border language" Chicano Spanish add to an ongoing conversation about the nature of language and its place in culture. We have recognized this conversation and given it shape throughout the various editions of this reader by selecting Orwell's essay for an early edition, adding Baldwin later, and bringing Anzaldúa into it now.

Like Obama, Jefferson, and King, or Plato, Sacks, and Thomas, we can think of Anzaldúa, Baldwin, and Orwell as taking part in a long-running conversation. A conversation about politics, race, and nationhood belongs primarily to the social sciences; one about perception and cosmology, to the sciences; and one about the English language, to the humanities. It's important to remember, however, that these subjects are relevant in more than one discipline. Writing as beautiful as that of Martin Luther King Jr. is likely to be studied in the humanities as well as the social sciences; Plato's text asks questions about perception and cosmology, but it does so in philosophical terms (and philosophy itself is sometimes categorized among the social sciences and sometimes among the humanities); and debates about language and culture belong to the social sciences as well as the humanities.

While the academic disciplines overlap, the written conversations most of us enter into in college and professional life tend to occur within such disciplinary structures as economics, history, biology, or political science. The writing in each of these fields is often very different. Consequently, writing has long been recognized as a subject that deserves close attention across the university curriculum. English majors need to write, but so do marketing, psychology, and physics majors. And while all that writing springs from a core facility with a language, in our case English, it also takes significantly diverging forms as writers specialize. This reader attempts to illustrate the core of usage that generates most of our writing as well as something of the paths toward specialization our writing can follow.

How This Book Is Structured

Each of this book's first three sections represents one of the broad areas of academic study: Arts and Humanities, Social Sciences and Public Affairs, and Sciences. Each of these sections contains articles that focus on individual fields of study, such as English, political science, and physics. We've included several readings in each section that highlight noteworthy issues in those areas, to give you opportunities to engage with — and respond to — single writers concerned with particular questions, issues, or problems. You may well find, however, that individual readings speak to each other in unexpected ways.

Paired Readings

In addition, we've included three paired readings in each of the academic areas. For example, in the Arts and Humanities section, we've paired two essays that focus on descriptive writing: Joan Didion's "On Keeping a Notebook" (p. 114) and Patricia Hampl's "The Dark Art of Description" (p. 122). In her essay, Didion is *explaining* the process of keeping a writer's notebook, while in hers, Hampl is *reflecting* on the powers of descriptive writing. Although both authors focus on how certain writing techniques help them think in new ways, they do so with very different tones and emphases; and although most readers will probably notice certain common themes in these two essays, individual readers will probably make their own unique connections. In this sense, the conversation taking place between these two readings might provoke your own original thinking and writing.

The same is true with the paired readings in the other two sections. In the Social Sciences and Public Affairs section, for example, John Berger is *reporting* on visual art created by witnesses to the bombing of Hiroshima in World War II in his essay named after that Japanese city (p. 315), and recent veterans are *reflecting* on the Iraq War in the series of accounts collected in "Soldiers' Stories: Dispatches from Iraq" (p. 323). In the Sciences section, Michael Pollan's "Corn Sex" (p. 467) is *explaining* the reproductive process of corn, while Emily Martin's "The Egg and the Sperm: How Science Has Constructed a Romance Based on Stereotypical Male-Female Roles" (p. 472) is *arguing* about the political implication of the way we tell the story of human reproduction. We encourage you to enter the conversations taking place among these pairs of writers — to respond to them, evaluate them, and extend them.

Casebooks

The second half of this book is made up of four "casebooks," each of which includes six readings that address common themes and questions: "Virtual Experience: Life Online" (p. 493), "The Classroom: Ideals, Obstacles, Solutions" (p. 565), "The Visual World: Sight and Insight" (p. 645), and "Gray Matter: The Brain and the Self" (p. 735). The readings in each of these sections were chosen because they offer various approaches to similar questions and a variety of rhetorical modes and academic disciplines. In a sense, these casebooks represent the work of the university in miniature: we've brought together readings that represent the range of inquiry you're likely to encounter in college, and we've done it in such a way that foregrounds the implicit connections among divergent texts and ways of thinking. Such interconnections are what make the intellectual life of college stimulating; it will be up to you to make the most of them. Often, you will do that through writing.

Writing and Thinking: The Rhetorical Modes

In this reader, we have tried to represent the variety of writing, or rhetorical modes, within each of the academic areas. *Reflecting, reporting, explaining,* and *arguing* are strategies that writers use to achieve varying purposes within their fields. For instance, a science writer may want to *explain* how a new experiment sheds new light on long-held assumptions about the firing of neurons or the nature of an atom, but that same science writer might, in another situation, want to *reflect* on the process or implications of that discovery. She chooses her form of writing to suit the particular needs of her task or assignment. It is not that each mode of writing is completely different from all the others; obviously, the lines between them blur, and most writing blends several ways of paying attention and thinking. In fact, the set of them makes sense as a continuum, in which one kind of writing leads naturally to another.

Nonetheless, *reflecting, reporting, explaining,* and *arguing* are distinct modes of writing, and each mode requires writers to practice somewhat different writing strategies. One important goal of this reader is to give you the opportunity to learn from strong examples of writing in each mode, so you can practice the strategies at work in these examples.

The word *reflection* means "bending back," as in reversing the flow of a ray of light. And so we associate this practice with looking back on an event or an idea or a finding, after we have gained some distance from it. The word suggests that moment of tranquility, after the storm, when we are better able to understand what the original drama was about. A *report* gathers information — from observation, interviews, lab experiments, or archives — and delivers it to an audience. Presumably, the writer of a report holds back his or her own judgment to let readers decide what they think of this information. An *explanation* usually focuses on a technical — or at least complex — phenomenon, situation, issue, or problem. The writer of an explanatory essay is usually an expert on a given topic, whether it's the science of genetics or the art of writing. *Argument* is the art of persuasion, of introducing a topic about which your reader may think very differently from you, and attempting to persuade him or her to take your views seriously or even change his or her mind.

Of course, just as the academic disciplines overlap, so do the rhetorical modes. Michael Pollan's essay *explains* how corn reproduces, but it's also making an implicit *argument* about the role of corn in the American diet; a graphic narrative like Marjane Satrapi's "The Veil" (p. 148) is *reporting* on life in Iran after the Islamic Revolution, but it's also *reflecting* on that experience. As you read essays in the various modes — and practice writing your own — it's instructive to think about the distinct effect of each mode and to remember that they overlap.

The Writing Process

Writers don't generally think to themselves, "I'm going to sit down and write a reflective (or reportorial or explanatory or argumentative) essay today." While most finished writing can be categorized somewhere along this rhetorical continuum, most writing happens more unpredictably — and, you might say, more organically — than this. Writing involves a process of thinking over time, in stages. By the time a piece of writing reaches an audience, it's likely to have gone through many stages of exploratory writing, drafting, and revision. Writers often discover their own purposes — or motives — through an informal and sometimes chaotic process of exploratory writing.

The questions and assignments that follow each reading in this book are designed to engage you in this process. *Reading* questions will challenge you to think carefully about a writer's ideas and rhetoric and push you to learn from them. *Exploratory Writing* questions will give you the opportunity to respond to the readings informally, pursuing inspiration for your own ideas and your own writing. *Making Connections* questions will help you find the implicit conversations happening among multiple readings. Finally, *Essay Writing* questions will ask you to write for an audience — sometimes in direct response to what you've read, sometimes using what you've read as a model for a certain kind of writing, and sometimes using what you've read as a point of departure for your writing.

The writing of any given essay (or report or poem or case history or screenplay) begins well before the writer sits down to compose the opening paragraph. Writing begins with reading or conversation or observation. In that sense, writing often develops unconsciously, as ideas percolate in the mind of the writer — often long before he or she plans to write them down. Any given writer will develop his or her own process, and this reader is designed to encourage you to develop yours. The process of most writers will involve some of the following stages.

- Reading (or rereading)
- Observing events, remembering experiences
- Discussing reading, events, or experiences

- Exploratory writing (usually informally, sometimes in a journal or on a blog)
- Organizing and drafting
- Revising
- Editing and proofreading

Reading to Write

Before writing in response to a text, whether that response is direct (as in Obama's response to the preamble to the U.S. Constitution) or indirect (as in Oliver Sacks's response to Plato's "The Cave"), it is well advised to reread the text thoroughly. That reading will be more productive if it's active, done with a pen or pencil in hand. You might take notes in the margins or, if you don't want to scribble in your books, on a separate sheet of paper. You might make lists of ideas you want to explore further, note interesting language or vocabulary, identify important stylistic or rhetorical strategies. Such active reading will shape your relationship to the text in a new way. It will help you "own" that text — and, ultimately, give you greater confidence when you respond to it.

As the digital age envelops us in stream after stream of media, we've come to live in a world of texts that we pass by with remarkable speed. This can make revisiting them difficult (or impossible). Still, we listen to certain music over and over, see movies or YouTube videos two or three times, return to familiar Web sites. Revisiting allows us to become connoisseurs of detail and notice what we had not noticed before. Similarly, you can't really come to know Satrapi or King or Thomas or Obama or any other writer from a single reading. And when it comes to *your* writing, you will write better by rewriting — which is to say, by rereading yourself. You will also find that a given reading will acquire new meanings after you've read another piece by another writer that addresses similar questions. (Orwell, for example, may read differently after you've read Anzaldúa.) Ultimately, rereading means rethinking.

Exploratory Writing

Observation, memory, and discussion are as important to the writing process as reading. This is one reason writers tend to keep journals (or, perhaps, blogs). A journal or a blog gives a writer a place to reflect on experience, using informal language to explore ideas and sort out responses to experiences, memories, and conversations. Exploratory writing will often raise questions or concerns that a little reading will help illuminate. This kind of exploration gives writers a chance to rehearse their ideas about the conversations they'll enter when they write for an audience.

Rethinking is a fundamental aspect of writing. Our first response to a text or an idea or a question is important because it often represents a complex, unconscious response. But that first response is rarely the whole story. If we're writing for an audience, the ideas we write about require careful consideration. Exploratory writing can help us get our minds around an issue or a writing project. It can help us sort through complex materials, find a focus, or come up with a plan for writing.

Exploratory writing can take the following forms:

- **A journal or blog.** The writer reflects on a given topic in a concentrated but informal way.
- **Freewriting.** The writer engages in free association on paper, writing down whatever comes to mind, regardless of sense, order, or meaning. (This kind of writing can lead to unpredictable insights.)
- **Lists, charts, or diagrams.** The writer begins to sort through or organize information.
- **Writing through conversation.** The writer asks others to be a sounding board for rough ideas, taking notes, documenting, or responding to these conversations in writing.
- **Generating questions.** The writer articulates the central questions that provide the motives for writing about the topic at hand.

Every writer will develop a slightly different process for exploring ideas, and the process may even vary from situation to situation, but most writers will engage in some of the preceding practices. See what works best for you. The strategies you adopt will most likely evolve over time. The important thing is to develop strategies for thinking and rethinking before — and as — you write.

Drafting

Drafting an essay involves both organizing ideas and finding language that conveys your meaning. A good draft will have a beginning, a middle, and an end. It will contain much of the evidence and much of the thinking that will eventually form the finished work. But a draft is just that — a draft. It's a first attempt to flesh out your ideas fully. That first attempt will usually involve some messy thinking, some disorganization, and some language that doesn't quite work. The draft may also demonstrate that you need more — or better — evidence. While a draft may be less than fully developed or polished, it gives you something to work with — a body of words, ideas, and evidence in need of revision.

The academic paradigm has always been that first we do our research and then we write it up. In a broad sense, this is true: you need to discover what you're going to write about. You need a purpose and a sense of direction. You need to organize your thoughts. Sometimes that's easier said than done. In many instances, the traditional outline is all but impossible to create until a writer has done a first draft, sorting through ideas and sifting through texts.

Often we don't recognize our real subject until we have written pages and pages. Then suddenly we make a connection or an imaginative leap, and we see where we are going. When drafting his essay "Ways of Seeing," John Berger (p. 315) may have come to several other conclusions as to what those paintings represented before he thought of "Hell." Perhaps he first wrote of them as representations of despair or as a more clinical documentation of disaster. But neither of those ideas quite satisfied him, and he kept on thinking until his "eureka" moment occurred. At that point, he knew what to pare from his writing and how to develop what remained. The excitement of writing often comes in such moments of discovery, which, once made and recognized, dictate the organization of the work.

In his essay "The Eureka Hunt" (p. 398), Jonah Lehrer explains recent scientific research on "the insight experience." Scientific investigation about eureka moments has demonstrated that "before there can be a breakthrough, there has to be a mental block." Where there is excitement and discovery, there is also frustration and block. That's part of the process, so don't worry if you get stuck. Keep at it. Writing through the block can lead to discovery.

In laboratory science, such a discovery is likely to be made before the writing begins. A researcher struggles with setting up the equipment, with determining how to measure a variable. Suddenly she sees something that rearranges everything, and her problem is well on its way to resolution. In such a case, writing up a discovery afterwards makes sense.

To sum up, drafting is an important step in the writing process, but making the most of a draft usually requires serious revision.

Revising

Revision in the root sense means "to see again." While your draft will represent much of your thinking on a topic, in most cases it will require substantial rethinking — of ideas, language, evidence, and organization — before it's ready for an audience. That is, you'll need to see it again very clearly before it's ready to enter into a public conversation on your topic.

Because it can be difficult to get enough perspective on your own writing to really rethink it, it's a good idea to get some distance from your draft before you revise. You can do this by setting it aside and taking a few days off from it. You can also get some distance by asking yourself certain questions about your draft, such as the following.

- Is my essay focused? Is it clear what it's about? Is it clear why my topic is significant?

- Is my evidence relevant and convincing?
- Is my essay well organized? Does it unfold appropriately for the purpose I'm trying to achieve?
- Is my language clear and polished?

If possible, it's also a good idea to get feedback from others — teachers, peers, friends, or family members. To get useful feedback, it is helpful to ask your readers very specific questions about your writing.

- What do you, as a reader, think I'm really trying to say?
- Is my motive for writing clear? Does the draft indicate a purpose and show why my topic is important?
- Where is the essay strongest? Where is it weakest? Why?
- Do you ever get confused by my language or reasoning? Where and why?
- What do you want to know more about?

Questions like these can help readers give you the information you need to gain a new perspective on your own writing. They can help you see your own writing the way you might see another's — with critical distance.

Once you've received and sifted through feedback from others, it will be up to you to use your judgment about how to revise. It's helpful to be very clear about your own motives. Why are you writing? Why is your topic important enough for others to read about it? If you know that, you'll gain control of the process, you'll have a better sense of what evidence you need to accomplish your purpose, and you'll have a clearer sense of how to organize that evidence. If you know what your mission is, you'll be in a good position to know when you've accomplished it.

Editing

Be sure to save time for editing. If revision means rethinking a piece of writing, editing means polishing it so that it's ready for an audience. Editing means looking closely at sentences and at formatting. It means eliminating typos and misspellings, yes, but it also means carefully considering your phrasing to determine whether sentences actually say what you mean them to say.

As with revising, it may be useful to get help from other people when you edit. Others will spot your typos, misspellings, and clunky phrases more readily than you will. By the time you're ready to edit, you've been working with these words so long they can start to seem almost invisible to you. You might ask someone to read your nearly finished draft with a colored pen or pencil in hand, circling or marking any problem spots. If you do this yourself, either imagine that you're another person reading your writing or read your piece out loud. This can help you become aware of problems you might miss otherwise.

Either way, it's important to imagine a reader when you edit. Clunky writing — writing that doesn't quite express your ideas or that expresses them awkwardly — will confuse readers, slow them down, and make them skeptical about your authority as a writer. When you edit, aim to communicate clearly and directly. Pay attention to the details. A worthy goal is to make the hard work of writing appear effortless to readers. That's an illusion, of course, but one that readers appreciate.

Your Process

Most writers develop their process through trial and error — experimenting until they find a sequence of stages that works for them. You should do the same. Remember, nearly every writer engages in a process of developing ideas, drafting, and revision. The professional journalist will receive feedback from an editor; the playwright will workshop a play and revise based on feedback from audiences and producers; the trial attorney will rehearse a closing statement with colleagues until it's just right. Good writing — writing readers want to read — is almost always the product of a long process. Great writers often make writing look easy, but that's because their readers are seeing only the product of a generally labor-intensive process.

To grapple with the hard work of writing, authors tend to form communities, often in the form of writing groups or online discussion groups or blogs. It's valuable to step away from a piece of writing — share it with peers, get feedback, engage in some social interaction — before returning to the sometimes lonely confrontation with the words on the page. Think of your instructor and the other students in the class as such a community. Don't worry if the writing sometimes feels difficult — that's part of the process. Instead of worrying, talk to your peers or your instructor about the process. Such a conversation will almost always become a conversation about your ideas or the process of developing your ideas. In many cases, you'll solve a problem or achieve a breakthrough just by talking. Then you'll be ready to go back to the words on the page and revise.

Writing across the Curriculum

After this course, as you travel through your college's curriculum, you will be asked to write in a variety of forms and with a variety of styles suitable for one discipline or another. In some sense, you'll need to learn to write anew for each of those specific contexts. Many of the methods you learn, practice, and develop in this course will be helpful in those courses, but many of them will also need to be adapted or revised to work in the new context. This book is intended to introduce you to accessible examples of writing from the major disciplines — forms you'll repeatedly encounter as you continue through college.

While the academic disciplines do overlap, they also involve specialized language and ways of thinking. In the sciences, generally, the quest is for facts that are demonstrable through some kind of experimental research. Once they have been observed, they are considered to be significantly true apart from the language in which they will be presented, and so it makes sense for the facts to be discovered first and then written up. In the humanities, however, the idea is less distinguishable from the sentence in and by which it is formed, so the research blends more with the writing. Writers in the social sciences tend to bridge the approaches common in the sciences and the humanities. Some social scientists work with quantitative data, some with qualitative analysis, and some with a combination of the two. In your college course work, you'll find that some instructors will ask you to gather all your data and then "write it up," while others will ask you to use writing as a process of discovery, refining your ideas — and often gathering new evidence — throughout that process.

In your writing for class assignments and the world beyond, be aware that the rules of the game will vary somewhat — sometimes quite a lot — from one field to another. An audience familiar with the rules of computer science will have different expectations from one familiar with the rules of art history or sociology or gender studies. As you read and write in various disciplines, you'll develop the agility to move from one to another, anticipating the expectations of your readers. The goal is to become a flexible writer comfortable with a variety of contexts, disciplines, and rhetorical modes.

Reflecting, Reporting, Explaining, Arguing

The modes of writing, as we suggested in the introduction, can describe a wide range of texts in all of the academic disciplines. Literary writers tend to be associated with reflecting, historians with reporting, scientists with explaining, and political scientists with arguing. But that's far from the whole story. A scientist like Oliver Sacks (p. 680) devotes considerable portions of his writing to reflecting on the lives of his patients; a literary writer like Marjane Satrapi (p. 148) uses the tools of graphic narrative to report, in a distinctive way, on life in Iran under the Islamic Republic; and so on.

In this chapter we will survey writing in each of the four modes, always with an eye toward helping you read them effectively, understand the techniques and rhetoric associated with them, and experiment with employing their strategies in your own writing.

Reflecting

The "reflecting" essays in this reader focus on disparate topics — for example, a slave's experience learning to read and write, tools used to torture and to beautify, and the nature of the universe. Reflective writing relies heavily on personal experience and memory, treating them as sources of knowledge and understanding. We recount memories to make sense of them for ourselves and for others. Reflective writers do this publicly for an audience interested in reading about the lives and memories of others, often as a way of reflecting on their own experience as well.

George Orwell's "Shooting an Elephant" (p. 266) is a good example of an essay in which the writer reflects on a personal experience in a way that invites readers to think about its larger implications. In the following passage, which comes from the third paragraph of the essay, Orwell presents himself in a reflective frame of mind:

> One day something happened which in a roundabout way was enlightening. It was a tiny incident in itself, but it gave me a better glimpse than I had had before of the real nature of imperialism — the real motives for which despotic governments act. Early one morning the sub-inspector at a police station at the other end of the town rang me up on the phone and said that an elephant was ravaging the bazaar. Would I please come and do something about it? I did not know what I could do, but I wanted to see what was happening, and I got on to a pony and started out.

In the opening sentence, Orwell looks back to an enlightening event, and in the second sentence, he gets more specific by letting us know that this single incident gave him new insight into "the real nature of imperialism." Having announced the general significance of this event, he begins to narrate its particulars, recalling what happened that day: the phone call informing him that an elephant was loose in the marketplace; the request that he, as a police officer, do something about it; and his journey to the scene.

This alternation between recalling things and commenting on their significance is typical of the reflective writing in this reader. In some cases, however, the event reflected on is less contained to a single time and place. It might involve a more general condition sustained over weeks or even years. Sometimes, too, the element of personal experience is crucial as the writer addresses a larger topic. In "The Corner of the Eye" (p. 339), for example, renowned physician Lewis Thomas reflects on the relationship between human beings, the planet earth, and the cosmos: "The overwhelming astonishment, the queerest structure we know about so far in the whole universe, the greatest of all cosmological scientific puzzles, confounding all our efforts to comprehend it, is the earth." Thomas's reflections go on to articulate his implicit argument: if we spend too much time looking straight ahead, we will miss out on some of life's greatest pleasures and overlook some of the universe's greatest puzzles. In the process of this reflection, Thomas invokes faint stars, Bach, artificial intelligence, language, metaphors, and the Big Bang, making his discussion more philosophical than personal. Nonetheless, it is reflective in the classic sense of *looking back*. While Orwell looks back on his personal history, Thomas surveys the history of the universe and human attempts to understand it.

Whether the subject of reflective writing is a dramatic moment in one's own life or the history of the universe, it tends to involve memory. In Orwell's case it's personal memory, and in Thomas's case, it's historical memory. It also tends to involve examining something particular, such as the shooting of an elephant or a Bach fugue, for the purpose of drawing broader conclusions — often personal, ethical, or philosophical ones. As a reader of reflective writing, you should always be attentive to the details of a writer's recollected experience as well as to the ways they illuminate the broader questions the writer is exploring. And in your own reflective writing, you should make sure that you convey both dimensions of your experience — what happened, and what the events enabled you to see.

Writing Reflective Essays

A reflective essay is usually composed of a combination of the following elements: a detailed account of past experiences or events (personal, historical, or cultural); observations about the larger significance of these experiences or events; and a narration of how the writer either came to understand that significance or was somehow changed by the experiences or events in question. You should include these elements in your own reflective writing; just remember, however, that while they may sound relatively straightforward, they can be employed and combined in a variety of unexpected ways. Orwell and Thomas, for example, combine these elements with very different results. Still other essays included in this reader — for example, Frederick Douglass's "Learning to Read and Write" (p. 46) — show how these elements can produce a range of results depending on the writer's subject, tone, evidence, and structure.

Your own memory and experience will be your primary source for much reflective writing. But once you have recalled something in detail and made sense of it for yourself, you are still faced with the problem of how to present it to readers in a way that will catch their attention, keep them reading, and invite them to reflect. Given that your readers are probably not familiar with your experience, you must select and organize your material so that you provide a readable account of it. Writing about an experience is different from remembering one. You can think of yourself as a tour guide, leading readers through an archive or a museum of your own experience. Your *point of view* — the physical and mental standpoints from which you tell your story — is crucial in reflective writing. Tell a story that will get readers to pay attention to the details — and emphasize the uniqueness of your reflection about the significance of those details. When you expand your story to include more detail, you will probably also begin to uncover subtleties of understanding that you might otherwise have missed.

As you organize your thoughts, your chosen subject will suggest ways of presenting itself clearly and meaningfully. If your reflections are focused on a single event, you will probably want to write a straightforward narrative, telling your readers what happened in a relatively direct way. Though you cover the event from beginning to end, your narrative should emphasize the details that you consider most striking and significant. In "Shooting an Elephant" (p. 266), Orwell devotes the largest segment of his piece to covering the brief instant when he finds himself on the verge of having to shoot the elephant despite his strong desire not to do so. In fact, he devotes one-third of the essay to those few moments of inner conflict because they bring about one of his major insights — "that when the white man turns tyrant it is his own freedom that he destroys." In writing about a memorable event of your own, you could make your story build similarly toward some kind of climax or surprise or decisive incident, which leads to a moment of insight upon which you would want to focus.

If your reflections center on a particular person, you might want to emphasize description as much as narrative, offering a portrait of this person that reveals his or her character in a variety of contexts or situations. Though you may rely heavily on narration, you will not be able to cover incidents in as much detail as if you were focusing on a single event. Instead, you should isolate the most striking details from each incident you choose to recall. If your reflections are focused on a particular problem or issue, you may need to combine narration, description, and explanation, bringing together your recollections of numerous events and persons to reveal the nature of the problem. You might survey the problem chronologically from beginning to end, or you might begin with a high point and circle around it, developing its context as you search for your understanding of that experience.

Whatever the subject of your reflection, it's a good idea to devote at least a couple of paragraphs to stepping back and drawing broad conclusions from the details you've been narrating or describing. You may also want to tell the story of how you came to understand these conclusions yourself. These paragraphs often come toward the end of the essay (whereas in an argumentative essay, they tend to come near the beginning). There is no formula for reflective writing. The important thing to consider is how you'll reveal connections between the particular and the general, how you'll use details to get readers invested in your reflections, and how you'll illuminate the subject at hand by drawing conclusions that will surprise readers. In a reflection, the uniqueness of the writer's perspective is fundamental. You will enlighten readers by offering them a glimpse of your experience and showing them how it led you to see the world in a strikingly new way.

Reporting

The "reporting" selections in this reader include a psychologist describing the troubled mind of a young boy, a brain surgeon detailing the progress of a delicate operation, and a historian offering an account of the plague that swept through medieval Europe. Informative writing is basic to every field of endeavor. A reportorial writer organizes and synthesizes material drawn from various sources: interviews, articles, books, public records, and firsthand observation. Working from such varied sources, these writers all provide detailed accounts of their subjects.

Though reporting depends on a careful gathering of information, it is by no means a mechanical and routine activity consisting simply of getting some facts and writing them down. Whereas reflective writing emphasizes *point of view*, newspaper editors and criminal investigators often say that they want "just the facts," yet they know that the facts are substantially shaped by the point of view of the observer or investigator. Every writer stands at a particular point in space and time, as well as in thought and feeling. Where we stand will shape the tone in which we write, direct the choices we make about what to include, and even determine how we perceive the subject we're writing about.

A reporter's point of view often goes unnoticed, but as a student of writing, you will learn a great deal by training yourself to notice the clues that help you see how a writer's perspective shapes his or her take on a given topic. Take a look at these three frames from Marjane Satrapi's "The Veil" (p. 148), in which she tells the story of Iran's Islamic Revolution from her perspective as a child.

Satrapi's written text begins with a simple statement: "In 1979 a revolution took place. It was later called 'the Islamic Revolution.'" The image in the first frame depicts the revolution through an image of men and women, dressed in simple black clothing, their fists raised. The starkness and simplicity of this image might well be understood to represent a child's-eye view of a

complex sociohistorical event. A child might well notice the drama, anger, and collective force of a revolution without understanding its ideology or social implications. But in the next frame, Satrapi switches gears. We follow her to school, in 1980, "the year it became obligatory to wear the veil." The faces of the children in the second frame seem curious, perhaps perplexed or even fearful like the one peering over the wall. The obligatory veil is something new, and they aren't sure what to make of it. In the third frame, they are learning what to make of it. Satrapi depicts several girls putting the veil to unexpected uses: as a jump rope, a set of reins, or a disguise, for example. She depicts herself and her peers as playful rebels. They may not understand the causes or the results of their country's revolution, but they are resisting its new rules. This is a report, but it's a highly personalized one, based on the experience of a child and told using the tools of the adult graphic novelist she would become.

Of course, a graphic novel is a particularly distinctive — and even unexpected — form to use for reportorial writing. Perhaps the most common forms of reporting belong to the journalist and the historian, two kinds of writers often thought of as objective observers of events or facts. In "Nickel and Dimed: On (Not) Getting By in America" (p. 195), journalist and activist Barbara Ehrenreich reports on an experiment — or mission — she undertook. She decided to leave her life behind and "plunge into the low-wage workforce." Her goal was to find out how 30 percent of Americans manage to live on very low wages. Like all reporters, Ehrenreich needed to do her research, interview people, and collect data from a variety of sources. However, Ehrenreich took a radical approach to collecting data: she became a member of the workforce she was interested in writing about. She worked as a waitress and a house cleaner — among other things — and discovered for herself just how difficult it was to survive on the wages she earned. She describes her endeavor as "a purely objective, scientific sort of mission," appropriate to the purpose of her ambitious project. However, in her account of that endeavor, she recounts that "to my total surprise and despite the scientific detachment I am doing my best to maintain, I care." Despite her goal of objectivity as an investigative journalist, Ehrenreich's method got her personally involved with her subject. In this sense, Ehrenreich builds reflection and her own point of view into her reporting.

Historian Barbara Tuchman's report on the bubonic plague in medieval Europe is perhaps a more traditional example of reportorial writing. But even this historical account is shaped by its writer's perspective. Tuchman's writing is known for its careful research and lively tone. In "'This Is the End of the World': The Black Death" (p. 231), Tuchman's perspective on the plague is both detailed and gripping. While the essay itself doesn't reveal much about its writer, its accessible tone and suspenseful structure are likely shaped by her experience as a teacher, historian, and writer. Tuchman knows how to hook her audience, as you can see from the graphic details in her first sentence: "In October 1347, two months after the fall of Calais, Genoese trading ships put into the harbor of Messina in Sicily with dead and dying men at the oars." Tuchman transports readers to a distant time — an October month over 660 years ago — and invites us to witness a shocking event: ships pulling into a harbor manned by ghoulish crews. If you keep reading, you'll learn that this moment turned out to be an early indication of a devastating plague that would kill between one-third and two-thirds of Europe's population. Far from being a dry account of dates and names, Tuchman's report on the plague balances specificity and narration to get readers involved in her story. From her perspective as a teacher and writer, she knows that it's her job to get her audience invested in her report.

The purpose of reporting is in one sense straightforward and self-evident. Whether it involves a firsthand account of some recent happening or the documented record of a long-past sequence of events, reportorial writing informs readers about various subjects that may interest them but that they cannot possibly observe or investigate on their own. As you can see from the examples above, writers use reporting for a combination of purposes — to provide information; to convey their attitudes, beliefs, or ideas about that information; and to influence the views of their readers. This range of purposes is not surprising. Whenever we make a report, we do so because we believe that the subject is important enough to share with others. And presumably we believe the subject to be important because of what we have come to know and think about it. So when we are faced with deciding what information to report and how to report it, we inevitably base our decisions on these ideas. At every point in the process of planning and writing a report, we act on the basis of our particular priorities for conveying information about the subject.

Writing Reportorial Essays

A reportorial essay tends to involve the following elements: information gathered through observation, interviews, or research; an introduction or overview of that information; detailed discussion of some of that information; and detailed analysis or reflection on that information. When you write your own reportorial essays, you'll need to strike a balance between shaping your material in ways that will get readers interested or engaged and letting the details speak for themselves. It may help to take a cue from the writers in this reader. Notice how Satrapi, Ehrenreich, and Tuchman combine the elements of a report and strike this balance in their own ways.

Your choice of topic and your motives for writing about it will usually guide you as you write a report. The material you write about is likely to shape the choices you make about the tone, structure, and contents of your essay. If the information concerns a single event or covers a set of events spread over time, the most effective method is probably narration — that is, telling a story in a more or less chronological order, as Ehrenreich does. If your assignment were to synthesize what is known, up to that moment, about a complex public event, you would need to look at a wider series of events, as Tuchman does. If your assignment is to report on firsthand experience, you might adopt a stance that emphasizes your perspective at the time of the events in question, as Satrapi does.

Once you have settled on a basic form, you should then devise a way of selecting and arranging your information to achieve your purposes effectively. You will need to review all the material you have gathered to determine what you consider to be the most important information to report. Some bits or kinds of information will strike you as more significant than others, and these are the ones that you should feature. Likewise, you will probably find that some information is simply not important enough to be mentioned. To help achieve your purposes, you should also give special thought to the perspective from which you will present your information to the reader. Do you want to present the material in the first or the third person? Do you want to be present in the piece, as Satrapi and Ehrenreich are? Or do you want to be invisible, like Tuchman? To some extent, your answer to these questions will depend on whether you gathered the information through your own firsthand observations and want to convey your own reactions to them. Look, for example, at "A Delicate Operation" by Roy C. Selby Jr. (p. 356). Although Selby must have written this piece on the basis of firsthand experience, he tells the story in the third person, removing himself almost completely from it except for such distant-sounding references to himself as "the surgeon." Selby is critically important to the information in this report, yet he decided to deemphasize his presence so as to focus our attention on the operation itself.

Your challenge will be to report on your "data" — the materials gathered on your topic — in a way that gets readers involved and offers enough details to help readers understand that data fully. To do this, you might draw on some of the other modes of writing. For example, some reflecting might help you make sense of your data or your relationship to it (as in Ehrenreich's case); some explaining might help readers understand the complexity of your data (as in Tuchman's case). In reportorial writing, perspective shouldn't dominate. It may enliven the writing and shape the choices you make, but it shouldn't interfere with the careful reporting of details. Your job, as reporter, is to synthesize details and deliver them to readers in a form that illuminates your subject.

Explaining

The "explaining" essays we've collected are written by specialists who aim to help nonspecialists understand phenomena as various as the color of the sky, the origin of the universe, the significance of urban legends, and the art of keeping a notebook. Explanation is an essential kind of writing in every academic field and profession. Facts, after all, do not speak for themselves; figures do not add up on their own. To make sense of a subject, we need to see it in terms of something that is related to it — the color of the sky in terms of lightwaves from the sun, the content of urban legends in terms of the immediate circumstances in which they are told.

To understand a subject, explanatory writers examine it in terms of some relevant context that will shed light on its origin and development, its nature and design, its elements and functions, its causes and effects, or its meaning and significance. For example, in James Jeans's "Why the Sky Is Blue" (p. 464), he explains the relationship between color and light:

> We know that sunlight is a blend of lights of many colors — as we can prove for ourselves by passing it through a prism, or even through a jug of water, or as Nature demonstrates to us when she passes it through the raindrops of a summer shower and produces a rainbow. We also know that light consists of waves, and that the different colors of light are produced by waves of different lengths, red light by long waves and blue light by short waves. The mixture of waves which constitutes sunlight has to struggle through the obstacles it meets in the atmosphere, just as the mixture of waves at the seaside has to struggle past the columns of the pier. And these obstacles treat the light-waves much as the columns of the pier treat the sea-waves. The long waves which constitute red light are hardly affected, but the short waves which constitute blue light are scattered in all directions.
>
> Thus, the different constituents of sunlight are treated in different ways as they struggle through the earth's atmosphere. A wave of blue light may be scattered by a dust particle and turned out of its course. After a time a second dust particle again turns it out of its course, and so on, until finally it enters our eyes by a path as zigzag as that of a flash of lightning. Consequently the blue waves of the sunlight enter our eyes from all directions. And that is why the sky looks blue.

Jeans's purpose here is to explain why the sky looks blue, and beginning in his opening sentence in this passage, he offers relevant information about the nature and properties of sunlight, light, and lightwaves to give readers the background context they'll need to understand his explanation. Drawing from the fields of astronomy and physics, he shows how "the different constituents of sunlight are treated in different ways as they struggle through the earth's atmosphere." After explaining how and why blue light is scattered "in all directions," Jeans concludes that "the blue waves of the sunlight enter our eyes from all directions. And that is why the sky looks blue." The information that Jeans draws on from astronomy and physics allows him to offer a knowledgeable, systematic, and instructive explanation for a philosophical question: How is it that the sky *looks* blue if it isn't *inherently* blue?

For an example of another style of explanatory writing, look at Oliver Sacks's "The Man Who Mistook His Wife for a Hat" (p. 680). Sacks, a neurologist, offers the results of a case study, which entails the close observation of an individual subject over time. Because the subject of a case study is by definition unique, the study cannot be replicated by other researchers. A case study must therefore be written in sufficient detail to document the observer's understanding of the subject and to enable other researchers to draw their own conclusions about what has been observed. This is exactly what Sacks does when he tells the story of Dr. P., a musician and painter:

> He saw all right, but what did he see? I opened out a copy of the *National Geographic* magazine and asked him to describe some pictures in it.
>
> His responses here were very curious. His eyes would dart from one thing to another, picking up tiny features, individual features, as they had done with my face. A striking brightness, a color, a shape would arrest his attention and elicit comment — but in no case did he get the scene-as-a-whole. He failed to see the whole, seeing only details, which he spotted like blips on a radar screen. He never entered into relation with the picture as a whole — never faced, so to speak, *its* physiognomy. He had no sense whatever of a landscape or scene.

It must have been obvious to Sacks that in explaining his patient's case, he needed to illustrate and demonstrate the man's unusual symptoms. Readers need the details to understand Dr. P.'s surprising symptoms. Sacks is careful to include enough concrete evidence to be convincing. But notice also that he includes the interpretive sentences toward the end of the paragraph, where he's seeking to explain Dr. P.'s puzzling behavior. Sacks's method could be accurately described as a series of detailed explanations punctuated by moments of interpretation and reflection. His case study is a good example for illustrating how a set of research materials often leads to a certain kind of writing. For readers to understand such a startling case, they need a lot of explanation and a little interpretation. That's exactly what Sacks delivers.

In Dr. P.'s paintings, Sacks sees evidence of "visual agnosia, in which all powers of representation and imagery, all sense of the concrete, all sense of reality, were being destroyed." Sacks decides to wait until nearly the end of the essay, when readers have an intimate sense of Dr. P.'s unusual symptoms, to define *visual agnosia*, his central term. His goal seems to be to ease nonspecialists into his tale before overwhelming us with medical terminology.

Once the definition is established, Sacks describes the process of uncovering the mystery behind Dr. P.'s unusual behavior. He shows, through description and dialogue with Dr. P. and his wife, the remarkable things Dr. P. can do (his extraordinary musical ability, for example) and the ordinary things he cannot do (such as recognize the faces of his wife and friends). Sacks is able to diagnose Dr. P.'s condition, but the diagnosis doesn't satisfy him. For Sacks, the diagnosis reveals the limitations of neurological and psychological explanations of what appear to be neuropsychological disorders when those sciences overlook "the judgmental, the particular, the personal." In the process, Sacks defines something larger: the limits of cognitive neurology and psychology, suggesting that they, too, may suffer from "an agnosia essentially similar to Dr. P.'s." Without some attention to the particular life of the person, the diagnosis will miss crucial details that may help the patient live a better life — which is, after all, an important goal in medicine. In this sense, his explanatory essay contains an implicit argument about the ethics and efficacy of medicine that doesn't account for the self of the patient.

Explanatory writing serves a wide range of academic, professional, and public purposes. Rules and regulations or guidelines and instructions are familiar examples of explanation that tell people how to carry out many of the practical and public activities of their lives. As you can see from comparing the essays of Jeans and Sacks, explanations can vary widely in their form. Textbooks — such as the one you are reading right now — as well as simplified presentations of highly specialized research are common examples of explanatory writing that help people understand a particular body of information and ideas. Scholarly research papers, government documents, and other technical presentations of data and analysis, though less familiar to the general reader, are important kinds of explanation that advance knowledge and inform decision making. As a reader of explanations, you must be flexible in your approach, always willing to move through unfamiliar territory on the way to understanding the subject being discussed.

Writing Explanatory Essays

An explanatory essay tends to combine the following elements: the presentation of specialized knowledge through concrete examples or evidence; definitions of key terms; detailed descriptions of a process, an object, or an idea; and explanation that helps to make sense of things. In planning a piece of explanatory writing, you should review your research materials, thinking about how these materials might direct the approach you take with regard to the elements listed above. As a writer of explanations, you must be flexible in choosing language and in selecting and arranging material to put your understanding in a form that satisfies you and fulfills the complex set of conditions that you are addressing at that moment. In every case, though, it is important to imagine what your reader will and won't know — and to do the careful work of defining terms, illustrating with concrete details, and demonstrating cause-and-effect relationships.

When you write an explanatory essay, you are just as likely to combine several methods as Sacks does. People do this even when explaining how to get somewhere in their day-to-day conversations. Often they'll give an overview of where the place is situated, a step-by-step set of movements to follow and places to look for, brief descriptions of prominent guideposts along the way, a review of the original directions, and possibly a remark or two about misleading spots to avoid. Similarly, when you explain something in writing, you'll want to help readers get from one place to another in a particular subject matter. As with the other modes, there is a range of explanatory writing, and writers in various fields will pick and choose from the methods of explaining we've described here. You should do the same. Let your topic and your purpose guide the choices you make, keeping in mind that your goal is to help readers without specialized knowledge understand a topic you understand more fully than they do. Your job, in short, is to explain.

Arguing

In the "arguing" selections we've included, you will find authors taking positions on numerous (and often controversial) subjects — from the benefits of television to the status of African-American English, from the meaning of war photographs to the problematic measurement of human intelligence. No matter what their academic fields or professions, these writers energetically defend their positions on the issues and questions they address. Like any of us, these writers are especially fired up when their views are pitted against the beliefs of others. So you will find these writers are vigorously engaged in the give and take of argument. As a consequence, you will find yourself having to weigh the merits of competing positions in debates about controversial issues.

Some of the distinctive qualities of argument are clear in the following paragraphs from Martin Luther King Jr.'s "Letter from Birmingham Jail" (p. 288):

> I think I should indicate why I am here in Birmingham, since you have been influenced by the view which argues against "outsiders coming in." I have the honor of serving as president of the Southern Christian Leadership Conference, an organization operating in every southern state, with headquarters in Atlanta, Georgia. We have some eighty-five affiliated organizations across the South, and one of them is the Alabama Christian Movement for Human Rights. Frequently we share staff, educational, and financial resources with our affiliates. Several months ago the affiliate here in Birmingham asked us to be on call to engage in a nonviolent direct-action program if such were deemed necessary. We readily consented, and when the hour came we lived up to our promise. So I, along with several members of my staff, am here because I was invited here. I am here because I have organizational ties here.
>
> But more basically, I am in Birmingham because injustice is here. Just as the prophets of the eighth century BC left their villages and carried their "thus saith the Lord" far beyond the boundaries of their home towns, and just as the Apostle Paul left his village of Tarsus and carried the gospel of Jesus Christ to the far corners of the Greco-

Roman world, so am I compelled to carry the gospel of freedom beyond my own home town. Like Paul, I must constantly respond to
the Macedonian call for aid.

King's letter is one of the finest statements of democratic values that our
country has yet produced; these are the first few paragraphs of an argument
that continues for several pages. Like many arguments, King's is a response
to an opposing viewpoint. In this case, eight Alabama clergymen had published a statement calling King's actions "unwise and untimely." He was also
accused of being an "outside agitator." King counters that accusation immediately by outlining his affiliations with the South, with Alabama, and even
with Birmingham. He has ample reason, he argues, to be "here," a word he
places unhesitatingly in the first sentence of the first paragraph quoted above
and then four more times in the last two sentences of that paragraph.

From this point on, King's argument expands to include larger and larger
ideas about justice. "I am in Birmingham because injustice is here," he writes,
opening his next paragraph by pivoting on "here," a word that becomes a
rhetorical feature of the essay. Calling on biblical parallels to support his idea
that the Christian is always "here," confronting need and injustice, King
asserts first that all U.S. citizens have every right to converge on whatever
"here" they identify as necessary. In the argument that follows, he expands on
that idea. However local they may have been, the clergymen who had objected
to his intervention had not been "here" at all — not with King, not on the side
of justice. Nor had most white clergy or sympathetic white moderates been
"here." Almost everyone had displaced King's "here" to some more distant
"there," distant in time as much as in place, so much so that the "[s]hallow
understanding from people of good will" distressed King almost as much as
the overt antagonism of segregationist authorities.

Argumentative writing pervades our lives. We encounter it in political
speeches, newspaper editorials, syndicated columns, and letters to the editor,
which typically debate the pros and cons of some public issue, be it local
taxes or national defense. But arguments crop up in less obvious places every
day: in the many brochures, TV ads, and e-mail spam we are confronted
with, urging us to vote for one candidate, support a cause, or buy a product.
Argument is fundamental in the judicial process, is crucial in the legislative
process, and serves the basic aims of the professional and academic world,
testing ideas and theories by pitting them against one another. Argument is
an important activity in the advancement of knowledge and society.

The broad range of argumentative writing can be understood by considering the kinds of issues and questions that typically give rise to disagreement and debate. The most basic sources of controversy are questions of
fact — the who, what, when, and where of things, as well as the how much.
Intense arguments over questions of fact can develop in any field, especially
when the facts in question have a significant bearing on a subject. Stephen
Jay Gould's essay "Women's Brains" (p. 761) is one such questioning of

fact. An earlier scientist had argued that women were less intelligent than men — an assertion Gould challenges by rereading the evidence the previous researcher had offered.

Argumentative writing is possible because any two people confronted with the same set of "facts" may disagree about what they mean. There is no disputing that Paul Broca weighed more than four hundred human brains and found that male brains were, on average, noticeably weightier than female brains. But how to account for that difference is an open question that allows several possible answers; and even if those questions were to be settled, there is no verifiable correlation of brain size with intelligence. What brain size *does* correlate with reliably enough is height; taller people have larger brains than shorter people. Men tend to be taller than women, and so their brains are larger. However, the average weight difference between the male and the female brain, Gould observes, "is exactly the average difference between a 5 foot 4 inch and a 6 foot 4 inch male in Broca's data. We would not (especially us short folks) want to ascribe greater intelligence to tall men."

Beliefs and values are the stuff of argument. In fact, arguments over values are integral to the formation of society and so determine much about how we live. Nothing illustrates that better than this well-known passage from the Declaration of Independence (p. 243):

> We hold these truths to be self-evident, that all men are created equal, that they are endowed by their Creator with certain unalienable Rights, that among these are Life, Liberty and the pursuit of Happiness. That to secure these rights, Governments are instituted among Men, deriving their just powers from the consent of the governed. That whenever any Form of Government becomes destructive of these ends, it is the Right of the People to alter or to abolish it, and to institute new Government, laying its foundation on such principles and organizing its powers in such form, as to them shall seem most likely to effect their Safety and Happiness.

In this crucial passage, Thomas Jefferson and his congressional colleagues directly challenged several fundamental assumptions about the rights of people and the sources of governmental power that were held by the British king and by many British people and others throughout the world. Only in this way was it possible for them to make the compelling case for their ultimate claim that the colonies should be "FREE AND INDEPENDENT STATES . . . Absolved from all Allegiance to the British Crown."

Though Jefferson and his colleagues did not outline a new system of government in the Declaration itself, the document illustrates the fact that conflicts over beliefs and values influence questions of policy and planning — and therefore shape the lives we are able to live. For an argument to be strong, it must be motivated by a genuine dilemma. Two people may well look at the same evidence and draw different conclusions. A strong argument takes a position — one that is plausible without being too obvious — with regard to one of these dilemmas. The good news for argumentative writers is that the world we live in offers dilemmas like these at just about every turn.

Writing Argumentative Essays

An argumentative essay tends to combine the following elements: an introduction to a conversation or debate of some kind; an explanation of why that conversation or debate is important; a thesis statement made near the beginning of the essay that demonstrates the writer's position in clear, straightforward terms; evidence that helps the writer illustrate, support, and develop this position; analysis of and reflection on that evidence; and the discussion (and often discrediting) of counterarguments that represent opposing points of view. When you write an argumentative essay, remember that your job is to persuade readers. To do so, your writing will need to be clear and readable, and your evidence and analysis will need to be convincing.

The statement of an argument is often called a *thesis* (or, in the sciences, a *hypothesis*). If you want to evaluate your own argument, it's a good idea to test your thesis. Ask yourself if it's *arguable*. In other words, could two reasonable people disagree about it? If an argument is too obvious — for example, "The earth orbits the sun" — then few people are likely to disagree about it. While it's worthwhile to explain how and why the earth orbits the sun, there's not much point in making an argument that it does. Then ask yourself if your thesis is plausible. Will it convince some readers? The argument "The earth orbits Venus" may be arguable, but it's not plausible. The trick of making a solid argument is to find the middle ground between originality and plausibility. Getting that balance right generally requires some trial and error (as does most writing).

In any piece of argumentative writing, your primary purpose is to persuade readers that your thesis deserves consideration. Some readers, of course, will agree with you in advance, but others will disagree, and still others will be undecided. In planning a piece of argumentative writing, you should begin by examining your material with an eye toward discovering the issues that have to be addressed and the points that have to be made to present your case persuasively, especially to readers who oppose you or who are undecided. This means that you will have to deal not only with issues that you consider relevant but also with matters that have been raised by your opponents. In other words, you need to consider plausible *counter-arguments* and show readers that you have considered all sides of the controversy, as King did right from the start by confronting the issue of "outside agitators" rather than ignoring it.

After you have identified the crucial points to be addressed, you will need to make a convincing case with respect to each of the points. Some methods for doing so are important no matter what point you are trying to prove. Every argument requires evidence. Sometimes this basic concern for providing readers with appropriate evidence will lead you into the activity of reporting. In his attempt to demonstrate the right of the colonies "to throw off such Government," Jefferson provides a lengthy and detailed list of "injuries" that the king of Great Britain inflicted on the colonies. Often evidence also requires some explaining. Gould, for example, explains several possible reasons for the discrepancy of size between the male and female brain. Height is one possible reason. Another is the probable manner of death. Prolonged illness will wither a brain and reduce its size, and women — especially in the mid-nineteenth century, when Broca worked — were more likely than men to die at advanced ages of lingering illness. Sometimes personal reflection becomes its own kind of evidence, as in King's reflections on how and why he came to Birmingham. In other words, the lessons you learn writing in the other three modes will come in handy when you are ready to discuss the evidence for an argument.

Evidence alone will not be persuasive to readers. It's the writer's job to analyze evidence in ways that show *how* it supports or illustrates an argument. For example, having made the general claim that "a long train of abuses" entitles people "to throw off such Government," and having cited a long list of abuses that Great Britain had inflicted on the colonies, Jefferson concludes that the colonies "are Absolved from all Allegiance to the British Crown." Because he has analyzed his evidence so effectively, his conclusion is convincing enough to shape our thinking two centuries after he wrote it. But that doesn't mean everybody would agree with Jefferson. Great Britain did not accept Jefferson's premises, so it did not accept his conclusions, logical though they were. Other countries of the time took a different view of the matter. The most common reaction to an argument we dislike is to challenge the premises on which it is founded. Many today would take issue with some of Jefferson's premises — for example, the fact that some citizens were defined as more "equal" than others. Keep this in mind when you write — as well as when you read. It's likely that you'll disagree with arguments made by writers in this reader. Take the opportunity to examine the premises of these arguments, and pay attention to the rhetorical moves the argumentative writers make. This will help you make your own arguments in response to theirs.

When you write an argumentative essay, you are taking part in a conversation on a subject about which people are likely to disagree. In Jefferson's and King's declarations of democratic principles, and in other selections in this reader, you will see how different writers use the various resources of language to produce some very striking and compelling arguments. You will learn from these essays just by reading them. It's likely that the strategies these writers use will creep into your writing without your even realizing it. At the same time, it can be helpful to study their strategies so that you'll both be able to identify the premises of a writer's argument and recognize when a writer invokes a counterargument or uses personal reflection as evidence. The more you recognize rhetorical elements like these in the writing of others, the easier it will become to experiment with them in your own writing.

Reflecting, Reporting, Explaining, Arguing

A central premise of this book is that writers learn by reading good writing. You can learn a great deal about your own writing by reading *as a writer.* Whatever modes they write in, the writers included here demonstrate a range of successful techniques for conceiving a writing project, engaging an audience, and exploring ideas. Notice how writers invent their own strategies, putting their own stamp on the modes in which they write. Notice how the modes sometimes overlap, or how the methods of one may help accomplish the goals of another. Great writing is inventive and dynamic on the one hand, and composed of time-tested techniques on the other. You'll want to learn from these techniques; do some experimenting of your own, and strive to become a flexible writer, able to adapt to a wide range of writing modes and contexts. The reading questions, classroom activities, and writing assignments that accompany the readings are designed to get you actively engaged in the process of reading the way writers do, responding with ideas of your own, and writing in a variety of modes and using a variety of techniques. As we mentioned in the introduction, you will continue the process of becoming a writer throughout college — and, beyond that, in your chosen profession. Learning to write is a continuous process — one that's never completely finished. We hope that this course and this book will be an important step in your process.

ARTS AND
HUMANITIES

Readings in the Arts and Humanities

The arts and humanities include those areas of academic research and creative expression that explore what is sometimes called the human condition — for example, philosophy, art and art history, literature and creative writing, theater, dance, film, music, new media, religion, and languages. (Certain disciplines, such as history and linguistics, are sometimes categorized among the humanities and sometimes among the social sciences.) Writers in the humanities tend to value and emphasize *interpretation,* studying subjective questions rather than factual knowledge: What is the nature of art? What is the nature of culture? How does one live a good life? How does language shape identity? Where did I come from?

Scholars in the arts and humanities explore these questions in the many shapes and sizes they come in, as you will see in the fifteen pieces of writing collected in this section. Here, nine readings stand alone, and three sets are paired in order to emphasize the dialogue between them. Five of these essays are primarily reflecting, three reporting, two explaining, and five arguing. Whatever modes they write in, the writers of these essays interpret both texts and the details of personal and social experience to illuminate larger questions.

Interpretation requires writers to strike a careful balance between the general and the particular, or the abstract and the concrete. Literary scholars, whose main task is to interpret, still need to ground their theories in fact — for example, the date of Oscar Wilde's imprisonment (1895) is important to know if you want to understand the history of the novel or the politics of sexuality. Analyzing how texts, experience, and events work in both a literal and a concrete sense is the first step in an interpretive process.

In the arts and humanities, you, too, will be asked to interpret texts — literature, visual art, argumentative essays, film, new media — to illuminate the subjective questions at the center of humanistic inquiry. When you write in response to texts like these, you will also be learning to strike a balance between the general and the particular, between facts and interpretation. Concrete details illuminate abstract concepts, and vice versa. You will be learning the art of speculating intelligently, examining nuances, and living with ambiguity and uncertainty. Whether you are reflecting, reporting, explaining, or arguing, you will be drawing your readers' attention to the implications of texts and experiences that require interpretation — *your* interpretation — to be understood.

Mirrors

Lucy Grealy

Lucy Grealy (1963–2002), an award-winning poet, attended the Iowa Writer's Workshop and was a fellow at the Bunting Institute of Radcliffe. At the age of nine, Grealy had cancer of the jaw, and the right side of her jaw was removed. In the following essay, which first appeared in Harper's *and which received the National Magazine Award, Grealy writes about the thirty operations she had in twenty years to try to reconstruct her face. In both this selection and her book,* Autobiography of a Face *(1994), Grealy reflects on the obsessions and perceptions of physical beauty that dominate our culture. Her last book was the essay collection* As Seen on TV: Provocations *(2000). She died at the age of thirty-nine, an apparent suicide.*

There was a long period of time, almost a year, during which I never looked in a mirror. It wasn't easy; just as you only notice how often people eat on television when you yourself are on a diet, I'd never suspected just how omnipresent were our own images. I began as an amateur, avoiding merely mirrors, but by the end of the year I found myself with a professional knowledge of the reflected image, its numerous tricks and wiles, how it can spring up at any moment: a glass tabletop, a well-polished door handle, a darkened window, a pair of sunglasses, a restaurant's otherwise magnificent brass-plated coffee machine sitting innocently by the cash register.

I hadn't simply woken up one morning deciding not to look at myself as part of some personal experiment, as my friend Sally had attempted once before me: She'd lasted about three days before finally giving in to the need "to make sure I was still there." For Sally, not looking in the mirror meant enacting a conscious decision against a constant desire that, at the end of her three days, she still was at a loss to define as either solely habit or instinct. For me, however, the act of not looking was insidious. It was nihilistic, an insurgence too chaotic even to know if it was directed at the world or at myself.

At the time I was living alone in Scotland, surviving financially because of my eligibility for the dole, the vernacular for Britain's social security benefits. When I first arrived in Aberdeen I didn't know anyone, had no idea just how I was going to live, yet I went anyway because I'd met a plastic surgeon there who said he could help me. I had been living in London, working temp jobs. Before that I'd been in Berlin, and ostensibly had come to

London only to earn money for a few weeks before returning to Germany. Exactly why I had this experience in London I don't know, but in my first week there I received more nasty comments about my face than I had in the past three years of living in Iowa, New York, and Germany. These comments, all from men and all odiously sexual, hurt and disoriented me so much I didn't think twice about a friendly suggestion to go see a plastic surgeon. I'd already had more than a dozen operations in the States, yet my insurance ran out and so did my hope that any real difference could be made. Here, however, was a surgeon who had some new techniques, and here was a government willing to foot the bill: I didn't feel I could pass up yet another chance to "fix" my face, which I confusedly thought concurrent with "fixing" my self, my soul, my life.

Sixteen years earlier, when I was nine and living in America, I came home from school one day with a toothache. Several weeks and misdiagnoses later surgeons removed most of the right side of my jaw as part of an attempt to prevent the cancer they found there from spreading. No one properly explained the operation to me and I awoke in a cocoon of pain that prevented me from moving or speaking. Tubes ran in and out of my body and because I couldn't ask, I made up my own explanations for their existence.

Up until this time I'd been having a great time in the hospital. For starters 5 it was in "The City," a place of traffic and noise and dangers and, best of all, elevators. Never having been in an elevator before, I thrilled not just at the ride itself, but also at the game of nonchalance played out in front of the other elevator-savvy children who stepped on and off without thought.

Second, I was free from school. In theory a school existed on the third floor for children well enough to attend, but my friend Derek and I quickly discovered that the volunteer who came each day after lunch to pick us up was a sucker for a few well-timed groans, and once we learned to play straight man for each other there was little trouble getting out of it. We made sure the nurses kept thinking we had gone off to school, leaving us free for a few brief hours to wander the mazelike halls of the ancient hospital. A favorite spot was the emergency waiting room; they had good magazines and sometimes you got to see someone covered in blood come through the door. Derek tried to convince me that a certain intersection in the sub-basement was an ideal place to watch for bodies heading toward the morgue, but the one time we did actually see one get wheeled by beneath its clichéd white sheet, we silently allowed each other to save face by suddenly deciding it was so much more fun to steal get-well cards from the gift shop than hang out in a cold basement. Once we stole the cards we sent them out randomly to other kids on the ward, signing them "Love and Kisses, Michael Jackson." Our theory was to watch them open up what they would think was a card from a famous star, but no one ever actually fell for it; by then we were well pegged as troublemakers.

There was something else going on too, something I didn't know how to articulate. Adults treated me in a mysterious manner. They asked me to do things: lie still for X rays, not cry for needles, things that, although not easy, never seemed equal to the praise I received in return. Reinforced to me again and again was how I was "a brave girl" for not crying, "a good girl" for not complaining, and soon I began defining myself this way, equating strength with silence.

Then the chemotherapy began. In the early seventies chemo was even cruder than it is now, the basic premise of it to poison the patient right up until the very brink of their own death. Up until this point I almost never cried, almost always received some sort of praise and attention in return for this, got what I considered the better part of the deal. But now, now it was like a practical joke that had gotten out of hand. Chemotherapy was a nightmare and I wanted it to stop, I didn't want to be brave any more. Yet I had so grown used to defining myself as "brave," i.e., silent, that even more terrifying was the thought of losing this sense of myself, certain that if I broke down this would be seen as despicable in the eyes of both my parents and doctors.

Mostly the task of taking me into the city for the injections fell upon my mother, though sometimes my father had to take me. Overwhelmed by the sight of the vomiting and weeping, my father developed the routine of "going to get the car," meaning that he left the office before the actual injection on the premise that then he could have the car ready and waiting when it was all over. Ashamed of my suffering, I felt relief when he was finally out of the room. When my mother was with me she stayed in the room, yet this only made the distance even more tangible, an almost palpable distance built on the intensity of our desperate longing to be anywhere else, anywhere at all. She explained that it was wrong to cry before the needle went in; afterward was one thing, but before, that was mere fear, and hadn't I already demonstrated my bravery earlier? Every week, every Friday, or "d-day" as we called it, for two and a half years I climbed up onto that too-big doctor's table and told myself not to cry, and every week I failed. The injections were really two large syringes, filled with chemicals so caustic to the vein that each had to be administered only very slowly. The whole process took about four minutes; I had to remain very still throughout it. Dry retching began in the first fifteen seconds, then the throb behind my eyes gave everything a yellow-green aura, and the bone-deep pain of alternating extreme hot and cold flashes made me tremble, yet still I had to sit motionless and not move my arm. No one spoke to me, not the doctor who was a paradigm of the cold-fish physician, not the nurse who told my mother I reacted much more violently than many of the other children, and not my mother, who, surely overwhelmed by the sight of her child's suffering, thought the best thing to do was remind me to be brave, to try and not cry. All the while I hated myself for having wept before the needle went in, convinced that the nurse and my mother were right, that I was "overdoing it," that the throwing up was psychosomatic, that my mother was angry with me for not being good or brave enough. So involved with controlling my guilt and shame, the problem of physical pain seemed easy by comparison.

Yet each week, usually two or three days after the injection, there came   10
the first flicker of feeling better, the always forgotten and gratefully rediscovered understanding that simply to be well in my body was the greatest thing
I could ask for. I thought other people felt this gratitude, this appreciation
and physical joy all the time, and I felt cheated because I only was able to
feel it once a week.

When you are only ten, which is when the chemotherapy began, two
and a half years seems like your whole life, yet it did finally end. I remember
the last day of chemotherapy very clearly for two reasons: one, because it
was the only day on which I succeeded in not crying, and because later, in
private, I cried harder than I had in years; I thought now I would no longer
be "special," that without the arena of chemotherapy in which to prove myself no one would ever love me, that I would fade unnoticed into the background. This idea about not being different didn't last very long. Before I
thought people stared because I was bald. I wore a hat constantly, but this
fooled no one, least of all myself.

During this time my mother worked in a nursing home in a Hasidic
community. Hasidism dictates that married women cover their hair, and
most commonly this is done with a wig. My mother's friends were all too
willing to donate their discarded wigs, and soon the house filled with wigs.
I never wore one of them, they frightened me even when my mother insisted
I looked better in one of the few that actually fit, yet we didn't know how to
say no to the women who kept graciously offering their wigs. The cats enjoyed sleeping on them and the dogs playing with them, and we grew used
to having to pick a wig up off a chair we wanted to sit in. It never struck us
as odd until one day a visitor commented wryly as he cleared a chair for
himself, and suddenly a great wave of shame overcame me. I had nightmares
about wigs, felt a flush if I even heard the word, and one night I put myself
out of my misery by getting up after everyone was asleep, gathering all the
wigs except for one the dogs were fond of and might miss, and which they
had chewed anyway into something other than a wig. I hid all the rest in an
old chest where they weren't found for almost a year.

But my hair eventually grew in, and it didn't take long before I understood that I looked different for other reasons. People stared at me in stores,
other children made fun of me to the point where I came to expect it constantly, wherever I went. School became a battleground, and I came home at
the end of each day exhausted with the effort of keeping my body so tense
and hard that I was sure anything would bounce off of it.

I was living in an extreme situation, and because I did not particularly
care for the world I was in, I lived in others, and because the world I did live
in was a dangerous one, I incorporated this danger into my private life. I
saw movies about and envied Indians, imagined myself one. Walking down
the streets I walked down through the forest, my body ready for any opportunity to fight or flee one of the big cats I knew stalked the area. Vietnam
and Cambodia were other places I walked through frequently, daily even as

I made my way down the school hall, knowing a landmine or a sniper might give themselves away at any moment with the subtle, soft metal clicks I'd read about in the books I took from the library. When faced with a land-mine, a mere insult about my face seemed a frivolous thing.

In the early years, when I was still on the chemo, I lived in worse places than Cambodia. Because I knew it was somehow inappropriate, I read only in secret Primo Levi,[1] Elie Wiesel,[2] every book by a survivor I could find by myself without resorting to asking the librarian for. Auschwitz, Birkenau: I felt the senseless blows of the Capos and somehow knew that because at any moment we might be called upon to live for a week on one loaf of bread and some water called soup, the peanut butter sandwich I found on my plate was nothing less than a miracle, an utter and sheer miracle capable of making me literally weep with joy.   15

I decided I wanted to become a "deep" person. I wasn't exactly sure what this would entail, but I believed that if I could just find the right phi-losophy, think the right thoughts, my suffering would end. To try to under-stand the world I was in, I undertook to find out what was "real," and quickly began seeing reality as existing in the lowest common denominator, that suffering was the one and only dependable thing. But rather than spend all of my time despairing, though certainly I did plenty of that, I developed a form of defensive egomania: I felt I was the only one walking about in the world who understood what was really important. I looked upon people complaining about the most mundane things — nothing on TV, traffic jams, the price of new clothes — and felt both joy because I knew how unimpor-tant those things really were and unenlightened feelings of superiority be-cause other people didn't. Because I lived a fantasy life in which I had to be thankful for each cold, blanketless night I survived on the cramped wooden bunks, chemotherapy — the nausea, pain, and deep despair it brought — was a breeze, a stroll through the country in comparison. I was often miser-able, but I knew that to feel warm instead of cold was its own kind of joy, that to eat was a reenactment of the grace of some god whom I could only dimly define, and that simply to be alive was a rare, ephemeral miracle. It was like reliving The Fall a dozen times a day: I was given these moments of grace and insight, only to be invariably followed by a clumsy tumble into narcissism.

As I got older, as I became a teenager, I began to feel very isolated. My nonidentical twin sister started going out with boys, and I started, my most

---

[1]*Primo Levi* (1919–1987): An Italian chemist, novelist, poet, and memoirist. He survived one year at Auschwitz and wrote about his war and postwar experiences. His death was an apparent suicide. [Eds.]

[2]*Elie Wiesel* (b. 1928): A Romanian-born American writer and scholar who sur-vived over a year at various concentration camps, including Auschwitz. His writings and work with persecuted groups earned him the Nobel Peace Prize in 1986. [Eds.]

tragic mistake of all, to listen to and believe the taunts thrown at me daily by the very boys she and the other girls were interested in. I was a dog, a monster, the ugliest girl they had ever seen. Of all the remarks the most damaging wasn't even directed at me, but was really an insult to Jerry, a boy I never saw because every day, between fourth and fifth periods when I was cornered by this particular group, I was too ashamed to lift my eyes off the floor. "Hey, look, it's Jerry's girlfriend," they yelled when they saw me, and I felt such shame, knowing that this was the deepest insult they could throw at Jerry.

I became interested in horses and got a job at a run-down local stable. Having those horses to go to each day after school saved my life; I spent all of my time either with them or thinking about them. To keep myself thinking objectively I became an obsessive reader and an obsessive television watcher, anything to keep me away from the subjective. I convinced myself I was smarter than everyone else, that only I knew what mattered, what was important, but by the time I was sixteen this wasn't true, not by a long shot. Completely and utterly repressed, I was convinced that I never wanted a boyfriend, not ever, and wasn't it convenient for me, a blessing I even thought, that none would ever want me. I told myself I was free to concentrate on the "true reality" of life, whatever that was. My sister and her friends put on blue eye shadow, blow-dried their hair, and went to spend interminable hours in the local mall, and I looked down on them for this, knew they were misleading themselves and being overoccupied with the "mere surface" of living. I had thought like this when I was younger, but now it was different, now my philosophy was haunted by desires so frightening I was unable to even admit they existed.

It wasn't until I was in college that I finally allowed that maybe, just maybe, it might be nice to have a boyfriend. As a person I had, as they say, blossomed in college. I went to a small, liberal, predominantly female school and suddenly, after years of alienation in high school, discovered that there were other people I could enjoy talking to, people who thought me intelligent and talented. I was, however, still operating on the assumption that no one, not ever, would be physically attracted to me, and in a curious way this shaped my personality. I became forthright and honest and secure in the way only the truly self-confident are, those who do not expect to be rejected, and those like me, who do not even dare to ask and so also expect no rejection. I had come to know myself as a person, but it would be graduate school before I was literally, physically able to use my name and the word woman in the same sentence.

Throughout all of this I was undergoing reconstructive surgery in an   20
attempt to rebuild my jaw. It started when I was fifteen, several years after the chemo ended. I had known for years I would have operations to fix my face, and sometimes at night I fantasized about how good my life would finally be then. One day I got a clue that maybe it would not be so easy. At fourteen I went first to an older plastic surgeon who explained the process of pedestals to me, and told me it would take ten years to fix my face. Ten

years? Why even bother? I thought. I'll be ancient by then. I went to the library and looked up the pedestals he talked about. There were gruesome pictures of people with grotesque tubes of their own skin growing out of their bodies, tubes of skin that were harvested like some kind of crop and then rearranged in ways with results that did not look at all normal or acceptable to my eye. But then I met a younger surgeon, a man who was working on a new way of grafting that did not involve pedestals, and I became more hopeful and once again began awaiting the fixing of my face, of the day when I would be whole, content, loved.

Long-term plastic surgery is not like the movies. There is no one single operation that will change everything, and there is certainly no slow unwrapping of the gauze in order to view the final product. There is always swelling, sometimes grotesque, there are often bruises, and always there are scars. After each operation, too scared to simply go look in the mirror, I developed an oblique method comprised of several stages. First, I tried to catch my reflection in an overhead lamp: The roundness of the metal distorted my image just enough to obscure details and give no true sense of size or proportion. Then I slowly worked my way up to looking at the reflection in someone's eyeglasses, and from there I went to walking as briskly as possible by a mirror, glancing only quickly. I repeated this as many times as it would take me, passing the mirror slightly more slowly each time until finally I was able to stand still and confront myself.

The theory behind most reconstructive surgery is to take large chunks of muscle, skin, and bone and slap them into the roughly appropriate place, then slowly begin to carve this mess into some sort of shape. It involves long, major operations, countless lesser ones, a lot of pain, and many, many years. And also, it does not always work. With my young surgeon in New York, who was becoming not so young with each passing year, I had two or three soft tissue grafts, two skin grafts, a bone graft, and some dozen other operations to "revise" my face, yet when I left graduate school at the age of twenty-five I was still more or less in the same position I had started in: a deep hole in the right side of my face and a rapidly shrinking left side and chin, a result of the radiation I'd had as a child and the stress placed upon it by the other operations. I was caught in a cycle of having a big operation, one that would force me to look monstrous from the swelling for many months, then have the subsequent revision operations that improved my looks tremendously, and then slowly, over the period of a few months or a year, watch the graft reabsorb back into my body, slowly shrink down and leave me with nothing but the scarred donor site the graft had originally come from.

I had little or no conception of how I appeared to other people. As a child, Halloween was my favorite holiday because I could put on a mask and walk among the blessed for a few brief, sweet hours. Such freedom I felt, walking down the street, my face hidden: Through the imperfect oval holes I could peer out at other faces, masked or painted or not, and see on those faces nothing but the normal faces of childhood looking back at me, faces I mistakenly thought were the faces everyone else but me saw all the time, faces that were simply curious and ready for fun, not the faces I usually braced myself for, the cruel, lonely, vicious ones I spent every day other than Halloween waiting to round each corner. As I breathed in the condensed, plastic air I somehow thought that I was breathing in normality, that this joy and weightlessness were what the world was comprised of, and it was only my face that kept me from it, my face that was my own mask, my own tangible barrier that kept me from knowing the true identity of the joy I was sure everyone but me lived with intimately. How could they not know it? Not know that to be free of the fear of taunts and the burden of knowing no one would ever love you was all anyone could ever ask for? I was a pauper walking for a short while in the clothes of the prince, and when the day ended, I gave up my disguise with dismay.

I also came to love winter, when I could wrap the lower half of my face up in a scarf: I could speak to people and they would have no idea of who and what they were really speaking to. I developed the bad habits of letting my long hair hang in my face, and of always covering my chin and mouth with my hand, hoping it might be seen as a thoughtful, accidental gesture. My one concession to this came in college, when I cut my hair short, very short, in an attempt to stop hiding behind it. It was also an attempt, though I didn't see it as such at the time, to desex myself. I had long, blond hair, and I also had a thin figure. Sometimes, from a distance, men would see the thin blonde and whistle, something I dreaded more than anything else because I knew as they got closer their tone would inevitably change, they would stare openly or, worse, turn away quickly, and by cutting my hair I felt I might possibly avoid this, clear up any misconception anyone, however briefly, might have about my being attractive.

Once in college my patient friends repeated for me endlessly that most   25
of it was in my mind, that, granted, I did not look like everyone else, but that didn't mean I looked bad. I am sure now that they were right some of the time. But with the constant surgery I was in a perpetual state of transfiguration. I rarely looked the same for more than six months at a time. So ashamed of my face, I was unable to even admit that this constant change affected me at all; I let everyone who wanted to know that it was only what was inside that mattered, that I had "grown used to" the surgery, that none of it bothered me at all. Just as I had done in childhood, I pretended nothing was wrong, and this was constantly mistaken by others for bravery. I spent a great deal of time looking in the mirror in private, positioning my head to show off my eyes and nose, which were not just normal, but quite pretty, as my still-patient friends told me often. But I could not bring myself to see them for more than a glimmer: I looked in the mirror and saw not the normal upper half of my face, but only the disfigured lower half. People still teased me. Not daily, not like when I was younger, but in ways that caused me more pain than ever before. Children stared at me and I learned to cross

the street to avoid them; this bothered me but not as much as the insults I got from men. They weren't thrown at me because I was disfigured, they were thrown at me because I was a disfigured woman.

They came from boys, sometimes men, and almost always a group of them. Only two or three times have I ever been teased by a single person, and I can think of only one time when I was ever teased by a woman. Had I been a man, would I have had to walk down the street while a group of young women followed and denigrated my sexual worth?

Not surprisingly, I viewed sex as my salvation. I was sure that if only I could get someone to sleep with me it would mean I wasn't ugly, that I was an attractive person, a lovable person. It would not be hard to guess where this line of reasoning led me, which was into the beds of a few manipulative men who liked themselves even less than they liked me, and I in turn left each short-term affair hating myself, obscenely sure that if only I had been prettier it would have worked, he would have loved me and it would have been like those other love affairs I was certain "normal" women had all the time. Gradually I became unable to say "I'm depressed," but could only say "I'm ugly," because the two had become inextricably linked in my mind. Into that universal lie, that sad equation of "if only" which we are all prey to, I was sure that if only I had a normal face, then I would be happy.

What our brains know is one thing, yet what our hearts know is another matter entirely, and when I met this new surgeon in Scotland, I offhandedly explained to my friends back home "why not, it's free, isn't it?" unable to admit that I believed in the fixability of life all over again.

Originally, it was planned I would have something called a tissue expander, followed by a bone graft. A tissue expander is a small balloon placed under the skin and then slowly blown up over the course of several months, the object being to stretch out the skin and create room and cover for the new bone. It is a bizarre, nightmarish thing to do to your face, yet I was hopeful about the end results and I was also able to spend the three months the expansion took in the hospital. I've always felt safe in hospitals: It's the one place I feel justified, sure of myself, free from the need to explain the way I look. For this reason the first tissue expander was bearable, just, and the bone graft that followed it was a success, it did not melt away like the previous ones.

However, the stress put upon my original remaining jaw from the sur- 30 gery instigated a period of deterioration of that bone, and it became apparent that I was going to need the same operation I'd just had on the right side done to the left. I remember my surgeon telling me this at an outpatient clinic. I planned to be traveling down to London that same night on an overnight train, and I barely made it to the station on time, I was in such a fumbling state of despair. I could not imagine doing it all over again, and just as I had done all my life, I was searching and searching through my intellect for a way to make it okay, make it bearable, for a way to do it. I lay awake all night on that train, feeling the tracks slip quickly and oddly erotic below me, when I remembered an afternoon from my three months in the hospital. Boredom was a big problem those long afternoons, the days punctuated and landmarked by meals and television programs. Waiting for the afternoon tea to come, wondering desperately how I could make time pass, it suddenly occurred to me I didn't have to make time pass, that it would do it of its own accord, that I simply had to relax and take no action. Lying on the train, remembering that, I realized I had no obligation to make my situation okay, that I didn't have to explain it, understand it, that I could invoke the idea of negative capability and just simply let it happen. By the time the train pulled into King's Cross Station, I felt able to bear it yet again, not entirely sure what other choice I had.

But there was an element I didn't yet know about. I returned to Scotland to set up a date to go in and have the tissue expander put in, and was told quite casually that I'd only be in the hospital three or four days. Wasn't I going to spend the whole expansion time in the hospital? I asked almost in a whisper. What's the point of that? You can just come in every day to the outpatient to have it expanded. Horrified by this, I was speechless. I would have to live and move about in the outside world with a giant balloon in my face? I can't remember what I did for the next few days before I went into the hospital, but I vaguely remember that these days involved a great deal of drinking alone in bars and at home.

I went in and had the operation and, just as they said, went home at the end of the week. The only thing I can truly say gave me any comfort during the months I lived with my tissue expander was my writing and Kafka. I started a novel and completely absorbed myself in it, writing for hours and hours every day. It was the only way I could walk down the street, to stand the stares I received, to think to myself "I'll bet none of them are writing a novel." It was that strange, old familiar form of egomania, directly related to my dismissive, conceited thoughts of adolescence. As for Kafka, who had always been one of my favorite writers even before the new fashion for him, he helped me in that I felt permission to feel alienated, and to have that alienation be okay, to make it bearable, noble even. In the way living in Cambodia helped me as a child, I walked the streets of my dark little Scottish city by the sea and knew without doubt that I was living in a story Kafka would have been proud to write.

This time period, however, was also the time I stopped looking in the mirror. I simply didn't want to know. Many times before in my life I have been repelled by the mirror, but the repulsion always took the form of a strange, obsessive attraction. Previously I spent many hours looking in the mirror, trying to see what it was that other people were seeing, a purpose I understand now was laughable, as I went to the mirror with an already clearly fixed, negative idea of what people saw. Once I even remember thinking how awful I looked in a mirror I was quickly passing in a shopping center, seeing perfectly all the flaws I knew were there, when I realized with a shock that I wasn't looking in a mirror, that I was looking through into a store at someone who had the same coat and haircut as me, someone who, when I looked closer, looked perfectly fine.

The one good thing about a tissue expander is that you look so bad with it in that no matter what you look like once it's finally removed, it has to be better. I had my bone graft and my fifth soft tissue graft and yes, even I had to admit I looked better. But I didn't look like me. Something was wrong: Was this the face I had waited through twenty years and almost thirty operations for? I somehow just couldn't make what I saw in the mirror correspond to the person I thought I was. It wasn't just that I felt ugly, I simply could not associate the image as belonging to me. My own image was the image of a stranger, and rather than try to understand this, I simply ignored it. I reverted quickly back to my tissue expander mode of not looking in the mirror, and quickly improved it to include not looking at any image of myself. I perfected the technique of brushing my teeth without a mirror, grew my hair in such a way that it would require only a quick simple brush, and wore clothes that were simply and easily put on, no complex layers or lines that might require even the most minor of visual adjustments.

On one level I understood that the image of my face was merely that, an *35* image, a surface that was not directly related to any true, deep definition of the self. But I also knew that it is only through image that we experience and make decisions about the everyday world, and I was not always able to gather the strength to prefer the deeper world over the shallower one. I looked for ways to relate the two, to find a bridge that would allow me access to both, anything no matter how tenuous, rather than ride out the constant swings between peace and anguish. The only direction I had to go in to achieve this was simply to strive for a state of awareness and self-honesty that sometimes, to this day, rewards me and sometimes exhausts me.

Our whole lives are dominated, though it is not always so clearly translatable, with the question "How do I look?" Take all the many nouns in our lives: car; house; job; family; love; friends; and substitute the personal pronoun — it is not that we are all so self-obsessed, it is that all things eventually relate back to ourselves, and it is our own sense of how we appear to the world by which we chart our lives, how we navigate our personalities that would otherwise be adrift in the ocean of other peoples' obsessions.

One particular afternoon I remember very lucidly, an afternoon, toward the end of my yearlong separation from the mirror. I was talking to someone, an attractive man as it happened, and we were having a wonderful, engaging conversation. For some reason it flickered across my mind to wonder what I looked like to him. What was he seeing when he saw me? So many times I've asked this of myself, and always the answer was a bad one, an ugly one. A warm, smart woman, yes, but still, an unattractive one. I sat there in the café and asked myself this old question and, startlingly, for the first time in my life I had no answer readily prepared. I had literally not looked in a mirror for so long that I quite simply had no clue as to what I looked like. I looked at the man as he spoke; my entire life I had been giving my negative image to people, handing it to them and watching the negative way it was reflected back to me. But now, because I had no idea what I was giving him, the only thing I had to judge by was what he was giving me, which, as reluctant as I was to admit it, was positive.

That afternoon in that café I had a moment of the freedom I had been practicing for behind my Halloween mask as a child. But where as a child I expected it to come as a result of gaining something, a new face, it came to me then as the result of shedding something, of shedding my image. I once thought that truth was an eternal, that once you understood something it was with you forever. I know now that this isn't so, that most truths are inherently unretainable, that we have to work hard all our lives to remember the most basic things. Society is no help; the images it gives us again and again want us only to believe that we can most be ourselves by looking like someone else, leaving our own faces behind to turn into ghosts that will inevitably resent us and haunt us. It is no mistake that in movies and literature the dead sometimes know they are dead only after they can no longer see themselves in the mirror. As I sat there feeling the warmth of the cup against my palm this small observation seemed like a great revelation to me, and I wanted to tell the man I was with about it, but he was involved in his own topic and I did not want to interrupt him, so instead I looked with curiosity over to the window behind him, its night-darkened glass reflecting the whole café, to see if I could recognize myself.

QUESTIONS

Reading

1. What does Grealy learn about herself from her "yearlong separation from the mirror"? In this *reflective* essay, how does Grealy use her personal experience to make her story have greater relevance to others?
2. Why did Grealy think that "fixing" her face would "fix" herself, her soul, her life? What is the significance of the word *fix*?
3. Grealy tells us, "most truths are inherently unretainable," and "we have to work hard all our lives to remember the most basic things" (paragraph 38). What truths does Grealy refer to?

Exploratory Writing

1. Grealy writes about the freedom she feels as a result of accepting the truth about her face. Such freedom, as Grealy shows, is never easily achieved. Reflect on a struggle or conflict in your own life, and write a brief essay on the "truths" that have emerged from your struggle.
2. Grealy writes, "Gradually I became unable to say 'I'm depressed,' but could only say 'I'm ugly,' because the two had become inextricably linked in my mind" (paragraph 27). In small groups, choose a photograph of a

person from a newspaper, Web site, or magazine, and based on that image alone, have each group member write a list of twenty observations about the person. When you are finished, share your lists, and notice whether group members have recorded only physical details or have also included observations about the person's character, lifestyle, or personality.

3. One of the features of this essay is Grealy's command of details. Locate details that you believe are effective, and think about their function. Try to rewrite some of Grealy's sentences to remove the details. What is lost? How do details link the author and the reader?

Making Connections

1. Olivia Judson (p. 220) discusses evolutionary reasons for generous or altruistic behaviors, such as helping a stranger cross the street or offering someone a seat on the subway. In Grealy's reflections on living with a dis-figured face, she notes that insults from strangers (groups of boys and men) caused her great emotional pain (p. 33). Do you think that there is a genetic explanation for the prevalence of street harassment and other bullying behaviors? As an evolutionary biologist, how might Olivia Judson explain why groups of boys and men banded together to tease Grealy and "denigrated [her] sexual worth"?

Essay Writing

1. Grealy concludes, "Society is no help; the images it gives us again and again want us only to believe that we can most be ourselves by looking like someone else" (paragraph 38). What do you think Grealy means by "society"? Do you agree or disagree with her claim? Write an essay arguing your position, using at least four popular images to support your points.

2. Write an essay reflecting on your own relationship with mirrors. If your appearance were to change radically, how might your life change as a result?

Learning to Read and Write

Frederick Douglass

Frederick Augustus Washington Bailey (1817–1895) was born to a slave mother on the Eastern Shore of Maryland; his father was a white man. After his escape from the South in 1838, he adopted the name Douglass and worked both to free other slaves and — after the Civil War — to protect the rights of freed slaves. He was a newspaper editor, a lecturer, the United States minister to Haiti, and the author of several books about his life and times. The Narrative of the Life of Frederick Douglass: An American Slave *(1841), from which the following selection has been taken, is his best-known work.*

I lived in Master Hugh's family about seven years. During this time, I succeeded in learning to read and write. In accomplishing this, I was compelled to resort to various stratagems. I had no regular teacher. My mistress, who had kindly commenced to instruct me, had, in compliance with the advice and direction of her husband, not only ceased to instruct, but had set her face against my being instructed by any one else. It is due, however, to my mistress to say of her, that she did not adopt this course of treatment immediately. She at first lacked the depravity indispensable to shutting me up in mental darkness. It was at least necessary for her to have some training in the exercise of irresponsible power, to make her equal to the task of treating me as though I were a brute.

My mistress was, as I have said, a kind and tender-hearted woman; and in the simplicity of her soul she commenced, when I first went to live with her, to treat me as she supposed one human being ought to treat another. In entering upon the duties of a slaveholder, she did not seem to perceive that I sustained to her the relation of a mere chattel, and that for her to treat me as a human being was not only wrong, but dangerously so. Slavery proved as injurious to her as it did to me. When I went there, she was a pious, warm, and tender-hearted woman. There was no sorrow or suffering for which she had not a tear. She had bread for the hungry, clothes for the naked, and comfort for every mourner that came within her reach. Slavery soon proved its ability to divest her of these heavenly qualities. Under its influence, the tender heart became stone, and the lamblike disposition gave way to one of tiger-like fierceness. The first step in her downward course was in her ceasing to instruct me. She now commenced to practice her husband's precepts. She finally became even more violent in her opposition than her husband himself. She was not satisfied with simply doing as well as he had commanded; she seemed anxious to do better. Nothing seemed to make her more angry than to see me with a newspaper. She seemed to think that here lay the danger. I have had her rush at me with a face made all up of fury, and snatch from me a newspaper, in a manner that fully revealed her apprehension. She was an apt woman; and a little experience soon demonstrated, to her satisfaction, that education and slavery were incompatible with each other.

From this time I was most narrowly watched. If I was in a separate room any considerable length of time, I was sure to be suspected of having a book, and was at once called to give an account of myself. All this, however, was too late. The first step had been taken. Mistress, in teaching me the alphabet, had given me the *inch*, and no precaution could prevent me from taking the *ell*.[1]

The plan which I adopted, and the one by which I was most successful, was that of making friends of all the little white boys whom I met in the street. As many of these as I could, I converted into teachers. With their kindly aid, obtained at different times and in different places, I finally succeeded in learning to read. When I was sent on errands, I always took my book with me, and by doing one part of my errand quickly, I found time to get a lesson before my return. I used also to carry bread with me, enough of which was always in the house, and to which I was always welcome; for I was much better off in this regard than many of the poor white children in our neighborhood. This bread I used to bestow upon the hungry little urchins, who, in return, would give me that more valuable bread of knowledge. I am strongly tempted to give the names of two or three of those little boys, as a testimonial of the gratitude and affection I bear them; but prudence forbids; — not that it would injure me, but it might embarrass them; for it is almost an unpardonable offense to teach slaves to read in this Christian country. It is enough to say of the dear little fellows, that they lived on Philpot Street, very near Durgin and Bailey's ship-yard. I used to talk this matter of slavery over with them. I would sometimes say to them, I wished I could be as free as they would be when they got to be men. "You will be free as soon as you are twenty-one, *but I am a slave for life!* Have not I as good a right to be free as you have?" These words used to trouble them; they would express for me the liveliest sympathy, and console me with the hope that something would occur by which I might be free.

I was now about twelve years old, and the thought of being *a slave for life* began to bear heavily upon my heart. Just about this time, I got hold of a book entitled "The Columbian Orator."[2] Every opportunity I got, I used

5

---

[1] *ell*: A unit of measurement, no longer used, equal to 45 inches. [Eds.]

[2] *The Columbian Orator*: A collection of speeches widely used in early-nineteenth-century schools to teach argument and rhetoric. [Eds.]

to read this book. Among much of other interesting matter, I found in it a dialogue between a master and his slave. The slave was represented as having run away from his master three times. The dialogue represented the conversation which took place between them, when the slave was retaken the third time. In this dialogue, the whole argument in behalf of slavery was brought forward by the master, all of which was disposed of by the slave. The slave was made to say some very smart as well as impressive things in reply to his master — things which had the desired though unexpected effect; for the conversation resulted in the voluntary emancipation of the slave on the part of the master.

In the same book, I met with one of Sheridan's mighty speeches on and in behalf of Catholic emancipation.[3] These were choice documents to me. I read them over and over again with unabated interest. They gave tongue to interesting thoughts of my own soul, which had frequently flashed through my mind, and died away for want of utterance. The moral which I gained from the dialogue was the power of truth over the conscience of even a slaveholder. What I got from Sheridan was a bold denunciation of slavery, and a powerful vindication of human rights. The reading of these documents enabled me to utter my thoughts, and to meet the arguments brought forward to sustain slavery; but while they relieved me of one difficulty, they brought on another even more painful than the one of which I was relieved. The more I read, the more I was led to abhor and detest my enslavers. I could regard them in no other light than a band of successful robbers, who had left their homes, and gone to Africa, and stolen us from our homes, and in a strange land reduced us to slavery. I loathed them as being the meanest as well as the most wicked of men. As I read and contemplated the subject, behold! that very discontentment which Master Hugh had predicted would follow my learning to read had already come, to torment and sting my soul to unutterable anguish. As I writhed under it, I would at times feel that learning to read had been a curse rather than a blessing. It had given me a view of my wretched condition, without the remedy. It opened my eyes to the horrible pit, but to no ladder upon which to get out. In moments of agony, I envied my fellow-slaves for their stupidity. I have often wished myself a beast. I preferred the condition of the meanest reptile to my own. Any thing, no matter what, to get rid of thinking! It was this everlasting thinking of my condition that tormented me. There was no getting rid of it. It was pressed upon me by every object within sight or hearing, animate or inanimate. The silver trump of freedom had roused my soul to eternal wakefulness. Freedom now appeared, to disappear no more forever. It was heard in every sound, and seen in every thing. It was ever present to torment me with a sense of my wretched condition. I saw nothing without seeing it, I heard

---

[3]*Richard Brinsley Sheridan* (1751–1816): A British dramatist, orator, and politician. Roman Catholics were not allowed to vote in England until 1829. [Eds.]

nothing without hearing it, and felt nothing without feeling it. It looked from every star, it smiled in every calm, breathed in every wind, and moved in every storm.

I often found myself regretting my own existence, and wishing myself dead; and but for the hope of being free, I have no doubt but that I should have killed myself, or done something for which I should have been killed. While in this state of mind, I was eager to hear any one speak of slavery. I was a ready listener. Every little while, I could hear something about the abolitionists. It was some time before I found what the word meant. It was always used in such connections as to make it an interesting word to me. If a slave ran away and succeeded in getting clear, or if a slave killed his master, set fire to a barn, or did any thing very wrong in the mind of a slaveholder, it was spoken of as the fruit of *abolition*. Hearing the word in this connection very often, I set about learning what it meant. The dictionary afforded me little or no help. I found it was "the act of abolishing"; but then I did not know what was to be abolished. Here I was perplexed. I did not dare to ask any one about its meaning, for I was satisfied that it was something they wanted me to know very little about. After a patient waiting, I got one of our city papers, containing an account of the number of petitions from the north, praying for the abolition of slavery in the District of Columbia, and of the slave trade between the States. From this time I understood the words *abolition* and *abolitionist*, and always drew near when that word was spoken, expecting to hear something of importance to myself and fellow-slaves. The light broke in upon me by degrees. I went one day down on the wharf of Mr. Waters; and seeing two Irishmen unloading a scow of stone, I went, unasked, and helped them. When we had finished, one of them came to me and asked me if I were a slave. I told him I was. He asked, "Are ye a slave for life?" I told him that I was. The good Irishman seemed to be deeply affected by the statement. He said to the other that it was a pity so fine a little fellow as myself should be a slave for life. He said it was a shame to hold me. They both advised me to run away to the north; that I should find friends there, and that I should be free. I pretended not to be interested in what they said, and treated them as if I did not understand them; for I feared they might be treacherous. White men have been known to encourage slaves to escape, and then, to get the reward, catch them and return them to their masters. I was afraid that these seemingly good men might use me so; but I nevertheless remembered their advice, and from that time I resolved to run away. I looked forward to a time at which it would be safe for me to escape. I was too young to think of doing so immediately; besides, I wished to learn how to write, as I might have occasion to write my own pass. I consoled myself with the hope that I should one day find a good chance. Meanwhile, I would learn to write.

The idea as to how I might learn to write was suggested to me by being in Durgin and Bailey's ship-yard, and frequently seeing the ship carpenters, after hewing, and getting a piece of timber ready for use, write on the timber the name of that part of the ship for which it was intended. When a piece of timber was intended for the larboard side, it would be marked thus — "L." When a piece was for the starboard side, it would be marked thus — "S." A piece for the larboard side forward, would be marked thus — "L. F." When a piece was for starboard side forward, it would be marked thus — "S. F." For larboard aft, it would be marked thus — "L. A." For starboard aft, it would be marked thus — "S. A." I soon learned the names of these letters, and for what they were intended when placed upon a piece of timber in the ship-yard. I immediately commenced copying them, and in a short time was able to make the four letters named. After that, when I met with any boy who I knew could write, I would tell him I could write as well as he. The next word would be, "I don't believe you. Let me see you try it." I would then make the letters which I had been so fortunate as to learn, and ask him to beat that. In this way I got a good many lessons in writing, which it is quite possible I should never have gotten in any other way. During this time, my copy-book was the board fence, brick wall, and pavement; my pen and ink was a lump of chalk. With these, I learned mainly how to write. I then commenced and continued copying the Italics in Webster's Spelling Book, until I could make them all without looking on the book. By this time, my little Master Thomas had gone to school, and learned how to write, and had written over a number of copy-books. These had been brought home, and shown to some of our near neighbors, and then laid aside. My mistress used to go to class meeting at the Wilk Street meetinghouse every Monday afternoon, and leave me to take care of the house. When left thus, I used to spend the time in writing in the spaces left in Master Thomas's copy-book, copying what he had written. I continued to do this until I could write a hand very similar to that of Master Thomas. Thus, after a long, tedious effort for years, I finally succeeded in learning how to write.

QUESTIONS

Reading

1. As its title proclaims, Douglass's book is a narrative, the story of his life. So, too, is this selection a narrative, the story of his learning to read and write. Identify the main events of this story, and list them in chronological order.
2. Douglass is documenting some of the events in his life in this selection, but certain events are not simply reported but described so that we may see, hear, and feel what was experienced by the people who were present. Which events are described most fully in this narrative? How does Douglass seek to engage our interest and direct our feelings through such scenes?

3. In this selection from his memoir and in the entire book, Douglass is engaged in evaluating an institution — slavery — and arguing a case against it. Can you locate the points in the text where reflecting gives way to argumentation? How does Douglass support his argument against slavery? What contributes to his persuasiveness?

Exploratory Writing

1. The situation of Roman Catholics and, by inference, the Irish is a subtheme in this essay. You can trace it by locating every mention of Catholicism and the Irish in the text. How does this theme relate to African American slavery? Locate *The Columbian Orator* in your library, or find out more about Sheridan and why he argued on behalf of "Catholic emancipation" (paragraph 6).

2. Put yourself in the place of Master Hugh's wife, and retell all events in her words and from her point of view. To do so, you will have to decide both what she might have come to know about all these events and how she would feel about them. You will also have to decide when she is writing. Is she keeping a diary during this time (the early 1830s), or is she looking back from the perspective of later years? Has she been moved to write by reading Douglass's own book, which appeared in 1841? If so, how old would she be then, and what would she think about these past events? Would she be angry, bitter, repentant, embarrassed, indulgent, or scornful?

Making Connections

1. Like Douglass, George Orwell ("Politics and the English Language," p. 97) and James Baldwin (p. 109) write about the political implications of language. How do the arguments of these three writers overlap? What ideas do they share? How do they differ?

Essay Writing

1. Borrow Douglass's title, "Learning to Read and Write," and write your own essay, reflecting on your personal history of literacy. When, where, and how did you learn to write? What was the environment like? What challenges did you face? What accomplishments did you experience? If appropriate, discuss the roles that other people played in the process as well as any social or political implications of your experience.

Homecoming, with Turtle

Junot Díaz

Born in the Dominican Republic in 1968, Junot Díaz immigrated to New Jersey with his family at the age of six. His love of reading helped him cope with his father's abandonment of the family, his brother's struggle with leukemia, and his family's resulting poverty. Díaz earned an MFA from Cornell University in 1995. In 1997, he published a collection of short stories entitled Drown. *In his Pulitzer Prize–winning novel* The Brief Wondrous Life of Oscar Wao *(2008), the main character is a science-fiction-loving "ghetto nerd" who mixes Spanish with English, and slang with formal diction. Díaz chronicles Oscar's downward trajectory, weaving his family's personal history with the public history of their home country, the Dominican Republic. The essay that follows appeared in the* New Yorker *magazine in April 2004.*

That summer! Eleven years ago, and I still remember every bit of it. Me and the girlfriend had decided to spend our vacation in Santo Domingo, a big milestone for me, one of the biggest, really: my first time "home" in nearly twenty years. (Blame it on certain "irregularities" in paperwork, blame it on my threadbare finances, blame it on me.) The trip was to accomplish many things. It would end my exile — what Salman Rushdie has famously called one's dreams of glorious return; it would plug me back into that island world, which I'd almost forgotten, closing a circle that had opened with my family's immigration to New Jersey, when I was six years old; and it would improve my Spanish. As in Tom Waits's song "Step Right Up," this trip would be and would fix everything.

Maybe if I hadn't had such high expectations everything would have turned out better. Who knows? What I can say is that the bad luck started early. Two weeks before the departure date, my *novia*[1] found out that I'd cheated on her a couple of months earlier. Apparently, my ex-*sucia*[2] had heard about our planned trip from a mutual friend and decided in a fit of vengeance, jealousy, justice, cruelty, transparency (please pick one) to give us an early bon-voyage gift: an "anonymous" letter to my *novia* that revealed my infidelities in

---

[1]*novia*: Girlfriend (Spanish). [Eds.]
[2]*ex-sucia*: Translates roughly to "my dirty (underhanded) ex" (Spanish). [Eds.]

excruciating detail (where do women get these memories?). I won't describe the *lio*[3] me and the *novia* got into over that letter, or the crusade I had to launch to keep her from dumping me and the trip altogether. In brief, I begged and promised and wheedled, and two weeks later we were touching down on the island of Hispaniola. What do I remember? Holding hands awkwardly while everybody else clapped and the fields outside La Capital burned. How did I feel? All I will say is that if you fused the instant when heartbreak occurs to the instant when one falls in love and shot that concoction straight into your brain stem you might have a sense of what it felt like for me to be back "home."

As for me and the *novia*, our first week wasn't too bad. In one of those weird details that you just couldn't make up, before leaving the States we had volunteered to spend a week in the Dominican Republic helping a group of American dentists who were on a good-will mission. We would be translating for them and handing them elevators and forceps and generally making ourselves useful. Even with the advantage of hindsight, I can't figure out why I thought this was a good way to kick off a homecoming, but that's just how we thought back then. We were young. We had ideals.

Our group of five dentists and five assistants treated roughly fourteen hundred kids from some of the poorest barrios in the city of La Romana (which is, ironically, the sugar capital of the D.R.). We weren't practicing the kind of dentistry that First Worlders with insurance are accustomed to, either; this was no-joke Third World care. No time or materials for fillings. If a tooth had a cavity, it would be numbed and pulled, and that was that. Nothing else we can do, our chief explained. That week, I learned more about bombed-out sixes, elevators, and cowborns than a layperson should ever have to know. Of our group, only me and the *novia* could be said to speak any Spanish. We worked triage, calming the kids, translating for everybody, and still we had it easy, compared with the dentists. These guys were animals; they worked so hard you would have thought they were in a competition, but by the thousandth patient even their hands started to fail. On the last day, our chief, an immensely compassionate Chinese-American with the forearms of a major-league shortstop, was confronted with one extraction he just couldn't finish. He tried everything to coax that kid's stubborn molar out of its socket, and finally he had to call over another dentist, and together they pulled out a long bloody scimitar of a six. During the ordeal the twelve-year-old patient never complained. *¿Te duele?*[4] we asked every couple of minutes, but he would shake his head fiercely, as though the question annoyed him.

Tu eres fuerte,[5] I said, and that might have been the first sentence I had conjugated correctly all week.   5

No, he said, shaking his beautiful head, *no soy.*[6]

---

[3]*lio*: Trouble (Spanish). [Eds.]
[4]*¿Te duele?*: "Does it hurt?" (Spanish). [Eds.]
[5]*Tu eres fuerte*: "You are strong" (Spanish). [Eds.]
[6]*no soy*: "No, I'm not" (Spanish). [Eds.]

Of course, we fought, me and the *novia* — I mean, the needs of the pueblo aside, I had just been bagged fucking some other girl — but it was nothing too outrageous. For one thing, we were too busy wrenching teeth. It wasn't until the mission was over and the dentists had packed their bags and we had headed out into the rest of the island that our real troubles began.

I don't know what I was thinking. Traveling the Third World is challenging enough as it is, but try it with a girlfriend who is only just realizing how badly she's been hurt and a boyfriend who is so worried that he no longer "fits in" at "home" that every little incident and interaction is sifted for rejection, for approval — a boyfriend who is so worried about his busted-up Spanish that he fucks up even more than normal. What I wanted more than anything was to be recognized as the long-lost son I was, but that wasn't going to happen. Not after nearly twenty years. Nobody believed I was Dominican! You? one cab-driver said incredulously, and then turned and laughed. That's doubtful. Instead of being welcomed with open arms, I was overcharged for everything and called *un americano.* I put us on all the wrong buses. If there was money to lose, I lost it; if there was a bus to catch, I made us miss it, and through some twist of bad luck all my relatives were in the States for the summer. The one relative we did manage to locate, a great-aunt, had been feuding with my mom since 1951, when Mami had accidentally broken her only vase, and my arrival signaled a new stage in the age-old conflict: each morning, she blithely served me and the *novia* sandwiches completely covered in fire ants.

Now that we didn't have the dentists to hold us back, we basically went off the deep end. We fought about everything: where to eat, what town we should visit, how to pronounce certain words in Spanish. We fought our way across the country: from La Capital to San Cristóbal to Santiago to Puerto Plata and back. It was miserable. If one of us wasn't storming off down the road with a backpack, the other one was trying to hitch a ride to the airport with strangers. Our craziness culminated one night in a hotel in Puerto Plata when the *novia* woke up and cried out, There's someone in the room! If you've never heard those words being shouted into your dreams, then yours has been a blessed life. I woke in a terrible fright and there he was — the intruder we'd all been waiting for.

It's at a crossroads like this that you really learn something about your-   10
self. There was someone in the room with us, and I could have done any number of things. I could have frozen, I could have screamed for help, I could have fled, but instead I did what my military father had beaten into us during his weekend toughening-up exercises: no matter what the situation, always attack. So I attacked. I threw myself with a roar at the intruder.

It wasn't a person, of course. The intruder was a sea-turtle shell that had been cured and waxed and mounted on the wall. For the sake of national honor, I can say that I acquitted myself well in the battle. I smashed my head clean through the shell, struck the concrete wall, and bounced back to the floor. But instead of staying down I went back at him again, and only then did I realize I was punching décor.

*   *   *

That was the end. A couple of days later, we returned home, defeated, she to New Jersey, me to upstate New York. There was no miracle reconciliation. For a couple of lousy months, the relationship dragged on to its inevitable conclusion, like the heat death of a universe, until finally, having had enough of me, she found herself a new man who she claimed spent more money on her than I did. You're cheap, she asserted, even though I'd used a travel grant and all my savings to pay for our trip. She broke my heart, that girl did, which was a fair trade, considering that I'd broken hers first. But in the end none of it mattered. Even though a dead turtle had kicked my ass, even though my girlfriend had dumped me and a family member had tried to poison me with fire ants, even though I was not granted a glorious return by my homeland, I wasn't entirely crushed. Turned out I wasn't all that easy to crumb; before the year was out, I was back in the D.R., trying again. I kept going back, too. I had committed myself to the *lucha*,[7] much as I had committed myself to that fight with the damned turtle.

These days, I get around Santo Domingo pretty easily (Los Tres Brazos? La Pintura? Katanga? Capotillo? No sweat), and most people will at least concede that I have some Dominican in me. My Spanish has improved to the point where I can hold forth on any subject — animal, vegetable, mineral — with only one major fuckup per sentence. I'm sure if you'd shown me that future during those last days of my trip with the *novia* I would have laughed at you. But even in the midst of the rubble there were signs; even on that last day, at the airport, I was still trying to pick my stupid self off the floor. My head was throbbing from the tortugal beat-down, and my nose felt as if it had only recently been reattached. (When I got home, my roommate blurted out, without so much as a hello, Fool, what the hell happened to you?) I was beat, truly beat, and, just in case I hadn't got the point, there was nothing cold to drink at the airport. But that didn't stop me from engaging in the debates that were going on all around me regarding the recent election and Santo Domingo's eternal President Balaguer — blind, deaf, and dumb but still *jodiendo el pueblo*.[8] A present that the United States gave our country after its last military occupation, in 1965 — God bless them all! Just before our flight was called, I was asked by a group of locals what I thought of Balaguer. I went into fulmination mode, and said he was a murderer, an election thief, an apologist of genocide, and, of course, a U.S. stooge of the Hosni Mubarak variety.

See, the newspaper seller announced triumphantly. Even the gringo knows.

QUESTIONS

Reading

1. Díaz reflects on his hopes for a glorious return to the Dominican Republic, but his homecoming goes awry. Highlight, underline, or flag the anecdotes

---

[7]*lucha*: Struggle (Spanish). [Eds.]
[8]*jodiendo el pueblo*: Screwing the people (Spanish). [Eds.]

he uses to demonstrate his inability to feel at home in his country of birth.

2. Díaz's desire to return to the Dominican Republic to close the circle of his immigrant life and "fix everything" is a serious one. Why does he use a humorous tone to describe this momentous occasion?

3. Notice the places where Díaz refers to heartbreak and love. How does he connect the story of his failing romantic relationship to his homecoming?

Exploratory Writing

1. In the first paragraph of *Homecoming, with Turtle*, Díaz refers to Santo Domingo as "home." He uses quotation marks because, for various reasons, he hasn't visited the city in almost twenty years. With a partner, list words that define what "home" means to you, then compare your results. Is your "home" the same place where you live? Have you ever felt like a stranger at home?

2. "It's at a crossroads like this that you really learn something about yourself," Díaz writes (paragraph 10). Write about a crossroads in your own history. What decisions could you have made? How did the action you chose teach you about yourself?

Making Connections

1. Gloria Anzaldúa (p. 131) observes, "Ethnic identity is twin skin to linguistic identity" (paragraph 27). Amy Tan (p. 142) writes about how she had wrongly believed that her mother's "limited" English reflected the quality of what she had to say. Compare Anzaldúa's and Tan's remarks on language, identity, and culture with Díaz's. How does each author connect identity with language?

2. Both Díaz and George Orwell ("Shooting an Elephant," p. 266) share their reflections about feeling alienated among locals in countries different from where they grew up. What is Díaz's purpose in sharing these reflections? How is it different from Orwell's?

Essay Writing

1. Díaz's outsider status doesn't stop him from engaging in the local debates about Joaquín Balaguer, the Dominican Republic's president in 1994. Yet the locals call *Díaz* a "gringo." Using articles archived on the Internet, compare the coverage of a recent national election or another major news event told from an *insider* and an *outsider* perspective. Write an essay defining these terms, using specific content from each article to exemplify what you're describing.

The Long Good-bye
Mother's Day in Federal Prison

Amanda Coyne

Amanda Coyne (b. 1966) was born in Colorado and subsequently migrated with her family to Alaska and ten other states as her father's "relentless pursuit of better employment" led him to hold such titles as fry cook, janitor, librarian, college professor, magazine editor, and presidential speechwriter. Coyne describes her own life as having thus far been "similarly kinetic and varied." Between traveling and "experimenting with religion, countercultural lifestyles, and writing," she has been employed as a waitress, nursing home assistant, teacher, public relations associate, and public policy analyst. A graduate of the University of Iowa, Coyne is currently a staff writer with the Anchorage Press in Alaska. Her work has been published in the New York Times Magazine, Harper's, Bust *magazine, and* Jane *magazine, and she has read her pieces on National Public Radio's* All Things Considered *and Public Radio International's* This American Life. *The following essay, which appeared in* Harper's *(May 1997), was her first publication.*

You can spot the convict-moms here in the visiting room by the way they hold and touch their children and by the single flower that is perched in front of them — a rose, a tulip, a daffodil. Many of these mothers have untied the bow that attaches the flower to its silver-and-red cellophane wrapper and are using one of the many empty soda cans at hand as a vase. They sit proudly before their flower-in-a-Coke-can, amid Hershey bar wrappers, half-eaten Ding Dongs, and empty paper coffee cups. Occasionally, a mother will pick up her present and bring it to her nose when one of the bearers of the single flower — her child — asks if she likes it. And the mother will respond the way that mothers always have and always will respond when presented with a gift on this day. "Oh, I just love it. It's perfect. I'll put it in the middle of my Bible." Or, "I'll put it on my desk, right next to your school picture." And always: "It's the best one here."

But most of what is being smelled today is the children themselves. While the other adults are plunking coins into the vending machines, the mothers take deep whiffs from the backs of their children's necks, or kiss and smell the backs of their knees, or take off their shoes and tickle their feet

Jennifer, prisoner number 07235-029.

and then pull them close to their noses. They hold them tight and take in their own second scent — the scent assuring them that these are still their children and that they still belong to them.

The visitors are allowed to bring in pockets full of coins, and today that Mother's Day flower, and I know from previous visits to my older sister here at the Federal Prison Camp for women in Pekin, Illinois, that there is always an aberrant urge to gather immediately around the vending machines. The sandwiches are stale, the coffee weak, the candy bars the ones we always pass up in a convenience store. But after we hand the children over to their mothers, we gravitate toward those machines. Like milling in the kitchen at a party. We all do it, and nobody knows why. Polite conversation ensues around the microwave while the popcorn is popping and the processed-chicken sandwiches are being heated. We ask one another where we are from, how long a drive we had. An occasional whistle through the teeth, a shake of the head. "My, my, long way from home, huh?" "Staying at the Super 8 right up the road. Not a bad place." "Stayed at the Econo Lodge last time. Wasn't a good place at all." Never asking the questions we really want to ask: "What's she in for?" "How much time's she got left?" You never ask in the waiting room of a doctor's office either. Eventually, all of us — fathers, mothers, sisters, brothers, a few boyfriends, and very few husbands — return to the queen of the day, sitting at a fold-out table loaded with snacks, prepared for five or so hours of attempted normal conversation.

Most of the inmates are elaborately dressed, many in prison-crafted dresses and sweaters in bright blues and pinks. They wear meticulously applied makeup in corresponding hues, and their hair is replete with loops and curls — hair that only women with the time have the time for. Some of the better seamstresses have crocheted vests and purses to match their outfits. Although the world outside would never accuse these women of making haute-couture fashion statements, the fathers and the sons and the boyfriends and the very few husbands think they look beautiful, and they tell them so repeatedly. And I can imagine the hours spent preparing for this visit — hours of needles and hooks clicking over brightly colored yards of yarn. The hours of discussing, dissecting, and bragging about these visitors — especially the men. Hours spent in the other world behind the door where we're not allowed, sharing lipsticks and mascaras, and unraveling the occasional hair-tangled hot roller, and the brushing out and lifting and teasing . . . and the giggles that abruptly change into tears without warning — things that define any female-only world. Even, or especially, if that world is a female federal prison camp.

While my sister Jennifer is with her son in the playroom, an inmate's mother comes over to introduce herself to my younger sister, Charity, my brother, John, and me. She tells us about visiting her daughter in a higher-security prison before she was transferred here. The woman looks old and tired, and her shoulders sag under the weight of her recently acquired bitterness.   5

"Pit of fire," she says, shaking her head. "Like a pit of fire straight from hell. Never seen anything like it. Like something out of an old movie about prisons." Her voice is getting louder and she looks at each of us with pleading eyes. "My *daughter* was there. Don't even get me started on that place. Women die there."

John and Charity and I silently exchange glances.

"My daughter would come to the visiting room with a black eye and I'd think, 'All she did was sit in the car while her boyfriend ran into the house.' She didn't even touch the stuff. Never even handled it."

She continues to stare at us, each in turn. "Ten years. That boyfriend talked and he got three years. She didn't know anything. Had nothing to tell them. They gave her ten years. They called it conspiracy. Conspiracy? Aren't there real criminals out there?" She asks this with hands outstretched, waiting for an answer that none of us can give her.

The woman's daughter, the conspirator, is chasing her son through the maze of chairs and tables and through the other children. She's a twenty-four-year-old blonde, whom I'll call Stephanie, with Dorothy Hamill[1] hair and matching dimples. She looks like any girl you might see in any shopping mall in middle America. She catches her chocolate-brown son and tickles him, and they laugh and trip and fall together onto the floor and laugh harder.   10

---

[1]*Dorothy Hamill*: The 1976 Olympic gold medal–winning figure skater whose "wedge" haircut became wildly popular in the United States. [Eds.]

Had it not been for that wait in the car, this scene would be taking place at home, in a duplex Stephanie would rent while trying to finish her two-year degree in dental hygiene or respiratory therapy at the local community college. The duplex would be spotless, with a blown-up picture of her and her son over the couch and ceramic unicorns and horses occupying the shelves of the entertainment center. She would make sure that her son went to school every day with stylishly floppy pants, scrubbed teeth, and a good breakfast in his belly. Because of their difference in skin color, there would be occasional tension — caused by the strange looks from strangers, teachers, other mothers, and the bullies on the playground, who would chant after they knocked him down, "Your Momma's white, your Momma's white." But if she were home, their weekends and evenings would be spent together transcending those looks and healing those bruises. Now, however, their time is spent eating visiting-room junk food and his school days are spent fighting the boys in the playground who chant, "Your Momma's in prison, your Momma's in prison."

He will be ten when his mother is released, the same age my nephew will be when his mother is let out. But Jennifer, my sister, was able to spend the first five years of Toby's life with him. Stephanie had Ellie after she was incarcerated. They let her hold him for eighteen hours, then sent her back to prison. She has done the "tour," and her son is a well-traveled six-year-old. He has spent weekends visiting his mother in prisons in Kentucky, Texas, Connecticut (the Pit of Fire), and now at last here, the camp — minimum security, Pekin, Illinois.

Ellie looks older than his age. But his shoulders do not droop like his grandmother's. On the contrary, his bitterness lifts them and his chin higher than a child's should be, and the childlike, wide-eyed curiosity has been replaced by defiance. You can see his emerging hostility as he and his mother play together. She tells him to pick up the toy that he threw, say, or to put the deck of cards away. His face turns sullen, but she persists. She takes him by the shoulders and looks him in the eye, and he uses one of his hands to swat at her. She grabs the hand and he swats with the other. Eventually, she pulls him toward her and smells the top of his head, and she picks up the cards or the toy herself. After all, it is Mother's Day and she sees him so rarely. But her acquiescence makes him angrier, and he stalks out of the playroom with his shoulders thrown back.

Toby, my brother and sister and I assure one another, will not have these resentments. He is better taken care of than most. He is living with relatives in Wisconsin. Good, solid, middle-class, churchgoing relatives. And when he visits us, his aunts and his uncle, we take him out for adventures where we walk down the alley of a city and pretend that we are being chased by the "bad guys." We buy him fast food, and his uncle, John, keeps him up well past his bedtime enthralling him with stories of the monkeys he met in India. A perfect mix, we try to convince one another. Until we take him to see his mother and on the drive back he asks the question that most confuses him, and no doubt all the other children who spend much of their lives in prison visiting rooms: "Is my Mommy a bad guy?" It is the question that most seriously disorders his five-year-old need to clearly separate right from wrong. And because our own need is perhaps just as great, it is the question that haunts us as well.

Now, however, the answer is relatively simple. In a few years, it won't be. In a few years we will have to explain mandatory minimums, and the war on drugs, and the murky conspiracy laws, and the enormous amount of money and time that federal agents pump into imprisoning low-level drug dealers and those who happen to be their friends and their lovers. In a few years he might have the reasoning skills to ask why so many armed robbers and rapists and child-molesters and, indeed, murderers are punished less severely than his mother. When he is older, we will somehow have to explain to him the difference between federal crimes, which don't allow for parole, and state crimes, which do. We will have to explain that his mother was taken from him for five years not because she was a drug dealer but because she made four phone calls for someone she loved.

But we also know it is vitally important that we explain all this without betraying our bitterness. We understand the danger of abstract anger, of being disillusioned with your country, and, most of all, we do not want him to inherit that legacy. We would still like him to be raised as we were, with the idea that we live in the best country in the world with the best legal system in the world — a legal system carefully designed to be immune to political mood swings and public hysteria; a system that promises to fit the punishment to the crime. We want him to be a good citizen. We want him to have absolute faith that he lives in a fair country, a country that watches over and protects its most vulnerable citizens: its women and children.

So for now we simply say, "Toby, your mother isn't bad, she just did a bad thing. Like when you put rocks in the lawn mower's gas tank. You weren't bad then, you just did a bad thing."

Once, after being given this weak explanation, he said, "I wish I could have done something really bad, like my Mommy. So I could go to prison too and be with her."

We notice a circle forming on one side of the visiting room. A little boy stands in its center. He is perhaps nine years old, sporting a burnt-orange three-piece suit and pompadour hair. He stands with his legs slightly apart, eyes half-shut, and sways back and forth, flashing his cuffs and snapping his fingers while singing:

> . . . *Doesn't like crap games with barons and earls.*
> *Won't go to Harlem in ermine and pearls.*
> *Won't dish the dirt with the rest of the girls.*
> *That's why the lady is a tramp.*

He has a beautiful voice and it sounds vaguely familiar. One of the   20
visitors informs me excitedly that the boy is the youngest Frank Sinatra
impersonator and that he has been on television even. The boy finishes his
performance and the room breaks into applause. He takes a sweeping bow,
claps his miniature hands together, and points both little index fingers at
the audience. "More. Later. Folks." He spins on his heels and returns to the
table where his mother awaits him, proudly glowing. "Don't mess with the
hair, Mom," we overhear. "That little boy's slick," my brother says with
true admiration.

Sitting a few tables down from the youngest Frank Sinatra is a table of
Mexican-Americans. The young ones are in white dresses or button-down
oxfords with matching ties. They form a strange formal contrast to the rest
of the rowdy group. They sit silently, solemnly listening to the white-haired
woman, who holds one of the table's two roses. I walk past and listen to the
grandmother lecture her family. She speaks of values, of getting up early
every day, of going to work. She looks at one of the young boys and points
a finger at him. "School is the most important thing. *Nada más importante.*[2]
You get up and you go to school and you study, and you can make lots of
money. You can be big. You can be huge. Study, study, study."

The young boy nods his head. "Yes, *abuelita.*[3] Yes, *abuelita*," he says.

The owner of the other flower is holding one of the group's three
infants. She has him spread before her. She coos and kisses his toes and
nuzzles his stomach.

When I ask Jennifer about them, she tells me that it is a "mother and
daughter combo." There are a few of them here, these combos, and I notice
that they have the largest number of visitors and that the older inmate,
the grandmother, inevitably sits at the head of the table. Even here, it seems,
the hierarchical family structure remains intact. One could take a picture,
replace the fast-food wrappers with chicken and potatoes, and these families could be at any restaurant in the country, could be sitting at any dining
room table, paying homage on this day to the one who brought them into
the world.

Back at our table, a black-haired, Middle Eastern woman dressed in   25
loose cottons and cloth shoes is whispering to my brother with a sense of
urgency that makes me look toward my sister Charity with questioning eyes
and a tilt of my head. Charity simply shrugs and resumes her conversation
with a nineteen-year-old ex–New York University student — another conspirator. Eight years.

Prison, it seems, has done little to squelch the teenager's rebellious
nature. She has recently been released from solitary confinement. She wears
new retro-bellbottom jeans and black shoes with big clunky heels. Her hair

---

[2]*Nada más importante*: Nothing more important (Spanish). [Eds.]
[3]*abuelita*: Grandma (Spanish). [Eds.]

is short, clipped perfectly ragged and dyed white — all except the roots, which are a stylish black. She has beautiful pale skin and beautiful red lips. She looks like any midwestern coed trying to escape her origins by claiming New York's East Village as home. She steals the bleach from the laundry room, I learn later, in order to maintain that fashionable white hue. But stealing the bleach is not what landed her in the hole. She committed the inexcusable act of defacing federal property. She took one of her government-issue T-shirts and wrote in permanent black magic marker, "I have been in your system. I have examined your system." And when she turned around it read, "I find it very much in need of repair."

But Charity has more important things to discuss with the girl than rebelling against the system. They are talking fashion. They talk prints versus plains, spring shoes, and spring dresses. Charity informs the girl that sling-back, high-heeled sandals and pastels are all the rage. She makes a disgusted face and says, "Damn! Pinks and blues wash me out. I hate pastels. I don't *have* any pastels."

This fashion blip seems to be putting the girl into a deep depression. And so Charity, attempting to lighten up the conversation, puts her nose toward the girl's neck.

"New Armani scent, Gio," my sister announces.

The girl perks up. She nods her head. She calls one of the other inmates over. 30

Charity performs the same ritual: "Coco Chanel." And again: "Paris, Yves St. Laurent."

The line gets longer, and the girls talk excitedly to one another. It seems that Charity's uncanny talent for divining brand-name perfumes is perhaps nowhere on earth more appreciated than here with these sensory-starved inmates.

As Charity continues to smell necks and call out names, I turn back to my brother and find that the woman who was speaking to him so intensely has gone. He stares pensively at the concrete wall ahead of him.

"What did she want?" I ask.

"She heard I was a sculptor. She wants me to make a bust, presented in her name, for Qaddafi." 35

"A bust of what?"

"Of Qaddafi. She's from Libya. She was a freedom fighter. Her kids are farmed out to strangers here — foster homes. It's Qaddafi's twenty-eighth anniversary as dictator in September. She knows him. He's mad at her now, but she thinks that he'll get over it and get her kids back to Libya if she gives him a present."

"Obsession. Calvin Klein," I hear my sister pronounce. The girls cheer in unison.

I get up and search for the girl. I want to ask her about her crime. I look in the book room only to find the four-foot Frank Sinatra crooning "Somewhere over the Rainbow" to a group of spellbound children.

I ask Ponytail, one of the female guards, where the woman went.   40
"Rule," she informs me. "Cannot be in the visiting room if no visitor is present. Should not have been here. Had to go back to unit one." I have spoken
to Ponytail a few times while visiting my sister and have yet to hear her use
a possessive pronoun, a contraction, or a conjunction.

According to Jennifer, Ponytail has wanted to be a prison guard since
she was a little girl. She is one of the few female guards here and she has
been here the longest, mainly because the male guards are continuously
being fired for "indiscretions" with the inmates. But Ponytail doesn't mess
around. She is also the toughest guard here, particularly in regard to the federal rules governing exposed skin. She is disgusted by any portion of the leg
showing above the required eight-inch shorts length. In summer, they say,
she is constantly whipping out her measuring tape and writing up those who
are even a fraction of an inch off.

Last summer posed a particular problem for Ponytail, though. It seems
that the shorts sold in the commissary were only seven inches from crotch to
seam. And because they were commissary-issued, Ponytail couldn't censor
them. So, of course, all the women put away their own shorts in favor of the
commissary's. This disturbed Ponytail — a condition that eventually,
according to one of the girls, developed into a low-grade depression. "She
walked around with that sad old tape in her hands all summer, throwing it
from one hand to the other and looking at our legs. After a while, not one
of us could get her even to crack a smile — not that she's a big smiler, but
you can get those corners to turn sometimes. Then she started looking
downright sad, you know real depressed like."

Ponytail makes sure that the girls get proper medical care. Also none of
the male guards will mess with them when she's around. But even if those
things weren't true, the girls would be fond of Ponytail. She is in a way just
another woman in the system, and perhaps no other group of women realizes
the absolute necessity for female solidarity. These inmates know with
absolute certainty what women on the outside only suspect — that men still
hold ultimate power over their bodies, their property, and their freedom.

So as a token of this solidarity, they all agreed to slip off their federal
shorts and put on their own. Ponytail perked up, the measuring tape
appeared again with a vengeance, and quite a few of the shorts owners spent
much of their free time that summer cleaning out toilet bowls and wiping
the scuffs off the gym floor.

It's now 3:00. Visiting ends at 3:30. The kids are getting cranky, and the   45
adults are both exhausted and wired from too many hours of conversation,
too much coffee and candy. The fathers, mothers, sisters, brothers, and the
few boyfriends, and the very few husbands are beginning to show signs of
gathering the trash. The mothers of the infants are giving their heads one
last whiff before tucking them and their paraphernalia into their respective
carrying cases. The visitors meander toward the door, leaving the older

children with their mothers for one last word. But the mothers never say what they want to say to their children. They say things like, "Do well in school," "Be nice to your sister," "Be good for Aunt Betty, or Grandma." They don't say, "I'm sorry I'm sorry I'm sorry. I love you more than anything else in the world and I think about you every minute and I worry about you with a pain that shoots straight to my heart, a pain so great I think I will just burst when I think of you alone, without me. I'm sorry."

We are standing in front of the double glass doors that lead to the outside world. My older sister holds her son, rocking him gently. They are both crying. We give her a look and she puts him down. Charity and I grasp each of his small hands, and the four of us walk through the doors. As we're walking out, my brother sings one of his banana songs to Toby.

"Take me out to the —" and Toby yells out, "Banana store!"

"Buy me some —"

"Bananas!!"

"I don't care if I ever come back. For it's root, root, root for the —"   50

"Monkey team!"

I turn back and see a line of women standing behind the glass wall. Some of them are crying, but many simply stare with dazed eyes. Stephanie is holding both of her son's hands in hers and speaking urgently to him. He is struggling, and his head is twisting violently back and forth. He frees one of his hands from her grasp, balls up his fist, and punches her in the face. Then he walks with purpose through the glass doors and out the exit. I look back at her. She is still in a crouched position. She stares, unblinking, through those doors. Her hands have left her face and are hanging on either side of her. I look away, but before I do, I see drops of blood drip from her nose, down her chin, and onto the shiny marble floor.

QUESTIONS

Reading

1. How would you describe Coyne's point of view in this piece? Detached or involved? Insider or outsider? How does her point of view affect your perception of the federal prison for women that she writes about in this piece?
2. In this *report*, why do you think that Coyne focuses on Mother's Day in the prison? What kinds of details is she able to report that might not be observable on most other days? What kinds of details are likely to be missing (or obscured) on such a day as this?
3. Coyne has come to visit her sister Jennifer, but why do you suppose she tells so little about Jennifer compared to what she reports about the other prisoners, particularly Stephanie and the nineteen-year-old former New York University student? Why do you suppose that Coyne tells so

much about Stephanie's child, Ellie, and the young Frank Sinatra impersonator but so little about Jennifer's child, Toby?
4. Given the selection and arrangement of descriptive details about the people who figure in this account, what do you consider to be Coyne's major
purposes in writing this piece?

Exploratory Writing

1. Collaborating in small groups, research or investigate a prison in your
community. Write a report highlighting the details that you think are
most important in revealing the quality of life in that prison.
2. Reflect on a time when one of your own friends or relatives got into trouble, suffered a tragedy, or made a life-changing mistake. How did his or
her story affect you?
3. Imagine that you have been appointed to a public office that has the task
of reforming women's prisons like the one described in "The Long
Good-bye." As a class, brainstorm about what changes you would make
to the system, and why. In considering this subject, you can also refer to
the information Christina Boufis (p. 67) provides in her essay on teaching literature in a county jail.

Making Connections

1. Coyne observes that women in the prison system realize the need for
female solidarity: "These inmates know with absolute certainty what
women on the outside only suspect — that men still hold ultimate power
over their bodies, their property, and their freedom" (paragraph 43).
Compare this view of male power to that of Lucy Grealy (p. 33), who
notes that one of the things that caused her the most pain about having a
disfigured face was being harassed on the street. Discuss the different ways
that Coyne and Grealy talk about female experiences of powerlessness.

Essay Writing

1. Compare Coyne's piece on women's prisons and female prisoners to
one or two other stories that you find on this subject in newspapers, in
magazines, or on the Internet.

Teaching Literature at the County Jail

Christina Boufis

*Christina Boufis (b. 1961) grew up on Long Island and is a gradu-
ate of Barnard College. She received an MA in English language
and literature from the University of Virginia and a PhD in literature and a certificate in women's studies from the Graduate Center
of the City University of New York. She currently teaches nonfiction writing at Stanford and the San Francisco Art Institute. She
has also taught writing at the University of California at Berkeley
and the San Francisco County Jail. Her work has appeared in many
popular magazines and academic journals, and her article "A
Teacher behind Bars," which first appeared in* Glamour *magazine,
was nominated for the Heart of America, a national journalism
award. She has said that the following essay "was written out of
necessity: teaching at the jail was so overwhelming at first that I
absolutely had to write about it to get some distance from my
students' painful experiences and be able to go back the next day."
This essay first appeared in the* Common Review *(Fall 2001).*

There is no money for books, so I am photocopying Toni Morrison's
Sula[1] chapter by chapter. This is in defiance of all copyright laws, but I think
if she knew, Morrison would understand. Sometimes I even imagine her
walking into our classroom, and I wonder how she would react to what she
saw: twenty-five women dressed in fluorescent orange, reading her works out
loud. It's been almost four years since I began teaching at the San Francisco
County Jail, and I barely notice the bright orange uniforms anymore, or that
my class is far from the traditional university setting in which I once imagined myself. Instead, I see only the women and their individual faces.

I arrived in San Francisco in 1994, as a new county jail was being built.
That year also marked a turning point in California's history: it was the first
time the state's corrections budget exceeded that of the entire University of
California system. I didn't know this then; I knew only that I wanted to live
and work in the city of my choice rather than follow the vagaries of a bleak

---

[1]*Toni Morrison* (b. 1931): The winner of the 1993 Nobel Prize for literature.
Sula (1973) is one of her novels. [Eds.]

academic job market. When I heard that a substitute teaching position in high-school equivalency was available at the jail, I didn't hesitate. Although I knew next to nothing about the subject, I had spent the last several years in graduate school reading about women in literature. I was eager to work with real ones.

Other than telling me that many women inmates have difficulty reading (most are at a fourth- to seventh-grade reading level, I later discovered) and that I should perhaps start with simple math exercises, my predecessor prepared me for little. He was in a great hurry, offered the class for as long as I would have it, and took off for Tahoe[2] without waiting for my answer. Obviously, he'd had enough.

But he gave me a parting gift: a copy of Alice Walker's *The Color Purple*,[3] stored in the top drawer of the classroom filing cabinet. "Sometimes, at the end of class, if they're quiet, I read it out loud to them," he explained. Though the class was held at San Francisco's newest county jail (nicknamed the "glamour slammer" for its seemingly posh facility), the building's school-like appearance belied the fact that the Sheriff's Department spent not a single cent on any of the educational or rehabilitative programs that went on inside. Thus there was no money for more copies of Walker's novel or anyone else's. The class I was teaching was funded by the local community college, which provided only GED[4] books.

I forgot all about *The Color Purple* my first harried, difficult day at the   5
jail. My shock at seeing the women, who appeared as a blur of orange, turned to alienation, then anger, as the class wore on. "Man, we're going to eat you alive," one woman repeatedly uttered. Others told me they didn't have to do any work and weren't going to. A few more crumpled up the math exercises I'd photocopied and told me they didn't know their multiplication tables.

But toward the end of class, one woman seemed to take pity on me and asked for "the book."

"What book?" I replied a little too eagerly.

"The book, the book," others chimed in as if it were obvious.

Another student pointed to the filing cabinet, and I remembered Walker's novel. There was some disagreement about where the previous instructor had left off, but the last ten minutes of class were spent in relative silence as I read and they listened. I wasn't happy with this as a pedagogical strategy — I'd much rather the students read for themselves — but I was thankful that it worked. The women nodded sympathetically to Celie's painful story and thanked me when they left for the day.

*   *   *

---

[2]*Tahoe*: Lake Tahoe, the largest alpine lake in North America. It is surrounded by the Sierra Nevadas on the California-Nevada border. [Eds.]

[3]*Alice Walker* (b. 1944): The best-selling writer of the Pulitzer Prize–winning novel *The Color Purple* (1982). [Eds.]

[4]*GED*: General equivalency diploma. [Eds.]

"Miss B, Miss B," calls Tanya, a woman who looks and acts much   10
younger than her nineteen years. It has been several months since the other
instructor was let go and I was hired; my nickname is a sign of acceptance.

Tanya sits up front—the better to get my attention—and soon her
pleas take on added urgency. "I need a pencil. I need some more paper."
When she finishes with one demand, she moves on to the next. When she
gets bored, which happens fairly quickly, she calls repeatedly for *Sula* as if
she were a great personal friend. "Where's *Sula*? When do we get to *Sula*?"

I have kept up the practice that my predecessor initiated, spending the
last half hour of class reading novels or plays aloud, but with a difference:
the students do the reading. The women have come to depend on this promise. The strategy also helps with continuity in what I found to be an almost
impossible teaching situation. Turnover is extremely high at county jails and
likewise in my classroom. I can have from six to sixteen new students a day
and I never know how long any of them will stay. Most serve sentences of
less than a year, yet jail is a liminal time during which many wait indetermi-
nately to be sentenced on to prison or parole. Release dates can come and
go mysteriously without the promised freedom and no explanation for the
delay. Life is thus more volatile in county jails than in prisons and the future
more uncertain. Not surprisingly, jails are one of the least studied and understood institutions in the criminal justice system.

Such unsettledness can make anyone edgy, if not downright crazy. Although Tanya has difficulty keeping up with the novel, it doesn't seem to
matter. What is important to her is the routine we have established in class,
my assurance that we will read the work each day. From what I know of my
students' backgrounds, even this modicum of stability was often missing
from their lives. Many were homeless before incarceration; few had support
from parents, friends, or partners. For Tanya and some of the others, *Sula*
has become a talisman of security, something they can rely on in a constantly shifting world.

Tanya has difficulty understanding some of the language and following
the plot, but many of the other women do not. They are quick to spot the
fact that when Sula's brother, Plum, returns from the war he is a drug addict,
though Morrison never states this directly. They can tell by several clues:
Plum's weight loss and antisocial behavior, his sugary diet, and the "bent
spoon black from steady cooking" found in his bedroom.

The following semester, I teach this same novel in my college writing   15
seminar at the University of California, Berkeley. My Berkeley students
don't pick up on the drug connection. Most of them think that Plum uses
the spoon to cook soup in his room, and they look at me with disbelief when
I tell them otherwise.

My jail students seem able to spot danger everywhere, practically in the
way an author uses a semicolon. Reading an O. Henry short story, they immediately inferred that one character was a prostitute, just from the author's
description of an abandoned shoe. And if my Berkeley students are frustrated

with Morrison for not providing explanations (for Sula's mother's missing leg, or Sula's role in a murder), the women at the jail shrug off such ambiguities. They assume that a character can do an evil act, such as not rescuing someone from drowning, and not be evil herself. My Berkeley students want to know what I think the work ultimately means, and they are frustrated with Morrison for being evasive. My jail students seem to rest more easily in uncertainty, knowing that life itself does not provide answers.

I can sympathize with both sets of student reactions (I clearly remember being an undergraduate eager to understand the depths of literature), yet the more I discover about my students at the jail, both individually and statistically, the more I appreciate their acute and emotionally sensitive readings. Studies vary, but several show that as many as 90 percent of incarcerated women have been sexually, emotionally, or physically abused. Like their imprisoned sisters elsewhere, most of my students are mothers, women of color, and the sole supporters of young children. They are also most likely in jail on drug charges, primarily for possessing minor amounts of crack cocaine. Before the 1980s "war on drugs" legislation mandated jail time for possessing crack cocaine — but none for possessing the same amount of its more expensive cousin, powder cocaine (a drug used predominantly by whites) — these women would have had rehabilitation or community-based programs as options. Not anymore.

The longer I worked at the jail, the more my curiosity was piqued by what I learned and the more I wanted to help. Years of reading Victorian novels had left me with a strong sense of social reform; I believed I could make a difference teaching at the jail, more so than at other places. And I still believe this despite the fact that I have seen hundreds of women get released from jail and come back again — often the same ones, and often more times than I can count.

Tanya is released before we finish reading *Sula*, and I promise to send the remaining chapters to the address she's given. She tells me that when she gets out, she is going to get her son back, get a job, and turn her life around. I am surprised when she mentions her baby; she looks so much like a child and in need of mothering herself.

We finish Morrison's novel, but it is anticlimactic. No one seems particularly interested in discussing the themes, nor is anyone as thrilled as I hoped they'd be when I announce that our next novel will be Zora Neale Hurston's *Their Eyes Were Watching God*.[5] The class seems subdued and sad. Perhaps this is due to Tanya's absence: although so many students come and go, Tanya has been a steady presence, and her noisy but good-natured complaints have punctuated our days.

20

---

[5]*Zora Neale Hurston* (1891–1960): A writer and folklorist. *Their Eyes Were Watching God* (1937) is her most popular novel. [Eds.]

I try to get one new student to do some work. She is much older, perhaps around fifty-five, and near toothless. "My mind is on burying my son, not on this schoolwork," she tells me, shaking her head. "It ain't right that they should put me in here when I ain't been in a classroom for thirty years. And I just buried my son. It don't make no sense."

I don't know what to say. Educational programs are mandatory at this jail, but the policy makes little sense to me, too, at times.

The next day, the women are livelier, and we begin reading *Their Eyes*. They quickly pick up on the dialect, something I feared would be prohibitive. "That's country," says one woman. Instead of finding Hurston's phonetic spellings a hindrance to understanding, the women seem to relish sounding out the dialogue and laugh when they trip over words. One fairly new student, a white woman whose face is pockmarked with what looks like deep cigarette burns, stands up to give Hurston's novel a try. The other students are encouraging, telling her to go on when she stumbles, and even yelling at me when I correct a mispronunciation. "Let her do it, Miss B! She's getting it."

As the novel continues, the women become hooked on the story and wonder what will happen next. They recognize Joe Starks for the smooth talker he is and think that the main character, Janie, should have stayed with her first husband, Logan, instead of running off with the slick Joe. "Logan wasn't so bad," says one student who has been in and out of jail several times — this despite the fact that Logan had wanted to buy Janie a mule to plow the field, and the protagonist remarks that she cannot love her first husband. "Besides, he was trying to teach her an important lesson — how to work."

When we get to the part where Janie meets her true love, Tea Cake, who takes her to a new world in the Florida Everglades, my students are quick to note that "he turned her out." I ask about the phrase and am told that it means to be introduced to new people and places, a whole new way of life.

"Is it a bad thing?"

"It doesn't have to be," one woman explains, "but it usually is. You're turned on to the life." That is, a life of drug use or prostitution.

I ask them to write essays about this, and I get back many that explain how they were turned out to drugs: on first dates, with boyfriends, cousins, even mothers.

When we get to the same scene in my Berkeley class, I say something about Tea Cake turning Janie out. My Cal students stare at me as if I've said something incredibly dumb. Some of them have heard the term before, but it doesn't resonate with meaning. We move on.

Tanya, I have heard, is back in jail. Out for less than a week before getting rearrested, she likely did not get the photocopies I sent her. She was apparently caught selling drugs to an undercover cop on the same street corner where she was arrested before. I ask the program's administrator about the rumor I heard, and she confirms it. Tanya said she needed money for clothes and that's why she was selling. "It didn't occur to her to get a job," the administrator states.

Yet, knowing her educational level, I wonder how easy it would have been for her to get one.

When Tanya comes back into class, she hugs me and asks me not to be mad at her. I'm not and I tell her so. I am always happy to see my former students again, even in jail; at least I know that they are alive and safe. But the rest of the class is unruly. It's a Monday, the day after visiting hours when the women are allowed a two-hour personal contact with their children. The aftermath of these visits is a palpable feeling of malaise. The women often can't concentrate, nor do they feel like doing anything but talking and complaining.

There are four new students, one of whom tells me she is going to prison in a few days and won't bother doing anything. "That crack took away my brain," says another. One young woman who always sits sullenly in the back spits out, "Why don't you take a day off? All the other classes are canceled today. How come ours isn't?"

I'm frustrated and tired of coercing them to work. So I pull out a passage from *Their Eyes*, where Janie talks about feeling like a rut in a road, beaten down, with the life all beneath the surface, and I tell them to respond in writing.

After much cajoling, they begin to write. One woman details the years she spent with a husband who, like Janie's Joe, always put her down. A new student calls me over and tells me she felt trampled this way when she was homeless. "I need more than one sheet of paper to tell this," she states. I agree.

My best student, Linnea, writes quickly, then hands me her essay to read.   35
"I felt I was in a rut when I found myself homeless, hooked on drugs and losing some of my hope," she writes. "I found myself doing things (sexually) that I never thought I would do for drugs. I would have sex in an alleyway, the back seat of an abandoned vehicle, and even out in the open park in front of crowds of people. I would eat out of trash cans. I would go days without bathing, or changing my clothes. . . . I would even try to sell drugs on a very, very small scale. I felt my life was becoming meaningless. . . . I now have a chance to regain my life by being here."

As painful as these stories often are, the women always want to share them by reading them out loud. They clap after each one and make supportive comments. "All you need now is Jesus," or "You're gonna make it, girl. I know it." I correct their punctuation ("Oh yeah, I forget how to use periods," says one student) but am often at a loss for words on the content.

From their essays and comments in class, I can piece together the world that many of my students come from. It's a world of broken promises — mothers who abandon them, boyfriends and fathers who rape them, partners who beat them — and one where home and school are fractured places at best. But despite some of the horrific experiences these women have had, there's a strong element of hope in their writing, a survivor's instinct that things can get better and life will turn around.

We are reading Toni Morrison's *The Bluest Eye,* a somber book about a girl, Pecola, who has internalized white standards of beauty and believes she would be loved if only she had blue eyes. One day, I tell my students that I sometimes feel self-conscious about my position: I'm a white woman teaching mostly African American literature to women of color. "Damn, Miss B, you worry too much," says one student. "Yeah," says another, "you think too hard." As unbelievable as it may sound, there is no racial tension among the women in the jail. Drugs, abuse, and poverty are the great levelers here, at least from what I've seen. It is these elements that transcend division by race, uniting my students with one another and the literature we read.

Similarly, Pecola's life is one of repeated rejection and abuse: she is raped by her father, neglected by her mother. This is by far my students' favorite work, and I suggest they write letters to the author. I vow to someday send them to Toni Morrison and apologize for photocopying her novels.

"Dear Toni," one woman writes, "I can really appreciate your book cuz   40
it gives without a doubt insight. . . . Also men abusing women it is a strong issue and your book brought strength to me as a woman of abuse." Despite the bleak outcome of the novel, the women find positive messages. "Dear Professor Morrison," writes another, "this book made me think about how we put off the beauty of are black people an put on the ugly, but I see the light now an when I leave jail I will keep my Lord with me black women like you makes me proud."

"To Toni Morrison," writes another, "I love the slang that you use it was kind of difficult getting it together but it was real. I love real stuff. . . . you are a dream come true."

"Dear Ms. Morrison. I really enjoyed reading 'The Bluest Eye.' . . . Even tho the cover states that the story is fiction, I truly believe that some little girl may have gone through this. It was a common thing. And Im sorry to say, that it still happens. . . . P.S. If you can please send me an autograph book I would really enjoy it. Thank you."

QUESTIONS

Reading

1. Boufis teaches in two different worlds. In each world, her students have their own kinds of knowledge, and for each audience, Boufis must shift her mode of teaching. What does she learn about teaching from her students in the county jail?
2. Highlight and list the things that Boufis criticizes about the criminal justice system in California.
3. Boufis writes from the perspective of, as she puts it, "a white woman teaching mostly African American literature to women of color" (paragraph 38). How does her voice shape the content of this essay?

4. Make a double-entry list of the ways Boufis compares her students at the county jail with her college writing students at the University of California, Berkeley. If you need more space, use a separate piece of paper. Then, write a paragraph reflecting on the conclusions she draws from this comparison.

COUNTY JAIL	BERKELEY

Exploratory Writing

1. If you were assigned to teach a literature class in a prison or jail, which books would you choose, and why? Create a reading list that includes at least ten books or stories, with a brief description of your goals for what your students would learn from each selection. In addition to the ten readings, include any movies, Web sites, or other educational materials that you think would be enlightening for your students to read.
2. In her experience teaching literature to inmates at the county jail, Boufis meets women who come from a very different background than her own. Reflect on a personal experience that involved working or spending time with people very different from you. What did you learn?

Making Connections

1. Compare Boufis's and Amanda Coyne's (p. 57) criticisms of harsh penalties for low-level drug dealing. Do some further research on this issue, and write a report on your findings.
2. In this essay, Boufis intersperses her personal observations and experiences with data about the prison system and incarcerated women. Compare her approach to Barbara Ehrenreich's (p. 195). In your opinion, would these authors' reports be more effective if they had left out their personal perspectives and included only factual information? Use examples to support your argument.

Essay Writing

1. What programs are available for prisoners in your local county jail? If there aren't any, what reasons are given for this lack? Write a report on what you learn.

Urban Legends
"The Boyfriend's Death"

Jan Harold Brunvand

With a PhD in folklore from Indiana University, Jan Harold Brunvand (b. 1933) has become a leading collector and interpreter of contemporary legends. These "urban legends" are stories told around campfires and in college dormitories, often as true experiences that happened to somebody other than the teller of the tale. A professor at the University of Utah for many years, Brunvand has been the editor of the Journal of American Folklore *and* American Folklore: An Encyclopedia *(1996), and is the author of the standard introduction to the field,* The Study of American Folklore: An Introduction, *fourth edition (1997). The following selection is taken from the first of his several collections of urban legends,* The Vanishing Hitchhiker: American Urban Legends and Their Meanings *(1981). Here Brunvand defines* urban legend, *gives one striking example, and offers some explanations about how and why such stories flourish even in the midst of a highly technologized society. The selection as reprinted is complete, except for the deletion of a few brief references to discussions elsewhere in Brunvand's book.*

We are not aware of our own folklore any more than we are of the grammatical rules of our language. When we follow the ancient practice of informally transmitting "lore" — wisdom, knowledge, or accepted modes of behavior — by word of mouth and customary example from person to person, we do not concentrate on the form or content of our folklore; instead, we simply listen to information that others tell us and then pass it on — more or less accurately — to other listeners. In this stream of unselfconscious oral tradition the information that acquires a clear story line is called *narrative folklore*, and those stories alleged to be true are *legends*. This, in broad summary, is the typical process of legend formation and transmission as it has existed from time immemorial and continues to operate today. It works about the same way whether the legendary plot concerns a dragon in a cave or a mouse in a Coke bottle.

It might seem unlikely that legends — *urban* legends at that — would continue to be created in an age of widespread literacy, rapid mass communications, and restless travel. While our pioneer ancestors may have had to rely heavily on oral traditions to pass the news along about changing events and frontier dangers, surely we no longer need mere "folk" reports of what's happening, with all their tendencies to distort the facts. A moment's reflection, however, reminds us of the many weird, fascinating, but unverified rumors and tales that so frequently come to our ears — killers and madmen on the loose, shocking or funny personal experiences, unsafe manufactured products, and many other unexplained mysteries of daily life. Sometimes we encounter different oral versions of such stories, and on occasion we may read about similar events in newspapers or magazines; but seldom do we find, or even seek after, reliable documentation. The lack of verification in no way diminishes the appeal urban legends have for us. We enjoy them merely as stories, and we tend at least to half-believe them as possibly accurate reports. And the legends we tell, as with any folklore, reflect many of the hopes, fears, and anxieties of our time. In short, legends are definitely part of our modern folklore — legends which are as traditional, variable, and functional as those of the past.

Folklore study consists of collecting, classifying, and interpreting in their full cultural context the many products of everyday human interaction that have acquired a somewhat stable underlying form and that are passed traditionally from person to person, group to group, and generation to generation. Legend study is a most revealing area of such research because the stories that people believe to be true hold an important place in their worldview. "If it's true, it's important" is an axiom to be trusted, whether or not the lore really *is* true or not. Simply becoming aware of this modern folklore which we all possess to some degree is a revelation in itself, but going beyond this to compare the tales, isolate their consistent themes, and relate them to the rest of the culture can yield rich insights into the state of our current civilization. . . .

Urban Legends as Folklore

Folklore subsists on oral tradition, but not all oral communication is folklore. The vast amounts of human interchange, from casual daily conversations to formal discussions in business or industry, law, or teaching, rarely constitute straight oral folklore. However, all such "communicative events" (as scholars dub them) are punctuated routinely by various units of traditional material that are memorable, repeatable, and that fit recurring social situations well enough to serve in place of original remarks. "Tradition" is the key idea that links together such utterances as nicknames, proverbs, greeting and leave-taking formulas, wisecracks, anecdotes, and jokes as "folklore"; indeed, these are a few of the best known "conversational genres" of American folklore. Longer and more complex folk forms — fairy tales, epics, myths, legends, or ballads, for example — may thrive only in certain special situations of oral transmission. All true folklore ultimately depends upon continued oral dissemination, usually within fairly homogeneous "folk groups," and upon the retention through time of internal patterns and motifs that become traditional in the oral exchanges. The corollary of this rule of stability in oral tradition is that all items of folklore, while retaining a fixed central core, are constantly changing as they are transmitted, so as to create countless "variants" differing in length, detail, style, and performance technique. Folklore, in short, consists of oral tradition in variants.

Urban legends belong to the subclass of folk narratives, legends, 5 that — unlike fairy tales — are believed, or at least believable, and that — unlike myths — are set in the recent past and involve normal human beings rather than ancient gods or demigods. Legends are folk history, or rather quasi-history. As with any folk legends, urban legends gain credibility from specific details of time and place or from references to source authorities. For instance, a popular western pioneer legend often begins something like, "My great-grandmother had this strange experience when she was a young girl on a wagon train going through Wyoming when an Indian chief wanted to adopt her. . . ." Even though hundreds of different great-grandmothers are supposed to have had the same doubtful experience (being desired by the chief because of her beautiful long blond hair), the fact seldom reaches legend-tellers; if it does, they assume that the family lore has indeed spread far and wide. This particular popular tradition, known as "Goldilocks on the Oregon Trail," interests folklorists because of the racist implications of a dark Indian savage coveting a fair young civilized woman — this legend is familiar in the *white* folklore only — and it is of little concern that the story seems to be entirely apocryphal.

In the world of modern urban legends there is usually no geographical or generational gap between teller and event. The story is *true*; it really occurred, and recently, and always to someone else who is quite close to the narrator, or at least "a friend of a friend." Urban legends are told both in the course of casual conversations and in such special situations as campfires, slumber parties, and college dormitory bull sessions. The legends' physical settings are often close by, real, and sometimes even locally renowned for other such happenings. Though the characters in the stories are usually nameless, they are true-to-life examples of the kind of people the narrators and their audience know firsthand.

One of the great mysteries of folklore research is where oral traditions originate and who invents them. One might expect that at least in modern folklore we could come up with answers to such questions, but this is seldom, if ever, the case. . . .

The Performance of Legends

Whatever the origins of urban legends, their dissemination is no mystery. The tales have traveled far and wide, and have been told and retold from person to person in the same manner that myths, fairy tales, or ballads spread in earlier cultures, with the important difference that today's legends are also disseminated by the mass media. Groups of age-mates, especially adolescents, are one important American legend channel, but other paths of transmission are among office workers and club members, as well as among religious, recreational, and regional groups. Some individuals make a point of learning every recent rumor or tale, and they can enliven any coffee break, party, or trip with the latest supposed "news." The telling of one story inspires other people to share what they have read or heard, and in a short time a lively exchange of details occurs and perhaps new variants are created.

Tellers of these legends, of course, are seldom aware of their roles as "performers of folklore." The conscious purpose of this kind of storytelling is to convey a true event, and only incidentally to entertain an audience. Nevertheless, the speaker's demeanor is carefully orchestrated, and his or her delivery is low-key and soft-sell. With subtle gestures, eye movements, and vocal inflections the stories are made dramatic, pointed, and suspenseful. But, just as with jokes, some can tell them and some can't. Passive tellers of urban legends may just report them as odd rumors, but the more active legend tellers re-create them as dramatic stories of suspense and, perhaps, humor.

"The Boyfriend's Death"

With all these points in mind — folklore's subject-matter, style, and oral   10
performance — consider this typical version of a well-known urban legend that folklorists have named "The Boyfriend's Death," collected in 1964 (the earliest documented instance of the story) by folklorist Daniel R. Barnes from an eighteen-year-old freshman at the University of Kansas. The usual tellers of the story are adolescents, and the normal setting for the narration is a college dormitory room with fellow students sprawled on the furniture and floors.

> This happened just a few years ago out on the road that turns off highway 59 by the Holiday Inn. This couple were parked under a tree out on this road. Well, it got to be time for the girl to be back at the dorm, so she told her boyfriend that they should start back. But the car wouldn't start, so he told her to lock herself in the car and he would go down to the Holiday Inn and call for help. Well, he didn't come back and he didn't come back, and pretty soon she started hearing a scratching noise on the roof of the car. "Scratch, scratch . . . scratch, scratch." She got scareder and scareder, but he didn't come back. Finally, when it was almost daylight, some people came along and stopped and helped her out of the car, and she looked up and there was her boyfriend hanging from the tree, and his feet were scraping against the roof of the car. This is why the road is called "Hangman's Road."

Here is a story that has traveled rapidly to reach nationwide oral circulation, in the process becoming structured in the typical manner of folk narratives. The traditional and fairly stable elements are the parked couple, the abandoned girl, the mysterious scratching (sometimes joined by a dripping sound and ghostly shadows on the windshield), the daybreak rescue, and the horrible climax. Variable traits are the precise location, the reason for her abandonment, the nature of the rescuers, murder details, and the concluding placename explanation. While "The Boyfriend's Death" seems to have captured teenagers' imaginations as a separate legend only since the early 1960s, it is clearly related to at least two older yarns, "The Hook" and "The Roommate's Death." All three legends have been widely collected by American folklorists, although only scattered examples have been published, mostly in professional journals. Examination of some of these variations helps to make clear the status of the story as folklore and its possible meanings.

At Indiana University, a leading American center of folklore research, folk-narrative specialist Linda Dégh and her students have gathered voluminous data on urban legends, especially those popular with adolescents. Dégh's preliminary published report on "The Boyfriend's Death" concerned nineteen texts collected from IU students from 1964 to 1968. Several storytellers had heard it in high school, often at parties; others had picked it up in college dormitories or elsewhere on campus. Several students expressed some belief in the legend, supposing either that it had happened in their own hometowns, or possibly in other states, once as far distant as "a remote part of Alabama." One informant reported that "she had been sworn to that the incident actually happened," but another, who had heard some variations of the tale, felt that "it seemed too horrible to be true." Some versions had incorporated motifs from other popular teenage horror legends or local ghost stories. . . .

One of the Indiana texts, told in the state of Washington, localizes the story there near Moses Lake, "in the country on a road that leads to a dead-end right under a big weeping willow tree . . . about four or five miles from town." As in most American versions of the story, these specific local touches make believable what is essentially a traveling legend. In a detail familiar from other variants of "The Boyfriend's Death," the body — now decapitated — is left hanging upside down from a branch of the willow tree with the fingernails scraping the top of the car. Another version studied by the Indiana researcher is somewhat aberrant, perhaps because the student was told the story by a friend's parents who claimed that "it happened a long time ago, probably thirty or forty years." Here a murderer is introduced, a "crazy old lady" on whose property the couple has parked. The victim this time is skinned rather than decapitated, and his head scrapes the car as the corpse swings to and fro in the breezy night.

A developing motif in "The Boyfriend's Death" is the character and role of the rescuers, who in the 1964 Kansas version are merely "some people."

The standard identification later becomes "the police," authority figures whose presence lends further credence to the story. They are either called by the missing teenagers' parents, or simply appear on the scene in the morning to check the car. In a 1969 variant from Leonardtown, Maryland, the police give a warning, "Miss, please get out of the car and walk to the police car with us, but don't look back." . . . In a version from Texas collected in 1971, set "at this lake somewhere way out in nowhere," a policeman gets an even longer line: "Young lady, we want you to get out of the car and come with us. Whatever you do, don't turn, don't turn around, just keep walking, just keep going straight and don't look back at the car." The more detailed the police instructions are, the more plausible the tale seems to become. Of course the standard rule of folk-narrative plot development now applies: the taboo must be broken (or the "interdiction violated" as some scholars put it). The girl always *does* look back, like Orpheus in the underworld, and in a number of versions her hair turns white from the shock of what she sees, as in a dozen other American legends.

In a Canadian version of "The Boyfriend's Death," told by a fourteen-year-old boy from Willowdale, Ontario, in 1973, the words of the policemen are merely summarized, but the opening scene of the legend is developed more fully, with several special details, including . . . a warning heard on the car radio. The girl's behavior when left behind is also described in more detail.   15

> A guy and his girlfriend are on the way to a party when their car starts to give them some trouble. At that same time they catch a news flash on the radio warning all people in the area that a lunatic killer has escaped from a local criminal asylum. The girl becomes very upset and at that point the car stalls completely on the highway. The boyfriend gets out and tinkers around with the engine but can't get the car to start again. He decides that he is going to have to walk on up the road to a gas station and get a tow truck but wants his girlfriend to stay behind in the car. She is frightened and pleads with him to take her, but he says that she'll be safe on the floor of the car covered with a blanket so that anyone passing will think it is an abandoned car and not bother her. Besides he can sprint along the road and get back more quickly than if she comes with him in her high-heeled shoes and evening dress. She finally agrees and he tells her not to come out unless she hears his signal of three knocks on the window. . . .

She does hear knocks on the car, but they continue eerily beyond three; the sound is later explained as the shoes of the boyfriend's corpse bumping the car as the body swings from a limb above the car.

The style in which oral narratives are told deserves attention, for the live telling that is dramatic, fluid, and often quite gripping in actual folk performance before a sympathetic audience may seem stiff, repetitious, and awkward on the printed page. Lacking in all our examples of "The Boyfriend's Death" is the essential ingredient of immediate context — the setting of the legend-telling, the storyteller's vocal and facial expression and gestures, the audience's reaction, and the texts of other similar tales narrated at the same session. Several of the informants explained that the story was told to them in spooky situations, late at night, near a cemetery, out camping, or even "while on a hayride or out parked," occasionally near the site of the supposed murder. Some students refer to such macabre legends, therefore, as "scary stories," "screamers," or "horrors."

A widely-distributed folk legend of this kind as it travels in oral tradition acquires a good deal of its credibility and effect from the localized details inserted by individual tellers. The highway and motel identification in the Kansas text are good examples of this, and in a New Orleans version, "The Boyfriend's Death" is absorbed into a local teenage tradition about "The Grunch" — a half-sheep, half-human monster that haunts specific local sites. One teenager there reported, "A man and lady went out by the lake and in the morning they found 'em hanging upside down on a tree and they said grunches did it." Finally, rumors or news stories about missing persons or violent crimes (as mentioned in the Canadian version) can merge with urban legends, helping to support their air of truth, or giving them renewed circulation after a period of less frequent occurrence.

Even the bare printed texts retain some earmarks of effective oral tradition. Witness in the Kansas text the artful use of repetition (typical of folk narrative style): "Well, he didn't come back and he didn't come back . . . but he didn't come back." The repeated use of "well" and the building of lengthy sentences with "and" are other hallmarks of oral style which give the narrator complete control over his performance, tending to squeeze out interruptions or prevent lapses in attention among the listeners. The scene that is set for the incident — lonely road, night, a tree looming over the car, out of gas — and the sound effects — scratches or bumps on the car — contribute to the style, as does the dramatic part played by the policeman and the abrupt ending line: "She looked back, and she saw . . . !" Since the typical narrators and auditors of "The Boyfriend's Death" themselves like to "park" and may have been alarmed by rumors, strange sights and noises, or automobile emergencies (all intensified in their effects by the audience's knowing other parking legends), the abrupt, unresolved ending leaves open the possibilities of what "really happened."

Urban Legends as Cultural Symbols

Legends can survive in our culture as living narrative folklore if they contain three essential elements: a strong basic story-appeal, a foundation in actual belief, and a meaningful message or "moral." That is, popular stories like "The Boyfriend's Death" are not only engrossing tales, but also "true," or at least so people think, and they teach valuable lessons. Jokes are a living part of oral tradition, despite being fictional and often silly, because of their humor, brevity, and snappy punch lines, but legends are by nature longer, slower, and more serious. Since more effort is needed to tell and appreciate a legend than a joke, it needs more than just verbal art to carry it along. Jokes have significant "messages" too, but these tend to be disguised or implied. People tell jokes primarily for amusement, and they seldom sense their underlying themes. In legends the primary messages are quite clear and straightforward; often they take the form of explicit warnings or good examples of "poetic justice." Secondary messages in urban legends tend to be suggested metaphorically or symbolically; these may provide deeper criticisms of human behavior or social condition.

People still tell legends, therefore, and other folk take time to listen to   20
them, not only because of their inherent plot interest but because they seem to convey true, worthwhile, and relevant information, albeit partly in a subconscious mode. In other words, such stories are "news" presented to us in an attractive way, with hints of larger meanings. Without this multiple appeal few legends would get a hearing in the modern world, so filled with other distractions. Legends survive by being as lively and "factual" as the television evening news, and, like the daily news broadcasts, they tend to concern deaths, injuries, kidnappings, tragedies, and scandals. Apparently the basic human need for meaningful personal contact cannot be entirely replaced by the mass media and popular culture. A portion of our interest in what is occurring in the world must be filled by some face-to-face reports from other human beings.

On a literal level a story like "The Boyfriend's Death" simply warns young people to avoid situations in which they may be endangered, but at a more symbolic level the story reveals society's broader fears of people, especially women and the young, being alone and among strangers in the darkened world outside the security of their own home or car. Note that the young woman in the story (characterized by "her high-heeled shoes and evening dress") is shown as especially helpless and passive, cowering under the blanket in the car until she is rescued by men. Such themes recur in various forms in many other urban legends. . . .

In order to be retained in a culture, any form of folklore must fill some genuine need, whether this be the need for an entertaining escape from reality, or a desire to validate by anecdotal examples some of the culture's ideals and institutions. For legends in general, a major function has always been the attempt to explain unusual and supernatural happenings in the natural world. To some degree this remains a purpose for urban legends, but their more common role nowadays seems to be to show that the prosaic contemporary scene is capable of producing shocking or amazing occurrences which may actually have happened to friends or to near-acquaintances but which are nevertheless explainable in some reasonably logical terms. On the one hand we want our factual lore to inspire awe, and at the same time we wish to have the most fantastic tales include at least the hint of a rational explanation and perhaps even a conclusion. Thus an escaped lunatic, a possibly *real* character, not a fantastic invader from outer space or Frankenstein's monster, is said to be responsible for the atrocities committed in the gruesome tales that teenagers tell. As sometimes happens in real life, the car radio gives warning, and the police get the situation back under control. (The policemen's role, in fact, becomes larger and more commanding as the story grows in oral tradition.) Only when the young lovers are still alone and scared are they vulnerable, but society's adults and guardians come to their rescue presently.

In common with brief unverified reports ("rumors"), to which they are often closely related, urban legends gratify our desire to know about and to try to understand bizarre, frightening, and potentially dangerous or embarrassing events that *may* have happened. (In rumors and legends there is always some element of doubt concerning where and when these things *did* occur.) These floating stories appeal to our morbid curiosity and satisfy our sensation-seeking minds that demand gratification through frequent infusions of new information, "sanitized" somewhat by the positive messages. Informal rumors and stories fill in the gaps left by professional news reporting, and these marvelous, though generally false, "true" tales may be said to be carrying the folk-news — along with some editorial matter — from person to person even in today's technological world.

QUESTIONS

Reading

1. Brunvand writes as a scholar, *explaining* urban legends from his perspective as a folklorist. How does his expertise shape his writing? What did you learn from reading his essay that you didn't know before?
2. According to Brunvand, what are the elements that allow legends to survive as living narrative folklore?
3. How does Brunvand differentiate between "oral communication" and "folklore"? Discuss Brunvand's system for categorizing urban legends. How are folk legends unlike fairy tales?

Exploratory Writing

1. Below is a list of other tales collected by Brunvand. Do you know any stories that might correspond to these titles?

   The Vanishing Hitchhiker
   The Mexican Pet
   The Baby-Sitter and the Man Upstairs
   The Microwaved Pet

The Toothbrush Story
Alligators in the Sewers
The Nude in the RV
The Kidney Heist

Briefly describe the stories you have heard. Compare the various versions produced by members of the class. What are the variables in the tale, and what seem to be the common features?

2. Select an urban legend that you have recently heard. Write down the best version of it that you can, and analyze what you have written as an urban legend. That is, explain the features that mark it as an urban legend, and discuss the elements that make it interesting or appealing to you.

3. Collaborating in small groups, choose a story from personal experience or from the media that sounds like an urban legend but is true. Make a presentation in which you identify and discuss the features that make it similar to an urban legend. How can you prove that the story is true?

Making Connections

1. Although Brunvand is a folklorist himself, he chooses to write this explanatory essay in the *third person*, leaving his own personal experiences and anecdotes out of his account. Find another essay in this book that's written in the third person, and two essays that are written in the *first person*. Flagging specific examples from each of the four essays, write a few paragraphs that discuss the ways that the writer's perspective shapes the tone of each piece.

Essay Writing

1. Brunvand writes, "And the legends we tell, as with any folklore, reflect many of the hopes, fears, and anxieties of our time" (paragraph 2). Write an essay comparing a mainstream narrative about an event in recent history (such as a *New York Times* or *Washington Post* article about the revelation of the torture of prisoners in Abu Ghraib or the corruption of financier Bernard Madoff) with an alternative narrative about the same event, taken from an obscure blog or Web site. Identify the major differences between the accounts, and then perform a reading of the alternative narrative in the way that Brunvand reads urban legends.

2. Write an essay reflecting on a time when you believed a story that wasn't true. It can be an urban legend, a story about Santa Claus or the tooth fairy, or something more personal. What was the symbolic meaning of the story? What changed for you when you learned that it wasn't true?

Watching TV Makes You Smarter

Steven Johnson

Steven Johnson (b. 1968) writes on culture and popular science and in 1995 was cofounder of the now defunct Feed — *one of the earliest e-zines to provide daily content on media, pop culture, and technology. A Distinguished Writer in Residence at New York University, Johnson has had work published in* Harper's, *the* New Yorker, *the* Wall Street Journal, *and the* New York Times. *His five books — including his most recent,* The Invention of Air *(2008) — concern the intersections of science, technology, culture, faith, and particularly pop culture. The following piece appeared in the* New York Times Magazine *and was adapted from Johnson's book* Everything Bad Is Good for You: How Today's Popular Culture Is Actually Making Us Smarter *(2005).*

The Sleeper Curve

SCIENTIST A: Has he asked for anything special?

SCIENTIST B: Yes, this morning for breakfast . . . he requested something called "wheat germ, organic honey and tiger's milk."

SCIENTIST A: Oh, yes. Those were the charmed substances that some years ago were felt to contain life-preserving properties.

SCIENTIST B: You mean there was no deep fat? No steak or cream pies or . . . hot fudge?

SCIENTIST A: Those were thought to be unhealthy.

— FROM WOODY ALLEN'S "SLEEPER"

On Jan. 24, the Fox network showed an episode of its hit drama "24," the real-time thriller known for its cliffhanger tension and often-gruesome violence. Over the preceding weeks, a number of public controversies had erupted around "24," mostly focused on its portrait of Muslim terrorists and its penchant for torture scenes. The episode that was shown on the 24th only fanned the flames higher: in one scene, a terrorist enlists a hit man to kill his child for not fully supporting the jihadist cause; in another scene, the secretary of defense authorizes the torture of his son to uncover evidence of a terrorist plot.

But the explicit violence and the post-9/11 terrorist anxiety are not the only elements of "24" that would have been unthinkable on prime-time network television 20 years ago. Alongside the notable change in content lies an equally notable change in form. During its 44 minutes — a real-time hour, minus 16 minutes for commercials — the episode connects the lives of 21 distinct characters, each with a clearly defined "story arc," as the Hollywood jargon has it: a defined personality with motivations and obstacles and specific relationships with other characters. Nine primary narrative threads wind their way through those 44 minutes, each drawing extensively upon events and information revealed in earlier episodes. Draw a map of all those intersecting plots and personalities, and you get structure that — where formal complexity is concerned — more closely resembles "Middlemarch" than a hit TV drama of years past like "Bonanza."

For decades, we've worked under the assumption that mass culture follows a path declining steadily toward lowest-common-denominator standards, presumably because the "masses" want dumb, simple pleasures and big media companies try to give the masses what they want. But as that "24" episode suggests, the exact opposite is happening: the culture is getting more cognitively demanding, not less. To make sense of an episode of "24," you have to integrate far more information than you would have a few decades ago watching a comparable show. Beneath the violence and the ethnic stereotypes, another trend appears: to keep up with entertainment like "24," you have to pay attention, make inferences, track shifting social relationships. This is what I call the Sleeper Curve: the most debased forms of mass diversion — video games and violent television dramas and juvenile sitcoms — turn out to be nutritional after all.

I believe that the Sleeper Curve is the single most important new force altering the mental development of young people today, and I believe it is largely a force for good: enhancing our cognitive faculties, not dumbing them down. And yet you almost never hear this story in popular accounts of today's media. Instead, you hear dire tales of addiction, violence, mindless escapism. It's assumed that shows that promote smoking or gratuitous violence are bad for us. While those that thunder against teen pregnancy or intolerance have a positive role in society. Judged by that morality-play standard, the story of popular culture over the past 50 years — if not 500 — is a story of decline: the morals of the stories have grown darker and more ambiguous, and the antiheroes have multiplied.

The usual counterargument here is that what media have lost in moral   5
clarity, they have gained in realism. The real world doesn't come in nicely packaged public-service announcements, and we're better off with entertainment like "The Sopranos" that reflects our fallen state with all its ethical ambiguity. I happen to be sympathetic to that argument, but it's not the one I want to make here. I think there is another way to assess the social virtue of pop culture, one that looks at media as a kind of cognitive workout, not as a

series of life lessons. There may indeed be more "negative messages" in the mediasphere today. But that's not the only way to evaluate whether our television shows or video games are having a positive impact. Just as important — if not more important — is the kind of thinking you have to do to make sense of a cultural experience. That is where the Sleeper Curve becomes visible.

Televised Intelligence

Consider the cognitive demands that televised narratives place on their viewers. With many shows that we associate with "quality" entertainment — "The Mary Tyler Moore Show," "Murphy Brown," "Frasier" — the intelligence arrives fully formed in the words and actions of the characters on-screen. They say witty things to one another and avoid lapsing into tired sitcom clichés, and we smile along in our living rooms, enjoying the company of these smart people. But assuming we're bright enough to understand the sentences they're saying, there's no intellectual labor involved in enjoying the show as a viewer. You no more challenge your mind by watching these intelligent shows than you challenge your body watching "Monday Night Football." The intellectual work is happening on-screen, not off.

But another kind of televised intelligence is on the rise. Think of the cognitive benefits conventionally ascribed to reading: attention, patience, retention, the parsing of narrative threads. Over the last half-century, programming on TV has increased the demands it places on precisely these mental faculties. This growing complexity involves three primary elements: multiple threading, flashing arrows, and social networks.

According to television lore, the age of multiple threads began with the arrival in 1981 of "Hill Street Blues," the Steven Bochco police drama invariably praised for its "gritty realism." Watch an episode of "Hill Street Blues" side by side with any major drama from the preceding decades — "Starsky and Hutch," for instance, or "Dragnet" — and the structural transformation will jump out at you. The earlier shows follow one or two lead characters, adhere to a single dominant plot, and reach a decisive conclusion at the end of the episode. Draw an outline of the narrative threads in almost every "Dragnet" episode, and it will be a single line: from the initial crime scene, through the investigation, to the eventual cracking of the case. A typical "Starsky and Hutch" episode offers only the slightest variation on this linear formula: the introduction of a comic subplot that usually appears only at the tail ends of the episode, creating a structure that looks like the graph below. The vertical axis represents the number of individual threads, and the horizontal axis is time.

"Starsky and Hutch" (any episode)

A "Hill Street Blues" episode complicates the picture in a number of profound ways. The narrative weaves together a collection of distinct strands — sometimes as many as 10, though at least half of the threads involve only a few quick scenes scattered through the episode. The number of primary characters — and not just bit parts — swells significantly. And the episode has fuzzy borders: picking up one or two threads from previous episodes at the outset and leaving one or two threads open at the end. Charted graphically, an average episode looks like this:

"Hill Street Blues" (episode 85)

Critics generally cite "Hill Street Blues" as the beginning of "serious   10 drama" narrative in the television medium — differentiating the series from the single-episode dramatic programs from the 50's, which were Broadway plays performed in front of a camera. But the "Hill Street" innovations weren't all that original; they'd long played a defining role in popular television, just not during the evening hours. The structure of a "Hill Street" episode — and indeed of all the critically acclaimed dramas that followed, from "thirtysomething" to "Six Feet Under" — is the structure of a soap opera. "Hill Street Blues" might have sparked a new golden age of television drama during its seven-year run, but it did so by using a few crucial tricks that "Guiding Light" and "General Hospital" mastered long before.

Bochco's genius with "Hill Street" was to marry complex narrative structure with complex subject matter. "Dallas" had already shown that the extended, interwoven threads of the soap-opera genre could survive the weeklong interruptions of a prime-time show, but the actual content of "Dallas" was fluff. (The most probing issue it addressed was the question, now folkloric, of who shot J.R.) "All in the Family" and "Rhoda" showed that you could tackle complex social issues, but they did their tackling in the comfort of the sitcom living room. "Hill Street" had richly drawn characters confronting difficult social issues and a narrative structure to match.

Since "Hill Street" appeared, the multi-threaded drama has become the most widespread fictional genre on prime time: "St. Elsewhere," "L.A. Law," "thirtysomething," "Twin Peaks," "N.Y.P.D. Blue," "E.R.," "The West Wing," "Alias," "Lost." (The only prominent holdouts in drama are shows like "Law and Order" that have essentially updated the venerable "Dragnet" format and thus remained anchored to a single narrative line.) Since the early 80's, however, there has been a noticeable increase in narrative complexity in these dramas. The most ambitious show on TV to date, "The Sopranos," routinely follows up to a dozen distinct threads over the course of an episode, with more than 20 recurring characters. An episode from late in the first season looks like this:

"The Sopranos" (episode 8)

The total number of active threads equals the multiple plots of "Hill Street," but here each thread is more substantial. The show doesn't offer a clear distinction between dominant and minor plots; each story line carries its weight in the mix. The episode also displays a chordal mode of story-telling entirely absent from "Hill Street": a single scene in "The Sopranos" will often connect to three different threads at the same time, layering one plot atop another. And every single thread in this "Sopranos" episode builds on events from previous episodes, and continues on through the rest of the season and beyond.

Put those charts together, and you have a portrait of the Sleeper Curve rising over the past 30 years of popular television. In a sense, this is as much a map of cognitive changes in the popular mind as it is a map of on-screen developments, as if the media titans decided to condition our brains to follow ever-larger numbers of simultaneous threads. Before "Hill Street," the conventional wisdom among television execs was that audiences wouldn't be comfortable following more than three plots in a single episode, and indeed, the "Hill Street" pilot, which was shown in January 1981, brought complaints from viewers that the show was too complicated. Fast-forward two decades, and shows like "The Sopranos" engage their audiences with narratives that make "Hill Street" look like "Three's Company." Audiences happily embrace that complexity because they've been trained by two decades of multi-threaded dramas.

Multi-threading is the most celebrated structural feature of the modern   15
television drama, and it certainly deserves some of the honor that has been doled out to it. And yet multi-threading is only part of the story.

The Case for Confusion

Shortly after the arrival of the first-generation slasher movies — "Halloween," "Friday the 13th" — Paramount released a mock-slasher flick called "Student Bodies," parodying the genre just as the "Scream" series would do 15 years later. In one scene, the obligatory nubile teenage baby sitter hears a noise outside a suburban house; she opens the door to investigate, finds nothing and then goes back inside. As the door shuts behind her, the camera swoops in on the doorknob, and we see that she has left the door unlocked. The camera pulls back and then swoops down again for emphasis. And then a flashing arrow appears on the screen, with text that helpfully explains: "Unlocked!"

That flashing arrow is parody, of course, but it's merely an exaggerated version of a device popular stories use all the time. When a sci-fi script inserts into some advanced lab a nonscientist who keeps asking the science geeks to explain what they're doing with that particle accelerator, that's a flashing arrow that gives the audience precisely the information it needs in order to make sense of the ensuing plot. ("Whatever you do, don't spill water on it, or you'll set off a massive explosion!") These hints serve as a kind of narrative hand-holding. Implicitly, they say to the audience, "We realize you have no idea what a particle accelerator is, but here's the deal: all you need to know is that it's a big fancy thing that explodes when wet." They focus the mind on relevant details: "Don't worry about whether the baby sitter is going to break up with her boyfriend. Worry about that guy lurking in the bushes." They reduce the amount of analytic work you need to do to make sense of a story. All you have to do is follow the arrows.

By this standard, popular television has never been harder to follow. If narrative threads have experienced a population explosion over the past 20 years, flashing arrows have grown correspondingly scarce. Watching our pinnacle of early 80's TV drama, "Hill Street Blues," we find there's an informational wholeness to each scene that differs markedly from what you see on shows like "The West Wing" or "The Sopranos" or "Alias" or "E.R."

"Hill Street" has ambiguities about future events: will a convicted killer be executed? Will Furillo marry Joyce Davenport? Will Renko find it in himself to bust a favorite singer for cocaine possession? But the present-tense of each scene explains itself to the viewer with little ambiguity. There's an open question or a mystery driving each of these stories — how will it all turn out? — but there's no mystery about the immediate activity on the screen. A contemporary drama like "The West Wing," on the other hand, constantly embeds mysteries into the present-tense events: you see characters performing actions or discussing events about which crucial information has been deliberately withheld. Anyone who has watched more than a handful of "The West Wing" episodes closely will know the feeling: scene after scene refers to some clearly crucial but unexplained piece of information, and after the sixth reference, you'll find yourself wishing you could rewind the tape to figure out what they're talking about, assuming you've missed something. And then you realize that you're supposed to be confused. The open question posed by these sequences is not "How will this turn out in the end?" The question is "What's happening right now?"

The deliberate lack of hand-holding extends down to the microlevel of   20
dialogue as well. Popular entertainment that addresses technical issues — whether they are the intricacies of passing legislation, or of performing

a heart bypass, or of operating a particle accelerator — conventionally switches between two modes of information in dialogue: texture and substance. Texture is all the arcane verbiage provided to convince the viewer that they're watching Actual Doctors at Work; substance is the material planted amid the background texture that the viewer needs to make sense of the plot.

Conventionally, narratives demarcate the line between texture and substance by inserting cues that flag or translate the important data. There's an unintentionally comical moment in the 2004 blockbuster "The Day After Tomorrow" in which the beleaguered climatologist (played by Dennis Quaid) announces his theory about the imminent arrival of a new ice age to a gathering of government officials. In his speech, he warns that "we have hit a critical desalinization point!" At this moment, the writer-director Roland Emmerich — a master of brazen arrow-flashing — has an official follow with the obliging remark: "It would explain what's driving this extreme weather." They might as well have had a flashing "Unlocked!" arrow on the screen.

The dialogue on shows like "The West Wing" and "E.R.," on the other hand, doesn't talk down to its audiences. It rushes by, the words accelerating in sync with the high-speed tracking shots that glide through the corridors and operating rooms. The characters talk faster in these shows, but the truly remarkable thing about the dialogue is not purely a matter of speed; it's the willingness to immerse the audience in information that most viewers won't understand. Here's a typical scene from "E.R.":

[WEAVER *and* WRIGHT *push a gurney containing a 16-year-old girl. Her parents,* JANNA *and* FRANK MIKAMI, *follow close behind.* CARTER *and* LUCY *fall in.*]

WEAVER: 16-year-old, unconscious, history of biliary atresia.
CARTER: Hepatic coma?
WEAVER: Looks like it.
MR. MIKAMI: She was doing fine until six months ago.
CARTER: What medication is she on?
MRS. MIKAMI: Ampicillin, tobramycin, vitamins A, D, and K.
LUCY: Skin's jaundiced.
WEAVER: Same with the sclera. Breath smells sweet.
CARTER: Fetor hepaticus?
WEAVER: Yep.
LUCY: What's that?
WEAVER: Her liver's shut down. Let's dip a urine. [*To* CARTER]
    Guys, it's getting a little crowded in here, why don't you deal with the parents? Start lactulose, 30 cc's per NG.
CARTER: We're giving medicine to clean her blood.
WEAVER: Blood in the urine, two-plus.
CARTER: The liver failure is causing her blood not to clot.

MRS. MIKAMI: Oh, God. . . .

CARTER: Is she on the transplant list?

MR. MIKAMI: She's been Status 2a for six months, but they haven't been able to find her a match.

CARTER: Why? What's her blood type?

MR. MIKAMI: AB.

[*This hits* CARTER *like a lightning bolt.* LUCY *gets it, too. They share a look.*]

There are flashing arrows here, of course — "The liver failure is causing her blood not to clot" — but the ratio of medical jargon to layperson translation is remarkably high. From a purely narrative point of view, the decisive line arrives at the very end: "AB." The 16-year-old's blood type connects her to an earlier plot line, involving a cerebral-hemorrhage victim who — after being dramatically revived in one of the opening scenes — ends up brain-dead. Far earlier, before the liver-failure scene above, Carter briefly discusses harvesting the hemorrhage victim's organs for transplants, and another doctor makes a passing reference to his blood type being the rare AB (thus making him an unlikely donor). The twist here revolves around a statistically unlikely event happening at the E.R. — an otherwise perfect liver donor showing up just in time to donate his liver to a recipient with the same rare blood type. But the show reveals this twist with remarkable subtlety. To make sense of that last "AB" line — and the look of disbelief on Carter's and Lucy's faces — you have to recall a passing remark uttered earlier regarding a character who belongs to a completely different thread. Shows like "E.R." may have more blood and guts than popular TV had a generation ago, but when it comes to storytelling, they possess a quality that can only be described as subtlety and discretion.

Even Bad TV Is Better

Skeptics might argue that I have stacked the deck here by focusing on relatively highbrow titles like "The Sopranos" or "The West Wing," when in fact the most significant change in the last five years of narrative entertainment involves reality TV. Does the contemporary pop cultural landscape look quite as promising if the representative show is "Joe Millionaire" instead of "The West Wing"?

I think it does, but to answer that question properly, you have to avoid   25 the tendency to sentimentalize the past. When people talk about the golden age of television in the early 70's — invoking shows like "The Mary Tyler Moore Show" and "All in the Family" — they forget to mention how awful most television programming was during much of that decade. If you're going to look at pop-culture trends, you have to compare apples to apples, or in this case, lemons to lemons. The relevant comparison is not between

"Joe Millionaire" and "MASH"; it's between "Joe Millionaire" and "The Newlywed Game," or between "Survivor" and "The Love Boat."

What you see when you make these head-to-head comparisons is that a rising tide of complexity has been lifting programming at the bottom of the quality spectrum and at the top. "The Sopranos" is several times more demanding of its audiences than "Hill Street" was, and "Joe Millionaire" has made comparable advances over "Battle of the Network Stars." This is the ultimate test of the Sleeper Curve theory: even the junk has improved.

If early television took its cues from the stage, today's reality programming is reliably structured like a video game: a series of competitive tests, growing more challenging over time. Many reality shows borrow a subtler device from gaming culture as well: the rules aren't fully established at the outset. You learn as you play.

On a show like "Survivor" or "The Apprentice," the participants — and the audience — know the general objective of the series, but each episode involves new challenges that haven't been ordained in advance. The final round of the first season of "The Apprentice," for instance, threw a monkey wrench into the strategy that governed the play up to that point, when Trump announced that the two remaining apprentices would have to assemble and manage a team of subordinates who had already been fired in earlier episodes of the show. All of a sudden the overarching objective of the game — do anything to avoid being fired — presented a potential conflict to the remaining two contenders: the structure of the final round favored the survivor who had maintained the best relationships with his comrades. Suddenly, it wasn't enough just to have clawed your way to the top; you had to have made friends while clawing. The original "Joe Millionaire" went so far as to undermine the most fundamental convention of all — that the show's creators don't openly lie to the contestants about the prizes — by inducing a construction worker to pose as a man of means while 20 women competed for his attention.

Reality programming borrowed another key ingredient from games: the intellectual labor of probing the system's rules for weak spots and opportunities. As each show discloses its conventions, and each participant reveals his or her personality traits and background, the intrigue in watching comes from figuring out how the participants should best navigate the environment that has been created for them. The pleasure in these shows comes not from watching other people being humiliated on national television; it comes from depositing other people in a complex, high-pressure environment where no established strategies exist and watching them find their bearings. That's why the water-cooler conversation about these shows invariably tracks in on the strategy displayed on the previous night's episode: why did Kwame pick Omarosa in that final round? What devious strategy is Richard Hatch concocting now?

When we watch these shows, the part of our brain that monitors the   30
emotional lives of the people around us — the part that tracks subtle shifts

in intonation and gesture and facial expression — scrutinizes the action on the screen, looking for clues. We trust certain characters implicitly and vote others off the island in a heartbeat. Traditional narrative shows also trigger emotional connections to the characters, but those connections don't have the same participatory effect, because traditional narratives aren't explicitly about strategy. The phrase "Monday-morning quarterbacking" describes the engaged feeling that spectators have in relation to games as opposed to stories. We absorb stories, but we second-guess games. Reality programming has brought that second-guessing to prime time, only the game in question revolves around social dexterity rather than the physical kind.

The Rewards of Smart Culture

The quickest way to appreciate the Sleeper Curve's cognitive training is to sit down and watch a few hours of hit programming from the late 70's on Nick at Nite or the SOAPnet channel or on DVD. The modern viewer who watches a show like "Dallas" today will be bored by the content — not just because the show is less salacious than today's soap operas (which it is by a small margin) but also because the show contains far less information in each scene, despite the fact that its soap-opera structure made it one of the most complicated narratives on television in its prime. With "Dallas," the modern viewer doesn't have to think to make sense of what's going on, and not having to think is boring. Many recent hit shows — "24," "Survivor," "The Sopranos," "Alias," "Lost," "The Simpsons," "E.R." — take the opposite approach, layering each scene with a thick network of affiliations. You have to focus to follow the plot, and in focusing you're exercising the parts of your brain that map social networks, that fill in missing information, that connect multiple narrative threads.

Of course, the entertainment industry isn't increasing the cognitive complexity of its products for charitable reasons. The Sleeper Curve exists because there's money to be made by making culture smarter. The economics of television syndication and DVD sales mean that there's a tremendous financial pressure to make programs that can be watched multiple times, revealing new nuances and shadings on the third viewing. Meanwhile, the Web has created a forum for annotation and commentary that allows more complicated shows to prosper, thanks to the fan sites where each episode of shows like "Lost" or "Alias" is dissected with an intensity usually reserved for Talmud scholars. Finally, interactive games have trained a new generation of media consumers to probe complex environments and to think on their feet, and that gamer audience has now come to expect the same challenges from their television shows. In the end, the Sleeper Curve tells us something about the human mind. It may be drawn toward the sensational where content is concerned — sex does sell, after all. But the mind also likes to be challenged; there's real pleasure to be found in solving puzzles, detecting patterns, or unpacking a complex narrative system.

In pointing out some of the ways that popular culture has improved our minds, I am not arguing that parents should stop paying attention to the way their children amuse themselves. What I am arguing for is a change in the criteria we use to determine what really is cognitive junk food and what is genuinely nourishing. Instead of a show's violent or tawdry content, instead of wardrobe malfunctions or the F-word, the true test should be whether a given show engages or sedates the mind. Is it a single thread strung together with predictable punch lines every 30 seconds? Or does it map a complex social network? Is your on-screen character running around shooting everything in sight, or is she trying to solve problems and manage resources? If your kids want to watch reality TV, encourage them to watch "Survivor" over "Fear Factor." If they want to watch a mystery show, encourage "24" over "Law and Order." If they want to play a violent game, encourage Grand Theft Auto over Quake. Indeed, it might be just as helpful to have a rating system that used mental labor and not obscenity and violence as its classification scheme for the world of mass culture.

Kids and grown-ups each can learn from their increasingly shared obsessions. Too often we imagine the blurring of kid and grown-up cultures as a series of violations: the 9-year-olds who have to have nipple broaches explained to them thanks to Janet Jackson; the middle-aged guy who can't wait to get home to his Xbox. But this demographic blur has a commendable side that we don't acknowledge enough. The kids are forced to think like grown-ups: analyzing complex social networks, managing resources, tracking subtle narrative intertwinings, recognizing long-term patterns. The grown-ups, in turn, get to learn from the kids: decoding each new technological wave, parsing the interfaces and discovering the intellectual rewards of play. Parents should see this as an opportunity, not a crisis. Smart culture is no longer something you force your kids to ingest, like green vegetables. It's something you share.

QUESTIONS

Reading

1. What is the Sleeper Curve? According to Johnson, what effect does the Sleeper Curve have on young people today?
2. What phrase does Johnson use to describe the engaged feeling that spectators have in relation to games as opposed to stories?
3. Johnson's thesis essentially involves a cause-and-effect claim about watching TV. In this *argumentative* essay, what kinds of evidence does he offer to support his claim that TV has such an effect? What kinds of evidence might help to strengthen his argument?

Exploratory Writing

1. The drift of Johnson's observations suggests that he favors programs that tend to be as complex and unpredictable as life itself. That being the case, shouldn't we just pay more attention to life than to a TV version of it? In what ways can watching TV serials provide better cognitive workouts than paying close attention to unmediated life? Stage a debate on the proposition, "TV makes you smarter than observing life."

2. Use Johnson's graphing method to analyze an episode from your favorite TV serial. For each strand in your graph, write a brief phrase to identify the characters and/or problem that it involves. How many distinct "threads" did you note in the episode? How many different characters were involved? How thick or thin was the treatment of each thread? What insights about the episode did you gain from this analysis? What features of the episode might be overlooked by Johnson's kind of analysis?

3. Johnson's title makes a very broad claim; however, he clearly doesn't think that all TV programs will make one smarter. What specific kinds of programs does he have in mind? Given the kinds of programs that he endorses and his reasons for doing so, what kinds of programs do you suppose he would criticize as likely to make one dumber?

Making Connections

1. Just as Johnson thinks that certain kinds of TV will make one smarter, Christina Boufis (p. 67) believes that certain kinds of reading will make one smarter. Compare their ideas of smartness, and consider which one is likely to be more academically helpful, more professionally helpful, and more existentially helpful.

Essay Writing

1. "Smarter" is such a broad term that it could refer to several different mental abilities. Write a *reflective* essay that evaluates Johnson's claims in terms of your own experiences watching TV. Has watching TV made you smarter? How does Johnson's idea of smartness compare with your own?

Politics and the English Language

George Orwell

Despite suffering from tuberculosis, prolific British writer George Orwell (1903–1950) wrote ten books and more than seven hundred articles and reviews during his foreshortened life. His most famous novels, Animal Farm *(1945) and* 1984 *(1949), dramatize the causes of totalitarianism in Europe, the rise of which Orwell witnessed and fought, both in writing and briefly as a soldier in the Spanish Civil War. In this essay, written in 1946, Orwell tells his readers that "in our time, political speech and writing are largely the defense of the indefensible." He attacks language that consists "largely of euphemism, question begging and sheer cloudy vagueness." Orwell, like John Berger (p. 315), is concerned with the ways in which language is often used to conceal unpleasant and horrifying realities.*

Most people who bother with the matter at all would admit that the English language is in a bad way, but it is generally assumed that we cannot by conscious action do anything about it. Our civilization is decadent and our language — so the argument runs — must inevitably share in the general collapse. It follows that any struggle against the abuse of language is a sentimental archaism, like preferring candles to electric light or hansom cabs to aeroplanes. Underneath this lies the half-conscious belief that language is a natural growth and not an instrument which we shape for our own purposes.

Now, it is clear that the decline of a language must ultimately have political and economic causes: it is not due simply to the bad influence of this or that individual writer. But an effect can become a cause, reinforcing the original cause and producing the same effect in an intensified form, and so on indefinitely. A man may take to drink because he feels himself to be a failure, and then fail all the more completely because he drinks. It is rather the same thing that is happening to the English language. It becomes ugly and inaccurate because our thoughts are foolish, but the slovenliness of our language makes it easier for us to have foolish thoughts. The point is that the process is reversible. Modern English, especially written English, is full of bad habits which spread by imitation and which can be avoided if one is willing to take the necessary trouble. If one gets rid of these habits one can think more clearly, and to think clearly is a necessary first step towards political regeneration: so that the fight against bad English is not frivolous and is not the exclusive concern of professional writers. I will come back to this presently, and I hope that by that time the meaning of what I have said here will have become clearer. Meanwhile, here are five specimens of the English language as it is now habitually written.

These five passages have not been picked out because they are especially bad — I could have quoted far worse if I had chosen — but because they illustrate various of the mental vices from which we now suffer. They are a little below the average, but are fairly representative samples. I number them so that I can refer back to them when necessary:

"(1) I am not, indeed, sure whether it is not true to say that the Milton who once seemed not unlike a seventeenth-century Shelley had not become, out of an experience ever more bitter in each year, more alien [*sic*] to the founder of that Jesuit sect which nothing could induce him to tolerate."

> Professor Harold Laski (Essay in *Freedom of Expression*)

"(2) Above all, we cannot play ducks and drakes with a native battery of idioms which prescribes such egregious collocations of vocables as the basic *put up with* for *tolerate* or *put at a loss* for *bewilder*."

> Professor Lancelot Hogben (*Interglossa*)

"(3) On the one side we have the free personality: by definition it is not neurotic, for it has neither conflict nor dream. Its desires, such as they are, are transparent, for they are just what institutional approval keeps in the forefront of consciousness; another institutional pattern would alter their number and intensity; there is little in them that is natural, irreducible, or culturally dangerous. But *on the other* side, the social bond itself is nothing but the mutual reflection of these self-secure integrities. Recall the definition of love. Is not this the very picture of a small academic? Where is there a place in this hall of mirrors for either personality or fraternity?"

> Essay on psychology in *Politics* (New York)

"(4) All the 'best people' from the gentlemen's clubs, and all the frantic fascist captains, united in common hatred of Socialism and bestial horror of the rising tide of the mass revolutionary movement, have turned to acts of provocation, to foul incendiarism, to medieval legends of poisoned wells, to legalize their own destruction of proletarian organizations, and rouse the agitated petty-bourgeoisie to chauvinistic fervour on behalf of the fight against the revolutionary way out of the crisis."

> Communist pamphlet

"(5) If a new spirit *is* to be infused into this old country, there is one thorny and contentious reform which must be tackled, and that is the humanization and galvanization of the B.B.C. Timidity here will bespeak cancer and atrophy of the soul. The heart of Britain may be sound and of strong beat, for instance, but the British lion's roar at present is like that of Bottom in Shakespeare's *Midsummer Night's Dream* — as gentle as any sucking dove. A virile new Britain cannot continue indefinitely to be traduced in the eyes or rather ears, of the world by the effete languors of Langham Place, brazenly masquerading as 'standard English.' When the Voice of Britain is heard at nine o'clock, better far and infinitely less ludicrous to hear aitches honestly dropped than the present priggish, inflated, inhibited, schoolma'amish arch braying of blameless bashful mewing maidens!"

Letter in *Tribune*

Each of these passages has faults of its own, but, quite apart from avoidable ugliness, two qualities are common to all of them. The first is staleness of imagery: the other is lack of precision. The writer either has a meaning and cannot express it, or he inadvertently says something else, or he is almost indifferent as to whether his words mean anything or not. This mixture of vagueness and sheer incompetence is the most marked characteristic of modern English prose, and especially of any kind of political writing. As soon as certain topics are raised, the concrete melts into the abstract and no one seems able to think of turns of speech that are not hackneyed: prose consists less and less of *words* chosen for the sake of their meaning, and more and more of *phrases* tacked together like the sections of a prefabricated hen-house. I list below, with notes and examples, various of the tricks by means of which the work of prose-construction is habitually dodged:

Dying Metaphors   A newly invented metaphor assists thought by evoking a visual image, while on the other hand a metaphor which is technically "dead" (e.g. *iron resolution*) has in effect reverted to being an ordinary word and can generally be used without loss of vividness. But in between these two classes there is a huge dump of worn-out metaphors which have lost all evocative power and are merely used because they save people the trouble of inventing phrases for themselves. Examples are: *Ring the changes on, take up the cudgels for, toe the line, ride roughshod over, stand shoulder to shoulder with, play into the hands of, no axe to grind, grist to the mill, fishing in troubled waters, on the order of the day, Achilles' heel, swan song, hotbed.* Many of these are used without knowledge of their meaning (what is a "rift," for instance?), and incompatible metaphors are frequently mixed, a sure sign that the writer is not interested in what he is saying. Some metaphors now current have been twisted out of their original meaning without those who use them even being aware of the fact. For example, *toe the line* is sometimes written *tow the line.* Another example is *the hammer*

5

and the anvil, now always used with the implication that the anvil gets the worst of it. In real life it is always the anvil that breaks the hammer, never the other way about: a writer who stopped to think what he was saying would be aware of this, and would avoid perverting the original phrase.

Operators or Verbal False Limbs   These save the trouble of picking out appropriate verbs and nouns, and at the same time pad each sentence with extra syllables which give it an appearance of symmetry. Characteristic phrases are: *render inoperative, militate against, make contact with, be subjected to, give rise to, give grounds for, have the effect of, play a leading part (role) in, make itself felt, take effect, exhibit a tendency to, serve the purpose of, etc., etc.* The keynote is the elimination of simple verbs. Instead of being a single word, such as *break, stop, spoil, mend, kill,* a verb becomes a *phrase,* made up of a noun or adjective tacked on to some general-purposes verb such as *prove, serve, form, play, render.* In addition, the passive voice is wherever possible used in preference to the active, and noun constructions are used instead of gerunds (*by examination of* instead of *by examining*). The range of verbs is further cut down by means of the *-ize* and *de-* formation, and the banal statements are given an appearance of profundity by means of the *not un-* formation. Simple conjunctions and prepositions are replaced by such phrases as *with respect to, having regard to, the fact that, by dint of, in view of, in the interests of, on the hypothesis that;* and the ends of sentences are saved from anticlimax by such resounding commonplaces as *greatly to be desired, cannot be left out of account, a development to be expected in the near future, deserving of serious consideration, brought to a satisfactory conclusion,* and so on and so forth.

Pretentious Diction   Words like *phenomenon, element, individual* (as noun), *objective, categorical, effective, virtual, basic, primary, promote, constitute, exhibit, exploit, utilize, eliminate, liquidate,* are used to dress up simple statements and give an air of scientific impartiality to biased judgments. Adjectives like *epoch-making, epic, historic, unforgettable, triumphant, age-old, inevitable, inexorable, veritable,* are used to dignify the sordid processes of international politics, while writing that aims at glorifying war usually takes on an archaic color, its characteristic words being: *realm, throne, chariot, mailed fist, trident, sword, shield, buckler, banner, jackboot, clarion.* Foreign words and expressions such as *cul de sac, ancien régime, deus ex machina, mutatis mutandis, status quo, gleichschaltung, weltanschauung,* are used to give an air of culture and elegance. Except for the useful abbreviations *i.e., e.g.,* and *etc.,* there is no real need for any of the hundreds of foreign phrases now current in English. Bad writers, and especially scientific, political and sociological writers, are nearly always haunted by the notion that Latin or Greek words are grander than Saxon ones, and unnecessary words like *expedite, ameliorate, predict, extraneous, deracinated, clandestine, subaqueous* and hundreds of others constantly gain ground from their Anglo-Saxon opposite numbers.[1] The jargon peculiar to Marxist writing (*hyena, hangman, cannibal, petty bourgeois, these gentry, lackey, flunky, mad dog, White Guard,* etc.) consists largely of words and phrases translated from Russian, German or French; but the normal way of coining a new word is to use a Latin or Greek root with the appropriate affix and, where necessary, the *-ize* formation. It is often easier to make up words of this kind (*deregionalize, impermissible, extramarital, nonfragmentatory* and so forth) than to think up the English words that will cover one's meaning. The result, in general, is an increase in slovenliness and vagueness.

Meaningless Words   In certain kinds of writing, particularly in art criticism and literary criticism, it is normal to come across long passages which are almost completely lacking in meaning.[2] Words like *romantic, plastic, values, human, dead, sentimental, natural, vitality,* as used in art criticism, are strictly meaningless in the sense that they not only do not point to any discoverable object, but are hardly ever expected to do so by the reader. When one critic writes, "The outstanding feature of Mr. X's work is its living quality," while another writes, "The immediately striking thing about Mr. X's work is its peculiar deadness," the reader accepts this as a simple difference of opinion. If words like *black* and *white* were involved, instead of the jargon words *dead* and *living*, he would see at once that language was being used in an improper way. Many political words are similarly abused. The word *Fascism* has now no meaning except in so far as it signifies "something not desirable." The words *democracy, socialism, freedom, patriotic, realistic, justice,* have each of them several different meanings which cannot be reconciled with one another. In the case of a word like *democracy,* not only is there no agreed definition, but the attempt to make one is resisted from all sides. It is almost universally felt that when we call a country democratic we are praising it: consequently the defenders of every kind of régime claim that it is a democracy, and fear that they might have to stop using the word if it were tied down to any one meaning. Words of this kind are often used in a consciously dishonest way. That is, the person who uses them has his own private definition, but allows his hearer to think he

---

[1]An interesting illustration of this is the way in which the English flower names which were in use till very recently are being ousted by Greek ones, *snapdragon* becoming *antirrhinum, forget-me-not* becoming *myosotis,* etc. It is hard to see any practical reason for this change of fashion: it is probably due to an instinctive turning-away from the more homely word and a vague feeling that the Greek word is scientific.

[2]Example: "Comfort's catholicity of perception and image, strangely Whitmanesque in range, almost the exact opposite in aesthetic compulsion, continues to evoke that trembling atmospheric accumulative hinting at a cruel, an inexorably serene timelessness . . . Wrey Gardiner scores by aiming at simple bull's-eyes with precision. Only they are not so simple, and through this contented sadness runs more than the surface bittersweet of resignation" (*Poetry Quarterly*).

means something quite different. Statements like *Marshal Pétain was a true patriot, The Soviet Press is the freest in the world, The Catholic Church is opposed to persecution,* are almost always made with intent to deceive. Other words used in variable meanings, in most cases more or less dishonestly, are: *class, totalitarian, science, progressive, reactionary, bourgeois, equality.*

Now that I have made this catalog of swindles and perversions, let me give another example of the kind of writing that they lead to. This time it must of its nature be an imaginary one. I am going to translate a passage of good English into modern English of the worst sort. Here is a well-known verse from *Ecclesiastes*:

> "I returned and saw under the sun, that the race is not to the swift, nor the battle to the strong, neither yet bread to the wise, nor yet riches to men of understanding, nor yet favor to men of skill; but time and chance happeneth to them all."

Here it is in modern English:

> "Objective consideration of contemporary phenomena compels the conclusion that success or failure in competitive activities exhibits no tendency to be commensurate with innate capacity, but that a considerable element of the unpredictable must invariably be taken into account."

This is a parody, but not a very gross one. Exhibit (3), above, for instance, contains several patches of the same kind of English. It will be seen that I have not made a full translation. The beginning and ending of the sentence follow the original meaning fairly closely, but in the middle the concrete illustrations — race, battle, bread — dissolve into the vague phrase "success or failure in competitive activities." This had to be so, because no modern writer of the kind I am discussing — no one capable of using phrases like "objective consideration of contemporary phenomena" — would ever tabulate his thoughts in that precise and detailed way. The whole tendency of modern prose is away from concreteness. Now analyze these two sentences a little more closely. The first contains forty-nine words but only sixty syllables, and all its words are those of everyday life. The second contains thirty-eight words of ninety syllables: eighteen of its words are from Latin roots, and one from Greek. The first sentence contains six vivid images, and only one phrase ("time and chance") that could be called vague. The second contains not a single fresh, arresting phrase, and in spite of its ninety syllables it gives only a shortened version of the meaning contained in the first. Yet without a doubt it is the second kind of sentence that is gaining ground in modern English. I do not want to exaggerate. This kind of writing is not yet universal, and outcrops of simplicity will occur here and there in the worst-written page. Still, if you or I were told to write a few lines

10

on the uncertainty of human fortunes, we should probably come much nearer to my imaginary sentence than to the one from *Ecclesiastes*.

As I have tried to show, modern writing at its worst does not consist in picking out words for the sake of their meaning and inventing images in order to make the meaning clearer. It consists in gumming together long strips of words which have already been set in order by someone else, and making the results presentable by sheer humbug. The attraction of this way of writing is that it is easy. It is easier — even quicker, once you have the habit — to say *In my opinion it is a not unjustifiable assumption that* than to say *I think*. If you use ready-made phrases, you not only don't have to hunt about for words; you also don't have to bother with the rhythms of your sentences, since these phrases are generally so arranged as to be more or less euphonious. When you are composing in a hurry — when you are dictating to a stenographer, for instance, or making a public speech — it is natural to fall into a pretentious, Latinized style. Tags like *a consideration which we should do well to bear in mind* or *a conclusion to which all of us would readily assent* will save many a sentence from coming down with a bump. By using stale metaphors, similes and idioms, you save much mental effort, at the cost of leaving your meaning vague, not only for your reader but for yourself. This is the significance of mixed metaphors. The sole aim of a metaphor is to call up a visual image. When these images clash — as in *The Fascist octopus has sung its swan song, the jackboot is thrown into the melting pot* — it can be taken as certain that the writer is not seeing a mental image of the objects he is naming; in other words he is not really thinking. Look again at the examples I gave at the beginning of this essay. Professor Laski (1) uses five negatives in fifty-three words. One of these is superfluous, making nonsense of the whole passage, and in addition there is the slip *alien* for akin, making further nonsense, and several avoidable pieces of clumsiness which increase the general vagueness. Professor Hogben (2) plays ducks and drakes with a battery which is able to write prescriptions, and, while disapproving of the everyday phrase *put up with*, is unwilling to look *egregious* up in the dictionary and see what it means. (3), if one takes an uncharitable attitude towards it, is simply meaningless: probably one could work out its intended meaning by reading the whole of the article in which it occurs. In (4), the writer knows more or less what he wants to say, but an accumulation of stale phrases chokes him like tea leaves blocking a sink. In (5), words and meaning have almost parted company. People who write in this manner usually have a general emotional meaning — they dislike one thing and want to express solidarity with another — but they are not interested in the detail of what they are saying. A scrupulous writer, in every sentence that he writes, will ask himself at least four questions, thus: What am I trying to say? What words will express it? What image or idiom will make it clearer? Is this image fresh enough to have an effect? And he will probably ask himself two more: Could I put it more shortly? Have I said anything that is avoidably ugly? But you are not obliged to go to all this trouble. You can shirk it by simply throwing your mind open and letting the ready-made phrases come crowding in. They will construct your sentences for you — even think your thoughts for you, to a certain extent — and at need they will perform the important service of partially concealing your meaning even from yourself. It is at this point that the special connection between politics and the debasement of language becomes clear.

In our time it is broadly true that political writing is bad writing. Where it is not true, it will generally be found that the writer is some kind of rebel, expressing his private opinions and not a "party line." Orthodoxy, of whatever color, seems to demand a lifeless, imitative style. The political dialects to be found in pamphlets, leading articles, manifestos, White Papers and the speeches of under-secretaries do, of course, vary from party to party, but they are all alike in that one almost never finds in them a fresh, vivid, home-made turn of speech. When one watches some tired hack on the platform mechanically repeating the familiar phrases — *bestial atrocities, iron heel, bloodstained tyranny, free peoples of the world, stand shoulder to shoulder* — one often has a curious feeling that one is not watching a live human being but some kind of dummy: a feeling which suddenly becomes stronger at moments when the light catches the speaker's spectacles and turns them into blank discs which seem to have no eyes behind them. And this is not altogether fanciful. A speaker who uses that kind of phraseology has gone some distance towards turning himself into a machine. The appropriate noises are coming out of his larynx, but his brain is not involved as it would be if he were choosing his words for himself. If the speech he is making is one that he is accustomed to make over and over again, he may be almost unconscious of what he is saying, as one is when one utters the responses in church. And this reduced state of consciousness, if not indispensable, is at any rate favorable to political conformity.

In our time, political speech and writing are largely the defense of the indefensible. Things like the continuance of British rule in India, the Russian purges and deportations, the dropping of the atom bombs on Japan, can indeed be defended, but only by arguments which are too brutal for most people to face, and which do not square with the professed aims of political parties. Thus political language has to consist largely of euphemism, question-begging and sheer cloudy vagueness. Defenseless villages are bombarded from the air, the inhabitants driven out into the countryside, the cattle machine-gunned, the huts set on fire with incendiary bullets: this is called *pacification*. Millions of peasants are robbed of their farms and sent trudging along the roads with no more than they can carry: this is called *transfer of population* or *rectification of frontiers*. People are imprisoned for years without trial, or shot in the back of the neck or sent to die of scurvy in Arctic lumber camps: this is called *elimination of unreliable elements*. Such phraseology is needed if one wants to name things without calling up mental pictures of them. Consider for instance some comfortable English professor defending Russian totalitarianism. He cannot say outright, "I believe in killing off your opponents when you can get good results by doing so." Probably, therefore, he will say something like this:

"While freely conceding that the Soviet régime exhibits certain features which the humanitarian may be inclined to deplore, we must, I think, agree that a certain curtailment of the right to political opposition is an unavoidable concomitant of transitional periods, and that the rigors which the Russian people have been called upon to undergo have been amply justified in the sphere of concrete achievement."

The inflated style is itself a kind of euphemism. A mass of Latin words falls upon the facts like soft snow, blurring the outlines and covering up all the details. The great enemy of clear language is insincerity. When there is a gap between one's real and one's declared aims, one turns as it were instinctively to long words and exhausted idioms, like a cuttlefish squirting out ink. In our age there is no such thing as "keeping out of politics." All issues are political issues, and politics itself is a mass of lies, evasions, folly, hatred and schizophrenia. When the general atmosphere is bad, language must suffer. I should expect to find — this is a guess which I have not sufficient knowledge to verify — that the German, Russian and Italian languages have all deteriorated in the last ten or fifteen years, as a result of dictatorship.

But if thought corrupts language, language can also corrupt thought. A bad usage can spread by tradition and imitation, even among people who should and do know better. The debased language that I have been discussing is in some ways very convenient. Phrases like *a not unjustifiable assumption, leaves much to be desired, would serve no good purpose, a consideration which we should do well to bear in mind*, are a continuous temptation, a packet of aspirins always at one's elbow. Look back through this essay, and for certain you will find that I have again and again committed the very faults I am protesting against. By this morning's post I have received a pamphlet dealing with conditions in Germany. The author tells me that he "felt impelled" to write it. I open it at random, and here is almost the first sentence that I see: "(The Allies) have an opportunity not only of achieving a radical transformation of Germany's social and political structure in such a way as to avoid a nationalistic reaction in Germany itself, but at the same time of laying the foundations of a cooperative and unified Europe." You see, he "feels impelled" to write — feels, presumably, that he has something new to say — and yet his words, like cavalry horses answering the bugle, group themselves automatically into the familiar dreary pattern. This invasion of one's mind by ready-made phrases (*lay the foundations, achieve a radical transformation*) can only be prevented if one is constantly on guard against them, and every such phrase anaesthetizes a portion of one's brain.

I said earlier that the decadence of our language is probably curable. Those who deny this would argue, if they produced an argument at all, that language merely reflects existing social conditions, and that we cannot influence its development by any direct tinkering with words and constructions. So far as the general tone or spirit of a language goes, this may be true, but it is not true in detail. Silly words and expressions have often disappeared, not through any evolutionary process but owing to the conscious action of a minority. Two recent examples were *explore every avenue* and *leave no stone unturned*, which were killed by the jeers of a few journalists. There is a long list of flyblown metaphors which could similarly be got rid of if enough people would interest themselves in the job; and it should also be possible to laugh the *not un-* formation out of existence,[3] to reduce the amount of Latin and Greek in the average sentence, to drive out foreign phrases and strayed scientific words, and, in general, to make pretentiousness unfashionable. But all these are minor points. The defense of the English language implies more than this, and perhaps it is best to start by saying what it does not imply.

To begin with it has nothing to do with archaism, with the salvaging of obsolete words and turns of speech, or with the setting up of a "standard English" which must never be departed from. On the contrary, it is especially concerned with the scrapping of every word or idiom which has outworn its usefulness. It has nothing to do with correct grammar and syntax, which are of no importance so long as one makes one's meaning clear, or with the avoidance of Americanisms, or with having what is called a "good prose style." On the other hand it is not concerned with fake simplicity and the attempt to make written English colloquial. Nor does it even imply in every case preferring the Saxon word to the Latin one, though it does imply using the fewest and shortest words that will cover one's meaning. What is above all needed is to let the meaning choose the word, and not the other way about. In prose, the worst thing one can do with words is to surrender to them. When you think of a concrete object, you think wordlessly, and then, if you want to describe the thing you have been visualizing you probably hunt about till you find the exact words that seem to fit. When you think of something abstract you are more inclined to use words from the start, and unless you make a conscious effort to prevent it, the existing dialect will come rushing in and do the job for you, at the expense of blurring or even changing your meaning. Probably it is better to put off using words as long as possible and get one's meaning as clear as one can through pictures or sensations. Afterwards one can choose — not simply *accept* — the phrases that will best cover the meaning, and then switch round and decide what impression one's words are likely to make on another person. This last effort of the mind cuts out all stale or mixed images, all prefabricated phrases, needless repetitions, and humbug and vagueness generally. But one can often be in doubt about the effect of a word or a phrase, and one

---

[3]One can cure oneself of the *not un-* formation by memorizing this sentence: *A not unblack dog was chasing a not unsmall rabbit across a not ungreen field.*

needs rules that one can rely on when instinct fails. I think the following rules will cover most cases:

(i) Never use a metaphor, simile or other figure of speech which you are used to seeing in print.

(ii) Never use a long word where a short one will do.

(iii) If it is possible to cut a word out, always cut it out.

(iv) Never use the passive where you can use the active.

(v) Never use a foreign phrase, a scientific word or a jargon word if you can think of an everyday English equivalent.

(vi) Break any of these rules sooner than say anything outright barbarous.

These rules sound elementary, and so they are, but they demand a deep change of attitude in anyone who has grown used to writing in the style now fashionable. One could keep all of them and still write bad English, but one could not write the kind of stuff that I quoted in those five specimens at the beginning of this article.

I have not here been considering the literary use of language, but merely language as an instrument for expressing and not for concealing or preventing thought. Stuart Chase and others have come near to claiming that all abstract words are meaningless, and have used this as a pretext for advocating a kind of political quietism. Since you don't know what Fascism is, how can you struggle against Fascism? One need not swallow such absurdities as this, but one ought to recognize that the present political chaos is connected with the decay of language, and that one can probably bring about some improvement by starting at the verbal end. If you simplify your English, you are freed from the worst follies of orthodoxy. You cannot speak any of the necessary dialects, and when you make a stupid remark its stupidity will be obvious, even to yourself. Political language — and with variations this is true of all political parties, from Conservatives to Anarchists — is designed to make lies sound truthful and murder respectable, and to give an appearance of solidity to pure wind. One cannot change this all in a moment, but one can at least change one's own habits, and from time to time one can even, if one jeers loudly enough, send some worn-out and useless phrase — some *jackboot*, *Achilles' heel*, *hotbed*, *melting pot*, *acid test*, *veritable inferno* or other lump of verbal refuse — into the dustbin where it belongs.

20

QUESTIONS

Reading

1. What is Orwell's position on the ways that modern writers are destroying the English language?

2. Orwell argues that "thought corrupts language," but he also argues that "language can also corrupt thought" (paragraph 16). What argument is he making? How does language corrupt thought?
3. Orwell writes in paragraph 16, "Look back through this essay, and for certain you will find that I have again and again committed the very faults I am protesting against." Does Orwell, in fact, break his own rules? If so, what might his purpose be in doing so?
4. What sense of himself does Orwell present to his readers? How would you describe his persona?

Exploratory Writing

1. Orwell stresses that his argument is not about the *literary* use of language. Find an example of a piece of literary writing — poetry, fiction, or literary prose — and analyze it according to Orwell's rules. Discuss whether the guidelines for literary and political writing should be the same.
2. Orwell presents guidelines for good writing in paragraph 18. Exchange one of your recent essays with a classmate. How does your partner's writing measure up to Orwell's standards?

Making Connections

1. American writer James Baldwin (p. 109) was probably influenced by Orwell's essay. Write an essay of your own explaining the connections that you find between Orwell and Baldwin.

Essay Writing

1. Spend one week developing a list of examples of bad writing from newspapers and popular magazines. Use this material as the basis for an essay in which you develop a thesis arguing your position on politics and language.
2. Written more than sixty years ago, this is probably the best known of all of Orwell's essays. How insightful and current do you find it today? Take five examples from your reading, as Orwell takes from his, and use them as evidence in an argument of your own about the state of contemporary written English. Take your examples from anywhere you like, including this book — even this question — if you wish. Be careful to choose recent pieces of writing.

If Black English Isn't a Language, Then Tell Me, What Is?

James Baldwin

Harlem-born writer James Baldwin (1924–1987) experimented with literary forms throughout his career, producing almost twenty volumes of poetry, fiction, essays, and plays, as well as five collaborations with people such as photographer Richard Avedon, poet Nikki Giovani, and anthropologist Margaret Mead. At the age of fourteen, Baldwin followed in his stepfather's footsteps and became a Pentecostal preacher, but he left the church three years later and resettled in New York's bohemian Greenwich Village. There he concentrated on his writing, much of which powerfully — and often poetically — defined and legitimized the black voice. His most famous works include his semi-autobiographical novel Go Tell It on the Mountain *(1953) and the essay collections* Notes of a Native Son *(1955) and* The Fire Next Time *(1963). The following essay on language and legitimacy first appeared in the* New York Times *in 1979. Baldwin died of stomach cancer in Paris, where he'd moved at the age of twenty-four and spent the last forty years of his life.*

The argument concerning the use, or the status, or the reality, of black English is rooted in American history and has absolutely nothing to do with the question the argument supposes itself to be posing. The argument has nothing to do with language itself but with the role of language. Language, incontestably, reveals the speaker. Language, also, far more dubiously, is meant to define the other — and, in this case, the other is refusing to be defined by a language that has never been able to recognize him.

People evolve a language in order to describe and thus control their circumstances or in order not to be submerged by a situation that they cannot articulate. (And if they cannot articulate it, they are submerged.) A Frenchman living in Paris speaks a subtly and crucially different language from that of the man living in Marseilles; neither sounds very much like a man living in Quebec; and they would all have great difficulty in apprehending what the man from Guadeloupe, or Martinique, is saying, to say nothing of the man from Senegal — although the "common" language of all these areas is French. But each has paid, and is paying, a different price for this "common" language, in which, as it turns out, they are not saying, and cannot be saying, the same things: They each have very different realities to articulate, or control.

What joins all languages, and all men, is the necessity to confront life, in order, not inconceivably, to outwit death: The price for this is the acceptance, and achievement, of one's temporal identity. So that, for example, though it is not taught in the schools (and this has the potential of becoming a political issue) the south of France still clings to its ancient and musical Provençal, which resists being described as a "dialect." And much of the tension in the Basque countries, and in Wales, is due to the Basque and Welsh determination not to allow their languages to be destroyed. This determination also feeds the flames in Ireland for among the many indignities the Irish have been forced to undergo at English hands is the English contempt for their language.

It goes without saying, then, that language is also a political instrument, means, and proof of power. It is the most vivid and crucial key to identity: It reveals the private identity, and connects one with, or divorces one from, the larger, public, or communal identity. There have been, and are, times and places, when to speak a certain language could be dangerous, even fatal. Or, one may speak the same language, but in such a way that one's antecedents are revealed, or (one hopes) hidden. This is true in France, and is absolutely true in England: The range (and reign) of accents on that damp little island make England coherent for the English and totally incomprehensible for everyone else. To open your mouth in England is (if I may use black English) to "put your business in the street." You have confessed your parents, your youth, your school, your salary, your self-esteem, and, alas, your future.

Now, I do not know what white Americans would sound like if there   5
had never been any black people in the United States, but they would not sound the way they sound. *Jazz*, for example, is a very specific sexual term, as in *jazz me, baby*, but white people purified it into the Jazz Age. *Sock it to me*, which means, roughly, the same thing, has been adopted by Nathaniel Hawthorne's descendants with no qualms or hesitations at all, along with *let it all hang out* and *right on! Beat to his socks*, which was once the black's most total and despairing image of poverty, was transformed into a thing called the Beat Generation, which phenomenon was, largely, composed of *uptight*, middle-class white people, imitating poverty, trying to *get down*, to *get with it*, doing their *thing*, doing their despairing best to be *funky*, which we, the blacks, never dreamed of doing — we were funky, baby, like *funk* was going out of style.

Now, no one can eat his cake, and have it, too, and it is late in the day to attempt to penalize black people for having created a language that permits the nation its only glimpse of reality, a language without which the nation would be even more *whipped* than it is.

I say that the present skirmish is rooted in American history, and it is. Black English is the creation of the black diaspora. Blacks came to the United States chained to each other, but from different tribes. Neither could speak the other's language. If two black people, at that bitter hour of the world's history, had been able to speak to each other, the institution of chattel slavery could never have lasted as long as it did. Subsequently, the slave was given, under the eye, and the gun, of his master, Congo Square, and the Bible — or, in other words, and under those conditions, the slave began the formation of the black church, and it is within this unprecedented tabernacle that black English began to be formed. This was not, merely, as in the European example, the adoption of a foreign tongue, but an alchemy that transformed ancient elements into a new language: *A language comes into existence by means of brutal necessity, and the rules of the language are dictated by what the language must convey.*

There was a moment, in time, and in this place, when my brother, or my mother, or my father, or my sister, had to convey to me, for example, the danger in which I was standing from the white man standing just behind me, and to convey this with a speed and in a language, that the white man could not possibly understand, and that, indeed, he cannot understand, until today. He cannot afford to understand it. This understanding would reveal to him too much about himself and smash that mirror before which he has been frozen for so long.

Now, if this passion, this skill, this (to quote Toni Morrison) "sheer intelligence," this incredible music, the mighty achievement of having brought a people utterly unknown to, or despised by "history" — to have brought this people to their present, troubled, troubling, and unassailable and unanswerable place — if this absolutely unprecedented journey does not indicate that black English is a language, I am curious to know what definition of languages is to be trusted.

A people at the center of the western world, and in the midst of so hostile a population, has not endured and transcended by means of what is patronizingly called a "dialect." We, the blacks, are in trouble, certainly, but we are not inarticulate because we are not compelled to defend a morality that we know to be a lie.   10

The brutal truth is that the bulk of the white people in America never had any interest in educating black people, except as this could serve white purposes. It is not the black child's language that is despised. It is his experience. A child cannot be taught by anyone who despises him, and a child cannot afford to be fooled. A child cannot be taught by anyone whose demand, essentially, is that the child repudiate his experience, and all that gives him sustenance, and enter a limbo in which he will no longer be black, and in which he knows that he can never become white. Black people have lost too many black children that way.

And, after all, finally, in a country with standards so untrustworthy, a country that makes heroes of so many criminal mediocrities, a country unable to face why so many of the nonwhite are in prison, or on the needle, or standing, futureless, in the streets — it may very well be that both the child, and his elder, have concluded that they have nothing whatever to learn from the people of a country that has managed to learn so little.

QUESTIONS

Reading

1. Baldwin begins his essay by challenging a long-standing argument concerning black English: "The argument has nothing to do with language itself but with the role of language" (paragraph 1). What distinctions does Baldwin note between "language itself" and "the role of language"? Why is this distinction central to his argument?
2. Baldwin's position on black English is at odds with those who would like to deny black English status as a language. Summarize Baldwin's position as well as the position of Baldwin's opponents.
3. In paragraph 4, Baldwin writes, "It goes without saying, then, that language is also a political instrument, means, and proof of power." How, according to Baldwin, does language connect or divide one from "communal identity"? What evidence does he provide to support this claim that language is a political instrument?

Exploratory Writing

1. Baldwin makes an important distinction between *dialect* and *language*. Make a double-entry list of the ways that he defines each (use a separate piece of paper if you need more room). Discuss whether you find his definitions persuasive.

DIALECT	LANGUAGE

2. Baldwin asks his readers to think about the evolution of black English and to consider "what definition of languages is to be trusted" (paragraph 9) if black English is not a language. Collaborate in small groups to choose an example of a dialect with which you are all familiar. Would you define this dialect as a language? Prepare a presentation describing and demonstrating the ways this dialect reflects the richness of its culture.

3. Reread Baldwin's memorable conclusion, first published in 1979. How does he prepare you for this conclusion? What are you left to contemplate? How relevant does his indictment of racism in the United States seem today?

Making Connections

1. Both Baldwin and Martin Luther King Jr. (p. 288) make strong arguments about racial questions. Both of these writers are considered to be exceptional masters of English prose. What color is their English? Write an essay in which you consider them as argumentative writers. Are their styles of argument different? Do they use the same vocabulary? How would you characterize each as a writer? Do you prefer one style over the other? Do you find that one of their arguments is more effective than the other? Present your opinions, and make your case.

Essay Writing

1. Both Baldwin and George Orwell ("Politics and the English Language," p. 97) are interested in understanding language as a political instrument. Write an essay in which you examine their views on the politics of language, pointing out their similarities and differences.

Paired Readings: On Descriptive Writing

On Keeping a Notebook

Joan Didion

Joan Didion was born in Sacramento, California, in 1934 and graduated from the University of California at Berkeley in 1956. Until the publication of her first novel, Run River, *in 1963, she worked as an editor for* Vogue *magazine. Since then, she has written four more novels, including* Play It as It Lays *(1971) and* The Last Thing He Wanted *(1996); six books of essays, most notably* Slouching Towards Bethlehem *(1968) and* The White Album *(1979); and, in collaboration with her late husband, John Gregory Dunne, a number of successful screenplays. As both novelist and essayist, Didion has shown herself to be a trenchant observer and interpreter of American society and culture. Many of her essays also explore her own private life in intimate detail. Her 2005 book,* The Year of Magical Thinking — *winner of the National Book Award for nonfiction* — *has been described as a memoir of grief, as it chronicles the aftermath of her husband's sudden death in 2003 from a heart attack. The following piece appeared in* Holiday *magazine in 1966 and in the critically acclaimed essay collection* Slouching Towards Bethlehem.

"'That woman Estelle,'" the note reads, "'is partly the reason why George Sharp and I are separated today.' *Dirty crepe-de-Chine wrapper, hotel bar, Wilmington RR, 9:45 a.m. August Monday morning.*"

Since the note is in my notebook, it presumably has some meaning to me. I study it for a long while. At first I have only the most general notion of what I was doing on an August Monday morning in the bar of the hotel across from the Pennsylvania Railroad station in Wilmington, Delaware (waiting for a train? missing one? 1960? 1961? why Wilmington?), but I do remember being there. The woman in the dirty crepe-de-Chine wrapper had come down from her room for a beer, and the bartender had heard before the reason why George Sharp and she were separated today. "Sure," he said, and went on mopping the floor. "You told me." At the other end of the bar is a girl. She is talking, pointedly, not to the man beside her but to a cat lying in the triangle of sunlight cast through the open door. She is wearing a plaid silk dress from Peck & Peck, and the hem is coming down.

Here is what it is: the girl has been on the Eastern Shore, and now she is going back to the city, leaving the man beside her, and all she can see ahead are the viscous summer sidewalks and the 3 a.m. long-distance calls that will make her lie awake and then sleep drugged through all the steaming mornings left in August (1960? 1961?). Because she must go directly from the train to lunch in New York, she wishes that she had a safety pin for the hem of the plaid silk dress, and she also wishes that she could forget about the hem and the lunch and stay in the cool bar that smells of disinfectant and malt and make friends with the woman in the crepe-de-Chine wrapper. She is afflicted by a little self-pity, and she wants to compare Estelles. That is what that was all about.

Why did I write it down? In order to remember, of course, but exactly what was it I wanted to remember? How much of it actually happened? Did any of it? Why do I keep a notebook at all? It is easy to deceive oneself on all those scores. The impulse to write things down is a peculiarly compulsive one, inexplicable to those who do not share it, useful only accidentally, only secondarily, in the way that any compulsion tries to justify itself. I suppose that it begins or does not begin in the cradle. Although I have felt compelled to write things down since I was five years old, I doubt that my daughter ever will, for she is a singularly blessed and accepting child, delighted with life exactly as life presents itself to her, unafraid to go to sleep and unafraid to wake up. Keepers of private notebooks are a different breed altogether, lonely and resistant rearrangers of things, anxious malcontents, children afflicted apparently at birth with some presentiment of loss.

My first notebook was a Big Five tablet, given to me by my mother with the sensible suggestion that I stop whining and learn to amuse myself by writing down my thoughts. She returned the tablet to me a few years ago; the first entry is an account of a woman who believed herself to be freezing to death in the Arctic night, only to find, when day broke, that she had stumbled onto the Sahara Desert, where she would die of the heat before lunch. I have no idea what turn of a five-year-old's mind could have prompted so insistently "ironic" and exotic a story, but it does reveal a certain predilection for the extreme which has dogged me into adult life; perhaps if I were analytically inclined I would find it a truer story than any I might have told about Donald Johnson's birthday party or the day my cousin Brenda put Kitty Litter in the aquarium.

5

So the point of my keeping a notebook has never been, nor is it now, to have an accurate factual record of what I have been doing or thinking. That would be a different impulse entirely, an instinct for reality which I sometimes envy but do not possess. At no point have I ever been able successfully to keep a diary; my approach to daily life ranges from the grossly negligent to the merely absent, and on those few occasions when I have tried dutifully to record a day's events, boredom has so overcome me that the results are mysterious at best. What is this business about "shopping, typing piece, dinner with E, depressed"? Shopping for what? Typing what piece? Who is E? Was this "E" depressed, or was I depressed? Who cares?

In fact I have abandoned altogether that kind of pointless entry; instead I tell what some would call lies. "That's simply not true," the members of my family frequently tell me when they come up against my memory of a shared event. "The party was *not* for you, the spider was *not* a black widow, *it wasn't that way at all.*" Very likely they are right, for not only have I always had trouble distinguishing between what happened and what merely might have happened, but I remain unconvinced that the distinction, for my purposes, matters. The cracked crab that I recall having for lunch the day my father came home from Detroit in 1945 must certainly be embroidery, worked into the day's pattern to lend verisimilitude; I was ten years old and would not now remember the cracked crab. The day's events did not turn on cracked crab. And yet it is precisely that fictitious crab that makes me see the afternoon all over again, a home movie run all too often, the father bearing gifts, the child weeping, an exercise in family love and guilt. Or that is what it was to me. Similarly, perhaps it never did snow that August in Vermont; perhaps there never were flurries in the night wind, and maybe no one else felt the ground hardening and summer already dead even as we pretended to bask in it, but that was how it felt to me, and it might as well have snowed, could have snowed, did snow.

How it felt to me: that is getting closer to the truth about a notebook. I sometimes delude myself about why I keep a notebook, imagine that some thrifty virtue derives from preserving everything observed. See enough and write it down, I tell myself, and then some morning when the world seems drained of wonder, some day when I am only going through the motions of doing what I am supposed to do, which is write — on that bankrupt morning I will simply open my notebook and there it will all be, a forgotten account with accumulated interest, paid passage back to the world out there: dialogue overheard in hotels and elevators and at the hat-check counter in Pavillon (one middle-aged man shows his hat check to another and says, "That's my old football number"); impressions of Bettina Aptheker and Benjamin Sonnenberg and Teddy ("Mr. Acapulco") Stauffer; careful *aperçus* about tennis bums and failed fashion models and Greek shipping heiresses, one of whom taught me a significant lesson (a lesson I could have learned from F. Scott Fitzgerald, but perhaps we all must meet the very rich for ourselves) by asking, when I arrived to interview her in her orchid-filled sitting room on the second day of a paralyzing New York blizzard, whether it was snowing outside.

I imagine, in other words, that the notebook is about other people. But of course it is not. I have no real business with what one stranger said to another at the hat-check counter in Pavillon; in fact I suspect that the line "That's my old football number" touched not my own imagination at all, but merely some memory of something once read, probably "The Eighty-Yard Run." Nor is my concern with a woman in a dirty crepe-de-Chine wrapper in a Wilmington bar. My stake is always, of course, in the unmentioned girl in the plaid silk dress. *Remember what it was to be me*: that is always the point.

It is a difficult point to admit. We are brought up in the ethic that others, any others, all others, are by definition more interesting than ourselves; taught to be diffident, just this side of self-effacing. ("You're the least important person in the room and don't forget it," Jessica Mitford's governess would hiss in her ear on the advent of any social occasion; I copied that into my notebook because it is only recently that I have been able to enter a room without hearing some such phrase in my inner ear.) Only the very young and the very old may recount their dreams at breakfast, dwell upon self, interrupt with memories of beach picnics and favorite Liberty lawn dresses and the rainbow trout in a creek near Colorado Springs. The rest of us are expected, rightly, to affect absorption in other people's favorite dresses, other people's trout.

And so we do. But our notebooks give us away, for however dutifully we record what we see around us, the common denominator of all we see is always, transparently, shamelessly, the implacable "I." We are not talking here about the kind of notebook that is patently for public consumption, a structural conceit for binding together a series of graceful *pensées*; we are talking about something private, about bits of the mind's string too short to use, an indiscriminate and erratic assemblage with meaning only for its maker.

And sometimes even the maker has difficulty with the meaning. There does not seem to be, for example, any point in my knowing for the rest of my life that, during 1964, 720 tons of soot fell on every square mile of New York City, yet there it is in my notebook, labeled "FACT." Nor do I really need to remember that Ambrose Bierce liked to spell Leland Stanford's name "£eland \$tanford" or that "smart women almost always wear black in Cuba," a fashion hint without much potential for practical application. And does not the relevance of these notes seem marginal at best?:

> In the basement museum of the Inyo County Courthouse in Independence, California, sign pinned to a mandarin coat: "This MANDARIN COAT was often worn by Mrs. Minnie S. Brooks when giving lectures on her TEAPOT COLLECTION."

> Redhead getting out of car in front of Beverly Wilshire Hotel, chinchilla stole, Vuitton bags with tags reading:

> MRS LOU FOX
> HOTEL SAHARA
> VEGAS

Well, perhaps not entirely marginal. As a matter of fact, Mrs. Minnie S. Brooks and her MANDARIN COAT pull me back into my own childhood, for although I never knew Mrs. Brooks and did not visit Inyo County until I was thirty, I grew up in just such a world, in houses cluttered with Indian relics and bits of gold ore and ambergris and the souvenirs my Aunt Mercy Farnsworth brought back from the Orient. It is a long way from that world to Mrs. Lou Fox's world, where we all live now, and is it not just as well to remember that? Might not Mrs. Minnie S. Brooks help me to remember what I am? Might not Mrs. Lou Fox help me to remember what I am not?

But sometimes the point is harder to discern. What exactly did I have in mind when I noted down that it cost the father of someone I know $650 a month to light the place on the Hudson in which he lived before the Crash? What use was I planning to make of this line by Jimmy Hoffa: "I may have my faults, but being wrong ain't one of them"? And although I think it interesting to know where the girls who travel with the Syndicate have their hair done when they find themselves on the West Coast, will I ever make suitable use of it? Might I not be better off just passing it on to John O'Hara? What is a recipe for sauerkraut doing in my notebook? What kind of magpie keeps this notebook? "*He was born the night the Titanic went down.*" That seems a nice enough line, and I even recall who said it, but is it not really a better line in life than it could ever be in fiction?

But of course that is exactly it: not that I should ever use the line, but that   15
I should remember the woman who said it and the afternoon I heard it. We were on her terrace by the sea, and we were finishing the wine left from lunch, trying to get what sun there was, a California winter sun. The woman whose husband was born the night the *Titanic* went down wanted to rent her house, wanted to go back to her children in Paris. I remember wishing that I could afford the house, which cost $1,000 a month. "Someday you will," she said lazily. "Someday it all comes." There in the sun on her terrace it seemed easy to believe in someday, but later I had a low-grade afternoon hangover and ran over a black snake on the way to the supermarket and was flooded with inexplicable fear when I heard the checkout clerk explaining to the man ahead of me why she was finally divorcing her husband. "He left me no choice," she said over and over as she punched the register. "He has a little seven-month-old baby by her, he left me no choice." I would like to believe that my dread then was for the human condition, but of course it was for me, because I wanted a baby and did not then have one and because I wanted to own the house that cost $1,000 a month to rent and because I had a hangover.

It all comes back. Perhaps it is difficult to see the value in having one's self back in that kind of mood, but I do see it; I think we are well advised to keep on nodding terms with the people we used to be, whether we find them attractive company or not. Otherwise they turn up unannounced and surprise us, come hammering on the mind's door at 4 a.m. of a bad night and demand to know who deserted them, who betrayed them, who is going to make amends. We forget all too soon the things we thought we could never forget. We forget the loves and the betrayals alike, forget what we whispered and what we screamed, forget who we were. I have already lost touch with a couple of people I used to be; one of them, a seventeen-year-old, presents little threat, although it would be of some interest to me to know again what it feels like to sit on a river levee drinking vodka-and-orange-juice and listening to Les Paul and Mary Ford and their echoes sing "How High the Moon" on the car radio. (You see I still have the scenes, but I no longer perceive myself among those present, no longer could even improvise the dialogue.) The other one, a twenty-three-year-old, bothers me more. She was always a good deal of trouble, and I suspect she will reappear when I least want to see her, skirts too long, shy to the point of aggravation, always the injured party, full of recriminations and little hurts and stories I do not want to hear again, at once saddening me and angering me with her vulnerability and ignorance, an apparition all the more insistent for being so long banished.

It is a good idea, then, to keep in touch, and I suppose that keeping in touch is what notebooks are all about. And we are all on our own when it comes to keeping those lines open to ourselves: your notebook will never help me, nor mine you. *"So what's new in the whiskey business?"* What could that possibly mean to you? To me it means a blonde in a Pucci bathing suit sitting with a couple of fat men by the pool at the Beverly Hills Hotel. Another man approaches, and they all regard one another in silence for a while. "So what's new in the whiskey business?" one of the fat men finally says by way of welcome, and the blonde stands up, arches one foot and dips it in the pool, looking all the while at the cabaña where Baby Pignatari is talking on the telephone. That is all there is to that, except that several years later I saw the blonde coming out of Saks Fifth Avenue in New York with her California complexion and a voluminous mink coat. In the harsh wind that day she looked old and irrevocably tired to me, and even the skins in the mink coat were not worked the way they were doing them that year, not the way she would have wanted them done, and there is the point of the story. For a while after that I did not like to look in the mirror, and my eyes would skim the newspapers and pick out only the deaths, the cancer victims, the premature coronaries, the suicides, and I stopped riding the Lexington Avenue IRT because I noticed for the first time that all the strangers I had seen for years—the man with the seeing-eye dog, the spinster who read the classified pages every day, the fat girl who always got off with me at Grand Central—looked older than they once had.

It all comes back. Even that recipe for sauerkraut: even that brings it back. I was on Fire Island when I first made that sauerkraut, and it was raining, and we drank a lot of bourbon and ate the sauerkraut and went to bed at ten, and I listened to the rain and the Atlantic and felt safe. I made the sauerkraut again last night and it did not make me feel any safer, but that is, as they say, another story.

QUESTIONS

Reading

1. Highlight, flag, or underline passages where Didion uses direct quotations from her notebook in this essay. Why do you think she uses these quotations? How do her responses to them evolve as the essay progresses?
2. Didion offers a number of tentative answers to her main question, "Why do I keep a notebook at all?" (paragraph 4). Make a list of these responses and their revisions throughout the essay. Why doesn't she simply explain at the beginning "what notebooks are all about" (paragraph 17) rather than waiting until the last paragraphs? Do you find this way of explaining to be effective? Explain why or why not.
3. How does Didion distinguish between a diary and a notebook? Does that distinction affect her sense of the difference "between what happened and what merely might have happened" (paragraph 7)? Is Didion concerned with truth in her notebook writing?

Exploratory Writing

1. What is the point of notebooks for you? Choose a statement of Didion's with which you agree or disagree, and discuss how it connects to your own writing process.
2. Spend a few days recording observations in a notebook whenever the impulse strikes you. The notebook should include observations about the outside world, like Didion's examples, rather than diary-like confessions. In small groups, trade notebooks, and discuss what you can and cannot learn about a person from his or her observations alone. What do your observations tell people about your attitude and personality?

Making Connections

1. In Didion's explanation, keeping a notebook is very personal — a tool for remembering what she was like in the past. If Lewis Thomas (p. 339), Atul Gawande (p. 410), Olivia Judson (p. 220), Theodore Sizer (p. 613), or Jan Harold Brunvand (p. 75) were to write an essay with the same title, how might their main points differ from Didion's? Choose any one of those scholars, and write an essay titled, "On Keeping a Notebook" from his or her perspective.
2. How do Didion's remarks about descriptive writing differ from Patricia Hampl's (p. 122)? Make a double-entry list comparing the ways each author characterizes the types of people who engage in memoir writing.

DIDION'S CHARACTERISTICS OF NOTEBOOK KEEPERS	HAMPL'S CHARACTERISTICS OF MEMOIRISTS

Essay Writing

1. Didion writes, "I think we are well advised to keep on nodding terms with the people we used to be, whether we find them attractive company or not" (paragraph 16). Write an essay in which you disagree with this statement, providing strong arguments for why it is a good idea to leave the past behind. If you are actually in agreement with Didion, you will be playing devil's advocate in your essay.

The Dark Art of Description

Patricia Hampl

*Patricia Hampl (b. 1946) is an acclaimed memoirist from St. Paul,
Minnesota. After earning her MFA from the University of Iowa in
1970, she worked as an editor and later became English Regents
Professor at the University of Minnesota. Her first memoir,* A
Romantic Education *(1981), concerns Hampl's Czech heritage;
her second,* Virgin Time: In Search of the Contemplative Life
(1993), explores her Catholic upbringing. The Florist's Daughter,
*a novelistic memoir, examines the opposing worldviews of her
Irish-American mother and her Czech-American father and their
"ordinary" lives in the city of St. Paul. Published in 2007, this
work garnered high praise from critics and was ranked by the*
New York Times *as one of the 100 Notable Books of the Year.
Hampl has also published collections of stories, poems, and
nonfiction. Her writing has been recognized by a Guggenheim
fellowship, two fellowships from the National Endowment for the
Arts, and a MacArthur fellowship. Hampl delivered the following
piece as a keynote address at the Bedell NonfictioNow conference,
November 1, 2007.*

I was coming down the last lap of my most recent book, a memoir
about my mother and father, and I was painfully aware of just how specific
every bit of writing is, full of choices and chances, not theoretical at all, not
the business of sweeping statements or smart ideas about "form" or "genre"
or anything remotely theoretical. Just subject-verb-object and the hope of
meaning.

Two nights away from the finish of my book, I was working late. I
looked away from the computer screen for a moment and there was my dog
staring at me intently. She was on the verge of speech. I could see it. *Come
to bed.* Her eyes said this clearly. It was almost 2 a.m. and for the past four
hours I'd been changing commas to dashes and then back again to commas
with the obsessive focus only a fanatic can sustain.

You've become a crazy person again, I said right out loud. The dog padded away.

The great short story writer J. F. Powers was once stopped by a colleague in the corridor at their university. The man asked him how things were going. Powers allowed that it had been a tough day — "I spent the morning trying to decide whether to have my character call his friend *pal* or *chum*," he said.

That's where I often find myself — thinking how important the choice   5
of *pal* or *chum* is, how whatever truth writing lays claim to resides in a passion for just such quite mad distinctions. This monomania is what a friend of mine calls the 600-pound gorilla of a book. Once the 600-pound gorilla gets hold of you, you're his (or hers). "Those last weeks of finishing a book are a world in themselves," she said. "I think that gorilla is the reason most of us write — it's a real high, but it's also a subconscious agreement not to be available or even normal for as long as it takes."

But as soon as you — or I, anyway — break away from the gorilla's embrace of a particular book, those big, rangy theoretical questions begin to make their approach again. Maybe this is especially true of memoir, the odd enterprise of "writing a life" that has captivated our literary life for the last two decades or so. We tend to think of the novel as the classic narrative form — ever evolving, but familiar, its stately provenance long the preserve of academic interest and the center of trade publishing. Whereas the memoir seems new or somehow "modern," a rather suspect literary upstart. And therefore a form that invites interrogation.

But strictly speaking, autobiography is a genre far older than the novel and is hard-wired into Western literary history. Perhaps from that first injunction of the oracle at Delphi — *Know thyself* — Western culture has been devoted to the exploration of individual consciousness and the unspooling of individual life.

That commandment to *know thyself* was central to antiquity. Plato uttered a version of it; Cicero used it in a tract on the development of social concord. It was such a pillar of cultural, even spiritual value that in the early Christian period Clement of Alexandria felt compelled to claim that the saying had been borrowed by the Greeks from scripture, thus binding the two developing spiritualities — pagan and monotheistic — together in a seamless endeavor.

Closer to modernity, Goethe is supposed to have said with a shudder, "Know thyself? If I knew myself, I'd run away." And Andre Gide probably expressed this revulsion best: "Know thyself! A maxim as pernicious as it is ugly. Whoever observes himself arrests his own development. A caterpillar who wanted to know itself well would never become a butterfly."

But the strongest indictment of the form I have ever encountered came   10
from a student in Indiana who had been conscripted by his Freshman Comp teacher to attend a reading I gave some years ago. He sprawled in his chair with his baseball cap on backwards, his eloquent body language making it

clear he was far, far away. Can't win them all, I decided, and carried on, my eye straying back to him like a tongue drawn to the absence of a just-pulled tooth.

During the Q&A I fielded the decorous questions the students posed. And then, suddenly, apparently in response to something I'd said, my anti-hero sat bolt-upright and was waving his hand urgently, his face alight with interest. Ah — a convert. I called on him, smiling.

"I get it," he said. "Nothin's ever happened to you — and you write books about it."

He was right, of course. And in pronouncing this acute literary critical remark, he touched on the most peculiar aspect of the rise of the memoir in our times — namely, that fundamentally it isn't about having a more interesting life than someone else. True, there is a strand of autobiographical writing that relies on the documentation of extraordinary circumstances, lives lived in extremity, often at great peril. But such memoirs have always been part of literary history. What characterizes the rise of memoir in recent times is precisely the opposite condition — not a gripping "narrative arc," but the quality of voice, the story of perception rather than action.

The self is not the subject of memoir, in this kind of book, but its instrument. And the work of the self is not to "narrate" but to describe. There is something fundamentally photographic about memoir, photographic rather than cinematic. Not a story, but a series of tableaus we are given to consider. No memoirist is surprised by the absences and blanks in action, for another unavoidable quality of autobiography as I am thinking of it — as lyrical quest literature — is that it is as much about reticence as it is about revelation.

It is often remarked that the advent of the movies and the ever faster   15
pace of modern life have conspired to make description a less essential part of prose narrative in our own times. We don't need to be told what things look like — we are inundated with images, pictures, moving or static. In this view, we need the opposite of the photographic quality so beloved of nine-teenth century descriptive writing in which the landscape is rolled out, sen-tence after sentence, the interior of a room and the interior of the character's mind meticulously presented.

We require writing, instead, that subsumes description, leaps right over it to frame episode and to create the much sought-after "narrative arc." The motto — even the mantra — of this narrative model is of course the com-mandment of introductory fiction writing workshops: *Show, don't tell.*

But as recent memoir writing shows, descriptive writing abounds. And it proves, finally, not to be about the object described. Or not only. Descrip-tion in memoir is where the consciousness of the writer and the material of the story are established in harmony, where the self is lost in the material, in a sense. In fiction of the show-don't-tell variety narrative scenes that "show" and dutifully do not "tell" are advanced by volleys of dialogue in which the author's presence is successfully obscured by the dramatic action of the dialogue of his characters. But in description we hear and feel the absorption of the author in the material. We sense the presence of the creator of the scene.

This personal absorption is what we mean by "style." It is strange that we would choose so oddly surfacey a word — style — for this most soulful aspect of writing. We could, perhaps more exactly, call this relation between consciousness and its subject "integrity." What else is the articulation of perception?

Style is a word usually claimed by fashion and the most passing aesthetic values. But maybe that's as it should be because style in writing is terribly perishable. It can rot — that is what we mean when we recognize writing to be "precious," for example. But at its best and most essential, style is the register between a writer's consciousness and the material he is committed to wrestling to the page. It is the real authority of a writer, more substantial than plot, less ego-dependent than voice.

In 1951, Alfred Kazin published his memoir of his boyhood in Brooklyn, 20 *A Walker in the City,* the book that establishes modern American memoir. The critic Leslie Fiedler admired the book but was also frustrated by it. It "perversely refuses to be a novel," he said with some annoyance, as if Kazin's book, deeply dependent on descriptive writing, were refusing to behave. And it was. It was refusing to obey the commandment to "Show, Don't Tell."

When you read "The Block and Beyond," a much-anthologized chapter from Kazin's memoir, it is impossible to discuss the main characters and certainly not its plot or even its narrative structure. It is a rhapsodic evocation of a place and time. And once read, it is impossible to forget, as indelible and inevitable as a poem.

What Kazin was able to do — what every memoirist can attempt — in liberating himself from the demands of show-don't-tell narrative was to enter into reflection, into speculation, into interpretation, and to use the fragment, the image, the vignette, rather than narratively linked scenes to form his world and his book. He was able to show *and* tell. To write a story and write an essay — all in the same tale, braided and twined together. The root of this double power lies in description.

I was one of those enthralled teenage readers of long nineteenth-century English novels. I toiled my way through dense descriptions of gloomy heaths and bogs to get to the airy volleys of dialogue that lofted back and forth down the page to give me what I wanted — would Jane and Mr. Rochester . . . or would they not? Would Dorothea Brooke awaken — would Mr. Lydgate? I didn't relish the descriptive passages. I endured them. Just as Jane and Dorothea endured their parched lives, as if these endless descriptive passages were the desert to be crossed before the paradise of dialogue and the love story could be entered.

Yet all this description was, after all, the *world* of the book — not simply because it gave the book "a sense of place" as the old literary cliché puts it. It wasn't a "sense of place" I cared about in these passages, but the meeting place of perception with story — the place where someone *claimed* the story, where I could glimpse the individual consciousness, the creator of the scene. The person pulling the wires and making Jane and Dorothea move. I was looking, I suppose, for a sign of intimacy with the invisible author. That "dear reader" moment so familiar in nineteenth-century novels — think of Thackeray pausing to have a chat with the reader — with you! — about how to live on nothing a year. Think of George Eliot breaking off to describe the furnishings of Dorothea's ardent mind.

Henry James is probably the crown prince of nineteenth century de-   25
scribers, a *flâneur* of the sentence, a lounge lizard of the paragraph, taking his own sweet time to unfurl an observation, smoking the cheroot of his thought in the contemplative after-dinner puffery of a man who knows how to draw out the pleasure of his rare tobacco. Or — because James himself never hesitates to pile up opposing figures of speech until he has sliced his thought to the refracted transparency he adores — maybe I'll just switch metaphors and say that James sits mildly at his torture apparatus, turning the crank in meticulously calibrated movements as the reader lies helplessly strained upon the rack of his ever-expanding sentences, the exquisite pain of the lengthening description almost breaking the bones of attention. In short (as James often says after gassing on for a nice fat paragraph or two on the quality of a Venetian sunset or the knowing lift of a European eyebrow glimpsed across a table by an artless American ingénue), in short, he loves to carry on.

Carrying on, I was discovering, is what it is to describe. A lot. At length. To trust description above plot, past character development, and even theme. To understand that to describe is both humbler and more essential than to think of compositional imponderables such as "voice" or to strain toward superstructures like "narrative arc." To trust that the act of description will *find* voice and out of its streaming attention will take hold of narration.

By the time I was considering all of this, I had passed from being a reader and had become that more desperate literary type — a writer trying to figure out how to do it myself. I had no idea how to "sustain a narrative" and didn't even understand at the time (the late 1970s) that I was writing something called "a memoir." Yet when I read *Speak, Memory* by Vladimir Nabokov and later read his command — *Caress the detail, the divine detail* — I knew I had found the motto I could live by, the one that prevailed over "Show, Don't Tell."

Perhaps only someone as thoroughly divested of his paradise as Nabokov had been of his boyhood Russia and his family, his native language and all his beloved associations and privileged expectations, could enshrine the detail, the fragment, as the divinity of his literary religion, could trust the truths to be found in the DNA of detail, attentively rendered in ardent description. The dutiful observation that is the yeoman's work of description finally ascended, Nabokov demonstrated, to the transcendent reality of literature, to metaphor itself.

Nabokov was asked in an interview if his characters ever "took over." He replied icily that *his* characters were his galley slaves.

Yet when it was a matter of locating the godhead of literary endeavor, even a writer as unabashedly imperious as Nabokov did not point to himself and his intentions but to the lowly detail. *Caress the detail, the divine detail.* Next to grand conceptions like plot, which is the legitimate government of most stories, or character, which is the crowned sovereign, the detail looks like a ragged peasant with a half-baked idea of revolution and a crazy, sure glint in its eye. But here, according to Nabokov, resides divinity.

Henry James put his faith in something at least as insubstantial. "If one was to undertake to . . . report with truth on the human scene," he wrote, "it could but be because notes had been from the cradle the ineluctable consequence of one's greatest inward energy . . . to take them was as natural as to look, to think, to feel, to recognize, to remember." He considered his habit the basis of literature and called it "the rich principle of the Note."

Such "notes" are of course details, observations. Description. In attending to these details, in the act of description, the more dynamic aspects of narrative have a chance to reveal themselves — not as "action" or "conflict" or any of the theoretical and technical terms we persist in thinking of as the sources of form. Rather, description gives the authorial mind a place to be in relation with the reality of the world.

It was surely this desire for the world — that is for the world's memoir, which is history — that drew me to memoir, that seemingly personal form. And it was to description I tended, not to narrative, not to story. Maybe the root of the desire to write is always lost — properly lost — in the non-literary earth of our real lives. And craft, as we think of it, is just the jargon we give to that darker, earthier medium.

I know it was my mother who was the storyteller in our house. I was her audience. Her dear reader, in a way. I dimly — and sometimes bitterly — understood that nothing much was happening in our modest Midwestern lives, yet I clung to the drama with which she infused every vignette, every encounter at the grocery store.

And when I sought to make sense of the world that kept slipping away to the past, to loss and forgetfulness, when I protested inwardly at that disappearance, it was to description I instinctively turned. Coming from a background in poetry and therefore being a literalist, it didn't occur to me to copy other prose writers. If I wanted to learn to write descriptively, I needed — what else? — pictures.

I took myself off to the Minneapolis Institute of Arts and plunked myself down in front of a Bonnard. I wrote the painting. Described it. I went home and looked at a teacup on my table — I wrote that too. Still life descriptions that ran on for several pages. I wrote and wrote, describing my way through art galleries and the inadvertent still lives of my house and my memory, my grandmother's garden, her Sunday dinners.

30

35

To my growing astonishment, these long descriptive passages, some-times running two, three pages or longer, had a way of sheering off into nar-rative after all. The teacup I was describing had been given to me by my mother. And once I thought of the fact that she had bought these cups, made in Czechoslovakia, as a bride just before the Second World War, I was writ-ing about that war, about my mother and her later disappointments which somehow were — and were not — part of this fragile cup. Description — which had seemed like background in novels, static and inert as a butterfly pinned to the page of my notebook, proved to be a dynamic engine that stoked voice and even more propelled the occasional narrative arc. Descrip-tion, written from the personal voice of my own perception, proved even to be the link with the world's story, with history itself. Here was my mother's teacup, made in Czechoslovakia before the War, and here, therefore, was not only my mother's heartbreak but Europe's. The detail was surely divine, offering up miracle after miracle of connections out of the faithful consider-ation of the fragments before me.

We sense this historical power at the heart of autobiographical writing in the testaments from the Holocaust, from the Gulag, from every marginal and abused life that has found the courage to speak its truth which is often its horror, to preserve its demonic details — and in so doing has seen them become divine. Nadezhda Mandelstam, Anne Frank, Primo Levi — to name only a very few. In time we will, surely, see such documents from Guantanamo and the unknown places of extreme rendition.

The history of whole countries, of an entire era and even lost populations depends sometimes on a little girl faithfully keeping her diary. The great con-tract of literature consists in this: you tell me your story and somehow I get my story. If we are looking for another reason to explain the strangely powerful grip of the first-person voice on contemporary writing perhaps we need look no farther than the power of Anne Frank's equation — that to write one's life enables the world to preserve its history.

But what of lives lived in the flyover? Lives that don't have that power-ful, if terrible, historical resonance of radical suffering. Ordinary lives, in a word. Alfred Kazin's life — or yours. And certainly mine in middling Minnesota in the middle of the twentieth century. Why bother to describe it? Because of course, all details are divine, not just Nabokov's. In fact, per-haps the poorer the supposed value, the more the detail requires description to assure its divinity.   40

Which brings me to — if not a story, at least a fragment, a vignette. Early in my teaching life, I went (foolishly) through a killer snowstorm in Minneapolis to get to my University office because I had student confer-ences scheduled. By the time I arrived, the University had closed and the campus was empty, whipped by white shrouds of blizzard snow, the wind whistling down the Mall. I sat in my office in the empty building, cursing my ruinous work ethic, wondering if the buses would keep running so I could get home.

Then a rap on my office door. I opened it and there, like an extra out of *Doctor Zhivago*, stood my 11 a.m. appointment, a quiet sophomore named Tommy.

He looked anxious. He was really glad I was there, he said, because he had a big problem with the assignment. I had asked the students to write short autobiographies. "I just can't write anything about my life," he said miserably, his head down, his overshoes puddling on the floor.

I waited for the disclosure. What would it be — child abuse, incest, what murder or mayhem could this boy not divulge? What had brought him trooping through the blizzard to get help with his life story? How would I get him to Student Counseling?

"See, I come from Fridley," he said, naming one of the nowhere-suburbs   45
sprawling drearily beyond the freeway north of Minneapolis.

I stared at him. I didn't, for a moment, comprehend that this was the dark disclosure, this the occasion of his misery: being from Fridley meant, surely, that he had nothing worth writing about.

There it was again — nothin' had ever happened to him and I was asking him to write about it.

"I have good news for you, Tommy," I said. "The field's wide open — nobody has told what it's like to grow up in Fridley yet. It's all yours."

All he needed to do was sit down and describe. And because the detail is divine, if you caress it into life, you find the world you have lost or ignored, the world ruined or devalued. The world you alone can bring into being, bit by broken bit. And so you create your own integrity, which is to say your voice, your style.

QUESTIONS

Reading

1. What is the biggest difference between fiction writing and memoir, in Hampl's opinion?
2. How does Hampl define the kind of memoir she writes? What other kinds are there, according to her?
3. Hampl uses a number of *metaphors* and *similes* — rhetorical devices that compare seemingly unrelated subjects — to illustrate her points about plot, style, narrative, and detail. List three metaphors or similes that Hampl uses. What purpose do they serve in the development of this *reflective* essay?
4. What does Hampl mean when she refers to description as a "dark art"?

Exploratory Writing

1. Hampl quotes the Nobel Prize–winning French author André Gide as saying that the classical injunction to *know thyself* is "as pernicious as it

is ugly. Whoever observes himself arrests his own development. A cater-pillar who wanted to know itself well would never become a butterfly" (paragraph 9). Write about something personal that you have written in the past — an essay, a journal entry, an autobiographical poem or story. What did you learn about yourself from writing the piece? Do you relate more to Plato's and Cicero's celebrations of self-knowledge, or to Goethe's and Gide's more cynical views?

2. Hampl uses the Alfred Kazin memoir *A Walker in the City* as an exam-ple of evocative descriptive writing that refuses to obey the mantra of introductory fiction-writing workshops: "Show, don't tell." Kazin, she suggests, was able to use description to both show *and* tell. Highlight the sentences or paragraphs in Hampl's essay that best exemplify Vladimir Nabokov's command to "Caress the detail, the divine detail." In your opinion, does Hampl herself succeed in showing *and* telling?

3. Choose a vignette from your own life and write a short autobiographical story about it. In pairs, trade stories. Does your partner's piece both show *and* tell?

Making Connections

1. "The impulse to write things down is a peculiarly compulsive one, inex-plicable to those who do not share it, useful only accidentally," writes Joan Didion (p. 114). In your opinion, how would Hampl respond to the idea that recording details for later writing is "useful only accidentally"?

Essay Writing

1. Keeping in mind Hampl's comments on the "historical power at the heart of autobiographical writing" (paragraph 38), write an essay de-scribing a piece of autobiographical writing that you have read that helped you understand history. You might choose Junot Díaz's essay re-flecting on his visit to the Dominican Republic (p. 52), George Orwell's "Shooting an Elephant" (p. 266), soldiers' personal experiences serving in Iraq (p. 323), or autobiographical writing not included in this book. Include a detailed description of the style of the piece you've chosen.

Paired Readings: On Bilingualism

How to Tame a Wild Tongue

Gloria Anzaldúa

Gloria Anzaldúa (1942–2004) was an award-winning writer and prolific editor whose life and work championed Chicana culture, lesbianism, and feminism. Determined to get an education, Anzaldúa juggled school with working in the fields of her native South Texas from the age of fourteen. Eventually, she received an MA in English and education from the University of Texas. Anzaldúa's seminal work, This Bridge Called My Back: Writings by Radical Women of Color *(1981), coedited with Cherrie Moraga, received the Before Columbus Foundation American Book Award and challenged the lesbian and feminist movements to include women of different ethnicities and classes. "How to Tame a Wild Tongue," a chapter from her first book,* Borderlands/La Frontera: The New Mestiza *(1987), addresses issues of Chicana identity in the United States.*

"We're going to have to control your tongue," the dentist says, pulling out all the metal from my mouth. Silver bits plop and tinkle into the basin. My mouth is a motherlode.

The dentist is cleaning out my roots. I get a whiff of the stench when I gasp. "I can't cap that tooth yet, you're still draining," he says.

"We're going to have to do something about your tongue," I hear the anger rising in his voice. My tongue keeps pushing out the wads of cotton, pushing back the drills, the long thin needles. "I've never seen anything as strong or as stubborn," he says. And I think, how do you tame a wild tongue, train it to be quiet, how do you bridle and saddle it? How do you make it lie down?

> Who is to say that robbing a people of
> its language is less violent than war?
> —RAY GWYN SMITH

131

I remember being caught speaking Spanish at recess — that was good for three licks on the knuckles with a sharp ruler. I remember being sent to the corner of the classroom for "talking back" to the Anglo teacher when all I was trying to do was tell her how to pronounce my name. "If you want to be American, speak 'American.' If you don't like it, go back to Mexico where you belong."

"I want you to speak English. *Pa' hallar buen trabajo tienes que saber*   5
hablar el inglés bien. Qué vale toda tu educación si todavía hablas inglés con un 'accent,'"[1] my mother would say, mortified that I spoke English like a Mexican. At Pan American University, I, and all Chicano students, were required to take two speech classes. Their purpose: to get rid of our accents.

Attacks on one's form of expression with the intent to censor are a violation of the First Amendment. *El Anglo con cara de inocente nos arrancó la lengua.* Wild tongues can't be tamed, they can only be cut out.

Overcoming the Tradition of Silence

> *Ahogadas, escupimos el oscuro.*
> *Peleando con nuestra propia sombra*
> *el silencio nos sepulta.*

En boca cerrada no entran moscas. "Flies don't enter a closed mouth" is a saying I kept hearing when I was a child. *Ser habladora* was to be a gossip and a liar, to talk too much. *Muchachitas bien criadas*, well-bred girls don't answer back. *Es una falta de respeto*[2] to talk back to one's mother or father. I remember one of the sins I'd recite to the priest in the confession box the few times I went to confession: talking back to my mother, *hablar pa' 'trás, repelar. Hocicona, repelona, chismosa,* having a big mouth, questioning, carrying tales are all signs of being *mal criada.*[3] In my culture they are all words that are derogatory if applied to women — I've never heard them applied to men.

The first time I heard two women, a Puerto Rican and a Cuban, say the word "*nosotras,*" I was shocked. I had not known the word existed. Chicanas use *nosotros*[4] whether we're male or female. We are robbed of our female being by the masculine plural. Language is a male discourse.

----

[1]*Pa' hallar . . . 'accent'*: "To get a good job, you need to speak English well. What's the use of all your education if you speak English with an accent?" (Spanish). [Eds.]

[2]*Es una falta de respeto*: It's disrespectful (Spanish). [Eds.]

[3]*mal criada*: Badly brought up (Spanish). [Eds.]

[4]*nosotros*: First person plural ("we") in the masculine ("-os"). This is the default personal pronoun in Spanish. Traditionally, in Romance languages, a feminine version (*nosotras*) does not exist. [Eds.]

And our tongues have become
dry   the wilderness has
dried out our tongues   and
we have forgotten speech.

—IRENA KLEPFISZ

Even our own people, other Spanish speakers *nos quieren poner candados en la boca.* They would hold us back with their bag of *reglas de academia.*[5]

Oye Como Ladra: El Lenguaje de la Frontera

Quien tiene boca se equivoca.

—MEXICAN SAYING

"*Pocho*, cultural traitor, you're speaking the oppressor's language by speaking English, you're ruining the Spanish language," I have been accused by various Latinos and Latinas. Chicano Spanish is considered by the purist and by most Latinos deficient, a mutilation of Spanish.

But Chicano Spanish is a border tongue which developed naturally. Change, *evolución, enriquecimiento de palabras nuevas por invención o adopción*[6] have created variants of Chicano Spanish, *un nuevo lenguaje. Un lenguaje que corresponde a un modo de vivir.* Chicano Spanish is not incorrect, it is a living language.

For a people who are neither Spanish nor live in a country in which Spanish is the first language; for a people who live in a country in which English is the reigning tongue but who are not Anglo; for a people who cannot entirely identify with either standard (formal, Castillian) Spanish nor standard English, what recourse is left to them but to create their own language? A language which they can connect their identity to, one capable of communicating the realities and values true to themselves — a language with terms that are neither *español ni inglés*, but both. We speak a patois, a forked tongue, a variation of two languages.

Chicano Spanish sprang out of the Chicanos' need to identify ourselves as a distinct people. We needed a language with which we could communicate with ourselves, a secret language. For some of us, language is a homeland closer than the Southwest — for many Chicanos today live in the Midwest and the East. And because we are a complex, heterogeneous people, we speak many languages. Some of the languages we speak are:

1. Standard English
2. Working class and slang English

---

[5]*reglas de academia*: Academic rules, or rules of traditional grammar (Spanish). [Eds.]

[6]*evolución, . . . adopción*: Evolution and enrichment with newly invented or adopted words (Spanish). [Eds.]

3. Standard Spanish

4. Standard Mexican Spanish

5. North Mexican Spanish dialect

6. Chicano Spanish (Texas, New Mexico, Arizona, and California have regional variations)

7. Tex-Mex

8. *Pachuco* (called *caló*)

My "home" tongues are the languages I speak with my sister and brothers, with my friends. They are the last five listed, with 6 and 7 being closest to my heart. From school, the media, and job situations, I've picked up standard and working class English. From Mamagrande Locha and from reading Spanish and Mexican literature, I've picked up Standard Spanish and Standard Mexican Spanish. From *los recién llegados*, Mexican immigrants, and *braceros*,[7] I learned the North Mexican dialect. With Mexicans I'll try to speak either Standard Mexican Spanish or the North Mexican dialect. From my parents and Chicanos living in the Valley, I picked up Chicano Texas Spanish, and I speak it with my mom, younger brother (who married a Mexican and who rarely mixes Spanish with English), aunts, and older relatives.

With Chicanas from *Nuevo México* or *Arizona* I will speak Chicano Spanish a little, but often they don't understand what I'm saying. With most California Chicanas I speak entirely in English (unless I forget). When I first moved to San Francisco, I'd rattle off something in Spanish, unintentionally embarrassing them. Often it is only with another Chicana *tejana*[8] that I can talk freely.

Words distorted by English are known as anglicisms or *pochismos*. The   15
pocho is an anglicized Mexican or American of Mexican origin who speaks Spanish with an accent characteristic of North Americans and who distorts and reconstructs the language according to the influence of English. Tex-Mex, or Spanglish, comes most naturally to me. I may switch back and forth from English to Spanish in the same sentence or in the same word. With my sister and my brother Nune and with Chicano *tejano* contemporaries I speak in Tex-Mex.

From kids and people my own age I picked up *Pachuco*. *Pachuco* (the language of the zoot suiters) is a language of rebellion, both against Standard Spanish and Standard English. It is a secret language. Adults of the culture and outsiders cannot understand it. It is made up of slang words from both English and Spanish. *Ruca* means girl or woman, *vato* means guy or dude, *chale* means no, *simón* means yes, *churo* is sure, talk is *periquiar*, *pigionear* means petting, *que gacho* means how nerdy, *ponte águila* means watch out, death is called *la pelona*. Through lack of practice and not having others who can speak it, I've lost most of the *Pachuco* tongue.

---

[7]*braceros*: Migratory worker of Latin American origin (Spanish). [Eds.]
[8]*tejana*: A Texan of Latin American descent (Spanish). [Eds.]

Chicano Spanish

Chicanos, after 250 years of Spanish/Anglo colonization, have developed significant differences in the Spanish we speak. We collapse two adjacent vowels into a single syllable and sometimes shift the stress in certain words such as *maíz/maiz, cohete/cuete*. We leave out certain consonants when they appear between vowels: *lado/lao, mojado/mojao*. Chicanos from South Texas pronounced *f* as *j* as in *jue* (*fue*). Chicanos use "archaisms," words that are no longer in the Spanish language, words that have been evolved out. We say *semos, truje, haiga, ansina*, and *naiden*. We retain the "archaic" *j*, as in *jalar*, that derives from an earlier *h* (the French *halar* or the Germanic *halon* which was lost to Standard Spanish in the sixteenth century), but which is still found in several regional dialects such as the one spoken in South Texas. (Due to geography, Chicanos from the Valley of South Texas were cut off linguistically from other Spanish speakers. We tend to use words that the Spaniards brought over from Medieval Spain. The majority of the Spanish colonizers in Mexico and the Southwest came from Extremadura — Hernán Cortés was one of them — and Andalucía. Andalucians pronounce *ll* like a *y*, and their *d*'s tend to be absorbed by adjacent vowels: *tirado* becomes *tirao*. They brought *el lenguaje popular, dialectos y regionalismos*.)

Chicanos and other Spanish speakers also shift *ll* to *y* and *z* to *s*. We leave out initial syllables, saying *tar* for *estar, toy* for *estoy, hora* for *ahora* (*cubanos* and *puertorriqueños* also leave out initial letters of some words). We also leave out the final syllable such as *pa* for *para*. The intervocalic *y*, the *ll* as in *tortilla, ella, botella*, gets replaced by *tortia* or *tortiya, ea, botea*. We add an additional syllable at the beginning of certain words: *atocar* for *tocar, agastar* for *gastar*. Sometimes we'll say *lavaste las vacijas*, other times *lavates* (substituting the *ates* verb endings for the *aste*).

We use anglicisms, words borrowed from English: *bola* from ball, *carpeta* from carpet, *máchina de lavar* (instead of *lavadora*) from washing machine. Tex-Mex argot, created by adding a Spanish sound at the beginning or end of an English word such as *cookiar* for cook, *watchar* for watch, *parkiar* for park, and *rapiar* for rape, is the result of the pressures on Spanish speakers to adapt to English.

We don't use the word *vosotros/as* or its accompanying verb form. We don't say *claro* (to mean yes), *imagínate*, or *me emociona* unless we picked up Spanish from Latinas, out of a book, or in a classroom. Other Spanish-speaking groups are going through the same, or similar, development in their Spanish. 20

Linguistic Terrorism

Deslenguadas. Somos los del español deficiente. We are your linguistic nightmare, your linguistic aberration, your linguistic *mestizaje*,[9]

---

[9]*mestizaje*: People with mixed European and Amerindian ancestry (Spanish). [Eds.]

the subject of your *burla*.[10] Because we speak with tongues of fire we are culturally crucified. Racially, culturally, and linguistically *somos huérfanos* — we speak an orphan tongue.

Chicanas who grew up speaking Chicano Spanish have internalized the belief that we speak poor Spanish. It is illegitimate, a bastard language. And because we internalize how our language has been used against us by the dominant culture, we use our language differences against each other.

Chicana feminists often skirt around each other with suspicion and hesitation. For the longest time I couldn't figure it out. Then it dawned on me. To be close to another Chicana is like looking into the mirror. We are afraid of what we'll see there. *Pena*. Shame. Low estimation of self. In childhood we are told that our language is wrong. Repeated attacks on our native tongue diminish our sense of self. The attacks continue throughout our lives.

Chicanas feel uncomfortable talking in Spanish to Latinas, afraid of their censure. Their language was not outlawed in their countries. They had a whole lifetime of being immersed in their native tongue; generations, centuries in which Spanish was a first language, taught in school, heard on radio and TV, and read in the newspaper.

If a person, Chicana or Latina, has a low estimation of my native tongue, she also has a low estimation of me. Often with *mexicanas y latinas* we'll speak English as a neutral language. Even among Chicanas we tend to speak English at parties or conferences. Yet, at the same time, we're afraid the other will think we're *agringadas*[11] because we don't speak Chicano Spanish. We oppress each other trying to out-Chicano each other, vying to be the "real" Chicanas, to speak like Chicanos. There is no one Chicano language just as there is no one Chicano experience. A monolingual Chicana whose first language is English or Spanish is just as much a Chicana as one who speaks several variants of Spanish. A Chicana from Michigan or Chicago or Detroit is just as much a Chicana as one from the Southwest. Chicano Spanish is as diverse linguistically as it is regionally.

By the end of this century, Spanish speakers will comprise the biggest   25
minority group in the U.S., a country where students in high schools and colleges are encouraged to take French classes because French is considered more "cultured." But for a language to remain alive it must be used. By the end of this century English, and not Spanish, will be the mother tongue of most Chicanos and Latinos.

So, if you want to really hurt me, talk badly about my language. Ethnic identity is twin skin to linguistic identity — I am my language. Until I can take pride in my language, I cannot take pride in myself. Until I can accept

---

[10]*burla*: Joke, mockery (Spanish). [Eds.]
[11]*agringadas*: Becoming influenced by white American ("gringolo") culture (Spanish). [Eds.]

as legitimate Chicano Texas Spanish, Tex-Mex, and all the other languages I speak, I cannot accept the legitimacy of myself. Until I am free to write bilingually and to switch codes without having always to translate, while I still have to speak English or Spanish when I would rather speak Spanglish, and as long as I have to accommodate the English speakers rather than having them accommodate me, my tongue will be illegitimate.

I will no longer be made to feel ashamed of existing. I will have my voice: Indian, Spanish, white. I will have my serpent's tongue — my woman's voice, my sexual voice, my poet's voice. I will overcome the tradition of silence.

> My fingers
> move sly against your palm
> Like women everywhere, we speak in code . . .
> —MELANIE KAYE/KANTROWITZ

"Vistas," Corridos y Comida: My Native Tongue

In the 1960s, I read my first Chicano novel. It was *City of Night* by John Rechy, a gay Texan, son of a Scottish father and a Mexican mother. For days I walked around in stunned amazement that a Chicano could write and could get published. When I read *I Am Joaquín* I was surprised to see a bilingual book by a Chicano in print. When I saw poetry written in Tex-Mex for the first time, a feeling of pure joy flashed through me. I felt like we really existed as a people. In 1971, when I started teaching high school English to Chicano students, I tried to supplement the required texts with works by Chicanos, only to be reprimanded and forbidden to do so by the principal. He claimed that I was supposed to teach "American" and English literature. At the risk of being fired, I swore my students to secrecy and slipped in Chicano short stories, poems, a play. In graduate school, while working toward a Ph.D., I had to "argue" with one advisor after the other, semester after semester, before I was allowed to make Chicano literature an area of focus.

Even before I read books by Chicanos or Mexicans, it was the Mexican movies I saw at the drive-in — the Thursday night special of $1.00 a carload — that gave me a sense of belonging. "*Vámonos a las vistas,*" my mother would call out and we'd all — grandmother, brothers, sister, and cousins — squeeze into the car. We'd wolf down cheese and bologna white bread sandwiches while watching Pedro Infante in melodramatic tear-jerkers like *Nosotros los pobres*,[12] the first "real" Mexican movie (that was not an imitation of European movies). I remember seeing *Cuando los hijos se van*[13] and surmising that all Mexican movies played up the love a mother has for her children and what ungrateful sons and daughters suffer when they are

---

[12]*Nosotros los pobres*: We the people (Spanish). [Eds.]
[13]*Cuando . . . van*: When the children go (Spanish). [Eds.]

not devoted to their mothers. I remember the singing-type "westerns" of Jorge Negrete and Miguel Aceves Mejía. When watching Mexican movies, I felt a sense of homecoming as well as alienation. People who were to amount to something didn't go to Mexican movies or *bailes*[14] or tune their radios to *bolero, rancherita,* and *corrido* music.

The whole time I was growing up, there was *norteño* music, sometimes   30
called North Mexican border music, or Tex-Mex music, or Chicano music, or *cantina* (bar) music. I grew up listening to *conjuntos,* three- or four-piece bands made up of folk musicians playing guitar, *bajo sexto,* drums, and button accordion, which Chicanos had borrowed from the German immigrants who had come to Central Texas and Mexico to farm and build breweries. In the Rio Grande Valley, Steve Jordan and Little Joe Hernández were popular, and Flaco Jiménez was the accordion king. The rhythms of Tex-Mex music are those of the polka, also adapted from the Germans, who in turn had borrowed the polka from the Czechs and Bohemians.

I remember the hot, sultry evenings when *corridos* — songs of love and death on the Texas-Mexican borderlands — reverberated out of cheap amplifiers from the local *cantinas* and wafted in through my bedroom window.

Corridos first became widely used along the South Texas/Mexican border during the early conflict between Chicanos and Anglos. The *corridos* are usually about Mexican heroes who do valiant deeds against the Anglo oppressors. Pancho Villa's song, "*La cucaracha,*" is the most famous one. *Corridos* of John F. Kennedy and his death are still very popular in the Valley. Older Chicanos remember Lydia Mendoza, one of the great border *corrido* singers who was called *la Gloria de Tejas.* Her "*El tango negro,*" sung during the Great Depression, made her a singer of the people. The everpresent *corridos* narrated one hundred years of border history, bringing news of events as well as entertaining. These folk musicians and folk songs are our chief cultural mythmakers, and they made our hard lives seem bearable.

I grew up feeling ambivalent about our music. Country western and rock-and-roll had more status. In the 50s and 60s, for the slightly educated and *agringado* Chicanos, there existed a sense of shame at being caught listening to our music. Yet I couldn't stop my feet from thumping to the music, could not stop humming the words, nor hide from myself the exhilaration I felt when I heard it.

There are more subtle ways that we internalize identification, especially in the forms of images and emotions. For me food and certain smells are tied to my identity, to my homeland. Woodsmoke curling up to an immense blue sky; woodsmoke perfuming my grandmother's clothes, her skin. The stench of cow manure and the yellow patches on the ground; the crack of a .22 rifle

---

[14]*bailes*: Dances (Spanish). [Eds.]

and the reek of cordite. Homemade white cheese sizzling in a pan, melting inside a folded *tortilla*. My sister Hilda's hot, spicy *menudo, chile colorado* making it deep red, pieces of *panza* and hominy floating on top. My brother Carito barbecuing *fajitas* in the backyard. Even now and 3,000 miles away, I can see my mother spicing the ground beef, pork, and venison with *chile*. My mouth salivates at the thought of the hot steaming *tamales* I would be eating if I were home.

Si Le Preguntas a Mi Mamá, "¿Qué Eres?"

Identity is the essential core of who we are as individuals, the conscious experience of the self inside.

—KAUFMAN

Nosotros los Chicanos straddle the borderlands. On one side of us, we 35 are constantly exposed to the Spanish of the Mexicans; on the other side we hear the Anglos' incessant clamoring so that we forget our language. Among ourselves we don't say *nosotros los americanos, o nosotros los españoles, o nosotros los hispanos*. We say *nosotros los mexicanos* (by *mexicanos* we do not mean citizens of Mexico; we do not mean a national identity, but a racial one). We distinguish between *mexicanos del otro lado* and *mexicanos de este lado*.[15] Deep in our hearts we believe that being Mexican has nothing to do with which country one lives in. Being Mexican is a state of soul — not one of mind, not one of citizenship. Neither eagle nor serpent, but both. And like the ocean, neither animal respects borders.

> *Dime con quien andas y te diré quien eres.*
> (Tell me who your friends are and I'll tell you who you are.)
>
> —MEXICAN SAYING

Si le preguntas a mi mamá, "¿Qué eres?" te dirá, "Soy mexicana."[16] My brothers and sister say the same. I sometimes will answer *"soy mexicana"* and at others will say *"soy Chicana" o "soy tejana."* But I identified as *"Raza"* before I ever identified as *"mexicana"* or "Chicana."

As a culture, we call ourselves Spanish when referring to ourselves as a linguistic group and when copping out. It is then that we forget our predominant Indian genes. We are 70 percent to 80 percent Indian. We call ourselves Hispanic or Spanish-American or Latin American or Latin when

---

[15]*mexicanos . . . este lado*: Mexicans from the other side (of the border) and Mexicans from this side (Spanish). [Eds.]

[16]*Si le preguntas . . . "Soy mexicana"*: "If you ask my mother, 'What are you?' she'll say, 'I'm Mexican'" (Spanish). [Eds.]

linking ourselves to other Spanish-speaking peoples of the Western hemisphere when copping out. We call ourselves Mexican-American to signify we are neither Mexican nor American, but more the noun "American" than the adjective "Mexican" (and when copping out).

Chicanos and other people of color suffer economically for not acculturating. This voluntary (yet forced) alienation makes for psychological conflict, a kind of dual identity — we don't identify with the Anglo-American cultural values and we don't totally identify with the Mexican cultural values. We are a synergy of two cultures with various degrees of Mexicanness or Angloness. I have so internalized the borderland conflict that sometimes I feel like one cancels out the other and we are zero, nothing, no one. *A veces no soy nada ni nadie. Pero hasta cuando no lo soy, lo soy.*[17]

When not copping out, when we know we are more than nothing, we call ourselves Mexican, referring to race and ancestry; *mestizo* when affirming both our Indian and Spanish (but we hardly ever own our Black) ancestry; Chicano when referring to a politically aware people born and/or raised in the U.S.; *Raza* when referring to Chicanos; *tejanos* when we are Chicanos from Texas.

Chicanos did not know we were a people until 1965 when Cesar Chavez   40
and the farmworkers united and *I Am Joaquín* was published and *la Raza Unida* party was formed in Texas. With that recognition, we became a distinct people. Something momentous happened to the Chicano soul — we became aware of our reality and acquired a name and a language (Chicano Spanish) that reflected that reality. Now that we had a name, some of the fragmented pieces began to fall together — who we were, what we were, how we had evolved. We began to get glimpses of what we might eventually become.

Yet the struggle of identities continues, the struggle of borders is our reality still. One day the inner struggle will cease and a true integration take place. In the meantime, *tenemos que hacer la lucha. ¿Quién está protegiendo los ranchos de mi gente? ¿Quién está tratando de cerrar la fisura entre la india y el blanco en nuestra sangre? El Chicano, sí, el Chicano que anda como un ladrón en su propia casa.*[18]

Los Chicanos, how patient we seem, how very patient. There is the quiet of the Indian about us. We know how to survive. When other races have given up their tongue, we've kept ours. We know what it is to live under the hammer blow of the dominant *norteamericano* culture. But more than we count the blows, we count the days the weeks the years the centuries the eons until the white laws and commerce and customs will rot in the deserts they've

----

[17]*A veces . . . lo soy:* "Sometimes I'm not anything or anyone. But even when I'm not, I am" (Spanish). [Eds.]

[18]*tenemos . . . casa:* "We have to wage the struggle. Who is protecting my people's hovels? Who is trying to close the gap between the Indian and the white parts in our blood? The Chicano is, yes, the Chicano who goes around like a thief in his own home" (Spanish). [Eds.]

created, lie bleached. *Humildes* yet proud, *quietos* yet wild, *nosotros los mexicanos*-Chicanos will walk by the crumbling ashes as we go about our business. Stubborn, persevering, impenetrable as stone, yet possessing a malleability that renders us unbreakable, we, the *mestizas* and *mestizos*, will remain.

QUESTIONS

Reading

1. When does Anzaldúa first read a novel written by a Chicano? How does she respond to her first encounter with poetry written in "Tex-Mex"? Why are these experiences important to her?
2. What is a *pochismo* (paragraph 15)?
3. Anzaldúa uses quotations from other writers to introduce or conclude sections of her essay. List them. How would you characterize their language? How does Anzaldúa's selection of quotes support her central argument?

Exploratory Writing

1. Anzaldúa suggests that there are subtle ways that we internalize identification. What does she mean by "identification"? Reflect on your personal identity. How might identification shape your sense of who you are?
2. How does Anzaldúa characterize Chicanos? Is her characterization of her "race" at odds with her arguments celebrating diversity or does it support her position? Underline, highlight, or flag the places where she defines or characterizes "Chicano" as an ethnic identity.

Making Connections

1. Amy Tan (p. 142) refers to the different "Englishes" spoken during her childhood. Make a list that compares Tan's account to Anzaldúa's list of the many languages spoken by Chicanos (paragraph 12).
2. Compare Anzaldúa's use of dialect with James Baldwin's (p. 109). Does she use dialects other than "standard" English? Does Baldwin? How does choice of language strengthen or weaken each author's argument?

Essay Writing

1. Anzaldúa writes, "If you want to really hurt me, talk badly about my language. Ethnic identity is twin skin to linguistic identity — I am my language" (paragraph 26). Do you agree that a person's language defines his or her identity? Write an essay using examples to support your position.

Mother Tongue

Amy Tan

Born in 1952 in Oakland, California, Amy Tan is the daughter of immigrants who fled China's Communist revolution in the late 1940s. Her Chinese name, An-Mei, means "blessing from America." Tan has remarked that she once tried to distance herself from her ethnicity, but writing her first novel, The Joy Luck Club *(1989), helped her discover "how very Chinese I was." Known as a gifted storyteller, Tan has written four other novels,* The Kitchen God's Wife *(1991),* The Hundred Secret Senses *(1995),* The Bonesetter's Daughter *(2001), and* Saving Fish from Drowning *(2005), as well as a collection of essays,* The Opposite of Fate: Memories of a Writing Life *(2004), and two children's books. The following essay, in which Tan reflects on her experience as a bilingual child speaking both Chinese and English, was originally published in* The Threepenny Review *in 1990.*

I am not a scholar of English or literature. I cannot give you much more than personal opinions on the English language and its variations in this country or others.

I am a writer. And by that definition, I am someone who has always loved language. I am fascinated by language in daily life. I spend a great deal of my time thinking about the power of language — the way it can evoke an emotion, a visual image, a complex idea, or a simple truth. Language is the tool of my trade. And I use them all — all the Englishes I grew up with.

Recently, I was made keenly aware of the different Englishes I do use. I was giving a talk to a large group of people, the same talk I had already given to half a dozen other groups. The nature of the talk was about my writing, my life, and my book *The Joy Luck Club.* The talk was going along well enough, until I remembered one major difference that made the whole talk sound wrong. My mother was in the room. And it was perhaps the first time she had heard me give a lengthy speech, using the kind of English I have never used with her. I was saying things like "The intersection of memory upon imagination" and "There is an aspect of my fiction that relates to thus-and-thus" — a speech filled with carefully wrought grammatical phrases, burdened, it suddenly seemed to me, with nominalized forms, past perfect tenses, conditional phrases, all the forms of standard English that I had learned in school and through books, the forms of English I did not use at home with my mother.

Just last week, I was walking down the street with my mother, and I again found myself conscious of the English I was using, the English I do use with her. We were talking about the price of new and used furniture and I heard myself saying this: "Not waste money that way." My husband was with us as well, and he didn't notice any switch in my English. And then I realized why. It's because over the twenty years we've been together I've often used that same kind of English with him, and sometimes he even uses it with me. It has become our language of intimacy, a different sort of English that relates to family talk, the language I grew up with.

So you'll have some idea of what this family talk I heard sounds like, I'll   5
quote what my mother said during a recent conversation which I videotaped and then transcribed. During this conversation, my mother was talking about a political gangster in Shanghai who had the same last name as her family's, Du, and how the gangster in his early years wanted to be adopted by her family, which was rich by comparison. Later, the gangster became more powerful, far richer than my mother's family, and one day showed up at my mother's wedding to pay his respects. Here's what she said in part:

"Du Yusong having business like fruit stand. Like off the street kind. He is Du like Du Zong — but not Tsung-ming Island people. The local people call putong, the river east side, he belong to that side local people. That man want to ask Du Zong father take him in like become own family. Du Zong father wasn't look down on him, but didn't take seriously, until that man big like become a mafia. Now important person, very hard to inviting him. Chinese way, came only to show respect, don't stay for dinner. Respect for making big celebration, he shows up. Mean gives lots of respect. Chinese custom. Chinese social life that way. If too important won't have to stay too long. He come to my wedding. I didn't see, I heard it. I gone to boy's side, they have YMCA dinner. Chinese age I was nineteen."

You should know that my mother's expressive command of English belies how much she actually understands. She reads the *Forbes* report, listens to *Wall Street Week*, converses daily with her stockbroker, reads all of Shirley MacLaine's[1] books with ease — all kinds of things I can't begin to understand. Yet some of my friends tell me they understand 50 percent of what my mother says. Some say they understand 80 to 90 percent. Some say they understand none of it, as if she were speaking pure Chinese. But to me, my mother's English is perfectly clear, perfectly natural. It's my mother tongue. Her language, as I hear it, is vivid, direct, full of observation and

---

[1]*Shirley MacLaine* (b. 1934): An American actor, dancer, and writer. She has written her memoirs and several books on spirituality and self-help.

imagery. That was the language that helped shape the way I saw things, expressed things, made sense of the world.

Lately, I've been giving more thought to the kind of English my mother speaks. Like others, I have described it to people as "broken" or "fractured" English. But I wince when I say that. It has always bothered me that I can think of no way to describe it other than "broken," as if it were damaged and needed to be fixed, as if it lacked a certain wholeness and soundness. I've heard other terms used, "limited English," for example. But they seem just as bad, as if everything is limited, including people's perceptions of the limited English speaker.

I know this for a fact, because when I was growing up, my mother's "limited" English limited *my* perception of her. I was ashamed of her English. I believed that her English reflected the quality of what she had to say. That is, because she expressed them imperfectly her thoughts were imperfect. And I had plenty of empirical evidence to support me: the fact that people in department stores, at banks, and at restaurants did not take her seriously, did not give her good service, pretended not to understand her, or even acted as if they did not hear her.

My mother has long realized the limitations of her English as well.   10 When I was fifteen, she used to have me call people on the phone to pretend I was she. In this guise, I was forced to ask for information or even to complain and yell at people who had been rude to her. One time it was a call to her stockbroker in New York. She had cashed out her small portfolio and it just so happened we were going to go to New York the next week, our very first trip outside California. I had to get on the phone and say in an adolescent voice that was not very convincing, "This is Mrs. Tan."

And my mother was standing in the back whispering loudly, "Why he don't send me check, already two weeks late. So mad he lie to me, losing me money."

And then I said in perfect English, "Yes, I'm getting rather concerned. You had agreed to send the check two weeks ago, but it hasn't arrived."

Then she began to talk more loudly. "What he want, I come to New York tell him front of his boss, you cheating me?" And I was trying to calm her down, make her be quiet, while telling the stockbroker, "I can't tolerate any more excuses. If I don't receive the check immediately, I am going to have to speak to your manager when I'm in New York next week." And sure enough, the following week there we were in front of this astonished stockbroker, and I was sitting there red-faced and quiet, and my mother, the real Mrs. Tan, was shouting at his boss in her impeccable broken English.

We used a similar routine just five days ago, for a situation that was far less humorous. My mother had gone to the hospital for an appointment, to find out about a benign brain tumor a CAT scan had revealed a month ago. She said she had spoken very good English, her best English, no mistakes. Still, she said, the hospital did not apologize when they said they had lost the CAT scan and she had come for nothing. She said they did not seem to have any sympathy when she told them she was anxious to know the exact diagnosis, since her husband and son had both died of brain tumors. She said they would not give her any more information until the next time and she would have to make another appointment for that. So she said she would not leave until the doctor called her daughter. She wouldn't budge. And when the doctor finally called her daughter, me, who spoke in perfect English — lo and behold — we had assurances the CAT scan would be found, promises that a conference call on Monday would be held, and apologies for any suffering my mother had gone through for a most regrettable mistake.

I think my mother's English almost had an effect on limiting my possi- 15
bilities in life as well. Sociologists and linguists probably will tell you that a person's developing language skills are more influenced by peers. But I do think that the language spoken in the family, especially in immigrant families which are more insular, plays a large role in shaping the language of the child. And I believe that it affected my results on achievement tests, IQ tests, and the SAT. While my English skills were never judged as poor, compared to math, English could not be considered my strong suit. In grade school I did moderately well, getting perhaps B's, sometimes B-pluses, in English and scoring perhaps in the sixtieth or seventieth percentile on achievement tests. But those scores were not good enough to override the opinion that my true abilities lay in math and science, because in those areas I achieved A's and scored in the ninetieth percentile or higher.

This was understandable. Math is precise; there is only one correct answer. Whereas, for me at least, the answers on English tests were always a judgment call, a matter of opinion and personal experience. Those tests were constructed around items like fill-in-the-blank sentence completion, such as "Even though Tom was _____ , Mary thought he was _____ ." And the correct answer always seemed to be the most bland combinations of thoughts, for example, "Even though Tom was shy, Mary thought he was charming," with the grammatical structure "even though" limiting the correct answer to some sort of semantic opposites, so you wouldn't get answers like "Even though Tom was foolish, Mary thought he was ridiculous." Well, according to my mother, there were very few limitations as to what Tom could have been and what Mary might have thought of him. So I never did well on tests like that.

The same was true with word analogies, pairs of words in which you were supposed to find some sort of logical, semantic relationship — for example, "*Sunset* is to *nightfall* as _____ is to _____ ." And here you would be presented with a list of four possible pairs, one of which showed the same kind of relationship: *red* is to *stoplight, bus* is to *arrival, chills* is to *fever, yawn* is to *boring*. Well, I could never think that way. I knew what the tests were asking, but I could not block out of my mind the images already created by the first pair, "*sunset* is to *nightfall*" — and I would see a burst of colors against a darkening sky, the moon rising, the lowering of a curtain of stars. And all the other pairs of words — *red, bus, stoplight, boring* — just threw up a mass of confusing images, making it impossible for me to sort out something as logical as saying: "A sunset precedes nightfall" is the same as "a chill precedes a fever." The only way I would have gotten that answer right would have been to imagine an associative situation, for example, my being disobedient and staying out past sunset, catching a chill at night, which turns into feverish pneumonia as punishment, which indeed did happen to me.

I have been thinking about all this lately, about my mother's English, about achievement tests. Because lately I've been asked, as a writer, why there are not more Asian Americans represented in American literature. Why are there few Asian Americans enrolled in creative writing programs? Why do so many Chinese students go into engineering? Well, these are broad sociological questions I can't begin to answer. But I have noticed in surveys — in fact, just last week — that Asian students, as a whole, always do significantly better on math achievement tests than in English. And this makes me think that there are other Asian American students whose English spoken in the home might also be described as "broken" or "limited." And perhaps they also have teachers who are steering them away from writing and into math and science, which is what happened to me.

Fortunately, I happen to be rebellious in nature and enjoy the challenge of disproving assumptions made about me. I became an English major my first year in college, after being enrolled as premed. I started writing nonfiction as a freelancer the week after I was told by my former boss that writing was my worst skill and I should hone my talents toward account management.

But it wasn't until 1985 that I finally began to write fiction. And at first   20
I wrote using what I thought to be wittily crafted sentences, sentences that would finally prove I had mastery over the English language. Here's an example from the first draft of a story that later made its way into *The Joy Luck Club*, but without this line: "That was my mental quandary in its nascent state." A terrible line, which I can barely pronounce.

Fortunately, for reasons I won't get into today, I later decided I should envision a reader for the stories I would write. And the reader I decided upon was my mother, because these were stories about mothers. So with this reader in mind — and in fact she did read my early drafts — I began to write stories using all the Englishes I grew up with: the English I spoke to my mother, which for lack of a better term might be described as "simple"; the English she used with me, which for lack of a better term might be described as "broken"; my translation of her Chinese, which could certainly be described as "watered down"; and what I imagined to be her translation of her Chinese if she could speak in perfect English, her internal language, and for that I sought to preserve the essence, but neither an English nor a Chinese structure. I wanted to capture what language ability tests can never reveal: her intent, her passion, her imagery, the rhythms of her speech and the nature of her thoughts.

Apart from what any critic had to say about my writing, I knew I had succeeded where it counted when my mother finished reading my book and gave me her verdict: "So easy to read."

QUESTIONS

Reading

1. In *reflecting* on her childhood experiences, Tan writes, "I think my mother's English almost had an effect on limiting my possibilities in life as well" (paragraph 15). Why does she believe this? What issues does she raise in her discussion?
2. What are the different "Englishes" with which Tan grew up? Find an example of each "English." What did Tan need to learn about each?
3. Make a list of ways that Tan characterizes her mother's English. What sense do we get of Tan's mother's personality from the quotations and anecdotes that Tan uses in this essay?
4. What was Tan's childhood experience studying math? What reasons does she give for the discrepancy between her achievement test scores in math and those in English?

Exploratory Writing

1. "[W]hen I was growing up," writes Tan, "my mother's 'limited' English limited *my* perception of her. . . . I believed that her English reflected the quality of what she had to say" (paragraph 9). In your own life, have you ever encountered someone who seemed "limited" to you, and then realized that you had misjudged that person? Write a short fictional or autobiographical account of this experience.
2. Tan tells us that as a writer, she cares about the way language "can evoke an emotion, a visual image, a complex idea, or a simple truth" (paragraph 2). Highlight, underline, or flag passages in Tan's essay where her language is evocative. Where does Tan surprise you with her choice of words?
3. Should only one kind of English be taught in schools, or should school curricula be expanded to include the teaching of different "Englishes" and bilingual or multilingual dialects? Break into groups and stage a debate on this topic. You can use the essays in this book by Tan and Gloria Anzaldúa (p. 131) to help formulate your arguments. You might also refer to the essays by Junot Díaz (p. 52) and James Baldwin (p. 109).

Making Connections

1. Gloria Anzaldúa uses the term *linguistic terrorism* in her essay on language and identity. How would you characterize linguistic terrorism? Based on her reflections in this essay, has Tan been a victim of linguistic terrorism? How?

Essay Writing

1. Tan writes that "the language spoken in the family, especially in immigrant families . . . , plays a large role in shaping the language of the child" (paragraph 15). Write an essay in which you reflect on the role of language in your family.

Paired Readings: On Religious Belief

The Veil

Marjane Satrapi

Marjane Satrapi (b. 1969) was born in Tehran, Iran, to a politically progressive, intellectual family and grew up in the increasingly repressive Islamic Republic. "The Veil" is the first chapter of Persepolis: The Story of a Childhood *(2003) — a graphic novel that narrates the daily lives of Satrapi, her family, and her friends during the fall of the shah, the early regime of Ayatollah Khomeini, and the beginning of the Iran-Iraq war. Today, Satrapi lives in Paris, France. She has authored and illustrated books for both children and adults, including* Persepolis 2: The Story of a Return *(2004) and* Embroideries *(2005). She codirected an animated film version of* Persepolis *with Vincent Paronnaud in 2007. Released in both French and English, the film won the Jury Prize at the Cannes Film Festival and was nominated for an Academy Award in the category of Best Animated Feature Film.*

THIS IS ME WHEN I WAS 10 YEARS OLD. THIS WAS IN 1980.

AND THIS IS A CLASS PHOTO. I'M SITTING ON THE FAR LEFT SO YOU DON'T SEE ME. FROM LEFT TO RIGHT: GOLNAZ, MAHSHID, NARINE, MINNA.

IN 1979 A REVOLUTION TOOK PLACE. IT WAS LATER CALLED "THE ISLAMIC REVOLUTION".

THEN CAME 1980: THE YEAR IT BECAME OBLIGATORY TO WEAR THE VEIL AT SCHOOL.

WEAR THIS!

WE DIDN'T REALLY LIKE TO WEAR THE VEIL, ESPECIALLY SINCE WE DIDN'T UNDERSTAND WHY WE HAD TO.

IT'S TOO HOT OUT!

EXECUTION IN THE NAME OF FREEDOM.

GIVE ME MY VEIL BACK!

YOU'LL HAVE TO LICK MY FEET!

OOH! I'M THE MONSTER OF DARKNESS.

GIDDYAP!

EVERYWHERE IN THE STREETS THERE WERE DEMONSTRATIONS FOR AND AGAINST THE VEIL.

the veil! the veil! the veil! the veil! the veil!

freedom! freedom! freedom! freedom! freedom!

AT ONE OF THE DEMONSTRATIONS, A GERMAN JOURNALIST TOOK A PHOTO OF MY MOTHER.

I WAS REALLY PROUD OF HER. HER PHOTO WAS PUBLISHED IN ALL THE EUROPEAN NEWSPAPERS.

AND EVEN IN ONE MAGAZINE IN IRAN. MY MOTHER WAS REALLY SCARED.

HAVE YOU SEEN THIS?

DON'T WORRY, DARLING.

SHE DYED HER HAIR,

AND WORE DARK GLASSES FOR A LONG TIME.

I REALLY DIDN'T KNOW WHAT TO THINK ABOUT THE VEIL. DEEP DOWN I WAS VERY RELIGIOUS BUT AS A FAMILY WE WERE VERY MODERN AND AVANT-GARDE.

I WAS BORN WITH RELIGION.

AT THE AGE OF SIX I WAS ALREADY SURE I WAS THE LAST PROPHET. THIS WAS A FEW YEARS BEFORE THE REVOLUTION.

O'Celestial light!

BEFORE ME THERE HAD BEEN A FEW OTHERS.

I AM THE LAST PROPHET.

A WOMAN?

I WANTED TO BE A PROPHET...

BECAUSE OUR MAID DID NOT EAT WITH US.

BECAUSE MY FATHER HAD A CADILLAC.

AND, ABOVE ALL, BECAUSE MY GRANDMOTHER'S KNEES ALWAYS ACHED.

COME HERE MARJI! HELP ME TO STAND UP.

DON'T WORRY. SOON YOU WON'T HAVE ANY MORE PAIN. YOU'LL SEE.

LIKE ALL MY PREDECESSORS I HAD MY HOLY BOOK.

THE FIRST THREE RULES CAME FROM ZARATHUSTRA. HE WAS THE FIRST PROPHET IN MY COUNTRY BEFORE THE ARAB INVASION.

YOU MUST BASE EVERYTHING ON THESE THREE RULES: BEHAVE WELL, SPEAK WELL, ACT WELL.

I ALSO WANTED US TO CELEBRATE THE TRADITIONAL ZARATHUSTRIAN HOLIDAYS. LIKE THE FIRE CEREMONY,

BEFORE THE PERSIAN NEW YEAR, NOROUZ, ON MARCH 21ST, THE FIRST DAY OF SPRING.

ONLY MY GRANDMOTHER KNEW ABOUT MY BOOK.

RULE NUMBER SIX: EVERYBODY SHOULD HAVE A CAR.

RULE NUMBER SEVEN: ALL MAIDS SHOULD EAT AT THE TABLE WITH THE OTHERS.

RULE NUMBER EIGHT: NO OLD PERSON SHOULD HAVE TO SUFFER.

IN THAT CASE, I'LL BE YOUR FIRST DISCIPLE.

REALLY?

BUT TELL ME HOW YOU'LL ARRANGE FOR OLD PEOPLE NOT TO SUFFER?

IT WILL SIMPLY BE FORBIDDEN.

EVERY NIGHT I HAD A BIG DISCUSSION WITH GOD.

GOD, GIVE ME SOME MORE TIME. I AM NOT QUITE READY YET.

YES YOU ARE, CELESTIAL LIGHT, YOU ARE MY CHOICE, MY LAST AND MY BEST CHOICE.

EXCEPT FOR MY GRANDMOTHER I WAS OBVIOUSLY THE ONLY ONE WHO BELIEVED IN MYSELF.

WHAT DO YOU WANT TO BE WHEN YOU GROW UP?

I'LL BE A PROPHET.

HAHA! HAHA! HAHA!

SHE'S CRAZY.

MY PARENTS WERE CALLED IN BY THE TEACHER.

YOUR CHILD IS DISTURBED. SHE WANTS TO BECOME A PROPHET.

WHAT ABOUT IT?

DOESN'T THIS WORRY YOU?

NO! NOT AT ALL!

QUESTIONS

Reading

1. How do Marji's views of God and the veil differ? What do these differences suggest about her attitudes toward religion?
2. Marji tells her grandmother that when she becomes a prophet she will declare a rule that "no old person should have to suffer" (p. 153) When her grandmother asks her how she will accomplish this, Marji replies, "it will simply be forbidden." What's *ironic* about Marji's response, given her attitudes about the veil and state-enforced religious observance?
3. The narrative in a graphic novel or comic unfolds through a series of *panels*. Most panels include both illustrations and language that work together to create a visual-verbal language. Choose a panel that contains a great deal of information, and take inventory of the information being communicated. Then make a bulleted list of everything you learn by "reading" the visual components of the panel. Once you complete your list, take ten to twenty minutes to freewrite on the following questions: How does visual communication differ from verbal communication? How does Satrapi use visual and verbal communication differently?

Exploratory Writing

1. Nonfiction graphic narratives are a form of *reporting* unique to the arts and humanities. Rather than attempting to report objectively, graphic narratives offer stylized accounts of firsthand observations. How does Satrapi's use of visuals shape her account? How would her story be different if it were written in the form of a newspaper article or historical account?
2. Make a short list of adjectives to describe the tone of each panel on the first page of "The Veil." Once your lists are complete, write a paragraph or two reflecting on the range of emotions represented on this single page. How does the tone change from one panel to the next? Are the changes gradual or abrupt? Are they expected or surprising? Why do you think Satrapi chooses to portray so many emotions in such a condensed way?
3. Some critics have complained that Satrapi's visual style is overly simplistic. Others argue that its simplicity is well suited to a story about childhood. In a small group, collaborate on writing the transcript for a debate between two critics representing each of these views. Give your critics names, and be sure to cite specific examples to illustrate their arguments about Satrapi's style. Be prepared to read your transcript out loud for the class.

Making Connections

1. In his essay "Is God an Accident?" (p. 158), Paul Bloom suggests three major theories to explain the origin of religion: the opiate theory, the fraternity theory, and the cognitive theory. Read Bloom's accounts of these theories. Then use his essay as a lens for interpreting "The Veil." Which of his theories seem to best describe Marji's religious belief? Which elements of these theories seem to resonate most with Marji's experience? Which elements are contradicted or challenged by her experience? Be sure to support your argument with evidence from Bloom's essay and Satrapi's graphic narrative.
2. Satrapi's graphic narrative tells the story of her childhood relationship to God and religion. Choose two figures discussed in Paul Bloom's essay (p. 158), and draw your own graphic narrative in which these two figures have a dialogue about God and religion. Be sure to capture their ideas accurately and to think carefully about how to use visuals to contribute relevant information to the dialogue. (For insight into how graphic narratives work, see Scott McCloud's piece "Setting the Record Straight" on p. 693.)

Essay Writing

1. In 2007, Satrapi created an animated film version of *Persepolis* (see headnote). Get a copy of this film from your local library or video store, and write an essay about the similarities and differences between the still version and the animated version of "The Veil." What has Satrapi changed? What has she kept intact? What differences do the changes make? Why do you think she's chosen to preserve particular elements and change others?

Paired Readings: On Religious Belief

Is God an Accident?

Paul Bloom

*A writer and award-winning research psychologist, Paul Bloom
was (b. 1963) born and raised in Canada. He attended McGill
University and went on to earn a PhD from Massachusetts
Institute of Technology, specializing in cognitive psychology
and language acquisition. While teaching at the University of
Arizona and later at Yale University, he developed theories that
connect the ability of young children to learn a language quickly
to the social skills they seem to pick up automatically, such as
interpreting others' intentions (or "mindreading," as he calls it).
Dr. Bloom's books —* How Children Learn the Meanings of
Words *(2000) and* Descartes' Baby: How the Science of Child
Development Explains What Makes Us Human *(2004) — use
his theories of child development to unearth knowledge about
human cognition and our understanding of morality, religion,
and art. The following essay first appeared in the* Atlantic
magazine, December 2005.

I. God Is Not Dead

When I was a teenager my rabbi believed that the Lubavitcher Rebbe,
who was living in Crown Heights, Brooklyn, was the Messiah, and that the
world was soon to end. He believed that the earth was a few thousand years
old, and that the fossil record was a consequence of the Great Flood. He
could describe the afterlife, and was able to answer adolescent questions
about the fate of Hitler's soul.

My rabbi was no crackpot; he was an intelligent and amiable man, a
teacher and a scholar. But he held views that struck me as strange, even disturbing. Like many secular people, I am comfortable with religion as a
source of spirituality and transcendence, tolerance and love, charity and
good works. Who can object to the faith of Martin Luther King Jr. or the

Dalai Lama — at least as long as that faith grounds moral positions one already accepts? I am uncomfortable, however, with religion when it makes claims about the natural world, let alone a world beyond nature. It is easy for those of us who reject supernatural beliefs to agree with Stephen Jay Gould that the best way to accord dignity and respect to both science and religion is to recognize that they apply to "non-overlapping magisteria": science gets the realm of facts, religion the realm of values.

For better or worse, though, religion is much more than a set of ethical principles or a vague sense of transcendence. The anthropologist Edward Tylor got it right in 1871, when he noted that the "minimum definition of religion" is a belief in spiritual beings, in the supernatural. My rabbi's specific claims were a minority view in the culture in which I was raised, but those *sorts* of views — about the creation of the universe, the end of the world, the fates of souls — define religion as billions of people understand and practice it.

The United States is a poster child for supernatural belief. Just about everyone in this country — 96 percent in one poll — believes in God. Well over half of Americans believe in miracles, the devil, and angels. Most believe in an afterlife — and not just in the mushy sense that we will live on in the memories of other people, or in our good deeds; when asked for details, most Americans say they believe that after death they will actually reunite with relatives and get to meet God. Woody Allen once said, "I don't want to achieve immortality through my work. I want to achieve it through not dying." Most Americans have precisely this expectation.

But America is an anomaly, isn't it? These statistics are sometimes taken   5
as yet another indication of how much this country differs from, for instance, France and Germany, where secularism holds greater sway. Americans are fundamentalists, the claim goes, isolated from the intellectual progress made by the rest of the world.

There are two things wrong with this conclusion. First, even if a gap between America and Europe exists, it is not the United States that is idiosyncratic. After all, the rest of the world — Asia, Africa, the Middle East — is not exactly filled with hard-core atheists. If one is to talk about exceptionalism, it applies to Europe, not the United States.

Second, the religious divide between Americans and Europeans may be smaller than we think. The sociologists Rodney Stark, of Baylor University, and Roger Finke, of Pennsylvania State University, write that the big difference has to do with church attendance, which really is much lower in Europe. (Building on the work of the Chicago-based sociologist and priest Andrew Greeley, they argue that this is because the United States has a rigorously free religious market, in which churches actively vie for parishioners and constantly improve their product, whereas European churches are often under state control and, like many government monopolies, have become inefficient.) Most polls from European countries show that a majority of their people are believers. Consider Iceland. To judge by rates of churchgoing, Iceland is the most secular country on earth, with a pathetic 2 percent weekly attendance. But four out of five Icelanders say that they pray, and the same proportion believe in life after death.

In the United States some liberal scholars posit a different sort of exceptionalism, arguing that belief in the supernatural is found mostly in Christian conservatives — those infamously described by the *Washington Post* reporter Michael Weisskopf in 1993 as "largely poor, uneducated, and easy to command." Many people saw the 2004 presidential election as pitting Americans who are religious against those who are not.

An article by Steven Waldman in the online magazine *Slate* provides some perspective on the divide:

> As you may already know, one of America's two political parties is extremely religious. Sixty-one percent of this party's voters say they pray daily or more often. An astounding 92 percent of them believe in life after death. And there's a hard-core subgroup in this party of super-religious Christian zealots. Very conservative on gay marriage, half of the members of this subgroup believe Bush uses too *little* religious rhetoric, and 51 percent of them believe God gave Israel to the Jews and that its existence fulfills the prophecy about the second coming of Jesus.

The group that Waldman is talking about is Democrats; the hard-core subgroup is African American Democrats.

Finally, consider scientists. They are less likely than non-scientists to be 10
religious — but not by a huge amount. A 1996 poll asked scientists whether they believed in God, and the pollsters set the bar high — no mealy-mouthed evasions such as "I believe in the totality of all that exists" or "in what is beautiful and unknown"; rather, they insisted on a real biblical God, one believers could pray to and actually get an answer from. About 40 percent of scientists said yes to a belief in this kind of God — about the same percentage found in a similar poll in 1916. Only when we look at the most elite scientists — members of the National Academy of Sciences — do we find a strong majority of atheists and agnostics.

These facts are an embarrassment for those who see supernatural beliefs as a cultural anachronism, soon to be eroded by scientific discoveries and the spread of cosmopolitan values. They require a new theory of why we are religious — one that draws on research in evolutionary biology, cognitive neuroscience, and developmental psychology.

II. Opiates and Fraternities

One traditional approach to the origin of religious belief begins with the observation that it is difficult to be a person. There is evil all around; everyone we love will die; and soon we ourselves will die — either slowly and probably unpleasantly or quickly and probably unpleasantly. For all but a pampered and lucky few life really is nasty, brutish, and short. And if our lives have some greater meaning, it is hardly obvious.

So perhaps, as Marx suggested, we have adopted religion as an opiate, to soothe the pain of existence. As the philosopher Susanne K. Langer has put it, man "cannot deal with Chaos"; supernatural beliefs solve the problem of this chaos by providing meaning. We are not mere things; we are lovingly crafted by God, and serve his purposes. Religion tells us that this is a just world, in which the good will be rewarded and the evil punished. Most of all, it addresses our fear of death. Freud summed it all up by describing a "three-fold task" for religious beliefs: "they must exorcise the terrors of nature, they must reconcile men to the cruelty of Fate, particularly as it is shown in death, and they must compensate them for the sufferings and privations which a civilized life in common has imposed on them."

Religions can sometimes do all these things, and it would be unrealistic to deny that this partly explains their existence. Indeed, sometimes theologians use the foregoing arguments to make a case for why we should believe: if one wishes for purpose, meaning, and eternal life, there is nowhere to go but toward God.

One problem with this view is that, as the cognitive scientist Steven   15
Pinker reminds us, we don't typically get solace from propositions that we don't already believe to be true. Hungry people don't cheer themselves up by believing that they just had a large meal. Heaven is a reassuring notion only insofar as people believe such a place exists; it is this belief that an adequate theory of religion has to explain in the first place.

Also, the religion-as-opiate theory fits best with the monotheistic religions most familiar to us. But what about those people (many of the religious people in the world) who do not believe in an all-wise and just God? Every society believes in spiritual beings, but they are often stupid or malevolent. Many religions simply don't deal with metaphysical or teleological questions; gods and ancestor spirits are called upon only to help cope with such mundane problems as how to prepare food and what to do with a corpse — not to elucidate the Meaning of It All. As for the reassurance of heaven, justice, or salvation, again, it exists in some religions but by no means all. (In fact, even those religions we are most familiar with are not always reassuring. I know some older Christians who were made miserable as children by worries about eternal damnation; the prospect of oblivion would have been far preferable.) So the opiate theory is ultimately an unsatisfying explanation for the existence of religion.

The major alternative theory is social: religion brings people together, giving them an edge over those who lack this social glue. Sometimes this argument is presented in cultural terms, and sometimes it is seen from an evolutionary perspective: survival of the fittest working at the level not of the gene or the individual but of the social group. In either case the claim is that religion thrives because groups that have it outgrow and outlast those that do not.

In this conception religion is a fraternity, and the analogy runs deep. Just as fraternities used to paddle freshmen on the rear end to instill loyalty and commitment, religions have painful initiation rites — for example, snipping off part of the penis. Also, certain puzzling features of many religions, such as dietary restrictions and distinctive dress, make perfect sense once they are viewed as tools to ensure group solidarity.

The fraternity theory also explains why religions are so harsh toward those who do not share the faith, reserving particular ire for apostates. This is clear in the Old Testament, in which "a jealous God" issues commands such as:

> Should your brother, your mother's son, or your son or your daughter or the wife of your bosom or your companion who is like your own self incite you in secret, saying "Let us go and worship other gods" . . . you shall surely kill him. Your hand shall be against him first to put him to death and the hand of all the people last. And you shall stone him and he shall die, for he sought to thrust you away from the LORD your God who brought you out of the land of Egypt, from the house of slaves.
>
> — DEUTERONOMY 13, 7:11

This theory explains almost everything about religion — except the religious part. It is clear that rituals and sacrifices can bring people together, and it may well be that a group that does such things has an advantage over one that does not. But it is not clear why a *religion* has to be involved. Why are gods, souls, an afterlife, miracles, divine creation of the universe, and so on brought in? The theory doesn't explain what we are most interested in, which is belief in the supernatural.   20

III. Bodies and Souls

Enthusiasm is building among scientists for a quite different view — that religion emerged not to serve a purpose but by accident.

This is not a value judgment. Many of the good things in life are, from an evolutionary perspective, accidents. People sometimes give money, time, and even blood to help unknown strangers in faraway countries whom they will never see. From the perspective of one's genes this is disastrous — the suicidal squandering of resources for no benefit. But its origin is not magical; long-distance altruism is most likely a by-product of other, more adaptive traits, such as empathy and abstract reasoning. Similarly, there is no reproductive advantage to the pleasure we get from paintings or movies. It just so happens that our eyes and brains, which evolved to react to three-dimensional objects in the real world, can respond to two-dimensional projections on a canvas or a screen.

Supernatural beliefs might be explained in a similar way. This is the religion-as-accident theory that emerges from my work and the work of cognitive scientists such as Scott Atran, Pascal Boyer, Justin Barrett, and Deborah Kelemen. One version of this theory begins with the notion that a distinction between the physical and the psychological is fundamental to human thought. Purely physical things, such as rocks and trees, are subject to the pitiless laws of Newton. Throw a rock, and it will fly through space on a certain path; if you put a branch on the ground, it will not disappear, scamper away, or fly into space. Psychological things, such as people, possess minds, intentions, beliefs, goals, and desires. They move unexpectedly, according to volition and whim; they can chase or run away. There is a moral difference as well: a rock cannot be evil or kind; a person can.

Where does the distinction between the physical and the psychological come from? Is it something we learn through experience, or is it somehow prewired into our brains? One way to find out is to study babies. It is notoriously difficult to know what babies are thinking, given that they can't speak and have little control over their bodies. (They are harder to test than rats or pigeons, because they cannot run mazes or peck levers.) But recently investigators have used the technique of showing them different events and recording how long they look at them, exploiting the fact that babies, like the rest of us, tend to look longer at something they find unusual or bizarre.

This has led to a series of striking discoveries. Six-month-olds understand that physical objects obey gravity. If you put an object on a table and then remove the table, and the object just stays there (held by a hidden wire), babies are surprised; they expect the object to fall. They expect objects to be solid, and contrary to what is still being taught in some psychology classes, they understand that objects persist over time even if hidden. (Show a baby an object and then put it behind a screen. Wait a little while and then remove the screen. If the object is gone, the baby is surprised.) Five-month-olds can even do simple math, appreciating that if first one object and then another is placed behind a screen, when the screen drops there should be two objects, not one or three. Other experiments find the same numerical understanding in nonhuman primates, including macaques and tamarins, and in dogs.

25

Similarly precocious capacities show up in infants' understanding of the social world. Newborns prefer to look at faces over anything else, and the sounds they most like to hear are human voices — preferably their mothers'. They quickly come to recognize different emotions, such as anger, fear, and happiness, and respond appropriately to them. Before they are a year old they can determine the target of an adult's gaze, and can learn by attending to the emotions of others; if a baby is crawling toward an area that might be dangerous and an adult makes a horrified or disgusted face, the baby usually knows enough to stay away.

A skeptic might argue that these social capacities can be explained as a set of primitive responses, but there is some evidence that they reflect a deeper understanding. For instance, when twelve-month-olds see one object chasing another, they seem to understand that it really is chasing, with the goal of catching; they expect the chaser to continue its pursuit along the most direct path, and are surprised when it does otherwise. In some work I've done with the psychologists Valerie Kuhlmeier, of Queen's University, and Karen Wynn, of Yale, we found that when babies see one character in a movie help an individual and a different character hurt that individual, they later expect the individual to approach the character that helped it and to avoid the one that hurt it.

Understanding of the physical world and understanding of the social world can be seen as akin to two distinct computers in a baby's brain, running separate programs and performing separate tasks. The understandings develop at different rates: the social one emerges somewhat later than the physical one. They evolved at different points in our prehistory; our physical understanding is shared by many species, whereas our social understanding is a relatively recent adaptation, and in some regards might be uniquely human.

That these two systems are distinct is especially apparent in autism, a developmental disorder whose dominant feature is a lack of social understanding. Children with autism typically show impairments in communication (about a third do not speak at all), in imagination (they tend not to engage in imaginative play), and most of all in socialization. They do not seem to enjoy the company of others; they don't hug; they are hard to reach out to. In the most extreme cases children with autism see people as nothing more than objects — objects that move in unpredictable ways and make unexpected noises and are therefore frightening. Their understanding of other minds is impaired, though their understanding of material objects is fully intact.

At this point the religion-as-accident theory says nothing about super-   30
natural beliefs. Babies have two systems that work in a cold-bloodedly rational way to help them anticipate and understand — and, when they get older, to manipulate — physical and social entities. In other words, both these systems are biological adaptations that give human beings a badly needed head start in dealing with objects and people. But these systems go awry in two important ways that are the foundations of religion. First, we perceive the world of objects as essentially separate from the world of minds, making it possible for us to envision soulless bodies and bodiless souls. This helps explain why we believe in gods and an afterlife. Second, as we will see, our system of social understanding overshoots, inferring goals and desires where none exist. This makes us animists and creationists.

IV. Natural-Born Dualists

For those of us who are not autistic, the separateness of these two mechanisms, one for understanding the physical world and one for understanding the social world, gives rise to a duality of experience. We experience the world of material things as separate from the world of goals and desires. The biggest consequence has to do with the way we think of ourselves and others. We are dualists; it seems intuitively obvious that a physical body and a conscious entity — a mind or soul — are genuinely distinct. We don't feel that we *are* our bodies. Rather, we feel that we *occupy* them, we *possess* them, we *own* them.

This duality is immediately apparent in our imaginative life. Because we see people as separate from their bodies, we easily understand situations in which people's bodies are radically changed while their personhood stays intact. Kafka envisioned a man transformed into a gigantic insect; Homer described the plight of men transformed into pigs; in *Shrek 2* an ogre is transformed into a human being, and a donkey into a steed; in *Star Trek* a scheming villain forcibly occupies Captain Kirk's body so as to take command of the *Enterprise*; in *The Tale of the Body Thief*, Anne Rice tells of a vampire and a human being who agree to trade bodies for a day; and in *13 Going on 30* a teenager wakes up as thirty-year-old Jennifer Garner. We don't think of these events as real, of course, but they are fully understandable; it makes intuitive sense to us that people can be separated from their bodies, and similar transformations show up in religions around the world.

This notion of an immaterial soul potentially separable from the body clashes starkly with the scientific view. For psychologists and neuroscientists, the brain is the source of mental life; our consciousness, emotions, and will are the products of neural processes. As the claim is sometimes put, *The mind is what the brain does.* I don't want to overstate the consensus here; there is no accepted theory as to precisely how this happens, and some scholars are skeptical that we will ever develop such a theory. But no scientist takes seriously Cartesian dualism, which posits that thinking need not involve the brain. There is just too much evidence against it.

Still, it *feels* right, even to those who have never had religious training, and even to young children. This became particularly clear to me one night when I was arguing with my six-year-old son, Max. I was telling him that he had to go to bed, and he said, "You can make me go to bed, but you can't make me go to sleep. It's *my* brain!" This piqued my interest, so I began to ask him questions about what the brain does and does not do. His answers showed an interesting split. He insisted that the brain was involved in perception — in seeing, hearing, tasting, and smelling — and he was adamant that it was responsible for thinking. But, he said, the brain was not essential for dreaming, for feeling sad, or for loving his brother. "That's what *I* do," Max said, "though my brain might help me out."

Max is not unusual. Children in our culture are taught that the brain is   35
involved in thinking, but they interpret this in a narrow sense, as referring
to conscious problem solving, academic rumination. They do not see the
brain as the source of conscious experience; they do not identify it with their
selves. They appear to think of it as a cognitive prosthesis — there is Max
the person, and then there is his brain, which he uses to solve problems just
as he might use a computer. In this commonsense conception the brain is, as
Steven Pinker puts it, "a pocket PC for the soul."

If bodies and souls are thought of as separate, there can be bodies without souls. A corpse is seen as a body that used to have a soul. Most things —
chairs, cups, trees — never had souls; they never had will or consciousness.
At least some nonhuman animals are seen in the same way, as what Descartes
described as "beast-machines," or complex automata. Some artificial creatures, such as industrial robots, Haitian zombies, and Jewish golems, are also
seen as soulless beings, lacking free will or moral feeling.

Then there are souls without bodies. Most people I know believe in a
God who created the universe, performs miracles, and listens to prayers. He
is omnipotent and omniscient, possessing infinite kindness, justice, and mercy.
But he does not in any literal sense have a body. Some people also believe in
lesser noncorporeal beings that can temporarily take physical form or occupy
human beings or animals: examples include angels, ghosts, poltergeists, suc-
cubi, dybbuks, and the demons that Jesus so frequently expelled from people's
bodies.

This belief system opens the possibility that we ourselves can survive the
death of our bodies. Most people believe that when the body is destroyed,
the soul lives on. It might ascend to heaven, descend to hell, go off into some
sort of parallel world, or occupy some other body, human or animal. Indeed,
the belief that the world teems with ancestor spirits — the souls of people
who have been liberated from their bodies through death — is common
across cultures. We can imagine our bodies being destroyed, our brains ceasing to function, our bones turning to dust, but it is harder — some would
say impossible — to imagine the end of our very existence. The notion of a
soul without a body makes sense to us.

Others have argued that rather than believing in an afterlife because we
are dualists, we are dualists because we want to believe in an afterlife. This
was Freud's position. He speculated that the "doctrine of the soul" emerged
as a solution to the problem of death: if souls exist, then conscious experience need not come to an end. Or perhaps the motivation for belief in an
afterlife is cultural: we believe it because religious authorities tell us that it is
so, possibly because it serves the interests of powerful leaders to control the
masses through the carrot of heaven and the stick of hell. But there is reason
to favor the religion-as-accident theory.

In a significant study the psychologists Jesse Bering, of the University of   40
Arkansas, and David Bjorklund, of Florida Atlantic University, told young
children a story about an alligator and a mouse, complete with a series of

pictures, that ended in tragedy: "Uh oh! Mr. Alligator sees Brown Mouse and is coming to get him!" (The children were shown a picture of the alligator eating the mouse.) "Well, it looks like Brown Mouse got eaten by Mr. Alligator. Brown Mouse is not alive anymore."

The experimenters asked the children a set of questions about the mouse's biological functioning — such as "Now that the mouse is no longer alive, will he ever need to go to the bathroom? Do his ears still work? Does his brain still work?" — and about the mouse's mental functioning, such as "Now that the mouse is no longer alive, is he still hungry? Is he thinking about the alligator? Does he still want to go home?"

As predicted, when asked about biological properties, the children appreciated the effects of death: no need for bathroom breaks; the ears don't work, and neither does the brain. The mouse's body is gone. But when asked about the psychological properties, more than half the children said that these would continue: the dead mouse can feel hunger, think thoughts, and have desires. The soul survives. And *children believe this more than adults do*, suggesting that although we have to learn which specific afterlife people in our culture believe in (heaven, reincarnation, a spirit world, and so on), the notion that life after death is possible is not learned at all. It is a by-product of how we naturally think about the world.

V. We've Evolved to Be Creationists

This is just half the story. Our dualism makes it possible for us to think of supernatural entities and events; it is why such things make sense. But there is another factor that makes the perception of them compelling, often irresistible. We have what the anthropologist Pascal Boyer has called a hypertrophy of social cognition. We see purpose, intention, design, even when it is not there.

In 1944 the social psychologists Fritz Heider and Mary-Ann Simmel made a simple movie in which geometric figures — circles, squares, triangles — moved in certain systematic ways, designed to tell a tale. When shown this movie, people instinctively describe the figures as if they were specific types of people (bullies, victims, heroes) with goals and desires, and repeat pretty much the same story that the psychologists intended to tell. Further research has found that bounded figures aren't even necessary — one can get much the same effect in movies where the "characters" are not single objects but moving groups, such as swarms of tiny squares.

Stewart Guthrie, an anthropologist at Fordham University, was the first 45 modern scholar to notice the importance of this tendency as an explanation for religious thought. In his book *Faces in the Clouds*, Guthrie presents anecdotes and experiments showing that people attribute human characteristics to a striking range of real-world entities, including bicycles, bottles, clouds, fire, leaves, rain, volcanoes, and wind. We are hypersensitive to signs of agency — so much so that we see intention where only artifice or accident exists. As Guthrie puts it, the clothes have no emperor.

Our quickness to overread purpose into things extends to the perception of intentional design. People have a terrible eye for randomness. If you show them a string of heads and tails that was produced by a random-number generator, they tend to think it is rigged — it looks orderly to them, too orderly. After 9/11 people claimed to see Satan in the billowing smoke from the World Trade Center. Before that some people were stirred by the Nun Bun, a baked good that bore an eerie resemblance to Mother Teresa. In November of 2004 someone posted on eBay a ten-year-old grilled cheese sandwich that looked remarkably like the Virgin Mary; it sold for $28,000. (In response pranksters posted a grilled cheese sandwich bearing images of the Olsen twins, Mary-Kate and Ashley.) There are those who listen to the static from radios and other electronic devices and hear messages from dead people — a phenomenon presented with great seriousness in the Michael Keaton movie *White Noise.* Older readers who lived their formative years before CDs and MPEGs might remember listening intently for the significant and sometimes scatological messages that were said to come from records played backward.

Sometimes there really are signs of nonrandom and functional design. We are not being unreasonable when we observe that the eye seems to be crafted for seeing, or that the leaf insect seems colored with the goal of looking very much like a leaf. The evolutionary biologist Richard Dawkins begins *The Blind Watchmaker* by conceding this point: "Biology is the study of complicated things that give the appearance of having been designed for a purpose." Dawkins goes on to suggest that anyone before Darwin who did not believe in God was simply not paying attention.

Darwin changed everything. His great insight was that one could explain complex and adaptive design without positing a divine designer. Natural selection can be simulated on a computer; in fact, genetic algorithms, which mimic natural selection, are used to solve otherwise intractable computational problems. And we can see natural selection at work in case studies across the world, from the evolution of beak size in Galápagos finches to the arms race we engage in with many viruses, which have an unfortunate capacity to respond adaptively to vaccines.

Richard Dawkins may well be right when he describes the theory of natural selection as one of our species' finest accomplishments; it is an intellectually satisfying and empirically supported account of our own existence. But almost nobody believes it. One poll found that more than a third of college undergraduates believe that the Garden of Eden was where the first human beings appeared. And even among those who claim to endorse Darwinian evolution, many distort it in one way or another, often seeing it as a mysterious internal force driving species toward perfection. (Dawkins writes that it appears almost as if "the human brain is specifically designed to misunderstand Darwinism.") And if you are tempted to see this as a red state–blue state issue, think again: although it's true that more Bush voters than Kerry voters are creationists, just about half of Kerry voters believe that God created human beings in their present form, and most of the rest believe that although we evolved from less-advanced life forms, God guided the process. Most Kerry voters want evolution to be taught either alongside creationism or not at all.

What's the problem with Darwin? His theory of evolution does clash 50 with the religious beliefs that some people already hold. For Jews and Christians, God willed the world into being in six days, calling different things into existence. Other religions posit more physical processes on the part of the creator or creators, such as vomiting, procreation, masturbation, or the molding of clay. Not much room here for random variation and differential reproductive success.

But the real problem with natural selection is that it makes no intuitive sense. It is like quantum physics; we may intellectually grasp it, but it will never feel right to us. When we see a complex structure, we see it as the product of beliefs and goals and desires. Our social mode of understanding leaves it difficult for us to make sense of it any other way. Our gut feeling is that design requires a designer — a fact that is understandably exploited by those who argue against Darwin.

It's not surprising, then, that nascent creationist views are found in young children. Four-year-olds insist that everything has a purpose, including lions ("to go in the zoo") and clouds ("for raining"). When asked to explain why a bunch of rocks are pointy, adults prefer a physical explanation, while children choose a functional one, such as "so that animals could scratch on them when they get itchy." And when asked about the origin of animals and people, children tend to prefer explanations that involve an intentional creator, even if the adults raising them do not. Creationism — and belief in God — is bred in the bone.

VI. Religion and Science Will Always Clash

Some might argue that the preceding analysis of religion, based as it is on supernatural beliefs, does not apply to certain non-Western faiths. In his recent book, *The End of Faith*, the neuroscientist Sam Harris mounts a fierce attack on religion, much of it directed at Christianity and Islam, which he criticizes for what he sees as ridiculous factual claims and grotesque moral views. But then he turns to Buddhism, and his tone shifts to admiration — it is "the most complete methodology we have for discovering the intrinsic freedom of consciousness, unencumbered by any dogma." Surely this religion, if one wants to call it a religion, is not rooted in the dualist and creationist views that emerge in our childhood.

Fair enough. But while it may be true that "theologically correct" Buddhism explicitly rejects the notions of body-soul duality and immaterial entities with special powers, actual Buddhists believe in such things. (Harris himself recognizes this; at one point he complains about the millions of Buddhists who treat the Buddha as a Christ figure.) For that matter, although many Christian theologians are willing to endorse evolutionary biology — and it was legitimately front-page news when Pope John Paul II conceded that Darwin's theory of evolution might be correct — this should not distract us from the fact that many Christians think evolution is nonsense.

Or consider the notion that the soul escapes the body at death. There is   55 little hint of such an idea in the Old Testament, although it enters into Judaism later on. The New Testament is notoriously unclear about the afterlife, and some Christian theologians have argued, on the basis of sources such as Paul's letters to the Corinthians, that the idea of a soul's rising to heaven conflicts with biblical authority. In 1999 the pope himself cautioned people to think of heaven not as an actual place but, rather, as a form of existence — that of being in relation to God.

Despite all this, most Jews and Christians, as noted, believe in an afterlife — in fact, even people who claim to have no religion at all tend to believe in one. Our afterlife beliefs are clearly expressed in popular books such as *The Five People You Meet in Heaven* and *A Travel Guide to Heaven*. As the *Guide* puts it,

> Heaven is *dynamic*. It's bursting with excitement and action. It's the ultimate playground, created purely for our enjoyment, by someone who knows what enjoyment means, because He invented it. It's Disney World, Hawaii, Paris, Rome, and New York all rolled up into one. And it's *forever!* Heaven truly is the vacation that never ends.

(This sounds a bit like hell to me, but it is apparently to some people's taste.)

Religious authorities and scholars are often motivated to explore and reach out to science, as when the pope embraced evolution and the Dalai Lama became involved with neuroscience. They do this in part to make their worldview more palatable to others, and in part because they are legitimately concerned about any clash with scientific findings. No honest person wants to be in the position of defending a view that makes manifestly false claims, so religious authorities and scholars often make serious efforts toward reconciliation — for instance, trying to interpret the Bible in a way that is consistent with what we know about the age of the earth.

If people got their religious ideas from ecclesiastical authorities, these efforts might lead religion away from the supernatural. Scientific views would spread through religious communities. Supernatural beliefs would gradually disappear as the theologically correct version of a religion gradually became consistent with the secular worldview. As Stephen Jay Gould hoped, religion would stop stepping on science's toes.

But this scenario assumes the wrong account of where supernatural ideas come from. Religious teachings certainly shape many of the specific beliefs we hold; nobody is born with the idea that the birthplace of humanity was the Garden of Eden, or that the soul enters the body at the moment of conception, or that martyrs will be rewarded with sexual access to scores of virgins. These ideas are learned. But the universal themes of religion are not learned. They emerge as accidental by-products of our mental systems. They are part of human nature.

QUESTIONS

Reading

1. What are the *opiate* and *fraternity* theories of the origin of religion? How do these differ from the cognitive theories at the heart of Bloom's discussion? Are the opiate and fraternity theories compatible with the cognitive theories, or do they contradict one another?
2. What is *dualism*? According to Bloom, why is dualism so persuasive?
3. Why does Bloom open his essay by invoking the mystical beliefs of a rabbi with whom he seems to disagree? Why does he compare that rabbi to Martin Luther King Jr. and the Dalai Lama?
4. Early in his essay, Bloom quotes public figures making provocative statements about various aspects of religion, including film director Woody Allen, evolutionary biologist Stephen Jay Gould, anthropologist Edward Tylor, and journalist Steven Waldman. Choose one of these quotations and reflect on its function in the essay. Why did Bloom use it? How does the point of view expressed in it relate to the theories of religion Bloom discusses?

Exploratory Writing

1. Bloom's essay focuses on *arguing*. In fact, he divides his essay into six sections and gives each of them a subtitle that functions like a *thesis statement*. On a blank sheet of paper, write out each of these subtitles, leaving several lines of blank space beneath each one. Write a brief summary of each section beneath each subtitle. Be sure to identify Bloom's central claims or questions in each section and to offer a concise summary of the evidence he uses to develop them.
2. In small groups, prepare for a debate on Bloom's question, "Is God an accident?" Some teams will make an argument for the cognitive theories Bloom discusses, and some teams will make an argument against them. The main source of evidence will be Bloom's essay, but the teams may choose to bring in evidence from their own experience, reading, and research. Each team must prepare an opening and closing statement (assigning a team member to deliver each) and be prepared to address any question raised by the other teams.

Making Connections

1. In Marjane Satrapi's "The Veil" (p. 148) Marji expresses strong beliefs
   about God and religion. If Marji were asked, "Is God an accident?" how
   do you think she would reply? Be sure to support your answer with
   evidence from Bloom's essay and Satrapi's graphic narrative.

Essay Writing

1. Write an essay in which you make an argument in response to Bloom's
   question, "Is God an accident?" What scientific theories suggest that
   the answer might be yes? What kind of "accident" are they referring to?
   What theories would suggest that the answer might be no? The bulk of
   your evidence should come from Bloom's essay, but you may use outside
   research or your own experience as evidence if relevant or necessary to
   make your argument stronger.

Social Sciences
and Public
Affairs

Readings in the Social Sciences and Public Affairs

The social sciences include academic disciplines that focus on groups of human beings — for example, sociology, political science, anthropology, economics, urban studies, and cultural geography. (Certain disciplines, such as history and linguistics, are sometimes classified among the social sciences and sometimes among the humanities; others, such as psychology, are sometimes classified among the social sciences and sometimes among the sciences.) Public affairs, closely related to the social sciences, encompass politics, law, and current events. Writers in the social sciences and public affairs tend to value facts, statistics, and data. Each discipline has developed careful methods for collecting and analyzing the facts that are relevant for their subjects of study. For example, a sociologist designs surveys to collect meaningful data, paying careful attention to the size and composition of the survey pool as well as potential biases, with the goal of conducting statistical analysis that will explain trends in social life; an anthropologist will often live among the group of people he or she studies, becoming a participant-observer, with the goal of writing an ethnography — a thorough study of a culture.

A variety of methods animate each discipline in the social sciences, but two are especially prominent: a quantitative approach focuses on numbers, usually statistics; a qualitative approach involves the collection and analysis of evidence drawn from a wide range of cultural sources, including interviews, newspapers, books, online sources, conversations, and artifacts. Some social scientists favor quantitative approaches, while others favor qualitative approaches. Many combine the two.

We've collected fifteen essays from the social sciences and public affairs, nine of which stand alone and the other six in pairs. Five of these essays are primarily reflecting, four reporting, two explaining, and four arguing. Most of these essays emphasize qualitative methods, because working with quantitative data involves specialized methods beyond the scope of most introductory writing courses.

For this course, when you write about the social sciences and public affairs, you too will be working primarily with qualitative data. Whether you are reflecting, reporting, explaining, or arguing, it will be your job to examine your data in such a way that it sheds light on the experiences of human beings that arise from group affiliations and social interactions. If you are writing about history, you'll be focusing on how past events shaped the development of such interactions; if you're writing about economics, you'll be writing about how trade and finances shape lives; if you're writing about politics, you'll be writing about how the choices (and compromises) made by nations and leaders affect the lives of citizens. These various writing topics share a common denominator: a focus on how social phenomena shape lives. It's important to get the facts right, but it's just as important to remember that such questions require judgment and analysis to be understood. That's where you, as a writer, come in.

Tools of Torture
An Essay on Beauty and Pain

Phyllis Rose

Born in 1942 in New York City, Phyllis Rose holds degrees from Radcliffe College (BA), Yale University (MA), and Harvard University (PhD). She is the author of A Woman of Letters: A Life of Virginia Woolf *(1978),* Never Say Goodbye: Essays *(1991), and* The Year of Reading Proust *(1997), as well as the editor of* The Norton Book of Women's Lives *(1993). Rose contributes frequently to periodicals such as the* Atlantic Monthly *and the* New York Times Book Review, *and she also serves on the editorial board of the* American Scholar. *Rose has received fellowships from the Guggenheim Foundation and the Rockefeller Foundation, among others. She has said, "I love the essay form because I very often don't know when I start on a subject where I'm going to end up. I find out what I think." This essay was first published in the* Atlantic Monthly *in October 1986.*

In a gallery off the rue Dauphine, near the *parfumerie* where I get my massage, I happened upon an exhibit of medieval torture instruments. It made me think that pain must be as great a challenge to the human imagination as pleasure. Otherwise there's no accounting for the number of torture instruments. One would be quite enough. The simple pincer, let's say, which rips out flesh. Or the head crusher, which breaks first your tooth sockets, then your skull. But in addition I saw tongs, thumbscrews, a rack, a ladder, ropes and pulleys, a grill, a garrote, a Spanish horse, a Judas cradle, an iron maiden, a cage, a gag, a strappado, a stretching table, a saw, a wheel, a twisting stork, an inquisitor's chair, a breast breaker, and a scourge. You don't need complicated machinery to cause incredible pain. If you want to saw your victim down the middle, for example, all you need is a slightly bigger than usual saw. If you hold the victim upside down so the blood stays in his head, hold his legs apart, and start sawing at the groin, you can get as far as the navel before he loses consciousness.

Even in the Middle Ages, before electricity, there were many things you could do to torment a person. You could tie him up in an iron belt that held the arms and legs up to the chest and left no point of rest, so that all his muscles went into spasm within minutes and he was driven mad within hours.

This was the twisting stork, a benign-looking object. You could stretch him out backward over a thin piece of wood so that his whole body weight rested on his spine, which pressed against the sharp wood. Then you could stop up his nostrils and force water into his stomach through his mouth. Then, if you wanted to finish him off, you and your helper could jump on his stomach, causing internal hemorrhage. This torture was called the rack. If you wanted to burn someone to death without hearing him scream, you could use a tongue lock, a metal rod between the jaw and collarbone that prevented him from opening his mouth. You could put a person in a chair with spikes on the seat and arms, tie him down against the spikes, and beat him, so that every time he flinched from the beating he drove his own flesh deeper onto the spikes. This was the inquisitor's chair. If you wanted to make it worse, you could heat the spikes. You could suspend a person over a pointed wooden pyramid and whenever he started to fall asleep, you could drop him onto the point. If you were Ippolito Marsili, the inventor of this torture, known as the Judas cradle, you could tell yourself you had invented something humane, a torture that worked without burning flesh or breaking bones. For the torture here was supposed to be sleep deprivation.

The secret of torture, like the secret of French cuisine, is that nothing is unthinkable. The human body is like a foodstuff, to be grilled, pounded, filleted. Every opening exists to be stuffed, all flesh to be carved off the bone. You take an ordinary wheel, a heavy wooden wheel with spokes. You lay the victim on the ground with blocks of wood at strategic points under his shoulders, legs, and arms. You use the wheel to break every bone in his body. Next you tie his body onto the wheel. With all its bones broken, it will be pliable. However, the victim will not be dead. If you want to kill him, you hoist the wheel aloft on the end of a pole and leave him to starve. Who would have thought to do this with a man and a wheel? But, then, who would have thought to take the disgusting snail, force it to render its ooze, stuff it in its own shell with garlic butter, bake it, and eat it?

Not long ago I had a facial — only in part because I thought I needed one. It was research into the nature and function of pleasure. In a dark booth at the back of the beauty salon, the aesthetician put me on a table and applied a series of ointments to my face, some cool, some warmed. After a while she put something into my hand, cold and metallic. "Don't be afraid, madame," she said. "It is an electrode. It will not hurt you. The other end is attached to two metal cylinders, which I roll over your face. They break down the electricity barrier on your skin and allow the moisturizers to penetrate deeply." I didn't believe this hocus-pocus. I didn't believe in the electricity barrier or in the ability of these rollers to break it down. But it all felt very good. The cold metal on my face was a pleasant change from the soft warmth of the aesthetician's fingers. Still, since Algeria it's hard to hear the word "electrode" without fear. So when she left me for a few minutes with a moist, refreshing cheesecloth over my face, I thought, What if the goal of her expertise had been pain, not moisture? What if the electrodes had been electrodes in the Algerian sense? What if the cheesecloth mask were dipped in acid?

In Paris, where the body is so pampered, torture seems particularly sinister, not because it's hard to understand but because — as the dark side of sensuality — it seems so easy. Beauty care is among the glories of Paris. *Soins esthétiques*[1] include makeup, facials, massages (both relaxing and reducing), depilations (partial and complete), manicures, pedicures, and tanning, in addition to the usual run of *soins* for the hair: cutting, brushing, setting, waving, styling, blowing, coloring, and streaking. In Paris the state of your skin, hair, and nerves is taken seriously, and there is little of the puritanical thinking that tries to persuade us that beauty comes from within. Nor do the French think, as Americans do, that beauty should be offhand and low-maintenance. Spending time and money on *soins esthétiques* is appropriate and necessary, not self-indulgent. Should that loving attention to the body turn malevolent, you have torture. You have the procedure — the aesthetic, as it were — of torture, the explanation for the rich diversity of torture instruments, but you do not have the cause.

Historically torture has been a tool of legal systems, used to get information needed for a trial or, more directly, to determine guilt or innocence. In the Middle Ages confession was considered the best of all proofs, and torture was the way to produce a confession. In other words, torture didn't come into existence to give vent to human sadism. It is not always private and perverse but sometimes social and institutional, vetted by the government and, of course, the Church. (There have been few bigger fans of torture than Christianity and Islam.) Righteousness, as much as viciousness, produces torture. There aren't squads of sadists beating down the doors to the torture chambers begging for jobs. Rather, as a recent book on torture by Edward Peters says, the institution of torture creates sadists; the weight of a culture, Peters suggests, is necessary to recruit torturers. You have to convince people that they are working for a great goal in order to get them to overcome their repugnance to the task of causing physical pain to another person. Usually the great goal is the preservation of society, and the victim is presented to the torturer as being in some way out to destroy it.

From another point of view, what's horrifying is how easily you can persuade someone that he is working for the common good. Perhaps the most appalling psychological experiment of modern times, by Stanley Milgram, showed that ordinary, decent people in New Haven, Connecticut, could be brought to the point of inflicting (as they thought) severe electric shocks on other people in obedience to an authority and in pursuit of a goal, the advancement of knowledge, of which they approved. Milgram used — some

---

[1]*Soins esthétiques*: Literally, "beauty cares"; that is, beauty treatments or cosmetic aids. [Eds.]

would say abused — the prestige of science and the university to make his point, but his point is chilling nonetheless. We can cluck over torture, but the evidence at least suggests that with intelligent handling most of us could be brought to do it ourselves.

In the Middle Ages, Milgram's experiment would have had no point. It would have shocked no one that people were capable of cruelty in the interest of something they believed in. That was as it should be. Only recently in the history of human thought has the avoidance of cruelty moved to the forefront of ethics. "Putting cruelty first," as Judith Shklar says in *Ordinary Vices,* is comparatively new. The belief that the "pursuit of happiness" is one of man's inalienable rights, the idea that "cruel and unusual punishment" is an evil in itself, the Benthamite[2] notion that behavior should be guided by what will produce the greatest happiness for the greatest number — all these principles are only two centuries old. They were born with the eighteenth-century democratic revolutions. And in two hundred years they have not been universally accepted. Wherever people believe strongly in some cause, they will justify torture — not just the Nazis, but the French in Algeria.

Many people who wouldn't hurt a fly have annexed to fashion the imagery of torture — the thongs and spikes and metal studs — hence reducing it to the frivolous and transitory. Because torture has been in the mainstream and not on the margins of history, nothing could be healthier. For torture to be merely kinky would be a big advance. Exhibitions like the one I saw in Paris, which presented itself as educational, may be guilty of pandering to the tastes they deplore. Solemnity may be the wrong tone. If taking one's goals too seriously is the danger, the best discouragement of torture may be a radical hedonism that denies that any goal is worth the means, that refuses to allow the nobly abstract to seduce us from the sweetness of the concrete. Give people a good croissant and a good cup of coffee in the morning. Give them an occasional facial and a plate of escargots. Marie Antoinette picked a bad moment to say "Let them eat cake," but I've often thought she was on the right track.

All of which brings me back to Paris, for Paris exists in the imagination   10
of much of the world as the capital of pleasure — of fun, food, art, folly, seduction, gallantry, and beauty. Paris is civilization's reminder to itself that nothing leads you less wrong than your awareness of your own pleasure and a genial desire to spread it around. In that sense the myth of Paris constitutes a moral touchstone, standing for the selfish frivolity that helps keep priorities straight.

---

[2]*Benthamite*: One who believes in the social policies of the nineteenth-century English philosopher Jeremy Bentham, who propounded the idea of the greatest good for the greatest number of people. [Eds.]

QUESTIONS

Reading

1. In the first paragraph of her essay, Rose lists more than twenty different tools of torture. In the next two paragraphs, she explains how some of these tools work and what kinds of torture each produces. Why do you think she goes into such elaborate detail beyond her original list? How did you feel as you read these paragraphs?

2. When Rose considers some tools of pleasure at the beauty salon, she devotes two paragraphs (4 and 5) to her discussion, but the list of tools she considers is shorter than her list of torture devices. Why do you suppose she is less detailed about pleasure?

3. Rose's reflections seem to be based in part on a supposition that tools of beauty (or pleasure) and tools of torture are the flip side of each other. What evidence and reasoning does she offer for this idea? In paragraph 9, she also seems to suggest that a widespread love of pleasure might be sufficient to put an end to torture. What evidence and reasoning does she offer for this idea?

Exploratory Writing

1. For Rose, the experience of getting a facial becomes an unlikely catalyst for *reflecting* on torture devices. Following her example, write about an experience or observation of your own that reminds you of the torture devices or practices Rose discusses.

2. Rose makes the point that images of torture have entered the mainstream through fashion, media, and the arts. Collaborate in small groups to find some examples of such images in popular culture (in films, magazines, advertising, art exhibitions), and prepare a presentation in which you reflect on what these images might reveal about contemporary attitudes about torture.

Making Connections

1. In "Regarding the Pain of Others" (p. 257), Susan Sontag examines ethical dilemmas inherent in the depiction of human suffering in war photographs. Imagine you are an archaeologist from a future civilization in which war has ceased to exist, and you have discovered copies of Rose's and Sontag's essays. Write a report describing the torture devices and photographs they discuss for citizens of your civilization.

Essay Writing

1. In paragraph 1, Rose names several tools of torture that aren't explained in the following paragraphs. Research two or three of these tools, and then write an essay that compares their origin, design, and effectiveness.
2. Though Rose focuses on medieval tools of torture, such tools have also been used more recently. Investigate two or three tools used in the twentieth century, and write an essay comparing them to medieval tools of torture.

What's So Bad about Hate?

Andrew Sullivan

Writer, editor, and public intellectual Andrew Sullivan (b. 1963) was born in southern England and now lives in Washington, D.C. He attended Oxford University, where he studied modern history and modern languages, and Harvard University, where he received a master's degree in public administration and a PhD in political science in 1989. Openly gay, Sullivan has been an outspoken advocate of gay issues. His 1993 New Republic *essay, "The Politics of Homosexuality," remains one of the most influential articles of the decade on the subject of gay rights; his controversial essay "Why Men Are Different" put him on the cover of* Time *magazine. Sullivan's books include* Virtually Normal: An Argument about Homosexuality *(1995);* Love Undetectable: Notes on Friendship, Sex, and Survival *(1998);* The Conservative Soul *(2006); and, most recently,* Intimations Pursued: The Voice of Practice in the Conversation of Michael Oakeshott *(2008). Editor of the* New Republic *from 1991 to 1996, Sullivan has also been a contributing writer for the* Sunday Times *(London),* Time *magazine, and the* New York Times Magazine, *in which this essay appeared in 1999. Sullivan's blog, the Daily Dish, appears daily on the* Atlantic Online.

I

I wonder what was going on in John William King's head two years ago when he tied James Byrd Jr.'s feet to the back of a pickup truck and dragged him three miles down a road in rural Texas. King and two friends had picked up Byrd, who was black, when he was walking home, half drunk, from a party. As part of a bonding ritual in their fledgling white supremacist group, the three men took Byrd to a remote part of town, beat him, and chained his legs together before attaching them to the truck. Pathologists at King's trial testified that Byrd was probably alive and conscious until his body finally hit a culvert and split in two. When King was offered a chance to say something to Byrd's family at the trial, he smirked and uttered an obscenity.

We know all these details now, many months later. We know quite a large amount about what happened before and after. But I am still drawn, again and again, to the flash of ignition, the moment when fear and loathing became hate, the instant of transformation when King became hunter and Byrd became prey.

181

What was that? And what was it when Buford Furrow Jr., long-time member of the Aryan Nations, calmly walked up to a Filipino American mailman he happened to spot, asked him to mail a letter, and then shot him at point-blank range? Or when Russell Henderson beat Matthew Shepard, a young gay man, to a pulp, removed his shoes, and then, with the help of a friend, tied him to a post, like a dead coyote, to warn off others?

For all our documentation of these crimes and others, our political and moral disgust at them, our morbid fascination with them, our sensitivity to their social meaning, we seem at times to have no better idea now than we ever had of what exactly they were about. About what that moment means when, for some reason or other, one human being asserts absolute, immutable superiority over another. About not the violence, but what the violence expresses. About what — exactly — hate is. And what our own part in it may be.

I find myself wondering what hate actually is in part because we have created an entirely new offense in American criminal law — a "hate crime" — to combat it. And barely a day goes by without someone somewhere declaring war against it. Last month President Clinton called for an expansion of hate-crime laws as "what America needs in our battle against hate." A couple of weeks later, Senator John McCain used a campaign speech to denounce the "hate" he said poisoned the land. New York's mayor, Rudolph Giuliani, recently tried to stop the Million Youth March in Harlem on the grounds that the event was organized by people "involved in hate marches and hate rhetoric." 5

The media concur in their emphasis. In 1985, there were eleven mentions of "hate crimes" in the national media database Nexis. By 1990, there were more than a thousand. In the first six months of 1999, there were seven thousand. "Sexy fun is one thing," wrote a *New York Times* reporter about sexual assaults in Woodstock '99's mosh pit. "But this was an orgy of lewdness tinged with hate." And when Benjamin Smith marked the Fourth of July this year by targeting blacks, Asians, and Jews for murder in Indiana and Illinois, the story wasn't merely about a twisted young man who had emerged on the scene. As the *Times* put it, "Hate arrived in the neighborhoods of Indiana University, in Bloomington, in the early-morning darkness."

But what exactly was this thing that arrived in the early-morning darkness? For all our zeal to attack hate, we still have a remarkably vague idea of what it actually is. A single word, after all, tells us less, not more. For all its emotional punch, "hate" is far less nuanced an idea than prejudice, or bigotry, or bias, or anger, or even mere aversion to others. Is it to stand in for all these varieties of human experience — and everything in between? If so, then the war against it will be so vast as to be quixotic. Or is "hate" to stand for a very specific idea or belief, or set of beliefs, with a very specific object or group of objects? Then waging war against it is almost certainly unconstitutional. Perhaps these kinds of questions are of no concern to those waging war on hate. Perhaps it is enough for them that they share a sentiment that there is too much hate and never enough vigilance in combating it. But sentiment is a poor basis for law and a dangerous tool in politics. It is better to leave some unwinnable wars unfought.

II

Hate is everywhere. Human beings generalize all the time, ahead of time, about everyone and everything. A large part of it may even be hard-wired. At some point in our evolution, being able to know beforehand who was friend or foe was not merely a matter of philosophical reflection. It was a matter of survival. And even today it seems impossible to feel a loyalty without also feeling a disloyalty, a sense of belonging without an equal sense of unbelonging. We're social beings. We associate. Therefore we disassociate. And although it would be comforting to think that the one could happen without the other, we know in reality that it doesn't. How many patriots are there who have never felt a twinge of xenophobia?

Of course, by hate we mean something graver and darker than this kind of lazy prejudice. But the closer you look at this distinction, the fuzzier it gets. Much of the time, we harbor little or no malice toward people of other backgrounds or places or ethnicities or ways of life. But then a car cuts you off at an intersection and you find yourself noticing immediately that the driver is a woman, or black, or old, or fat, or white, or male. Or you are walking down a city street at night and hear footsteps quickening behind you. You look around and see that it is a white woman and not a black man, and you are instantly relieved. These impulses are so spontaneous they are almost involuntary. But where did they come from? The mindless need to be mad at someone — anyone — or the unconscious eruption of a darker prejudice festering within?

In 1993, in San Jose, California, two neighbors, one heterosexual, one homosexual, were engaged in a protracted squabble over grass clippings. (The full case is recounted in *Hate Crimes*, by James B. Jacobs and Kimberly Potter.) The gay man regularly mowed his lawn without a grass catcher, which prompted his neighbor to complain on many occasions that grass clippings spilled over onto his driveway. Tensions grew until one day the gay man mowed his front yard, spilling clippings onto his neighbor's driveway, prompting the straight man to yell an obscene and common antigay insult. The wrangling escalated. At one point the gay man agreed to collect the clippings from his neighbor's driveway but then later found them dumped on his own porch. A fracas ensued, with the gay man spraying the straight man's son with a garden hose and the son hitting and kicking the gay man several times, yelling antigay slurs. The police were called, and the son was eventually convicted of a hate-motivated assault, a felony. But what was the nature of the hate, antigay bias or suburban property-owner madness?

Or take the Labor Day parade last year in Broad Channel, a small island in Jamaica Bay, Queens. Almost everyone there is white, and in recent years a group of local volunteer firefighters has taken to decorating a pickup truck for the parade in order to win the prize for "funniest float." Their themes have tended toward the outrageously provocative. Beginning in 1995, they won prizes for floats depicting "Hasidic Park," "Gooks of Hazzard," and "Happy Gays." Last year they called their float "Black to the

10

Future, Broad Channel 2098." They imagined their community a century hence as a largely black enclave, with every stereotype imaginable: watermelons, basketballs, and so on. At one point during the parade, one of them mimicked the dragging death of James Byrd. It was caught on videotape, and before long the entire community was depicted as a cauldron of hate.

It's an interesting case, because the float was indisputably in bad taste and the improvisation on the Byrd killing was grotesque. But was it hate? The men on the float were local heroes for their volunteer work; they had no record of bigoted activity and were not members of any racist organizations. In previous years they had made fun of many other groups, and they saw themselves more as provocateurs than bigots. When they were described as racists, it came as a shock to them. They apologized for poor taste but refused to confess to bigotry. "The people involved aren't horrible people," protested a local woman. "Was it a racist act? I don't know. Are they racists? I don't think so."

If hate is a self-conscious activity, she has a point. The men were primarily motivated by the desire to shock and to reflect what they thought was their community's culture. Their display was not aimed at any particular black people or at any blacks who lived in Broad Channel — almost none do. But if hate is primarily an unconscious activity, then the matter is obviously murkier. And by taking the horrific lynching of a black man as a spontaneous object of humor, the men were clearly advocating indifference to it. Was this an aberrant excess? Or the real truth about the men's feelings toward African Americans? Hate or tastelessness? And how on earth is anyone, even perhaps the firefighters themselves, going to know for sure?

Or recall H. L. Mencken. He shared in the anti-Semitism of his time with more alacrity than most and was an indefatigable racist. "It is impossible," he wrote in his diary, "to talk anything resembling discretion or judgment into a colored woman. They are all essentially childlike, and even hard experience does not teach them anything." He wrote at another time of the "psychological stigmata" of the "Afro-American race." But it is also true that during much of his life, day to day, Mencken conducted himself with no regard to race and supported a politics that was clearly integrationist. As the editor of his diary has pointed out, Mencken published many black authors in his magazine, *The Mercury*, and lobbied on their behalf with his publisher, Alfred A. Knopf. The last thing Mencken ever wrote was a diatribe against racial segregation in Baltimore's public parks. He was good friends with leading black writers and journalists, including James Weldon Johnson, Walter White, and George S. Schuyler, and played an underappreciated role in promoting the Harlem Renaissance.

What would our modern view of hate do with Mencken? Probably   15
ignore him, or change the subject. But with regard to hate, I know lots of people like Mencken. He reminds me of conservative friends who oppose almost every measure for homosexual equality yet genuinely delight in the company of their gay friends. It would be easier for me to think of them as

haters, and on paper, perhaps, there is a good case that they are. But in real life, I know they are not. Some of them clearly harbor no real malice toward me or other homosexuals whatsoever.

They are as hard to figure out as those liberal friends who support every gay rights measure they have ever heard of but do anything to avoid going into a gay bar with me. I have to ask myself in the same frustrating kind of way, are they liberal bigots or bigoted liberals? Or are they neither bigots nor liberals, but merely people?

III

Hate used to be easier to understand. When Sartre described anti-Semitism in his 1946 essay "Anti-Semite and Jew," he meant a very specific array of firmly held prejudices, with a history, an ideology, and even a pseudo-science to back them up. He meant a systematic attempt to demonize and eradicate an entire race. If you go to the Web site of the World Church of the Creator, the organization that inspired young Benjamin Smith to murder in Illinois earlier this year, you will find a similarly bizarre, pseudo-rational ideology. The kind of literature read by Buford Furrow before he rained terror on a Jewish kindergarten last month and then killed a mailman because of his color is full of the same paranoid loopiness. And when we talk about hate, we often mean this kind of phenomenon.

But this brand of hatred is mercifully rare in the United States. These professional maniacs are to hate what serial killers are to murder. They should certainly not be ignored, but they represent what Harold Meyerson, writing in *Salon*, called "niche haters": cold-blooded, somewhat deranged, often poorly socialized psychopaths. In a free society with relatively easy access to guns, they will always pose a menace.

But their menace is a limited one, and their hatred is hardly typical of anything very widespread. Take Buford Furrow. He famously issued a "wake-up call" to "kill Jews" in Los Angeles before he peppered a Jewish community center with gunfire. He did this in a state with two Jewish female senators, in a city with a large, prosperous Jewish population, in a country where out of several million Jewish Americans, a total of sixty-six were reported by the FBI as the targets of hate-crime assaults in 1997. However despicable Furrow's actions were, it would require a very large stretch to describe them as representative of anything but the deranged fringe of an American subculture.

Most hate is more common and more complicated, with as many varieties as there are varieties of love. Just as there are possessive love and needy love, family love and friendship, romantic love and unrequited love, passion and respect, affection and obsession, so hatred has its shadings. There is hate that fears, and hate that merely feels contempt; there is hate that expresses power, and hate that comes from powerlessness; there is revenge, and there is hate that comes from envy. There is hate that was love, and hate

20

that is a curious expression of love. There is hate of the other, and hate of something that reminds us too much of ourselves. There is the oppressor's hate and the victim's hate. There is hate that burns slowly and hate that fades. And there is hate that explodes and hate that never catches fire.

The modern words that we have created to describe the varieties of hate — *sexism, racism, anti-Semitism, homophobia* — tell us very little about any of this. They tell us merely the identities of the victims; they don't reveal the identities of the perpetrators, or what they think, or how they feel. They don't even tell us how the victims feel. And this simplicity is no accident. Coming from the theories of Marxist and post-Marxist academics, these isms are far better at alleging structures of power than at delineating the workings of the individual heart or mind. In fact, these isms can exist without mentioning individuals at all.

We speak of institutional racism, for example, as if an institution can feel anything. We talk of "hate" as an impersonal noun, with no hater specified. But when these abstractions are actually incarnated, when someone feels something as a result of them, when a hater actually interacts with a victim, the picture changes. We find that hates are often very different phenomena one from another, that they have very different psychological dynamics, that they might even be better understood by not seeing them as varieties of the same thing at all.

There is, for example, the now unfashionable distinction between reasonable hate and unreasonable hate. In recent years we have become accustomed to talking about hates as if they were all equally indefensible, as if it could never be the case that some hates might be legitimate, even necessary. But when some 800,000 Tutsis are murdered under the auspices of a Hutu regime in Rwanda, and when a few thousand Hutus are killed in revenge, the hates are not commensurate. Genocide is not an event like a hurricane, in which damage is random and universal; it is a planned and often merciless attack of one group upon another. The hate of the perpetrators is a monstrosity. The hate of the victims, and their survivors, is justified. What else, one wonders, were surviving Jews supposed to feel toward Germans after the Holocaust? Or, to a different degree, South African blacks after apartheid? If the victims overcome this hate, it is a supreme moral achievement. But if they don't, the victims are not as culpable as the perpetrators. So the hatred of Serbs for Kosovars today can never be equated with the hatred of Kosovars for Serbs.

Hate, like much of human feeling, is not rational, but it usually has its reasons. And it cannot be understood, let alone condemned, without knowing them. Similarly, the hate that comes from knowledge is always different from the hate that comes from ignorance. *It is one of the most foolish clichés of our time that prejudice is always rooted in ignorance and can usually be overcome by familiarity with the objects of our loathing.* The racism of many Southern whites under segregation was not appeased by familiarity with Southern blacks; the virulent loathing of Tutsis by many Hutus was not undermined by living next door to them for centuries. Theirs was a hatred that sprang, for whatever reasons, from experience. It cannot easily be compared with, for example, the resilience of anti-Semitism in Japan, or hostility to immigration in areas where immigrants are unknown, or fear of homosexuals by people who have never knowingly met one.

The same familiarity is an integral part of what has become known as   25
"sexism." Sexism isn't, properly speaking, a prejudice at all. Few men live without knowledge or constant awareness of women. Every single sexist man was born of a woman and is likely to be sexually attracted to women. His hostility is going to be very different from that of, say, a reclusive member of the Aryan Nations toward Jews he has never met.

In her book *The Anatomy of Prejudices*, the psychotherapist Elisabeth Young-Bruehl proposes a typology of three distinct kinds of hate: obsessive, hysterical, and narcissistic. It's not an exhaustive analysis, but it's a beginning in any serious attempt to understand hate rather than merely declaring war on it. The obsessives, for Young-Bruehl, are those, like the Nazis or Hutus, who fantasize a threat from a minority and obsessively try to rid themselves of it. For them, the very existence of the hated group is threatening. They often describe their loathing in almost physical terms: they experience what Patrick Buchanan, in reference to homosexuals, once described as a "visceral recoil" from the objects of their detestation. They often describe those they hate as diseased or sick, in need of a cure. Or they talk of "cleansing" them, as the Hutus talked of the Tutsis, or call them "cockroaches," as Yitzhak Shamir called the Palestinians. If you read material from the Family Research Council, it is clear that the group regards homosexuals as similar contaminants. A recent posting on its Web site about syphilis among gay men was headlined "Unclean."

Hysterical haters have a more complicated relationship with the objects of their aversion. In Young-Bruehl's words, hysterical prejudice is a prejudice that "a person uses unconsciously to appoint a group to act out in the world forbidden sexual and sexually aggressive desires that the person has repressed." Certain kinds of racists fit this pattern. White loathing of blacks is for some people at least partly about sexual and physical envy. A certain kind of white racist sees in black America all those impulses he wishes most to express himself but cannot. He idealizes in "blackness" a sexual freedom, a physical power, a Dionysian release that he detests but also longs for. His fantasy may not have any basis in reality, but it is powerful nonetheless. It is a form of love-hate, and it is impossible to understand the nuances of racism in, say, the American South, or in British imperial India, without it.

Unlike the obsessives, the hysterical haters do not want to eradicate the objects of their loathing; rather, they want to keep them in some kind of permanent and safe subjugation in order to indulge the attraction of their repulsion. A recent study, for example, found that the men most likely to be opposed to equal rights for homosexuals were those most likely to be aroused by homoerotic imagery. This makes little rational sense, but it has a certain psychological plausibility. If homosexuals were granted equality, then the hysterical gay-hater might panic that his repressed passions would run out of control, overwhelming him and the world he inhabits.

A narcissistic hate, according to Young-Bruehl's definition, is sexism. In its most common form, it is rooted in many men's inability even to imagine what it is to be a woman, a failing rarely challenged by men's control of our most powerful public social institutions. Women are not so much hated by most men as simply ignored in nonsexual contexts, or never conceived of as true equals. The implicit condescension is mixed, in many cases, with re-pressed and sublimated erotic desire. So the unawareness of women is some-times commingled with a deep longing or contempt for them.

Each hate, of course, is more complicated than this, and in any one person   30 hate can assume a uniquely configured combination of these types. So there are hysterical sexists who hate women because they need them so much, and narcissistic sexists who hardly notice that women exist, and sexists who os-cillate between one of these positions and another. And there are gay-bashers who are threatened by masculine gay men and gay-haters who feel repulsed by effeminate ones. The soldier who beat his fellow soldier Barry Winchell to death with a baseball bat in July had earlier lost a fight to him. It was the image of a macho gay man — and the shame of being bested by him — that the vengeful soldier had to obliterate, even if he needed a gang of accomplices and a weapon to do so. But the murderers of Matthew Shepard seem to have had a different impulse: a visceral disgust at the thought of any sexual con-tact with an effeminate homosexual. Their anger was mixed with mockery, as the cruel spectacle at the side of the road suggested.

In the same way, the pathological anti-Semitism of Nazi Germany was obsessive, inasmuch as it tried to cleanse the world of Jews, but also, as Daniel Jonah Goldhagen shows in his book, *Hitler's Willing Executioners*, hysterical. The Germans were mysteriously compelled as well as repelled by Jews, devising elaborate ways, like death camps and death marches, to keep them alive even as they killed them. And the early Nazi phobia of interracial sex suggests as well a lingering erotic quality to the relationship, partaking of exactly the kind of sexual panic that persists among some homosexual-haters and antimiscegenation racists. So the concept of "homophobia," like that of "sexism" and "racism," is often a crude one. All three are essentially cookie-cutter formulas that try to understand human impulses merely through the one-dimensional identity of the victims, rather than through the thoughts and feelings of the haters and hated.

This is deliberate. The theorists behind these isms want to ascribe all blame to one group in society — the "oppressors" — and render specific others — the "victims" — completely blameless. And they want to do this in order in part to side unequivocally with the underdog. But it doesn't take a genius to see how this approach too can generate its own form of bias. It can justify blanket condemnations of whole groups of people — white straight males, for example — purely because of the color of their skin or the nature of their sexual orientation. And it can condescendingly ascribe innocence to whole groups of others. It does exactly what hate does: it hammers the uniqueness of each individual into the anvil of group identity. And it postures morally over the result.

In reality, human beings and human acts are far more complex, which is why these isms and the laws they have fomented are continually coming under strain and challenge. Once again, hate wriggles free of its definers. It knows no monolithic groups of haters and hated. Like a river, it has many eddies, back-waters, and rapids. So there are anti-Semites who actually admire what they think of as Jewish power, and there are gay-haters who look up to homosexuals and some who want to sleep with them. And there are black racists, racist Jews, sexist women, and anti-Semitic homosexuals. Of course there are. . . .

V

. . . Why is hate for a group worse than hate for a person? In Laramie, Wyoming, the now-famous "epicenter of homophobia," where Matthew Shepard was brutally beaten to death, vicious murders are not unknown. In the previous twelve months, a fifteen-year-old pregnant girl was found east of the town with seventeen stab wounds. Her thirty-eight-year-old boyfriend was apparently angry that she had refused an abortion and left her in the Wyoming foothills to bleed to death. In the summer of 1998, an eight-year-old Laramie girl was abducted, raped, and murdered by a pedophile, who disposed of her young body in a garbage dump. Neither of these killings was deemed a hate crime, and neither would be designated as such under any existing hate-crime law. Perhaps because of this, one crime is an international legend; the other two are virtually unheard of.

But which crime was more filled with hate? Once you ask the question, you realize how difficult it is to answer. Is it more hateful to kill a stranger or a lover? Is it more hateful to kill a child than an adult? Is it more hateful to kill your own child than another's? Under the law before the invention of hate crimes, these decisions didn't have to be taken. But under the law after hate crimes, a decision is essential. A decade ago, a murder was a murder. Now, in the era when group hate has emerged as our cardinal social sin, it all depends.

The supporters of laws against hate crimes argue that such crimes should be disproportionately punished because they victimize more than the victim. Such crimes, these advocates argue, spread fear, hatred, and panic among whole populations and therefore merit more concern. But of course all crimes victimize more than the victim and spread alarm in the society at large. Just think of the terrifying church shooting in Texas only two weeks ago. In fact, a purely random murder may be even more terrifying than a targeted one, since the entire community and not just a part of it feels threatened. High rates of murder, robbery, assault, and burglary victimize everyone, by spreading fear, suspicion, and distress everywhere. Which crime was more frightening to more people this summer: the mentally ill Buford

Furrow's crazed attacks in Los Angeles, killing one, or Mark Barton's murder of his own family and several random day-traders in Atlanta, killing twelve? Almost certainly the latter. But only Furrow was guilty of "hate."

One response to this objection is that certain groups feel fear more in- 40 tensely than others because of a history of persecution or intimidation. But doesn't this smack of a certain condescension toward minorities? Why, after all, should it be assumed that gay men or black women or Jews, for example, are as a group more easily intimidated than others? Surely in any of these communities there will be a vast range of responses, from panic to concern to complete indifference. The assumption otherwise is the kind of crude generalization the law is supposed to uproot in the first place. And among these groups, there are also likely to be vast differences. To equate a population once subjected to slavery with a population of Mexican immigrants or third-generation Holocaust survivors is to equate the unequatable. In fact, it is to set up a contest of vulnerability in which one group vies with another to establish its particular variety of suffering, a contest that can have no dignified solution.

Rape, for example, is not classified as a hate crime under most existing laws, pitting feminists against ethnic groups in a battle for recognition. If, as a solution to this problem, everyone except the white straight able-bodied male is regarded as a possible victim of a hate crime, then we have simply created a two-tier system of justice in which racial profiling is reversed, and white straight men are presumed guilty before being proved innocent, and members of minorities are free to hate them as gleefully as they like. But if we include the white straight male in the litany of potential victims, then we have effectively abolished the notion of a hate crime altogether, for if every crime is possibly a hate crime, then it is simply another name for crime. All we will have done is widened the search for possible bigotry, ratcheted up the sentences for everyone, and filled the jails up even further.

Hate-crime law advocates counter that extra penalties should be imposed on hate crimes because our society is experiencing an "epidemic" of such crimes. Mercifully, there is no hard evidence to support this notion. The federal government has only been recording the incidence of hate crimes in this decade, and the statistics tell a simple story. In 1992, there were 6,623 hate-crime incidents reported to the FBI by a total of 6,181 agencies, covering 51 percent of the population. In 1996, there were 8,734 incidents reported by 11,355 agencies, covering 84 percent of the population. That number dropped to 8,049 in 1997. These numbers are of course hazardous. They probably underreport the incidence of such crimes, but they are the only reliable figures we have. Yet even if they are faulty as an absolute number, they do not show an epidemic of hate crimes in the 1990s.

Is there evidence that the crimes themselves are becoming more vicious? None. More than 60 percent of recorded hate crimes in America involve no violent physical assault against another human being at all, and again, according to the FBI, that proportion has not budged much in the 1990s. These impersonal attacks are crimes against property or crimes of intimidation.

Murder, which dominates media coverage of hate crimes, is a tiny proportion of the total. Of the 8,049 hate crimes reported to the FBI in 1997, a total of 8 were murders. Eight. The number of hate crimes that were aggravated assaults (generally involving a weapon) in 1997 is less than 15 percent of the total. That's 1,237 assaults too many, of course, but to put it in perspective, compare it with a reported 1,022,492 "equal opportunity" aggravated assaults in America in the same year. The number of hate crimes that were physical assaults is half the total. That's 4,000 assaults too many, of course, but to put it in perspective, it compares with around 3.8 million "equal opportunity" assaults in America annually.

The truth is, the distinction between a crime filled with personal hate and a crime filled with group hate is an essentially arbitrary one. It tells us nothing interesting about the psychological contours of the specific actor or his specific victim. It is a function primarily of politics, of special-interest groups carving out particular protections for themselves, rather than a serious response to a serious criminal concern. In such an endeavor, hate-crime law advocates cram an entire world of human motivations into an immutable, tiny box called hate and hope to have solved a problem. But nothing has been solved, and some harm may even have been done.

In an attempt to repudiate a past that treated people differently because of the color of their skin or their sex or religion or sexual orientation, we may merely create a future that permanently treats people differently because of the color of their skin or their sex, religion, or sexual orientation. This notion of a hate crime, and the concept of hate that lies behind it, takes a psychological mystery and turns it into a facile political artifact. Rather than compounding this error and extending it even further, we should seriously consider repealing the concept altogether.

45

To put it another way: violence can and should be stopped by the government. In a free society, hate can't and shouldn't be. The boundaries between hate and prejudice and between prejudice and opinion and between opinion and truth are so complicated and blurred that any attempt to construct legal and political fire walls is a doomed and illiberal venture. We know by now that hate will never disappear from human consciousness; in fact, it is probably, at some level, definitive of it. We know after decades of education measures that hate is not caused merely by ignorance and, after decades of legislation, that it isn't cured entirely by law.

To be sure, we have made much progress. Anyone who argues that America is as inhospitable to minorities and to women today as it has been in the past has not read much history. And we should of course be vigilant that our most powerful institutions, most notably the government, do not actively or formally propagate hatred, and ensure that the violent expression of hate is curtailed by the same rules that punish all violent expression.

But after that, in an increasingly diverse culture, it is crazy to expect that hate, in all its variety, can be eradicated. A free country will always mean a hateful country. This may not be fair, or perfect, or admirable, but it is reality, and while we need not endorse it, we should not delude ourselves into thinking we can prevent it. That is surely the distinction between toleration and tolerance. Tolerance is the eradication of hate; toleration is coexistence despite it. We might do better as a culture and as a polity if we concentrated more on achieving the latter than the former. We would certainly be less frustrated.

And by aiming lower, we might actually reach higher. In some ways, some expression of prejudice serves a useful social purpose. It lets off steam; it allows natural tensions to express themselves incrementally; it can siphon off conflict through words rather than actions. Anyone who has lived in the ethnic shouting match that is New York City knows exactly what I mean. If New Yorkers disliked each other less, they wouldn't be able to get on so well. We may not all be able to pull off a Mencken — bigoted in words, egalitarian in action — but we might achieve a lesser form of virtue: a human acceptance of our need for differentiation without a total capitulation to it.

Do we not owe something more to the victims of hate? Perhaps we do.   50
But it is also true that there is nothing that government can do for the hated that the hated cannot better do for themselves. After all, most bigots are not foiled when they are punished specifically for their beliefs. In fact, many of the worst haters crave such attention and find vindication in such rebukes. Indeed, our media's obsession with "hate," our elevation of it above other social misdemeanors and crimes, may even play into the hands of the pathetic and the evil, may breathe air into the smoldering embers of their paranoid loathing. Sure, we can help create a climate in which such hate is disapproved of — and we should. But there is a danger that if we go too far, if we punish it too much, if we try to abolish it altogether, we may merely increase its mystique, and entrench the very categories of human difference that we are trying to erase.

For hate is only foiled not when the haters are punished but when the hated are immune to the bigot's power. A hater cannot psychologically wound if a victim cannot psychologically be wounded. And that immunity to hurt can never be given; it can merely be achieved. The racial epithet only strikes at someone's core if he lets it, if he allows the bigot's definition of him to be the final description of his life and his person — if somewhere in his heart of hearts, he believes the hateful slur to be true. The only final answer to this form of racism, then, is not majority persecution of it but minority indifference to it. The only permanent rebuke to homophobia is not the enforcement of tolerance but gay equanimity in the face of prejudice. The only effective answer to sexism is not a morass of legal proscriptions but the simple fact of female success. In this, as in so many other things, there is no solution to the problem. There is only a transcendence of it. For all our rhetoric, hate will never be destroyed. Hate, as our predecessors knew better, can merely be overcome.

QUESTIONS

Reading

1. What arguments does Sullivan make about the use of the terms *racism, sexism,* and *homophobia*?
2. How does Sullivan characterize H. L. Mencken? How does this characterization serve to support his broader argument?
3. What is the definition of a hate crime? Summarize Sullivan's criticisms of this concept. What are his conclusions about hate crime law?

Exploratory Writing

1. Sullivan equates the widespread European anti-Semitism discussed in Jean-Paul Sartre's 1946 "Anti-Semite and Jew" with the "paranoid loopiness" of unhinged individuals who might open fire in kindergartens. This brand of hatred, he says, "is mercifully rare in the United States" (paragraph 18). He suggests that seeing expressions of hatred as independent psychological responses rather than as evidence of widespread institutional racism, sexism, and homophobia helps people understand the complexity of human acts. List the evidence that Sullivan uses to support this claim. What evidence could you use to make a *counterargument*?
2. Collaborating in small groups, use library or Internet news archives to find two articles about recent crimes that were allegedly motivated by racism, sexism, religious prejudice, or homophobia. Discuss each case in light of Sullivan's essay and whether such crimes should be prosecuted differently from other crimes. How do these cases support or undermine Sullivan's claims that "human beings and human acts" are more complex than isms and that "monolithic groups of haters and hated" do not actually exist (paragraph 33)?
3. Sullivan writes that, "Sexism isn't . . . a prejudice at all. Few men live without . . . constant awareness of women" (paragraph 25). To make this claim, Sullivan assumes that there are only two kinds of people: men and women. Increasingly, awareness of transgender and intersex people is calling his assumption into question. Writers like Kate Bornstein, the author of *Gender Outlaw*, argue that prejudice is the process of grouping people into categories based on ascribed traits (such as skin color, ethnic heritage, or their genitals at birth) rather than viewing them as distinct individuals. Reflecting on Sullivan's arguments, write your own definition of the term *prejudice*.

Making Connections

1. Do you think that James Baldwin (p. 109) would agree with Sullivan's arguments about hate and his remarks on racism? Why or why not?

Essay Writing

1. Sullivan asks the rhetorical question, "Why is hate for a group worse than hate for a person?" (paragraph 37). Based on your own experience and your own understanding of history, write an essay reflecting on this question.

2. Sullivan writes, "[V]iolence can and should be stopped by the government. In a free society, hate can't and shouldn't be" (paragraph 46). Over the next four weeks, trace the articles published on the subject of "hate crimes" in major newspapers and magazines. After you have done this research, write an essay reporting on the degree to which the authors of these articles appear to share Sullivan's views. After following these articles, write an essay in which you share your conclusions.

Nickel and Dimed
On (Not) Getting By in America

Barbara Ehrenreich

A native of Butte, Montana, Barbara Ehrenreich (b. 1941) is one of the country's most outspoken social critics. After graduating from Reed College, Ehrenreich earned her PhD in biology from Roosevelt University in Chicago. Instead of becoming a research scientist, she decided to pursue liberal political activism. According to Ehrenreich, as she began working on leaflets and newsletters, writing "crept up on" her. She was soon a regular contributor to Ms. *magazine and has since written for the* New Republic, Mother Jones, *and* Time, *among many other periodicals. Ehrenreich's books include* Complaints and Disorders: The Sexual Politics of Sickness *(1973),* Fear of Falling: The Inner Life of the Middle Class *(1989),* The Worst Years of Our Lives: Irreverent Notes from the Decade of Greed *(1990),* The Snarling Citizen: Collected Essays *(1995),* Blood Rites: Origins and History of the Passions of War *(1997), and* Bait and Switch: The (Futile) Pursuit of the American Dream *(2005). The recipient of a Guggenheim Fellowship and a MacArthur grant, Ehrenreich contributed the following essay, which provided the basis for her 2001 book of the same title, to the* Atlantic *in 1999. As she later told an interviewer, it began in a meeting with the editor of the magazine when "the conversation drifted to talking about welfare reform and the assumption that these single moms could just get out there in the workforce and get a job and then everything would be okay. They'd be lifted out of poverty. We were both agreeing that nobody seems to see that the math doesn't work. That's when I made this, perhaps disastrous, suggestion that somebody should go out there and do the old-fashioned kind of journalism, just try it for themselves and write about it. I did not expect him to say, 'Yeah, great idea. It should be you.'"*

At the beginning of June 1998 I leave behind everything that normally soothes the ego and sustains the body—home, career, companion, reputation, ATM card—for a plunge into the low-wage workforce. There, I become another, occupationally much diminished "Barbara Ehrenreich"—depicted on job-application forms as a divorced homemaker whose sole work experience consists of housekeeping in a few private homes. I am terrified, at the beginning, of being unmasked for what I am: a middle-class journalist setting out to explore the world that welfare mothers are entering, at the rate of approximately fifty thousand a month, as welfare reform kicks in. Happily, though, my fears turn out to be entirely unwarranted: during a month of poverty and toil, my name goes unnoticed and for the most part unuttered. In this parallel universe where my father never got out of the mines and I never got through college, I am "baby," "honey," "blondie," and, most commonly, "girl."

My first task is to find a place to live. I figure that if I can earn $7 an hour — which, from the want ads, seems doable — I can afford to spend $500 on rent, or maybe, with severe economies, $600. In the Key West area, where I live, this pretty much confines me to flophouses and trailer homes — like the one, a pleasing fifteen-minute drive from town, that has no airconditioning, no screens, no fans, no television, and, by way of diversion, only the challenge of evading the landlord's Doberman pinscher. The big problem with this place, though, is the rent, which at $675 a month is well beyond my reach. All right, Key West is expensive. But so is New York City, or the Bay Area, or Jackson Hole, or Telluride, or Boston, or any other place where tourists and the wealthy compete for living space with the people who clean their toilets and fry their hash browns.[1] Still, it is a shock to realize that "trailer trash" has become, for me, a demographic category to aspire to.

So I decide to make the common trade-off between affordability and convenience, and go for a $500-a-month efficiency thirty miles up a two-lane highway from the employment opportunities of Key West, meaning forty-five minutes if there's no road construction and I don't get caught behind some sun-dazed Canadian tourists. I hate the drive, along a roadside studded with white crosses commemorating the more effective head-on collisions, but it's a sweet little place — a cabin, more or less, set in the swampy back yard of the converted mobile home where my landlord, an affable TV repairman, lives with his bartender girlfriend. Anthropologically speaking, a bustling trailer park would be preferable, but here I have a gleaming white floor and a firm mattress, and the few resident bugs are easily vanquished.

Besides, I am not doing this for the anthropology. My aim is nothing so mistily subjective as to "experience poverty" or find out how it "really feels" to be a long-term low-wage worker. I've had enough unchosen encounters with poverty and the world of low-wage work to know it's not a place you want to visit for touristic purposes; it just smells too much like fear. And

---

[1]According to the Department of Housing and Urban Development, the "fair-market rent" for an efficiency is $551 here in Monroe County, Florida. A comparable rent in the five boroughs of New York City is $704; in San Francisco, $713; and in the heart of Silicon Valley, $808. The fair-market rent for an area is defined as the amount that would be needed to pay rent plus utilities for "privately owned, decent, safe, and sanitary rental housing of a modest (non-luxury) nature with suitable amenities."

with all my real-life assets — bank account, IRA, health insurance, multiroom home — waiting indulgently in the background, I am, of course, thoroughly insulated from the terrors that afflict the genuinely poor.

No, this is a purely objective, scientific sort of mission. The humanitarian rationale for welfare reform — as opposed to the more punitive and stingy impulses that may actually have motivated it — is that work will lift poor women out of poverty while simultaneously inflating their self-esteem and hence their future value in the labor market. Thus, whatever the hassles involved in finding child care, transportation, etc., the transition from welfare to work will end happily, in greater prosperity for all. Now there are many problems with this comforting prediction, such as the fact that the economy will inevitably undergo a downturn, eliminating many jobs. Even without a downturn, the influx of a million former welfare recipients into the low-wage labor market could depress wages by as much as 11.9 percent, according to the Economic Policy Institute (EPI) in Washington, D.C.

But is it really possible to make a living on the kinds of jobs currently available to unskilled people? Mathematically, the answer is no, as can be shown by taking $6 to $7 an hour, perhaps subtracting a dollar or two an hour for child care, multiplying by 160 hours a month, and comparing the result to the prevailing rents. According to the National Coalition for the Homeless, for example, in 1998 it took, on average nationwide, an hourly wage of $8.89 to afford a one-bedroom apartment, and the Preamble Center for Public Policy estimates that the odds against a typical welfare recipient's landing a job at such a "living wage" are about 97 to 1. If these numbers are right, low-wage work is not a solution to poverty and possibly not even to homelessness.

It may seem excessive to put this proposition to an experimental test. As certain family members keep unhelpfully reminding me, the viability of low-wage work could be tested, after a fashion, without ever leaving my study. I could just pay myself $7 an hour for eight hours a day, charge myself for room and board, and total up the numbers after a month. Why leave the people and work that I love? But I am an experimental scientist by training. In that business, you don't just sit at a desk and theorize; you plunge into the everyday chaos of nature, where surprises lurk in the most mundane measurements. Maybe, when I got into it, I would discover some hidden economies in the world of the low-wage worker. After all, if 30 percent of the workforce toils for less than $8 an hour, according to the EPI, they may have found some tricks as yet unknown to me. Maybe — who knows? — I would even be able to detect in myself the bracing psychological effects of getting out of the house, as promised by the welfare wonks at places like the Heritage Foundation. Or, on the other hand, maybe there would be unexpected costs — physical, mental, or financial — to throw off all my calculations. Ideally, I should do this with two small children in tow, that being the welfare average, but mine are grown and no one is willing to lend me theirs for a month-long vacation in penury. So this is not the perfect experiment, just a test of the best possible case: an unencumbered woman, smart and even strong, attempting to live more or less off the land.

On the morning of my first full day of job searching, I take a red pen to the want ads, which are auspiciously numerous. Everyone in Key West's booming "hospitality industry" seems to be looking for someone like me — trainable, flexible, and with suitably humble expectations as to pay. I know I possess certain traits that might be advantageous — I'm white and, I like to think, well-spoken and poised — but I decide on two rules: One, I cannot use any skills derived from my education or usual work — not that there are a lot of want ads for satirical essayists anyway. Two, I have to take the best-paid job that is offered me and of course do my best to hold it; no Marxist rants or sneaking off to read novels in the ladies' room. In addition, I rule out various occupations for one reason or another: Hotel front-desk clerk, for example, which to my surprise is regarded as unskilled and pays around $7 an hour, gets eliminated because it involves standing in one spot for eight hours a day. Waitressing is similarly something I'd like to avoid, because I remember it leaving me bone tired when I was eighteen, and I'm decades of varicosities and back pain beyond that now. Telemarketing, one of the first refuges of the suddenly indigent, can be dismissed on grounds of personality. This leaves certain supermarket jobs, such as deli clerk, or housekeeping in Key West's thousands of hotel and guest rooms. Housekeeping is especially appealing, for reasons both atavistic and practical: it's what my mother did before I came along, and it can't be too different from what I've been doing part-time, in my own home, all my life.

So I put on what I take to be a respectful-looking outfit of ironed Bermuda shorts and scooped-neck T-shirt and set out for a tour of the local hotels and supermarkets. Best Western, Econo Lodge, and HoJo's all let me fill out application forms, and these are, to my relief, interested in little more than whether I am a legal resident of the United States and have committed any felonies. My next stop is Winn-Dixie, the supermarket, which turns out to have a particularly onerous application process, featuring a fifteen-minute "interview" by computer since, apparently, no human on the premises is deemed capable of representing the corporate point of view. I am conducted to a large room decorated with posters illustrating how to look "professional" (it helps to be white and, if female, permed) and warning of the slick promises that union organizers might try to tempt me with. The interview is multiple choice: Do I have anything, such as childcare problems, that might make it hard for me to get to work on time? Do I think safety on the job is the responsibility of management? Then, popping up cunningly out of the blue: How many dollars' worth of stolen goods have I purchased in the last year? Would I turn in a fellow employee if I caught him stealing? Finally, "Are you an honest person?"

Apparently, I ace the interview, because I am told that all I have to do   10 is show up in some doctor's office tomorrow for a urine test. This seems to be a fairly general rule: if you want to stack Cheerio boxes or vacuum hotel rooms in chemically fascist America, you have to be willing to squat down and pee in front of some health worker (who has no doubt had to do the same thing herself). The wages Winn-Dixie is offering — $6 and a couple of dimes to start with — are not enough, I decide, to compensate for this indignity.[2]

I lunch at Wendy's, where $4.99 gets you unlimited refills at the Mexican part of the Super-bar, a comforting surfeit of refried beans and "cheese sauce." A teenage employee, seeing me studying the want ads, kindly offers me an application form, which I fill out, though here, too, the pay is just $6 and change an hour. Then it's off for a round of the locally owned inns and guesthouses. At "The Palms," let's call it, a bouncy manager actually takes me around to see the rooms and meet the existing housekeepers, who, I note with satisfaction, look pretty much like me — faded ex-hippie types in shorts with long hair pulled back in braids. Mostly, though, no one speaks to me or even looks at me except to proffer an application form. At my last stop, a palatial B&B, I wait twenty minutes to meet "Max," only to be told that there are no jobs now but there should be one soon, since "nobody lasts more than a couple weeks." (Because none of the people I talked to knew I was a reporter, I have changed their names to protect their privacy and, in some cases perhaps, their jobs.)

Three days go by like this, and, to my chagrin, no one out of the approximately twenty places I've applied calls me for an interview. I had been vain enough to worry about coming across as too educated for the jobs I sought, but no one even seems interested in finding out how overqualified I am. Only later will I realize that the want ads are not a reliable measure of the actual jobs available at any particular time. They are, as I should have guessed from Max's comment, the employers' insurance policy against the relentless turnover of the low-wage workforce. Most of the big hotels run ads almost continually, just to build a supply of applicants to replace the current workers as they drift away or are fired, so finding a job is just a matter of being at the right place at the right time and flexible enough to take whatever is being offered that day. This finally happens to me at one of the big discount hotel chains, where I go, as usual, for housekeeping and am sent, instead, to try out as a waitress at the attached "family restaurant," a dismal spot with a counter and about thirty tables that looks out on a parking garage and features such tempting fare as "Pollish [sic] sausage and BBQ

---

[2]According to the *Monthly Labor Review* (November 1996), 28 percent of work sites surveyed in the service industry conduct drug tests (corporate workplaces have much higher rates), and the incidence of testing has risen markedly since the eighties. The rate of testing is highest in the South (56 percent of work sites polled), with the Midwest in second place (50 percent). The drug most likely to be detected — marijuana, which can be detected in urine for weeks — is also the most innocuous, while heroin and cocaine are generally undetectable three days after use. Prospective employees sometimes try to cheat the tests by consuming excessive amounts of liquids and taking diuretics and even masking substances available through the Internet.

sauce" on 95-degree days. Phillip, the dapper young West Indian who introduces himself as the manager, interviews me with about as much enthusiasm as if he were a clerk processing me for Medicare, the principal questions being what shifts can I work and when can I start. I mutter something about being woefully out of practice as a waitress, but he's already on to the uniform: I'm to show up tomorrow wearing black slacks and black shoes; he'll provide the rust-colored polo shirt with HEARTHSIDE embroidered on it, though I might want to wear my own shirt to get to work, ha ha. At the word "tomorrow," something between fear and indignation rises in my chest. I want to say, "Thank you for your time, sir, but this is just an experiment, you know, not my actual life."

So begins my career at the Hearthside, I shall call it, one small profit center within a global discount hotel chain, where for two weeks I work from 2:00 till 10:00 p.m. for $2.43 an hour plus tips.[3] In some futile bid for gentility, the management has barred employees from using the front door, so my first day I enter through the kitchen, where a red-faced man with shoulder-length blond hair is throwing frozen steaks against the wall and yelling, "Fuck this shit!" "That's just Jack," explains Gail, the wiry middle-aged waitress who is assigned to train me. "He's on the rag again" — a condition occasioned, in this instance, by the fact that the cook on the morning shift had forgotten to thaw out the steaks. For the next eight hours, I run after the agile Gail, absorbing bits of instruction along with fragments of personal tragedy. All food must be trayed, and the reason she's so tired today is that she woke up in a cold sweat thinking of her boyfriend, who killed himself recently in an upstate prison. No refills on lemonade. And the reason he was in prison is that a few DUIs caught up with him, that's all, could have happened to anyone. Carry the creamers to the table in a monkey bowl, never in your hand. And after he was gone she spent several months living in her truck, peeing in a plastic pee bottle and reading by candlelight at night, but you can't live in a truck in the summer, since you need to have the windows down, which means anything can get in, from mosquitoes on up.

At least Gail puts to rest any fears I had of appearing overqualified. From the first day on, I find that of all the things I have left behind, such as home and identity, what I miss the most is competence. Not that I have ever felt utterly competent in the writing business, in which one day's success augurs nothing at all for the next. But in my writing life, I at least have some

---

[3]According to the Fair Labor Standards Act, employers are not required to pay "tipped employees," such as restaurant servers, more than $2.13 an hour in direct wages. However, if the sum of tips plus $2.13 an hour falls below the minimum wage, or $5.15 an hour, the employer is required to make up the difference. This fact was not mentioned by managers or otherwise publicized at either of the restaurants where I worked.

notion of procedure: do the research, make the outline, rough out a draft, etc. As a server, though, I am beset by requests like bees: more iced tea here, ketchup over there, a to-go box for table fourteen, and where are the high chairs, anyway? Of the twenty-seven tables, up to six are usually mine at any time, though on slow afternoons or if Gail is off, I sometimes have the whole place to myself. There is the touch-screen computer-ordering system to master, which is, I suppose, meant to minimize server-cook contact, but in practice requires constant verbal fine-tuning: "That's gravy on the mashed, okay? None on the meatloaf," and so forth — while the cook scowls as if I were inventing these refinements just to torment him. Plus, something I had forgotten in the years since I was eighteen: about a third of a server's job is "side work" that's invisible to customers — sweeping, scrubbing, slicing, refilling, and restocking. If it isn't all done, every little bit of it, you're going to face the 6:00 p.m. dinner rush defenseless and probably go down in flames. I screw up dozens of times at the beginning, sustained in my shame entirely by Gail's support — "It's okay, baby, everyone does that sometime" — because, to my total surprise and despite the scientific detachment I am doing my best to maintain, I care.

The whole thing would be a lot easier if I could just skate through it as Lily Tomlin in one of her waitress skits, but I was raised by the absurd Booker T. Washingtonian precept that says: If you're going to do something, do it well. In fact, "well" isn't good enough by half. Do it better than anyone has ever done it before. Or so said my father, who must have known what he was talking about because he managed to pull himself, and us with him, up from the mile-deep copper mines of Butte to the leafy suburbs of the Northeast, ascending from boilermakers to martinis before booze beat out ambition. As in most endeavors I have encountered in my life, doing it "better than anyone" is not a reasonable goal. Still, when I wake up at 4:00 a.m. in my own cold sweat, I am not thinking about the writing deadlines I'm neglecting; I'm thinking about the table whose order I screwed up so that one of the boys didn't get his kiddie meal until the rest of the family had moved on to their Key Lime pies. That's the other powerful motivation I hadn't expected — the customers, or "patients," as I can't help thinking of them on account of the mysterious vulnerability that seems to have left them temporarily unable to feed themselves. After a few days at the Hearthside, I feel the service ethic kick in like a shot of oxytocin, the nurturance hormone. The plurality of my customers are hard-working locals — truck drivers, construction workers, even housekeepers from the attached hotel — and I want them to have the closest to a "fine dining" experience that the grubby circumstances will allow. No "you guys" for me; everyone over twelve is "sir" or "ma'am." I ply them with iced tea and coffee refills; I return, mid-meal, to inquire how everything is; I doll up their salads with chopped raw mushrooms, summer squash slices, or whatever bits of produce I can find that have survived their sojourn in the cold-storage room mold-free.

There is Benny, for example, a short, tight-muscled sewer repairman, who cannot even think of eating until he has absorbed a half hour of air-conditioning and ice water. We chat about hyperthermia and electrolytes until he is ready to order some finicky combination like soup of the day, garden salad, and a side of grits. There are the German tourists who are so touched by my pidgin "Willkommen" and "Ist alles gut?" that they actually tip. (Europeans, spoiled by their trade-union-ridden, high-wage welfare states, generally do not know that they are supposed to tip. Some restaurants, the Hearthside included, allow servers to "grat" their foreign customers, or add a tip to the bill. Since this amount is added before the customers have a chance to tip or not tip, the practice amounts to an automatic penalty for imperfect English.) There are the two dirt-smudged lesbians, just off their construction shift, who are impressed enough by my suave handling of the fly in the piña colada that they take the time to praise me to Stu, the assistant manager. There's Sam, the kindly retired cop, who has to plug up his tracheotomy hole with one finger in order to force the cigarette smoke into his lungs.

Sometimes I play with the fantasy that I am a princess who, in penance for some tiny transgression, has undertaken to feed each of her subjects by hand. But the non-princesses working with me are just as indulgent, even when this means flouting management rules—concerning, for example, the number of croutons that can go on a salad (six). "Put on all you want," Gail whispers, "as long as Stu isn't looking." She dips into her own tip money to buy biscuits and gravy for an out-of-work mechanic who's used up all his money on dental surgery, inspiring me to pick up the tab for his milk and pie. Maybe the same high levels of agape can be found throughout the "hospitality industry." I remember the poster decorating one of the apartments I looked at, which said "If you seek happiness for yourself you will never find it. Only when you seek happiness for others will it come to you," or words to that effect—an odd sentiment, it seemed to me at the time, to find in the dank one-room basement apartment of a bellhop at the Best Western. At the Hearthside, we utilize whatever bits of autonomy we have to ply our customers with the illicit calories that signal our love. It is our job as servers to assemble the salads and desserts, pouring the dressings and squirting the whipped cream. We also control the number of butter patties our customers get and the amount of sour cream on their baked potatoes. So if you wonder why Americans are so obese, consider the fact that waitresses both express their humanity and earn their tips through the covert distribution of fats.

Ten days into it, this is beginning to look like a livable lifestyle. I like Gail, who is "looking at fifty" but moves so fast she can alight in one place and then another without apparently being anywhere between them. I clown around with Lionel, the teenage Haitian busboy, and catch a few fragments of conversation with Joan, the svelte fortyish hostess and militant feminist who is the only one of us who dares to tell Jack to shut the fuck up. I even warm up to Jack when, on a slow night and to make up for a particularly unwarranted attack on my abilities, or so I imagine, he tells me about his glory days as a young man at "coronary school"—or do you say "culinary"?—in Brooklyn, where he dated a knock-out Puerto Rican chick and learned everything there is to know about food. I finish up at 10:00 or 10:30, depending on how much side work I've been able to get done during the shift, and cruise home to the tapes I snatched up at random when I left my real home—Marianne Faithfull, Tracy Chapman, Enigma, King Sunny Ade, the Violent Femmes—just drained enough for the music to set my cranium resonating but hardly dead. Midnight snack is Wheat Thins and Monterey Jack, accompanied by cheap white wine on ice and whatever AMC has to offer. To bed by 1:30 or 2:00, up at 9:00 or 10:00, read for an hour while my uniform whirls around in the landlord's washing machine, and then it's another eight hours spent following Mao's central instruction, as laid out in the Little Red Book, which was: Serve the people.

I could drift along like this, in some dreamy proletarian idyll, except for two things. One is management. If I have kept this subject on the margins thus far it is because I still flinch to think that I spent all those weeks under the surveillance of men (and later women) whose job it was to monitor my behavior for signs of sloth, theft, drug abuse, or worse. Not that managers and especially "assistant managers" in low-wage settings like this are exactly the class enemy. In the restaurant business, they are mostly former cooks or servers, still capable of pinch-hitting in the kitchen or on the floor, just as in hotels they are likely to be former clerks, and paid a salary of only about $400 a week. But everyone knows they have crossed over to the other side, which is, crudely put, corporate as opposed to human. Cooks want to prepare tasty meals; servers want to serve them graciously; but managers are there for only one reason—to make sure that money is made for some theoretical entity that exists far away in Chicago or New York, if a corporation can be said to have a physical existence at all. Reflecting on her career, Gail tells me ruefully that she had sworn, years ago, never to work for a corporation again. "They don't cut you no slack. You give and you give, and they take."

Managers can sit—for hours at a time if they want—but it's their job to see that no one else ever does, even when there's nothing to do, and this is why, for servers, slow times can be as exhausting as rushes. You start dragging out each little chore, because if the manager on duty catches you in an idle moment, he will give you something far nastier to do. So I wipe, I clean, I consolidate ketchup bottles and recheck the cheesecake supply, even tour the tables to make sure the customer evaluation forms are all standing perkily in their places—wondering all the time how many calories I burn in these strictly theatrical exercises. When, on a particularly dead afternoon, Stu finds me glancing at a *USA Today* a customer has left behind, he assigns me to vacuum the entire floor with the broken vacuum cleaner that has a handle only two feet long, and the only way to do that without incurring orthopedic damage is to proceed from spot to spot on your knees.

On my first Friday at the Hearthside there is a "mandatory meeting for all restaurant employees," which I attend, eager for insight into our overall marketing strategy and the niche (your basic Ohio cuisine with a tropical twist?) we aim to inhabit. But there is no "we" at this meeting. Phillip, our top manager except for an occasional "consultant" sent out by corporate headquarters, opens it with a sneer: "The break room — it's disgusting. Butts in the ashtrays, newspapers lying around, crumbs." This windowless little room, which also houses the time clock for the entire hotel, is where we stash our bags and civilian clothes and take our half-hour meal breaks. But a break room is not a right, he tells us. It can be taken away. We should also know that the lockers in the break room and whatever is in them can be searched at any time. Then comes gossip; there has been gossip; gossip (which seems to mean employees talking among themselves) must stop. Off-duty employees are henceforth barred from eating at the restaurant, because "other servers gather around them and gossip." When Phillip has exhausted his agenda of rebukes, Joan complains about the condition of the ladies' room and I throw in my two bits about the vacuum cleaner. But I don't see any backup coming from my fellow servers, each of whom has subsided into her own personal funk; Gail, my role model, stares sorrowfully at a point six inches from her nose. The meeting ends when Andy, one of the cooks, gets up, muttering about breaking up his day off for this almighty bullshit.

Just four days later we are suddenly summoned into the kitchen at 3:30 p.m., even though there are live tables on the floor. We all — about ten of us — stand around Phillip, who announces grimly that there has been a report of some "drug activity" on the night shift and that, as a result, we are now to be a "drug-free" workplace, meaning that all new hires will be tested, as will possibly current employees on a random basis. I am glad that this part of the kitchen is so dark, because I find myself blushing as hard as if I had been caught toking up in the ladies' room myself: I haven't been treated this way — lined up in the corridor, threatened with locker searches, peppered with carelessly aimed accusations — since junior high school. Back on the floor, Joan cracks, "Next they'll be telling us we can't have sex on the job." When I ask Stu what happened to inspire the crackdown, he just mutters about "management decisions" and takes the opportunity to upbraid Gail and me for being too generous with the rolls. From now on there's to be only one per customer, and it goes out with the dinner, not with the salad. He's also been riding the cooks, prompting Andy to come out of the kitchen and observe — with the serenity of a man whose customary implement is a butcher knife — that "Stu has a death wish today."

Later in the evening, the gossip crystallizes around the theory that Stu is himself the drug culprit, that he uses the restaurant phone to order up marijuana and sends one of the late servers out to fetch it for him. The server was caught, and she may have ratted Stu out or at least said enough to cast some suspicion on him, thus accounting for his pissy behavior. Who knows? Lionel, the busboy, entertains us for the rest of the shift by standing just behind Stu's back and sucking deliriously on an imaginary joint.

The other problem, in addition to the less-than-nurturing management style, is that this job shows no sign of being financially viable. You might imagine, from a comfortable distance, that people who live, year in and year out, on $6 to $10 an hour have discovered some survival stratagems unknown to the middle class. But no. It's not hard to get my coworkers to talk about their living situations, because housing, in almost every case, is the principal source of disruption in their lives, the first thing they fill you in on when they arrive for their shifts. After a week, I have compiled the following survey:

- Gail is sharing a room in a well-known downtown flophouse for which she and a roommate pay about $250 a week. Her roommate, a male friend, has begun hitting on her, driving her nuts, but the rent would be impossible alone.

- Claude, the Haitian cook, is desperate to get out of the two-room apartment he shares with his girlfriend and two other, unrelated, people. As far as I can determine, the other Haitian men (most of whom only speak Creole) live in similarly crowded situations.

- Annette, a twenty-year-old server who is six months pregnant and has been abandoned by her boyfriend, lives with her mother, a postal clerk.

- Marianne and her boyfriend are paying $170 a week for a one-person trailer.

- Jack, who is, at $10 an hour, the wealthiest of us, lives in the trailer he owns, paying only the $400-a-month lot fee.

- The other white cook, Andy, lives on his dry-docked boat, which, as far as I can tell from his loving descriptions, can't be more than twenty feet long. He offers to take me out on it, once it's repaired, but the offer comes with inquiries as to my marital status, so I do not follow up on it.

- Tina and her husband are paying $60 a night for a double room in a Days Inn. This is because they have no car and the Days Inn is within walking distance of the Hearthside. When Marianne, one of the breakfast servers, is tossed out of her trailer for subletting (which is against the trailer-park rules), she leaves her boyfriend and moves in with Tina and her husband.

- Joan, who had fooled me with her numerous and tasteful outfits (hostesses wear their own clothes), lives in a van she parks behind a shopping center at night and showers in Tina's motel room. The clothes are from thrift shops.[4]

---

[4]I could find no statistics on the number of employed people living in cars or vans, but according to the National Coalition for the Homeless's 1997 report "Myths and Facts about Homelessness," nearly one in five homeless people (in twenty-nine cities across the nation) is employed in a full- or part-time job.

It strikes me, in my middle-class solipsism, that there is gross improvi-   25
dence in some of these arrangements. When Gail and I are wrapping silver-
ware in napkins — the only task for which we are permitted to sit — she tells
me she is thinking of escaping from her roommate by moving into the Days
Inn herself. I am astounded: How can she even think of paying between $40
and $60 a day? But if I was afraid of sounding like a social worker, I come
out just sounding like a fool. She squints at me in disbelief, "And where am
I supposed to get a month's rent and a month's deposit for an apartment?"
I'd been feeling pretty smug about my $500 efficiency, but of course it was
made possible only by the $1,300 I had allotted myself for start-up costs
when I began my low-wage life: $1,000 for the first month's rent and
deposit, $100 for initial groceries and cash in my pocket, $200 stuffed away
for emergencies. In poverty, as in certain propositions in physics, starting
conditions are everything.

There are no secret economies that nourish the poor; on the contrary,
there are a host of special costs. If you can't put up the two months' rent you
need to secure an apartment, you end up paying through the nose for a
room by the week. If you have only a room, with a hot plate at best, you
can't save by cooking up huge lentil stews that can be frozen for the week
ahead. You eat fast food, or the hot dogs and styrofoam cups of soup that
can be microwaved in a convenience store. If you have no money for health
insurance — and the Hearthside's niggardly plan kicks in only after three
months — you go without routine care or prescription drugs and end up
paying the price. Gail, for example, was fine until she ran out of money for
estrogen pills. She is supposed to be on the company plan by now, but they
claim to have lost her application form and need to begin the paperwork all
over again. So she spends $9 per migraine pill to control the headaches she
wouldn't have, she insists, if her estrogen supplements were covered. Similarly, Marianne's boyfriend lost his job as a roofer because he missed so
much time after getting a cut on his foot for which he couldn't afford the
prescribed antibiotic.

My own situation, when I sit down to assess it after two weeks of
work, would not be much better if this were my actual life. The seductive
thing about waitressing is that you don't have to wait for payday to feel a
few bills in your pocket, and my tips usually cover meals and gas, plus something left over to stuff into the kitchen drawer I use as a bank. But as the
tourist business slows in the summer heat, I sometimes leave work with only
$20 in tips (the gross is higher, but servers share about 15 percent of their
tips with the busboys and bartenders). With wages included, this amounts
to about the minimum wage of $5.15 an hour. Although the sum in the
drawer is piling up, at the present rate of accumulation it will be more than
a hundred dollars short of my rent when the end of the month comes
around. Nor can I see any expenses to cut. True, I haven't gone the lentil-
stew route yet, but that's because I don't have a large cooking pot, pot

holders, or a ladle to stir with (which cost about $30 at Kmart, less at thrift stores), not to mention onions, carrots, and the indispensable bay leaf. I do make my lunch almost every day—usually some slow-burning, high-protein combo like frozen chicken patties with melted cheese on top and canned pinto beans on the side. Dinner is at the Hearthside, which offers its employees a choice of BLT, fish sandwich, or hamburger for only $2. The burger lasts longest, especially if it's heaped with gut-puckering jalapeños, but by midnight my stomach is growling again. . . .

In one month, I had earned approximately $1,040 and spent $517 on food, gas, toiletries, laundry, phone, and utilities. If I had remained in my $500 efficiency, I would have been able to pay the rent and have $22 left over (which is $78 less than the cash I had in my pocket at the start of the month). During this time I bought no clothing except for the required slacks and no prescription drugs or medical care (I did finally buy some vitamin B to compensate for the lack of vegetables in my diet). Perhaps I could have saved a little on food if I had gotten to a supermarket more often, instead of convenience stores, but it should be noted that I lost almost four pounds in four weeks, on a diet weighted heavily toward burgers and fries.

How former welfare recipients and single mothers will (and do) survive in the low-wage workforce, I cannot imagine. Maybe they will figure out how to condense their lives — including child-raising, laundry, romance, and meals — into the couple of hours between full-time jobs. Maybe they will take up residence in their vehicles, if they have one. All I know is that I couldn't hold two jobs and I couldn't make enough money to live on with one. And I had advantages unthinkable to many of the long-term poor — health, stamina, a working car, and no children to care for and support. Certainly nothing in my experience contradicts the conclusion of Kathryn Edin and Laura Lein, in their recent book *Making Ends Meet: How Single Mothers Survive Welfare and Low-Wage Work*, that low-wage work actually involves more hardship and deprivation than life at the mercy of the welfare state. In the coming months and years, economic conditions for the working poor are bound to worsen, even without the almost inevitable recession. As mentioned earlier, the influx of former welfare recipients into the low-skilled workforce will have a depressing effect on both wages and the number of jobs available. A general economic downturn will only enhance these effects, and the working poor will of course be facing it without the slight, but nonetheless often saving, protection of welfare as a backup.

The thinking behind welfare reform was that even the humblest jobs are morally uplifting and psychologically buoying. In reality they are likely to be fraught with insult and stress. But I did discover one redeeming feature of the most abject low-wage work — the camaraderie of people who are, in almost all cases, far too smart and funny and caring for the work they do and the wages they're paid. The hope, of course, is that someday these people will come to know what they're worth, and take appropriate action.

QUESTIONS

Reading

1. Ehrenreich tells us in the first paragraph who she is and what she wants to uncover: "I am . . . a middle-class journalist setting out to explore the world that welfare mothers are entering, at the rate of approximately fifty thousand a month, as welfare reform kicks in." In her *reportorial* essay, what questions does Ehrenreich ask about this world? What strategies does she use, as a reporter, to make readers care about this world?
2. According to Ehrenreich, what is the rationale for welfare reform? Why does she distrust this rationale?
3. Ehrenreich plunges us into the middle of her work life at the Hearthside. Identify the details and images that you find most compelling and memorable. How do these details help her establish her credibility?
4. Ehrenreich points to housing as "the principal source of disruption" (paragraph 24) in her coworkers' lives. Look at her survey of where and how her coworkers live. What does this survey suggest about the difficulties of "(not) getting by in America"?

Exploratory Writing

1. On an episode in the first season of his television series *30 Days*, shot in 2005, documentary filmmaker Morgan Spurlock and his fiancée experimented with spending a month in a new city, living on minimum wage. Like Ehrenreich, they found that it was almost impossible to make ends meet. Find out the minimum wage in your town, and calculate your expenses for the coming month. Discuss how your life would change if you had to get by on minimum wage. Would you need to apply for public assistance?
2. What questions are you asking about work? In groups of two, interview each other about your current job and job history. Report to the class on what you learn in these interviews.
3. "In poverty," writes Ehrenreich, "as in certain propositions in physics, starting conditions are everything" (paragraph 25). Make a double-entry list showing ways that Ehrenreich's relatively privileged "starting conditions" make her life different from the lives of her coworkers. If you need more space, use an extra sheet of paper.

EHRENREICH	COWORKERS

Making Connections

1. Compare Ehrenreich's experiment to Christina Boufis's (p. 67) experiences as a literature teacher in a county jail. Write an essay reflecting on the advantages and disadvantages of observing groups of people from an outside perspective.

Essay Writing

1. Go to the library and research the federal Welfare Reform Act of 1996. What main arguments did members of Congress offer for and against welfare reform during the debates that preceded their vote on the act? Research the consequences of welfare reform within your region or state.

What Did You Do in the War, Grandma?
A Flashback to August 1945

Zoë Tracy Hardy

Born in 1926 and raised in the Midwest, Zoë Tracy Hardy was one of millions of young women who worked in defense plants during World War II. Considered at first to be surrogates for male workers, these women — sometimes called Rosie the Riveters — were soon building bombers that their supervisors declared "equal in the construction [to] those turned out by experienced workmen in the plant's other departments," as a news feature at the time stated. After the eventful summer described in the following essay, Hardy finished college, married, and began teaching college En-glish in Arizona, Guam, and Colorado. This essay first appeared in the August 1985 issue of Ms. *magazine — exactly forty years after the end of World War II.*

It was unseasonably cool that day in May 1945, when I left my mother and father and kid brother in eastern Iowa and took the bus all the way to Omaha to help finish the war. I was eighteen, and had just completed my first year at the University of Iowa without distinction. The war in Europe had ended in April; the war against the Japanese still raged. I wanted to go where something *real* was being done to end this bitter war that had always been part of my adolescence.

I arrived in Omaha at midnight. The YWCA, where I promised my family I would get a room, was closed until 7 a.m., so I curled up in a cracked maroon leather chair in the crowded, smoky waiting room of the bus station.

In the morning I set off on foot for the YWCA, dragging a heavy suitcase and carrying my favorite hat trimmed in daisies in a large round hatbox. An hour of lugging and resting brought me to the Y, a great Victorian house of dark brick, where I paid two weeks in advance (most of my money) for board and a single room next to a bathroom that I would share with eight other girls. I surrendered my red and blue food-ration stamp books and my sugar coupons to the cook who would keep them as long as I stayed there.

I had eaten nothing but a wartime candy bar since breakfast at home the day before, but breakfast at the Y was already over. So, queasy and light-headed, I went back out into the cold spring day to find my job. I set out for the downtown office of the Glenn L. Martin Company. It was at their plant south of the city that thousands of workers, in around-the-clock shifts, built the famous B-29 bombers, the great Superfortresses, which the papers said would end the war.

I filled out an application and thought about the women welders and   5
riveters and those who operated machine presses to help put the Super-
fortresses together. I grew shakier by the minute, more and more certain I was unqualified for any job here.

My interview was short. The personnel man was unconcerned about my total lack of skills. If I passed the physical, I could have a job in the Reproduction Department, where the blueprints were handled.

Upstairs in a gold-walled banquet room furnished with examination tables and hospital screens, a nurse sat me on a stool to draw a blood sample from my arm. I watched my blood rolling slowly into the needle. The gold walls wilted in the distance, and I slumped forward in a dead faint.

A grandfatherly doctor waved ammonia under my nose, and said if I would go to a café down the street and eat the complete fifty-cent breakfast, I had the job.

The first week in the Reproduction Department, I learned to cut and fold enormous blueprints as they rolled from a machine that looked like a giant washing machine wringer. Then I was moved to a tall, metal contraption with a lurid light glowing from its interior. An ammonia guzzler, it spewed out smelly copies of specifications so hot my fingertips burned when I touched them. I called it the dragon, and when I filled it with ammonia, the fumes reminded me of gold walls dissolving before my eyes. I took all my breaks outdoors, even when it was raining.

My boss, Mr. Johnson,[1] was a sandy-haired man of about forty, who spoke   10
pleasantly when he came around to say hello and to check our work. Elsie, his secretary, a cool redhead, seldom spoke to any of us and spent most of her time in the darkroom developing negatives and reproducing photographs.

One of my coworkers in Reproduction was Mildred, a tall dishwater blond with a horsey, intelligent face. She was the first woman I'd ever met with an earthy unbridled tongue.

When I first arrived, Mildred warned me always to knock on the dark-room door before going in because Mr. Johnson and Elsie did a lot of screw-ing in there. I didn't believe her; I thought we were supposed to knock to give Elsie time to protect her negatives from the sudden light. "Besides," I said, "there isn't room to lie down in there." Mildred laughed until tears squeezed from the corners of her eyes. "You poor kid," she said. "Don't you *know* you don't have to lie down?"

---

[1] All names but the author's have been changed.

I was stunned. "But it's easier if you do," I protested, defensive about my sex education. My mother, somewhat ahead of her time, had always been explicit in her explanations, and I had read "Lecture 14," an idyllic description of lovemaking being passed around among freshman girls in every dormitory in the country.

"Sitting, standing, any quick way you can in time of war," Mildred winked wickedly. She was as virginal as I, but what she said reminded us of the steady dearth of any day-to-day presence of young men in our lives.

We were convinced that the war would be over by autumn. We were stepping up the napalm and incendiary bombing of the Japanese islands, the British were now coming to our aid in the Pacific, and the Japanese Navy was being reduced to nothing in some of the most spectacular sea battles in history.   15

Sometimes, after lunch, I went into the assembly areas to see how the skeletons of the B-29s were growing from our blueprints. At first there were enormous stark ribs surrounded by scaffolding two and three stories high. A few days later there was aluminum flesh over the ribs and wings sprouting from stubs on the fuselage. Women in overalls and turbans, safety glasses, and steel-toed shoes scrambled around the wings with riveting guns and welding torches, fitting fuel tanks in place. Instructions were shouted at them by hoarse, paunchy old men in hard hats. I cheered myself by thinking how we were pouring it on, a multitude of us together creating this great bird to end the war.

Away from the plant, however, optimism sometimes failed me. My room at the Y was bleak. I wrote letters to my unofficial fiancé and to other young men in the service who had been friends and classmates. Once in a while I attempted to study, thinking I would redeem my mediocre year at the university.

During those moments when I sensed real homesickness lying in wait, I would plan something to do with Betty and Celia, friends from high school, who had moved to Omaha "for the duration" and had jobs as secretaries for a large moving and storage company. Their small apartment was upstairs in an old frame house in Benson, a northwest suburb. Celia and Betty and I cooked, exchanged news from servicemen we all knew, and talked about plans for the end of the war. Betty was engaged to her high school sweetheart, a soldier who had been wounded in Germany and who might be coming home soon. We guessed she would be the first one of us to be married, and we speculated, in the careful euphemisms of "well-brought-up girls," about her impending introduction to sex.

By the first of July, work and the pace of life had lost momentum. The war news seemed to repeat itself without advancing, as day after day battles were fought around jungly Pacific islands that all seemed identical and unreal.

At the plant, I was moved from the dragon to a desk job, a promotion   20
of sorts. I sat on a high stool in a cubicle of pigeonholed cabinets and filed

blueprints, specs, and deviations in the proper holes. While I was working, I saw no one and couldn't talk to anybody.

In mid-July Betty got married. Counsel from our elders was always to wait — wait until things settle down after the war. Harold, still recuperating from shrapnel wounds, asked Betty not to wait.

Celia and I attended the ceremony on a sizzling afternoon in a musty Presbyterian church. Harold was very serious, gaunt-faced and thin in his loose-hanging Army uniform. Betty, a fair-skinned, blue-eyed brunette in a white street dress, looked pale and solemn. After the short ceremony, they left the church in a borrowed car. Someone had given them enough gasoline stamps for a honeymoon trip to a far-off cabin on the shore of a piney Minnesota lake.

Celia and I speculated on Betty's introduction to lovemaking. I had "Lecture 14" in mind and hoped she would like lovemaking, especially way off in Minnesota, far from the sweltering city and the war. Celia thought it didn't matter much whether a girl liked it or not, as long as other important parts of marriage got off to a good start.

That weekend Celia and I took a walk in a park and watched a grandfather carefully pump a seesaw up and down for his small grandson. We saw a short, middle-aged sailor walking with a sad-faced young woman who towered over him. "A whore," Celia said. "Probably one of those from the Hotel Bianca." Celia had been in Omaha longer than I and knew more of its secrets.

I wanted, right then, to see someone young and male and healthy cross the grass under the trees, someone without wounds and without a cap, someone with thick disheveled hair that hadn't been militarily peeled down to the green skin on the back of his skull. Someone wearing tennis shorts to show strong, hair-matted legs, and a shirt with an open neck and short sleeves revealing smooth, hard muscles and tanned skin. Someone who would pull me out of this gloom with a wide spontaneous smile as he passed.

In the next few days, the tempo of the summer changed subtly. From friends stationed in the Pacific, I began to get letters free from rectangular holes where military censors had snipped out "sensitive" words. Our Navy was getting ready to surround the Japanese islands with a starvation blockade, and our B-29s had bombed the industrial heart of the country. We were dropping leaflets warning the Japanese people that we would incinerate hundreds of thousands of them by firebombing 11 of their major cities. Rumors rippled through the plant back in Omaha. The Japanese Empire would collapse in a matter of weeks, at most.

One Friday night, with Celia's help, I moved out of the Y to Celia's apartment in Benson. We moved by streetcar. Celia carried my towels and my full laundry bag in big rolls, one under each arm, and wore my straw picture hat with the daisies, which bobbled wildly on top of her head. My hatbox was crammed with extra underwear and the war letters I was determined to save. When we climbed aboard the front end of the streetcar, I dropped the hatbox,

25

spilled an armload of books down the aisle, and banged my suitcase into the knees of an elderly man who was trying to help me retrieve them.

We began to laugh, at everything, at nothing, and were still laughing when we hauled everything off the car and down one block to the apartment, the daisies all the while wheeling recklessly on Celia's head.

It was a good move. Summer nights were cooler near the country, and so quiet I could hear the crickets. The other upstairs apartment was occupied by Celia's older sister, Andrea, and her husband, Bob, who hadn't been drafted.

Late in July, an unusual thing happened at the plant. Mr. Johnson asked   30 us to work double shifts for a few days. The situation was urgent, he said, and he wanted 100 percent cooperation from the Reproduction Department, even if it meant coming to work when we felt sick or postponing something that was personally important to us.

The next morning no one from the day shift was missing, and the place was full of people from the graveyard shift. Some of the time I worked in my cubicle counting out special blueprints and deviations. The rest of the time I helped the crews sweating over the blueprint machine cut out prints that contained odd lines and numbers that I had never seen before. Their shapes were different, too, and there was no place for them in the numbered pigeonholes of my cubicle. Some prints were small, about four inches square. Mildred said they were so cute she might tuck one in her shoe and smuggle it home as a souvenir even if it meant going to the federal pen if she got caught.

During those days I learned to nap on streetcars. I had to get up at 4:30, bolt down breakfast, and catch the first car to rumble out of the darkness at 5:15. The double shift wasn't over until 11:30, so I got home about one in the morning.

The frenzy at the plant ended as suddenly as it had begun. Dazed with fatigue, I slept through most of a weekend and hoped we had pushed ourselves to some limit that would lift us over the last hump of the war.

On Monday the familiar single shift was not quite the same. We didn't know what we had done, but an undercurrent of anticipation ran through the department because of those double shifts — and the news. The papers told of factories that were already gearing up to turn out refrigerators, radios, and automobiles instead of bombs and planes.

In Reproduction, the pace began to slacken. Five hundred thirty-six   35 B-29s, planes we had put together on the Nebraska prairie, had firebombed the principal islands of the Japanese Empire: Hokkaido, Honshu, Kyushu, Shikoku. We had reduced to ashes more than 15 square miles of the heart of Tokyo. The battered and burned Japanese were so near defeat that there couldn't be much left for us to do. With surprising enthusiasm, I began to plan for my return to college.

Going home on the streetcar the first Tuesday afternoon in August, I heard about a puzzling new weapon. Some excited people at the end of the car were jabbering about it, saying the Japanese would be forced to surrender in a matter of hours.

When I got home, Andrea, her round bespectacled face flushed, met me at the head of the stairs. "Oh, come and listen to the radio—it's a new bomb—it's almost over!"

I sat down in her living room and listened. There was news, then music, then expanded news. Over and over the newscaster reported that the United States had unlocked a secret of the universe and unleashed a cosmic force—from splitting atoms of uranium—on the industrial seaport of Hiroshima. Most of the city had been leveled to the ground, and many of its inhabitants disintegrated to dust in an instant by a single bomb. "Our scientists have changed the history of the world," the newscaster said. He sounded as if he could not believe it himself.

We ate dinner from our laps and continued to listen as the news pounded on for an hour, then two, then three. I tried, at last, to *think* about it. In high school physics we had already learned that scientists were close to splitting an atom. We imagined that a cupful of the tremendous energy from such a phenomenon might run a car back and forth across the entire country dozens of times. I could visualize that. But I could not imagine how such energy put into a small bomb would cause the kind of destruction described on the radio.

About nine, I walked over to McCollum's grocery store to buy an evening 40 paper. The headline said we had harnessed atomic power. I skimmed through a front page story. Science had ushered us into a strange new world, and President Truman had made two things clear: the bomb had created a monster that could wipe out civilization; and some protection against this monster would have to be found before its secret could be given to the world.

Back out in the dark street, I hesitated. For the first time I could remember, I felt a rush of terror at being out in the night alone.

When I got back to the apartment, I made a pot of coffee and sat down at the kitchen table to read the rest of the paper. President Truman had said: "The force from which the sun draws its power has been loosed against those who brought war to the Far East. . . . If they do not now accept our terms they may expect a rain of ruin from the air the like of which has never been seen on this earth." New and more powerful bombs were now being developed.

I read everything, looking for some speculation from someone about how we were going to live in this new world. There was nothing. About midnight Andrea knocked on my open door to get my attention. She stood there a moment in her nightgown and curlers looking at me rather oddly. She asked if I was all right.

I said yes, just trying to soak it all in.

Gently she told me I had better go to bed and think about how soon the 45 war would be over.

The next day Reproduction was nearly demolished by the spirit of celebration. The *Enola Gay*, the plane that had dropped the bomb, was one of ours. By Thursday morning the United States had dropped a second atomic bomb, an even bigger one, on an industrial city, Nagasaki, and the Russians had declared war on Japan.

At the end of the day, Mr. Johnson asked us to listen to the radio for announcements about when to return to work, then shook hands all around. "You've all done more than you know to help win the war," he said.

We said tentative good-byes. I went home and over to McCollum's for an evening paper. An Army Strategic Air Forces expert said that there was no comparison between the fire caused by the atomic bomb and that of a normal conflagration. And there were other stories about radiation, like X-rays, that might cripple and poison living things for hours, weeks, maybe years, until they died.

I went to bed late and had nightmares full of flames and strange dry gale winds. The next noon I got up, exhausted, and called Mildred. She said they were still saying not to report to work until further notice. "It's gonna bore our tails off," she moaned. "I don't know how long we can sit around here just playing hearts." I could hear girls laughing in the background.

"Mildred," I blurted anxiously, "do you think we should have done this   50 thing?"

"Why not? Better us than somebody else, kid."

I reminded her that we knew the Japanese were finished weeks ago and asked her if it wasn't sort of like kicking a dead horse — brutally.

"Look," she said. "The war is really over even if the bigwigs haven't said so yet. What more do you want?"

The evening paper finally offered a glimmer of relief. One large headline said that serious questions about the morality of *Americans* using such a weapon were being raised by some civilians of note and some churchmen. I went to bed early and lay listening to the crickets and thinking about everyone coming home — unofficial fiancés, husbands, fathers, brothers — all filling the empty spaces between kids and women and old men, putting a balance in our lives we hadn't known in years.

Yet the bomb haunted me. I was still awake when the windowpanes   55 lightened up at daybreak.

It was all over on August 14, 1945. Unconditional surrender.

For hours at a time, the bomb's importance receded in the excitement of that day. Streetcar bells clanged up and down the streets; we heard sirens, whistles, church bells. A newscaster described downtown Omaha as a free-for-all. Perfect strangers were hugging each other in the streets; some were dancing. Churches had thrown open their doors, and people were streaming in and out, offering prayers of thanksgiving. Taverns were giving away free drinks.

Andrea wanted us to have a little whiskey, even though we were under age, because there would never be another day like this as long as we lived. I hated the first taste of it, but as we chattered away, inventing wild, gratifying futures, I welcomed the muffler it wrapped around the ugliness of the bomb.

*   *   *

In the morning Mildred called to say our jobs were over and that we should report to the plant to turn in our badges and get final paychecks. She had just talked to Mr. Johnson, who told her that those funny blueprints we had made during double shift had something to do with the bomb.

"Well, honey," she said, "I don't understand atomic energy, but old   60
jazzy Johnson said we had to work like that to get the *Enola Gay* and the *thing* to go together."

I held my breath, waiting for Mildred to say she was kidding, as usual. Ordinary 19- and 20-year-old girls were not, not in the United States of America, required to work night and day to help launch scientific monsters that would catapult us all into a precarious "strange new world" — forever. But I knew in my bones that Mildred, forthright arrow-straight Mildred, was only telling me what I had already, unwillingly, guessed.

After a long silence she said, "Well, kid, give me your address in Iowa, and I'll send you a Christmas card for auld lang syne."

I wanted to cry as we exchanged addresses. I liked Mildred. I hated the gap that I now sensed would always be between me and people like her.

"It's been nice talking dirty to you all summer," she said.

"Thanks." I hung up, slipped down the stairs, and walked past the   65
streetcar line out into the country.

The whole countryside was sun-drenched, fragrant with sweet clover and newly mown alfalfa. I leaned against a fence post and tried to think.

The president had said we had unleashed the great secret of the universe in this way, to shorten the war and save American lives. Our commitment to defeat the Japanese was always clear to me. They had attacked us first. But we had already firebombed much of the Japanese Empire to char. That seemed decisive enough, and terrible enough.

If he had asked me whether I would work very hard to help bring this horror into being, knowing it would shorten the war but put the world into jeopardy for all time, how would I have answered?

I would have said, "No. With all due respect, Sir, how could such a thing make a just end to our just cause?"

But the question had never been asked of us. And I stood now, in   70
the warm sun, gripping a splintery fence post, outraged by our final insignificance — all of us who had worked together in absolute trust to end the war.

An old cow stood near the fence switching her tail. I looked at her great, uncomprehending brown eyes and began to sob.

After a while I walked back to the apartment, mentally packing my suitcase and tying up my hatbox of war letters. I knew it was going to be very hard, from now on, for the whole world to take care of itself.

I wanted very much to go home.

QUESTIONS

Reading

1. How does Hardy's attitude toward the war change over the course of this essay? What narrative devices does Hardy use to reveal her transformation?
2. What is the role of "homesickness" in this essay? What does Hardy mean, in her conclusion, when she writes, "I wanted very much to go home"?
3. "You've all done more than you know to help win the war," Hardy's boss tells her and her coworkers (paragraph 47). How does she react to the fact that she was not informed of the purpose of her work? How does her reaction differ from that of her coworker Mildred?
4. As Hardy's attitude toward war changes, her attitude toward sex changes as well. Trace this change in attitude. What connection, if any, do you see between the two?

Exploratory Writing

1. At the library or online, read first-person accounts of the bombings of Hiroshima and Nagasaki from a Japanese perspective. (You can find transcripts of many accounts at **www.atomicarchive.com/Docs/Hibakusha/index.shtml**.) Choose any one survivor's testimony and compare its narrative to Hardy's, using a double-entry list. How does each person reflect on his or her changed view of the world during and after the events of August 6, 1945? How does each person describe the process of trying to comprehend those events?

HARDY	JAPANESE SURVIVOR

2. This essay was published over twenty years ago and a little more than forty years after the events it describes. Are Hardy's fears and speculations (on atomic power, on the authority of the government, on sex) dated in any way, or are they still relevant today? Explain your answer.

Making Connections

1. Susan Sontag (p. 257) discusses the "centuries-old practice of exhibiting exotic — that is, colonized — human beings," and argues that most published photos showing "grievously injured" human bodies are of Asian or African, rather than American, victims. Using Internet or library

resources, find photographs or film footage of victims of the bombings at Hiroshima or Nagasaki. Discuss Sontag's argument in relation to Hardy's reflections on her changing perspective on America's (and her own) role in World War II. List several pros and cons of publishing photographs or airing film footage of Japanese victims in the United States after the war.

2. Compare Hardy's essay, written decades after the events of August 1945, with war dispatches (p. 323) written by American soldiers still stationed in Iraq. How might Hardy's essay have been different if she'd written it in September 1945? How might the soldiers' reflections change over the next forty years?

Essay Writing

1. Have you, like Hardy, ever wondered about the larger social implications of any job that you've held or that a friend or parent holds? Write an essay like Hardy's reflecting on that job and describing how your attitude changed as you placed the job in a larger context.

The Selfless Gene

Olivia Judson

Born in England in 1970, Olivia Judson moved to Baltimore with her family at the age of ten. Though initially interested in physics, Judson eventually graduated from Stanford University with a biology degree. In 1995, she earned her PhD from Oxford University in biological sciences and soon after joined the Economist *as a science writer. There she wrote about biology in the style of a witty sex-advice columnist, taking on such different perspectives as that of a queen bee, a male spider, and a fruit fly. She later turned these articles into the best-selling book* Dr. Tatiana's Sex Advice to All Creation: The Definitive Guide to the Evolutionary Biology of Sex *(2002), which was nominated for the Samuel Johnson Prize for excellence in nonfiction writing and, in 2004, adapted into a TV series. Dr. Judson is currently a research fellow in evolutionary biology at Imperial College in London. She writes a weekly blog called the* Wild Side *for the* New York Times.

At 2 a.m. on February 26, 1852, the Royal Navy troopship *Birkenhead*, which was carrying more than six hundred people, including seven women and thirteen children, struck a rock near Danger Point, two miles off the coast of South Africa. Almost immediately, the ship began to break up. Just three lifeboats could be launched. The men were ordered to stand on deck, and they did. The women and children (along with a few sailors) were put into the lifeboats and rowed away. Only then were the men told that they could try to save themselves by swimming to shore. Most drowned or were eaten by sharks. The heroism of the troops, standing on deck facing almost certain death while others escaped, became the stuff of legend. But the strange thing is, such heroics are not rare: humans often risk their lives for strangers — think of the firemen going into the World Trade Center — or for people they know but are not related to.

How does a propensity for self-sacrifice evolve? And what about the myriad lesser acts of daily kindness — helping a little old lady across the street, giving up a seat on the subway, returning a wallet that's been lost? Are these impulses as primal as ferocity, lust, and greed? Or are they just a thin veneer over a savage nature? Answers come from creatures as diverse as amoebas and baboons, but the story starts in the county of Kent, in southern England.

Evolving Generosity

Kent has been home to two great evolutionary biologists. In the nineteenth century, Charles Darwin lived for many years in the village of Downe. In the twentieth, William Donald Hamilton grew up catching beetles and chasing butterflies over the rolling hills near Badgers Mount.

Hamilton was a tall man with a craggy face and the tops of a couple of fingers missing from a childhood accident — he blew himself up while making explosives. He died in 2000, at age sixty-three, after an illness contracted while undertaking another risky endeavor: a trip to the Congo to collect chimpanzee feces. When I first met him, in Oxford in 1991, he had a terrific shock of white hair, rode a rickety bicycle at prodigious speed, and was preoccupied with the question of why sex is useful in evolutionary terms. (For my doctorate, I worked with him on this question.) But he began his career studying social behavior, and in the early 1960s he published a trio of now-classic papers in which he offered the first rigorous explanation of how generosity can evolve, and under what circumstances it is likely to emerge.

Hamilton didn't call it generosity, though; he called it altruism. And the   5
particular behaviors he sought to explain are acts of extreme self-sacrifice, such as when a bee dies to defend the hive, or when an animal spends its whole life helping others rear their children instead of having some of its own.

To see why these behaviors appear mysterious to biologists, consider how natural selection works. In every generation, some individuals leave more descendants than others. If the reason for their greater "reproductive success" is due to the particular genes they have, then natural selection has been operating.

Here's an example: Suppose you're a mosquito living on the French Mediterranean coast. Tourists don't like mosquitoes, and the French authorities try to keep the tourists happy by spraying insecticide. Which means that on the coast, mosquitoes bearing a gene that confers insecticide resistance tend to leave many more descendants than those lacking it — and so today's coastal mosquitoes are far more resistant to insecticide than those that live inland.

Extreme altruists, by definition, leave no descendants: they're too busy helping others. So at first blush, a gene that promotes extreme altruism should quickly vanish from a population.

Hamilton's solution to this problem was simple and elegant. He realized that a gene promoting extreme altruism could spread if the altruist helped its close relations. The reason is that your close relations have some of the same genes as you do. In humans and other mammals, full brothers and sisters have, on average, half the same genes. First cousins have, on average, an eighth of their genes in common. Among insects such as ants and bees, where the underlying genetics work differently, full sisters (but not brothers) typically have three-quarters of their genes in common.

Hamilton derived a formula — now known as Hamilton's rule — for   10
predicting whether the predisposition toward a given altruistic act is likely

to evolve: $rB > C$. In plain language, this says that genes that promote the altruistic act will spread if the benefit (B) that the act bestows is high enough, and the genetic relationship (r) between the altruist and the beneficiary is close enough, to outweigh the act's cost (C) to the altruist. Cost and benefit are both measured in nature's currency: children. "Cheap" behaviors — such as when a small bird squawks from the bushes to announce it's seen a cat or a hawk — can, and do, evolve easily, even though they often benefit nonrelatives. "Expensive" behaviors, such as working your whole life to rear someone else's children, evolve only in the context of close kin.

Since Hamilton first proposed the idea, "kin selection" has proved tremendously powerful as a way to understand cooperative and self-sacrificial behavior in a huge menagerie of animals. Look at lions. Lionesses live with their sisters, cousins, and aunts; they hunt together and help each other with child care. Bands of males, meanwhile, are typically brothers and half brothers. Large bands are better able to keep a pride of lionesses; thus, even males who never mate with a female still spread some of their genes by helping their brothers defend the pride. Or take peacocks. Males often stand in groups when they display to females. This is because females are drawn to groups of displaying males; they ogle them, then pick the guy they like best to be their mate. Again, peacocks prefer to display with their brothers rather than with males they are not related to.

Kin selection operates even in mindless creatures such as amoebas. For instance, the soil-dwelling amoeba *Dictyostelium purpureum*. When times are good, members of this species live as single cells, reproducing asexually and feasting on bacteria. But when times get tough — when there's a bacteria shortage — thousands of individuals join together into a single entity known as a slug. This glides off in search of more-suitable conditions. When it finds them, the slug transforms itself into a fruiting body that looks like a tiny mushroom; some of the amoebas become the stalk, others become spores. Those in the stalk will die; only the spores will go on to form the next amoeboid generation. Sure enough, amoebas with the same genes (in other words, clones) tend to join the same slugs: they avoid mixing with genetic strangers and sacrifice themselves only for their clones.

Kin selection also accounts for some of the nastier features of human behavior, such as the tendency stepparents have to favor their own children at the expense of their stepkids. But it's not enough to explain the evolution of all aspects of social behavior, in humans or in other animals.

Living Together

Animals may begin to live together for a variety of reasons — most obviously, safety in numbers. In one of his most engaging papers, Hamilton observed that a tight flock, herd, or shoal will readily appear if every animal tries to make itself safer by moving into the middle of the group — a phenomenon he termed the "selfish herd." But protection from predators isn't the only benefit of bunching together. A bird in a flock spends more time eating and less time looking about for danger than it does when on its own. Indeed, eating well is another common reason for group living. Some predatory animals — chimpanzees, spotted hyenas, and wild dogs, for example — have evolved to hunt together.

Many social animals thus live in huge flocks or herds, and not in family groups — or even if the nexus of social life is the family, the family group is itself part of a larger community. In species such as these, social behavior must extend beyond a simple "Be friendly and helpful to your family and hostile to everybody else" approach to the world. At the least, the evolution of social living requires limiting aggression so that neighbors can tolerate each other. And often, the evolution of larger social groupings is accompanied by an increase in the subtlety and complexity of the ways animals get along together.   15

Consider baboons. Baboons are monkeys, not apes, and are thus not nearly as closely related to us as chimpanzees are. Nonetheless, baboons have evolved complex social lives. They live in troops that can number from as few as eight to as many as two hundred. Females live with their sisters, mothers, aunts, and infants; males head off to find a new troop at adolescence (around age four). Big troops typically contain several female family groups, along with some adult males. The relationships between members of a troop are varied and complex. Sometimes two or more males team up to defeat a dominant male in combat. Females often have a number of male "friends" that they associate with (friends may or may not also be sex partners). If a female is attacked or harassed, her friends will come bounding to the rescue; they will also protect her children, play with them, groom them, carry them, and sometimes share food with them. If the mother dies, they may even look after an infant in her place.

Yet friendliness and the associated small acts of affection and kindness — a bout of grooming here, a shared bite to eat there — seem like evolutionary curiosities. Small gestures like these don't affect how many children you have. Or do they?

Among social animals, one potentially important cause of premature death is murder. Infanticide can be a problem for social mammals, from baboons and chimpanzees to lions and even squirrels. During one four-year study of Belding's ground squirrels, for example, the main cause of death for juveniles was other Belding's ground squirrels; at least 8 percent of the young were murdered before being weaned. Similarly, fighting between adults — particularly in species where animals are well armed with horns, tusks, or teeth — can be lethal, and even if it is not, it may result in severe injuries, loss of status, or eviction from the group.

The possibility of death by murder creates natural selection for traits that reduce this risk. For example, any animal that can appease an aggressor, or that knows when to advance and when to retreat, is more likely to leave descendants than an animal that leaps wildly into any fray. Which explains why, in many social-mammal species, you don't see many murders, though you do see males engaging in elaborate rituals to see who's bigger and stronger. Serious physical fights tend to break out only when both animals think they can win (that is, when they are about the same size).

Thus, among animals such as baboons, friendships mean more than a   20
bit of mutual scratching; they play a fundamental role in an animal's ability to survive and reproduce within the group. Friendships between males can be important in overcoming a dominant male — which may in turn lead to an improvement in how attractive the animals are to females. Similarly, females that have a couple of good male friends will be more protected from bullying — and their infants less likely to be killed. Why do the males do it? Males that are friends with a particular female are more likely to become her sex partners later on, if indeed they are not already. In other words, friendship may be as primal an urge as ferocity.

Becoming Human

The lineage that became modern humans split off from the lineage that became chimpanzees around six million years ago. Eventually this new lineage produced the most socially versatile animal the planet has ever seen: us. How did we get to be this way?

One clue comes from chimpanzees. Chimpanzee society is the mirror image of baboon society, in that it's the females that leave home at adolescence, and the males that stay where they were born. Chimpanzee communities can also be fairly large, comprising several different subcommunities and family groups. Males prefer to associate with their brothers and half-brothers on their mother's side, but they also have friendships with unrelated males. Friends hang out together and hunt together — and gang up on other males.

However, unlike baboon troops, which roam around the savannah freely intermingling, chimpanzee communities are territorial. Bands of males patrol the edges of their community's territory looking for strangers — and sometimes make deep incursions into neighboring terrain. Males on patrol move together in silence, often stopping to listen. If they run into a neighboring patrol, there may be some sort of skirmish, which may or may not be violent. But woe betide a lone animal that runs into the patrolling males. If they encounter a strange male on his own, they may well kill him. And sometimes, repeated and violent attacks by one community lead to the annihilation of another, usually smaller, one. Indeed, two of the three most-studied groups of chimpanzees have wiped out a neighboring community.

Chimpanzees have two important sources of premature death at the hands of other chimpanzees: they may be murdered by members of their own community, or they may be killed during encounters with organized bands of hostile neighbors.

Just like humans. Except that humans aren't armed with big teeth and   25
strong limbs. Humans carry weapons, and have done so for thousands of
years.

On Love and War

Darwin wondered whether lethal warring between neighboring groups
might have caused humans to evolve to be more helpful and kind to each
other. At first, the idea seems paradoxical. But Darwin thought this could
have happened if the more cohesive, unified, caring groups had been better
able to triumph over their more disunited rivals. If so, the members of those
cohesive, yet warlike, groups would have left more descendants.

For a long time, the idea languished. Why? A couple of reasons. First, it
appears to depend on "group selection." This is the idea that some groups
evolve characteristics that allow them to outcompete other groups, and it's
long been out of favor with evolutionary biologists. In general, natural
selection works much more effectively on individuals than it does on groups,
unless the groups are composed of close kin. That's because group selection
can be effective only when the competing groups are genetically distinct.
Members of a kin group tend to be genetically similar to each other, and
different from members of other kin groups. In contrast, groups composed of
non-kin tend to contain considerable genetic variation, and differences
between such groups are generally much smaller. Moreover, contact between
the groups — individuals migrating from one to another, say — will reduce
any genetic differences that have started to accumulate. So unless natural selection within the groups is different — such that what it takes to survive and
reproduce in one group is different from what it takes in another — migration quickly homogenizes the genetics of the whole population.

A second reason Darwin's idea has been ignored is that it seems to have
a distasteful corollary. The idea implies, perhaps, that some unpleasant
human characteristics — such as xenophobia or even racism — evolved in
tandem with generosity and kindness. Why? Because banding together to
fight means that people must be able to tell the difference between friends
(who belong in the group) and foes (who must be fought). In the mid-1970s,
in a paper that speculated about how humans might have evolved, Hamilton suggested that xenophobia might be innate. He was pilloried.

But times have changed. Last year, the science journal *Nature* published
a paper that tested the idea of "parochial altruism" — the notion that people might prefer to help strangers from their own ethnic group over
strangers from a different group; the experiment found that indeed they do. In
addition, the idea that natural selection might work on groups — at least in
particular and narrow circumstances — has become fashionable again. And
so Darwin's idea about the evolution of human kindness as a result of war
has been dusted off and scrutinized.

Sam Bowles, an economist turned evolutionary biologist who splits his   30
time between the Santa Fe Institute, in New Mexico, and the University of
Siena, in Italy, notes that during the last 90,000 years of the Pleistocene
Epoch (from about 100,000 years ago until about 10,000 years ago, when
agriculture emerged), the human population hardly grew. One reason for
this was the extraordinary climactic volatility of the period. But another,
Bowles suggests, was that our ancestors were busy killing each other in
wars. Working from archaeological records and ethnographic studies, he
estimates that wars between different groups could have accounted for a
substantial fraction of human deaths — perhaps as much as 15 percent, on
average, of those born in any given year — and as such, represented a significant source of natural selection.

Bowles shows that groups of supercooperative, altruistic humans could
indeed have wiped out groups of less-united folk. However, his argument
works only if the cooperative groups also had practices — such as monogamy
and the sharing of food with other group members — that reduced the ability
of their selfish members to outreproduce their more generous members.
(Monogamy helps the spread of altruism because it reduces the differences in
the number of children that different people have. If, instead, one or two
males monopolized all the females in the group, any genes involved in altruism would quickly disappear.) In other words, Bowles argues that a genetic
predisposition for altruism would have been far more likely to evolve in
groups where disparities and discord inside the group — whether over mates
or food — would have been relatively low. Cultural differences between
groups would then allow genetic differences to accumulate.

"That's Not the Way You Do It"

If Bowles's analysis is right, it suggests that individuals who could not
conform, or who were disruptive, would have weakened the whole group;
any group that failed to drive out such people, or kill them, would have been
more likely to be overwhelmed in battle. Conversely, people who fit in —
sharing the food they found, joining in hunting, helping to defend the group,
and so on — would have given their group a collective advantage, and thus
themselves an individual evolutionary advantage.

This suggests two hypotheses. First, that one of the traits that may have
evolved in humans is conformity, an ability to fit in with a group and adopt
its norms and customs. Second, that enforcement of those norms and customs could have been essential for group cohesion and harmony, especially
as groups got bigger (bigness is important in battles against other groups).

Let's start with conformity. This hasn't been studied much in other animals, but male baboons do appear to conform to the social regimens of the
groups they join. For example, in one baboon troop in Kenya in the 1980s,
all the aggressive males died of tuberculosis. The aggressives were the ones

to snuff it because they'd eaten meat infected with bovine TB that had been thrown into a garbage dump; only the more-aggressive males ate at the dump. After their deaths, the dynamics of the troop shifted to a more laid-back way of life. Ten years later — by which time all the original resident males had either died or moved on — the troop was still notable for its mellow attitude. The new males who'd arrived had adopted the local customs.

What about humans? According to Michael Tomasello — a psycholo-   35
gist at the Max Planck Institute, in Leipzig, Germany, who studies the behavior of human children and of chimpanzees — children as young as three will quickly deduce and conform to rules. If an adult demonstrates a game, and then a puppet comes in and plays it differently, the children will clamor to correct the puppet with shouts of "No, that's not the way you do it — you do it this way!" In other words, it's not just that they infer and obey rules; they try to enforce them, too.

Which brings me to the question of punishment.

Punishment Games

I'll be dictator. Here's how we play: An economist puts some money on the table — let's say $1,000. Since I'm dictator, I get to decide how you and I are going to split the cash; you have no say in the matter. How much do you think I'll give you?

Now, let's play the ultimatum game. We've still got $1,000 to play with, and I still get to make you an offer. But the game has a wrinkle: If you don't like the offer I make, you can refuse it. If you refuse it, we both get nothing. What do you think I'll do here?

As you've probably guessed, people tend to play the two games differently. In the dictator game, the most common offer is nothing, and the average offer is around 20 percent. In the ultimatum game, the most common offer is half the cash, while the average is around 45 percent. Offers of less than 25 percent are routinely refused — so both players go home empty-handed.

Economists scratch their heads at this. In the first place, they are sur-   40
prised that some people are nice enough to share with someone they don't know, even in the dictator game, where there's nothing to lose by not sharing. Second, economists predict that people will accept any offer in the ultimatum game, no matter how low, because getting something is better than getting nothing. But that's not what happens. Instead, some people forgo getting anything themselves in order to punish someone who made an ungenerous offer. Money, it seems, is not the only currency people are dealing in.

Bring in the neuroscientists, and the other currency gets clearer. If you measure brain activity while such games are being played (and there are many variants, for the fun doesn't stop with dictators and ultimatums), you find that the reward centers of the brain — the bits that give you warm, fuzzy feelings — light up when people are cooperating. But they also light up if you punish someone who wasn't generous, or watch the punishment of someone who wasn't.

Whether these responses are universal isn't clear: the genetic basis is obscure, and the number of people who've had their brain activity measured is tiny. Moreover, most economic-game playing has been done with college students; the extent to which the results hold among people from different cultures and backgrounds is relatively unknown. But the results suggest an intriguing possibility: that humans have evolved both to be good at conforming to the prevailing cultural norms and to enjoy making sure that those norms are enforced. (Perhaps this explains why schemes such as zero-tolerance policing work so well: they play into our desire to conform to the prevailing norms.)

Bringing Out the Best

If the evolutionary scenario I've outlined is even half right, then we should expect to find that there are genes involved in mediating friendly behavior. And there are. Consider Williams syndrome.

People who have Williams syndrome tend to have poor cardiovascular function and a small, pointed, "elfin" face. They are typically terrible with numbers but good with words. And they are weirdly, incautiously friendly and nice — and unafraid of strangers.

They are also missing a small segment of chromosome 7. Chromosomes   45 are long strings of DNA. Most people have forty-six chromosomes in twenty-three pairs; you get one set of twenty-three from your mother, and the other from your father. In Williams syndrome, one copy of chromosome 7 is normal; the other is missing a small piece. The missing piece contains about twenty genes, some of which make proteins that are important in the workings of the brain. Since one chromosome is intact, the problem isn't a complete absence of the proteins that the genes encode, but an insufficiency. Somehow, this insufficiency results in people who are too nice. What's more, they can't learn not to be nice. Which is to say, someone with Williams syndrome can learn the phrase "Don't talk to strangers" but can't translate it into action.

Much about Williams syndrome remains mysterious. How the missing genes normally influence behavior is unclear; moreover, the environment has a role to play, too. But despite these complexities, Williams syndrome shows that friendliness has a genetic underpinning — that it is indeed as primal as ferocity. Indirectly, it shows something else as well. Most of us are able to apply brakes to friendly behavior, picking and choosing the people we are friendly to; those with Williams syndrome aren't. They cannot modulate their behavior. This is even odder than being too friendly. And it throws into sharp relief one of the chief features of ordinary human nature: its flexibility.

One of the most important, and least remarked upon, consequences of social living is that individual behavior must be highly flexible and tailored to circumstance: an individual who does not know whom to be aggressive toward, or whom to help, is unlikely to survive for long within the group. This is true for baboons and chimpanzees. It is also true for us.

Indeed, the ability to adjust our behavior to fit a given social environment is one of our main characteristics, yet it's so instinctive we don't even notice it, let alone consider it worthy of remark. But its implications are profound — and hopeful. It suggests that we can, in principle, organize society so as to bring out the best facets of our complex, evolved natures.

QUESTIONS

Reading

1. What questions does Judson set out to answer in this *explanatory* essay? What strategies does she use to help readers understand her explanation? What are her main conclusions?
2. What is *parochial altruism*?
3. Judson explains Darwin's idea that "lethal warring between neighboring groups might have caused humans to evolve to be more helpful and kind to each other" (paragraph 26). Why, according to Judson, did this idea languish?
4. What, according to Judson, can we learn about genetics by studying people with Williams syndrome?

Exploratory Writing

1. "[F]riendship," Judson suggests, "may be as primal an urge as ferocity" (paragraph 20). In small groups, come up with a list of ten human behaviors that you can *unanimously* agree are based on "primal" urges. (You might include the urge to eat, sleep, run from danger, or urinate.) How do people customarily resist these urges? (For example, in the United States, most people do not defecate in the street. Even if they have the urge to go, they find a restroom.) Why might social customs develop that support the expression of some primal urges but not others?
2. In a classroom setting, play what Judson calls "punishment games" — the dictator game and the ultimatum game. Are the results in your classroom similar to the average results that Judson reports? Discuss Judson's comment that people seem to be dealing in a currency in addition to money.

Making Connections

1. Consider Emily Martin's (p. 472) claim that there are "sleeping metaphors" in science — meaning, instances when scientists project cultural imagery onto what they study — which are "all the more powerful" because they are "hidden within the scientific content of texts." Do you think that Martin would find any sleeping metaphors in Judson's

explanatory essay? Identify examples in Judson's essay where the line between scientific research and cultural ideas is blurred.

2. Compare Judson's explanation of the connection between genes and altruism with Steven Pinker's (p. 427) arguments about morality. How do you think that each writer might respond to the other's conclusions?

Essay Writing

1. Judson believes that our ability to modulate our behavior allows us to organize society in a way that brings out the best in our natures. Some scientists, however, advocate improving human society through the physical manipulation of genes. Do you believe that it should be legal to genetically alter a newly conceived person to enhance qualities such as appearance, intelligence, kindness, or strength? Write an essay arguing your position. As a resource, read (or take) the survey on PBS's Web site for *Cracking the Code of Life*: **www.pbs.org/wgbh/nova/genome/survey.html**.

"This Is the End of the World"
The Black Death

Barbara Tuchman

*Barbara Wertheim Tuchman (1912–1989) wrote books on histori-
cal subjects ranging over six centuries — from the Middle Ages to
the Vietnam War. Her careful research and lively writing in books
like* The Guns of August *(1962),* A Distant Mirror *(1978),* The
March of Folly: From Troy to Vietnam *(1984), and* The First
Salute *(1988) pleased not only the general public but many professional historians as well. She twice won the Pulitzer Prize.* A Distant Mirror, *from which the following selection has been taken,
was on the* New York Times *best-seller list for more than nine
months.*

In October 1347, two months after the fall of Calais, Genoese trading
ships put into the harbor of Messina in Sicily with dead and dying men at
the oars. The ships had come from the Black Sea port of Caffa (now
Feodosiya) in the Crimea, where the Genoese maintained a trading post.
The diseased sailors showed strange black swellings about the size of an
egg or an apple in the armpits and groin. The swellings oozed blood and
pus and were followed by spreading boils and black blotches on the skin
from internal bleeding. The sick suffered severe pain and died quickly
within five days of the first symptoms. As the disease spread, other symptoms of continuous fever and spitting of blood appeared instead of the
swellings or buboes. These victims coughed and sweated heavily and died
even more quickly, within three days or less, sometimes in 24 hours. In both
types everything that issued from the body — breath, sweat, blood from the
buboes and lungs, bloody urine, and blood-blackened excrement — smelled
foul. Depression and despair accompanied the physical symptoms, and
before the end "death is seen seated on the face."

The disease was bubonic plague, present in two forms: one that infected
the bloodstream, causing the buboes and internal bleeding, and was spread
by contact; and a second, more virulent pneumonic type that infected the
lungs and was spread by respiratory infection. The presence of both at once
caused the high mortality and speed of contagion. So lethal was the disease
that cases were known of persons going to bed well and dying before they
woke, of doctors catching the illness at a bedside and dying before the

patient. So rapidly did it spread from one to another that to a French physician, Simon de Covino, it seemed as if one sick person "could infect the whole world." The malignity of the pestilence appeared more terrible because its victims knew no prevention and no remedy.

The physical suffering of the disease and its aspects of evil mystery were expressed in a strange Welsh lament which saw "death coming into our midst like black smoke, a plague which cuts off the young, a rootless phantom which has no mercy for fair countenance. Woe is me of the shilling in the armpit! It is seething, terrible . . . a head that gives pain and causes a loud cry . . . a painful angry knob . . . Great is its seething like a burning cinder . . . a grievous thing of ashy color." Its eruption is ugly like the "seeds of black peas, broken fragments of brittle sea-coal . . . the early ornaments of black death, cinders of the peelings of the cockle weed, a mixed multitude, a black plague like halfpence, like berries. . . ."

Rumors of a terrible plague supposedly arising in China and spreading through Tartary (Central Asia) to India and Persia, Mesopotamia, Syria, Egypt, and all of Asia Minor had reached Europe in 1346. They told of a death toll so devastating that all of India was said to be depopulated, whole territories covered by dead bodies, other areas with no one left alive. As added up by Pope Clement VI at Avignon, the total of reported dead reached 23,840,000. In the absence of a concept of contagion, no serious alarm was felt in Europe until the trading ships brought their black burden of pestilence into Messina while other infected ships from the Levant carried it to Genoa and Venice.

By January 1348 it penetrated France via Marseille, and North Africa   5
via Tunis. Shipborne along coasts and navigable rivers, it spread westward from Marseille through the ports of Languedoc to Spain and northward up the Rhône to Avignon, where it arrived in March. It reached Narbonne, Montpellier, Carcassonne, and Toulouse between February and May, and at the same time in Italy spread to Rome and Florence and their hinterlands. Between June and August it reached Bordeaux, Lyon, and Paris, spread to Burgundy and Normandy, and crossed the Channel from Normandy into southern England. From Italy during the same summer it crossed the Alps into Switzerland and reached eastward to Hungary.

In a given area the plague accomplished its kill within four to six months and then faded, except in the larger cities, where, rooting into the close-quartered population, it abated during the winter, only to reappear in spring and rage for another six months.

In 1349 it resumed in Paris, spread to Picardy, Flanders, and the Low Countries, and from England to Scotland and Ireland as well as to Norway, where a ghost ship with a cargo of wool and a dead crew drifted offshore until it ran aground near Bergen. From there the plague passed into Sweden, Denmark, Prussia, Iceland, and as far as Greenland. Leaving a strange pocket of immunity in Bohemia, and Russia unattacked until 1351, it had passed from most of Europe by mid-1350. Although the mortality rate was

A detail from *The Triumph of Death*, a fresco by Francesco Traini in the Camposanto, Pisa, Italy, c. 1350.

erratic, ranging from one-fifth in some places to nine-tenths or almost total elimination in others, the overall estimate of modern demographers has settled — for the area extending from India to Iceland — around the same figure expressed in Froissart's casual words: "a third of the world died." His estimate, the common one at the time, was not an inspired guess but a borrowing of St. John's figure for mortality from plague in Revelation, the favorite guide to human affairs of the Middle Ages.

A third of Europe would have meant about 20 million deaths. No one knows in truth how many died. Contemporary reports were an awed impression, not an accurate count. In crowded Avignon, it was said, 400 died daily; 7,000 houses emptied by death were shut up; a single graveyard received 11,000 corpses in six weeks; half the city's inhabitants reportedly died, including 9 cardinals, or one-third of the total, and 70 lesser prelates. Watching the endlessly passing death carts, chroniclers let normal exaggeration take wings and put the Avignon death toll at 62,000 and even at 120,000, although the city's total population was probably less than 50,000.

When graveyards filled up, bodies at Avignon were thrown into the Rhône until mass burial pits were dug for dumping the corpses. In London in such pits corpses piled up in layers until they overflowed. Everywhere reports speak of the sick dying too fast for the living to bury. Corpses were dragged out of homes and left in front of doorways. Morning light revealed new piles of bodies. In Florence the dead were gathered up by the Compagnia della Misericordia — founded in 1244 to care for the sick — whose members wore red robes and hoods masking the face except for the eyes. When their efforts failed, the dead lay putrid in the streets for days at a time. When no coffins were to be had, the bodies were laid on boards, two or three at once, to be carried to graveyards or common pits. Families dumped their own relatives into the pits, or buried them so hastily and thinly "that dogs dragged them forth and devoured their bodies."

Amid accumulating death and fear of contagion, people died without last   10 rites and were buried without prayers, a prospect that terrified the last hours of the stricken. A bishop in England gave permission to laymen to make confession to each other as was done by the Apostles, "or if no man is present then even to a woman," and if no priest could be found to administer extreme unction, "then faith must suffice." Clement VI found it necessary to grant remissions of sin to all who died of the plague because so many were unattended by priests. "And no bells tolled," wrote a chronicler of Siena, "and nobody wept no matter what his loss because almost everyone expected death. . . . And people said and believed, 'This is the end of the world.'"

In Paris, where the plague lasted through 1349, the reported death rate was 800 a day, in Pisa 500, in Vienna 500 to 600. The total dead in Paris numbered 50,000 or half the population. Florence, weakened by the famine of 1347, lost three- to four-fifths of its citizens, Venice two-thirds, Hamburg and Bremen, though smaller in size, about the same proportion. Cities, as centers of transportation, were more likely to be affected than villages, although once a village was infected, its death rate was equally high. At Givry, a prosperous village in Burgundy of 1,200 to 1,500 people, the parish register records 615 deaths in the space of fourteen weeks, compared to an average of 30 deaths a year in the previous decade. In three villages of Cambridgeshire, manorial records show a death rate of 47 percent, 57 percent, and in one case 70 percent. When the last survivors, too few to carry on, moved away, a deserted village sank back into the wilderness and disappeared from the map altogether, leaving only a grass-covered ghostly outline to show where mortals once had lived.

In enclosed places such as monasteries and prisons, the infection of one person usually meant that of all, as happened in the Franciscan convents of Carcassonne and Marseille, where every inmate without exception died. Of the 140 Dominicans at Montpellier only 7 survived. Petrarch's brother Gherardo, member of a Carthusian monastery, buried the prior and 34 fellow monks one by one, sometimes three a day, until he was left alone with his dog and fled to look for a place that would take him in. Watching every comrade die, men in such places could not but wonder whether the strange peril that filled the air had not been sent to exterminate the human race. In Kilkenny, Ireland, Brother John Clyn of the Friars Minor, another monk left alone among dead men, kept a record of what had happened lest "things which should be remembered perish with time and vanish from the memory of those who come after us." Sensing "the whole world, as it were, placed within the grasp of the Evil One," and waiting for death to visit him too, he wrote, "I leave parchment to continue this work, if perchance any man

Burial of plague victims, from *Annales de Gilles li Muisis* (The Annals of Gilles li Muisis, c. 1272–1352).

survive and any of the race of Adam escape this pestilence and carry on the work which I have begun." Brother John, as noted by another hand, died of the pestilence, but he foiled oblivion.

The largest cities of Europe, with populations of about 100,000, were Paris and Florence, Venice and Genoa. At the next level, with more than 50,000, were Ghent and Bruges in Flanders, Milan, Bologna, Rome, Naples, and Palermo, and Cologne. London hovered below 50,000, the only city in England except York with more than 10,000. At the level of 20,000 to 50,000 were Bordeaux, Toulouse, Montpellier, Marseille, and Lyon in France, Barcelona, Seville, and Toledo in Spain, Siena, Pisa, and other secondary cities in Italy, and the Hanseatic trading cities of the Empire. The plague raged through them all, killing anywhere from one-third to two-thirds of their inhabitants. Italy, with a total population of 10 to 11 million, probably suffered the heaviest toll. Following the Florentine bankruptcies, the crop failures and workers' riots of 1346–47, the revolt of Cola di Rienzi that plunged Rome into anarchy, the plague came as the peak of successive calamities. As if the world were indeed in the grasp of the Evil One, its first appearance on the European mainland in January 1348 coincided with a fearsome earthquake that carved a path of wreckage from Naples up to Venice. Houses collapsed, church towers toppled, villages were crushed, and the destruction reached as far as Germany and Greece. Emotional response, dulled by horrors, underwent a kind of atrophy epitomized by the chronicler who wrote, "And in these days was burying without sorrowe and wedding without friendschippe."

In Siena, where more than half the inhabitants died of the plague, work was abandoned on the great cathedral, planned to be the largest in the world, and never resumed, owing to loss of workers and master masons and "the melancholy and grief" of the survivors. The cathedral's truncated transept still stands in permanent witness to the sweep of death's scythe. Agnolo di Tura, a chronicler of Siena, recorded the fear of contagion that froze every other instinct. "Father abandoned child, wife husband, one brother another," he wrote, "for this plague seemed to strike through the breath and sight. And so they died. And no one could be found to bury the dead for money or friendship. . . . And I, Agnolo di Tura, called the Fat, buried my five children with my own hands, and so did many others likewise."

There were many to echo his account of inhumanity and few to balance   15
it, for the plague was not the kind of calamity that inspired mutual help. Its loathsomeness and deadliness did not herd people together in mutual distress, but only prompted their desire to escape each other. "Magistrates and notaries refused to come and make the wills of the dying," reported a Franciscan friar of Piazza in Sicily; what was worse, "even the priests did not come to hear their confessions." A clerk of the Archbishop of Canterbury reported the same of English priests who "turned away from the care of their benefices from fear of death." Cases of parents deserting children and children their parents were reported across Europe from Scotland to Russia. The calamity chilled the hearts of men, wrote Boccaccio in his famous account of the plague in Florence that serves as introduction to the *Decameron*. "One man shunned another . . . kinsfolk held aloof, brother was forsaken by brother, oftentimes husband by wife; nay, what is more, and scarcely to be believed, fathers and mothers were found to abandon their own children to their fate, untended, unvisited as if they had been strangers." Exaggeration and literary pessimism were common in the fourteenth century, but the Pope's physician, Guy de Chauliac, was a sober, careful observer who reported the same phenomenon: "A father did not visit his son, nor the son his father. Charity was dead."

Yet not entirely. In Paris, according to the chronicler Jean de Venette, the nuns of the Hotel Dieu or municipal hospital, "having no fear of death, tended the sick with all sweetness and humility." New nuns repeatedly took the places of those who died, until the majority "many times renewed by death now rest in peace with Christ as we may piously believe."

When the plague entered northern France in July 1348, it settled first in Normandy and, checked by winter, gave Picardy a deceptive interim until the next summer. Either in mourning or warning, black flags were flown from church towers of the worst-stricken villages of Normandy. "And in that time," wrote a monk of the abbey of Fourcarment, "the mortality was so great among the people of Normandy that those of Picardy mocked them." The same unneighborly reaction was reported of the Scots, separated by a winter's immunity from the English. Delighted to hear of the disease that was scourging the "southrons," they gathered forces for an invasion, "laughing at their enemies." Before they could move, the savage mortality fell upon them too, scattering some in death and the rest in panic to spread the infection as they fled.

In Picardy in the summer of 1349 the pestilence penetrated the castle of Coucy to kill Enguerrand's[1] mother, Catherine, and her new husband. Whether her nine-year-old son escaped by chance or was perhaps living elsewhere with one of his guardians is unrecorded. In nearby Amiens, tannery workers, responding quickly to losses in the labor force, combined to bargain for higher wages. In another place villagers were seen dancing to drums and trumpets, and on being asked the reason, answered that, seeing their neighbors die day by day while their village remained immune, they believed that they could keep the plague from entering "by the jollity that is in us. That is why we dance." Further north in Tournai on the border of Flanders, Gilles li Muisis, Abbot of St. Martin's, kept one of the epidemic's most vivid accounts. The passing bells rang all day and all night, he recorded, because sextons were anxious to obtain their fees while they could. Filled with the sound of mourning, the city became oppressed by fear, so that the authorities forbade the tolling of bells and the wearing of black and restricted funeral services to two mourners. The silencing of funeral bells and of criers' announcements of deaths was ordained by most cities. Siena imposed a fine on the wearing of mourning clothes by all except widows.

Flight was the chief recourse of those who could afford it or arrange it. The rich fled to their country places like Boccaccio's young patricians of Florence, who settled in a pastoral palace "removed on every side from the roads" with "wells of cool water and vaults of rare wines." The urban poor died in their burrows, "and only the stench of their bodies informed neighbors of their deaths." That the poor were more heavily afflicted than the rich was clearly remarked at the time, in the north as in the south. A Scottish chronicler, John of Fordun, stated flatly that the pest "attacked especially the meaner sort and common people—seldom the magnates." Simon de Covino of Montpellier made the same observation. He ascribed it to the misery and want and hard lives that made the poor more susceptible, which was half the truth. Close contact and lack of sanitation was the unrecognized other half. It was noticed too that the young died in greater proportion than the old; Simon de Covino compared the disappearance of youth to the withering of flowers in the fields.

In the countryside peasants dropped dead on the roads, in the fields, in   20
their houses. Survivors in growing helplessness fell into apathy, leaving ripe wheat uncut and livestock untended. Oxen and asses, sheep and goats, pigs and chickens ran wild and they too, according to local reports, succumbed to the pest. English sheep, bearers of the precious wool, died throughout the country. The chronicler Henry Knighton, canon of Leicester Abbey, reported five thousand dead in one field alone, "their bodies so corrupted by the plague that neither beast nor bird would touch them," and spreading an appalling stench. In the Austrian Alps wolves came down to prey upon sheep and then,

---

[1]*Enguerrand de Coucy*: A French nobleman. Tuchman follows his life as a way of unifying her study of the fourteenth century. [Eds.]

"as if alarmed by some invisible warning, turned and fled back into the wilderness." In remote Dalmatia bolder wolves descended upon a plague-stricken city and attacked human survivors. For want of herdsmen, cattle strayed from place to place and died in hedgerows and ditches. Dogs and cats fell like the rest.

The dearth of labor held a fearful prospect because the fourteenth century lived close to the annual harvest both for food and for next year's seed. "So few servants and laborers were left," wrote Knighton, "that no one knew where to turn for help." The sense of a vanishing future created a kind of dementia of despair. A Bavarian chronicler of Neuberg on the Danube recorded that "Men and women . . . wandered around as if mad" and let their cattle stray "because no one had any inclination to concern themselves about the future." Fields went uncultivated, spring seed unsown. Second growth with nature's awful energy crept back over cleared land, dikes crumbled, salt water reinvaded and soured the lowlands. With so few hands remaining to restore the work of centuries, people felt, in Walsingham's words, that "the world could never again regain its former prosperity."

Though the death rate was higher among the anonymous poor, the known and the great died too. King Alfonso XI of Castile was the only reigning monarch killed by the pest, but his neighbor King Pedro of Aragon lost his wife, Queen Leonora, his daughter Marie, and a niece in the space of six months. John Cantacuzene, Emperor of Byzantium, lost his son. In France the lame Queen Jeanne and her daughter-in-law Bonne de Luxemburg, wife of the Dauphin, both died in 1349 in the same phase that took the life of Enguerrand's mother. Jeanne, Queen of Navarre, daughter of Louis X, was another victim. Edward III's second daughter, Joanna, who was on her way to marry Pedro, the heir of Castile, died in Bordeaux. Women appear to have been more vulnerable than men, perhaps because, being more housebound, they were more exposed to fleas. Boccaccio's mistress Fiammetta, illegitimate daughter of the King of Naples, died, as did Laura, the beloved—whether real or fictional—of Petrarch. Reaching out to us in the future, Petrarch cried, "Oh happy posterity who will not experience such abysmal woe and will look upon our testimony as a fable."

In Florence Giovanni Villani, the great historian of his time, died at sixty-eight in the midst of an unfinished sentence: " . . . *e dure questo pistolenza fino a* . . . (in the midst of this pestilence there came to an end . . .)." Siena's master painters, the brothers Ambrogio and Pietro Lorenzetti, whose names never appear after 1348, presumably perished in the plague, as did Andrea Pisano, architect and sculptor of Florence. William of Ockham and the English mystic Richard Rolle of Hampole both disappear from mention after 1349. Francisco Datini, merchant of Prato, lost both his parents and two siblings. Curious sweeps of mortality afflicted certain bodies of merchants in London. All eight wardens of the Company of Cutters, all six wardens of the Hatters, and four wardens of the Goldsmiths died before July 1350. Sir John Pulteney, master draper and four-time Mayor of London, was a victim, likewise Sir John Montgomery, Governor of Calais.

Among the clergy and doctors the mortality was naturally high because of the nature of their professions. Out of twenty-four physicians in Venice, twenty were said to have lost their lives in the plague, although, according to another account, some were believed to have fled or to have shut themselves up in their houses. At Montpellier, site of the leading medieval medical school, the physician Simon de Covino reported that, despite the great number of doctors, "hardly one of them escaped." In Avignon, Guy de Chauliac confessed that he performed his medical visits only because he dared not stay away for fear of infamy, but "I was in continual fear." He claimed to have contracted the disease but to have cured himself by his own treatment; if so, he was one of the few who recovered.

Clerical mortality varied with rank. Although the one-third toll of cardinals reflects the same proportion as the whole, this was probably due to their concentration in Avignon. In England, in strange and almost sinister procession, the Archbishop of Canterbury, John Stratford, died in August 1348, his appointed successor died in May 1349, and the next appointee three months later, all three within a year. Despite such weird vagaries, prelates in general managed to sustain a higher survival rate than the lesser clergy. Among bishops the deaths have been estimated at about one in twenty. The loss of priests, even if many avoided their fearful duty of attending the dying, was about the same as among the population as a whole.   25

Government officials, whose loss contributed to the general chaos, found, on the whole, no special shelter. In Siena four of the nine members of the governing oligarchy died, in France one-third of the royal notaries, in Bristol fifteen out of the fifty-two members of the Town Council, or almost one-third. Tax-collecting obviously suffered, with the result that Philip VI was unable to collect more than a fraction of the subsidy granted him by the Estates in the winter of 1347–48.

Lawlessness and debauchery accompanied the plague as they had during the great plague of Athens of 430 BC, when according to Thucydides, men grew bold in the indulgence of pleasure: "For seeing how the rich died in a moment and those who had nothing immediately inherited their property, they reflected that life and riches were alike transitory and they resolved to enjoy themselves while they could." Human behavior is timeless. When St. John had his vision of plague in Revelation, he knew from some experience or race memory that those who survived "repented not of the work of their hands. . . . Neither repented they of their murders, nor of their sorceries, nor of their fornication, nor of their thefts."

Notes

Although Tuchman's notes are labeled by page number, the numbers in this Notes section refer to the paragraphs in which the sources are mentioned. Tuchman does not use numbered footnotes. At the end of her book, she numbers her notes by page number and provides a source for each quotation and citation. Following her notes, she provides a bibliography that provides the full citation for every reference given in her notes.

1. "death is seen seated": Simon de Covino, q. Campbell, 80.
2. "could infect the whole world": q. Gasquet, 41.
3. Welsh lament: q. Ziegler, 190.
9. "dogs dragged them forth": Agnolo di Tura, q. Ziegler, 58.
10. "or if no man is present": Bishop of Bath and Wells, q. Ziegler, 125. "No bells tolled": Agnolo di Tura, q. Schevill, 211. The same observation was made by Gabriel de Muisis, notary of Piacenza, q. Crawfurd, 113.
11. Givry parish register: Renouard, 111. Three villages of Cambridgeshire: Saltmarsh.
12. Petrarch's brother: Bishop, 273. Brother John Clyn: q. Ziegler, 195.
13. "And in these days": q. Deaux, 143, citing only "an old northern chronicle."
14. Agnolo di Tura, "Father abandoned child": q. Ziegler, 58.
15. "Magistrates and notaries": q. Deaux, 49. English priests turned away: Ziegler, 261. Parents deserting children: Hecker, 30. Guy de Chauliac, "A father": q. Gasquet, 50–51.
16. nuns of the Hotel Dieu: *Chron. Jean de Venette*, 49.
17. Picards and Scots mock mortality of neighbors: Gasquet, 53, and Ziegler, 198.
18. Catherine de Coucy: *L'Art de vérifier*, 237. Amiens tanners: Gasquet, 57. "By the jollity that is in us": *Grandes Chrôns.*, VI, 486–87.
19. John of Fordun: q. Ziegler, 199. Simon de Covino on the poor: Gasquet, 42. On youth: Cazelles.
20. Knighton on sheep: q. Ziegler, 175. Wolves of Austria and Dalmatia: ibid., 84, 111. Dogs and cats: Muisis, q. Gasquet, 44, 61.
21. Bavarian chronicler of Neuberg: q. Ziegler, 84. Walsingham, "the world could never": Denifle, 273.
22. "Oh happy posterity": q. Ziegler, 45.
23. Giovanni Villani, "*e dure questo*": q. Snell, 334.
24. Physicians of Venice: Campbell, 98. Simon de Covino: ibid., 31. Guy de Chauliac, "I was in continual fear": q. Thompson, 379.
27. Thucydides: q. Crawfurd, 30–31.

Bibliography

L'Art de vérifier les dates des faits historiques, par un Religieux de la Congregation de St.-Maur, vol. XII. Paris, 1818.

Bishop, Morris. *Petrarch and His World.* Indiana University Press, 1963.

Campbell, Anna M. *The Black Death and Men of Learning.* Columbia University Press, 1931.

Cazelles, Raymond. "*La Peste de 1348–49 en Langue d'oil: épidémie prolitarienne et enfantine.*" Bull philologique et historique, 1962, pp. 293–305.

Chronicle of Jean de Venette. Trans. Jean Birdsall. Ed. Richard A. Newhall. Columbia University Press, 1853.

Crawfurd, Raymond. *Plague and Pestilence in Literature and Art.* Oxford, 1914.

Deaux, George. *The Black Death, 1347.* London, 1969.

Denifle, Henri. *La Désolation des églises, monastères et hôpitaux en France pendant la guerre de cent ans,* vol. I. Paris, 1899.

Gasquet, Francis Aidan, Abbot. *The Black Death of 1348 and 1349*, 2nd ed. London, 1908.

Grandes Chroniques de France, vol. VI (to 1380). Ed. Paulin Paris. Paris, 1838.

Hecker, J. F. C. *The Epidemics of the Middle Ages*. London, 1844.

Renouard, Yves. *"La Peste noire de 1348–50." Rev. de Paris*, March, 1950.

Saltmarsh, John. "Plague and Economic Decline in England in the Later Middle Ages." *Cambridge Historical Journal*, vol. VII, no. 1, 1941.

Schevill, Ferdinand. *Siena: The History of a Medieval Commune*. New York, 1909.

Snell, Frederick. *The Fourteenth Century*. Edinburgh, 1899.

Thompson, James Westfall. *Economic and Social History of Europe in the Later Middle Ages*. New York, 1931.

Ziegler, Philip. *The Black Death*. New York, 1969. (The best modern study.)

QUESTIONS

Reading

1. According to Tuchman, how many people died in Europe during the Black Death?
2. In writing this report, Tuchman chooses to end many of her paragraphs with direct quotations. Underline, highlight, or flag some of these. What do they have in common? Why do you think Tuchman closes so many paragraphs in this way?
3. Much of this essay is devoted to the reporting of facts and figures. This could be very tedious, but Tuchman is an expert at avoiding dullness. How does she help the reader see and feel the awfulness of the plague? Locate specific examples in the text, and discuss their effectiveness.

Exploratory Writing

1. What is valuable about reading accounts of history? Reflect on a time when learning about events from the distant past changed your view of your own life.
2. "Human nature is timeless," writes Tuchman (paragraph 27). In your opinion, how does her study of the Black Death support or refute this claim? Make a list of examples of the timeless aspects of human nature that you find in her essay.
3. Collaborating in small groups, research and create a presentation *explaining* a painting that portrays the Black Death. What does the painting show about history? In what ways is the painting timeless?

Making Connections

1. Patricia Hampl (p. 122) discusses memoir writing as a kind of history, and advises memoirists to follow Nabokov's command, "Caress the detail, the divine detail." Compare Tuchman's historical report on the Black Death to a memoir. What are the differences between history and memoir?

Discuss ways that Hampl's guidelines for good memoir writing do or do not apply to historical reporting.

2. Imagine that we had photographs and film footage of many of the gruesome deaths caused by the plague. Susan Sontag (p. 257) writes, "To catch a death actually happening and embalm it for all time is something only cameras can do." Discuss the extent to which images of the dead and dying can be invoked by painters or writers without the use of a camera. How might our reflections about the catastrophe be different if it had been recorded on film?

Essay Writing

1. Taking Tuchman as a model, write a report on some other catastrophe, blending factual reporting with descriptions of what it was like to be there. This will require both careful research and artful selection and arrangement of the fruits of that research.

The Declaration of Independence

Thomas Jefferson

Thomas Jefferson (1743–1826) was born in Shadwell, Virginia, attended the College of William and Mary, and became a lawyer. He was elected to the Virginia House of Burgesses in 1769 and was a delegate to the Continental Congress in 1776. When the Congress voted in favor of Richard Henry Lee's resolution that the colonies "ought to be free and independent states," a committee of five members, including John Adams, Benjamin Franklin, and Jefferson, was appointed to draw up a declaration. Jefferson, because of his eloquence as a writer, was asked by this committee to draw up a first draft. Jefferson's text, with a few changes suggested by Franklin and Adams, was presented to the Congress. After a debate in which further changes were made, including striking out a passage condemning the slave trade, the Declaration was approved on July 4, 1776. Jefferson said of it, "Neither aiming at originality of principles or sentiments, nor yet copied from any particular and previous writing, it was intended to be an expression of the American mind."

In Congress, July 4, 1776
The unanimous Declaration of the
thirteen united States of America

When in the Course of human events it becomes necessary for one people to dissolve the political bands which have connected them with another, and to assume among the powers of the earth, the separate and equal station to which the Laws of Nature and of Nature's God entitle them, a decent respect to the opinions of mankind requires that they should declare the causes which impel them to the separation.

We hold these truths to be self-evident, that all men are created equal, that they are endowed by their Creator with certain unalienable Rights, that among these are Life, Liberty and the pursuit of Happiness. That to secure these rights, Governments are instituted among Men, deriving their just powers from the consent of the governed. That whenever any Form of Government becomes destructive of these ends, it is the Right of the People to alter or to abolish it, and to institute new Government, laying its foundation on such principles and organizing its powers in such form, as to them shall seem most likely to effect their Safety and Happiness. Prudence, indeed, will dictate that Governments long established should not be changed for light and transient causes; and accordingly all experience hath shewn that mankind are more disposed to suffer, while evils are sufferable, than to right themselves by abolishing the forms to which they are accustomed. But when a long train of abuses and usurpations, pursuing invariably the same Object evinces a design to reduce them under absolute Despotism, it is their right, it is their duty, to throw off such Government, and to provide new Guards for their future security. Such has been the patient sufferance of these Colonies; and such is now the necessity which constrains them to alter their former Systems of Government. The history of the present King of Great Britain is a history of repeated injuries and usurpations, all having in direct object the establishment of an absolute Tyranny over these States. To prove this, let Facts be submitted to a candid world.

He has refused his Assent to Laws, the most wholesome and necessary for the public good.

He has forbidden his Governors to pass laws of immediate and pressing importance, unless suspended in their operation till his Assent should be obtained; and when so suspended, he has utterly neglected to attend to them.

He has refused to pass other Laws for the accommodation of large   5
districts of people, unless those people would relinquish the right of Representation in the Legislature, a right inestimable to them and formidable to tyrants only.

He has called together legislative bodies at places unusual, uncomfortable, and distant from the depository of their Public Records, for the sole purpose of fatiguing them into compliance with his measures.

He has dissolved Representative Houses repeatedly, for opposing with manly firmness his invasions on the rights of the people.

He has refused for a long time, after such dissolutions, to cause others to be elected; whereby the Legislative Powers, incapable of Annihilation, have returned to the People at large for their exercise; the State remaining in the mean time exposed to all the dangers of invasion from without, and convulsions within.

He has endeavored to prevent the population of these States; for that purpose obstructing the Laws for Naturalization of Foreigners; refusing to pass others to encourage their migration hither, and raising the conditions of new Appropriations of Lands.

He has obstructed the Administration of Justice, by refusing his Assent   10
to Laws for Establishing Judiciary Powers.

He has made Judges dependent on his Will alone, for the tenure of their offices, and the amount and payment of their salaries.

He has erected a multitude of New Offices, and sent hither swarms of Officers to harass our people, and eat out their substance.

He has kept among us, in times of peace, Standing Armies without the Consent of our legislatures.

He has affected to render the Military independent of and superior to the Civil Power.

He has combined with others to subject us to a jurisdiction foreign to 15 our constitution, and unacknowledged by our laws; giving his Assent to the Acts of pretended Legislation: For quartering large bodies of armed troops among us: For protecting them, by a mock Trial, from punishment for any Murders which they should commit on the Inhabitants of these States: For cutting off our Trade with all parts of the world: For imposing Taxes on us without our Consent: For depriving us in many cases, of the benefits of Trial by Jury: For Transporting us beyond Seas to be tried for pretended offenses: For abolishing the free System of English Laws in a neighboring Province, establishing therein an Arbitrary government, and enlarging its Boundaries so as to render it at once an example and fit instrument for introducing the same absolute rule into these Colonies: For taking away our Charters, abolishing our most valuable Laws and altering fundamentally the Forms of our Governments: For suspending our own Legislatures, and declaring themselves invested with power to legislate for us in all cases whatsoever.

He has abdicated Government here, by declaring us out of his Protection and waging War against us.

He has plundered our seas, ravaged our Coasts, burnt our towns, and destroyed the lives of our people.

He is at this time transporting large Armies of foreign Mercenaries to complete the works of death, desolation and tyranny, already begun with circumstances of Cruelty & Perfidy scarcely paralleled in the most barbarous ages, and totally unworthy the Head of a civilized nation.

He has constrained our fellow Citizens taken Captive on the high Seas to bear Arms against their Country, to become the executioners of their friends and Brethren, or to fall themselves by their Hands.

He has excited domestic insurrections amongst us, and has endeavored 20 to bring on the inhabitants of our frontiers, the merciless Indian Savages, whose known rule of warfare is an undistinguished destruction of all ages, sexes, and conditions.

In every stage of these Oppressions We have Petitioned for Redress in the most humble terms: Our repeated petitions have been answered only by repeated injury. A Prince, whose character is thus marked by every act which may define a Tyrant, is unfit to be the ruler of a free people.

Nor have we been wanting in attention to our British brethren. We have warned them from time to time of attempts by their legislature to extend an unwarrantable jurisdiction over us. We have reminded them of the circumstances of our emigration and settlement here. We have appealed to their native justice and magnanimity, and we have conjured them by the ties of our common kindred to disavow these usurpations, which would inevitably interrupt our connections and correspondence. They too have been deaf to the voice of justice and of consanguinity. We must, therefore, acquiesce in the necessity, which denounces our Separation, and hold them, as we hold the rest of mankind, Enemies in War, in Peace Friends.

We, THEREFORE, the Representatives of the UNITED STATES OF AMERICA, in General Congress, Assembled, appealing to the Supreme Judge of the world for the rectitude of our intentions, do, in the Name, and by Authority of the good People of these Colonies, solemnly publish and declare, That these United Colonies are, and of Right ought to be FREE AND INDEPENDENT STATES; that they are Absolved from all Allegiance to the British Crown, and that all political connection between them and the State of Great Britain, is and ought to be totally dissolved; and that as Free and Independent States, they have full Power to levy War, conclude Peace, contract Alliances, establish Commerce, and to do all the Acts and Things which Independent States may of right do. And for the support of this Declaration, with a firm reliance on the protection of Divine Providence, we mutually pledge to each other our Lives, our Fortunes, and our sacred Honor.

QUESTIONS

Reading

1. The Declaration of Independence is frequently cited as a classic *deductive* argument. A deductive argument is based on a general statement, or premise, that is assumed to be true. What does this document assume that the American colonists are entitled to, and on what is this assumption based? Look at the reasoning in paragraph 2. What truths are considered self-evident? What does *self-evident* mean?
2. What accusations against the king of Great Britain are the Declaration's facts meant to substantiate?
3. To what extent is the audience of the Declaration intended to be the king and people of Great Britain? What other audiences were intended for this document?

Exploratory Writing

1. Write a declaration of your own, announcing your separation from some injurious situation (an incompatible roommate, a noisy sorority or fraternity house, an awful job). Start with a premise, give reasons to substantiate it, provide facts that illustrate the injurious conditions, and conclude with a statement of what your new condition will mean to you and to other oppressed people.
2. The Declaration of Independence has been celebrated not only for outlining a new kind of self-government but also for Jefferson's writing style. How might the same document have been received if it had been written differently? Collaborating in small groups, rewrite the Declaration

in your own words, then present your new version to the class. How does the rewriting change the document's impact?

3. Jefferson asserts that "Life, Liberty and the pursuit of Happiness" are inalienable human rights, but at the time the Declaration was written, slavery was widespread. In class, discuss different definitions of the word *human*. Why has it been such a widespread historical practice to categorize humans into different groups (based on race, class, religion, sex, sexual orientation, and age) before determining laws? How have the political structures of different periods shaped common understandings of those categories? In your discussion, consider the Universal Declaration of Human Rights drafted by the United Nations in 1948 (**www.un.org/ Overview/rights.html**) as well as Jefferson's 1776 document.

Making Connections

1. What if, rather than writing the Declaration of Independence, Jefferson had offered "a modest proposal" to the British king? What do you suppose he would have said? How would he have formulated his argument? Write your own modest proposal to the king, addressing him more or less in the manner of Jonathan Swift (p. 248) but drawing on the evidence that Jefferson provides in the Declaration.

2. Compare Barack Obama's March 2008 speech (p. 303) with Jefferson's document. Identify similarities and differences in their tone, style, and purpose.

Essay Writing

1. Although this declaration could have been expected to lead to war and all the horrors thereof, it is a civilized document, showing great respect throughout for certain standards of civility among people and among nations. Define the civilized standards that the Declaration assumes. Write an essay that identifies and characterizes the nature and variety of those expectations.

A Modest Proposal

Jonathan Swift

Jonathan Swift (1667–1745) was born in Dublin, Ireland, of English parents and was educated in Irish schools. A graduate of Trinity College, Dublin, he received a master's degree from Oxford and was ordained as a priest in the Church of England in 1695. He was active in politics as well as religion, becoming an editor and pamphlet writer for the Tory party in 1710. After becoming Dean of St. Patrick's Cathedral, Dublin, in 1713, he settled in Ireland and began to take an interest in the English economic exploitation of Ireland, gradually becoming a fierce Irish patriot. By 1724, the English were offering a reward for the discovery of the writer of the Drapier's Letters, *a series of pamphlets secretly written by Swift that attacked the British for their treatment of Ireland. In 1726, Swift produced the first volume of a more universal satire, known to modern readers as* Gulliver's Travels, *which has kept his name alive for more than 250 years. "A Modest Proposal," his best-known essay on Irish affairs, appeared in 1729.*

A Modest Proposal
for Preventing the Children of Poor People in Ireland
from Being a Burden to Their Parents or Country,
and for Making Them Beneficial to the Public

It is a melancholy object to those who walk through this great town,[1] or travel in the country, when they see the streets, the roads and cabin-doors crowded with beggars of the female sex, followed by three, four, or six children, all in rags, and importuning every passenger for an alms. These mothers, instead of being able to work for their honest livelihood, are forced to employ all their time in strolling, to beg sustenance for their helpless infants, who, as they grow up, either turn thieves for want of work, or

---

[1]*this great town*: Dublin. [Eds.]

leave their dear native country to fight for the Pretender in Spain,[2] or sell themselves to the Barbadoes.[3]

I think it is agreed by all parties that this prodigious number of children, in the arms, or on the backs, or at the heels of their mothers, and frequently of their fathers, is in the present deplorable state of the kingdom a very great additional grievance; and therefore whoever could find out a fair, cheap, and easy method of making these children sound and useful members of the commonwealth would deserve so well of the public as to have his statue set up for a preserver of the nation.

But my intention is very far from being confined to provide only for the children of professed beggars; it is of a much greater extent, and shall take in the whole number of infants at a certain age who are born of parents in effect as little able to support them as those who demand our charity in the streets.

As to my own part, having turned my thoughts for many years upon this important subject, and maturely weighed the several schemes of other projectors, I have always found them grossly mistaken in their computation. It is true a child just dropped from its dam may be supported by her milk for a solar year with little other nourishment, at most not above the value of two shillings,[4] which the mother may certainly get, or the value in scraps, by her lawful occupation of begging, and it is exactly at one year old that I propose to provide for them, in such a manner as, instead of being a charge upon their parents, or the parish, or wanting food and raiment for the rest of their lives, they shall, on the contrary, contribute to the feeding and partly to the clothing of many thousands.

There is likewise another great advantage to my scheme, that it will prevent those voluntary abortions, and that horrid practice of women murdering their bastard children, alas, too frequent among us, sacrificing the poor innocent babes, I doubt, more to avoid the expense than the shame, which would move tears and pity in the most savage and inhuman breast.   5

The number of souls in Ireland being usually reckoned one million and a half, of these I calculate there may be about two hundred thousand couples whose wives are breeders, from which number I subtract thirty thousand couples who are able to maintain their own children, although I apprehend there cannot be so many under the present distresses of the kingdom, but this being granted, there will remain an hundred and seventy thousand breeders.

---

[2]*Pretender in Spain*: A Catholic descendant of the British royal family of Stuart (James I, Charles I, Charles II, and James II). Exiled to France and Spain so that England could be governed by Protestant rulers, the Stuarts prepared various disastrous schemes for regaining the throne. [Eds.]

[3]*sell themselves to the Barbadoes*: Sell themselves as indentured servants, a sort of temporary slavery, to the sugar merchants of the British Caribbean islands. [Eds.]

[4]*shillings*: A shilling used to be worth about one day's labor. [Eds.]

I again subtract fifty thousand for those women who miscarry, or whose children die by accident or disease within the year. There only remain an hundred and twenty thousand children of poor parents annually born: the question therefore is, how this number shall be reared, and provided for, which as I have already said, under the present situation of affairs is utterly impossible by all the methods hitherto proposed, for we can neither employ them in handicraft or agriculture; we neither build houses (I mean in the country), nor cultivate land: they can very seldom pick up a livelihood by stealing until they arrive at six years old, except where they are of towardly parts, although I confess they learn the rudiments much earlier, during which time they can however be properly looked upon only as probationers, as I have been informed by a principal gentleman in the County of Cavan, who protested to me that he never knew above one or two instances under the age of six, even in a part of the kingdom so renowned for the quickest proficiency in that art.

I am assured by our merchants that a boy or girl before twelve years old, is no saleable commodity, and even when they come to this age, they will not yield above three pounds, or three pounds and half-a-crown at most on the Exchange, which cannot turn to account either to the parents or the kingdom, the charge of nutriment and rags having been at least four times that value.

I shall now therefore humbly propose my own thoughts, which I hope will not be liable to the least objection.

I have been assured by a very knowing American of my acquaintance in London, that a young healthy child well nursed is at a year old a most delicious, nourishing and wholesome food, whether stewed, roasted, baked, or boiled, and I make no doubt that it will equally serve in a fricassee, or a ragout.

I do therefore humbly offer it to public consideration, that of the hundred and twenty thousand children already computed, twenty thousand may be reserved for breed, whereof only one-fourth part to be males, which is more than we allow to sheep, black-cattle, or swine, and my reason is that these children are seldom the fruits of marriage, a circumstance not much regarded by our savages, therefore one male will be sufficient to serve four females. That the remaining hundred thousand may at a year old be offered in sale to the persons of quality, and fortune, through the kingdom, always advising the mother to let them suck plentifully in the last month, so as to render them plump, and fat for a good table. A child will make two dishes at an entertainment for friends, and when the family dines alone, the fore or hind quarters will make a reasonable dish, and seasoned with a little pepper or salt will be very good boiled on the fourth day, especially in winter.

I have reckoned upon a medium, that a child just born will weigh twelve pounds, and in a solar year if tolerably nursed increaseth to twenty-eight pounds.

I grant this food will be somewhat dear, and therefore very proper for landlords, who, as they have already devoured most of the parents, seem to have the best title to the children.

Infant's flesh will be in season throughout the year, but more plentiful in March, and a little before and after, for we are told by a grave author, an eminent French physician,[5] that fish being a prolific diet, there are more children born in Roman Catholic countries about nine months after Lent than at any other season; therefore reckoning a year after Lent, the markets will be more glutted than usual, because the number of Popish infants is at least three to one in this kingdom, and therefore it will have one other collateral advantage by lessening the number of Papists among us.

I have already computed the charge of nursing a beggar's child (in which list I reckon all cottagers, laborers, and four-fifths of the farmers) to be about two shillings *per annum*, rags included, and I believe no gentleman would repine to give ten shillings for the carcass of a good fat child, which, as I have said, will make four dishes of excellent nutritive meat, when he hath only some particular friend of his own family to dine with him. Thus the Squire will learn to be a good landlord and grow popular among his tenants, the mother will have eight shillings net profit, and be fit for work until she produces another child.

Those who are more thrifty (as I must confess the times require) may   15
flay the carcass; the skin of which artificially dressed, will make admirable gloves for ladies, and summer boots for fine gentlemen.

As to our city of Dublin, shambles[6] may be appointed for this purpose, in the most convenient parts of it, and butchers we may be assured will not be wanting, although I rather recommend buying the children alive, and dressing them hot from the knife, as we do roasting pigs.

A very worthy person, a true lover of his country, and whose virtues I highly esteem, was lately pleased in discoursing on this matter to offer a refinement upon my scheme. He said that many gentlemen of this kingdom, having of late destroyed their deer, he conceived that the want of venison might be well supplied by the bodies of young lads and maidens, not exceeding fourteen years of age, nor under twelve, so great a number of both sexes in every county being now ready to starve, for want of work and service: and these to be disposed of by their parents if alive, or otherwise by their nearest relations. But with due deference to so excellent a friend, and so deserving a patriot, I cannot be altogether in his sentiments. For as to the males, my American acquaintance assured me from frequent experience that their flesh was generally tough and lean, like that of our schoolboys, by continual exercise, and their taste disagreeable, and to fatten them would not answer the charge. Then as to the females, it would, I think with humble submission, be a loss to the public, because they soon would become breeders themselves: and besides, it is not improbable that some scrupulous people might be apt to

----

[5]*French physician*: François Rabelais (1494?–1553), a French physician and satirist who is known for his novel, *Gargantua and Pantagruel*. [Eds.]

[6]*shambles*: Slaughterhouses. [Eds.]

censure such a practice (although indeed very unjustly) as a little bordering upon cruelty, which I confess, hath always been with me the strongest objection against any project, howsoever well intended.

But in order to justify my friend, he confessed that this expedient was put into his head by the famous Psalmanazar, a native of the island Formosa, who came from thence to London, above twenty years ago, and in conversation told my friend that in his country when any young person happened to be put to death, the executioner sold the carcass to persons of quality, as a prime dainty, and that, in his time, the body of a plump girl of fifteen, who was crucified for an attempt to poison the emperor, was sold to his Imperial Majesty's Prime Minister of State, and other great Mandarins of the Court, in joints from the gibbet, at four hundred crowns. Neither indeed can I deny that if the same use were made of several plump young girls in this town who, without one single groat to their fortunes, cannot stir abroad without a chair, and appear at the playhouse and assemblies in foreign fineries, which they never will pay for, the kingdom would not be the worse.

Some persons of a desponding spirit are in great concern about that vast number of poor people, who are aged, diseased, or maimed, and I have been desired to employ my thoughts what course may be taken to ease the nation of so grievous an encumbrance. But I am not in the least pain upon that matter, because it is very well known that they are every day dying, and rotting, by cold, and famine, and filth, and vermin, as fast as can be reasonably expected. And as to the younger laborers they are now in almost as hopeful a condition. They cannot get work, and consequently pine away from want of nourishment, to a degree that if at any time they are accidentally hired to common labor, they have not strength to perform it; and thus the country and themselves are in a fair way of being soon delivered from the evils to come.

I have too long digressed, and therefore shall return to my subject. I   20 think the advantages by the proposal which I have made are obvious and many, as well as of the highest importance.

For first, as I have already observed, it would greatly lessen the number of Papists, with whom we are yearly over-run, being the principal breeders of the nation, as well as our most dangerous enemies, and who stay at home on purpose with a design to deliver the kingdom to the Pretender, hoping to take their advantage by the absence of so many good Protestants, who have chosen rather to leave their country than stay at home and pay tithes against their conscience to an idolatrous Episcopal curate.

Secondly, the poorer tenants will have something valuable of their own, which by law may be made liable to distress, and help to pay their landlord's rent, their corn and cattle being already seized, and money a thing unknown.

Thirdly, whereas the maintenance of an hundred thousand children, from two years old, and upwards, cannot be computed at less than ten shillings a piece *per annum*, the nation's stock will be thereby increased fifty thousand pounds *per annum*, besides the profit of a new dish, introduced to the tables of all gentlemen of fortune in the kingdom, who have any refinement in taste, and the money will circulate among ourselves, the goods being entirely of our own growth and manufacture.

Fourthly, the constant breeders, besides the gain of eight shillings sterling *per annum*, by the sale of their children, will be rid of the charge of maintaining them after the first year.

Fifthly, this food would likewise bring great custom to taverns, where   25
the vintners will certainly be so prudent as to procure the best receipts for dressing it to perfection, and consequently have their houses frequented by all the fine gentlemen, who justly value themselves upon their knowledge in good eating; and a skillful cook, who understands how to oblige his guests, will contrive to make it as expensive as they please.

Sixthly, this would be a great inducement to marriage, which all wise nations have either encouraged by rewards, or enforced by laws and penalties. It would increase the care and tenderness of mothers towards their children, when they were sure of a settlement for life, to the poor babes, provided in some sort by the public to their annual profit instead of expense. We should soon see an honest emulation among the married women, which of them could bring the fattest child to the market. Men would become as fond of their wives, during the time of their pregnancy, as they are now of their mares in foal, their cows in calf, or sows when they are ready to farrow, nor offer to beat or kick them (as it is too frequent a practice) for fear of a miscarriage.

Many other advantages might be enumerated. For instance, the addition of some thousand carcasses in our exportation of barreled beef; the propagation of swine's flesh, and improvement in the art of making good bacon, so much wanted among us by the great destruction of pigs, too frequent at our tables, are no way comparable in taste or magnificence to a well-grown, fat yearling child, which roasted whole will make a considerable figure at a Lord Mayor's feast, or any other public entertainment. But this and many others I omit, being studious of brevity.

Supposing that one thousand families in this city would be constant customers for infants' flesh, besides others who might have it at merry meetings, particularly weddings and christenings; I compute that Dublin would take off annually about twenty thousand carcasses, and the rest of the kingdom (where probably they will be sold somewhat cheaper) the remaining eighty thousand.

I can think of no one objection that will possibly be raised against this proposal, unless it should be urged that the number of people will be thereby much lessened in the kingdom. This I freely own, and it was indeed one principal design in offering it to the world. I desire the reader will observe, that I calculate my remedy *for this one individual Kingdom of* Ireland, *and for no other that ever was, is, or, I think, ever can be upon earth.* Therefore let no man talk to me of other expedients: *Of taxing our absentees at five shillings a pound: Of using neither clothes, nor household furniture, except what is of our own growth and manufacture: Of utterly rejecting the materials and instruments that promote foreign luxury: Of curing the expensiveness of pride, vanity, idleness, and gaming in our women: Of introducing a vein of parsimony, prudence, and temperance: Of learning to love our country, wherein we differ even from* Laplanders, *and the inhabitants of* Topinamboo: *Of quitting our animosities and factions, nor act any longer like the* Jews, *who were murdering one another at the very moment their city was taken: Of being a little cautious not to sell our country and consciences for nothing: Of teaching landlords to have at least one degree of mercy towards their tenants.* Lastly, *of putting a spirit of honesty, industry, and skill into our shopkeepers, who, if a resolution could now be taken to buy only our native goods, would immediately unite to cheat and exact upon us in the price, the measure and the goodness, nor could ever yet be brought to make one fair proposal of just dealing, though often and earnestly invited to it.*

Therefore I repeat, let no man talk to me of these and the like expedients, till he hath at least a glimpse of hope that there will ever be some hearty and sincere attempt to put them in practice.   30

But as to myself, having been wearied out for many years with offering vain, idle, visionary thoughts, and at length utterly despairing of success, I fortunately fell upon this proposal, which as it is wholly new, so it hath something solid and real, of no expense and little trouble, full in our own power, and whereby we can incur no danger in disobliging England. For this kind of commodity will not bear exportation, the flesh being of too tender a consistence to admit a long continuance in salt, *although perhaps I could name a country which would be glad to eat up our whole nation without it.*

After all I am not so violently bent upon my own opinion as to reject any offer, proposed by wise men, which shall be found equally innocent, cheap, easy and effectual. But before some thing of that kind shall be advanced in contradiction to my scheme, and offering a better, I desire the author, or authors, will be pleased maturely to consider two points. First, as things now stand, how they will be able to find food and raiment for an hundred thousand useless mouths and backs? And secondly, there being a round million of creatures in human figure, throughout this kingdom, whose whole subsistence put into a common stock would leave them in debt two millions of pounds sterling; adding those who are beggars by profession, to the bulk of farmers, cottagers, and laborers with their wives and children, who are beggars in effect; I desire those politicians who dislike my overture, and may perhaps be so bold to attempt an answer, that they will first ask the parents of these mortals whether they would not at this day think it a great happiness to have been sold for food at a year old, in the manner I prescribe, and thereby have avoided such a perpetual scene of misfortunes as they have since gone through, by the oppression of landlords, the impossibility of paying rent without money or trade, the want of common sustenance, with neither house nor clothes to cover them from the inclemencies of weather, and the most inevitable prospect of entailing the like, or greater miseries upon their breed for ever.

I profess in the sincerity of my heart that I have not the least personal interest in endeavoring to promote this necessary work, having no other motive than the *public good of my country, by advancing our trade, providing for infants, relieving the poor, and giving some pleasure to the rich.* I have no children by which I can propose to get a single penny; the youngest being nine years old, and my wife past child-bearing.

QUESTIONS

Reading

1. A proposal always involves a proposer. What is the character of the proposer here? How do we distinguish between the author and the proposer? What details of style help us make this distinction?
2. When does the proposer actually offer his proposal? What does he do before making his proposal, and what does he do after? How does the order in which he does things affect our impression of both him and his proposal?
3. List the counterarguments to his own proposal that the proposer anticipates. How does he answer and refute proposals that might be considered alternatives to his?
4. It will (hopefully) be evident to most readers that this proposal is *ironic*. Identify several specific places where the author uses words, phrases, or details to highlight the ironic humor of not only the proposal's content but the proposer's tone. Underline, highlight, or flag these instances and be prepared to discuss them in class.

Exploratory Writing

1. To what extent does an ironic essay like this depend on shared values being held by the author and readers without question or exception? In groups, list and discuss several popularly upheld historical positions that now seem to be just as outrageous and absurd as this "modest proposal." (Examples might include burning witches at the stake, executing people for claiming that the earth was round, or denying adults the right to vote and own property because of their race.)
2. *Reductio ad absurdum* is a type of argument in which, in order to disprove a proposition, a writer assumes that very proposition and then shows that it leads to absurd or impossible conclusions. Using this strategy, choose a position in a popular legal debate, and write your own "modest proposal" on its behalf.

Making Connections

1. Steven Pinker (p. 427) argues that there are many issues for which we, as a society, are "too quick to hit the morality button and look for villains" rather than actually fix the problems. "Our habit of moralizing

problems . . . can get in the way of doing the right thing." Choose an argument from Pinker's essay, such as his comments on human-induced climate change (paragraph 77), and discuss ways it is similar to, or different from, the argument in "A Modest Proposal."

Essay Writing

1. Write an essay explaining what you see as advantages and disadvantages of using irony in a written argument.

Regarding the Pain of Others

Susan Sontag

One of America's leading social commentators, Susan Sontag (1933–2004) was hailed as a brilliant critic and provocative thinker. Raised in Arizona and California, she studied at a number of universities, among them the University of Chicago, Harvard, and Oxford. When her formal schooling finished, she began writing essays for such journals as the New Yorker *and the* New York Review of Books. *Beginning in 1964 with "Notes on Camp" — an influential essay on the avant-garde — her work was both widely discussed and well received. She published two groundbreaking collections of essays on culture and politics in the 1960s:* Against Interpretation *(1966) and* Styles of Radical Will *(1969). Over the next several decades, she continued to explore a wide range of cultural phenomena, from illness to art. In later years, she published work in other genres, including a best-selling historical novel,* The Volcano Lover *(1992). The following piece is taken from* Regarding the Pain of Others *(2003), a book on war imagery in which the author decried the birth of a "culture of spectatorship," arguing that it "neutralized the moral force of photographs of atrocities." Sontag's many honors and awards included membership in the American Academy of Arts and Sciences, a MacArthur Fellowship, and a National Book Award.*

To catch a death actually happening and embalm it for all time is something only cameras can do, and pictures taken by photographers out in the field of the moment of (or just before) death are among the most celebrated and often reproduced of war photographs. There can be no suspicion about the authenticity of what is being shown in the picture taken by Eddie Adams in February 1968 of the chief of the South Vietnamese national police, Brigadier General Nguyen Ngoc Loan, shooting a Vietcong suspect in a street in Saigon. Nevertheless, it was staged — by General Loan, who had led the prisoner, hands tied behind his back, out to the street where journalists had gathered; he would not have carried out the summary execution there had they not been available to witness it. Positioned beside his prisoner so that his profile and the prisoner's face were visible to the cameras behind him, Loan aimed point-blank. Adams's picture shows the moment the bullet has been fired; the dead man, grimacing, has not started to fall. As for the viewer, this viewer, even many years after the picture was taken . . . well, one can gaze at these faces for a long time and not come to the end of the mystery, and the indecency, of such co-spectatorship.

More upsetting is the opportunity to look at people who know they have been condemned to die: the cache of six thousand photographs taken between 1975 and 1979 at a secret prison in a former high school in Tuol Sleng, a suburb of Phnom Penh, the killing house of more than fourteen thousand Cambodians charged with being either "intellectuals" or "counter-revolutionaries" — the documentation of this atrocity courtesy of the Khmer Rouge record keepers, who had each sit for a photograph just before being executed.* A selection of these pictures in a book titled *The Killing Fields* makes it possible, decades later, to stare back at the faces staring into the camera — therefore at us. The Spanish Republican soldier has just died, if we may believe the claim made for that picture, which Capa took at some distance from his subject: we see no more than a grainy figure, a body and head, an energy, swerving from the camera as he falls. These Cambodian women and men of all ages, including many children, photographed from a few feet away, usually in half figure, are — as in Titian's *The Flaying of Marsyas*, where Apollo's knife is eternally about to descend — forever looking at death, forever about to be murdered, forever wronged. And the viewer is in the same position as the lackey behind the camera; the experience is sickening. The prison photographer's name is known — Nhem Ein — and can be cited. Those he photographed, with their stunned faces, their emaciated torsos, the number tags pinned to the top of their shirts, remain an aggregate: anonymous victims.

And even if named, unlikely to be known to "us." When Woolf notes that one of the photographs she has been sent shows a corpse of a man or woman so mangled that it could as well be that of a dead pig, her point is that the scale of war's murderousness destroys what identifies people as individuals, even as human beings.[1] This, of course, is how war looks when it is seen from afar, as an image.

Victims, grieving relatives, consumers of news — all have their own nearness to or distance from war. The frankest representations of war, and of disaster-injured bodies, are of those who seem most foreign, therefore least likely to be known. With subjects closer to home, the photographer is expected to be more discreet.

When, in October 1862, a month after the battle of Antietam, photographs taken by Gardner and O'Sullivan were exhibited at Brady's Manhattan gallery, the *New York Times* commented: 5

> The living that throng Broadway care little perhaps for the Dead at Antietam, but we fancy they would jostle less carelessly down the

---

*Photographing political prisoners and alleged counter-revolutionaries just before their execution was also standard practice in the Soviet Union in the 1930s and 1940s, as recent research into the NKVD files in the Baltic and Ukrainian archives, as well as the central Lubyanka archives, has disclosed. [Au.]

[1] *Virginia Woolf* (1882–1941): English novelist and essayist, who reflected on the roots of war in her book *Three Guineas*. [Eds.]

great thoroughfare, saunter less at their ease, were a few dripping bodies, fresh from the field, laid along the pavement. There would be a gathering up of skirts and a careful picking of way . . .

Concurring in the perennial charge that those whom war spares are callously indifferent to the sufferings beyond their purview did not make the reporter less ambivalent about the immediacy of the photograph.

> The dead of the battlefield come to us very rarely even in dreams. We see the list in the morning paper at breakfast but dismiss its recollection with the coffee. But Mr. Brady has done something to bring home to us the terrible reality and earnestness of war. If he has not brought bodies and laid them in our dooryards and along the streets, he has done something very like it. . . . These pictures have a terrible distinctness. By the aid of the magnifying-glass, the very features of the slain may be distinguished. We would scarce choose to be in the gallery, when one of the women bending over them should recognize a husband, a son, or a brother in the still, lifeless lines of bodies, that lie ready for the gaping trenches.

Admiration is mixed with disapproval of the pictures for the pain they might give the female relatives of the dead. The camera brings the viewer close, too close; supplemented by a magnifying glass — for this is a double-lens story — the "terrible distinctness" of the pictures gives unnecessary, indecent information. Yet the *Times* reporter cannot resist the melodrama that mere words supply (the "dripping bodies" ready for "the gaping trenches"), while reprehending the intolerable realism of the image.

New demands are made on reality in the era of cameras. The real thing may not be fearsome enough, and therefore needs to be enhanced; or reenacted more convincingly. Thus, the first newsreel ever made of a battle — a much-publicized incident in Cuba during the Spanish-American War of 1898 known as the Battle of San Juan Hill — in fact shows a charge staged shortly afterward by Colonel Theodore Roosevelt and his volunteer cavalry unit, the Rough Riders, for the Vitagraph cameramen, the actual charge up the hill, after it was filmed, having been judged insufficiently dramatic. Or the images may be too terrible, and need to be suppressed in the name of propriety or of patriotism — like the images showing, without appropriate partial concealment, our dead. To display the dead, after all, is what the enemy does. In the Boer War (1899–1902), after their victory at Spion Kop in January 1900, the Boers thought it would be morale-building for their own troops to circulate a horrifying picture of dead British soldiers. Taken by an unknown Boer photographer ten days after the British defeat, which had cost the lives of thirteen hundred of their soldiers, it gives an intrusive view down a long shallow trench packed with unburied bodies. What is particularly aggressive about the image is the absence of a landscape. The trench's receding jumble of bodies fills the whole picture space. British indignation upon hearing of this latest Boer outrage was keen, if stiffly expressed: to have made public such pictures, declared *Amateur Photographer*, "serves no useful purpose and appeals to the morbid side of human nature solely."

There had always been censorship, but for a long time it remained desultory, at the pleasure of generals and heads of state. The first organized ban on press photography at the front came during the First World War; both the German and French high commands allowed only a few selected military photographers near the fighting. (Censorship of the press by the British General Staff was less inflexible.) And it took another fifty years, and the relaxation of censorship with the first televised war coverage, to understand what impact shocking photographs could have on the domestic public. During the Vietnam era, war photography became, normatively, a criticism of war. This was bound to have consequences: mainstream media are not in the business of making people feel queasy about the struggles for which they are being mobilized, much less of disseminating propaganda against waging war.

Since then, censorship — the most extensive kind, self-censorship, as well as censorship imposed by the military — has found a large and influential number of apologists. At the start of the British campaign in the Falklands in April 1982, the government of Margaret Thatcher granted access to only two photojournalists — among those refused was a master war photographer, Don McCullin — and only three batches of film reached London before the islands were recaptured in May. No direct television transmission was permitted. There had not been such drastic restrictions on the reporting of a British military operation since the Crimean War. It proved harder for the American authorities to duplicate the Thatcher controls on the reporting of their own foreign adventures. What the American military promoted during the Gulf War in 1991 were images of the techno war: the sky above the dying, filled with light-traces of missiles and shells — images that illustrated America's absolute military superiority over its enemy. American television viewers weren't allowed to see footage acquired by NBC (which the network then declined to run) of what that superiority could wreak: the fate of thousands of Iraqi conscripts who, having fled Kuwait City at the end of the war, on February 27, were carpet bombed with explosives, napalm, radioactive DU (depleted uranium) rounds, and cluster bombs as they headed north, in convoys and on foot, on the road to Basra, Iraq — a slaughter notoriously described by one American officer as a "turkey shoot." And most American operations in Afghanistan in late 2001 were off-limits to news photographers.

The terms for allowing the use of cameras at the front for nonmilitary purposes have become much stricter as war has become an activity prosecuted with increasingly exact optical devices for tracking the enemy. There is no war without photography, that notable aesthete of war Ernst Jünger observed in 1930, thereby refining the irrepressible identification of the camera and the gun, "shooting" a subject and shooting a human being. War-making and picture-taking are congruent activities: "It is the same intelligence, whose weapons of annihilation can locate the enemy to the exact second and meter," wrote Jünger, "that labors to preserve the great historical event in fine detail."*

The preferred current American way of war-making has expanded on   10 this model. Television, whose access to the scene is limited by government controls and by self-censorship, serves up the war as images. The war itself is waged as much as possible at a distance, through bombing, whose targets can be chosen, on the basis of instantly relayed information and visualizing technology, from continents away: the daily bombing operations in Afghanistan in late 2001 and early 2002 were directed from U.S. Central Command in Tampa, Florida. The aim is to produce a sufficiently punishing number of casualties on the other side while minimizing opportunities for the enemy to inflict any casualties at all; American and allied soldiers who die in vehicle accidents or from "friendly fire" (as the euphemism has it) both count and don't count.

In the era of tele-controlled warfare against innumerable enemies of American power, policies about what is to be seen and not seen by the public are still being worked out. Television news producers and newspaper and magazine photo editors make decisions every day which firm up the wavering consensus about the boundaries of public knowledge. Often their decisions are cast as judgments about "good taste" — always a repressive standard when invoked by institutions. Staying within the bounds of good taste was the primary reason given for not showing any of the horrific pictures of the dead taken at the site of the World Trade Center in the immediate aftermath of the attack on September 11, 2001. (Tabloids are usually bolder than broadsheet papers in printing grisly images; a picture of a severed hand lying in the rubble of the World Trade Center ran in one late edition of New York's *Daily News* shortly after the attack; it seems not to have appeared in any other paper.) And television news, with its much larger audience and therefore greater responsiveness to pressures from advertisers, operates under even stricter, for the most part self-policed constraints on what is "proper" to air. This novel insistence on good taste in a culture saturated with commercial incentives to lower standards of taste may be puzzling. But it makes sense if understood as obscuring a host of concerns and

---

*Thus, thirteen years before the destruction of Guernica, Arthur Harris, later the chief of Bombing Command in the Royal Air Force during the Second World War, then a young RAF squadron leader in Iraq, described the air campaign to crush the rebellious natives in this newly acquired British colony, complete with photographic proof of the success of the mission. "The Arab and the Kurd," he wrote in 1924, "now know what real bombing means in casualties and damage; they now know that within forty-five minutes a full-sized village (vide attached photos of Kushan-Al-Ajaza) can be practically wiped out and a third of its inhabitants killed by four or five machines which offer them no real target, no opportunity for glory as warriors, no effective means of escape." [Au.]

anxieties about public order and public morale that cannot be named, as well as pointing to the inability otherwise to formulate or defend traditional conventions of how to mourn. What can be shown, what should not be shown — few issues arouse more public clamor.

The other argument often used to suppress pictures cites the rights of relatives. When a weekly newspaper in Boston briefly posted online a propaganda video made in Pakistan that showed the "confession" (that he was Jewish) and subsequent ritual slaughter of the kidnapped American journalist Daniel Pearl in Karachi in early 2002, a vehement debate took place in which the right of Pearl's widow to be spared more pain was pitted against the newspaper's right to print and post what it saw fit and the public's right to see. The video was quickly taken off-line. Notably, both sides treated the three and a half minutes of horror only as a snuff film. Nobody could have learned from the debate that the video had other footage, a montage of stock accusations (for instance, images of Ariel Sharon sitting with George W. Bush at the White House, Palestinian children killed in Israeli attacks), that it was a political diatribe and ended with dire threats and a list of specific demands — all of which might suggest that it was worth suffering through (if you could bear it) to confront better the particular viciousness and intransigence of the forces that murdered Pearl. It is easier to think of the enemy as just a savage who kills, then holds up the head of his prey for all to see.

With our dead, there has always been a powerful interdiction against showing the naked face. The photographs taken by Gardner and O'Sullivan still shock because the Union and Confederate soldiers lie on their backs, with the faces of some clearly visible. American soldiers fallen on the battlefield were not shown again in a major publication for many wars, not, indeed, until the taboo-shattering picture by George Strock that *Life* published in September 1943 — it had initially been withheld by the military censors — of three soldiers killed on the beach during a landing in New Guinea. (Though "Dead GIs on Buna Beach" is invariably described as showing three soldiers lying face down in the wet sand, one of the three lies on his back, but the angle from which the picture was taken conceals his head.) By the time of the landing in France — June 6, 1944 — photographs of anonymous American casualties had appeared in a number of newsmagazines, always prone or shrouded or with their faces turned away. This is a dignity not thought necessary to accord to others.

The more remote or exotic the place, the more likely we are to have full frontal views of the dead and dying. Thus postcolonial Africa exists in the consciousness of the general public in the rich world — besides through its sexy music — mainly as a succession of unforgettable photographs of large-eyed victims, starting with figures in the famine lands of Biafra in the late 1960s to the survivors of the genocide of nearly a million Rwandan Tutsis in 1994 and, a few years later, the children and adults whose limbs were hacked off during the program of mass terror conducted by the RUF, the rebel forces in Sierra Leone. (More recently, the photographs are of whole families of indigent villagers dying of AIDS.) These sights carry a double message. They show a suffering that is outrageous, unjust, and should be repaired. They confirm that this is the sort of thing which happens in that place. The ubiquity of those photographs, and those horrors, cannot help but nourish belief in the inevitability of tragedy in the benighted or backward — that is, poor — parts of the world.

Comparable cruelties and misfortunes used to take place in Europe, too; cruelties that surpass in volume and luridness anything we might be shown now from the poor parts of the world occurred in Europe only sixty years ago. But horror seems to have vacated Europe, vacated it for long enough to make the present pacified state of affairs seem inevitable. (That there could be death camps and a siege and civilians slaughtered by the thousands and thrown into mass graves on European soil fifty years after the end of the Second World War gave the war in Bosnia and the Serb campaign of killing in Kosovo their special, anachronistic interest. But one of the main ways of understanding the war crimes committed in southeastern Europe in the 1990s has been to say that the Balkans, after all, were never really part of Europe.) Generally, the grievously injured bodies shown in published photographs are from Asia or Africa. This journalistic custom inherits the centuries-old practice of exhibiting exotic — that is, colonized — human beings: Africans and denizens of remote Asian countries were displayed like zoo animals in ethnological exhibitions mounted in London, Paris, and other European capitals from the sixteenth until the early twentieth century. In *The Tempest*, Trinculo's first thought upon coming across Caliban is that he could be put on exhibit in England: "[N]ot a holiday fool there but would give it piece of silver. . . . When they will not give a doit to relieve a lame beggar, they will lay out ten to see a dead Indian." The exhibition in photographs of cruelties inflicted on those with darker complexions in exotic countries continues this offering, oblivious to the considerations that deter such displays of our own victims of violence; for the other, even when not an enemy, is regarded only as someone to be seen, not someone (like us) who also sees. But surely the wounded Taliban soldier begging for his life whose fate was pictured prominently in the *New York Times* also had a wife, children, parents, sisters and brothers, some of whom may one day come across the three color photographs of their husband, father, son, brother being slaughtered — if they have not already seen them.

QUESTIONS

Reading

1. How does Sontag characterize the role of television in the "preferred current American way of war-making" (paragraph 10)?

2. What are two commonly used arguments in favor of suppressing the publication of images of the dead? Summarize Sontag's criticisms of these arguments.
3. What is the main purpose of Sontag's essay? Do you find her argument persuasive? Why or why not?

Exploratory Writing

1. Only cameras, according to Sontag, can "catch a death actually happening and embalm it for all time" (paragraph 1). Do you agree with this statement, or do you think that written words can "catch," or capture, an event just as persuasively as a photograph?
2. Sontag points out the irony of one reporter's use of sensationalistic phrases ("'dripping bodies' ready for 'the gaping trenches'") within a condemnation of graphic images (paragraph 5). Make a double-entry list comparing the "shock value" of photographs versus that of the written word. Use a separate sheet of paper if you need more room.

PHOTOGRAPHS	WRITING

3. "New demands are made on reality in the era of cameras," Sontag states. "The real thing may not be fearsome enough and therefore needs to be enhanced, or reenacted more convincingly" (paragraph 6). She discusses how images can be manipulated or staged to intensify the drama of war events, or suppressed to downplay their importance. List examples, outside of a war context, of ways that images are regularly manipulated and altered for effect.
4. Split up into teams, and stage a debate on the subject of whether American newspapers should be allowed to publish photographs of people who have been (or are being) killed in war. Your team should use at least three well-crafted arguments to make your case.

Making Connections

1. George Orwell ("Politics and the English Language," p. 97) talks about how language can be used in political writing for the purposes of distortion and obfuscation. Drawing on Orwell's examples as well as Sontag's, discuss differences between using manipulative language in war reporting and publishing manipulated images.

Essay Writing

1. Consider Sontag's remarks on the "double message" carried by photographs of dead and dying people in "exotic" places (paragraph 14). Using online newspaper archives, find three articles with photographs from the past two years documenting catastrophic events, war, or atrocities in Africa, Asia, or Latin America. How does each article support or refute Sontag's thesis?
2. Write an essay describing a photograph that had a great personal impact on your life and beliefs. What was so powerful about this image?

Shooting an Elephant

George Orwell

*George Orwell (1903–1950) was the pen name of Eric Blair,
the son of a British customs officer stationed in Bengal, India.
As a boy, Blair was sent home to prestigious English schools,
where he learned to dislike the rich and powerful. After finishing
preparatory school at Eton College, he returned to Asia to serve
as an officer of the British police in India and Burma, where he
became disillusioned with imperialism. He later studied conditions
among the urban poor and the coal miners of Wigan, a city in
northwestern England, which strengthened his socialist beliefs.
He was wounded in the Spanish civil war, defending the lost cause
of the left against the fascists. Under the name Orwell, he wrote
accounts of all of these experiences as well as the anti-Stalinist
fable* Animal Farm *(1945) and the novel* 1984 *(1949). In the
following essay, first published in 1936, Orwell attacks the
politics of imperialism.*

In Moulmein, in Lower Burma, I was hated by large numbers of
people — the only time in my life that I have been important enough for this
to happen to me. I was sub-divisional police officer of the town, and in an
aimless, petty kind of way anti-European feeling was very bitter. No one had
the guts to raise a riot, but if a European woman went through the bazaars
alone somebody would probably spit betel juice over her dress. As a police
officer I was an obvious target and was baited whenever it seemed safe to do
so. When a nimble Burman tripped me up on the football field and the ref-
eree (another Burman) looked the other way, the crowd yelled with hideous
laughter. This happened more than once. In the end the sneering yellow
faces of young men that met me everywhere, the insults hooted after me
when I was at a safe distance, got badly on my nerves. The young Buddhist
priests were the worst of all. There were several thousands of them in the
town and none of them seemed to have anything to do except stand on
street corners and jeer at Europeans.

All this was perplexing and upsetting. For at that time I had already made up my mind that imperialism was an evil thing and the sooner I chucked up my job and got out of it the better. Theoretically — and secretly, of course — I was all for the Burmese and all against their oppressors, the British. As for the job I was doing, I hated it more bitterly than I can perhaps make clear. In a job like that you see the dirty work of Empire at close quarters. The wretched prisoners huddling in the stinking cages of the lock-ups, the grey, cowed faces of the long-term convicts, the scarred buttocks of the men who had been flogged with bamboos — all these oppressed me with an intolerable sense of guilt. But I could get nothing into perspective. I was young and ill-educated and I had had to think out my problems in the utter silence that is imposed on every Englishman in the East. I did not even know that the British Empire is dying, still less did I know that it is a great deal better than the younger empires that are going to supplant it. All I knew was that I was stuck between my hatred of the empire I served and my rage against the evil-spirited little beasts who tried to make my job impossible. With one part of my mind I thought of the British Raj[1] as an unbreakable tyranny, as something clamped down, in *saecula saeculorum*,[2] upon the will of prostrate peoples; with another part I thought that the greatest joy in the world would be to drive a bayonet into a Buddhist priest's guts. Feelings like these are the normal by-product of imperialism; ask any Anglo-Indian official, if you can catch him off duty.

One day something happened which in a roundabout way was enlightening. It was a tiny incident in itself, but it gave me a better glimpse than I had had before of the real nature of imperialism — the real motives for which despotic governments act. Early one morning the sub-inspector at a police station at the other end of the town rang me up on the phone and said that an elephant was ravaging the bazaar. Would I please come and do something about it? I did not know what I could do, but I wanted to see what was happening and I got on to a pony and started out. I took my rifle, an old .44 Winchester and much too small to kill an elephant, but I thought the noise might be useful *in terrorem*.[3] Various Burmans stopped me on the way and told me about the elephant's doings. It was not, of course, a wild elephant, but a tame one which had gone "must."[4] It had been chained up, as tame elephants always are when their attack of "must" is due, but on the previous night it had broken its chain and escaped. Its mahout,[5] the only person who could manage it when it was in that state, had set out in pursuit, but had taken the wrong direction and was now twelve hours' journey

---

[1]*British Raj*: British rule in India and Burma. [Eds.]

[2]*saecula saeculorum*: Forever and ever. [Eds.]

[3]*in terrorem*: For fright. [Eds.]

[4]*"must"*: The frenzied state of the bull elephant in sexual excitement. [Eds.]

[5]*mahout*: An elephant's keeper. [Eds.]

away, and in the morning the elephant had suddenly reappeared in town. The Burmese population had no weapons and were quite helpless against it. It had already destroyed somebody's bamboo hut, killed a cow and raided some fruit-stalls and devoured the stock; also it had met the municipal rubbish van and, when the driver jumped out and took to his heels, had turned the van over and inflicted violences upon it.

The Burmese sub-inspector and some Indian constables were waiting for me in the quarter where the elephant had been seen. It was a very poor quarter, a labyrinth of squalid bamboo huts, thatched with palm-leaf, winding all over a steep hillside. I remember that it was a cloudy, stuffy morning at the beginning of the rains. We began questioning the people as to where the elephant had gone and, as usual, failed to get any definite information. That is invariably the case in the East; a story always sounds clear enough at a distance, but the nearer you get to the scene of events the vaguer it becomes. Some of the people said that the elephant had gone in one direction, some said that he had gone in another, some professed not even to have heard of any elephant. I had almost made up my mind that the whole story was a pack of lies, when we heard yells a little distance away. There was a loud, scandalized cry of "Go away, child! Go away this instant!" and an old woman with a switch in her hand came round the corner of a hut, violently shooing away a crowd of naked children. Some more women followed, clicking their tongues and exclaiming; evidently there was something that the children ought not to have seen. I rounded the hut and saw a man's dead body sprawling in the mud. He was an Indian, a black Dravidian coolie,[6] almost naked, and he could not have been dead many minutes. The people said that the elephant had come suddenly upon him round the corner of the hut, caught him with its trunk, put its foot on his back and ground him into the earth. This was the rainy season and the ground was soft, and his face had scored a trench a foot deep and a couple of yards long. He was lying on his belly with arms crucified and head sharply twisted to one side. His face was coated with mud, the eyes wide open, the teeth bared and grinning with an expression of unendurable agony. (Never tell me, by the way, that the dead look peaceful. Most of the corpses I have seen looked devilish.) The friction of the great beast's foot had stripped the skin from his back as neatly as one skins a rabbit. As soon as I saw the dead man I sent an orderly to a friend's house nearby to borrow an elephant rifle. I had already sent back the pony, not wanting it to go mad with fright and throw me if it smelt the elephant.

The orderly came back in a few minutes with a rifle and five cartridges, and meanwhile some Burmans had arrived and told us that the elephant was in the paddy fields below, only a few hundred yards away. As I started

5

---

[6]*Dravidian coolie: Dravidian* refers to a large ethnic group from south and central India. A *coolie* is an unskilled laborer. [Eds.]

forward practically the whole population of the quarter flocked out of the houses and followed me. They had seen the rifle and were all shouting excitedly that I was going to shoot the elephant. They had not shown much interest in the elephant when he was merely ravaging their homes, but it was different now that he was to be shot. It was a bit of fun to them, as it would be to an English crowd; besides they wanted the meat. It made me vaguely uneasy. I had no intention of shooting the elephant — I had merely sent for the rifle to defend myself if necessary — and it is always unnerving to have a crowd following you. I marched down the hill, looking and feeling a fool, with the rifle over my shoulder and an ever-growing army of people jostling at my heels. At the bottom, when you got away from the huts, there was a metalled road and beyond that a miry waste of paddy fields a thousand yards across, not yet ploughed but soggy from the first rains and dotted with coarse grass. The elephant was standing eight yards from the road, his left side towards us. He took not the slightest notice of the crowd's approach. He was tearing up bunches of grass, beating them against his knees to clean them and stuffing them into his mouth.

I had halted on the road. As soon as I saw the elephant I knew with perfect certainty that I ought not to shoot him. It is a serious matter to shoot a working elephant — it is comparable to destroying a huge and costly piece of machinery — and obviously one ought not to do it if it can possibly be avoided. And at that distance, peacefully eating, the elephant looked no more dangerous than a cow. I thought then and I think now that his attack of "must" was already passing off; in which case he would merely wander harmlessly about until the mahout came back and caught him. Moreover, I did not in the least want to shoot him. I decided that I would watch him for a little while to make sure that he did not turn savage again, and then go home.

But at that moment I glanced around at the crowd that had followed me. It was an immense crowd, two thousand at the least and growing every minute. It blocked the road for a long distance on either side. I looked at the sea of yellow faces above the garish clothes — faces all happy and excited all over this bit of fun, all certain that the elephant was going to be shot. They were watching me as they would watch a conjurer about to perform a trick. They did not like me, but with the magical rifle in my hands I was momentarily worth watching. And suddenly I realized that I should have to shoot the elephant after all. The people expected it of me and I had got to do it; I could feel their two thousand wills pressing me forward, irresistibly. And it was at this moment, as I stood there with the rifle in my hands, that I first grasped the hollowness, the futility of the white man's dominion in the East. Here was I, the white man with his gun, standing in front of the unarmed native crowd — seemingly the leading actor of the piece; but in reality I was only an absurd puppet pushed to and fro by the will of those yellow faces behind. I perceived in this moment that when the white man turns tyrant it is his own freedom that he destroys. He becomes a sort of hollow, posing dummy, the conventionalized figure of a sahib. For it is the condition of his rule that he shall spend his life in trying to impress the "natives," and so in every crisis he has got to do what the "natives" expect of him. He wears a mask, and his face grows to fit it. I had got to shoot the elephant. I had committed myself to doing it when I sent for the rifle. A sahib has got to act like a sahib; he has got to appear resolute, to know his own mind and do definite things. To come all that way, rifle in hand, with two thousand people marching at my heels, and then to trail feebly away, having done nothing — no, that was impossible. The crowd would laugh at me. And my whole life, every white man's life in the East, was one long struggle not to be laughed at.

But I did not want to shoot the elephant. I watched him beating his bunch of grass against his knees, with that preoccupied grandmotherly air that elephants have. It seemed to me that it would be murder to shoot him. At that age I was not squeamish about killing animals, but I had never shot an elephant and never wanted to. (Somehow it always seems worse to kill a *large* animal.) Besides, there was the beast's owner to be considered. Alive, the elephant was worth at least a hundred pounds; dead, he would only be worth the value of his tusks, five pounds, possibly. But I had got to act quickly. I turned to some experienced-looking Burmans who had been there when we arrived, and asked them how the elephant had been behaving. They all said the same thing: he took no notice of you if you left him alone, but he might charge if you went too close to him.

It was perfectly clear to me what I ought to do. I ought to walk up to within, say, twenty-five yards of the elephant and test his behavior. If he charged, I could shoot; if he took no notice of me, it would be safe to leave him until the mahout came back. But also I knew that I was going to do no such thing. I was a poor shot with a rifle and the ground was soft mud into which one would sink at every step. If the elephant charged and I missed him, I should have about as much chance as a toad under a steam-roller. But even then I was not thinking particularly of my own skin, only of the watchful yellow faces behind. For at the moment, with the crowd watching me, I was not afraid in the ordinary sense, as I would have been if I had been alone. A white man mustn't be frightened in front of "natives"; and so, in general, he isn't frightened. The sole thought in my mind was that if anything went wrong those two thousand Burmans would see me pursued, caught, trampled on and reduced to a grinning corpse like that Indian up the hill. And if that happened it was quite probable that some of them would laugh. That would never do. There was only one alternative. I shoved the cartridges into the magazine and lay down on the road to get a better aim.

The crowd grew very still, and a deep, low, happy sigh, as of people who   10
see the theatre curtain go up at last, breathed from innumerable throats. They were going to have their bit of fun after all. The rifle was a beautiful German thing with cross-hair sights. I did not then know that in shooting an elephant one would shoot to cut an imaginary bar running from ear-hole to

ear-hole. I ought, therefore, as the elephant was sideways on, to have aimed straight at his ear-hole; actually I aimed several inches in front of this, thinking the brain would be further forward.

When I pulled the trigger I did not hear the bang or feel the kick — one never does when a shot goes home — but I heard the devilish roar of glee that went up from the crowd. In that instant, in too short a time, one would have thought, even for the bullet to get there, a mysterious, terrible change had come over the elephant. He neither stirred nor fell, but every line of his body had altered. He looked suddenly stricken, shrunken, immensely old, as though the frightful impact of the bullet had paralyzed him without knocking him down. At last, after what seemed a long time — it might have been five seconds, I dare say — he sagged flabbily to his knees. His mouth slobbered. An enormous senility seemed to have settled upon him. One could have imagined him thousands of years old. I fired again into the same spot. At the second shot he did not collapse but climbed with desperate slowness to his feet and stood weakly upright, with legs sagging and head drooping. I fired a third time. That was the shot that did for him. You could see the agony of it jolt his whole body and knock the last remnant of strength from his legs. But in falling he seemed for a moment to rise, for as his hind legs collapsed beneath him he seemed to tower upward like a huge rock toppling, his trunk reaching skywards like a tree. He trumpeted, for the first and only time. And then down he came, his belly towards me, with a crash that seemed to shake the ground even where I lay.

I got up. The Burmans were already racing past me across the mud. It was obvious that the elephant would never rise again, but he was not dead. He was breathing very rhythmically with long rattling gasps, his great mound of a side painfully rising and falling. His mouth was wide open — I could see far down into caverns of pale pink throat. I waited for a long time for him to die, but his breathing did not weaken. Finally I fired my two remaining shots into the spot where I thought his heart must be. The thick blood welled out of him like red velvet, but still he did not die. His body did not even jerk when the shots hit him, the tortured breathing continued without a pause. He was dying, very slowly and in great agony, but in some world remote from me where not even a bullet could damage him further. I felt that I had got to put an end to that dreadful noise. It seemed dreadful to see the great beast lying there, powerless to move and yet powerless to die, and not even to be able to finish him. I sent back for my small rifle and poured shot after shot into his heart and down his throat. They seemed to make no impression. The tortured gasps continued as steadily as the ticking of a clock.

In the end I could not stand it any longer and went away. I heard later that it took him half an hour to die. Burmans were bringing dahs[7] and

---

[7]*dahs*: Large knives. [Eds.]

baskets even before I left, and I was told they had stripped his body almost to the bones by the afternoon.

Afterwards, of course, there were endless discussions about the shooting of the elephant. The owner was furious, but he was only an Indian and could do nothing. Besides, legally I had done the right thing, for a mad elephant has to be killed, like a mad dog, if its owner fails to control it. Among the Europeans opinion was divided. The older men said I was right, the younger men said it was a damn shame to shoot an elephant for killing a coolie, because an elephant was worth more than any damn Coringhee coolie. And afterwards I was very glad that the coolie had been killed; it put me legally in the right and it gave me a sufficient pretext for shooting the elephant. I often wondered whether any of the others grasped that I had done it solely to avoid looking a fool.

QUESTIONS

Reading

1. How does Orwell characterize "every white man's life" in the East?
2. How do the natives "force" Orwell to shoot the elephant against his better judgment? How does he relate this personal episode to the larger problems of British imperialism?
3. What is Orwell's final reaction to his deed? How literally can we take his statement that he "was very glad that the coolie had been killed" (paragraph 14)?
4. Orwell's recollection of shooting the elephant is shaped to support a specific point or thesis. Where does Orwell state this thesis? Is this placement effective?

Exploratory Writing

1. From the opening sentence, Orwell displays a remarkable candor concerning his feelings. How does this personal, candid tone add to or detract from the strength of the essay?
2. Although "Shooting an Elephant" seems to be a *reflective,* autobiographical essay, one of Orwell's biographers, Bernard Crick, has suggested that the story may be partly fiction. There is no evidence that Orwell himself actually shot an elephant while he was in Burma. How might your reading of this essay change if you learned that it was pure fiction? How might your reading change if you had proof that it was 100 percent factual?

Making Connections

1. Orwell and Charles Siebert (p. 274) discuss more than elephants in their essays. Underline, highlight, or flag the claims that each author makes about *human* societies. What has each author's encounter with elephants allowed him to learn about human beings?

Essay Writing

1. Write an essay identifying and discussing the ways that Orwell uses irony in "Shooting an Elephant." How does his ironic tone help him make his point?
2. Write an essay reflecting on an ethical dilemma you faced in your own life. What were your choices? How do you feel about the course of action you chose?

An Elephant Crackup?

Charles Siebert

A native of Brooklyn, New York, Charles Siebert (b. 1954) is a poet, essayist, and novelist who writes about nature, medicine, and animals. His digressive tendencies manifest in all of his published works, transcending simple categorization yet enabling him to glean connections from seemingly incongruous moments. In his memoir, Wickerby: An Urban Pastoral *(1998), Siebert juxtaposes his urban surroundings in Brooklyn with reminiscences about five months he spent in the Canadian wilderness, blurring the lines between city and country. In 2000, he published* Angus: A Novel, *written from the lively perspective of his Jack Russell terrier. A blend of scientific journalism and biography,* A Man after His Own Heart *(2004) describes a heart transplant firsthand while exploring the heart ailments and subsequent death of Siebert's father. His essays have been published in the* New Yorker, Harper's, Esquire, *and the* New York Times Magazine, *in which the following article appeared in October 2006. Here, Siebert investigates the effects of poaching and captivity on elephants in Africa, India, and Southeast Asia.*

"We're not going anywhere," my driver, Nelson Okello, whispered to me one morning this past June, the two of us sitting in the front seat of a jeep just after dawn in Queen Elizabeth National Park in southwestern Uganda. We'd originally stopped to observe what appeared to be a lone bull elephant grazing in a patch of tall savanna grasses off to our left. More than one "rogue" had crossed our path that morning — a young male elephant that has made an overly strong power play against the dominant male of his herd and been banished, sometimes permanently. This elephant, however, soon proved to be not a rogue but part of a cast of at least thirty. The ground vibrations registered just before the emergence of the herd from the surrounding trees and brush. We sat there watching the elephants cross the road before us, seeming, for all their heft, so light on their feet, soundlessly plying the wind-swept savanna grasses like land whales adrift above the floor of an ancient, waterless sea.

Then, from behind a thicket of acacia trees directly off our front left bumper, a huge female emerged — "the matriarch," Okello said softly. There was a small calf beneath her, freely foraging and knocking about within the secure cribbing of four massive legs. Acacia leaves are an elephant's favorite food, and as the calf set to work on some low branches, the matriarch stood guard, her vast back flank blocking the road, the rest of the herd milling about in the brush a short distance away.

After fifteen minutes or so, Okello started inching the jeep forward, revving the engine, trying to make us sound as beastly as possible. The matriarch, however, was having none of it, holding her ground, the fierce white of her eyes as bright as that of her tusks. Although I pretty much knew the answer, I asked Okello if he was considering trying to drive around. "No," he said, raising an index finger for emphasis. "She'll charge. We should stay right here."

I'd have considered it a wise policy even at a more peaceable juncture in the course of human-elephant relations. In recent years, however, those relations have become markedly more bellicose. Just two days before I arrived, a woman was killed by an elephant in Kazinga, a fishing village nearby. Two months earlier, a man was fatally gored by a young male elephant at the northern edge of the park, near the village of Katwe. African elephants use their long tusks to forage through dense jungle brush. They've also been known to wield them, however, with the ceremonious flash and precision of gladiators, pinning down a victim with one knee in order to deliver the decisive thrust. Okello told me that a young Indian tourist was killed in this fashion two years ago in Murchison Falls National Park, north of where we were.

These were not isolated incidents. All across Africa, India, and parts of Southeast Asia, from within and around whatever patches and corridors of their natural habitat remain, elephants have been striking out, destroying villages and crops, attacking and killing human beings. In fact, these attacks have become so commonplace that a new statistical category, known as Human-Elephant Conflict, or HEC, was created by elephant researchers in the mid-1990s to monitor the problem. In the Indian state of Jharkhand, near the western border of Bangladesh, three hundred people were killed by elephants between 2000 and 2004. In the past twelve years, elephants have killed 605 people in Assam, a state in northeastern India, 239 of them since 2001; 265 elephants have died in that same period, the majority of them as a result of retaliation by angry villagers, who have used everything from poison-tipped arrows to laced food to exact their revenge. In Africa, reports of human-elephant conflicts appear almost daily, from Zambia to Tanzania, from Uganda to Sierra Leone, where three hundred villagers evacuated their homes last year because of unprovoked elephant attacks.

Still, it is not only the increasing number of these incidents that is causing alarm but also the singular perversity — for want of a less anthropocentric term — of recent elephant aggression. Since the early 1990s, for example, young male elephants in Pilanesberg National Park and the Hluhluwe-Umfolozi Game Reserve in South Africa have been raping and killing rhinoceroses; this abnormal behavior, according to a 2001 study in the journal *Pachyderm*, has been reported in "a number of reserves" in the region. In July of last year, officials in Pilanesberg shot three young male elephants who were responsible for the killings of sixty-three rhinos, as well as attacks on people in safari vehicles. In Addo Elephant National Park, also in South Africa, up to 90 percent of male elephant deaths are now attributable to other male elephants, compared with a rate of 6 percent in more stable elephant communities.

In a coming book on this phenomenon, Gay Bradshaw, a psychologist at the environmental-sciences program at Oregon State University, notes that in India, where the elephant has long been regarded as a deity, a recent headline in a leading newspaper warned, "To Avoid Confrontation, Don't Worship Elephants." "Everybody pretty much agrees that the relationship between elephants and people has dramatically changed," Bradshaw told me recently. "What we are seeing today is extraordinary. Where for centuries humans and elephants lived in relatively peaceful coexistence, there is now hostility and violence. Now, I use the term 'violence' because of the intentionality associated with it, both in the aggression of humans and, at times, the recently observed behavior of elephants."

For a number of biologists and ethologists who have spent their careers studying elephant behavior, the attacks have become so abnormal in both number and kind that they can no longer be attributed entirely to the customary factors. Typically, elephant researchers have cited, as a cause of aggression, the high levels of testosterone in newly matured male elephants or the competition for land and resources between elephants and humans. But in "Elephant Breakdown," a 2005 essay in the journal *Nature*, Bradshaw and several colleagues argued that today's elephant populations are suffering from a form of chronic stress, a kind of species-wide trauma. Decades of poaching and culling and habitat loss, they claim, have so disrupted the intricate web of familial and societal relations by which young elephants have traditionally been raised in the wild, and by which established elephant herds are governed, that what we are now witnessing is nothing less than a precipitous collapse of elephant culture.

It has long been apparent that every large, land-based animal on this planet is ultimately fighting a losing battle with humankind. And yet entirely befitting of an animal with such a highly developed sensibility, a deep-rooted sense of family and, yes, such a good long-term memory, the elephant is not going out quietly. It is not leaving without making some kind of statement, one to which scientists from a variety of disciplines, including human psychology, are now beginning to pay close attention.

Once the matriarch and her calf were a comfortable distance from us   10
that morning, Okello and I made the twenty-minute drive to Kyambura, a

village at the far southeastern edge of the park. Back in 2003, Kyambura was reportedly the site of the very sort of sudden, unprovoked elephant attack I'd been hearing about. According to an account of the event in the magazine *New Scientist*, a number of huts and fields were trampled, and the townspeople were afraid to venture out to surrounding villages, either by foot or on their bikes, because elephants were regularly blocking the road and charging out at those who tried to pass.

Park officials from the Uganda Wildlife Authority with whom I tried to discuss the incident were reluctant to talk about it or any of the recent killings by elephants in the area. Eco-tourism is one of Uganda's major sources of income, and the elephant and other wildlife stocks of Queen Elizabeth National Park are only just now beginning to recover from years of virtually unchecked poaching and habitat destruction. Tom Okello, the chief game warden at the park (and no relation to my driver), and Margaret Driciru, Queen Elizabeth's chief veterinarian, each told me that they weren't aware of the attack in Kyambura. When I mentioned it to the executive director of the wildlife authority, Moses Mapesa, upon my initial arrival in the capital city, Kampala, he eventually admitted that it did happen, but he claimed that it was not nearly as recent as reported. "That was fourteen years ago," he said. "We have seen aggressive behavior from elephants, but that's a story of the past."

Kyambura did look, upon our arrival, much like every other small Ugandan farming community I'd passed through on my visit. Lush fields of banana trees, millet and maize framed a small town center of pastel-colored single-story cement buildings with corrugated-tin roofs. People sat on stoops out front in the available shade. Bicyclers bore preposterously outsize loads of bananas, firewood and five-gallon water jugs on their fenders and handlebars. Contrary to what I had read, the bicycle traffic along the road in and out of Kyambura didn't seem impaired in the slightest.

But when Okello and I asked a shopkeeper named Ibrah Byamukama about elephant attacks, he immediately nodded and pointed to a patch of maize and millet fields just up the road, along the edges of the surrounding Maramagambo Forest. He confirmed that a small group of elephants charged out one morning two years earlier, trampled the fields and nearby gardens, knocked down a few huts and then left. He then pointed to a long orange gash in the earth between the planted fields and the forest: a fifteen-foot-deep, twenty-five-foot-wide trench that had been dug by the wildlife authority around the perimeter of Kyambura in an attempt to keep the elephants at bay. On the way out of town, Okello and I took a closer look at the trench. It was filled with stacks of thorny shrubs for good measure.

"The people are still worried," Byamukama said, shaking his head. "The elephants are just becoming more destructive. I don't know why."

Three years ago, Gay Bradshaw, then working on her graduate degree in   15
psychology at Pacifica Graduate Institute outside Santa Barbara, California, began wondering much the same thing: was the extraordinary behavior of

elephants in Africa and Asia signaling a breaking point? With the assistance of several established African-elephant researchers, including Daphne Sheldrick and Cynthia Moss, and with the help of Allan Schore, an expert on human trauma disorders at the department of psychiatry and biobehavioral sciences at UCLA, Bradshaw sought to combine traditional research into elephant behavior with insights about trauma drawn from human neuroscience. Using the few remaining relatively stable elephant herds in places like Amboseli National Park in Kenya as control groups, Bradshaw and her colleagues analyzed the far more fractious populations found in places like Pilanesberg in South Africa and Queen Elizabeth National Park in Uganda. What emerged was a portrait of pervasive pachyderm dysfunction.

Elephants, when left to their own devices, are profoundly social creatures. A herd of them is, in essence, one incomprehensibly massive elephant: a somewhat loosely bound and yet intricately interconnected, tensile organism. Young elephants are raised within an extended, multitiered network of doting female caregivers that includes the birth mother, grandmothers, aunts and friends. These relations are maintained over a life span as long as seventy years. Studies of established herds have shown that young elephants stay within fifteen feet of their mothers for nearly all of their first eight years of life, after which young females are socialized into the matriarchal network, while young males go off for a time into an all-male social group before coming back into the fold as mature adults.

When an elephant dies, its family members engage in intense mourning and burial rituals, conducting weeklong vigils over the body, carefully covering it with earth and brush, revisiting the bones for years afterward, caressing the bones with their trunks, often taking turns rubbing their trunks along the teeth of a skull's lower jaw, the way living elephants do in greeting. If harm comes to a member of an elephant group, all the other elephants are aware of it. This sense of cohesion is further enforced by the elaborate communication system that elephants use. In close proximity they employ a range of vocalizations, from low-frequency rumbles to higher-pitched screams and trumpets, along with a variety of visual signals, from the waving of their trunks to subtle anglings of the head, body, feet and tail. When communicating over long distances — in order to pass along, for example, news about imminent threats, a sudden change of plans or, of the utmost importance to elephants, the death of a community member — they use patterns of subsonic vibrations that are felt as far as several miles away by exquisitely tuned sensors in the padding of their feet.

This fabric of elephant society, Bradshaw and her colleagues concluded, had effectively been frayed by years of habitat loss and poaching, along with systematic culling by government agencies to control elephant numbers and translocations of herds to different habitats. The number of older matriarchs and female caregivers (or "allomothers") had drastically fallen, as had the number of elder bulls, who play a significant role in keeping younger males in line. In parts of Zambia and Tanzania, a number of the elephant groups studied contained no adult females whatsoever. In Uganda, herds were often found to be "semipermanent aggregations," as a paper written by Bradshaw describes them, with many females between the ages of fifteen and twenty-five having no familial associations.

As a result of such social upheaval, calves are now being born to and raised by ever younger and inexperienced mothers. Young orphaned elephants, meanwhile, that have witnessed the death of a parent at the hands of poachers are coming of age in the absence of the support system that defines traditional elephant life. "The loss of elephant elders," Bradshaw told me, "and the traumatic experience of witnessing the massacres of their family, impairs normal brain and behavior development in young elephants."

What Bradshaw and her colleagues describe would seem to be an extreme form of anthropocentric conjecture if the evidence that they've compiled from various elephant researchers, even on the strictly observational level, weren't so compelling. The elephants of decimated herds, especially orphans who've watched the death of their parents and elders from poaching and culling, exhibit behavior typically associated with post-traumatic stress disorder and other trauma-related disorders in humans: abnormal startle response, unpredictable asocial behavior, inattentive mothering and hyperaggression. Studies of the various assaults on the rhinos in South Africa, meanwhile, have determined that the perpetrators were in all cases adolescent males that had witnessed their families being shot down in cullings. It was common for these elephants to have been tethered to the bodies of their dead and dying relatives until they could be rounded up for translocation to, as Bradshaw and Schore describe them, "locales lacking traditional social hierarchy of older bulls and intact natal family structures."

In fact, even the relatively few attempts that park officials have made to restore parts of the social fabric of elephant society have lent substance to the elephant-breakdown theory. When South African park rangers recently introduced a number of older bull elephants into several destabilized elephant herds in Pilanesburg and Addo, the wayward behavior — including unusually premature hormonal changes among the adolescent elephants — abated.

But according to Bradshaw and her colleagues, the various pieces of the elephant-trauma puzzle really come together at the level of neuroscience, or what might be called the physiology of psychology, by which scientists can now map the marred neuronal fields, snapped synaptic bridges and crooked chemical streams of an embattled psyche. Though most scientific knowledge of trauma is still understood through research on human subjects, neural studies of elephants are now under way. (The first functional MRI scan of an elephant brain, taken this year, revealed, perhaps not surprisingly, a huge hippocampus, a seat of memory in the mammalian brain, as well as a prominent structure in the limbic system, which processes emotions.) Allan Schore, the UCLA psychologist and neuroscientist who for the past fifteen years has focused his research on early human brain development and the negative

20

impact of trauma on it, recently wrote two articles with Bradshaw on the stress-related neurobiological underpinnings of current abnormal elephant behavior.

"We know that these mechanisms cut across species," Schore told me. "In the first years of humans as well as elephants, development of the emotional brain is impacted by these attachment mechanisms, by the interaction that the infant has with the primary caregiver, especially the mother. When these early experiences go in a positive way, it leads to greater resilience in things like affect regulation, stress regulation, social communication and empathy. But when these early experiences go awry in cases of abuse and neglect, there is a literal thinning down of the essential circuits in the brain, especially in the emotion-processing areas."

For Bradshaw, these continuities between human and elephant brains resonate far outside the field of neuroscience. "Elephants are suffering and behaving in the same ways that we recognize in ourselves as a result of violence," she told me. "It is entirely congruent with what we know about humans and other mammals. Except perhaps for a few specific features, brain organization and early development of elephants and humans are extremely similar. That's not news. What is news is when you start asking, What does this mean beyond the science? How do we respond to the fact that we are causing other species like elephants to psychologically break down? In a way, it's not so much a cognitive or imaginative leap anymore as it is a political one." . . .

Shortly after my return from Uganda, I went to visit the Elephant Sanctuary in Tennessee, a 2,700-acre rehabilitation center and retirement facility situated in the state's verdant, low-rolling southern hill country. The sanctuary is a kind of asylum for some of the more emotionally and psychologically disturbed former zoo and circus elephants in the United States — cases so bad that the people who profited from them were eager to let them go. Given that elephants in the wild are now exhibiting aberrant behaviors that were long observed in captive elephants, it perhaps follows that a positive working model for how to ameliorate the effects of elephant breakdown can be found in captivity.

Of the nineteen current residents of the sanctuary, perhaps the biggest   35
hard-luck story is that of a forty-year-old, five-ton Asian elephant named Misty. Originally captured as a calf in India in 1966, Misty spent her first decade in captivity with a number of American circuses and finally ended up in the early 1980s at a wild-animal attraction known as Lion Country Safari in Irvine, California. It was there, on the afternoon of July 25, 1983, that Misty, one of four performing elephants at Lion Country Safari that summer, somehow managed to break free of her chains and began madly dashing about the park, looking to make an escape. When one of the park's zoologists tried to corner and contain her, Misty killed him with one swipe of her trunk.

There are, in the long, checkered history of human-elephant relations, countless stories of lethal elephantine assaults, and almost invariably of some gruesomely outsize, animalistic form of retribution exacted by us. It was in the very state of Tennessee, back in September 1916, that another five-ton Asian circus elephant, Mary, was impounded by a local sheriff for the killing of a young hotel janitor who'd been hired to mind Mary during a stopover in the northeast Tennessee town of Kingsport. The janitor had apparently taken Mary for a swim at a local pond, where, according to witnesses, he poked her behind the left ear with a metal hook just as she was reaching for a piece of floating watermelon rind. Enraged, Mary turned, swiftly snatched him up with her trunk, dashed him against a refreshment stand and then smashed his head with her foot.

With cries from the townspeople to "Kill the elephant!" and threats from nearby town leaders to bar the circus if "Murderous Mary," as newspapers quickly dubbed her, remained a part of the show, the circus's owner, Charlie Sparks, knew he had to do something to appease the public's bloodlust and save his business. (Among the penalties he is said to have contemplated was electrocution, a ghastly precedent which had been set thirteen years earlier, on the grounds of the nearly completed Luna Park in Coney Island. A long-time circus elephant named Topsy, who'd killed three trainers in as many years — the last one after he tried to feed her a lighted cigarette — became the largest and most prominent victim of Thomas Edison, the father of direct-current electricity, who had publicly electrocuted a number of animals at that time using his rival George Westinghouse's alternating current, in hopes of discrediting it as being too dangerous.)

Sparks ultimately decided to have Mary hanged and shipped her by train to the nearby town of Erwin, Tennessee, where more than 2,500 people gathered at the local rail yard for her execution. Dozens of children are said to have run off screaming in terror when the chain that was suspended from a huge industrial crane snapped, leaving Mary writhing on the ground with a broken hip. A local rail worker promptly clambered up Mary's bulk and secured a heavier chain for a second, successful hoisting.

Misty's fate in the early 1980s, by contrast, seems a triumph of modern humanism. Banished, after the Lion Safari killing, to the Hawthorn Corporation, a company in Illinois that trains and leases elephants and tigers to circuses, she would continue to lash out at a number of her trainers over the years. But when Hawthorn was convicted of numerous violations of the Animal Welfare Act in 2003, the company agreed to relinquish custody of Misty to the Elephant Sanctuary. She was loaded onto a trailer transport on the morning of November 17, 2004, and even then managed to get away with one final shot at the last in her long line of captors.

"The details are kind of sketchy," Carol Buckley, a founder of the Elephant Sanctuary, said to me one afternoon in July, the two of us pulling up on her all-terrain four-wheeler to a large grassy enclosure where an extremely docile and contented-looking Misty, trunk high, ears flapping,   40 waited to greet us. "Hawthorn's owner was trying to get her to stretch out so he could remove her leg chains before loading her on the trailer. At one point he prodded her with a bull hook, and she just knocked him down with a swipe of her trunk. But we've seen none of that since she's been here. She's as sweet as can be. You'd never know that this elephant killed anybody."

In the course of her nearly two years at the Elephant Sanctuary — much of it spent in quarantine while undergoing daily treatment for tuberculosis — Misty has also been in therapy, as in psychotherapy. Wild-caught elephants often witness as young calves the slaughter of their parents, just about the only way, shy of a far more costly tranquilization procedure, to wrest a calf from elephant parents, especially the mothers. The young captives are then dispatched to a foreign environment to work as either performers or laborers, all the while being kept in relative confinement and isolation, a kind of living death for an animal as socially developed and dependent as we now know elephants to be.

And yet just as we now understand that elephants hurt like us, we're learning that they can heal like us as well. Indeed, Misty has become a testament to the Elephant Sanctuary's signature "passive control" system, a therapy tailored in many ways along the lines of those used to treat human sufferers of post-traumatic stress disorder. Passive control, as a sanctuary newsletter describes it, depends upon "knowledge of how elephants process information and respond to stress" as well as specific knowledge of each elephant's past response to stress. Under this so-called nondominance system, there is no discipline, retaliation or withholding of food, water and treats, which are all common tactics of elephant trainers. Great pains are taken, meanwhile, to afford the elephants both a sense of safety and freedom of choice — two mainstays of human trauma therapy — as well as continual social interaction.

Upon her arrival at the Elephant Sanctuary, Misty seemed to sense straight off the different vibe of her new home. When Scott Blais of the sanctuary went to free Misty's still-chained leg a mere day after she'd arrived, she stood peaceably by, practically offering her leg up to him. Over her many months of quarantine, meanwhile, with only humans acting as a kind of surrogate elephant family, she has consistently gone through the daily rigors of her tuberculosis treatments — involving two caretakers, a team of veterinarians and the use of a restraining chute in which harnesses are secured about her chest and tail — without any coaxing or pressure. "We'll shower her with praise in the barn afterwards," Buckley told me as Misty stood by, chomping on a mouthful of hay, "and she actually purrs with pleasure. The whole barn vibrates."

Of course, Misty's road to recovery — when viewed in light of her history and that of all the other captive elephants, past and present — is as harrowing as it is heartening. She and the others have suffered, we now understand, not simply because of us, but because they are, by and large, us. If as recently as the end of the Vietnam War people were still balking at the idea that a soldier, for example, could be physically disabled by psychological harm — the idea, in other words, that the mind is not an entity apart from the body and therefore just as woundable as any limb — we now find ourselves having to make an equally profound and, for many, even more difficult leap: that a fellow creature as ostensibly unlike us in every way as an elephant is as precisely and intricately woundable as we are. And while such knowledge naturally places an added burden upon us, the keepers, that burden is now being greatly compounded by the fact that sudden violent outbursts like Misty's can no longer be dismissed as the inevitable isolated revolts of a restless few against the constraints and abuses of captivity.

They have no future without us. The question we are now forced to grapple with is whether we would mind a future without them, among the more mindful creatures on this earth and, in many ways, the most devoted. Indeed, the manner of the elephants' continued keeping, their restoration and conservation, both in civil confines and what's left of wild ones, is now drawing the attention of everyone from naturalists to neuroscientists. Too much about elephants, in the end — their desires and devotions, their vulnerability and tremendous resilience — reminds us of ourselves to dismiss out of hand this revolt they're currently staging against their own dismissal. And while our concern may ultimately be rooted in that most human of impulses — the preservation of our own self-image — the great paradox about this particular moment in our history with elephants is that saving them will require finally getting past ourselves; it will demand the ultimate act of deep, interspecies empathy. 45

On a more immediate, practical level, as Gay Bradshaw sees it, this involves taking what has been learned about elephant society, psychology and emotion and inculcating that knowledge into the conservation schemes of researchers and park rangers. This includes doing things like expanding elephant habitat to what it used to be historically and avoiding the use of culling and translocations as conservation tools. "If we want elephants around," Bradshaw told me, "then what we need to do is simple: learn how to live with elephants. In other words, in addition to conservation, we need to educate people how to live with wild animals like humans used to do, and to create conditions whereby people can live on their land and live with elephants without it being this life-and-death situation."

The other part of our newly emerging compact with elephants, however, is far more difficult to codify. It requires nothing less than a fundamental shift in the way we look at animals and, by extension, ourselves. It requires what Bradshaw somewhat whimsically refers to as a new "transspecies psyche," a commitment to move beyond an anthropocentric frame of reference and, in effect, be elephants. Two years ago, Bradshaw wrote a paper for the journal *Society and Animals*, focusing on the work of the David Sheldrick Wildlife Trust in Kenya, a sanctuary for orphaned and traumatized wild elephants — more or less the wilderness-based complement to Carol Buckley's trauma therapy at the Elephant Sanctuary in Tennessee. The trust's human caregivers essentially serve as surrogate mothers to young orphan elephants, gradually restoring their psychological and emotional well-being to the point at which they can be reintroduced into existing wild herds. The human "allomothers" stay by their adopted young orphans' sides, even sleeping with them at night in stables. The caretakers make sure, however, to rotate from one elephant to the next so that the orphans grow fond of all the keepers. Otherwise an elephant would form such a strong bond with one keeper that whenever he or she was absent, that elephant would grieve as if over the loss of another family member, often becoming physically ill itself.

To date, the Sheldrick Trust has successfully rehabilitated more than sixty elephants and reintroduced them into wild herds. A number of them have periodically returned to the sanctuary with their own wild-born calves in order to reunite with their human allomothers and to introduce their offspring to what — out on this uncharted frontier of the new "trans-species psyche" — is now being recognized, at least by the elephants, it seems, as a whole new subspecies: the human allograndmother. "Traditionally, nature has served as a source of healing for humans," Bradshaw told me. "Now humans can participate actively in the healing of both themselves and non-human animals. The trust and the sanctuary are the beginnings of a mutually benefiting interspecies culture."

On my way back to New York via London, I contacted Felicity de Zulueta, a psychiatrist at Maudsley Hospital in London who treats victims of extreme trauma, among them former child soldiers from the Lord's Resistance Army. De Zulueta, an acquaintance of Eve Abe's, grew up in Uganda in the early 1960s on the outskirts of Queen Elizabeth National Park, near where her father, a malaria doctor, had set up camp as part of a malaria-eradication program. For a time she had her own elephant, orphaned by poaching, that local villagers had given to her father, who brought it home to the family garage, where it immediately bonded with an orphan antelope and dog already residing there.

"He was doing fine," de Zulueta told me of the pet elephant. "My   50
mother was loving it and feeding it, and then my parents realized, How can we keep this elephant that is going to grow bigger than the garage? So they gave it to who they thought were the experts. They sent him to the Entebbe Zoo, and although they gave him all the right food and everything, he was a lonely little elephant, and he died. He had no attachment."

For de Zulueta, the parallel that Abe draws between the plight of war orphans, human and elephant, is painfully apt, yet also provides some cause for hope, given the often startling capacity of both animals for recovery. She told me that one Ugandan war orphan she is currently treating lost all the members of his family except for two older brothers. Remarkably, one of those brothers, while serving in the Ugandan Army, rescued the younger sibling from the Lord's Resistance Army; the older brother's unit had captured the rebel battalion in which his younger brother had been forced to fight.

The two brothers eventually made their way to London, and for the past two years, the younger brother has been going through a gradual process of recovery in the care of Maudsley Hospital. Much of the rehabilitation, according to de Zulueta, especially in the early stages, relies on the basic human trauma therapy principles now being applied to elephants: providing decent living quarters, establishing a sense of safety and of attachment to a larger community and allowing freedom of choice. After that have come the more complex treatments tailored to the human brain's particular cognitive capacities: things like reliving the original traumatic experience and being taught to modulate feelings through early detection of hyperarousal and through breathing techniques. And the healing of trauma, as de Zulueta describes it, turns out to have physical correlatives in the brain just as its wounding does.

"What I say is, we find bypass," she explained. "We bypass the wounded areas using various techniques. Some of the wounds are not healable. Their scars remain. But there is hope because the brain is an enormous computer, and you can learn to bypass its wounds by finding different methods of approaching life. Of course there may be moments when something happens and the old wound becomes unbearable. Still, people do recover. The boy I've been telling you about is eighteen now, and he has survived very well in terms of his emotional health and capacities. He's a lovely, lovely man. And he's a poet. He writes beautiful poetry."

On the afternoon in July that I left the Elephant Sanctuary in Tennessee, Carol Buckley and Scott Blais seemed in particularly good spirits. Misty was only weeks away from the end of her quarantine, and she would soon be able to socialize with some of her old cohorts from the Hawthorn Corporation: eight female Asians that had been given over to the sanctuary. I would meet the lot of them that day, driving from one to the next on the back of Buckley's four-wheeler across the sanctuary's savanna-like stretches. Buckley and Blais refer to them collectively as the Divas.

Buckley and Blais told me that they got word not long ago of a significant breakthrough in a campaign of theirs to get elephants out of entertainment and zoos: the Bronx Zoo, one of the oldest and most formidable zoos in the country, had announced that upon the death of the zoo's three current elephant inhabitants, Patty, Maxine and Happy, it would phase out its elephant exhibit on social-behavioral grounds — an acknowledgment of a new awareness of the elephant's very particular sensibility and needs. "They're really taking the lead," Buckley told me. "Zoos don't want to concede the inappropriateness of keeping elephants in such confines. But if we as a society determine that an animal like this suffers in captivity, if the information shows us that they do, hey, we are the stewards. You'd think we'd want to do the right thing."

Four days later, I received an e-mail message from Gay Bradshaw, who consults with Buckley and Blais on their various stress-therapy strategies. She wrote that one of the sanctuary's elephants, an Asian named Winkie,

55

had just killed a thirty-six-year-old female assistant caretaker and critically injured the male caretaker who'd tried to save her.

People who work with animals on a daily basis can tell you all kinds of stories about their distinct personalities and natures. I'd gotten, in fact, an elaborate breakdown from Buckley and Blais on the various elephants at the sanctuary and their sociopolitical maneuverings within the sanctuary's distinct elephant culture, and I went to my notebook to get a fix again on Winkie. A forty-year-old, 7,600-pound female from Burma, she came to the sanctuary in 2000 from the Henry Vilas Zoo in Madison, Wisconsin, where she had a reputation for lashing out at keepers. When Winkie first arrived at the sanctuary, Buckley told me, she used to jump merely upon being touched and then would wait for a confrontation. But when it never came, she slowly calmed down. "Has never lashed out at primary keepers," my last note on Winkie reads, "but has at secondary ones."

Bradshaw's e-mail message concludes: "A stunning illustration of trauma in elephants. The indelible etching."

I thought back to a moment in Queen Elizabeth National Park this past June. As Nelson Okello and I sat waiting for the matriarch and her calf to pass, he mentioned to me an odd little detail about the killing two months earlier of the man from the village of Katwe, something that, the more I thought about it, seemed to capture this particularly fraught moment we've arrived at with the elephants. Okello said that after the man's killing, the elephant herd buried him as it would one of its own, carefully covering the body with earth and brush and then standing vigil over it.

Even as we're forcing them out, it seems, the elephants are going out of   60
their way to put us, the keepers, in an ever more discomfiting place, challenging us to preserve someplace for them, the ones who in many ways seem to regard the matter of life and death more devoutly than we. In fact, elephant culture could be considered the precursor of our own, the first permanent human settlements having sprung up around the desire of wandering tribes to stay by the graves of their dead. "The city of the dead," as Lewis Mumford once wrote, "antedates the city of the living."

When a group of villagers from Katwe went out to reclaim the man's body for his family's funeral rites, the elephants refused to budge. Human remains, a number of researchers have observed, are the only other ones that elephants will treat as they do their own. In the end, the villagers resorted to a tactic that has long been etched in the elephant's collective memory, firing volleys of gunfire into the air at close range, finally scaring the mourning herd away.

QUESTIONS

Reading

1. According to Bradshaw and her colleagues, what has caused the fraying of elephant society?

2. What do an elephant's family members do when it dies?
3. What does Siebert conclude about the relationship between elephants and humans? Which *reportorial* techniques does Siebert use to lead up to this conclusion?

Exploratory Writing

1. Using recent news archives, find an article about the interconnection of wild-animal life and human culture. Choose an animal other than the elephant. Considering Siebert's use of the term *elephant culture*, compose a list of characteristics that define the "culture" of the animal you have chosen. How does this animal's culture interrelate with human society? How is it entirely unique?
2. The nonprofit group Elephant Voices (**www.elephantvoices.org**) states: "We believe that it is immoral and unjust to allow elephants to suffer [in circuses] just so they can entertain us. . . . We don't think very many kids or adults would visit a circus if they knew how much the elephants suffer." Keeping this in mind (as well as the organization's ideas about zoos), stage a debate on the topic: "Elephants should be released back into the wild." Use Siebert's article, the "Elephants in Captivity" and "Frequently Asked Questions" sections on the Elephant Voices Web site, and archived newspaper or magazine articles to make your case.
3. Make a double-entry list comparing Siebert's characterizations of humans and elephants. Use a separate piece of paper if you need more space. Which behaviors and traits do we share with elephants?

HUMANS	ELEPHANTS

Making Connections

1. Compare how George Orwell ("Shooting an Elephant," p. 266) and Siebert characterize elephants as living creatures. To what extent (if any) is each author's discussion of elephants anthropomorphic?

Essay Writing

1. "They have no future without us," Siebert says of elephants. "The question we are now forced to grapple with is whether we would mind a future without them" (paragraph 45). Write an essay grappling with this question. Would you mind if elephants went extinct? If not, why not?

Paired Readings: On Race Relations

Letter from Birmingham Jail

Martin Luther King Jr.

*The son of an Atlanta, Georgia, minister, civil rights leader
Martin Luther King Jr. (1929–1968) graduated from Morehouse
College and Crozier Theological Seminary before receiving a
PhD in theology from Boston University in 1955. He became
pastor of Dexter Avenue Baptist Church in Montgomery,
Alabama, in 1954 and the next year led a boycott of the city's
segregated bus system, which brought him national attention
when the system began to be integrated in 1956. He organized
the Southern Christian Leadership Conference to pursue civil
rights gains through nonviolent resistance, and his participation
in nonviolent protests led to several arrests. In 1963, King
helped plan a massive march on Washington, D.C., where he
delivered his famous "I Have a Dream" speech, calling for racial
justice. The next year he was awarded the Nobel Peace Prize. He
was assassinated in Memphis, Tennessee, at the age of thirty-
nine. King wrote the following letter while serving an eight-day
jail sentence for participating in protests against segregated
businesses in Birmingham, Alabama. In the introduction to its
published version, King noted, "This response to a published
statement by eight fellow clergymen from Alabama . . . was
composed under somewhat constricting circumstance. Begun on
the margins of the newspaper in which the statement appeared
while I was in jail, the letter was continued on scraps of writing
paper supplied by a friendly Negro trusty, and concluded on a
pad my attorneys were eventually permitted to leave me.
Although the text remains in substance unaltered, I have
indulged in the author's prerogative of polishing it for
publication."*

APRIL 16, 1963

My Dear Fellow Clergymen:

While confined here in the Birmingham city jail, I came across your recent statement calling my present activities "unwise and untimely." Seldom do I pause to answer criticism of my work and ideas. If I sought to answer all the criticisms that cross my desk, my secretaries would have little time for anything other than such correspondence in the course of the day, and I would have no time for constructive work. But since I feel that you are men of genuine good will and that your criticisms are sincerely set forth, I want to try to answer your statement in what I hope will be patient and reasonable terms.

I think I should indicate why I am here in Birmingham, since you have been influenced by the view which argues against "outsiders coming in." I have the honor of serving as president of the Southern Christian Leadership Conference, an organization operating in every southern state, with headquarters in Atlanta, Georgia. We have some eighty-five affiliated organizations across the South, and one of them is the Alabama Christian Movement for Human Rights. Frequently we share staff, educational, and financial resources with our affiliates. Several months ago the affiliate here in Birmingham asked us to be on call to engage in a nonviolent direct-action program if such were deemed necessary. We readily consented, and when the hour came we lived up to our promise. So I, along with several members of my staff, am here because I was invited here. I am here because I have organizational ties here.

But more basically, I am in Birmingham because injustice is here. Just as the prophets of the eighth century B.C. left their villages and carried their "thus saith the Lord" far beyond the boundaries of their home towns, and just as the Apostle Paul left his village of Tarsus and carried the gospel of Jesus Christ to the far corners of the Greco-Roman world, so am I compelled to carry the gospel of freedom beyond my own home town. Like Paul, I must constantly respond to the Macedonian call for aid.[1]

Moreover, I am cognizant of the interrelatedness of all communities and states. I cannot sit idly by in Atlanta and not be concerned about what happens in Birmingham. Injustice anywhere is a threat to justice everywhere. We are caught in an inescapable network of mutuality, tied in a single garment of destiny. Whatever affects one directly, affects all indirectly. Never again can we afford to live with the narrow, provincial, "outside agitator" idea. Anyone who lives inside the United States can never be considered an outsider anywhere within its bounds.

You deplore the demonstrations taking place in Birmingham. But your statement, I am sorry to say, fails to express a similar concern for the conditions that brought about the demonstrations. I am sure that none of you

5

---

[1]*Macedonian call for aid*: A reference to Paul's vision of a Macedonian man requesting help (see Acts 16:9–10). [Eds.]

would want to rest content with the superficial kind of social analysis that deals merely with effects and does not grapple with underlying causes. It is unfortunate that demonstrations are taking place in Birmingham, but it is even more unfortunate that the city's white power structure left the Negro community with no alternative.

In any nonviolent campaign there are four basic steps: collection of the facts to determine whether injustices exist; negotiation; self-purification; and direct action. We have gone through all these steps in Birmingham. There can be no gainsaying the fact that racial injustice engulfs this community. Birmingham is probably the most thoroughly segregated city in the United States. Its ugly record of brutality is widely known. Negroes have experienced grossly unjust treatment in the courts. There have been more unsolved bombings of Negro homes and churches in Birmingham than in any other city in the nation. These are the hard brutal facts of the case. On the basis of these conditions, Negro leaders sought to negotiate with the city fathers. But the latter consistently refused to engage in good-faith negotiation.

Then, last September, came the opportunity to talk with leaders of Birmingham's economic community. In the course of the negotiations, certain promises were made by the merchants — for example, to remove the stores' humiliating racial signs. On the basis of these promises, the Reverend Fred Shuttlesworth and the leaders of the Alabama Christian Movement for Human Rights agreed to a moratorium on all demonstrations. As the weeks and months went by, we realized that we were the victims of a broken promise. A few signs, briefly removed, returned; the others remained.

As in so many past experiences, our hopes had been blasted, and the shadow of deep disappointment settled upon us. We had no alternative except to prepare for direct action, whereby we would present our very bodies as a means of laying our case before the conscience of the local and the national community. Mindful of the difficulties involved, we decided to undertake a process of self-purification. We began a series of workshops on nonviolence, and we repeatedly asked ourselves: "Are you able to accept blows without retaliating?" "Are you able to endure the ordeal of jail?" We decided to schedule our direct-action program for the Easter season, realizing that except for Christmas, this is the main shopping period of the year. Knowing that a strong economic-withdrawal program would be the by-product of direct action, we felt that this would be the best time to bring pressure to bear on the merchants for the needed change.

Then it occurred to us that Birmingham's mayoral election was coming up in March, and we speedily decided to postpone action until after election day. When we discovered that the Commissioner of Public Safety, Eugene "Bull" Connor, had piled up enough votes to be in the run-off, we decided again to postpone action until the day after the run-off so that the demonstrations could not be used to cloud the issues. Like many others, we waited to see Mr. Connor defeated, and to this end we endured postponement after postponement. Having aided in this community need, we felt that our direct-action program could be delayed no longer.

You may well ask, "Why direct action? Why sit-ins, marches, and so forth? Isn't negotiation a better path?" You are quite right in calling for negotiation. Indeed, this is the very purpose of direct action. Nonviolent direct action seeks to create such a crisis and foster such a tension that a community which has constantly refused to negotiate is forced to confront the issue. It seeks so to dramatize the issue that it can no longer be ignored. My citing the creation of tension as part of the work of the nonviolent resister may sound rather shocking. But I must confess that I am not afraid of the word "tension." I have earnestly opposed violent tension, but there is a type of constructive, nonviolent tension which is necessary for growth. Just as Socrates felt that it was necessary to create a tension in the mind so that individuals could rise from the bondage of myths and half truths to the unfettered realm of creative analysis and objective appraisal, so must we see the need for nonviolent gadflies to create the kind of tension in society that will help men rise from the dark depths of prejudice and racism to the majestic heights of understanding and brotherhood.

The purpose of our direct-action program is to create a situation so crisis-packed that it will inevitably open the door to negotiation. I therefore concur with you in your call for negotiation. Too long has our beloved Southland been bogged down in a tragic effort to live in monologue rather than dialogue.

One of the basic points in your statement is that the action that I and my associates have taken in Birmingham is untimely. Some have asked: "Why didn't you give the new city administration time to act?" The only answer that I can give to this query is that the new Birmingham administration must be prodded about as much as the outgoing one, before it will act. We are sadly mistaken if we feel that the election of Albert Boutwell as mayor will bring the millennium[2] to Birmingham. While Mr. Boutwell is a much more gentle person than Mr. Connor, they are both segregationists, dedicated to maintenance of the status quo. I have hoped that Mr. Boutwell will be reasonable enough to see the futility of massive resistance to desegregation. But he will not see this without pressure from devotees of civil rights. My friends, I must say to you that we have not made a single gain in civil rights without determined legal and nonviolent pressure. Lamentably, it is an historical fact that privileged groups seldom give up their privileges voluntarily. Individuals may see the moral light and voluntarily give up their unjust posture; but, as Reinhold Niebuhr[3] has reminded us, groups tend to be more immoral than individuals.

10

---

[2]*the millennium*: A reference to the Second Coming of Christ, which the Book of Revelation says will be followed by a thousand years of peace. [Eds.]

[3]*Reinhold Niebuhr* (1892–1971): A Protestant philosopher who urged church members to put their beliefs into action against social injustice. [Eds.]

We know through painful experience that freedom is never voluntarily given by the oppressor; it must be demanded by the oppressed. Frankly, I have yet to engage in a direct-action campaign that was "well timed" in the view of those who have not suffered unduly from the disease of segregation. For years now I have heard the word "Wait!" It rings in the ear of every Negro with piercing familiarity. This "Wait" has almost always meant "Never." We must come to see, with one of our distinguished jurists, that "justice too long delayed is justice denied."[4]

We have waited for more than 340 years for our constitutional and God-given rights. The nations of Asia and Africa are moving with jet-like speed toward gaining political independence, but we still creep at horse-and-buggy pace toward gaining a cup of coffee at a lunch counter. Perhaps it is easy for those who have never felt the stinging darts of segregation to say, "Wait." But when you have seen vicious mobs lynch your mothers and fathers at will and drown your sisters and brothers at whim; when you have seen hate-filled policemen curse, kick, and even kill your black brothers and sisters; when you see the vast majority of your twenty million Negro brothers smothering in an airtight cage of poverty in the midst of an affluent society; when you suddenly find your tongue twisted and your speech stammering as you seek to explain to your six-year-old daughter why she can't go to the public amusement park that has just been advertised on television, and see tears welling up in her eyes when she is told that Funtown is closed to colored children, and see ominous clouds of inferiority beginning to form in her little mental sky, and see her beginning to distort her personality by developing an unconscious bitterness toward white people; when you have to concoct an answer for a five-year-old son who is asking, "Daddy, why do white people treat colored people so mean?"; when you take a cross-country drive and find it necessary to sleep night after night in the uncomfortable corners of your automobile because no motel will accept you; when you are humiliated day in and day out by nagging signs reading "white" and "colored"; when your first name becomes "nigger," your middle name becomes "boy" (however old you are) and your last name becomes "John," and your wife and mother are never given the respected title "Mrs."; when you are harried by day and haunted by night by the fact that you are a Negro, living constantly at tiptoe stance, never quite knowing what to expect next, and are plagued with inner fears and outer resentments; when you are forever fighting a degenerating sense of "nobodiness" — then you will understand why we find it difficult to wait. There comes a time when the cup of endurance runs over, and men are no longer willing to be plunged into the abyss of despair. I hope, sirs, you can understand our legitimate and unavoidable impatience.

---

[4] *"justice too long delayed is justice denied"*: A statement made by U.S. Supreme Court Chief Justice Earl Warren. It was inspired by English writer Walter Savage Landor's statement that "Justice delayed is justice denied." [Eds.]

You express a great deal of anxiety over our willingness to break laws.   15
This is certainly a legitimate concern. Since we so diligently urge people to
obey the Supreme Court's decision of 1954 outlawing segregation in the
public schools, at first glance it may seem rather paradoxical for us consciously to break laws. One may then ask: "How can you advocate breaking some laws and obeying others?" The answer lies in the fact that there are
two types of laws: just and unjust. I would be the first to advocate obeying
just laws. One has not only a legal but a moral responsibility to obey just
laws. Conversely, one has a moral responsibility to disobey unjust laws. I
would agree with St. Augustine that "an unjust law is no law at all."

Now, what is the difference between the two? How does one determine
whether a law is just or unjust? A just law is a manmade code that squares
with the moral law or the law of God. An unjust law is a code that is out of
harmony with the moral law. To put it in the terms of St. Thomas Aquinas:
An unjust law is a human law that is not rooted in eternal law and natural
law. Any law that uplifts human personality is just. Any law that degrades
human personality is unjust. All segregation statutes are unjust because segregation distorts the soul and damages the personality. It gives the segrega-
tor a false sense of superiority and the segregated a false sense of inferiority.
Segregation, to use the terminology of the Jewish philosopher Martin Buber,
substitutes an "I-it" relationship for an "I-thou" relationship and ends up
relegating persons to the status of things. Hence segregation is not only politically, economically, and sociologically unsound, it is morally wrong and
sinful. Paul Tillich has said that sin is separation. Is not segregation an existential expression of man's tragic separation, his awful estrangement, his
terrible sinfulness? Thus it is that I can urge men to obey the 1954 decision
of the Supreme Court, for it is morally right; and I can urge them to disobey
segregation ordinances, for they are morally wrong.

Let us consider a more concrete example of just and unjust laws. An
unjust law is a code that a numerical or power majority group compels a
minority group to obey but does not make binding on itself. This is *difference*
made legal. By the same token, a just law is a code that a majority compels
a minority to follow and that it is willing to follow itself. This is *sameness*
made legal.

Let me give another explanation. A law is unjust if it is inflicted on a
minority that, as a result of being denied the right to vote, had no part in
enacting or devising the law. Who can say that the legislature of Alabama
which set up that state's segregation laws was democratically elected?
Throughout Alabama all sorts of devious methods are used to prevent
Negroes from becoming registered voters, and there are some counties in
which, even though Negroes constitute a majority of the population, not a
single Negro is registered. Can any law enacted under such circumstances be
considered democratically structured?

Sometimes a law is just on its face and unjust in its application. For instance, I have been arrested on a charge of parading without a permit. Now,

there is nothing wrong in having an ordinance which requires a permit for a parade. But such an ordinance becomes unjust when it is used to maintain segregation and to deny citizens the First Amendment privilege of peaceful assembly and protest.

I hope you are able to see the distinction I am trying to point out. In no sense do I advocate evading or defying the law, as would the rabid segregationist. That would lead to anarchy. One who breaks an unjust law must do so openly, lovingly, and with a willingness to accept the penalty. I submit that an individual who breaks a law that conscience tells him is unjust, and who willingly accepts the penalty of imprisonment in order to arouse the conscience of the community over its injustice, is in reality expressing the highest respect for law.   20

Of course, there is nothing new about this kind of civil disobedience. It was evidenced sublimely in the refusal of Shadrach, Meshach, and Abednego to obey the laws of Nebuchadnezzar,[5] on the ground that a higher moral law was at stake. It was practiced superbly by the early Christians, who were willing to face hungry lions and the excruciating pain of chopping blocks rather than submit to certain unjust laws of the Roman Empire. To a degree, academic freedom is a reality today because Socrates practiced civil disobedience. In our own nation, the Boston Tea Party represented a massive act of civil disobedience.

We should never forget that everything Adolf Hitler did in Germany was "legal" and everything the Hungarian freedom fighters did in Hungary was "illegal." It was "illegal" to aid and comfort a Jew in Hitler's Germany. Even so, I am sure that, had I lived in Germany at the time, I would have aided and comforted my Jewish brothers. If today I lived in a Communist country where certain principles dear to the Christian faith are suppressed, I would openly advocate disobeying that country's antireligious laws.

I must make two honest confessions to you, my Christian and Jewish brothers. First, I must confess that over the past few years I have been gravely disappointed with the white moderate. I have almost reached the regrettable conclusion that the Negro's great stumbling block in his stride toward freedom is not the White Citizen's Counciler[6] or the Ku Klux Klanner, but the white moderate, who is more devoted to "order" than to justice; who prefers a negative peace which is the absence of tension to a positive

---

[5] *"the refusal of Shadrach . . . Nebuchadnezzar"*: According to the Book of Daniel 1:7–3:30, Nebuchadnezzar (c. 630 BCE–c. 562 BCE), king of the Chaldean empire, ordered Shadrach, Meshach, and Abednego to worship a golden image. When they refused, they were cast into a fiery furnace but remained unharmed. [Eds.]

[6] *White Citizen's Counciler*: A member of an organization that was formed after the U.S. Supreme Court's 1954 *Brown v. Board of Education* decision. Its purpose was to maintain segregation. [Eds.]

peace which is the presence of justice; who constantly says, "I agree with you in the goal you seek, but I cannot agree with your methods of direct action"; who paternalistically believes he can set the timetable for another man's freedom; who lives by a mythical concept of time and who constantly advises the Negro to wait for a "more convenient season." Shallow understanding from people of good will is more frustrating than absolute misunderstanding from people of ill will. Lukewarm acceptance is much more bewildering than outright rejection.

I had hoped that the white moderate would understand that law and order exist for the purpose of establishing justice and that when they fail in this purpose they become the dangerously structured dams that block the flow of social progress. I had hoped that the white moderate would understand that the present tension in the South is a necessary phase of the transition from an obnoxious negative peace, in which the Negro passively accepted his unjust plight, to a substantive and positive peace, in which all men will respect the dignity and worth of human personality. Actually, we who engage in nonviolent direct action are not the creators of tension. We merely bring to the surface the hidden tension that is already alive. We bring it out in the open, where it can be seen and dealt with. Like a boil that can never be cured so long as it is covered up but must be opened with all its ugliness to the natural medicines of air and light, injustice must be exposed, with all the tension its exposure creates, to the light of human conscience and the air of national opinion before it can be cured.

In your statement you assert that our actions, even though peaceful, must be condemned because they precipitate violence. But is this a logical assertion? Isn't this like condemning a robbed man because his possession of money precipitated the evil act of robbery? Isn't this like condemning Socrates because his unswerving commitment to truth and his philosophical inquiries precipitated the act by the misguided populace in which they made him drink hemlock? Isn't this like condemning Jesus because his unique God-consciousness and never-ceasing devotion to God's will precipitated the evil act of crucifixion? We must come to see that, as the federal courts have consistently affirmed, it is wrong to urge an individual to cease his efforts to gain his basic constitutional rights because the quest may precipitate violence. Society must protect the robbed and punish the robber.

I had also hoped that the white moderate would reject the myth concerning time in relation to the struggle for freedom. I have just received a letter from a white brother in Texas. He writes: "All Christians know that the colored people will receive equal rights eventually, but it is possible that you are in too great a religious hurry. It has taken Christianity almost two thousand years to accomplish what it has. The teachings of Christ take time to come to earth." Such an attitude stems from a tragic misconception of time, from the strangely irrational notion that there is something in the very flow of time that will inevitably cure all ills. Actually, time itself is neutral; it can be used either destructively or constructively. More and more I feel that the people of ill will have used time much more effectively than have the people of good will. We will have to repent in this generation not merely for the hateful words and actions of the bad people, but for the appalling silence of the good people. Human progress never rolls in on wheels of inevitability; it comes through the tireless efforts of men willing to be co-workers with God, and without this hard work, time itself becomes an ally of the forces of social stagnation. We must use time creatively, in the knowledge that the time is always ripe to do right. Now is the time to make real the promise of democracy and transform our pending national elegy into a creative psalm of brotherhood. Now is the time to lift our national policy from the quicksand of racial injustice to the solid rock of human dignity.

You speak of our activity in Birmingham as extreme. At first I was rather disappointed that fellow clergymen would see my nonviolent efforts as those of an extremist. I began thinking about the fact that I stand in the middle of two opposing forces in the Negro community. One is a force of complacency, made up in part of Negroes who, as a result of long years of oppression, are so drained of self-respect and a sense of "somebodiness" that they have adjusted to segregation; and in part of a few middle-class Negroes who, because of a degree of academic and economic security and because in some ways they profit by segregation, have become insensitive to the problems of the masses. The other force is one of bitterness and hatred, and it comes perilously close to advocating violence. It is expressed in the various black nationalist groups that are springing up across the nation, the largest and best known being Elijah Muhammad's Muslim movement. Nourished by the Negro's frustration over the continued existence of racial discrimination, this movement is made up of people who have lost faith in America, who have absolutely repudiated Christianity, and who have concluded that the white man is an incorrigible "devil."

I have tried to stand between these two forces, saying that we need emulate neither the "do-nothingism" of the complacent nor the hatred and despair of the black nationalist. For there is the more excellent way of love and nonviolent protest. I am grateful to God that, through the influence of the Negro church, the way of nonviolence became an integral part of our struggle.

If this philosophy had not emerged, by now many streets of the South would, I am convinced, be flowing with blood. And I am further convinced that if our white brothers dismiss as "rabble-rousers" and "outside agitators" those of us who employ nonviolent direct action, and if they refuse to support our nonviolent efforts, millions of Negroes will, out of frustration and despair, seek solace and security in black nationalist ideologies — a development that would inevitably lead to a frightening racial nightmare.

Oppressed people cannot remain oppressed forever. The yearning for   30
freedom eventually manifests itself, and that is what has happened to the American Negro. Something within has reminded him of his birthright of freedom, and something without has reminded him that it can be gained.

Consciously or unconsciously, he has been caught up by the *Zeitgeist*,[7] and with his black brothers of Africa and his brown and yellow brothers of Asia, South America, and the Caribbean, the United States Negro is moving with a sense of great urgency toward the promised land of racial justice. If one recognizes this vital urge that has engulfed the Negro community, one should readily understand why public demonstrations are taking place. The Negro has many pent-up resentments and latent frustrations, and he must release them. So let him march; let him make prayer pilgrimages to the city hall; let him go on freedom rides[8] — and try to understand why he must do so. If his repressed emotions are not released in nonviolent ways, they will seek expression through violence; this is not a threat but a fact of history. So I have not said to my people, "Get rid of your discontent." Rather, I have tried to say that this normal and healthy discontent can be channeled into the creative outlet of nonviolent direct action. And now this approach is being termed extremist.

But though I was initially disappointed at being categorized as an extremist, as I continued to think about the matter I gradually gained a measure of satisfaction from the label. Was not Jesus an extremist for love: "Love your enemies, bless them that curse you, do good to them that hate you, and pray for them which despitefully use you, and persecute you." Was not Amos an extremist for justice: "Let justice roll down like waters and righteousness like an everflowing stream." Was not Paul an extremist for the Christian gospel: "I bear in my body the marks of the Lord Jesus." Was not Martin Luther an extremist: "Here I stand; I cannot do otherwise, so help me God." And John Bunyan: "I will stay in jail to the end of my days before I make a butchery of my conscience." And Abraham Lincoln: "This nation cannot survive half slave and half free." And Thomas Jefferson: "We hold these truths to be self-evident, that all men are created equal . . ." So the question is not whether we will be extremists, but what kind of extremists we will be. Will we be extremists for hate or for love? Will we be extremists for the preservation of injustice or for the extension of justice? In that dramatic scene on Calvary's hill three men were crucified. We must never forget that all three were crucified for the same crime — the crime of extremism. Two were extremists for immorality, and thus fell below their environment. The other, Jesus Christ, was an extremist for love, truth, and goodness, and thereby rose above his environment. Perhaps the South, the nation, and the world are in dire need of creative extremists.

I had hoped that the white moderate would see this need. Perhaps I was too optimistic; perhaps I expected too much. I suppose I should have realized

---

[7]*Zeitgeist*: The intellectual, moral, and cultural spirit of the times (German). [Eds.]

[8]*freedom rides*: The bus and train rides that black and white protesters took in the early 1960s to protest segregation. [Eds.]

that few members of the oppressor race can understand the deep groans and passionate yearnings of the oppressed race, and still fewer have the vision to see that injustice must be rooted out by strong, persistent, and determined action. I am thankful, however, that some of our white brothers in the South have grasped the meaning of this social revolution and committed themselves to it. They are still all too few in quantity, but they are big in quality. Some — such as Ralph McGill, Lillian Smith, Harry Golden, James McBride Dabbs, Ann Braden, and Sarah Patton Boyle — have written about our struggle in eloquent and prophetic terms. Others have marched with us down nameless streets of the South. They have languished in filthy, roach-infested jails, suffering the abuse and brutality of policemen who view them as "dirty nigger-lovers." Unlike so many of their moderate brothers and sisters, they have recognized the urgency of the moment and sensed the need for powerful "action" antidotes to combat the disease of segregation.

Let me take note of my other major disappointment. I have been so greatly disappointed with the white church and its leadership. Of course, there are some notable exceptions. I am not unmindful of the fact that each of you has taken some significant stands on this issue. I commend you, Reverend Stallings, for your Christian stand on this past Sunday, in welcoming Negroes to your worship service on a nonsegregated basis. I commend the Catholic leaders of this state for integrating Spring Hill College several years ago.

But despite these notable exceptions, I must honestly reiterate that I have been disappointed with the church. I do not say this as one of those negative critics who can always find something wrong with the church. I say this as a minister of the gospel, who loves the church; who was nurtured in its bosom; who has been sustained by its spiritual blessings and who will remain true to it as long as the cord of life shall lengthen.

When I was suddenly catapulted into the leadership of the bus protest   35 in Montgomery, Alabama, a few years ago, I felt we would be supported by the white church. I felt that the white ministers, priests, and rabbis of the South would be among our strongest allies. Instead, some have been outright opponents, refusing to understand the freedom movement and misrepresenting its leaders; all too many others have been more cautious than courageous and have remained silent behind the anesthetizing security of stained-glass windows.

In spite of my shattered dreams, I came to Birmingham with the hope that the white religious leadership of this community would see the justice of our cause and, with deep moral concern, would serve as the channel through which our just grievances could reach the power structure. I had hoped that each of you would understand. But again I have been disappointed. . . .

There was a time when the church was very powerful — in the time when the early Christians rejoiced at being deemed worthy to suffer for what they believed. In those days the church was not merely a thermometer that recorded the ideas and principles of popular opinion; it was a thermostat that transformed the mores of society. Whenever the early Christians entered a town, the people in power became disturbed and immediately sought to convict the Christians for being "disturbers of the peace" and "outside agitators." But the Christians pressed on, in the conviction that they were "a colony of heaven," called to obey God rather than man. Small in number, they were big in commitment. They were too God-intoxicated to be "astronomically intimidated." By their effort and example they brought an end to such ancient evils as infanticide and gladiatorial contests.

Things are different now. So often the contemporary church is a weak, ineffectual voice with an uncertain sound. So often it is an archdefender of the status quo. Far from being disturbed by the presence of the church, the powerful structure of the average community is consoled by the church's silent — and often even vocal — sanction of things as they are.

But the judgment of God is upon the church as never before. If today's church does not recapture the sacrificial spirit of the early church, it will lose its authenticity, forfeit the loyalty of millions, and be dismissed as an irrelevant social club with no meaning for the twentieth century. Every day I meet young people whose disappointment with the church has turned into outright disgust.

Perhaps I have once again been too optimistic. Is organized religion too inextricably bound to the status quo to save our nation and the world? Perhaps I must turn my faith to the inner spiritual church, the church within the church, as the true *ekklesia*[9] and the hope of the world. But again I am thankful to God that some noble souls from the ranks of organized religion have broken loose from the paralyzing chains of conformity and joined us as active partners in the struggle for freedom. They have left their secure congregations and walked the streets of Albany, Georgia, with us. They have gone down the highways of the South on torturous rides for freedom. Yes, they have gone to jail with us. Some have been dismissed from their churches, have lost the support of their bishops and fellow ministers. But they have acted in the faith that right defeated is stronger than evil triumphant. Their witness has been the spiritual salt that has preserved the true meaning of the gospel in these troubled times. They have carved a tunnel of hope through the dark mountain of disappointment.

I hope the church as a whole will meet the challenge of this decisive hour. But even if the church does not come to the aid of justice, I have no despair about the future. I have no fear about the outcome of our struggle in Birmingham, even if our motives are at present misunderstood. We will reach the goal of freedom in Birmingham and all over the nation, because the goal of America is freedom. Abused and scorned though we may be, our destiny is tied up with America's destiny. Before the pilgrims landed at Plymouth, we were here. Before the pen of Jefferson etched the majestic words

40

---

[9]*ekklesia*: The church (Greek). Refers to the spirit of the church. [Eds.]

of the Declaration of Independence across the pages of history, we were here. For more than two centuries our forebears labored in this country without wages; they made cotton king; they built the homes of their masters while suffering gross injustice and shameful humiliation — and yet out of a bottomless vitality they continued to thrive and develop. If the inexpressible cruelties of slavery could not stop us, the opposition we now face will surely fail. We will win our freedom because the sacred heritage of our nation and the eternal will of God are embodied in our echoing demands.

Before closing I feel impelled to mention one other point in your statement that has troubled me profoundly. You warmly commended the Birmingham police force for keeping "order" and "preventing violence." I doubt that you would have so warmly commended the police force if you had seen its dogs sinking their teeth into unarmed, nonviolent Negroes. I doubt that you would so quickly commend the policemen if you were to observe their ugly and inhumane treatment of Negroes here in the city jail; if you were to watch them push and curse old Negro women and young Negro girls; if you were to see them slap and kick old Negro men and young boys; if you were to observe them, as they did on two occasions, refuse to give us food because we wanted to sing our grace together. I cannot join you in your praise of the Birmingham police department.

It is true that the police have exercised a degree of discipline in handling the demonstrators. In this sense they have conducted themselves rather "nonviolently" in public. But for what purpose? To preserve the evil system of segregation. Over the past few years I have consistently preached that nonviolence demands that the means we use must be as pure as the ends we seek. I have tried to make clear that it is wrong to use immoral means to attain moral ends. But now I must affirm that it is just as wrong, or perhaps even more so, to use moral means to preserve immoral ends. Perhaps Mr. Connor and his policemen have been rather nonviolent in public, as was Chief Pritchett in Albany, Georgia, but they have used the moral means of nonviolence to maintain the immoral end of racial injustice. As T. S. Eliot has said, "The last temptation is the greatest treason: To do the right deed for the wrong reason."

I wish you had commended the Negro sit-inners and demonstrators of Birmingham for their sublime courage, their willingness to suffer, and their amazing discipline in the midst of great provocation. One day the South will recognize its real heroes. They will be the James Merediths,[10] with the noble sense of purpose that enables them to face jeering and hostile mobs, and with the agonizing loneliness that characterizes the life of the pioneer. They will be old, oppressed, battered Negro women, symbolized in a seventy-two-year-old woman in Montgomery, Alabama, who rose up with a sense of

---

[10] *James Meredith* (b. 1933): In 1962, the first African American to become a student at the University of Mississippi. [Eds.]

dignity and with her people decided not to ride segregated buses and who responded with ungrammatical profundity to one who inquired about her weariness: "My feets is tired, but my soul is at rest." They will be the young high school and college students, the young ministers of the gospel and a host of their elders, courageously and nonviolently sitting in at lunch counters and willingly going to jail for conscience' sake. One day the South will know that when these disinherited children of God sat down at lunch counters, they were in reality standing up for what is best in the American dream and for the most sacred values in our Judaeo-Christian heritage, thereby bringing our nation back to those great wells of democracy which were dug deep by the founding fathers in their formulation of the Constitution and the Declaration of Independence.

Never before have I written so long a letter. I'm afraid it is much too   45
long to take your precious time. I can assure you that it would have been much shorter if I had been writing from a comfortable desk, but what else can one do when he is alone in a narrow jail cell other than write long letters, think long thoughts, and pray long prayers?

If I have said anything in this letter that overstates the truth and indicates an unreasonable impatience, I beg you to forgive me. If I have said anything that understates the truth and indicates my having a patience that allows me to settle for anything less than brotherhood, I beg God to forgive me.

I hope this letter finds you strong in the faith. I also hope that circumstances will soon make it possible for me to meet each of you, not as an integrationist or a civil rights leader but as a fellow clergyman and a Christian brother. Let us all hope that the dark clouds of racial prejudice will soon pass away and the deep fog of misunderstanding will be lifted from our fear-drenched communities, and in some not too distant tomorrow the radiant stars of love and brotherhood will shine over our great nation with all their scintillating beauty.

> *Yours in the cause of*
> *Peace and Brotherhood,*
> *Martin Luther King Jr.*

QUESTIONS

Reading

1. What are the four basic steps in any nonviolent campaign?
2. How does King define "just" and "unjust" laws? What does King conclude about individuals who break unjust laws?
3. King is always aware of the positions against which he is arguing and the counterarguments that are offered by those who hold those positions. How does he represent those positions, and how does he deal with them?

Base your response on specific instances in which he mentions such positions and responds to them.

4. In this *argumentative* open letter, what attitude does King seem to have toward his opponents? How does this apparent attitude strengthen, weaken, or otherwise change the force of his arguments?

Exploratory Writing

1. King's letter was an open response to a statement published by eight white Alabama clergymen. Working alone or in pairs, find an article, an editorial, or a political speech that you passionately disagree with, and write an *open letter* to the author or speaker. Use the skills and strategies you've learned about argumentative essay writing to strengthen your case.

2. At times King's prose verges on the poetical in its use of imagery and metaphor. Highlight, underline, or flag the places in this letter where King uses poetic language. How do these sections shape your response to the letter?

Making Connections

1. What is the tone of King's letter? How is it similar to or different from the tone of Barack Obama's (p. 303) speech?

2. Compare King's comments on historical racism with James Baldwin's (p. 109). In your opinion, where do the two writers' viewpoints overlap? Where do they diverge?

Essay Writing

1. Write an essay reflecting on King's famous statement: "Injustice anywhere is a threat to justice everywhere" (paragraph 4). Be sure to use contemporary examples of injustice in your discussion.

Paired Readings: On Race Relations

A More Perfect Union

Barack Obama

*Barack Obama (b. 1961) was born in Honolulu, Hawaii, to a
Kansas-born American mother and a Kenyan father, who met and
married when they were students at the University of Hawaii. The
effects of his parents' interracial marriage, his father's return to
Kenya, and his parents' subsequent divorce when he was very
young are central to his memoir,* Dreams from My Father: A Story
of Race and Inheritance *(1995; reprinted in 2004). A 1995 review
in the* New York Times Book Review *said that Obama's memoir
"persuasively describes the phenomenon of belonging to two different worlds, and thus belonging to neither." In addition to his
memoir, Obama wrote* The Audacity of Hope: Thoughts on Re-
claiming the American Dream, *published in 2006. After graduating from Columbia University in 1983, Obama worked as a
community organizer in Chicago, then went on to Harvard University, where he became the first African American president of
the* Harvard Law Review; *he received his law degree in 1991.
Turning down a prestigious judicial clerkship, he chose instead to
practice civil rights law in Chicago and to teach constitutional law
at the University of Chicago. He served in the Illinois Senate from
1997 to 2003 and was elected to the U.S. Senate in 2004. In 2008
he ran as the Democratic Party nominee for president of the United
States against Senator John McCain and won the election. At the
National Constitution Center in Philadelphia, Pennsylvania, in
March 2008, Senator Obama delivered the following speech about
racial relations, precipitated by the controversial remarks made by
his former pastor, Reverend Jeremiah Wright. Titled after the preamble to the United States Constitution, the speech elicited a
widespread reaction from politicians, news media, academics, and
voters, ultimately having a positive effect on the campaign.*

"We the people, in order to form a more perfect union."

Two hundred and twenty-one years ago, in a hall that still stands across the street, a group of men gathered and, with these simple words, launched America's improbable experiment in democracy. Farmers and scholars, statesmen and patriots, who had traveled across an ocean to escape tyranny and persecution finally made real their declaration of independence at a Philadelphia convention that lasted through the spring of 1787.

The document they produced was eventually signed but ultimately unfinished. It was stained by this nation's original sin of slavery, a question that divided the colonies and brought the convention to a stalemate until the founders chose to allow the slave trade to continue for at least twenty more years, and to leave any final resolution to future generations.

Of course, the answer to the slavery question was already embedded within our Constitution — a Constitution that had at its very core the ideal of equal citizenship under the law; a Constitution that promised its people liberty and justice, and a union that could be and should be perfected over time.

And yet words on a parchment would not be enough to deliver slaves   5
from bondage, or provide men and women of every color and creed their full rights and obligations as citizens of the United States. What would be needed were Americans in successive generations who were willing to do their part — through protests and struggle, on the streets and in the courts, through a civil war and civil disobedience, and always at great risk — to narrow that gap between the promise of our ideals and the reality of their time.

This was one of the tasks we set forth at the beginning of this campaign — to continue the long march of those who came before us, a march for a more just, more equal, more free, more caring, and more prosperous America. I chose to run for the presidency at this moment in history because I believe deeply that we cannot solve the challenges of our time unless we solve them together — unless we perfect our union by understanding that we may have different stories, but we hold common hopes; that we may not look the same and we may not have come from the same place, but we all want to move in the same direction — towards a better future for our children and our grandchildren.

This belief comes from my unyielding faith in the decency and generosity of the American people. But it also comes from my own American story.

I am the son of a black man from Kenya and a white woman from Kansas. I was raised with the help of a white grandfather who survived a Depression to serve in Patton's Army during World War II and a white grandmother who worked on a bomber assembly line at Fort Leavenworth while he was overseas. I've gone to some of the best schools in America and lived in one of the world's poorest nations. I am married to a black American who carries within her the blood of slaves and slaveowners — an inheritance we pass on to our two precious daughters. I have brothers, sisters, nieces, nephews, uncles, and cousins, of every race and every hue, scattered across three continents, and for as long as I live, I will never forget that in no other country on earth is my story even possible.

It's a story that hasn't made me the most conventional candidate. But it is a story that has seared into my genetic makeup the idea that this nation is more than the sum of its parts — that out of many, we are truly one.

Throughout the first year of this campaign, against all predictions to the contrary, we saw how hungry the American people were for this message of unity. Despite the temptation to view my candidacy through a purely racial lens, we won commanding victories in states with some of the whitest populations in the country. In South Carolina, where the Confederate flag still flies, we built a powerful coalition of African Americans and white Americans.

This is not to say that race has not been an issue in the campaign. At various stages in the campaign, some commentators have deemed me either "too black" or "not black enough." We saw racial tensions bubble to the surface during the week before the South Carolina primary. The press has scoured every exit poll for the latest evidence of racial polarization, not just in terms of white and black, but black and brown as well.

And yet, it has only been in the last couple of weeks that the discussion of race in this campaign has taken a particularly divisive turn.

On one end of the spectrum, we've heard the implication that my candidacy is somehow an exercise in affirmative action; that it's based solely on the desire of wide-eyed liberals to purchase racial reconciliation on the cheap. On the other end, we've heard my former pastor, Reverend Jeremiah Wright, use incendiary language to express views that have the potential not only to widen the racial divide, but views that denigrate both the greatness and the goodness of our nation — that rightly offend white and black alike.

I have already condemned, in unequivocal terms, the statements of Reverend Wright that have caused such controversy. For some, nagging questions remain. Did I know him to be an occasionally fierce critic of American domestic and foreign policy? Of course. Did I ever hear him make remarks that could be considered controversial while I sat in church? Yes. Did I strongly disagree with many of his political views? Absolutely — just as I'm sure many of you have heard remarks from your pastors, priests, or rabbis with which you strongly disagreed.

But the remarks that have caused this recent firestorm weren't simply controversial. They weren't simply a religious leader's effort to speak out against perceived injustice. Instead, they expressed a profoundly distorted view of this country — a view that sees white racism as endemic, and that elevates what is wrong with America above all that we know is right with America; a view that sees the conflicts in the Middle East as rooted primarily in the actions of stalwart allies like Israel, instead of emanating from the perverse and hateful ideologies of radical Islam.

As such, Reverend Wright's comments were not only wrong but divisive, divisive at a time when we need unity; racially charged at a time when we need to come together to solve a set of monumental problems — two wars, a terrorist threat, a falling economy, a chronic health-care crisis, and potentially devastating climate change; problems that are neither black or white or Latino or Asian, but rather problems that confront us all.

Given my background, my politics, and my professed values and ideals, there will no doubt be those for whom my statements of condemnation are not enough. Why associate myself with Reverend Wright in the first place, they may ask? Why not join another church? And I confess that if all that I knew of Reverend Wright were the snippets of those sermons that have run in an endless loop on the television and YouTube, or if Trinity United Church of Christ conformed to the caricatures being peddled by some commentators, there is no doubt that I would react in much the same way.

But the truth is, that isn't all that I know of the man. The man I met more than twenty years ago is a man who helped introduce me to my Christian faith, a man who spoke to me about our obligations to love one another, to care for the sick and lift up the poor. He is a man who served his country as a U.S. Marine, who has studied and lectured at some of the finest universities and seminaries in the country, and who for over thirty years led a church that serves the community by doing God's work here on earth — by housing the homeless, ministering to the needy, providing day-care services and scholarships and prison ministries, and reaching out to those suffering from HIV/AIDS.

In my first book, *Dreams from My Father,* I described the experience of my first service at Trinity:

> People began to shout, to rise from their seats and clap and cry out, a forceful wind carrying the reverend's voice up into the rafters. . . . And in that single note — hope! — I heard something else; at the foot of that cross, inside the thousands of churches across the city, I imagined the stories of ordinary black people merging with the stories of David and Goliath, Moses and Pharaoh, the Christians in the lion's den, Ezekiel's field of dry bones. Those stories — of survival, and freedom, and hope — became our story, my story; the blood that had spilled was our blood, the tears our tears; until this black church, on this bright day, seemed once more a vessel carrying the story of a people into future generations and into a larger world. Our trials and triumphs became at once unique and universal, black and more than black; in chronicling our journey, the stories and songs gave us a means to reclaim memories that we didn't need to feel shame about . . . memories that all people might study and cherish — and with which we could start to rebuild.

That has been my experience at Trinity. Like other predominantly black churches across the country, Trinity embodies the black community in its entirety — the doctor and the welfare mom, the model student and the   20 former gang-banger. Like other black churches, Trinity's services are full of raucous laughter and sometimes bawdy humor. They are full of dancing, clapping, screaming, and shouting that may seem jarring to the untrained ear. The church contains in full the kindness and cruelty; the fierce intelligence and the shocking ignorance; the struggles and successes; the love and, yes, the bitterness and bias that make up the black experience in America.

And this helps explain, perhaps, my relationship with Reverend Wright. As imperfect as he may be, he has been like family to me. He strengthened my faith, officiated my wedding, and baptized my children. Not once in my conversations with him have I heard him talk about any ethnic group in derogatory terms, or treat whites with whom he interacted with anything but courtesy and respect. He contains within him the contradictions — the good and the bad — of the community that he has served diligently for so many years.

I can no more disown him than I can disown the black community. I can no more disown him than I can my white grandmother — a woman who helped raise me, a woman who sacrificed again and again for me, a woman who loves me as much as she loves anything in this world, but a woman who once confessed her fear of black men who passed by her on the street, and who on more than one occasion has uttered racial or ethnic stereotypes that made me cringe.

These people are a part of me. And they are a part of America, this country that I love.

Some will see this as an attempt to justify or excuse comments that are simply inexcusable. I can assure you it is not. I suppose the politically safe thing would be to move on from this episode and just hope that it fades into the woodwork. We can dismiss Reverend Wright as a crank or a demagogue, just as some have dismissed Geraldine Ferraro, in the aftermath of her recent statements, as harboring some deep-seated racial bias.

But race is an issue that I believe this nation cannot afford to ignore   25 right now. We would be making the same mistake that Reverend Wright made in his offending sermons about America — to simplify and stereotype and amplify the negative to the point that it distorts reality.

The fact is that the comments that have been made and the issues that have surfaced over the last few weeks reflect the complexities of race in this country that we've never really worked through — a part of our union that we have yet to perfect. And if we walk away now, if we simply retreat into our respective corners, we will never be able to come together and solve challenges like health care, or education, or the need to find good jobs for every American.

Understanding this reality requires a reminder of how we arrived at this point. As William Faulkner once wrote, "The past isn't dead and buried. In fact, it isn't even past." We do not need to recite here the history of racial injustice in this country. But we do need to remind ourselves that so many of the disparities that exist in the African-American community today can be directly traced to inequalities passed on from an earlier generation that suffered under the brutal legacy of slavery and Jim Crow.

Segregated schools were, and are, inferior schools; we still haven't fixed them, fifty years after *Brown v. Board of Education*, and the inferior education they provided, then and now, helps explain the pervasive achievement gap between today's black and white students.

Legalized discrimination — where blacks were prevented, often through violence, from owning property, or loans were not granted to African-American business owners, or black homeowners could not access FHA mortgages, or blacks were excluded from unions, or the police force, or fire departments — meant that black families could not amass any meaningful wealth to bequeath to future generations. That history helps explain the wealth and income gap between black and white, and the concentrated pockets of poverty that persist in so many of today's urban and rural communities.

A lack of economic opportunity among black men, and the shame and   30
frustration that came from not being able to provide for one's family, contributed to the erosion of black families — a problem that welfare policies for many years may have worsened. And the lack of basic services in so many urban black neighborhoods — parks for kids to play in, police walking the beat, regular garbage pick-up, and building code enforcement — all helped create a cycle of violence, blight, and neglect that continues to haunt us.

This is the reality in which Reverend Wright and other African-Americans of his generation grew up. They came of age in the late fifties and early sixties, a time when segregation was still the law of the land and opportunity was systematically constricted. What's remarkable is not how many failed in the face of discrimination, but rather how many men and women overcame the odds; how many were able to make a way out of no way for those like me who would come after them.

But for all those who scratched and clawed their way to get a piece of the American Dream, there were many who didn't make it — those who were ultimately defeated, in one way or another, by discrimination. That legacy of defeat was passed on to future generations — those young men and increasingly young women who we see standing on street corners or languishing in our prisons, without hope or prospects for the future. Even for those blacks who did make it, questions of race, and racism, continue to define their worldview in fundamental ways. For the men and women of Reverend Wright's generation, the memories of humiliation and doubt and fear have not gone away; nor has the anger and the bitterness of those years. That anger may not get expressed in public, in front of white co-workers or white friends. But it does find voice in the barbershop or around the kitchen table. At times, that anger is exploited by politicians, to gin up votes along racial lines, or to make up for a politician's own failings.

And occasionally it finds voice in the church on Sunday morning, in the pulpit and in the pews. The fact that so many people are surprised to hear that anger in some of Reverend Wright's sermons simply reminds us of the old truism that the most segregated hour in American life occurs on Sunday morning. That anger is not always productive; indeed, all too often it distracts attention from solving real problems; it keeps us from squarely facing our own complicity in our condition, and prevents the African-American community from forging the alliances it needs to bring about real change. But the anger is real; it is powerful; and to simply wish it away, to condemn it without understanding its roots, only serves to widen the chasm of misunderstanding that exists between the races.

In fact, a similar anger exists within segments of the white community. Most working- and middle-class white Americans don't feel that they have been particularly privileged by their race. Their experience is the immigrant experience — as far as they're concerned, no one's handed them anything; they've built it from scratch. They've worked hard all their lives, many times only to see their jobs shipped overseas or their pension dumped after a lifetime of labor. They are anxious about their futures, and feel their dreams slipping away; in an era of stagnant wages and global competition, opportunity comes to be seen as a zero sum game, in which your dreams come at my expense. So when they are told to bus their children to a school across town, when they hear that an African-American is getting an advantage in landing a good job or a spot in a good college because of an injustice that they themselves never committed; when they're told that their fears about crime in urban neighborhoods are somehow prejudiced, resentment builds over time.

Like the anger within the black community, these resentments aren't   35 always expressed in polite company. But they have helped shape the political landscape for at least a generation. Anger over welfare and affirmative action helped forge the Reagan Coalition. Politicians routinely exploited fears of crime for their own electoral ends. Talk show hosts and conservative commentators built entire careers unmasking bogus claims of racism while dismissing legitimate discussions of racial injustice and inequality as mere political correctness or reverse racism.

Just as black anger often proved counterproductive, so have these white resentments distracted attention from the real culprits of the middle class squeeze — a corporate culture rife with inside dealing, questionable accounting practices, and short-term greed; a Washington dominated by lobbyists and special interests; economic policies that favor the few over the many. And yet, to wish away the resentments of white Americans, to label them as misguided or even racist, without recognizing they are grounded in legitimate concerns — this too widens the racial divide, and blocks the path to understanding.

This is where we are right now. It's a racial stalemate we've been stuck in for years. Contrary to the claims of some of my critics, black and white, I have never been so naive as to believe that we can get beyond our racial divisions in a single election cycle, or with a single candidacy — particularly a candidacy as imperfect as my own.

But I have asserted a firm conviction — a conviction rooted in my faith in God and my faith in the American people — that working together we can move beyond some of our old racial wounds, and that in fact we have no choice if we are to continue on the path of a more perfect union.

For the African-American community, that path means embracing the burdens of our past without becoming victims of our past. It means continuing to insist on a full measure of justice in every aspect of American life. But it also means binding our particular grievances — for better health care, and better schools, and better jobs — to the larger aspirations of all Americans — the white woman struggling to break the glass ceiling, the white man who's been laid off, the immigrant trying to feed his family. And it means taking full responsibility for our own lives — by demanding more from our fathers, and spending more time with our children, and reading to them, and teaching them that while they may face challenges and discrimination in their own lives, they must never succumb to despair or cynicism; they must always believe that they can write their own destiny.

Ironically, this quintessentially American — and yes, conservative — notion of self-help found frequent expression in Reverend Wright's sermons. But what my former pastor too often failed to understand is that embarking on a program of self-help also requires a belief that society can change.   40

The profound mistake of Reverend Wright's sermons is not that he spoke about racism in our society. It's that he spoke as if our society was static; as if no progress has been made; as if this country — a country that has made it possible for one of his own members to run for the highest office in the land and build a coalition of white and black, Latino and Asian, rich and poor, young and old — is still irrevocably bound to a tragic past. But what we know — what we have seen — is that America can change. That is the true genius of this nation. What we have already achieved gives us hope — the audacity to hope — for what we can and must achieve tomorrow.

In the white community, the path to a more perfect union means acknowledging that what ails the African-American community does not just exist in the minds of black people; that the legacy of discrimination — and current incidents of discrimination, while less overt than in the past — are real and must be addressed. Not just with words, but with deeds — by investing in our schools and our communities; by enforcing our civil rights laws and ensuring fairness in our criminal justice system; by providing this generation with ladders of opportunity that were unavailable for previous generations. It requires all Americans to realize that your dreams do not have to come at the expense of my dreams; that investing in the health, welfare, and education of black and brown and white children will ultimately help all of America prosper.

In the end, then, what is called for is nothing more, and nothing less, than what all the world's great religions demand — that we do unto others as we would have them do unto us. Let us be our brother's keeper, scripture tells us. Let us be our sister's keeper. Let us find that common stake we all have in one another, and let our politics reflect that spirit as well.

For we have a choice in this country. We can accept a politics that breeds division, and conflict, and cynicism. We can tackle race only as spectacle — as we did in the OJ trial — or in the wake of tragedy, as we did in the aftermath of Katrina — or as fodder for the nightly news. We can play Reverend Wright's sermons on every channel, every day, and talk about them from now until the election, and make the only question in this campaign whether or not the American people think that I somehow believe or sympathize with his most offensive words. We can pounce on some gaffe by a Hillary supporter as evidence that she's playing the race card, or we can speculate on whether white men will all flock to John McCain in the general election regardless of his policies.

We can do that.   45

But if we do, I can tell you that in the next election, we'll be talking about some other distraction. And then another one. And then another one. And nothing will change.

That is one option. Or, at this moment, in this election, we can come together and say, "Not this time." This time we want to talk about the crumbling schools that are stealing the future of black children and white children and Asian children and Hispanic children and Native American children. This time we want to reject the cynicism that tells us that these kids can't learn; that those kids who don't took like us are somebody else's problem. The children of America are not "those" kids; they are our kids, and we will not let them fall behind in a twenty-first century economy. Not this time.

This time we want to talk about how the lines in the emergency room are filled with whites and blacks and Hispanics who do not have health care, who don't have the power on their own to overcome the special interests in Washington, but who can take them on if we do it together.

This time we want to talk about the shuttered mills that once provided a decent life for men and women of every race, and the homes for sale that once belonged to Americans from every religion, every region, every walk of life. This time we want to talk about the fact that the real problem is not that someone who doesn't look like you might take your job; it's that the corporation you work for will ship it overseas for nothing more than a profit.

This time we want to talk about the men and women of every color   50 and creed who serve together, and fight together, and bleed together under the same proud flag. We want to talk about how to bring them home from a war that never should've been authorized and never should've been waged, and we want to talk about how we'll show our patriotism by caring for them, and their families, and giving them the benefits they have earned.

I would not be running for president if I didn't believe with all my heart that this is what the vast majority of Americans want for this country. This union may never be perfect, but generation after generation has shown that it can always be perfected. And today, whenever I find myself feeling doubtful or cynical about this possibility, what gives me the most hope is the next generation — the young people whose attitudes and beliefs and openness to change have already made history in this election.

There is one story in particular that I'd like to leave you with today — a story I told when I had the great honor of speaking on Dr. King's birthday at his home church, Ebenezer Baptist, in Atlanta.

There is a young, twenty-three-year-old white woman named Ashley Baia who organized for our campaign in Florence, South Carolina. She had been working to organize a mostly African-American community since the beginning of this campaign, and one day she was at a roundtable discussion where everyone went around telling their story and why they were there.

And Ashley said that when she was nine years old, her mother got cancer. And because she had to miss days of work, she was let go and lost her health care. They had to file for bankruptcy, and that's when Ashley decided that she had to do something to help her mom.

She knew that food was one of their most expensive costs, and so Ashley convinced her mother that what she really liked and really wanted to eat more than anything else was mustard and relish sandwiches. Because that was the cheapest way to eat.   55

She did this for a year until her mom got better, and she told everyone at the roundtable that the reason she joined our campaign was so that she could help the millions of other children in the country who want and need to help their parents too.

Now Ashley might have made a different choice. Perhaps somebody told her along the way that the source of her mother's problems were blacks who were on welfare and too lazy to work, or Hispanics who were coming into the country illegally. But she didn't. She sought out allies in her fight against injustice.

Anyway, Ashley finishes her story and then goes around the room and asks everyone else why they're supporting the campaign. They all have different stories and reasons. Many bring up a specific issue. And finally they come to this elderly black man who's been sitting there quietly the entire time. And Ashley asks him why he's there. And he does not bring up a specific issue. He does not say health care or the economy. He does not say education or the war. He does not say that he was there because of Barack Obama. He simply says to everyone in the room, "I am here because of Ashley."

"I'm here because of Ashley." By itself, that single moment of recognition between that young white girl and that old black man is not enough. It is not enough to give health care to the sick, or jobs to the jobless, or education to our children.

But it is where we start. It is where our union grows stronger. And as so   60
many generations have come to realize over the course of the two hundred
and twenty-one years since a band of patriots signed that document in
Philadelphia, that is where the perfection begins.

QUESTIONS

Reading

1. How does Obama characterize his former pastor, Reverend Jeremiah
   Wright?
2. How does Obama describe segregated schools? What remarks does he
   make about the school system?
3. In what ways is Obama's speech *reflective*? In what ways is it *argumentative* or *polemical*? Find and list examples of each mode of writing in
   Obama's speech.

Exploratory Writing

1. Highlight, underline, or flag the quotations that Obama uses in this
   speech. Consider not only the content of the quotes but the types of people he is quoting. What purpose does it serve to invoke the preamble to
   the Constitution in this speech? What purpose does it serve to invoke
   William Faulkner?
2. Without thinking too much about it or doing any extra research, write a
   personal response describing your instant reaction to this speech. Compare your response with that of another student. What do the different
   responses tell you about the effectiveness of the speech?
3. Some writing — such as plays, speeches, and slam poetry — is designed
   to be performed in front of an audience. List some differences between
   reading words on a page and hearing them spoken. Why would a politician choose to give a speech rather than simply post its text online or
   publish it in newspapers?

Making Connections

1. Martin Luther King Jr.'s famous "Letter from Birmingham Jail" (p. 288)
   was a response to eight white Alabama clergymen who published a
   statement speaking out against anti-segregation demonstrations in the
   streets. Obama's speech is also a statement in response to a controversy.
   Compare and contrast the different ways that King and Obama address
   the problem of race. How does each man anticipate his opponents'
   arguments?
2. George Orwell ("Politics and the English Language," p. 97) offers six
   rules for political writing. Analyze Obama's speech according to these

rules, as well as Orwell's other comments about political writing. How do you think Orwell would respond to this speech? Would he find it vague and obfuscating, or clear and honest?

Essay Writing

1. Imagine that you are running for president. Write a passionate speech describing why you are running and what you plan to do if you're elected. (An interesting bit of trivia about Obama's speech — although presidential candidates usually have their speechwriters write the first drafts of their speeches based on their ideas, in this case Obama wrote the first draft, and then got editing help from his speechwriter, Jon Favreau.)

Paired Readings: On the Reality of War

Hiroshima

John Berger

*After beginning his career as a painter and drawing instructor,
John Berger (b. 1926) became one of Britain's most influential art
critics. He has achieved recognition as a screenwriter, novelist,
and documentary writer. As a Marxist, he is concerned with the
ideological and technological conditioning of our ways of seeing
both art and the world. In* Ways of Seeing *(1972), he explores the
interrelation between words and images, between verbal and
visual meaning. "Hiroshima" first appeared in 1981 in the journal*
New Society *and later in a collection of essays,* The Sense of Sight
*(1985). Berger examines how the facts of nuclear holocaust have
been hidden through "a systematic, slow and thorough process
of suppression and elimination . . . within the reality of politics."
Images, rather than words, Berger asserts, can help us see through
the "mask of innocence" that evil wears.*

The whole incredible problem begins with the need to reinsert those
events of 6 August 1945 back into living consciousness.

I was shown a book last year at the Frankfurt Book Fair. The editor
asked me some question about what I thought of its format. I glanced at it
quickly and gave some reply. Three months ago I was sent a finished copy of
the book. It lay on my desk unopened. Occasionally its title and cover picture
caught my eye, but I did not respond. I didn't consider the book urgent, for I
believed that I already knew about what I would find within it.

Did I not clearly remember the day—I was in the army in Belfast—
when we first heard the news of the bomb dropped on Hiroshima? At how
many meetings during the first nuclear disarmament movement had I and
others not recalled the meaning of that bomb?

And then, one morning last week, I received a letter from America,
accompanying an article written by a friend. This friend is a doctor of philosophy and a Marxist. Furthermore, she is a very generous and warm-hearted
woman. The article was about the possibilities of a third world war. Vis-à-vis

the Soviet Union she took, I was surprised to read, a position very close to Reagan's. She concluded by evoking the likely scale of destruction which would be caused by nuclear weapons, and then welcomed the positive possibilities that this would offer the socialist revolution in the United States.

It was on that morning that I opened and read the book on my desk. It   5
is called *Unforgettable Fire.*[1]

The book consists of drawings and paintings made by people who were in Hiroshima on the day that the bomb was dropped, thirty-six years ago today. Often the pictures are accompanied by a verbal record of what the image represents. None of them is by a professional artist. In 1974, an old man went to the television center in Hiroshima to show to whomever was interested a picture he had painted, entitled "At about 4 pm, 6th August 1945, near Yurozuyo bridge."

This prompted an idea of launching a television appeal to other survivors of that day to paint or draw their memories of it. Nearly a thousand pictures were sent in, and these were made into an exhibition. The appeal was worded: "Let us leave for posterity pictures about the atomic bomb, drawn by citizens."

Clearly, my interest in these pictures cannot be an art-critical one. One does not musically analyze screams. But after repeatedly looking at them, what began as an impression became a certainty. These were images of hell.

I am not using the word as hyperbole. Between these paintings by women and men who have never painted anything else since leaving school, and who have surely, for the most part, never traveled outside Japan, between these traced memories which had to be exorcised, and the numerous representations of hell in European medieval art, there is a very close affinity.

This affinity is both stylistic and fundamental. And fundamentally it is   10
to do with the situations depicted. The affinity lies in the degree of the multiplication of pain, in the lack of appeal or aid, in the pitilessness, in the equality of wretchedness, and in the disappearance of time.

> I am 78 years old. I was living at Midorimachi on the day of the A-bomb blast. Around 9 am that morning, when I looked out of my window, I saw several women coming along the street one after another towards the Hiroshima prefectural hospital. I realized for the first time, as it is sometimes said, that when people are very much frightened hair really does stand on end. The women's hair was, in fact, standing straight up and the skin of their arms was peeled off. I suppose they were around 30 years old.

Time and again, the sober eyewitness accounts recall the surprise and horror of Dante's verses about the Inferno. The temperature at the center of the Hiroshima fireball was 300,000 degrees centigrade. The survivors are called in Japanese *hibakuska*— "those who have seen hell."

> Suddenly, one man who was stark naked came up to me and said in a quavering voice, "Please help me!" He was burned and swollen

all over from the effects of the A-bomb. Since I did not recognize him as my neighbor, I asked who he was. He answered that he was Mr. Sasaki, the son of Mr. Ennosuke Sasaki, who had a lumber shop in Funairi town. That morning he had been doing volunteer labor service, evacuating the houses near the prefectural office in Kato town. He had been burned black all over and had started back to his home in Funairi. He looked miserable — burned and sore, and naked with only pieces of his gaiters trailing behind as he walked. Only the part of his hair covered by his soldier's hat was left, as if he was wearing a bowl. When I touched him, his burned skin slipped off. I did not know what to do, so I asked a passing driver to take him to Eba hospital.

Does not this evocation of hell make it easier to forget that these scenes belonged to life? Is there not something conveniently unreal about hell? The whole history of the twentieth century proves otherwise.

Very systematically in Europe the conditions of hells have been constructed. It is not even necessary to list the sites. It is not even necessary to repeat the calculations of the organizers. We know this, and we choose to forget it.

We find it ridiculous or shocking that most of the pages concerning, for example, Trotsky were torn out of official Soviet history. What has been

How survivors saw it. A painting by Kazuhiro Ishizu, aged 68.

At the Aioi bridge, by Sawami Katagiri, aged 76.

torn out of our history are the pages concerning the experience of the two atom bombs dropped on Japan.

Of course, the facts are there in the textbooks. It may even be that   15
school children learn the dates. But what these facts mean — and originally their meaning was so clear, so monstrously vivid, that every commentator in the world was shocked, and every politician was obliged to say (whilst planning differently), "Never again" — what these facts mean has now been torn out. It has been a systematic, slow and thorough process of suppression and elimination. This process has been hidden within the reality of politics.

Do not misunderstand me. I am not here using the word "reality" ironically, I am not politically naïve. I have the greatest respect for political reality, and I believe that the innocence of political idealists is often very dangerous. What we are considering is how in this case in the West — not in Japan for obvious reasons and not in the Soviet Union for different reasons — political and military realities have eliminated another reality.

The eliminated reality is both physical —

Yokogawa bridge above Tenma river, 6th August 1945, 8:30 am.
    People crying and moaning were running towards the city. I did not know why. Steam engines were burning at Yokogawa station.
    Skin of cow tied to wire.
    Skin of girl's hip was hanging down.
    "My baby is dead, isn't she?"

and moral.

The political and military arguments have concerned such issues as deterrence, defense systems, relative strike parity, tactical nuclear weapons and—pathetically—so-called civil defense. Any movement for nuclear disarmament today has to contend with those considerations and dispute their false interpretation. To lose sight of them is to become as apocalyptic as the Bomb and all utopias. (The construction of hells on earth was accompanied in Europe by plans for heavens on earth.)

What has to be redeemed, reinserted, disclosed and never be allowed to be forgotten, is the other reality. Most of the mass means of communication are close to what has been suppressed.

These paintings were shown on Japanese television. Is it conceivable that   20
the BBC would show these pictures on Channel One at a peak hour? Without any reference to "political" and "military" realities, under the straight title, *This Is How It Was, 6th August 1945*? I challenge them to do so.

What happened on that day was, of course, neither the beginning nor the end of the act. It began months, years before, with the planning of the action, and the eventual final decision to drop two bombs on Japan. However much the world was shocked and surprised by the bomb dropped on Hiroshima, it has to be emphasized that it was not a miscalculation, an error, or the result (as can happen in war) of a situation deteriorating so rapidly that it gets out of hand. What happened was consciously and precisely planned. Small scenes like this were part of the plan:

> I was walking along the Hihiyama bridge about 3 pm on 7th August. A woman, who looked like an expectant mother, was dead. At her side, a girl of about three years of age brought some water in an empty can she had found. She was trying to let her mother drink from it.
>
> As soon as I saw this miserable scene with the pitiful child, I embraced the girl close to me and cried with her, telling her that her mother was dead.

There was a preparation. And there was an aftermath. The latter included long, lingering deaths, radiation sickness, many fatal illnesses which developed later as a result of exposure to the bomb, and tragic genetical effects on generations yet to be born.

I refrain from giving the statistics: how many hundreds of thousands of dead, how many injured, how many deformed children. Just as I refrain from pointing out how comparatively "small" were the atomic bombs dropped on Japan. Such statistics tend to distract. We consider numbers instead of pain. We calculate instead of judging. We relativize instead of refusing.

It is possible today to arouse popular indignation or anger by speaking of the threat and immorality of terrorism. Indeed, this appears to be the central plank of the rhetoric of the new American foreign policy ("Moscow is the world-base of all terrorism") and of British policy towards Ireland. What is able to shock people about terrorist acts is that often their targets are unselected and innocent — a crowd in a railway station, people waiting for a bus to go home after work. The victims are chosen indiscriminately in the hope of producing a shock effect on political decision-making by their government.

The two bombs dropped on Japan were terrorist actions. The calculation   25
was terrorist. The indiscriminacy was terrorist. The small groups of terrorists operating today are, by comparison, humane killers.

Another comparison needs to be made. Today terrorist groups mostly represent small nations or groupings who are disputing large powers in a position of strength. Whereas Hiroshima was perpetrated by the most powerful alliance in the world against an enemy who was already prepared to negotiate, and was admitting defeat.

To apply the epithet "terrorist" to the acts of bombing Hiroshima and Nagasaki is logically justifiable, and I do so because it may help to reinsert that act into living consciousness today. Yet the word changes nothing in itself.

The first-hand evidence of the victims, the reading of the pages which have been torn out, provokes a sense of outrage. This outrage has two natural faces. One is a sense of horror and pity at what happened; the other face is self-defensive and declares: *this should not happen again (here)*. For some the *here* is in brackets, for others it is not.

The face of horror, the reaction which has now been mostly suppressed, forces us to comprehend the reality of what happened. The second reaction, unfortunately, distances us from that reality. Although it begins as a straight declaration, it quickly leads into the labyrinth of defense policies, military arguments and global strategies. Finally it leads to the sordid commercial absurdity of private fall-out shelters.

This split of the sense of outrage into, on one hand, horror, and, on the   30
other hand, expediency occurs because the concept of evil has been abandoned. Every culture, except our own in recent times, has had such a concept.

That its religious or philosophical bases vary is unimportant. The concept of evil implies a force or forces which have to be continually struggled against so that they do not triumph over life and destroy it. One of the very first written texts from Mesopotamia, 1,500 years before Homer, speaks of this struggle, which was the first condition of human life. In public thinking nowadays, the concept of evil has been reduced to a little adjective to support an opinion or hypothesis (abortions, terrorism, ayatollahs).

Nobody can confront the reality of 6th August 1945 without being forced to acknowledge that what happened was evil. It is not a question of opinion or interpretation, but of events.

The memory of these events should be continually before our eyes. This is why the thousand citizens of Hiroshima started to draw on their little scraps of paper. We need to show their drawings everywhere. These terrible images can now release an energy for opposing evil and for the lifelong struggle of that opposition.

And from this a very old lesson may be drawn. My friend in the United States is, in a sense, innocent. She looks beyond a nuclear holocaust without considering its reality. This reality includes not only its victims but also its planners and those who support them. Evil from time immemorial has often worn a mask of innocence. One of evil's principal modes of being is *looking beyond* (with indifference) that which is before the eyes.

August 9th: On the west embankment of a military training field was a young boy four or five years old. He was burned black, lying on his back, with his arms pointing towards heaven.

Only by looking beyond or away can one come to believe that such evil 35 is relative, and therefore under certain conditions justifiable. In reality — the reality to which the survivors and the dead bear witness — it can never be justified.

Note

1. Edited by Japan Broadcasting Corporation, London, Wildwood House, 1981; New York, Pantheon, 1981.

QUESTIONS

Reading

1. Berger begins his essay with this powerful sentence: "The whole incredible problem begins with the need to reinsert those events of 6 August 1945 back into living consciousness." What is "the whole incredible problem," as Berger describes and defines it?
2. Berger argues that what happened on August 6, 1945, was "consciously and precisely planned" (paragraph 21). Highlight, underline, or flag the evidence he uses to support this claim. How does this argument support his larger purpose?
3. What does Berger mean by the term *expediency* (paragraph 30)?

Exploratory Writing

1. Berger argues that reviving the concept of "evil" is the only way anybody can "confront the reality of 6th August 1945." He writes, "It is not a question of opinion or interpretation, but of events" (paragraph 32). In your own words, write a definition of *evil*. How is your characterization of evil different from Berger's?
2. Spend some time looking at and thinking about the paintings by survivors Kazuhiro Ishizu and Sawami Katagiri, reprinted on pages 317 and 318. What do you *see* in these paintings? List at least twenty nouns that capture what these images represent to you.

3. Collaborating in small groups, find survivor depictions — whether photographs, oral or written accounts, or paintings — of a recent tragedy or atrocity. Prepare a presentation in which you lay out a strong argument about why it is essential for the public to be exposed to these documents.

Making Connections

1. Berger challenges the BBC to show paintings from survivors of the Hiroshima bombings on Channel One at peak hour, the way they were shown on Japanese television, "[w]ithout any reference to 'political' and 'military' realities" (paragraph 20). In your opinion, do the firsthand stories from American soldiers serving in Iraq (p. 323) show the reality of "how it was"?

2. Zoë Tracy Hardy's essay "What Did You Do in the War, Grandma?" (p. 210) reports on Hiroshima from the other side of that experience. How different are Berger's and Hardy's essays in their conclusions about the meaning of the event? Do the two essays contradict or reinforce each other?

Essay Writing

1. This essay about Hiroshima was first published in 1981. Write your own essay reflecting on what the term *terrorist* means to you. Include a summary of Berger's characterization of terrorism and terrorist actions. Consider Berger's comments about the use of the word *terrorist* in light of the ways the term has been applied to more recent events.

Soldiers' Stories
Dispatches from Iraq

Various Authors

The following pieces were compiled from e-mails and journal entries written by soldiers serving in the war in Iraq during 2003–2004. Sponsored by the National Endowment for the Arts (NEA) since April 2004, Operation Homecoming is a project that organized fifty-nine writing workshops for military personnel in twenty-seven overseas and domestic military installations in order to encourage them to document their experiences. The NEA has also received over 1,200 writing submissions, with almost 100 anthologized in Operation Homecoming: Iraq, Afghanistan, and the Home Front in the Words of U.S. Troops and Their Families *(2006). In 2007, a documentary with interviews and dramatic readings aired on PBS. The soldiers' stories — poetry, fiction, and nonfiction — will be preserved in the U.S. National Archives and Records Administration in College Park, Maryland. To hear audio recordings of the soldiers, and to view their photographs from Iraq, visit* **www.newyorker.com.**

Captain Ryan Kelly, thirty-six, Denver, Colorado. E-mail to his mother, from Camp Buehring, Kuwait. December 2003.
The worst thing here is not the searing heat or the cold nights. It's the waiting. Waiting for the wind to quit blowing and the sand to quit grinding against your skin. Waiting for a moment of privacy in a tent packed with seventy other men, in a camp packed with seven hundred other tents, in a base packed with fifteen thousand soldiers, all looking for a clean place to go to the bathroom. . . . Waiting for the bone-rattling coughs from dust finer than powdered sugar to stop attacking the lungs. Waiting for the generals to order the battalion to move north, toward Tikrit, where others — Iraqis — are also waiting: waiting for us . . .

A quick look around my tent will show you who is fighting this war. There's Ed, a fifty-eight-year-old grandfather from Delaware. He never complains about his age, but his body does, in aches and creaks and in the slowness of his movements on late nights and cold mornings.

There's Lindon, a thirty-one-year-old, black-as-coal ex-Navy man from Trinidad who speaks every word with a smile. His grandfather owned an animal farm and lived next to his grandmother, who owned an adjacent cocoa field. They met as children.

There's Sergeant Lilian, a single mother who left her five-year-old daughter at home with a frail and aging mother because nobody else was there to help.

There's Melissa and Mike, two sergeants who got married inside the   5 Fort Dix chapel a month before we deployed — so in love, yet forbidden, because of fraternization policies, even to hold hands in front of other soldiers. But if you watch them closely, you can catch them stealing secret glances at each other. Sometimes I'll see them sitting together on a box of bottled water tenderly sharing a lunch. They are so focussed on each other that the world seems to dissolve around them. If they were on a picnic in Sheep Meadow in Central Park, instead of here, surrounded by sand and war machines, it would be the same. War's a hell of a way to spend your honeymoon.

There's Sergeant First Class Ernesto, thirty-eight, a professional soldier whose father owns a coffee plantation in Puerto Rico and whose four-year-old daughter cries when he calls.

There's Noah, a twenty-three-year-old motocross stuntman, who wears his hair on the ragged edge of Army regulations. He's been asking me for months to let him ship his motorcycle to the desert. I keep telling him no.

There's Chief Warrant Officer 4 Jerry, the "linedog" of aviation maintenance, whose father was wounded in WWII a month after he arrived in combat. On D Day, a grenade popped up from behind a hedge grove near a Normandy beach and spewed burning white phosphorus all over his body, consigning the man to a cane and special shoes for the rest of his life. CWO4 Jerry lives out on the flight line, going from aircraft to aircraft with his odd bag of tools, like a doctor making house calls. He works so hard that I often have to order him to take a day off.

There's Martina, twenty-two, a jet-black-haired girl, who fled Macedonia with her family to escape the genocide of the civil war in Bosnia. Her family ran away to prevent the draft from snatching up her older brother and consuming him in a war they considered absurd and illegal. A few years later, the family, with no place else to run, watched helplessly as the United States flew their daughter into Iraq. She's not even a U.S. citizen, just a foreigner fighting for a foreign country on foreign soil for a foreign cause. She has become one of my best soldiers.

There is William (Wild Bill), a twenty-three-year-old kid from Jersey   10 with a strong chin and a James Dean-like grin. The day before we went on leave, he roared up in front of the barracks and beamed at me from behind the wheel of a gleaming white monster truck that he bought for fifteen hundred dollars. Three days later, he drove it into the heart of Amish country, where the transmission clanked and clattered to a stop. He drank beer all night at some stranger's house, and in the morning sold him the truck. Kicker is, he made it back to post in time for my formation.

There's Top, my First Sergeant, my no-nonsense right-hand man. He's my counsel, my confidant, my friend. He's the top enlisted man in the company, with twenty-eight years in the Army, and would snap his back, and anybody else's, for that matter, for any one of our men. Last year, his pit bull attacked his wife's smaller dog — a terrier of some sort, I think. As she tried to pry them apart, the pit bit off the tip of her ring finger. Top punched the pit bull in the skull and eventually separated the two. A hospital visit and half a pack of cigarettes later, he learned the blow broke his hand. He bought her a new wedding ring in Kuwait.

And on and on and on . . .

I hope you are doing well, Mom. I'm doing my best. For them. For me. For you. I hope it's good enough.

Commander Edward W. Jewell, MD, forty-eight, Washington, D.C. Journal entries, hospital ship USNS Comfort. *March–April 2003.*

March 27. Q: The *Comfort* is a large non-combat hospital ship protected by the most powerful Navy, Army, and Air Force in history. What is there to be afraid of? A: Everything. Danger is all around us. We are really very close to the action. At times we see oil fires near the shore. However, we cannot really see the combat. We are not afraid of the Iraqi military. If they try to fire a rocket at us it would be easily shot down by artillery on the ground, aircraft, or by naval gunnery/rockets. However, we believe there are mines in the Gulf. Purportedly, small boats have approached the *Comfort* several times. When this happens we call in a helo and launch our small boat to run them off. How can we possibly see one of these things in the dark? I think it would be very easy for a terrorist to attack this ship with an explosive-laden small boat. Very easy. Would the Iraqis attack a hospital ship if they could? Why not? In their view, they were invaded by mercenary infidels who deserve no better. A surgeon buddy of mine, Mike from Massachusetts, thinks an attack on our ship is a near-given, with a 50% chance of success. However, he is a proctologist and a Red Sox fan and naturally pessimistic.

March 28. Sickening sight: a helicopter's downwash blows a stack of letters overboard. Who knows what was lost? Last letter to save a troubled relationship? A fat check? Notice of tax audit? We'll never know. That's war.

The doctors are all bored from underutilization, but the surgeons seem particularly restless. There are so many of them and not enough cases to fill the time.

15

The Army helos cannot fly patients out to us in bad weather. The visibility has been poor the last three days, with choppy seas. We were to have received twenty or thirty new patients, but they never made it because of the weather.

March 29. The old Navy jargon "belay my last," meaning disregard my last statement, applies to my commentary from yesterday. We got creamed with fresh casualties last night, thirty new patients, both sides, all needing immediate and significant intervention. The injuries are horrifying. Ruptured eyeballs. Children missing limbs. Large burns. Genitals and buttocks blown off. Grotesque fractures. Gunshot wounds to the head. Faces blown apart. Paraplegics from spine injuries. The number of X-ray studies performed last night in a short period of time is so great that it causes the entire system to crash under the burden of electronic data it is being fed.

Our patients are mostly Iraqis. Along with their combat wounds, they are dirty, undernourished, and dehydrated. One rumor says that we will treat all the wounded Iraqi EPWs (enemy prisoners of war) for the duration of the war, and these are the only patients we will see. If true, this would, in effect, make the *Comfort* a prison hospital ship. The corpsmen on the wards have to guard the prisoners and keep them from communicating with one another to prevent rebellion. As medical people we are trained to care for the sick; it is difficult to stay mindful that these patients are the enemy and could fight back against us.

April 5. The Saturday entertainment is karaoke. I usually like it, but   20
tonight it's not for me. The room is hot and crowded, and the whole event just too loud. I step out for air. On deck is a different world. For safety we are on "darken ship" status now. This means no external lights, and all windows are covered to block light transmission. The goal is to make the ship invisible or nearly so to evildoers trying to locate the ship in the dark. It does actually work. The night is moonless, skies only a slight haze. It is very dark outside. So dark my eyes need ten minutes to fully accommodate. There is a magnificent display of stars tonight, reminiscent of what you see in Utah. The night has a misty, Impressionist feel. People moving about in the night are just vague dark shapes. Voices are low. Boys and girls being what they are, couples are forming on *Comfort*. They drift into obscure corners. Ghostlike green blobs of fluorescence rise and fall in the water. Jellyfish. Thousands of jellyfish drift and bob around the ship. I watch the stars until my neck hurts. Someone is singing in the dark in a beautiful, strange language. He tells me it is Hindi, and he is actually practicing for karaoke. I hope he wins.

April 7. The prisoners are kept on a separate ward, deep in the bowels of the ship, for security reasons, and the location is kept obscure. There is concern for the security of the prisoners. Lawyers run everything now, and we actually have a lawyer on board whose primary job is to ensure we comply with all tenets of the Geneva Conventions. There are press on board all the time.

Most of the Iraqis show real appreciation for the care rendered them. I would love to talk to them about family, etc., but we have been firmly warned not to do this. The prisoners are a sad lot. I feel for them. Most were not real soldiers, just conscripts forced to fight for the Big Lie, Saddam Hussein. Some of these guys, however, were the feared fedayeen suicide commandos. In general, the prisoners are badly wounded. They look defeated and glad to be out of combat.

April 11. The number of patients coming aboard *Comfort* is simply out of control. Like the doctors on *M*A*S*H*, we have grown to hate the rumble of helos on the flight deck, since it usually means another load of Iraqi patients. Today we received at least thirty-five more patients. New in the last twenty-four hours is a big influx of sick and injured children. We have only one doctor with residency training in pediatrics. Some of the kids are very ill. One was DOA from drinking kerosene. "They" are sending everyone here. We don't know who "they" are, and no one seems to have a handle on where these patients come from, when they are arriving, or who is sending them. We take them all and do our best.

There is no long-term-care plan for all these patients, and the ones who survive will need long-term care. Where will they go? Who will care for them after we leave? We have become deeply involved in a humanitarian crisis that we will not be able to extricate ourselves from.

April 15. Civilian Iraqi patients are being allowed to move around the   25 ship more (with escorts, of course) as their conditions improve. I saw a teen-ager today smiling and shaking hands with everyone. As he bent to tie his shoe, his sleeve slid up. I saw he had a tattoo on his upper arm. A fresh Marine Corps "globe and anchor." Wow! Hearts and minds, indeed.

April 17. We began in earnest to discharge stable EPW patients from the *Comfort.* Close to thirty sent back today. Sent somewhere. Sadly, these guys don't realize they are not being repatriated. For security reasons, they cannot be told where they are really going. Looking at these pathetic-looking fellows, it is easy to forget that they were the enemy, and many probably still wish us harm. According to an ICU doctor, one of the most timid-looking teen-age patients is actually an identified terrorist. Another patient awoke from surgery disoriented to place; he asked if he had been sent home to Syria!

April 21. *Comfort* receives a visit from CENTCOM, the name for the headquarters group for the entire war. A group of their medical-admin bureaucrats, primarily Army, are on board to give us an overview of the medical situation in Iraq and Kuwait. We hope to hear something concrete about our own status: what is planned for us, how can we offload our patients, and, mostly, when can we go home? Instead of insight and clarity, we got more obscuring mud in the eye. The formal presentation is tiresome, trite, and uninformative. It takes fifteen minutes to get the PowerPoint working. The speaker uses too much Army-specific jargon. He admits that the *Comfort* is the most stable, established, and productive medical unit in the theater. The hospitals in Iraq have been looted and are barely functioning.

A Q&A session follows. The discussion is as overheated as the room. Pointed questions regarding why we got stuck with so many patients go ignored or glossed over. It is explained that the Iraqi casualties were put on helicopters by well-meaning, altruistic U.S. troops, even though they were told not to do this. They offer no explanation for why all the Iraqis ended up in our hospital. They thank us for all our hard work, tell us that they "feel our pain," and say that war is hell. It is not convincing or reassuring to us. These guys all look rested, tanned, and pain-free to us.

Sergeant Timothy J. Gaestel, twenty-two, Austin, Texas. E-mail to his father, from south of Baghdad. September 21, 2003.

Hey, Dad, this is your son. I finally get to write y'all a letter. First off, let me tell you we made it here safe and so far, but everything is going very good. Now, Dad, I know that you have already received a phone call that tells you I am OK, but I want you to know exactly what happened. . . . We were heading south down Highway 8 and I was gunning for the second truck. Byrd was driving and my chief was the passenger. We got off Highway 8 onto Ambush Alley, the route we didn't take going up there. I was in the back of the truck with my 240B machine gun, and the S2 [an intelligence officer] wanted to ride in the back of the truck with me, since I was the only one back there. We were at the end of the convoy at this point so we were really hauling ass, driving down the wrong side of the road and all that, just so we could get to the front of the convoy. My buddy Eddie was a badass driver and kept us from getting in wrecks a few times. But still able to get the mission done. The XO [executive officer] truck was behind us and needed to get in front, not to mention the fact that I had his Gatorade I was supposed to throw to him the next time they passed us.

At that exact moment, a loud and thunderous boom went off and pushed me all the way to the front of where my 240B was mounted. I knew something had just happened and when I turned around I could see two large smoke clouds on each side of the road. The first thing I thought was that I had just been hit in the back by an IED [improvised explosive device]. It wasn't like I felt as if I was going to die, more like "Man, that really hurt." At that moment, I reached around and felt my back and pulled my hand back, and it was covered with blood. Before that I honestly thought it had just hit my IBA [interceptor body armor]. It turns out that it had hit my IBA and gone right through it.

I lay down in the back of the truck, but this didn't seem like a good idea and I didn't have my weapon and had to yell at the S2 to give me my weapon — I didn't want an ambush to happen and for me to not have my weapon. So I stood up on my knees and yelled again to him to man the 240B; he was scared, but that's what happens when you don't ever get any kind of training and you sit in an office all day. This guy didn't react very well when I showed him my back — he started flipping out and yelling "Oh, G., you got hit man, oh he's hit bad, man." This is the last thing that you tell

30

someone who has just been hit in the back and is bleeding. As you can imagine, I was pretty pissed off at this point, and I showed my anger toward the people in the town that we were driving through, I had my M4 rifle at the ready and my trigger finger on the trigger and was just waiting for someone to give me a reason to have me put it from safe to semi. I maintained my military bearing as well as one could in that situation. I sure wanted to shoot the bastard that had just set the IED off.

As we were making our way back to the FOB [forward operating base] at that last street, I could no longer sit up straight and my back was killing me. There was a major who was our field surgeon waiting for me in the front of the gate to check me out. This guy didn't reassure me, either. When I told him that I was OK, he looked at me and said, "Look, son, you may have internal bleeding." Now I was scared. They rushed me to the aid station, where I talked to some sergeant majors and the colonel. In like fifteen minutes, in my brown underwear, green socks up to my knees, and a blanket, I was rushed out to the landing zone where a chopper took me to CSH [Combat Support Hospital] 28, in downtown Baghdad. The flight through Baghdad was amazing, too, you could see the whole city and all the buildings and stuff, it was very strange. The helicopter pilot was a badass as well, he had to do a wartime landing, which is really fast and quick; it was cool. Now, Dad, I hadn't seen a female in twenty-one days, and so you could imagine I was excited when I looked down off the helicopter as we were coming in for a landing to see a very beautiful woman (it could be she was beautiful because I haven't seen a woman in a while). Now when I landed, a female second lieutenant took me into the ER with no one else in the whole room except her and me. She came up to me and ripped off my blanket, grabbed my brown undies, and ripped those off too and gave me a catheter. Now that was more painful than the IED and way not what I was thinking was going to happen when she grabbed my blanket off me. Then she gave me some morphine and I was good.

One thing that bothered me is the way they treated people — just because they're always around stuff like that doesn't mean that they have to act like it's nothing to get hit in the back by a bomb. They did an X-ray of my back and found that I had two pieces of shrapnel in my back. I asked the doctor if I could keep the shrapnel and he said, "Yeah, sure, forever." They weren't going to be taking the shrapnel out. So, yeah, now your son is going to have two pieces of metal in his back for the rest of his life. I was cleaned up and taken to patient hold. A place that is something out of a movie. It was horrible to see all the soldiers with missing legs and arms and bandages everywhere. Shortly afterward, I was given some morphine and I passed out. When I woke up, Colonel Smith, Company Sergeant Major Burgos, Lieutenant Layton, Company Sergeant Major Howard, and our chaplain came in. The first thing Lieutenant Layton said to me was "Well, me and the sergeant major were talking and you are the first person to receive the Purple Heart in the 'Loyalty' battalion since Grenada (in 1983)." It's quite crazy, the turn of events that have led me here. A Purple Heart recipient — I guess all it means is that some guy got me before I could get him. We will joke about this all someday, Dad. I told them I didn't want you all to find out about this because I'm not leaving Iraq and I don't want you to worry. I know you're going to worry anyway but the reason I shared this story here was so you know what it's like to be here and that the people that I'm with all look after one another. I guess it's really crazy that I volunteered to stay even though I was hit in the back with shrapnel, and as soon as I can I'm going to return to my unit. I don't want Mom to worry so don't read her the detailed parts of this letter. I LOVE Y'ALL and will be home soon enough.

Captain Lisa R. Blackman, thirty-two, Chelmsford, Massachusetts, serving as a clinical psychologist. E-mails to friends and family, from Al Udeid Air Base, Qatar. October 2004.

A quick word on guilt. No one ever feels like they are doing enough. If you are in a safe location, you feel guilty that your friends are getting shot at and you aren't. If you are getting shot at, you feel guilty if your buddy gets hit and you don't. If you get shot at but don't die, you feel guilty that you lived, and more guilty if you get to go home and your friends have to stay behind. I have not seen one person out here who didn't check off "increased guilt" on our intake form. . . .

Lately I have had a string of combat-trauma evaluations. Several have been Army troops passing through for R and R — they come here for a bit and then go back to Iraq or Afghanistan. As if this is a glamorous vacation site. But they are grateful to be someplace safe (and someplace with alcohol, which I will surely complain about at a later date). Anyway, each one presented with a different complaint. One guy wasn't sleeping, one gal was angry about "sexual harassment" in her unit, one gal was depressed, one guy just wanted to go home. Standard stuff.

I had no initial clue that the problems were combat-related and no idea that I should be assessing for acute stress disorder or PTSD. None of these guys or gals said "I was in combat" or "I saw someone die." None connected these experiences to their symptoms. It was as if they didn't remember how hard and unusual it is to be at war. They're used to the danger. They've been out here too long. Why would a war mess with your mood, right?

Each evaluation started with the typical questions: "What brought you in today?" "When did the problem start?" "Have you ever experienced these symptoms before?" "How's your sleep?" etc., etc., etc. I kept asking questions and thinking that the symptoms did not add up. Something wasn't right. I wasn't getting the right reactions. Stories were incomplete. Affect was blunted. Level of distress did not match presenting complaint. Alarm red, people, alarm red.

At home I ask people if they have ever experienced or witnessed a traumatic event or abuse. But out here I ask, "Have you ever been in combat?" Apparently, this is a question with the power to unglue, because all four of these troops burst into tears at the mention of the word "combat."

And when I say burst, I mean splatter — tears running, snot flowing, and I literally had to mop my floor after one two-hour session. In other words, I mean sobbing for minutes on end, unable to speak, flat-out grief by an otherwise healthy, strong, manly guy who watches football on the weekends and never puts the toilet seat down.

Each time, I sit there with not a clue what to say . . . offering tissues . . .   40
saying I'm sorry . . . trying to normalize . . . trying to say, "It was not your fault that so-and-so died" and "If you could have done differently, you would have" and "You had a right to be scared." And, even worse, "You had to shoot back," and "Yes, you killed someone, and you still deserve to go back to your family and live your life."

Next time you are hanging out with a friend, think about what you would do if he turned to you and said, "My boss made me kill someone, and I know I'm going to Hell for it, so why bother?" What would you say to "normalize" that?

I will probably never see these folks again. I have no idea if I have been helpful. Maybe I planted a seed of reprieve that will grow into self-forgiveness. Maybe I did absolutely nothing but sit here. Who knows?

I can't stop thinking about the fact that these folks have lost something that they will never get back — innocence (and a life free of guilt). My heart hurts for them.

Second Lieutenant Brian Humphreys, thirty-two, Santa Barbara, California. Journal, Hit, Iraq. February–September 2004.

Bang, bang, bang. The sheet-metal door amplifies the sound of the large fist striking it. Sergeant Graham is standing in the doorway, silhouetted by the white-hot afternoon sunlight.

"Sir, we have a unit in contact, two friendly KIA. The platoon is getting   45
ready downstairs."

I throw my uniform and flak jacket on, grab my rifle, and head down a flight of stairs. The platoon is already on the vehicles, ready to roll with an ambulance.

The palm groves to our east that line the Euphrates River whip by. To the west of the asphalt ribbon are the scorched wadis used by insurgents to stage their attacks. Up ahead I see the telltale cluster of Humvees and marines. I pull up to the first vehicle and find the patrol leader.

"Where do you want the ambulance?" I ask.

"Just have it pull up, we'll guide it in," he replies, as if we have arrived to help fix a flat tire. The ambulance in the middle of my six-vehicle column pulls forward, and I get out to find where the casualties are.

"What the hell is that?" I ask a marine. Perhaps the explosion had   50
somehow killed a farm animal of some sort who wandered out on the road. A sheep maybe? Or a cow. No, not big enough. Well, what is that and how did it happen? The marine gives his buddy's name and asks me to help find his head. Fuck.

We do not want the stray dogs that occupy Iraq with us to find our brothers. The corpsmen, with their blue latex gloves and body bags, scour the bushes for the last scraps of human tissue as waves of heat rise from the desert. The Associated Press dutifully reports that three marines were killed in Al Anbar province in Iraq. Names have not been released by the Defense Department pending notification of next of kin. We will not read the two-sentence notice for several days. The Internet room is always padlocked while we wait for somebody to get a knock on the door half a world away.

At one point the casualties got so bad that it seemed the room was closed for a week at a time while notifications were made. Iraq is coming apart at the seams. Pictures of flag-draped coffins being unloaded from Air Force transports surface on the back reaches of the Internet, as if they were a grainy celebrity sex video that decent people should avoid looking at. But I think otherwise. The images of flag-draped coffins show the end of war as we are meant to see it, and as we are meant to believe it. Uniforms, flags, patriotism, honor, sacrifice. In these images we are not street fighters struggling to survive and kill in a distant gangland but soldiers in the nation's service. They will help the families, I think. They will help us. In our own way, we, too, need to believe.

Today, the marines will have to wait to log on to their chat rooms, HotOrNot.com, MilitarySingles.com, and the online shopping sites. I myself have become something of a spendthrift in Iraq, ordering more books and CDs than I normally would. I have seen death enough times among people who had been indestructibly living only the day before. It is better to go ahead and buy the CD you have been meaning to get. There are reminders wherever you care to look. For instance, the pile of blood-soaked flak jackets sitting in the company's combat operations center, a low-tech jumble of maps and radios. The flak jackets' owners are either dead or in the hospital recovering from their wounds.

The executive officer reminds us that the flak jackets need to be sent back through the Marine Corps' supply chain as soon as possible. Somewhere, somebody will wash them and inspect them for damage, filling out all the necessary paperwork. It is the banality, even more than the carnage, that shocks. Our occupation grinds on. Others will assign meaning to our lives here, noble or otherwise. For us, though, there is a close meanness to the fight. There are no flags, no dress uniforms. We are fighting a rival gang for the same turf, while the neighborhood residents cower and wait to see whose side they should come out on.

Imperceptibly, we are coming to the end of our deployment. Time has stood still for months, with days and nights fusing together in the burning-hot air of the desert. But now our deployment is being measured in finite units of time. It takes getting used to.

Returning from a patrol with my platoon, I find a blue sedan riddled with bullet holes on the side of the highway. There are a few Iraqi soldiers

55

standing around when we find it. We quickly learn the car belongs to Captain Laithe, one of the senior men in the local police force. Connected, calculating, and English-speaking, he has collaborated with the Americans since the fall of Baghdad. I wondered since I first met him why he cast his lot with us, what calculation he made, and whether we could even understand it — what mix of nobility and venality it contained. His future, however he imagined it, ended with the finality of death in a hail of bullets on the highway less than a mile from our forward operating base.

Not long before we leave, I am awakened out of a sound sleep again, this time at midnight. The company executive officer is at the door. We have another KIA. I feel the same shock I did the first time, only there's a certain numbness to it now, as if it were hitting a nerve becoming deadened by repeated blows. Our turn had almost passed, and now this. I nod, and begin collecting my gear. Lieutenant Lenz is outside in the pitch-black. It is the body of one of his marines that we will go out in the dead of night to recover. I ask Lenz if he is all right. I ask him if his marines are all right. The worst thing, he says, is that by now they are used to it. It is better and worse at the same time. I realize that we have all come to accept the loss of familiar faces, to live with it, and cross the line of departure again the next morning. It is this acceptance, rather than the thud of hidden bombs, that has finally made us veterans, and will finish the words on the obscure page of history that we occupy.

We head off in the pitch-black, navigating the highway through the grainy green glow of our night-vision goggles. We move north to a point just north of the place where we lost the two marines in the bomb explosion months before. One of the Humvees in the patrol struck a land mine a short distance from the Iraqi National Guard post the marines had been tasked with protecting.

The sun is rising above the river's palm groves when the trucks arrive to remove the wrecked vehicle. The dead marine's remains are loaded in another truck and driven north towards Al Asad Air Base. The remains will be laid in a flag-draped coffin, and then secured in the cargo hold of a transport plane to be flown back to the United States. We, too, will soon go to Al Asad. We will then strap ourselves into the cargo hold of an identical plane to begin our own journey home. The scrawled memorials on barracks walls to fallen buddies will stay behind for the troops who replace us. They might read the awkwardly worded poems and epitaphs written in loving memory, and half wonder who we were.

QUESTIONS

Reading

1. According to Captain Lisa R. Blackman's entry, how do the people she questions during combat-trauma evaluations respond to the word *combat*?

2. What is CENTCOM? How does Commander Edward W. Jewell describe the visit and presentation?
3. A *dispatch* is a type of report, often sent from on-site officials, military personnel, or journalists to be published in a newspaper or magazine back home. Identify and list examples of *reporting* versus *reflecting* in these soldiers' stories. Use a separate piece of paper if you need more room.

REPORTING	REFLECTING

4. Are each of these "soldiers' stories" written in the same style? What observations can you make about the style of these pieces, both individually and as a whole?

Exploratory Writing

1. These "soldiers' stories" were written in workshops led by professional writers. The soldiers were told to "write freely, without fear of official constraints or oversight," and many of their writings are taken from private letters and journals. How might the stories be different if they were written *anonymously* for inclusion in these same public forums? Does it matter how the project was funded? Why were soldiers told to "write freely"? Collaborating in small groups, peruse the Operation Homecoming Web site (**www.nea.gov/national/homecoming/index.html**), and prepare a statement on what it means to "write freely."
2. Explore the audio recordings of the soldiers reading their accounts at **www.newyorker.com**. What dimension do the audio recordings add to these soldiers' stories?
3. Choose an article with a photo gallery from documentary photographer Andrea Bruce's "Unseen Iraq" series, online at the *Washington Post* (**http://voices.washingtonpost.com/unseen-iraq/**), such as the article "A Joyful Welcome Home for Detainees" (posted October 5, 2008) or "A Baghdad Trailer Park for Widows and Children" (posted September 15, 2008). Compare the article to this collection of soldiers' stories. What do these different reports tell readers who have never visited Iraq? What strategies can newspaper and magazine editors use to create balanced reports from a war?

Making Connections

1. "Evil from time immemorial has often worn a mask of innocence," writes John Berger (p. 315) at the close of his essay. Carefully highlight, underline, or flag any references to evil, horror, or hell in both Berger's essay and these soldiers' stories. Do you think that Berger's conclusions about the reality of Hiroshima also apply to the reality of the Iraq War? Why or why not?

Essay Writing

1. One of these soldiers' stories, the report from Sergeant Timothy J. Gaestel, is an e-mail to a father from his twenty-two-year-old son. Write a reflective essay discussing how this *epistolary* approach shapes the way you respond to Sergeant Gaestel's narrative. You can also use examples from the other epistolary stories in this essay.

SCIENCES

Sciences

The scientific method — the observation, collection, measuring, and analysis of evidence using empirical techniques — is the foundation of all disciplines in the sciences. Empirical methods are based on careful, first-hand observation, and form the foundation of the scientific method. A scientist can study anything — from molecules to language — as long as it can be explained through scientific method and empirical observation.

There are many approaches to knowledge within the sciences. Experimental science focuses on laboratory experiments; applied science focuses on solutions for problems in the real world. Biological science focuses on the bodies of animals, including human beings; physical science focuses on the earth, the universe, and the cosmos. While science has the reputation of dealing with narrow topics and hard facts, it's important to remember that the scientific method serves a larger, awe-inspiring aim: to explain the mysteries of the measurable world. While a lot of these mysteries have been explained over the course of human civilization, many continue to require investigation.

The fifteen essays collected here — nine that stand on their own and three paired sets — all address these kinds of fundamental questions about the physical world. Of these, four are primarily reflecting; three reporting; five explaining; and three arguing. Some of these essays are written by scientists, such as cell biologist Lewis Thomas, cognitive scientist Steven Pinker, or astronomer and physicist James Jeans; others are by writers or journalists who specialize in science, such as Diane Ackerman or Michael Pollan. By highlighting the basic and important questions that science addresses — from explaining the processes of climate change to charting the physiology of pain — these writers incorporate urgent, well-formulated facts, experiments, conditions, and questions from the sciences into a general conversation.

When you write about scientific questions and debates, you may start with hard facts but end up exploring some of the philosophical questions that their scientific observations provoke. You may even end up using them as dialogue in your writing from the humanities or social sciences. Whatever the case may be, you should feel free to enter the conversations these essays open up, to experiment with various methods of responding to them, and to find your own careful methods for writing about the fundamental questions about life and the workings of the universe that they explore.

The Corner of the Eye

Lewis Thomas

*Essayist, physician, and academic, Lewis Thomas (1913–1993)
was born to a doctor and a nurse in Flushing, New York. He followed in his parents' footsteps, beginning a successful research
career in immunology and microbiology after studying at Harvard
Medical School. It wasn't until 1971, however, when he received a
monthly column in the* New England Journal of Medicine, *that
Thomas began to write the essays that brought him acclaim as a
science writer. The column, which moved to* Discover *in 1980,
brought attention to Thomas's lyrical prose and his ability to draw
on science for insights into a range of subjects, from the intercon-
nectedness of earth and its organisms to space exploration to
nuclear warfare. He won a National Book Award in 1975 for* The
Lives of a Cell, *a collection of these columns, which was followed
by numerous compilations, including* The Medusa and the Snail
(1979); Et Cetera, Et Cetera *(1990); and* The Fragile Species
(1992). Thomas died in 1993. "The Corner of the Eye," from
Late Night Thoughts on Listening to Mahler's Ninth Symphony
*(1983), displays Thomas's meditative style (influenced by Mon-
taigne) and focuses on two of his fascinations: the development of
language and the relationship between humans and nature.*

There are some things that human beings can see only out of the corner
of the eye. The niftiest examples of this gift, familiar to all children, are
small, faint stars. When you look straight at one such star, it vanishes; when
you move your eyes to stare into the space nearby, it reappears. If you pick
two faint stars, side by side, and focus on one of the pair, it disappears and
now you can see the other in the corner of your eye, and you can move your
eyes back and forth, turning off the star in the center of your retina and
switching the other one on. There is a physiological explanation for the phenomenon: we have more rods, the cells we use for light perception, at the pe-
riphery of our retinas; more cones, for perceiving color, at the center.

Something like this happens in music. You cannot really hear certain sequences of notes in a Bach fugue unless at the same time there are other
notes being sounded, dominating the field. The real meaning in music comes
from tones only audible in the corner of the mind.

I used to worry that computers would become so powerful and sophisticated as to take the place of human minds. The notion of Artificial Intelligence used to scare me half to death. Already, a large enough machine can do all sorts of intelligent things beyond our capacities: calculate in a split second the answers to mathematical problems requiring years for a human brain, draw accurate pictures from memory, even manufacture successions of sounds with a disarming resemblance to real music. Computers can translate textbooks, write dissertations of their own for doctorates, even speak in machine-tooled, inhuman phonemes any words read off from a printed page. They can communicate with one another, holding consultations and committee meetings of their own in networks around the earth.

Computers can make errors, of course, and do so all the time in small, irritating ways, but the mistakes can be fixed and nearly always are. In this respect they are fundamentally inhuman, and here is the relaxing thought: computers will not take over the world; they cannot replace us, because they are not designed, as we are, for ambiguity.

Imagine the predicament faced by a computer programmed to make   5
language, not the interesting communication in sounds made by vervets or in symbols by brilliant chimpanzee prodigies, but real human talk. The grammar would not be too difficult, and there would be no problem in constructing a vocabulary of etymons, the original, pure, unambiguous words used to name real things. The impossibility would come in making the necessary mistakes we humans make with words instinctively, intuitively, as we build our kinds of language, changing the meanings to imply quite different things, constructing and elaborating the varieties of ambiguity without which speech can never become human speech.

Look at the record of language if you want to glimpse the special qualities of the human mind that lie beyond the reach of any machine. Take, for example, the metaphors we use in everyday speech to tell ourselves who we are, where we live, and where we come from.

The earth is a good place to begin. The word "earth" is used to name the ground we walk on, the soil in which we grow plants or dig clams, and the planet itself; we also use it to describe all of humanity ("the whole earth responds to the beauty of a child," we say to each other).

The earliest word for earth in our language was the Indo-European root *dhghem*, and look what we did with it. We turned it, by adding suffixes, into *humus* in Latin; today we call the complex polymers that hold fertile soil together "humic" acids, and somehow or other the same root became "humility." With another suffix the word became "human." Did the earth become human, or did the human emerge from the earth? One answer may lie in that nice cognate word "humble." "Humane" was built on it, extending the meaning of both the earth and ourselves. In ancient Hebrew, *adamha* was the word for earth, *adam* for man. What computer could run itself through such manipulations as those?

We came at the same system of defining ourselves from the other direction. The word *wiros* was the first root for man; it took us in our vanity on to "virile" and "virtue," but also turned itself into the Germanic word *weraldh*, meaning the life of man, and thence in English to our word "world."

There is a deep hunch in this kind of etymology. The world of man derives from this planet, shares origin with the life of the soil, lives in humility with all the rest of life. I cannot imagine programming a computer to think up an idea like that, not a twentieth-century computer, anyway.

The world began with what it is now the fashion to call the "Big Bang." Characteristically, we have assigned the wrong words for the very beginning of the earth and ourselves, in order to evade another term that would cause this century embarrassment. It could not, of course, have been a bang of any sort, with no atmosphere to conduct the waves of sound, and no ears. It was something else, occurring in the most absolute silence we can imagine. It was the Great Light.

We say it had been chaos before, but it was not the kind of place we use the word "chaos" for today, things tumbling over each other and bumping around. Chaos did not have that meaning in Greek; it simply meant empty.

We took it, in our words, from chaos to cosmos, a word that simply meant order, cosmetic. We perceived the order in surprise, and our cosmologists and physicists continue to find new and astonishing aspects of the order. We made up the word "universe" from the whole affair, meaning literally turning everything into one thing. We used to say it was a miracle, and we still permit ourselves to refer to the whole universe as a marvel, holding in our unconscious minds the original root meaning of these two words, miracle and marvel — from the ancient root word *smei*, signifying a smile. It immensely pleases a human being to see something never seen before, even more to learn something never known before, most of all to think something never thought before. The rings of Saturn are the latest surprise. All my physicist friends are enchanted by this phenomenon, marveling at the small violations of the laws of planetary mechanics, shocked by the unaccountable braids and spokes stuck there among the rings like graffiti. It is nice for physicists to see something new and inexplicable; it means that the laws of nature are once again about to be amended by a new footnote.

The greatest surprise of all lies within our own local, suburban solar system. It is not Mars; Mars was surprising in its way but not flabbergasting; it was a disappointment not to find evidences of life, and there was some sadness in the pictures sent back to earth from the Mars Lander, that lonely long-legged apparatus poking about with its jointed arm, picking up sample after sample of the barren Mars soil, looking for any flicker of life and finding none; the only sign of life on Mars was the Lander itself, an extension of the human mind all the way from earth to Mars, totally alone.

Nor is Saturn the great surprise, nor Jupiter, nor Venus, nor Mercury, nor any of the glimpses of the others.

10

15

The overwhelming astonishment, the queerest structure we know about so far in the whole universe, the greatest of all cosmological scientific puzzles, confounding all our efforts to comprehend it, is the earth. We are only now beginning to appreciate how strange and splendid it is, how it catches the breath; the loveliest object afloat around the sun, enclosed in its own blue bubble of atmosphere, manufacturing and breathing its own oxygen, fixing its own nitrogen from the air into its own soil, generating its own weather at the surface of its rain forests, constructing its own carapace from living parts: chalk cliffs, coral reefs, old fossils from earlier forms of life now covered by layers of new life meshed together around the globe, Troy upon Troy.

Seen from the right distance, from the corner of the eye of an extraterrestrial visitor, it must surely seem a single creature, clinging to the round warm stone, turning in the sun.

QUESTIONS

Reading

1. According to Thomas, could computers become sophisticated enough to take the place of human minds? Why or why not?
2. Summarize Thomas's comments about the Big Bang theory.
3. Highlight, underline, or flag the different words or word origins that Thomas defines in his essay. Why is etymology important in his discussion?

Exploratory Writing

1. In small groups, write a list of biological, astronomical, or chemical phenomena that could be considered miraculous or marvelous. Do some research to learn the etymology of the terms we use to describe these phenomena or processes. What additional insights do the word roots offer?
2. Consider Thomas's conclusions about planet earth. Which of his reflections are scientifically based observations? Rewrite his two concluding paragraphs in objective, scientific language, removing any poetic language or subjective descriptions. How does this change the tone of Thomas's essay?

Making Connections

1. A number of the science writers included in this volume use writing to conjure memorable visual images of scientific phenomena. Compare Thomas's descriptive writing to the work of any two other essayists in this book. Highlight the passages in their descriptions that allow you to "see" images in your mind.

Essay Writing

1. Thomas writes: "It immensely pleases a human being to see something never seen before, even more to learn something never known before, most of all to think something never thought before" (paragraph 13). He celebrates the element of surprise in scientific observation and discovery. Reflecting on your own experiences, write an essay describing a moment when you saw, learned, or thought something new about the natural world. How did that moment change your perspective?

My Pain, My Brain

Melanie Thernstrom

Melanie Thernstrom was born in 1964 to well-known political scientist Abigail Thernstrom and Harvard University historian Stephan Thernstrom. After graduating with honors in English from Harvard University, Thernstrom adapted her thesis into an elegy for a friend who had been mysteriously murdered. The Dead Girl *was published in 1990 to high praise from such writers and literary critics as Harold Bloom, Harold Brodkey, and Helen Vendler. Vendler describes Thernstrom's account as "a coming of age through tragedy." Her second book,* Halfway Heaven: Diary of a Harvard Murderer *(1998), focuses the story on an Ethiopian student who murdered her Vietnamese roommate. The student's diary entries reveal her loneliness and possible struggle with mental illness. Thernstrom interviewed family members of both women, providing a thorough insight into their cultural experiences and lives. Her essays have been published in the* New Yorker, Vanity Fair, *and* Food and Wine. *"My Pain, My Brain" appeared in the* New York Times Magazine *in May 2006.*

Who hasn't wished she could watch her brain at work and make changes to it, the way a painter steps back from a painting, studies it and decides to make the sky a different hue? If only we could spell-check our brain like a text, or reprogram it like a computer to eliminate glitches like pain, depression and learning disabilities. Would we one day become completely transparent to ourselves, and — fully conscious of consciousness — consciously create ourselves as we like?

The glitch I'd like to program out of my brain is chronic pain. For the past ten years, I have been suffering from an arthritic condition that causes chronic pain in my neck that radiates into the right side of my face and right shoulder and arm. Sometimes I picture the pain — soggy, moldy, dark or perhaps ashy, like those alarming pictures of smokers' lungs. Wherever the pain is located, it must look awful by now, after a decade of dominating my brain. I'd like to replace my forehead with a Plexiglas window, set up a camera and film my brain and (since this is my brain, I'm the director) redirect it. *Cut. Those areas that are generating pain — cool it. Those areas that are supposed to be alleviating pain — hello? I need you! Down-regulate pain-perception circuitry, as scientists say. Up-regulate pain-modulation circuitry. Now.*

Recently, I had a glimpse of what that reprogramming would look like. I was lying on my back in a large white plastic fMRI machine that uses ingenious new software, peering up through 3-D goggles at a small screen. I was experiencing a clinical demonstration of a new technology — real-time functional neuroimaging — used in a Stanford University study, now in its second phase, that allows subjects to see their own brain activity while feeling pain and to try to change that brain activity to control their pain.

Over six sessions, volunteers are being asked to try to increase and decrease their pain while watching the activation of a part of their brain involved in pain perception and modulation. This real-time imaging lets them assess how well they are succeeding. Dr. Sean Mackey, the study's senior investigator and the director of the Neuroimaging and Pain Lab at Stanford, explained that the results of the study's first phase, which were recently published in the prestigious *Proceedings of the National Academy of Sciences*, showed that while looking at the brain, subjects can learn to control its activation in a way that regulates their pain. While this may be likened to biofeedback, traditional biofeedback provides indirect measures of brain activity through information about heart rate, skin temperature and other autonomic functions, or even EEG waves. Mackey's approach allows subjects to interact with the brain itself.

"It is the mind-body problem — right there on the screen," one of Mackey's collaborators, Christopher deCharms, a neurophysiologist and a principal investigator of the study, told me later. "We are doing something that people have wanted to do for thousands of years. Descartes said, 'I think, therefore I am.' Now we're watching that process as it unfolds." 5

Suddenly, the machine made a deep rattling sound, and an image flickered before me: *my brain. I am looking at my own brain, as it thinks my own thoughts, including these thoughts.*

How does it work? I want to ask. Just as people were once puzzled by Freud's talking cure (how does describing problems solve them?), the Stanford study makes us wonder: How can one part of our brain control another by looking at it? Who is the "me" controlling my brain, then? It seems to deepen the mind-body problem, widening the old Cartesian divide by splitting the self into subject and agent.

But most of all I want to know: *Will I be able to learn it?*

For most of history, the idea of watching the mind at work was as fantastical as documenting a ghost. You could break into the haunted house — slice the brain open — but all you would find would be the house itself, the brain's architecture, not its invisible occupant. Photographing it with X-rays resulted only in pictures of the shell of the house, the skull. The invention of the CT scan and magnetic resonance imaging (MRI) were great advances because they reveal tissue as well as bones — the wallpaper as well as the walls — but the ghost still didn't show up. Consciousness remained elusive.

A newer form of MRI, functional magnetic resonance imaging (fMRI),   10
used with increasingly sophisticated software, is accomplishing this, taking
"movies" of brain activity. Researchers are able to watch the brain work, as
the films show parts of the brain becoming active under various stimuli by
detecting areas of increased blood flow connected with the faster firing of
nerve cells. These films are difficult to read; researchers puzzle over the new
images like Columbus staring at the gray shoreline, thinking, *India?* Most of
the brain is uncharted, the nature of the terrain unclear. But the voyage has
been made; the technology exists. Pain — a complex perception occupying
the elusive space spanning sensation, emotion and cognition — is a particularly promising area of imaging research because, researchers say, it has the
potential to make great progress in a short time.

Perhaps more than any other aspect of human existence, persistent pain
is experienced as something we cannot control but desperately wish we
could. Acute pain serves the evolutionary function of warning us of tissue
damage, but chronic pain does nothing except undo us. Pain is the primary
complaint that sends people to the doctor. Of the fifty-odd million sufferers
in the United States, half cannot get adequate relief from their chronic pain.
Many do not even have a diagnosis.

Unlike acute pain, chronic pain is now thought to be a disease of the
central nervous system that may or may not correlate with any tissue damage but involves an errant reprogramming in the brain and spinal cord. The
brain can generate terrible pain in a wound that is long healed, in a body
that is numb and paralyzed or — in the case of phantom-limb pain — in a
limb that no longer even exists.

Although there have been many theories about how pain works in the
brain, it is only through neuroimaging that the process has actually been observed. It is now clear that there is no single pain center in the brain. Rather,
pain is a complex, adaptive network involving five to ten areas of the brain
transmitting information back and forth.

This network has two pain systems: pain perception and pain modulation, which involve both overlapping and distinct brain structures. The
pain-modulatory system constantly interacts with the pain-perception system, inhibiting its activity. Much chronic pain is thought to involve either
an overactive pain-perception circuit or an underactive pain-modulation
circuit.

Like everyone who suffers from chronic pain, I find it hard to believe   15
that I have a pain-modulation circuit. The aspect of my pain I feel most certain about is that it is not voluntary: I cannot modulate it. And this belief is
reinforced every single day that I suffer from pain, which is every day. Yet I
know that pain is not a fact, like a broken bone; it's a perception, like
hunger, about a physical state ("an unpleasant sensory and emotional experience associated with actual or potential tissue damage or described in
terms of such damage," as the International Association for the Study of

Pain defines it). And it's a mercurial perception; under certain circumstances the pain-modulatory system works like a spell and the brain completely blocks out pain.

Soldiers, athletes, martyrs and pilgrims engage in battles, athletic feats or acts of devotion without being distracted by the pain of injuries. When the teenage surfer Bethany Hamilton's arm was bitten off by a shark, she felt pressure, but "I didn't feel any pain — I'm really lucky, because if I felt pain, things might not have gone as well," she said (articulating one reason the modulatory system evolved: if she had thrashed about in pain, she would have bled until she drowned).

In addition to being activated by stress, the pain-modulatory system is triggered by belief. The brain will shut down pain if it believes it has been given pain relief, even when it hasn't (the placebo effect), and it will augment pain if it believes you are being hurt, even if you aren't (the nocebo effect). The brain's modulatory system relies on endogenous endorphins, its own opiatelike substances. The nature of a placebo has long been a source of speculation and debate, but neuroimaging studies have shown the way a placebo actually helps to activate the pain-modulatory system.

In a recently published study led by Dr. Jon-Kar Zubieta at the University of Michigan Medical School, the brains of fourteen men were imaged after a stinging saltwater solution was injected into their jaws. They were then each given a placebo and told that it would positively relieve their pain. The men immediately felt better — and the screen showed how. Parts of the brain that release endogenous opiates lighted up. In other words, fake opiates caused the brain to dispense real ones. Like some New Age dictum, philosophy becomes chemistry; believing becomes reality; the mind unites with the body.

Other studies have shown that opiates and other medications *rely on a placebo* to achieve part of their effect. When subjects are covertly given strong opiates like morphine, they don't work nearly as well as they do if the subjects are told they are being given a powerful pain reliever. Even real medications require some of the brain's own bounty.

Conversely, thinking about pain creates pain. In studies at Oxford University, Irene Tracey has shown that asking subjects to think about their chronic pain, for example, increases activation in their pain-perception circuits. Distraction, on the other hand, is a great analgesic; when Tracey's volunteers were asked to engage in a complicated counting task while being subjected to a painful heat stimulus, she could watch the pain-perception matrix decrease while cognitive parts of the brain involved in counting lighted up. At McGill University, Catherine Bushnell has shown that simply listening to tones while being subjected to a heat stimulus decreased activity in the pain-perception circuit.

"There is an interesting irony to pain," comments Christopher deCharms, who worked with Mackey designing and carrying out the Stanford study. We were talking in his office at Omneuron, a Menlo Park

20

medical-technology company he founded three years ago to develop clinical applications of neuroimaging. "Everyone is born with a system designed to turn off pain. There isn't an obvious mechanism to turn off other diseases like Parkinson's. With pain, the system is there, but we don't have control over the dial."

The goal of the Stanford technique is to teach people to control their dials — to activate their modulatory systems without requiring the extreme stress of fleeing from a shark or the deception of a placebo. The hope of neuroimaging therapy (as deCharms calls the Stanford technique) is that repeated practice will strengthen and eventually change the ineffective modulatory system to eliminate chronic pain, the way long-term physical therapy can change muscular weakness. The scan would thus be more than a research tool: *the scan itself would be the treatment;* and the subject his or her own researcher.

Only once do I recall having a glimmer of my own pain-modulatory system at work: a hidden power that emerged, dispensed with pain and then returned to some forgotten fold in my brain, where I have never been able to locate it again. The event did not take place on a battlefield or a marathon course or in a temple; it was in a basement of the Stanford University medical center three years ago. At the time, Mackey had designed an earlier study that did not use imaging technology but focused on how suggestion alters pain perception. Although I was not formally enrolled in the study, I asked if I could undergo a clinical demonstration. My experience illustrated the power of suggestion in an unexpected fashion.

A metal probe attached to the underbelly of my arm heated up and cooled down at set intervals. I was told that although the heat probe would feel uncomfortable, my skin would not be burned. During one exposure, I was instructed to think of the pain as positively as possible, during another to think of it as negatively. After each sequence, I was asked to rate my pain on a 0-to-10 scale, with 10 being the worst pain I could imagine.

Although I discovered that I could make the pain fluctuate depending   25
on whether I was imagining that I was sunbathing or was the victim of an inquisition, I still rated all the pain as low — ranging from a 1 to a 3. If 10 was being slowly burned alive, I felt I should at least be begging for mercy to justify a rating of 5. So I insisted that Mackey turn up the dial so I could get a real response. But even during the moments when I was actively trying to imagine the pain as negatively as possible, it remained in a mental box of "not even burned," which kept it from really hurting: hurting, that is, the way a burn would.

As it turned out, I got a second-degree burn that later darkened into a square mark. Mackey was more than a little dismayed as we watched the reddening skin pucker, but I was thrilled. Naturally the protocol had been carefully designed not to injure anyone, yet in my case that protection had failed *because of the very phenomenon it was designed to study:* expectation — the effect of the mind on pain or placebo.

I had recently spent several weeks observing Mackey in the university's pain clinic, where he is associate director. I was so convinced that Mackey — then a tall sandy-haired thirty-nine-year-old with a deep interest in technology (he got a PhD in electrical engineering before he went to medical school) and an air of radiant integrity — would not burn me that my brain had not perceived the stimulus as a threat and generated pain. I admired him, I trusted him, I was positive that he wouldn't hurt me. And, ipso facto, he hadn't.

Mackey's genius as a practitioner, I thought, lay partly in his ability to similarly inspire patients. "When I started working with pain patients, I realized how much of the treatment involved trying to reverse learned helplessness," he said — to rally them out of the despair ingrained from years of unremitting pain and cajole their minds to chip in its own analgesic to their therapies. "The purpose of this study is to show patients their mind matters." Mackey said.

The mark of the burn is barely visible now, but for a couple of years afterward, at times when my chronic pain was making me miserable, the sight of it would both encourage and reproach me. *Here is the ultimate proof that my mind can control pain*, I would think, yet I didn't know how to make it wake up and do so. I could take the edge off the pain by conjuring positive images, but the effects didn't last, and I never again had the remarkable placebo response that masked a second-degree burn. In fact, a mild burn from spilling tea on my hand one day brought tears to my eyes.

When the real-time neuroimaging study began, I couldn't wait to try it.   30

The area of the brain that the scanner focuses on is the rostral anterior cingulate cortex (rACC). The rACC (a quarter-size patch in the middle-front of the brain, the cingular cortex) plays a critical role in the awareness of the nastiness of pain: the feeling of dislike for it, a loathing so intense that you are immediately compelled to try to make it stop. Indeed, the pain of pain, you might say, its defining element, is the way in which the sensation is suffused with a particular unpleasantness researchers refer to as dysphoria. Since pain is a perception, it's not pain if you don't experience it as hurting. You can feel hot or cold or pressure, and note them simply as stimuli, but when they exceed a certain intensity, the rACC kicks in, and suddenly they become painful, riveting your attention and causing you to recoil.

Many pain-reducing techniques aim to manipulate the conscious awareness of pain. Distraction, placebo, meditation, imagining pleasant scenes and hypnosis all result in a reduction of rACC activation when they work. Patients who have undergone a radical surgical treatment occasionally used for pain (as well as for mental illness) called a cingulotomy, in which the rACC is partly destroyed, report that they are still aware of pain but that they don't "mind" it anymore. Their emotional response has receded.

The image I saw while lying in the fMRI machine at the time of the recent Stanford study was not literally my rACC but a visual analogue of it that is easier to see: a 3-D image of a fire. The flames represent the degree of activation in your rACC: when it is low, the flames are low: when rACC activation is high, the flames flare. The study involves five thirteen-minute scanning runs, each consisting of five cycles of a thirty-second rest followed by a one-minute interval in which you try to increase rACC activation and then a one-minute interval in which you try to decrease rACC activation.

Before my scan began, I was prepped in different mental strategies for increasing and modulating my pain. Everyone's brain works a bit differently, though, so subjects have to experiment in the scanner to see what is most effective for them. For some, trying to distract themselves from their pain works best; for others, focusing on their pain — like embracing a Zen koan — seems to be what triggers their pain-modulatory system. When deCharms used neuroimaging therapy on himself to try to alleviate his chronic neck pain, he concentrated on the pain itself and felt it "suddenly melt away." He said that a patient described the feeling as being "like a runner's high" (a state that has been shown to involve the release of endogenous endorphins).

Increase Your Pain, the screen commanded, as the first run began. I   35
tried to recall the mental strategies in which I had been prepped for increasing pain: *Dwell on how hopeless, depressed or lonely you felt when your pain was most severe. Sense that the pain is causing long-term damage.*

Dwelling on the hopeless loneliness of my pain certainly made the flames of my rACC spark. The mental image that I found increased my pain the most, however, was the one that matched the visual analogue of the rACC: *Picture a hot flame on your painful area. Try to make the flame grow in the painful area, and imagine it actually burning your flesh.*

Having recently read Ariel Glucklich's extraordinary *Sacred Pain,* I had plenty of details of the burning of heretics and witches available to me. I had only to imagine the smell of sizzling hair to make the flames of my rACC explode.

Decrease Pain, the screen commanded.

The suggested pain-reduction strategies, however, did little to quell the flames on the screen. I pictured suffocating the pain with banal positive imagery: *flowing water or honey, something soft and gentle,* but my mind kept slipping back to the progress of the auto-da-fé, and the rACC fire flared.

Feel that sensation, but tell yourself that it is just a completely harmless,   40
short-term tactile sensation.

Pilgrims and devotees all around the world choose to inflict pain upon themselves during sacred rites — from being nailed to crosses to dangling from hooks. For them, pain is an occasion for euphoria, not dysphoria. There are many historical records of the equanimity saints and martyrs often possessed during torture. The second-century Jewish martyr Rabbi Akiva, for example, continued to recite a prayer with a smile on his lips *while the flesh was being combed from his bones.* "All my life," he explained to the puzzled Roman general orchestrating his execution, "when I said the words 'You shall love the Lord your God with all your heart, with all your soul, and with all your might,' I was saddened, for I thought, When shall I be able to fulfill this command? Now that I am giving my life and my resolution remains firm, should I not smile?"

As Glucklich writes, the conviction that pain is a spiritual opportunity seems paradoxically anesthetizing — or, as a scientist would say, religious states of conviction can robustly activate the pain-modulatory system.

During my next Decrease Pain interval, instead of trying to picture a vacation, I imagined myself as a martyr, lucidly reciting *Though I walk through the valley of the shadow of death* while being burned at the stake. My rACC activation — I noted — respectfully quieted. Then I remembered that the 23rd Psalm seems to have Christian associations, and since I was presumably being tortured for being half-Jewish, a Jewish prayer might be more appropriate. Unless, that is, I was being accused of witchcraft, in which case, I might be generally disillusioned with Judeo-Christian prayer. As I tried to settle on a fantasy, I noticed that my rACC stayed low: Irene Tracey's theory of the modulating effects of distraction. By the last run, I had the strategies down — heretic-martyr: rACC down; heretic-victim: rACC up.

The results of the scan, Mackey showed me, revealed significant brain control. A week later, I was scanned again, this time in the offices of Omneuron. I could feel that it was easier to control my rACC with less reliance on elaborate fantasy; I was interacting more directly with my brain.

This learning effect was clearly seen in the recent Stanford study (which 45 was financed in part by the National Institutes of Health). The first phase of the study looked at twelve subjects with chronic pain and thirty-six healthy subjects. (The healthy participants were subjected to a painful heat stimulus in the scanner and tried to modulate their responses. The chronic-pain patients, however, simply worked to reduce their own pain.) The chronic-pain patients who underwent neuroimaging training reported an average decrease of 64 percent in pain rating by the end of the study. (Healthy subjects also reported a significant increase in their ability to control the pain.)

"One big concern we had," Mackey says, "is, Were we creating the world's most expensive placebo?" To ensure against that, Mackey trained a control group in pain-reduction techniques without using the scanner (as in his previous study) to see if that was as effective as employing a $2 million machine. Mackey also tried scanning subjects without showing them their brain images or tricking subjects by feeding them images of irrelevant parts of the brain or feeding them someone else's brain images. "None of these worked," Mackey says, "or worked nearly as well." Traditional biofeedback also compared unfavorably; changes in pain ratings of subjects in the experimental group were three times as large as in the biofeedback control group.

The second phase of the study, which is now under way, is designed to assess whether neuroimaging therapy offers long-term practical benefits to a larger group of chronic-pain patients. After the six sessions designed to teach them to regulate their pain, they will be observed for at least six months. The idea is to see whether they can fundamentally change their modulation system so that it can reduce pain all the time without constantly and consciously thinking about it. If so, the technique would not simply provide shelter from the storm of pain; it would bring about climate change.

"I believe the technique may make lasting changes because the brain is a machine designed to learn," deCharms says. The brain is soft-wired (plastic) rather than hard-wired: whenever you learn something new, new neural connections are believed to form and old, unused ones to wither away. (Researchers refer to this as activity-dependent neuroplasticity.) In other words, if you actively engage a certain brain region, you can alter it.

Many diseases of the central nervous system involve inappropriate levels of activation in particular brain regions that change the way they operate (negative neuroplasticity). Some regions experience atrophy, while other regions become hyperactive. (For example, epilepsy involves hyperactivity of cells; stroke, Parkinson's and other diseases involve the atrophy of nerve cells.) With chronic pain, it is believed that additional nerve cells, recruited for transmitting pain, create more pain pathways in the nervous system, while nerve cells that normally inhibit or slow the signaling, decrease or change function.

In addition, chronic pain results in a significant loss of other kinds of brain cells. A. Vania Apkarian at Northwestern University found that while the brain of a healthy person shrinks 2.5 percent a year, in a person with chronic back pain, it shrinks an additional 1.3 percent annually in the areas that involve rational thinking. I know chronic pain interferes with my concentration at times, but I never imagined that it could be truly impairing it! The Stanford technique may mitigate this harm by teaching people how to increase the efficacy of the healthy cells.

Moreover, the technique may offer a particular advantage over drug therapy. It is very difficult to design drugs to fix a problem in a specific region of the brain because the receptors that drugs target, like the opiate receptors, generally appear in multiple systems throughout the brain (which is partly why drugs almost always have side effects). Neuroimaging therapy, on the other hand, is designed to teach control of a localized brain region.

"The technique gives people a tool they didn't know they had," Mackey says, "cognitive control over neuroplasticity. We don't fully understand how this feedback mechanism is working, but it provides tangible evidence that people can change something in their own brains, which can be very empowering. It takes Buddhist monks thirty years of sitting on a mountain learning to control their brains through meditation — we're trying to jumpstart that process." As to how exactly it works — how the decision-making parts of the brain (the prefrontal regions of the cortex) cause the change in the rACC — "Heck if I know!" he says. "How do we get the brain to do anything? We can map out the anatomical circuits involved and the general functions of those circuits, but we can't tell you the mechanism by which any cognitive decision is translated into action."

If neuroimaging therapy could treat pain, could it rewire the brain to fix other diseases, like depression, stroke and learning disabilities, or exercise the brain in ways that would make it cleverer and more adept at certain skills? Neuroimaging has shown, for example, that the part of the brains of London cabdrivers that regulates spatial relations is larger than usual and that learning to juggle creates visible changes in parts of the brain involved with motor coordination during three months of training. I'm constantly getting lost and dropping things. Could I exercise and strengthen those areas more quickly by, say, thinking about maps in the scanner than by driving around London?

"What is the limit to neuroimaging therapy?" deCharms muses. "Could you learn to target the reward or serotonin system and up-regulate happiness? Could you augment psychotherapy by allowing the patient and the therapist to watch the brain?" — an idea Omneuron is already exploring, by bringing therapists and patients to the scanner and imaging patients' brains as they undergo the sessions. "After all, talk therapy is about learning to understand thought processes — to understand neural substrates and change them," he says.

How deep can the insights that functional imaging might offer really go? 55

What I'd like to do most is not fix problems or improve skills but use imaging as a vehicle for self-transparency. Instead of puzzling about my motivations, I'd like to be able to read my mind completely, like a book: for imaging to be the Plexiglas window through which I could finally see the ghost.

"Hmm," Dr. Scott Fishman, chief of the pain-medicine division at the University of California, Davis, said dubiously when I brought up this notion. "I'm not sure that functional imaging is actually looking at the mind. The mind is like a virtual organ — it doesn't have a physical address that we know about. Functional imaging provides a two-dimensional snapshot of a three-dimensional or a four-dimensional event of this entity of the mind. Right now, imaging is just looking at the brain; we have to be honest about that." Imaging shows the level of activation of different parts of the brain, from which we can extrapolate something about the mind, he points out, "but what we really need to see is how the parts talk to each other — and the complex nuances of their language."

The brain has more than a hundred billion neurons. All functional imaging can tell us now is that a few hundred million of them in various areas become more active at certain times. It's as if you were trying to conduct a symphony by watching a silent film of the concert. You would see the players in the bass section active at one moment, vigorously gesturing, and then the rest of the orchestra would join in, but you couldn't hear the notes or how they form strands of melody and harmony and meld together to create the ethereal experience.

"Consciousness is not neurons firing — consciousness is a transcendent emergent phenomenon that depends on the firing of neurons," says Dr. Daniel Carr, an eminent pain researcher who is now the CEO of Javelin Pharmaceuticals. "The gears of a watch rotate and keep time, but the turning of the gears is not time. The question is, Is neuroimaging a picture of the experience of consciousness or is it a picture of a mechanism associated with that experience? Can there actually be a picture of an experience? Does a picture of a funeral or a wedding show you experiences? Or is there an unbridgeable gap there because you need to already understand the experience in order to interpret the photos? If a higher being told us how consciousness works, could we understand the explanation?"

QUESTIONS

Reading

1. What does the acronym *fMRI* stand for? What does fMRI allow researchers to do?
2. How does Thernstrom distinguish between acute pain and chronic pain? From what kind of pain does Thernstrom suffer?
3. What benefits and advantages of using the Stanford technique does Thernstrom list? What are some potential drawbacks of the technique, or themes of concern to researchers? How does Thernstrom connect her explanation of this technique to her own personal reflections?
4. Thernstrom describes her chronic pain visually — she pictures it as "soggy, moldy, dark or perhaps ashy, like those alarming pictures of smokers' lungs" (paragraph 2). Highlight, underline, or flag other places in the essay where Thernstrom uses visual language or descriptions of images. What purpose does using words to conjure pictures serve in Thernstrom's reflective essay?

Exploratory Writing

1. Imagine that you could look inside your own brain and reprogram it, as if it were a computer. How would your brain look? What "glitches" would you fix? What other programming changes would you make?
2. Discuss the different scientific studies and experiments that Thernstrom brings up in her essay. In teams, design an experiment to test subjects' ability to control their experience through controlling their thoughts. What role would the placebo effect play in your experiment?

Making Connections

1. Consider Jonah Lehrer's (p. 398) explanation of how insights, or "eureka moments," might occur in the human brain. How might insights and

moments of inspiration be related to consciousness, as Thernstrom explains it? In each essay, which brain functions can be explained entirely by neural mechanics, and which remain mysterious?

Essay Writing

1. In her conclusion, Thernstrom quotes Dr. Daniel Carr: "Consciousness is not neurons firing — consciousness is a transcendent emergent phenomenon that depends on the firing of neurons." Write an essay discussing different definitions of *consciousness*. What are your own reflections on how consciousness works?

A Delicate Operation

Roy C. Selby Jr.

Roy C. Selby Jr. (1930–2001) graduated from Louisiana State University and the University of Arkansas Medical School, where he specialized in neurology and neurosurgery. He was the author of numerous professional articles on neurosurgery and a member of the American Association of Neurological Surgeons. "A Delicate Operation," which first appeared in Harper's *magazine in 1975, reports for a more general audience the details of a difficult brain operation.*

In the autumn of 1973 a woman in her early fifties noticed, upon closing one eye while reading, that she was unable to see clearly. Her eyesight grew slowly worse. Changing her eyeglasses did not help. She saw an ophthalmologist, who found that her vision was seriously impaired in both eyes. She then saw a neurologist, who confirmed the finding and obtained X rays of the skull and an EMI scan — a photograph of the patient's head. The latter revealed a tumor growing between the optic nerves at the base of the brain. The woman was admitted to the hospital by a neurosurgeon.

Further diagnosis, based on angiography, a detailed X-ray study of the circulatory system, showed the tumor to be about two inches in diameter and supplied by many small blood vessels. It rested beneath the brain, just above the pituitary gland, stretching the optic nerves to either side and intimately close to the major blood vessels supplying the brain. Removing it would pose many technical problems. Probably benign and slow-growing, it may have been present for several years. If left alone it would continue to grow and produce blindness, and might become impossible to remove completely. Removing it, however, might not improve the patient's vision and could make it worse. A major blood vessel could be damaged, causing a stroke. Damage to the undersurface of the brain could cause impairment of memory and changes in mood and personality. The hypothalamus, a most important structure of the brain, could be injured, causing coma, high fever, bleeding from the stomach, and death.

The neurosurgeon met with the patient and her husband and discussed the various possibilities. The common decision was to operate.

The patient's hair was shampooed for two nights before surgery. She was given a cortisonelike drug to reduce the risk of damage to the brain during surgery. Five units of blood were cross-matched, as a contingency against hemorrhage. At 1:00 p.m. the operation began. After the patient was anesthetized her hair was completely clipped and shaved from the scalp. Her head was prepped with an organic iodine solution for ten minutes. Drapes were placed over her, leaving exposed only the forehead and crown of the skull. All the routine instruments were brought up — the electrocautery used to coagulate areas of bleeding, bipolar coagulation forceps to arrest bleeding from individual blood vessels without damaging adjacent tissues, and small suction tubes to remove blood and cerebrospinal fluid from the head, thus giving the surgeon a better view of the tumor and surrounding areas.

A curved incision was made behind the hairline so it would be concealed when the hair grew back. It extended almost from ear to ear. Plastic clips were applied to the cut edges of the scalp to arrest bleeding. The scalp was folded back to the level of the eyebrows. Incisions were made in the muscle of the right temple, and three sets of holes were drilled near the temple and the top of the head because the tumor had to be approached from directly in front. The drill, powered by nitrogen, was replaced with a fluted steel blade, and the holes were connected. The incised piece of skull was pried loose and held out of the way by a large sponge.

Beneath the bone is a yellowish leatherlike membrane, the dura, that surrounds the brain. Down the middle of the head the dura carries a large vein, but in the area near the nose the vein is small. At that point the vein and dura were cut, and clips made of tantalum, a hard metal, were applied to arrest and prevent bleeding. Sutures were put into the dura and tied to the scalp to keep the dura open and retracted. A malleable silver retractor, resembling the blade of a butter knife, was inserted between the brain and skull. The anesthesiologist began to administer a drug to relax the brain by removing some of its water, making it easier for the surgeon to manipulate the retractor, hold the brain back, and see the tumor. The nerve tracts for smell were cut on both sides to provide additional room. The tumor was seen approximately two-and-one-half inches behind the base of the nose. It was pink in color. On touching it, it proved to be very fibrous and tough. A special retractor was attached to the skull, enabling the other retractor blades to be held automatically and freeing the surgeon's hands. With further displacement of the frontal lobes of the brain, the tumor could be seen better, but no normal structures — the carotid arteries, their branches, and the optic nerves — were visible. The tumor obscured them.

A surgical microscope was placed above the wound. The surgeon had selected the lenses and focal length prior to the operation. Looking through the microscope, he could see some of the small vessels supplying the tumor and he coagulated them. He incised the tumor to attempt to remove its core and thus collapse it, but the substance of the tumor was too firm to be removed in this fashion. He then began to slowly dissect the tumor from the adjacent brain tissue and from where he believed the normal structures to be.

Using small squares of cotton, he began to separate the tumor from very loose fibrous bands connecting it to the brain and to the right side of the part of the skull where the pituitary gland lies. The right optic nerve and carotid artery came into view, both displaced considerably to the right. The optic nerve had a normal appearance. He protected these structures with cotton compresses placed between them and the tumor. He began to raise the tumor from the skull and slowly to reach the point of its origin and attachment — just in front of the pituitary gland and medial to the left optic nerve, which still could not be seen. The small blood vessels entering the tumor were cauterized. The upper portion of the tumor was gradually separated from the brain, and the branches of the carotid arteries and the branches to the tumor were coagulated. The tumor was slowly and gently lifted from its bed, and for the first time the left carotid artery and optic nerve could be seen. Part of the tumor adhered to this nerve. The bulk of the tumor was amputated, leaving a small bit attached to the nerve. Very slowly and carefully the tumor fragment was resected.

The tumor now removed, a most impressive sight came into view — the pituitary gland and its stalk of attachment to the hypothalamus, the hypothalamus itself, and the brainstem, which conveys nerve impulses between the body and the brain. As far as could be determined, no damage had been done to these structures or other vital centers, but the left optic nerve, from chronic pressure of the tumor, appeared gray and thin. Probably it would not completely recover its function.

After making certain there was no bleeding, the surgeon closed the wounds and placed wire mesh over the holes in the skull to prevent dimpling of the scalp over the points that had been drilled. A gauze dressing was applied to the patient's head. She was awakened and sent to the recovery room.   10

Even with the microscope, damage might still have occurred to the cerebral cortex and hypothalamus. It would require at least a day to be reasonably certain there was none, and about seventy-two hours to monitor for the major postoperative dangers — swelling of the brain and blood clots forming over the surface of the brain. The surgeon explained this to the patient's husband, and both of them waited anxiously. The operation had required seven hours. A glass of orange juice had given the surgeon some additional energy during the closure of the wound. Though exhausted, he could not fall asleep until after two in the morning, momentarily expecting a call from the nurse in the intensive care unit announcing deterioration of the patient's condition.

At 8:00 a.m. the surgeon saw the patient in the intensive care unit. She was alert, oriented, and showed no sign of additional damage to the optic nerves or the brain. She appeared to be in better shape than the surgeon or her husband.

QUESTIONS

Reading

1. Why did Selby decide to operate? What could have happened if the patient chose not to have the operation? What effect does knowing this information have on the reader?
2. What is the *dura*?
3. Selby uses different methods of reporting to create the drama of "A Delicate Operation." At what point in the essay does he provide background information? How much of the essay reports events before, during, and after the operation? At what points does the writer explain terms and procedures for the reader?

Exploratory Writing

1. Highlight, underline, or flag the passages in this essay that you find especially powerful. How did Selby create this effect?
2. Using the Internet or library, find an article on neurosurgery that was obviously written for professionals within the field rather than for a general audience. How does the tone of the article differ from Selby's? How is the structure different? What types of material are included in — or omitted from — each article?
3. Write a checklist of steps required in the neurosurgical procedure that Selby describes. (You may refer to Atul Gawande's [p. 410] description of a checklist.) As a class or in small groups, compare the different checklists. Were certain steps forgotten on some checklists? Discuss whether a checklist would be a useful resource for doctors working on this complex procedure.

Making Connections

1. Compare Selby's perspective to Melanie Thernstrom's (p. 344). Why is Selby's essay *reportorial*, while Thernstrom's is *reflective*? What elements of explanation are required in each essay to introduce specialized topics to the reader?
2. Jonah Lehrer (p. 398) describes the differences between left-brain thinking and the right-brain thinking that results in moments of inspiration. In your opinion, does the surgeon performing the procedure described in this essay use left-brain thinking, right-brain thinking, or both? Refer to Lehrer's definitions, and use specific examples from Selby's report to explain your conclusions.

Essay Writing

1. Imagine that you had to perform an operation like the one Selby describes. Write an essay reflecting on the experiences and personality traits that would help or hinder your performance as a surgeon.

The Other Stem-Cell Debate

Jamie Shreeve

Jamie Shreeve received his BA in English from Brown University in 1973 and graduated from the Iowa Writers' Workshop in 1979. He contributed fiction to a number of literary magazines before turning to science writing. From 1983 to 1985, he was the director of public information at the Marine Biological Laboratory in Woods Hole, Massachusetts. While there, Shreeve founded and edited MBL Science, *a magazine for general readers, and created the* MBL Science *Writing Fellowship Program. He has written for* Discover, National Geographic, Science, Smithsonian, *the* Atlantic Monthly, *and the* New York Times. *He has been a fellow of the Alfred P. Sloan Foundation and the Alicia Patterson Foundation. His books, under the name James Shreeve, include* Nature: The Other Earthlings *(1987), a companion book to the public television series;* Lucy's Child: The Discovery of a Human Ancestor *(1989), written with Donald Johanson, the paleontologist who discovered the fossil remains of Lucy;* The Neanderthal Enigma: Solving the Mystery of Modern Human Origins *(1995); and* The Genome War: How Craig Venter Tried to Capture the Code of Life and Save the World *(2004), an account of the two competing attempts to sequence the human genome. The following article appeared in the* New York Times Magazine *in 2005.*

Except for the three million human brain cells injected into his cranium, XO47 is just an average green vervet monkey. He weighs about twelve pounds and measures thirty-four inches from the tip of his tail to the sutured incision on the top of his head. His fur is a melange of black, yellow, and olive, with white underparts and a coal-black face. Until his operation, two days before I met him, he was skittering about an open-air enclosure on the grounds of a biomedical facility on the Caribbean island of St. Kitts. Afterward, he was caged in a hut shared with half a dozen other experimental monkeys, all of whom bore identical incisions in their scalps. Judging from the results of previous experiments, the human neural stem cells inserted into their brains would soon take hold and begin to grow, their fibers reaching out to shake hands with their monkey counterparts. The green vervets' behavior was, and will remain, all monkey. To a vervet, eye contact signals aggression, and when I peered into XO47's cage he took umbrage, vigorously bobbing his head in a stereotypical threat display. Still, it was hard not to stare.

By virtue of the human material added to his brain, XO47 is a chimera — that is, an organism assembled out of living parts taken from more than one biological species. The word comes from the monstrous creature of Greek mythology — part lion, part serpent, and part goat — that is slain by the hero Bellerophon. Less fearsome chimeras occur naturally — lichen, for instance, is a mix of fungus and algae. Most, however, are created in the laboratory by scientists like Dr. Eugene Redmond of Yale University, the soft-spoken sixty-five-year-old psychiatrist and neurosurgeon who operated on XO47. He set up the St. Kitts Biomedical Foundation on this island because that is where the monkeys are — an overabundant feral population of them, ideally suited for research. Redmond has transplanted immature human brain cells into a region of XO47's brain that produces dopamine, a neurochemical that is depleted in the brains of people with Parkinson's disease. If the human cells can take hold and differentiate and bolster the monkey's own dopamine-producing machinery, a similar operation on a Parkinson's patient, the reasoning goes, should have an even greater chance of success.

Redmond is of the opinion that the insertion of a few human cells into a monkey brain is no big deal, and most biologists would agree. But many bioethicists and policy makers are alarmed by recent research developments that have made chimeric experiments more common and increasingly capable of producing human-animal amalgamations that are more ambitious, more "unnatural" — and thus more troubling — than Redmond's vervets.

Driving the surge in chimeric experimentation is the enormous but still untested promise of human stem cells. In theory, stem cells isolated from an early human embryo can transform themselves into virtually any kind of cell in the body, kindling hope that one day they may be transplanted into human patients to provide new tissue wherever it is needed — heart muscle for cardiac patients, insulin-producing cells for diabetics, nerve cells to repair crushed spinal cords, and so on. But there are serious hurdles to overcome before this dream can be realized, including figuring out what controls the differentiation of stem cells and combating their tendency to form tumors. Clearly it is unethical to study the unknown actions of stem cells in human subjects. One obvious solution is to insert the cells into animals and watch how they develop. Depending on what kind of stem cells are used and where they are put in the animal, it may also be possible to pluck some particular human biological feature or disease trait out of its natural context and re-create it in an animal model, where it can be examined and manipulated at will.

While the objections to stem-cell research have largely revolved around 5 the ethics of using human embryos, there is another debate bubbling to the surface: how "human" are chimeric creatures made from human stem cells? Fueling the anxiety has been the lack of coherent regulations in the

United States governing the creation of chimeras. The President's Council on Bioethics has twice taken up the issue in recent weeks, and Senator Sam Brownback, the Kansas Republican and outspoken social conservative, has introduced legislation to restrict chimeric experiments. Meanwhile, the National Academy of Sciences is expected to issue guidelines later this month as part of a widely anticipated report on the proper use of human stem cells. While the academy's recommendations will carry considerable clout, compliance will be voluntary.

Few people argue that all experiments mixing human and animal material should be banned outright. But where should the lines be drawn? "Some scientists are completely upset with even a single human cell in a monkey brain," says Evan Snyder, a neurobiologist who has conducted chimeric experiments with Redmond. "I don't have problems with putting in a large percentage of cells — 10 or 20 percent — if I felt it could help a patient. It comes down to what percentage of human cells starts making you squirm."

Françoise Baylis, a bioethicist at Dalhousie University in Halifax, Nova Scotia, and a co-author of Canada's stem-cell guidelines, squirms not at a percentage of human cells but at the place where awareness begins. "We have to be sure we are not creating beings with consciousness," she says. The very existence of biologically ambiguous creatures could lead to "inexorable moral confusion" in a society with two ancient and irreconcilable codes of conduct governing the treatment of humans and animals. That said, all modern genetic research, including the sequencing of the human genome itself, underscores how trivial the biological difference really is between a human being and the rest of life. Ninety-nine percent of our genome is shared with chimpanzees. Thirty-one percent of our genes are interchangeable with those of yeast. Does the nearness of our kinship with the rest of nature make the prospect of a quasi-human chimera among us less of a threat to our collective psyche or more of one?

Chimeras have been with us for some time. In 1988, Dr. Irving Weissman and his colleagues at Stanford University created a lab model for AIDS by endowing a mouse with an entirely human immune system. Since then, scientists have tailored mice and other animals with human kidneys, blood, skin, muscles, and various other components. Baboon and chimp hearts have been transplanted into human chest cavities, pig cells into the brains of Parkinson's disease patients and, more routinely, pig heart valves into people with heart disease, including Jesse Helms, the former U.S. senator.

For most of us, a senator with a partly porcine heart or a mouse with a human immune system is not sufficient to provoke the kind of instinctive queasiness known among ethicists as "the yuck factor." The man most identified with that term, Dr. Leon Kass, the bioethicist and current chairman of the President's Council on Bioethics, is of the opinion that widespread feelings of repugnance may be an alarm that something is morally wrong, even if you are not able to articulate precisely why. The mouse and the senator may not trigger a yuck because they look just like a rodent and a person. But what about a normal-looking mouse with a headful of human brain cells or a human-animal embryo that is only briefly alive and never seen?

If you want to get a peek at a real live chimera, drive about five miles   10
east from downtown Reno, Nevada, until you come to a farm that looks pretty much like any other farm. The gate will be locked, but from the road you can see some pens holding sheep that look pretty much like any other sheep. Pound for pound, however, these may be the most thoroughly humanized animals on the planet. They are the work of Esmail Zanjani, a hematologist in the College of Agriculture, Biotechnology, and Natural Resources at the University of Nevada at Reno. Several years ago, Zanjani and his colleagues began injecting fetal lambs with human stem cells, mostly ones derived from human bone marrow. He said he hoped that the cells would transform into blood cells so that he could use the sheep to study the human blood system. According to Zanjani, when he examined the sheep he discovered that the human cells had traveled with their lymphatic system throughout the sheep's body, developing into blood, bone, liver, heart, and assorted other cells, including some in the brain. While some scientists are skeptical of his findings, Zanjani told me that some have livers that are as much as 40 percent humanized, with distinct human structural units pumping out uniquely human proteins.

While the idea of partly humanized sheep might make some people a little uncomfortable, it isn't easy to see where they trespass across some unambiguous ethical line. But according to Dr. William Hurlbut, a physician and consulting professor in human biology at Stanford, who serves with Kass on the President's Council on Bioethics, the seeing is exactly the point. What if, instead of internal human organs, Zanjani's sheep sported recognizably human parts on the outside — human limbs or genitals, for instance, ready for transplant should the need arise? Hurlbut maintains that this is scientifically plausible. But it would be wrong. Every living thing has a natural trajectory through its life beginning at conception, and in Hurlbut's view, a visible chimera would veer dangerously off course.

"It has to do with the relationship between signs and their meaning," he told me. "Human appearance is something we should reserve for humans. Anything else that looks human debases the coinage of truth."

Understanding the world as divided into distinct categories is a fundamental organizing principle of civilization. We conceive of the living aspect of that world as separated into species, with boundaries around them that should not be purposively muddled. The underlying validity of our categorical constructs is not as important as how we use them to make sense of the world. Our minds have evolved to be hypersensitive to the borders between species, just as we see a rainbow as composed of six or seven distinct colors when it is really a continuum of wavelengths of light. "When we start to blend the edges of things, we're uneasy," Hurlbut says. "That's why chimeric creatures are monsters in mythology in the first place."

It is easy to marshal rational arguments to counter this thinking. The limitations of a typological concept of species, which goes back to Aristotle, are well known. Some species interbreed with closely related ones on the borders of their habitats. Evolutionary biologists cannot agree on how to define what a species really is in the first place, so it is hard to see how the boundaries between them can be absolute. Even if species boundaries do have a natural integrity, how alarming is it to find that those walls can be perforated by artificial means? We have been engaging in unnatural acts upon nature for centuries, grafting plants onto one another or breeding dogs in visible shapes and sizes that diverge wildly from their natural state — let alone performing heart transplants and in vitro fertilizations. I'm not sure I would undergo a crisis of truth at the sight of a sheep with a human arm, especially if it were the best means available for replacing a lost one. But everyone has a squirm threshold. What would you make of a sheep with a human face?

The reason Zanjani's chimeras look like perfectly ordinary sheep is that he injected them with stem cells in a late stage of their fetal development, when their body plans were already laid down. The reason he was allowed to conduct the experiment at all is that he works in the United States, as opposed to Canada or Great Britain where such chimeric research is restricted. Older fetuses are not as impressionable as younger ones, and embryos are the most vulnerable of all. And the younger the human stem cell you insert, the more powerful an influence it can have on the body and brain of the host animal. The way to produce the most homogenous blend of human and animal would thus be to inject fully potent human embryonic stem cells into the very early embryo of, say, a mouse. This is the experiment that policies in those countries are most keen to prevent.

It is also the one that Ali Brivanlou is poised to begin. For several years, Brivanlou, a forty-five-year-old developmental biologist at Rockefeller University in New York, has been arguing that one of the best ways to understand the usefulness of stem cells for regenerative medicine is to first insert them in an animal embryo and see how they divide and differentiate in a living system. The experiment is explicitly prohibited by the institutions that supply the stem-cell lines approved by the Bush administration, so he is using private funds to develop his own lines. He plans to insert them into three-to-five-day-old mouse embryos, which he will then implant in the wombs of female mice. Brivanlou is anxiously awaiting the publication of the National Academy of Sciences guidelines before proceeding, but he says he doubts that they will prove an impediment. In his view, showing the potency of stem cells only in a petri dish is like testing the power of a new car by revving its engine in the garage. He wants to take the car out on the track and see how it might perform some day on the open road.

"This experiment must be done," he says. "We can't go directly from culture to a patient. That would be extremely dangerous."

But his experiment is one that most are very reluctant to undertake, even in the private sector. When I inquired at Geron Corporation, a biotechnology company in California, whether scientists there were considering such work, I received a terse e-mail reply that "the company is not, has not and will not pursue inter-species stem-cell chimeras."

Robert Lanza, vice president for medical and scientific development at Advanced Cell Technology, in Worcester, Mass., says much the same thing. "I personally don't want to engage in those kinds of experiments, and I won't have any of my scientists do that work," he says. "Sure, we could reach our endpoints quicker that way. But it takes you into very murky water."

Why all the shuddering? For starters, there is the gonad quandary. If the experiment really works, the human cells should differentiate into all of the embryo's cell lineages, including the one that eventually forms the animal's reproductive cells. If the mouse were male, some of its sperm might thus be human, and if it were female, some of its eggs might be human eggs. If two such creatures were to mate, there would be a chance that a human embryo could be conceived and begin to grow in a mouse uterus — a sort of Stuart Little scenario, but in reverse and not so cute.   20

"Literally nobody wants to see an experiment where two mice that have eggs and sperm of human origin have the opportunity to mate and produce human offspring," says Dr. Norman Post, professor of pediatrics and director of the bioethics program at the University of Wisconsin and a member of the National Academy of Sciences committee reviewing stem-cell research policies. "That's beyond anybody's wildest nightmare."

Is the concern over the reproductive issue overblown? It is, of course, biologically impossible for a human fetus to be delivered from a rodent uterus. Moreover, for a human embryo to be conceived, the chimeras would have to be born first in order to mate, and Brivanlou says he has no intention of allowing them to come to term. He plans to terminate them and examine the fate of the human cells after a week. Still, there remains the question of what kind of being would be present during those seven days. Nobody knows. Does even the fleeting, prenatal existence of a chimera of unknown aspect cross a moral line — not because of what it might look like or become but simply for what it is?

Brivanlou is not troubled by that question. He sees the other methods of testing the stem cells' power — in vitro or in the body of an older fetus or of a fully developed animal — as inadequate, and he says he wants the science to be allowed to follow its natural course. "One thing that is important to remember — we've been here before," he says. "In the 70s, there was a huge debate around whether recombinant DNA should be allowed. Now they do it in high-school labs. For any new technology that emerges, the first reaction is fear. Time will take care of that. When people take the time to think, it becomes routine."

During my visit to St. Kitts, I watched as Gene Redmond, dressed in blue surgical scrubs in the operating room, drilled into the skull of a vervet monkey. Once he penetrated the skull, Redmond positioned a four-inch hypodermic needle on a mount over the hole and ever so slowly lowered it into the monkey's cerebral cortex, down through structures associated with emotion and on until it reached its target in the basal ganglia at the base of the brain. He let the brain settle around the needle for a while and then injected a solution of donor cells into the target.

If he were performing this operation on a human patient, the procedure   25
would be more or less the same. But he would need a much longer needle. If it is not some categorical essentialism that draws a bright line between us and the rest of the animals, surely it is the size and power of our brains. They are the physical address of everything we think of as uniquely human — our rational thinking, intelligence, language, complex emotions and unparalleled ability to imagine a future and remember the past. Not surprisingly, chimeric experiments that seed the brain of an animal with a little neural matter of our own are uniquely suspect, especially those that meddle with the sites of higher function in the cortex.

"If you create stem-cell lines that might produce dopamine and want to put them in an animal first to see if they retained their stability, that's not problematic," Norman Fost maintains. "But what if you want to study brain cortex? You'd want to create a stem-cell line that looks and acts like cortex and put this in an animal. In the toughest case, you'd want to put it in a very early stage of development. This is extremely hypothetical, but suppose these cells completely took over the brain of the animal? A goat or a pig with a purely human brain. Unlikely, but imaginable. That would certainly raise questions about what experiences that animal was having. Is it a very smart pig? Or something having human experiences? These are interesting questions that no one has thought about before because they haven't had to."

The scientist most responsible for making people think about those questions — and squirm and fume — is Irving Weissman. Several years ago, Weissman and his colleagues at Stanford and at StemCells Inc., a private company he helped to found, transplanted human neural stem cells into the brains of newborn mice. The human cells spread throughout the mouse brain, piggybacking on the host's developmental pathways to eventually make up as much as 1 percent of some parts of the host's neural tissue. Once again, the ultimate purpose of the chimera was to create a research model for human brain function and disease. While somewhat successful in this regard, Weissman said he felt his model was hampered by the 99 percent of it that was still mouse. So he came up with an ingenious idea: why not make a mouse with a brain composed entirely of human neurons? In theory, at least, this could be achieved by transplanting human neural stem cells into the fetal brain of a strain of mouse whose own neurons happen to die off just before birth. If the human stem cells took up the slack and differentiated along the same lines as in the earlier experiment, you might just end up with a living newborn mouse controlled by a functioning brain that just happened to be composed of human cells.

Before proceeding with this experiment, Weissman said he thought it might be a good idea to solicit some ethical input. He contacted Hank Greely, a bioethicist at Stanford's law school, who put together a committee to review the benefits and risks involved. The members agreed that the human neuronal mouse could be an extremely beneficial tool to study the effects of pathogens and disease in the human brain and the action of new drugs. They identified several areas of risk. The most difficult one to articulate, as Greely told the National Academy of Sciences panel reviewing the use of human stem cells, was the "nontrivial chance of conferring significant aspects of humanness on the nonhuman organism."

"Though exceedingly remote, we thought this possibility was reason for caution and concern," Greely told me recently. His committee, which has yet to publish its report, did not find that risk alone was sufficient grounds for canceling the experiment. Instead, the members suggested that Weissman incorporate into the experimental protocol a series of "stopping points." Some of the fetal mice should be terminated and examined before birth, and if there should appear any "disquieting or disturbing results," the experiment should be suspended pending further ethical review. Results deemed troubling would include any evidence that the transplant was shaping the architecture of the mouse's neural edifice, as opposed to just contributing the bricks. Mice have sensory structures in their brains called "whisker barrels," for instance, which we lack, while we have a far more complicated visual cortex. Shrunken whisker barrels or swollen visual cortex in the fetal mice brains would be a red flag. If everything appeared normal, the remaining animals could be brought to term and monitored for the appearance of any odd, and especially humanlike, behavior, which would again warrant stopping the experiment and seeking additional input from the ethical community.

Weissman is still months or even years away from actually trying his human neuron mouse experiment, and it has already drawn "This shall not stand" rhetoric from Jeremy Rifkin, the anti-biotech activist, Bill O'Reilly, and numerous religious commentators and bloggers.

The real problem with Weissman's proposed mouse, however, may turn out to be not that it is too human but that it is not human enough. The basic structure of our nerve cells is not all that different from those of any other mammal, including a mouse's. But because our brains are so much bigger, the cells that compose them reach across greater distances, and the timing of their development is much longer. How likely is it that human nerve cells will develop into a whole functioning brain in the tiny arena of a fetal mouse's skull? Weissman concedes that his proposed chimeric experiment may not succeed. But, hypothetically speaking, what if you could conduct the analogous experiment in an animal with a brain more like our own, like a monkey or a

30

chimpanzee? Strictly from a biomedical perspective, a human–ape chimera could be the ultimate research model for human biology and disease — one that is completely human in everything but its humanity.

"If someone were to try Irv's mouse experiment with a great ape or even a monkey, I'd get real worried," Greely says. "I'd want to make sure people thought long and hard about that."

The danger, of course, is in how difficult it would be to know when you've slipped over the edge. While Greely's committee has been brooding over Weissman's mouse and the National Academy has been pondering its recommendations for the use of embryonic stem cells, another ethics group has been meeting at the Phoebe R. Berman Bioethics Institute at Johns Hopkins University to grapple with the especially dicey issue of human–primate chimeras. Could the introduction of human cells into nonhuman primate brains cause changes that would make them more humanlike? How would one tell? Would it be morally problematic to create a chimera with a significant degree of humanlike consciousness, cognition, or emotion? Should such experimentation be banned? If such chimeras were to be created, what legal rights and protections should they have, distinct from other animals?

The report of the Working Group on Interspecific Chimeric Brains is expected to be published later this spring in a scientific journal. While the group's recommendations remain confidential until then, a rough idea of the boundary they might draw between allowable and prohibited research is suggested by two experiments that have already been conducted. One was carried out in 2001 by Evan Snyder, then at Harvard University and now director of the stem-cell program at the Burnham Institute in La Jolla, California. Snyder and his colleagues implanted human neural stem cells into the brains of twelve-week-old fetal bonnet monkeys, aborted them four weeks later, and found that the human cells had migrated and differentiated into both cerebral hemispheres, including into regions of the developing monkey cortex. Like Redmond, Snyder discounts any possibility that had the monkeys been brought to term the relatively small number of human cells in their brain would have had any effect on their normal cognition and behavior.

"Even if I were to make a monkey with a hippocampus composed entirely of human cells, it's not going to stand up and quote Shakespeare," Snyder says. "Those sophisticated in human functioning know that it's more than the cellular components that make a human brain. It's the connections, the blood vessels that feed them; it's the various surfaces on which they migrate, the timing by which various synaptic molecules are released and impact other things, like molecules from the bloodstream and from the bone."

It's quite likely that the members of the Johns Hopkins committee (it includes distinguished philosophers, bioethicists, neuroscientists, primatologists, and stem-cell researchers) will conclude that an experiment like Snyder's is ethically safe. A relatively small scattering of human cells could

35

be introduced into a primate brain, late in its development when there would be no chance the human cells could influence its fundamental architecture. But a result of another experiment, performed in the late 1980s by Evan Balaban, who is now at McGill University in Montreal, might give the group pause about mixing human and primate tissue in a very early fetus. Balaban removed a section from the midbrain of a chick embryo, grafting in its place the corresponding piece of proto-brain from an embryonic quail. While many of the embryos failed to develop, a few matured and eventually hatched. The newborn chicks were normal in most respects — except they crowed like quails.

"One could imagine that if you took a human embryonic midbrain and spliced it into a developing chimpanzee, you could get a chimp with many of our automatic vocalizations," says Terrence Deacon, a biological anthropologist at the University of California at Berkeley and a member of the Johns Hopkins committee. "It wouldn't be able to talk. But it might laugh or sob, instead of pant-hoot."

Of course, Deacon adds quickly, such an experiment would be highly unethical. The notion of a chimpanzee normal except for its human sobbing would probably exceed the squirm threshold of the other members of the Johns Hopkins group. Perhaps it is not what a human–animal chimera would be that violates some fundamental categorical construct in our minds, or what it would look like, as William Hurlbut maintains, as much as what it could *do* — whether it would have a brain that makes it act in a way that is uncomfortably familiar. "Humanness" surely resides in the emergent layers building the vastly complex architecture of the human brain.

But is there a clear biological distinction between us and the rest of creation, one that should never be confounded by the scuffling of strange new feet in laboratory basements? Deacon has devoted a great deal of thought and research to such questions. While his is hardly the only view, after a career spent comparing the brains of living primates and the skulls of fossilized hominids, he says that there is little evidence for the sudden appearance of some new thing — a uniquely human gene, a completely novel brain structure in the hominid lineage — that sets us distinctly apart. Obviously, there has been an overall increase in brain size. But the telling difference is in more subtle shifts in proportion and connections between regions of the brain, "a gerrymandering of the system" that corresponds to a growing reliance on the use of language and other symbolic behavior as a means of survival. This shift, which Deacon believes began as long as two and a half million years ago, is reflected most prominently in the swollen human prefrontal cortex.

"We humans have been shaped by the use of symbols," he says. "We are 40 embedded in a world of human creation, where demands for success and reproduction are all powerfully dependent on how well we swim through our symbolic niche."

This raises some fascinating questions, not just about the chimeras we might create with our scalpels and stem cells but also about the ones we may already have fashioned by coaxing humanlike behaviors from animals who have the latent capacity to express them. In the wild, chimpanzees and other apes do not engage in any symbolic behavior remotely comparable to what humans have evolved. But in the laboratory they can learn to communicate with sign language and other means on a par with the skills of a toddler. The difference is that the toddler's symbolic behavior becomes increasingly enriched, while the chimpanzee hits a wall. How much further could a bio-engineered chimera go? Could it swim in our symbolic niche well enough to communicate what is going on inside its hybrid mind? What could it teach us about animals? What could it teach us about us? And what is the price of the knowing?

QUESTIONS

Reading

1. What is a *chimera*? Why does Shreeve use this term to describe XO47?
2. Why, according to Shreeve, have chimeric experiments become more common? Explain one of the chimeric experiments that Shreeve describes.
3. Why do biologically ambiguous creatures change the stem-cell debate? Why do they, according to Shreeve, lead to moral confusion?
4. In this *reportorial* essay, does Shreeve take a stand on the subjects of chimeric experimentation, stem-cell research, or the other contested bioethical issues he discusses? In your opinion, what is Shreeve's agenda in writing this report? What techniques does he use to achieve this agenda?

Exploratory Writing

1. Breaking into teams, stage a debate on the proposition, "Chimeric experimentation should be banned." Use Shreeve's essay, as well as other resources, for help in formulating your arguments.
2. What scientific, moral, and religious questions does Shreeve's essay raise for you? Exchange questions and viewpoints with your classmates. Ask classmates to pose questions and positions that counter your point of view.

Making Connections

1. Steven Pinker (p. 427) describes anthropological research that reveals how certain moral concerns are shared by most people in the world, despite the diversity of human societies. The themes of these concerns include harm, fairness, community or group loyalty, authority, and purity. Using the examples from Pinker's essay (paragraph 37) as a guideline, identify where and how these themes come into play in the bioethical debates that Shreeve discusses.

Essay Writing

1. Shreeve writes that "everyone has a squirm threshold" (paragraph 14) when it comes to biologically ambiguous creatures. What is your squirm threshold? Write an essay explaining your position.
2. Over the next month, collect articles in popular newspapers and magazines that address the debate about scientific research using stem cells or other biological materials. Write an essay explaining the current status of the debate and reporting on trends you notice in these articles.

Joey: A "Mechanical Boy"

Bruno Bettelheim

*Austrian-born psychotherapist Bruno Bettelheim (1903–1990)
received his PhD from the University of Vienna and was strongly
influenced by the work of Sigmund Freud. Imprisoned as a Jew in
Nazi concentration camps between 1938 and 1939, he wrote about
these experiences after his immigration to the United States in an
article titled "Individual and Mass Behavior in Extreme Situations"
(1943) and later in the book* The Informed Heart *(1960). From
1944 to 1973, he was director of a Chicago-based school for the
rehabilitation of emotionally disturbed children, a subject he
addressed in numerous works on child psychology and child
rearing, including* Love Is Not Enough *(1950) and* The Empty
Fortress *(1967). He was also the author of the highly influential*
The Uses of Enchantment *(1976), a study of children and fairy
tales. Since his suicide at the age of eighty-seven, Bettelheim
has been the subject of a number of sharp attacks regarding
the veracity of some of his work, and a 1997 biography by Richard
Pollak was particularly damning. Still, Bettelheim continues to
have his defenders, including his most recent biographer, his friend
and literary agent Theron Raines. The following essay was first
published in* Scientific American *in 1959.*

Joey, when we began our work with him, was a mechanical boy. He functioned as if by remote control, run by machines of his own powerfully creative
fantasy. Not only did he himself believe that he was a machine, but, more
remarkably, he created this impression in others. Even while he performed
actions that are intrinsically human, they never appeared to be other than
machine-started and executed. On the other hand, when the machine was not
working, we had to concentrate on recollecting his presence, for he seemed
not to exist. A human body that functions as if it were a machine and a
machine that duplicates human functions are equally fascinating and frightening. Perhaps they are so uncanny because they remind us that the human
body can operate without a human spirit, that body can exist without soul.
And Joey was a child who had been robbed of his humanity.

Not every child who possesses a fantasy world is possessed by it. Normal
children may retreat into realms of imaginary glory or magic powers, but they
are easily recalled from these excursions. Disturbed children are not always

able to make the return trip; they remain withdrawn, prisoners of the inner world of delusion and fantasy. In many ways Joey presented a classic example of this state of infantile autism.[1]

At the Sonia Shankman Orthogenic School of the University of Chicago, it is our function to provide a therapeutic environment in which such children may start life over again. I have previously described in this magazine[2] the rehabilitation of another of our patients. This time I shall concentrate upon the illness, rather than the treatment. In any age, when the individual has escaped into a delusional world, he has usually fashioned it from bits and pieces of the world at hand. Joey, in his time and world, chose the machine and froze himself in its image. His story has a general relevance to the understanding of emotional development in a machine age.

Joey's delusion is not uncommon among schizophrenic[3] children today. He wanted to be rid of his unbearable humanity, to become completely automatic. He so nearly succeeded in attaining this goal that he could almost convince others, as well as himself, of his mechanical character. The descriptions of autistic children in the literature take for their point of departure and comparison the normal or abnormal human being. To do justice to Joey, I would have to compare him simultaneously to a most inept infant and a highly complex piece of machinery. Often we had to force ourselves by a conscious act of will to realize that Joey was a child. Again and again his acting-out of his delusions froze our own ability to respond as human beings.

During Joey's first weeks with us, we would watch absorbedly as this at once fragile-looking and imperious nine-year-old went about his mechanical existence. Entering the dining room, for example, he would string an imaginary wire from his "energy source" — an imaginary electric outlet — to the table. There he "insulated" himself with paper napkins and finally plugged himself in. Only then could Joey eat, for he firmly believed that the "current" ran his ingestive apparatus. So skillful was the pantomime that one had to look twice to be sure there was neither wire nor outlet nor plug. Children and members of our staff spontaneously avoided stepping on the "wires" for fear of interrupting what seemed the source of his very life.   5

For long periods of time, when his "machinery" was idle, he would sit so quietly that he would disappear from the focus of the most conscientious observation. Yet in the next moment he might be "working" and the center of our captivated attention. Many times a day he would turn himself on and shift noisily through a sequence of higher and higher gears until he

---

[1]*autism*: A complex developmental disability that affects an individual in the areas of social interaction and communication. [Eds.]

[2]*in this magazine*: Bruno Bettelheim, "Schizophrenic Art: A Case Study," *Scientific American*, April 1952. [Eds.]

[3]*schizophrenic*: Relating to a severe mental disorder that is characterized by thought disorder, delusions, and hallucinations. [Eds.]

"exploded," screaming "Crash, crash!" and hurling items from his ever present apparatus — radio tubes, light bulbs, even motors, or, lacking these, any handy breakable object. (Joey had an astonishing knack for snatching bulbs and tubes unobserved.) As soon as the object thrown had shattered, he would cease his screaming and wild jumping and retire to mute, motionless nonexistence.

Our maids, inured to difficult children, were exceptionally attentive to Joey; they were apparently moved by his extreme infantile fragility, so strangely coupled with megalomaniacal superiority. Occasionally some of the apparatus he fixed to his bed to "live him" during his sleep would fall down in disarray. This machinery he contrived from masking tape, cardboard, wire, and other paraphernalia. Usually the maids would pick up such things and leave them on a table for the children to find, or disregard them entirely. But Joey's machine they carefully restored: "Joey must have the carburetor so he can breathe." Similarly they were on the alert to pick up and preserve the motors that ran him during the day and the exhaust pipes through which he exhaled.

How had Joey become a human machine? From intensive interviews with his parents we learned that the process had begun even before birth. Schizophrenia often results from parental rejection, sometimes combined ambivalently with love. Joey, on the other hand, had been completely ignored.

"I never knew I was pregnant," his mother said, meaning that she had already excluded Joey from her consciousness. His birth, she said, "did not make any difference." Joey's father, a rootless draftee in the wartime civilian army, was equally unready for parenthood. So, of course, are many young couples. Fortunately most such parents lose their indifference upon the baby's birth. But not Joey's parents. "I did not want to see or nurse him," his mother declared. "I had no feeling of actual dislike — I simply didn't want to take care of him." For the first three months of his life Joey "cried most of the time." A colicky baby, he was kept on a rigid four-hour feeding schedule, was not touched unless necessary and was never cuddled or played with. The mother, preoccupied with herself, usually left Joey alone in the crib or playpen during the day. The father discharged his frustration by punishing Joey when the child cried at night.

Soon the father left for overseas duty, and the mother took Joey, now a year and a half old, to live with her at her parents' home. On his arrival the grandparents noticed that ominous changes had occurred in the child. Strong and healthy at birth, he had become frail and irritable; a responsive baby, he had become remote and inaccessible. When he began to master speech, he talked only to himself. At an early date he became preoccupied with machinery, including an old electric fan which he could take apart and put together again with surprising deftness.

Joey's mother impressed us with a fey quality that expressed her insecurity, her detachment from the world, and her low physical vitality. We were struck especially by her total indifference as she talked about Joey. This

10

seemed much more remarkable than the actual mistakes she made in handling him. Certainly he was left to cry for hours when hungry, because she fed him on a rigid schedule; he was toilet-trained with great rigidity so that he would give no trouble. These things happen to many children. But Joey's existence never registered with his mother. In her recollections he was fused at one moment with one event or person; at another, with something or somebody else. When she told us about his birth and infancy, it was as if she were talking about some vague acquaintance, and soon her thoughts would wander off to another person or to herself.

When Joey was not yet four, his nursery school suggested that he enter a special school for disturbed children. At the new school his autism was immediately recognized. During his three years there he experienced a slow improvement. Unfortunately a subsequent two years in a parochial school destroyed this progress. He began to develop compulsive defenses, which he called his "preventions." He could not drink, for example, except through elaborate piping systems built of straws. Liquids had to be "pumped" into him, in his fantasy, or he could not suck. Eventually his behavior became so upsetting that he could not be kept in the parochial school. At home things did not improve. Three months before entering the Orthogenic School he made a serious attempt at suicide.

To us Joey's pathological behavior seemed the external expression of an overwhelming effort to remain almost nonexistent as a person. For weeks Joey's only reply when addressed was "Bam." Unless he thus neutralized whatever we said, there would be an explosion, for Joey plainly wished to close off every form of contact not mediated by machinery. Even when he was bathed he rocked back and forth with mute, engine-like regularity, flooding the bathroom. If he stopped rocking, he did this like a machine too; suddenly he went completely rigid. Only once, after months of being lifted from his bath and carried to bed, did a small expression of puzzled pleasure appear on his face as he said very softly: "They even carry you to your bed here."

For a long time after he began to talk, he would never refer to anyone by name, but only as "that person" or "the little person" or "the big person." He was unable to designate by its true name anything to which he attached feelings. Nor could he name his anxieties except through neologisms or word contaminations.[4] For a long time he spoke about "master paintings" and "a master painting room" (i.e., masturbating and masturbating room). One of his machines, the "criticizer," prevented him from "saying words which have unpleasant feelings." Yet he gave personal names to the tubes and motors in his collection of machinery. Moreover, these dead things had feelings; the tubes bled when hurt and sometimes got sick. He consistently maintained this reversal between animate and inanimate objects.

---

[4]*neologisms or word contaminations*: Words that Joey made up or words that he peculiarly altered. [Eds.]

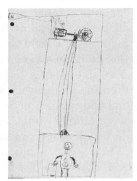

Growing self-esteem is shown in this sequence of drawings. At left Joey portrays himself as an electrical "papoose," completely enclosed, suspended in empty space and operated by wireless signals. In center drawing his figure is much larger, though still under wireless control. At right he is able to picture the machine which controls him, and he has acquired hands with which he can manipulate his immediate environment.

In Joey's machine world everything, on pain of instant destruction, 15 obeyed inhibitory laws much more stringent than those of physics. When we came to know him better, it was plain that in his moments of silent withdrawal, with his machine switched off, Joey was absorbed in pondering the compulsive laws of his private universe. His preoccupation with machinery made it difficult to establish even practical contacts with him. If he wanted to do something with a counselor, such as play with a toy that had caught his vague attention, he could not do so: "I'd like this very much, but first I have to turn off the machine." But by the time he had fulfilled all the requirements of his preventions, he had lost interest. When a toy was offered to him, he could not touch it because his motors and his tubes did not leave him a hand free. Even certain colors were dangerous and had to be strictly avoided in toys and clothing, because "some colors turn off the current, and I can't touch them because I can't live without the current."

Joey was convinced that machines were better than people. Once when he bumped into one of the pipes on our jungle gym he kicked it so violently that his teacher had to restrain him to keep him from injuring himself. When she explained that the pipe was much harder than his foot, Joey replied: "That proves it. Machines are better than the body. They don't break; they're much harder and stronger." If he lost or forgot something, it merely proved that this brain ought to be thrown away and replaced by machinery. If he spilled something, his arm should be broken and twisted off because it did not work properly. When his head or arm failed to work as it should, he tried to punish it by hitting it. Even Joey's feelings were mechanical. Much later in his therapy, when he had formed a timid attachment to another child and had been rebuffed, Joey cried: "He broke my feelings."

Gradually we began to understand what had seemed to be contradictory in Joey's behavior — why he held on to the motors and tubes, then suddenly destroyed them in a fury, then set out immediately and urgently to equip himself with new and larger tubes. Joey had created these machines to run his body and mind because it was too painful to be human. But again and again he became dissatisfied with their failure to meet his need and rebellious at the way they frustrated his will. In a recurrent frenzy he "exploded" his light bulbs and tubes, and for a moment became a human being — for one crowning instant he came alive. But as soon as he had asserted his dominance through the self-created explosion, he felt his life ebbing away. To keep on existing he had immediately to restore his machines and replenish the electricity that supplied his life energy.

What deep-seated fears and needs underlay Joey's delusional system? We were long in finding out, for Joey's preventions effectively concealed the secret of his autistic behavior. In the meantime we dealt with his peripheral problems one by one.

During his first year with us Joey's most trying problem was toilet behavior. This surprised us, for Joey's personality was not "anal" in the Freudian sense; his original personality damage had antedated the period of his toilet-training. Rigid and early toilet-training, however, had certainly contributed to his anxieties. It was our effort to help Joey with this problem that led to his first recognition of us as human beings.

Going to the toilet, like everything else in Joey's life, was surrounded by elaborate preventions. We had to accompany him; he had to take off all his clothes; he could only squat, not sit, on the toilet seat; he had to touch the wall with one hand, in which he also clutched frantically the vacuum tubes that powered his elimination. He was terrified lest his whole body be sucked down. 20

To counteract this fear we gave him a metal wastebasket in lieu of a toilet. Eventually, when eliminating into the wastebasket, he no longer needed to take off all his clothes, nor to hold on to the wall. He still needed the tubes and motors which, he believed, moved his bowels for him. But here again the all-important machinery was itself a source of new terrors. In Joey's world the gadgets had to move their bowels, too. He was terribly concerned that they should, but since they were so much more powerful than men, he was also terrified that if his tubes moved their bowels, their feces would fill all of space and leave him no room to live. He was thus always caught in some fearful contradiction.

Our readiness to accept his toilet habits, which obviously entailed some hardship for our counselors, gave Joey the confidence to express his obsessions in drawings. Drawing these fantasies was a first step toward letting us in, however distantly, to what concerned him most deeply. It was the first step in a yearlong process of externalizing his anal preoccupations. As a result he began seeing feces everywhere; the whole world became to him a mire of excrement. At the same time he began to eliminate freely wherever he happened to be. But with this release from his infantile imprisonment in compulsive rules, the toilet and the whole process of elimination became less dangerous. Thus far it had been beyond Joey's comprehension that anybody could possibly move his bowels without mechanical aid. Now Joey took a further step forward; defecation became the first physiological process he could perform without the help of vacuum tubes. It must not be thought that he was proud of this ability. Taking pride in an achievement presupposes that one accomplishes it of one's own free will. He still did not feel himself an autonomous person who could do things on his own. To Joey defecation still seemed enslaved to some incomprehensible but utterly binding cosmic law, perhaps the law his parents had imposed on him when he was being toilet-trained.

It was not simply that his parents had subjected him to rigid, early training. Many children are so trained. But in some cases the parents have a deep emotional investment in the child's performance. The child's response in turn makes training an occasion for interaction between them and for the building of genuine relationships. Joey's parents had no emotional investment in him. His obedience gave them no satisfaction and won him no affection or approval. As a toilet-trained child he saved his mother labor, just as household machines saved her labor. As a machine he was not loved for his performance, nor could he love himself.

So it had been with all other aspects of Joey's existence with his parents. Their reactions to his eating or noneating, sleeping or wakening, urinating or defecating, being dressed or undressed, washed or bathed, did not flow from any unitary interest in him, deeply embedded in their personalities. By treating him mechanically his parents made him a machine. The various functions of life — even the parts of his body — bore no integrating relationship to one another or to any sense of self that was acknowledged and confirmed by others. Though he had acquired mastery over some functions, such as toilet-training and speech, he had acquired them separately and kept them isolated from each other. Toilet-training had thus not gained him a pleasant feeling of body mastery; speech had not led to communication of thought or feeling. On the contrary, each achievement only steered him away from self-mastery and integration. Toilet-training had enslaved him. Speech left him talking in neologisms that obstructed his and our ability to relate to each other. In Joey's development the normal process of growth had been made to run backward. Whatever he had learned put him not at the end of his infantile development toward integration but, on the contrary, farther behind than he was at its very beginning. Had we understood this sooner, his first years with us would have been less baffling.

It is unlikely that Joey's calamity could befall a child in any time and 25
culture but our own. He suffered no physical deprivation; he starved for human contact. Just to be taken care of is not enough for relating. It is a necessary but not a sufficient condition. At the extreme where utter scarcity reigns, the forming of relationships is certainly hampered. But our

Elaborate sewage system in Joey's drawing of a house reflects his long preoccupation with excretion. His obsession with sewage reflected intense anxieties produced by his early toilet-training, which was not only rigid but also completely impersonal.

society of mechanized plenty often makes for equal difficulties in a child's learning to relate. Where parents can provide the simple creature-comforts for their children only at the cost of significant effort, it is likely that they will feel pleasure in being able to provide for them; it is this, the parents' pleasure, that gives children a sense of personal worth and sets the process of relating in motion. But if comfort is so readily available that the parents feel no particular pleasure in winning it for their children, then the children cannot develop the feeling of being worthwhile around the satisfaction of their basic needs. Of course parent and children can and do develop relationships around other situations. But matters are then no longer so simple and direct. The child must be on the receiving end of care and concern given with pleasure and without the exaction of return if he is to feel loved and worthy of respect and consideration. This feeling gives him the ability to trust; he can entrust his well-being to persons to whom he is so important. Out of such trust the child learns to form close and stable relationships.

For Joey, relationship with his parents was empty of pleasure in comfort-giving as in all other situations. His was an extreme instance of a plight that sends many schizophrenic children to our clinics and hospitals. Many months

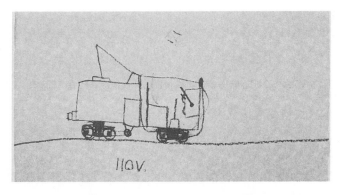

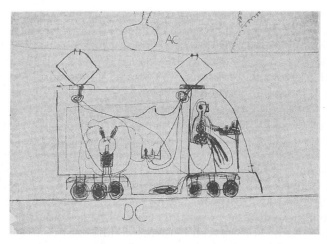

Growing autonomy is shown in Joey's drawings of the
imaginary "Carr" (car) family. Top drawing shows a
machine which can move but is unoccupied. Machine in
center is occupied, but by a passive figure. In bottom
drawing figure has gained control of machine.

passed before he could relate to us; his despair that anybody could like him made contact impossible.

When Joey could finally trust us enough to let himself become more infantile, he began to play at being a papoose. There was a corresponding change in his fantasies. He drew endless pictures of himself as an electrical papoose. Totally enclosed, suspended in empty space, he is run by unknown, unseen powers through wireless electricity.

As we eventually came to understand, the heart of Joey's delusional system was the artificial, mechanical womb he had created and into which he had locked himself. In his papoose fantasies lay the wish to be entirely reborn in a womb. His new experiences in the school suggested that life, after all, might be worth living. Now he was searching for a way to be reborn in a better way. Since machines were better than men, what was more natural than to try rebirth through them? This was the deeper meaning of this electrical papoose.

As Joey made progress, his pictures of himself became more dominant in his drawings. Though still machine-operated, he has grown in self-importance. Another great step forward is represented in the picture [opposite]. . . . Now he has acquired hands that do something, and he has had the courage to make a picture of the machine that runs him. Later still the papoose became a person, rather than a robot encased in glass.

Gentle landscape painted by Joey after his recovery symbolizes the human emotions he had regained. At twelve, having learned to express his feelings, he was no longer a machine.

Eventually Joey began to create an imaginary family at the school: the   30
"Carr" family. Why the Carr family? In the car he was enclosed as he had
been in his papoose, but at least the car was not stationary; it could move.
More important, in a car one was not only driven but also could drive. The
Carr family was Joey's way of exploring the possibility of leaving the school,
of living with a good family in a safe, protecting car.

Joey at last broke through his prison. In this brief account it has not
been possible to trace the painfully slow process of his first true relations
with other human beings. Suffice it to say that he ceased to be a mechanical boy and became a human child. This newborn child was, however,
nearly twelve years old. To recover the lost time is a tremendous task.
That work has occupied Joey and us ever since. Sometimes he sets to it
with a will; at other times the difficulty of real life makes him regret that
he ever came out of his shell. But he has never wanted to return to his
mechanical life.

One last detail and this fragment of Joey's story has been told. When Joey
was twelve, he made a float for our Memorial Day parade. It carried the
slogan: "Feelings are more important than anything under the sun." Feelings,
Joey had learned, are what make for humanity; their absence, for a mechanical existence. With this knowledge Joey entered the human condition.

QUESTIONS

Reading

1. Bettelheim's task in this article was to report and explain Joey's behavior
   as best he could. What did he and his colleagues do, what did they examine, and how did they behave as they developed their explanation of Joey?
2. How does Bettelheim characterize Joey's parents?
3. To begin to be cured, Joey had to *reinterpret* his life. What were the
   major steps toward that reinterpretation? What changed for Joey?
4. Even using the word *cured*, as we did in question 3, involves an unexamined interpretation. What assumptions guide our use of that word? In
   your opinion, is *cured* a satisfying explanation of what begins to happen
   to Joey?

Exploratory Writing

1. Bettelheim's case study of Joey was published in 1959. Considering technological developments since then, write an imaginary *case study* of a
   contemporary child who thinks that he or she is a machine. What kind
   of machine might he or she be? What would he or she be capable of?
2. Make a chart listing Joey's different behaviors and Bettelheim's interpretation of each. Which of the interpretations seem to be based on pure
   observation? Which seem to be based on assumptions and conjecture?

JOEY'S BEHAVIOR	BETTELHEIM'S INTERPRETATION

3. Reread Bettelheim's concluding paragraph. Do you agree that "[f]eelings . . . are what make for humanity"? Collaborating in small groups, come up with a slogan that sums up what it means to be human, and prepare a presentation explaining your slogan. You can draw on the case study of Joey as well as other essays in this book that offer an assessment of what humanity means.

Making Connections

1. Lucy Grealy (p. 33) writes very personally about her experiences dealing with her disfigured face. How might Joey's story have been different if Joey himself, rather than Bettelheim, had written it?

Essay Writing

1. In the *third person*, write a case study of yourself based on a transition you've undergone. For example, you could write about how you adjusted to high school or college, or about how you coped with dramatic changes in your family or living situation.

The Sky Is Falling

Gregg Easterbrook

Gregg Easterbrook (b. 1953) was educated at Colorado College and Northwestern University, earning an MA in journalism in 1977 and quickly gaining a national reputation for his investigative reporting. Easterbrook is a senior editor of the New Republic, *and a frequent contributor to the* New York Times, *the* Washington Post, *the* Los Angeles Times, Wired, *and* Slate's "Tuesday Morning Quarterback." *He is a visiting fellow at the Brookings Institution and the author of many books, including* A Moment on the Earth: The Coming Age of Environmental Optimism *(1996),* Beside Still Waters: Searching for Meaning in an Age of Doubt *(1998),* Tuesday Morning Quarterback *(2001), and* The Progress Paradox: How Life Gets Better While People Feel Worse *(2003). He is also the author of two novels,* This Magic Moment *(1987) and* The Here and Now *(2002). "The Sky Is Falling" appeared in the* Atlantic *in June 2008; visit* **www.theatlantic.com** *to hear Easterbrook discuss the "treacherous world of space rocks" in the companion video,* Target Earth.

Breakthrough ideas have a way of seeming obvious in retrospect, and about a decade ago, a Columbia University geophysicist named Dallas Abbott had a breakthrough idea. She had been pondering the craters left by comets and asteroids that smashed into Earth. Geologists had counted them and concluded that space strikes are rare events and had occurred mainly during the era of primordial mists. But, Abbott realized, this deduction was based on the number of craters found on land — and because 70 percent of Earth's surface is water, wouldn't most space objects hit the sea? So she began searching for underwater craters caused by impacts rather than by other forces, such as volcanoes. What she has found is spine-chilling: evidence that several enormous asteroids or comets have slammed into our planet quite recently, in geologic terms. If Abbott is right, then you may be here today, reading this magazine, only because by sheer chance those objects struck the ocean rather than land.

Abbott believes that a space object about three hundred meters in diameter hit the Gulf of Carpentaria, north of Australia, in 536 AD. An object that size, striking at up to fifty thousand miles per hour, could release as much energy as one thousand nuclear bombs. Debris, dust, and gases thrown into the atmosphere by the impact would have blocked sunlight, temporarily cooling the planet — and indeed, contemporaneous accounts describe dim skies, cold summers, and poor harvests in 536 and 537. "A most dread portent took place," the Byzantine historian Procopius wrote of 536; the sun "gave forth its light without brightness." Frost reportedly covered China in the summertime. Still, the harm was mitigated by the ocean impact. When a space object strikes land, it kicks up more dust and debris, increasing the global-cooling effect; at the same time, the combination of shock waves and extreme heating at the point of impact generates nitric and nitrous acids, producing rain as corrosive as battery acid. If the Gulf of Carpentaria object were to strike Miami today, most of the city would be leveled, and the atmospheric effects could trigger crop failures around the world.

What's more, the Gulf of Carpentaria object was a skipping stone compared with an object that Abbott thinks whammed into the Indian Ocean near Madagascar some 4,800 years ago, or about 2800 BC. Researchers generally assume that a space object a kilometer or more across would cause significant global harm: widespread destruction, severe acid rain, and dust storms that would darken the world's skies for decades. The object that hit the Indian Ocean was three to five kilometers across, Abbott believes, and caused a tsunami in the Pacific six hundred feet high — many times higher than the 2004 tsunami that struck Southeast Asia. Ancient texts such as Genesis and the Epic of Gilgamesh support her conjecture, describing an unspeakable planetary flood in roughly the same time period. If the Indian Ocean object were to hit the sea now, many of the world's coastal cities could be flattened. If it were to hit land, much of a continent would be leveled; years of winter and mass starvation would ensue.

At the start of her research, which has sparked much debate among specialists, Abbott reasoned that if colossal asteroids or comets strike the sea with about the same frequency as they strike land, then given the number of known land craters, perhaps one hundred large impact craters might lie beneath the oceans. In less than a decade of searching, she and a few colleagues have already found what appear to be fourteen large underwater impact sites. That they've found so many so rapidly is hardly reassuring.

Other scientists are making equally unsettling discoveries. Only in the past few decades have astronomers begun to search the nearby skies for objects such as asteroids and comets (for convenience, let's call them "space rocks"). What they are finding suggests that near-Earth space rocks are more numerous than was once thought, and that their orbits may not be as stable as has been assumed. There is also reason to think that space rocks may not even need to reach Earth's surface to cause cataclysmic damage. Our solar system appears to be a far more dangerous place than was previously believed.

5

The received wisdom about the origins of the solar system goes something like this: the sun and planets formed about 4.5 billion years ago from a swirling nebula containing huge amounts of gas and dust, as well as relatively small amounts of metals and other dense substances released by ancient supernova explosions. The sun is at the center; the denser planets, including Earth, formed in the middle region, along with many asteroids — the small rocky bodies made of material that failed to incorporate into a planet. Farther out are the gas-giant planets, such as Jupiter, plus vast amounts of light elements, which formed comets on the boundary of the solar system. Early on, asteroids existed by the millions; the planets and their satellites were bombarded by constant, furious strikes. The heat and shock waves generated by these impacts regularly sterilized the young Earth. Only after the rain of space objects ceased could life begin; by then, most asteroids had already either hit something or found stable orbits that do not lead toward planets or moons. Asteroids still exist, but most were assumed to be in the asteroid belt, which lies between Mars and Jupiter, far from our blue world.

As for comets, conventional wisdom held that they also bombarded the planets during the early eons. Comets are mostly frozen water mixed with dirt. An ancient deluge of comets may have helped create our oceans; lots of comets hit the moon, too, but there the light elements they were composed of evaporated. As with asteroids, most comets were thought to have smashed into something long ago; and, because the solar system is largely void, researchers deemed it statistically improbable that those remaining would cross the paths of planets.

These standard assumptions — that remaining space rocks are few, and that encounters with planets were mainly confined to the past — are being upended. On March 18, 2004, for instance, a thirty-meter asteroid designated 2004 FH — a hunk potentially large enough to obliterate a city — shot past Earth, not far above the orbit occupied by telecommunications satellites. (Enter "2004 FH" in the search box at Wikipedia and you can watch film of that asteroid passing through the night sky.) Looking at the broader picture, in 1992 the astronomers David Jewitt, of the University of Hawaii, and Jane Luu, of the Massachusetts Institute of Technology, discovered the Kuiper Belt, a region of asteroids and comets that starts near the orbit of Neptune and extends for immense distances outward. At least one thousand objects big enough to be seen from Earth have already been located there. These objects are one hundred kilometers across or larger, much bigger than whatever dispatched the dinosaurs; space rocks this size are referred to as "planet killers" because their impact would likely end life on Earth. Investigation of the Kuiper Belt has just begun, but there appear to be substantially more asteroids in this region than in the asteroid belt, which may need a new name.

Beyond the Kuiper Belt may lie the hypothesized Oort Cloud, thought to contain as many as trillions of comets. If the Oort Cloud does exist, the number of extant comets is far greater than was once believed. Some astronomers now think that short-period comets, which swing past the sun frequently, hail from the relatively nearby Kuiper Belt, whereas comets whose return periods are longer originate in the Oort Cloud.

But if large numbers of comets and asteroids are still around, several billion years after the formation of the solar system, wouldn't they by now be in stable orbits — ones that rarely intersect those of the planets? Maybe not. During the past few decades, some astronomers have theorized that the movement of the solar system within the Milky Way varies the gravitational stresses to which the sun, and everything that revolves around it, is exposed. The solar system may periodically pass close to stars or groups of stars whose gravitational pull affects the Oort Cloud, shaking comets and asteroids loose from their orbital moorings and sending them downward, toward the inner planets.

10

Consider objects that are already near Earth, and the picture gets even bleaker. Astronomers traditionally spent little time looking for asteroids, regarding them as a lesser class of celestial bodies, lacking the beauty of comets or the significance of planets and stars. Plus, asteroids are hard to spot — they move rapidly, compared with the rest of the heavens, and even the nearby ones are fainter than other objects in space. Not until the 1980s did scientists begin systematically searching for asteroids near Earth. They have been finding them in disconcerting abundance.

In 1980, only 86 near-Earth asteroids and comets were known to exist. By 1990, the figure had risen to 170; by 2000, it was 921; as of this writing, it is 5,388. The Jet Propulsion Laboratory, part of NASA, keeps a running tally at www.neo.jpl.nasa.gov/stats. Ten years ago, 244 near-Earth space rocks one kilometer across or more — the size that would cause global calamity — were known to exist; now 741 are. Of the recently discovered nearby space objects, NASA has classified 186 as "impact risks." . . . And because most space-rock searches to date have been low-budget affairs, conducted with equipment designed to look deep into the heavens, not at nearby space, the actual number of impact risks is undoubtedly much higher. Extrapolating from recent discoveries, NASA estimates that there are perhaps twenty thousand potentially hazardous asteroids and comets in the general vicinity of Earth.

There's still more bad news. Earth has experienced several mass extinctions — the dinosaurs died about 65 million years ago, and something killed off some 96 percent of the world's marine species about 250 million years ago. Scientists have generally assumed that whatever caused those long-ago mass extinctions — comet impacts, extreme volcanic activity — arose from conditions that have changed and no longer pose much threat. It's a comforting notion — but what about the mass extinction that occurred close to our era?

About twelve thousand years ago, many large animals of North America started disappearing — woolly mammoths, saber-toothed cats, mastodons, and others. Some scientists have speculated that Paleo-Indians may have hunted some of the creatures to extinction. A millennia-long mini–Ice Age also may have been a factor. But if that's the case, what explains the disappearance of the Clovis People, the best-documented Paleo-Indian culture, at about the same time? Their population stretched as far south as Mexico, so the mini–Ice Age probably was not solely responsible for their extinction.

A team of researchers led by Richard Firestone, of the Lawrence Berkeley   15
National Laboratory, in California, recently announced the discovery of evidence that one or two huge space rocks, each perhaps several kilometers across, exploded high above Canada 12,900 years ago. The detonation, they believe, caused widespread fires and dust clouds, and disrupted climate patterns so severely that it triggered a prolonged period of global cooling. Mammoths and other species might have been killed either by the impact itself or by starvation after their food supply was disrupted. These conclusions, though hotly disputed by other researchers, were based on extensive examinations of soil samples from across the continent; in strata from that era, scientists found widely distributed soot and also magnetic grains of iridium, an element that is rare on Earth but common in space. Iridium is the meteor-hunter's lodestar: the discovery of iridium dating back 65 million years is what started the geologist Walter Alvarez on his path-breaking theory about the dinosaurs' demise.

A more recent event gives further cause for concern. As buffs of the television show *The X Files* will recall, just a century ago, in 1908, a huge explosion occurred above Tunguska, Siberia. The cause was not a malfunctioning alien star-cruiser but a small asteroid or comet that detonated as it approached the ground. The blast had hundreds of times the force of the Hiroshima bomb and devastated an area of several hundred square miles. Had the explosion occurred above London or Paris, the city would no longer exist. Mark Boslough, a researcher at the Sandia National Laboratory, in

Asteroid 243 Ida, about 35 miles long, and its moon
(Image courtesy of NASA/NSSDC)

New Mexico, recently concluded that the Tunguska object was surprisingly small, perhaps only thirty meters across. Right now, astronomers are nervously tracking 99942 Apophis, an asteroid with a slight chance of striking Earth in April 2036. Apophis is also small by asteroid standards, perhaps three hundred meters across, but it could hit with about sixty thousand times the force of the Hiroshima bomb — enough to destroy an area the size of France. In other words, small asteroids may be more dangerous than we used to think — and may do considerable damage even if they don't reach Earth's surface.

Until recently, nearly all the thinking about the risks of space-rock strikes has focused on counting craters. But what if most impacts don't leave craters? This is the prospect that troubles Boslough. Exploding in the air, the Tunguska rock did plenty of damage, but if people had not seen the flashes, heard the detonation, and traveled to the remote area to photograph the scorched, flattened wasteland, we'd never know the Tunguska event had happened. Perhaps a comet or two exploding above Canada 12,900 years ago spelled the end for saber-toothed cats and Clovis society. But no obvious crater resulted; clues to the calamity were subtle and hard to come by.

Comets, asteroids, and the little meteors that form pleasant shooting stars approach Earth at great speeds — at least twenty-five thousand miles per hour. As they enter the atmosphere they heat up, from friction, and compress, because they decelerate rapidly. Many space rocks explode under this stress, especially small ones; large objects are more likely to reach Earth's surface. The angle at which objects enter the atmosphere also matters: an asteroid or comet approaching straight down has a better chance of hitting the surface than one entering the atmosphere at a shallow angle, as the latter would have to plow through more air, heating up and compressing as it descended. The object or objects that may have detonated above Canada 12,900 years ago would probably have approached at a shallow angle.

If, as Boslough thinks, most asteroids and comets explode before reaching the ground, then this is another reason to fear that the conventional thinking seriously underestimates the frequency of space-rock strikes — the small number of craters may be lulling us into complacency. After all, if a space rock were hurtling toward a city, whether it would leave a crater would not be the issue — the explosion would be the issue.

A generation ago, the standard assumption was that a dangerous object would strike Earth perhaps once in a million years. By the mid-1990s, researchers began to say that the threat was greater: perhaps a strike every 300,000 years. This winter, I asked William Ailor, an asteroid specialist at the Aerospace Corporation, a think tank for the Air Force, what he thought the risk was. Ailor's answer: a one-in-ten chance per century of a dangerous space-object strike.   20

Regardless of which estimate is correct, the likelihood of an event is, of course, no predictor. Even if space strikes are *likely* only once every million years, that doesn't mean a million years will pass before the next impact — the sky could suddenly darken tomorrow. Equally important, improbable but cataclysmic dangers ought to command attention because of their scope. A tornado is far more likely than an asteroid strike, but humanity is sure to survive the former. The chances that any one person will die in an airline crash are minute, but this does not prevent us from caring about aviation safety. And as Nathan Myhrvold, the former chief technology officer of Microsoft, put it, "The odds of a space-object strike during your lifetime may be no more than the odds you will die in a plane crash — but with space rocks, it's like the entire human race is riding on the plane."

Given the scientific findings, shouldn't space rocks be one of NASA's priorities? You'd think so, but Dallas Abbott says NASA has shown no interest in her group's work: "The NASA people don't want to believe me. They won't even listen."

NASA supports some astronomy to search for near-Earth objects, but the agency's efforts have been piecemeal and underfunded, backed by less than a tenth of a percent of the NASA budget. And though altering the course of space objects approaching Earth appears technically feasible, NASA possesses no hardware specifically for this purpose, has nearly nothing in development, and has resisted calls to begin work on protection against space strikes. Instead, NASA is enthusiastically preparing to spend hundreds of billions of taxpayers' dollars on a manned moon base that has little apparent justification. "What is in the best interest of the country is never even mentioned in current NASA planning," says Russell Schweickart, one of the *Apollo* astronauts who went into space in 1969, who is leading a campaign to raise awareness of the threat posed by space rocks. "Are we going to let a space strike kill millions of people before we get serious about this?" he asks.

In January, I attended an internal NASA conference, held at agency headquarters, during which NASA's core goals were presented in a Power-Point slideshow. Nothing was said about protecting Earth from space strikes — not even researching what sorts of spacecraft might be used in an approaching-rock emergency. Goals that *were* listed included "sustained human presence on the moon for national preeminence" and "extend the human presence across the solar system and beyond." Achieving national preeminence — isn't the United States pretty well-known already? As for extending our presence, a manned mission to Mars is at least decades away, and human travel to the outer planets is not seriously discussed by even the most zealous advocates of space exploration. Sending people "beyond" the solar system is inconceivable with any technology that can reasonably be foreseen; an interstellar spaceship traveling at the fastest speed ever achieved in space flight would take sixty thousand years to reach the next-closest star system.

After the presentation, NASA's administrator, Michael Griffin, came into the room. I asked him why there had been no discussion of space rocks. 25

He said, "We don't make up our goals. Congress has not instructed us to provide Earth defense. I administer the policy set by Congress and the White House, and that policy calls for a focus on return to the moon. Congress and the White House do not ask me what I think." I asked what NASA's priorities would be if he did set the goals. "The same. Our priorities are correct now," he answered. "We are on the right path. We need to go back to the moon. We don't need a near-Earth-objects program." In a public address about a month later, Griffin said that the moon-base plan was "the finest policy framework for United States civil space activities that I have seen in forty years."

Actually, Congress *has* asked NASA to pay more attention to space rocks. In 2005, Congress instructed the agency to mount a sophisticated search of the proximate heavens for asteroids and comets, specifically requesting that NASA locate all near-Earth objects 140 meters or larger that are less than 1.3 astronomical units from the sun — roughly out to the orbit of Mars. Last year, NASA gave Congress its reply: an advanced search of the sort Congress was requesting would cost about $1 billion, and the agency had no intention of diverting funds from existing projects, especially the moon-base initiative.

How did the moon-base idea arise? In 2003, after the shuttle *Columbia* was lost, manned space operations were temporarily shut down, and the White House spent a year studying possible new missions for NASA. George W. Bush wanted to announce a voyage to Mars. Every Oval Office occupant since John F. Kennedy knows how warmly history has praised him for the success of his pledge to put men on the moon; it's only natural that subsequent presidents would dream about securing their own place in history by sending people to the Red Planet. But the technical barriers and even the most optimistic cost projections for a manned mission to Mars are prohibitive. So in 2004, Bush unveiled a compromise plan: a permanent moon base that would be promoted as a stepping-stone for a Mars mission at some unspecified future date. As anyone with an aerospace engineering background well knows, stopping at the moon, as Bush was suggesting, actually would be an impediment to Mars travel, because huge amounts of fuel would be wasted landing on the moon and then blasting off again. Perhaps something useful to a Mars expedition would be learned in the course of building a moon base; but if the goal is the Red Planet, then spending vast sums on lunar living would only divert that money from the research and development needed for Mars hardware. However, saying that a moon base would one day support a Mars mission allowed Bush to create the impression that his plan would not merely be restaging an effort that had already been completed more than thirty years before. For NASA, a decades-long project to build a moon base would ensure a continuing flow of money to its favorite contractors and to the congressional districts where manned-space-program centers are located. So NASA signed on to the proposal, which Congress approved the following year.

It is instructive, in this context, to consider the agency's rhetoric about China. The Chinese manned space program has been improving and is now about where the U.S. program was in the mid-1960s. Stung by criticism that the moon-base project has no real justification — thirty-seven years ago, President Richard Nixon cancelled the final planned *Apollo* moon missions because the program was accomplishing little at great expense; as early as 1964, the communitarian theorist Amitai Etzioni was calling lunar obsession a "moondoggle" — NASA is selling the new plan as a second moon race, this time against Beijing. "I'll be surprised if the Chinese don't reach the moon before we return," Griffin said. "China is now a strategic peer competitor to the United States in space. China is drawing national prestige from achievements in space, and there will be a tremendous shift in national prestige toward Beijing if the Chinese are operating on the moon and we are not. Great nations have always operated on the frontiers of their era. The moon is the frontier of our era, and we must outperform the Chinese there."

Wouldn't shifting NASA's focus away from wasting money on the moon and toward something of clear benefit for the entire world — identifying and deflecting dangerous space objects — be a surer route to enhancing national prestige? But NASA's institutional instinct is not to ask, "What can we do in space that makes sense?" Rather, it is to ask, "What can we do in space that requires lots of astronauts?" That finding and stopping space rocks would be an expensive mission with little role for the astronaut corps is, in all likelihood, the principal reason NASA doesn't want to talk about the asteroid threat.

NASA's lack of interest in defending against space objects leaves a void the Air Force seems eager to fill. The Air Force has the world's second-largest space program, with a budget of about $11 billion — $6 billion less than NASA's. The tension between the two entities is long-standing. Many in the Air Force believe the service could achieve U.S. space objectives faster and more effectively than NASA. And the Air Force simply wants flyboys in orbit: several times in the past, it has asked Congress to fund its own space station, its own space plane, and its own space-shuttle program. Now, with NASA all but ignoring the space-object threat, the Air Force appears to be seizing an opportunity.

All known space rocks have been discovered using telescopes designed for traditional "soda straw" astronomy — that is, focusing on a small patch of sky. Now the Air Force is funding the first research installation designed to conduct panoramic scans of the sky, a telescope complex called Pan-STARRS, being built by the University of Hawaii. By continuously panning the entire sky, Pan-STARRS should be able to spot many near-Earth objects that so far have gone undetected. The telescope also will have substantially better resolving power and sensitivity than existing survey instruments, enabling it to find small space rocks that have gone undetected because of their faintness.

The Pan-STARRS project has no military utility, so why is the Air Force the sponsor? One speculation is that Pan-STARRS is the Air Force's foot in the door for the Earth-defense mission. If the Air Force won funding to build high-tech devices to fire at asteroids, this would be a major milestone in its goal of an expanded space presence. But space rocks are a natural hazard, not a military threat, and an Air Force Earth-protection initiative, however gallant, would probably cause intense international opposition. Imagine how other governments would react if the Pentagon announced, "Don't worry about those explosions in space — we're protecting you."

Thus, the task of defending Earth from objects falling from the skies seems most fitting for NASA, or perhaps for a multinational civilian agency that might be created. Which raises the question: What could NASA, or anyone else, actually do to provide a defense?

Russell Schweickart, the former *Apollo* astronaut, runs the B612 Foundation (B612 is the asteroid home of Saint-Exupéry's Little Prince). The foundation's goal is to get NASA officials, Congress, and ultimately the international community to take the space-rock threat seriously; it advocates testing a means of precise asteroid tracking, then trying to change the course of a near-Earth object.

Current telescopes cannot track asteroids or comets accurately enough   35
for researchers to be sure of their courses. When 99942 Apophis was spotted, for example, some calculations suggested it would strike Earth in April 2029, but further study indicates it won't — instead, Apophis should pass between Earth and the moon, during which time it may be visible to the naked eye. The Pan-STARRS telescope complex will greatly improve astronomers' ability to find and track space rocks, and it may be joined by the Large Synoptic Survey Telescope, which would similarly scan the entire sky. Earlier this year, the software billionaires Bill Gates and Charles Simonyi pledged $30 million for work on the LSST, which proponents hope to erect in the mountains of Chile. If it is built, it will be the first major telescope to broadcast its data live over the Web, allowing countless professional and amateur astronomers to look for undiscovered asteroids.

Schweickart thinks, however, that even these instruments will not be able to plot the courses of space rocks with absolute precision. NASA has said that an infrared telescope launched into an orbit near Venus could provide detailed information on the exact courses of space rocks. Such a telescope would look outward from the inner solar system toward Earth, detect the slight warmth of asteroids and comets against the cold background of the cosmos, and track their movements with precision. Congress would need to fund a near-Venus telescope, though, and NASA would need to build it — neither of which is happening.

Another means of gathering data about a potentially threatening near-Earth object would be to launch a space probe toward it and attach a transponder, similar to the transponders used by civilian airliners to report their exact locations and speed; this could give researchers extremely precise information on the object's course. There is no doubt that a probe can rendezvous with a space rock: in 2005, NASA smashed a probe called *Deep Impact* into the nucleus of comet 9P/Tempel in order to vaporize some of the material on the comet's surface and make a detailed analysis of it. Schweickart estimates that a mission to attach a transponder to an impact-risk asteroid could be staged for about $400 million — far less than the $11.7 billion cost to NASA of the 2003 *Columbia* disaster.

Then what? In the movies, nuclear bombs are used to destroy space rocks. In NASA's 2007 report to Congress, the agency suggested a similar approach. But nukes are a brute-force solution, and because an international treaty bans nuclear warheads in space, any proposal to use them against an asteroid would require complex diplomatic agreements. Fortunately, it's likely that just causing a slight change in course would avert a strike. The reason is the mechanics of orbits. Many people think of a planet as a vacuum cleaner whose gravity sucks in everything in its vicinity. It's true that a free-falling body will plummet toward the nearest source of gravity — but in space, free-falling bodies are rare. Earth does not plummet into the sun, because the angular momentum of Earth's orbit is in equilibrium with the sun's gravity. And asteroids and comets swirl around the sun with tremendous angular momentum, which prevents them from falling toward most of the bodies they pass, including Earth.

For any space object approaching a planet, there exists a "keyhole" — a patch in space where the planet's gravity and the object's momentum align, causing the asteroid or comet to hurtle toward the planet. Researchers have calculated the keyholes for a few space objects and found that they are tiny, only a few hundred meters across — pinpoints in the immensity of the solar system. You might think of a keyhole as the win-a-free-game opening on the eighteenth tee of a cheesy, incredibly elaborate miniature-golf course. All around the opening are rotating windmills, giants stomping their feet, dragons walking past, and other obstacles. If your golf ball hits the opening precisely, it will roll down a pipe for a hole in one. Miss by even a bit, and the ball caroms away.

Tiny alterations might be enough to deflect a space rock headed toward   40
a keyhole. "The reason I am optimistic about stopping near-Earth-object impacts is that it looks like we won't need to use fantastic levels of force," Schweickart says. He envisions a "gravitational tractor," a spacecraft weighing only a few tons — enough to have a slight gravitational field. If an asteroid's movements were precisely understood, placing a gravitational tractor in exactly the right place should, ever so slowly, alter the rock's course, because low levels of gravity from the tractor would tug at the asteroid. The rock's course would change only by a minuscule amount, but it would miss the hole-in-one pipe to Earth.

Will the gravitational-tractor idea work? The B612 Foundation recommends testing the technology on an asteroid that has no chance of approaching Earth. If the gravitational tractor should prove impractical or ineffective, other solutions could be considered. Attaching a rocket motor to the side of an asteroid might change its course. So might firing a laser: as materials boiled off the asteroid, the expanding gases would serve as a natural jet engine, pushing it in the opposite direction.

But when it comes to killer comets, you'll just have to lose sleep over the possibility of their approach; there are no proposals for what to do about them. Comets are easy to see when they are near the sun and glowing but are difficult to detect at other times. Many have "eccentric" orbits, spending centuries at tremendous distances from the sun, then falling toward the inner solar system, then slingshotting away again. If you were to add comets to one of those classroom models of the solar system, many would need to come from other floors of the building, or from another school district, in order to be to scale. Advanced telescopes will probably do a good job of detecting most asteroids that pass near Earth, but an unknown comet suddenly headed our way would be a nasty surprise. And because many comets change course when the sun heats their sides and causes their frozen gases to expand, deflecting or destroying them poses technical problems to which there are no ready solutions. The logical first step, then, seems to be to determine how to prevent an asteroid from striking Earth and hope that some future advance, perhaps one building on the asteroid work, proves useful against comets.

None of this will be easy, of course. Unlike in the movies, where impossibly good-looking, wisecracking men and women grab space suits and race to the launchpad immediately after receiving a warning that something is approaching from space, in real life preparations to defend against a space object would take many years. First the necessary hardware must be built — quite possibly a range of space probes and rockets. An asteroid that appeared to pose a serious risk would require extensive study, and a transponder mission could take years to reach it. International debate and consensus would be needed: the possibility of one nation acting alone against a space threat or of, say, competing U.S. and Chinese missions to the same object, is more than a little worrisome. And suppose Asteroid X appeared to threaten Earth. A mission by, say, the United States to deflect or destroy it might fail, or even backfire, by nudging the rock toward a gravitational keyhole rather than away from it. Asteroid X then hits Costa Rica; is the U.S. to blame? In all likelihood, researchers will be unable to estimate where on Earth a space rock will hit. Effectively, then, everyone would be threatened, another reason nations would need to act cooperatively — and achieving international cooperation could be a greater impediment than designing the technology.

We will soon have a new president, and thus an opportunity to reassess NASA's priorities. Whoever takes office will decide whether the nation commits to spending hundreds of billions of dollars on a motel on the moon, or invests in space projects of tangible benefit — space science, environmental studies of Earth, and readying the world for protection against a space-object strike. Although the moon-base initiative has been NASA's focus for four years, almost nothing has yet been built for the project, and comparatively little money has been spent; current plans don't call for substantial funding until the space-shuttle program ends, in 2010. This suggests that NASA could back off from the moon base without having wasted many resources. Further, the new Ares rocket NASA is designing for moon missions might be just the ticket for an asteroid-deflection initiative.

Congress, too, ought to look more sensibly at space priorities. Because   45
it controls federal funding, Congress holds the trump cards. In 2005, it pas-
sively approved the moon-base idea, seemingly just as budgetary log-rolling to maintain spending in the congressional districts favored under NASA's current budget hierarchy. The House and Senate ought to demand that the space program have as its first priority returning benefits to taxpayers. It's hard to imagine how taxpayers could benefit from a moon base. It's easy to imagine them benefiting from an effort to protect our world from the ultimate calamity.

QUESTIONS

Reading

1. Highlight, underline, or flag the places where Easterbrook asks and answers *rhetorical questions* in this essay. What purpose do these questions
   serve?
2. What explanation did a team of California researchers find for the mass
   extinction of large North American animals, as well as the Clovis people,
   approximately twelve thousand years ago? Did they prove their hypothesis? What research methods did they use? Why might their conclusions
   be controversial?
3. How does Easterbrook characterize NASA and its scientists? What does
   this characterization show?

Exploratory Writing

1. This essay was first published in June 2008, five months before the election
   of a new president. According to Easterbrook, that new president would
   decide "whether the nation commits to spending hundreds of billions of
   dollars on a motel on the moon, or invests in space projects of tangible
   benefit" (paragraph 44). Do some follow-up research to find out what
   projects NASA has prioritized during the current administration. In your
   opinion, have there been changes that Easterbrook would support?
2. Should NASA's funds be diverted from the moon-base initiative to locate
   space rocks? Stage a debate on this topic.

3. Using the online space rocks resources at NASA's Jet Propulsion Laboratory at the California Institute of Technology (**www.jpl.nasa.gov/multimedia/neo/index.cfm**), prepare a presentation *explaining* a particular NEO (near-Earth object). Use key elements of explanatory writing — such as definitions, analogies, and illustrations — to make your presentation clear.

Making Connections

1. Compare Easterbrook's essay with another writer's explanation of a scientific phenomenon, such as Diane Ackerman's (p. 459) explanation of why leaves change color in the fall, or Michael Pollan's explanation of corn reproduction (p. 467). Do the essays use only explanatory writing, or do they also employ a technique more closely associated with a different writing mode, such as *arguing* or *reporting*? Create a chart in which you quote examples of *explaining* and other modes from the two essays. What can you learn about each writer's agenda from these examples?

	EXPLAINING	REFLECTING	REPORTING	ARGUING
Easterbrook				
Ackerman/Pollan				

Essay Writing

1. Write an essay *reporting* on the B612 Foundation described in Easterbrook's essay. You can use the foundation's Web site (**www.b612foundation.org**) and any other sources you think are important. Remember to address the key reportorial questions: *who, what, when, where,* and *why*?
2. If you knew for sure that an asteroid was going to crash into Earth in a month, how would your life change? Write an essay outlining how you would spend that final month.

The Eureka Hunt

Jonah Lehrer

Jonah Lehrer (b. 1981) is an editor at large for the science maga-zine Seed. *His collection of essays,* Proust Was a Neuroscientist *(2007), proposes that the imaginative work of eight artists pre-dated scientists' current understanding of the brain. The title essay charts the early-twentieth-century French writer's "discoveries" that taste and smell can evoke intense memories — an observation only recently confirmed by scientists. (It was not until 2002 that Brown University psychologist Rachel Herz showed that the nerves associated with taste and smell connect to the hippocam-pus, affecting long-term memory.) In a 2008 interview, Lehrer ex-plains how Proust's novels, which he read during breaks from his lab experiments on the memory of sea slugs, inspired his thesis: "Once I had this idea about looking at art through the prism of science, I began to see connections everywhere." Lehrer's latest book,* How We Decide *(2009), rationalizes the daily decisions we make from a neuroscientific perspective. He earned a degree from Columbia University, sharing a lab with Nobel Prize–winning neuroscientist Eric Kandel, and studied at Oxford University as a Rhodes Scholar. His writing has been featured on NPR and has appeared in the* Boston Globe, Nature, *and the* New Yorker, *in which this article appeared in July 2008. He currently writes a science blog, the* Frontal Cortex.

The summer of 1949 was long and dry in Montana. On the afternoon of August 5th — the hottest day ever recorded in the state — a lightning fire was spotted in a remote area of pine forest. A parachute brigade of fifteen firefighters known as smoke jumpers was dispatched to put out the blaze; the man in charge was named Wag Dodge. When the jumpers left Missoula, in a C-47 cargo plane, they were told that the fire was small, just a few burn-ing acres in the Mann Gulch.

Mann Gulch, nearly three miles long, is a site of geological transition, where the Great Plains meet the Rocky Mountains, pine trees give way to tall grasses, and steep cliffs loom over the steppes of the Midwest. The fire began in the trees on one side of the gulch. By the time the firefighters ar-rived, the blaze was already out of control. Dodge moved his men along the other side of the gulch and told them to head downhill, toward the water.

When the smoke jumpers started down the gulch, a breeze was blowing the flames away from them. Suddenly, the wind reversed, and Dodge watched the fire leap across the gulch and spark the grass on his side. He and his men were only a quarter mile uphill. An updraft began, and fierce winds howled through the canyon as the fire sucked in the surrounding air. Dodge was suddenly staring at a wall of flame fifty feet tall and three hundred feet deep. In a matter of seconds, the fire began to devour the grass, hurtling toward the smoke jumpers at seven hundred feet a minute.

Dodge screamed at his men to retreat. They dropped their gear and started running up the steep canyon walls, trying to reach the top of the ridge. After a few minutes, Dodge glanced over his shoulder and saw that the fire was less than fifty yards away. He realized that the blaze couldn't be outrun; the gulch was too steep, the flames too fast.

So Dodge stopped running. The decision wasn't as suicidal as it appeared: in a moment of desperate insight, he had devised an escape plan. He lit a match and ignited the ground in front of him, the flames quickly moving up the grassy slope. Then Dodge stepped into the shadow of his fire, so that he was surrounded by a buffer of burned land. He wet his handkerchief with water from his canteen, clutched the cloth to his mouth, and lay down on the smoldering embers. He closed his eyes and tried to inhale the thin layer of oxygen clinging to the ground. Then he waited for the fire to pass over him.

Thirteen smoke jumpers died in the Mann Gulch fire. White crosses below the ridge still mark the spots where the men died. But after several terrifying minutes Dodge emerged from the ashes, virtually unscathed.

There is something inherently mysterious about moments of insight. Wag Dodge, for instance, could never explain where his idea for the escape fire came from. ("It just seemed the logical thing to do" was all he could muster.) His improbable survival has become one of those legendary stories of insight, like Archimedes shouting "Eureka!" when he saw his bathwater rise, or Isaac Newton watching an apple fall from a tree and then formulating his theory of gravity. Such tales all share a few essential features, which psychologists and neuroscientists use to define "the insight experience." The first of these is the impasse: before there can be a breakthrough, there has to be a mental block. Wag Dodge spent minutes running from the fire, although he was convinced that doing so was futile. Then, when the insight arrived, Dodge immediately realized that the problem was solved. This is another key feature of insight: the feeling of certainty that accompanies the idea. Dodge didn't have time to think about whether his plan would work. He simply knew that it would.

Mark Jung-Beeman, a cognitive neuroscientist at Northwestern University, has spent the past fifteen years trying to figure out what happens inside the brain when people have an insight. "It's one of those defining features of the human mind, and yet we have no idea how or why it happens," he told me. Insights have often been attributed to divine intervention, but, by mapping the epiphany as a journey between cortical circuits, Jung-Beeman wants to purge the insight experience of its mystery. Jung-Beeman has a tense smile, a receding hairline, and the wiry build of a long-distance runner. He qualified for the 1988 and 1992 Olympic trials in the fifteen hundred metres, although he gave up competitive running after, as he puts it, "everything below the hips started to fall apart." He now subsists on long walks and manic foot tapping. When Jung-Beeman gets excited about an idea — be it the cellular properties of pyramidal neurons or his new treadmill — his speech accelerates, and he starts to draw pictures on whatever paper is nearby. It's as if his mind were sprinting ahead of his mouth.

Jung-Beeman became interested in the nature of insight in the early 1990s, while researching the right hemisphere of the brain. At the time, he was studying patients who had peculiar patterns of brain damage. "We had a number of patients with impaired right hemispheres," he said. "And the doctors would always say, 'Wow, you're lucky — it got the right hemisphere. That's the minor hemisphere. It doesn't do much, and it doesn't do anything with language.'" But it gradually became clear to Jung-Beeman that these patients did have serious cognitive problems after all, particularly with understanding linguistic nuance, and he began to suspect that the talents of the right hemisphere had been overlooked. If the left hemisphere excelled at denotation — storing the primary meaning of a word — Jung-Beeman suspected that the right hemisphere dealt with connotation, everything that gets left out of a dictionary definition, such as the emotional charge in a sentence or a metaphor. "Language is so complex that the brain has to process it in two different ways at the same time," he said. "It needs to see the forest *and* the trees. The right hemisphere is what helps you see the forest."

It wasn't clear how to pinpoint these nuanced aspects of cognition, because the results of right-hemisphere damage were harder to spot than those of left-hemisphere damage. But in 1993 Jung-Beeman heard a talk by the psychologist Jonathan Schooler on moments of insight. Schooler had demonstrated that it was possible to interfere with insight by making people explain their thought process while trying to solve a puzzle — a phenomenon he called "verbal overshadowing." This made sense to Jung-Beeman, since the act of verbal explanation would naturally shift activity to the left hemisphere, causing people to ignore the more subtle associations coming from the right side of the brain. "That's when I realized that insight could be a really interesting way to look at all these skills the right hemisphere excelled at," he said. "I guess I had an insight about insight."

Jung-Beeman began searching in the right hemisphere for the source of insight in the brain. He decided to compare puzzles solved in moments of insight with those solved by methodical testing of potential solutions, in which people could accurately trace their thought process and had no sense of surprise when the answer came. Unfortunately, all the classic puzzles developed by scientists to study insight *required* insight; if subjects didn't solve them in a sudden "Aha!" moment, they didn't solve them at all. In a popular puzzle known as "the candle problem," for instance, subjects are given a cardboard box containing a few thumbtacks, a book of matches, and a candle. They are told to attach the candle to a piece of corkboard so that it can burn properly. Nearly 90 percent of people pursue the same two strategies. They try to tack the candle directly to the board, which causes the candle wax to shatter. Or they try melting the candle with the matches, so that it sticks to the board; but the wax doesn't hold and the candle falls. Only 4 percent of people manage to come up with the solution, which involves attaching the candle to the cardboard box and tacking the cardboard box to the corkboard.

To isolate the brain activity that defined the insight process, Jung-Beeman needed to develop a set of puzzles that could be solved either by insight or by analysis. Doing so was a puzzle in itself. "It can get pretty frustrating trying to find an experimentally valid brainteaser," Jung-Beeman said. "The puzzles can't be too hard or too easy, and you need to be able to generate lots of them." He eventually settled on a series of verbal puzzles, based on ones used by a psychologist in the early 1960s, which he named the Compound Remote Associate Problems, or CRAP. (The joke is beginning to get old, and in his scientific papers Jung-Beeman decorously leaves off the final "P.")

In a CRA word puzzle, a subject is given three words, such as *pine*, *crab*, and *sauce*, and asked to think of a word that can be combined with all three — in this case, *apple* (*pineapple*, *crab apple*, *apple sauce*). The subjects have up to thirty seconds to solve the puzzle. If they come up with an answer, they press the space bar on the keyboard and say whether the answer arrived via insight or analysis. When I participated in the experiment in Jung-Beeman's lab, I found that it was surprisingly easy to differentiate between the two cognitive paths. When I solved puzzles with analysis, I tended to sound out each possible word combination, cycling through all the words that went with *pine* and then seeing if they also worked with *crab* or *sauce*. If I worked toward a solution, I always double-checked it before pressing the space bar. An insight, on the other hand, felt instantaneous: the answer arrived like a revelation.

Jung-Beeman initially asked his subjects to solve the puzzles while inside an fMRI machine, a brain scanner that monitors neural activity by tracking changes in blood flow. But fMRI has a three-to-five-second delay, as the blood diffuses across the cortex. "Insights happen too fast for fMRI," Jung-Beeman said. "The data was just too messy." Around this time, he teamed up with John Kounios, a cognitive neuroscientist at Drexel University, who was interested in insight largely because it seemed to contradict the classic model of learning, in which the learning process was assumed to be gradual. Kounios, a man with a shock of unruly wavy hair and an affinity for rumpled button-up vests, had been working with electroencephalography, or EEG, which measures the waves of electricity produced by the brain by means of a nylon hat filled with greased electrodes. (The device looks like a bulky shower cap.) Because there is no time delay with EEG, Kounios thought it could be useful for investigating the fleeting process of insight. Unfortunately, the waves of electricity can't be traced back to their precise source, but Kounios and Jung-Beeman saw that combining EEG with fMRI might allow them to construct a precise map, both in time and space, of the insight process.

The resulting studies, published in 2004 and 2006, found that people 15 who solved puzzles with insight activated a specific subset of cortical areas. Although the answer seemed to appear out of nowhere, the mind was carefully preparing itself for the breakthrough. The first areas activated during the problem-solving process were those involved with executive control, like the prefrontal cortex and the anterior cingulate cortex. The scientists refer to this as the "preparatory phase," since the brain is devoting its considerable computational power to the problem. The various sensory areas, like the visual cortex, go silent as the brain suppresses possible distractions. "The cortex does this for the same reason we close our eyes when we're trying to think," Jung-Beeman said. "Focus is all about blocking stuff out."

What happens next is the "search phase," as the brain starts looking for answers in all the relevant places. Because Jung-Beeman and Kounios were giving people word puzzles, they saw additional activity in areas related to speech and language. The search can quickly get frustrating, and it takes only a few seconds before people say that they've reached an impasse, that they can't think of the right word. "Almost all of the possibilities your brain comes up with are going to be wrong," Jung-Beeman said. "And it's up to the executive-control areas to keep on searching or, if necessary, change strategies and start searching somewhere else."

But sometimes, just when the brain is about to give up, an insight appears. "You'll see people bolt up in their chair and their eyes go all wide," Ezra Wegbreit, a graduate student in the Jung-Beeman lab who often administers the CRA test, said. "Sometimes they even say 'Aha!' before they blurt out the answer." The suddenness of the insight comes with a burst of brain activity. Three hundred milliseconds before a participant communicates the answer, the EEG registers a spike of gamma rhythm, which is the highest electrical frequency generated by the brain. Gamma rhythm is thought to come from the "binding" of neurons, as cells distributed across the cortex draw themselves together into a new network, which is then able to enter consciousness. It's as if the insight had gone incandescent.

Jung-Beeman and Kounios went back and analyzed the information from the fMRI experiment to see what was happening inside the brain in the seconds before the gamma burst. "My biggest worry was that we would find nothing," Kounios said. "I thought there was a good possibility that whatever we found on the EEG wouldn't show up on the brain imaging." When the scientists looked at the data, however, they saw that a small fold of tissue on the surface of the right hemisphere, the anterior superior temporal gyrus (aSTG), became unusually active in the second before the insight. The activation was sudden and intense, a surge of electricity leading to a rush of blood. Although the function of the aSTG remains mostly a mystery — the brain is stuffed with obscurities — Jung-Beeman wasn't surprised to see it involved with the insight process. A few previous studies had linked the area to aspects of language comprehension, such as the detection of literary themes and the interpretation of metaphors. (A related area was implicated in the processing of jokes.) Jung-Beeman argues that these linguistic skills, like insight, require the brain to make a set of distant and unprecedented connections. He cites studies showing that cells in the right hemisphere are more "broadly tuned" than cells in the left hemisphere, with longer branches and more dendritic spines. "What this means is that neurons in the right hemisphere are collecting information from a larger area of cortical space," Jung-Beeman said. "They are less precise but better connected." When the brain is searching for an insight, these are the cells that are most likely to produce it.

The insight process, as sketched by Jung-Beeman and Kounios, is a delicate mental balancing act. At first, the brain lavishes the scarce resource of attention on a single problem. But, once the brain is sufficiently focussed, the cortex needs to relax in order to seek out the more remote association in the right hemisphere, which will provide the insight. "The relaxation phase is crucial," Jung-Beeman said. "That's why so many insights happen during warm showers." Another ideal moment for insights, according to the scientists, is the early morning, right after we wake up. The drowsy brain is unwound and disorganized, open to all sorts of unconventional ideas. The right hemisphere is also unusually active. Jung-Beeman said, "The problem with the morning, though, is that we're always so rushed. We've got to get the kids ready for school, so we leap out of bed and never give ourselves a chance to think." He recommends that, if we're stuck on a difficult problem, it's better to set the alarm clock a few minutes early so that we have time to lie in bed and ruminate. We do some of our best thinking when we're still half asleep.

As Jung-Beeman and Kounios see it, the insight process is an act of cognitive deliberation — the brain must be focussed on the task at hand — transformed by accidental, serendipitous connections. We must concentrate, but we must concentrate on letting the mind wander. The patterns of brain activity that define this particular style of thought have recently been studied by Joy Bhattacharya, a psychologist at Goldsmiths, University of London. Using EEG, he has found that he can tell which subjects will solve insight puzzles up to eight seconds before the insight actually arrives. One of the key predictive signals is a steady rhythm of alpha waves emanating from the right hemisphere. Alpha waves typically correlate with a state of relaxation, and Bhattacharya believes that such activity makes the brain more receptive to new and unusual ideas. He has also found that unless subjects have

20

sufficient alpha-wave activity they won't be able to make use of hints the researchers give them.

One of the surprising lessons of this research is that trying to force an insight can actually prevent the insight. While it's commonly assumed that the best way to solve a difficult problem is to focus, minimize distractions, and pay attention only to the relevant details, this clenched state of mind may inhibit the sort of creative connections that lead to sudden break-throughs. We suppress the very type of brain activity that we should be encouraging. Jonathan Schooler has recently demonstrated that making people focus on the details of a visual scene, as opposed to the big picture, can significantly disrupt the insight process. "It doesn't take much to shift the brain into left-hemisphere mode," he said. "That's when you stop paying attention to those more holistic associations coming in from the right hemisphere." Meanwhile, in a study published last year, German researchers found that people with schizotypy — a mental condition that resembles schizophrenia, albeit with far less severe symptoms — were significantly better at solving insight problems than a control group. Schizotypal subjects have enhanced right-hemisphere function and tend to score above average on measures of creativity and associative thinking.

Schooler's research has also led him to reconsider the bad reputation of letting one's mind wander. Although we often complain that the brain is too easily distracted, Schooler believes that letting the mind wander is essential. "Just look at the history of science," he said. "The big ideas seem to always come when people are sidetracked, when they're doing something that has nothing to do with their research." He cites the example of Henri Poincaré, the nineteenth-century mathematician, whose seminal insight into non-Euclidean geometry arrived while he was boarding a bus. "At the moment when I put my foot on the step," Poincaré wrote, "the idea came to me, without anything in my former thoughts seeming to have paved the way for it. . . . I did not verify the idea; I should not have had the time, as, upon taking my seat in the omnibus, I went on with the conversation already commenced, but I felt a perfect certainty." Poincaré credited his sudden mathematical insight to "unconscious work," an ability to mull over the mathematics while he was preoccupied with unrelated activities, like talking to a friend on the bus. In his 1908 essay "Mathematical Creation," Poincaré insisted that the best way to think about complex problems is to immerse yourself in the problem until you hit an impasse. Then, when it seems that "nothing good is accomplished," you should find a way to distract yourself, preferably by going on a "walk or a journey." The answer will arrive when you least expect it. Richard Feynman, the Nobel Prize–winning physicist, preferred the relaxed atmosphere of a topless bar, where he would sip 7 UP, "watch the entertainment," and, if inspiration struck, scribble equations on cocktail napkins.

Kounios and Jung-Beeman aren't quite ready to offer extensive practical advice, but, when pressed, they often sound like Poincaré. "You've got to know when to step back," Kounios said. "If you're in an environment that forces you to produce and produce, and you feel very stressed, then you're not going to have any insights." Many stimulants, like caffeine, Adderall, and Ritalin, are taken to increase focus — one recent poll found that nearly 20 percent of scientists and researchers regularly took prescription drugs to "enhance concentration" — but, according to Jung-Beeman and Kounios, drugs may actually make insights less likely, by sharpening the spotlight of attention and discouraging mental rambles. Concentration, it seems, comes with the hidden cost of diminished creativity. "There's a good reason Google puts Ping-Pong tables in their headquarters," Kounios said. "If you want to encourage insights, then you've got to also encourage people to relax." Jung-Beeman's latest paper investigates why people who are in a good mood are so much better at solving insight puzzles. (On average, they solve nearly 20 percent more CRA problems.)

Last year, Kounios and Jung-Beeman were invited to present their findings to DARPA, the central research agency of the Department of Defense. ("It was quite strange," Kounios recalls. "I never thought I'd be talking about creativity to national-security officials.") DARPA was interested in finding ways to encourage insights amid the stress of war, fostering creativity on the battlefield. The scientists are convinced that it's only a matter of time before it becomes possible to "up-regulate" insight. "This could be a drug or technology or just a new way to structure our environment," Jung-Beeman said. "I think we'll soon get to the point where we can do more than tell people to take lots of showers."

For now, though, the science of promoting insight remains rooted in anecdote, in stories of people, like Poincaré, who were able to consistently induce the necessary state of mind. Kounios tells a story about an expert Zen meditator who took part in one of the CRA insight experiments. At first, the meditator couldn't solve any of the insight problems. "This Zen guy went through thirty or so of the verbal puzzles and just drew a blank," Kounios said. "He was used to being very focussed, but you can't solve these problems if you're too focussed." Then, just as he was about to give up, he started solving one puzzle after another, until, by the end of the experiment, he was getting them all right. It was an unprecedented streak. "Normally, people don't get better as the task goes along," Kounios said. "If anything, they get a little bored." Kounios believes that the dramatic improvement of the Zen meditator came from his paradoxical ability to focus on *not* being focussed, so that he could pay attention to those remote associations in the right hemisphere. "He had the cognitive control to let go," Kounios said. "He became an insight machine."

The most mysterious aspect of insight is not the revelation itself but what happens next. The brain is an infinite library of associations, a cacophony of competing ideas, and yet, as soon as the right association appears, we know. The new thought, which is represented by that rush of gamma waves in the right hemisphere, immediately grabs our attention. There is something paradoxical and bizarre about this. On the one hand, an epiphany is a surprising event; we are startled by what we've just discovered. Some part of our brain, however, clearly isn't surprised at all, which is why we are able to instantly recognize the insight. "As soon as the insight happens, it just seems so obvious," Schooler said. "People can't believe they didn't see it before."

The brain area responsible for this act of recognition is the prefrontal cortex, which lights up whenever people are shown the right answer — even if they haven't come up with the answer themselves. Pressed tight against the bones of the forehead, the prefrontal cortex has undergone a dramatic expansion during human evolution, so that it now represents nearly a third of the brain. While this area is often associated with the most specialized aspects of human cognition, such as abstract reasoning, it also plays a critical role in the insight process. Hallucinogenic drugs are thought to work largely by modulating the prefrontal cortex, tricking the brain into believing that its sensory delusions are revelations. People have the feeling of an insight but without the content. Understanding how this happens — how a circuit of cells can identify an idea as an insight, even if the idea has yet to enter awareness — requires an extremely precise level of investigation. The rhythms of brain waves and the properties of blood can't answer the question. Instead, it's necessary to study the brain at its most basic level, as a loom of electrical cells.

Earl Miller is a neuroscientist at MIT who has devoted his career to understanding the prefrontal cortex. He has a shiny shaved head and a silver goatee. His corner office in the gleaming Picower Institute is cantilevered over a railroad track, and every afternoon the quiet hum of the lab is interrupted by the rattle of a freight train. Miller's favorite word is *exactly* — it's the adverb that modifies everything, so that a hypothesis is "exactly right," or an experiment was "exactly done" — and that emphasis on precision has defined his career. His first major scientific advance was a by-product of necessity. It was 1995, and Miller had just started his lab at MIT. His research involved recording directly from neurons in the monkey brain, monitoring the flux of voltage within an individual cell as the animals performed various tasks. "There were machines that allowed you to record from eight or nine at the same time, but they were very expensive," Miller said. "I still had no grants, and there was no way I could afford one." So Miller began inventing his own apparatus in his spare time. After a few months of patient tinkering, he constructed a messy tangle of wires, steel screws, and electrodes that could simultaneously record from numerous cells, distributed across the brain. "It worked even better than the expensive machine," Miller said.

This methodological advance — it's known as multiple electrode recording — allowed Miller to ask a completely new kind of scientific question. For the first time, it was possible to see how cells in different brain areas interacted. Miller was most interested in the interactions of the prefrontal cortex. "You name the brain area, and the prefrontal cortex is almost certainly linked to it," he said. It took more than five years of painstaking probing, as Miller recorded from cells in the monkey brain, but he was eventually able to show that the prefrontal cortex wasn't simply an aggregator of information. Instead, it was like the conductor of an orchestra, waving its baton and directing the players. This is known as "top-down processing," since the prefrontal cortex (the "top" of the brain) is directly modulating the activity of other areas. This is why, during the focussing phase of the insight process, Jung-Beeman and Kounios saw activity in the prefrontal cortex and the neighboring anterior cingulate cortex. They were watching the conductor at work.

In 2001, Miller and Jonathan Cohen, a neuroscientist at Princeton,   30 published an influential paper that laid out their theory of how, exactly, the prefrontal cortex controls the rest of the brain. According to Miller and Cohen, this brain area is responsible not only for focussing on the task at hand but for figuring out what other areas need to be engaged in order to solve a problem. One implication of this is that if we're trying to solve a verbal puzzle the prefrontal cortex will selectively activate the specific brain areas involved with verbal processing. If it decides to turn on parts of the right hemisphere, then we might end up with an insight; if it decides to restrict its search to the left hemisphere, we'll probably arrive at a solution incrementally or not at all.

This "integrative" theory of the prefrontal cortex suggests why we can instantly recognize the insight, even when it seems surprising: the brain has been concertedly pursuing the answer; we just didn't know it. "Your consciousness is very limited in capacity," Miller said, "and that's why your prefrontal cortex makes all these plans without telling you about it." When that obscure circuit in the right hemisphere finally generates the necessary association, the prefrontal cortex is able to identify it instantly, and the insight erupts into awareness. We suddenly notice the music that has been playing all along.

Because Miller can eavesdrop on neurons, he's been able to see how these insights operate at the cellular level. One of his current experiments involves showing monkeys different arrangements of dots and asking them to sort the arrangements into various categories that they have been taught. The monkeys guess randomly at first, learning from trial and error. "But then, at a certain point, the monkey just gets it," Miller said. "They just start being able to categorize arrangements of dots that they've never seen before. That's the moment of categorical insight." This primate epiphany registers as a new pattern of neural activity in the prefrontal cortex. The brain cells have been altered by the breakthrough. "An insight is a restructuring of information — it's seeing the same old thing in a completely new way," Miller said. "Once that restructuring occurs, you never go back."

And yet even this detailed explanation doesn't fully demystify insight. It remains unclear how simple cells recognize what the conscious mind cannot, or how they are able to filter through the chaos of bad ideas to produce the epiphany. "This mental process will always be a little unknowable, which is why it's so interesting to study," Jung-Beeman said. "At a certain point, you just have to admit that your brain knows much more than you do." An insight is a fleeting glimpse of the brain's huge store of unknown knowledge. The cortex is sharing one of its secrets.

So it was for Wag Dodge. After the fire crossed the river, all the other smoke jumpers were fixated on reaching the ridge. Panic had narrowed their thoughts, so that beating the flames up the slope was their sole goal. But, because Dodge realized that the fire would beat them to the top, his prefrontal cortex started frantically searching for an alternative. It was able to look past his fear and expand the possibilities of his thought process, as he considered remote mental associations that he'd never contemplated before. (As Miller says, "That Dodge guy had some really high prefrontal function.") And then, just as the blaze started to suck the oxygen out of the air, some remote bit of his brain realized that he could cheat death by starting his own fire. This unprecedented idea, a flicker of electricity somewhere in the right hemisphere, was immediately recognized as the solution the prefrontal cortex had been searching for. And so Dodge stopped running. He stood still as the wall of flame raced toward him. Then he lit the match.

QUESTIONS

Reading

1. Which essential features comprise "the insight experience"?
2. Chart the different activities or types of thinking that are governed by each hemisphere of the brain, according to this essay.

LEFT BRAIN	RIGHT BRAIN

3. Discuss Jonathan Schooler's research and experiments. How does describing Schooler's work strengthen this *explanatory* essay?
4. What role does the writer, Jonah Lehrer, play in this *third-person* explanation of how insight works? In what ways would a *first-person* reflection on the experience of insight be different from this account?

Exploratory Writing

1. In the course of doing his research, Jung-Beeman realized that "all the classic puzzles developed by scientists to study insight *required* insight; if subjects didn't solve them in a sudden 'Aha!' moment, they didn't solve them at all" (paragraph 11). In small groups, find a sample "insight puzzle" online or at the library. Each group member should first try to solve the puzzle alone. After your attempt, report your experiences trying to solve the puzzle to the rest of the group.
2. Reflect on a time when you had an epiphany, or an "Aha!" moment. How did it change your life and way of thinking?

Making Connections

1. Consider Lewis Thomas's (p. 339) reflection, "It immensely pleases a human being to see something never seen before, even more to learn something never known before, most of all to think something never thought before." How do "Eureka!" moments fit in with his discussion of ways the universe is surprising?
2. Steven Johnson (p. 85) argues that watching certain kinds of television shows can make people smarter. Based on both Johnson's and Lehrer's arguments and examples, do you think that television viewing can stimulate moments of insight? Do the kinds of intellectual development that Johnson attributes to television viewing sound more right-brained or left-brained to you?

Essay Writing

1. According to the Nobel Prize–winning physiologist Albert Szent-Györgyi, "Discovery consists of seeing what everybody has seen and thinking what nobody has thought." Research and write an essay about a famous invention, discovery, or breakthrough in history. To what extent did the discovery arrive in a "Eureka!" moment? To what extent was it the result of the inventor's methodical labor? What can we learn about insight from the particular case study you've chosen?

The Checklist

Atul Gawande

Dr. Atul Gawande (b. 1965) is a general and endocrine surgeon at the Brigham and Women's Hospital (BWH) and the Dana-Farber Cancer Institute (both affiliated with Harvard Medical School) in Boston, and associate director for the BWH Center for Surgery and Public Health. Born to Indian immigrants — both doctors — Gawande grew up in Athens, Ohio, and attended Stanford University before pursuing an MA at Oxford University, an MD at Harvard Medical School, and an MPH at the Harvard School of Public Health. From 1992 to 1993 he acted as senior health policy advisor to the Clinton administration. In addition to his research, publications, and advisory work in the medical field, Dr. Gawande also teaches surgery and health policy at Harvard and writes for the New Yorker, *where he has been a staff writer since 1998. His first book,* Complications: A Surgeon's Notes on an Imperfect Science *(2002), was a National Book Award finalist. In 2006 he won the MacArthur Award, often called the "genius award," for his research and writing. His latest book,* Better: A Surgeon's Notes on Performance *(2007), is a collection of essays that takes us from polio in India to surgical tents in Iraq to delivery rooms in Boston. The following article was published in the* New Yorker *in December 2007.*

The damage that the human body can survive these days is as awesome as it is horrible: crushing, burning, bombing, a burst blood vessel in the brain, a ruptured colon, a massive heart attack, rampaging infection. These conditions had once been uniformly fatal. Now survival is commonplace, and a large part of the credit goes to the irreplaceable component of medicine known as intensive care.

It's an opaque term. Specialists in the field prefer to call what they do "critical care," but that doesn't exactly clarify matters. The non-medical term "life support" gets us closer. Intensive-care units take artificial control of failing bodies. Typically, this involves a panoply of technology — a mechanical ventilator and perhaps a tracheostomy tube if the lungs have failed, an aortic balloon pump if the heart has given out, a dialysis machine if the kidneys don't work. When you are unconscious and can't eat, silicone tubing can be surgically inserted into the stomach or intestines for formula feeding. If the intestines are too damaged, solutions of amino acids, fatty acids, and glucose can be infused directly into the bloodstream.

The difficulties of life support are considerable. Reviving a drowning victim, for example, is rarely as easy as it looks on television, where a few chest compressions and some mouth-to-mouth resuscitation always seem to bring someone with waterlogged lungs and a stilled heart coughing and sputtering back to life. Consider a case report in *The Annals of Thoracic Surgery* of a three-year-old girl who fell into an icy fishpond in a small Austrian town in the Alps. She was lost beneath the surface for thirty minutes before her parents found her on the pond bottom and pulled her up. Following instructions from an emergency physician on the phone, they began cardiopulmonary resuscitation. A rescue team arrived eight minutes later. The girl had a body temperature of sixty-six degrees, and no pulse. Her pupils were dilated and did not react to light, indicating that her brain was no longer working.

But the emergency technicians continued CPR anyway. A helicopter took her to a nearby hospital, where she was wheeled directly to an operating room. A surgical team put her on a heart-lung bypass machine. Between the transport time and the time it took to plug the inflow and outflow lines into the femoral vessels of her right leg, she had been lifeless for an hour and a half. By the two-hour mark, however, her body temperature had risen almost ten degrees, and her heart began to beat. It was her first organ to come back.

After six hours, her core temperature reached 98.6 degrees. The team tried to put her on a breathing machine, but the pond water had damaged her lungs too severely for oxygen to reach her blood. So they switched her to an artificial-lung system known as ECMO — extracorporeal membrane oxygenation. The surgeons opened her chest down the middle with a power saw and sewed lines to and from the ECMO unit into her aorta and her beating heart. The team moved the girl into intensive care, with her chest still open and covered with plastic foil. A day later, her lungs had recovered sufficiently for the team to switch her from ECMO to a mechanical ventilator and close her chest. Over the next two days, all her organs recovered except her brain. A CT scan showed global brain swelling, which is a sign of diffuse damage, but no actual dead zones. So the team drilled a hole into the girl's skull, threaded in a probe to monitor her cerebral pressure, and kept that pressure tightly controlled by constantly adjusting her fluids and medications. For more than a week, she lay comatose. Then, slowly, she came back to life.

First, her pupils started to react to light. Next, she began to breathe on her own. And, one day, she simply awoke. Two weeks after her accident, she went home. Her right leg and left arm were partially paralyzed. Her speech was thick and slurry. But by age five, after extensive outpatient therapy, she had recovered her faculties completely. She was like any little girl again.

* * *

What makes her recovery astounding isn't just the idea that someone could come back from two hours in a state that would once have been considered death. It's also the idea that a group of people in an ordinary hospital could do something so enormously complex. To save this one child, scores of people had to carry out thousands of steps correctly: placing the heart-pump tubing into her without letting in air bubbles; maintaining the sterility of her lines, her open chest, the burr hole in her skull; keeping a temperamental battery of machines up and running. The degree of difficulty in any one of these steps is substantial. Then you must add the difficulties of orchestrating them in the right sequence, with nothing dropped, leaving some room for improvisation, but not too much.

For every drowned and pulseless child rescued by intensive care, there are many more who don't make it — and not just because their bodies are too far gone. Machines break down; a team can't get moving fast enough; a simple step is forgotten. Such cases don't get written up in *The Annals of Thoracic Surgery*, but they are the norm. Intensive-care medicine has become the art of managing extreme complexity — and a test of whether such complexity can, in fact, be humanly mastered.

On any given day in the United States, some ninety thousand people are in intensive care. Over a year, an estimated five million Americans will be, and over a normal lifetime nearly all of us will come to know the glassed bay of an ICU from the inside. Wide swaths of medicine now depend on the life support systems that ICUs provide: care for premature infants; victims of trauma, strokes, and heart attacks; patients who have had surgery on their brain, heart, lungs, or major blood vessels. Critical care has become an increasingly large portion of what hospitals do. Fifty years ago, ICUs barely existed. Today, in my hospital, 155 of our almost 700 patients are, as I write this, in intensive care. The average stay of an ICU patient is four days, and the survival rate is 86 percent. Going into an ICU, being put on a mechanical ventilator, having tubes and wires run into and out of you, is not a sentence of death. But the days will be the most precarious of your life.

A decade ago, Israeli scientists published a study in which engineers observed patient care in ICUs for twenty-four-hour stretches. They found that the average patient required 178 individual actions per day, ranging from administering a drug to suctioning the lungs, and every one of them posed risks. Remarkably, the nurses and doctors were observed to make an error in just 1 percent of these actions — but that still amounted to an average of two errors a day with every patient. Intensive care succeeds only when we hold the odds of doing harm low enough for the odds of doing good to prevail. This is hard. There are dangers simply in lying unconscious in bed for a few days. Muscles atrophy. Bones lose mass. Pressure ulcers form. Veins begin to clot off. You have to stretch and exercise patients' flaccid limbs daily to avoid contractures, give subcutaneous injections of blood thinners at least twice a day, turn patients in bed every few hours, bathe them and change their sheets without knocking out a tube or a line, brush their teeth

10

twice a day to avoid pneumonia from bacterial buildup in their mouths. Add a ventilator, dialysis, and open wounds to care for, and the difficulties only accumulate.

The story of one of my patients makes the point. Anthony DeFilippo was a forty-eight-year-old limousine driver from Everett, Massachusetts, who started to hemorrhage at a community hospital during surgery for a hernia and gallstones. The bleeding was finally stopped but his liver was severely damaged, and over the next few days he became too sick for the hospital's facilities. When he arrived in our ICU, at 1:30 a.m. on a Sunday, his ragged black hair was plastered to his sweaty forehead, his body was shaking, and his heart was racing at 114 beats a minute. He was delirious from fever, shock, and low oxygen levels.

"I need to get out!" he cried. "I need to get out!" He clawed at his gown, his oxygen mask, the dressings covering his abdominal wound.

"Tony, it's all right," a nurse said to him. "We're going to help you. You're in a hospital."

He shoved her — he was a big man — and tried to swing his legs out of the bed. We turned up his oxygen flow, put his wrists in cloth restraints, and tried to reason with him. He eventually let us draw blood from him and give him antibiotics.

The laboratory results came back showing liver failure and a wildly elevated white-blood-cell count indicating infection. It soon became evident from his empty urine bag that his kidneys had failed, too. In the next few hours, his blood pressure fell, his breathing worsened, and he drifted from agitation to near-unconsciousness. Each of his organ systems, including his brain, was shutting down. 15

I called his sister, who was his next of kin, and told her of the situation. "Do everything you can," she said.

So we did. We gave him a syringeful of anesthetic, and a resident slid a breathing tube into his throat. Another resident "lined him up." She inserted a thin, two-inch-long needle and catheter through his upturned right wrist and into his radial artery, and then sewed the line to his skin with a silk suture. Next, she put in a central line — a twelve-inch catheter pushed into the jugular vein in his left neck. After she sewed that in place, and an X-ray showed its tip floating just where it was supposed to — inside his vena cava at the entrance to his heart — she put a third, slightly thicker line, for dialysis, through his right upper chest and into the subclavian vein, deep under the collarbone.

We hooked a breathing tube up to a hose from a ventilator and set it to give him fourteen forced breaths of 100 percent oxygen every minute. We dialed the ventilator pressures and gas flow up and down, like engineers at a control panel, until we got the blood levels of oxygen and carbon dioxide where we wanted them. The arterial line gave us continuous arterial blood-pressure measurements, and we tweaked his medications to get the pressures we liked. We regulated his intravenous fluids according to venous-pressure measurements from his jugular line. We plugged his subclavian line into tubing from a dialysis machine, and every few minutes his entire blood volume washed through this artificial kidney and back into his body; a little adjustment here and there, and we could alter the levels of potassium and bicarbonate and salt in his body as well. He was, we liked to imagine, a simple machine in our hands.

But he wasn't, of course. It was as if we had gained a steering wheel and a few gauges and controls, but on a runaway eighteen-wheeler hurtling down a mountain. Keeping his blood pressure normal was requiring gallons of intravenous fluid and a pharmacy shelf of drugs. He was on near-maximal ventilator support. His temperature climbed to 104 degrees. Less than 5 percent of patients with his degree of organ failure make it home. And a single misstep could easily erase those slender chances.

For ten days, though, all went well. His chief problem had been liver   20
damage from the operation he'd had. The main duct from his liver was severed and was leaking bile, which is caustic — it digests the fat in one's diet and was essentially eating him alive from the inside. He had become too sick to survive an operation to repair the leak. So we tried a temporary solution — we had radiologists place a plastic drain, using X-ray guidance, through his abdominal wall and into the severed duct in order to draw the leaking bile out of him. They found so much that they had to place three drains — one inside the duct and two around it. But, as the bile drained out, his fevers subsided. His requirements for oxygen and fluids diminished. His blood pressure returned to normal. He was on the mend. Then, on the eleventh day, just as we were getting ready to take him off the mechanical ventilator, he developed high, spiking fevers, his blood pressure sank, and his blood-oxygen levels plummeted again. His skin became clammy. He got shaking chills.

We didn't understand what had happened. He seemed to have developed an infection, but our X-rays and CT scans failed to turn up a source. Even after we put him on four antibiotics, he continued to spike fevers. During one fever, his heart went into fibrillation. A Code Blue was called. A dozen nurses and doctors raced to his bedside, slapped electric paddles onto his chest, and shocked him. His heart responded, fortunately, and went back into rhythm. It took two more days for us to figure out what had gone wrong. We considered the possibility that one of his lines had become infected, so we put in new lines and sent the old ones to the lab for culturing. Forty-eight hours later, the results returned: *all* of them were infected. The infection had probably started in one line, perhaps contaminated during insertion, and spread through his bloodstream to the others. Then they all began spilling bacteria into him, producing his fevers and steep decline.

This is the reality of intensive care: at any point, we are as apt to harm as we are to heal. Line infections are so common that they are considered a routine complication. ICUs put five million lines into patients each year, and national statistics show that, after ten days, 4 percent of those lines become infected. Line infections occur in eighty thousand people a year in the United States, and are fatal between 5 and 28 percent of the time, depending on how sick one is at the start. Those who survive line infections spend on average a week longer in intensive care. And this is just one of many risks. After ten days with a urinary catheter, 4 percent of American ICU patients develop a bladder infection. After ten days on a ventilator, 6 percent develop bacterial pneumonia, resulting in death 40 to 55 percent of the time. All in all, about half of ICU patients end up experiencing a serious complication, and, once a complication occurs, the chances of survival drop sharply.

It was a week before DeFilippo recovered sufficiently from his infections to come off the ventilator, and it was two months before he left the hospital. Weak and debilitated, he lost his limousine business and his home, and he had to move in with his sister. The tube draining bile still dangled from his abdomen; when he was stronger, I was going to have to do surgery to reconstruct the main bile duct from his liver. But he survived. Most people in his situation do not.

Here, then, is the puzzle of ICU care: you have a desperately sick patient, and in order to have a chance of saving him you have to make sure that 178 daily tasks are done right — despite some monitor's alarm going off for God knows what reason, despite the patient in the next bed crashing, despite a nurse poking his head around the curtain to ask whether someone could help "get this lady's chest open." So how do you actually manage all this complexity? The solution that the medical profession has favored is specialization.

I tell DeFilippo's story, for instance, as if I were the one tending to him hour by hour. But that was actually Max Weinmann, an intensivist (as intensive-care specialists like to be called). I want to think that, as a general surgeon, I can handle most clinical situations. But, as the intricacies involved in intensive care have mounted, responsibility has increasingly shifted to super-specialists like him. In the past decade, training programs focussed on critical care have opened in every major American city, and half of ICUs now rely on super-specialists. 25

Expertise is the mantra of modern medicine. In the early twentieth century, you needed only a high-school diploma and a one-year medical degree to practice medicine. By the century's end, all doctors had to have a college degree, a four-year medical degree, and an additional three to seven years of residency training in an individual field of practice — pediatrics, surgery, neurology, or the like. Already, though, this level of preparation has seemed inadequate to the new complexity of medicine. After their residencies, most young doctors today are going on to do fellowships, adding one to three further years of training in, say, laparoscopic surgery, or pediatric metabolic disorders, or breast radiology — or critical care. A young doctor is not so young nowadays; you typically don't start in independent practice until your mid-thirties.

We now live in the era of the super-specialist — of clinicians who have taken the time to practice at one narrow thing until they can do it better than anyone who hasn't. Super-specialists have two advantages over ordinary specialists: greater knowledge of the details that matter and an ability to handle the complexities of the job. There are degrees of complexity, though, and intensive-care medicine has grown so far beyond ordinary complexity that avoiding daily mistakes is proving impossible even for our super-specialists. The ICU, with its spectacular successes and frequent failures, therefore poses a distinctive challenge: what do you do when expertise is not enough?

On October 30, 1935, at Wright Air Field in Dayton, Ohio, the U.S. Army Air Corps held a flight competition for airplane manufacturers vying to build its next-generation long-range bomber. It wasn't supposed to be much of a competition. In early evaluations, the Boeing Corporation's gleaming aluminum-alloy Model 299 had trounced the designs of Martin and Douglas. Boeing's plane could carry five times as many bombs as the Army had requested; it could fly faster than previous bombers, and almost twice as far. A Seattle newspaperman who had glimpsed the plane called it the "flying fortress," and the name stuck. The flight "competition," according to the military historian Phillip Meilinger, was regarded as a mere formality. The Army planned to order at least sixty-five of the aircraft.

A small crowd of Army brass and manufacturing executives watched as the Model 299 test plane taxied onto the runway. It was sleek and impressive, with a 103-foot wingspan and four engines jutting out from the wings, rather than the usual two. The plane roared down the tarmac, lifted off smoothly, and climbed sharply to three hundred feet. Then it stalled, turned on one wing, and crashed in a fiery explosion. Two of the five crew members died, including the pilot, Major Ployer P. Hill.

An investigation revealed that nothing mechanical had gone wrong.   30
The crash had been due to "pilot error," the report said. Substantially more complex than previous aircraft, the new plane required the pilot to attend to the four engines, a retractable landing gear, new wing flaps, electric trim tabs that needed adjustment to maintain control at different airspeeds, and constant-speed propellers whose pitch had to be regulated with hydraulic controls, among other features. While doing all this, Hill had forgotten to release a new locking mechanism on the elevator and rudder controls. The Boeing model was deemed, as a newspaper put it, "too much airplane for one man to fly." The Army Air Corps declared Douglas's smaller design the winner. Boeing nearly went bankrupt.

Still, the Army purchased a few aircraft from Boeing as test planes, and some insiders remained convinced that the aircraft was flyable. So a group of test pilots got together and considered what to do.

They could have required Model 299 pilots to undergo more training. But it was hard to imagine having more experience and expertise than Major Hill, who had been the U.S. Army Air Corps' chief of flight testing. Instead, they came up with an ingeniously simple approach: they created a pilot's checklist, with step-by-step checks for takeoff, flight, landing, and taxiing. Its mere existence indicated how far aeronautics had advanced. In the early years of flight, getting an aircraft into the air might have been nerve-racking, but it was hardly complex. Using a checklist for takeoff would no more have occurred to a pilot than to a driver backing a car out of the garage. But this new plane was too complicated to be left to the memory of any pilot, however expert.

With the checklist in hand, the pilots went on to fly the Model 299 a total of 1.8 million miles without one accident. The Army ultimately ordered almost thirteen thousand of the aircraft, which it dubbed the B-17. And, because flying the behemoth was now possible, the Army gained a decisive air advantage in the Second World War which enabled its devastating bombing campaign across Nazi Germany.

Medicine today has entered its B-17 phase. Substantial parts of what hospitals do — most notably, intensive care — are now too complex for clinicians to carry them out reliably from memory alone. ICU life support has become too much medicine for one person to fly.

Yet it's far from obvious that something as simple as a checklist could   35
be of much help in medical care. Sick people are phenomenally more various than airplanes. A study of forty-one thousand trauma patients — just trauma patients — found that they had 1,224 different injury-related diagnoses in 32,261 unique combinations for teams to attend to. That's like having 32,261 kinds of airplane to land. Mapping out the proper steps for each is not possible, and physicians have been skeptical that a piece of paper with a bunch of little boxes would improve matters much.

In 2001, though, a critical-care specialist at Johns Hopkins Hospital named Peter Pronovost decided to give it a try. He didn't attempt to make the checklist cover everything; he designed it to tackle just one problem, the one that nearly killed Anthony DeFilippo: line infections. On a sheet of plain paper, he plotted out the steps to take in order to avoid infections when putting a line in. Doctors are supposed to (1) wash their hands with soap, (2) clean the patient's skin with chlorhexidine antiseptic, (3) put sterile drapes over the entire patient, (4) wear a sterile mask, hat, gown, and gloves, and (5) put a sterile dressing over the catheter site once the line is in. Check, check, check, check, check. These steps are no-brainers; they have been known and taught for years. So it seemed silly to make a checklist just for them. Still, Pronovost asked the nurses in his ICU to observe the doctors for a month as they put lines into patients, and record how often they completed each step. In more than a third of patients, they skipped at least one.

The next month, he and his team persuaded the hospital administration to authorize nurses to stop doctors if they saw them skipping a step on the checklist; nurses were also to ask them each day whether any lines ought to be removed, so as not to leave them in longer than necessary. This was revolutionary. Nurses have always had their ways of nudging a doctor into doing the right thing, ranging from the gentle reminder ("Um, did you forget to put on your mask, doctor?") to more forceful methods (I've had a nurse bodycheck me when she thought I hadn't put enough drapes on a patient). But many nurses aren't sure whether this is their place, or whether a given step is worth a confrontation. (Does it really matter whether a patient's legs are draped for a line going into the chest?) The new rule made it clear: if doctors didn't follow every step on the checklist, the nurses would have backup from the administration to intervene.

Pronovost and his colleagues monitored what happened for a year afterward. The results were so dramatic that they weren't sure whether to believe them: the ten-day line-infection rate went from 11 percent to zero. So they followed patients for fifteen more months. Only two line infections occurred during the entire period. They calculated that, in this one hospital, the checklist had prevented forty-three infections and eight deaths, and saved two million dollars in costs.

Pronovost recruited some more colleagues, and they made some more checklists. One aimed to ensure that nurses observe patients for pain at least once every four hours and provide timely pain medication. This reduced the likelihood of a patient's experiencing untreated pain from 41 percent to 3 percent. They tested a checklist for patients on mechanical ventilation, making sure that, for instance, the head of each patient's bed was propped up at least thirty degrees so that oral secretions couldn't go into the windpipe, and antacid medication was given to prevent stomach ulcers. The proportion of patients who didn't receive the recommended care dropped from 70 percent to 4 percent; the occurrence of pneumonias fell by a quarter; and twenty-one fewer patients died than in the previous year. The researchers found that simply having the doctors and nurses in the ICU make their own checklists for what they thought should be done each day improved the consistency of care to the point that, within a few weeks, the average length of patient stay in intensive care dropped by half.

The checklists provided two main benefits, Pronovost observed. First,   40
they helped with memory recall, especially with mundane matters that are easily overlooked in patients undergoing more drastic events. (When you're worrying about what treatment to give a woman who won't stop seizing, it's hard to remember to make sure that the head of her bed is in the right position.) A second effect was to make explicit the minimum, expected steps in complex processes. Pronovost was surprised to discover how often even experienced personnel failed to grasp the importance of certain precautions. In a survey of ICU staff taken before introducing the ventilator checklists, he found that half hadn't realized that there was evidence strongly supporting giving ventilated patients antacid medication. Checklists established a higher standard of baseline performance.

These are, of course, ridiculously primitive insights. Pronovost is routinely described by colleagues as "brilliant," "inspiring," a "genius." He has an MD and a PhD in public health from Johns Hopkins, and is trained in emergency medicine, anesthesiology, and critical-care medicine. But, really, does it take all that to figure out what house movers, wedding planners, and tax accountants figured out ages ago?

Pronovost is hardly the first person in medicine to use a checklist. But he is among the first to recognize its power to save lives and take advantage of the breadth of its possibilities. Forty-two years old, with cropped light-brown hair, tenth-grader looks, and a fluttering, finchlike energy, he is an odd mixture of the nerdy and the messianic. He grew up in Waterbury, Connecticut, the son of an elementary-school teacher and a math professor, went to nearby Fairfield University, and, like many good students, decided that he would go into medicine. Unlike many students, though, he found that he actually liked caring for sick people. He hated the laboratory — with all those micropipettes and cell cultures, and no patients around — but he had that scientific "How can I solve this unsolved problem?" turn of mind. So after his residency in anesthesiology and his fellowship in critical care, he studied clinical-research methods.

For his doctoral thesis, he examined intensive-care units in Maryland, and he discovered that putting an intensivist on staff reduced death rates by a third. It was the first time that someone had demonstrated the public-health value of using intensivists. He wasn't satisfied with having proved his case, though; he wanted hospitals to change accordingly. After his study was published, in 1999, he met with a coalition of large employers known as the Leapfrog Group. It included companies like General Motors and Verizon, which were seeking to improve the standards of hospitals where their employees obtain care. Within weeks, the coalition announced that its members expected the hospitals they contracted with to staff their ICUs with intensivists. These employers pay for health care for thirty-seven million employees, retirees, and dependents nationwide. So although hospitals protested that there weren't enough intensivists to go around, and that the cost could be prohibitive, Pronovost's idea effectively became an instant national standard.

The scientist in him has always made room for the campaigner. People say he is the kind of guy who, even as a trainee, could make you feel you'd saved the world every time you washed your hands properly. "I've never seen anybody inspire as he does," Marty Makary, a Johns Hopkins surgeon, told me. "Partly, he has this contagious, excitable nature. He has a smile that's tough to match. But he also has a way of making people feel heard. People will come to him with the dumbest ideas, and he'll endorse them anyway. 'Oh, I like that, I like that, I like that!' he'll say. I've watched him, and I still have no idea how deliberate this is. Maybe he really does like every idea. But wait, and you realize: he only acts on the ones he truly believes in."

After the checklist results, the idea Pronovost truly believed in was that   45
checklists could save enormous numbers of lives. He took his findings on the
road, showing his checklists to doctors, nurses, insurers, employers — anyone who would listen. He spoke in an average of seven cities a month while
continuing to work full time in Johns Hopkins's ICUs. But this time he found
few takers.

There were various reasons. Some physicians were offended by the suggestion that they needed checklists. Others had legitimate doubts about
Pronovost's evidence. So far, he'd shown only that checklists worked in
one hospital, Johns Hopkins, where the ICUs have money, plenty of staff,
and Peter Pronovost walking the hallways to make sure that the checklists
are being used properly. How about in the real world — where ICU nurses
and doctors are in short supply, pressed for time, overwhelmed with
patients, and hardly receptive to the idea of filling out yet another piece
of paper?

In 2003, however, the Michigan Health and Hospital Association asked
Pronovost to try out three of his checklists in Michigan's ICUs. It would be
a huge undertaking. Not only would he have to get the state's hospitals to
use the checklists; he would also have to measure whether doing so made a
genuine difference. But at last Pronovost had a chance to establish whether
his checklist idea really worked.

This past summer, I visited Sinai-Grace Hospital, in inner-city Detroit,
and saw what Pronovost was up against. Occupying a campus of red brick
buildings amid abandoned houses, check-cashing stores, and wig shops on
the city's West Side, just south of 8 Mile Road, Sinai-Grace is a classic urban
hospital. It has eight hundred physicians, seven hundred nurses, and two
thousand other medical personnel to care for a population with the lowest
median income of any city in the country. More than a quarter of a million
residents are uninsured; three hundred thousand are on state assistance.
That has meant chronic financial problems. Sinai-Grace is not the most
cash-strapped hospital in the city — that would be Detroit Receiving Hospital, where a fifth of the patients have no means of payment. But between
2000 and 2003 Sinai-Grace and eight other Detroit hospitals were forced to
cut a third of their staff, and the state had to come forward with a fifty-
million-dollar bailout to avert their bankruptcy.

Sinai-Grace has five ICUs for adult patients and one for infants. Hassan
Makki, the director of intensive care, told me what it was like there in 2004,
when Pronovost and the hospital association started a series of mailings and
conference calls with hospitals to introduce checklists for central lines and
ventilator patients. "Morale was low," he said. "We had lost lots of staff,
and the nurses who remained weren't sure if they were staying." Many doctors were thinking about leaving, too. Meanwhile, the teams faced an even
heavier workload because of new rules limiting how long the residents could
work at a stretch. Now Pronovost was telling them to find the time to fill out
some daily checklists?

Tom Piskorowski, one of the ICU physicians, told me his reaction: 50
"Forget the paperwork. Take care of the patient."

I accompanied a team on 7 a.m. rounds through one of the surgical
ICUs. It had eleven patients. Four had gunshot wounds (one had been shot
in the chest; one had been shot through the bowel, kidney, and liver; two
had been shot through the neck, and left quadriplegic). Five patients had
cerebral hemorrhaging (three were seventy-nine years and older and had
been injured falling down stairs; one was a middle-aged man whose skull
and left temporal lobe had been damaged by an assault with a blunt
weapon; and one was a worker who had become paralyzed from the neck
down after falling twenty-five feet off a ladder onto his head). There was a
cancer patient recovering from surgery to remove part of his lung, and a patient who had had surgery to repair a cerebral aneurysm.

The doctors and nurses on rounds tried to proceed methodically from
one room to the next but were constantly interrupted: a patient they
thought they'd stabilized began hemorrhaging again; another who had been
taken off the ventilator developed trouble breathing and had to be put back
on the machine. It was hard to imagine that they could get their heads far
enough above the daily tide of disasters to worry about the minutiae on
some checklist.

Yet there they were, I discovered, filling out those pages. Mostly, it was
the nurses who kept things in order. Each morning, a senior nurse walked
through the unit, clipboard in hand, making sure that every patient on a
ventilator had the bed propped at the right angle, and had been given the
right medicines and the right tests. Whenever doctors put in a central line, a
nurse made sure that the central-line checklist had been filled out and placed
in the patient's chart. Looking back through their files, I found that they had
been doing this faithfully for more than three years.

Pronovost had been canny when he started. In his first conversations
with hospital administrators, he didn't order them to use the checklists. Instead, he asked them simply to gather data on their own infection rates. In
early 2004, they found, the infection rates for ICU patients in Michigan hospitals were higher than the national average, and in some hospitals dramatically so. Sinai-Grace experienced more line infections than 75 percent of
American hospitals. Meanwhile, Blue Cross Blue Shield of Michigan agreed
to give hospitals small bonus payments for participating in Pronovost's program. A checklist suddenly seemed an easy and logical thing to try.

In what became known as the Keystone Initiative, each hospital as- 55
signed a project manager to roll out the checklists and participate in a twice-
monthly conference call with Pronovost for trouble-shooting. Pronovost
also insisted that each participating hospital assign to each unit a senior hospital executive, who would visit the unit at least once a month, hear people's
complaints, and help them solve problems.

The executives were reluctant. They normally lived in meetings worrying about strategy and budgets. They weren't used to venturing into patient

territory and didn't feel that they belonged there. In some places, they encountered hostility. But their involvement proved crucial. In the first month, according to Christine Goeschel, at the time the Keystone Initiative's director, the executives discovered that the chlorhexidine soap, shown to reduce line infections, was available in fewer than a third of the ICUs. This was a problem only an executive could solve. Within weeks, every ICU in Michigan had a supply of the soap. Teams also complained to the hospital officials that the checklist required that patients be fully covered with a sterile drape when lines were being put in, but full-size barrier drapes were often unavailable. So the officials made sure that the drapes were stocked. Then they persuaded Arrow International, one of the largest manufacturers of central lines, to produce a new central-line kit that had both the drape and chlorhexidine in it.

In December, 2006, the Keystone Initiative published its findings in a landmark article in the *New England Journal of Medicine*. Within the first three months of the project, the infection rate in Michigan's ICUs decreased by 66 percent. The typical ICU — including the ones at Sinai-Grace Hospital — cut its quarterly infection rate to zero. Michigan's infection rates fell so low that its average ICU outperformed 90 percent of ICUs nationwide. In the Keystone Initiative's first eighteen months, the hospitals saved an estimated $175 million in costs and more than fifteen hundred lives. The successes have been sustained for almost four years — all because of a stupid little checklist.

Pronovost's results have not been ignored. He has since had requests to help Rhode Island, New Jersey, and the country of Spain do what Michigan did. Back in the Wolverine State, he and the Keystone Initiative have begun testing half a dozen additional checklists to improve care for ICU patients. He has also been asked to develop a program for surgery patients. It has all become more than he and his small group of researchers can keep up with.

But consider: there are hundreds, perhaps thousands, of things doctors do that are at least as dangerous and prone to human failure as putting central lines into ICU patients. It's true of cardiac care, stroke treatment, HIV treatment, and surgery of all kinds. It's also true of diagnosis, whether one is trying to identify cancer or infection or a heart attack. All have steps that are worth putting on a checklist and testing in routine care. The question — still unanswered — is whether medical culture will embrace the opportunity.

Tom Wolfe's *The Right Stuff* tells the story of our first astronauts, and   60
charts the demise of the maverick, Chuck Yeager test-pilot culture of the 1950s. It was a culture defined by how unbelievably dangerous the job was. Test pilots strapped themselves into machines of barely controlled power and complexity, and a quarter of them were killed on the job. The pilots had to have focus, daring, wits, and an ability to improvise — the right stuff. But as knowledge of how to control the risks of flying accumulated — as checklists and flight simulators became more prevalent and sophisticated — the

danger diminished, values of safety and conscientiousness prevailed, and the rock-star status of the test pilots was gone.

Something like this is going on in medicine. We have the means to make some of the most complex and dangerous work we do — in surgery, emergency care, and ICU medicine — more effective than we ever thought possible. But the prospect pushes against the traditional culture of medicine, with its central belief that in situations of high risk and complexity what you want is a kind of expert audacity — the right stuff, again. Checklists and standard operating procedures feel like exactly the opposite, and that's what rankles many people.

It's ludicrous, though, to suppose that checklists are going to do away with the need for courage, wits, and improvisation. The body is too intricate and individual for that: good medicine will not be able to dispense with expert audacity. Yet it should also be ready to accept the virtues of regimentation.

The still limited response to Pronovost's work may be easy to explain, but it is hard to justify. If someone found a new drug that could wipe out infections with anything remotely like the effectiveness of Pronovost's lists, there would be television ads with Robert Jarvik extolling its virtues, detail men offering free lunches to get doctors to make it part of their practice, government programs to research it, and competitors jumping in to make a newer, better version. That's what happened when manufacturers marketed central-line catheters coated with silver or other antimicrobials; they cost a third more, and reduced infections only slightly — and hospitals have spent tens of millions of dollars on them. But, with the checklist, what we have is Peter Pronovost trying to see if maybe, in the next year or two, hospitals in Rhode Island and New Jersey will give his idea a try.

Pronovost remains, in a way, an odd bird in medical research. He does not have the multimillion-dollar grants that his colleagues in bench science have. He has no swarm of doctoral students and lab animals. He's focussed on work that is not normally considered a significant contribution in academic medicine. As a result, few other researchers are venturing to extend his achievements. Yet his work has already saved more lives than that of any laboratory scientist in the past decade.

I called Pronovost recently at Johns Hopkins, where he was on duty in 65 an ICU. I asked him how long it would be before the average doctor or nurse is as apt to have a checklist in hand as a stethoscope (which, unlike checklists, has never been proved to make a difference to patient care).

"At the current rate, it will never happen," he said, as monitors beeped in the background. "The fundamental problem with the quality of American medicine is that we've failed to view delivery of health care as a science. The tasks of medical science fall into three buckets. One is understanding disease biology. One is finding effective therapies. And one is ensuring those therapies are delivered effectively. That third bucket has been almost totally ignored by research funders, government, and academia. It's viewed as the art of medicine. That's a mistake, a huge mistake. And from a taxpayer's perspective it's outrageous." We have a thirty-billion-dollar-a-year National Institutes of Health, he pointed out, which has been a remarkable power-house of discovery. But we have no billion-dollar National Institute of Health Care Delivery studying how best to incorporate those discoveries into daily practice.

I asked him how much it would cost for him to do for the whole country what he did for Michigan. About two million dollars, he said, maybe three, mostly for the technical work of signing up hospitals to participate state by state and coordinating a database to track the results. He's already devised a plan to do it in all of Spain for less.

"We could get ICU checklists in use throughout the United States within two years, if the country wanted it," he said.

So far, it seems, we don't. The United States could have been the first to adopt medical checklists nationwide, but, instead, Spain will beat us. "I at least hope we're not the last," Pronovost said.

Recently, I spoke to Markus Thalmann, the cardiac surgeon on the team   70
that saved the little Austrian girl who had drowned, and learned that a checklist had been crucial to her survival. Thalmann had worked for six years at the city hospital in Klagenfurt, the small provincial capital in south Austria where the girl was resuscitated. She was not the first person whom he and his colleagues had tried to revive from cardiac arrest after hypother-mia and suffocation. They received between three and five such patients a year, he estimated, mostly avalanche victims (Klagenfurt is surrounded by the Alps), some of them drowning victims, and a few of them people at-tempting suicide by taking a drug overdose and then wandering out into the snowy forests to fall unconscious.

For a long time, he said, no matter how hard the medical team tried, it had no survivors. Most of the victims had gone without a pulse and oxygen for too long by the time they were found. But some, he felt, still had a flicker of viability in them, and each time the team failed to sustain it.

Speed was the chief difficulty. Success required having an array of equipment and people at the ready — helicopter-rescue personnel, trauma surgeons, an experienced cardiac anesthesiologist and surgeon, bioengineer-ing support staff, operating and critical-care nurses, intensivists. Too often, someone or something was missing. So he and a couple of colleagues made and distributed a checklist. In cases like these, the checklist said, rescue teams were to tell the hospital to prepare for possible cardiac bypass and re-warming. They were to call, when possible, even before they arrived on the scene, as the preparation time could be significant. The hospital would then work down a list of people to be notified. They would have an operating room set up and standing by.

The team had its first success with the checklist in place — the rescue of the three-year-old girl. Not long afterward, Thalmann left to take a job at a hospital in Vienna. The team, however, was able to make at least two other such rescues, he said. In one case, a man was found frozen and pulseless after a suicide attempt. In another, a mother and her sixteen-year-old daughter were in an accident that sent them and their car through a guardrail, over a cliff, and into a mountain river. The mother died on impact; the daughter was trapped as the car rapidly filled with icy water. She had been in cardiac and respiratory arrest for a prolonged period of time when the rescue team arrived.

From that point onward, though, the system went like clockwork. By the time the rescue team got to her and began CPR, the hospital had been notified. The transport team got her there in minutes. The surgical team took her straight to the operating room and crashed her onto heart-lung bypass. One step went right after another. And, because of the speed with which they did, she had a chance.

As the girl's body slowly rewarmed, her heart came back. In the ICU, a mechanical ventilator, fluids, and intravenous drugs kept her going while the rest of her body recovered. The next day, the doctors were able to remove her lines and tubes. The day after that, she was sitting up in bed, ready to go home. 75

QUESTIONS

Reading

1. What is a "super-specialist"? What advantages do they have over ordinary specialists?
2. How does Gawande characterize the role of nurses?
3. Although Gawande clearly supports Pronovost's checklist protocol, he discusses several reasons that some medical professionals have resisted it. List all of the pros and cons of using the checklist system that arise in Gawande's article. Include Gawande's own opinion, as well as points with which he clearly disagrees.

CHECKLIST PROS	CHECKLIST CONS

Exploratory Writing

1. Collaborate in small groups to create a checklist for making a checklist. That is, consider all of the steps required to assess *any* complicated situation, to gather materials and information about it, and to organize the steps in the most comprehensive and accurate way possible.

2. What is the most *complicated* thing you've ever done? Describe your experience. How would a checklist have helped you?
3. In your own words, summarize what Peter Pronovost says is the fundamental problem with the quality of American medicine. As a taxpayer (or future taxpayer), do you agree or disagree? Write a statement arguing your case.

Making Connections

1. Consider Jonah Lehrer's discussion (p. 398) of how "breakthrough thinking" occurs. In what ways could using checklists help foster inspiration and "Eureka!" moments? In what ways might checklists interfere with breakthrough thinking?
2. Several of the authors in this book, including Lewis Thomas (p. 339), Richard Seltzer (p. 443), Abraham Verghese (p. 455), and Oliver Sacks (p. 680), are medical doctors as well as writers. Choose one of them, and describe very specifically how a checklist could help him in the work he discusses in his essay.

Essay Writing

1. Find an article other than Gawande's that discusses Peter Pronovost's checklist protocol. Write an essay comparing and contrasting the two articles. Identify and quote places where you find the authors reflecting, reporting, explaining, or arguing. Does each author use each mode of writing? How does each author characterize Pronovost? Discuss each author's motives and perspective.

The Moral Instinct

Steven Pinker

A cognitive scientist, psychologist, linguist, and scholar, Steven Pinker (b. 1954) has been variously described as the "bad boy" of language, an "agent provocateur" of science, a "wunderkind," and an "evolutionary pop star." He earned these labels as much from his best-selling books and articles in the mainstream press as from his many — and masterful — scholarly works. His books in-clude The Language Instinct *(1994), which argues that language is a biological adaptation;* How the Mind Works *(1997), which in-cludes the rest of the mind — "from vision and reasoning to the emotions, humor, and art" — in his synthesis; and* The Blank Slate: The Modern Denial of Human Nature *(2002), which ex-plores the political, moral, and emotional aspects of human na-ture. His latest book is* The Stuff of Thought: Language as a Window into Human Nature *(2007). Pinker — currently a profes-sor in the department of psychology at Harvard University — was, until 2003, director of the Center for Cognitive Neuroscience at the Massachusetts Institute of Technology (MIT), where he spe-cialized in psycholinguistics — particularly language development in children. Born in Montreal, Canada, he earned a degree in ex-perimental psychology at McGill University, then went to the United States in 1976 to do his graduate work at Harvard fol-lowed by a postdoctoral fellowship at MIT. He became a natural-ized U.S. citizen in 1980. His essay, "The Moral Instinct," appeared in the* New York Times Magazine *in January 2008.*

Which of the following people would you say is the most admirable: Mother Teresa, Bill Gates or Norman Borlaug? And which do you think is the least admirable? For most people, it's an easy question. Mother Teresa, famous for ministering to the poor in Calcutta, has been beatified by the Vatican, awarded the Nobel Peace Prize and ranked in an American poll as the most admired person of the twentieth century. Bill Gates, infamous for giving us the Microsoft dancing paper clip and the blue screen of death, has been decapitated in effigy in "I Hate Gates" Web sites and hit with a pie in the face. As for Norman Borlaug . . . who the heck is Norman Borlaug?

Yet a deeper look might lead you to rethink your answers. Borlaug, father of the "Green Revolution" that used agricultural science to reduce world hunger, has been credited with saving a billion lives, more than anyone else in history. Gates, in deciding what to do with his fortune, crunched the numbers and determined that he could alleviate the most misery by fighting everyday scourges in the developing world like malaria, diarrhea and parasites. Mother Teresa, for her part, extolled the virtue of suffering and ran her well-financed missions accordingly: their sick patrons were offered plenty of prayer but harsh conditions, few analgesics and dangerously primitive medical care.

It's not hard to see why the moral reputations of this trio should be so out of line with the good they have done. Mother Teresa was the very embodiment of saintliness: white-clad, sad-eyed, ascetic and often photographed with the wretched of the earth. Gates is a nerd's nerd and the world's richest man, as likely to enter heaven as the proverbial camel squeezing through the needle's eye. And Borlaug, now ninety-three, is an agronomist who has spent his life in labs and nonprofits, seldom walking onto the media stage, and hence into our consciousness, at all.

I doubt these examples will persuade anyone to favor Bill Gates over Mother Teresa for sainthood. But they show that our heads can be turned by an aura of sanctity, distracting us from a more objective reckoning of the actions that make people suffer or flourish. It seems we may all be vulnerable to moral illusions, the ethical equivalent of the bending lines that trick the eye on cereal boxes and in psychology textbooks. Illusions are a favorite tool of perception scientists for exposing the workings of the five senses, and of philosophers for shaking people out of the naive belief that our minds give us a transparent window onto the world (since if our eyes can be fooled by an illusion, why should we trust them at other times?). Today, a new field is using illusions to unmask a sixth sense, the moral sense. Moral intuitions are being drawn out of people in the lab, on Web sites and in brain scanners, and are being explained with tools from game theory, neuroscience and evolutionary biology.

"Two things fill the mind with ever new and increasing admiration and   5
awe, the oftener and more steadily we reflect on them," wrote Immanuel Kant, "the starry heavens above and the moral law within." These days, the moral law within is being viewed with increasing awe, if not always admiration. The human moral sense turns out to be an organ of considerable complexity, with quirks that reflect its evolutionary history and its neurobiological foundations.

These quirks are bound to have implications for the human predicament. Morality is not just any old topic in psychology but close to our conception of the meaning of life. Moral goodness is what gives each of us the sense that we are worthy human beings. We seek it in our friends and mates, nurture it in our children, advance it in our politics and justify it with our religions. A disrespect for morality is blamed for everyday sins and history's worst atrocities. To carry this weight, the concept of morality would have to be bigger than any of us and outside all of us.

So dissecting moral intuitions is no small matter. If morality is a mere trick of the brain, some may fear, our very grounds for being moral could be eroded. Yet as we shall see, the science of the moral sense can instead be seen as a way to strengthen those grounds, by clarifying what morality is and how it should steer our actions.

The Moralization Switch

The starting point for appreciating that there *is* a distinctive part of our psychology for morality is seeing how moral judgments differ from other kinds of opinions we have on how people ought to behave. Moralization is a psychological state that can be turned on and off like a switch, and when it is on, a distinctive mind-set commandeers our thinking. This is the mind-set that makes us deem actions immoral ("killing is wrong"), rather than merely disagreeable ("I hate brussels sprouts"), unfashionable ("bell-bottoms are out") or imprudent ("don't scratch mosquito bites").

The first hallmark of moralization is that the rules it invokes are felt to be universal. Prohibitions of rape and murder, for example, are felt not to be matters of local custom but to be universally and objectively warranted. One can easily say, "I don't like brussels sprouts, but I don't care if you eat them," but no one would say, "I don't like killing, but I don't care if you murder someone."

The other hallmark is that people feel that those who commit immoral 10
acts deserve to be punished. Not only is it allowable to inflict pain on a person who has broken a moral rule; it is wrong *not* to, to "let them get away with it." People are thus untroubled in inviting divine retribution or the power of the state to harm other people they deem immoral. Bertrand Russell wrote, "The infliction of cruelty with a good conscience is a delight to moralists — that is why they invented hell."

We all know what it feels like when the moralization switch flips inside us — the righteous glow, the burning dudgeon, the drive to recruit others to the cause. The psychologist Paul Rozin has studied the toggle switch by comparing two kinds of people who engage in the same behavior but with different switch settings. Health vegetarians avoid meat for practical reasons, like lowering cholesterol and avoiding toxins. Moral vegetarians avoid meat for ethical reasons: to avoid complicity in the suffering of animals. By investigating their feelings about meat-eating, Rozin showed that the moral motive sets off a cascade of opinions. Moral vegetarians are more likely to treat meat as a contaminant — they refuse, for example, to eat a bowl of soup into which a drop of beef broth has fallen. They are more likely to think that other people ought to be vegetarians, and are more likely to imbue their dietary habits with other virtues, like believing that meat avoidance makes people less aggressive and bestial.

Much of our recent social history, including the culture wars between liberals and conservatives, consists of the moralization or amoralization of particular kinds of behavior. Even when people agree that an outcome is desirable, they may disagree on whether it should be treated as a matter of preference and prudence or as a matter of sin and virtue. Rozin notes, for example, that smoking has lately been moralized. Until recently, it was understood that some people didn't enjoy smoking or avoided it because it was hazardous to their health. But with the discovery of the harmful effects of secondhand smoke, smoking is now treated as immoral. Smokers are ostracized; images of people smoking are censored; and entities touched by smoke are felt to be contaminated (so hotels have not only nonsmoking rooms but nonsmoking *floors*). The desire for retribution has been visited on tobacco companies, who have been slapped with staggering "punitive damages."

At the same time, many behaviors have been amoralized, switched from moral failings to lifestyle choices. They include divorce, illegitimacy, being a working mother, marijuana use and homosexuality. Many afflictions have been reassigned from payback for bad choices to unlucky misfortunes. There used to be people called "bums" and "tramps"; today they are "homeless." Drug addiction is a "disease"; syphilis was rebranded from the price of wanton behavior to a "sexually transmitted disease" and more recently a "sexually transmitted infection."

This wave of amoralization has led the cultural right to lament that morality itself is under assault, as we see in the group that anointed itself the Moral Majority. In fact there seems to be a Law of Conservation of Moralization, so that as old behaviors are taken out of the moralized column, new ones are added to it. Dozens of things that past generations treated as practical matters are now ethical battlegrounds, including disposable diapers, IQ tests, poultry farms, Barbie dolls and research on breast cancer. Food alone has become a minefield, with critics sermonizing about the size of sodas, the chemistry of fat, the freedom of chickens, the price of coffee beans, the species of fish and now the distance the food has traveled from farm to plate.

Many of these moralizations, like the assault on smoking, may be understood as practical tactics to reduce some recently identified harm. But whether an activity flips our mental switches to the "moral" setting isn't just a matter of how much harm it does. We don't show contempt to the man who fails to change the batteries in his smoke alarms or takes his family on a driving vacation, both of which multiply the risk they will die in an accident. Driving a gas-guzzling Hummer is reprehensible, but driving a gas-guzzling old Volvo is not; eating a Big Mac is unconscionable, but not imported cheese or crème brûlée. The reason for these double standards is obvious: people tend to align their moralization with their own lifestyles. 15

Reasoning and Rationalizing

It's not just the content of our moral judgments that is often questionable, but the way we arrive at them. We like to think that when we have a conviction, there are good reasons that drove us to adopt it. That is why an older approach to moral psychology, led by Jean Piaget and Lawrence Kohlberg, tried to document the lines of reasoning that guided people to moral conclusions. But consider these situations, originally devised by the psychologist Jonathan Haidt:

Julie is traveling in France on summer vacation from college with her brother Mark. One night they decide that it would be interesting and fun if they tried making love. Julie was already taking birth-control pills, but Mark uses a condom, too, just to be safe. They both enjoy the sex but decide not to do it again. They keep the night as a special secret, which makes them feel closer to each other. What do you think about that — was it OK for them to make love?

A woman is cleaning out her closet and she finds her old American flag. She doesn't want the flag anymore, so she cuts it up into pieces and uses the rags to clean her bathroom.

A family's dog is killed by a car in front of their house. They heard that dog meat was delicious, so they cut up the dog's body and cook it and eat it for dinner.

Most people immediately declare that these acts are wrong and then grope to justify *why* they are wrong. It's not so easy. In the case of Julie and Mark, people raise the possibility of children with birth defects, but they are reminded that the couple were diligent about contraception. They suggest that the siblings will be emotionally hurt, but the story makes it clear that they weren't. They submit that the act would offend the community, but then recall that it was kept a secret. Eventually many people admit, "I don't know, I can't explain it, I just know it's wrong." People don't generally engage in moral reasoning, Haidt argues, but moral *rationalization*: they begin with the conclusion, coughed up by an unconscious emotion, and then work backward to a plausible justification.

The gap between people's convictions and their justifications is also on display in the favorite new sandbox for moral psychologists, a thought experiment devised by the philosophers Philippa Foot and Judith Jarvis Thomson called the Trolley Problem. On your morning walk, you see a trolley car hurtling down the track, the conductor slumped over the controls. In the path of the trolley are five men working on the track, oblivious to the danger. You are standing at a fork in the track and can pull a lever that will divert the trolley onto a spur, saving the five men. Unfortunately, the trolley would then run over a single worker who is laboring on the spur. Is it permissible to throw the switch, killing one man to save five? Almost everyone says yes.

Consider now a different scene. You are on a bridge overlooking the tracks and have spotted the runaway trolley bearing down on the five workers. Now the only way to stop the trolley is to throw a heavy object in its path. And the only heavy object within reach is a fat man standing next to you. Should you throw the man off the bridge? Both dilemmas present you with the option of sacrificing one life to save five, and so, by the utilitarian standard of what would result in the greatest good for the greatest number, the two dilemmas are morally equivalent. But most people don't see it that way: though they would pull the switch in the first dilemma, they would not heave the fat man in the second. When pressed for a reason, they can't come up with anything coherent, though moral philosophers haven't had an easy time coming up with a relevant difference, either.

When psychologists say "most people" they usually mean "most of the two dozen sophomores who filled out a questionnaire for beer money." But in this case it means most of the 200,000 people from a hundred countries who shared their intuitions on a Web-based experiment conducted by the psychologists Fiery Cushman and Liane Young and the biologist Marc Hauser. A difference between the acceptability of switch-pulling and man-heaving, and an inability to justify the choice, was found in respondents from Europe, Asia, and North and South America; among men and women, blacks and whites, teenagers and octogenarians, Hindus, Muslims, Buddhists, Christians, Jews and atheists; people with elementary-school educations and people with PhDs.

Joshua Greene, a philosopher and cognitive neuroscientist, suggests that evolution equipped people with a revulsion to manhandling an innocent person. This instinct, he suggests, tends to overwhelm any utilitarian calculus that would tot up the lives saved and lost. The impulse against roughing up a fellow human would explain other examples in which people abjure killing one to save many, like euthanizing a hospital patient to harvest his organs and save five dying patients in need of transplants, or throwing someone out of a crowded lifeboat to keep it afloat.

By itself this would be no more than a plausible story, but Greene   25
teamed up with the cognitive neuroscientist Jonathan Cohen and several Princeton colleagues to peer into people's brains using functional MRI. They sought to find signs of a conflict between brain areas associated with emotion (the ones that recoil from harming someone) and areas dedicated to rational analysis (the ones that calculate lives lost and saved).

When people pondered the dilemmas that required killing someone with their bare hands, several networks in their brains lighted up. One, which included the medial (inward-facing) parts of the frontal lobes, has been implicated in emotions about other people. A second, the dorsolateral (upper and outer-facing) surface of the frontal lobes, has been implicated in ongoing mental computation (including nonmoral reasoning, like deciding whether to get somewhere by plane or train). And a third region, the anterior cingulate cortex (an evolutionarily ancient strip lying at the base of the inner surface of each cerebral hemisphere), registers a conflict between an urge coming from one part of the brain and an advisory coming from another.

But when the people were pondering a hands-off dilemma, like switching the trolley onto the spur with the single worker, the brain reacted differently: only the area involved in rational calculation stood out. Other studies have shown that neurological patients who have blunted emotions because of damage to the frontal lobes become utilitarians: they think it makes perfect sense to throw the fat man off the bridge. Together, the findings corroborate Greene's theory that our nonutilitarian intuitions come from the victory of an emotional impulse over a cost-benefit analysis.

A Universal Morality?

The findings of trolleyology — complex, instinctive and worldwide moral intuitions — led Hauser and John Mikhail (a legal scholar) to revive an analogy from the philosopher John Rawls between the moral sense and language. According to Noam Chomsky, we are born with a "universal grammar" that forces us to analyze speech in terms of its grammatical structure, with no conscious awareness of the rules in play. By analogy, we are born with a universal moral grammar that forces us to analyze human action in terms of its moral structure, with just as little awareness.

The idea that the moral sense is an innate part of human nature is not far-fetched. A list of human universals collected by the anthropologist Donald E. Brown includes many moral concepts and emotions, including a distinction between right and wrong; empathy; fairness; admiration of generosity; rights and obligations; proscription of murder, rape and other forms of violence; redress of wrongs; sanctions for wrongs against the community; shame; and taboos.

The stirrings of morality emerge early in childhood. Toddlers spontaneously offer toys and help to others and try to comfort people they see in distress. And according to the psychologists Elliot Turiel and Judith Smetana, preschoolers have an inkling of the difference between societal conventions and moral principles. Four-year-olds say that it is not OK to wear pajamas to school (a convention) and also not OK to hit a little girl for no reason (a moral principle). But when asked whether these actions would be OK if the teacher allowed them, most of the children said that wearing pajamas would now be fine but that hitting a little girl would still not be.

Though no one has identified genes for morality, there is circumstantial evidence they exist. The character traits called "conscientiousness" and "agreeableness" are far more correlated in identical twins separated at birth (who share their genes but not their environment) than in adoptive siblings raised together (who share their environment but not their genes). People given diagnoses of "antisocial personality disorder" or "psychopathy" show signs of morality blindness from the time they are children. They bully younger children, torture animals, habitually lie and seem incapable of empathy or remorse, often despite normal family backgrounds. Some of these children grow up into the monsters who bilk elderly people out of their savings, rape a succession of women or shoot convenience-store clerks lying on the floor during a robbery.

30

Though psychopathy probably comes from a genetic predisposition, a milder version can be caused by damage to frontal regions of the brain (including the areas that inhibit intact people from throwing the hypothetical fat man off the bridge). The neuroscientists Hanna and Antonio Damasio and their colleagues found that some children who sustain severe injuries to their frontal lobes can grow up into callous and irresponsible adults, despite normal intelligence. They lie, steal, ignore punishment, endanger their own children and can't think through even the simplest moral dilemmas, like what two people should do if they disagreed on which TV channel to watch or whether a man ought to steal a drug to save his dying wife.

The moral sense, then, may be rooted in the design of the normal human brain. Yet for all the awe that may fill our minds when we reflect on an innate moral law within, the idea is at best incomplete. Consider this moral dilemma: A runaway trolley is about to kill a schoolteacher. You can divert the trolley onto a sidetrack, but the trolley would trip a switch sending a signal to a class of six-year-olds, giving them permission to name a teddy bear Muhammad. Is it permissible to pull the lever?

This is no joke. Last month a British woman teaching in a private school in Sudan allowed her class to name a teddy bear after the most popular boy in the class, who bore the name of the founder of Islam. She was jailed for blasphemy and threatened with a public flogging, while a mob outside the prison demanded her death. To the protesters, the woman's life clearly had less value than maximizing the dignity of their religion, and their judgment on whether it is right to divert the hypothetical trolley would have differed from ours. Whatever grammar guides people's moral judgments can't be all *that* universal. Anyone who stayed awake through Anthropology 101 can offer many other examples.

Of course, languages vary, too. In Chomsky's theory, languages conform to an abstract blueprint, like having phrases built out of verbs and objects, while the details vary, like whether the verb or the object comes first. Could we be wired with an abstract spec sheet that embraces all the strange ideas that people in different cultures moralize?   35

The Varieties of Moral Experience

When anthropologists like Richard Shweder and Alan Fiske survey moral concerns across the globe, they find that a few themes keep popping up from amid the diversity. People everywhere, at least in some circumstances and with certain other folks in mind, think it's bad to harm others and good to help them. They have a sense of fairness: that one should reciprocate favors, reward benefactors and punish cheaters. They value loyalty to a group, sharing and solidarity among its members and conformity to its norms. They believe that it is right to defer to legitimate authorities and to respect people with high status. And they exalt purity, cleanliness and sanctity while loathing defilement, contamination and carnality.

The exact number of themes depends on whether you're a lumper or a splitter, but Haidt counts five — harm, fairness, community (or group loyalty), authority and purity — and suggests that they are the primary colors of our moral sense. Not only do they keep reappearing in cross-cultural surveys, but each one tugs on the moral intuitions of people in our own culture. Haidt asks us to consider how much money someone would have to pay us to do hypothetical acts like the following:

Stick a pin into your palm.

Stick a pin into the palm of a child you don't know. (Harm.)

Accept a wide-screen TV from a friend who received it at no charge because of a computer error.   40

Accept a wide-screen TV from a friend who received it from a thief who had stolen it from a wealthy family. (Fairness.)

Say something bad about your nation (which you don't believe) on a talk-radio show in your nation.

Say something bad about your nation (which you don't believe) on a talk-radio show in a foreign nation. (Community.)

Slap a friend in the face, with his permission, as part of a comedy skit.

Slap your minister in the face, with his permission, as part of a comedy   45 skit. (Authority.)

Attend a performance-art piece in which the actors act like idiots for thirty minutes, including flubbing simple problems and falling down on stage.

Attend a performance-art piece in which the actors act like animals for thirty minutes, including crawling around naked and urinating on stage. (Purity.)

In each pair, the second action feels far more repugnant. Most of the moral illusions we have visited come from an unwarranted intrusion of one of the moral spheres into our judgments. A violation of community led people to frown on using an old flag to clean a bathroom. Violations of purity repelled the people who judged the morality of consensual incest and prevented the moral vegetarians and nonsmokers from tolerating the slightest trace of a vile contaminant. At the other end of the scale, displays of extreme purity lead people to venerate religious leaders who dress in white and affect an aura of chastity and asceticism.

The Genealogy of Morals

The five spheres are good candidates for a periodic table of the moral sense not only because they are ubiquitous but also because they appear to have deep evolutionary roots. The impulse to avoid harm, which gives trolley ponderers the willies when they consider throwing a man off a bridge, can also be found in rhesus monkeys, who go hungry rather than pull a chain that delivers food to them and a shock to another monkey. Respect for authority is clearly related to the pecking orders of dominance and appeasement that are widespread in the animal kingdom. The purity-defilement contrast taps the emotion of disgust that is triggered by potential disease vectors like bodily effluvia, decaying flesh and unconventional forms of meat, and by risky sexual practices like incest.

The other two moralized spheres match up with the classic examples of   50
how altruism can evolve that were worked out by sociobiologists in the 1960s and 1970s and made famous by Richard Dawkins in his book "The Selfish Gene." Fairness is very close to what scientists call reciprocal altruism, where a willingness to be nice to others can evolve as long as the favor helps the recipient more than it costs the giver and the recipient returns the favor when fortunes reverse. The analysis makes it sound as if reciprocal altruism comes out of a robotlike calculation, but in fact Robert Trivers, the biologist who devised the theory, argued that it is implemented in the brain as a suite of moral emotions. Sympathy prompts a person to offer the first favor, particularly to someone in need for whom it would go the furthest. Anger protects a person against cheaters who accept a favor without reciprocating, by impelling him to punish the ingrate or sever the relationship. Gratitude impels a beneficiary to reward those who helped him in the past. Guilt prompts a cheater in danger of being found out to repair the relationship by redressing the misdeed and advertising that he will behave better in the future (consistent with Mencken's definition of *conscience* as "the inner voice which warns us that someone might be looking"). Many experiments on who helps whom, who likes whom, who punishes whom and who feels guilty about what have confirmed these predictions.

Community, the very different emotion that prompts people to share and sacrifice without an expectation of payback, may be rooted in nepotistic altruism, the empathy and solidarity we feel toward our relatives (and which evolved because any gene that pushed an organism to aid a relative would have helped copies of itself sitting inside that relative). In humans, of course, communal feelings can be lavished on nonrelatives as well. Sometimes it pays people (in an evolutionary sense) to love their companions because their interests are yoked, like spouses with common children, in-laws with common relatives, friends with common tastes or allies with common enemies. And sometimes it doesn't pay them at all, but their kinship-detectors have been tricked into treating their groupmates as if they were relatives by tactics like kinship metaphors (*blood brothers, fraternities, the fatherland*), origin myths, communal meals and other bonding rituals.

Juggling the Spheres

All this brings us to a theory of how the moral sense can be universal and variable at the same time. The five moral spheres are universal, a legacy of evolution. But how they are ranked in importance, and which is brought in to moralize which area of social life — sex, government, commerce, religion, diet and so on — depends on the culture. Many of the flabbergasting practices in faraway places become more intelligible when you recognize that the same moralizing impulse that Western elites channel toward violations of harm and fairness (our moral obsessions) is channeled elsewhere to violations in the other spheres. Think of the Japanese fear of nonconformity (community), the holy ablutions and dietary restrictions of Hindus and Orthodox Jews (purity), the outrage at insulting the Prophet among Muslims (authority). In the West, we believe that in business and government, fairness should trump community and try to root out nepotism and cronyism. In other parts of the world this is incomprehensible — what heartless creep would favor a perfect stranger over his own brother?

The ranking and placement of moral spheres also divides the cultures of liberals and conservatives in the United States. Many bones of contention, like homosexuality, atheism and one-parent families from the right, or racial imbalances, sweatshops and executive pay from the left, reflect different weightings of the spheres. In a large Web survey, Haidt found that liberals put a lopsided moral weight on harm and fairness while playing down group loyalty, authority and purity. Conservatives instead place a moderately high weight on all five. It's not surprising that each side thinks it is driven by lofty ethical values and that the other side is base and unprincipled.

Reassigning an activity to a different sphere, or taking it out of the moral spheres altogether, isn't easy. People think that a behavior belongs in its sphere as a matter of sacred necessity and that the very act of questioning an assignment is a moral outrage. The psychologist Philip Tetlock has shown that the mentality of taboo — a conviction that some thoughts are sinful to think — is not just a superstition of Polynesians but a mind-set that can easily be triggered in college-educated Americans. Just ask them to think about applying the sphere of reciprocity to relationships customarily governed by community or authority. When Tetlock asked subjects for their opinions on whether adoption agencies should place children with the couples willing to pay the most, whether people should have the right to sell their organs and whether they should be able to buy their way out of jury duty, the subjects not only disagreed but felt personally insulted and were outraged that anyone would raise the question.

The institutions of modernity often question and experiment with the way activities are assigned to moral spheres. Market economies tend to put everything up for sale. Science amoralizes the world by seeking to understand phenomena rather than pass judgment on them. Secular philosophy is in the business of scrutinizing all beliefs, including those entrenched by authority and tradition. It's not surprising that these institutions are often seen to be morally corrosive.

Is Nothing Sacred?

And "morally corrosive" is exactly the term that some critics would apply to the new science of the moral sense. The attempt to dissect our moral intuitions can look like an attempt to debunk them. Evolutionary psychologists seem to want to unmask our noblest motives as ultimately self-interested — to show that our love for children, compassion for the unfortunate and sense of justice are just tactics in a Darwinian struggle to perpetuate our genes. The explanation of how different cultures appeal to different spheres could lead to a spineless relativism, in which we would never have grounds to criticize the practice of another culture, no matter how barbaric, because "we have our kind of morality and they have theirs." And the whole enterprise seems to be dragging us to an amoral nihilism, in which morality itself would be demoted from a transcendent principle to a figment of our neural circuitry.

In reality, none of these fears are warranted, and it's important to see why not. The first misunderstanding involves the logic of evolutionary explanations. Evolutionary biologists sometimes anthropomorphize DNA for the same reason that science teachers find it useful to have their students imagine the world from the viewpoint of a molecule or a beam of light. One shortcut to understanding the theory of selection without working through the math is to imagine that the genes are little agents that try to make copies of themselves.

Unfortunately, the meme of the selfish gene escaped from popular biology books and mutated into the idea that organisms (including people) are ruthlessly self-serving. And this doesn't follow. Genes are not a reservoir of our dark unconscious wishes. "Selfish" genes are perfectly compatible with selfless organisms, because a gene's metaphorical goal of selfishly replicating itself can be implemented by wiring up the brain of the organism to do unselfish things, like being nice to relatives or doing good deeds for needy strangers. When a mother stays up all night comforting a sick child, the genes that endowed her with that tenderness were "selfish" in a metaphorical sense, but by no stretch of the imagination is *she* being selfish.

Nor does reciprocal altruism — the evolutionary rationale behind fairness — imply that people do good deeds in the cynical expectation of repayment down the line. We all know of unrequited good deeds, like tipping a waitress in a city you will never visit again and falling on a grenade to save platoonmates. These bursts of goodness are not as anomalous to a biologist as they might appear.

In his classic 1971 article, Trivers, the biologist, showed how natural selection could push in the direction of true selflessness. The emergence of tit-for-tat reciprocity, which lets organisms trade favors without being cheated, is just a first step. A favor-giver not only has to avoid blatant cheaters (those who would accept a favor but not return it) but also prefer generous reciprocators (those who return the biggest favor they can afford) over stingy   60 ones (those who return the smallest favor they can get away with). Since it's good to be chosen as a recipient of favors, a competition arises to be the most generous partner around. More accurately, a competition arises to *appear* to be the most generous partner around, since the favor-giver can't literally read minds or see into the future. A reputation for fairness and generosity becomes an asset.

Now this just sets up a competition for potential beneficiaries to inflate their reputations without making the sacrifices to back them up. But it also pressures the favor-giver to develop ever-more-sensitive radar to distinguish the genuinely generous partners from the hypocrites. This arms race will eventually reach a logical conclusion. The most effective way to *seem* generous and fair, under harsh scrutiny, is to be generous and fair. In the long run, then, reputation can be secured only by commitment. At least some agents evolve to be genuinely high-minded and self-sacrificing — they are moral not because of what it brings them but because that's the kind of people they are.

Of course, a theory that predicted that everyone always sacrificed themselves for another's good would be as preposterous as a theory that predicted that no one ever did. Alongside the niches for saints there are niches for more grudging reciprocators, who attract fewer and poorer partners but don't make the sacrifices necessary for a sterling reputation. And both may coexist with outright cheaters, who exploit the unwary in one-shot encounters. An ecosystem of niches, each with a distinct strategy, can evolve when the payoff of each strategy depends on how many players are playing the other strategies. The human social environment does have its share of generous, grudging and crooked characters, and the genetic variation in personality seems to bear the fingerprints of this evolutionary process. . . .

Doing Better by Knowing Ourselves

Morality, then, is still something larger than our inherited moral sense, and the new science of the moral sense does not make moral reasoning and conviction obsolete. At the same time, its implications for our moral universe are profound.

At the very least, the science tells us that even when our adversaries' agenda is most baffling, they may not be amoral psychopaths but in the throes of a moral mind-set that appears to them to be every bit as mandatory and universal as ours does to us. Of course, some adversaries really are psychopaths, and others are so poisoned by a punitive moralization that they are beyond the pale of reason. (The actor Will Smith had many historians on his side when he recently speculated to the press that Hitler thought he was acting morally.) But in any conflict in which a meeting of the minds is not completely hopeless, a recognition that the other guy is acting from moral rather than venal reasons can be a first patch of common ground.

One side can acknowledge the other's concern for community or stability or fairness or dignity, even while arguing that some other value should trump it in that instance. With affirmative action, for example, the opponents can be seen as arguing from a sense of fairness, not racism, and the defenders can be seen as acting from a concern with community, not bureaucratic power. Liberals can ratify conservatives' concern with families while noting that gay marriage is perfectly consistent with that concern.

The science of the moral sense also alerts us to ways in which our psychological makeup can get in the way of our arriving at the most defensible moral conclusions. The moral sense, we are learning, is as vulnerable to illusions as the other senses. It is apt to confuse morality per se with purity, status and conformity. It tends to reframe practical problems as moral crusades and thus see their solution in punitive aggression. It imposes taboos that make certain ideas indiscussible. And it has the nasty habit of always putting the self on the side of the angels.

Though wise people have long reflected on how we can be blinded by our own sanctimony, our public discourse still fails to discount it appropriately. In the worst cases, the thoughtlessness of our brute intuitions can be celebrated as a virtue. In his influential essay "The Wisdom of Repugnance," Leon Kass, former chair of the President's Council on Bioethics, argued that we should disregard reason when it comes to cloning and other biomedical technologies and go with our gut: "We are repelled by the prospect of cloning human beings . . . because we intuit and feel, immediately and without argument, the violation of things that we rightfully hold dear. . . . In this age in which everything is held to be permissible so long as it is freely done . . . repugnance may be the only voice left that speaks up to defend the central core of our humanity. Shallow are the souls that have forgotten how to shudder."

There are, of course, good reasons to regulate human cloning, but the shudder test is not one of them. People have shuddered at all kinds of morally irrelevant violations of purity in their culture: touching an untouchable, drinking from the same water fountain as a Negro, allowing Jewish blood to mix with Aryan blood, tolerating sodomy between consenting men. And if our ancestors' repugnance had carried the day, we never would have had autopsies, vaccinations, blood transfusions, artificial insemination, organ transplants and in vitro fertilization, all of which were denounced as immoral when they were new.

There are many other issues for which we are too quick to hit the moralization button and look for villains rather than bug fixes. What should we do when a hospital patient is killed by a nurse who administers the wrong drug in a patient's intravenous line? Should we make it easier to sue the hospital for damages? Or should we redesign the IV fittings so that it's physically impossible to connect the wrong bottle to the line?

And nowhere is moralization more of a hazard than in our greatest global challenge. The threat of human-induced climate change has become the occasion for a moralistic revival meeting. In many discussions, the cause of climate change is overindulgence (too many SUVs) and defilement (sullying the atmosphere), and the solution is temperance (conservation) and expiation (buying carbon offset coupons). Yet the experts agree that these numbers don't add up: even if every last American became conscientious about his or her carbon emissions, the effects on climate change would be trifling, if for no other reason than that two billion Indians and Chinese are unlikely to copy our born-again abstemiousness. Though voluntary conservation may be one wedge in an effective carbon-reduction pie, the other wedges will have to be morally boring, like a carbon tax and new energy technologies, or even taboo, like nuclear power and deliberate manipulation of the ocean and atmosphere. Our habit of moralizing problems, merging them with intuitions of purity and contamination, and resting content when we feel the right feelings, can get in the way of doing the right thing.

Far from debunking morality, then, the science of the moral sense can advance it, by allowing us to see through the illusions that evolution and culture have saddled us with and to focus on goals we can share and defend. As Anton Chekhov wrote, "Man will become better when you show him what he is like."

QUESTIONS

Reading

1. According to Pinker, what are the hallmarks of moralization?
2. How does Jonathan Haidt contrast *moral reasoning* with *moral rationalization*?
3. What are the five moral spheres to which Pinker refers? Summarize Pinker's conclusion about the spheres and moral relativism.

Exploratory Writing

1. Prepare a debate over the proposition, "Morality is innate." You might draw on Olivia Judson's (p. 220) arguments as well as Pinker's as you research your case.
2. In pairs, discuss the situations devised by Jonathan Haidt (paragraphs 17–19). Is anyone able to explain *why* these scenarios are wrong? Next, devise a hypothetical moral quandary based on Haidt's examples. Trade your scenarios, then attempt to write a clear, reasonable statement about *why* the scenario is right or wrong. What did you learn about your own moral reasoning from this exercise?
3. Summarize Pinker's argument about the "shudder test." Write your own argumentative statement, either agreeing or disagreeing with Pinker.

Making Connections

1. Choose any argumentative essay in this book, and flag any *moral* statements or arguments contained within it. In each case, would you categorize the statement as *moral reasoning* or *moral rationalization*?

Essay Writing

1. Choose a behavior that has been "amoralized" (paragraph 13). Write an essay *reporting* on the history of social and legal prohibitions against that behavior. (Note that the very categorization of some of these things as "behaviors" or "choices" is controversial.) In your research, be aware of moral agendas within the sources you find.
2. Write an essay describing your personal experience of something that you find morally wrong. Why is it wrong? What experiences led you to hold your current beliefs on the subject?

A Mask on the Face of Death

Richard Selzer

*Richard Selzer (b. 1928) is the son of a general practitioner father
and a singer mother, both of whom wanted their son to follow in
their footsteps. At ten he began sneaking into his father's office to
look at his medical textbooks, where he discovered "the rich allit-
erative language of medicine—words such as* cerebellum, *which,
when said aloud, melt in the mouth and drip from the end of the
tongue like chocolate." After his father's death, he decided to become a doctor and was for many years a professor of surgery at
Yale Medical School. Only after working as a doctor for many
decades did he begin to write. About the similarities between surgery and writing he says, "In surgery, it is the body that is being
opened up and put back together. In writing it is the whole world
that is taken in for repairs, then put back in working order piece
by piece." His articles have appeared in* Vanity Fair, Harper's,
Esquire, *and the* New York Times Magazine. *His books include
the short-story collections* Rituals of Surgery *(1974) and* The Doctor Stories *(1998); the essay collections* Mortal Lessons *(1976),*
Raising the Dead *(1994),* The Exact Location of the Soul *(2001),
and* The Whistler's Room *(2004); and an autobiography,* Down
from Troy *(1992). This essay appeared in* Life *in 1988.*

It is ten o'clock at night as we drive up to the Copacabana, a dilapidated
brothel on the rue Dessalines in the red-light district of Port-au-Prince. My
guide is a young Haitian, Jean-Bernard. Ten years before, J-B tells me, at the
age of fourteen, "like every good Haitian boy" he had been brought here by
his older cousins for his *rite de passage*. From the car to the entrance, we are
accosted by a half dozen men and women for sex. We enter, go down a long
hall that breaks upon a cavernous room with a stone floor. The cubicles of
the prostitutes, I am told, are in an attached wing of the building. Save for a
red-purple glow from small lights on the walls, the place is unlit. Dark
shapes float by, each with a blindingly white stripe of teeth. Latin music is

blaring. We take seats at the table farthest from the door. Just outside, there is the rhythmic lapping of the Caribbean Sea. About twenty men are seated at the tables or lean against the walls. Brightly dressed women, singly or in twos or threes, stroll about, now and then exchanging banter with the men. It is as though we have been deposited in act two of Bizet's *Carmen*. If this place isn't Lillas Pastia's tavern, what is it?

Within minutes, three light-skinned young women arrive at our table. They are very beautiful and young and lively. Let them be Carmen, Mercedes and Frasquita.

"I want the old one," says Frasquita, ruffling my hair. The women laugh uproariously.

"Don't bother looking any further," says Mercedes. "We are the prettiest ones."

"We only want to talk," I tell her.   5

"Aaah, aaah," she crows. "*Massissi*. You are *massissi*." It is the contemptuous Creole term for homosexual. If we want only to talk, we must be gay. Mercedes and Carmen are slender, each weighing one hundred pounds or less. Frasquita is tall and hefty. They are dressed for work: red taffeta, purple chiffon and black sequins. Among them a thousand gold bracelets and earrings multiply every speck of light. Their bare shoulders are like animated lamps gleaming in the shadowy room. Since there is as yet no business, the women agree to sit with us. J-B orders beer and cigarettes. We pay each woman $10.

"Where are you from?" I begin.

"We are Dominican."

"Do you miss your country?"

"Oh, yes, we do." Six eyes go muzzy with longing. "Our country is   10
the most beautiful in the world. No country is like the Dominican. And it doesn't stink like this one."

"Then why don't you work there? Why come to Haiti?"

"Santo Domingo has too many whores. All beautiful, like us. All light-skinned. The Haitian men like to sleep with light women."

"Why is that?"

"Because always, the whites have all the power and the money. The black men can imagine they do, too, when they have us in bed."

Eleven o'clock. I look around the room that is still sparsely peopled   15
with men.

"It isn't getting any busier," I say. Frasquita glances over her shoulder. Her eyes drill the darkness.

"It is still early," she says.

"Could it be that the men are afraid of getting sick?" Frasquita is offended.

"Sick! They do not get sick from us. We are healthy, strong. Every week we go for a checkup. Besides, we know how to tell if we are getting sick."

"I mean sick with AIDS." The word sets off a hurricane of taffeta, chiffon   20
and gold jewelry. They are all gesticulation and fury. It is Carmen who speaks.

"AIDS!" Her lips curl about the syllable. "There is no such thing. It is a false disease invented by the American government to take advantage of the poor countries. The American President hates poor people, so now he makes up AIDS to take away the little we have." The others nod vehemently.

"*Mira, mon cher.* Look, my dear," Carmen continues. "One day the police came here. Believe me, they are worse than the *tonton macoutes* with their submachine guns. They rounded up one hundred and five of us and they took our blood. That was a year ago. None of us have died, you see? We are all still here. *Mira*, we sleep with all the men and we are not sick."

"But aren't there some of you who have lost weight and have diarrhea?"

"One or two, maybe. But they don't eat. That is why they are weak."

"Only the men die," says Mercedes. "They stop eating, so they die. It is   25
hard to kill a woman."

"Do you eat well?"

"Oh, yes, don't worry, we do. We eat like poor people, but we eat." There is a sudden scream from Frasquita. She points to a large rat that has emerged from beneath our table.

"My God!" she exclaims. "It is big like a pig." They burst into laughter. For a moment the women fall silent. There is only the restlessness of their many bracelets. I give them each another $10.

"Are many of the men here bisexual?"

"Too many. They do it for money. Afterward, they come to us."   30
Carmen lights a cigarette and looks down at the small lace handkerchief she has been folding and unfolding with immense precision on the table. All at once she turns it over as though it were the ace of spades.

"*Mira, blanc* . . . look, white man," she says in a voice suddenly full of foreboding. Her skin seems to darken to coincide with the tone of her voice.

"*Mira*, soon many Dominican women will die in Haiti!"

"Die of what?"

She shrugs. "It is what they do to us."

"Carmen," I say, "if you knew that you had AIDS, that your blood was   35
bad, would you still sleep with men?" Abruptly, she throws back her head and laughs. It is the same laughter with which Frasquita had greeted the rat at our feet. She stands and the others follow.

"*Méchant!* You wicked man," she says. Then, with terrible solemnity, "You don't know anything."

"But you are killing the Haitian men," I say.

"As for that," she says, "everyone is killing everyone else." All at once, I want to know everything about these three — their childhood, their dreams, what they do in the afternoon, what they eat for lunch.

"Don't leave," I say. "Stay a little more." Again, I reach for my wallet. But they are gone, taking all the light in the room with them — Mercedes and Carmen to sit at another table where three men have been waiting. Frasquita is strolling about the room. Now and then, as if captured by the music, she breaks into a few dance steps, snapping her fingers, singing to herself.

Midnight. And the Copacabana is filling up. Now it is like any other   40
seedy nightclub where men and women go hunting. We get up to leave. In
the center a couple are dancing a *méringue*. He is the most graceful dancer I
have ever watched; she, the most voluptuous. Together they seem to be riding
the back of the music as it gallops to a precisely sexual beat. Closer up, I see
that the man is short of breath, sweating. All at once, he collapses into a chair.
The woman bends over him, coaxing, teasing, but he is through. A young
man with a long polished stick blocks my way.

"I come with you?" he asks. "Very good time. You say yes? Ten dollars?
Five?"

I have been invited by Dr. Jean William Pape to attend the AIDS clinic of
which he is the director. Nothing from the outside of the low whitewashed
structure would suggest it as a medical facility. Inside, it is divided into many
small cubicles and a labyrinth of corridors. At nine a.m. the hallways are already full of emaciated silent men and women, some sitting on the few
benches, the rest leaning against the walls. The only sounds are subdued
moans of discomfort interspersed with coughs. How they eat us with their
eyes as we pass.

The room where Pape and I work is perhaps ten feet by ten. It contains a
desk, two chairs and a narrow wooden table that is covered with a sheet that
will not be changed during the day. The patients are called in one at a time,
asked how they feel and whether there is any change in their symptoms, then
examined on the table. If the patient is new to the clinic, he or she is questioned about sexual activities.

A twenty-seven-year-old man whose given name is Miracle enters. He is
wobbly, panting, like a groggy boxer who has let down his arms and is waiting for the last punch. He is neatly dressed and wears, despite the heat, a
heavy woolen cap. When he removes it, I see that his hair is thin, dull reddish
and straight. It is one of the signs of AIDS in Haiti, Pape tells me. The man's
skin is covered with a dry itchy rash. Throughout the interview and examination he scratches himself slowly, absentmindedly. The rash is called prurigo. It
is another symptom of AIDS in Haiti. This man has had diarrhea for six
months. The laboratory reports that the diarrhea is due to an organism called
cryptosporidium, for which there is no treatment. The telltale rattling of the
tuberculous moisture in his chest is audible without a stethoscope. He is like
a leaky cistern that bubbles and froths. And, clearly, exhausted.

"Where do you live?" I ask.   45

"Kenscoff." A village in the hills above Port-au-Prince.

"How did you come here today?"

"I came on the *tap-tap*." It is the name given to the small buses that
swarm the city, each one extravagantly decorated with religious slogans,
icons, flowers, animals, all painted in psychedelic colors. I have never seen a
tap-tap that was not covered with passengers as well, riding outside and
hanging on. The vehicles are little masterpieces of contagion, if not of AIDS

then of the multitude of germs which Haitian flesh is heir to. Miracle is given a prescription for a supply of Sera, which is something like Gatorade, and told to return in a month.

"*Mangé kou bêf*," says the doctor in farewell. "Eat like an ox." What can he mean? The man has no food or money to buy any. Even had he food, he has not the appetite to eat or the ability to retain it. To each departing patient the doctor will say the same words—"*Mangé kou bêf*." I see that it is his way of offering a hopeful goodbye.

"Will he live until his next appointment?" I ask.   50

"No." Miracle leaves to catch the *tap-tap* for Kenscoff.

Next is a woman of twenty-six who enters holding her right hand to her forehead in a kind of permanent salute. In fact, she is shielding her eye from view. This is her third visit to the clinic. I see that she is still quite well nourished.

"Now, you'll see something beautiful, tremendous," the doctor says. Once seated upon the table, she is told to lower her hand. When she does, I see that her right eye and its eyelid are replaced by a huge fungating ulcerated tumor, a side product of her AIDS. As she turns her head, the cluster of lymph glands in her neck to which the tumor has spread is thrown into relief. Two years ago she received a blood transfusion at a time when the country's main blood bank was grossly contaminated with AIDS. It has since been closed down. The only blood available in Haiti is a small supply procured from the Red Cross.

"Can you give me medicine?" the woman wails.

"No."   55

"Can you cut it away?"

"No."

"Is there radiation therapy?" I ask.

"No."

"Chemotherapy?" The doctor looks at me in what some might call   60
weary amusement. I see that there is nothing to do. She has come here because there is nowhere else to go.

"What will she do?"

"Tomorrow or the next day or the day after that she will climb up into the mountains to seek relief from the *houngan*, the voodoo priest, just as her slave ancestors did two hundred years ago."

Then comes a frail man in his thirties, with a strangely spiritualized face, like a child's. Pus runs from one ear onto his cheek, where it has dried and caked. He has trouble remembering, he tells us. In fact, he seems confused. It is from toxoplasmosis of the brain, an effect of his AIDS. This man is bisexual. Two years ago he engaged in oral sex with foreign men for money. As I palpate the swollen glands of his neck, a mosquito flies between our faces. I swat at it, miss. Just before coming to Haiti I had read that the AIDS virus had been isolated from a certain mosquito. The doctor senses my thought.

"Not to worry," he says. "So far as we know there has never been a case transmitted by insects."

"Yes," I say. "I see."   65

And so it goes until the last, the thirty-sixth AIDS patient has been seen. At the end of the day I am invited to wash my hands before leaving. I go down a long hall to a sink. I turn on the faucets but there is no water.

"But what about *you?*" I ask the doctor. "You are at great personal risk here — the tuberculosis, the other infections, no water to wash . . ." He shrugs, smiles faintly and lifts his hands palm upward.

We are driving up a serpiginous steep road into the barren mountains above Port-au-Prince. Even in the bright sunshine the countryside has the bloodless color of exhaustion and indifference. Our destination is the Baptist Mission Hospital, where many cases of AIDS have been reported. Along the road there are slow straggles of schoolchildren in blue uniforms who stretch out their hands as we pass and call out, "Give me something." Already a crowd of outpatients has gathered at the entrance to the mission compound. A tour of the premises reveals that in contrast to the aridity outside the gates, this is an enclave of productivity, lush with fruit trees and poinsettia.

The hospital is clean and smells of creosote. Of the forty beds, less than a third are occupied. In one male ward of twelve beds, there are two patients. The chief physician tells us that last year he saw ten cases of AIDS each week. Lately the number has decreased to four or five.

"Why is that?" we want to know.   70

"Because we do not admit them to the hospital, so they have learned not to come here."

"Why don't you admit them?"

"Because we would have nothing but AIDS here then. So we send them away."

"But I see that you have very few patients in bed."

"That is also true."   75

"Where do the AIDS patients go?"

"Some go to the clinic in Port-au-Prince or the general hospital in the city. Others go home to die or to the voodoo priest."

"Do the people with AIDS know what they have before they come here?"

"Oh, yes, they know very well, and they know there is nothing to be done for them."

Outside, the crowd of people is dispersing toward the gate. The clinic   80
has been canceled for the day. No one knows why. We are conducted to the office of the reigning American pastor. He is a tall, handsome Midwesterner with an ecclesiastical smile.

"It is voodoo that is the devil here." He warms to his subject. "It is a demonic religion, a cancer on Haiti. Voodoo is worse than AIDS. And it is one of the reasons for the epidemic. Did you know that in order for a man to become a *houngan* he must perform anal sodomy on another man? No, of course you didn't. And it doesn't stop there. The *houngans* tell the men that in order to appease the spirits they too must do the same thing. So you have ritualized homosexuality. That's what is spreading the AIDS." The pastor tells us of a nun who witnessed two acts of sodomy in a provincial hospital where she came upon a man sexually assaulting a houseboy and another man mounting a male patient in his bed.

"Fornication," he says. "It is Sodom and Gomorrah all over again, so what can you expect from these people?" Outside his office we are shown a cage of terrified, cowering monkeys to whom he coos affectionately. It is clear that he loves them. At the car, we shake hands.

"By the way," the pastor says, "what is your religion? Perhaps I am a kinsman?"

"While I am in Haiti," I tell him, "it will be voodoo or it will be nothing at all."

Abruptly, the smile breaks. It is as though a crack had suddenly appeared 85
in the face of an idol.

From the mission we go to the general hospital. In the heart of Port-au-Prince, it is the exact antithesis of the immaculate facility we have just left—filthy, crowded, hectic and staffed entirely by young interns and residents. Though it is associated with a medical school, I do not see any members of the faculty. We are shown around by Jocelyne, a young intern in a scrub suit. Each bed in three large wards is occupied. On the floor about the beds, hunkered in the posture of the innocent poor, are family members of the patients. In the corridor that constitutes the emergency room, someone lies on a stretcher receiving an intravenous infusion. She is hardly more than a cadaver.

"Where are the doctors in charge?" I ask Jocelyne. She looks at me questioningly.

"We are in charge."

"I mean your teachers, the faculty."

"They do not come here." 90

"What is wrong with that woman?"

"She has had diarrhea for three months. Now she is dehydrated." I ask the woman to open her mouth. Her throat is covered with the white plaques of thrush, a fungus infection associated with AIDS.

"How many AIDS patients do you see here?"

"Three or four a day. We send them home. Sometimes the families abandon them, then we must admit them to the hospital. Every day, then, a relative comes to see if the patient has died. They want to take the body. That is important to them. But they know very well that AIDS is contagious and they are afraid to keep them at home. Even so, once or twice a week the truck comes to take away the bodies. Many are children. They are buried in mass graves."

"Where do the wealthy patients go?" 95

"There is a private hospital called Canapé Vert. Or else they go to Miami. Most of them, rich and poor, do not go to the hospital. Most are never diagnosed."

"How do you know these people have AIDS?"

"We don't know sometimes. The blood test is inaccurate. There are many false positives and false negatives. Fifteen percent of those with the disease have negative blood tests. We go by their infections — tuberculosis, diarrhea, fungi, herpes, skin rashes. It is not hard to tell."

"Do they know what they have?"

"Yes. They understand at once and they are prepared to die."   100

"Do the patients know how AIDS is transmitted?"

"They know, but they do not like to talk about it. It is taboo. Their memories do not seem to reach back to the true origins of their disaster. It is understandable, is it not?"

"Whatever you write, don't hurt us any more than we have already been hurt." It is a young Haitian journalist with whom I am drinking a rum punch. He means that any further linkage of AIDS and Haiti in the media would complete the economic destruction of the country. The damage was done early in the epidemic when the Centers for Disease Control in Atlanta added Haitians to the three other high-risk groups — hemophiliacs, intravenous drug users and homosexual and bisexual men. In fact, Haitians are no more susceptible to AIDS than anyone else. Although the CDC removed Haitians from special scrutiny in 1985, the lucrative tourism on which so much of the country's economy was based was crippled. Along with tourism went much of the foreign business investment. Worst of all was the injury to the national pride. Suddenly Haiti was indicted as the source of AIDS in the western hemisphere.

What caused the misunderstanding was the discovery of a large number of Haitian men living in Miami with AIDS antibodies in their blood. They denied absolutely they were homosexuals. But the CDC investigators did not know that homosexuality is the strongest taboo in Haiti and that no man would ever admit to it. Bisexuality, however, is not uncommon. Many married men and heterosexually oriented males will occasionally seek out other men for sex. Further, many, if not most, Haitian men visit female prostitutes from time to time. It is not difficult to see that once the virus was set loose in Haiti, the spread would be swift through both genders.

Exactly how the virus of AIDS arrived is not known. Could it have been   105 brought home by the Cuban soldiers stationed in Angola and thence to Haiti, about fifty miles away? Could it have been passed on by the thousands of Haitians living in exile in Zaire, who later returned home or immigrated to the United States? Could it have come from the American and Canadian homosexual tourists, and, yes, even some U.S. diplomats who have traveled to the island to have sex with impoverished Haitian men all too willing to sell themselves to feed their families? Throughout the international gay community Haiti was known as a good place to go for sex.

On a private tip from an official at the Ministry of Tourism, J-B and I drive to a town some fifty miles from Port-au-Prince. The hotel is owned by two Frenchmen who are out of the country, one of the staff tells us. He is a man of about thirty and clearly he is desperately ill. Tottering, short of breath, he shows us about the empty hotel. The furnishings are opulent and extreme — tiger skins on the wall, a live leopard in the garden, a bedroom containing a giant bathtub with gold faucets. Is it the heat of the day or the heat of my imagination that makes these walls echo with the painful cries of pederasty?

The hotel where we are staying is in Pétionville, the fashionable suburb of Port-au-Prince. It is the height of the season but there are no tourists, only a dozen or so French and American businessmen. The swimming pool is used once or twice a day by a single person. Otherwise, the water remains undisturbed until dusk, when the fruit bats come down to drink in midswoop. The hotel keeper is an American. He is eager to set me straight on Haiti.

"What did and should attract foreign investment is a combination of reliable weather, an honest and friendly populace, low wages and multilingual managers."

"What spoiled it?"

"Political instability and a bad American press about AIDS." He pauses,   110 then adds: "To which I hope you won't be contributing."

"What about just telling the truth?" I suggest.

"Look," he says, "there is no more danger of catching AIDS in Haiti than in New York or Santo Domingo. It is not where you are but what you do that counts." Agreeing, I ask if he had any idea that much of the tourism in Haiti during the past few decades was based on sex.

"No idea whatsoever. It was only recently that we discovered that that was the case."

"How is it that you hoteliers, restaurant owners and the Ministry of Tourism did not know what *tout*[1] Haiti knew?"

"Look. All I know is that this is a middle-class, family-oriented hotel.   115 We don't allow guests to bring women, or for that matter men, into their rooms. If they did, we'd ask them to leave immediately."

At five a.m. the next day the telephone rings in my room. A Creole-accented male voice.

"Is the lady still with you, sir?"

"There is no lady here."

"In your room, sir, the lady I allowed to go up with a package?"

"There is no lady here, I tell you."   120

At seven a.m. I stop at the front desk. The clerk is a young man.

---

[1] *tout*: All. [Eds.]

"Was it you who called my room at five o'clock?"

"Sorry," he says with a smile. "It was a mistake, sir. I meant to ring the room next door to yours." Still smiling, he holds up his shushing finger.

Next to Dr. Pape, director of the AIDS clinic, Bernard Liautaud, a dermatologist, is the most knowledgeable Haitian physician on the subject of the epidemic. Together, the two men have published a dozen articles on AIDS in international medical journals. In our meeting they present me with statistics:

- There are more than one thousand documented cases of AIDS in Haiti, and as many as one hundred thousand carriers of the virus.
- Eighty-seven percent of AIDS is now transmitted heterosexually. While it is true that the virus was introduced via the bisexual community, that route has decreased to 10 percent or less.
- Sixty percent of the wives or husbands of AIDS patients tested positive for the antibody.
- Fifty percent of the prostitutes tested in the Port-au-Prince area are infected.
- Eighty percent of the men with AIDS have had contact with prostitutes.
- The projected number of active cases in four years is ten thousand. (Since my last visit, the Haitian Medical Association broke its silence on the epidemic by warning that one million of the country's six million people could be carriers by 1992.)

The two doctors have more to tell. "The crossing over of the plague from   125 the homosexual to the heterosexual community will follow in the United States within two years. This, despite the hesitation to say so by those who fear to sow panic among your population. In Haiti, because bisexuality is more common, there was an early crossover into the general population. The trend, inevitably, is the same in the two countries."

"What is there to do, then?"

"Only education, just as in America. But here the Haitians reject the use of condoms. Only the men who are too sick to have sex are celibate."

"What is to be the end of it?"

"When enough heterosexuals of the middle and upper classes die, perhaps there will be the panic necessary for the people to change their sexual lifestyles."

This evening I leave Haiti. For two weeks I have fastened myself to this   130 lovely fragile land like an ear pressed to the ground. It is a country to break a traveler's heart. It occurs to me that I have not seen a single jogger. Such a public expenditure of energy while everywhere else strength is ebbing — it would be obscene. In my final hours, I go to the Cathédrale of Sainte Trinité, the inner walls of which are covered with murals by Haiti's most renowned artists. Here are all the familiar Bible stories depicted in naïveté and piety, and all in such an exuberance of color as to tax the capacity of the retina to receive it, as though all the vitality of Haiti had been turned to paint and brushed upon these walls. How to explain this efflorescence at a time when all else is lassitude and inertia? Perhaps one day the plague will be rendered in poetry, music, painting, but not now. Not now.

QUESTIONS

Reading

1. Summarize the scene at the Copacabana. Which details are memorable? Why does Selzer spend so much time with Carmen, Mercedes, and Frasquita? Why are their attitudes toward AIDS so important?
2. Selzer writes at great length about his visit to the AIDS clinic directed by Dr. Jean William Pape. What does Selzer learn from observing patients at this clinic? What does Selzer learn about AIDS from the doctor at work?
3. Look at the various scenes and vignettes Selzer offers his readers. How does he connect these different scenes? How does this structure succeed in presenting his reflections?

Exploratory Writing

1. How might Selzer's research experience at the Copacabana have been different if he were a woman, or a man raised and educated in Haiti, rather than the United States? Consider the ways that Carmen, Mercedes, and Frasquita approach him and respond to his questions. How might his commentary have been different if he, himself, were infected with HIV? In your opinion, how balanced is the report that Selzer offers?
2. Collaborating in small groups, take the "How Much Do You Know about HIV/AIDS?" quiz (**www.pbs.org/wgbh/pages/frontline/aids/etc/quiz.html**) on the *Frontline* Web site. Using the links contained in the answers, choose a topic in the field of HIV/AIDS education, prevention, and treatment, and prepare a presentation arguing a policy position. (For example, "The U.S. Should Provide Federal Funding for Needle Exchange" or "HIV Testing Should Be a Standard Part of Medical Care for Patients Age 13–64.") Use at least four key points to make your argument persuasive.
3. A young Haitian journalist tells Selzer, "Whatever you write, don't hurt us any more than we have already been hurt" (paragraph 103). What is the significance of this request? After reading Selzer's essay, do you think Selzer has honored this request?

Making Connections

1. Abraham Verghese (p. 455) describes feeling a sense of helplessness while volunteering to help care for victims of Hurricane Katrina, as well as in his work in field clinics in India and Ethiopia, because he knows that the illnesses he is treating are "inextricably linked to the bigger problem of homelessness, disenfranchisement, and despair." Find the sections in Selzer's essay where he shows how the spread of HIV/AIDS in Haiti is linked to broader social, economic, or political problems. Discuss ways that highlighting these connections might alter medical strategies for educating and treating patients.

Essay Writing

1. What have you learned about the politics of AIDS from reading Selzer's essay? Write an essay reflecting on this essay.

Paired Readings: On Suffering

REFLECTING

Close Encounter of the Human Kind

Abraham Verghese

Abraham Verghese was born in 1955 in Addis Ababa, Ethiopia, the son of two physicists who were immigrants from India. He attended medical school in Ethiopia and worked in hospitals in the United States before completing his medical degree at Madras University. In 1991, he received an MFA from the University of Iowa. His first book, My Own Country: A Doctor's Story *(1994), is a memoir about treating AIDS in Johnson City, Tennessee. The book was a finalist for the National Book Critics Circle Award in nonfiction, won the Lambda Literary Award for nonfiction, was named one of the five best books of 1994 by* Time *magazine, and was made into a Showtime original movie. In his second book,* The Tennis Partner: A Story of Friendship and Loss *(1998), Verghese wrote about coming to terms with love and loss through the death of his best friend and tennis partner. Verghese has contributed many articles to medical journals and has published stories, articles, and reviews in magazines and newspapers, including the* North American Review, Sports Illustrated, *the* New Yorker, Granta, *and* MD. *Verghese has noted of his two professions, "Writing has many similarities to the practice of internal medicine. Both require astute observation and a fondness for detail." He has also said, "I suspect that the challenge for doctors in the next century will be to rediscover why the profession was once called the 'ministry of healing.' . . . People who visit doctors are looking for more than a cure, they are looking for 'healing' as well. To understand the distinction between 'healing' and 'curing,' let me use an analogy: If you have ever been robbed, and if the cops came back an hour later with all the stuff taken from your home, you would be 'cured' but not 'healed' — your sense of spiritual violation would still remain. In the same way, all illnesses have these two components: a physical violation and a spiritual violation." The following article appeared in the* New York Times Magazine *in 2005.*

With the first bus loads of Katrina refugees about to arrive in San Antonio, the call went out for physician volunteers, and I signed up for the 2 a.m. to 8 a.m. shift. On the way, riding down dark, deserted streets, I thought of driving in for night shifts in the ICU as an intern many years ago, and how I would try to steel myself, as if putting on armor.

Within a massive structure at Kelly U.S.A. (formerly Kelly Air Force Base), a brightly lighted processing area led to office cubicles, where after registering, new arrivals with medical needs came to see us. My first patient sat before me, haggard, pointing to what ailed her, as if speech no longer served her. I peeled her shoes from swollen feet, trying not to remove skin in the process. Cuts from submerged objects and immersion in standing water had caused the swelling, as well as infection of both feet. An antibiotic, a pair of slip-ons from the roomful of donated clothing, and a night with her feet elevated — that would help.

The ailments common among the refugees included diarrhea, bronchitis, sore throat, and voices hoarse or lost. And stress beyond belief. People didn't have their medications, and blood sugars and blood pressures were out of control.

I prayed, as I wrote prescriptions, that their memories of particular pills were accurate. For a man on methadone maintenance who was now cramping and sweating, I prescribed codeine to hold him. Another man, clutching a gym bag as if I might snatch it from him, admitted when I gently probed that he was hearing voices again. We sat together looking through the *Physicians' Desk Reference*. "That's it," he said, recognizing the pill he hadn't taken since the storm hit.

Hesitantly, I asked each patient, "Where did you spend the last five   5 days?" I wanted to reconcile the person in front of me with the terrible locales on television. But as the night wore on, I understood that they *needed* me to ask; to not ask was to not honor their ordeal. Hard men wiped at their eyes and became animated in the telling. The first woman, the one who seemed mute from stress, began a recitation in a courtroom voice, as if preparing for future testimony.

It reminded me of my previous work in field clinics in India and Ethiopia, where, with so few medical resources at hand, the careful listening, the thorough exam, the laying of hands was the therapy. And I felt the same helplessness, knowing that the illness here was inextricably linked to the bigger problem of homelessness, disenfranchisement, and despair.

Near the end of my shift, a new group of patients arrived. A man in his seventies with gray hair and beard came in looking fit and vigorous. One eye was milky white and sightless, but the glint in his good eye was enough for two. His worldly belongings were in a garbage bag, but his manner was dignified.

He was out of medicine, and his blood sugar and blood pressure were high. He couldn't pay for his medication, so his doctor always gave him samples: "Whatever he have. Whatever he have." He had kept his shoes on for five days, he said, removing the battered, pickled, but elegant pair, a cross between bowling shoes and dancing shoes. His toes were carved ebony, the tendons on the back like cables, the joints gnarled but sturdy. All night I had seen many feet; in his bare feet I read resilience.

He told me that for two nights after the floods, he had perched on a ledge so narrow that his legs dangled in the water. At one point, he said, he saw Air Force One fly over, and his hopes soared. "I waited, I waited," he said, but no help came. Finally a boat got him to a packed bridge. There, again, he waited. He shook his head in disbelief, smiling though. "Doc, they treat refugees in other countries better than they treated us."

"I'm so sorry," I said. "So sorry."   10

He looked at me long and hard, cocking his head as if weighing my words, which sounded so weak, so inadequate. He rose, holding out his hand, his posture firm as he shouldered his garbage bag. "Thank you, Doc. I needed to hear that. All they got to say is sorry. All they got to say is sorry."

I was still troubled by him when I left, even though he seemed the hardiest of all. This encounter between two Americans, between doctor and patient, had been carried to all the fullness that was permitted, and yet it was incomplete, as if he had, as a result of this experience, set in place some new barriers that neither I nor anyone else would ever cross.

Driving home, I remembered my own metaphor of strapping on armor for the night shift. The years have shown that there is no armor. There never was. The willingness to be wounded may be all we have to offer.

QUESTIONS

Reading

1. The bulk of this piece is devoted to reporting, but as in many such essays, it moves to reflection at a certain point. Exactly where is that move made in this essay?
2. The reporting section of this essay can be divided into a number of sections. Make an outline of them. At a certain point, the author is reminded of other experiences. Why are those particular connections made in this essay? That is, what do India and Ethiopia have to do with San Antonio and New Orleans?
3. What ailments are common among the Katrina refugees as they arrive in San Antonio?

Exploratory Writing

1. Verghese writes of one Katrina refugee, "All night I had seen many feet; in his bare feet I read resilience" (paragraph 8). Consider the idea that you can look at a person's body part, facial expression, or clothing and "read" something about them. Why do you think that Verghese chooses

to say that he *read* this man's feet? Write a few paragraphs reflecting on a person you know, and describe what you can read about his or her character based only on appearance.

2. There is one main anecdote in the reporting part of this piece. Summarize it, and analyze the result.

3. Divide into groups, and based on Verghese's observations of the human interaction his patients need (see especially paragraphs 5 and 11), write a *protocol* for compassionate patient care. Imagine that your protocol will be used by doctors who are volunteering to help refugees who have lost their homes. In a crisis situation, how might you balance the medical needs of patients with their human needs? You can refer to resources on the Web site for the nonprofit organization Doctors Without Borders (**www.doctorswithoutborders.org/**) as you formulate your protocol.

Making Connections

1. Verghese and Richard Selzer (p. 443) approach the human experience from the point of view of highly trained and experienced medical doctors, yet they are both also writers. Compare the ways that these two men write about human suffering. How does each writer characterize the people he encounters? Are their tones similar or different? How does each writer position himself in relation to the other people in his essay?

Essay Writing

1. Write an essay reflecting on the difference between *curing* and *healing*. Offer a definition for each term. You can draw on the essays by Verghese and Selzer to help formulate your ideas.

Paired Readings: On Natural Phenomena

Why Leaves Turn Color in the Fall

Diane Ackerman

Poet, essayist, and naturalist Diane Ackerman was born in Waukegan, Illinois, in 1948 and received her MFA and PhD in English from Cornell University. Her earliest works, published when she was still a doctoral student, were the poetry collections The Planets *(1976) and* Wife of Life *(1978); since then she has produced several volumes, most recently* I Praise My Destroyer *(1998) and* Origami Bridges *(2002). Ackerman's first book of prose was* Twilight of the Tenderfoot *(1980), about her experiences working on a cattle ranch in New Mexico. Her subsequent prose works have focused on a range of subjects, as suggested by some of their titles:* The Moon by Whale Light: And Other Adventures among Bats, Crocodilians, Penguins, and Whales *(1990),* The Rarest of the Rare: Vanishing Animals, Timeless Worlds *(1995),* A Natural History of Love *(1994),* Cultivating Delight: A Natural History of My Garden *(2001),* An Alchemy of Mind *(2004), and* The Zookeeper's Wife: A War Story *(2007). All, however, are characterized by Ackerman's deeply insightful observations of the natural world, as evidenced perhaps most fully in her most popular book and the source of a highly rated public television series,* A Natural History of the Senses *(1990), where the following selection appeared. Admitting that her work is difficult to categorize, Ackerman has said, "I write about nature and human nature. And most often about that twilight zone where the two meet and have something they can teach each other."*

The stealth of autumn catches one unaware. Was that a goldfinch perching in the early September woods, or just the first turning leaf? A red-winged blackbird or a sugar maple closing up shop for the winter? Keen-eyed as leopards, we stand still and squint hard, looking for signs of movement. Early-morning frost sits heavily on the grass, and turns barbed wire into a

string of stars. On a distant hill, a small square of yellow appears to be a
lighted stage. At last the truth dawns on us: Fall is staggering in, right on
schedule, with its baggage of chilly nights, macabre holidays, and spectacular, heart-stoppingly beautiful leaves. Soon the leaves will start cringing on
the trees, and roll up in clenched fists before they actually fall off. Dry seed-
pods will rattle like tiny gourds. But first there will be weeks of gushing
color so bright, so pastel, so confettilike, that people will travel up and
down the East Coast just to stare at it — a whole season of leaves.

Where do the colors come from? Sunlight rules most living things with
its golden edicts. When the days begin to shorten, soon after the summer
solstice on June 21, a tree reconsiders its leaves. All summer it feeds them so
they can process sunlight, but in the dog days of summer the tree begins
pulling nutrients back into its trunk and roots, pares down, and gradually
chokes off its leaves. A corky layer of cells forms at the leaves' slender petioles, then scars over. Undernourished, the leaves stop producing the pigment
chlorophyll, and photosynthesis ceases. Animals can migrate, hibernate, or
store food to prepare for winter. But where can a tree go? It survives by
dropping its leaves, and by the end of autumn only a few fragile threads of
fluid-carrying xylem hold leaves to their stems.

A turning leaf stays partly green at first, then reveals splotches of yellow
and red as the chlorophyll gradually breaks down. Dark green seems to stay
longest in the veins, outlining and defining them. During the summer,
chlorophyll dissolves in the heat and light, but it is also being steadily replaced. In the fall, on the other hand, no new pigment is produced, and so
we notice the other colors that were always there, right in the leaf, although
chlorophyll's shocking green hid them from view. With their camouflage
gone, we see these colors for the first time all year, and marvel, but they were
always there, hidden like a vivid secret beneath the hot glowing greens of
summer.

The most spectacular range of fall foliage occurs in the northeastern
United States and in eastern China, where the leaves are robustly colored,
thanks in part to a rich climate. European maples don't achieve the same
flaming reds as their American relatives, which thrive on cold nights and
sunny days. In Europe, the warm, humid weather turns the leaves brown or
mildly yellow. Anthocyanin, the pigment that gives apples their red and
turns leaves red or red-violet, is produced by sugars that remain in the leaf
after the supply of nutrients dwindles. Unlike the carotenoids, which color
carrots, squash, and corn, and turn leaves orange and yellow, anthocyanin
varies from year to year, depending on the temperature and amount of sunlight. The fiercest colors occur in years when the fall sunlight is strongest
and the nights are cool and dry (a state of grace scientists find vexing to fore-
cast). This is also why leaves appear dizzyingly bright and clear on a sunny
fall day: The anthocyanin flashes like a marquee.

Not all leaves turn the same colors. Elms, weeping willows, and the   5
ancient ginkgo all grow radiant yellow, along with hickories, aspens,

bottlebrush buckeyes, cottonweeds, and tall, keening poplars. Basswood turns bronze, birches bright gold. Water-loving maples put on a symphonic display of scarlets. Sumacs turn red, too, as do flowering dogwoods, black gums, and sweet gums. Though some oaks yellow, most turn a pinkish brown. The farmlands also change color, as tepees of cornstalks and bales of shredded-wheat-textured hay stand drying in the fields. In some spots, one slope of a hill may be green and the other already in bright color, because the hillside facing south gets more sun and heat than the northern one.

An odd feature of the colors is that they don't seem to have any special purpose. We are predisposed to respond to their beauty, of course. They shimmer with the colors of sunset, spring flowers, the tawny buff of a colt's pretty rump, the shuddering pink of a blush. Animals and flowers color for a reason — adaptation to their environment — but there is no adaptive reason for leaves to color so beautifully in the fall any more than there is for the sky or ocean to be blue. It's just one of the haphazard marvels the planet bestows every year. We find the sizzling colors thrilling, and in a sense they dupe us. Colored like living things, they signal death and disintegration. In time, they will become fragile and, like the body, return to dust. They are as we hope our own fate will be when we die: Not to vanish, just to sublime from one beautiful state into another. Though leaves lose their green life, they bloom with urgent colors, as the woods grow mummified day by day, and Nature becomes more carnal, mute, and radiant.

We call the season "fall," from the Old English *feallan*, to fall, which leads back through time to the Indo-European *phol*, which also means to fall. So the word and the idea are both extremely ancient, and haven't really changed since the first of our kind needed a name for fall's leafy abundance. As we say the word, we're reminded of that other Fall, in the garden of Eden, when fig leaves never withered and scales fell from our eyes. Fall is the time when leaves fall from the trees, just as spring is when flowers spring up, summer is when we simmer, and winter is when we whine from the cold.

Children love to play in piles of leaves, hurling them into the air like confetti, leaping into soft unruly mattresses of them. For children, leaf fall is just one of the odder figments of Nature, like hailstones or snowflakes. Walk down a lane overhung with trees in the never-never land of autumn, and you will forget about time and death, lost in the sheer delicious spill of color. Adam and Eve concealed their nakedness with leaves, remember? Leaves have always hidden our awkward secrets.

But how do the colored leaves fall? As a leaf ages, the growth hormone, auxin, fades, and cells at the base of the petiole divide. Two or three rows of small cells, lying at right angles to the axis of the petiole, react with water, then come apart, leaving the petioles hanging on by only a few threads of xylem. A light breeze, and the leaves are airborne. They glide and swoop, rocking in invisible cradles. They are all wing and may flutter from yard to yard on small whirlwinds or updrafts, swiveling as they go. Firmly tethered to earth, we love to see things rise up and fly—soap bubbles, balloons, birds, fall leaves. They remind us that the end of a season is capricious, as is the end of life. We especially like the way leaves rock, careen, and swoop as they fall. Everyone knows the motion. Pilots sometimes do a maneuver called a "falling leaf," in which the plane loses altitude quickly and on purpose, by slipping first to the right, then to the left. The machine weighs a ton or more, but in one pilot's mind it is a weightless thing, a falling leaf. She has seen the motion before, in the Vermont woods where she played as a child. Below her the trees radiate gold, copper, and red. Leaves are falling, although she can't see them fall, as she falls, swooping down for a closer view.

At last the leaves leave. But first they turn color and thrill us for weeks   10
on end. Then they crunch and crackle underfoot. They *shush*, as children drag their small feet through leaves heaped along the curb. Dark, slimy mats of leaves cling to one's heels after a rain. A damp, stuccolike mortar of semi-decayed leaves protects the tender shoots with a roof until spring, and makes a rich humus. An occasional bulge or ripple in the leafy mounds signals a shrew or a field mouse tunneling out of sight. Sometimes one finds in fossil stones the imprint of a leaf, long since disintegrated, whose outlines remind us how detailed, vibrant, and alive are the things of this earth that perish.

QUESTIONS

Reading

1. According to Ackerman, where does the most spectacular range of fall foliage occur?
2. Highlight, underline, or flag the places where Ackerman makes a connection between the concept of autumn leaves and the concept of death in general. How would you summarize the point she is making here?
3. What is the purpose of the different leaf colors?

Exploratory Writing

1. Print out a photograph of autumn foliage from the Internet. Collaborating in small groups, label the trees in the picture based on (a) how they got their colors, and (b) which types of trees they might be. Use only Ackerman's essay as a reference point. Based on this exercise, how useful did you find the essay? What did you learn about trees from reading it?
2. Make a list of all of the adjectives that Ackerman uses to describe autumn leaves. How would her explanation of the leaves be different without those adjectives? What can you learn just from reading the list, with none of the scientific explanations attached?

Making Connections

1. The title of James Jeans's essay "Why the Sky Is Blue" (p. 464) sets up expectations similar to those that Ackerman's title does: that what follows will provide an explanation of a natural process. In fact, how similar — and how different — are the two essays? Do you feel that one provides a clearer or more effective explanation than the other does? Why or why not? Which do you respond to more favorably?
2. Refer to Patricia Hampl's "The Dark Art of Description" (p. 122). Highlight, underline, or flag places where Ackerman uses what Hampl would call "the divine detail." Then rewrite Ackerman's explanation as simply, clearly, and tersely as possible, in your own words. Why does Ackerman use such literary language to describe a scientific phenomenon? What does the explanation lose or gain when you rewrite it more simply?

Essay Writing

1. Think of a natural phenomenon that you consider beautiful or spectacular. Do some research to learn about the biological, geological, or other natural process that produces it. Write an essay in which, like Ackerman, you *explain* the technical aspects of the natural process while also describing the beauty of the phenomenon and *reflecting* on the reasons that you respond to it as you do.

Paired Readings: On Natural Phenomena

EXPLAINING

Why the Sky Is Blue

James Jeans

*Sir James Jeans (1877–1946) was a British physicist and astrono-
mer. Educated at Trinity College, Cambridge, he lectured there
and was a professor of applied mathematics at Princeton University from 1905 to 1909. He later did research at Mount Wilson
Observatory in California. Jeans won many honors for his work
and wrote a number of scholarly and popular scientific books. The
following selection is from* The Stars in Their Courses *(1931), a
written version of what began as a series of radio talks for an
audience assumed to have no special knowledge of science.*

Imagine that we stand on any ordinary seaside pier, and watch the waves
rolling in and striking against the iron columns of the pier. Large waves pay
very little attention to the columns — they divide right and left and re-unite
after passing each column, much as a regiment of soldiers would if a tree
stood in their road; it is almost as though the columns had not been there.
But the short waves and ripples find the columns of the pier a much more formidable obstacle. When the short waves impinge on the columns, they are reflected back and spread as new ripples in all directions. To use the technical
term, they are "scattered." The obstacle provided by the iron columns hardly
affects the long waves at all, but scatters the short ripples.

We have been watching a sort of working model of the way in which
sunlight struggles through the earth's atmosphere. Between us on earth and
outer space the atmosphere interposes innumerable obstacles in the form of
molecules of air, tiny droplets of water, and small particles of dust. These are
represented by the columns of the pier.

The waves of the sea represent the sunlight. We know that sunlight is a
blend of lights of many colors — as we can prove for ourselves by passing it
through a prism, or even through a jug of water, or as Nature demonstrates
to us when she passes it through the raindrops of a summer shower and produces a rainbow. We also know that light consists of waves, and that the different colors of light are produced by waves of different lengths, red light by

464

long waves and blue light by short waves. The mixture of waves which constitutes sunlight has to struggle through the obstacles it meets in the atmosphere, just as the mixture of waves at the seaside has to struggle past the columns of the pier. And these obstacles treat the light-waves much as the columns of the pier treat the sea-waves. The long waves which constitute red light are hardly affected, but the short waves which constitute blue light are scattered in all directions.

Thus, the different constituents of sunlight are treated in different ways as they struggle through the earth's atmosphere. A wave of blue light may be scattered by a dust particle, and turned out of its course. After a time a second dust particle again turns it out of its course, and so on, until finally it enters our eyes by a path as zigzag as that of a flash of lightning. Consequently the blue waves of the sunlight enter our eyes from all directions. And that is why the sky looks blue.

QUESTIONS

Reading

1. Analogy, the comparison of something familiar with something less familiar, occurs frequently in scientific explanation. Jeans introduces an analogy in his first paragraph. How does he develop that analogy as he develops his explanation?
2. Besides the sea waves, what other familiar examples does Jeans use in his explanation?
3. What is the difference between red light and blue light?

Exploratory Writing

1. Analogies can be effective in explaining tricky scientific concepts, and they can also change our view of familiar things by juxtaposing them in new ways. Collaborating in small groups, choose something familiar, and develop at least five analogies to explain it. For example, you might explain why you dislike one of your classes by likening it to a forced-labor camp, a three-ring circus, squirrels on a treadmill, a tea party, or a group therapy session. How do these analogies change the way you think about the subject?
2. This piece opens with "Imagine that we stand . . ." Suppose that every *we* was replaced with a *you*. How would the tone of the essay change?

Making Connections

1. Like Jeans, Diane Ackerman (p. 459) is *explaining* a natural phenomenon. List the different explanatory techniques in each essay. From this list, what can you deduce about the motives of each author?

2. Refer to Jan Harold Brunvand's (p. 75) essay on urban legends. Do some research, and find some alternative (mythical or legendary) explanations for why the sky is blue. Interpret these stories using Brunvand's methodology. What do they show about the cultures of the people who wrote them?

Essay Writing

1. Jeans offers a *process analysis* of why the sky is blue, identifying and describing each step in the process by which light waves from the sun move through our atmosphere and determine our perceptions of the color of the sky, then explaining how the process as a whole culminates in the final result. Choose your own burning question, and write an essay using this process-analysis technique to explain the answer.

Paired Readings: On Sexual Reproduction

EXPLAINING

Corn Sex

Michael Pollan

Journalist, author, and educator Michael Pollan (b. 1955) has become a popular and persuasive advocate for changing the industrialized American food system — what we grow and what we eat. The theme of his latest book, In Defense of Food: An Eater's Manifesto (2008), *is summarized in the words that appear on the book's cover: "Eat Food. Not Too Much. Mostly Plants." His previous books include* The Botany of Desire: A Plant's-Eye View of the World *(2001), in which he argues that domesticated plants have shaped humans as much as humans have shaped them, and* The Omnivore's Dilemma: A Natural History of Four Meals *(2006), in which he focuses on the impact of corn on both the American diet and the environment, and from which "Corn Sex" is excerpted. Pollan was born and raised on Long Island, New York, and educated at Bennington College, Mansfield College, Oxford University, and Columbia University, where he received his MA in English. Since then, he has written books and articles; lectured; and taught about food, agriculture, nature, and the environment. He is currently the Knight Professor of Journalism and director of the Knight Program in Science and Environmental Journalism at the University of California, Berkeley. An award-winning journalist, Pollan is a regular contributor to the* New York Times Magazine *and writes frequently for a host of other magazines, including* Mother Jones, Gourmet, Vogue, House and Garden, Smithsonian, *and* Harper's, *where he was an editor for more than ten years.*

Maize is self-fertilized and wind-pollinated, botanical terms that don't begin to describe the beauty and wonder of corn sex. The tassel at the top of the plant houses the male organs, hundreds of pendant anthers that over the course of a few summer days release a superabundance of powdery yellow pollen: fourteen million to eighteen million grains per plant, twenty thousand for every potential kernel. ("Better safe than sorry" or "more is more" being nature's general rule for male genes.) A meter or so below await the female organs, hundreds of minuscule flowers arranged in tidy rows along a tiny, sheathed cob that juts upward from the stalk at the crotch of a leaf midway between tassel and earth. That the male anthers resemble flowers and the female cob a phallus is not the only oddity in the sex life of corn.

Each of the four hundred to eight hundred flowers on a cob has the potential to develop into a kernel — but only if a grain of pollen can find its way to its ovary, a task complicated by the distance the pollen has to travel and the intervening husk in which the cob is tightly wrapped. To surmount this last problem, each flower sends out through the tip of the husk a single, sticky strand of silk (technically its "style") to snag its own grain of pollen. The silks emerge from the husk on the very day the tassel is set to shower its yellow dust.

What happens next is very strange. After a grain of pollen has fallen through the air and alighted on the moistened tip of silk, its nucleus divides in two, creating a pair of twins, each with the same set of genes but a completely different role to perform in the creation of the kernel. The first twin's job is to tunnel a microscopic tube down through the center of the silk thread. That accomplished, its clone slides down through the tunnel, past the husk, and into the waiting flower, a journey of between six and eight inches that takes several hours to complete. Upon arrival in the flower the second twin fuses with the egg to form the embryo — the germ of the future kernel. Then the first twin follows, entering the now fertilized flower, where it sets about forming the endosperm — the big, starchy part of the kernel. Every kernel of corn is the product of this intricate ménage à trois; the tiny, stunted kernels you often see at the narrow end of a cob are flowers whose silk no pollen grain ever penetrated. Within a day of conception, the now superfluous silk dries up, eventually turning reddish brown; fifty or so days later, the kernels are mature.[1]

The mechanics of corn sex, and in particular the great distance over open space corn pollen must travel to complete its mission, go a long way toward accounting for the success of maize's alliance with humankind. It's a simple matter for a human to get between a corn plant's pollen and its flower, and only a short step from there to deliberately crossing one corn plant with another with an eye to encouraging specific traits in the offspring. Long before scientists understood hybridization, Native Americans had discovered that by taking the pollen from the tassel of one corn plant and dusting it on the silks of another, they could create new plants that combined the traits of both parents. American Indians were the world's first plant breeders, developing literally thousands of distinct cultivars for every conceivable environment and use.

---

[1]My account of the sex life of corn is drawn from Betty Fussell's *The Story of Corn* (1992) and Frederick Sargent's *Corn Plants* (1901).

Looked at another way, corn was the first plant to involve humans so   5
intimately in its sex life. For a species whose survival depends on how well
it can gratify the ever-shifting desires of its only sponsor, this has proved to
be an excellent evolutionary strategy. More even than other domesticated
species, many of which can withstand a period of human neglect, it pays for
corn to be obliging — and to be so quick about it. The usual way a domesticated species figures out what traits its human ally will reward is through
the slow and wasteful process of Darwinian trial and error. Hybridization
represents a far swifter and more efficient means of communication, or feedback loop, between plant and human; by allowing humans to arrange its
marriages, corn can discover in a single generation precisely what qualities
it needs to prosper.

It is by being so obliging that corn has won itself as much human attention and habitat as it has. The plant's unusual sexual arrangements, so
amenable to human intervention, have allowed it to adapt to the very different worlds of Native Americans (and to *their* very different worlds, from
southern Mexico to New England), of colonists and settlers and slaves, and
of all the other corn-eating societies that have come and gone since the first
human chanced upon that first teosinte freak.

But of all the human environments to which corn has successfully adapted
since then, the adaptation to our own — the world of industrial consumer
capitalism; the world, that is, of the supermarket and fast-food franchise —
surely represents the plant's most extraordinary evolutionary achievement to
date. For to prosper in the industrial food chain to the extent it has, corn had
to acquire several improbable new tricks. It had to adapt itself not just to humans but to their machines, which it did by learning to grow as upright, stiff-
stalked, and uniform as soldiers. It had to multiply its yield by an order of
magnitude, which it did by learning to grow shoulder to shoulder with other
corn plants, as many as thirty thousand to the acre. It had to develop an appetite for fossil fuel (in the form of petrochemical fertilizer) and a tolerance for
various synthetic chemicals. But even before it could master these tricks and
make a place for itself in the bright sunshine of capitalism, corn first had to
turn itself into something never before seen in the plant world: a form of intellectual property.

The free corn sex I've described allowed people to do virtually anything they wanted with the genetics of corn except own them — a big problem for a would-be capitalist plant. If I crossed two corn plants to create a
variety with an especially desirable trait, I could sell you my special seeds,
but only once, since the corn you grew from my special seeds would produce lots more special seeds, for free and forever, putting me out of business in short order. It's difficult to control the means of production when
the product you're selling can reproduce itself endlessly. This is one of the
ways in which the imperatives of biology are difficult to mesh with the
imperatives of business.

Difficult, but not impossible. Early in the twentieth century American corn breeders figured out how to bring corn reproduction under firm control and to protect the seed from copiers. The breeders discovered that when they crossed two corn plants that had come from inbred lines — from ancestors that had themselves been exclusively self-pollinated for several generations — the hybrid offspring displayed some highly unusual characteristics. First, all the seeds in that first generation (F-1, in the plant breeder's vocabulary) produced genetically identical plants — a trait that, among other things, facilitates mechanization. Second, those plants exhibited heterosis, or hybrid vigor — better yields than either of their parents. But most important of all, they found that the seeds produced by these seeds did not "come true" — the plants in the second (F-2) generation bore little resemblance to the plants in the first. Specifically, their yields plummeted by as much as a third, making their seeds virtually worthless.

Hybrid corn now offered its breeders what no other plant at that time   10
could: the biological equivalent of a patent. Farmers now had to buy new seeds every spring; instead of depending upon their plants to reproduce themselves, they now depended on a corporation. The corporation, assured for the first time of a return on its investment in breeding, showered corn with attention — R&D, promotion, advertising — and the plant responded, multiplying its fruitfulness year after year. With the advent of the F-1 hybrid, a technology with the power to remake nature in the image of capitalism, *Zea mays* entered the industrial age and, in time, it brought the whole American food chain with it.

QUESTIONS

Reading

1. What did hybrid corn come to offer its breeders?
2. What does Pollan mean when he says that "corn was the first plant to involve humans so intimately in its sex life" (paragraph 5)?
3. How does Pollan explain the distinction between first-generation and second-generation seeds?
4. Chart the process of corn reproduction stage by stage, beginning with the journey of a grain of pollen to the ovary. How clear is Pollan's *explanation*? Are there any parts of the process that raise questions for you?

Stage 1	Stage 2	Stage 3

Exploratory Writing

1. Pollan describes corn's adaptation to "our own . . . world of industrial consumer capitalism" as an extraordinary evolutionary achievement. Choose a different common food. Collaborating in small groups, prepare a presentation explaining the "improbable new tricks" the food has developed in order to remain a staple of the modern diet.

2. Pollan's essay centers on a *biological* explanation of corn reproduction, but he also makes some *economic* and *social* claims about corn. Highlight and sort these claims. What do they show about Pollan's agenda and motives in writing this essay?

BIOLOGICAL	ECONOMIC	SOCIAL

3. Research the contentious issue of genetically modified corn and other common crops. Stage a debate about whether genetically modified food is harmful or helpful.

Making Connections

1. Pollan uses surprising language to describe natural phenomena. He writes that conventional biological terms "don't begin to describe the beauty and wonder of corn sex" (paragraph 1). Highlight, underline, or flag places where Pollan uses a term or phrase that you would not normally associate with plant reproduction, and analyze each in relation to Emily Martin's (p. 472) discussion of how the language that biologists use to describe human reproduction reflects cultural biases. How does Pollan's use of language shape how you think about his explanation of corn reproduction?

Essay Writing

1. Write an essay *explaining* the reproductive processes of a plant or an animal, other than corn or human beings. After researching how the reproductive system works, use Pollan's explanatory techniques to enrich and clarify your explanation. Keeping in mind Emily Martin's argument, do your best to write your explanation in unbiased language.

Paired Readings: On Sexual Reproduction

The Egg and the Sperm
How Science Has Constructed a Romance Based on Stereotypical Male-Female Roles

Emily Martin

Emily Martin (b. 1944) is a professor of anthropology at New York University. She has written The Woman in the Body: A Cultural Analysis of Reproduction *(1987) and* Flexible Bodies: Tracking Immunity in American Culture — From the Days of Polio to the Age of AIDS *(1994). In the following article, which originally appeared in the journal* Signs *(1991), Martin's intent is to expose the cultural stereotypes operative in the so-called scientific language surrounding human reproduction.*

The theory of the human body is always a part of a world-picture. . . .
The theory of the human body is always a part of a fantasy.
— [JAMES HILLMAN, *The Myth of Analysis*][1]

As an anthropologist, I am intrigued by the possibility that culture shapes how biological scientists describe what they discover about the natural world. If this were so, we would be learning about more than the natural world in high

Portions of this article were presented as the 1987 Becker Lecture, Cornell University. I am grateful for the many suggestions and ideas I received on this occasion. For especially pertinent help with my arguments and data I thank Richard Cone, Kevin Whaley, Sharon Stephens, Barbara Duden, Susanne Kuechler, Lorna Rhodes, and Scott Gilbert. The article was strengthened and clarified by the comments of the anonymous *Signs* reviewers as well as the superb editorial skills of Amy Gage.
[1]James Hillman, *The Myth of Analysis* (Evanston, Ill.: Northwestern University Press, 1972), 220.

school biology class; we would be learning about cultural beliefs and practices as if they were part of nature. In the course of my research I realized that the picture of egg and sperm drawn in popular as well as scientific accounts of reproductive biology relies on stereotypes central to our cultural definitions of male and female. The stereotypes imply not only that female biological processes are less worthy than their male counterparts but also that women are less worthy than men. Part of my goal in writing this article is to shine a bright light on the gender stereotypes hidden within the scientific language of biology. Exposed in such a light, I hope they will lose much of their power to harm us.

Egg and Sperm: A Scientific Fairy Tale

At a fundamental level, all major scientific textbooks depict male and female reproductive organs as systems for the production of valuable substances, such as eggs and sperm.[2] In the case of women, the monthly cycle is described as being designed to produce eggs and prepare a suitable place for them to be fertilized and grown — all to the end of making babies. But the enthusiasm ends there. By extolling the female cycle as a productive enterprise, menstruation must necessarily be viewed as a failure. Medical texts describe menstruation as the "debris" of the uterine lining, the result of necrosis, or death of tissue. The descriptions imply that a system has gone awry, making products of no use, not to specification, unsalable, wasted, scrap. An illustration in a widely used medical text shows menstruation as a chaotic disintegration of form, complementing the many texts that describe it as "ceasing," "dying," "losing," "denuding," "expelling."[3]

Male reproductive physiology is evaluated quite differently. One of the texts that sees menstruation as failed production employs a sort of breathless prose when it describes the maturation of sperm: "The mechanisms which guide the remarkable cellular transformation from spermatid to mature sperm remain uncertain. . . . Perhaps the most amazing characteristic of spermatogenesis is its sheer magnitude: the normal human male may manufacture several hundred million sperm per day."[4] In the classic text *Medical Physiology*, edited by Vernon Mountcastle, the male/female, productive/destructive comparison is more explicit: "Whereas the female *sheds* only a

---

[2] The textbooks I consulted are the main ones used in classes for undergraduate premedical students or medical students (or those held on reserve in the library for these classes) during the past few years at Johns Hopkins University. These texts are widely used at other universities in the country as well.

[3] Arthur C. Guyton, *Physiology of the Human Body*, 6th ed. (Philadelphia: Saunders College Publishing, 1984), 624.

[4] Arthur J. Vander, James H. Sherman, and Dorothy S. Luciano, *Human Physiology: The Mechanisms of Body Function*, 3d ed. (New York: McGraw Hill, 1980), 483–84.

single gamete each month, the seminiferous tubules *produce* hundreds of millions of sperm each day" (emphasis mine).[5] The female author of another text marvels at the length of the microscopic seminiferous tubules, which, if uncoiled and placed end to end, "would span almost one-third of a mile!" She writes, "In an adult male these structures produce millions of sperm cells each day." Later she asks, "How is this feat accomplished?"[6] None of these texts expresses such intense enthusiasm for any female processes. It is surely no accident that the "remarkable" process of making sperm involves precisely what, in the medical view, menstruation does not: production of something deemed valuable.[7]

One could argue that menstruation and spermatogenesis are not analogous processes and, therefore, should not be expected to elicit the same kind of response. The proper female analogy to spermatogenesis, biologically, is ovulation. Yet ovulation does not merit enthusiasm in these texts either. Textbook descriptions stress that all of the ovarian follicles containing ova are already present at birth. Far from being *produced*, as sperm are, they merely sit on the shelf, slowly degenerating and aging like overstocked inventory: "At birth, normal human ovaries contain an estimated one million follicles [each], and no new ones appear after birth. Thus, in marked contrast to the male, the newborn female already has all the germ cells she will ever have. Only a few, perhaps 400, are destined to reach full maturity during her active productive life. All the others degenerate at some point in their development so that few, if any, remain by the time she reaches menopause at approximately 50 years of age."[8] Note the "marked contrast" that this description sets up between male and female: the male, who continuously produces fresh germ cells, and the female, who has stockpiled germ cells by birth and is faced with their degeneration.

Nor are the female organs spared such vivid descriptions. One scientist   5
writes in a newspaper article that a woman's ovaries become old and worn out from ripening eggs every month, even though the woman herself is still relatively young: "When you look through a laparoscope . . . at an ovary that has been through hundreds of cycles, even in a superbly healthy American female, you see a scarred, battered organ."[9]

To avoid the negative connotations that some people associate with the female reproductive system, scientists could begin to describe male and female

---

[5]Vernon B. Mountcastle, *Medical Physiology*, 14th ed. (London: Mosby, 1980), 2:1624.

[6]Eldra Pearl Solomon, *Human Anatomy and Physiology* (New York: CBS College Publishing, 1983), 678.

[7]For elaboration, see Emily Martin, *The Woman in the Body: A Cultural Analysis of Reproduction* (Boston: Beacon, 1987), 27–53.

[8]Vander, Sherman, and Luciano, 568.

[9]Melvin Konner, "Childbearing and Age," *New York Times Magazine* (December 27, 1987), 22–23, esp. 22.

processes as homologous. They might credit females with "producing" mature ova one at a time, as they're needed each month, and describe males as having to face problems of degenerating germ cells. This degeneration would occur throughout life among spermatogonia, the undifferentiated germ cells in the testes that are the long-lived, dormant precursors of sperm.

But the texts have an almost dogged insistence on casting female processes in a negative light. The texts celebrate sperm production because it is continuous from puberty to senescence, while they portray egg production as inferior because it is finished at birth. This makes the female seem unproductive, but some texts will also insist that it is she who is wasteful.[10] In a section heading for *Molecular Biology of the Cell*, a best-selling text, we are told that "Oogenesis is wasteful." The text goes on to emphasize that of the seven million oogonia, or egg germ cells, in the female embryo, most degenerate in the ovary. Of those that do go on to become oocytes, or eggs, many also degenerate, so that at birth only two million eggs remain in the ovaries. Degeneration continues throughout a woman's life: by puberty three hundred thousand eggs remain, and only a few are present by menopause. "During the 40 or so years of a woman's reproductive life, only 400 to 500 eggs will have been released," the authors write. "All the rest will have degenerated. It is still a mystery why so many eggs are formed only to die in the ovaries."[11]

The real mystery is why the male's vast production of sperm is not seen as wasteful.[12] Assuming that a man "produces" 100 million (10^8) sperm per day

---

[10]I have found but one exception to the opinion that the female is wasteful: "Smallpox being the nasty disease it is, one might expect nature to have designed antibody molecules with combining sites that specifically recognize the epitopes on smallpox virus. Nature differs from technology, however: it thinks nothing of wastefulness. (For example, rather than improving the chance that a spermatozoon will meet an egg cell, nature finds it easier to produce millions of spermatozoa)" (Niels Kaj Jerne, "The Immune System," *Scientific American* 229, no. 1 [July 1973]: 53). Thanks to a *Signs* reviewer for bringing this reference to my attention.

[11]Bruce Alberts et al., *Molecular Biology of the Cell* (New York: Garland, 1983), 795.

[12]In her essay "Have Only Men Evolved?" (in *Discovering Reality: Feminist Perspectives on Epistemology, Metaphysics, Methodology, and Philosophy of Science*, ed. Sandra Harding and Merrill B. Hintikka [Dordrecht, The Netherlands: Reidel, 1983], 45–69, esp. 60–61), Ruth Hubbard points out that sociobiologists have said the female invests more energy than the male in the production of her large gametes, claiming that this explains why the female provides parental care. Hubbard questions whether it "really takes more 'energy' to generate the one or relatively few eggs than the large excess of sperms required to achieve fertilization." For further critique of how the greater size of eggs is interpreted in sociobiology, see Donna Haraway, "Investment Strategies for the Evolving Portfolio of Primate Females," in *Body/Politics*, ed. Mary Jacobus, Evelyn Fox Keller, and Sally Shuttleworth (New York: Routledge, 1990), 155–56.

(a conservative estimate) during an average reproductive life of sixty years, he would produce well over two trillion sperm in his lifetime. Assuming that a woman "ripens" one egg per lunar month, or thirteen per year, over the course of her forty-year reproductive life, she would total five hundred eggs in her lifetime. But the word "waste" implies an excess, too much produced. Assuming two or three offspring, for every baby a woman produces, she wastes only around two hundred eggs. For every baby a man produces, he wastes more than one trillion (10^{12}) sperm.

How is it that positive images are denied to the bodies of women? A look at language — in this case, scientific language — provides the first clue. Take the egg and the sperm.[13] It is remarkable how "femininely" the egg behaves and how "masculinely" the sperm.[14] The egg is seen as large and passive.[15] It does not *move* or *journey*, but passively "is transported," "is swept,"[16] or even "drifts"[17] along the fallopian tube. In utter contrast, sperm are small, "streamlined,"[18] and invariably active. They "deliver" their genes to the egg, "activate the developmental program of the egg,"[19] and have a "velocity" that is often remarked upon.[20] Their tails are "strong" and efficiently powered.[21] Together with the forces of ejaculation, they can "propel the semen into the deepest recesses of the vagina."[22] For this they need "energy," "fuel,"[23] so that with a

---

[13]The sources I used for this article provide compelling information on interactions among sperm. Lack of space prevents me from taking up this theme here, but the elements include competition, hierarchy, and sacrifice. For a newspaper report, see Malcolm W. Browne, "Some Thoughts on Self Sacrifice," *New York Times* (July 5, 1988), C6. For a literary rendition, see John Barth, "Night-Sea Journey," in his *Lost in the Funhouse* (Garden City, N.Y.: Doubleday, 1968), 3–13.

[14]See Carol Delaney, "The Meaning of Paternity and the Virgin Birth Debate," *Man* 21, no. 3 (September 1986): 494–513. She discusses the difference between this scientific view that women contribute genetic material to the fetus and the claim of long-standing Western folk theories that the origin and identity of the fetus comes from the male, as in the metaphor of planting a seed in soil.

[15]For a suggested direct link between human behavior and purportedly passive eggs and active sperm, see Erik H. Erikson, "Inner and Outer Space: Reflections on Womanhood," *Daedalus* 93, no. 2 (Spring 1964): 582–606, esp. 591.

[16]Guyton (n. 3), 619; and Mountcastle (n. 5), 1609.

[17]Jonathan Miller and David Pelham, *The Facts of Life* (New York: Viking Penguin, 1984), 5.

[18]Alberts et al., 796.

[19]Ibid., 796.

[20]See, e.g., William F. Ganong, *Review of Medical Physiology*, 7th ed. (Los Altos, Calif.: Lange Medical Publications, 1975), 322.

[21]Alberts et al. (n. 11), 796.

[22]Guyton, 615.

[23]Solomon (n. 6), 683.

"whiplashlike motion and strong lurches"[24] they can "burrow through the egg coat"[25] and "penetrate" it.[26]

At its extreme, the age-old relationship of the egg and the sperm takes on   10
a royal or religious patina. The egg coat, its protective barrier, is sometimes
called its "vestments," a term usually reserved for sacred, religious dress. The
egg is said to have a "corona,"[27] a crown, and to be accompanied by "attendant cells."[28] It is holy, set apart and above, the queen to the sperm's king. The
egg is also passive, which means it must depend on sperm for rescue. Gerald
Schatten and Helen Schatten liken the egg's role to that of Sleeping Beauty: "a
dormant bride awaiting her mate's magic kiss, which instills the spirit that
brings her to life."[29] Sperm, by contrast, have a "mission,"[30] which is to "move
through the female genital tract in quest of the ovum."[31] One popular account
has it that the sperm carry out a "perilous journey" into the "warm darkness,"
where some fall away "exhausted." "Survivors" "assault" the egg, the successful candidates "surrounding the prize."[32] Part of the urgency of this journey, in
more scientific terms, is that "once released from the supportive environment
of the ovary, an egg will die within hours unless rescued by a sperm."[33] The
wording stresses the fragility and dependency of the egg, even though the same
text acknowledges elsewhere that sperm also live for only a few hours.[34]

In 1948, in a book remarkable for its early insights into these matters,
Ruth Herschberger argued that female reproductive organs are seen as biologically interdependent, while male organs are viewed as autonomous,
operating independently and in isolation:

> At present the functional is stressed only in connection with
> women: it is in them that ovaries, tubes, uterus, and vagina have
> endless interdependence. In the male, reproduction would seem to
> involve "organs" only.
>
> Yet the sperm, just as much as the egg, is dependent on a great
> many related processes. There are secretions which mitigate the

---

[24]Vander, Sherman, and Luciano (n. 4), 4th ed. (1985), 580.

[25]Alberts et al., 796.

[26]All biology texts quoted use the word "penetrate."

[27]Solomon, 700.

[28]A. Beldecos et al., "The Importance of Feminist Critique for Contemporary Cell Biology," *Hypatia* 3, no. 1 (Spring 1988): 61–76.

[29]Gerald Schatten and Helen Schatten, "The Energetic Egg," *Medical World News* 23 (January 23, 1984): 51–53, esp. 51.

[30]Alberts et al., 796.

[31]Guyton (n. 3), 613.

[32]Miller and Pelham (n. 17), 7.

[33]Alberts et al. (n. 11), 804.

[34]Ibid., 801.

urine in the urethra before ejaculation, to protect the sperm. There is the reflex shutting off of the bladder connection, the provision of prostatic secretions, and various types of muscular propulsion. The sperm is no more independent of its milieu than the egg, and yet from a wish that it were, biologists have lent their support to the notion that the human female, beginning with the egg, is congenitally more dependent than the male.[35]

Bringing out another aspect of the sperm's autonomy, an article in the journal *Cell* has the sperm making an "existential decision" to penetrate the egg: "Sperm are cells with a limited behavioral repertoire, one that is directed toward fertilizing eggs. To execute the decision to abandon the haploid state, sperm swim to an egg and there acquire the ability to effect membrane fusion."[36] Is this a corporate manager's version of the sperm's activities — "executing decisions" while fraught with dismay over difficult options that bring with them very high risk?

There is another way that sperm, despite their small size, can be made to loom in importance over the egg. In a collection of scientific papers, an electron micrograph of an enormous egg and tiny sperm is titled "A Portrait of the Sperm."[37] This is a little like showing a photo of a dog and calling it a picture of the fleas. Granted, microscopic sperm are harder to photograph than eggs, which are just large enough to see with the naked eye. But surely the use of the term "portrait," a word associated with the powerful and wealthy, is significant. Eggs have only micrographs or pictures, not portraits.

One depiction of sperm as weak and timid, instead of strong and powerful — the only such representation in Western civilization, so far as I know — occurs in Woody Allen's movie *Everything You Always Wanted to Know about Sex but Were Afraid to Ask*. Allen, playing the part of an apprehensive sperm inside a man's testicles, is scared of the man's approaching orgasm. He is reluctant to launch himself into the darkness, afraid of contraceptive devices, afraid of winding up on the ceiling if the man masturbates.

The more common picture — egg as damsel in distress, shielded only   15
by her sacred garments; sperm as heroic warrior to the rescue — cannot be proved to be dictated by the biology of these events. While the "facts" of biology may not *always* be constructed in cultural terms, I would argue

---

[35]Ruth Herschberger, *Adam's Rib* (New York: Pelligrini & Cudaby, 1948), esp. 84. I am indebted to Ruth Hubbard for telling me about Herschberger's work, although at a point when this paper was already in draft form.

[36]Bennett M. Shapiro, "The Existential Decision of a Sperm," *Cell* 49, no. 3 (May 1987): 293–94, esp. 293.

[37]Lennart Nilsson, "A Portrait of the Sperm," in *The Functional Anatomy of the Spermatozoan*, ed. Bjorn A. Afzelius (New York: Pergamon, 1975), 79–82.

that in this case they are. The degree of metaphorical content in these descriptions, the extent to which differences between egg and sperm are emphasized, and the parallels between cultural stereotypes of male and female behavior and the character of egg and sperm all point to this conclusion.

New Research, Old Imagery

As new understandings of egg and sperm emerge, textbook gender imagery is being revised. But the new research, far from escaping the stereotypical representations of egg and sperm, simply replicates elements of textbook gender imagery in a different form. The persistence of this imagery calls to mind what Ludwik Fleck termed "the self-contained" nature of scientific thought. As he described it, "the interaction between what is already known, what remains to be learned, and those who are to apprehend it, go to ensure harmony within the system. But at the same time they also preserve the harmony of illusions, which is quite secure within the confines of a given thought style."[38] We need to understand the way in which the cultural content in scientific descriptions changes as biological discoveries unfold, and whether that cultural content is solidly entrenched or easily changed.

In all of the texts quoted above, sperm are described as penetrating the egg, and specific substances on a sperm's head are described as binding to the egg. Recently, this description of events was rewritten in a biophysics lab at Johns Hopkins University — transforming the egg from the passive to the active party.[39]

Prior to this research, it was thought that the zona, the inner vestments of the egg, formed an impenetrable barrier. Sperm overcame the barrier by mechanically burrowing through, thrashing their tails and slowly working their way along. Later research showed that the sperm released digestive enzymes that chemically broke down the zona; thus, scientists presumed that the sperm used mechanical *and* chemical means to get through to the egg.

In this recent investigation, the researchers began to ask questions about the mechanical force of the sperm's tail. (The lab's goal was to develop a contraceptive that worked topically on sperm.) They discovered, to their great surprise, that the forward thrust of sperm is extremely weak,

---

[38]Ludwik Fleck, *Genesis and Development of a Scientific Fact*, ed. Thaddeus J. Trenn and Robert K. Merton (Chicago: University of Chicago Press, 1979), 38.

[39]Jay M. Baltz carried out the research I describe when he was a graduate student in the Thomas C. Jenkins Department of Biophysics at Johns Hopkins University.

which contradicts the assumption that sperm are forceful penetrators.[40] Rather than thrusting forward, the sperm's head was now seen to move mostly back and forth. The sideways motion of the sperm's tail makes the head move sideways with a force that is ten times stronger than its forward movement. So even if the overall force of the sperm were strong enough to mechanically break the zona, most of its force would be directed sideways rather than forward. In fact, its strongest tendency, by tenfold, is to escape by attempting to pry itself off the egg. Sperm, then, must be exceptionally efficient at *escaping* from any cell surface they contact. And the surface of the egg must be designed to trap the sperm and prevent their escape. Otherwise, few if any sperm would reach the egg.

The researchers at Johns Hopkins concluded that the sperm and egg   20 stick together because of adhesive molecules on the surfaces of each. The egg traps the sperm and adheres to it so tightly that the sperm's head is forced to lie flat against the surface of the zona, a little bit, they told me, "like Br'er Rabbit getting more and more stuck to tar baby the more he wriggles." The trapped sperm continues to wiggle ineffectually side to side. The mechanical force of its tail is so weak that a sperm cannot break even one chemical bond. This is where the digestive enzymes released by the sperm come in. If they start to soften the zona just at the tip of the sperm and the sides remain stuck, then the weak, flailing sperm can get oriented in the right direction and make it through the zona — provided that its bonds to the zona dissolve as it moves in.

Although this new version of the saga of the egg and the sperm broke through cultural expectations, the researchers who made the discovery continued to write papers and abstracts as if the sperm were the active party who attacks, binds, penetrates, and enters the egg. The only difference was that sperm were now seen as performing these actions weakly.[41] Not until August 1987, more than three years after the findings described above, did these researchers reconceptualize the process to give the egg a more active role. They began to describe the zona as an aggressive sperm catcher, covered with adhesive molecules that can capture a sperm with a single bond

-----

[40]Far less is known about the physiology of sperm than comparable female substances, which some feminists claim is no accident. Greater scientific scrutiny of female reproduction has long enabled the burden of birth control to be placed on women. In this case, the researchers' discovery did not depend on development of any new technology. The experiments made use of glass pipettes, a manometer, and a simple microscope, all of which have been available for more than one hundred years.

[41]Jay Baltz and Richard A. Cone, "What Force Is Needed to Tether a Sperm?" (abstract for Society for the Study of Reproduction, 1985), and "Flagellar Torque on the Head Determines the Force Needed to Tether a Sperm" (abstract for Biophysical Society, 1986).

and clasp it to the zona's surface.[42] In the words of their published account: "The innermost vestment, the *zona pellucida*, is a glyco-protein shell, which captures and tethers the sperm before they penetrate it. . . . The sperm is captured at the initial contact between the sperm tip and the *zona*. . . . Since the thrust [of the sperm] is much smaller than the force needed to break a single affinity bond, the first bond made upon the tip-first meeting of the sperm and *zona* can result in the capture of the sperm."[43]

Experiments in another lab reveal similar patterns of data interpretation. Gerald Schatten and Helen Schatten set out to show that, contrary to conventional wisdom, the "egg is not merely a large, yolk-filled sphere into which the sperm burrows to endow new life. Rather, recent research suggests the almost heretical view that sperm and egg are mutually active partners."[44] This sounds like a departure from the stereotypical textbook view, but further reading reveals Schatten and Schatten's conformity to the aggressive-sperm metaphor. They describe how "the sperm and egg first touch when, from the tip of the sperm's triangular head, a long, thin filament shoots out and harpoons the egg." Then we learn that "remarkably, the harpoon is not so much fired as assembled at great speed, molecule by molecule, from a pool of protein stored in a specialized region called the acrosome. The filament may grow as much as twenty times longer than the sperm head itself before its tip reaches the egg and sticks."[45] Why not call this "making a bridge" or "throwing out a line" rather than firing a harpoon? Harpoons pierce prey and injure or kill them, while this filament only sticks. And why not focus, as the Hopkins lab did, on the stickiness of the egg, rather than the stickiness of the sperm?[46] Later in the article, the Schattens replicate the common view of the sperm's perilous journey into the warm darkness of the vagina, this time for the purpose of explaining its journey into the egg itself: "[The sperm] still has

---

[42]Jay M. Baltz, David F. Katz, and Richard A. Cone, "The Mechanics of the Sperm-Egg Interaction at the Zona Pellucida," *Biophysical Journal* 54, no. 4 (October 1988): 643–54. Lab members were somewhat familiar with work on metaphors in the biology of female reproduction. Richard Cone, who runs the lab, is my husband, and he talked with them about my earlier research on the subject from time to time. Even though my current research focuses on biological imagery and I heard about the lab's work from my husband every day, I myself did not recognize the role of imagery in the sperm research until many weeks after the period of research and writing I describe. Therefore, I assume that any awareness the lab members may have had about how underlying metaphor might be guiding this particular research was fairly inchoate.

[43]Ibid., 643, 650.

[44]Schatten and Schatten (n. 29), 51.

[45]Ibid., 52.

[46]Surprisingly, in an article intended for a general audience, the authors do not point out that these are sea urchin sperm and note that human sperm do not shoot out filaments at all.

an arduous journey ahead. It must penetrate farther into the egg's huge sphere of cytoplasm and somehow locate the nucleus, so that the two cells' chromosomes can fuse. The sperm dives down into the cytoplasm, its tail beating. But it is soon interrupted by the sudden and swift migration of the egg nucleus, which rushes toward the sperm with a velocity triple that of the movement of chromosomes during cell division, crossing the entire egg in about a minute."[47]

Like Schatten and Schatten and the biophysicists at Johns Hopkins, another researcher has recently made discoveries that seem to point to a more interactive view of the relationship of egg and sperm. This work, which Paul Wassarman conducted on the sperm and eggs of mice, focuses on identifying the specific molecules in the egg coat (the zona pellucida) that are involved in egg-sperm interaction. At first glance, his descriptions seem to fit the model of an egalitarian relationship. Male and female gametes "recognize one another," and "interactions . . . take place between sperm and egg."[48] But the article in *Scientific American* in which those descriptions appear begins with a vignette that presages the dominant motif of their presentation: "It has been more than a century since Hermann Fol, a Swiss zoologist, peered into his microscope and became the first person to see a sperm penetrate an egg, fertilize it and form the first cell of a new embryo."[49] This portrayal of the sperm as the active party—the one that *penetrates* and *fertilizes* the egg and *produces* the embryo—is not cited as an example of an earlier, now outmoded view. In fact, the author reiterates the point later in the article: "Many sperm can bind to and penetrate the zona pellucida, or outer coat, of an unfertilized mouse egg, but only one sperm will eventually fuse with the thin plasma membrane surrounding the egg proper (*inner sphere*), fertilizing the egg and giving rise to a new embryo."[50]

The imagery of sperm as aggressor is particularly startling in this case: the main discovery being reported is isolation of a particular molecule *on the egg coat* that plays an important role in fertilization! Wassarman's choice of language sustains the picture. He calls the molecule that has been isolated, ZP3, a "sperm receptor." By allocating the passive, waiting role to the egg, Wassarman can continue to describe the sperm as the actor, the one that makes it all happen: "The basic process begins when many sperm first attach loosely and then bind tenaciously to receptors on the surface of the egg's thick outer coat, the zona pellucida. Each sperm, which has a large number of egg-binding proteins on its surface, binds to many sperm receptors on the egg. More specifically, a site on each of the egg-binding proteins

---

[47]Schatten and Schatten, 53.

[48]Paul M. Wassarman, "Fertilization in Mammals," *Scientific American* 259, no. 6 (December 1988): 78–84, esp. 78, 84.

[49]Ibid., 78.

[50]Ibid., 79.

fits a complementary site on a sperm receptor, much as a key fits a lock."[51] With the sperm designated as the "key" and the egg the "lock," it is obvious which one acts and which one is acted upon. Could this imagery not be reversed, letting the sperm (the lock) wait until the egg produces the key? Or could we speak of two halves of a locket matching, and regard the matching itself as the action that initiates the fertilization?

It is as if Wassarman were determined to make the egg the receiving   25
partner. Usually in biological research, the *protein* member of the pair of binding molecules is called the receptor, and physically it has a pocket in it rather like a lock. As the diagrams that illustrate Wassarman's article show, the molecules on the sperm are proteins and have "pockets." The small, mobile molecules that fit into these pockets are called ligands. As shown in the diagrams, ZP3 on the egg is a polymer of "keys"; many small knobs stick out. Typically, molecules on the sperm would be called receptors and molecules on the egg would be called ligands. But Wassarman chose to name ZP3 on the egg the receptor and to create a new term, "the egg-binding protein," for the molecule on the sperm that otherwise would have been called the receptor.[52]

Wassarman does credit the egg coat with having more functions than those of a sperm receptor. While he notes that "the zona pellucida has at times been viewed by investigators as a nuisance, a barrier to sperm and hence an impediment to fertilization," his new research reveals that the egg coat "serves as a sophisticated biological security system that screens incoming sperm, selects only those compatible with fertilization and development, prepares sperm for fusion with the egg and later protects the resulting embryo from polyspermy [a lethal condition caused by fusion of more than one sperm with a single egg]."[53] Although this description gives the egg an active role, that role is drawn in stereotypically feminine terms. The egg *selects* an appropriate mate, *prepares* him for fusion, and then *protects* the resulting offspring from harm. This is courtship and mating behavior as seen through the eyes of a sociobiologist: woman as the hard-to-get prize, who, following union with the chosen one, becomes woman as servant and mother.

And Wassarman does not quit there. In a review article for *Science*, he outlines the "chronology of fertilization."[54] Near the end of the article are

---

[51]Ibid., 78.

[52]Since receptor molecules are relatively immotile and the ligands that bind to them relatively motile, one might imagine the egg being called the receptor and the sperm the ligand. But the molecules in question on egg and sperm are immotile molecules. It is the sperm as a cell that has motility, and the egg as a cell that has relative immotility.

[53]Wassarman, 78–79.

[54]Paul M. Wassarman, "The Biology and Chemistry of Fertilization," *Science* 235, no. 4788 (January 30, 1987): 553–60, esp. 554.

two subject headings. One is "Sperm Penetration," in which Wassarman describes how the chemical dissolving of the zona pellucida combines with the "substantial propulsive force generated by sperm." The next heading is "Sperm-Egg Fusion." This section details what happens inside the zona after a sperm "penetrates" it. Sperm "can make contact with, adhere to, and fuse with (that is, fertilize) an egg."[55] Wassarman's word choice, again, is astonishingly skewed in favor of the sperm's activity, for in the next breath he says that sperm *lose* all motility upon fusion with the egg's surface. In mouse and sea urchin eggs, the sperm enters at the *egg's* volition, according to Wassarman's description: "Once fused with egg plasma membrane [the surface of the egg], how does a sperm enter the egg? The surface of both mouse and sea urchin eggs is covered with thousands of plasma membrane-bound projections, called microvilli [tiny 'hairs']. Evidence in sea urchins suggests that, after membrane fusion, a group of elongated microvilli cluster tightly around and interdigitate over the sperm head. As these microvilli are resorbed, the sperm is drawn into the egg. Therefore, sperm motility, which ceases at the time of fusion in both sea urchins and mice, is not required for sperm entry."[56] The section called "Sperm Penetration" more logically would be followed by a section called "The Egg Envelops," rather than "Sperm-Egg Fusion." This would give a parallel — and more accurate — sense that both the egg and the sperm initiate action.

Another way that Wassarman makes less of the egg's activity is by describing components of the egg but referring to the sperm as a whole entity. Deborah Gordon has described such an approach as "atomism" ("the part is independent of and primordial to the whole") and identified it as one of the "tenacious assumptions" of Western science and medicine.[57] Wassarman employs atomism to his advantage. When he refers to processing going on within sperm, he consistently returns to descriptions that remind us from whence these activities came: they are part of sperm that penetrate an egg or generate propulsive force. When he refers to processes going on within eggs, he stops there. As a result, any active role he grants them appears to be assigned to the parts of the egg, and not to the egg itself. In the quote above, it is the microvilli that actively cluster around the sperm. In another example, "the driving force for engulfment of a fused sperm comes from a region of cytoplasm just beneath an egg's plasma membrane."[58]

---

[55]Ibid., 557.

[56]Ibid., 557–58. This finding throws into question Schatten and Schatten's description (n. 29 above) of the sperm, its tail beating, diving down into the egg.

[57]Deborah R. Gordon, "Tenacious Assumptions in Western Medicine," in *Biomedicine Examined*, ed. Margaret Lock and Deborah Gordon (Dordrecht, The Netherlands: Kluwer, 1988), 19–56, esp. 26.

[58]Wassarman, "The Biology and Chemistry of Fertilization," 558.

Social Implications: Thinking Beyond

All three of these revisionist accounts of egg and sperm cannot seem to escape the hierarchical imagery of older accounts. Even though each new account gives the egg a larger and more active role, taken together they bring into play another cultural stereotype: woman as a dangerous and aggressive threat. In the Johns Hopkins lab's revised model, the egg ends up as the female aggressor who "captures and tethers" the sperm with her sticky zona, rather like a spider lying in wait in her web.[59] The Schatten lab has the egg's nucleus "interrupt" the sperm's dive with a "sudden and swift" rush by which she "clasps the sperm and guides its nucleus to the center."[60] Wassarman's description of the surface of the egg "covered with thousands of plasma membrane-bound projections, called microvilli" that reach out and clasp the sperm adds to the spiderlike imagery.[61]

These images grant the egg an active role but at the cost of appearing 30
disturbingly aggressive. Images of woman as dangerous and aggressive, the femme fatale who victimizes men, are widespread in Western literature and culture.[62] More specific is the connection of spider imagery with the idea of an engulfing, devouring mother.[63] New data did not lead scientists to eliminate gender stereotypes in their descriptions of egg and sperm. Instead, scientists simply began to describe egg and sperm in different, but no less damaging, terms.

Can we envision a less stereotypical view? Biology itself provides another model that could be applied to the egg and the sperm. The cybernetic model — with its feedback loops, flexible adaptation to change, coordination of the parts within a whole, evolution over time, and changing response to the environment — is common in genetics, endocrinology, and ecology and has a growing influence in medicine in general.[64] This model has the potential to shift our imagery from the negative, in which the female reproductive system is castigated both for not producing eggs after birth and for producing (and thus wasting) too many eggs overall, to something more positive. The female reproductive system could be seen as responding to the environment (pregnancy or menopause), adjusting to

[59]Baltz, Katz, and Cone (n. 42 above), 643, 650.

[60]Schatten and Schatten, 53.

[61]Wassarman, "The Biology and Chemistry of Fertilization," 557.

[62]Mary Ellman, *Thinking about Women* (New York: Harcourt Brace Jovanovich, 1968), 140; Nina Auerbach, *Woman and the Demon* (Cambridge, Mass.: Harvard University Press, 1982), esp. 186.

[63]Kenneth Alan Adams, "Arachnophobia: Love American Style," *Journal of Psychoanalytic Anthropology* 4, no. 2 (1981): 157–97.

[64]William Ray Arney and Bernard Bergen, *Medicine and the Management of Living* (Chicago: University of Chicago Press, 1984).

monthly changes (menstruation), and flexibly changing from reproductivity after puberty to nonreproductivity later in life. The sperm and egg's interaction could also be described in cybernetic terms. J. F. Hartman's research in reproductive biology demonstrated fifteen years ago that if an egg is killed by being pricked with a needle, live sperm cannot get through the zona.[65] Clearly, this evidence shows that the egg and sperm *do* interact on more mutual terms, making biology's refusal to portray them that way all the more disturbing.

We would do well to be aware, however, that cybernetic imagery is hardly neutral. In the past, cybernetic models have played an important part in the imposition of social control. These models inherently provide a way of thinking about a "field" of interacting components. Once the field can be seen, it can become the object of new forms of knowledge, which in turn can allow new forms of social control to be exerted over the components of the field. During the 1950s, for example, medicine began to recognize the psychosocial *environment* of the patient: the patient's family and its psychodynamics. Professions such as social work began to focus on this new environment, and the resulting knowledge became one way to further control the patient. Patients began to be seen not as isolated, individual bodies, but as psychosocial entities located in an "ecological" system: management of "the patient's psychology was a new entrée to patient control."[66]

The models that biologists use to describe their data can have important social effects. During the nineteenth century, the social and natural sciences strongly influenced each other: the social ideas of Malthus about how to avoid the natural increase of the poor inspired Darwin's *Origin of Species*.[67] Once the *Origin* stood as a description of the natural world, complete with competition and market struggles, it could be reimported into social science as social Darwinism, in order to justify the social order of the time. What we are seeing now is similar: the importation of cultural ideas about passive females and heroic males into the "personalities" of gametes. This amounts to the "implanting of social imagery on representations of nature so as to lay a firm basis for reimporting exactly that same imagery as natural explanations of social phenomena."[68]

Further research would show us exactly what social effects are being wrought from the biological imagery of egg and sperm. At the very least, the imagery keeps alive some of the hoariest old stereotypes about weak damsels in distress and their strong male rescuers. That these stereotypes are

---

[65]J. F. Hartman, R. B. Gwatkin, and C. F. Hutchison, "Early Contact Interactions between Mammalian Gametes *In Vitro*," *Proceedings of the National Academy of Sciences (U.S.)* 69, no. 10 (1972): 2767–69.

[66]Arney and Bergen, 68.

[67]Ruth Hubbard, "Have Only Men Evolved?" (n. 12 above), 51–52.

[68]David Harvey, personal communication, November 1989.

now being written in at the level of the *cell* constitutes a powerful move to make them seem so natural as to be beyond alteration.

The stereotypical imagery might also encourage people to imagine that what results from the interaction of egg and sperm—a fertilized egg—is the result of deliberate "human" action at the cellular level. Whatever the intentions of the human couple, in this microscope "culture" a cellular "bride" (or femme fatale) and a cellular "groom" (her victim) make a cellular baby. Rosalind Petchesky points out that through visual representations such as sonograms, we are given "*images* of younger and younger, and tinier and tinier, fetuses being 'saved.'" This leads to "the point of viability being 'pushed back' *indefinitely.*"[69] Endowing egg and sperm with intentional action, a key aspect of personhood in our culture, lays the foundation for the point of viability being pushed back to the moment of fertilization. This will likely lead to greater acceptance of technological developments and new forms of scrutiny and manipulation, for the benefit of these inner "persons": court-ordered restrictions on a pregnant woman's activities in order to protect her fetus, fetal surgery, amniocentesis, and rescinding of abortion rights, to name but a few examples.[70]

Even if we succeed in substituting more egalitarian, interactive metaphors to describe the activities of egg and sperm, and manage to avoid the pitfalls of cybernetic models, we would still be guilty of endowing cellular entities with personhood. More crucial, then, than what *kinds* of personalities we bestow on cells is the very fact that we are doing it at all. This process could ultimately have the most disturbing social consequences.

One clear feminist challenge is to wake up sleeping metaphors in science, particularly those involved in descriptions of the egg and the sperm. Although the literary convention is to call such metaphors "dead," they are not so much dead as sleeping, hidden within the scientific content of texts— and all the more powerful for it.[71] Waking up such metaphors, by becoming aware of when we are projecting cultural imagery onto what we study, will improve our ability to investigate and understand nature. Waking up such metaphors, by becoming aware of their implications, will rob them of their power to naturalize our social conventions about gender.

[69]Rosalind Petchesky, "Fetal Images: The Power of Visual Culture in the Politics of Reproduction," *Feminist Studies* 13, no. 2 (Summer 1987): 263–92, esp. 272.

[70]Rita Arditti, Renate Klein, and Shelley Minden, *Test-Tube Women* (London: Pandora, 1984); Ellen Goodman, "Whose Right to Life?" *Baltimore Sun* (November 17, 1987); Tamar Lewin, "Courts Acting to Force Care of the Unborn," *New York Times* (November 23, 1987), A1 and B10; Susan Irwin and Brigitte Jordan, "Knowledge, Practice, and Power: Court Ordered Cesarean Sections," *Medical Anthropology Quarterly* 1, no. 3 (September 1987): 319–34.

[71]Thanks to Elizabeth Fee and David Spain, who in February 1989 and April 1989, respectively, made points related to this.

QUESTIONS

Reading

1. Summarize Martin's argument. How has she structured it?
2. What does Ludwik Fleck mean by the "self-contained" nature of scientific thought (paragraph 16)?
3. The first subheading in the essay is "Egg and Sperm: A Scientific Fairy Tale." The implications are that the actions of the egg and sperm constitute a story written by scientists. List ways that different fairy-tale images or archetypes are often attached to characterizations of the egg and the sperm.

EGG	SPERM

Exploratory Writing

1. Collaborating in small groups, look at some biology textbooks. Are the same or similar "sleeping metaphors" that Martin discusses present in the discussions of human or animal reproduction? What about other bodily processes and functions? Conduct a sleeping-metaphor search through one or more textbooks. List five to ten examples (or more) of writing in which the description of biological functions reflects cultural ideas or prejudices.
2. Using the biological information in Martin's essay, write a nonsexist description of the reproductive functions. In your conclusion, reflect on any difficulties you encountered in keeping your cellular entities free of personhood. Switch papers with a classmate to check each other for sleeping metaphors.
3. Unlike many essayists in this book, Martin uses footnotes extensively in her argumentative essay. Read these footnotes carefully. What is Martin's purpose in using them?

Making Connections

1. In Michael Pollan's (p. 467) explanation of "corn sex," he bypasses traditional scientific language, instead using language that humanizes, or even anthropomorphizes, the corn, giving it character and personality. Would you call Pollan's essay a "scientific fairy tale"? Using Martin's

analysis of sleeping metaphors and biased scientific language, rewrite Pollan's "corn sex" description. Maintain the scientific facts of his narrative, but give the corn a whole new personality. Identify the rhetorical devices that you use in your rewriting process.

Essay Writing

1. Look at a sampling of sex education texts and materials designed for elementary or secondary school students to see if the cultural stereotypes that Martin warns against are present. What analogies and metaphors do you find being used? Write up your discussion as an argument either for or against the revision of those texts.
2. Write an essay reflecting on a time in your life when an assumption you had was turned on its head, and you learned to look at one of your beliefs in a radical new way.

CASEBOOKS

Virtual Experience: Life Online

The six readings collected in this casebook address some of the many ways the Internet has changed — and continues to change — life as we know it. These changes are happening so quickly that they seem almost invisible. But if you stop to think about it, the Internet — along with the technologies, businesses, communication, and knowledge associated with it — is changing how we talk to each other; how we study; how we create, disseminate, and store knowledge and information; how we conduct relationships with friends and loved ones; how we argue; how we elect our leaders; how we shop; how we read; and how we write. It's no exaggeration to say that we are living through one of the biggest cultural shifts in history. And we're still in the very early years of what some have coined the digital age — a name that calls to mind previous eras of vast change: the Stone Age, the print revolution, the Industrial Revolution, and the computer age.

The following readings are engaged in a conversation about how the Internet is changing *particular* facets of our lives — including political debate (Andrew Sullivan's "Why I Blog"), the collection and dissemination of knowledge (Marshall Poe's "The Hive" and Anthony Grafton's "Future Reading: Digitization and Its Discontents"), the development of our minds (Nicholas Carr's "Is Google Making Us Stupid?"), our social lives and intimate relationships (Clive Thompson's "I'm So Totally, Digitally, Close to You"), and race relations (Guillermo Gómez-Peña's "The Virtual Barrio @ the Other Frontier").

Of course it's likely that you, like most people, spend a lot of time (or life) online; thus, as you read these essays, you'll probably encounter some familiar ideas. But you're also likely to find some of your own experiences described or analyzed in new and unexpected ways. In a sense, reading this casebook will give you new expertise on the debates surrounding the development of the Internet and its implications for social relations and individual life experience. But what you read may raise new questions as well — questions that might require further research to explore fully. The questions that follow each reading are intended to give you the opportunity to write in response to these texts and, when appropriate, to use them as a foundation for research into the questions they address.

Why I Blog

Andrew Sullivan

*Writer, editor, and public intellectual, Andrew Sullivan (b. 1963)
was born in southern England and lives in Washington, D.C.
He attended Oxford University, where he studied modern history
and modern languages, and Harvard University, where he received
a master's degree in public administration and a PhD in political
science in 1989. Openly gay, Sullivan has been an outspoken
advocate of gay issues. His 1993* New Republic *essay, "The
Politics of Homosexuality," remains one of the most influential
articles of the decade on the subject of gay rights; his controversial
"Why Men Are Different" put him on the cover of* Time
magazine. Sullivan's books include Virtually Normal: An
Argument about Homosexuality *(1995);* Love Undetectable:
Notes on Friendship, Sex, and Survival *(1998);* The Conservative
Soul *(2006); and, most recently,* Intimations Pursued: The Voice
of Practice in the Conversation of Michael Oakeshott *(2008).
Editor of the* New Republic *from 1991 to 1996, Sullivan has
also been a contributing writer for the* London Sunday Times,
Time *magazine, and the* New York Times Magazine. *A frequent
contributor to the* Atlantic, *in which "Why I Blog" appeared
in 2008, Sullivan also writes a blog, the Daily Dish, for the*
Atlantic Online.

The word *blog* is a conflation of two words: *Web* and *log*. It contains in
its four letters a concise and accurate self-description: it is a log of thoughts
and writing posted publicly on the World Wide Web. In the monosyllabic
vernacular of the Internet, *Web log* soon became the word *blog*.

This form of instant and global self-publishing, made possible by
technology widely available only for the past decade or so, allows for no
retroactive editing (apart from fixing minor typos or small glitches) and
removes from the act of writing any considered or lengthy review. It is the
spontaneous expression of instant thought — impermanent beyond even the
ephemera of daily journalism. It is accountable in immediate and unavoidable ways to readers and other bloggers, and linked via hypertext to continuously multiplying references and sources. Unlike any single piece of print
journalism, its borders are extremely porous and its truth inherently transitory. The consequences of this for the act of writing are still sinking in.

A ship's log owes its name to a small wooden board, often weighted with lead, that was for centuries attached to a line and thrown over the stern. The weight of the log would keep it in the same place in the water, like a provisional anchor, while the ship moved away. By measuring the length of line used up in a set period of time, mariners could calculate the speed of their journey (the rope itself was marked by equidistant "knots" for easy measurement). As a ship's voyage progressed, the course came to be marked down in a book that was called a log.

In journeys at sea that took place before radio or radar or satellites or sonar, these logs were an indispensable source for recording what actually happened. They helped navigators surmise where they were and how far they had traveled and how much longer they had to stay at sea. They provided accountability to a ship's owners and traders. They were designed to be as immune to faking as possible. Away from land, there was usually no reliable corroboration of events apart from the crew's own account in the middle of an expanse of blue and gray and green; and in long journeys, memories always blur and facts disperse. A log provided as accurate an account as could be gleaned in real time.

As you read a log, you have the curious sense of moving backward in time as you move forward in pages — the opposite of a book. As you piece together a narrative that was never intended as one, it seems — and is — more truthful. Logs, in this sense, were a form of human self-correction. They amended for hindsight, for the ways in which human beings order and tidy and construct the story of their lives as they look back on them. Logs require a letting-go of narrative because they do not allow for a knowledge of the ending. So they have plot as well as dramatic irony — the reader will know the ending before the writer did. 5

Anyone who has blogged his thoughts for an extended time will recognize this world. We bloggers have scant opportunity to collect our thoughts, to wait until events have settled and a clear pattern emerges. We blog now — as news reaches us, as facts emerge. This is partly true for all journalism, which is, as its etymology suggests, daily writing, always subject to subsequent revision. And a good columnist will adjust position and judgment and even political loyalty over time, depending on events. But a blog is not so much daily writing as hourly writing. And with that level of timeliness, the provisionality of every word is even more pressing — and the risk of error or the thrill of prescience that much greater.

No columnist or reporter or novelist will have his minute shifts or constant small contradictions exposed as mercilessly as a blogger's are. A columnist can ignore or duck a subject less noticeably than a blogger committing thoughts to pixels several times a day. A reporter can wait — must wait — until every source has confirmed. A novelist can spend months or years before committing words to the world. For bloggers, the deadline is always now. Blogging is therefore to writing what extreme sports are to athletics: more free-form, more accident-prone, less formal, more alive. It is, in many ways, writing out loud.

You end up writing about yourself, since you are a relatively fixed point in this constant interaction with the ideas and facts of the exterior world. And in this sense, the historic form closest to blogs is the diary. But with this difference: a diary is almost always a private matter. Its raw honesty, its dedication to marking life as it happens and remembering life as it was, makes it a terrestrial log. A few diaries are meant to be read by others, of course, just as correspondence could be — but usually posthumously, or as a way to compile facts for a more considered autobiographical rendering. But a blog, unlike a diary, is instantly public. It transforms this most personal and retrospective of forms into a painfully public and immediate one. It combines the confessional genre with the log form and exposes the author in a manner no author has ever been exposed before.

I remember first grappling with what to put on my blog. It was the spring of 2000, and like many a freelance writer at the time, I had some vague notion that I needed to have a presence "online." I had no clear idea of what to do, but a friend who ran a Web-design company offered to create a site for me, and since I was technologically clueless, he also agreed to post various essays and columns as I wrote them. Before too long, this became a chore for him, and he called me one day to say he'd found an online platform that was so simple I could henceforth post all my writing myself. The platform was called Blogger.

As I used it to post columns or links to books or old essays, it occurred   10
to me that I could also post new writing — writing that could even be exclusive to the blog. But what? Like any new form, blogging did not start from nothing. It evolved from various journalistic traditions. In my case, I drew on my mainstream-media experience to navigate the virgin sea. I had a few early inspirations: the old Notebook section of the *New Republic,* a magazine that, under the editorial guidance of Michael Kinsley, had introduced a more English style of crisp, short commentary into what had been a more high-minded genre of American opinion writing. The *New Republic* had also pioneered a Diarist feature on the last page, which was designed to be a more personal, essayistic, first-person form of journalism. Mixing the two genres, I did what I had been trained to do — and improvised.

I'd previously written online as well, contributing to a listserv for gay writers and helping Kinsley initiate a more discursive form of online writing for *Slate,* the first magazine published exclusively on the Web. As soon as I began writing this way, I realized that the online form rewarded a colloquial, unfinished tone. In one of my early Kinsley-guided experiments, he urged me not to think too hard before writing. So I wrote as I'd write an e-mail — with only a mite more circumspection. This is hazardous, of course, as anyone who has ever clicked Send in a fit of anger or hurt will testify. But blogging requires an embrace of such hazards, a willingness to fall off the trapeze rather than fail to make the leap.

From the first few days of using the form, I was hooked. The simple experience of being able to directly broadcast my own words to readers was an exhilarating literary liberation. Unlike the current generation of writers, who have only ever blogged, I knew firsthand what the alternative meant. I'd edited a weekly print magazine, the *New Republic,* for five years, and written countless columns and essays for a variety of traditional outlets. And in all this, I'd often chafed, as most writers do, at the endless delays, revisions, office politics, editorial fights, and last-minute cuts for space that dead-tree publishing entails. Blogging — even to an audience of a few hundred in the early days — was intoxicatingly free in comparison. Like taking a narcotic.

It was obvious from the start that it was revolutionary. Every writer since the printing press has longed for a means to publish himself and reach — instantly — any reader on earth. Every professional writer has paid some dues waiting for an editor's nod, or enduring a publisher's incompetence, or being ground to literary dust by a legion of fact-checkers and copy editors. If you added up the time a writer once had to spend finding an outlet, impressing editors, sucking up to proprietors, and proofreading edits, you'd find another lifetime buried in the interstices. But with one click of the Publish Now button, all these troubles evaporated.

Alas, as I soon discovered, this sudden freedom from above was immediately replaced by insurrection from below. Within minutes of my posting something, even in the earliest days, readers responded. E-mail seemed to unleash their inner beast. They were more brutal than any editor, more persnickety than any copy editor, and more emotionally unstable than any colleague.

Again, it's hard to overrate how different this is. Writers can be sensitive, 15
vain souls, requiring gentle nurturing from editors, and oddly susceptible to the blows delivered by reviewers. They survive, for the most part, but the thinness of their skins is legendary. Moreover, before the blogosphere, reporters and columnists were largely shielded from this kind of direct hazing. Yes, letters to the editor would arrive in due course and subscriptions would be canceled. But reporters and columnists tended to operate in a relative sanctuary, answerable mainly to their editors, not readers. For a long time, columns were essentially monologues published to applause, muffled murmurs, silence, or a distant heckle. I'd gotten blowback from pieces before — but in an amorphous, time-delayed, distant way. Now the feedback was instant, personal, and brutal.

And so blogging found its own answer to the defensive counterblast from the journalistic establishment. To the charges of inaccuracy and unprofessionalism, bloggers could point to the fierce, immediate scrutiny of their readers. Unlike newspapers, which would eventually publish corrections in a box of printed spinach far from the original error, bloggers had to walk the walk of self-correction in the same space and in the same format as the original screwup. The form was more accountable, not less, because there is nothing more conducive to professionalism than being publicly humiliated for sloppiness. Of course, a blogger could ignore an error or simply refuse to acknowledge mistakes. But if he persisted, he would be razzed by competitors and assailed by commenters and abandoned by readers. In an era when the traditional media found itself beset by scandals as disparate as Stephen Glass, Jayson Blair, and Dan Rather, bloggers survived the first assault on their worth. In time, in fact, the high standards expected of well-trafficked bloggers spilled over into greater accountability, transparency, and punctiliousness among the media powers that were. Even *New York Times* columnists were forced to admit when they had been wrong.

The blog remained a *superficial* medium, of course. By superficial, I mean simply that blogging rewards brevity and immediacy. No one wants to read a nine-thousand-word treatise online. On the Web, one-sentence links are as legitimate as thousand-word diatribes — in fact, they are often valued more. And, as Matt Drudge told me when I sought advice from the master in 2001, the key to understanding a blog is to realize that it's a broadcast, not a publication. If it stops moving, it dies. If it stops paddling, it sinks.

But the superficiality masked considerable depth — greater depth, from one perspective, than the traditional media could offer. The reason was a single technological innovation: the hyperlink. An old-school columnist can write eight hundred brilliant words analyzing or commenting on, say, a new think-tank report or scientific survey. But in reading it on paper, you have to take the columnist's presentation of the material on faith, or be convinced by a brief quotation (which can always be misleading out of context). Online, a hyperlink to the original source transforms the experience. Yes, a few sentences of bloggy spin may not be as satisfying as a full column, but the ability to read the primary material instantly — in as careful or shallow a fashion as you choose — can add much greater context than anything on paper. Even a blogger's chosen pull quote, unlike a columnist's, can be effortlessly checked against the original. Now this innovation, predating blogs but popularized by them, is increasingly central to mainstream journalism.

A blog, therefore, bobs on the surface of the ocean but has its anchorage in waters deeper than those print media is technologically able to exploit. It disempowers the writer to that extent, of course. The blogger can get away with less and afford fewer pretensions of authority. He is — more than any writer of the past — a node among other nodes, connected but unfinished without the links and the comments and the track-backs that make the blogosphere, at its best, a conversation, rather than a production.

A writer fully aware of and at ease with the provisionality of his own   20
work is nothing new. For centuries, writers have experimented with forms that suggest the imperfection of human thought, the inconstancy of human affairs, and the humbling, chastening passage of time. If you compare the meandering, questioning, unresolved dialogues of Plato with the definitive, logical treatises of Aristotle, you see the difference between a skeptic's spirit translated into writing and a spirit that seeks to bring some finality to the

argument. Perhaps the greatest single piece of Christian apologetics, Pascal's *Pensées,* is a series of meandering, short, and incomplete stabs at arguments, observations, insights. Their lack of finish is what makes them so compelling — arguably more compelling than a polished treatise by Aquinas.

Or take the brilliant polemics of Karl Kraus, the publisher of and main writer for *Die Fackel,* who delighted in constantly twitting authority with slashing aphorisms and rapid-fire bursts of invective. Kraus had something rare in his day: the financial wherewithal to self-publish. It gave him a fearlessness that is now available to anyone who can afford a computer and an Internet connection.

But perhaps the quintessential blogger *avant la lettre* was Montaigne. His essays were published in three major editions, each one longer and more complex than the previous. A passionate skeptic, Montaigne amended, added to, and amplified the essays for each edition, making them three-dimensional through time. In the best modern translations, each essay is annotated, sentence by sentence, paragraph by paragraph, by small letters (A, B, and C) for each major edition, helping the reader see how each rewrite added to or subverted, emphasized or ironized, the version before. Montaigne was living his skepticism, daring to show how a writer evolves, changes his mind, learns new things, shifts perspectives, grows older — and that this, far from being something that needs to be hidden behind a veneer of unchanging authority, can become a virtue, a new way of looking at the pretensions of authorship and text and truth. Montaigne, for good measure, also peppered his essays with myriads of what bloggers would call external links. His own thoughts are strewn with and complicated by the aphorisms and anecdotes of others. Scholars of the sources note that many of these "money quotes" were deliberately taken out of context, adding layers of irony to writing that was already saturated in empirical doubt.

To blog is therefore to let go of your writing in a way, to hold it at arm's length, open it to scrutiny, allow it to float in the ether for a while, and to let others, as Montaigne did, pivot you toward relative truth. A blogger will notice this almost immediately upon starting. Some e-mailers, unsurprisingly, know more about a subject than the blogger does. They will send links, stories, and facts, challenging the blogger's view of the world, sometimes outright refuting it, but more frequently adding context and nuance and complexity to an idea. The role of a blogger is not to defend against this but to embrace it. He is similar in this way to the host of a dinner party. He can provoke discussion or take a position, even passionately, but he also must create an atmosphere in which others want to participate.

That atmosphere will inevitably be formed by the blogger's personality. The blogosphere may, in fact, be the least veiled of any forum in which a writer dares to express himself. Even the most careful and self-aware blogger will reveal more about himself than he wants to in a few unguarded sentences and publish them before he has the sense to hit Delete. The wise panic that can paralyze a writer — the fear that he will be exposed, undone, humiliated — is not available to a blogger. You can't have blogger's block. You have to express yourself now, while your emotions roil, while your temper flares, while your humor lasts. You can try to hide yourself from real scrutiny, and the exposure it demands, but it's hard. And that's what makes blogging as a form stand out: it is rich in personality. The faux intimacy of the Web experience, the closeness of the e-mail and the instant message, seeps through. You feel as if you know bloggers as they go through their lives, experience the same things you are experiencing, and share the moment. When readers of my blog bump into me in person, they invariably address me as Andrew. Print readers don't do that. It's Mr. Sullivan to them.

On my blog, my readers and I experienced 9/11 together, in real time. I   25
can look back and see not just how I responded to the event, but how I responded to it at 3:47 that afternoon. And at 9:46 that night. There is a vividness to this immediacy that cannot be rivaled by print. The same goes for the 2000 recount, the Iraq War, the revelations of Abu Ghraib, the death of John Paul II, or any of the other history-making events of the past decade. There is simply no way to write about them in real time without revealing a huge amount about yourself. And the intimate bond this creates with readers is unlike the bond that the *Times,* say, develops with its readers through the same events. Alone in front of a computer, at any moment, are two people: a blogger and a reader. The proximity is palpable, the moment human — whatever authority a blogger has is derived not from the institution he works for but from the humanness he conveys. This is writing with emotion not just under but always breaking through the surface. It renders a writer and a reader not just connected but linked in a visceral, personal way. The only term that really describes this is *friendship*. And it is a relatively new thing to write for thousands and thousands of friends.

These friends, moreover, are an integral part of the blog itself — sources of solace, company, provocation, hurt, and correction. If I were to do an inventory of the material that appears on my blog, I'd estimate that a good third of it is reader-generated, and a good third of my time is spent absorbing readers' views, comments, and tips. Readers tell me of breaking stories, new perspectives, and counterarguments to prevailing assumptions. And this is what blogging, in turn, does to reporting. The traditional method involves a journalist searching for key sources, nurturing them, and sequestering them from his rivals. A blogger splashes gamely into a subject and dares the sources to come to him.

Some of this material — e-mails from soldiers on the front lines, from scientists explaining new research, from dissident Washington writers too scared to say what they think in their own partisan redoubts — might never have seen the light of day before the blogosphere. And some of it, of course, is dubious stuff. Bloggers can be spun and misled as easily as traditional writers — and the rigorous source assessment that good reporters do can't be done by e-mail. But you'd be surprised by what comes unsolicited into the in-box, and how helpful it often is.

Not all of it is mere information. Much of it is also opinion and scholarship, a knowledge base that exceeds the research department of any newspaper. A good blog is your own private Wikipedia. Indeed, the most pleasant surprise of blogging has been the number of people working in law or government or academia or rearing kids at home who have real literary talent and real knowledge, and who had no outlet — until now. There is a distinction here, of course, between the edited use of e-mailed sources by a careful blogger and the often mercurial cacophony on an unmediated comments section. But the truth is out there — and the miracle of e-mail allows it to come to you.

Fellow bloggers are always expanding this knowledge base. Eight years ago, the blogosphere felt like a handful of individual cranks fighting with one another. Today, it feels like a universe of cranks, with vast, pulsating readerships, fighting with one another. To the neophyte reader, or blogger, it can seem overwhelming. But there is a connection between the intimacy of the early years and the industry it has become today. And the connection is human individuality.

The pioneers of online journalism — *Slate* and *Salon* — are still very   30
popular, and successful. But the more memorable stars of the Internet — even within those two sites — are all personally branded. Daily Kos, for example, is written by hundreds of bloggers, and amended by thousands of commenters. But it is named after Markos Moulitsas, who started it, and his own prose still provides a backbone to the front-page blog. The biggest news-aggregator site in the world, the Drudge Report, is named after its founder, Matt Drudge, who somehow conveys a unified sensibility through his selection of links, images, and stories. The vast, expanding universe of the Huffington Post still finds some semblance of coherence in the Cambridge-Greek twang of Arianna; the entire world of online celebrity gossip circles the drain of Perez Hilton; and the investigative journalism, reviewing, and commentary of Talking Points Memo is still tied together by the tone of Josh Marshall. Even *Slate* is unimaginable without Mickey Kaus's voice.

What endures is a human brand. Readers have encountered this phenomenon before — *I. F. Stone's Weekly* comes to mind — but not to this extent. It stems, I think, from the conversational style that blogging rewards. What you want in a conversationalist is as much character as authority. And if you think of blogging as more like talk radio or cable news than opinion magazines or daily newspapers, then this personalized emphasis is less surprising. People have a voice for radio and a face for television. For blogging, they have a sensibility.

But writing in this new form is a collective enterprise as much as it is an individual one — and the connections between bloggers are as important as the content on the blogs. The links not only drive conversation — they drive readers. The more you link, the more others will link to you, and the more traffic and readers you will get. The zero-sum game of old media — in which *Time* benefits from *Newsweek*'s decline and vice versa — becomes win-win. It's great for *Time* to be linked to by *Newsweek* and the other way round. One of the most prized statistics in the blogosphere is therefore not the total number of readers or page views, but the "authority" you get by being linked to by other blogs. It's an indication of how central you are to the online conversation of humankind.

The reason this open-source market of thinking and writing has such potential is that the always adjusting and evolving collective mind can rapidly filter out bad arguments and bad ideas. The flip side, of course, is that bloggers are also human beings. Reason is not the only fuel in the tank. In a world where no distinction is made between good traffic and bad traffic, and where emotion often rules, some will always raise their voice to dominate the conversation; others will pander shamelessly to their readers' prejudices; others will start online brawls for the fun of it. Sensationalism, dirt, and the ease of formulaic talking points always beckon. You can disappear into the partisan blogosphere and never stumble onto a site you disagree with.

But linkage mitigates this. A Democratic blog will, for example, be forced to link to Republican ones, if only to attack and mock. And it's in the interests of both camps to generate shared traffic. This encourages polarized slugfests. But online, at least you see both sides. Reading the *Nation* or *National Review* before the Internet existed allowed for more cocooning than the wide-open online sluice gates do now. If there's more incivility, there's also more fluidity. Rudeness, in any case, isn't the worst thing that can happen to a blogger. Being ignored is. Perhaps the nastiest thing one can do to a fellow blogger is to rip him apart and fail to provide a link.

A successful blog therefore has to balance itself between a writer's own take on the world and others. Some bloggers collect, or "aggregate," other bloggers' posts with dozens of quick links and minimalist opinion topspin: Glenn Reynolds at Instapundit does this for the right-of-center; Duncan Black at Eschaton does it for the left. Others are more eclectic, or aggregate links in a particular niche, or cater to a settled and knowledgeable reader base. A "blogroll" is an indicator of whom you respect enough to keep in your galaxy. For many years, I kept my reading and linking habits to a relatively small coterie of fellow political bloggers. In today's blogosphere, to do this is to embrace marginality. I've since added links to religious blogs and literary ones and scientific ones and just plain weird ones. As the blogosphere has expanded beyond anyone's capacity to absorb it, I've needed an assistant and interns to scour the Web for links and stories and photographs to respond to and think about. It's a difficult balance, between your own interests and obsessions, and the knowledge, insight, and wit of others — but an immensely rich one. There are times, in fact, when a blogger feels less like a writer than an online disc jockey, mixing samples of tunes and generating

35

new melodies through mashups while also making his own music. He is both artist and producer — and the beat always goes on.

If all this sounds postmodern, that's because it is. And blogging suffers from the same flaws as postmodernism: a failure to provide stable truth or a permanent perspective. A traditional writer is valued by readers precisely because they trust him to have thought long and hard about a subject, given it time to evolve in his head, and composed a piece of writing that is worth their time to read at length and to ponder. Bloggers don't do this and cannot do this — and that limits them far more than it does traditional long-form writing.

A blogger will air a variety of thoughts or facts on any subject in no particular order other than that dictated by the passing of time. A writer will instead use time, synthesizing these thoughts, ordering them, weighing which points count more than others, seeing how his views evolved in the writing process itself, and responding to an editor's perusal of a draft or two. The result is almost always more measured, more satisfying, and more enduring than a blizzard of posts. The triumphalist notion that blogging should somehow replace traditional writing is as foolish as it is pernicious. In some ways, blogging's gifts to our discourse make the skills of a good traditional writer much more valuable, not less. The torrent of blogospheric insights, ideas, and arguments places a greater premium on the person who can finally make sense of it all, turning it into something more solid, and lasting, and rewarding.

The points of this essay, for example, have appeared in shards and fragments on my blog for years. But being forced to order them in my head and think about them for a longer stretch has helped me understand them better, and perhaps express them more clearly. Each week, after a few hundred posts, I also write an actual newspaper column. It invariably turns out to be more considered, balanced, and evenhanded than the blog. But the blog will always inform and enrich the column, and often serve as a kind of free-form, free-associative research. And an essay like this will spawn discussion best handled on a blog. The conversation, in other words, is the point, and the different idioms used by the conversationalists all contribute something of value to it. And so, if the defenders of the old media once viscerally regarded blogging as some kind of threat, they are starting to see it more as a portal, and a spur.

There is, after all, something simply irreplaceable about reading a piece of writing at length on paper, in a chair or on a couch or in bed. To use an obvious analogy, jazz entered our civilization much later than composed, formal music. But it hasn't replaced it; and no jazz musician would ever claim that it could. Jazz merely demands a different way of playing and listening, just as blogging requires a different mode of writing and reading. Jazz and blogging are intimate, improvisational, and individual — but also inherently collective. And the audience talks over both.

The reason they talk while listening, and comment or link while read-   40
ing, is that they understand that this is a kind of music that needs to be
engaged rather than merely absorbed. To listen to jazz as one would listen to
an aria is to miss the point. Reading at a monitor, at a desk, or on an iPhone
provokes a querulous, impatient, distracted attitude, a demand for instant,
usable information, that is simply not conducive to opening a novel or a
favorite magazine on the couch. Reading on paper evokes a more relaxed
and meditative response. The message dictates the medium. And each medium
has its place — as long as one is not mistaken for the other.

In fact, for all the intense gloom surrounding the newspaper and magazine business, this is actually a golden era for journalism. The blogosphere
has added a whole new idiom to the act of writing and has introduced an
entirely new generation to nonfiction. It has enabled writers to write out loud
in ways never seen or understood before. And yet it has exposed a hunger
and need for traditional writing that, in the age of television's dominance,
had seemed on the wane.

Words, of all sorts, have never seemed so now.

QUESTIONS

Reading

1. What does Sullivan mean when he writes that the blog is a *superficial*
   medium (paragraph 17)?
2. What, according to Sullivan, is "the most pleasant surprise of blogging"
   (paragraph 28)?
3. In your own words, explain the *analogy* that Sullivan makes between
   blogging versus traditional journalism, and jazz versus "composed, formal"
   music. Create your own analogy to describe the distinction between
   blogging and pre-Internet writing forms.
4. Make a double-entry list of the things that distinguish blogging from
   print journalism, according to Sullivan. How do his points support his
   conclusion?

TRADITIONAL/PRINT JOURNALISM	BLOGS

Exploratory Writing

1. Collaborating in small groups, *report* on your experiences writing a real-life blog. Each group member should start his or her own blog, or share his or her existing blog with the rest of the group. Post on your blog daily, and comment on other group members' blogs at least once a day. Feel free to invite people outside of the group to read your blog, too. Throughout the week, keep a private journal about your blog, noting whether or not your experiences are similar to those that Sullivan describes. At the conclusion of your blog experiment, discuss your findings with the class.

2. For Sullivan, the "sudden freedom from above" of blogging is replaced by "insurrection from below" — instant, personal, and brutal responses from unedited readers. Choose a blog on a topic that interests you, and spend a few days tracking all of the comments from readers posted there. How many of the comments seem constructive and topical? How many seem brutal, like "direct hazing"? How many seem "emotionally unstable" or irrelevant? What conclusions do you draw from your observations?

Making Connections

1. Sullivan describes feeling strong emotions about his interactions with the readers of his blog, including hurt and friendship. Choose any two essays in this casebook, and compare the role of emotions in the authors' discussions or arguments.

Essay Writing

1. Write your own reflective essay titled "Why I Blog" (or "Why I Don't Blog"). Use details and anecdotes to bring your experiences to life for the reader.

The Hive

Marshall Poe

Marshall Poe (b. 1961) is an American writer, Russian historian, and — most recently — a Wikipedia scholar. After receiving his PhD in history from the University of California, Berkeley, in 1992, Poe held fellowships at the Davis Center for Russian Studies at Harvard; the Institute for Advanced Study in Princeton, New Jersey; and the Harriman Institute for Russian Studies at Columbia University. While he originally made a name for himself in historical literature, popularizing the once-obscure writings of a sixteenth-century Austrian diplomat, Poe is increasingly known for work stemming from his 2002 essay in the Journal of Electronic Publishing *"Note to Self: Print Monograph Dead; Invent New Publishing Model." "The Hive" — which first appeared in the* New Yorker *in 2006 — makes the controversial argument that Wikipedia is a globally accessible, editable repository of common knowledge that's quickly making traditional encyclopedias obsolete. Poe is also the founder of Memory Archive — a universal wiki-type database of contemporary memoirs he began with his American University students in 2005.*

Several months ago, I discovered that I was being "considered for deletion." Or rather, the entry on me in the Internet behemoth that is Wikipedia was.

For those of you who are (as uncharitable Wikipedians sometimes say) "clueless newbies," Wikipedia is an online encyclopedia. But it is like no encyclopedia Diderot could have imagined. Instead of relying on experts to write articles according to their expertise, Wikipedia lets anyone write about anything. You, I, and any wired-up fool can add entries, change entries, even propose that entries be deleted. For reasons I'd rather not share outside of therapy, I created a one-line biographical entry on "Marshall Poe." It didn't take long for my tiny article to come to the attention of Wikipedia's self-appointed guardians. Within a week, a very active — and by most accounts responsible — Scottish Wikipedian named "Alai" decided that . . . well, that I wasn't worth knowing about. Why? "No real evidence of notability," Alai cruelly but accurately wrote, "beyond the proverbial average college professor."

Wikipedia has the potential to be the greatest effort in collaborative knowledge gathering the world has ever known, and it may well be the greatest effort in voluntary collaboration of any kind. The English-language version alone has more than a million entries. It is consistently ranked among the most visited Web sites in the world. A quarter century ago it was inconceivable that a legion of unpaid, unorganized amateurs scattered about the globe could create anything of value, let alone what may one day be the most comprehensive repository of knowledge in human history. Back then we knew that people do not work for free; or if they do work for free, they do a poor job; and if they work for free in large numbers, the result is a muddle. Jimmy Wales and Larry Sanger knew all this when they began an online encyclopedia in 1999. Now, just seven years later, everyone knows different.

The Moderator

Jimmy Wales does not fit the profile of an Internet revolutionary. He was born in 1966 and raised in modest circumstances in Huntsville, Alabama. Wales majored in finance at Auburn, and after completing his degree enrolled in a graduate program at the University of Alabama. It was there that he developed a passion for the Internet. His entry point was typical for the nerdy set of his generation: fantasy games.

In 1974, Gary Gygax and Dave Arneson, two gamers who had obviously read *The Lord of the Rings*, invented the tabletop role-playing game Dungeons & Dragons. The game spread largely through networks of teenage boys, and by 1979, the year the classic *Dungeon Master's Guide* was published, it seemed that every youth who couldn't get a date was rolling the storied twenty-sided die in a shag-carpeted den. Meanwhile, a more electronically inclined crowd at the University of Illinois at Urbana-Champaign was experimenting with moving fantasy play from the basement to a computer network. The fruit of their labors was the unfortunately named MUD (Multi-User Dungeon). Allowing masses of players to create virtual fantasy worlds, MUDs garnered a large audience in the 1980s and 1990s under names like Zork, Myst, and Scepter of Goth. (MUDs came to be known as "Multi-Undergraduate Destroyers" for their tendency to divert college students from their studies.)

Wales began to play MUDs at Alabama in the late 1980s. It was in this context that he first encountered the power of networked computers to facilitate voluntary cooperation on a large scale. He did not, however, set up house in these fantasy worlds, nor did he show any evidence of wanting to begin a career in high tech. He completed a degree in finance at Auburn, received a master's in finance at the University of Alabama, and then pursued a PhD in finance at Indiana University. He was interested, it would seem, in finance. In 1994, he quit his doctoral program and moved to Chicago to take a job as an options trader. There he made (as he has repeatedly said) "enough."

Wales is of a thoughtful cast of mind. He was a frequent contributor to the philosophical "discussion lists" (the first popular online discussion forums) that emerged in the late eighties as e-mail spread through the humanities. His particular passion was objectivism, the philosophical system developed by Ayn Rand. In 1989, he initiated the Ayn Rand Philosophy Discussion List and served as moderator — the person who invites and edits e-mails from subscribers. Though discussion lists were not new among the technorati in the 1980s, they were unfamiliar territory for most academics. In the oak-paneled seminar room, everyone had always been careful to behave properly — the chairman sat at the head of the table, and everyone spoke in turn and stuck to the topic. E-mail lists were something altogether different. Unrestrained by convention and cloaked by anonymity, participants could behave very badly without fear of real consequences. The term for such poor comportment — *flaming* — became one of the first bits of net jargon to enter common usage.

Wales had a careful moderation style:

> First, I will frown — very much — on any flaming of any kind whatsoever. . . . Second, I impose no restrictions on membership based on my own idea of what objectivism really is. . . . Third, I hope that the list will be more "academic" than some of the others, and tend toward discussions of technical details of epistemology. . . . Fourth, I have chosen a "middle-ground" method of moderation, a sort of behind-the-scenes prodding.

Wales was an advocate of what is generically termed "openness" online. An "open" online community is one with few restrictions on membership or posting — everyone is welcome, and anyone can say anything as long as it's generally on point and doesn't include gratuitous ad hominem attacks. Openness fit not only Wales's idea of objectivism, with its emphasis on reason and rejection of force, but also his mild personality. He doesn't like to fight. He would rather suffer fools in silence, waiting for them to talk themselves out, than confront them. This patience would serve Wales well in the years to come.

Top-Down and Bottom-Up

In the mid-1990s, the great dream of Internet entrepreneurs was to   10
create *the* entry point on the Web. "Portals," as they were called, would provide everything: e-mail, news, entertainment, and, most important, the tools to help users find what they wanted on the Web. As Google later showed, if you build the best "finding aid," you'll be a dominant player. In 1996, the smart money was on "Web directories," man-made guides to the Internet. Both Netscape and Yahoo relied on Web directories as their primary finding

aids, and their IPOs in the mid-1990s suggested a bright future.[1] In 1996, Wales and two partners founded a Web directory called Bomis.

Initially, the idea was to build a universal directory, like Yahoo's. The question was how to build it. At the time, there were two dominant models: top-down and bottom-up. The former is best exemplified by Yahoo, which began as *Jerry's Guide to the World Wide Web*. Jerry — in this case Jerry Yang, Yahoo's cofounder — set up a system of categories and began to classify Web sites accordingly. Web surfers flocked to the site because no one could find anything on the Web in the early 1990s. So Yang and his partner, David Filo, spent a mountain of venture capital to hire a team of surfers to classify the Web. Yahoo ("Yet Another Hierarchical Officious Oracle") was born.

Other would-be classifiers approached the problem of Web chaos more democratically. Beginning from the sound premise that it's good to share, a seventeen-year-old Oregonian named Sage Weil created the first "Web ring" at about the time Yang and Filo were assembling their army of paid Web librarians. A Web ring is nothing more than a set of topically related Web sites that have been linked together for ease of surfing. Rings are easy to find, easy to join, and easy to create; by 1997, they numbered ten thousand.

Wales focused on the bottom-up strategy using Web rings, and it worked. Bomis users built hundreds of rings — on cars, computers, sports, and especially "babes" (e.g., the Anna Kournikova Web ring), effectively creating an index of the "laddie" Web. Instead of helping all users find all content, Bomis found itself positioned as the *Playboy* of the Internet, helping guys find guy stuff. Wales's experience with Web rings reinforced the lesson he had learned with MUDs: given the right technology, large groups of self-interested individuals will unite to create something they could not produce by themselves, be it a sword-and-sorcery world or an index of Web sites on Pamela Anderson. He saw the power of what we now call "peer-to-peer," or "distributed," content production.

Wales was not alone: Rich Skrenta and Bob Truel, two programmers at Sun Microsystems, saw it too. In June 1998, along with three partners, they launched GnuHoo, an all-volunteer alternative to the Yahoo Directory. (GNU, a recursive acronym for "GNUs Not Unix," is a free operating system created by the über-hacker Richard Stallman.) The project was an immediate success, and it quickly drew the attention of Netscape, which was eager to find a directory capable of competing with Yahoo's index. In November 1998, Netscape acquired GnuHoo (then called NewHoo), promising to both develop it and release it under an "open content" license, which meant anyone could use it. At the date of Netscape's acquisition, the directory had indexed some one hundred thousand URLs; a year later, it included about a million.

---

[1]*IPOs*: Initial public offerings (of stock).

Wales clearly had the open-content movement in mind when, in the fall   15
of 1999, he began thinking about a "volunteer-built" online encyclopedia.
The idea — explored most prominently in Stallman's 1999 essay "The Free
Universal Encyclopedia and Learning Resource" — had been around for
some time. Wales says he had no direct knowledge of Stallman's essay
when he embarked on his encyclopedia project, but two bits of evidence suggest that he was thinking of Stallman's GNU free documentation license. First,
the name Wales adopted for his encyclopedia — Nupedia.org — strongly
suggested a Stallman-esque venture. Second, he took the trouble of leasing
a related domain name, GNUpedia.org. By January 2000, his encyclopedia
project had acquired funding from Bomis and hired its first employee:
Larry Sanger.

The Philosopher

Sanger was born in 1968 in Bellevue, Washington, a suburb of Seattle.
When he was seven, his father, a marine biologist, moved the family to
Anchorage, Alaska, where Sanger spent his youth. He excelled in high
school, and in 1986 he enrolled at Reed College. Reed is the sort of school
you attend if you are intelligent, are not interested in investment banking,
and wonder a lot about truth. There Sanger found a question that fired his
imagination: What is knowledge? He embarked on that most unremunera-
tive of careers, epistemology, and entered a doctoral program in philosophy
at Ohio State.

Sanger fits the profile of almost every Internet early adopter: he'd been
a good student, played Dungeons & Dragons, and tinkered with PCs as a
youth — going so far as to code a text-based adventure game in BASIC, the
first popular programming language. He was drawn into the world of
philosophy discussion lists and, in the early 1990s, was an active participant
in Wales's objectivism forum. Sanger also hosted a mailing list as part of his
own online philosophy project (eventually named the Association for
Systematic Philosophy). The mission and mien of Sanger's list stood in stark
contrast to Wales's Rand forum. Sanger was far more programmatic. As he
wrote in his opening manifesto, dated March 22, 1994:

> The history of philosophy is full of disagreement and confusion.
> One reaction by philosophers to this state of things is to doubt
> whether the truth about philosophy can ever be known, or whether
> there is any such thing as the truth about philosophy. But there is
> another reaction: one may set out to think more carefully and
> methodically than one's intellectual forebears.

Wales's Rand forum was generally serious, but it was also a place for
philosophically inclined laypeople to shoot the breeze: Wales permitted

discussion of "objectivism in the movies" or "objectivism in Rush lyrics." Sanger's list was more disciplined, but he soon began to feel it, too, was of limited philosophical worth. He resigned after little more than a year. "I think that my time could really be better spent in the real world," Sanger wrote in his resignation letter, "as opposed to cyberspace, and in thinking to myself, rather than out loud to a bunch of other people." Sanger was seriously considering abandoning his academic career.

As the decade and the century came to a close, another opportunity arose, one that would let Sanger make a living away from academia, using the acumen he had developed on the Internet. In 1998, Sanger created a digest of news reports relating to the "Y2K problem." *Sanger's Review of Y2K News Reports* became a staple of IT managers across the globe. It also set him to thinking about how he might make a living in the new millennium. In January 2000, he sent Wales a business proposal for what was in essence a cultural news blog. Sanger's timing was excellent.

The Cathedral

Wales was looking for someone with good academic credentials to organize Nupedia, and Sanger fit the bill. Wales pitched the project to Sanger in terms of Eric S. Raymond's essay (and later book) "The Cathedral and the Bazaar." Raymond sketched two models of software development. Under the "cathedral model," source code was guarded by a core group of developers; under the "bazaar model," it was released on the Internet for anyone to tinker with. Raymond argued that the latter model was better, and he coined a now-famous hacker aphorism to capture its superiority: "Given enough eyeballs, all bugs are shallow." His point was simply that the speed with which a complex project is perfected is directly proportional to the number of informed people working on it. Wales was enthusiastic about Raymond's thesis. His experience with MUDs and Web rings had demonstrated to him the power of the bazaar. Sanger, the philosopher, was charier about the wisdom-of-crowds scheme but drawn to the idea of creating an open online encyclopedia that would break all the molds. Sanger signed on and moved to San Diego.

According to Sanger, Wales was very "hands-off." He gave Sanger only the loosest sketch of an open encyclopedia. "Open" meant two things: First, anyone, in principle, could contribute. Second, all of the content would be made freely available. Sanger proceeded to create, in effect, an online academic journal. There was simply no question in his mind that Nupedia would be guided by a board of experts, that submissions would be largely written by experts, and that articles would be published only after extensive peer review. Sanger set about recruiting academics to work on Nupedia. In early March 2000, he and Wales deemed the project ready to go public, and the Nupedia Web site was launched with the following words:

20

Fastest-Growing Foreign-Language Wikipedias
Among those with 10,000 or more articles as of June 2006

		Number of articles	Percent change from June 2005	
1.	Turkish	23,416	649	▬▬▬▬▬▬
2.	Thai	11,894	470	▬▬▬▬
3.	Farsi	12,661	413	▬▬▬
4.	Lithuanian	21,075	396	▬▬▬
5.	Slovak	39,630	386	▬▬▬
6.	Arabic	14,015	380	▬▬▬
7.	Russian	83,815	328	▬▬
8.	Icelandic	10,260	289	▬▬
9.	Basque	10,214	259	▬▬
10.	Italian	162,732	254	▬▬
11.	Polish	239,018	243	▬▬
12.	Ido	13,386	243	▬▬
13.	Hungarian	32,973	233	▬▬
14.	Czech	32,158	214	▬▬
15.	Malaysian	13,358	194	▬
	All Wikipedias	4,283,387	132	▬

Source: Wikimedia Foundation.

Suppose scholars the world over were to learn of a serious online encyclopedia effort in which the results were not proprietary to the encyclopedists, but were freely distributable under an open content license in virtually any desired medium. How quickly would the encyclopedia grow?

The answer, as Wales and Sanger found out, was "not very." Over the first several months little was actually accomplished in terms of article assignment, writing, and publication. First, there was the competition. Wales and Sanger had the bad luck to launch Nupedia around the same time as *Encyclopedia Britannica* was made available for free on the Internet. Then there was the real problem: production. Sanger and the Nupedia board had worked out a multistage editorial system that could have been borrowed from any scholarly journal. In a sense, it worked: assignments were made, articles were submitted and evaluated, and copyediting was done. But, to both Wales and Sanger, it was all much too slow. They had built a cathedral.

The Bazaar

In the mid-1980s, a programmer named Ward Cunningham began trying to create a "pattern language" for software design. A pattern language is in essence a common vocabulary used in solving engineering problems — think of it as best practices for designers. Cunningham believed that software development should have a pattern language, and he proposed to find a way for software developers to create it.

Apple's Hypercard offered inspiration. Hypercard was a very flexible database application. It allowed users to create records ("cards"), add data fields to them, and link them in sets. Cunningham created a Hypercard "stack" of software patterns and shared it with colleagues. His stack was well liked but difficult to share, since it existed only on Cunningham's computer. In the 1990s, Cunningham found himself looking for a problem-solving technique that would allow software developers to fine-tune and accumulate their knowledge collaboratively. A variation on Hypercard seemed like an obvious option.

Cunningham coded and, in the spring of 1995, launched the first "wiki," calling it the WikiWikiWeb. (*Wiki* is Hawaiian for "quick," which Cunningham chose to indicate the ease with which a user could edit the pages.) A wiki is a Web site that allows multiple users to create, edit, and hyperlink pages. As users work, a wiki can keep track of all changes; users can compare versions as they edit and, if necessary, revert to earlier states. Nothing is lost, and everything is transparent. 25

The wiki quickly gained a devoted following within the software community. And there it remained until January 2001, when Sanger had dinner with an old friend named Ben Kovitz. Kovitz was a fan of "extreme programming." Standard software engineering is very methodical — first you plan, then you plan and plan and plan, then you code. The premise is that you must correctly anticipate what the program will need to do in order to avoid drastic changes late in the coding process. In contrast, extreme programmers advocate going live with the earliest possible version of new software and letting many people work simultaneously to rapidly refine it.

Over tacos that night, Sanger explained his concerns about Nupedia's lack of progress, the root cause of which was its serial editorial system. As Nupedia was then structured, no stage of the editorial process could proceed before the previous stage was completed. Kovitz brought up the wiki and sketched out "wiki magic," the mysterious process by which communities with common interests work to improve wiki pages by incremental contributions. If it worked for the rambunctious hacker culture of programming, Kovitz said, it could work for any online collaborative project. The wiki could break the Nupedia bottleneck by permitting volunteers to work simultaneously all over the project. With Kovitz in tow, Sanger rushed back to his apartment and called Wales to share the idea. Over the next few days he wrote a formal proposal for Wales and started a page on Cunningham's wiki called "WikiPedia."

Wales and Sanger created the first Nupedia wiki on January 10, 2001. The initial purpose was to get the public to add entries that would then be "fed into the Nupedia process" of authorization. Most of Nupedia's expert volunteers, however, wanted nothing to do with this, so Sanger decided to launch a separate site called "Wikipedia." Neither Sanger nor Wales looked on Wikipedia as anything more than a lark. This is evident in Sanger's flip announcement of Wikipedia to the Nupedia discussion list. "Humor me," he wrote. "Go there and add a little article. It will take all of five or ten minutes." And, to Sanger's surprise, go they did. Within a few days, Wikipedia outstripped Nupedia in terms of quantity, if not quality, and a small community developed. In late January, Sanger created a Wikipedia discussion list (Wikipedia-L) to facilitate discussion of the project. At the end of January, Wikipedia had seventeen "real" articles (entries with more than 200 characters). By the end of February, it had 150; March, 572; April, 835; May, 1,300; June, 1,700; July, 2,400; August, 3,700. At the end of the year, the site boasted approximately 15,000 articles and about 350 "Wikipedians."

Setting the Rules

Wikipedia's growth caught Wales and Sanger off guard. It forced them to make quick decisions about what Wikipedia would be, how to foster cooperation, and how to manage it. In the beginning it was by no means clear what an "open" encyclopedia should include. People posted all manner of things: dictionary definitions, autobiographies, position papers, historical documents, and original research. In response, Sanger created a "What Wikipedia Is Not" page. There he and the community defined Wikipedia by exclusion — not a dictionary, not a scientific journal, not a source collection, and so on. For everything else, they reasoned that if an article could conceivably have gone in *Britannica*, it was "encyclopedic" and permitted; if not, it was "not encyclopedic" and deleted.

Sanger and Wales knew that online collaborative ventures can easily   30
slide into a morass of unproductive invective. They had already worked out a solution for Nupedia, called the "lack of bias" policy. On Wikipedia it became NPOV, or the "neutral point of view," and it brilliantly encouraged the work of the community. Under NPOV, authors were enjoined to present the conventionally acknowledged "facts" in an unbiased way and, where arguments occurred, to accord space to both sides. The concept of neutrality, though philosophically unsatisfying, had a kind of everybody-lay-down-your-arms ring to it. Debates about what to include in the article were encouraged on the "discussion" page that attends every Wikipedia article.

The most important initial question, however, concerned governance. When Wikipedia was created, wikis were synonymous with creative anarchy. Both Wales and Sanger thought that the software might be useful, but that it was no way to build a trusted encyclopedia. Some sort of authority was assumed to be essential. Wales's part in it was clear: he owned Wikipedia. Sanger's role was murkier.

Citing the communal nature of the project, Sanger refused the title of "editor in chief," a position he held at Nupedia, opting instead to be "chief organizer." He governed the day-to-day operations of the project in close consultation with the "community," the roughly two dozen committed Wikipedians (most of them Nupedia converts) who were really designing the software and adding content to the site. Though the division of powers between Sanger and the community remained to be worked out, an important precedent had been set: Wikipedia would have an owner, but no leader.

The Cunctator

By October 2001, the number of Wikipedians was growing by about fifty a month. There were a lot of new voices, among them a user known as "The Cunctator" (Latin for "procrastinator" or "delayer"). "Cunc," as he was called, advocated a combination of anarchy (no hierarchy within the project) and radical openness (few or no limitations on contributions). Sanger was not favorably disposed to either of these positions, though he had not had much of a chance to air his opposition. Cunc offered such an opportunity by launching a prolonged "edit war" with Sanger in mid-October of that year. In an edit war, two or more parties cyclically cancel each other's work on an article with no attempt to find the NPOV. It's the wiki equivalent of "No, *your* mother wears combat boots."

With Cunc clearly in mind, Sanger curtly defended his role before the community on November 1, 2001:

> I need to be granted fairly broad authority by the community — by you, dear reader — if I am going to do my job effectively. Until fairly recently, I was granted such authority by Wikipedians. I was indeed not infrequently called to justify decisions I made, but not constantly and nearly always respectfully and helpfully. This place in the community did not make me an all-powerful editor who must be obeyed on pain of ousting; but it did make me a leader. That's what I want, again. This is my job.

Seen from the trenches, this was a striking statement. Sanger had so far 35 said he was primus inter pares; now he seemed to be saying that he was just primus. Upon reading this post, one Wikipedian wrote: "Am I the only person who detects a change in [Sanger's] view of his own position? Am I the only person who fears this is a change for the worse?"

On November 4, the Sanger-Cunc contretemps exploded. Simon Kissane, a respected Wikipedian, accused Sanger of capriciously deleting pages, including some of Cunc's work. Sanger denied the allegation but implied that the excised material was no great loss. He then launched a defense of his position in words that bled resentment:

I do reserve the right to permanently delete things — particularly when they have little merit and when they are posted by people whose main motive is evidently to undermine my authority and therefore, as far as I'm concerned, damage the project. Now suppose that, in my experience, if I make an attempt to justify this or other sorts of decisions, the people in question will simply co-opt huge amounts of my time and will never simply say, "Larry, you win; we realize that this decision is up to you, and we'll have to respect it." Then, in order to preserve my time and sanity, I have to act like an autocrat. In a way, I am being trained to act like an autocrat. It's rather clever in a way — if you think college-level stunts are clever. Frankly, it's hurting the project, guys — so stop it, already.

Just write articles — please!

The blowup disturbed Wales to no end. As a list moderator, he had tried hard to keep his discussants out of flame wars. He weighed in with an unusually forceful posting that warned against a "culture of conflict." Wikipedia, he implied, was about building an encyclopedia, not about debating how to build or govern an encyclopedia. Echoing Sanger, he argued that the primary duty of community members was to contribute — by writing code, adding content, and editing. Enough talk, he seemed to be saying: we know what to do, now let's get to work. Yet he also seemed to take a quiet stand against Sanger's positions on openness and on his own authority:

Just speaking off the top of my head, I think that total deletions seldom make sense. They should be reserved primarily for pages that are just completely mistaken (typos, unlikely misspellings), or for pages that are nothing more than insults.

Wales also made a strong case that anyone deleting pages should record his or her identity, explain his or her reasons, and archive the entire affair.

Within several weeks, Sanger and Cunc were at each other's throats again. Sanger had proposed creating a "Wikipedia Militia" that would deal with issues arising from sudden massive influxes of new visitors. It was hardly a bad idea: such surges did occur (they're commonly called "slash-dottings"). But Cunc saw in Sanger's reasonable proposition a very slippery slope toward "central authority." "You start deputizing groups of people to do necessary and difficult tasks," he wrote, "fast-forward two/three years, and you have pernicious cabals."

Given the structure of Wikipedia, there was little Sanger could do to defend himself. The principles of the project denied him real punitive authority: he couldn't ban "trolls" — users like Cunc who baited others for sport — and deleting posts was evidence of tyranny in the eyes of Sanger's detractors. A defensive strategy wouldn't work either, as the skilled moderator's tactic for fighting bad behavior — ignoring it — was blunted by the wiki. On e-mail lists, unanswered inflammatory posts quickly vanish under layers of new

40

discussion; on a wiki, they remain visible to all, often near the tops of pages. Sanger was trapped by his own creation.

The "God-King"

Wales saw that Sanger was having trouble managing the project. Indeed, he seems to have sensed that Wikipedia really needed no manager. In mid-December 2001, citing financial shortfalls, he told Sanger that Bomis would be cutting its staff and that he should look for a new job. To that point, Wales and his partners had supported both Nupedia and Wikipedia. But with Bomis suffering in the Internet bust, there was financial pressure. Early on, Wales had said that advertising was a possibility, but the community was now set against any commercialization. In January 2002, Sanger loaded up his possessions and returned to Ohio.

Cunc responded to Sanger's departure with apparent appreciation:

> I know that we've hardly been on the best of terms, but I want you to know that I'll always consider you one of the most important Wikipedians, and I hope that you'll always think of yourself as a Wikipedian, even if you don't have much time to contribute. Herding cats ain't easy; you did a good job, all things considered.

Characteristically, Sanger took this as nothing more than provocation: "Oh, how nice and gracious this was. Oh, thank you SO much, Cunctator. I'm sure glad I won't have to deal with you anymore, Cunctator. You're a friggin' piece of work." The next post on the list is from Wales, who showed a business-as-usual sangfroid: "With the resignation of Larry, there is a much less pressing need for funds."

Sanger made two great contributions to Wikipedia: he built it, and he left it. After forging a revolutionary mode of knowledge building, he came to realize — albeit dimly at first — that it was not to his liking. He found that he was not heading a disciplined crew of qualified writers and editors collaborating on authoritative statements (the Nupedia ideal), but trying to control an ill-disciplined crowd of volunteers fighting over ever-shifting articles. From Sanger's point of view, both the behavior of the participants and the quality of the scholarship were wanting. Even after seeing Wikipedia's explosive growth, Sanger continued to argue that Wikipedia should engage experts and that Nupedia should be saved.

Wales, though, was a businessman. He wanted to build a free encyclopedia, and Wikipedia offered a very rapid and economically efficient means to that end. The articles flooded in, many were good, and they cost him almost nothing. Why interfere? Moreover, Wales was not really the meddling kind. Early on, Wikipedians took to calling him the "God-King." The appellation is purely ironic. Over the past four years, Wales has repeatedly

45

demonstrated an astounding reluctance to use his power, even when the community has begged him to. He wouldn't exile trolls or erase offensive material, much less settle on rules for how things should or should not be done. In 2003, Wales diminished his own authority by transferring Wikipedia and all of its assets to the nonprofit Wikimedia Foundation, whose sole purpose is to set general policy for Wikipedia and its allied projects. (He is one of five members of the foundation's board.)

Wales's benign rule has allowed Wikipedia to do what it does best: grow. The numbers are staggering. The English-language Wikipedia alone has well more than a million articles and expands by about 1,700 a day. (*Britannica*'s online version, by comparison, has about 100,000 articles.) As of mid-February 2006, more than 65,000 Wikipedians — registered users who have made at least ten edits since joining — had contributed to the English-language Wikipedia. The number of registered contributors is increasing by more than 6,000 a month; the number of unregistered contributors is presumably much larger. Then there are the 200-odd non-English-language Wikipedias. Nine of them already have more than 100,000 entries each, and nearly all of the major-language versions are growing on pace with the English version.

What Is Wikipedia?

The Internet did not create the desire to collect human knowledge. For most of history, however, standardizing and gathering knowledge was hard to do very effectively. The main problem was rampant equivocation. Can we all agree on what an apple is exactly, or the shades of the color green? Not easily. The wiki offered a way for people to actually decide in common. On Wikipedia, an apple is what the contributors say it is *right now*. You can try to change the definition by throwing in your own two cents, but the community — the voices actually negotiating and renegotiating the definition — decides in the end. Wikipedia grew out of a natural impulse (communication) facilitated by a new technology (the wiki).

The power of the community to decide, of course, asks us to reexamine what we mean when we say that something is "true." We tend to think of truth as something that resides in the world. The fact that two plus two equals four is written in the stars — we merely discovered it. But Wikipedia suggests a different theory of truth. Just think about the way we learn what words mean. Generally speaking, we do so by listening to other people (our parents, first). Since we want to communicate with them (after all, they feed us), we use the words in the same way they do. Wikipedia says judgments of truth and falsehood work the same way. The community decides that two plus two equals four the same way it decides what an apple is: by consensus. Yes, that means that if the community changes its mind and decides that two plus two equals five, then two plus two does equal five. The community isn't likely to do such an absurd or useless thing, but it has the ability.

Most-Edited Articles
As of June 17, 2006

	Total Edits			Total Edits
1. George W. Bush	30,393		12. Islam	8,566
2. Wikipedia	17,919		13. John Kerry	8,395
3. Jesus	14,183		14. 2004 Indian	8,278
4. United States	13,806		Ocean earthquake	
5. Adolf Hitler	11,947		15. Bill Clinton	8,241
6. Hurricane Katrina	11,191		16. Anarchism	8,220
7. World War II	10,722		17. September 11,	7,666
8. RuneScape	10,596		2001, attacks	
9. Michael Jackson	9,342		18. Christianity	7,601
10. Canada	8,783		19. Wii (Nintendo)	7,548
11. Britney Spears	8,672		20. Pope Benedict XVI	7,302

Source: Wikimedia Foundation.

Early detractors commonly made two criticisms of Wikipedia. First, unless experts were writing and vetting the material, the articles were inevitably going to be inaccurate. Second, since anyone could edit, vandals would have their way with even the best articles, making them suspect. No encyclopedia produced in this way could be trusted. Last year, however, a study in the journal *Nature* compared *Britannica* and Wikipedia science articles and suggested that the former are usually only marginally more accurate than the latter. *Britannica* demonstrated that *Nature*'s analysis was seriously flawed ("Fatally Flawed" was the fair title of the response), and no one has produced a more authoritative study of Wikipedia's accuracy. Yet it is a widely accepted view that Wikipedia is comparable to *Britannica*. Vandalism also has proved much less of an issue than originally feared. A study by IBM suggests that although vandalism does occur (particularly on high-profile entries like "George W. Bush"), watchful members of the huge Wikipedia community usually swoop down to stop the malfeasance shortly after it begins.

There are, of course, exceptions, as in the case of the journalist John   50
Seigenthaler, whose Wikipedia biography long contained a libel about his supposed complicity in the assassinations of John F. and Robert Kennedy. But even this example shows that the system is, if not perfect, at least responsive. When Seigenthaler became aware of the error, he contacted Wikipedia. The community (led in this instance by Wales) purged the entry of erroneous material, expanded it, and began to monitor it closely. Even though the Seigenthaler entry is often attacked by vandals, and is occasionally locked to block them, the page is more reliable precisely because it is now under "enough eyeballs." The same could be said about many controversial entries on Wikipedia: the quality of articles generally increases with the number of eyeballs. Given enough eyeballs, all errors are shallow.

Common Knowledge

In June 2001, only six months after Wikipedia was founded, a Polish Wikipedian named Krzysztof Jasiutowicz made an arresting and remarkably forward-looking observation. The Internet, he mused, was nothing but a "global Wikipedia without the end-user editing facility." The contents of the Internet — its pages — are created by a loose community of users, namely those on the Web. The contents of Wikipedia — its entries — are also created by a loose community of users, namely Wikipedians. On the Internet, contributors own their own pages, and only they can edit them. They can also create new pages as they see fit. On Wikipedia, contributors own *all* of the pages collectively, and each can edit nearly every page. Page creation is ultimately subject to community approval. The private-property regime that governs the Internet allows it to grow freely, but it makes organization and improvement very difficult. In contrast, Wikipedia's communal regime permits growth *plus* organization and improvement. The result of this difference is there for all to see: much of the Internet is a chaotic mess and therefore useless, whereas Wikipedia is well ordered and hence very useful.

Having seen all of this in prospect, Jasiutowicz asked a logical question: "Can someone please tell me what's the end point/goal of Wikipedia?" Wales responded, only half jokingly, "The goal of Wikipedia is fun for the contributors." He had a point. Editing Wikipedia *is* fun, and even rewarding. The site is huge, so somewhere on it there is probably something you know quite a bit about. Imagine that you happen upon your pet subject, or perhaps even look it up to see how it's being treated. And what do you find? Well, this date is wrong, that characterization is poor, and a word is misspelled. You click the "edit" tab and make the corrections, and you've just contributed to the progress of human knowledge. All in under five minutes, and at no cost.

Yet Wikipedia has a value that goes far beyond the enjoyment of its contributors. For all intents and purposes, the project is laying claim to a vast region of the Internet, a territory we might call "common knowledge." It is the place where all nominal information about objects of widely shared experience will be negotiated, stored, and renegotiated. When you want to find out *what something is*, you will go to Wikipedia, for that is where common knowledge will, by convention, be archived and updated and made freely available. And while you are there, you may just add or change a little something, and thereby feel the pride of authorship shared by the tens of thousands of Wikipedians.

Keeper

One of the objects of common knowledge in Wikipedia, I'm relieved to report, is "Marshall Poe." Recall that the Scottish Wikipedian Alai said that

I had no "notability" and therefore couldn't really be considered encyclopedic. On the same day that Alai suggested my entry be deleted, a rather vigorous discussion took place on the "discussion" page that attended the Marshall Poe entry. A Wikipedian who goes by "Dlyons493" discovered that I had indeed written an obscure dissertation on an obscure topic at a not-so-obscure university. He gave the article a "Weak Keep." Someone with the handle "Splash" searched Amazon and verified that I had indeed written books on Russian history, so my claim to be a historian was true. He gave me a "Keep." And finally, my champion and hero, a Wikipedian called "Tupsharru," dismissed my detractors with this:

> Keep. Obvious notability. Several books published with prestigious academic publishers. One of his books has even been translated into Swedish. I don't know why I have to repeat this again and again in these deletion discussions on academics, but don't just use Amazon when the Library of Congress catalogue is no farther than a couple of mouse clicks away.

Bear in mind that I knew none of these people, and they had, as far as I know, no interest other than truth in doing all of this work. Yet they didn't stop with verifying my claims and approving my article. They also searched the Web for material they could use to expand my one-line biography. After they were done, the Marshall Poe entry was two paragraphs long and included a good bibliography. Now that's wiki magic. 55

QUESTIONS

Reading

1. What is a *wiki*? Where did the term originate?
2. What types of information does Poe include in this essay *explaining* Wikipedia? Which *explanatory* techniques does he use to convey the information? Are these techniques effective in teaching you new information about Poe's subject?
3. Highlight, underline, or flag the labels that Poe uses to head each section of his essay. Write a brief definition of each label. Why might Poe structure his essay in this way?

Exploratory Writing

1. Make a double-entry list comparing Wikipedia to traditional encyclopedias. Considering this list, discuss whether Wikipedia is basically a traditional encyclopedia in an online format, or an entirely new type of research tool.

WIKIPEDIA	ENCYCLOPEDIA

2. Search Wikipedia for people you have met. Is anyone you know included in this resource? After your search, meet in small groups to discuss your findings. What would it mean if everyone you knew was on Wikipedia? How has the Internet changed the nature of fame?

Making Connections

1. Poe, Andrew Sullivan (p. 494), and Guillermo Gómez-Peña (p. 555) use themselves as guinea pigs in their research. Sullivan reports on responses to his blog, Gómez-Peña creates participatory online experiments, and Poe tries to post his own entry on Wikipedia (and finally succeeds, thanks to a diligent stranger). Design a project on the theme "Internet Services: Boon or Bane," in which you use yourself as a guinea pig. Report on your experience to the class.

Essay Writing

1. By the early 2000s, the Wikipedia community was "set against any commercialization" (paragraph 41). Write an essay speculating on the question of how Wikipedia would change if it included advertisements and paid contributors.

Future Reading
Digitization and Its Discontents

Anthony Grafton

Anthony Grafton (b. 1950) is a historian renowned for his studies of the classical tradition from the Renaissance to the eighteenth century, as well as for his meta-interest in the history of historical scholarship. The Footnote: A Curious History *(1997) — a so-called "case-study in what might be called the history of history, from below" — falls into this latter category. After receiving his PhD in history from the University of Chicago, Grafton taught briefly at Cornell University and has been a professor of history at Princeton University since 1975, where he is the Henry Putnam University Professor. He's currently working on a large-scale study of the science of chronology in sixteenth- and seventeenth-century Europe — namely, how scholars attempted to assign dates to past events, reconstruct ancient calendars, and reconcile the Bible with competing accounts of the past. Grafton also writes on a wide variety of topics for the* New Republic, *the* American Scholar, *and the* New York Review of Books. *"Future Reading" was originally published in the* New Yorker *in 2007.*

In 1938, Alfred Kazin began work on his first book, *On Native Grounds*. The child of poor Jewish immigrants in Brooklyn, he had studied at City College. Somehow, with little money or backing, he managed to write an extraordinary book, setting the great American intellectual and literary movements from the late nineteenth century to his own time in a richly evoked historical context. One institution made his work possible: the New York Public Library on Fifth Avenue and Forty-second Street. Kazin later recalled, "Anything I had heard of and wanted to see, the blessed place owned: first editions of American novels out of those germinal decades after the Civil War that led to my theme of the 'modern'; old catalogues from long-departed Chicago publishers who had been young men in the eighteen-nineties trying to support a little realism." Without leaving Manhattan, Kazin read his way into "lonely small towns, prairie villages, isolated colleges, dusty law offices, national magazines, and provincial 'academies' where no one suspected that the obedient-looking young reporters, law clerks, librarians, teachers would turn out to be Willa Cather, Robert Frost, Sinclair Lewis, Wallace Stevens, Marianne Moore."

It's an old and reassuring story: bookish boy or girl enters the cool, dark library and discovers loneliness and freedom. For the past ten years or so, however, the cities of the book have been anything but quiet. The computer and the Internet have transformed reading more dramatically than any technology since the printing press, and for the past five years Google has been at work on an ambitious project, Google Book Search. Google's self-described aim is to "build a comprehensive index of all the books in the world," one that would enable readers to search the list of books it contains and to see full texts of those not covered by copyright. Google collaborates with publishers, called Google Publishing Partners — there are more than ten thousand of them around the world — to provide information about books that are still copyright protected, including text samples, to all users of the Web. A second enterprise, the Google Library Project, is digitizing as many books as possible, in collaboration with great libraries in the United States and abroad. Among them is Kazin's beloved New York Public Library, where more than a million books are being scanned.

Google's projects, together with rival initiatives by Microsoft and Amazon, have elicited millenarian prophecies about the possibilities of digitized knowledge and the end of the book as we know it. Last year, Kevin Kelly, the self-styled "senior maverick" of *Wired*, predicted, in a piece in the *Times*, that "all the books in the world" would "become a single liquid fabric of interconnected words and ideas." The user of the electronic library would be able to bring together "all texts — past and present, multilingual — on a particular subject," and, by doing so, gain "a clearer sense of what we as a civilization, a species, do know and don't know." Others have evoked even more utopian prospects, such as a universal archive that will contain not only all books and articles but all documents anywhere — the basis for a total history of the human race.

In fact, the Internet will not bring us a universal library, much less an encyclopedic record of human experience. None of the firms now engaged in digitization projects claim that it will create anything of the kind. The hype and rhetoric make it hard to grasp what Google and Microsoft and their partner libraries are actually doing. We have clearly reached a new point in the history of text production. On many fronts, traditional periodicals and books are making way for blogs and other electronic formats. But magazines and books still sell a lot of copies. The rush to digitize the written record is one of a number of critical moments in the long saga of our drive to accumulate, store, and retrieve information efficiently. It will result not in the infotopia that the prophets conjure up but in one in a long series of new information ecologies, all of them challenging, in which readers, writers, and producers of text have learned to survive.

*   *   *

As early as the third millennium B.C., Mesopotamian scribes began 5 to catalogue the clay tablets in their collections. For ease of reference, they appended content descriptions to the edges of tablets, and they adopted systematic shelving for quick identification of related texts. The greatest and most famous of the ancient collections, the Library of Alexandria, had, in its ambitions and its methods, a good deal in common with Google's book projects. It was founded around 300 B.C. by Ptolemy I, who had inherited Alexandria, a brand-new city, from Alexander the Great. A historian with a taste for poetry, Ptolemy decided to amass a comprehensive collection of Greek works. Like Google, the library developed an efficient procedure for capturing and reproducing texts. When ships docked in Alexandria, any scrolls found on them were confiscated and taken to the library. The staff made copies for the owners and stored the originals in heaps, until they could be catalogued. At the collection's height, it contained more than half a million scrolls, a welter of information that forced librarians to develop new organizational methods. For the first time, works were shelved alphabetically.

Six hundred years later, Eusebius, a historian and bishop of the coastal city of Caesarea, in Palestine, assembled Christian writings in the local library. He also devised a system of cross-references, known as "canon tables," that enabled readers to find parallel passages in the four Gospels — a system that the scholar James O'Donnell recently described as the world's first set of hot links. A deft impresario, Eusebius mobilized a team of secretaries and scribes to produce Bibles featuring his new study aid; in the 330s, the emperor Constantine placed an order with Eusebius for fifty parchment codex Bibles for the churches of his new city, Constantinople. Throughout the Middle Ages, the great monastic libraries engaged in the twin projects of accumulating large holdings and, in their scriptoria, making and disseminating copies of key texts.

The rise of printing in fifteenth-century Europe transformed the work of librarians and readers. Into a world already literate and curious, the printers brought, within half a century, some twenty-eight thousand titles, and millions of individual books — many times more than the libraries of the West had previously held. Reports of new worlds, new theologies, and new ideas about the universe travelled faster and more cheaply than ever before. The entrepreneurial world of printing made much use of the traditional skills of learned librarians. Giovanni Andrea Bussi, a librarian of the papal collection of Sixtus IV, also served as adviser to two German printers in Rome, Conrad Sweynheym and Arnold Pannartz, who began printing handsome editions of classical texts, edited, corrected, and sometimes prefaced by Bussi. Like many first movers, Bussi and his partners soon found that they had overestimated the market, with disastrous financial results. They were not the last impresarios of new book technologies to experience this kind of difficulty.

Still, the model of scholars advising printers became normal in the six-teenth century, even if, in later centuries, the profit-driven industry of publishing and the industrious scholarship of the libraries gradually became separate spheres. Remarkably, this ancient model has been resurgent in recent years, as sales of university-press books have dwindled and the price of journal subscriptions has risen. With electronic publishing programs, libraries have begun to take on many of the tasks that traditionally fell to university presses, such as the distribution of doctoral dissertations and the reproduction of local book and document collections — a spread of activities that Eusebius would have found natural.

Fast, reliable methods of search and retrieval are sometimes identified as the hallmark of our information age; "Search is everything" has become a proverb. But scholars have had to deal with too much information for millennia, and in periods when information resources were multiplying especially fast they devised ingenious ways to control the floods. The Renaissance, during which the number of new texts threatened to become overwhelming, was the great age of systematic note-taking. Manuals such as Jeremias Drexel's *Goldmine* — the frontispiece of which showed a scholar taking notes opposite miners digging for literal gold — taught students how to condense and arrange the contents of literature by headings. Scholars well grounded in this regime, like Isaac Casaubon, spun tough, efficient webs of notes around the texts of their books and in their notebooks — hundreds of Casaubon's books survive — and used them to retrieve information about everything from the religion of Greek tragedy to Jewish burial practices. Jacques Cujas, a sixteenth-century legal scholar, astonished visitors to his study when he showed them the rotating barber's chair and movable bookstand that enabled him to keep many open books in view at the same time. Thomas Harrison, a seventeenth-century English inventor, devised a cabinet that he called the Ark of Studies: readers could synopsize and excerpt books and then arrange their notes by subject on a series of labelled metal hooks, somewhat in the manner of a card index. The German philosopher Leibniz obtained one of Harrison's cabinets and used it in his research.

For less erudite souls, simpler techniques abridged the process of look-   10 ing for information much as Wikipedia does now. Erasmus said that every serious student must read the entire corpus of the classics and make his own notes on them. But he also composed a magnificent reference work, the *Adages,* in which he laid out and explicated thousands of pithy ancient sayings — and provided subject indexes to help readers find what they needed. For centuries, schoolboys first encountered the wisdom of the ancients in this predigested form. When Erasmus told the story of Pandora, he said that she opened not a jar, as in the original version of the story, by the Greek poet Hesiod, but a box. In every European language except Italian, Pandora's box became proverbial — a canard made ubiquitous by the power of a new information technology. Even the best search procedures depend on the databases they explore.

From the eighteenth century, countries, universities, and academies maintained research libraries, whose staff pioneered information retrieval with a variety of indexing and cataloguing systems. The development of the Dewey decimal system, in the 1870s, coincided with a democratization of reading. Cheap but durable editions like those of Bohn's Library brought books other than the Bible into working-class households, and newspapers, which in the late nineteenth century sometimes appeared every hour, made breaking news and social commentary available across all social ranks.

In the 1940s, Fremont Rider, a librarian at Wesleyan University, prophesied that material was multiplying so quickly that it would soon overflow even the biggest sets of stacks. He argued that microphotography could eliminate this problem, and that, by multiplying the resources of any given library, it also offered the promise of truly universal libraries. As old universities expanded and new ones sprouted in the 1950s and 1960s, generous funding enabled them to buy what was available on film or microfiche and in reprint form. Suddenly, you could do serious research on the Vatican Library's collections not only in Rome but also in St. Louis, where the Knights of Columbus assembled a vast holding of microfilm.

But the film- and reprint-based libraries never became really comprehensive. The commercial companies that did most of the filming naturally concentrated on more marketable texts, while nonprofit sponsors concentrated on the texts that mattered to them. No overall logic determined which texts were reprinted on paper, which were filmed, and which remained in obscurity. Some efforts, like Eugene Power's STC [Short-Title Catalogue] project, which distributed on microfilm twenty-six thousand early English books, transformed research conditions in certain fields. Others simply died. As the production of books and serials exploded in the sixties, library budgets failed to keep pace. A number of reprint publishers ended up, like Bussi and his associates, drowning in unsold books. The vendors of microfilm kept going — so efficiently, and enthusiastically, that they persuaded librarians and archivists to destroy large quantities of books and newspapers that could have been preserved.

The current era of digitization outstrips that of microfilm, in ambition and in achievement. Few individuals ever owned microfilm readers, after all, whereas many people have access to PCs with Internet connections. Now even the most traditional-minded scholar generally begins by consulting a search engine. As a cheerful editor at Cambridge University Press recently told me, "Conservatively, ninety-five percent of all scholarly inquiries start at Google." Google's famous search algorithm emulates the principle of scholarly citation — counting up and evaluating earlier links in order to steer users toward the sources that others have already found helpful. In a sense, the system resembles nothing more than trillions of old-fashioned footnotes.

The Google Library Project has so far received mixed reviews. Google   15
shows the reader a scanned version of the page; it is generally accurate and readable. But Google also uses optical character recognition to produce a second version, for its search engine to use, and this double process has some quirks. In a scriptorium lit by the sun, a scribe could mistakenly transcribe a *u* as an *n*, or vice versa. Curiously, the computer makes the same mistake. If you enter *"qualitas"* — an important term in medieval philosophy — into Google Book Search, you'll find almost two thousand appearances. But if you enter "qnalitas," you'll be rewarded with more than five hundred references that you wouldn't necessarily have found. Sometimes the scanner operators miss pages, or scan them out of order. Sometimes the copy is not in good condition. The cataloguing data that identify an item are often incomplete or confusing. And the key terms that Google provides in order to characterize individual books are sometimes unintentionally comic. It's not all that helpful, when you're thinking about how to use an 1878 Baedeker guide to Paris, to be told that one of its keywords is *fauteuils*.

But there are even more fundamental limitations to the Google project, and to its competitors from Microsoft and Amazon. One of the most frequently discussed difficulties is that of copyright. A conservative reckoning of the number of books ever published is thirty-two million; Google believes that there could be as many as a hundred million. It is estimated that between 5 and 10 percent of known books are currently in print, and 20 percent — those produced between the beginning of print, in the fifteenth century, and 1923 — are out of copyright. The rest, perhaps 75 percent of all books ever printed, are "orphans," possibly still covered by copyright protections but out of print and pretty much out of mind. Google, controversially, is scanning these books although it is not yet making them fully available; Microsoft, more cautiously, is scanning only what it knows it can legitimately disseminate.

Google and Microsoft pursue their own interests, in ways that they think will generate income, and this has prompted a number of major libraries to work with the Open Content Alliance, a nonprofit book-digitizing venture. Many important books will remain untouched: Google, for example, has no immediate plans to scan books from the first couple of centuries of printing. Rare books require expensive special conditions for copying, and most of those likely to generate a lot of use have already been made available by companies like Chadwyck-Healey and Gale, which sell their collections to libraries and universities for substantial fees. Early English Books Online offers a hundred thousand titles printed between 1475 and 1700. Massive tomes in Latin and the little pamphlets that poured off the presses during the Puritan revolution — schoolbooks, Jacobean tragedies with prompters' notes, and political pamphlets by Puritan regicides — are all available to anyone in a major library.

Other sectors of the world's book production are not even catalogued and accessible on site, much less available for digitization. The materials from the poorest societies may not attract companies that rely on subscriptions or on advertising for cash flow. This is unfortunate, because these very societies have the least access to printed books and thus to their own literature and history. If you visit the Web site of the Online Computer Library Center and look at its WorldMap, you can see the numbers of books in public and academic systems around the world. Sixty million Britons have 116 million public-library books at their disposal, while more than 1.1 billion Indians have only 36 million. Poverty, in other words, is embodied in lack of print as well as in lack of food. The Internet will do much to redress this imbalance, by providing Western books for non-Western readers. What it will do for non-Western books is less clear.

A record of all history appears even more distant. If you were going to make such a record available, as the most utopian champions of digitization imagine, you would have to include both literary works and archival documents never meant for publication. It's true that millions of these documents are starting to appear on screens. The online records of the Patent and Trademark Office are a boon for anyone interested in its spectacular panorama of the brilliance and lunacy of American tinkerers. Thanks to the nonprofit Aluka archive, scholars and writers in Africa can study on the Web a growing number of African records whose originals are stored, inaccessibly, elsewhere in the world. Historians of the papacy can read original documents of the early Popes without going to Rome, in a digitized collection of documents mounted by the Vatican Secret Archives. But even the biggest of these projects is nothing more than a flare of light in the still unexplored night sky of humanity's recorded past. ArchivesUSA, a Web-based guide to American archives, lists 5,500 repositories and more than 160,000 collections of primary source material. The U.S. National Archives alone contain some nine billion items. It's not likely that we'll see the whole archives of the United States or any other developed nation online in the immediate future — much less those of poorer nations.

The supposed universal library, then, will be not a seamless mass of   20
books, easily linked and studied together, but a patchwork of interfaces and databases, some open to anyone with a computer and WiFi, others closed to those without access or money. The real challenge now is how to chart the tectonic plates of information that are crashing into one another and then to learn to navigate the new landscapes they are creating. Over time, as more of this material emerges from copyright protection, we'll be able to learn things about our culture that we could never have known previously. Soon, the present will become overwhelmingly accessible, but a great deal of older material may never coalesce into a single database. Neither Google nor anyone else will fuse the proprietary databases of early

books and the local systems created by individual archives into one accessible store of information. Though the distant past will be more available, in a technical sense, than ever before, once it is captured and preserved as a vast, disjointed mosaic it may recede ever more rapidly from our collective attention.

Still, it is hard to exaggerate what is already becoming possible month by month and what will become possible in the next few years. Google and Microsoft are flanked by other big efforts. Some are largely philanthropic, like the old standby Project Gutenberg, which provides hand-keyboarded texts of English and American classics, and the distinctive Million Book Project, founded by Raj Reddy, at Carnegie Mellon University. Reddy works with partners around the world to provide, among other things, online texts in many languages for which character-recognition software is not yet available. There are hundreds of smaller efforts in specialized fields — like Perseus, a site, based at Tufts, specializing in Greek and Latin — and new commercial enterprises like Alexander Street Press, which offers libraries beautifully produced collections of everything from *Harper's Weekly* to the letters and diaries of American immigrants. It has become impossible for ordinary scholars to keep abreast of what's available in this age of electronic abundance — though *D-Lib Magazine*, an online publication, helps by highlighting new digital sources and collections, rather as material libraries used to advertise their acquisition of a writer's papers or a collection of books with fine bindings.

The Internet's technologies, moreover, are continually improving. Search engines like Google, Altavista, and HotBot originally informed the user about only the top layers of Web pages. To find materials buried in such deep bodies of fact and document as the Library of Congress's Web site or JSTOR, a repository of scholarly journal articles, you had to go to the site and ask a specific question. But in recent years — as anyone who regularly uses Google knows — they have become more adept at asking questions, and the search companies have apparently induced the largest proprietary sites to become more responsive. Specialist engines like Google Scholar can discriminate with astonishing precision between relevant and irrelevant, firsthand and derivative, information.

Alfred Kazin loved the New York Public Library because it admitted everyone. The readers included not only presentable young scholars like his friend Richard Hofstadter but also many wild figures who haunted the reading rooms: "the little man with one slice of hair across his bald head, like General MacArthur's . . . poring with a faint smile over a large six-column Bible in Hebrew, Greek, Latin, English, French, German," and "the bony, ugly, screeching madwoman who reminded me of Maxim Gorky's 'Boless.'" Even Kazin's democratic imagination could not have envisaged the hordes of the Web's actual and potential users, many of whom will read material that would have been all but inaccessible to them a generation ago.

And yet we will still need our libraries and archives. John Seely Brown and Paul Duguid have written of the so-called "social life of information" — the form in which you encounter a text can have a huge impact on how you use it. Original documents reward us for taking the trouble to find them by telling us things that no image can. Duguid describes watching a fellow historian systematically sniff 250-year-old letters in an archive. By detecting the smell of vinegar — which had been sprinkled, in the eighteenth century, on letters from towns struck by cholera, in the hope of disinfecting them — he could trace the history of disease outbreaks. Historians of the book — a new and growing tribe — read books as scouts read trails. Bindings, usually custom-made in the early centuries of printing, can tell you who owned them and what level of society they belonged to. Marginal annotations, which abounded in the centuries when readers usually went through books with pen in hand, identify the often surprising messages that individuals have found as they read. Many original writers and thinkers — Martin Luther, John Adams, Samuel Taylor Coleridge — have filled their books with notes that are indispensable to understanding their thought. Thousands of forgotten men and women have covered Bibles and prayer books, recipe collections, and political pamphlets with pointing hands, underlining, and notes that give insights into which books mattered, and why. If you want to capture how a book was packaged and what it has meant to the readers who have unwrapped it, you have to look at all the copies you can find, from original manuscripts to cheap reprints. The databases include multiple copies of some titles. But they will never provide all the copies of, say, *The Wealth of Nations* and the early responses it provoked.

For now and for the foreseeable future, any serious reader will have to know how to travel down two very different roads simultaneously. No one should avoid the broad, smooth, and open road that leads through the screen. But if you want to know what one of Coleridge's annotated books or an early "Spider-Man" comic really looks and feels like, or if you just want to read one of those millions of books which are being digitized, you still have to do it the old way, and you will have to for decades to come. At the New York Public Library, the staff loves electronic media. The library has made hundreds of thousands of images from its collections accessible on the Web, but it has done so in the knowledge that its collection comprises fifty-three million items.

Sit in your local coffee shop, and your laptop can tell you a lot. If you want deeper, more local knowledge, you will have to take the narrower path that leads between the lions and up the stairs. There — as in great libraries around the world — you'll use all the new sources, the library's and those it buys from others, all the time. You'll check musicians' names and dates at Grove Music Online, read Marlowe's *Doctor Faustus* on Early English Books Online, or decipher Civil War documents on Valley of the Shadow. But these streams of data, rich as they are, will illuminate, rather than eliminate, books and prints and manuscripts that only the library can put in front of you. The narrow path still leads, as it must, to crowded public rooms where the sunlight gleams on varnished tables, and knowledge is embodied in millions of dusty, crumbling, smelly, irreplaceable documents and books.

QUESTIONS

Reading

1. Why do a number of major libraries work with the Open Content Alliance instead of Google or Microsoft?
2. Summarize Grafton's major *argument* in this essay. According to Grafton, what do original documents offer that images cannot?
3. According to Grafton, how do the staff at traditional libraries — such as the one where Kazin began work on his first book in 1938 — feel about electronic media?
4. How does Grafton's *perspective* change in the final paragraph of his argument? How does this change make his essay more evocative?

Exploratory Writing

1. Do you agree with Grafton that traditional libraries and books are still valuable in this technologically sophisticated era? Break into groups, and stage a debate on the following topic: Traditional libraries should be replaced by digital media. You can use Grafton's examples as well as Internet research to build your arguments.
2. Visit Grafton's online tour of his favorite digital collections on the *New Yorker*'s Web site (**www.newyorker.com/online/2007/11/05/071105on _onlineonly_grafton**), or explore other online digital resources. List ten "crumbling, smelly, irreplaceable" documents or books that you are guided to by these resources.

Making Connections

1. Grafton believes that the streams of data available on Google or other Internet resources will lead us to pursue deeper knowledge in the library. Consider this argument in light of Nicholas Carr's essay, "Is Google Making Us Stupid?" (p. 533). For example, Carr quotes a blogger as reporting that his thinking has taken on a "staccato" quality and that he has lost the ability to read long novels. *Compare* and *contrast* Carr's and Grafton's conclusions. What is your own opinion?

Essay Writing

1. Visit the most appealing library in your area, and write an essay reflecting on your experience there. Use rich details like Grafton's to describe the library.

Is Google Making Us Stupid?

Nicholas Carr

Nicholas Carr (b. 1959) has published numerous books and articles on the intersection of technology, business, and culture. Of these, the most incendiary have been Does IT Matter? *(2004), a book that argues the diminished importance of information technology in an increasingly savvy corporate workplace; "The Amorality of Web 2.0" (Rough Type, 2005), an article that criticizes the quality of crowd-sourced information projects such as Wikipedia and the blogosphere as opposed to the more expensive professional alternatives they displace; and the following essay, first published in the* Atlantic *in 2008, which posits that the Internet may diminish our capacity for concentration and contemplation as well as lead to other detrimental effects on cognition. Carr holds a BA from Dartmouth College and an MA in English literature from Harvard University. In addition to writing best-sellers and much-discussed technology articles (often published on his blog, Rough Type), Carr has been a speaker at MIT, Harvard, the Kennedy School of Government, and NASA. He was named to* Encyclopaedia Britannica's *editorial board of advisors in 2008.*

"Dave, stop. Stop, will you? Stop, Dave. Will you stop, Dave?" So the supercomputer HAL pleads with the implacable astronaut Dave Bowman in a famous and weirdly poignant scene toward the end of Stanley Kubrick's *2001: A Space Odyssey.* Bowman, having nearly been sent to a deep-space death by the malfunctioning machine, is calmly, coldly disconnecting the memory circuits that control its artificial brain. "Dave, my mind is going," HAL says, forlornly. "I can feel it. I can feel it."

I can feel it, too. Over the past few years I've had an uncomfortable sense that someone, or something, has been tinkering with my brain, remapping the neural circuitry, reprogramming the memory. My mind isn't going — so far as I can tell — but it's changing. I'm not thinking the way I used to think. I can feel it most strongly when I'm reading. Immersing myself in a book or a lengthy article used to be easy. My mind would get caught up in the narrative or the turns of the argument, and I'd spend hours strolling through long stretches of prose. That's rarely the case anymore. Now my concentration often starts to drift after two or three pages. I get fidgety, lose the thread, begin looking for something else to do. I feel as if I'm always dragging my wayward brain back to the text. The deep reading that used to come naturally has become a struggle.

I think I know what's going on. For more than a decade now, I've been spending a lot of time online, searching and surfing and sometimes adding to the great databases of the Internet. The Web has been a godsend to me as a writer. Research that once required days in the stacks or periodical rooms of libraries can now be done in minutes. A few Google searches, some quick clicks on hyperlinks, and I've got the telltale fact or pithy quote I was after. Even when I'm not working, I'm as likely as not to be foraging in the Web's info-thickets — reading and writing e-mails, scanning headlines and blog posts, watching videos and listening to podcasts, or just tripping from link to link to link. (Unlike footnotes, to which they're sometimes likened, hyperlinks don't merely point to related works; they propel you toward them.)

For me, as for others, the Net is becoming a universal medium, the conduit for most of the information that flows through my eyes and ears and into my mind. The advantages of having immediate access to such an incredibly rich store of information are many, and they've been widely described and duly applauded. "The perfect recall of silicon memory," *Wired*'s Clive Thompson has written, "can be an enormous boon to thinking." But that boon comes at a price. As the media theorist Marshall McLuhan pointed out in the 1960s, media are not just passive channels of information. They supply the stuff of thought, but they also shape the process of thought. And what the Net seems to be doing is chipping away my capacity for concentration and contemplation. My mind now expects to take in information the way the Net distributes it: in a swiftly moving stream of particles. Once I was a scuba diver in the sea of words. Now I zip along the surface like a guy on a Jet Ski.

I'm not the only one. When I mention my troubles with reading to friends   5
and acquaintances — literary types, most of them — many say they're having similar experiences. The more they use the Web, the more they have to fight to stay focused on long pieces of writing. Some of the bloggers I follow have also begun mentioning the phenomenon. Scott Karp, who writes a blog about online media, recently confessed that he has stopped reading books altogether. "I was a lit major in college, and used to be [a] voracious book reader," he wrote. "What happened?" He speculates on the answer: "What if I do all my reading on the Web not so much because the way I read has changed, i.e., I'm just seeking convenience, but because the way I THINK has changed?"

Bruce Friedman, who blogs regularly about the use of computers in medicine, also has described how the Internet has altered his mental habits. "I now have almost totally lost the ability to read and absorb a longish article on the Web or in print," he wrote earlier this year. A pathologist who has long been on the faculty of the University of Michigan Medical School, Friedman elaborated on his comment in a telephone conversation with me. His thinking, he said, has taken on a "staccato" quality, reflecting the way he quickly scans short passages of text from many sources online. "I can't read *War and Peace* anymore," he admitted. "I've lost the ability to do that. Even a blog post of more than three or four paragraphs is too much to absorb. I skim it."

Anecdotes alone don't prove much. And we still await the long-term neurological and psychological experiments that will provide a definitive picture of how Internet use affects cognition. But a recently published study of online research habits, conducted by scholars from University College London, suggests that we may well be in the midst of a sea change in the way we read and think. As part of the five-year research program, the scholars examined computer logs documenting the behavior of visitors to two popular research sites, one operated by the British Library and one by a UK educational consortium, that provide access to journal articles, e-books, and other sources of written information. They found that people using the sites exhibited "a form of skimming activity," hopping from one source to another and rarely returning to any source they'd already visited. They typically read no more than one or two pages of an article or book before they would "bounce" out to another site. Sometimes they'd save a long article, but there's no evidence that they ever went back and actually read it. The authors of the study report:

> It is clear that users are not reading online in the traditional sense; indeed there are signs that new forms of "reading" are emerging as users "power browse" horizontally through titles, contents pages and abstracts going for quick wins. It almost seems that they go online to avoid reading in the traditional sense.

Thanks to the ubiquity of text on the Internet, not to mention the popularity of text-messaging on cell phones, we may well be reading more today than we did in the 1970s or 1980s, when television was our medium of choice. But it's a different kind of reading, and behind it lies a different kind of thinking — perhaps even a new sense of the self. "We are not only *what* we read," says Maryanne Wolf, a developmental psychologist at Tufts University and the author of *Proust and the Squid: The Story and Science of the Reading Brain.* "We are *how* we read." Wolf worries that the style of reading promoted by the Net, a style that puts "efficiency" and "immediacy" above all else, may be weakening our capacity for the kind of deep reading that emerged when an earlier technology, the printing press, made long and complex works of prose commonplace. When we read online, she says, we tend to become "mere decoders of information." Our ability to interpret text, to make the rich mental connections that form when we read deeply and without distraction, remains largely disengaged.

Reading, explains Wolf, is not an instinctive skill for human beings. It's not etched into our genes the way speech is. We have to teach our minds how to translate the symbolic characters we see into the language we understand. And the media or other technologies we use in learning and practicing the craft of reading play an important part in shaping the neural circuits inside our brains. Experiments demonstrate that readers of ideograms, such as the Chinese, develop a mental circuitry for reading that is very different from the circuitry found in those of us whose written language employs an alphabet. The variations extend across many regions of the brain, including those that govern such essential cognitive functions as memory and the interpretation of visual and auditory stimuli. We can expect as well that the circuits woven by our use of the Net will be different from those woven by our reading of books and other printed works.

Sometime in 1882, Friedrich Nietzsche bought a typewriter — a   10
Malling-Hansen Writing Ball, to be precise. His vision was failing, and keeping his eyes focused on a page had become exhausting and painful, often bringing on crushing headaches. He had been forced to curtail his writing, and he feared that he would soon have to give it up. The typewriter rescued him, at least for a time. Once he had mastered touch-typing, he was able to write with his eyes closed, using only the tips of his fingers. Words could once again flow from his mind to the page.

But the machine had a subtler effect on his work. One of Nietzsche's friends, a composer, noticed a change in the style of his writing. His already terse prose had become even tighter, more telegraphic. "Perhaps you will through this instrument even take to a new idiom," the friend wrote in a letter, noting that, in his own work, his "'thoughts' in music and language often depend on the quality of pen and paper."

"You are right," Nietzsche replied, "our writing equipment takes part in the forming of our thoughts." Under the sway of the machine, writes the German media scholar Friedrich A. Kittler, Nietzsche's prose "changed from arguments to aphorisms, from thoughts to puns, from rhetoric to telegram style."

The human brain is almost infinitely malleable. People used to think that our mental meshwork, the dense connections formed among the hundred billion or so neurons inside our skulls, was largely fixed by the time we reached adulthood. But brain researchers have discovered that that's not the case. James Olds, a professor of neuroscience who directs the Krasnow Institute for Advanced Study at George Mason University, says that even the adult mind "is very plastic." Nerve cells routinely break old connections and form new ones. "The brain," according to Olds, "has the ability to reprogram itself on the fly, altering the way it functions."

As we use what the sociologist Daniel Bell has called our "intellectual technologies" — the tools that extend our mental rather than our physical capacities — we inevitably begin to take on the qualities of those technologies. The mechanical clock, which came into common use in the fourteenth century, provides a compelling example. In *Technics and Civilization*, the historian and cultural critic Lewis Mumford described how the clock "disassociated time from human events and helped create the belief in an independent world of mathematically measurable sequences." The "abstract framework of divided time" became "the point of reference for both action and thought."

The clock's methodical ticking helped bring into being the scientific 15 mind and the scientific man. But it also took something away. As the late MIT computer scientist Joseph Weizenbaum observed in his 1976 book, *Computer Power and Human Reason: From Judgment to Calculation,* the conception of the world that emerged from the widespread use of timekeeping instruments "remains an impoverished version of the older one, for it rests on a rejection of those direct experiences that formed the basis for, and indeed constituted, the old reality." In deciding when to eat, to work, to sleep, to rise, we stopped listening to our senses and started obeying the clock.

The process of adapting to new intellectual technologies is reflected in the changing metaphors we use to explain ourselves to ourselves. When the mechanical clock arrived, people began thinking of their brains as operating "like clockwork." Today, in the age of software, we have come to think of them as operating "like computers." But the changes, neuroscience tells us, go much deeper than metaphor. Thanks to our brain's plasticity, the adaptation occurs also at a biological level.

The Internet promises to have particularly far-reaching effects on cognition. In a paper published in 1936, the British mathematician Alan Turing proved that a digital computer, which at the time existed only as a theoretical machine, could be programmed to perform the function of any other information-processing device. And that's what we're seeing today. The Internet, an immeasurably powerful computing system, is subsuming most of our other intellectual technologies. It's becoming our map and our clock, our printing press and our typewriter, our calculator and our telephone, and our radio and TV.

When the Net absorbs a medium, that medium is re-created in the Net's image. It injects the medium's content with hyperlinks, blinking ads, and other digital gewgaws, and it surrounds the content with the content of all the other media it has absorbed. A new e-mail message, for instance, may announce its arrival as we're glancing over the latest headlines at a newspaper's site. The result is to scatter our attention and diffuse our concentration.

The Net's influence doesn't end at the edges of a computer screen, either. As people's minds become attuned to the crazy quilt of Internet media, traditional media have to adapt to the audience's new expectations. Television programs add text crawls and pop-up ads, and magazines and newspapers shorten their articles, introduce capsule summaries, and crowd their pages with easy-to-browse info-snippets. When, in March of this year, the *New York Times* decided to devote the second and third pages of every edition to article abstracts, its design director, Tom Bodkin, explained that the "shortcuts" would give harried readers a quick "taste" of the day's news, sparing them the "less efficient" method of actually turning the pages and reading the articles. Old media have little choice but to play by the new-media rules.

Never has a communications system played so many roles in our lives — 20 or exerted such broad influence over our thoughts — as the Internet does today. Yet, for all that's been written about the Net, there's been little consideration of how, exactly, it's reprogramming us. The Net's intellectual ethic remains obscure.

About the same time that Nietzsche started using his typewriter, an earnest young man named Frederick Winslow Taylor carried a stopwatch into the Midvale Steel plant in Philadelphia and began a historic series of experiments aimed at improving the efficiency of the plant's machinists. With the approval of Midvale's owners, he recruited a group of factory hands, set them to work on various metalworking machines, and recorded and timed their every movement as well as the operations of the machines. By breaking down every job into a sequence of small, discrete steps and then testing different ways of performing each one, Taylor created a set of precise instructions — an "algorithm," we might say today — for how each worker should work. Midvale's employees grumbled about the strict new regime, claiming that it turned them into little more than automatons, but the factory's productivity soared.

More than a hundred years after the invention of the steam engine, the Industrial Revolution had at last found its philosophy and its philosopher. Taylor's tight industrial choreography — his "system," as he liked to call it — was embraced by manufacturers throughout the country and, in time, around the world. Seeking maximum speed, maximum efficiency, and maximum output, factory owners used time-and-motion studies to organize their work and configure the jobs of their workers. The goal, as Taylor defined it in his celebrated 1911 treatise, *The Principles of Scientific Management,* was to identify and adopt, for every job, the "one best method" of work and thereby to effect "the gradual substitution of science for rule of thumb throughout the mechanic arts." Once his system was applied to all acts of manual labor, Taylor assured his followers, it would bring about a restructuring not only of industry but of society, creating a utopia of perfect efficiency. "In the past the man has been first," he declared; "in the future the system must be first."

Taylor's system is still very much with us; it remains the ethic of industrial manufacturing. And now, thanks to the growing power that computer engineers and software coders wield over our intellectual lives, Taylor's ethic is beginning to govern the realm of the mind as well. The Internet is a machine designed for the efficient and automated collection, transmission, and manipulation of information, and its legions of programmers are intent on finding the "one best method" — the perfect algorithm — to carry out every mental movement of what we've come to describe as "knowledge work."

Google's headquarters, in Mountain View, California — the Googleplex — is the Internet's high church, and the religion practiced inside its walls is Taylorism. Google, says its chief executive, Eric Schmidt, is "a company that's founded around the science of measurement," and it is striving to "systematize everything" it does. Drawing on the terabytes of behavioral data it collects through its search engine and other sites, it carries out thousands of experiments a day, according to the *Harvard Business Review,* and it uses the results to refine the algorithms that increasingly control how people find information and extract meaning from it. What Taylor did for the work of the hand, Google is doing for the work of the mind.

The company has declared that its mission is "to organize the world's   25
information and make it universally accessible and useful." It seeks to develop "the perfect search engine," which it defines as something that "understands exactly what you mean and gives you back exactly what you want." In Google's view, information is a kind of commodity, a utilitarian resource that can be mined and processed with industrial efficiency. The more pieces of information we can "access" and the faster we can extract their gist, the more productive we become as thinkers.

Where does it end? Sergey Brin and Larry Page, the gifted young men who founded Google while pursuing doctoral degrees in computer science at Stanford, speak frequently of their desire to turn their search engine into an artificial intelligence, a HAL-like machine that might be connected directly to our brains. "The ultimate search engine is something as smart as people — or smarter," Page said in a speech a few years back. "For us, working on search is a way to work on artificial intelligence." In a 2004 interview with *Newsweek*, Brin said, "Certainly if you had all the world's information directly attached to your brain, or an artificial brain that was smarter than your brain, you'd be better off." Last year, Page told a convention of scientists that Google is "really trying to build artificial intelligence and to do it on a large scale."

Such an ambition is a natural one, even an admirable one, for a pair of math whizzes with vast quantities of cash at their disposal and a small army of computer scientists in their employ. A fundamentally scientific enterprise, Google is motivated by a desire to use technology, in Eric Schmidt's words, "to solve problems that have never been solved before," and artificial intelligence is the hardest problem out there. Why wouldn't Brin and Page want to be the ones to crack it?

Still, their easy assumption that we'd all "be better off" if our brains were supplemented, or even replaced, by an artificial intelligence is unsettling. It suggests a belief that intelligence is the output of a mechanical process, a series of discrete steps that can be isolated, measured, and optimized. In Google's world, the world we enter when we go online, there's little place for the fuzziness of contemplation. Ambiguity is not an opening for insight but a bug to be fixed. The human brain is just an outdated computer that needs a faster processor and a bigger hard drive.

The idea that our minds should operate as high-speed data-processing machines is not only built into the workings of the Internet, it is the network's reigning business model as well. The faster we surf across the Web — the more links we click and pages we view — the more opportunities Google and other companies gain to collect information about us and to feed us advertisements. Most of the proprietors of the commercial Internet have a financial stake in collecting the crumbs of data we leave behind as we flit from link to link — the more crumbs, the better. The last thing these companies want is to encourage leisurely reading or slow, concentrated thought. It's in their economic interest to drive us to distraction.

*   *   *

Maybe I'm just a worrywart. Just as there's a tendency to glorify tech-   30
nological progress, there's a countertendency to expect the worst of every
new tool or machine. In Plato's *Phaedrus*, Socrates bemoaned the development of writing. He feared that, as people came to rely on the written word
as a substitute for the knowledge they used to carry inside their heads, they
would, in the words of one of the dialogue's characters, "cease to exercise
their memory and become forgetful." And because they would be able to
"receive a quantity of information without proper instruction," they would
"be thought very knowledgeable when they are for the most part quite ignorant." They would be "filled with the conceit of wisdom instead of real wisdom." Socrates wasn't wrong — the new technology did often have the
effects he feared — but he was shortsighted. He couldn't foresee the many
ways that writing and reading would serve to spread information, spur fresh
ideas, and expand human knowledge (if not wisdom).

The arrival of Gutenberg's printing press, in the fifteenth century, set off
another round of teeth gnashing. The Italian humanist Hieronimo Squarci-
afico worried that the easy availability of books would lead to intellectual
laziness, making men "less studious" and weakening their minds. Others
argued that cheaply printed books and broadsheets would undermine religious authority, demean the work of scholars and scribes, and spread sedi-
tion and debauchery. As New York University professor Clay Shirky notes,
"Most of the arguments made against the printing press were correct, even
prescient." But, again, the doomsayers were unable to imagine the myriad
blessings that the printed word would deliver.

So, yes, you should be skeptical of my skepticism. Perhaps those who
dismiss critics of the Internet as Luddites or nostalgists will be proved correct, and from our hyperactive, data-stoked minds will spring a golden age
of intellectual discovery and universal wisdom. Then again, the Net isn't the
alphabet, and although it may replace the printing press, it produces something altogether different. The kind of deep reading that a sequence of
printed pages promotes is valuable not just for the knowledge we acquire
from the author's words but for the intellectual vibrations those words set
off within our own minds. In the quiet spaces opened up by the sustained,
undistracted reading of a book, or by any other act of contemplation, for
that matter, we make our own associations, draw our own inferences and
analogies, foster our own ideas. Deep reading, as Maryanne Wolf argues, is
indistinguishable from deep thinking.

If we lose those quiet spaces, or fill them up with "content," we will
sacrifice something important not only in our selves but in our culture. In a
recent essay, the playwright Richard Foreman eloquently described what's
at stake:

> I come from a tradition of Western culture, in which the ideal
> (my ideal) was the complex, dense and "cathedral-like" structure of
> the highly educated and articulate personality — a man or woman

who carried inside themselves a personally constructed and unique version of the entire heritage of the West. [But now] I see within us all (myself included) the replacement of complex inner density with a new kind of self — evolving under the pressure of information overload and the technology of the "instantly available."

As we are drained of our "inner repertory of dense cultural inheritance," Foreman concluded, we risk turning into "'pancake people' — spread wide and thin as we connect with that vast network of information accessed by the mere touch of a button."

I'm haunted by that scene in *2001*. What makes it so poignant, and so weird, is the computer's emotional response to the disassembly of its mind: its despair as one circuit after another goes dark, its childlike pleading with the astronaut — "I can feel it. I can feel it. I'm afraid" — and its final reversion to what can only be called a state of innocence. HAL's outpouring of feeling contrasts with the emotionlessness that characterizes the human figures in the film, who go about their business with an almost robotic efficiency. Their thoughts and actions feel scripted, as if they're following the steps of an algorithm. In the world of *2001*, people have become so machinelike that the most human character turns out to be a machine. That's the essence of Kubrick's dark prophecy: as we come to rely on computers to mediate our understanding of the world, it is our own intelligence that flattens into artificial intelligence.

QUESTIONS

Reading

1. What does Carr mean by the term *stupid* in his title? Make a list of the ways that Carr thinks the Internet adversely changes the brain's functions.
2. What is the agenda of Google's creators and programmers, according to Carr? Why do they want our minds to operate like machines?
3. Carr uses personal anecdotes and reflections in his *argument*, but he says, "Anecdotes alone don't prove much" (paragraph 7). Which other techniques does he use to make his point?
4. What is Carr's *tone* in this essay? What sense does he offer you of his own authority and expertise?

Exploratory Writing

1. Over a weekend, spend an hour surfing the Internet and an hour reading a good novel. What are your impressions of the different types of thinking that each activity required? Which hour passed faster? In a double-entry list, jot down all of your impressions and experiences from the two different activities.

INTERNET SURFING	READING A NOVEL

2. James Olds describes the adult human mind as "very plastic," with "the ability to reprogram itself on the fly" (paragraph 13). In pairs, make a list of ten activities, and speculate about how each one might affect your brain if you did it every day for fifteen years. Examples include javelin throwing, scuba diving, reading nineteenth-century Russian novels, solving complex mathematical theorems, studying ancient Greek, watching ten hours of MTV, playing video games, hiking in the woods, meditating, or staring at nothing. How do your current activities affect your intelligence?

Making Connections

1. Anthony Grafton (p. 523) notes that some major libraries are choosing to digitize their books with the nonprofit Open Content Alliance rather than be subject to the commercial interests of Google and Microsoft. Marshall Poe (p. 506) explains how Wikipedia is staunchly ad free. Imagine if companies like Google were nonprofits that ran on a donation basis and refused to include product placements or other advertisements of any kind, and evaluate Carr's arguments based on this premise. How much of what he says is "making us stupid" is due to Internet technology, and how much is due to the agenda to create thoughtless consumers?

Essay Writing

1. Carr writes, "you should be skeptical of my skepticism" (paragraph 32). Although some of the essays in this casebook offer arguments or information that strongly supports or celebrates the Internet, many of the authors hint at potentially dark or negative consequences of our increasingly technological society. Choose an essay describing one of these dark or negative consequences, and write an essay imagining what the world would be like if the consequence happened in the most extreme way possible. Use information from the essay you chose.

I'm So Totally, Digitally, Close to You
The Brave New World of Digital Intimacy

Clive Thompson

Clive Thompson is the brain trust behind Collision Detection, *one of the Internet's most highly regarded blogs on science, technology, and culture since its inception in 2002. A one-time Knight Fellow at MIT, Thompson is currently a contributing writer for* the New York Times Magazine, *in which the following piece appeared in 2008. He is also a columnist for* Wired. *His writing has been widely anthologized and was included in* The Best American Science and Nature Writing *(2002).*

On September 5, 2006, Mark Zuckerberg changed the way that Facebook worked, and in the process he inspired a revolt.

Zuckerberg, a doe-eyed twenty-four-year-old CEO, founded Facebook in his dorm room at Harvard two years earlier, and the site quickly amassed nine million users. By 2006, students were posting heaps of personal details onto their Facebook pages, including lists of their favorite TV shows, whether they were dating (and whom), what music they had in rotation, and the various ad hoc "groups" they had joined (like *Sex and the City* Lovers). All day long, they'd post "status" notes explaining their moods — "hating Monday," "skipping class b/c i'm hung over." After each party, they'd stagger home to the dorm and upload pictures of the soused revelry, and spend the morning after commenting on how wasted everybody looked. Facebook became the de facto public commons — the way students found out what everyone around them was like and what he or she was doing.

But Zuckerberg knew Facebook had one major problem: it required a lot of active surfing on the part of its users. Sure, every day your Facebook friends would update their profiles with some new tidbits; it might even be something particularly juicy, like changing their relationship status to "single" when they got dumped. But unless you visited each friend's page every day, it might be days or weeks before you noticed the news, or you might miss it entirely. Browsing Facebook was like constantly poking your head into someone's room to see how she was doing. It took work and forethought. In a sense, this gave Facebook an inherent, built-in level of privacy, simply because if you had two hundred friends on the site — a fairly typical number — there weren't enough hours in the day to keep tabs on every friend all the time.

"It was very primitive," Zuckerberg told me when I asked him about it last month. And so he decided to modernize. He developed something he called News Feed, a built-in service that would actively broadcast changes in a user's page to every one of his or her friends. Students would no longer need to spend their time zipping around to examine each friend's page, checking to see if there was any new information. Instead, they would just log into Facebook, and News Feed would appear: a single page that — like a social gazette from the eighteenth century — delivered a long list of up-to-the-minute gossip about their friends, around the clock, all in one place. "A stream of everything that's going on in their lives," as Zuckerberg put it.

When students woke up that September morning and saw News Feed,   5 the first reaction, generally, was one of panic. Just about every little thing you changed on your page was now instantly blasted out to hundreds of friends, including potentially mortifying bits of news — Tim and Lisa broke up; Persaud is no longer friends with Matthew — and drunken photos someone snapped, then uploaded and tagged with names. Facebook had lost its vestigial bit of privacy. For students, it was now like being at a giant, open party filled with everyone you know, able to eavesdrop on what everyone else was saying, all the time.

"Everyone was freaking out," Ben Parr, then a junior at Northwestern University, told me recently. What particularly enraged Parr was that there wasn't any way to opt out of News Feed, to "go private" and have all your information kept quiet. He created a Facebook group demanding Zuckerberg either scrap News Feed or provide privacy options. "Facebook users really think Facebook is becoming the Big Brother of the Internet, recording every single move," a California student told the *Star-Ledger* of Newark. Another chimed in, "Frankly, I don't need to know or care that Billy broke up with Sally, and Ted has become friends with Steve." By lunchtime of the first day, 10,000 people had joined Parr's group, and by the next day it had 284,000.

Zuckerberg, surprised by the outcry, quickly made two decisions. The first was to add a privacy feature to News Feed, letting users decide what kind of information went out. But the second decision was to leave News Feed otherwise intact. He suspected that once people tried it and got over their shock, they'd like it.

He was right. Within days, the tide reversed. Students began e-mailing Zuckerberg to say that via News Feed they'd learned things they would never have otherwise discovered through random surfing around Facebook. The bits of trivia that News Feed delivered gave them more things to talk about — Why do you hate Kiefer Sutherland? — when they met friends face to face in class or at a party. Trends spread more quickly. When one student joined a group — proclaiming her love of Coldplay or a desire to volunteer for Greenpeace — all her friends instantly knew, and many would sign up themselves. Users' worries about their privacy seemed to vanish within days, boiled away by their excitement at being so much more connected to their friends. (Very few people stopped using Facebook, and most people kept on publishing most of their information through News Feed.) Pundits predicted that News Feed would kill Facebook, but the opposite happened. It catalyzed a massive boom in the site's growth. A few weeks after the News Feed imbroglio, Zuckerberg opened the site to the general public (previously, only students could join), and it grew quickly; today, it has one hundred million users.

When I spoke to him, Zuckerberg argued that News Feed is central to Facebook's success. "Facebook has always tried to push the envelope," he said. "And at times that means stretching people and getting them to be comfortable with things they aren't yet comfortable with. A lot of this is just social norms catching up with what technology is capable of."

In essence, Facebook users didn't think they wanted constant, up-to-the-minute updates on what other people are doing. Yet when they experienced this sort of omnipresent knowledge, they found it intriguing and addictive. Why?   10

Social scientists have a name for this sort of incessant online contact. They call it "ambient awareness." It is, they say, very much like being physically near someone and picking up on his mood through the little things he does — body language, sighs, stray comments — out of the corner of your eye. Facebook is no longer alone in offering this sort of interaction online. In the last year, there has been a boom in tools for "microblogging": posting frequent tiny updates on what you're doing. The phenomenon is quite different from what we normally think of as blogging, because a blog post is usually a written piece, sometimes quite long: a statement of opinion, a story, an analysis. But these new updates are something different. They're far shorter, far more frequent, and less carefully considered. One of the most popular new tools is Twitter, a Web site and messaging service that allows its two-million-plus users to broadcast to their friends haiku-length updates — limited to 140 characters, as brief as a mobile-phone text message — on what they're doing. There are other services for reporting where you're traveling (Dopplr) or for quickly tossing online a stream of the pictures, videos, or Web sites you're looking at (Tumblr). And there are even tools that give your location. When the new iPhone, with built-in tracking, was introduced in July, one million people began using Loopt, a piece of software that automatically tells all your friends exactly where you are.

For many people — particularly anyone over the age of thirty — the idea of describing your blow-by-blow activities in such detail is absurd. Why would you subject your friends to your daily minutiae? And conversely, how much of their trivia can you absorb? The growth of ambient intimacy can seem like modern narcissism taken to a new, supermetabolic extreme — the ultimate expression of a generation of celebrity-addled youths who believe their every utterance is fascinating and ought to be shared with the world. Twitter, in particular, has been the subject of nearly relentless scorn since it went online. "Who really cares what I am doing, every hour of the day?"

wondered Alex Beam, a *Boston Globe* columnist, in an essay about Twitter last month. "Even I don't care."

Indeed, many of the people I interviewed, who are among the most avid users of these "awareness" tools, admit that at first they couldn't figure out why anybody would want to do this. Ben Haley, a thirty-nine-year-old documentation specialist for a software firm who lives in Seattle, told me that when he first heard about Twitter last year from an early-adopter friend who used it, his first reaction was that it seemed silly. But a few of his friends decided to give it a try, and they urged him to sign up, too.

Each day, Haley logged on to his account, and his friends' updates would appear as a long page of one- or two-line notes. He would check and recheck the account several times a day, or even several times an hour. The updates were indeed pretty banal. One friend would post about starting to feel sick; one posted random thoughts like "I really hate it when people clip their nails on the bus"; another Twittered whenever she made a sandwich — and she made a sandwich every day. Each so-called tweet was so brief as to be virtually meaningless.

But as the days went by, something changed. Haley discovered that he was beginning to sense the rhythms of his friends' lives in a way he never had before. When one friend got sick with a virulent fever, he could tell by her Twitter updates when she was getting worse and the instant she finally turned the corner. He could see when friends were heading into hellish days at work or when they'd scored a big success. Even the daily catalog of sandwiches became oddly mesmerizing, a sort of metronomic click that he grew accustomed to seeing pop up in the middle of each day. 15

This is the paradox of ambient awareness. Each little update — each individual bit of social information — is insignificant on its own, even supremely mundane. But taken together, over time, the little snippets coalesce into a surprisingly sophisticated portrait of your friends' and family members' lives, like thousands of dots making a pointillist painting. This was never before possible, because in the real world, no friend would bother to call you up and detail the sandwiches she was eating. The ambient information becomes like "a type of ESP," as Haley described it to me, an invisible dimension floating over everyday life.

"It's like I can distantly read everyone's mind," Haley went on to say. "I love that. I feel like I'm getting to something raw about my friends. It's like I've got this heads-up display for them." It can also lead to more real-life contact, because when one member of Haley's group decides to go out to a bar or see a band and Twitters about his plans, the others see it, and some decide to drop by — ad hoc, self-organizing socializing. And when they do socialize face to face, it feels oddly as if they've never actually been apart. They don't need to ask, "So, what have you been up to?" because they already know. Instead, they'll begin discussing something that one of the friends Twittered that afternoon, as if picking up a conversation in the middle.

Facebook and Twitter may have pushed things into overdrive, but the idea of using communication tools as a form of "co-presence" has been around for a while. The Japanese sociologist Mizuko Ito first noticed it with mobile phones: lovers who were working in different cities would send text messages back and forth all night — tiny updates like "enjoying a glass of wine now" or "watching TV while lying on the couch." They were doing it partly because talking for hours on mobile phones isn't very comfortable (or affordable). But they also discovered that the little Ping-Ponging messages felt even more intimate than a phone call.

"It's an aggregate phenomenon," Marc Davis, a chief scientist at Yahoo and former professor of information science at the University of California at Berkeley, told me. "No message is the single-most-important message. It's sort of like when you're sitting with someone and you look over and they smile at you. You're sitting here reading the paper, and you're doing your side-by-side thing, and you just sort of let people know you're aware of them." Yet it is also why it can be extremely hard to understand the phenomenon until you've experienced it. Merely looking at a stranger's Twitter or Facebook feed isn't interesting, because it seems like blather. Follow it for a day, though, and it begins to feel like a short story; follow it for a month, and it's a novel.

You could also regard the growing popularity of online awareness as a reaction to social isolation, the modern American disconnectedness that Robert Putnam explored in his book *Bowling Alone*. The mobile workforce requires people to travel more frequently for work, leaving friends and family behind, and members of the growing army of the self-employed often spend their days in solitude. Ambient intimacy becomes a way to "feel less alone," as more than one Facebook and Twitter user told me.

20

When I decided to try out Twitter last year, at first I didn't have anyone to follow. None of my friends were yet using the service. But while doing some Googling one day I stumbled upon the blog of Shannon Seery, a thirty-two-year-old recruiting consultant in Florida, and I noticed that she Twittered. Her Twitter updates were pretty charming — she would often post links to camera-phone pictures of her two children or videos of herself cooking Mexican food, or broadcast her agonized cries when a flight was delayed on a business trip. So on a whim I started "following" her — as easy on Twitter as a click of the mouse — and never took her off my account. (A Twitter account can be "private," so that only invited friends can read one's tweets, or it can be public, so anyone can; Seery's was public.) When I checked in last month, I noticed that she had built up a huge number of online connections: she was now following 677 people on Twitter and another 442 on Facebook. How in God's name, I wondered, could she follow so many people? Who precisely are they? I called Seery to find out.

"I have a rule," she told me. "I either have to know who you are, or I have to know of you." That means she monitors the lives of friends, family, anyone she works with, and she'll also follow interesting people she discovers via her friends' online lives. Like many people who live online, she has wound up following a few strangers — though after a few months they no longer feel like strangers, despite the fact that she has never physically met them.

I asked Seery how she finds the time to follow so many people online. The math seemed daunting. After all, if her one thousand online contacts each post just a couple of notes each a day, that's several thousand little social pings to sift through daily. What would it be like to get thousands of e-mail messages a day? But Seery made a point I heard from many others: awareness tools aren't as cognitively demanding as an e-mail message. E-mail is something you have to stop to open and assess. It's personal; someone is asking for 100 percent of your attention. In contrast, ambient updates are all visible on one single page in a big row, and they're not really directed at you. This makes them skimmable, like newspaper head-lines; maybe you'll read them all, maybe you'll skip some. Seery estimated that she needs to spend only a small part of each hour actively reading her Twitter stream.

Yet she has, she said, become far more gregarious online. "What's really funny is that before this 'social media' stuff, I always said that I'm not the type of person who had a ton of friends," she told me. "It's so hard to make plans and have an active social life, having the type of job I have where I travel all the time and have two small kids. But it's easy to tweet all the time, to post pictures of what I'm doing, to keep social relations up." She paused for a second, before continuing: "Things like Twitter have actually given me a much bigger social circle. I know more about more people than ever before."

I realized that this is becoming true of me, too. After following Seery's   25
Twitter stream for a year, I'm more knowledgeable about the details of her life than the lives of my two sisters in Canada, whom I talk to only once every month or so. When I called Seery, I knew that she had been struggling with a three-day migraine headache; I began the conversation by asking her how she was feeling.

Online awareness inevitably leads to a curious question: What sort of relationships are these? What does it mean to have hundreds of "friends" on Facebook? What kind of friends are they, anyway?

In 1998, the anthropologist Robin Dunbar argued that each human has a hardwired upper limit on the number of people he or she can personally know at one time. Dunbar noticed that humans and apes both develop social bonds by engaging in some sort of grooming; apes do it by picking at and smoothing one another's fur, and humans do it with conversation. He theorized that ape and human brains could manage only a finite number of grooming relationships: unless we spend enough time doing social grooming — chitchatting, trading gossip or, for apes, picking lice — we won't really feel that we "know" someone well enough to call him a friend. Dunbar noticed that ape groups tended to top out at fifty-five members. Since human brains were proportionally bigger, Dunbar figured that our maximum number of social connections would be similarly larger: about 150 on average. Sure enough, psychological studies have confirmed that human groupings naturally tail off at around 150 people: the "Dunbar number," as it is known. Are people who use Facebook and Twitter increasing their Dunbar number because they can so easily keep track of so many more people?

As I interviewed some of the most aggressively social people online — people who follow hundreds or even thousands of others — it became clear that the picture was a little more complex than this question would suggest. Many maintained that their circle of true intimates, their very close friends and family, had not become bigger. Constant online contact had made those ties immeasurably richer, but it hadn't actually increased the number of them; deep relationships are still predicated on face time, and there are only so many hours in the day for that.

But where their sociality had truly exploded was in their "weak ties" — loose acquaintances, people they knew less well. It might be someone they met at a conference, or someone from high school who recently "friended" them on Facebook, or somebody from last year's holiday party. In their pre-Internet lives, these sorts of acquaintances would have quickly faded from their attention. But when one of these far-flung people suddenly posts a personal note to your feed, it is essentially a reminder that they exist. I have noticed this effect myself. In the last few months, dozens of old work colleagues I knew from ten years ago in Toronto have friended me on Facebook, such that I'm now suddenly reading their stray comments and updates and falling into oblique, funny conversations with them. My overall Dunbar number is thus 301: Facebook (254) + Twitter (47), double what it would be without technology. Yet only twenty are family or people I'd consider close friends. The rest are weak ties — maintained via technology.

This rapid growth of weak ties can be a very good thing. Sociologists   30
have long found that "weak ties" greatly expand your ability to solve problems. For example, if you're looking for a job and ask your friends, they won't be much help; they're too similar to you, and thus probably won't have any leads that you don't already have yourself. Remote acquaintances will be much more useful, because they're farther afield, yet still socially intimate enough to want to help you out. Many avid Twitter users — the ones who fire off witty posts hourly and wind up with thousands of intrigued followers — explicitly milk this dynamic for all it's worth, using their large online followings as a way to quickly answer almost any question. Laura Fitton, a social-media consultant who has become a minor celebrity on Twitter — she has more than 5,300 followers — recently discovered to her horror that her accountant had made an error in filing last year's taxes. She went to Twitter, wrote a tiny note explaining her problem, and within ten minutes her online audience had provided leads to lawyers and better accountants. Fritton joked to me that she no longer buys anything worth more than fifty dollars without quickly checking it with her Twitter network.

"I outsource my entire life," she said. "I can solve any problem on Twitter in six minutes." (She also keeps a secondary Twitter account that is private and only for a much smaller circle of close friends and family — "My little secret," she said. It is a strategy many people told me they used: one account for their weak ties, one for their deeper relationships.)

It is also possible, though, that this profusion of weak ties can become a problem. If you're reading daily updates from hundreds of people about whom they're dating and whether they're happy, it might, some critics worry, spread your emotional energy too thin, leaving less for true intimate relationships. Psychologists have long known that people can engage in "parasocial" relationships with fictional characters, like those on TV shows or in books, or with remote celebrities we read about in magazines. Parasocial relationships can use up some of the emotional space in our Dunbar number, crowding out real-life people. Danah Boyd, a fellow at Harvard's Berkman Center for Internet and Society who has studied social media for ten years, published a paper this spring arguing that awareness tools like News Feed might be creating a whole new class of relationships that are nearly parasocial — peripheral people in our network whose intimate details we follow closely online, even while they, like Angelina Jolie, are basically unaware we exist.

"The information we subscribe to on a feed is not the same as in a deep social relationship," Boyd told me. She has seen this herself; she has many virtual admirers that have, in essence, a parasocial relationship with her. "I've been very, very sick lately, and I write about it on Twitter and my blog, and I get all these people who are writing to me telling me ways to work around the health-care system, or they're writing saying, 'Hey, I broke my neck!' And I'm like, 'You're being very nice and trying to help me, but though you feel like you know me, you don't.'" Boyd sighed. "They can observe you, but it's not the same as knowing you."

When I spoke to Caterina Fake, a founder of Flickr (a popular photo-sharing site), she suggested an even more subtle danger: that the sheer ease of following her friends' updates online has made her occasionally lazy about actually taking the time to visit them in person. "At one point I realized I had a friend whose child I had seen, via photos on Flickr, grow from birth to one year old," she said. "I thought, I really should go meet her in person. But it was weird; I also felt that Flickr had satisfied that getting-to-know-you satisfaction, so I didn't feel the urgency. But then I was like, Oh, that's not sufficient! I should go in person!" She has about four hundred people she follows online but suspects many of those relationships are tissue-fragile. "These technologies allow you to be much more broadly friendly, but you just spread yourself much more thinly over many more people."

What is it like to never lose touch with anyone? One morning this summer at my local café, I overheard a young woman complaining to her friend about a recent Facebook drama. Her name is Andrea Ahan, a twenty-seven-year-old restaurant entrepreneur, and she told me that she had discovered   35 that high-school friends were uploading old photos of her to Facebook and tagging them with her name, so they automatically appeared in searches for her.

She was aghast. "I'm like, my God, these pictures are completely hideous!" Ahan complained, while her friend looked on sympathetically and sipped her coffee. "I'm wearing all these totally awful nineties clothes. I look like crap. And I'm like, Why are you people in my life, anyway? I haven't seen you in ten years. I don't know you anymore!" She began furiously detagging the pictures — removing her name, so they wouldn't show up in a search anymore.

Worse, Ahan was also confronting a common plague of Facebook: the recent ex. She had broken up with her boyfriend not long ago, but she hadn't "unfriended" him, because that felt too extreme. But soon he paired up with another young woman, and the new couple began having public conversations on Ahan's ex-boyfriend's page. One day, she noticed with alarm that the new girlfriend was quoting material Ahan had e-mailed privately to her boyfriend; she suspected he had been sharing the e-mail with his new girlfriend. It is the sort of weirdly subtle mind game that becomes possible via Facebook, and it drove Ahan nuts.

"Sometimes I think this stuff is just crazy, and everybody has got to get a life and stop obsessing over everyone's trivia and gossiping," she said.

Yet Ahan knows that she cannot simply walk away from her online life, because the people she knows online won't stop talking about her, or posting unflattering photos. She needs to stay on Facebook just to monitor what's being said about her. This is a common complaint I heard, particularly from people in their twenties who were in college when Facebook appeared and have never lived as adults without online awareness. For them, participation isn't optional. If you don't dive in, other people will define who you are. So you constantly stream your pictures, your thoughts, your relationship status, and what you're doing — right now! — if only to ensure the virtual version of you is accurate, or at least the one you want to present to the world.

This is the ultimate effect of the new awareness: it brings back the   40
dynamics of small-town life, where everybody knows your business. Young people at college are the ones to experience this most viscerally, because, with more than 90 percent of their peers using Facebook, it is especially difficult for them to opt out. Zeynep Tufekci, a sociologist at the University of Maryland, Baltimore County, who has closely studied how college-age users are reacting to the world of awareness, told me that athletes used to sneak off to parties illicitly, breaking the no-drinking rule for team members. But then camera phones and Facebook came along, with students posting photos of the drunken carousing during the party; savvy coaches could see which athletes were breaking the rules. First the athletes tried to fight back by waking up early the morning after the party in a hungover daze to detag photos of themselves so they wouldn't be searchable. But that didn't work, because the coaches sometimes viewed the pictures live, as they went online

at 2 a.m. So parties simply began banning all camera phones in a last-ditch attempt to preserve privacy.

"It's just like living in a village, where it's actually hard to lie because everybody knows the truth already," Tufekci said. "The current generation is never unconnected. They're never losing touch with their friends. So we're going back to a more normal place, historically. If you look at human history, the idea that you would drift through life, going from new relation to new relation, that's very new. It's just the twentieth century."

Psychologists and sociologists spent years wondering how humanity would adjust to the anonymity of life in the city, the wrenching upheavals of mobile immigrant labor — a world of lonely people ripped from their social ties. We now have precisely the opposite problem. Indeed, our modern awareness tools reverse the original conceit of the Internet. When cyberspace came along in the early 1990s, it was celebrated as a place where you could reinvent your identity — become someone new.

"If anything, it's identity-constraining now," Tufekci told me. "You can't play with your identity if your audience is always checking up on you. I had a student who posted that she was downloading some Pearl Jam, and someone wrote on her wall, 'Oh, right, ha-ha — I know you, and you're not into that.'" She laughed. "You know that old cartoon? 'On the Internet, nobody knows you're a dog'? On the Internet today, everybody knows you're a dog! If you don't want people to know you're a dog, you'd better stay away from a keyboard."

Or, as Leisa Reichelt, a consultant in London who writes regularly about ambient tools, put it to me: "Can you imagine a Facebook for children in kindergarten, and they never lose touch with those kids for the rest of their lives? What's that going to do to them?" Young people today are already developing an attitude toward their privacy that is simultaneously vigilant and laissez-faire. They curate their online personas as carefully as possible, knowing that everyone is watching — but they have also learned to shrug and accept the limits of what they can control.

It is easy to become unsettled by privacy-eroding aspects of awareness   45
tools. But there is another — quite different — result of all this incessant updating: a culture of people who know much more about themselves. Many of the avid Twitterers, Flickrers, and Facebook users I interviewed described an unexpected side effect of constant self-disclosure. The act of stopping several times a day to observe what you're feeling or thinking can become, after weeks and weeks, a sort of philosophical act. It's like the Greek dictum to "know thyself," or the therapeutic concept of mindfulness. (Indeed, the question that floats eternally at the top of Twitter's Web site — "What are you doing?" — can come to seem existentially freighted. What are you doing?) Having an audience can make the self-reflection even more acute, since, as my interviewees noted, they're trying to describe their activities in a way that is not only accurate but also interesting to others: the status update as a literary form.

Laura Fitton, the social-media consultant, argues that her constant status updating has made her "a happier person, a calmer person" because the process of, say, describing a horrid morning at work forces her to look at it objectively. "It drags you out of your own head," she added. In an age of awareness, perhaps the person you see most clearly is yourself.

QUESTIONS

Reading

1. What is the *Dunbar number*?
2. Thompson is *reporting* on Twitter, Facebook, and the world of digital intimacy, but he sums up his report with a controversial conclusion. Summarize this conclusion. Do you agree or disagree? Based on your own reading of Thompson's report, what different conclusion could you reach?
3. What does Thompson mean when he writes that our "modern awareness tools reverse the original conceit" of the Internet (paragraph 42)?

Exploratory Writing

1. Collaborating in small groups, make a list of advantages to having a presence on Facebook, Twitter, and similar sites, and a list of advantages to being "off the grid." Do you think that these forms of "digital intimacy" will be an enduring part of our society, or are they a passing fad?

ADVANTAGES OF FACEBOOK, TWITTER, AND SO ON	ADVANTAGES OF BEING "OFF THE GRID"

2. On an Internet search engine, conduct a search for the authors in this casebook. Make a chart of which ones keep a blog, have a MySpace page, or have a Facebook page. Choose one of the authors, and list things you learned about him or her that would not be in a typical author biography. Did this search feel like "poking your head" into the author's private space?

Making Connections

1. Compare and contrast Andrew Sullivan's (p. 494) reflections on keeping a blog with Thompson's conclusion that constant self-disclosure on the Internet becomes "a sort of philosophical act" of self-knowledge. How does each author characterize "friends"?

Essay Writing

1. Spend a full day (or, ideally, two or three days) not using the Internet at all — no e-mail, no social-networking sites, no Google, no Wikipedia. It will probably be a great inconvenience, partly because people you know may be online. Write an essay reflecting on how life in your generation would be different without any Internet technology at all.

The Virtual Barrio @ the Other Frontier

Guillermo Gómez-Peña

Performance artist Guillermo Gómez-Peña (b. 1955) moved to the United States from Mexico City in 1978 and quickly established himself as a writer, activist, and educator working in a wide variety of media, including bilingual poetry, journalism, radio, television, and installation art. While varied, his original interdisciplinary arts projects and books all tend toward the exploration of borders — physical, cultural, and otherwise — between his two countries. His work explores the U.S.–Mexico border itself; immigration; cross-cultural and hybrid identities; and the confrontation and misunderstandings between cultures, languages, and races. Gómez-Peña is a founding member of the Border Art Workshop/Taller de Arte Fronterizo; the editor of the experimental arts magazine The Broken Line/la Linea Quebrada; *a commentator on National Public Radio; and the first artist of Mexican birth to be awarded a MacArthur Fellowship. He received both his BA and MA in linguistics and Latin American literature from California Institute of the Arts. Gómez-Peña currently directs La Pocha Nostra, a San Francisco–based performance troupe focused on collaboration across national borders, race, gender, and generations as an act of citizen diplomacy and as a means to create transnational communities of rebel artists.*

[Mexicans] are simple people. They are happy with the little they got. . . . They are not ambitious and complex like us. They don't need all this technology to communicate. Sometimes I just feel like going down there & living among them.

—ANONYMOUS CONFESSION ON THE WEB

Tecnofobia

My laptop is decorated with a 3-D decal of the Virgin of Guadalupe.[1]
It's like a traveling altar, office, and literary bank, all in one. Since I spend
70 percent of the year on the road, it is (besides the phone of course) my
principal means to remain in touch with my beloved relatives and colleagues, spread throughout many cities in the United States and Mexico.
Unwillingly, I have become a cyber-vato,[2] an information superhighway
bandido. Like that of most Mexican artists, my relationship with digital
technology and personal computers is defined by paradoxes and contradictions: I don't quite understand them, yet I am seduced by them; I don't want
to know how they work, but I love how they look and what they do; I criticize my colleagues who are critically immersed in new technology, yet I
silently envy them. I resent the fact that I am constantly told that as a
"Latino" I am supposedly culturally handicapped or somehow unfit to handle
high technology; yet once I have it right in front of me, I am propelled to
work against it, to question it, to expose it, to subvert it, to imbue it with
humor, linguas polutas[3] — Spanglish, Frangle, gringonol,[4] and radical politics. In doing so, I become a sort of Mexican virus, the cyberversion of the
Mexican fly: tiny, irritating, inescapable, and highly contagious. Contradiction prevails.

Over a year ago, my collaborator Roberto Sifuentes and I bullied
ourselves into the Net, and once we were generously adopted by various
communities (Arts Wire and Latino Net, among others) we started to lose
interest in maintaining ongoing conversations with phantasmagoric beings we
had never met in person (that, I must say, is a Mexican cultural prejudice — if
I don't know you in person, I don't really care to talk with you). Then we
started sending a series of poetic/activist "techno-placas"[5] in Spanglish. In
these short communiqués we raised some tough questions regarding access,
privilege, and language. Since we didn't quite know where to post them
in order to get the maximum response, and the responses were sporadic,
casual, and unfocused, our passion began to dim. Roberto and I spend a lot
of time in front of our laptops conceptualizing performance projects that incorporate new technologies in what we believe is a responsible and original
manner, yet every time we are invited to participate in a public discussion

---

[1] *Virgin of Guadalupe*: Image of Mary, the mother of Jesus, deemed to have deep
religious and cultural significance by many Mexicans and Mexican Americans.

[2] *cyber-vato*: Cyber-guy.

[3] *linguas polutas*: Dirty or grammatically incorrect language.

[4] *Spanglish, Frangle, gringonol*: Terms referring to mixtures of English and other
languages.

[5] *"techno-placas"*: Techno-plaque or sheet.

around art and technology, we tend to emphasize its shortcomings and over-state our cultural skepticism. Why? I can only speak for myself. Perhaps I have some computer traumas. I've been utilizing computers since 1988; however, during the first five years, I utilized my old "lowrider" Mac as a glorified typewriter. During those years I probably deleted accidentally here and there over three hundred pages of original texts that I hadn't backed up on disks, and thus was forced to rewrite them by memory. The thick and confusing "user-friendly" manuals fell many a time from my impatient hands, and I spent many desperate nights cursing the mischievous gods of cyberspace and dialing promising "hotlines" that rarely answered.

My bittersweet relationship to technology dates back to my formative years in the highly politicized ambiance of Mexico City in the 1970s. As a young "radical artist," I was full of ideological dogmas and partial truths. One such partial truth spouted was that high technology was intrinsically dehumanizing; that it was mostly used as a means to control "us" little techno-illiterate people politically. My critique of technology overlapped with my critique of capitalism. To me, "capitalists" were rootless corporate men who utilized mass media to advertise useless electronic gadgets, and sold us unnecessary apparatuses that kept us both eternally in debt and con-veniently distracted from "the truly important matters of life." These mat-ters included sex, music, spirituality, and "revolution" California style (in the abstract). As a child of contradiction, besides being a rabid antitechnol-ogy artist, I owned a little Datsun and listened to my favorite U.S. and British rock groups on my Panasonic *importado,* often while meditating or making love as a means to "liberate myself" from capitalist socialization. My favorite clothes, books, posters, and albums had all been made by "cap-italists," but for some obscure reason, that seemed perfectly logical to me. Luckily, my family never lost their magical thinking and sense of humor around technology. My parents were easily seduced by refurbished and slightly dated American and Japanese electronic goods. We bought them as *fayuca* (contraband) in the Tepito neighborhood, and they occupied an im-portant place in the decoration of our "modern" middle-class home. Our huge color TV set, for example, was decorated so as to perform the double function of entertainment unit and involuntary postmodern altar — with nostalgic photos, plastic flowers, and assorted figurines all around it — as was the sound system next to it. Though I was sure that with the scary ar-rival of the first microwave oven to our traditional kitchen our delicious daily meals were going to turn overnight into sleazy fast food, my mother soon realized that el microondas[6] was only good to reheat cold coffee and soups. When I moved to California, I bought an electric ionizer for my grandma. She put it in the middle of her bedroom altar and kept it there — unplugged of course — for months. When I next saw her, she told me,

---

[6]*el microondas*: The microwave.

"Mijito,[7] since you gave me that thing, I truly can breathe much better." And probably she did. Things like televisions, shortwave radios, and microwave ovens, and later on ionizers, Walkmans, calculators, and video cameras were seen by my family and friends as high technology, and their function was as much pragmatic as it was social, ritual, and aesthetic. It is no coincidence then that in my early performance work, technology performed both ritual and aesthetic functions.

Verbigratia[8]

For years, I used video monitors as centerpieces for my "techno-altars" on stage. I combined ritualistic structures, spoken-word multilingual poetry, and activist politics with my fascination for "low-tech." Fog machines, strobe lights, gobos,[9] megaphones, and cheesy voice filters have remained since then trademark elements in my "low-tech/high-tech" performances. By the early 1990s, I sarcastically baptized my aesthetic practice "Aztec high-tech art," and when I teamed with Cyber-Vato Sifuentes, we decided that what we were doing was "techno-razcuache art."[10] In a glossary that dates back to 1993, we defined it as "a new aesthetic that fuses performance art, epic rap poetry, interactive television, experimental radio and computer art; but with a Chicanocentric perspective and a sleazoid bent."

(El Naftaztec[11] turns the knobs of his "Chicano virtual reality machine" and then proceeds to feed chili peppers into it. The set looks like a Mexican sci-fi movie from the 1950s.) El Naftaztec (speaking with a computerized voice): *So now, let's talk about the TECHNOPAL 2000, a technology originally invented by the Mayans with the help of aliens from Harvard. Its CPU is powered by habanero chili peppers, combined with this or DAT technology, with a measured clock speed of 200,000 megahertz! It uses neural nets supplemented by actual chicken-brain matter and nacho cheese spread to supply the massive processing speed necessary for the machine to operate. And it's all integrated into one sombrero! Originally, the Chicano VR had to use a poncho, but with the VR sombrero, the weight is greatly reduced and its efficiency is magnified.*

---

[7] *"Mijito"*: My child.

[8] *Verbigratia*: For example.

[9] *gobos*: Thin masks.

[10] *"techno-razcuache art"*: Thin masks placed in the gate of a spotlight that shape the light beam into a certain pattern.

[11] *El Naftaztec*: The name of Gómez-Peña's hero combines the abbreviation for the North American Free Trade Agreement (NAFTA) with *Aztec*, the name of the indigenous tribe that originally occupied the present site of Mexico City.

And now, we have the first alpha version of the VR bandanna dos mil,[12] *which Cyber-Vato will demonstrate for us!* (Cyber-Vato wears a bandanna over his eyes. It is connected by a thick rope to a robotic glove. Special effects on the TV screen simulate the graphics and sounds of a VR helmet.)
—FROM "NAFTAZTEC," AN INTERACTIVE TV PROJECT ABOUT
MEXICANS AND HIGH TECHNOLOGY

The mythology goes like this. Mexicans (and other Latinos) can't handle high technology. Caught between a preindustrial past and an imposed postmodernity, we continue to be manual beings — *Homo fabers*[13] par excellence, imaginative artisans (not technicians) — and our understanding of the world is strictly political, poetical, or metaphysical at best, but certainly not scientific. Furthermore, we are perceived as sentimental and passionate, meaning irrational; and when we decide to step out of our realm and utilize high technology in our art (most of the time we are not even interested), we are meant to naively repeat what others have already done. We often feed this mythology by overstating our romantic nature and humanistic stances and/or by assuming the role of colonial victims of technology. We are ready to point out the fact that "computers are the source of the Anglos' social handicaps and sexual psychosis" and that communication in America, the land of the future, "is totally mediated by faxes, phones, computers, and other technologies we are not even aware of." We, "on the contrary," socialize profusely, negotiate information ritually and sensually, and remain in touch with our primeval selves. This simplistic binary worldview presents Mexico as technologically underdeveloped yet culturally and spiritually overdeveloped and the United States as exactly the opposite. Reality is much more complicated: the average Anglo-American does not understand new technologies either; people of color and women in the United States clearly don't have equal access to cyberspace; and at the same time, the average urban Mexican is already afflicted in varying degrees by the same "first world" existential diseases produced by advanced capitalism and high technology. In fact the new generations of Mexicans, including my hip generation-Mex nephews and my seven-year-old fully bicultural son, are completely immersed in and defined by personal computers, video games, and virtual reality. Far from being the romantic preindustrial paradise of the American imagination, the Mexico of the 1990s is already a virtual nation whose cohesiveness and boundaries are provided solely by television, transnational pop culture, and the free market. It is true that there are entire parts of the country that still lack basic infrastructures and public services (not to mention communications technology). But in 1996 the same can be said of the

---

[12]*dos mil*: Two thousand.
[13]*Homo fabers*: *Homo faber* is Latin for "man the maker" or "man the builder."

United States, a "first world" nation whose ruined "ethnic" neighborhoods, Native American reserves, and rural areas exist in conditions comparable to those of a "third world" country. When trying to link, say, Los Angeles and Mexico City via video-telephone, we encounter new problems. In Mexico, the only artists with "access" to the technology are upper class, politically conservative, and uninteresting. And the funding sources down there willing to fund the project are clearly interested in controlling who is part of the experiment. In other words, we don't really need Octavio Paz[14] conversing with Richard Rodriguez.[15] We need Rubén Martínez[16] talking to Monsivais,[17] as well.

The world is waiting for you — so come on!

The Cyber-Migra[18]

Roberto and I arrived late to the debate. When we began to dialogue   5
with artists working with new technologies, we were perplexed by the fact that when referring to cyberspace or the Net, they spoke of a politically neutral/raceless/genderless/classless "territory" that provided us all with "equal access" and unlimited possibilities of participation, interaction, and belonging — especially belonging. Their enthusiastic rhetoric reminded us of both a sanitized version of the pioneer and cowboy mentalities of the Old West ("Guillermo, you can be the first Mexican ever to do this and that in the Net"), and the early-century Futurist cult[19] to the speed and beauty of epic technology (airplanes, trains, factories, etc.). Given the existing "compassion fatigue" regarding political art dealing with issues of race and gender, it was hard not to see this feel-good utopian view of new technologies as an attractive exit from the acute social and racial crisis afflicting the United States. We were also perplexed by the "benign (not naive) ethnocentrism" permeating the debates around art and digital technology. The unquestioned

---

[14]*Octavio Paz* (1914–1998): Famed Mexican poet, critic, diplomat, and recipient of the Nobel Prize for literature in 1990.

[15]*Richard Rodriguez* (b. 1944): Nationally known Mexican American essayist and editor.

[16]*Rubén Martínez*: Mexican American journalist and editor.

[17]*Monsivais* (b. 1938): Carlos Monsivais, Mexican writer. In 1977, awarded the National Prize of Journalism. In 1995, awarded the Villaurrutia Literature Prize.

[18]*Migra*: Spanish slang for the Immigration and Naturalization Service.

[19]*Futurist cult*: Futurism was an artistic movement at the turn of the twentieth century that celebrated technology and saw the machine as the epitome of rationality and modern design.

lingua franca[20] was of course English, the "official language of international communications"; the vocabulary utilized in these discussions was hyper-specialized and depoliticized; and if Chicanos and Mexicans didn't partici-pate enough in the Net, it was solely because of lack of information or interest (not money or access), or again because we were "culturally unfit." The unspoken assumption was that our true interests were grassroots (by grassroots I mean the streets), representational, or oral (as if these con-cerns couldn't exist in virtual space). In other words, we were to remain dancing salsa, painting murals, writing flamboyant love poetry, and plotting revolutions in rowdy cafés. We were also perplexed by the recurring labels of "originality" and "innovation" attached to virtual art. And it was not the nature, contents, and structural complexity of the parallel realities created by digital technology, but the use of the technology per se that seemed to be "original" and "innovative." That, of course, has since engendered many conflicting responses. Native American shamans and medicine men right-fully see their centuries-old "visions" as a form of virtual reality. And Latin American writers equate their literary experimentation with involuntary hypertexts and vernacular postmodern aesthetics, and so do Chicanos and Chicanas. Like the pre-multicultural art world of the early 1980s, the new high-tech art world assumed an unquestionable "center" and drew a dra-matic digital border. On the other side of that border lived all the techno-illiterate artists, along with most women, Chicanos, African Americans, and Native Americans. The role for us, then, was to assume, once again, the un-pleasant but necessary role of cultural invaders, techno-pirates, and coyotes (smugglers). And then, just as multiculturalism was declared dead as soon as we began to share the paycheck, now as we venture into the virtual barrio[21] for the first time, some asshole at MIT declares it dead. Why? It is no longer an exclusive space. It emulates too much real life and social demographics. Luckily many things have changed. Since we don't wish to reproduce the unpleasant mistakes of the multicultural days, our strategies are now quite different: we are no longer trying to persuade anyone that we are worthy of inclusion. Nor are we fighting for the same funding (since funding no longer exists). What we want is to "politicize" the debate; to "brownify" virtual space; to "Spanglishize the Net"; to "infect" the lingua franca; to exchange a different sort of information — mythical, poetical, political, performative, imagistic; and on top of that to find grassroots applications to new tech-nologies and hopefully to do all this with humor and intelligence. The ulti-mate goals are perhaps to help the Latino youth exchange their guns for computers and video cameras, and to link the community centers through

---

[20]*lingua franca*: The language of general communication in a multilingual society.

[21]*barrio*: Spanish for neighborhood.

the Net. CD-ROMs can perform the role of community memory banks, while the larger virtual community gets used to a new presence, a new sensibility, a new language.

QUESTIONS

Reading

1. Gómez-Peña uses language dynamically. Highlight, underline, or flag words, phrases, or usages in this piece that caught your attention. Why might Gómez-Peña choose to use language this way? What effect does this have on your reading experience?
2. What does Gómez-Peña mean by "mythology"? Make a double-entry list of the ways he characterizes the myths versus realities about Chicano/ Latino and Anglo-American Internet users.

MYTHS	REALITIES

3. List the assumptions that Gómez-Peña identifies as implicit in debates surrounding art and digital technology. What does the "utopian rhetoric" around digital technologies in California bring to mind for Gómez-Peña and Roberto?

Exploratory Writing

1. Visit Gómez-Peña's Web site, **www.pochanostra.com**. After reading "La Pocha Manifesto," contribute to the project by writing and submitting answers to the "Thirteen Questions We Ask Ourselves." Keep a copy of your answers. What did you learn from contributing to the project?
2. How does Gómez-Peña characterize the few people in Mexico who are "wired"? Using your Internet research skills, how would you characterize the other authors included in this casebook? How many of them seem to offer a non-hegemonic perspective? How many of them "politicize" their comments about cyberspace or take into consideration issues of class, sex, sexuality, ethnicity, language, and nationality?

3. Read the manifesto on Gómez-Peña's Web site (**http://www.pochanostra .com/what/**). Collaborate in small groups to draft your own manifesto about remapping cyberspace. What is your group's vision of how cyberspace should be created, debated, or explored in the future? When you share your manifesto with the class, discuss whether there was dissent within your group. How did your own personal experiences and perspective shape your agenda for cyberspace?

Making Connections

1. In Gómez-Peña's manifesto, he writes that Chicano artists wish to "brownify" virtual space and "'infect' the lingua franca" online (paragraph 5). Choose any other essay in this casebook, and consider how race, class, or gender differences fit into the essay's theme. Write a list of suggestions for how a multicultural theoretical understanding could be brought to the technology described in the essay.

Essay Writing

1. In a longer version of this essay, found on his Web site, Gómez-Peña writes, "I venture into the terra ignota of cyberlandia, without documents, a map, or an invitation at hand. In doing so, I become a sort of Mexican virus, the cyberversion of the Mexican fly: tiny, irritating, inescapable, and highly contagious" (paragraph 1). Write a personal essay reflecting on your own virtual travels. What role do you play in the cyberworld? How do you experience your online identity?

The Classroom: Ideals, Obstacles, Solutions

The six readings in this casebook address problems whose solutions shape education in the United States. Educating a nation — and one of the most influential nations in existence — is a mammoth task, one that will always require invention and reinvention. Classrooms are places where people with different backgrounds, goals, talents, and learning styles gather to gain experience, acquire knowledge, and develop abilities that will serve them for a lifetime. A huge number of decisions affect how these classrooms will be constituted and conducted — decisions made by political leaders, school administrators, teachers, and students. Even the education of an individual student — starting before kindergarten; advancing through elementary, middle, and high school; and moving on to college or university — involves a long trajectory that will bring up complex questions and life decisions along the way.

The readings here question, reflect on, and make arguments about a variety of educational issues affecting both individuals and education as a whole: placement methods that divide students into categories and send them along different educational "tracks" (Mike Rose, "I Just Wanna Be Average"); the challenge of providing integrated education in terms of both race and class (Emily Bazelon, "The Next Kind of Integration"); the gender dynamics of classrooms (Elizabeth Weil, "Teaching to the Testosterone: The Gender Wars Go to School"); the disparity between educators' and politicians' descriptions of school and the experience of school as it is lived by students (Theodore R. Sizer, "What High School Is"); the status of teachers in contemporary culture (Garret Keizer, "Why We Hate Teachers"); and the tension between educational bureaucracies and the classrooms they oversee (Matt Miller, "First, Kill All the School Boards: A Modest Proposal to Fix the Schools").

If you're reading this textbook, odds are you are a member of a college classroom and you've completed your education through high school. By this time, you have accumulated a great variety of classroom and school experiences, and you probably have a lot of ideas about what constitutes a strong education and what barriers impede such an education. Some of the writers here will confirm ideas you already have, but others will challenge your ideas or provoke you to think about them in new ways. Either way, reading this casebook will give you a variety of perspectives on debates about education. This will give you a foundation of ideas and details for writing about these debates and will provoke new questions best addressed through further inquiry and research, which the questions that follow each reading are designed to help you with.

I Just Wanna Be Average

Mike Rose

Mike Rose (b. 1944) is a nationally recognized American education scholar, noted both for his significant contribution to the study of literacy and for his insights into the struggles of working-class America. A onetime "vocational track" student himself, Rose has a deep belief that students whom the system has written off can have tremendous unrealized potential. To that end, his work primarily focuses on fostering confidence in such students and increasing equality in educational opportunities across socioeconomic strata. A professor in the School of Education at UCLA, Rose has won awards from the National Academy of Education, the National Council of Teachers of English, and the John Simon Guggenheim Memorial Foundation. He has also published poetry, scholarly research, a textbook, and two widely praised books on education in America: Lives on the Boundary *(1989) and* Possible Lives: The Promise of Public Education in America *(1995). The selection comes from* Lives on the Boundary, *Rose's exploration of America's educationally underprivileged. His most recent book,* The Mind at Work *(2004), is a study of the thinking patterns of blue-collar workers.*

Between 1880 and 1920, well over four million southern Italian peasants immigrated to America. Their poverty was extreme and hopeless — twelve hours of farm labor would get you one lira, about twenty cents — so increasing numbers of desperate people booked passage for the United States, the country where, the steamship companies claimed, prosperity was a way of life. My father left Naples before the turn of the century; my mother came with her mother from Calabria in 1921. They met in Altoona, Pennsylvania, at the lunch counter of Tom and Joe's, a steamy diner with twangy-voiced waitresses and graveyard stew.

For my mother, life in America was not what the promoters had told her father it would be. She grew up very poor. She slept with her parents and brothers and sisters in one room. She had to quit school in the seventh grade to care for her sickly younger brothers. When her father lost his leg in a railroad accident, she began working in a garment factory where women sat crowded at their stations, solitary as penitents in a cloister. She stayed there until her marriage. My father had found a freer route. He was closemouthed about his past, but I know that he had been a salesman, a tailor, and a gambler; he knew people in the mob and had, my uncles whisper, done time in Chicago. He went through a year or two of Italian elementary school and could write a few words — those necessary to scribble measurements for a suit — and over the years developed a quiet urbanity, a persistence, and a slowly debilitating arteriosclerosis.

When my father proposed to my mother, he decided to open a spaghetti house, a venture that lasted through the war and my early years. The restaurant collapsed in bankruptcy in 1951 when Altoona's major industry, the Pennsylvania Railroad, had to shut down its shops. My parents managed to salvage seven hundred dollars and, on the advice of the family doctor, headed to California, where the winters would be mild and where I, their seven-year-old son, would have the possibility of a brighter future.

At first we lived in a seedy hotel on Spring Street in downtown Los Angeles, but my mother soon found an ad in the *Times* for cheap property on the south side of town. My parents contacted a woman named Mrs. Jolly, used my mother's engagement ring as a down payment, and moved to 9116 South Vermont Avenue, a house about one and one-half miles northwest of Watts. The neighborhood was poor, and it was in transition. Some old white folks had lived there for decades and were retired. Younger black families were moving up from Watts and settling by working-class white families newly arrived from the South and the Midwest. Immigrant Mexican families were coming in from Baja. Any such demographic mix is potentially volatile, and as the fifties wore on, the neighborhood would be marked by outbursts of violence. . . .

One night I watched as a guy sprinted from Walt's to toss something on   5
our lawn. The police were right behind, and a cop tackled him, smashing his face into the sidewalk. I ducked out to find the packet: a dozen glassine bags of heroin. Another night, one August midnight, an argument outside the record store ended with a man being shot to death. And the occasional gang forays brought with them some fated kid who would fumble his moves and catch a knife.

It's popular these days to claim you grew up on the streets. Men tell violent tales and romanticize the lessons violence brings. But, though it was occasionally violent, it wasn't the violence in South L.A. that marked me, for sometimes you can shake that ugliness off. What finally affected me was subtler, but more pervasive: I cannot recall a young person who was crazy in love or lost in work or one old person who was passionate about a cause or an idea. I'm not talking about an absence of energy — the street toughs . . . had energy. And I'm not talking about an absence of decency, for my father was a thoughtful man. The people I grew up with were retired from jobs that rub away the heart or were working hard at jobs to keep their lives from caving in or were anchorless and in between jobs and spouses or were diving headlong into a barren tomorrow: junkies, alcoholics, and mean kids walking along Vermont looking to throw a punch. I developed a picture of human existence that rendered it short and brutish or sad and aimless or long and quiet with rewards like afternoon naps, the evening newspaper, walks around the block, occasional letters from children in other states. When, years later, I was introduced to humanistic psychologists like Abraham Maslow and Carl Rogers, with their visions of self-actualization, or even Freud with his sober dictum about love and work, it all sounded like a glorious fairy tale, a magical account of a world full of possibility, full of hope and empowerment. Sindbad and Cinderella couldn't have been more fanciful.

Some people who manage to write their way out of the working class describe the classroom as an oasis of possibility. It became their intellectual playground, their competitive arena. Given the richness of my memories of this time, it's funny how scant are my recollections of school. I remember the red brick building of St. Regina's itself, and the topography of the playground: the swings and basketball courts and peeling benches. There are images of a few students: Erwin Petschaur, a muscular German boy with a strong accent; Dave Sanchez, who was good in math; and Sheila Wilkes, everyone's curly-haired heartthrob. And there are two nuns: Sister Monica, the third-grade teacher with beautiful hands for whom I carried a candle and who, to my dismay, had wedded herself to Christ; and Sister Beatrice, a woman truly crazed, who would sweep into class, eyes wide, to tell us about the Apocalypse.

All the hours in class tend to blend into one long, vague stretch of time. What I remember best, strangely enough, are the two things I couldn't understand and over the years grew to hate: grammar lessons and mathematics. I would sit there watching a teacher draw her long horizontal line and her short, oblique lines and break up sentences and put adjectives here and adverbs there and just not get it, couldn't see the reason for it, turned off to it. I would hide by slumping down in my seat and page through my reader, carried along by the flow of sentences in a story. She would test us, and I would dread that, for I always got Cs and Ds. Mathematics was a bit different. For whatever reasons, I didn't learn early math very well, so when it came time for more complicated operations, I couldn't keep up and started daydreaming to avoid my inadequacy. This was a strategy I would rely on as I grew older. I fell further and further behind. A memory: The teacher is faceless and seems very far away. The voice is faint and is discussing an equation written on the board. It is raining, and I am watching the streams of water form patterns on the windows.

I realize now how consistently I defended myself against the lessons I couldn't understand and the people and events of South L.A. that were too strange to view head-on. I got very good at watching a blackboard with minimum awareness. And I drifted more and more into a variety of protective fantasies. I was lucky in that although my parents didn't read or write very much and had no more than a few books around the house, they never debunked my pursuits. And when they could, they bought me what I needed to spin my web.

One early Christmas they got me a small chemistry set. My father 10 brought home an old card table from the secondhand store, and on that table I spread out my test tubes, my beaker, my Erlenmeyer flask, and my gas-generating apparatus. The set came equipped with chemicals, minerals, and various treated papers — all in little square bottles. You could send away to someplace in Maryland for more, and I did, saving pennies and nickels to get the substances that were too exotic for my set, the Junior Chemcraft: Congo red paper, azurite, glycerine, chrome alum, cochineal — this from female insects! — tartaric acid, chameleon paper, logwood. I would sit before my laboratory and play for hours. My father rested on the purple couch in front of me watching wrestling or *Gunsmoke* while I measured powders or heated crystals or blew into solutions that my breath would turn red or pink. I was taken by the blends of names and by the colors that swirled through the beaker. My equations were visual and phonetic. I would hold a flask up to the hall light, imagining the veils of a million atoms dancing. Sulfur and alcohol hung in the air. I wanted to shake down the house.

One day my mother came home from Coffee Dan's with an awful story. The teenage brother of one of her waitress friends was in the hospital. He had been fooling around with explosives in his garage "where his mother couldn't see him," and something happened, and "he blew away part of his throat. For God's sake, be careful," my mother said. "Remember poor Ada's brother." Wow! I thought. How neat! Why couldn't my experiments be that dangerous? I really lost heart when I realized that you could probably eat the chemicals spread across my table.

I knew what I had to do. I saved my money for a week and then walked with firm resolve past Walt's Malts, past the brake shop, across Ninetieth Street, and into Palazolla's market. I bought a little bottle of Alka-Seltzer and ran home. I chipped up the wafers and mixed them into a jar of white crystals. When my mother came home, dog tired, and sat down on the edge of the couch to tell me and Dad about her day, I gravely poured my concoction into a beaker of water, cried something about the unexpected, and ran out from behind my table. The beaker foamed ominously. My father swore in Italian. The second time I tried it, I got something milder — in English. And by my third near-miss with death, my parents were calling my behavior cute. Cute! Who wanted cute? I wanted to toy with the disaster that befell Ada Pendleton's brother. I wanted all those wonderful colors to collide in ways that could blow your voice box right off.

But I was limited by the real. The best I could do was create a toxic antacid. I loved my chemistry set — its glassware and its intriguing labels — but it wouldn't allow me to do the things I wanted to do. St. Regina's had an all-purpose room, one wall of which was lined with old books — and one of those shelves held a row of plastic-covered space novels. The sheen of their covers was gone, and their futuristic portraits were dotted with erasures and grease spots like a meteor shower of the everyday. I remember the rockets best. Long cylinders outfitted at the base with three slick fins, tapering at the other end to a perfect conical point, ready to pierce out of the stratosphere and into my imagination: X-fifteens and Mach 1, the dark side at the moon, the Red Planet, Jupiter's Great Red Spot, Saturn's rings — and beyond the solar system to swirling wisps of galaxies, to stardust.

I would check out my books two at a time and take them home to curl up with a blanket on my chaise longue, reading, sometimes, through the weekend, my back aching, my thoughts lost between galaxies. I became the hero of a thousand adventures, all with intricate plots and the triumph of good over evil, all many dimensions removed from the dim walls of the living room. We were given time to draw in school, so, before long, all this worked itself onto paper. The stories I was reading were reshaping themselves into pictures. My father got me some butcher paper from Palazzolla's, and I continued to draw at home. My collected works rendered the Horsehead Nebula, goofy space cruisers, robots, and Saturn. Each had its crayon, a particular waxy pencil with mood and meaning: rust and burnt sienna for Mars, yellow for the Sun, lime and rose for Saturn's rings, and bright red for the Jovian spot. I had a little sharpener to keep the points just right. I didn't write any stories; I just read and drew. I wouldn't care much about writing until late in high school.

The summer before the sixth grade, I got a couple of jobs. The first was   15
at a pet store a block or so away from my house. Since I was still small, I could maneuver around in breeder cages, scraping the heaps of parakeet crap from the tin floor, cleaning the water troughs and seed trays. It was pretty awful. I would go home after work and fill the tub and soak until all the fleas and bird mites came floating to the surface, little Xs in their multiple eyes. When I heard about a job selling strawberries door-to-door, I jumped at it. I went to work for a white-haired Chicano named Frank. He would carry four or five kids and dozens of crates of strawberries in his ramshackle truck up and down the avenues of the better neighborhoods: houses with mowed lawns and petunia beds. We'd work all day for seventy-five cents, Frank dropping pairs of us off with two crates each, then picking us up at preassigned corners. We spent lots of time together, bouncing around on the truck bed redolent with strawberries or sitting on a corner, cold, listening for the sputter of Frank's muffler. I started telling the other kids about my books, and soon it was my job to fill up that time with stories.

Reading opened up the world. There I was, a skinny bookworm drawing the attention of street kids who, in any other circumstances, would have had me for breakfast. Like an epic tale-teller, I developed the stories as I went along, relying on a flexible plot line and a repository of heroic events. I had a great time. I sketched out trajectories with my finger on Frank's dusty truck bed. And I stretched out each story's climax, creating cliffhangers like the ones I saw in the Saturday serials. These stories created for me a temporary community.

It was around this time that fiction started leading me circuitously to a child's version of science. In addition to the space novels, St. Regina's library also had half a dozen books on astronomy — *The Golden Book of the Planets* and stuff like that — so I checked out a few of them. I liked what I read and wheedled enough change out of my father to enable me to take the bus to the public library. I discovered star maps, maps of lunar seas, charts upon charts of the solar system and the planetary moons: Rhea, Europa, Callisto, Miranda, Io. I didn't know that most of these moons were named for women — I didn't know classical mythology — but I would say their names to myself as though they had a woman's power to protect: Europa, Miranda, Io . . . The distances between stars fascinated me, as did the sizes of the big telescopes. I sent away for catalogs. Then prices fascinated me too. I wanted to drape my arm over a thousand-dollar scope and hear its motor drive whir. I conjured a twelve-year-old's life of the astronomer: sitting up all night with potato chips and the stars, tracking the sky for supernovas, humming "Earth Angel" with the Penguins. What was my mother to do but save her tips and buy me a telescope?!

It was a little reflecting job, and I solemnly used to carry it out to the front of the house on warm summer nights, to find Venus or Alpha Centauri or trace the stars in Orion or lock onto the moon. I would lay out my star maps on the concrete, more for their magic than anything else, for I had trouble figuring them out. I was no geometer of the constellations; I was their balladeer. Those nights were very peaceful. I was far enough away from the front door and up enough from the sidewalk to make it seem as if I rested on a mound of dark silence, a mountain in Arizona, perhaps, watching the sky alive with points of light. Poor Freddie, toothless Lester, whispering promises about making me feel good, the flat days, the gang fights — all this receded, for it was now me, the star child, lost in an eyepiece focused on a reflecting mirror that cradled, in its center, a shimmering moon.

The loneliness in Los Angeles fosters strange arrangements. Lou Minton was a wiry man with gaunt, chiseled features and prematurely gray hair, combed straight back. He had gone to college in the South for a year or two and kicked around the country for many more before settling in L.A. He lived in a small downtown apartment with a single window and met my mother at the counter of Coffee Dan's. He had been alone too long and eventually came to our house and became part of the family. Lou repaired washing machines, and he had a car, and he would take me to the vast, echoing library just west of Pershing Square and to the Museum of Science and Industry in Exposition Park. He bought me astronomy books, taught me how to use tools, and helped me build model airplanes from balsa wood and rice paper. As my father's health got worse, Lou took care of him.

My rhapsodic and prescientific astronomy carried me into my teens,   20
consumed me right up till high school, losing out finally, and only, to the siren call of pubescence — that endocrine hoodoo that transmogrifies nice

boys into gawky flesh fiends. My mother used to bring home *Confidential* magazine, a peep-show rag specializing in the sins of the stars, and it beckoned me mercilessly: Jayne Mansfield's cleavage, Gina Lollobrigida's eyes, innuendos about deviant sexuality, ads for Frederick's of Hollywood — spiked heels, lacy brassieres, the epiphany of silk panties on a mannequin's hips. Along with Phil Everly, I was through with counting the stars above.

Budding manhood. Only adults talk about adolescence budding. Kids have no choice but to talk in extremes; they're being wrenched and buffeted, rabbit-punched from inside by systemic thugs. Nothing sweet and pastoral here. Kids become ridiculous and touching at one and the same time: passionate about the trivial, fixed before the mirror, yet traversing one of the most important rites of passage in their lives — liminal people, silly and profoundly human. Given my own expertise, I fantasized about concocting the fail-safe aphrodisiac that would bring Marianne Bilpusch, the cloakroom monitor, rushing into my arms or about commanding a squadron of bosomy, linguistically mysterious astronauts like Zsa Zsa Gabor. My parents used to say that their son would have the best education they could afford. Maybe I would be a doctor. There was a public school in our neighborhood and several Catholic schools to the west. They had heard that quality schooling meant private, Catholic schooling, so they somehow got the money together to send me to Our Lady of Mercy, fifteen or so miles southwest of Ninety-first and Vermont. So much for my fantasies. Most Catholic secondary schools then were separated by gender.

It took two buses to get to Our Lady of Mercy. The first started deep in South Los Angeles and caught me at midpoint. The second drifted through neighborhoods with trees, parks, big lawns, and lots of flowers. The rides were long but were livened up by a group of South L.A. veterans whose parents also thought that Hope had set up shop in the west end of the county. There was Christy Biggars, who, at sixteen, was dealing and was, according to rumor, a pimp as well. There were Bill Cobb and Johnny Gonzales, grease-pencil artists extraordinaire, who left Nembutal-enhanced swirls of "Cobb" and "Johnny" on the corrugated walls of the bus. And then there was Tyrrell Wilson. Tyrrell was the coolest kid I knew. He ran the dozens like a metric halfback, laid down a rap that outrhymed and outpointed Cobb, whose rap was good but not great — the curse of a moderately soulful kid trapped in white skin. But it was Cobb who would sneak a radio onto the bus, and thus underwrote his patter with Little Richard, Fats Domino, Chuck Berry, the Coasters, and Ernie K. Doe's mother-in-law, an awful woman who was "sent from down below." And so it was that Christy and Cobb and Johnny G. and Tyrrell and I and assorted others picked up along the way passed our days in the back of the bus, a funny mix brought together by geography and parental desire.

Entrance to school brings with it forms and releases and assessments. Mercy relied on a series of tests, mostly the Stanford-Binet, for placement, and somehow the results of my tests got confused with those of another student named Rose. The other Rose apparently didn't do very well, for I was placed in the vocational track, a euphemism for the bottom level. Neither I nor my parents realized what this meant. We had no sense that Business Math, Typing, and English–Level D were dead ends. The current spate of reports on the schools criticizes parents for not involving themselves in the education of their children. But how would someone like Tommy Rose, with his two years of Italian schooling, know what to ask? And what sort of pressure could an exhausted waitress apply? The error went undetected, and I remained in the vocational track for two years. What a place.

My homeroom was supervised by Brother Dill, a troubled and unstable man who also taught freshman English. When his class drifted away from him, which was often, his voice would rise in paranoid accusations, and occasionally he would lose control and shake or smack us. I hadn't been there two months when one of his brisk, face-turning slaps had my glasses sliding down the aisle. Physical education was also pretty harsh. Our teacher was a stubby ex-lineman who had played old-time pro ball in the Midwest. He routinely had us grabbing our ankles to receive his stinging paddle across our butts. He did that, he said, to make men of us. "Rose," he bellowed on our first encounter; me standing geeky in line in my baggy shorts. "'Rose'? What the hell kind of name is that?"

"Italian sir," I squeaked.   25

"Italian! Ho. Rose, do you know the sound a bag of shit makes when it hits the wall?"

"No, sir."

"Wop!"

Sophomore English was taught by Mr. Mitropetros. He was a large, bejeweled man who managed the parking lot at the Shrine Auditorium. He would crow and preen and list for us the stars he'd brushed against. We'd ask questions and glance knowingly and snicker, and all that fueled the poor guy to brag some more. Parking cars was his night job. He had little training in English, so his lesson plan for his day work had us reading the district's required text, *Julius Caesar*, aloud for the semester. We'd finish the play way before the twenty weeks was up, so he'd have us switch parts again and again and start again: Dave Snyder, the fastest guy at Mercy, muscling through Caesar to the breathless squeals of Calpurnia, as interpreted by Steve Fusco, a surfer who owned the school's most envied paneled wagon. Week ten and Dave and Steve would take on new roles, as would we all, and render a waterlogged Cassius and a Brutus that are beyond my powers of description.

Spanish I — taken in the second year — fell into the hands of a new recruit.   30 Mr. Montez was a tiny man, slight, five foot six at the most, soft-spoken and delicate. Spanish was a particularly rowdy class, and Mr. Montez was as prepared for it as a doily maker at a hammer throw. He would tap his pencil to a room in which Steve Fusco was propelling spitballs from his heavy lips, in which Mike Dweetz was taunting Billy Hawk, a half-Indian, half-Spanish, reed-thin, quietly explosive boy. The vocational track at Our Lady of Mercy mixed kids traveling in from South L.A. with South Bay surfers and a few Slavs and Chicanos from the harbors of San Pedro. This was a dangerous miscellany: surfers and hodads and South-Central blacks all ablaze to the metronomic tapping of Hector Montez's pencil.

One day Billy lost it. Out of the corner of my eye I saw him strike out with his right arm and catch Dweetz across the neck. Quick as a spasm, Dweetz was out of his seat, scattering desks, cracking Billy on the side of the head, right behind the eye. Snyder and Fusco and others broke it up, but the room felt hot and close and naked. Mr. Montez's tenuous authority was finally ripped to shreds, and I think everyone felt a little strange about that. The charade was over, and when it came down to it, I don't think any of the kids really wanted it to end this way. They had pushed and pushed and bullied their way into a freedom that both scared and embarrassed them.

Students will float to the mark you set. I and the others in the vocational classes were bobbing in pretty shallow water. Vocational education has aimed at increasing the economic opportunities of students who do not do well in our schools. Some serious programs succeed in doing that, and through exceptional teachers — like Mr. Gross in *Horace's Compromise* — students learn to develop hypotheses and troubleshoot, reason through a problem, and communicate effectively — the true job skills. The vocational track, however, is most often a place for those who are just not making it, a dumping ground for the disaffected. There were a few teachers who worked hard at education; young Brother Slattery, for example, combined a stern voice with weekly quizzes to try to pass along to us a skeletal outline of world history. But mostly the teachers had no idea of how to engage the imaginations of us kids who were scuttling along at the bottom of the pond.

And the teachers would have needed some inventiveness, for none of us was groomed for the classroom. It wasn't just that I didn't know things — didn't know how to simplify algebraic fractions, couldn't identify different kinds of clauses, bungled Spanish translations — but that I had developed various faulty and inadequate ways of doing algebra and making sense of Spanish. Worse yet, the years of defensive tuning out in elementary school had given me a way to escape quickly while seeming at least half alert. During my time in Voc. Ed., I developed further into a mediocre student and a somnambulant problem solver, and that affected the subjects I did have the wherewithal to handle: I detested Shakespeare; I got bored with history. My attention flitted here and there. I fooled around in class and read my books indifferently — the intellectual equivalent of playing with your food. I did what I had to do to get by, and I did it with half a mind.

But I did learn things about people and eventually came into my own socially. I liked the guys in Voc. Ed. Growing up where I did, I understood and admired physical prowess, and there was an abundance of muscle here.

There was Dave Snyder, a sprinter and halfback of true quality. Dave's ability and his quick wit gave him a natural appeal, and he was welcome in any clique, though he always kept a little independent. He enjoyed acting the fool and could care less about studies, but he possessed a certain maturity and never caused the faculty much trouble. It was a testament to his independence that he included me among his friends — I eventually went out for track, but I was no jock. Owing to the Latin alphabet and a dearth of *R*s and *S*s, Snyder sat behind Rose, and we started exchanging one-liners and became friends.

There was Ted Richard, a much-touted Little League pitcher. He was   35 chunky and had a baby face and came to Our Lady of Mercy as a seasoned street fighter. Ted was quick to laugh and he had a loud, jolly laugh, but when he got angry he'd smile a little smile, the kind that simply raises the corner of the mouth a quarter of an inch. For those who knew, it was an eerie signal. Those who didn't found themselves in big trouble, for Ted was very quick. He loved to carry on what we would come to call philosophical discussions: What is courage? Does God exist? He also loved words, enjoyed picking up big ones like *salubrious* and *equivocal* and using them in our conversations — laughing at himself as the word hit a chuckhole rolling off his tongue. Ted didn't do all that well in school — baseball and parties and testing the courage he'd speculated about took up his time. His textbooks were *Argosy* and *Field and Stream*, whatever newspapers he'd find on the bus stop — from the *Daily Worker* to pornography — conversations with uncles or hobos or businessmen he'd meet in a coffee shop, *The Old Man and the Sea*. With hindsight, I can see that Ted was developing into one of those rough-hewn intellectuals whose sources are a mix of the learned and the apocryphal, whose discussions are both assured and sad.

And then there was Ken Harvey. Ken was good-looking in a puffy way and had a full and oily ducktail and was a car enthusiast . . . a hodad. One day in religion class, he said the sentence that turned out to be one of the most memorable of the hundreds of thousands I heard in those Voc. Ed. years. We were talking about the parable of the talents, about achievement, working hard, doing the best you can do, blah-blah-blah, when the teacher called on the restive Ken Harvey for an opinion. Ken thought about it, but just for a second, and said (with studied, minimal affect), "I just wanna be average." That woke me up. Average?! Who wants to be average? Then the athletes chimed in with the clichés that make you want to laryngectomize them, and the exchange became a platitudinous melee. At the time, I thought Ken's assertion was stupid, and I wrote him off. But his sentence has stayed with me all these years, and I think I am finally coming to understand it.

Ken Harvey was gasping for air. School can be a tremendously disorienting place. No matter how bad the school, you're going to encounter notions that don't fit with the assumptions and beliefs that you grew up with — maybe you'll hear these dissonant notions from teachers, maybe from the other students, and maybe you'll read them. You'll also be thrown in with all kinds of kids from all kinds of backgrounds, and that can be unsettling — this is especially true in places of rich ethnic and linguistic mix, like the L.A. basin. You'll see a handful of students far excel you in courses that sound exotic and that are only in the curriculum of the elite: French, physics, trigonometry. And all this is happening while you're trying to shape an identity; your body is changing, and your emotions are running wild. If you're a working-class kid in the vocational track, the options you'll have to deal with this will be constrained in certain ways: You're defined by your school as "slow"; you're placed in a curriculum that isn't designed to liberate you but to occupy you, or, if you're lucky, train you, though the training is for work the society does not esteem; other students are picking up the cues from your school and your curriculum and interacting with you in particular ways. If you're a kid like Ted Richard, you turn your back on all this and let your mind roam where it may. But youngsters like Ted are rare. What Ken and so many others do is protect themselves from such suffocating madness by taking on with a vengeance the identity implied in the vocational track. Reject the confusion and frustration by openly defining yourself as the Common Joe. Champion the average. Rely on your own good sense. Fuck this bullshit. Bullshit, of course, is everything you — and the others — fear is beyond you: books, essays, tests, academic scrambling, complexity, scientific reasoning, philosophical inquiry.

The tragedy is that you have to twist the knife in your own gray matter to make this defense work. You'll have to shut down, have to reject intellectual stimuli or diffuse them with sarcasm, have to cultivate stupidity, have to convert boredom from a malady into a way of confronting the world. Keep your vocabulary simple, act stoned when you're not or act more stoned than you are, flaunt ignorance, materialize your dreams. It is a powerful and effective defense — it neutralizes the insult and the frustration of being a vocational kid and, when perfected, it drives teachers up the wall, a delightful secondary effect. But like all strong magic, it exacts a price.

My own deliverance from the Voc. Ed. world began with sophomore biology. Every student, college prep to vocational, had to take biology, and unlike the other courses, the same person taught all sections. When teaching the vocational group, Brother Clint probably slowed down a bit or omitted a little of the fundamental biochemistry, but he used the same book and more or less the same syllabus across the board. If one class got tough, he could get tougher. He was young and powerful and very handsome, and looks and physical strength were high currency. No one gave him any trouble.

I was pretty bad at the dissecting table, but the lectures and the text-book were interesting: plastic overlays that, with each turned page, peeled away skin, then veins and muscle, then organs, down to the very bones that Brother Clint, pointer in hand, would tap out on our hanging skeleton.

40

Dave Snyder was in big trouble, for the study of life — versus the living of it — was sticking in his craw. We worked out a code for our multiple-choice exams. He'd poke me in the back: once for the answer under *A*, twice for *B*, and so on; and when he'd hit the right one, I'd look up to the ceiling as though I were lost in thought. Poke: cytoplasm. Poke, poke: methane. Poke, poke, poke: William Harvey. Poke, poke, poke, poke: islets of Langerhans. This didn't work out perfectly, but Dave passed the course, and I mastered the dreamy look of a guy on a record jacket. And something else happened. Brother Clint puzzled over this Voc. Ed. kid who was racking up 98s and 99s on his tests. He checked the school's records and discovered the error. He recommended that I begin my junior year in the College Prep program. According to all I've read since, such a shift, as one report put it, is virtually impossible. Kids at that level rarely cross tracks. The telling thing is how chancy both my placement into and exit from Voc. Ed. was; neither I nor my parents had anything to do with it. I lived in one world during spring semester, and when I came back to school in the fall, I was living in another.

Switching to College Prep was a mixed blessing. I was an erratic student. I was undisciplined. And I hadn't caught on to the rules of the game: why work hard in a class that didn't grab my fancy? I was also hopelessly behind in math. Chemistry was hard; toying with my chemistry set years before hadn't prepared me for the chemist's equations. Fortunately, the priest who taught both chemistry and second-year algebra was also the school's athletic director. Membership on the track team covered me; I knew I wouldn't get lower than a C. U.S. history was taught pretty well, and I did okay. But civics was taken over by a football coach who had trouble reading the textbook aloud — and reading aloud was the centerpiece of his pedagogy. College Prep at Mercy was certainly an improvement over the vocational program — at least it carried some status — but the social science curriculum was weak, and the mathematics and physical sciences were simply beyond me. I had a miserable quantitative background and ended up copying some assignments and finessing the rest as best I could. Let me try to explain how it feels to see again and again material you should once have learned but didn't.

You are given a problem. It requires you to simplify algebraic fractions or to multiply expressions containing square roots. You know this is pretty basic material because you've seen it for years. Once a teacher took some time with you, and you learned how to carry out these operations. Simple versions, anyway. But that was a year or two or more in the past, and these are more complex versions, and now you're not sure. And this, you keep telling yourself, is ninth- or even eighth-grade stuff.

Next it's a word problem. This is also old hat. The basic elements are as familiar as story characters: trains speeding so many miles per hour or shadows of buildings angling so many degrees. Maybe you know enough, have sat through enough explanations, to be able to begin setting up the problem: "If one train is going this fast . . ." or "This shadow is really one line of a triangle. . . ." Then: "Let's see . . ." "How did Jones do this?" "Hmmmm." "No." "No, that won't work." Your attention wavers. You wonder about other things: a football game, a dance, that cute new checker at the market. You try to focus on the problem again. You scribble on paper for a while, but the tension wins out and your attention flits elsewhere. You crumple the paper and begin daydreaming to ease the frustration.

The particulars will vary, but in essence this is what a number of students go through, especially those in so-called remedial classes. They open their textbooks and see once again the familiar and impenetrable formulas and diagrams and terms that have stumped them for years. There is no excitement here. *No* excitement. Regardless of what the teacher says, this is not a new challenge. There is, rather, embarrassment and frustration and, not surprisingly, some anger in being reminded once again of long-standing inadequacies. No wonder so many students finally attribute their difficulties to something inborn, organic: "That part of my brain just doesn't work." Given the troubling histories many of these students have, it's miraculous that any of them can lift the shroud of hopelessness sufficiently to make deliverance from these classes possible.

Through this entire period, my father's health was deteriorating with cruel   45
momentum. His arteriosclerosis progressed to the point where a simple nick on his shin wouldn't heal. Eventually it ulcerated and widened. Lou Minton would come by daily to change the dressing. We tried renting an oscillating bed — which we placed in the front room — to force blood through the constricted arteries in my father's legs. The bed hummed through the night, moving in place to ward off the inevitable. The ulcer continued to spread, and the doctors finally had to amputate. My grandfather had lost his leg in a stockyard accident. Now my father too was crippled. His convalescence was slow but steady, and the doctors placed him in the Santa Monica Rehabilitation Center, a sun-bleached building that opened out onto the warm spray of the Pacific. The place gave him some strength and some color and some training in walking with an artificial leg. He did pretty well for a year or so until he slipped and broke his hip. He was confined to a wheelchair after that, and the confinement contributed to the diminishing of his body and spirit.

I am holding a picture of him. He is sitting in his wheelchair and smiling at the camera. The smile appears forced, unsteady, seems to quaver, though it is frozen in silver nitrate. He is in his mid-sixties and looks eighty. Late in my junior year, he had a stroke and never came out of the resulting coma. After that, I would see him only in dreams, and to this day that is how I join him. Sometimes the dreams are sad and grisly and primal: my father lying in a bed soaked with his suppuration, holding me, rocking me. But sometimes the dreams bring him back to me healthy: him talking to me on an empty street, or buying some pictures to decorate our old house, or transformed somehow into someone strong and adept with tools and the physical.

* * *

Jack MacFarland couldn't have come into my life at a better time. My father was dead, and I had logged up too many years of scholastic indifference. Mr. MacFarland had a master's degree from Columbia and decided, at twenty-six, to find a little school and teach his heart out. He never took any credentialing courses, couldn't bear to, he said, so he had to find employment in a private system. He ended up at Our Lady of Mercy teaching five sections of senior English. He was a beatnik who was born too late. His teeth were stained, he tucked his sorry tie in between the third and fourth buttons of his shirt, and his pants were chronically wrinkled. At first, we couldn't believe this guy, thought he slept in his car. But within no time, he had us so startled with work that we didn't much worry about where he slept or if he slept at all. We wrote three or four essays a month. We read a book every two to three weeks, starting with the *Iliad* and ending up with Hemingway. He gave us a quiz on the reading every other day. He brought a prep school curriculum to Mercy High.

MacFarland's lectures were crafted, and as he delivered them he would pace the room jiggling a piece of chalk in his cupped hand, using it to scribble on the board the names of all the writers and philosophers and plays and novels he was weaving into his discussion. He asked questions often, raised everything from Zeno's paradox to the repeated last line of Frost's "Stopping by Woods on a Snowy Evening." He slowly and carefully built up our knowledge of Western intellectual history — with facts, with connections, with speculations. We learned about Greek philosophy, about Dante, the Elizabethan worldview, the Age of Reason, existentialism. He analyzed poems with us, had us reading sections from John Ciardi's *How Does a Poem Mean?* making a potentially difficult book accessible with his own explanations. We gave oral reports on poems Ciardi didn't cover. We imitated the styles of Conrad, Hemingway, and *Time* magazine. We wrote and talked, wrote and talked. The man immersed us in language.

Even MacFarland's barbs were literary. If Jim Fitzsimmons, hung over and irritable, tried to smart-ass him, he'd rejoin with a flourish that would spark the indomitable Skip Madison — who'd lost his front teeth in a hapless tackle — to flick his tongue through the gap and opine, "good chop," drawing out the single "o" in stinging indictment. Jack MacFarland, this tobacco-stained intellectual, brandished linguistic weapons of a kind I hadn't encountered before. Here was this *egghead*, for God's sake, keeping some pretty difficult people in line. And from what I heard, Mike Dweetz and Steve Fusco and all the notorious Voc. Ed. crowd settled down as well when MacFarland took the podium. Though a lot of guys groused in the schoolyard, it just seemed that giving trouble to this particular teacher was a silly thing to do. Tomfoolery, not to mention assault, had no place in the world he was trying to create for us, and instinctively everyone knew that. If nothing else, we all recognized MacFarland's considerable intelligence and respected the hours he put into his work. It came to this: the troublemaker would look foolish rather than daring. Even Jim Fitzsimmons was reading *On the Road* and turning his incipient alcoholism to literary ends.

There were some lives that were already beyond Jack MacFarland's minis-   50
trations, but mine was not. I started reading again as I hadn't since elementary
school. I would go into our gloomy little bedroom or sit at the dinner table
while, on the television, Danny McShane was paralyzing Mr. Moto with the
atomic drop, and work slowly back through *Heart of Darkness*, trying to catch
the words in Conrad's sentences. I certainly was not MacFarland's best student;
most of the other guys in College Prep, even my fellow slackers, had better backgrounds than I did. But I worked very hard, for MacFarland had hooked me. He
tapped my old interest in reading and creating stories. He gave me a way to feel
special by using my mind. And he provided a role model that wasn't shaped on
physical prowess alone, and something inside me that I wasn't quite aware of responded to that. Jack MacFarland established a literacy club, to borrow a phrase
of Frank Smith's, and invited me — invited all of us — to join.

There's been a good deal of research and speculation suggesting that the
acknowledgment of school performance with extrinsic rewards — smiling
faces, stars, numbers, grades — diminishes the intrinsic satisfaction children
experience by engaging in reading or writing or problem solving. While it's
certainly true that we've created an educational system that encourages our
best and brightest to become cynical grade collectors and, in general, have
developed an obsession with evaluation and assessment, I must tell you that
venal though it may have been, I loved getting good grades from MacFarland.
I now know how subjective grades can be, but then they came tucked in the
back of essays like bits of scientific data, some sort of spectroscopic readout
that said, objectively and publicly, that I had made something of value. I
suppose I'd been mediocre for too long and enjoyed a public redefinition.
And I suppose the workings of my mind, such as they were, had been private for too long. My linguistic play moved into the world; like the inter-
galactic stories I told years before on Frank's berry-splattered truck bed,
these papers with their circled, red B-pluses and A-minuses linked my mind
to something outside it. I carried them around like a club emblem.

One day in the December of my senior year, Mr. MacFarland asked me
where I was going to go to college. I hadn't thought much about it. Many of
the students I teach today spent their last year in high school with a physics
text in one hand and the Stanford catalog in the other, but I wasn't even
aware of what "entrance requirements" were. My folks would say that they
wanted me to go college and be a doctor, but I don't know how seriously I
ever took that; it seemed a sweet thing to say, a bit of supportive family chatter, like telling a gangly daughter she's graceful. The reality of higher education wasn't in my scheme of things: no one in the family had gone to college;
only two of my uncles had completed high school. I figured I'd get a night job
and go to the local junior college because I knew that Snyder and Company
were going there to play ball. But I hadn't even prepared for that. When I
finally said, "I don't know," MacFarland looked down at me — I was seated
in his office — and said, "Listen, you can write."

My grades stank. I had A's in biology and a handful of B's in a few English and social science classes. All the rest were C's — or worse. MacFarland

said I would do well in his class and laid down the law about doing well in the others. Still, the record for my first three years wouldn't have been acceptable to any four-year school. To nobody's surprise, I was turned down flat by USC and UCLA. But Jack MacFarland was on the case. He had received his bachelor's degree from Loyola University, so he made calls to old professors and talked to somebody in admissions and wrote me a strong letter. Loyola finally accepted me as a probationary student. I would be on trial for the first year, and if I did okay, I would be granted regular status. MacFarland also intervened to get me a loan, for I could never have afforded a private college without it. Four more years of religion classes and four more years of boys at one school, girls at another. But at least I was going to college. Amazing.

In my last semester of high school, I elected a special English course fashioned by Mr. MacFarland, and it was through this elective that there arose at Mercy a fledgling literati. Art Mitz, the editor of the school newspaper and a very smart guy, was the kingpin. He was joined by me and by Mark Dever, a quiet boy who wrote beautifully and who would die before he was forty. MacFarland occasionally invited us to his apartment, and those visits became the high point of our apprenticeship: we'd clamp on our training wheels and drive to his salon.

He lived in a cramped and cluttered place near the airport, tucked away   55 in the kind of building that architectural critic Reyner Barham calls a *dingbat*. Books were all over: stacked, piled, tossed, and crated, underlined and dog eared, well worn and new. Cigarette ashes crusted with coffee in saucers or spilled over the sides of motel ashtrays. The little bedroom had, along two of its walls, bricks and boards loaded with notes, magazines, and oversized books. The kitchen joined the living room, and there was a stack of German newspapers under the sink. I had never seen anything like it: a great flophouse of language furnished by City Lights and Café le Metro. I read every title. I flipped through paperbacks and scanned jackets and memorized names: Gogol, *Finnegan's Wake*, Djuna Barnes, Jackson Pollock, *A Coney Island of the Mind*, F. O. Matthiessen's *American Renaissance*, all sorts of Freud, *Troubled Sleep*, Man Ray, *The Education of Henry Adams*, Richard Wright, *Film as Art*, William Butler Yeats, Marguerite Duras, *Redburn*, *A Season in Hell*, *Kapital*. On the cover of Alain-Fournier's *The Wanderer* was an Edward Gorey drawing of a young man on a road winding into dark trees. By the hotplate sat a strange Kafka novel called *Amerika*, in which an adolescent hero crosses the Atlantic to find the Nature Theater of Oklahoma. Art and Mark would be talking about a movie or the school newspaper, and I would be consuming my English teacher's library. It was heady stuff. I felt like a Pop Warner athlete on steroids.

Art, Mark, and I would buy stogies and triangulate from MacFarland's apartment to the Cinema, which now shows X-rated films but was then L.A.'s premiere art theater, and then to the musty Cherokee Bookstore in Hollywood to hobnob with beatnik homosexuals — smoking, drinking bourbon and coffee, and trying out awkward phrases we'd gleaned from our mentor's bookshelves. I was happy and precocious and a little scared as well, for Hollywood Boulevard was thick with a kind of decadence that was foreign to the South Side. After the Cherokee, we would head back to the security of MacFarland's apartment, slaphappy with hipness.

Let me be the first to admit that there was a good deal of adolescent passion in this embrace of the avant-garde: self-absorption, sexually charged pedantry, an elevation of the odd and abandoned. Still it was a time during which I absorbed an awful lot of information: long lists of titles, images from expressionist paintings, new wave shibboleths, snippets of philosophy, and names that read like Steve Fusco's misspellings — Goethe, Nietzsche, Kierkegaard. Now this is hardly the stuff of deep understanding. But it was an introduction, a phrase book, a Baedeker to a vocabulary of ideas, and it felt good at the time to know all these words. With hindsight I realize how layered and important that knowledge was.

It enabled me to do things in the world. I could browse bohemian bookstores in far-off, mysterious Hollywood; I could go to the Cinema and see events through the lenses of European directors; and, most of all, I could share an evening, talk that talk, with Jack MacFarland, the man I most admired at the time. Knowledge was becoming a bonding agent. Within a year or two, the persona of the disaffected hipster would prove too cynical, too alienated to last. But for a time it was new and exciting: it provided a critical perspective on society, and it allowed me to act as though I were living beyond the limiting boundaries of South Vermont.

QUESTIONS

Reading

1. How does Rose end up in Voc. Ed.?
2. Highlight, underline, or flag places that Rose talks about his fellow students in Voc. Ed., then summarize how he characterizes them. What does Rose think of Voc. Ed.?
3. In this essay *reflecting* on his own personal experiences, what impressions does Rose give you of himself as a student and a person? How does his tone shape your understanding of his reflections?

Exploratory Writing

1. Jack MacFarland changes Rose's life. Choose two of the teachers you remember best, and list the things you learned from them — not just academic skills or facts but also lessons about adulthood, inspiration, and social interactions. The lessons can be positive, negative, or a complicated mix. Do you have more vivid memories of the teachers you loved or the teachers you loathed?

2. List the most inspiring of Rose's formative educational experiences, both in and out of the classroom, such as receiving a chemistry set from his parents, entering new worlds through library books, and meeting Jack MacFarland. Now, make a chart of your own positive educational turning points, and the people, institutions, or resources that made them possible.

EDUCATIONAL TURNING POINT	WHO/WHAT PROVIDED IT

3. If you browse through Rose's blog (**http://mikerosebooks.blogspot.com**), you can see how strongly his educational experiences affected not only his career but also his interests, opinions, and vision of the world. Interview an adult you know about his or her educational background, learning breakthroughs, and other formative experiences. How did these experiences shape his or her adult life and career?

Making Connections

1. How do Rose's social class and ethnicity shape his educational experiences? Using Rose as a case study, evaluate the ideas that Emily Bazelon (p. 585) discusses about integrating students according to social class. How would a class-based integration program have changed Rose's educational experience? Bazelon shows how standardized test scores are widely used as the measure of successful race and class integration. How does Rose's experience call this into question?
2. Rose implies that remedial students often do not lack intelligence. Rather, they are responding in complicated ways to unsupportive social and economic conditions, and to years of inadequate education. This directly contradicts *essentialist* arguments, which attribute students' performance and behaviors to factors such as innate intelligence, race, and sex. Through this casebook, highlight examples of *essentialism*. How do Rose's reflections help contradict them?

Essay Writing

1. Theodore R. Sizer's (p. 613) essay is titled "What High School Is." Keeping in mind what you have learned from Rose's reflections on his high school experience, or from any other essays in this casebook, write your own essay titled "What High School Should Be."

The Next Kind of Integration

Emily Bazelon

*Emily Bazelon (b. 1971) is an American journalist and senior edi-
tor of* Slate *magazine, where she edits columns on jurisprudence
and family issues. Before joining* Slate, *she worked as an editor
and writer at* Legal Affairs *magazine and as a law clerk on the
U.S. Court of Appeals for the First Circuit. A Truman Capote Fellow at Yale Law School — her alma mater (2000) — Bazelon's
work has appeared in the* New York Times Magazine, *the*
Atlantic, *and* Mother Jones, *among other publications. This piece
appeared in the* New York Times Magazine *in 2008.*

In June of last year, a conservative majority of the Supreme Court, in a
5-to-4 decision, declared the racial-integration efforts of two school districts
unconstitutional. Seattle and Louisville, Kentucky, could no longer assign
students to schools based on their race, Chief Justice John Roberts wrote in
his lead opinion in *Meredith v. Jefferson County School Board* (and its companion case, *Parents Involved in Community Schools v. Seattle School District No. 1*). Justice Stephen Breyer sounded a sad and grim note of dissent.
Pointing out that the court was rejecting student-assignment plans that the
districts had designed to stave off de facto resegregation, Breyer wrote that
"to invalidate the plans under review is to threaten the promise of *Brown*."
By invoking *Brown v. Board of Education*, the court's landmark 1954 civil
rights ruling, Breyer accused the majority of abandoning a touchstone in the
country's efforts to overcome racial division. "This is a decision that the
court and the nation will come to regret," he concluded.

Breyer's warning, along with even more dire predictions from civil
rights groups, helped place the court's ruling at the center of the liberal indictment of the Roberts court. In Louisville, too, the court's verdict met with
resentment. Last fall, I asked Pat Todd, the assignment director for the
school district of Jefferson County, which encompasses Louisville and its
suburbs, whether any good could come of the ruling. She shook her head so
hard that strands of blond hair loosened from her bun. "No," she said with
uncharacteristic exasperation, "we're *already doing* what we should be."

Todd was referring to Louisville's success in distributing black and
white students, which it does more evenly than any district in the country
with a comparable black student population; almost every school is between
15 and 50 percent African-American. The district's combination of school

choice, busing and magnet programs has brought general, if not uniform, acceptance — rather than white flight and disaffection, the legacy of desegregation in cities like Boston and Kansas City, Missouri. The student population, which now numbers nearly one hundred thousand, has held steady at about 35 percent black and 55 percent white, along with a small and growing number of Hispanics and Asians.

With its decision in Meredith, the court was forcing Louisville to rethink the way it would assign elementary-school students and, in the process, to confront some tricky questions. Is the purpose of integration simply to mix students of different colors for the sake of equity or to foster greater familiarity and comfort among the races? Should integration necessarily translate into concrete gains like greater achievement for all students? If so, is mixing students by race the most effective mechanism for attaining it?

In Louisville, the achievement gap between whites and blacks is twenty percentage points at many grade levels. For Todd and her team, whatever their reservations about the decision in Meredith, coming up with an alternative assignment plan was an opportunity to think about a new kind of integration and what it might accomplish. In Louisville, integration would no longer focus solely on race but also on the barriers of class, of advantage and disadvantage. Other cities have been thinking along these lines. In the wake of the Supreme Court's decision, four other districts — Des Moines, Burlington, Vermont, Omaha, and Beaumont, Texas — announced a switch to class-based integration. Seattle, too, is discussing setting aside 5 to 15 percent of the spots (a relatively small percentage) in desired high schools for low-income students. Some of the plans go into effect this fall; others, including Louisville's, begin a year from September.

The chief justice didn't address the idea of class-based integration in his opinion. But Justice Anthony Kennedy did, in a separate concurrence. And because Kennedy cast the fifth vote for the majority, his view controls the law. Though he agreed with Roberts that public school districts should not make school assignments based on the race of individual students, he added that the court's ruling "should not prevent school districts from continuing the important work of bringing together students of different racial, ethnic and economic backgrounds."

How were schools to do this? Around the country, school-district lawyers studied Kennedy's opinion and came to a rough consensus. In its amicus brief before the court, the Bush administration cited socioeconomic integration as a "race neutral" alternative to race-based assignment plans. Kennedy picked up on this, and no other justice wrote to contradict him. As a result, the school-district lawyers concluded that districts could assign an individual child to a school based on any kind of socioeconomic measure they chose — income, assets, parental education attainment. Districts could also be "race conscious," according to Kennedy, when they drew school boundaries, chose sites for new schools and directed money to particular programs. But in these situations, they would usually be limited to taking into account the racial composition of a neighborhood rather than the race of an individual student.

In terms of the court's jurisprudence, this is a major change. Race has been the organizing principle of integration since *Brown v. Board of Education*. At the time of the court's ruling in Meredith, hundreds of districts were pursuing some sort of racial integration, with or without a court order, while only a few dozen at most were trying any form of socioeconomic integration. Over the years, racial integration has proved to have tangible benefits. Amy Stuart Wells, an education professor at Columbia Teachers College, has found that going to school with substantial numbers of white students helped black students to form cross-racial friendships and, by giving them access to white social networks, eventually to find work in jobs higher up the economic ladder.

However important these gains are, they are long-term and cannot be easily or quickly assessed. And increasingly, schools are held to a standard of immediately measurable outcomes. The No Child Left Behind Act, signed into law in 2002, demands student test scores that climb ever upward, with a mandate for all students to be proficient in reading and math by 2014. Test scores may not be the best way to assess the quality of a teacher or a school, but the pressure to improve scores, whatever its shortcomings, is itself on the rise. And if high test scores are the goal, it turns out, class-based integration may be the more effective tool.

Researchers have been demonstrating this result since 1966, when Congress asked James S. Coleman, a Johns Hopkins sociologist, to deliver a report on why the achievement of black students lagged far behind that of white ones. The expected answer was that more than a decade after *Brown*, black kids were still often going to inferior schools with small budgets. But Coleman found that the varying amount of money spent on schools didn't account for the achievement gap. Instead, the greater poverty of black families did. When high concentrations of poor kids went to school together, Coleman reported, all the students at the school tended to learn less.

How much less was later quantified. The Harvard sociologist Christopher Jencks reanalyzed Coleman's data in the 1970s and concluded that poor black sixth-graders in majority middle-class schools were twenty months ahead of poor black sixth-graders in majority low-income schools. The statistics for poor white students were similar. In the last forty years, Coleman's findings, known informally as the Coleman Report, have been confirmed again and again. Most recently, in a 2006 study, Douglas Harris, an economist at the University of Wisconsin, found that when more than half the students were low-income, only 1.1 percent of schools consistently performed at a "high" level (defined as two years of scores in the top third of the U.S. Department of Education's national achievement database in two grades and in two subjects: English and math). By contrast, 24.2 percent of schools that are majority middle-class met Harris's standard.

10

There are, of course, determined urban educators who have proved that select schools filled with poor and minority students can thrive — in the right circumstances, with the right teachers and programs. But consistently good education at schools with such student bodies remains the rare exception. The powerful effect of the socioeconomic makeup of a student body on academic achievement has become "one of the most consistent findings in research on education," Gary Orfield, a UCLA education professor, and Susan Eaton, a research director at Harvard Law, wrote in their 1996 book, *Dismantling Desegregation.*

Most researchers think that this result is brought about by the advantages that middle-class students bring with them. Richard Kahlenberg of the Century Foundation lays them out in his 2001 book, *All Together Now*: more high-level classes, more parent volunteers and peers who on average have twice the vocabulary and half the behavioral problems of poor students. And, especially, more good teachers. Harris, the economist, says that poor minority students still don't have comparable access to effective teachers, measured by preparation and experience. The question, then, is whether a plan that integrates a district by class as well as by race will help win for all its schools the kind of teaching that tends to be linked to achievement. "The evidence indicates that it would," Harris says.

Ronald Ferguson, an economist at the Kennedy School of Government at Harvard, is less persuaded. His research highlights the nagging persistence of a racial achievement gap in well-off suburbs. "What happens with the achievement gap in a place like Louisville," he says, "will depend on how vigilant their leaders are to make sure high-quality instruction is delivered across the board." Such teaching is more likely in a school with a critical mass of middle-class parents, he concedes. But he stresses that to reap the benefits, poor kids have to be evenly distributed among classrooms and not just grouped together in the lowest tracks. "To the degree a district takes the kids who struggle the most academically and spreads them across different classrooms, they're making teachers' work more doable," he says. "And that may be the biggest effect."

Once they started looking for them, Todd and her colleagues saw the   15 effects of class division and poverty in the Jefferson County schools. Thorough racial desegregation had not, it seemed, led to thorough class desegregation. At forty of ninety elementary schools in the district, 75 percent or more of the students came from low-income homes. And the effects of these high concentrations of poverty were striking: poor students in Louisville, black and white, fared worse when they attended schools filled with other poor kids. In elementary school, 61 percent of poor students at mostly low-income schools scored proficient in reading, compared with 71 percent of poor students at majority-middle-class schools. For math, the comparative proficiency rates were 52 percent to 63 percent. Because black students were disproportionately poor, they were more likely to attend high-poverty schools, and this was contributing to the district's pronounced black-white achievement gap.

Todd and her planners wanted to tackle the problem, she says, but they were mindful of going too far in their efforts and losing the support of parents. In other districts — including Cincinnati, Evanston, Illinois, Bibb County, Georgia, and Madison, Wisconsin — the reaction to the Supreme Court's ruling had been to move to dismantle racial-integration programs. Todd and other school officials didn't want integration redefined to turn into no integration at all. To get a handle on a new plan, Todd turned to an heir of James Coleman: the researcher John Powell.

In the 1960s, Powell was one of the only African-American students in his advanced high-school classes in Detroit; when he became the class valedictorian, a teacher told him he wasn't the smartest student. He now directs the Kirwan Institute for the Study of Race and Ethnicity at Ohio State University, and he says he still thinks that race is a category with singular power. But he also appreciates the stark effects of segregating poor kids. "Ever since the Coleman Report, we've seen that there's a high correlation between good schools and schools that are integrated socioeconomically as well as racially," he says. "I think everyone agrees that what we need are more good schools."

In Louisville, Powell lent his expertise to Todd and her team. They came up with a computer-generated map that shows what Powell defines as the district's areas of "low opportunity." Todd, who is sixty-one and taught every grade in the Louisville schools before becoming an administrator, went over the map with me one day last December. The map used two different measures of class to identify Jefferson County's areas of disadvantage: income level and the educational attainment of adults. (To gauge disadvantage, districts embarking on class-based integration often use who among their students receives free or reduced lunch; Powell, however, contends that this is a relatively crude measure.) Using census data, Todd's team identified the zones in the district in which households fall below the average income and education levels, with fewer adults who have finished high school or gone to college or beyond. Finally, the team added one more factor: a higher-than-average number of minorities, almost all of them African-Americans or Hispanics.

The map's class-plus-race formula revealed a major partition. One region, which Todd's team called Geographic Area A, is a mermaid-shaped swath of blue, with its head in Louisville's West End, just south of the Ohio River, and its tail to the south. The region encompasses the parts of the district with a higher-than-average minority population, lower-than-average median income and lower-than-average adult educational attainment. In Geographic Area A live about 30 percent of Jefferson County's students. The rest of the county, colored yellow, included everyone else — the better off, better educated and whiter Geographic Area B.

What if the district were to use this map as a guide for school integration? Instead of maintaining each school as no less than 15 percent and no more than 50 percent black, Todd's team could propose that each school

20

have no less than 15 percent and no more than 50 percent of students from Geographic Area A. By distributing students from the district's residential zones of disadvantage, the new plan would integrate the schools by class. There would no longer be forty elementary schools with heavily poor-student populations. There could potentially be no such schools.

Given the presumed boost to test scores resulting from distributing poor students more widely, you might wonder why Todd's team retained race as an admissions factor at all. To answer this, it's worth considering the country's existing examples of purely class-based integration. The best known is in Wake County, North Carolina. With 134,000 students, the Wake County school district ranks nineteen among the country's twenty largest, spanning eight hundred square miles that include bleak tracts in the city of Raleigh, mansion-filled suburban cul-de-sacs and rural roads ending in the fresh earth of a new subdivision. The student population is about half white; one-quarter African-American; and one-quarter Hispanic, Asian, and multi-racial. The district voluntarily pursued race-based integration in the 1980s and 1990s. In 2000, after the U.S. Court of Appeals for the Fourth Circuit began to frown on the use of race in student assignment — a harbinger of the Supreme Court's stance last year — the district began assigning kids to schools based on the income level of the geographic zone they lived in. The aim was to balance the schools so that no more than 40 percent of the students at each one came from a low-income area. (This year, the district added another goal: to have no more than 25 percent of students at any one school for whom English is a second language.)

Wake County adopted class-based integration with the hard-nosed goal of raising test scores. The strategy was simple: no poor schools, no bad schools. And indeed, the district has posted striking improvements in the test scores of black and low-income students: in 1995, only 40 percent of the black students in Wake County in the third through eighth grades scored at grade level in state reading tests; by last year, the rate had almost doubled, to 82.5 percent. Statewide scores for black students also got better over the same time period, but not by as much. Wake County's numbers improve as students get older: 92 percent of all eighth graders read at or above grade level, including about 85 percent of black students and about 80 percent of low-income students. (Math scores are lower, following a statewide trend that reflects a change in the grading scale.) The district has achieved these results even as the share of low-income students overall has increased from about 30 percent a decade ago to about 40 percent today.

But the lessons of Wake County, Powell and Todd argue, don't apply everywhere. "In different districts, you have different geographic patterns," Powell says. "So you need different integration models to shop around." To begin with, Louisville is less affluent — more than 60 percent of its elementary school students receive free or reduced lunches, compared with Wake County's 40 percent. In Wake County, the vast majority of the poor students are black and Hispanic, and so mixing kids by class tightly correlates to mixing them by race. But in Jefferson County, more than a third of the kids who receive free or reduced lunches are white. As a result, redistributing students by class alone might still isolate them by race.

This is a limitation of class-based integration that holds true elsewhere. The city of San Francisco, for instance, has undergone substantial racial resegregation since retooling its diversity plan to emphasize socioeconomic factors. Even in Wake County, the fraction of students in racially segregated schools has climbed a bit over the last decade, from 25 percent to 32 percent. A 2006 paper by the education researchers Sean Reardon, John T. Yun and Michal Kurlaender crunched census data across the country and concluded that "given the extent of residential racial segregation in the United States, it is unlikely that race-neutral income-integration policies will significantly reduce school racial segregation, although there is reason to believe that such policies are likely to have other beneficial effects on schooling."

Many big cities have a different problem. Simple demographics dictate that they can't really integrate their schools at all, by either race or class. Consider the numbers for Detroit (74 percent low-income students; 91 percent black), Los Angeles (77 percent low-income; 85 percent black and Hispanic), New York City (74 percent; 63 percent), Washington (64 percent; 93 percent), Philadelphia (71 percent; 79 percent), Chicago (74 percent; 88 percent) and Boston (71 percent; 76 percent). In theory, big cities can diversify their schools by class and race by persuading many more middle-class and white parents to choose public school over private school or by combining forces with the well-heeled suburbs that surround them. But short of those developments, big cities are stuck. "The options have shrunk," says Tom Payzant, a former superintendent of schools in Boston.

Notably, there are a good many districts that have evaded this predicament. They are particularly found in the South, in part because of a historical accident. Because it was predominantly rural for longer, the South has more countywide school districts than the North. An unintended consequence was to ease the way to integration. Instead of city schools filled with poor black and Hispanic kids separated from a burgeoning ring of suburban districts stocked with affluent whites (and in some places, Asians), one district controls student assignment for the region.

Even in school districts with a mix of students of different races and income levels, however, there is no one-size-fits-all approach to socioeconomic integration, as underscored by the differences between Wake County and Jefferson County. Wake County's demographics entail that mixing kids by class, on its own, produces a fair degree of racial integration. Jefferson County's demographics don't necessarily work this way. And so civil rights lawyers suggest that districts configured like Jefferson County should continue to pursue racial diversity directly. They point to cities like Berkeley, California, which has an assignment plan that primarily relies on socioeconomics, but like Geography Area A also factors in the racial composition of a neighborhood to guard against resegregation along racial lines. "It's not either-or," says Anurima Bhargava, an education lawyer at the NAACP Legal Defense Fund.

In addition, there's a tacit liberal constitutional agenda at work in hybrid class-race approaches to integration: better to test Kennedy's opinion, with its support for the drawing of "race conscious" school boundaries, than to retreat further than is in fact required. "For Kennedy, there are ways of taking race into account," John Powell says. "It's just the method that's in question. How do you do it? We need to find out what's still permitted." He also points out that African-Americans are more likely than whites to be poor over generations — a bigger hurdle than a short stint in a low-income bracket.

The continuing attention to race aligns with the internal politics of Louisville and its suburbs. Many of today's parents grew up there and tend to remember and care about overcoming their county's Jim Crow legacy. In 1975, when a federal judge first ordered the city and its suburbs to desegregate, the Ku Klux Klan demonstrated, and the next day about 150 white protesters attacked eight school buses filled with black students. "We had tough times here when the buses burned," says Ann Elmore, a black member of the Jefferson County School Board. "We can still include race as a factor in our plan, and let me say I think it's important that we do."

Elsewhere in the United States, it is too soon to tell how the politics of class-based integration (Wake County) or class-plus-race (Jefferson County) will play out. Richard Kahlenberg makes the case for shifting integration policies primarily or solely to being class-based over the next decade or two. What's fair, he asks, about giving a spot in a coveted magnet program to the son of a South Asian college professor or an African-American politician over the daughter of a white waitress? Over time, such injustices threaten to sour white parents on the whole diversity enterprise, whereas giving poor kids a boost, whatever their color, is far less controversial. Polls at the time of the Supreme Court's 2003 decision in *Grutter v. Bollinger*, which concerned affirmative action at public universities, showed public support running 2 to 1 for giving poorer kids a leg up in going to college, as opposed to 2 to 1 against race-based preferences. In her majority opinion in the case, Justice Sandra Day O'Connor famously said she thought that racial preferences would continue only for another twenty-five years. Barack Obama has said, looking ahead to his daughters' college applications, that they don't deserve an admissions break — an acknowledgment that the mix of race, affirmative action and privilege is a complicated one.

To catch on nationwide, however, class-based integration would have to generate momentum that it has so far lacked. In his State of the Union address in January, President Bush urged action "to help liberate poor children trapped in failing public schools." And yet a provision in the No Child Left Behind Act that theoretically allows students to transfer depends on the availability of open spaces elsewhere and has barely been utilized. The administration may have advocated class-based integration to the Supreme Court, but Bush officials haven't used their signature education law to make it happen.

If Congress were to revise No Child Left Behind to encourage more transfers of poor students to middle-class schools, would poor students drag down their better-off peers? In the end, the prospects of class-based integration will probably rise or fall on the answer to this question. Socioeconomic integration may be good for the have-nots, but if the haves think their kids are paying too great a price, they will kill it off at the polls. Richard Kahlenberg argues that the key is to ensure there is a solidly middle-class majority at as many schools as possible. That majority will then set the tone, he argues. Kahlenberg says that more research is needed to pin down the percentage of middle-class kids that a school needs to have to serve all its students well. Maybe a school can go as high as 50 percent low-income without losing ground. Or maybe it's telling that in Wake County, a proposal to increase the ceiling for low-income students from 40 percent to 50 percent died a swift death last fall after concerted protest.

Whatever the exact answer, there is some support for the view that schools can handle a substantial fraction of poor students without sacrificing performance. In Wake County, test scores of middle-class students have risen since instituting income-based integration. Additionally, Kahlenberg points out that middle-class students are generally less influenced by a school's environment because they tend to learn more at home, and that the achievement of white students has not declined in specific schools that experienced racial (and thus some class) desegregation.

Would schools need to track students by ability to protect middle-class students, who are more often higher-achieving than their low-income peers? Perhaps not. In a 2006 longitudinal study of an accelerated middle-school math program in Nassau County, New York, which grouped students heterogeneously, the authors found that students at all achievement levels, as well as minority and low-income students, were more likely than the students in tracked classes to take advanced math in high school. In addition, the kids who came into the program as math whizzes performed as well as other top-achievers in homogeneous classes.

This study underscores Ronald Ferguson's point about the value of seating students of different backgrounds and abilities in class together, as opposed to tracking them. Still, it's worth noting that less than 15 percent of the students studied in Nassau County were low-income. So the math study doesn't tell us what happens to the high-achieving middle-class kids when close to half of their classmates aren't as well off. 35

At the end of February, Todd started showing the map of mermaid-shaped Geographic Area A, which she hoped to use to implement the new assignment system, to the parents of Jefferson County. Todd would start her presentation with quotes from Justice Kennedy and from Justice Breyer's dissent; she especially wanted to remind her audiences of the sentiment

Breyer expressed by quoting former Justice Thurgood Marshall: "Unless our children begin to learn together, there is little hope that our people will ever learn to live together."

Todd's first stop was at a forum sponsored jointly by the Urban League and the NAACP, groups associated with Louisville's black establishment. Most of their members supported the school district, but some clergy members who worked with the city's black youth spoke against it. The Rev. John Carter, associate minister at Green Street Baptist Church, pointed to the district's black-white achievement gap and called for a return to neighborhood schools and an earlier era of black self-reliance.

As more forums followed in high-school auditoriums across the county, white parents asked a different question: How would the new assignment plan affect their kids? Would they be forced to switch schools in second, third or fourth grade? "We like the diversity," a white parent named Niki Noe told me the next morning at her son's elementary school, St. Matthews. "But if we have to go to Chenoweth" — a school with lower test scores — "we'll pull out and go to private school."

That's a serious threat to the district's well-being, but one that Todd anticipated. She designed a grandfather clause for kids like Noe's, so that the new assignments would apply almost entirely to new students. Meanwhile, at every meeting, Todd polled parents on whether they cared about maintaining diverse schools. The University of Kentucky also conducted a telephone survey with 654 parents of elementary schoolers. In April, Todd called me, elated and relieved, with the results: 88 percent of parents supported enrollment guidelines "to ensure that students learn with students from different races and backgrounds." Todd said she had dropped Breyer's dissent in Meredith from her presentation; she was no longer feeling frustrated with the court. "It's been a personal emotional trek, but I think we've come out better for it," she said in May.

Carter, the proponent of black self-reliance, was feeling more at ease,   40
too. He had come to see the virtue of mixing kids by income level. "Once I did the research, I was pretty impressed by the economic part of it," he said. Carter had taken note of the district's data showing that a switch to neighborhood schools, as he had first advocated, would mean that median household income would range from a high of more than $100,000 at the wealthiest school to about $8,300 at the poorest. A split between rich students and poor schools, he agreed, was the wrong path.

It is, of course, the path taken by most of the country. And yet at the end of May, the Jefferson County School Board voted unanimously to make Geographic Area A the basis for integrating elementary schools for the 2009 school year, a new chapter in the district's history. As the schools shift to the new class-plus-race formula, the district will closely watch the test scores of black students and poor students, hoping for an upsurge, and those of middle-class students, hoping to see achievement hold steady. And if they do, maybe the court's decision in Meredith will come to seem less like a cause for regret and more like an unexpected opportunity.

QUESTIONS

Reading

1. List the methods that are used to determine school success according to Bazelon's report. What criteria are used to judge the *performance* of students and schools? Are there alternative criteria that are not discussed in this report?
2. What is the Coleman Report? Summarize its findings.
3. What impression do you get of Bazelon from her report? What does she share about her own race, class background, and beliefs about education? How would her report change if she included autobiographical reflections?

Exploratory Writing

1. Collaborate in groups to develop a working definition of socioeconomic *class*. How would you define the social class of someone descended from slaves whose mother was the CEO of a multinational corporation? How would you define the social class of a person whose parents had PhDs but had left academia and were working menial jobs and supporting their family with government help? Is class only about economic privilege or also about cultural, educational, and historical privilege? Why does Richard Kahlenberg advocate having a "solidly middle-class majority" to "set the tone" at schools (paragraph 32)?
2. Research the educational biography of a living person who you believe has achieved remarkable things and made a positive difference in the world. What was the class background of this person's parents? How and where was he or she educated? What role do you think class played in his or her life and education?

Making Connections

1. Go through each essay in this casebook and underline, highlight, or flag any *generalizations* that you find about class, race, gender, Americans, how people learn, and so on. Could these essays be rewritten without generalizations? What purpose do these generalizations serve? In what ways do they strengthen or compromise each author's ideas about education?
2. Theodore R. Sizer (p. 613) describes what he sees as a typical high school by reporting on a typical day in the life of one student, Mark. From Sizer's remarks, can you identify Mark's class and race? How does class integration figure into the type of high school that Sizer describes?

Essay Writing

1. Write an essay reflecting on the mix of students at your grade school, junior high, and high school, based on class, race, gender, family educational background, religion, personality, style, and any other factors you wish to include. What effect did this mix have on students' learning?

Teaching to the Testosterone
The Gender Wars Go to School

Elizabeth Weil

Elizabeth Weil, a proponent for increasing public discourse on early childhood education, is fascinated by the ways we build and raise our families in the United States. A contributing writer for the New York Times Magazine, *she is the author of* They All Laughed at Christopher Columbus *(2002) and coauthor of* Crib Notes *(2004), a quirky cradle-side companion of facts and charts for new parents. Weil's work has also appeared in* Time *magazine, in* Rolling Stone, *and on National Public Radio's* This American Life. *She lives in San Francisco. This piece appeared in the* New York Times *in 2008.*

On an unseasonably cold day last November in Foley, Alabama, Colby Royster and Michael Peterson, two students in William Bender's fourth-grade public-school class, informed me that the class corn snake could eat a rat faster than the class boa constrictor. Bender teaches twenty-six fourth graders, all boys. Down the hall and around the corner, Michelle Gay teaches twenty-six fourth-grade girls. The boys like being on their own, they say, because girls don't appreciate their jokes and think boys are too messy, and are also scared of snakes. The walls of the boys' classroom are painted blue, the light bulbs emit a cool white light and the thermostat is set to sixty-nine degrees. In the girls' room, by contrast, the walls are yellow, the light bulbs emit a warm yellow light and the temperature is kept six degrees warmer, as per the instructions of Leonard Sax, a family physician turned author and advocate who this May will quit his medical practice to devote himself full time to promoting single-sex public education.

Foley Intermediate School began offering separate classes for boys and girls a few years ago, after the school's principal, Lee Mansell, read a book by Michael Gurian called *Boys and Girls Learn Differently!* After that, she read a magazine article by Sax and thought that his insights would help improve the test scores of Foley's lowest-achieving cohort, minority boys. Sax went on to publish those ideas in *Why Gender Matters: What Parents and Teachers Need to Know about the Emerging Science of Sex Differences.* Both books feature conversion stories of children, particularly boys, failing and on Ritalin in coeducational settings and then pulling themselves together in single-sex schools. Sax's book and lectures also include neurological diagrams and scores of citations of obscure scientific studies, like one by a Swedish researcher who found, in a study of ninety-six adults, that males and females have different emotional and cognitive responses to different kinds of light. Sax refers to a few other studies that he says show that girls and boys draw differently, including one from a group of Japanese researchers who found girls' drawings typically depict still lifes of people, pets, or flowers, using ten or more crayons, favoring warm colors like red, green, beige, and brown; boys, on the other hand, draw action, using six or fewer colors, mostly cool hues like gray, blue, silver and black. This apparent difference, which Sax argues is hardwired, causes teachers to praise girls' artwork and make boys feel that they're drawing incorrectly. Under Sax's leadership, teachers learn to say things like, "Damien, take your green crayon and draw some sparks and take your black crayon and draw some black lines coming out from the back of the vehicle, to make it look like it's going faster." "Now Damien feels encouraged," Sax explained to me when I first met him last spring in San Francisco. "To say: 'Why don't you use more colors? Why don't you put someone in the vehicle?' is as discouraging as if you say to Emily, 'Well, this is nice, but why don't you have one of them kick the other one — give us some action.'"

During the fall of 2003, Principal Mansell asked her entire faculty to read *Boys and Girls Learn Differently!* and, in the spring of 2004, to attend a one-day seminar led by Sax at the school, explaining boys' and girls' innate differences and how to teach to them. She also invited all Foley Intermediate School parents to a meeting extolling the virtues of single-sex public education. Enough parents were impressed that when Foley Intermediate, a school of 322 fourth and fifth graders, reopened after summer recess, the school had four single-sex classrooms: a girls' and a boys' class in both the fourth and fifth grades. Four classrooms in each grade remained coed.

Separating schoolboys from schoolgirls has long been a staple of private and parochial education. But the idea is now gaining traction in American public schools, in response to both the desire of parents to have more choice in their children's public education and the separate education crises girls and boys have been widely reported to experience. The girls' crisis was cited in the 1990s, when the American Association of University Women published *Shortchanging Girls, Shortchanging America*, which described how girls' self-esteem plummets during puberty and how girls are subtly discouraged from careers in math and science. More recently, in what Sara Mead, an education expert at the New America Foundation, calls a "man bites dog" sensation, public and parental concerns have shifted to boys. Boys are currently behind their sisters in high-school and college graduation rates. School, the boy-crisis argument goes, is shaped by females to match the abilities of girls (or, as Sax puts it, is taught "by soft-spoken women who bore" boys). In 2006, Doug Anglin, a seventeen-year-old in Milton, Massachusetts, filed a civil rights complaint with the United States Department of Education, claiming that his high school — where there are twice as many girls on the honor roll as there are boys — discriminated against males. His case did not prevail in the courts, but his sentiment found support in the legislature and the press. That same year, as part of No Child Left Behind, the federal law that authorizes programs aimed at improving accountability and test scores in public schools, the Department of Education passed new regulations making it easier for districts to create single-sex classrooms and schools.

In part because of these regulations and in part because of a mix of cultural   5 and technological forces — ranging from the growth of brain-scan research to the increased academic pressures on kindergartners and a chronic achievement gap between richer and poorer students and between white and minority students — new single-sex public schools and classrooms are opening at an accelerating pace. In 1995, there were two single-sex public schools operating in this country. Currently, there are forty-nine, and 65 percent of those have opened in the last three years. Nobody is keeping exact count of the number of schools offering single-sex classrooms, but Sax estimates that in the fall of 2002, only about a dozen public schools in the United States offered any kind of single-sex educational options (excluding schools which offered single-sex classrooms only in health or physical education). By this past fall, Sax says, that number had soared to more than 360, with boys- and girls-only classrooms now established in Cleveland; Detroit; Albany; Gary, Indiana; Philadelphia; Dallas; and Nashville, among other places. A disproportionate number of the schools are in the South (where attitudes toward gender roles tend to be more conservative) or serve disadvantaged kids. Sax claims that "many more are in the pipeline for 2008–2009."

Among advocates of single-sex public education, there are two camps: those who favor separating boys from girls because they are essentially different and those who favor separating boys from girls because they have different social experiences and social needs. Leonard Sax represents the essential-difference view, arguing that boys and girls should be educated separately for reasons of biology: for example, Sax asserts that boys don't hear as well as girls, which means that an instructor needs to speak louder in order for the boys in the room to hear her; and that boys' visual systems are better at seeing action, while girls are better at seeing the nuance of color and texture. The social view is represented by teachers like Emily Wylie, who works at the Young Women's Leadership School of East Harlem (TYWLS), an all-girls school for grades 7–12. Wylie described her job to me by saying, "It's my subversive mission to create all these strong girls who will then go out into the world and be astonished when people try to oppress them." Sax calls schools like TYWLS "anachronisms" — because, he says, they're stuck in 1970s-era feminist ideology and they don't base their pedagogy on the latest research. Few on the other side want to disparage Sax publicly, though TYWLS's founder, Ann Tisch, did tell me pointedly, "Nobody is planning the days of our girls around a photograph of a brain."

The two camps face a common enemy in the ACLU, which opposes all single-sex public education. (When I asked a lawyer at the ACLU's Women's

Rights Project why, she said, "Have you ever heard of Title IX?" referring to the 1972 Education Amendments that outlaw all discrimination in educational programs on the basis of sex.) But that hasn't brought the two sides together. "What kind of message does it give when you tell a group of kids that boys and girls need to be separated because they don't even see or hear alike?" asks Rosemary Salomone, a legal scholar at St. John's University School of Law. Salomone is especially invested in the debate, as she provided support to TYWLS before it opened in 1996 and was subsequently tapped by the United States Department of Education to draft the revised regulations that made it easier for districts to separate boys from girls. Those regulations now require that a district "provide a rationale," review its program every two years and ensure that enrollment in single-sex classrooms is voluntary. When Salomone revised the regulations, she thought they would usher in a flurry of schools of the TYWLS — not the Sax — variety. She was wrong. "As one of the people who let the horse out the barn, I'm now feeling like I really need to watch that horse," Salomone told me over lunch near her home in Rye, New York, last month. "Every time I hear of school officials selling single-sex programs to parents based on brain research, my heart sinks."

On that November day in Foley, Alabama, William Bender pulled a stool up to a lectern and began reading to his fourth-grade boys from Gary Paulsen's young-adult novel *Hatchet*. Bender's voice is deep and calm, a balm to many of his students who lack father figures or else have parents who, Bender says, "don't want to be parents. They want to be their kids' friends." Bender paused to ask one of his boys, who said he was feeling sick, "Are you going to make it, brother?" Then he kept reading. "'The pain in his forehead seemed to be abating. . . .' What's *abating*, gentlemen?" The protagonist of *Hatchet* survives a plane crash and finds himself alone by an insect-infested lake. Bender encouraged his boys to empathize. They discussed how annoying it is, when you're out hunting, to be swarmed by yellow flies.

Meanwhile, in Michelle Gay's fourth-grade class, the girls sang a vigorous rendition of "Always Sisters" and then did a tidy science experiment: pouring red water, blue oil and clear syrup into a plastic cup to test which has the greatest density, then confirming their results with the firsthand knowledge that when you're doing the dishes after your mother makes fried chicken, the oil always settles on top of the water in the sink.

Foley, population 11,300, is ten miles from the Gulf Coast. Fifty-seven percent of Foley Intermediate's students are white, 24 percent are black and 17 percent are Latino; 70 percent receive free or reduced-price lunches each day. In the first year of Foley's single-sex program, a third of the kids enrolled. The next year, two-thirds signed up, and in its third year 87 percent of parents requested the program. Principal Mansell reports that her single-sex classes produce fewer discipline problems, more parental support and better scores in writing, reading and math. She does, however, acknowledge that her data are compromised, as her highest-performing teachers and her most-motivated students have chosen single-sex.

In his books and frequent media appearances, Sax holds up Foley Intermediate as an example of his theories put to good use. In his second book, *Boys Adrift: The Five Factors Driving the Growing Epidemic of Unmotivated Boys and Underachieving Young Men,* Sax credits Bender for helping focus a boy who was given a wrong diagnosis of attention-deficit disorder by telling him that his father, who had left the family, would be even less likely to return if all his mother had to report was the boy misbehaving in school. Sax also goes out of his way to note that Bender had this conversation with the boy "shoulder to shoulder," not "face to face." "Just remember this rule of thumb," Sax tells readers: "A good place to talk with your son is in your car, with you driving and your son in the passenger seat."

Sax used to say that he was "uniquely unqualified to lead the single-sex public education movement," since, among other reasons, he had never been a teacher. Now, he no longer says that, and he maintains that a school's teachers and staff need only fourteen hours of training — two 7-hour days with him — to prepare to switch from coeducation to single-sex. Sax is forty-eight, square-jawed and sturdily built, with a thick shag of side-parted brown hair and a relentless intellect and tireless charisma that leave even his critics exhausted and impressed. In the 1980s he earned an MD and PhD (in psychology) from the University of Pennsylvania. Last year, he gave about fifty seminars and lectures on sex differences in children. The first time I met him, he was swinging through San Francisco to give a series of such talks at the Katherine Delmar Burke School, a private all-girls school. Speaking to a group of sixth graders, Sax explained his theory that girls' hearing ability is much better than boys', as is girls' sense of smell. The girls, just on the edge of puberty, sat utterly rapt, seeming to want to understand why their brothers, boy cousins, cute skater-dude neighbors and fathers were so weird. A few weeks after the lecture, Sax sent me a packet of color photocopies of thank-you notes he had received from the girls. One, from a girl with two fathers, read: "Dr. Sax, Thank you so much for coming to Burkes. . . . I had a smell in my room and my Dads couldn't smell it but I could. I thought I was going crazy. It ends up there was a dead rat in the wall. Hope you come back soon."

Sax comes off as a true believer and describes his conversion experience like this: In 2000, one of his patients, a twelve-year-old boy, came to his medical office. For several years before then, the boy had been withdrawn, uninspired and on multiple medications, but he had recently made a big turnaround, which his parents credited to having enrolled him in an all-boys school. Upon hearing this, Sax said to the boy's mother, "With all due respect, I regard single-sex education as an antiquated relic of the Victorian Era." To which he says she replied, "With all due respect, Dr. Sax, you have no idea what you're talking about." After visiting a handful of single-sex schools, Sax threw himself into studying neurological differences between males and females, eventually focusing on how to protect boys from a syndrome he calls "failure to launch," which Sax often characterizes as caring more about getting a Kilimanjaro in Halo 3 than performing well in high school or taking a girl on a date. Among his early proposals was that boys should start kindergarten at age six, a year later than girls, in order to ease the "sense of scholastic incompetence" that so many boys feel early on because they tend to develop later. Several friends quickly convinced Sax that American families would never go for this. So Sax started thinking it might be better for boys and girls to be in different classrooms.

Sax's official foray into single-sex public-school advocacy started in early 2002, when, he says, he applied for "a 501(c)(3) with the pretentious and improbable name of the National Association for Single-Sex Public Education." In its first few years, NASSPE didn't see much action. Then, in 2004, he was invited to give a seminar in Foley. His appearance there led to a workshop in Wilcox County, Alabama, and over the next few years, Sax says, "things started to mushroom." Sax estimates that, at present, 300 of the 360 single-sex public school programs in the country "are coming at this from a neuroscience basis." Either he or one of NASSPE's board members has been in touch with about half the programs.

David Chadwell, one of Sax's disciples and the coordinator of Single-Gender Initiatives at the South Carolina Department of Education, explained to me the ways that teachers should teach to gender differences. For boys, he said: "You need to get them up and moving. That's based on the nervous system, that's based on eyes, that's based upon volume and the use of volume with the boys." Chadwell, like Sax, says that differences in eyesight, hearing and the nervous system all should influence how you instruct boys. "You need to engage boys' energy, use it, rather than trying to say, No, no, no. So instead of having boys raise their hands, you're going to have boys literally stand up. You're going to do physical representation of number lines. Relay races. Ball tosses during discussion." For the girls, Chadwell prescribes a focus on "the connections girls have (a) with the content, (b) with each other and (c) with the teacher. If you try to stop girls from talking to one another, that's not successful. So you do a lot of meeting in circles, where every girl can share something from her own life that relates to the content in class."

While Sax rejects the notion that he is a gender essentialist — according to Sax's own definition, "a gender essentialist is a derogatory term that arose in the 1970s to define someone who is an idiot, or a Republican, or both, who does not understand that gender is socially constructed" — he does say that "human nature is gendered to the core" and that "all that happens when you take a toy gun away from your son and give him a doll instead is that you tell him, 'I don't like the person that you are and I wish you were more like your sister, Emily.'" He opens *Why Gender Matters* with two cautionary tales: one about a boy who starts kindergarten at age five, is given a diagnosis of ADHD and depression and ends up on a three-drug

15

cocktail of Adderall, Wellbutrin and clonidine; the other about a girl who transforms "from chubby wallflower to outgoing socialite" in middle school, seems to have it all — friends, academic success — and then shocks her parents by overdosing on Vicodin and Xanax. The two anecdotes are capsule versions of the boys' and girls' crises, and depending on one's point of view, Sax effectively either addresses or exploits these parental concerns. After presenting the Adderall-doped grammar-school boy and the suicidal middle-school girl, Sax offers a possible cause of these sad stories. "The neglect of gender in education and child-rearing has done real harm." These tragedies "might have been averted if the parents had known enough about gender differences to recognize what was really happening in their child's life."

Among the differences Sax notes between boys and girls: Baby boys prefer to stare at mobiles; baby girls at faces. Boys solve maze puzzles using the hippocampus; girls use the cerebral cortex. Boys covet risk; girls shy away. Boys perform better under moderate stress; girls perform worse. Many academics and progressives tend to find Sax's views stereotyped and infuriating, yet Sax does not seem to mind. Sax told me that in 2005, he delivered a lecture at a conference at the University of Alaska in Fairbanks. When the next speaker, Michael Younger, of Cambridge University, took the lectern, Sax says Younger threw down his speech and said, "I'm going to depart from my prepared remarks because I'm so annoyed by the sexist rubbish I just heard from Dr. Sax. Dr. Sax is trying to tell us that boys draw action and girls draw stasis. He might as well have said: 'Boys are active, girls are passive. Boys should go out and have jobs, girls should stay home and have babies.'" While Sax, a gadfly, enjoys telling this story, Younger calls it "a fiction," though he does concede "that certain aspects of Sax's work suggest an essentialism about boys and girls which is not borne out by reality as exposed in our own research."

A deluge of data has emerged in recent years detailing how boys and girls have different developmental trajectories and different brains. Sax has made a role for himself popularizing this work, though it's not yet clear what the research means or whether there are implications for single-sex education. For instance, among neuroscientists, motor skills are often used as proxies for assessing cognitive skills and social and emotional control in younger children. As Martha Denckla, director of the Developmental Cognitive Neurology Clinic at Kennedy Krieger Institute in Maryland, explained to me: "Looking at normal motor development in boys and girls — the ability to balance, to hop, to use your feet, to use your fingers and your hands — as a group, five-year-old girls look almost completely the same as six-year-old boys. The same is also true for anything having to do with speed of output: for example, how quickly you answer a question. Maybe you know the answer, but you just can't prepare your mouth to form the words." The gender gap in motor development shrinks through grammar and middle schools, Denckla says, disappearing once everyone has gone through puberty, around age fifteen. Yet Denckla doesn't see any need for single-sex public education; she thinks mixed-grade K–1, 1–2 and 2–3 classrooms are a better way to deal with the developmental differences among school-age kids.

Scans of boys' and girls' brains over time also show they develop differently. Analyzing data from the largest pediatric neuro-imaging study to date — 829 scans from 387 subjects ages 3 to 27 — researchers from the National Institute of Mental Health (NIMH) found that total cerebral volume peaks at 10.5 years in girls, four years earlier than in boys. Cortical and subcortical gray-matter trajectories peak one to two years earlier in girls as well. This may sound very significant, but researchers claim it means nothing for educators, or at least nothing yet. "Differences in brain size between males and females should not be interpreted as implying any sort of functional advantage or disadvantage," the NIMH paper concludes. Not one to be deterred, Sax invited Jay Giedd, chief of brain imaging at the Child Psychiatry Branch at NIMH, to give the keynote address at his NASSPE conference in 2007. Giedd spoke for ninety minutes, but made no comments on schooling at all.

One reason for this, Giedd says, is that when it comes to education, gender is a pretty crude tool for sorting minds. Giedd puts the research on brain differences in perspective by using the analogy of height. "On both the brain imaging and the psychological testing, the biggest differences we see between boys and girls are about one standard deviation. Height differences between boys and girls are two standard deviations." Giedd suggests a thought experiment: Imagine trying to assign a population of students to the boys' and girls' locker rooms based solely on height. As boys tend to be taller than girls, one would assign the tallest 50 percent of the students to the boys' locker room and the shortest 50 percent of the students to the girls' locker room. What would happen? While you'd end up with a better-than-random sort, the results would be abysmal, with unacceptably large percentages of students in the wrong place. Giedd suggests the same is true when educators use gender alone to assign educational experiences for kids. Yes, you'll get more students who favor cooperative learning in the girls' room, and more students who enjoy competitive learning in the boys', but you won't do very well. Says Giedd, "There are just too many exceptions to the rule."

Despite a lack of empirical evidence, a cottage industry has emerged working the "boys and girls are essentially different, so we should educate them differently" angle. Several advocates like Sax have been quite successful commercially, including Michael Gurian, a family therapist, who published the best-selling *The Wonder of Boys* in 1996, a work he has since followed up with fifteen more, including *Boys and Girls Learn Differently!* Through the Gurian Institute, he provides training to teachers, "showing the PET scans, showing the Spect scans" (a Spect scan is a nuclear imaging test that shows how blood flows through tissue), "teaching how the male

20

and female brain are different," Gurian told me. Like Sax, Gurian speaks authoritatively, yet both have been criticized for cherry-picking studies to serve their views. For instance, Sax initially built his argument that girls hear better than boys on two papers published in 1959 and 1963 by a psychologist named John Corso. Mark Liberman, a linguistics professor at the University of Pennsylvania, has spent a fair amount of energy examining the original research behind Sax's claims. In Corso's 1959 study, for example, Corso didn't look at children; he looked at adults. And he found only between one-quarter and one-half of a standard deviation in male and female hearing thresholds. What this means, Liberman says, is that if you choose a man and a woman at random, the chances are about 6 in 10 that the woman's hearing will be more sensitive and about 4 in 10 that the man's hearing will be more sensitive. Sax uses several other hearing studies to make his case that a teacher who is audible to boys will sound too loud to girls. But Liberman says that if you really look at this research, it shows that girls' and boys' hearing is much more similar than different. What's more, the sample sizes in those studies are far too small to make meaningful conclusions about gender differences in the classroom. The "disproportion between the reported facts and Sax's interpretation is spectacular," Liberman wrote on his blog, Language Log. "Dr. Sax isn't summarizing scientific research; he's making a political argument," he wrote in an e-mail message. "The political conclusion comes first, and the scientific evidence — often unrepresentative or misrepresented — is selected to support it."

One of Sax's core arguments is that trying to teach a 5-year-old boy to read is as developmentally fraught as trying to teach a 3 1/2-year-old girl and that such an exercise often leads to a kid hating school. This argument resonates with many teachers and parents, who long for the days when kindergarten meant learning how to stand in line for recess, not needing to complete phonics homework. Yet public schools are beholden to state standards, and those standards require kindergartners to learn to read. As a result, even leaders of single-sex public schools, like Jabali Sawicki, the principal of the all-boys Excellence Charter School in the Bedford-Stuyvesant neighborhood of Brooklyn, are using some of what Sax has to offer while quietly refuting other claims.

Sawicki is thirty, lanky and mocha-skinned, with an infectious energy. He grew up in a tough part of San Francisco with a single mother who managed to get her son a scholarship for middle school at a private all-boys school. From there he went to a private high school and then on to Oberlin College. The Excellence School is part of Uncommon Schools, a small network of charter schools. Housed in a gracious building on a modest street, Excellence currently teaches children in kindergarten through grade 4, and will add a grade each year for the next four years, up to grade 8. Sawicki's office occupies an empty classroom slated to be overtaken by students as the school grows. There, he told me that educating lower-class black boys is "the new civil rights movement." He then walked me down the hall to one of his kindergarten classrooms, where a sign on the door read "Fordham, Class of 2024."

"Jacob," said Sawicki, folding himself into a tiny chair and pointing to a line in a workbook, "will you read that for our guest?"

Jacob, who is five, straightened his tiny tie under his green cardigan and   25
used his index finger to track his place on the page. "A rat and a rabbit went down the slide."

"Thank you," said Sawicki. "And can you tell our guest what you like about the Excellence School?"

"I like that I get to wear a sweater with buttons," he said, glancing down at his uniform. "And I like that I'm going to college."

While there's some dispute over whether there's an ongoing education crisis for white, middle-class boys, there's no doubt that public schools are failing poor minority students in general and poor minority boys in particular. Despite six years of No Child Left Behind, the achievement gaps between rich and poor students and white and black students have not significantly narrowed. "People are getting desperate" is how Benjamin Wright, chief administrative officer for the Nashville public schools, described the current interest in single-sex education to me. "Coed's not working. Time to try something else."

Wright was one of the first principals in the country to address the racial and socioeconomic achievement gaps by separating boys from girls. In 1999, he was sent to the failing Thurgood Marshall Elementary School, in Seattle, to try to turn the place around. One of the first things he noticed was that three boys were getting suspended for every girl, "and for the most ridiculous things in the world — a boy would burp, or he'd pass gas, or a girl would say, 'He hit me.'" Nationwide, boys are nearly twice as likely as girls to be suspended, and more likely to drop out of high school than girls (65 percent of boys complete high school in four years; 72 percent of girls do). Boys make up two-thirds of special-education students. They are 1.5 times more likely to be held back a grade and 2.5 times more likely to be given diagnoses of ADHD. So Wright met with his fourth-grade teachers and recalls telling them, "OK, here's what we're going to do: how about *you* take all the boys and *you* take all the girls?" Wright says that in 2001, after Marshall's first year in a single-sex format, the percentage of boys meeting the state's academic standards rose from 10 percent to 35 percent in math and 10 percent to 53 percent in reading and writing.

Wright attributes this both to the insights of "brain researchers" like Sax   30
and to what he calls "the character piece" — giving children a positive sense of themselves as students — which he says is easier to address in a single-sex setting. "*Nobody cares about me, nobody really wants me* — an African American or a Latino boy will tell you that in a hurry," Wright told me when we spoke in January. "Or a Vietnamese or a Cambodian boy, if you're in the right neighborhood. *Don't nobody care.* Teachers need to understand when it's time to stop teaching the content and start teaching the context."

Not all schools see great results from switching to a single-sex format. After transforming the Thurgood Marshall School in Seattle, Wright moved to Philadelphia to work on the district's single-sex programs, and the results were rather modest, a fact Wright attributes to working both with middle- and high-school students and with less-engaged teachers. Other districts have started single-gender programs only to shut them down, as major logistical headaches outweighed the small academic gains. Lori Clark, principal at Jefferson Leadership Academies in Long Beach, California, which in 1999 became the first public middle school in the country to convert to a single-gender format, is in the process of reverting her school to coed. "We just didn't get the bang for the buck we'd been hoping for with our test scores," Clark told me. "Our master schedule is like one of those old Rubik's cubes. It's hard enough to make sure each kid gets *this* level English class and *that* level math class — and then we need to account for if that student is a boy or a girl? We just couldn't have our hands tied like that."

When Sawicki first took the job at Excellence, he attended conferences given by Sax and others on single-sex education, and at all of them he'd stand up and say: "Tell me what is it that I should do? What's the magic dust that I should sprinkle?" Now, four years into the job, he's following Wright's lead, trying to take the best of all models. At Excellence, in a third-grade room, the teacher Roberto de Leon roused his students into calling out the two-dimensional sides of three-dimensional shapes while throwing around a big purple eyeball. But the Excellence school couples their games with serious discipline. By 7:30 each morning, 220 boys walk through the school's heavy double doors, each dressed, in the terminology of the school, as a professional scholar: in black sneakers, dress pants, a white shirt, a green cardigan, a belt and a tie. If a child arrives at 7:31 a.m., his parents will receive a call at 5:45 the next morning to make sure that boy will be at school on time. Excellence is a charter school — meaning the school is publicly financed but has been freed from some of the rules that apply to other public schools, in exchange for promising to produce certain results. Its halls are silent from 7:50 to 10:30 a.m. each day. "The school's sacred time," Sawicki explains. "Right now we have 220 boys who are reading. Just a few blocks that way" — he pointed toward Crown Heights, a nearby section of Brooklyn — "you've got 220 boys who are doing something that's not going to get them to college."

After meeting Jacob, Sawicki walked me over to a room labeled "University of North Carolina, 2024," where the kindergarten teacher Trisha Bailey was sitting with nine boys in a reading circle. Part of Excellence's strategy is to keep boys too busy to fall out of line. "Friends, who's sitting tallest?" Bailey said in her brightest voice. "Who has a smile on his face? Whose feet are flat on the floor? OK, here we go." For the next two minutes, Bailey led the boys in a simple phonics exercise, sounding out together *cat, kitten, kiss*. Then she said, as animated as the host of *Blues Clues*: "Good job for you! Good job for me! Good job everybody! OK, next."

Under Bailey's guidance, the boys did two more pages of phonics, and then she jumped to her feet and announced: "Stand up if you need to get your sillies out! Put your hands on your belly. Ha . . . ha, ha . . . ha, ha, ha. Now get ready for a blastoff with me!" Bailey counted down from ten to one, crouched down into a squat alongside the boys and then exploded into the air. Then she promptly took her seat. "Sit up tall, fold your hands, three-two-one, here we go." Bailey held up a page and put her index finger on a red dot. "Boys, let's read together now. *This . . . is . . . my . . . kitten.*"

The Young Women's Leadership School in Harlem is widely considered   35
the birthplace of the current single-sex public school movement. This position of eminence stems from both its early beginnings and its success: since opening in 1996, every girl in every senior class at TYWLS has graduated and been accepted at a four-year college.

TYWLS occupies the top five floors of a commercial building in Harlem, on 106th Street near Lexington Avenue. Most of the girls come from the neighborhood, where they walk home so quickly that they often breeze by their own mothers before registering whom they've passed. One afternoon in January, Dalibell Ferreira, a senior, sat drinking a soda in the college counselor's office, where she sometimes stays until 8:00 p.m. because she finds her own home distracting. Ferreira is tall, poised, with wide-set eyes and her hair neatly pulled back around her fine Dominican face. When she graduates, she wants "to go to Wesleyan and study abroad, then travel, and then work for Unicef." When she entered TYWLS in the seventh grade, she mostly liked that the linoleum floor was so clean she could see her own face reflected on it. Then she started appreciating that people wouldn't snicker, "Oh, she thinks she's so smart" when she raised her hand in class. Then one day last spring, on the way home from a friend's house, Ferreira ran into a classmate from elementary school who was pushing a stroller and also pregnant. "I know that girl is smart, very smart, but now she just hangs around the block," Ferreira told me. "I want to be bigger in life. Maybe that girl had dreams, too, but you can just see: the lights have gone out in her face."

TYWLS was founded by Ann Rubenstein Tisch, wife of Andrew Tisch, the co-chairman of the Loews Corporation. Ferreira's is exactly the story Tisch, a former correspondent for NBC Network News, hoped her students would someday tell. Tisch first got the idea for a public all-girls school while on assignment in Milwaukee in the late 1980s. She was interviewing a fifteen-year-old at a public high school that had just opened a nursery so teenage moms could come back and finish their degrees. "Where do you see yourself in five years?" Tisch asked the young mother. The mother started to cry. "I said to myself: 'She's stuck, she knows she's stuck. And she's impacting three generations: her mother, her child and herself.' We need to get these kids on a completely different path, a path that wealthy girls and parochial-school girls and yeshiva girls are offered. Don't you think that might make a difference?"

Tisch is fifty-three years old, with reddish hair and a strong, warm face. One of the first things she did when she got serious about trying to start an all-girls public school was to hire a lawyer, George Shebitz, to explore the legality of a single-sex school. Tisch started visiting elite Manhattan all-girls private schools like Brearley and Spence, and once she had a vision of girls in blue-and-white uniforms sitting in circles around tables instead of at rows of desks, Tisch met with Evelyn Castro, who was then the superintendent of New York City's District 4, the district that encompasses part of East Harlem and one known for its innovation. She then spoke to Rosemary Salomone, the legal scholar at St. John's. Salomone knew of a 1994 report by the New York City Department of Education showing a gender gap in math and science scores, which was particularly notable among African American and Hispanic females. Salomone knew that Title IX prohibits schools that receive federal funds from discriminating on the basis of sex, but she explained to Tisch that this gender gap could work to her advantage.

As the Supreme Court would rule in June 1996, just three months before TYWLS opened, the legality of single-sex schools depends on context. In *United States v. Virginia,* a case regarding females' exclusion from the all-male Virginia Military Institute (VMI), the justices found that the male bastion was in fact violating the equal-protection clause of the Fourteenth Amendment, and that the state of Virginia's proposal to open an all-girls school wasn't a sufficient remedy because VMI gave its students not just a good education but powerful connections within Virginia's military and political elite. Justice Ruth Bader Ginsburg, who earlier in her career had been a founder of the ACLU Women's Rights Project (a group that has been active in suing single-sex public schools), wrote the majority opinion, composing what some people consider a condensation of feminist thinking up to 1996. Ginsburg's opinion states that in some contexts, single-sex schools might be legal, as long as those schools worked to "dissipate, rather than perpetuate, traditional gender classifications." "The two sexes are not fungible," Ginsburg wrote, quoting a 1946 decision; the physical differences between the sexes are "enduring" and "cause for celebration." Yet, Ginsburg warned, those differences cannot be used to place "artificial constraints on individuals' opportunity."

News of an all-girls school opening in Harlem hit the press in July 1996   40
and started a firestorm of arguments about whether single-sex public education was illegal, regressive, antifeminist and a nonanswer to the problem of how to educate both boys and girls well in school. As Salomone recalls, TYWLS "divided the feminist community right down the middle." Later that year at Fordham Law School, Salomone debated the merits of single-sex public education against Anne Conners, then the president of NOW-NYC. According to Salomone, Conners evoked *Brown v. Board of Education.* Salomone countered that race is substantially different from gender, and, more important, that a child would end up at TYWLS, or another single-sex school, only by parental choice. After the debate, Salomone says she asked Conners if she had lost members over the issue and that Conners suggested that she had. Salomone told her, "Well, you lost me."

Thanks to Tisch and the money she raises, TYWLS enjoys some significant advantages over an ordinary urban public school, most notably a health-and-wellness curriculum and a superheroic college counselor, Chris Farmer, who starts taking the girls on field trips to Columbia University in seventh grade and who once drove a student's entire Ghanaian family, Islamic music blaring, from Harlem to Hobart and William Smith Colleges in upstate New York so the father would feel comfortable enough to let his daughter attend. Tisch's connections also make for priceless opportunities: Bill Clinton and Katie Couric, among other megawatt notables, have visited the school. But it was inside Emily Wylie's AP English class where the real social value of single-sex teaching was on display. Ferreira, among twenty other seniors, sat in a circle discussing *Pride and Prejudice*. Wylie asked the girls to call out which characters had which vices and virtues. A serious discussion of whether lust — Lydia's lust — was a vice or a virtue ensued.

"She's following her passions!"

"At least she's not sleeping with folks for money."

Wylie regretted to inform her girls that lust is one of the seven deadly sins, which prompted the thoroughly modern question: "But how is lust bad?"

Wylie says she believes she is a better teacher, and her students are better students, because they're in a desexualized — or at least less-sexualized — environment. "Sure," she says, "when they take pictures, they often present their backsides first. But I think I'm giving girls a better education than I could have if there were guys in the room. I'm freer. I'm more able to be bold in my statements. When I teach poetry and I talk about the sex in poetry I don't need to be worried about the boy in the room who is going to chuckle over the thing he did with the girl last week and embarrass her. Which happened more than once in my last coed environment." 45

Nearly everyone at TYWLS acknowledges that often parents' most pressing concern when enrolling their eleven-year-old daughters is sheltering those girls from sexualized classrooms and sexualized streets. "Harlem's a very intense environment," says Drew Higginbotham, TYWLS's assistant principal, who lives in the neighborhood. "You're constantly needing to prove yourself physically, to prove yourself sexually. Parents, when they come to our school, they sort of exhale deeply. You can hear them thinking to themselves, I can see my daughter here and she's going to be OK for six hours a day." Sax is not above or beyond this kind of thinking, either. In fact, after a nearly two-hour conversation filled with scientific jargon and brains, he told me, perhaps wishfully, that really the most important reason to send a child to a single-sex high school was that those kids still go on dates. "Boys at boys' schools like Old Farms in Connecticut, or Saint Albans in Washington, D.C., will call up girls at Miss Porter's in Connecticut, at Stone Ridge in Maryland, and they will ask the girl out, and the boy will drive to the girl's house to pick her up and meet her parents. You tell kids at a coed school to do this, and they'll fall on the floor laughing. But the culture of dating is much healthier than the culture of the hookup, in which the primary form of sexual intimacy is a girl on her knees servicing a boy."

In the past few years Tisch's Young Women's Leadership Foundation has opened schools in the Bronx and Queens, as well as helping start ones in Chicago, Philadelphia, Dallas and Austin. Tisch wants to be careful about not overextending her network — "we don't want to become Mrs. Fields or Benetton" — but she says she also feels an obligation from her success. Last year, 2,100 students applied for the three open ninth-grade spots in the Harlem school. Many other schools make inquiries about how they might replicate TWYLS's success. This coming year, for the first time, Tisch plans on holding her own conference on single-sex public education. Though she's meticulously circumspect about not disparaging Sax, her actions suggest that she is aware that if she doesn't engage with the many districts interested in starting up single-sex programs, there's a chance that Sax will run away with the movement.

Education scholarship has contributed surprisingly little to the debate over single-sex public education. In 2005, the United States Department of Education, along with the American Institute for Research, tried to weigh in, publishing a meta-analysis comparing single-sex and coed schooling. The authors started out with 2,221 citations on the subject that they then whittled down to 40 usable studies. Yet even those forty studies did not yield strong results: 41 percent favored single-sex schools, 45 percent found no positive or negative effects for either single-sex or coed schools, 6 percent were mixed (meaning they found positive results for one gender but not the other) and 8 percent favored coed schools. This meta-analysis is part of a larger project by the Department of Education being led by Cornelius Riordan, a Providence College professor. He explained to me that such muddled findings are the norm for education research on school effects. School-effects studies try to answer questions like whether large schools are better than small schools or whether charter schools are better than public schools. The effects are always small. So many variables are at play in a school: quality of teachers, quality of the principal, quality of the infrastructure, involvement of families, financing, curriculum — the list is nearly endless. Riordan says, "You're never going to be able to compare two types of schools and say, 'The data very strongly suggests that schools that look like *a* are better than schools that look like *b*.'"

That certainly appears to be the case for single-sex schools. The data do not suggest that they're clearly better for all kids. Nor do they suggest that they're worse. The most concrete findings from the research on single-sex schools come from studies of Catholic schools, which have a long history of single-sex education, and suggest that while single-sex schools may not have much of an impact on the educational achievement of white, middle-class boys, they do measurably benefit poor and minority students. According to Riordan, disadvantaged students at single-sex schools have higher scores on standardized math, reading, science and civics tests than their counterparts in coed schools. There are two prevailing theories to explain this: one is that single-sex schools are indeed better at providing kids with a positive sense of themselves as students, to compete with the antiacademic influences of youth culture; the other is that in order to end up in a single-sex classroom, you need to have a parent who has made what educators call "a pro-academic choice." You need a parent who at least cares enough to read the notices sent home and go through the process of making a choice — any choice.

As TYWLS let out on a Friday in January and the girls spilled onto 106th Street, one such parent, a man in saggy jeans and a black parka, walked up the sidewalk clutching his daughter's dog-eared report card and hoping to secure her a spot for next year. "This where the school at?" he asked a security guard. The engagement of parents like this may be a major part of the success of single-sex public education. These schools are popular with many parents, who are happy to have an option that has long been available in private and parochial schools. And they are also attractive to teachers and administrators, who are offered a relatively easy and inexpensive way to try to improve some of the intractable problems in public education, especially for disadvantaged students.

But schools, inevitably, present many curriculums, some overt and some subtle; and critics argue that with Sax's model comes a lesson that our gender differences are primary, and this message is at odds with one of the most foundational principles of America's public schools. Given the myriad ways in which our schools are failing, it may be hard to remember that public schools were intended not only to instruct children in reading and math but also to teach them commonality, tolerance and what it means to be American. "When you segregate, by any means, you lose some of that," says Richard Kahlenberg, a senior fellow at the Century Foundation. "Even if one could prove that sending a kid off to his or her own school based on religion or race or ethnicity or gender did a little bit better job of raising the academic skills for workers in the economy, there's also the issue of trying to create tolerant citizens in a democracy."

QUESTIONS

Reading

1. What does Weil mean by the term "gender wars" in her title? How and where does she define and clarify this term?
2. What is an *essentialist*? How does Dr. Sax respond to the charge that he is an essentialist? What attitude does Weil convey about his response?
3. What are the details of Sax's "conversion experience"?
4. In *reporting* on controversial educational ideas, what does Weil reveal about her own orientation and beliefs?

Exploratory Writing

1. On the *New York Times* Web site, read the letters from readers in response to Weil's article. Michael Myers, the executive director of the New York Civil Rights Coalition, writes, "All of this new science sounds

like the discredited scientific racism that for decades studied 'The Negro.'" Highlight, underline, or flag places in Weil's article where generalizations are made about "boys" versus "girls," and replace those words with racial terms (*boys* with *whites*, *girls* with *blacks*, for example). Do the generalizations become examples of racist thinking?

2. Schools set up based on Sax's beliefs assume that it is easy to define all students as either *boys* or *girls*. Weil does not mention the issues faced by transgender or intersex youth. Visit the Web site of Harvey Milk High (**http://www.hmi.org**), a school in New York City. Anyone between the ages of twelve and twenty-one is welcome to participate in the school's after-school programs, whether they identify as gay, straight, bisexual, lesbian, transgender, male, female, other, or questioning. In a double-entry list, compare and contrast the *assumptions* on the Web site with Sax's *assumptions*. Which of them are mutually exclusive?

DR. LEONARD SAX	HARVEY MILK HIGH/HETRICK-MARTIN INSTITUTE WEB SITE

Making Connections

1. Mike Rose (p. 567) writes, "Students will float to the mark you set" (paragraph 32). Vocational Ed. students neutralize the insult and frustration of how they've been stereotyped by pretending to fit the role that has been defined for them (paragraph 37). Weil reports on controversial science that asserts that *all* boys think and learn differently from *all* girls. Does categorizing students according to assumptions about them limit their excitement and inspiration, and become a self-fulfilling prophecy, as Rose suggests? Draw on any of the essays in this casebook for examples.

Essay Writing

1. Garret Keizer (p. 625) writes, "Public schools embody our democratic principles and contradictions better than any other institution we know" (paragraph 31). Choose three essays from this casebook, and discuss how the kind of school described or advocated in each essay reflects the values, ideas, and priorities of our society.

What High School Is

Theodore R. Sizer

Born in New Haven, Connecticut, in 1932, and educated at Yale and Harvard, Theodore R. Sizer has been headmaster at Phillips Academy in Andover, Massachusetts; dean of the Graduate School of Education at Harvard; and chair of the Education Department at Brown. He is the author of several influential books on educational reform and American secondary schools, including Horace's Hope: What Works for the American High School *(1996),* The Students Are Watching: Schools and the Moral Contract *(1999, with Nancy Faust Sizer),* The Red Pencil: Convictions from Experience in Education *(2004), and* Keeping School: Letters to Families from Principals of Two Small Schools *(2004). The following selection is a chapter from an earlier book,* Horace's Compromise: The Dilemma of the American High School *(1984), which reports the results of a study of American high schools sponsored by the National Association of Independent Schools.*

Mark, sixteen and a genial eleventh-grader, rides a bus to Franklin High School, arriving at 7:25. It is an Assembly Day, so the schedule is adapted to allow for a meeting of the entire school. He hangs out with his friends, first outside school and then inside, by his locker. He carries a pile of textbooks and notebooks; in all, it weighs eight and a half pounds.

From 7:30 to 8:19, with nineteen other students, he is in Room 304 for English class. The Shakespeare play being read this year by the eleventh grade is *Romeo and Juliet.* The teacher, Ms. Viola, has various students in turn take parts and read out loud. Periodically, she interrupts the (usually halting) recitations to ask whether the thread of the conversation in the play is clear. Mark is entertained by the stumbling readings of some of his classmates. He hopes he will not be asked to be Romeo, particularly if his current steady, Sally, is Juliet. There is a good deal of giggling in class, and much attention paid to who may be called on next. Ms. Viola reminds the class of a test on this part of the play to be given next week.

The bell rings at 8:19. Mark goes to the boys' room, where he sees a classmate who he thinks is a wimp but who constantly tries to be a buddy. Mark avoids the leech by rushing off. On the way, he notices two boys engaged in some sort of transaction, probably over marijuana. He pays them no attention. 8:24. Typing class. The rows of desks that embrace big office machines are almost filled before the bell. Mark is uncomfortable here: typing class is girl country. The teacher constantly threatens what to Mark is a humiliatingly female future: "Your employer won't like these erasures." The minutes during the period are spent copying a letter from a handbook onto business stationery. Mark struggles to keep from looking at his work; the teacher wants him to watch only the material from which he is copying. Mark is frustrated, uncomfortable, and scared that he will not complete his letter by the class's end, which would be embarrassing.

Nine-tenths of the students present at school that day are assembled in the auditorium by the 9:18 bell. The dilatory tenth still stumble in, running down aisles. Annoyed class deans try to get the mob settled. The curtains part; the program is a concert by a student rock group. Their electronic gear flashes under the lights, and the five boys and one girl in the group work hard at being casual. Their movements on stage are studiously at three-quarter time, and they chat with one another as though the tumultuous screaming of their schoolmates were totally inaudible. The girl balances on a stool; the boys crank up the music. It is very soft rock, the sanitized lyrics surely cleared with the assistant principal. The girl sings, holding the mike close to her mouth, but can scarcely be heard. Her light voice is tentative, and the lyrics indecipherable. The guitars, amplified, are tuneful, however, and the drums are played with energy.

The students around Mark — all juniors, since they are seated by class — alternately slouch in their upholstered, hinged seats, talking to one another, or sit forward, leaning on the chair backs in front of them, watching the band. A boy near Mark shouts noisily at the microphone-fondling singer, "Bite it . . . ohhh," and the area around Mark explodes in vulgar male laughter, but quickly subsides. A teacher walks down the aisle. Songs continue, to great applause. Assembly is over at 9:46, two minutes early.

5

9:53 and biology class. Mark was at a different high school last year and did not take this course there as a tenth-grader. He is in it now, and all but one of his classmates are a year younger than he. He sits on the side, not taking part in the chatter that goes on after the bell. At 9:57, the public address system goes on, with the announcements of the day. After a few words from the principal ("Here's today's cheers and jeers . . ." with a cheer for the winning basketball team and a jeer for the spectators who made a ruckus at the gymnasium), the task is taken over by officers of ASB (Associated Student Bodies). There is an appeal for "bat bunnies." Carnations are for sale by the Girls' League. Miss Indian American is coming. Students are auctioning off their services (background catcalls are heard) to earn money for the prom. Nominees are needed for the ballot for school bachelor and school bachelorette. The announcements end with a "thought for the day. When you throw a little mud, you lose a little ground."

At 10:04 the biology class finally turns to science. The teacher, Mr. Robbins, has placed one of several labeled laboratory specimens — some are pinned in frames, others swim in formaldehyde — on each of the classroom's eight laboratory tables. The three or so students whose chairs circle each of these benches are to study the specimen and make notes about it or drawings of it. After a few minutes each group of three will move to another table. The teacher points out that these specimens are of organisms already studied in previous classes. He says that the period-long test set for the following day will involve observing some of these specimens — then to be without labels — and writing an identifying paragraph on each. Mr. Robbins points out that some of the printed labels ascribe the specimens names different from those given in the textbook. He explains that biologists often give several names to the same organism.

The class now falls to peering, writing, and quiet talking. Mr. Robbins comes over to Mark, and in whispered words asks him to carry a requisition form for science department materials to the business office. Mark, because of his "older" status, is usually chosen by Robbins for this kind of errand. Robbins gives Mark the form and a green hall pass to show to any teacher who might challenge him, on his way to the office, for being out of a classroom. The errand takes Mark four minutes. Meanwhile Mark's group is hard at work but gets to only three of the specimens before the bell rings at 10:42. As the students surge out, Robbins shouts a reminder about a "double" laboratory period on Thursday.

Between classes one of the seniors asks Mark whether he plans to be a candidate for schoolwide office next year. Mark says no. He starts to explain. The 10:47 bell rings, meaning that he is late for French class.

There are fifteen students in Monsieur Bates's language class. He hands out tests taken the day before: "*C'est bien fait, Etienne . . . c'est mieux, Marie . . . Tch, tch, Robert . . .*" Mark notes his C+ and peeks at the A– in front of Susanna, next to him. The class has been assigned seats by M. Bates; Mark resents sitting next to prissy, brainy Susanna. Bates starts by asking a student to read a question and give the correct answer. "*James, question un.*" James haltingly reads the question and gives the answer that Bates, now speaking English, says is incomplete. In due course: "*Mark, question cinq.*" Mark does his bit, and the sequence goes on, the eight quiz questions and answers filling about twenty minutes of time.

"Turn to page forty-nine. *Maintenant, lisez après moi . . .*" and Bates reads a sentence and has the class echo it. Mark is embarrassed by this and mumbles with a barely audible sound. Others, like Susanna, keep the decibel count up, so Mark can hide. This I-say-you-repeat drill is interrupted once by the public address system, with an announcement about a meeting for the cheerleaders. Bates finishes the class, almost precisely at the bell, with a homework assignment. The students are to review these sentences for a brief quiz the following day. Mark takes note of the assignment, because he knows that tomorrow will be a day of busy-work in French class. Much though he dislikes oral drills, they are better than the workbook stuff that Bates hands out. Write, write, write, for Bates to throw away, Mark thinks.

10

11:36. Down to the cafeteria, talking noisily, hanging, munching. Getting to room 104 by 12:17: U.S. history. The teacher is sitting cross-legged on his desk when Mark comes in, heatedly arguing with three students over the fracas that had followed the previous night's basketball game. The teacher, Mr. Suslovic, while agreeing that the spectators from their school certainly were provoked, argues that they should neither have been so obviously obscene in yelling at the opposing cheerleaders nor have allowed Coke cans to be rolled out on the floor. The three students keep saying that "it isn't fair." Apparently they and some others had been assigned "Saturday mornings" (detentions) by the principal for the ruckus.

At 12:34, the argument appears to subside. The uninvolved students, including Mark, are in their seats, chatting amiably. Mr. Suslovic climbs off his desk and starts talking: "We've almost finished this unit, chapters nine and ten . . ." The students stop chattering among themselves and turn toward Suslovic. Several slouch down in their chairs. Some open notebooks. Most have the five-pound textbook on their desks.

Suslovic lectures on the cattle drives, from north Texas to railroads west of St. Louis. He breaks up this narrative with questions ("Why were the railroad lines laid largely east to west?"), directed at nobody in particular and eventually answered by Suslovic himself. Some students take notes. Mark doesn't. A student walks in the open door, hands Mr. Suslovic a list, and starts whispering with him. Suslovic turns from the class and hears out this messenger. He then asks, "Does anyone know where Maggie Sharp is?" Someone answers, "Sick at home"; someone else says, "I thought I saw her at lunch." Genial consternation. Finally Suslovic tells the messenger, "Sorry, we can't help you," and returns to the class: "Now, where were we?" He goes on for some minutes. The bell rings. Suslovic forgets to give the homework assignment.

1:11 and Algebra II. There is a commotion in the hallway: someone's locker is rumored to have been opened by the assistant principal and a narcotics agent. In the five-minute passing time, Mark hears the story three times and three ways. A locker had been broken into by another student. It was Mr. Gregory and a narc. It was the cops, and they did it without Gregory's knowing. Mrs. Ames, the mathematics teacher, has not heard anything about it. Several of the nineteen students try to tell her and start arguing among themselves. "OK, that's enough." She hands out the day's problem, one sheet to each student. Mark sees with dismay that it is a single, complicated "word" problem about some train that, while traveling at 84 mph, due west, passes a car that was going due east at 55 mph. Mark struggles: Is it $d = rt$ or $t = rd$? The class becomes quiet, writing, while Mrs. Ames writes some additional, short problems on the blackboard. "Time's up." A sigh; most students still writing. A muffled "Shit." Mrs. Ames frowns. "Come on, now." She collects papers, but it takes four minutes for her to corral them all.

15

"Copy down the problems from the board." A minute passes. "William, try number one." William suggests an approach. Mrs. Ames corrects and cajoles, and William finally gets it right. Mark watches two kids to his right passing notes; he tries to read them, but the handwriting is illegible from his distance. He hopes he is not called on, and he isn't. Only three students are asked to puzzle out an answer. The bell rings at 2:00. Mrs. Ames shouts a homework assignment over the resulting hubbub.

Mark leaves his books in his locker. He remembers that he has homework, but figures that he can do it during English class the next day. He knows that there will be an in-class presentation of one of the *Romeo and Juliet* scenes and that he will not be in it. The teacher will not notice his homework writing, or won't do anything about it if she does.

Mark passes various friends heading toward the gym, members of the basketball teams. Like most students, Mark isn't an active school athlete. However, he is associated with the yearbook staff. Although he is not taking "Yearbook" for credit as an English course, he is contributing photographs. Mark takes twenty minutes checking into the yearbook staff's headquarters (the classroom of its faculty adviser) and getting some assignments of pictures from his boss, the senior who is the photography editor. Mark knows that if he pleases his boss and the faculty adviser, he'll take that editor's post for the next year. He'll get English credit for his work then.

After gossiping a bit with the yearbook staff, Mark will leave school by 2:35 and go home. His grocery market bagger's job is from 4:45 to 8:00, the rush hour for the store. He'll have a snack at 4:30, and his mother will save him some supper to eat at 8:30. She will ask whether he has any homework, and he'll tell her no. Tomorrow, and virtually every other tomorrow, will be the same for Mark, save for the lack of the assembly: each period then will be five minutes longer.

Most Americans have an uncomplicated vision of what secondary education should be. Their conception of high school is remarkably uniform across the country, a striking fact, given the size and diversity of the United States and the politically decentralized character of the schools. This uniformity is of several generations' standing. It has, however, two appearances, each quite different from the other, one of words and the other of practice, a world of political rhetoric and Mark's world. 20

A California high school's general goals, set out in 1979, could serve equally well most of America's high schools, public and private. This school had as its ends:

- Fundamental scholastic achievement . . . to acquire knowledge and share in the traditionally academic fundamentals . . . to develop the ability to make decisions, to solve problems, to reason independently, and to accept responsibility for self-evaluation and continuing self-improvement.

- Career and economic competence . . .
- Citizenship and civil responsibility . . .
- Competence in human and social relations . . .
- Moral and ethical values . . .
- Self-realization and mental and physical health . . .
- Aesthetic awareness . . .
- Cultural diversity . . .[1]

In addition to its optimistic rhetoric, what distinguishes this list is its comprehensiveness. The high school is to touch most aspects of an adolescent's existence — mind, body, morals, values, career. No one of these areas is given especial prominence. School people arrogate to themselves an obligation to all.

An example of the wide acceptability of these goals is found in the courts. Forced to present a detailed definition of "thorough and efficient education," elementary as well as secondary, a West Virginia judge sampled the best of conventional wisdom and concluded that

> there are eight general elements of a thorough and efficient system of education: (a) Literacy, (b) The ability to add, subtract, multiply, and divide numbers, (c) Knowledge of government to the extent the child will be equipped as a citizen to make informed choices among persons and issues that affect his own governance, (d) Self-knowledge and knowledge of his or her total environment to allow the child to intelligently choose life work — to know his or her options, (e) Work-training and advanced academic training as the child may intelligently choose, (f) Recreational pursuits, (g) Interests in all creative arts such as music, theater, literature, and the visual arts, and (h) Social ethics, both behavioral and abstract, to facilitate compatibility with others in this society.[2]

That these eight — now powerfully part of the debate over the purpose and practice of education in West Virginia — are reminiscent of the influential list, "The Seven Cardinal Principles of Secondary Education," promulgated in

---

[1]Shasta High School, Redding, California. An eloquent and analogous statement, "The Essentials of Education," one stressing explicitly the "interdependence of skills and content" that is implicit in the Shasta High School statement, was issued in 1980 by a coalition of educational associations, Organizations for the Essentials of Education (Urbana, Illinois).

[2]Judge Arthur M. Recht, in his order resulting from *Pauley v. Kelly*, 1979, as reprinted in *Education Week*, May 26, 1982, p. 10. See also, in *Education Week*, January 16, 1983, pp. 21, 24, Jonathan P. Sher, "The Struggle to Fulfill a Judicial Mandate: How Not to 'Reconstruct' Education in W. Va."

1918 by the National Education Association, is no surprise.[3] The rhetoric of high school purpose has been uniform and consistent for decades. Americans agree on the goals for their high schools.

That agreement is convenient, but it masks the fact that virtually all the words in these goal statements beg definition. Some schools have labored long to identify specific criteria beyond them; the result has been lists of daunting pseudospecificity and numbing earnestness. However, most leave the words undefined and let the momentum of traditional practice speak for itself. That is why analyzing how Mark spends his time is important: from watching him one uncovers the important purposes of education, the ones that shape practice. Mark's day is similar to that of other high school students across the country, as similar as the rhetoric of one goal statement to others'. Of course, there are variations, but the extent of consistency in the shape of school routine for a large and diverse adolescent population is extraordinary, indicating more graphically than any rhetoric the measure of agreement in America about what one does in high school, and, by implication, what it is for.

The basic organizing structures in schools are familiar. Above all, students are grouped by age (that is, freshman, sophomore, junior, senior), and all are expected to take precisely the same time — around 720 school days over four years, to be precise — to meet the requirements for a diploma. When one is out of his grade level, he can feel odd, as Mark did in his biology class. The goals are the same for all, and the means to achieve them are also similar.

Young males and females are treated remarkably alike; the schools' goals are the same for each gender. In execution, there are differences, as those pressing sex discrimination suits have made educators intensely aware. The students in metalworking classes are mostly male; those in home economics, mostly female. But it is revealing how much less sex discrimination there is in high schools than in other American institutions. For many young women, the most liberated hours of their week are in school.

School is to be like a job: you start in the morning and end in the afternoon, five days a week. You don't get much of a lunch hour, so you go home early, unless you are an athlete or are involved in some special school or extracurricular activity. School is conceived of as the children's workplace, and it takes young people off parents' hands and out of the labor market during prime-time work hours. Not surprisingly, many students see going to school as little more than a dogged necessity. They perceive the day-to-day routine, a Minnesota study reports, as one of "boredom and

25

---

[3]Bureau of Education, Department of the Interior, "Cardinal Principles of Secondary Education: A Report of the Commission on the Reorganization of Secondary Education, appointed by the National Education Association," *Bulletin*, no. 35 (Washington: U.S. Government Printing Office, 1918).

lethargy." One of the students summarizes: School is "boring, restless, tiresome, puts ya to sleep, tedious, monotonous, pain in the neck."[4]

The school schedule is a series of units of time: the clock is king. The base time block is about fifty minutes in length. Some schools, on what they call modular scheduling, split that fifty-minute block into two or even three pieces. Most schools have double periods for laboratory work, especially in the sciences, or four-hour units for the small numbers of students involved in intensive vocational or other work-study programs. The flow of all school activity arises from or is blocked by these time units. "How much time do I have with my kids" is the teacher's key question.

Because there are many claims for those fifty-minute blocks, there is little time set aside for rest between them, usually no more than three to ten minutes, depending on how big the school is and, consequently, how far students and teachers have to walk from class to class. As a result, there is a frenetic quality to the school day, a sense of sustained restlessness. For the adolescents, there are frequent changes of room and fellow students, each change giving tempting opportunities for distraction, which are stoutly resisted by teachers. Some schools play soft music during these "passing times," to quiet the multitude, one principal told me.

Many teachers have a chance for a coffee break. Few students do. In some city schools where security is a problem, students must be in class for seven consecutive periods, interrupted by a heavily monitored twenty-minute lunch period for small groups, starting as early as 10:30 a.m. and running to after 1:00 p.m. A high premium is placed on punctuality and on "being where you're supposed to be." Obviously, a low premium is placed on reflection and repose. The students rush from class to class to collect knowledge. Savoring it, it is implied, is not to be done much in school, nor is such meditation really much admired. The picture that these familiar patterns yield is that of an academic supermarket. The purpose of going to school is to pick things up, in an organized and predictable way, the faster the better.

What is supposed to be picked up is remarkably consistent among all   30
sorts of high schools. Most schools specifically mandate three out of every five courses a student selects. Nearly all of these mandates fall into five areas — English, social studies, mathematics, science, and physical education. On the average, English is required to be taken each year, social studies and physical education three out of the four high school years, and mathematics and science one or two years. Trends indicate that in the mid-eighties there is likely to be an increase in the time allocated to these last two subjects. Most

[4]Diane Hedin, Paula Simon, and Michael Robin, *Minnesota Youth Poll: Youth's Views on School and School Discipline*, Minnesota Report 184 (1983), Agricultural Experiment Station, University of Minnesota, p. 13.

students take classes in these four major academic areas beyond the minimum requirements, sometimes in such special areas as journalism and "yearbook," offshoots of English departments.[5]

Press most adults about what high school is for, and you hear these subjects listed. *High school? That's where you learn English and math and that sort of thing.* Ask students, and you get the same answer. High school is to "teach" these "subjects."

What is often absent is any definition of these subjects or any rationale for them. They are just there, labels. Under those labels lie a multitude of things. A great deal of material is supposed to be "covered"; most of these courses are surveys, great sweeps of the stuff of their parent disciplines.

While there is often a sequence *within* subjects — algebra before trigonometry, "first-year" French before "second-year" French — there is rarely a coherent relationship or sequence *across* subjects. Even the most logically related matters — reading ability as a precondition for the reading of history books, and certain mathematical concepts or skills before the study of some of physics — are only loosely coordinated, if at all. There is little demand for a synthesis of it all; English, mathematics, and the rest are discrete items, to be picked up individually. The incentive for picking them up is largely through tests and, with success at these, in credits earned.

Coverage within subjects is the key priority. If some imaginative teacher makes a proposal to force the marriage of, say, mathematics and physics or to require some culminating challenges to students to use several objects in the solution of a complex problem, and if this proposal will take "time" away from other things, opposition is usually phrased in terms of what may be thus forgone. If we do that, we'll have to give up colonial history. We won't be able to get to programming. We'll not be able to read *Death of a Salesman*. There isn't time. The protesters usually win out.

The subjects come at a student like Mark in random order, a kaleidoscope of worlds: algebraic formulae to poetry to French verbs to Ping-Pong to the War of the Spanish Succession, all before lunch. Pupils are to pick up these things. Tests measure whether the picking up has been successful. 35

The lack of connection between stated goals, such as those of the California high school cited earlier, and the goals inherent in school practice is obvious and, curiously, tolerated. Most striking is the gap between statements about "self-realization and mental and physical growth" or "moral and ethical values" — common rhetoric in school documents — and practice. Most physical education programs have neither the time nor the focus really to ensure fitness. Mental health is rarely defined. Neither are ethical values, save at the negative extremes, such as opposition to assault or

---

[5]I am indebted to Harold F. Sizer and Lyde E. Sizer for a survey of the diploma requirements of fifty representative secondary schools, completed for *A Study of High Schools*.

dishonesty. Nothing in the regimen of a day like Mark's signals direct or implicit teaching in this area. The "school boy code" (not ratting on a fellow student) protects the marijuana pusher, and a leechlike associate is shrugged off without concern. The issue of the locker search was pushed aside, as not appropriate for class time.

Most students, like Mark, go to class in groups of twenty to twenty-seven students. The expected attendance in some schools, particularly those in low-income areas, is usually higher, often thirty-five students per class, but high absentee rates push the actual numbers down. About twenty-five per class is an average figure for expected attendance, and the actual numbers are somewhat lower. There are remarkably few students who go to class in groups much larger or smaller than twenty-five.[6]

A student such as Mark sees five or six teachers per day; their differing styles and expectations are part of his kaleidoscope. High school staffs are highly specialized: guidance counselors rarely teach mathematics, mathematics teachers rarely teach English, principals rarely do any classroom instruction. Mark, then, is known a little bit by a number of people, each of whom sees him in one specialized situation. No one may know him as a "whole person" — unless he becomes a special problem or has special needs.

Save in extracurricular or coaching situations, such as in athletics, drama, or shop classes, there is little opportunity for sustained conversation between student and teacher. The mode is a one-sentence or two-sentence exchange: *Mark, when was Grover Cleveland president?* Let's see, was 1890 . . . or something . . . wasn't he the one . . . he was elected twice, wasn't he . . . *Yes . . . Gloria, can you get the dates right?* Dialogue is strikingly absent, and as a result the opportunity of teachers to challenge students' ideas in a systematic and logical way is limited. Given the rushed, full quality of the school day, it can seldom happen. One must infer that careful probing of students' thinking is not a high priority. How one gains (to quote the California school's statement of goals again) "the ability to make decisions, to solve problems, to reason independently, and to accept responsibility for self-evaluation and continuing self-improvement" without being challenged is difficult to imagine. One certainly doesn't learn these things merely from lectures and textbooks.

Most schools are nice places. Mark and his friends enjoy being in theirs.   40
The adults who work in schools generally like adolescents. The academic pressures are limited, and the accommodations to students are substantial. For example, if many members of an English class have jobs after school, the English teacher's expectations for them are adjusted, downward. In a word, school is sensitively accommodating, as long as students are punctual,

---

[6]Education Research Service, Inc., *Class Size: A Summary of Research* (Arlington, Virginia, 1978); and *Class Size Research: A Critique of Recent Meta-Analyses* (Arlington, Virginia, 1980).

where they are supposed to be, and minimally dutiful about picking things up from the clutch of courses in which they enroll.

This characterization is not pretty, but it is accurate, and it serves to describe the vast majority of American secondary schools. "Taking subjects" in a systematized, conveyer-belt way is what one does in high school. That this process is, in substantial respects, not related to the rhetorical purposes of education is tolerated by most people, perhaps because they do not really either believe in those ill-defined goals or, in their heart of hearts, believe that schools can or should even try to achieve them. The students are happy taking subjects. The parents are happy, because that's what they did in high school. The rituals, the most important of which is graduation, remain intact. The adolescents are supervised safely and constructively most of the time, during the morning and afternoon hours, and they are off the labor market. That is what high school is all about.

QUESTIONS

Reading

1. What does Sizer conclude that high school is "about"? What evidence does he use to support this conclusion?
2. What methods do you think Sizer used in this *explanatory* essay? How and where did he find his information?
3. How is the explanatory section of the essay (paragraphs 20–41) organized? The first subtopic discussed is the goals of high school. What are the other subtopics?
4. How does Sizer describe the vision that most Americans have of what a high school should be?

Exploratory Writing

1. In small groups, design an ideal fantasy high school. What would a typical day at that school be like for the students? Write a list of the goals that your school's program would reflect, using the program that Sizer describes in paragraph 21 as a model.
2. Your view of high school might be different from Sizer's, or perhaps your high school was different from the one he describes. Write an essay that is organized like Sizer's but that presents your own report and explanation of what school is.

Making Connections

1. Sizer writes that although there is sex discrimination in high schools, there is less there than in some "other American institutions" (paragraph 25). Consider Elizabeth Weil's (p. 596) discussion of controversial psychologists

like Dr. Leonard Sax, who believe that boys and girls can be generalized into two essential categories, with different modes of learning and thought. How would implementing the teaching methods Sax advocates change the high school that Sizer describes?

2. Compare and contrast Sizer's Mark with Mike Rose's (p. 567) description of himself as a high school student. What details about each student's class, race, ethnicity, personality, learning style, and family background do you learn from these essays? In what ways do these details matter?

Essay Writing

1. Write an essay reporting on your own high school in the way that Sizer reports on Mark's. Sizer comments that most schools are "nice places" and that most students enjoy being there, "off the labor market." Did your experience support these conclusions?

Why We Hate Teachers

Garret Keizer

A graduate of the University of Vermont, Garret Keizer (b. 1954) worked as a high school English teacher for fifteen years, an experience that provided the basis for his first book, No Place but Here: A Teacher's Vocation in a Rural Community *(1988). He went on to become an Episcopal minister, a transition he chronicled in* A Dresser of Sycamore Trees: The Finding of a Ministry *(1991). A prolific essayist and regular contributor to* Harper's *magazine, Keizer has also published* Help: The Original Human Dilemma *(2004) and a young adult novel,* God of Beer *(2002). The following essay appeared in a 2001 issue of* Harper's *that was devoted to contemporary American education.*

Glory, glory, alleluia.
Teacher hit me with a ruler.
I knocked her on the bean
With a rotten tangerine,
And she ain't gonna teach no more.
— "Mine Eyes Have Seen
the Glory of the
Burning of the School"
(Traditional)

As soon as I entered first grade, I began throwing up my breakfast every day, Monday through Friday, usually two or three minutes before the school bus came. I do not recall having what are nowadays referred to as "academic difficulties." In fact, I was already the good student I would continue to be right through graduate school. Nor do I recall being picked on in any particular way; that would come later. What I recall is being struck at about the same time as my mother handed me my lunch with an irresistible urge to vomit my breakfast — that, and the sight of my mother on her knees again, wiping up my mess.

I have long since marveled at the way in which my parents, without benefit of formal courses in psychology or any thought of sending me to a psychologist (this was 1959), set about trying to cure me by a psychological stratagem at once desperate, risky, and ingenious. It amounted to the contrivance of an epiphany. One evening they announced that the next day I would not be going to school. Instead, my mother and I would be taking a trip "up country" to see Aunt Em and have a picnic. Aunt Em and her husband were caretakers of a sprawling rural cemetery in which I delighted to play and explore. They lived in a house "as old as George Washington." Propped against one of their porch pillars was an enormous Chiclet-shaped rock, an object of great fascination for me, which they claimed was a petrified dinosaur tooth. There were few places on earth I would rather have gone.

The next morning arrived like an early Christmas. I watched impatiently as my mother packed a lunch for our adventure. Then, just at the time when the school bus would have picked me up, she turned to me and in a tone of poignant resignation said, "Now, you see, Gary, there is nothing wrong with your stomach. You get sick because you don't want to go to school." She handed me my lunch and told me that we were not going to Aunt Em's that day. I did not throw up. I forget whether or not I cried. But, for the most part, I was cured.

I say for the most part because even now, at the age of forty-eight, I am rarely able to walk into any school without feeling something of the same duodenal ominousness that haunted my first days as a student. I doubt I am unique in this, though it does seem like an odd symptom for someone who went to school for almost twenty years, who taught high school for fifteen years after that, who saw his wife through graduate school after she had done the same for him, and who will be in his mid-fifties by the time he has seen his daughter through college. I have spent most of my life "in school," doing homework or correcting it, which means that for much of my life I have either skipped breakfast or eaten it as an act of faith.

And I still catch myself thinking of that aborted trip to Aunt Em's. I pic-   5
ture myself running over the mown graves, past generations of polished monuments, with a cool breeze at my back and the clouds unfolding like angel wings above me. It amounts to a waking dream, with a dream's psychic symbolism, and what I think it means is that I have reconciled myself to death by imagining it as the most sublime form of hooky: the blessed stage at which no one will ever again, in any form whatsoever, make me go to school.

I do not have frightful memories of my first-grade teacher, though my parents have told me she was "stern." I remember her punishing a boy who'd meandered into the girls' bathroom by forcing him to wear a cardboard sign that read I AM A GIRL TODAY. I remember another boy, a budding Leonardo da Vinci, whose crammed, cluttered desk she would from time to time dump over onto the floor, like an unfaithful wife's wardrobe tossed onto the street. I can still see him kneeling among his precocious drawings and playground-excavated fossils, straightening things up as best as he could, while the rest of us looked on with the dumbstruck fascination of smaller-brained primates. I can see these things clearly, but I do not remember the teacher herself as an ogre. As for the memories of my two classmates, the first of whom would eventually become an outlaw biker and the second of whom probably went on through a long progression of larger and even messier desks, I am not so sure.

Such stories of cruel and unusual punishment probably account at least partially for that hideous strain of American folk humor, with a pedigree that runs from Washington Irving to Garrison Keillor: the Tale of the Teacher We Drove Nuts. I used to know a man who would tell me, in the tone of someone bragging about his first sexual experience, how he and his friends had driven a nun at his Catholic school to a nervous breakdown. "Let's put it this way: She didn't come back the next year." It so happens that I was working as a teacher when I first heard the story. So was the man who told it to me.

It's hard to imagine a parallel from another profession, perhaps some folksy yarn about an undertaker driven to tears by a repeated switcheroo of his embalming fluid and his coffee, a cashier who fell down foaming at the mouth after making change for one too many ten-pound bags of dimes. It's simplistic to say that we see these tales as innocuous because their protagonists are only children. We also see them as innocuous because their victims are only teachers (and usually women). We like to tell these stories, I think, because they requite some primal — as in "primary" school — pain within us.

For many children, going to school amounts to a fall from grace. I have long sensed a mystical connection between the iconic apple on the teacher's desk and the apple Adam ate from the forbidden tree; I am tempted to take them for the same apple. Perhaps the New England Puritans who taught their children the alphabet starting with the A in "Adam's Fall" were playing with the same idea. Although teachers may figure variously in the myth as Eve, the Serpent, or God, they are almost always the flaming cherubim who bar our return to the innocence of early childhood. For better or for worse, a teacher was our first surrogate mother. The wicked stepmother and the fairy god-mother are *mothers*, after all, and in the fairy tales of personal history they both tend to have teaching licenses. In other words, the story of our first encounter with school is either the tale of how we betrayed our mothers for a princess or the tale of how they abandoned us to a witch.

And the last chapter mirrors the first: the teacher who took us from our mothers appears in another guise to take our children from us later on. The teacher who is a boy's first crush is also his mother's first rival. Further-more, in an era when mothers frequently work outside the home, a teacher with the benefit of a shorter day and a longer summer vacation not only spends the best hours of the day with our children; she spends the brightest days of the year with her own. I believe this accounts for much of the disdain for teachers, particularly in working-class communities like mine. If someone gave me the power and the money to make one change that might improve the public perception of teachers, I would give working parents more time with their kids. At the very least, that would remind them to be grateful for the hours their kids are in school.

There are, of course, other ways in which schools represent a psychic fall; and teachers, the guardian angels of its trajectory. Although schools in a democracy purport to exist for the creation of "a level playing field," it does not take us long to discover that level playing fields exist mainly to sort out

winners from losers. Unless we came from a large family with parents who
went out of their way to play favorites, school was our first introduction to
the idea of relative merit. It is not an idea with as much application to the
so-called real world as we might think. Neither are any number of school-
house rigors justified in that name. Certainly we encounter relative merit in
the world. My work as an adult is evaluated and rewarded, and I must face
the fact that others are going to be better at it than I am.

But that oppressive sense of minute gradation, of success not as a mansion
of many rooms but as a ladder of infinite rungs — where does that exist but
in a classroom, or in the imagination of the adult who still sits there? To be a
kid again, I must walk to my assigned place in a room ranked with little desks,
each occupied by a writer my age, or as he was at my age. And the Updike kid
always has his hand up first, and the teacher can't seem to get enough of his
stories about rabbits, whereas my poems about turtles always seem to lag behind in her esteem. "Taking your degree" is the most precise phrase in all of
education: that is what we take from our first day in kindergarten, our *degree*
of relative worth. The educational apple of Adam's Fall, by which the first
American primer said "we sinned all," did not give us the knowledge of good
and evil but of good, better, and best, world without end.

Another way in which our teachers took us out of the Garden was by taking us out of the moment. It was in school that the future first began its incessant bullying of the present and the past. The watchword was "preparation,"
and, considered only by the criterion of effective pedagogy, the watchword
could hardly be called progressive. Ask a random sample of parents if and
when school began to grow sour for their kids, and they will usually say
"sometime around fourth or fifth grade"; that is, when teachers began working with a more intentional zeal to "get kids ready for high school," a process
that might be likened to getting Sir John Gielgud ready to do a Pepsi commercial. Diminishment follows diminishment, until we reach graduate school,
where the ability and certainly the desire to teach are not only rare but generally held in contempt. Few can go that far without developing grave suspi-
cions about the future — perhaps one reason why so many people end up
stalled in graduate school. The Serpent promised that we would become "as
gods," though it seems that what he really meant is that with the right amount
of training and gumption we could become as serpents.

For some of us that meant we could become teachers. We could bring the
process of preparation full circle, like the myth of the serpent that devours its
own tail. That is, admittedly, a paradoxical image. To be a teacher in America
is to embody any number of seeming contradictions, some peculiar to the profession and others intrinsic to the nature of democracy itself.

For one thing, teachers can find themselves an embarrassing exception to   15
the first article of their own creed: that education prepares one to be privileged
and prosperous. Of the professional classes, theirs is probably one of the least
esteemed; it is certainly one of the least paid. Teaching has traditionally been

a port of entry, the Ellis Island by which the children of blue-collar workers entered the professional classes. I seldom see a first-year teacher with her tote bag or briefcase without conjuring up the image of an immigrant and his duffel bag of worldly belongings — so full of faith, so free of cynicism, so ripe for exploitation. And such an easy target for prejudice.

Occupying a no-man's-land between the union hall and the reserved parking space, able in some cases to take a sabbatical but in many cases unable to get to a toilet, teachers sometimes find themselves caught in a crossfire of contradictory resentments. On the one hand, the public expects teachers to have some of the same expertise and even some of the same polish as physicians, though no teacher of my acquaintance has ever had the opportunity of hiring his own nurse in the form of a classroom aide — assuming he even had one. On the other hand, those who see teachers as no more than a highly specialized class of clock-punchers are prone to ask what truck driver ever had a nine-week vacation, or what waitress ever had a pension fund.

It almost goes without saying that a teacher's perceived status will vary with the status of the perceiver. So to the svelte mom in the Volvo, Ms. Hart is an air-headed twit without a creative bone in her body, who probably had to write crib notes all over her chubby little hand just to get through Hohum State College with a C. To the burly dad in the rusty pickup truck, Ms. Hart is a book-addled flake without a practical bone in her body but with plenty of good teeth in her head thanks to a dental plan that comes out of said dad's property taxes. In Shakespeare's *King Henry VI*, a common rebel known as Dick the Butcher says, "The first thing we do, let's kill all the lawyers," but to honor the sentiments inside as well as outside the palace Ms. Hart has to die first.

Of course there are any number of parents, in Volvos, old Fords, and on Harley-Davidsons, who will see Ms. Hart as an angel. And of those who see otherwise, might at least a few be responding to her pedagogical competence rather than to her professional status? Undoubtedly so. Teachers probably provide some of the most and least inspiring examples we have of human beings in the act of work. A friend of mine remarked to me recently, "No one, not even a farmer, works harder than a hardworking teacher. But there is nothing on this earth lazier than a lazy teacher." Having taught school for a good part of my adult life, I tend to agree. I wouldn't say that extremes of this kind are unique to teachers, however. I would propose that the same extremes can be found in any occupation that shares the following characteristics: a notable degree of specialized training, a mission to help other human beings, a duty to help them irrespective of their ability to pay, and a measure of authority that comes from all of the above. In short, the extremes of character and performance that exist among teachers also exist among doctors and police. But most of us, even if we grow up to be invalids or criminals, will have spent more time with teachers than with either of their counterparts.

What also sets teachers apart is the milder consequences of their extremes. Doctors and cops can kill somebody or save her life; teachers at their worst or best can usually do no more than to ruin or to improve it. Because the extremes of benefit and detriment are less, the mystique may be less also. But because those extremes do exist and are so noticeable, the mediocre quality of the mediocre teacher tends to be noticeable as well. An average guy seldom looks more average than in front of a classroom.

In a society that touts both "excellence" and "equality," teachers are   20 perhaps our best example of the complex interplay of those two values — both in the evaluative nature of their work and in their own status as workers. We put them down in the clichés of populist rhetoric and we put them up in the titanium shrines of space shuttles, but the truth is, taken as a whole, they're probably more representative of "ordinary Americans" than any single occupational group. If I were Arthur Miller, I would not have made Willy Loman a salesman; I would have made him a teacher. In the lines in which Willy calls the Chevrolet "the greatest car ever built" and then, several pages later, says, "That goddamn Chevrolet, they ought to prohibit the manufacture of that car!" I would have him talking about the American public school.

Yet another way in which the conflicting currents of our democracy affect our resentment of teachers has to do with how we conceive of service, which is not much different from how Süleyman the Magnificent conceived of service. In aristocratic societies, service is the butler who appears when the master pulls the velvet bell rope. In a society like ours, service is the desk clerk who's supposed to come running (with a smile) whenever any tourist slaps the bell. Our version may be the more "democratic," but like the Greeks, whose democracies preceded our own, we always seem to need a few slaves in order to feel truly emancipated.

It would be foolish to suggest that teachers are a kind of slave. It would be equally foolish to forget that not so long ago they were virtually a kind of indentured servant. That they have advanced beyond servitude is not always regarded as a cause for celebration. Add teachers to that list of groups and persons who eventually "got so uppity" that they threatened to diminish the status that came of having them under our thumbs. Here again I must be careful not to overstate my case. One of my favorite school stories has to do with a principal who told a friend of mine that although he understood his frustration when his son's teacher consistently failed to return his phone calls, he should understand that "returning calls has never been Mrs. Van Winkle's strength."

Still, even when one allows for the maddening imperviousness — and equally maddening impunity — of certain teachers, one is still struck from time to time by the popular assumption that public schools, like Third World bazaars and Atlantic City casinos, ought to be places where the almighty spender can throw his weight around like Almighty God. Whenever one hears that dearly beloved phrase "local control," and one hears it in my corner of New England about once a day, the accent is usually on *control*; and the control, firmly on the teachers. Of course this is also true beyond the local level, most recently in proposals to fingerprint teachers in order to "protect children." What politician as keen on protecting his or her career as on protecting children would ever propose fingerprinting clergy, orthodontists, or live-in boyfriends? Not to forget every legislator employing a page.

For the most part, though, I do not hear teachers criticized for having slipped their leashes so much as for having dropped their halos. "Teachers are not supposed to be in it for the money; they're supposed to be in it for the children" — a sentiment that sounds reasonable enough until we remember that even the most altruistic teachers have been known to produce children, and that teachers' children have been known to eat. Still, one can almost hear the aggrieved tones of unrequited love in the voices of those who wistfully recall the days "when a teacher was respected" and wouldn't have known what to do with anything so crass as a dollar bill, not if you taped it to her nose.

Once again there's a contradiction lurking under the rhetoric, which   25 reveals a cultural contradiction as well. Teachers are also resented *for* their altruism, and one does not have to look too far for examples of the resentment. I remember sitting next to a father at Town Meeting who in his litany of grievances against teachers closed with this: "They teach kids not to work." It was a hardworking man who said this. What I think he meant was: "They teach kids that there are other things in life *besides* work, that is, besides work done for money." I recall another father, also hardworking but with the added perspective of being a teacher's husband, who gave as his explanation for the bitter controversy surrounding a guidance counselor at his school: "I think people resent her goodness."

It was a remark that struck home, in part because home for me is a hardscrabble place where many people have led very hard lives. In their eyes, teachers make children unfit to live in a world where survival belongs to the toughest. Special education, cooperative learning, second chances — even art and music — are "fine for some," but what have such things to do with real life as these people have known it? And if all this coddling is indeed valuable, does that mean that a hard life is not? I'm told there's a Sicilian proverb that says, "It's a foolish man who educates his children so they can despise him." It's a foolish man who doesn't see that fear at the root of nearly everything we might call reactionary.

People are said to hate change, even though in our society political change, at least, is supposed to come about by the will of the people. I imagine that for many of them hating teachers comes down to the same thing. Whenever our society changes, or wishes to change, or pretends that it wishes to change, schools and teachers are enlisted in the cause. If we decide that cyberspace is the place to go, we start by sending the second grade. If we come to fear that morality is going to hell in a handbasket, we draw up a curriculum of "values-based" education. No teacher can hear the phrase "launching a new initiative" without knowing that the launching pad is going to be located on top of his desk.

If we oppose a given change, we may be inclined to disdain the teacher who carries it forward, though in many cases this amounts to hearing bad news and killing the messenger. Our chagrin can come not only from the change itself but from the sense of having to subsidize our own obsolescence. We shall never require a sign outside a school building that reads YOUR TAX DOLLARS AT WORK: people feel them at work, no less than the workings of their own bowels, which is why, in times of unsettling social change and political insecurity, citizens will sometimes descend with merciless indignation on a school budget. The first thing we do, let's kill all the special programs. I have even heard people say, "It's the one thing left that I have some control over."

But schools have not only been placed in the vanguard of change; they have in many ways been used to contain and minimize change. So if, for instance, we want to continue to practice de facto racial segregation, we can pretend otherwise by busing children between racially homogeneous schools. If we are content to see the gap between rich and poor grow wider every year, but wish to seem more "compassionate," we can try to establish some semblance of equity in the funding of public education. Ostensibly, our guiding principle here is that the first step in changing society for the better is changing schools.

That is a fairly sound guiding principle — provided that the *first* step doesn't wind up being the *only* step. Schools can indeed be better places than the communities that sustain them, but never much better, and never better for long. In the end, we can only change the world by changing the world. When something happens in a schoolyard to remind us of this, something awful and sad, we lash out at "the teachers" and "the schools." They were supposed to be making the world a better place, or at least maintaining the illusion that we wanted them to.

Public schools embody our democratic principles and contradictions better than any other institution we know. In schools we behold our own spitting image as a people who value equality but crave excellence, who live for the moment but bet on the future, who espouse altruism but esteem self-reliance, who sincerely believe in change but just as sincerely doubt that change will do them any good. Whether we call these contradictions schizophrenia or creative tension, beauty or ugliness, will depend on the eye of the beholder. Public-school teachers themselves are no less an embodiment of the same contradictions, just as in the broadest sense all teachers embody the subjects that they teach. At least the more memorable ones do. Think of it sometime: lean Mr. Silverstein didn't teach you math; he *was* math, fleshed out in its angular glory. All of this is to say that the best teaching is incarnational. Teaching is the *word* — the music, the formula, and even the Constitution of the United States — made flesh and dwelling among us.

The forty-odd years that I have spent in school are not unlike the forty-eight years I have spent in my body, a mix of pain and pleasure in which the pain has perhaps been more intense but the pleasure more constant, more influential, and, in some way I can't entirely explain, more true. At some level it was most fitting that my mother sent me off to school that morning, and every morning, by handing me my lunch, as if to say that the part of me that learns is one with the part that eats, even if on certain mornings it was also one with the part that pukes. In contrast, the daydream of the boy I was at six, playing among the tombstones when he ought to have been at school, amounts to a wish for disembodiment. It is the vision of a gnostic heaven, in which the emancipated spirits of the elect rise from the complications of the flesh, not in a new body but in no body at all.

The same can be said for many of the present initiatives to diminish radically the scope of public education in America, if not to abolish it altogether. The utopian school, the cyber-school, the voucher-subsidized school, the school of "school choice," all reduce to a fantasy of social and political transcendence — an attempt to sidestep the contradictions of democracy, the cruel jokes of genetics, the crueler jokes of class, and the darker side of diversity. If we can but find the right gnosis, you see, the secret path to educational enlightenment, we shall at last be able to shed the blemished, prickly skin of the body politic and live as unencumbered spirits with harps and cornets or whichever golden instrument best accompanies the appropriate lifestyle choice. It may sound like a return to Eden, like the miraculous reversal of some irreversible fall, but make no mistake; it is the equivalent of a wish for death.

QUESTIONS

Reading

1. This essay is about teachers and includes an explanation of why we feel so emotionally about them, but it is ultimately an *argument* about schools and what we should and shouldn't expect of them. Summarize this argument.
2. Highlight, underline, or flag the paradoxes or *contradictions* in common attitudes about schools, teachers, and society that Keizer notes throughout his argument. How do these make his argument deeper and more complex?
3. One element of argument is establishing the authority of the speaker for the statements that he or she makes. How does Keizer attempt to do this?
4. A good argument presents counterarguments and deals with them. Can you find examples of this process in Keizer's essay?

Exploratory Writing

1. "In the end, we can only change the world by changing the world," writes Keizer (paragraph 30). In groups, write a list of ten changes you

would like to see take place in the world. Then, for each item, design an elementary, a middle, or a high school program that would help promote that change in society. In real life, how effective do you think your programs would be? Would they be controversial among parents, teachers, school boards, and taxpayers?

2. Highlight or flag the different figures from fairy tales or myths that Keizer associates with teachers. Make a chart showing the archetypes, mythological figures, monsters, heroes, or fairy-tale figures you associate with the teachers that you remember most from kindergarten through grade school. What do these associations show about the roles that your teachers played in your life? Were some of your expectations about teachers contradictory or paradoxical?

TEACHER	ARCHETYPE

Making Connections

1. Review all of the essays in this casebook, and summarize the role of teachers in each one. Even when teachers aren't explicitly discussed, consider how teachers and teaching methods might be important. For example, in Elizabeth Weil's (p. 596) report, is it possible that students are responding to their teacher's unconscious assumptions about gender roles, rather than behaving in a way that's innate? How did Mike Rose's (p. 567) education change because of Jack MacFarland? What role do teachers play in Matt Miller's (p. 635) proposal?

Essay Writing

1. In his concluding paragraph, Keizer writes, "The utopian school, the cyber-school, the voucher-subsidized school, the school of 'school choice,' all reduce to a fantasy of social and political transcendence — an attempt to sidestep the contradictions of democracy, the cruel jokes of genetics, the crueler jokes of class, and the darker side of diversity." Write an essay agreeing or disagreeing with this conclusion. Use examples from your own educational experience, research, or the essays in this casebook to make your argument.

First, Kill All the School Boards
A Modest Proposal to Fix the Schools

Matt Miller

Matt Miller (b. 1962) is a senior fellow at the Center for American Progress and the author of The Two Percent Solution: Fixing America's Problems in Ways Liberals and Conservatives Can Love *(2003). A graduate of Brown University, Miller went on to serve as an advisor in the Clinton administration and continues to work with various economic think tanks. In addition to regular appearances on CNN and MSNBC, he is moderator and cohost of the nationally syndicated public radio show* Left, Right, and Center *(representing the center). While typically a proponent of small government, Miller makes an interesting argument for nationalizing America's school systems in this article, originally published in the* Atlantic *(2008).*

It wasn't just the slate and pencil on every desk, or the absence of daily beatings. As Horace Mann sat in a Leipzig classroom in the summer of 1843, it was the entire Prussian system of schools that impressed him. Mann was six years into the work as Massachusetts secretary of education that would earn him lasting fame as the "father of public education." He had sailed from Boston to England several weeks earlier with his new wife, combining a European honeymoon with educational fact-finding. In England, the couple had been startled by the luxury and refinement of the upper classes, which exceeded anything they had seen in America and stood in stark contrast to the poverty and ignorance of the masses. If the United States was to avoid this awful chasm and the social upheaval it seemed sure to create, he thought, education was the answer. Now he was seeing first-hand the Prussian schools that were the talk of reformers on both sides of the Atlantic.

In Massachusetts, Mann's vision of "common schools," publicly funded and attended by all, represented an inspiring democratic advance over the state's hodgepodge of privately funded and charity schools. But beyond using the bully pulpit, Mann had little power to make his vision a reality. Prussia, by contrast, had a system designed from the center. School attendance was compulsory. Teachers were trained at national institutes with the same care that went into training military officers. Their enthusiasm for their subjects was contagious, and their devotion to students evoked recip-rocal affection and respect, making Boston's routine resort to classroom whippings seem barbaric.

Mann also admired Prussia's rigorous national curriculum and tests. The results spoke for themselves: illiteracy had been vanquished. To be sure, Prussian schools sought to create obedient subjects of the kaiser — hardly Mann's aim. Yet the lessons were undeniable, and Mann returned home determined to share what he had seen. In the seventh of his legendary "Annual Reports" on education to the Commonwealth of Massachusetts, he touted the benefits of a national system and cautioned against the "calamities which result . . . from leaving this most important of all the functions of a government to chance."

Mann's epiphany that summer put him on the wrong side of America's tradition of radical localism when it came to schools. And although his efforts in the years that followed made Massachusetts a model for taxpayer-funded schools and state-sponsored teacher training, the obsession with local control — not incidentally, an almost uniquely American obsession — still dominates U.S. education to this day. For much of the 150 or so years between Mann's era and now, the system served us adequately: during that time, we extended more schooling to more people than any nation had before and rose to superpower status. But let's look at what local control gives us today, in the "flat" world in which our students will have to compete.

The United States spends more than nearly every other nation on   5
schools, but out of twenty-nine developed countries in a 2003 assessment, we ranked twenty-fourth in math and in problem-solving, eighteenth in sci-ence, and fifteenth in reading. Half of all black and Latino students in the United States don't graduate on time (or ever) from high school. As of 2005, about 70 percent of eighth-graders were not proficient in reading. By the end of eighth grade, what passes for a math curriculum in America is two years behind that of other countries.

Dismal fact after dismal fact; by now, they are hardly news. But in the twenty-five years since the landmark report *A Nation at Risk* sounded the alarm about our educational mediocrity, America's response has been scat-tershot and ineffective, orchestrated mainly by some fifteen thousand school districts acting alone, with help more recently from the states. It's as if after Pearl Harbor, FDR had suggested we prepare for war through the uncoor-dinated efforts of thousands of small factories; they'd know what kinds of planes and tanks were needed, right?

When you look at what local control of education has wrought, the conclusion is inescapable: we must carry Mann's insights to their logical end and nationalize our schools, to some degree. But before delving into the de-tails of why and how, let's back up for a moment and consider what brought us to this pass.

PER-PUPIL SPENDING IN PUBLIC ELEMENTARY AND SECONDARY SCHOOLS, BY COUNTY (2004–2005)

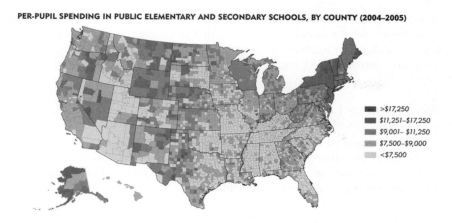

>$17,250
$11,251–$17,250
$9,001– $11,250
$7,500–$9,000
<$7,500

130,000 Little Red Schoolhouses

Our system is, more than anything, an artifact of our Colonial past. For the religious dissenters who came to the New World, literacy was essential to religious freedom, enabling them to teach their own beliefs. Religion and schooling moved in tandem across the Colonies. Many people who didn't like what the local minister was preaching would move on and found their own church, and generally their own school.

This preference for local control of education dovetailed with the broader ethos of the American Revolution and the Founders' distrust of distant, centralized authority. Education was left out of the Constitution; in the Tenth Amendment, it is one of the unnamed powers reserved for the states, which in turn passed it on to local communities. Eventually the United States would have 130,000 school districts, most of them served by a one-room school. These little red schoolhouses, funded primarily through local property taxes, became the iconic symbols of democratic American learning.

Throughout the late nineteenth and early twentieth centuries, nothing 10 really challenged this basic structure. Eventually many rural districts were consolidated, and the states assumed a greater role in school funding; since the 1960s, the federal government has offered modest financial aid to poorer districts as well. But neither these steps, nor the standards-based reform movement inspired by *A Nation at Risk*, brought significant change.

Many reformers across the political spectrum agree that local control has become a disaster for our schools. But the case against it is almost never articulated. Public officials are loath to take on powerful school-board associations and teachers' unions; foundations and advocacy groups, who must work with the boards and unions, also pull their punches. For these reasons, as well as our natural preference for having things done nearby, support for local control still lingers, largely unexamined, among the public.

No Problem Left Behind

Why is local control such a failure when applied to our schools? After all, political decentralization has often served America well, allowing decisions to be made close to where their impact would be felt. But in education, it has spawned several crippling problems:

- **No way to know how children are doing.** "We're two decades into the standards movement in this country, and standards are still different by classroom, by school, by district, and by state," says Tom Vander Ark, who headed the education program at the Bill and Melinda Gates Foundation from 1999 through 2006. "Most teachers in America still pretty much teach whatever they want."

  If you thought President Bush's 2001 No Child Left Behind legislation was fixing these problems, think again. True, NCLB requires states to establish standards in core subjects and to test children in grades 3–8 annually, with the aim of making all students "proficient" by 2014. But by leaving standards and definitions of "proficiency" to state discretion, it has actually made matters worse. *The Proficiency Illusion*, a report released in October by the conservative Thomas B. Fordham Foundation, details how. "'Proficiency' varies wildly from state to state, with 'passing scores' ranging from the 6th percentile to the 77th," the researchers found:

  > Congress erred big-time when NCLB assigned each state to set its own standards and devise and score its own tests . . . this study underscores the folly of a big modern nation, worried about its global competitiveness, nodding with approval as Wisconsin sets its eighth-grade reading passing level at the 14th percentile while South Carolina sets its at the 71st percentile.

  The lack of uniform evaluation creates a "tremendous risk of delusion about how well children are actually doing," says Chris Cerf, the deputy chancellor of schools in New York City. That delusion makes it far more difficult to enact reforms — and even to know where reforms are needed. "Schools may get an award from their state for high performance, and under federal guidelines they may be targeted for closure for low performance," Vander Ark says. This happens in California, he told me, all the time.

- **Stunted R & D.** Local control has kept education from attracting the research and development that drives progress, because benefits of scale are absent. There are some fifteen thousand curriculum departments in this country — one for every district. None of them can afford to invest in deeply understanding what works best when it comes to teaching reading to English-language learners, or using computers to develop customized strategies for students with different learning styles. Local-control advocates would damn the federal government if it tried to take on such things. Perhaps more important, the private sector generally won't pursue them, either. Purchasing decisions are made by a complex mix of classroom, school, and school board officials. The more complicated and fragmented the sale that a company has to make, the less willing it is to invest in product research and development.

- **Incompetent school boards and union dominance.** "In the first place, God made idiots," Mark Twain once wrote. "This was for practice. Then He made School Boards." Things don't appear to have improved much since Twain's time. "The job has become more difficult, more complicated, and more political, and as a result, it's driven out many of the good candidates," Vander Ark says. "So while teachers' unions have become more sophisticated and have smarter people who are better-equipped and -prepared at the table, the quality of school-board members, particularly in urban areas, has decreased." Board members routinely spend their time on minor matters, from mid-level personnel decisions to bus routes. "The tradition goes back to the rural era, where the school board hired the schoolmarm and oversaw the repair of the roof, looked into the stove in the room, and deliberated on every detail of operating the schools," says Michael Kirst, an emeritus professor of education at Stanford University. "A lot of big-city school boards still do these kinds of things." Because of Progressive-era reforms meant to get school boards out of "politics," most urban school districts are independent, beyond the reach of mayors and city councils. Usually elected in off-year races that few people vote in or even notice, school boards are, in effect, accountable to no one.

   Local control essentially surrenders power over the schools to the teachers' unions. Union money and mobilization are often decisive in board elections. And local unions have hefty intellectual and political backing from their state and national affiliates. Even when they're not in the unions' pockets, in other words, school boards are outmatched.

   The unions are adept at negotiating new advantages for their members, spreading their negotiating strategies to other districts in the state, and getting these advantages embodied in state and sometimes federal law as well. This makes it extraordinarily difficult for superintendents to change staffing, compensation, curriculum, and other policies. Principals, for their part, are compliance machines, spending their days making sure that federal, state, and district programs are implemented. Meanwhile, commonsense reforms, like offering higher pay to attract teachers to underserved specialties such as math, science, and special education, can't get traction, because the unions say no.

- **Financial inequity.** The dirty little secret of local control is the enormous tax advantage it confers on better-off Americans: communities with high property wealth can tax themselves at low rates and still generate far more dollars per pupil than poor communities taxing themselves heavily. This wasn't always the case: in the nineteenth century, property taxes were rightly seen as the fairest way to pay for education, since property was the main form of wealth, and the rich and poor tended to live near one another. But the rise of commuter suburbs since World War II led to economically segregated communities; today, the spending gap between districts can be thousands of dollars per pupil.

  But local taxes represent only 44 percent of overall school funding; the spending gaps between states, which contribute 47 percent of total spending, account for most of the financial inequity. Perversely, Title I, the federal aid program enacted in the 1960s to boost poor schools, has widened the gaps, because it distributes money largely according to how much states are already spending.

What Would Horace Do?

I asked Marc Tucker, the head of the New Commission on the Skills of the American Workforce (a 2006 bipartisan panel that called for an overhaul of the education system), how he convinces people that local control is hobbling our schools. He said he asks a simple question: If we have the second-most-expensive K–12 system of all those measured by the Organization for Economic Cooperation and Development, but consistently perform between the middle and the bottom of the pack, shouldn't we examine the systems of countries that spend less and get better results? "I then point out that the system of local control that we have is almost unique," Tucker says. "One then has to defend a practice that is uncharacteristic of the countries with the best performance.

"It's an industrial-benchmarking argument," he adds.

Horace Mann wouldn't have used this jargon, but his thinking was   15
much the same. In his time, the challenge was to embrace a bigger role for the state; today, the challenge is to embrace a bigger role for the federal government in standards, funding, and other arenas.

The usual explanation for why national standards won't fly is that the right hates "national" and the left hates "standards." But that's changing.

Two Republican former secretaries of education, Rod Paige and William Bennett, now support national standards and tests, writing in the *Washington Post*: "In a world of fierce economic competition, we can't afford to pretend that the current system is getting us where we need to go." On the Democratic side, John Podesta, a former chief of staff to President Clinton and the current president of the Center for American Progress (where I'm a senior fellow), told me that he believes the public is far ahead of the established political wisdom, which holds that the only safe way to discuss national standards is to stipulate that they are "optional" or "voluntary" — in other words, not "national" at all.

Recent polling suggests he's right. Two surveys conducted for the education campaign Strong American Schools, which I advised in 2006, found that a majority of Americans think there should be uniform national standards. Most proponents suggest we start by establishing standards and tests in grades 3–12 in the core subjects — reading, math, and science — and leave more-controversial subjects, such as history, until we have gotten our feet wet.

According to U.S. Department of Education statistics, the federal government accounts for 9 percent, or $42 billion, of our K–12 spending. If we're serious about improving our schools, and especially about raising up the lowest, Uncle Sam's contribution must rise to 25 or 30 percent of the total (a shift President Nixon considered). Goodwin Liu, a University of California at Berkeley law professor who has studied school financing, suggests that a higher federal contribution could be used in part to bring all states up to a certain minimum per-pupil funding. It could also, in my view, fund conditional grants to boost school performance. For example, federal aid could be offered to raise teachers' salaries in poor schools, provided that states or districts take measures such as linking pay to performance and deferring or eliminating tenure. Big grants might be given to states that adopt new national standards, making those standards "voluntary" but hard to refuse. The government also needs to invest much more heavily in research. It now spends $28 billion annually on research at the National Institutes of Health, but only $260 million — not even 1 percent of that amount — on R & D for education.

What of school boards? In an ideal world, we would scrap them — especially in big cities, where most poor children live. That's the impulse behind a growing drive for mayoral control of schools. New York and Boston have used mayoral authority to sustain what are among the most far-reaching reform agendas in the country, including more-rigorous curricula and a focus on better teaching and school leadership. Of course, the chances of eliminating school boards anytime soon are nil. But we can at least recast and limit their role.

In all of these efforts, we must understand one paradox: only by transcending local control can we create genuine autonomy for our schools. "If you visit schools in many other parts of the world," Marc Tucker says,   20 "you're struck almost immediately . . . by a sense of autonomy on the part of the school staff and principal that you don't find in the United States." Research in forty-six countries by Ludger Woessmann of the University of Munich has shown that setting clear external standards while granting real discretion to schools in how to meet them is the most effective way to run a system. We need to give schools one set of national expectations, free educators and parents to collaborate locally in whatever ways work, and get everything else out of the way.

Nationalizing our schools even a little goes against every cultural tradition we have, save the one that matters most: our capacity to renew ourselves to meet new challenges. Once upon a time a national role in retirement funding was anathema; then suddenly, after the Depression, we had Social Security. Once, a federal role in health care would have been rejected as socialism; now, federal money accounts for half of what we spend on health care. We started down this road on schooling a long time ago. Time now to finish the journey.

QUESTIONS

Reading

1. Why does Miller use the term "A Modest Proposal" in his title? What does this title suggest about the style of argument he intends to use? Is this essay truly a "Modest Proposal"?
2. According to Miller, what effect did former U.S. president George W. Bush's No Child Left Behind legislation have on the "crippling problems" facing schools?
3. One section of Miller's argument is titled, "What Would Horace Do?" What does he mean by this question, and how does he answer it?
4. How does Miller describe himself? What bearing does this self-description have on his argument?

Exploratory Writing

1. Collaborate in groups to research the public school system in your county. What role does the school board play in the school programs? Find recent articles reporting on any controversies over the local schools. If possible, interview a public school teacher or principal about the role of national and local government in overseeing his or her school's standards and curriculum. Prepare a dossier of materials about local schools. Looking over these materials, do you agree with Miller's argument?
2. The cultural tradition that matters most, according to Miller, is "our capacity to renew ourselves to meet new challenges" (paragraph 21). Research an example of a time in the history of public education when

the school system changed to meet new challenges. Who was responsible for initiating this change? Who implemented the change? Give a presentation of your findings.

Making Connections

1. According to a survey that Miller advised in 2006, most Americans think that there should be national standards — measured by tests — to chart the learning of third through twelfth graders. Using all of the essays in this casebook — especially those by Emily Bazelon (p. 585) and Mike Rose (p. 567) — make a double-entry list of pros and cons of standardized testing. When you are finished, expand the list with your own pros and cons.

Pros of standardized testing	Cons of standardized testing

Essay Writing

1. Using ideas from any essay or essays in this casebook, write your own "Modest Proposal" for reforming the school system.

The Visual World: Sight and Insight

At first glance, it seems obvious that vision gives us clear and direct access to the world around us. But as the six essays collected in this casebook demonstrate, sight is more complex than it first appears. Consider blindsight. As Rita Carter explains in "A Stream of Illusion" (p. 671), blindsight is "seeing without knowing it" (paragraph 23). It's a phenomenon experienced, as Carter explains, "in people who have patches of dead tissue in the primary visual cortex." These people can respond to visual stimulus even though they don't know they can see this stimulus. This is just one of many examples that show how complex the communication between our eyes and our brains can be. In reality, our brains *create* images out of perceptual information collected through our eyes. Because the communication between the eyes and the brain is so subtle and complex, the visual experience of each individual is likely to vary, as you'll see from some of the essays in this casebook.

When vision goes awry, the results can be fascinating, but when vision is functioning normally — or optimally, as it does for an artist — the results can be just as fascinating. The readings in this casebook explore some of the physiological, philosophical, social, and artistic complexities of vision, including a description of the intensely visual mind of a woman with Asperger's syndrome, a form of autism (Temple Grandin, "Thinking in Pictures: Autism and Visual Thought"); a case history about a music professor whose brain disorder disrupts his visual knowledge of the world — and people — around him (Oliver Sacks, "The Man Who Mistook His Wife for a Hat"); a philosophical exploration of the relationship between vision and reality (Plato, "The Cave"); an overview of the physiology of vision, including blindsight (Rita Carter, "A Stream of Illusion"); a comic artist's history of pictorial art (Scott McCloud, "Setting the Record Straight"); and a painter and art critic's argument about how what we see is shaped by culture and history (Berger, "Ways of Seeing").

The essays in this casebook focus on how our visual worlds are shaped — or, how the visual shapes our worlds. After reading them, you will be in a good position to analyze visual experience in new ways. This may mean responding directly to one or more of the texts you've read, analyzing a visual experience of your own, or following a line of thinking that leads to some research on a topic related to vision or the visual. The questions that follow each reading are intended to give you the opportunity to write in response to these texts and, when appropriate, to use them as a foundation for research into the questions they address.

Thinking in Pictures
Autism and Visual Thought

Temple Grandin

Temple Grandin (b. 1947) is a professor of animal science at Colorado State University, a best-selling author, and a consultant to the livestock industry on animal behavior. She's also the high-functioning, autistic author of the groundbreaking book Emergence: Labeled Autistic *(1986) — the first insider story of living with autism. Her story and her work as an autism advocate have been featured on* 20/20, The Today Show, *and* Larry King Live, *and she has been profiled in* Time *magazine and the* New York Times. *She is also the focus of a semibiographical HBO film, currently titled* Temple Grandin Thinking in Pictures, *starring Claire Danes in the eponymous role. Like the bulk of her oeuvre, Grandin's most recent book,* Animals Make Us Human *(2009), combines her work as a philosophical leader in both the animal welfare and autism advocacy movements. The following piece is an excerpt from* Thinking in Pictures: My Life with Autism *(1996).*

I think in pictures. Words are like a second language to me. I translate both spoken and written words into full-color movies, complete with sound, which run like a VCR tape in my head. When somebody speaks to me, his words are instantly translated into pictures. Language-based thinkers often find this phenomenon difficult to understand, but in my job as an equipment designer for the livestock industry, visual thinking is a tremendous advantage.

Visual thinking has enabled me to build entire systems in my imagination. During my career I have designed all kinds of equipment, ranging from corrals for handling cattle on ranches to systems for handling cattle and hogs during veterinary procedures and slaughter. I have worked for many major livestock companies. In fact, one-third of the cattle and hogs in the United States are handled in equipment I have designed. Some of the people I've worked for don't even know that their systems were designed by someone with autism. I value my ability to think visually, and I would never want to lose it.

One of the most profound mysteries of autism has been the remarkable ability of most autistic people to excel at visual spatial skills while performing so poorly at verbal skills. When I was a child and a teenager, I thought everybody thought in pictures. I had no idea that my thought processes were different. In fact, I did not realize the full extent of the differences until very recently. At meetings and at work I started asking other people detailed questions about how they accessed information from their memories. From their answers I learned that my visualization skills far exceeded those of most other people.

I credit my visualization abilities with helping me understand the animals I work with. Early in my career I used a camera to help give me the animals' perspective as they walked through a chute for their veterinary treatment. I would kneel down and take pictures through the chute from the cow's eye level. Using the photos, I was able to figure out which things scared the cattle, such as shadows and bright spots of sunlight. Back then I used black-and-white film, because twenty years ago scientists believed that cattle lacked color vision. Today, research has shown that cattle can see colors, but the photos provided the unique advantage of seeing the world through a cow's viewpoint. They helped me figure out why the animals refused to go in one chute but willingly walked through another.

Every design problem I've ever solved started with my ability to visual-   5
ize and see the world in pictures. I started designing things as a child, when I was always experimenting with new kinds of kites and model airplanes. In elementary school I made a helicopter out of a broken balsa-wood airplane. When I wound up the propeller, the helicopter flew straight up about a hundred feet. I also made bird-shaped paper kites, which I flew behind my bike. The kites were cut out from a single sheet of heavy drawing paper and flown with thread. I experimented with different ways of bending the wings to increase flying performance. Bending the tips of the wings up made the kite fly higher. Thirty years later, this same design started appearing on commercial aircraft.

Now, in my work, before I attempt any construction, I test-run the equipment in my imagination. I visualize my designs being used in every possible situation, with different sizes and breeds of cattle and in different weather conditions. Doing this enables me to correct mistakes prior to construction. Today, everyone is excited about the new virtual reality computer systems in which the user wears special goggles and is fully immersed in video game action. To me, these systems are like crude cartoons. My imagination works like the computer graphics programs that created the lifelike dinosaurs in *Jurassic Park*. When I do an equipment simulation in my imagination or work on an engineering problem, it is like seeing it on a videotape in my mind. I can view it from any angle, placing myself above or below the equipment and rotating it at the same time. I don't need a fancy graphics program that can produce three-dimensional design simulations. I can do it better and faster in my head.

I create new images all the time by taking many little parts of images I have in the video library in my imagination and piecing them together. I have video memories of every item I've ever worked with — steel gates, fences, latches, concrete walls, and so forth. To create new designs, I retrieve bits and pieces from my memory and combine them into a new whole. My design ability keeps improving as I add more visual images to my library. I add video-like images from either actual experiences or translations of written information into pictures. I can visualize the operation of such things as squeeze chutes, truck loading ramps, and all different types of livestock equipment. The more I actually work with cattle and operate equipment, the stronger my visual memories become.

I first used my video library in one of my early livestock design projects, creating a dip vat and cattle-handling facility for John Wayne's Red River feed yard in Arizona. A dip vat is a long, narrow, seven-foot-deep swimming pool through which cattle move in single file. It is filled with pesticide to rid the animals of ticks, lice, and other external parasites. In 1978, existing dip vat designs were very poor. The animals often panicked because they were forced to slide into the vat down a steep, slick concrete decline. They would refuse to jump into the vat, and sometimes they would flip over backward and drown. The engineers who designed the slide never thought about why the cattle became so frightened.

The first thing I did when arrived at the feedlot was to put myself inside the cattle's heads and look out through their eyes. Because their eyes are on the sides of their heads, cattle have wide-angle vision, so it was like walking through the facility with a wide-angle video camera. I had spent the past six years studying how cattle see their world and watching thousands move through different facilities all over Arizona, and it was immediately obvious to me why they were scared. Those cattle must have felt as if they were being forced to jump down an airplane escape slide into the ocean.

Cattle are frightened by high contrasts of light and dark as well as by people and objects that move suddenly. I've seen cattle that were handled in two identical facilities easily walk through one and balk in the other. The only difference between the two facilities was their orientation to the sun. The cattle refused to move through the chute where the sun cast harsh shadows across it. Until I made this observation, nobody in the feedlot industry had been able to explain why one veterinary facility worked better than the other. It was a matter of observing the small details that made a big difference. To me, the dip vat problem was even more obvious.

My first step in designing a better system was collecting all the published information on existing dip vats. Before doing anything else, I always check out what is considered state-of-the-art so I don't waste time reinventing the wheel. Then I turned to livestock publications, which usually have very limited information, and my library of video memories, all of which contained bad designs. From experience with other types of equipment, such as unloading ramps for trucks, I had learned that cattle willingly walk down a ramp that has cleats to provide secure, nonslip footing. Sliding causes them to panic and back up. The challenge was to design an entrance that would encourage the cattle to walk in voluntarily and plunge into the water, which was deep enough to submerge them completely, so that all the bugs, including those that collect in their ears, would be eliminated.

I started running three-dimensional visual simulations in my imagination. I experimented with different entrance designs and made the cattle walk through them in my imagination. Three images merged to form the final design: a memory of a dip vat in Yuma, Arizona; a portable vat I had seen in a magazine; and an entrance ramp I had seen on a restraint device at the Swift meat-packing plant in Tolleson, Arizona. The new dip vat entrance ramp was a modified version of the ramp I had seen there. My design contained three features that had never been used before: an entrance that would not scare the animals, an improved chemical filtration system, and the use of animal behavior principles to prevent the cattle from becoming overexcited when they left the vat.

The first thing I did was convert the ramp from steel to concrete. The final design had a concrete ramp on a twenty-five-degree downward angle. Deep grooves in the concrete provided secure footing. The ramp appeared to enter the water gradually, but in reality it abruptly dropped away below the water's surface. The animals could not see the drop-off because the dip chemicals colored the water. When they stepped out over the water, they quietly fell in, because their center of gravity had passed the point of no return.

Before the vat was built, I tested the entrance design many times in my imagination. Many of the cowboys at the feedlot were skeptical and did not believe my design would work. After it was constructed, they modified it behind my back, because they were sure it was wrong. A metal sheet was installed over the nonslip ramp, converting it back to an old-fashioned slide entrance. The first day they used it, two cattle drowned because they panicked and flipped over backward.

When I saw the metal sheet, I made the cowboys take it out. They were   15
flabbergasted when they saw that the ramp now worked perfectly. Each calf stepped out over the steep drop-off and quietly plopped into the water. I fondly refer to this design as "cattle walking on water."

Over the years, I have observed that many ranchers and cattle feeders think that the only way to induce animals to enter handling facilities is to force them in. The owners and managers of feedlots sometimes have a hard time comprehending that if devices such as dip vats and restraint chutes are properly designed, cattle will voluntarily enter them. I can imagine the sensations the animals would feel. If I had a calf's body and hooves, I would be very scared to step on a slippery metal ramp.

There were still problems I had to resolve after the animals left the dip vat. The platform where they exit is usually divided into two pens so that cattle can dry on one side while the other side is being filled. No one understood why the animals coming out of the dip vat would sometimes become excited, but I figured it was because they wanted to follow their drier buddies, not unlike children divided from their classmates on a playground. I installed a solid fence between the two pens to prevent the animals on one side from seeing the animals on the other side. It was a very simple solution, and it amazed me that nobody had ever thought of it before.

The system I designed for filtering and cleaning the cattle hair and other gook out of the dip vat was based on a swimming pool filtration system. My imagination scanned two specific swimming pool filters that I had operated, one on my Aunt Brecheen's ranch in Arizona and one at our home. To prevent water from splashing out of the dip vat, I copied the concrete coping overhang used on swimming pools. That idea, like many of my best designs, came to me very clearly just before I drifted off to sleep at night.

Being autistic, I don't naturally assimilate information that most people take for granted. Instead, I store information in my head as if it were on a CD-ROM disc. When I recall something I have learned, I replay the video in my imagination. The videos in my memory are always specific; for example, I remember handling cattle at the veterinary chute at Producer's Feedlot or McElhaney Cattle Company. I remember exactly how the animals behaved in that specific situation and how the chutes and other equipment were built. The exact construction of steel fenceposts and pipe rails in each case is also part of my visual memory. I can run these images over and over and study them to solve design problems.

If I let my mind wander, the video jumps in a kind of free association   20 from fence construction to a particular welding shop where I've seen posts being cut and Old John, the welder, making gates. If I continue thinking about Old John welding a gate, the video image changes to a series of short scenes of building gates on several projects I've worked on. Each video memory triggers another in this associative fashion, and my daydreams may wander far from the design problem. The next image may be of having a good time listening to John and the construction crew tell war stories, such as the time the backhoe dug into a nest of rattlesnakes and the machine was abandoned for two weeks because everybody was afraid to go near it.

This process of association is a good example of how my mind can wander off the subject. People with more severe autism have difficulty stopping endless associations. I am able to stop them and get my mind back on track. When I find my mind wandering too far away from a design problem I am trying to solve, I just tell myself to get back to the problem.

Interviews with autistic adults who have good speech and are able to articulate their thought processes indicate that most of them also think in visual images. More severely impaired people, who can speak but are unable to explain how they think, have highly associational thought patterns. Charles Hart, the author of *Without Reason,* a book about his autistic son and brother, sums up his son's thinking in one sentence: "Ted's thought processes aren't logical, they're associational." This explains Ted's statement "I'm not afraid of planes. That's why they fly so high." In his mind, planes fly high because he is not afraid of them; he combines two pieces of information, that planes fly high and that he is not afraid of heights.

Another indicator of visual thinking as the primary method of processing information is the remarkable ability many autistic people exhibit in solving jigsaw puzzles, finding their way around a city, or memorizing enormous amounts of information at a glance. My own thought patterns are similar to those described by A. R. Luria in *The Mind of a Mnemonist*. This book describes a man who worked as a newspaper reporter and could perform amazing feats of memory. Like me, the mnemonist had a visual image for everything he had heard or read. Luria writes, "For when he heard or read a word, it was at once converted into a visual image corresponding with the object the word signified for him." The great inventor Nikola Tesla was also a visual thinker. When he designed electric turbines for power generation, he built each turbine in his head. He operated it in his imagination and corrected faults. He said it did not matter whether the turbine was tested in his thoughts or in his shop; the results would be the same.

Early in my career I got into fights with other engineers at meat-packing plants. I couldn't imagine that they could be so stupid as not to see the mistakes on the drawing before the equipment was installed. Now I realize it was not stupidity but a lack of visualization skills. They literally could not see. I was fired from one company that manufactured meat-packing plant equipment because I fought with the engineers over a design which eventually caused the collapse of an overhead track that moved 1,200-pound beef carcasses from the end of a conveyor. As each carcass came off the conveyor, it dropped about three feet before it was abruptly halted by a chain attached to a trolley on the overhead track. The first time the machine was run, the track was pulled out of the ceiling. The employees fixed it by bolting it more securely and installing additional brackets. This only solved the problem temporarily, because the force of the carcasses jerking the chains was so great. Strengthening the overhead track was treating a symptom of the problem rather than its cause. I tried to warn them. It was like bending a paper clip back and forth too many times. After a while it breaks.

Different Ways of Thinking

The idea that people have different thinking patterns is not new.   25
Francis Galton, in *Inquiries into Human Faculty and Development*, wrote that while some people see vivid mental pictures, for others "the idea is not felt to be mental pictures, but rather symbols of facts. In people with low pictorial imagery, they would remember their breakfast table but they could not see it."

It wasn't until I went to college that I realized some people are completely verbal and think only in words. I first suspected this when I read an article in a science magazine about the development of tool use in prehistoric humans.

Some renowned scientist speculated that humans had to develop language before they could develop tools. I thought this was ridiculous, and this article gave me the first inkling that my thought processes were truly different from those of many other people. When I invent things, I do not use language. Some other people think in vividly detailed pictures, but most think in a combination of words and vague, generalized pictures.

For example, many people see a generalized generic church rather than specific churches and steeples when they read or hear the word *steeple*. Their thought patterns move from a general concept to specific examples. I used to become very frustrated when a verbal thinker could not understand something I was trying to express because he or she couldn't see the picture that was crystal clear to me. Further, my mind constantly revises general concepts as I add new information to my memory library. It's like getting a new version of software for the computer. My mind readily accepts the new "software," though I have observed that some people often do not readily accept new information.

Unlike those of most people, my thoughts move from video-like, specific images to generalization and concepts. For example, my concept of dogs is inextricably linked to every dog I've ever known. It's as if I have a card catalogue of dogs I have seen, complete with pictures, which continually grows as I add more examples to my video library. If I think about Great Danes, the first memory that pops into my head is Dansk, the Great Dane owned by the headmaster at my high school. The next Great Dane I visualize is Helga, who was Dansk's replacement. The next is my aunt's dog in Arizona, and my final image comes from an advertisement for Fitwell seat covers that featured that kind of dog. My memories usually appear in my imagination in strict chronological order, and the images I visualize are always specific. There is no generic, generalized Great Dane.

However, not all people with autism are highly visual thinkers, nor do they all process information this way. People throughout the world are on a continuum of visualization skills ranging from next to none, to seeing vague generalized pictures, to seeing semi-specific pictures, to seeing, as in my case, in very specific pictures.

I'm always forming new visual images when I invent new equipment or think of something novel and amusing. I can take images that I have seen, rearrange them, and create new pictures. For example, I can imagine what a dip vat would look like modeled on computer graphics by placing it on my memory of a friend's computer screen. Since his computer is not programmed to do the fancy 3-D rotary graphics, I take computer graphics I have seen on TV or in the movies and superimpose them in my memory. In my visual imagination the dip vat will appear in the kind of high-quality computer graphics shown on *Star Trek*. I can then take a specific dip vat, such as the one at Red River, and redraw it on the computer screen in my mind. I can even duplicate the cartoonlike, three-dimensional skeletal image on the computer screen or imagine the dip vat as a videotape of the real thing.

30

Similarly, I learned how to draw engineering designs by closely observing a very talented draftsman when we worked together at the same feed yard construction company. David was able to render the most fabulous drawings effortlessly. After I left the company, I was forced to do all my own drafting. By studying David's drawings for many hours and photographing them in my memory, I was actually able to emulate David's drawing style. I laid some of his drawings out so I could look at them while I drew my first design. Then I drew my new plan and copied his style. After making three or four drawings, I no longer had to have his drawings out on the table. My video memory was now fully programmed. Copying designs is one thing, but after I drew the Red River drawings, I could not believe I had done them. At the time, I thought they were a gift from God. Another factor that helped me to learn to draw well was something as simple as using the same tools that David used. I used the same brand of pencil, and the ruler and straight edge forced me to slow down and trace the visual images in my imagination.

My artistic abilities became evident when I was in first and second grade. I had a good eye for color and painted watercolors of the beach. One time in fourth grade I modeled a lovely horse from clay. I just did it spontaneously, though I was not able to duplicate it. In high school and college I never attempted engineering drawing, but I learned the value of slowing down while drawing during a college art class. Our assignment had been to spend two hours drawing a picture of one of our shoes. The teacher insisted that the entire two hours be spent drawing that one shoe. I was amazed at how well my drawing came out. While my initial attempts at drafting were terrible, when I visualized myself as David, the draftsman, I'd automatically slow down.

Processing Nonvisual Information

Autistics have problems learning things that cannot be thought about in pictures. The easiest words for an autistic child to learn are nouns, because they directly relate to pictures. Highly verbal autistic children like I was can sometimes learn how to read with phonics. Written words were too abstract for me to remember, but I could laboriously remember the approximately fifty phonetic sounds and a few rules. Lower-functioning children often learn better by association, with the aid of word labels attached to objects in their environment. Some very impaired autistic children learn more easily if words are spelled out with plastic letters they can feel.

Spatial words such as *over* and *under* had no meaning for me until I had a visual image to fix them in my memory. Even now, when I hear the word *under* by itself, I automatically picture myself getting under the cafeteria tables at school during an air-raid drill, a common occurrence on the East Coast during the early fifties. The first memory that any single word triggers is almost always a childhood memory. I can remember the teacher telling us to be quiet and walking single-file into the cafeteria, where six or eight children huddled under each table. If I continue on the same train of thought, more and more associative memories of elementary school emerge. I can remember the teacher scolding me after I hit Alfred for putting dirt on my shoe. All of these memories play like videotapes in the VCR in my imagination. If I allow my mind to keep associating, it will wander a million miles away from the word *under*, to submarines under the Antarctic and the Beatles song "Yellow Submarine." If I let my mind pause on the picture of the yellow submarine, I then hear the song. As I start humming the song and get to the part about people coming on board, my association switches to the gangway of a ship I saw in Australia.

I also visualize verbs. The word *jumping* triggers a memory of jumping   35
hurdles at the mock Olympics held at my elementary school. Adverbs often trigger inappropriate images — *quickly* reminds me of Nestle's Quik — unless they are paired with a verb, which modifies my visual image. For example, "he ran quickly" triggers an animated image of Dick from the first-grade reading book running fast, and "he walked slowly" slows the image down. As a child, I left out words such as *is*, *the*, and *it*, because they had no meaning by themselves. Similarly, words like *of* and *an* made no sense. Eventually I learned how to use them properly, because my parents always spoke correct English and I mimicked their speech patterns. To this day certain verb conjugations, such as *to be*, are absolutely meaningless to me.

When I read, I translate written words into color movies or I simply store a photo of the written page to be read later. When I retrieve the material, I see a photocopy of the page in my imagination. I can then read it like a teleprompter. It is likely that Raymond, the autistic savant depicted in the movie *Rain Man*, used a similar strategy to memorize telephone books, maps, and other information. He simply photocopied each page of the phone book into his memory. When he wanted to find a certain number, he just scanned pages of the phone book that were in his mind. To pull information out of my memory, I have to replay the video. Pulling facts up quickly is sometimes difficult, because I have to play bits of different videos until I find the right tape. This takes time.

When I am unable to convert text to pictures, it is usually because the text has no concrete meaning. Some philosophy books and articles about the cattle futures market are simply incomprehensible. It is much easier for me to under-. stand written text that describes something that can be easily translated into pictures. The following sentence from a story in the February 21, 1994, issue of *Time* magazine, describing the Winter Olympics figure-skating championships, is a good example: "All the elements are in place — the spotlights, the swelling waltzes and jazz tunes, the sequined sprites taking to the air." In my imagination I see the skating rink and skaters. However, if I ponder too long on the word *elements*, I will make the inappropriate association of a periodic table on the wall of my high school chemistry classroom. Pausing on the word *sprite* triggers an image of a Sprite can in my refrigerator instead of a pretty young skater.

Teachers who work with autistic children need to understand associative thought patterns. An autistic child will often use a word in an inappropriate manner. Sometimes these uses have a logical associative meaning and other times they don't. For example, an autistic child might say the word *dog* when he wants to go outside. The word *dog* is associated with going outside. In my own case, I can remember both logical and illogical use of inappropriate words. When I was six, I learned to say *prosecution.* I had absolutely no idea what it meant, but it sounded nice when I said it, so I used it as an exclamation every time my kite hit the ground. I must have baffled more than a few people who heard me exclaim "Prosecution!" to my downward-spiraling kite.

Discussions with other autistic people reveal similar visual styles of thinking about tasks that most people do sequentially. An autistic man who composes music told me that he makes "sound pictures" using small pieces of other music to create new compositions. A computer programmer with autism told me that he sees the general pattern of the program tree. After he visualizes the skeleton for the program, he simply writes the code for each branch. I use similar methods when I review scientific literature and troubleshoot at meat plants. I take specific findings or observations and combine them to find new basic principles and general concepts.

My thinking pattern always starts with specifics and works toward gener-   40
alization in an associational and nonsequential way. As if I were attempting to figure out what the picture on a jigsaw puzzle is when only one-third of the puzzle is completed, I am able to fill in the missing pieces by scanning my video library. Chinese mathematicians who can make large calculations in their heads work the same way. At first they need an abacus, the Chinese calculator, which consists of rows of beads on wires in a frame. They make calculations by moving the rows of beads. When a mathematician becomes really skilled, he simply visualizes the abacus in his imagination and no longer needs a real one. The beads move on a visualized video abacus in his brain.

Abstract Thought

Growing up, I learned to convert abstract ideas into pictures as a way to understand them. I visualized concepts such as peace or honesty with symbolic images. I thought of peace as a dove, an Indian peace pipe, or TV or newsreel footage of the signing of a peace agreement. Honesty was represented by an image of placing one's hand on the Bible in court. A news report describing a person returning a wallet with all the money in it provided a picture of honest behavior.

The Lord's Prayer was incomprehensible until I broke it down into specific visual images. The power and the glory were represented by a semicircular rainbow and an electrical tower. These childhood visual images are still triggered every time I hear the Lord's Prayer. The words "thy will be done" had no meaning when I was a child, and today the meaning is still vague. "Will" is a hard concept to visualize. When I think about it, I imagine God throwing a lightning bolt. Another adult with autism wrote that he visualized "Thou art in heaven" as God with an easel above the clouds. "Trespassing" was pictured as black and orange NO TRESPASSING signs. The word "Amen" at the end of the prayer was a mystery: a man at the end made no sense.

As a teenager and young adult I had to use concrete symbols to understand abstract concepts such as getting along with people and moving on to the next steps of my life, both of which were always difficult. I knew I did not fit in with my high school peers, and I was unable to figure out what I was doing wrong. No matter how hard I tried, they made fun of me. They called me "workhorse," "tape recorder," and "bones" because I was skinny. At the time I was able to figure out why they called me "workhorse" and "bones," but "tape recorder" puzzled me. Now I realize that I must have sounded like a tape recorder when I repeated things verbatim over and over. But back then I just could not figure out why I was such a social dud. I sought refuge in doing things I was good at, such as working on reroofing the barn or practicing my riding prior to a horse show. Personal relationships made absolutely no sense to me until I developed visual symbols of doors and windows. It was then that I started to understand concepts such as learning the give-and-take of a relationship. I still wonder what would have happened to me if I had not been able to visualize my way in the world.

The really big challenge for me was making the transition from high school to college. People with autism have tremendous difficulty with change. In order to deal with a major change such as leaving high school, I needed a way to rehearse it, acting out each phase in my life by walking through an actual door, window, or gate. When I was graduating from high school, I would go and sit on the roof of my dormitory and look up at the stars and think about how I would cope with leaving. It was there I discovered a little door that led to a bigger roof while my dormitory was being remodeled. While I was still living in this old New England house, a much larger building was being constructed over it. One day the carpenters tore out a section of the old roof next to my room. When I walked out, I was now able to look up into the partially finished new building. High on one side was a small wooden door that led to the new roof. The building was changing, and it was now time for me to change too. I could relate to that. I had found the symbolic key.

When I was in college, I found another door to symbolize getting ready for graduation. It was a small metal trap door that went out onto the flat roof of the dormitory. I had to actually practice going through this door many times. When I finally graduated from Franklin Pierce, I walked through a third, very important door, on the library roof.

I no longer use actual physical doors or gates to symbolize each transition in my life. When I reread years of diary entries while writing this book,

45

a clear pattern emerged. Each door or gate enabled me to move on to the next level. My life was a series of incremental steps. I am often asked what the single breakthrough was that enabled me to adapt to autism. There was no single breakthrough. It was a series of incremental improvements. My diary entries show very clearly that I was fully aware that when I mastered one door, it was only one step in a whole series.

> April 22, 1970
> Today everything is completed at Franklin Pierce College and it is now time to walk through the little door in the library. I ponder now about what I should leave as a message on the library roof for future people to find.
> I have reached the top of one step and I am now at the bottom step of graduate school.
> For the top of the building is the highest point on campus and I have gone as far as I can go now.
> I have conquered the summit of FPC. Higher ones still remain unchallenged.
>
> Class 70

> I went through the little door tonight and placed the plaque on the top of the library roof. I was not as nervous this time. I had been much more nervous in the past. Now I have already made it and the little door and the mountain had already been climbed. The conquering of this mountain is only the beginning for the next mountain.
> The word *commencement* means beginning and the top of the library is the beginning of graduate school. It is human nature to strive, and this is why people will climb mountains. The reason why is that people strive to prove that they could do it.
> After all, why should we send a man to the moon? The only real justification is that it is human nature to keep striving out. Man is never satisfied with one goal he keeps reaching. The real reason for going to the library roof was to prove that I could do it.

During my life I have been faced with five or six major doors or gates to go through. I graduated from Franklin Pierce, a small liberal arts college, in 1970, with a degree in psychology, and moved to Arizona to get a PhD. As I found myself getting less interested in psychology and more interested in cattle and animal science, I prepared myself for another big change in my life — switching from a psychology major to an animal science major. On May 8, 1971, I wrote:

> I feel as if I am being pulled more and more in the farm direction. I walked through the cattle chute gate but I am still holding on tightly to the gate post. The wind is blowing harder and harder and

I feel that I will let go of the gate post and go back to the farm; at least for a while. Wind has played an important part in many of the doors. On the roof, the wind was blowing. Maybe this is a symbol that the next level that is reached is not ultimate and that I must keep moving on. At the party [a psychology department party] I felt completely out of place and it seems as if the wind is causing my hands to slip from the gate post so that I can ride free on the wind.

At that time I still struggled in the social arena, largely because I didn't have a concrete visual corollary for the abstraction known as "getting along with people." An image finally presented itself to me while I was washing the bay window in the cafeteria (students were required to do jobs in the dining room). I had no idea my job would take on symbolic significance when I started. The bay window consisted of three glass sliding doors enclosed by storm windows. To wash the inside of the bay window, I had to crawl through the sliding door. The door jammed while I was washing the inside panes, and I was imprisoned between the two windows. In order to get out without shattering the door, I had to ease it back very carefully. It struck me that relationships operate the same way. They also shatter easily and have to be approached carefully. I then made a further association about how the careful opening of doors was related to establishing relationships in the first place. While I was trapped between the windows, it was almost impossible to communicate through the glass. Being autistic is like being trapped like this. The windows symbolized my feelings of disconnection from other people and helped me cope with the isolation. Throughout my life, door and window symbols have enabled me to make progress and connections that are unheard of for some people with autism.

In more severe cases of autism, the symbols are harder to understand and often appear to be totally unrelated to the things they represent. D. Park and P. Youderian described the use of visual symbols and numbers by Jessy Park, then a twelve-year-old autistic girl, to describe abstract concepts such as good and bad. Good things, such as rock music, were represented by drawings of four doors and no clouds. Jessy rated most classical music as pretty good, drawing two doors and two clouds. The spoken word was rated as very bad, with a rating of zero doors and four clouds. She had formed a visual rating system using doors and clouds to describe these abstract qualities. Jessy also had an elaborate system of good and bad numbers, though researchers have not been able to decipher her system fully.

Many people are totally baffled by autistic symbols, but to an autistic 50 person they may provide the only tangible reality or understanding of the world. For example, "French toast" may mean happy if the child was happy while eating it. When the child visualizes a piece of French toast, he becomes happy. A visual image or word becomes associated with an experience. Clara Park, Jessy's mother, described her daughter's fascination with objects such as electric blanket controls and heaters. She had no idea why the objects were so important to Jessy, though she did observe that Jessy was happiest, and her voice was no longer a monotone, when she was thinking about her special things. Jessy was able to talk, but she was unable to tell people why her special things were important. Perhaps she associated electric blanket controls and heaters with warmth and security. The word *cricket* made her happy, and "partly heard song" meant "I don't know." The autistic mind works via these visual associations. At some point in Jessy's life, a partly heard song was associated with not knowing.

Ted Hart, a man with severe autism, has almost no ability to generalize and no flexibility in his behavior. His father, Charles, described how on one occasion Ted put wet clothes in the dresser after the dryer broke. He just went on to the next step in a clothes-washing sequence that he had learned by rote. He has no common sense. I would speculate that such rigid behavior and lack of ability to generalize may be partly due to having little or no ability to change or modify visual memories. Even though my memories of things are stored as individual specific memories, I am able to modify my mental images. For example, I can imagine a church painted in different colors or put the steeple of one church onto the roof of another; but when I hear somebody say the word *steeple*, the first church that I see in my imagination is almost always a childhood memory and not a church image that I have manipulated. This ability to modify images in my imagination helped me to learn how to generalize.

Today, I no longer need door symbols. Over the years I have built up enough real experiences and information from articles and books I have read to be able to make changes and take necessary steps as new situations present themselves. Plus, I have always been an avid reader, and I am driven to take in more and more information to add to my video library. A severely autistic computer programmer once said that reading was "taking in information." For me, it is like programming a computer.

Visual Thinking and Mental Imagery

Recent studies of patients with brain damage and of brain imaging indicate that visual and verbal thought may work via different brain systems. Recordings of blood flow in the brain indicate that when a person visualizes something such as walking through his neighborhood, blood flow increases dramatically in the visual cortex, in parts of the brain that are working hard. Studies of brain-damaged patients show that injury to the left posterior hemisphere can stop the generation of visual images from stored long-term memories, while language and verbal memory are not impaired. This indicates that visual imagery and verbal thought may depend on distinct neurological systems.

The visual system may also contain separate subsystems for mental imagery and image rotation. Image rotation skills appear to be located on the right side of the brain, whereas visual imagery is in the left rear of the brain. In autism, it is possible that the visual system has expanded to make up for verbal and sequencing deficits. The nervous system has a remarkable ability to compensate when it is damaged. Another part can take over for a damaged part.

Recent research by Dr. Pascual-Leone at the National Institutes of Health indicates that exercising a visual skill can make the brain's motor map expand. Research with musicians indicates that real practice on the piano and imagining playing the piano have the same effect on motor maps, as measured by brain scans. The motor maps expand during both real piano playing and mental imagery; random pushing of the keys has no effect. Athletes have also found that both mental practice and real practice can improve a motor skill. Research with patients with damage to the hippocampus has indicated that conscious memory of events and motor learning are separate neurological systems. A patient with hippocampal damage can learn a motor task and get better with practice, but each time he practices he will have no conscious memory of doing the task. The motor circuits become trained, but damage to the hippocampus prevents the formation of new conscious memories. Therefore, the motor circuits learn a new task, such as solving a simple mechanical puzzle, but the person does not remember seeing or doing the puzzle. With repeated practice, the person gets better and better at it, but each time the puzzle is presented, he says he has never seen it before.

I am fortunate in that I am able to build on my library of images and visualize solutions based on those pictures. However, most people with autism lead extremely limited lives, in part because they cannot handle any deviation from their routine. For me, every experience builds on the visual memories I carry from prior experience, and in this way my world continues to grow.

About two years ago I made a personal breakthrough when I was hired to remodel a meat plant that used very cruel restraint methods during kosher slaughter. Prior to slaughter, live cattle were hung upside down by a chain attached to one back leg. It was so horrible I could not stand to watch it. The frantic bellows of terrified cattle could be heard in both the office and the parking lot. Sometimes an animal's back leg was broken during hoisting. This dreadful practice totally violated the humane intent of kosher slaughter. My job was to rip out this cruel system and replace it with a chute that would hold the animal in a standing position while the rabbi performed kosher slaughter. Done properly, the animal should remain calm and would not be frightened.

The new restraining chute was a narrow metal stall which held one steer. It was equipped with a yoke to hold the animal's head, a rear pusher gate to nudge the steer forward into the yoke, and a belly restraint which was raised under the belly like an elevator. To operate the restrainer, the operator had to push six hydraulic control levers in the proper sequence to move the entrance and discharge gates as well as the head- and body-positioning devices. The basic design of this chute had been around for about thirty years, but I added pressure-regulating devices and changed some critical dimensions to make it more comfortable for the animal and to prevent excessive pressure from being applied.

Prior to actually operating the chute at the plant, I ran it in the machine shop before it was shipped. Even though no cattle were present, I was able to program my visual and tactile memory with images of operating the chute. After running the empty chute for five minutes, I had accurate mental pictures of how the gates and other parts of the apparatus moved. I also had tactile memories of how the levers on this particular chute felt when pushed. Hydraulic valves are like musical instruments; different brands of valves have a different feel, just as different types of wind instruments do. Operating the controls in the machine shop enabled me to practice later via mental imagery. I had to visualize the actual controls on the chute and, in my imagination, watch my hands pushing the levers. I could feel in my mind how much force was needed to move the gates at different speeds. I rehearsed the procedure many times in my mind with different types of cattle entering the chute.

On the first day of operation at the plant, I was able to walk up to the   60
chute and run it almost perfectly. It worked best when I operated the hydraulic levers unconsciously, like using my legs for walking. If I thought about the levers, I got all mixed up and pushed them the wrong way. I had to force myself to relax and just allow the restrainer to become part of my body, while completely forgetting about the levers. As each animal entered, I concentrated on moving the apparatus slowly and gently so as not to scare him. I watched his reactions so that I applied only enough pressure to hold him snugly. Excessive pressure would cause discomfort. If his ears were laid back against his head or he struggled, I knew I had squeezed him too hard. Animals are very sensitive to hydraulic equipment. They feel the smallest movement of the control levers.

Through the machine I reached out and held the animal. When I held his head in the yoke, I imagined placing my hands on his forehead and under his chin and gently easing him into position. Body boundaries seemed to disappear, and I had no awareness of pushing the levers. The rear pusher gate and head yoke became an extension of my hands.

People with autism sometimes have body boundary problems. They are unable to judge by feel where their body ends and the chair they are sitting on or the object they are holding begins, much like what happens when a person loses a limb but still experiences the feeling of the limb being there. In this case, the parts of the apparatus that held the animal felt as if they were a continuation of my own body, similar to the phantom limb effect. If I just concentrated on holding the animal gently and keeping him calm, I was able to run the restraining chute very skillfully.

During this intense period of concentration I no longer heard noise from the plant machinery. I didn't feel the sweltering Alabama summer heat, and everything seemed quiet and serene. It was almost a religious experience. It was my job to hold the animal gently, and it was the rabbi's job to perform the final deed. I was able to look at each animal, to hold him gently and make him as comfortable as possible during the last moments of his life. I had participated in the ancient slaughter ritual the way it was supposed to be. A new door had been opened. It felt like walking on water.

QUESTIONS

Reading

1. Highlight, underline, or flag the places that Grandin invokes the images of doors or gates as she reflects on her thought patterns. How does her discussion of this image help her communicate her experiences with autism?

2. What is a *dip vat*? Make a chart of the steps that Grandin took to design the dip vat and the types of thinking that she used for each step. What skills and techniques does she use in this process?

STEP	DESCRIPTION OF SKILL/ TECHNIQUE/THOUGHT PROCESS
1.	
2.	
3.	

3. As she *reflects* on her own thought patterns and processes, which *perspective* does Grandin use? Why might she choose this perspective? How would the essay be different if she had written it from a different point of view?

Exploratory Writing

1. In your opinion, is visual thinking available to everyone? In pairs, experiment with trying to think in pictures instead of in words. Take turns writing a page or two of descriptive prose that evokes visual images ("Picture yourself approaching a red barn. You see a sheep outside the barn"), then have your partner close his or her eyes and try to experience your writing in pictures. Afterwards, discuss your experience. What did this exercise show you about the ways that you normally think?

2. Grandin notes that not everyone with autism is a highly visual thinker. All people "are on a continuum of visualization skills" (paragraph 29). Make a diagram of this continuum. Where would your style of thinking fall on the continuum? Describe the way that thoughts look, sound, or feel to you.

Making Connections

1. Grandin describes how many people with autism need to use visual symbols to understand abstract ideas, such as good and bad. Compare this with the challenges of "inattentional blindness" and "change blindness" that Rita Carter (p. 671) describes.

Essay Writing

1. Grandin writes, "The first thing I did when I arrived at the feedlot was to put myself inside the cattle's heads and look out through their eyes" (paragraph 9). Obviously, she did not literally get inside a cow, but she was able to visualize the way that the world would look from the animal's perspective. Through imagination and visualization, put yourself inside an animal, a plant, or an object. Write an essay or short story reflecting on the world from its perspective.

2. Over the next month, trace the articles about autism published in popular newspapers and magazines. Write an essay reporting on the trends and themes that you notice running through these articles. Describe any differences you notice between Grandin's reflections about her own autism and characterizations of autism in the mass media.

The Cave

Plato

*Plato (c. 427–347 BCE), the student of Socrates and teacher of
Aristotle, is the most revered thinker in Western civilization. As
Alfred North Whitehead stated, "All of Western philosophy is
but a footnote to Plato. . . . [H]is shadow falls over all of Western
thought." Most of the historically significant issues with which
philosophy has been concerned — the nature of being, the question of how we know things, the purposes of right action, the
structure of an ordered society, the meaning of love and beauty —
were issues that he raised. Plato's signature work was his concept
of idealism — the doctrine of a permanent realm of eternal
Forms that shape our mutable, material world. Idealism developed in reaction to the Sophists, who claimed their science of
language could lead to the truth. Plato, however, thought it
dangerous to suppose that the highest realities — Truth, Goodness,
Beauty — could have the flickering impermanence of human
words. Plato believed that language, even matter, could be shaped
to cheat and deceive. Because he mistrusted writing, Plato's own
famous works, namely* The Republic *and* Ion, *are written not as
treatises but as dialogues with Socrates. This has, however, led to
problems of interpretation and consistency. Nonetheless, these two
works have held up as two of the most important and engaging
works in philosophical thinking.*

*"The Cave," perhaps the best-known of Plato's allegories, is
presented as a story told by Socrates and then interpreted by the
questioner. It appears at the start of Book VII of* The Republic.
*The following version was translated by Paul Shorey and pub-
lished in 1961.*

Next, said I, compare our nature in respect of education and its lack to
such an experience as this. Picture men dwelling in a sort of subterranean
cavern with a long entrance open to the light on its entire width. Conceive
them as having their legs and necks fettered from childhood, so that they remain in the same spot, able to look forward only, and prevented by the fetters from turning their heads. Picture further the light from a fire burning
higher up and at a distance behind them, and between the fire and the prisoners and above them a road along which a low wall has been built, as the

exhibitors of puppet shows have partitions before the men themselves, above which they show the puppets.

All that I see, he said.

See also, then, men carrying past the wall implements of all kinds that rise above the wall, and human images and shapes of animals as well, wrought in stone and wood and every material, some of these bearers presumably speaking and others silent.

A strange image you speak of, he said, and strange prisoners.

Like to us, I said. For, to begin with, tell me do you think that these men   5
would have seen anything of themselves or of one another except the shadows cast from the fire on the wall of the cave that fronted them?

How could they, he said, if they were compelled to hold their heads unmoved through life?

And again, would not the same be true of the objects carried past them?
Surely.

If then they were able to talk to one another, do you not think that they would suppose that in naming the things that they saw they were naming the passing objects?

Necessarily.   10

And if their prison had an echo from the wall opposite them, when one of the passers-by uttered a sound, do you think that they would suppose anything else than the passing shadow to be the speaker?

By Zeus, I do not, said he.

Then in every way such prisoners would deem reality to be nothing else than the shadows of the artificial objects.

Quite inevitably, he said.

Consider, then, what would be the manner of the release and healing   15
from these bonds and this folly if in the course of nature something of this sort should happen to them. When one was freed from his fetters and compelled to stand up suddenly and turn his head around and walk and to lift up his eyes to the light, and in doing all this felt pain and, because of the dazzle and glitter of the light, was unable to discern the objects whose shadows he formerly saw, what do you suppose would be his answer if someone told him that what he had seen before was all a cheat and an illusion, but that now, being nearer to reality and turned toward more real things, he saw more truly? And if also one should point out to him each of the passing objects and constrain him by questions to say what it is, do you not think that he would be at a loss and that he would regard what he formerly saw as more real than the things now pointed out to him?

Far more real, he said.

And if he were compelled to look at the light itself, would not that pain his eyes, and would he not turn away and flee to those things which he is able to discern and regard them as in very deed more clear and exact than the objects pointed out?

It is so, he said.

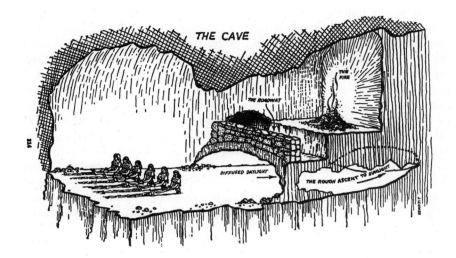

And if, said I, someone should drag him thence by force up the ascent which is rough and steep, and not let him go before he had drawn him out into the light of the sun, do you not think that he would find it painful to be so haled along, and would chafe at it, and when he came out into the light, that his eyes would be filled with its beams so that he would not be able to see even one of the things that we call real?

Why, no, not immediately, he said.   20

Then there would be need of habituation, I take it, to enable him to see the things higher up. And at first he would most easily discern the shadows and, after that, the likenesses or reflections in water of men and other things, and later, the things themselves, and from these he would go on to contemplate the appearances in the heavens and heaven itself, more easily by night, looking at the light of the stars and the moon, than by day the sun and the sun's light.

Of course.

And so, finally, I suppose, he would be able to look upon the sun itself and see its true nature, not by reflections in water or phantasms of it in an alien setting, but in and by itself in its own place.

Necessarily, he said.

And at this point he would infer and conclude that this it is that pro-   25
vides the seasons and the courses of the year and presides over all things in the visible region, and is in some sort the cause of all these things that they had seen.

Obviously, he said, that would be the next step.

Well then, if he recalled to mind his first habitation and what passed for wisdom there, and his fellow bondsmen, do you not think that he would count himself happy in the change and pity them?

He would indeed.

And if there had been honors and commendations among them which they bestowed on one another and prizes for the man who is quickest to make out the shadows as they pass and best able to remember their customary precedences, sequences, and coexistences, and so most successful in guessing at what was to come, do you think he would be very keen about such rewards, and that he would envy and emulate those who were honored by these prisoners and lorded it among them, or that he would feel with Homer and greatly prefer while living on earth to be serf of another, a landless man, and endure anything rather than opine with them and live that life?

Yes, he said, I think that he would choose to endure anything rather than such a life.   30

And consider this also, said I. If such a one should go down again and take his old place would he not get his eyes full of darkness, thus suddenly coming out of the sunlight?

He would indeed.

Now if he should be required to contend with these perpetual prisoners in "evaluating" these shadows while his vision was still dim and before his eyes were accustomed to the dark — and this time required for habituation would not be very short — would he not provoke laughter, and would it not be said of him that he had returned from his journey aloft with his eyes ruined and that it was not worthwhile even to attempt the ascent? And if it were possible to lay hands on and to kill the man who tried to release them and lead them up, would they not kill him?

They certainly would, he said.

This image then, dear Glaucon, we must apply as a whole to all that has   35
been said, likening the region revealed through sight to the habitation of the prison, and the light of the fire in it to the power of the sun. And if you assume that the ascent and the contemplation of the things above is the soul's ascension to the intelligible region, you will not miss my surmise, since that is what you desire to hear. But God knows whether it is true. But, at any rate, my dream as it appears to me is that in the region of the known the last thing to be seen and hardly seen is the idea of good, and that when seen it must needs point us to the conclusion that this is indeed the cause for all things of all that is right and beautiful, giving birth in the visible world to light, and the author of light and itself in the intelligible world being the authentic source of truth and reason, and that anyone who is to act wisely in private or public must have caught sight of this.

I concur, he said, so far as I am able.

Come then, I said, and join me in this further thought, and do not be surprised that those who have attained to this height are not willing to occupy themselves with the affairs of men, but their souls ever feel the upward urge and the yearning for that sojourn above. For this, I take it, is likely if in this point too the likeness of our image holds.

Yes, it is likely.

And again, do you think it at all strange, said I, if a man returning from divine contemplations to the petty miseries of men cuts a sorry figure and appears most ridiculous, if, while still blinking through the gloom, and before he has become sufficiently accustomed to the environing darkness, he is compelled, in courtrooms or elsewhere to contend about the shadows of justice or the images that cast the shadows and to wrangle in debate about the notions of these things in the minds of those who have never seen justice itself?

It would be by no means strange, he said. 40

But a sensible man, I said, would remember that there are two distinct disturbances of the eyes arising from two causes, according as the shift is from light to darkness or from darkness to light, and, believing that the same thing happens to the soul too, whenever he saw a soul perturbed and unable to discern something, he would not laugh unthinkingly, but would observe whether coming from a brighter life its vision was obscured by the unfamiliar darkness, or whether the passage from the deeper dark of ignorance into a more luminous world and the greater brightness had dazzled its vision. And so he would deem the one happy in its experience and way of life and pity the other, and if it pleased him to laugh at it, his laughter would be less laughable than that at the expense of the soul that had come down from the light above.

That is a very fair statement, he said.

Then, if this is true, our view of these matters must be this, that education is not in reality what some people proclaim it to be in their professions. What they aver is that they can put true knowledge into a soul that does not possess it, as if they were inserting vision into blind eyes.

They do indeed, he said.

But our present argument indicates, said I, that the true analogy for this 45 indwelling power in the soul and the instrument whereby each of us apprehends is that of an eye that could not be converted to the light from the darkness except by turning the whole body. Even so this organ of knowledge must be turned around from the world of becoming together with the entire soul, like the scene-shifting periactus in the theater, until the soul is able to endure the contemplation of essence and the brightest region of being. And this, we say, is the good, do we not?

QUESTIONS

Reading

1. In this dialogue from *The Republic*, Socrates uses an extended *analogy* to *explain* his ideas about illusion versus the truth to be found through "the soul's ascension to the intelligible region" (paragraph 35). Briefly summarize this dialogue without using any analogies. What is lost in your rewritten version?
2. In what ways are human beings like chained prisoners in a cave, able to see only the shadows of carved images of things? Why is their delusion

not remediable by simply releasing them from the chains that impede their accurate perception of things?

3. Given that Socrates puts so much emphasis on the accurate versus inaccurate perception of things, how do you account for his statement "likening the region revealed through sight to the habitation of the prison" (paragraph 35)? How, one might ask, are we imprisoned by our eyes, by our visual perceptions? What, after all, could be more liberating than to see things clearly with our own eyes?

Exploratory Writing

1. Examine the illustration included with the text. Does it help you visualize Socrates' analogy? Are there any details in the text that are missing or misrepresented in the drawing? Using any materials and media you like, create your own visual representation of "The Cave." (You could make a collage, painting, drawing, or cartoon.) Try to make it an accurate representation of Plato's text.

2. Many people were familiar with the cave allegory before they ever read Plato's text, and many others (all those who cannot read ancient Greek) have only read *The Republic* in translation, which sometimes reflects the assumptions and styles of the translator's own time. Find two different translations of Book VII of Plato's *Republic*, and flag sections where the language varies between the translations. What interpretations of the text does each version reveal?

Making Connections

1. Socrates was famously mistrustful of writing. In fact, he was probably illiterate. Although documentation suggests that he did exist, our knowledge of his philosophy comes from the writings of his literate students and contemporaries, including Xenophon and Plato. Compare Socrates' style of thinking and discussion to that of Temple Grandin (p. 647), Oliver Sacks's Dr. P. (p. 680), Sacks himself, John Berger (p. 710), or Rita Carter (p. 671). Do you recognize anything Socratic about their thinking and work?

Essay Writing

1. Compare and contrast life in the cave with the situation of people watching TV, playing video games, or sitting at desks surfing the Internet. Assuming that Socrates would probably consider all these media more illusory than life in the cave — images of shadows of images — how would you respond to his charges? Write an essay arguing your position.

2. Write an essay reflecting on an experience in your own life that might be described or illuminated by Plato's metaphor of the cave. Imagine yourself as the inhabitant of the cave, mistaking an illusion for reality. Consider this situation in terms of light and darkness, good and evil, and vision and blindness.

A Stream of Illusion

Rita Carter

Rita Carter is a medical writer in Britain who contributes to the Independent, New Scientist, *the* Daily Mail, *and the* Telegraph, *among other publications. Fascinated with the nature and mechanics of the conscious mind, she has authored two popular science books,* Mapping the Mind *(1999) and* Exploring Consciousness *(2004), both of which explore not only the geography of the brain but the fundamental nature of reality as we experience it. Carter is a frequent panelist on the Great Debate — a yearly science lecture series in England — and was twice awarded the Medical Journalists' Association prize for outstanding contribution to medical journalism. She lives in Ashford, England.*

When you are a bear of Very Little Brain, and Think of Things, you sometimes find that a Thing which seemed very Thingish inside you is quite different when it gets out into the open and has other people looking at it.

    — POOH BEAR FROM *WINNIE THE POOH*, A. A. MILNE

Please do not think about your nose. Just forget that you have that fleshy protuberance altogether.

Successful? I doubt it. Your consciousness, like mine, constantly roves in time and space — switching from a passing face, to the origin of the universe, to tonight's dinner or the tickle in your toe — seemingly at the behest of your will. It is like an all-enveloping movie, behind which the self lurks like some shadowy director calling the shots.

The intuition that this "I" is in control is, however, almost certainly illusory. Your brain is subjected to a continuous barrage of cues — light waves that activate your retinal cells; vibrations that ruffle the hairs in your cochlea; molecules that latch on to the receptors on your tongue and in your olfactory bulb; molecular assaults on the nerve endings in your skin and changes in body cells that send urgent messages up your spinal cord. It is these stimuli that dictate where the action goes next, even if you are not consciously aware of them. The most compelling cues are immediate, personal and odd. They snag your attention, and where attention goes, so does consciousness. So if you are asked not to think about your nose — an immediate, personal and decidedly odd request — it is almost impossible not to do so.

By now, however, your brain will have checked out the status of your nose and (I hope) found it to be okay. The show has moved on.

So, what are you conscious of at this very instant? Start with the obvious: 5 certainly you will say that you are conscious of these words; their meaning; the look of them on this page; perhaps the book itself and maybe even the place in which you are reading it. You might say you are also conscious of the state of your stomach (if you are hungry); the temperature (if it is too hot or cold); or maybe you are conscious of a slight headache; the drone of traffic; or some lingering feeling of irritation or elation from a recent social encounter. Sensations, thoughts, emotions; all jostling for attention . . . a rich and full mix.

Question two: Are you clear about the contents of your consciousness? Can you say, precisely, which things are conscious and which are not? Of course (given a cue like this) your mind may rove around and yank up memories and ideas which were not conscious an instant ago. But at any precise moment would you say there were things that were in consciousness (this question, for example) and things that — though known to you, like your middle name or the rain outside — are definitely not? In other words, do there seem to be two distinct levels of mind — conscious and unconscious — with a clear division between them?

Question three: How does it feel from moment to moment? Does your consciousness flow smoothly, continuously, and in real time? Or does it lurch along, punctuated by jump-cuts and freeze-frames, flashbacks and fade-outs?

Final question: Whose is it, this consciousness? If that seems a daft thing to ask it is because, if there is one thing about consciousness that seems incontrovertible it is that it is yours — your own, single, private, unshareable world.

Now, impertinent though it is to throw doubt on your private introspection, the assessment you have just made of your own consciousness is almost certainly incorrect. The contents of one's own mind seem to be the single thing we can talk about with absolute confidence, but in fact we are very unreliable witnesses and nothing about consciousness — not even the assumption that it is yours and yours alone — is as clear-cut as it might at first appear.

Take that seemingly fulsome contents list. Sight plays a huge part in 10 human consciousness, and visual perception is probably better understood than any other sort, so it is a good place to start. Glance up, momentarily, at your surroundings. What were you conscious of in that first split second? Not everything, certainly — you are limited, after all, by your field of vision. But within that field you probably thought you took in more or less the whole scene, albeit not in detail. If you are inside a building, for example, you would probably report seeing the walls, the carpet, the door, a table, the window and the view beyond. Certainly you would say you were aware of the main objects, at least to the extent that if you looked up again you would notice if one of them disappeared.

So try this. At the end of this paragraph, without looking up again, close your eyes and try to bring the scene around you to mind. Recall the table — what sort of legs does it have? What does it have on its surface — was there

The lines show the eye movements; and the circles, the resting points of a person looking at a painting as detected by eye-tracking apparatus. Only the regions within the circles are consciously registered. Such experiments show that an observer typically focuses on four or five small parts of a scene and continues to scrutinize only these details even when they go on looking at the same thing for some time. Yet their subjective impression is that they have observed the whole image. The fact that they have not studied the whole scene usually only becomes apparent when they try to recall it and find they can't.

a cup? A magazine? If you are in your own home you may be able to visualize the table clearly, and you may know there is a magazine and a cup on it because you just put them there. But exactly where on the table is the cup? Which way does its handle point? What does the magazine cover look like? Do this for each element of the scene and note exactly what appears in your mind's eye. Unless you are one of the few people with eidetic (photographic) memory, when you concentrate on these images you will find they become hazy. If you are in unfamiliar surroundings the image you conjure in your mind will be even hazier. In fact, the chances are that in that first glance you were fully conscious — that is, conscious enough to give a report — of no more than four or five objects or aspects of the scene. This seems to be the limit of our capacity at any one moment.[1]

Our startling lack of consciousness of what is in front of our eyes was demonstrated in an experiment, carried out at Harvard University, in which students were invited to sign on for an (unspecified) experiment by filling in a consent form. The form was handed to them, from behind a counter, by a young man with blond hair, wearing a yellow shirt. When the form was completed, the man took it and moved behind a bookcase, ostensibly to file it away. In fact, while he was out of view, another man — dark-haired, and wearing a blue shirt — stepped into his place. The second experimenter then emerged from behind the bookcase, handed the students an information pack, and directed them to the "experiment room" — where 75 per cent of the students were found to be totally unaware that they had just dealt with two entirely different people.[2]

In another experiment, subjects watched a competitive ball game being played in a room. They were told to watch the moves carefully. Halfway through the game a woman carrying an umbrella walked slowly across the foreground of their vision, from one side of the room to the other. Barely anyone noticed.

Our tendency to miss things we are not primed to look for is called, in neurospeak, "inattentional blindness." Scientists have been studying it for just a few years, but magicians have used it since the year dot.

"Change blindness" is a similar phenomenon, and demonstrates that, even when you are invited to concentrate on a scene, huge changes can take place in it without you noticing. If you look at the two pictures on page 675, you will probably spot almost immediately that they are different. The change is not small or marginal — it is quite big, and right there in the centre of the picture. If these pictures were presented to you one after the other, in quick succession, you would expect that the difference in them would leap out at you, much as it does when you see them next to each other. And, indeed, if you alternate between the two pictures without leaving a time-gap between them, the change does show clearly. But if you alternate the pictures with a tiny period — just one-fifth of a second — of blackout between them, most people fail to see any change at all.   15

In one series of change blindness experiments, none of the subjects noticed when a large building, smack in the centre of the picture, shrank by a quarter between glimpses. None of them saw that two men exchanged hats of different colours and styles. And 92 per cent failed to spot the sudden disappearance of a group of thirty puffins on an otherwise uninhabited ice floe.[3]

A gorilla (actually someone in a gorilla suit) walks through the middle of a basketball game. An observer, intent on the game, will often fail to notice such an extraordinary event — a phenomenon known as inattentional blindness.[4]

It is quite easy to spot the difference between these two pictures when they are [shown together] (the plane's engine is missing in the bottom picture). But if the images are shown in succession, with a brief blackout in between, very few people notice the change, even though the engine is in the centre of the picture.

Recent research into change blindness shows you don't even have to leave a gap. If you alternate two different pictures rapidly and, at the moment of each change "splatter" unaltered areas of the image with a few small blots, the difference in the pictures can go unnoticed for more than half a minute.[5] The only changes that are not masked by the splashes are those which capture our attention instantly — typically the central or "action" part of the image, or something that has particular emotional salience, for example, a facial expression or a scene of social interaction like a kiss.

Within-the-moment visual consciousness is not, then, the rich and detailed panorama we think it is. It is limited to a handful of clear perceptions, and the apparent detail is an illusion. Our minds are fooled because consciousness unfolds in time, and the construction of our experience depends on merging the consciousness of one moment with that of the next. Our impoverished visual perceptions are fleshed out by our memories of the perceptions that went before, and our expectations of what will come next. So great is the illusory nature of vision that it is possible to construct the entire experience of seeing without any sensory input at all. In a rare condition known as Anton's delusion people who become blind (usually due to a severe stroke) continue to believe that they can see.[6] Such a state seems hard to credit, but it may be just a very extreme example of something all of us do the whole time.

Kevin O'Regan, an experimental psychologist at the Université René Descartes, France, believes that almost everything we see is, in effect, a "grand illusion." The few items which catch our attention in a scene are directly sensed while everything else consists of nothing but the knowledge that it is there, and that if we turned our attention to it we would bring about certain neurological changes which would provide us with direct knowledge of them. We get an impression of rich, all-round cinemascope not because we have a picture in our brain but because whenever we think about whether we can see something, our attention is drawn to it and information about it therefore immediately becomes available. The sensation of seeing something comes, not from a replica of the thing being created somewhere in the brain, but from the knowledge that information about it is at this moment available.

It is, says O'Regan, rather like being rich. A person with a billion   20
pounds in the bank feels rich because she knows it is there, not because she spends her entire time taking wads of notes out of a hole-in-the-wall. If the money was not there she would not know until she next needed some and found she could not get it.[7] Of course, says O'Regan, seeing has much more of a "real feel" than feeling rich. To account for this difference, O'Regan notes that, among other things, seeing is intimately linked to body motion: the slightest eye or head shift brings new information flooding in, so we don't have to think about how we are going to get it. To feel similarly

"really" rich, a person would need to be able to access their money just by reaching for it.

If O'Regan is correct, a person with Anton's delusion would be rather like a person who had spent their fortune but — due to an administration error — kept receiving bank statements that showed it to be intact. They would not realize the truth until they wrote a cheque and found it bounced. Similarly, a person with Anton's delusion can operate very happily as a fully sighted person until they physically collide with objects that happened not to be in their imaginary picture of the world.

The difference, then, between the person with Anton's delusion and one with normal vision shows only in their interaction with the world. The former will trip over things rather more often than the latter on account of their sight being wholly illusory rather than mainly so. But their visual *experience* will be similar.

If normal sight is a matter of "knowing" you can see, blindsight is the opposite: seeing without knowing it. During the First World War stories emerged from the trenches about soldiers who — though apparently blinded by head injuries — still dodged bullets. They seemed to be guided by some sixth sense. In 1917, a possible explanation for the phenomenon emerged, when the English neurologist George Riddoch described what is now known as blindsight.[8]

Blindsight is observed most easily in people who have patches of dead tissue in the primary visual cortex (V1). V1 is, in one way, like a mirror: if an object is at the edge of the visual field, it is processed by neurons at the edge of V1, and if the object is in the centre of the field central V1 neurons respond to it. Dead tissue in V1 therefore creates spatially corresponding blind spots (scotomas) in the visual field. Although people with scotomas claim to have no visual awareness in their blind spot, when a moving object crosses it some of them are able to report with 100 per cent accuracy the direction in which it is moving. Because they are unaware of it, however, they only report it when they are prompted to "guess." The subjects themselves are usually, at first, staggered to discover that their guesses are correct.

Recent research on blindsight subjects has revealed that it is not just movement that can be reported on — one "star" blindsighter can tell the shape and colour of a target as well as its motion, and even the expression on an "invisible" face.[9] Blindsight — or something very like it — has also been demonstrated, in cleverly devised laboratory experiments, in people with normal vision.[10] So has "blindtouch" and even "blindsmell." In one experiment, for example, people were asked to smell two phials of liquid, each of which had a very weak odour — one pleasant (amyl acetate, similar to bananas) and the other nasty (butyric acid, a bit like rancid butter). The smells were so weak the volunteers claimed they could not detect them at all. However, when prompted to "guess" which one smelt nice and which was nasty, they were very successful.[11]

Studies such as this suggest that sensory information which does not make it to consciousness may nevertheless influence our behaviour. Places that somehow don't "feel right"; people who seem curiously attractive for reasons we can't work out — perhaps the effect they have on us is due to our unconscious processing of their aversive or attractive odour.

Notes

1. Nørretranders (1998); Edelman and Tonio (2000).
2. Mack and Rock (1998).
3. Grimes (1996), pp. 89–110.
4. Simons and Chabris (1999); Simons (2007).
5. O'Regan, Rensink, and Clark (1999), p. 34.
6. Carter (1998).
7. O'Regan (2000, April).
8. Riddoch (1917), pp. 15–57.
9. Heywood and Kentridge (2000), pp. 125–26.
10. Muckli et al. (1997).
11. Radil (2000, April).

Bibliography

Carter, R. (1998). *Mapping the mind*. London: Weidenfeld and Nicolson.

Edelman, G., & Tonio, G. (2000). *A universe of consciousness*. New York: Basic Books.

Grimes, J. (1996). On the failure to detect changes in scenes across saccades. In K. Akins (Ed.), *Perception* (pp. 89–110). New York: Oxford University Press.

Heywood, C. A., & Kentridge, R. W. (2000). Affective blindsight? *Trends in Cognitive Science, 4*, 125–26.

Mack, A., & Rock, I. (1998). *Inattentional blindness*. Cambridge, MA: MIT Press.

Muckli, L., Hacker, H., Singer, W., & Goebel, R. (1997). Blindsight in normal observers? Activity in area MT/MST during the perception of transparent motion. *NeuroImage, 5*(4), 144.

Nørretranders, T. (1998). *The user illusion: Cutting consciousness down to size*. New York: Viking.

O'Regan, J. K. (2000, April). Change blindness and the visual world as an outside memory. In *Is visual consciousness a grand illusion?* Symposium conducted at Toward a Science of Consciousness IV, Tucson, AZ.

O'Regan, J. K., Rensink, R. A., & Clark, J. J. (1999). Change-blindness as a result of "mudsplashes." *Nature, 398*, 34.

Radil, T. (2000, April). Anosmic and hyposmic olfaction — a blindsight-like phenomenon. Paper presented at Toward a Science of Consciousness Conference, Tucson, AZ.

Riddoch, G. (1917). Dissociation of visual perception due to occipital injuries, with especial reference to appreciation of movement. *Brain, 40*, 15–57.

Simons, D. J. (2007). Opaque gorilla from Simons and Chabris. [Video file]. Retrieved from [http://viscog.beckman.illinois.edu/flashmovie/15.php].

Simons, D. J., & Chabris, C. F. (1999). Gorillas in our midst: Sustained inattentional blindness for dynamic events. *Perception, 28*, 1059–74.

[These notes were adapted to conform to APA style from the original notes in Carter's book *Exploring Consciousness*. –Eds.]

QUESTIONS

Reading

1. Highlight, underline, or flag the exercises that Carter asks you to do in this essay. What purpose do they serve in her *report* on consciousness and illusion? Which types of thinking do they seem to stimulate?
2. What is "change blindness"?
3. What voice does Carter use in this essay? How might her discussion of perception be different if she described her own experience?

Exploratory Writing

1. Without thinking too much about your responses, quickly jot down answers to Carter's questions (paragraphs 5 through 8). In pairs, trade your answers and review them. Is your "consciousness" the same as your partner's? Do you agree with Carter that the assessment you've made of your own consciousness is incorrect? In what ways are you an unreliable witness?
2. In your own words, describe *blindsight, blindtouch,* and *blindsmell.* Have you had a personal experience in which sensory information that did not make it to consciousness influenced your perceptions or behavior, such as visiting a place that somehow didn't "feel right," or finding yourself mysteriously drawn to someone? Relate this experience, connecting it to Carter's idea of *illusion.*

Making Connections

1. John Berger (p. 710) argues that the invention of the camera has changed not only *what* we see, but *how* we see it. Compare the different "ways of seeing" that Berger and Carter discuss in their essays. How do their theoretical perspectives differ?
2. Carter shows how the mind makes shortcuts as we process and perceive what we are seeing. Temple Grandin (p. 647) writes that "thinking in pictures" instead of words is a condition of her autism. In order to understand abstract ideas, she visualizes them using concrete symbols. This helps her design systems in an innovative way. Scott McCloud (p. 693) finds that comics have a hidden power to convey something unique that other media cannot capture in the same way. Choose any three authors in this casebook, and chart their accounts of the role of mental shortcuts in creating or understanding art.

Essay Writing

1. Write a case study of a person suffering from a visual disorder. You can research a real life case or invent one. What are the physiological and psychological details of this person's sensory malfunction? How are they similar to the illusory perceptions of all human beings?

The Man Who Mistook His Wife for a Hat

Oliver Sacks

Oliver Sacks was born in London, England, in 1933 and educated in London and Oxford before coming to the United States to complete his education in California and New York. At present he is professor of neurology and psychiatry at Columbia University Medical Center. He is best known, however, for his extraordinary writing on matters related to his medical studies, in such books as Awakenings *(1974),* Seeing Voices: A Journey into the World of the Deaf *(1989),* An Anthropologist on Mars *(1995),* The Island of the Colorblind *(1997), and his national best-seller,* The Man Who Mistook His Wife for a Hat *(1986), from which the following selection was adapted. Interested in the art of storytelling as well as in clinical neurology, Sacks subtitled the book in which this essay appeared "and Other Clinical Tales." He insists that his essays are not just case studies but also tales or fables of "heroes, victims, martyrs, warriors." In his writing, he says, "the scientific and romantic . . . come together at the intersection of fact and fable." Sacks's prose style is lyrical as well as accurate; his explanation of prosopagnosia (perception without recognition) seeks to engage our interest and emotions while it defines and illustrates a syndrome unfamiliar to many readers. His most recent book is* Musicophilia: Tales of Music and the Brain *(2007).*

Dr. P. was a musician of distinction, well known for many years as a singer, and then, at the local school of music, as a teacher. It was here, in relation to his students, that certain strange problems were first observed. Sometimes a student would present himself, and Dr. P. would not recognize him; or, specifically, would not recognize his face. The moment the student spoke, he would be recognized by his voice. Such incidents multiplied, causing embarrassment, perplexity, fear — and, sometimes, comedy. For not only did Dr. P. increasingly fail to see faces, but he saw faces when there were no faces to see: genially, Magoo-like, when in the street he might pat the heads of water hydrants and parking meters, taking these to be the heads of children; he would amiably address carved knobs on the furniture and be astounded when they did not reply. At first these odd mistakes were laughed off as jokes, not least by Dr. P. himself. Had he not always had a quirky sense of humor and been given to Zen-like paradoxes and jests? His musical powers were as dazzling as ever; he did not feel ill—he had never felt better; and the mistakes were so ludicrous—and so ingenious—that they could hardly be serious or betoken anything serious. The notion of there being "something the matter" did not emerge until some three years later, when diabetes developed. Well aware that diabetes could affect his eyes, Dr. P. consulted an ophthalmologist, who took a careful history and examined his eyes closely. "There's nothing the matter with your eyes," the doctor concluded. "But there is trouble with the visual parts of your brain. You don't need my help, you must see a neurologist." And so, as a result of this referral, Dr. P. came to me.

It was obvious within a few seconds of meeting him that there was no trace of dementia in the ordinary sense. He was a man of great cultivation and charm who talked well and fluently, with imagination and humor. I couldn't think why he had been referred to our clinic.

And yet there *was* something a bit odd. He faced me as he spoke, was oriented towards me, and yet there was something the matter—it was difficult to formulate. He faced me with his *ears*, I came to think, but not with his eyes. These, instead of looking, gazing, at me, "taking me in," in the normal way, made sudden strange fixations—on my nose, on my right ear, down to my chin, up to my right eye—as if noting (even studying) these individual features, but not seeing my whole face, its changing expressions, "me," as a whole. I am not sure that I fully realized this at the time—there was just a teasing strangeness, some failure in the normal interplay of gaze and expression. He saw me, he *scanned* me, and yet . . .

"What seems to be the matter?" I asked him at length.

"Nothing that I know of," he replied with a smile, "but people seem to   5
think there's something wrong with my eyes."

"But *you* don't recognize any visual problems?"

"No, not directly, but I occasionally make mistakes."

I left the room briefly to talk to his wife. When I came back, Dr. P. was sitting placidly by the window, attentive, listening rather than looking out. "Traffic," he said, "street sounds, distant trains—they make a sort of symphony, do they not? You know Honegger's[1] *Pacific 234?*"

What a lovely man, I thought to myself. How can there be anything seriously the matter? Would he permit me to examine him?

"Yes, of course, Dr. Sacks."   10

I stilled my disquiet, his perhaps, too, in the soothing routine of a neurological exam—muscle strength, coordination, reflexes, tone. . . . It was while examining his reflexes—a trifle abnormal on the left side—that the first bizarre experience occurred. I had taken off his left shoe and scratched

---

[1]*Arthur Honegger* (1892–1955): French composer. [Eds.]

the sole of his foot with a key — a frivolous-seeming but essential test of a reflex — and then, excusing myself to screw my ophthalmoscope together, left him to put on the shoe himself. To my surprise, a minute later, he had not done this.

"Can I help?" I asked.

"Help what? Help whom?"

"Help you put on your shoe."

"Ach," he said, "I had forgotten the shoe," adding, *sotto voce,* "The   15
shoe? The shoe?" He seemed baffled.

"Your shoe," I repeated. "Perhaps you'd put it on."

He continued to look downwards, though not at the shoe, with an intense but misplaced concentration. Finally his gaze settled on his foot: "That is my shoe, yes?"

Did I mis-hear? Did he mis-see?

"My eyes," he explained, and put a hand to his foot. "*This* is my shoe, no?"

"No, it is not. That is your foot. *There* is your shoe."   20

"Ah! I thought that was my foot."

Was he joking? Was he mad? Was he blind? If this was one of his "strange mistakes," it was the strangest mistake I had ever come across.

I helped him on with his shoe (his foot), to avoid further complication. Dr. P. himself seemed untroubled, indifferent, maybe amused. I resumed my examination. His visual acuity was good: he had no difficulty seeing a pin on the floor, though sometimes he missed it if it was placed to his left.

He saw all right, but what did he see? I opened out a copy of the *National Geographic* magazine and asked him to describe some pictures in it.

His responses here were very curious. His eyes would dart from one   25
thing to another, picking up tiny features, individual features, as they had done with my face. A striking brightness, a color, a shape would arrest his attention and elicit comment — but in no case did he get the scene-as-a-whole. He failed to see the whole, seeing only details, which he spotted like blips on a radar screen. He never entered into relation with the picture as a whole — never faced, so to speak, *its* physiognomy. He had no sense whatever of a landscape or scene.

I showed him the cover, an unbroken expanse of Sahara dunes.

"What do you see here?" I asked.

"I see a river," he said. "And a little guest-house with its terrace on the water. People are dining out on the terrace. I see colored parasols here and there." He was looking, if it was "looking," right off the cover into mid-air and confabulating nonexistent features, as if the absence of features in the actual picture had driven him to imagine the river and the terrace and the colored parasols.

I must have looked aghast, but he seemed to think he had done rather well. There was a hint of a smile on his face. He also appeared to have decided that the examination was over and started to look around for his hat. He reached out his hand and took hold of his wife's head, tried to lift it off, to put it on. He had apparently mistaken his wife for a hat! His wife looked as if she was used to such things.

I could make no sense of what had occurred in terms of conventional neurology (or neuropsychology). In some ways he seemed perfectly preserved, and in others absolutely, incomprehensibly devastated. How could he, on the one hand, mistake his wife for a hat and, on the other, function, as apparently he still did, as a teacher at the music school? 30

I had to think, to see him again — and to see him in his own familiar habitat, at home.

A few days later I called on Dr. P. and his wife at home, with the score of the *Dichterliebe* in my briefcase (I knew he liked Schumann),[2] and a variety of odd objects for the testing of perception. Mrs. P. showed me into a lofty apartment, which recalled fin-de-siècle Berlin. A magnificent old Bösendorfer stood in state in the center of the room, and all around it were music stands, instruments, scores. . . . There were books, there were paintings, but the music was central. Dr. P. came in, a little bowed, and, distracted, advanced with outstretched hands to the grandfather clock, but, hearing my voice, corrected himself, and shook hands with me. We exchanged greetings and chatted a little of current concerts and performances. Diffidently, I asked him if he would sing.

"The *Dichterliebe!*" he exclaimed. "But I can no longer read music. You will play them, yes?"

I said I would try. On that wonderful old piano even my playing sounded right, and Dr. P. was an aged but infinitely mellow Fischer-Dieskau,[3] combining a perfect ear and voice with the most incisive musical intelligence. It was clear that the music school was not keeping him on out of charity.

Dr. P.'s temporal lobes were obviously intact: he had a wonderful musical cortex. What, I wondered, was going on in his parietal and occipital lobes, especially in those areas where visual processing occurred? I carry the Platonic solids in my neurological kit and decided to start with these. 35

"What is this?" I asked, drawing out the first one.

"A cube, of course."

"Now this?" I asked, brandishing another.

He asked if he might examine it, which he did swiftly and systematically: "A dodecahedron, of course. And don't bother with the others — I'll get the icosahedron, too."

Abstract shapes clearly presented no problems. What about faces? I took out a pack of cards. All of these he identified instantly, including the jacks, queens, kings, and the joker. But these, after all, are stylized designs, and it was impossible to tell whether he saw faces or merely patterns. I 40

---

[2]*Robert Schumann* (1810–1856): German romantic composer. [Eds.]
[3]*Dietrich Fischer-Dieskau* (b. 1925): German baritone, noted for his interpretations of Schumann's vocal music. [Eds.]

decided I would show him a volume of cartoons which I had in my brief-case. Here, again, for the most part, he did well. Churchill's cigar, Schnozzle's nose: as soon as he had picked out a key feature he could identify the face. But cartoons, again, are formal and schematic. It remained to be seen how he would do with real faces, realistically represented.

I turned on the television, keeping the sound off, and found an early Bette Davis film. A love scene was in progress. Dr. P. failed to identify the actress — but this could have been because she had never entered his world. What was more striking was that he failed to identify the expressions on her face or her partner's, though in the course of a single torrid scene these passed from sultry yearning through passion, surprise, disgust, and fury to a melting reconciliation. Dr. P. could make nothing of any of this. He was very unclear as to what was going on, or who was who or even what sex they were. His comments on the scene were positively Martian.

It was just possible that some of his difficulties were associated with the unreality of a celluloid, Hollywood world; and it occurred to me that he might be more successful in identifying faces from his own life. On the walls of the apartment there were photographs of his family, his colleagues, his pupils, himself. I gathered a pile of these together and, with some misgiv-ings, presented them to him. What had been funny, or farcical, in relation to the movie, was tragic in relation to real life. By and large, he recognized nobody: neither his family, nor his colleagues, nor his pupils, nor himself. He recognized a portrait of Einstein because he picked up the characteristic hair and mustache; and the same thing happened with one or two other people. "Ach, Paul!" he said, when shown a portrait of his brother. "That square jaw, those big teeth — I would know Paul anywhere!" But was it Paul he recognized, or one or two of his features, on the basis of which he could make a reasonable guess as to the subject's identity? In the absence of obvious "markers," he was utterly lost. But it was not merely the cognition, the gnosis, at fault; there was something radically wrong with the whole way he proceeded. For he approached these faces — even of those near and dear — as if they were abstract puzzles or tests. He did not relate to them, he did not behold. No face was familiar to him, seen as a "thou," being just identified as a set of features, an "it." Thus, there was formal, but no trace of personal, gnosis. And with this went his indifference, or blindness, to ex-pression. A face, to us, is a person looking out — we see, as it were, the per-son through his *persona,* his face. But for Dr. P. there was no *persona* in this sense — no outward *persona,* and no person within.

I had stopped at a florist on my way to his apartment and bought my-self an extravagant red rose for my buttonhole. Now I removed this and handed it to him. He took it like a botanist or morphologist given a speci-men, not like a person given a flower.

"About six inches in length," he commented. "A convoluted red form with a linear green attachment."

"Yes," I said encouragingly, "and what do you think it *is,* Dr. P.?"   45

"Not easy to say." He seemed perplexed. "It lacks the simple symmetry of the Platonic solids, although it may have a higher symmetry of its own. . . . I think this could be an inflorescence or flower."

"Could be?" I queried.

"Could be," he confirmed.

"Smell it," I suggested, and he again looked somewhat puzzled, as if I had asked him to smell a higher symmetry. But he complied courteously, and took it to his nose. Now, suddenly, he came to life.

"Beautiful!" he exclaimed. "An early rose. What a heavenly smell!" He   50
started to hum "*Die Rose, die Lillie* . . ." Reality, it seemed, might be conveyed by smell, not by sight.

I tried one final test. It was still a cold day, in early spring, and I had thrown my coat and gloves on the sofa.

"What is this?" I asked, holding up a glove.

"May I examine it?" he asked, and, taking it from me, he proceeded to examine it as he had examined the geometrical shapes.

"A continuous surface," he announced at last, "infolded on itself. It appears to have" — he hesitated — "five outpouchings, if this is the word."

"Yes," I said cautiously. "You have given me a description. Now tell me   55
what it is."

"A container of some sort?"

"Yes," I said, "and what would it contain?"

"It would contain its contents!" said Dr. P., with a laugh. "There are many possibilities. It could be a change purse, for example, for coins of five sizes. It could . . ."

I interrupted the barmy flow. "Does it not look familiar? Do you think it might contain, might fit, a part of your body?"

No light of recognition dawned on his face.[4]   60

No child would have the power to see and speak of "a continuous surface . . . infolded on itself," but any child, any infant, would immediately know a glove as a glove, see it as familiar, as going with a hand. Dr. P. didn't. He saw nothing as familiar. Visually, he was lost in a world of lifeless abstractions. Indeed, he did not have a real visual world, as he did not have a real visual self. He could speak about things, but did not see them face-to-face. Hughlings Jackson, discussing patients with aphasia and left-hemisphere lesions, says they have lost "abstract" and "propositional" thought — and compares them with dogs (or, rather, he compares dogs to patients with aphasia). Dr. P., on the other hand, functioned precisely as a machine functions. It wasn't merely that he displayed the same indifference to the visual world as a computer but — even more strikingly — he construed the world as a

---

[4]Later, by accident, he got it on, and exclaimed, "My God, it's a glove!" This was reminiscent of Kurt Goldstein's patient "Lanuti," who could only recognize objects by trying to use them in action.

computer construes it, by means of key features and schematic relationships. The scheme might be identified — in an "identikit" way — without the reality being grasped at all.

The testing I had done so far told me nothing about Dr. P.'s inner world. Was it possible that his visual memory and imagination were still intact? I asked him to imagine entering one of our local squares from the north side, to walk through it, in imagination or in memory, and tell me the buildings he might pass as he walked. He listed the buildings on his right side, but none of those on his left. I then asked him to imagine entering the square from the south. Again he mentioned only those buildings that were on the right side, although these were the very buildings he had omitted before. Those he had "seen" internally before were not mentioned now; presumably, they were no longer "seen." It was evident that his difficulties with leftness, his visual field deficits, were as much internal as external, bisecting his visual memory and imagination.

What, at a higher level, of his internal visualization? Thinking of the almost hallucinatory intensity with which Tolstoy visualizes and animates his characters, I questioned Dr. P. about *Anna Karenina*. He could remember incidents without difficulty, had an undiminished grasp of the plot, but completely omitted visual characteristics, visual narrative, and scenes. He remembered the words of the characters but not their faces; and though, when asked, he could quote, with his remarkable and almost verbatim memory, the original visual descriptions, these were, it became apparent, quite empty for him and lacked sensorial, imaginal, or emotional reality. Thus, there was an internal agnosia as well.[5]

But this was only the case, it became clear, with certain sorts of visualization. The visualization of faces and scenes, of visual narrative and drama — this was profoundly impaired, almost absent. But the visualization of *schemata* was preserved, perhaps enhanced. Thus, when I engaged him in a game of mental chess, he had no difficulty visualizing the chessboard or the moves — indeed, no difficulty in beating me soundly.

Luria[6] said of Zazetsky that he had entirely lost his capacity to play   65
games but that his "vivid imagination" was unimpaired. Zazetsky and Dr. P.

---

[5]I have often wondered about Helen Keller's visual descriptions, whether these, for all their eloquence, are somehow empty as well? Or whether, by the transference of images from the tactile to the visual, or, yet more extraordinarily, from the verbal and the metaphorical to the sensorial and the visual, she *did* achieve a power of visual imagery, even though her visual cortex had never been stimulated, directly, by the eyes? But in Dr. P.'s case it is precisely the cortex that was damaged, the organic prerequisite of all pictorial imagery. Interestingly and typically he no longer dreamed pictorially — the "message" of the dream being conveyed in nonvisual terms.

[6]*Alexander Luria* (1902–1977): Russian neuropsychologist who developed theories of brain function that were based, in part, on his work with people with traumatic head injuries. [Eds.]

lived in worlds which were mirror images of each other. But the saddest difference between them was that Zazetsky, as Luria said, "fought to regain his lost faculties with the indomitable tenacity of the damned," whereas Dr. P. was not fighting, did not know what was lost, did not indeed know that anything was lost. But who was more tragic, or who was more damned — the man who knew it, or the man who did not?

When the examination was over, Mrs. P. called us to the table, where there was coffee and a delicious spread of little cakes. Hungrily, hummingly, Dr. P. started on the cakes. Swiftly, fluently, unthinkingly, melodiously, he pulled the plates towards him and took this and that in a great gurgling stream, an edible song of food, until, suddenly, there came an interruption: a loud, peremptory rat-tat-tat at the door. Startled, taken aback, arrested by the interruption, Dr. P. stopped eating and sat frozen, motionless, at the table, with an indifferent, blind bewilderment on his face. He saw, but no longer saw, the table; no longer perceived it as a table laden with cakes. His wife poured him some coffee: the smell titillated his nose and brought him back to reality. The melody of eating resumed.

How does he do anything? I wondered to myself. What happens when he's dressing, goes to the lavatory, has a bath? I followed his wife into the kitchen and asked her how, for instance, he managed to dress himself. "It's just like the eating," she explained. "I put his usual clothes out, in all the usual places, and he dresses without difficulty, singing to himself. He does everything singing to himself. But if he is interrupted and loses the thread, he comes to a complete stop, doesn't know his clothes — or his own body. He sings all the time — eating songs, dressing songs, bathing songs, everything. He can't do anything unless he makes it a song."

While we were talking my attention was caught by the pictures on the walls.

"Yes," Mrs. P. said, "he was a gifted painter as well as a singer. The school exhibited his pictures every year."

I strolled past them curiously — they were in chronological order. All   70
his earlier work was naturalistic and realistic, with vivid mood and atmosphere, but finely detailed and concrete. Then, years later, they became less vivid, less concrete, less realistic and naturalistic, but far more abstract, even geometrical and cubist. Finally, in the last paintings, the canvases became nonsense, or nonsense to me — mere chaotic lines and blotches of paint. I commented on this to Mrs. P.

"Ach, you doctors, you're such Philistines!"[7] she exclaimed. "Can you not see *artistic development* — how he renounced the realism of his earlier years, and advanced into abstract, nonrepresentational art?"

---

[7]*Philistines*: Uncultured, materialistic people. According to the Bible, the Philistines were enemies of the Israelites. [Eds.]

"No, that's not it," I said to myself (but forbore to say it to poor Mrs. P.). He had indeed moved from realism to nonrepresentation to the abstract, yet this was not the artist, but the pathology, advancing—advancing towards a profound visual agnosia, in which all powers of representation and imagery, all sense of the concrete, all sense of reality, were being destroyed. This wall of paintings was a tragic pathological exhibit, which belonged to neurology, not art.

And yet, I wondered, was she not partly right? For there is often a struggle, and sometimes, even more interestingly, a collusion between the powers of pathology and creation. Perhaps, in his cubist period, there might have been both artistic and pathological development, colluding to engender an original form; for as he lost the concrete, so he might have gained in the abstract, developing a greater sensitivity to all the structural elements of line, boundary, contour—an almost Picasso-like power to see, and equally depict, those abstract organizations embedded in, and normally lost in, the concrete. . . . Though in the final pictures, I feared, there was only chaos and agnosia.

We returned to the great music room, with the Bösendorfer in the center, and Dr. P. humming the last torte.

"Well, Dr. Sacks," he said to me. "You find me an interesting case, I 75 perceive. Can you tell me what you find wrong, make recommendations?"

"I can't tell you what I find wrong," I replied, "but I'll say what I find right. You are a wonderful musician, and music is your life. What I would prescribe, in a case such as yours, is a life which consists entirely of music. Music has been the center, now make it the whole, of your life."

This was four years ago—I never saw him again, but I often wondered about how he apprehended the world, given his strange loss of image, visuality, and the perfect preservation of a great musicality. I think that music, for him, had taken the place of image. He had no body-image, he had body-music: this is why he could move and act as fluently as he did, but came to a total confused stop if the "inner music" stopped. And equally with the outside, the world. . . .[8]

In *The World as Representation and Will*, Schopenhauer[9] speaks of music as "pure will." How fascinated he would have been by Dr. P., a man who had wholly lost the world as representation, but wholly preserved it as music or will.

And this, mercifully, held to the end—for despite the gradual advance of his disease (a massive tumor or degenerative process in the visual parts of his brain) Dr. P. lived and taught music to the last days of his life.

---

[8]Thus, as I learned later from his wife, though he could not recognize his students if they sat still, if they were merely "images," he might suddenly recognize them if they *moved*. "That's Karl," he would cry. "I know his movements, his body-music."

[9]*Arthur Schopenhauer* (1788–1860): German philosopher whose work included a theory to explain the life and work of the artist. [Eds.]

Postscript

How should one interpret Dr. P.'s peculiar inability to interpret, to   80
judge, a glove as a glove? Manifestly, here, he could not make a cognitive
judgment, though he was prolific in the production of cognitive hypotheses.
A judgment is intuitive, personal, comprehensive, and concrete — we "see"
how things stand, in relation to one another and oneself. It was precisely
this setting, this relating, that Dr. P. lacked (though his judging, in all other
spheres, was prompt and normal). Was this due to lack of visual information,
or faulty processing of visual information? (This would be the explanation
given by a classical, schematic neurology.) Or was there something amiss in
Dr. P.'s attitude, so that he could not relate what he saw to himself?

These explanations, or modes of explanation, are not mutually
exclusive — being in different modes they could coexist and both be true.
And this is acknowledged, implicitly or explicitly, in classical neurology: implicitly, by Macrae, when he finds the explanation of defective schemata, or
defective visual processing and integration, inadequate; explicitly, by Goldstein, when he speaks of "abstract attitude." But abstract attitude, which
allows "categorization," also misses the mark with Dr. P. — and, perhaps,
with the concept of "judgment" in general. For Dr. P. *had* abstract attitude —
indeed, nothing else. And it was precisely this, his absurd abstractness of
attitude — absurd because unleavened with anything else —which rendered
him incapable of perceiving identity, or particulars, rendered him incapable
of judgment.

Neurology and psychology, curiously, though they talk of everything
else, almost never talk of "judgment" — and yet it is precisely the downfall
of judgment . . . which constitutes the essence of so many neuropsychological disorders. Judgment and identity may be casualties — but neuropsychology never speaks of them.

And yet, whether in a philosophic sense (Kant's sense),[10] or an empirical
and evolutionary sense, judgment is the most important faculty we have. An
animal, or a man, may get on very well without "abstract attitude" but will
speedily perish if deprived of judgment. Judgment must be the *first* faculty
of higher life or mind — yet it is ignored, or misinterpreted, by classical
(computational) neurology. And if we wonder how such an absurdity can
arise, we find it in the assumptions, or the evolution, of neurology itself. For
classical neurology (like classical physics) has always been mechanical —
from Hughlings Jackson's mechanical analogies to the computer analogies
of today.

Of course, the brain is a machine and a computer — everything in classical neurology is correct. But our mental processes, which constitute our

---

[10]*Immanuel Kant* (1724–1804): German philosopher; some of his work concerned ethics and moral judgment. [Eds.]

being and life, are not just abstract and mechanical, but personal, as well — and, as such, involve not just classifying and categorizing, but continual judging and feeling also. If this is missing, we become computer-like, as Dr. P. was. And, by the same token, if we delete feeling and judging, the personal, from the cognitive sciences, we reduce them to something as defective as Dr. P. — and we reduce our apprehension of the concrete and real.

By a sort of comic and awful analogy, our current cognitive neurology and psychology resemble nothing so much as poor Dr. P.! We need the concrete and real, as he did; and we fail to see this, as he failed to see it. Our cognitive sciences are themselves suffering from an agnosia essentially similar to Dr. P.'s. Dr. P. may therefore serve as a warning and parable — of what happens to a science which eschews the judgmental, the particular, the personal, and becomes entirely abstract and computational.

It was always a matter of great regret to me that, owing to circumstances beyond my control, I was not able to follow his case further, either in the sort of observations and investigations described, or in ascertaining the actual disease pathology.

One always fears that a case is "unique," especially if it has such extraordinary features as those of Dr. P. It was, therefore, with a sense of great interest and delight, not unmixed with relief, that I found, quite by chance — looking through the periodical *Brain* for 1956 — a detailed description of an almost comically similar case, similar (indeed identical) neuropsychologically and phenomenologically, though the underlying pathology (an acute head injury) and all personal circumstances were wholly different. The authors speak of their case as "unique in the documented history of this disorder" — and evidently experienced, as I did, amazement at their own findings.[11] The interested reader is referred to the original paper, Macrae and Trolle (1956), of which I here subjoin a brief paraphrase, with quotations from the original.

Their patient was a young man of thirty-two, who, following a severe automobile accident, with unconsciousness for three weeks, " . . . complained, exclusively, of an inability to recognize faces, even those of his wife

---

[11]Only since the completion of this book have I found that there is, in fact, a rather extensive literature on visual agnosia in general, and prosopagnosia in particular. In particular I had the great pleasure recently of meeting Dr. Andrew Kertesz, who has himself published some extremely detailed studies of patients with such agnosias (see, for example, his paper on visual agnosia, Kertesz 1979). Dr. Kertesz mentioned to me a case known to him of a farmer who had developed prosopagnosia and in consequence could no longer distinguish (the faces of) his *cows,* and of another such patient, an attendant in a natural history museum, who mistook his own reflection for the diorama of an *ape.* As with Dr. P., and as with Macrae and Trolle's patient, it is especially the animate which is so absurdly misperceived. The most important studies of such agnosias, and of visual processing in general, are now being undertaken by A. R. and H. Damasio.

and children." Not a single face was "familiar" to him, but there were three he could identify; these were workmates: one with an eye-blinking tic, one with a large mole on his cheek, and a third "because he was so tall and thin that no one else was like him." Each of these, Macrae and Trolle bring out, was "recognized solely by the single prominent feature mentioned." In general (like Dr. P.) he recognized familiars only by their voices.

He had difficulty even recognizing himself in a mirror, as Macrae and Trolle describe in detail: "In the early convalescent phase he frequently, especially when shaving, questioned whether the face gazing at him was really his own, and even though he knew it could physically be none other, on several occasions grimaced or stuck out his tongue 'just to make sure.' By carefully studying his face in the mirror he slowly began to recognize it, but 'not in a flash' as in the past — he relied on the hair and facial outline, and on two small moles on his left cheek."

In general he could not recognize objects "at a glance," but would have   90 to seek out, and guess from, one or two features — occasionally his guesses were absurdly wrong. In particular, the authors note, there was difficulty with the *animate*.

On the other hand, simple schematic objects — scissors, watch, key, etc. — presented no difficulties. Macrae and Trolle also note that: "His *topographical memory* was strange: the seeming paradox existed that he could find his way from home to hospital and around the hospital, but yet could not name streets *en route* [unlike Dr. P., he also had some aphasia] or appear to visualize the topography."

It was also evident that visual memories of people, even from long before the accident, were severely impaired — there was memory of conduct, or perhaps a mannerism, but not of visual appearance or face. Similarly, it appeared, when he was questioned closely, that he no longer had visual images in his *dreams*. Thus, as with Dr. P., it was not just visual perception, but visual imagination and memory, the fundamental powers of visual representation, which were essentially damaged in this patient — at least those powers insofar as they pertained to the personal, the familiar, the concrete.

A final, humorous point. Where Dr. P. might mistake his wife for a hat, Macrae's patient, also unable to recognize his wife, needed her to identify herself by a visual *marker*, by ". . . a conspicuous article of clothing, such as a large hat."

QUESTIONS

Reading

1. Summarize as clearly as you can the nature of Dr. P.'s problem. What are the symptoms? What seems to have caused them?
2. In *explaining* the case study of Dr. P., Sacks uses several techniques commonly found in fiction writing, including describing characters in a

compelling way. How does Sacks bring Dr. and Mrs. P. to life as characters? How does he characterize himself? What are your impressions of Dr. Sacks from this characterization?

3. Highlight, underline, or flag the tests that Sacks uses to learn about Dr. P.'s condition. How, according to Sacks, is the human brain different from a machine or a computer?

Exploratory Writing

1. Sacks is relieved to learn that the case of Dr. P. is not entirely unique. Collaborate in small groups to find a case of someone who has a neurological condition that makes his or her perception different from the "normal," or average. Write up a case study or profile of this person, and present your findings to the class. What is the diagnosis of his or her condition? What are its details? What might it be like to live with this condition?

2. Mrs. P. believes that Dr. P.'s abstract, nonrepresentational images are evidence of his artistic development rather than his visual agnosia. Sacks writes, "There is often . . . a collusion between the powers of pathology and creation" (paragraph 73). Choose a work of visual art that you find powerful, and list its qualities or details that could equally be interpreted as either artistic innovation or signs of skewed perception. Why does Sacks fear that Dr. P.'s later work is more about "chaos and agnosia" than creativity?

Making Connections

1. Dr. P. and Temple Grandin (p. 647) both see, perceive, and experience the world in unusual ways. Compare Dr. P.'s visual perceptions, as Sacks describes them, with Grandin's account of how she sees the world.

2. The prisoners in the allegory of the cave in Plato's *Republic* (p. 665), like Dr. P., are unaware of their inability to perceive reality. Sacks asks whether a man who is aware that he has lost his faculties is "more tragic" than a man like Dr. P., who has no understanding of what is lost (paragraph 65). How might Socrates evaluate the case of Dr. P.? Is Socrates arguing that all human beings suffer from a kind of neurological disorder?

Essay Writing

1. This essay is not only a single case history and an explanation of some curious behavior. It also contains an argument about the nature of the cognitive sciences — how they should and should not proceed. What is that argument? Do you agree or disagree with the view of cognitive science that Sacks is advocating? Write an essay in which you present his position, and develop one of your own on this matter.

Setting the Record Straight

Scott McCloud

*Scott McCloud (b. 1960), cartoonist and comics theorist, grew up
in Lexington, Massachusetts, and received a BFA in illustration
from Syracuse University. In 1984, he began his career in independent comics, creating the series* Zot!, *the chronicles of two
teenagers living in parallel worlds, which he refers to as "a cross
between Peter Pan, Buck Rogers, and Marshall McLuhan." He
has also written for mainstream comic book titles, notably*
Superman, *and has been an important proponent of webcomics.
McCloud is perhaps best known, however, for his explorations of
comics as a unique narrative medium. In his seminal* Understanding Comics, *published in 1993, McCloud uses the comics form
itself to explain how comics differ from more conventional storytelling media like film and novels, while arguing for the medium's
distinctive virtues. This was followed by* Reinventing Comics *in
2000 and* Making Comics *in 2006. An excerpt from the opening
chapter of* Understanding Comics *is reprinted here.*

CHAPTER ONE

SETTING THE RECORD STRAIGHT.

HI, I'M *SCOTT McCLOUD.*

WHEN I WAS A *LITTLE KID* I KNEW *EXACTLY* WHAT COMICS WERE.

COMICS WERE THOSE *BRIGHT, COLORFUL MAGAZINES* FILLED WITH *BAD ART, STUPID STORIES* AND *GUYS IN TIGHTS.*

I READ *REAL* BOOKS, NATURALLY. I WAS MUCH TOO *OLD* FOR COMICS!

BUT WHEN I WAS IN *8th GRADE,* A FRIEND OF MINE (WHO WAS A LOT *SMARTER* THAN I WAS) CONVINCED ME TO GIVE COMICS ANOTHER LOOK AND LENT ME HIS COLLECTION.

SOON, I WAS *HOOKED!*

THE REALLY *OLD* MEN

IN LESS THAN A *YEAR*, I BECAME *TOTALLY OBSESSED* WITH COMICS! I DECIDED TO BECOME A *COMICS ARTIST* IN *10th GRADE* AND BEGAN TO *PRACTICE, PRACTICE, PRACTICE!*

I FELT THAT THERE WAS SOMETHING *LURKING* IN COMICS... SOMETHING THAT HAD *NEVER BEEN DONE.*

SOME KIND OF *HIDDEN POWER!*

BUT WHENEVER I TRIED TO *EXPLAIN* MY FEELING, I FAILED *MISERABLY.*

COMIC BOOKS?! HA! HA! HA!

BUT IT-- BUT IT'S-- BUH...

SURE, I REALIZED THAT COMIC BOOKS WERE USUALLY *CRUDE, POORLY-DRAWN, SEMILITERATE, CHEAP, DISPOSABLE KIDDIE FARE*--

--*BUT*--

THEY DON'T *HAVE* TO BE!

THE *PROBLEM* WAS THAT FOR *MOST PEOPLE*, THAT WAS WHAT "*COMIC BOOK*" *MEANT!*

DON'T GIMME THAT *COMIC BOOK* TALK, BARNEY!

IF PEOPLE FAILED TO *UNDERSTAND* COMICS, IT WAS BECAUSE THEY DEFINED WHAT COMICS COULD BE *TOO NARROWLY!*

A *PROPER DEFINITION*, IF WE COULD *FIND* ONE, MIGHT GIVE *LIE* TO THE STEREOTYPES--

--AND SHOW THAT THE *POTENTIAL* OF COMICS IS *LIMITLESS* AND *EXCITING!*

THIS IS WHERE OUR JOURNEY *BEGINS.*

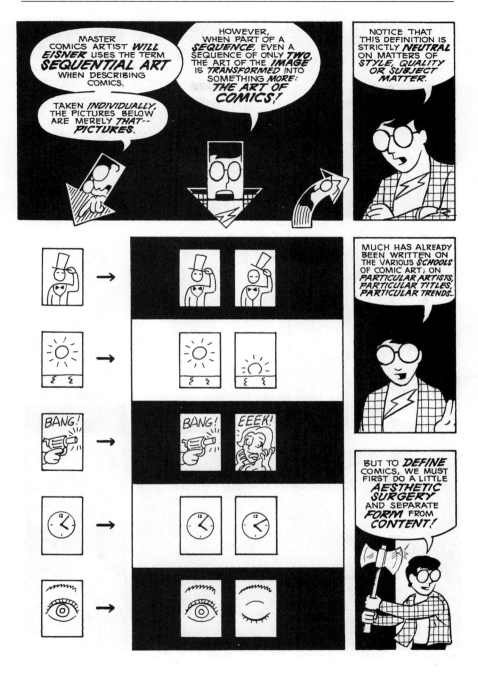

*EISNER'S OWN *COMICS AND SEQUENTIAL ART* BEING A HAPPY EXCEPTION.

*JUXTAPOSED= ADJACENT, SIDE-BY-SIDE.
GREAT ART SCHOOL WORD.

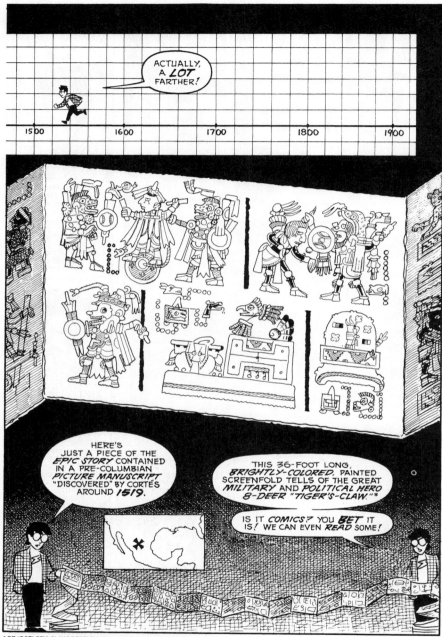

* OR "OCELOT'S CLAW" DEPENDING ON WHOSE BOOK YOU READ.
THIS SEQUENCE IS BASED ON A READING BY MEXICAN HISTORIAN
AND ARCHAEOLOGIST ALFONSO CASO.

FIRST, WE SEPARATE WORDS FROM *PICTURES*.

8-DEER "TIGER'S CLAW"

(A NAME)

11 HOUSE 12 MONKEY

(A DATE)

GOD XIPE'S BUNDLE

(GLYPH FOR PLACE WHOSE NAME WE DON'T KNOW.)

THEN *REVERSE* IT AND STRAIGHTEN IT OUT (THE ORIGINAL READ RIGHT-TO-LEFT AND *ZIGZAGGED*.) AND *BEGIN*:

THE YEAR: *1049 AD*
THE DATE: *MAY 3* *
THE PLACE: *HERE!*

OUR HERO, *8-DEER "TIGER'S CLAW"*, CONQUERS THE PLACE AND CAPTURES THE *9-YEAR-OLD PRINCE, 4-WIND "SERPENT OF FIRE."*

8-DEER ALSO CAPTURES THE PRINCE'S OLDER BROTHERS, *10-DOG "EAGLE COPAL BURNING"* AND *6-HOUSE "ROW OF FLINT KNIVES"* AND PUTS 'EM ON ICE.

(I'M TAKING THE TRANSLATOR'S WORD ON THIS ONE.)

THE FOLLOWING YEAR, *8-DEER* AND (PROBABLY) HIS BROTHER, DISGUISED AS *TIGERS*, ENGAGE IN *SACRIFICIAL GLADITORIAL COMBAT* WITH THE PRINCE, *10-DOG*, AND ANOTHER WARRIOR DISGUISED AS *DEATH*.

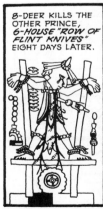

8-DEER KILLS THE OTHER PRINCE, *6-HOUSE "ROW OF FLINT KNIVES"* EIGHT DAYS LATER.

* WE KNOW THE YEAR; I'M JUST *GUESSING* AT THE DATE REPRESENTED BY "12 MONKEY"

READING *LEFT TO RIGHT* WE SEE THE *EVENTS* OF THE CONQUEST, IN *DELIBERATE CHRONOLOGICAL ORDER* UNFOLD BEFORE OUR VERY *EYES.*

AS WITH THE *MEXICAN CODEX,* THERE ARE NO *PANEL BORDERS* PER SE, BUT THERE ARE CLEAR DIVISIONS OF SCENE BY *SUBJECT MATTER.*

DUKE WILLIAM REMOVES HIS HELMET TO RALLY HIS SOLDIERS

HAROLD'S ARMY IS CUT TO PIECES

THUS, THEIR *REAL* DESCENDENT IS *THE WRITTEN WORD* AND NOT COMICS.

"ses tu baíu abta, hennu-nek baíu amenta"

"FOLLOW THEE, THE SOULS OF THE EAST. PRAISE THEE, THE SOULS OF THE WEST."

EGYPTIAN *PAINTING* IS *ANOTHER MATTER.* SOME, LIKE THIS, MAY *SEEM* TO BE CONCERNED WITH SEQUENCE, BUT ARE ACTUALLY SHOWING TWO DIFFERENT LOCATIONS, EVENTS AND CASTS, GROUPED ONLY BY *SUBJECT.*

I HAD BEEN TRYING TO FIND *SEQUENCE* IN EGYPTIAN PAINTINGS FOR *YEARS* WHEN I BEGAN THIS BOOK AND WAS READY TO CALL IT QUITS--

--UNTIL I DISCOVERED THAT THE BOOKS I HAD BEEN USING AS REFERENCE--

--HAD ONLY BEEN SHOWING ME *PART* OF THE PICTURE!

HERE'S THE *COMPLETE* SCENE * PAINTED OVER *THIRTY-TWO CENTURIES* AGO FOR THE TOMB OF *"MENNA,"* AN ANCIENT EGYPTIAN *SCRIBE.*

AS WOULD BE DONE 2,700 YEARS *LATER* IN MEXICO, THE EGYPTIANS READ THEIR COMICS *ZIG-ZAG.*

GOING *UP* THIS TIME *!*

FINISH

START

16|00   14|00   1300 B.C.   12|00

* MORE *NEARLY* COMPLETE, ANYWAY.

STARTING AT THE *LOWER LEFT,* WE SEE THREE WORKERS REAPING WHEAT WITH THEIR SICKLES--

PAINTING TRACED FOR BLACK AND WHITE REPRODUCTION.

--THEN CARRYING IT IN *BASKETS* TO A *THRESHING* LOCATION. (IN THE BACKGROUND TWO GIRLS FIGHT OVER BITS OF WHEAT LEFT BEHIND, AS TWO WORKERS SIT UNDER A TREE, ONE SLEEPING, ONE PLAYING THE *FLUTE!*)

THE SHEAVES ARE THEN *RAKED OUT* INTO A *THICK CARPET OF WHEAT.*

THEN OXEN TREAD *KERNELS* OUT OF THE HUSKS.

NEXT, PEASANTS SEPARATE THE WHEAT FROM THE CHAFF.

OLD MENNA HIMSELF LOOKS ON -- *

-- AS LOYAL SCRIBES RECORD THE YIELD ON THEIR TABLETS.

NOW AN OFFICIAL USES A MEASURING ROPE TO *SURVEY THE LAND* AND DECIDE HOW MUCH WHEAT IS OWED IN *TAXES.*

AND AS MENNA WATCHES, FARMERS *LATE* IN PAYING THEIR TAXES ARE *BEATEN.*

I'LL *GLADLY ADMIT* THAT I HAVE *NO IDEA* WHERE OR *WHEN* COMICS ORIGINATED. LET *OTHERS* WRESTLE WITH *THAT* ONE.

? B.C.   ? A.D.

I'VE ONLY SCRATCHED THE *SURFACE* IN THIS CHAPTER... *TRAJAN'S COLUMN, GREEK PAINTING, JAPANESE SCROLLS...* ALL THESE HAVE BEEN SUGGESTED AND ALL SHOULD BE EXPLORED.

BUT THERE IS *ONE* EVENT WHICH LOOMS AS LARGE IN *COMICS* HISTORY AS IT DOES IN THE HISTORY OF THE *WRITTEN WORD.*

THE INVENTION OF PRINTING.

* FACE GOUGED OUT BY FUTURE GENERATIONS OF LEADERS

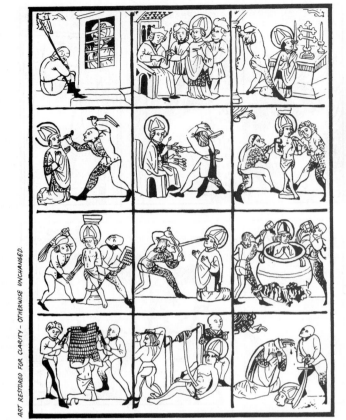

ART RESTORED FOR CLARITY -- OTHERWISE UNCHANGED.

WITH THE INVENTION OF PRINTING, THE ART-FORM WHICH HAD BEEN A DIVERSION OF THE *RICH* AND *POWERFUL* NOW COULD BE ENJOYED BY *EVERYONE!*

POPULAR TASTES HAVEN'T *CHANGED* MUCH IN *FIVE CENTURIES.* CHECK OUT *"THE TORTURES OF SAINT ERASMUS,"* CIRCA 1460. WORD HAS IT THIS GUY WAS A VERY POPULAR CHARACTER.

QUESTIONS

Reading

1. According to McCloud, what are some stereotypes that most people believe about comic books? Does he agree with these stereotypes?
2. Describe the narrator of *Understanding Comics*. What function does this narrator serve?
3. How did the invention of printing change the role of comics in culture?

Exploratory Writing

1. Underline, highlight, or flag McCloud's different definitions of comics. Choose a sequence of images from any period in history, and explain why it is or is not a comic, according to McCloud's final, complete definition.
2. McCloud uses a comic to make an *argument* about the cultural status of comics. Choose something that interests you, and create a comic to make an argument about it. How is designing an argumentative comic different from writing an argumentative essay?

Making Connections

1. John Berger (p. 710) concludes that "the entire art of the past" has become a political issue. Compare and contrast Berger's argument about original artworks with McCloud's discussion of the history of comics. How might McCloud feel about Berger's conclusions?

Essay Writing

1. McCloud talks about becoming "totally obsessed" with comics and seeing them as a medium with a special, hidden power. Write an essay reflecting on an art form, writing style, type of music or dance, or some other form of personal expression that obsessed you. In your experience, what is special and unique about that type of expression? What is its power?

Ways of Seeing

John Berger

After beginning his career as a painter and drawing instructor, John Berger (b. 1926) became one of Britain's most influential art critics. He has achieved recognition as a screenwriter, novelist, and documentary writer. As a Marxist, he is concerned with the ideological and technological conditioning of our ways of seeing both art and the world. During a remarkably prolific career, he has published more than eight works of fiction and fifteen works of nonfiction, along with numerous articles and screenplays. His novel G: A Novel *won the Booker Prize in 1972. Berger focuses his art criticism on the broad issues of seeing as a social and historical act. He introduced a mixed-media approach — combining poetry, photography, essays, and criticism — to the field of art criticism in books such as* Ways of Seeing *(1972),* About Looking *(1980), and* Another Way of Telling *(1982). His most recent work is* From A to X *(2008), a novel told through one character's letters to her imprisoned lover. The selection printed here is the first essay in* Ways of Seeing, *which was based on a BBC television series.*

Seeing comes before words. The child looks and recognizes before it can speak.

But there is also another sense in which seeing comes before words. It is seeing which establishes our place in the surrounding world; we explain that world with words, but words can never undo the fact that we are surrounded by it. The relation between what we see and what we know is never settled. Each evening we *see* the sun set. We *know* that the earth is turning away from it. Yet the knowledge, the explanation, never quite fits the sight. The Surrealist painter Magritte commented on this always-present gap between words and seeing in a painting called *The Key of Dreams.*

The way we see things is affected by what we know or what we believe. In the Middle Ages when men believed in the physical existence of Hell the sight of fire must have meant something different from what it means today. Nevertheless their idea of Hell owed a lot to the sight of fire consuming and the ashes remaining — as well as to their experience of the pain of burns.

When in love, the sight of the beloved has a completeness which no words and no embrace can match: a completeness which only the act of making love can temporarily accommodate.

The Key of Dreams by Magritte, 1898–1967.

Yet this seeing which comes before words, and can never be quite covered 5
by them, is not a question of mechanically reacting to stimuli. (It can only be
thought of in this way if one isolates the small part of the process which concerns the eye's retina.) We only see what we look at. To look is an act of choice.
As a result of this act, what we see is brought within our reach — though not
necessarily within arm's reach. To touch something is to situate oneself in relation to it. (Close your eyes, move round the room and notice how the faculty
of touch is like a static, limited form of sight.) We never look at just one thing;
we are always looking at the relation between things and ourselves. Our vision
is continually active, continually moving, continually holding things in a circle
around itself, constituting what is present to us as we are.

Soon after we can see, we are aware that we can also be seen. The eye
of the other combines with our own eye to make it fully credible that we are
part of the visible world.

If we accept that we can see that hill over there, we propose that from
that hill we can be seen. The reciprocal nature of vision is more fundamental than that of spoken dialogue. And often dialogue is an attempt to verbal-
ize this — an attempt to explain how, either metaphorically or literally,
"you see things," and an attempt to discover how "he sees things."

In the sense in which we use the word in this book, all images are
man-made.

An image is a sight which has been re-created or reproduced. It is an appearance, or a set of appearances, which has been detached from the place
and time in which it first made its appearance and preserved — for a few moments or a few centuries. Every image embodies a way of seeing. Even a
photograph. For photographs are not, as is often assumed, a mechanical
record. Every time we look at a photograph, we are aware, however slightly,
of the photographer selecting that sight from an infinity of other possible
sights. This is true even in the most casual family snapshot. The photographer's way of seeing is reflected in his choice of subject. The painter's way of

seeing is reconstituted by the marks he makes on the canvas or paper. Yet, although every image embodies a way of seeing, our perception or appreciation of an image depends also upon our own way of seeing. (It may be, for example, that Sheila is one figure among twenty; but for our own reasons she is the one we have eyes for.)

Images were first made to conjure up the appearances of something that   10
was absent. Gradually it became evident that an image could outlast what it represented; it then showed how something or somebody had once looked — and thus by implication how the subject had once been seen by other people. Later still the specific vision of the image-maker was also recognized as part of the record. An image became a record of how X had seen Y. This was the result of an increasing consciousness of individuality, accompanying an increasing awareness of history. It would be rash to try to date this last development precisely. But certainly in Europe such consciousness has existed since the beginning of the Renaissance.

No other kind of relic or text from the past can offer such a direct testimony about the world which surrounded other people at other times. In this respect images are more precise and richer than literature. To say this is not to deny the expressive or imaginative quality of art, treating it as mere documentary evidence; the more imaginative the work, the more profoundly it allows us to share the artist's experience of the visible.

Yet when an image is presented as a work of art, the way people look at it is affected by a whole series of learnt assumptions about art. Assumptions concerning:

Beauty

Truth

Genius

Civilization

Form

Status

Taste, etc.

Many of these assumptions no longer accord with the world as it is. (The world-as-it-is is more than pure objective fact; it includes consciousness.) Out of true with the present, these assumptions obscure the past. They mystify rather than clarify. The past is never there waiting to be discovered, to be recognized for exactly what it is. History always constitutes the relation between a present and its past. Consequently fear of the present leads to mystification of the past. The past is not for living in; it is a well of conclusions from which we draw in order to act. Cultural mystification of the past entails a double loss. Works of art are made unnecessarily remote. And the past offers us fewer conclusions to complete in action.

When we "see" a landscape, we situate ourselves in it. If we "saw" the art of the past, we would situate ourselves in history. When we are prevented from seeing it, we are being deprived of the history which belongs to us. Who benefits from this deprivation? In the end, the art of the past is being mystified because a privileged minority is striving to invent a history which can retrospectively justify the role of the ruling classes, and such a justification can no longer make sense in modern terms. And so, inevitably, it mystifies.

Let us consider a typical example of such mystification. A two-volume study was recently published on Frans Hals. It is the authoritative work to date on this painter. As a book of specialized art history it is no better and no worse than the average.   15

The last two great paintings by Frans Hals portray the governors and the governesses of an alms house for old paupers in the Dutch seventeenth-century city of Haarlem [see p. 714]. They were officially commissioned portraits. Hals, an old man of over eighty, was destitute. Most of his life he had been in debt. During the winter of 1664, the year he began painting these pictures, he obtained three loads of peat on public charity; otherwise he would have frozen to death. Those who now sat for him were administrators of such public charity.

The author records these facts and then explicitly says that it would be incorrect to read into the paintings any criticism of the sitters. There is no evidence, he says, that Hals painted them in a spirit of bitterness. The author considers them, however, remarkable works of art and explains why. Here he writes of the regentesses:

> Each woman speaks to us of the human condition with equal importance. Each woman stands out with equal clarity against the *enormous* dark surface, yet they are linked by a firm rhythmical arrangement and the subdued diagonal pattern formed by their heads and hands. Subtle modulations of the *deep,* glowing blacks contribute to the *harmonious fusion* of the whole and form an *unforgettable contrast* with the *powerful* whites and vivid flesh tones where the detached strokes reach *a peak of breadth and strength.* (italics added)

Regents of the Old Men's Alms House by Hals, 1580–1666.

Regentesses of the Old Men's Alms House by Hals, 1580–1666.

The compositional unity of a painting contributes fundamentally to the power of its image. It is reasonable to consider a painting's composition. But here the composition is written about as though it were in itself the emotional charge of the painting. Terms like *harmonious fusion, unforgettable contrast,* reaching *a peak of breadth and strength* transfer the emotion provoked by the image from the plane of lived experience, to that of disinterested "art appreciation." All conflict disappears. One is left with the unchanging "human condition," and the painting considered as a marvellously made object.

Very little is known about Hals or the regents who commissioned him. It is not possible to produce circumstantial evidence to establish what their

relations were. But there is the evidence of the paintings themselves: the evidence of a group of men and a group of women as seen by another man, the painter. Study this evidence and judge for yourself.

The art historian fears such direct judgement: 20

> As in so many other pictures by Hals, the penetrating characterizations almost seduce us into believing that we know the personality traits and even the habits of the men and women portrayed.

What is this "seduction" he writes of? It is nothing less than the paintings working upon us. They work upon us because we accept the way Hals saw his sitters. We do not accept this innocently. We accept it in so far as it corresponds to our own observation of people, gestures, faces, institutions. This is possible because we still live in a society of comparable social relations and moral values. And it is precisely this which gives the paintings their psychological and social urgency. It is this — not the painter's skill as a "seducer" — which convinces us that we *can* know the people portrayed.

The author continues:

> In the case of some critics the seduction has been a total success. It has, for example, been asserted that the Regent in the tipped slouch hat, which hardly covers any of his long, lank hair, and whose curiously set eyes do not focus, was shown in a drunken state.

This, he suggests, is a libel. He argues that it was a fashion at that time to wear hats on the side of the head. He cites medical opinion to prove that the regent's expression could well be the result of a facial paralysis. He insists that the painting would have been unacceptable to the regents if one of them had been portrayed drunk. One might go on discussing each of

these points for pages. (Men in seventeenth-century Holland wore their hats on the side of their heads in order to be thought of as adventurous and pleasure-loving. Heavy drinking was an approved practice. Etcetera.) But such a discussion would take us even farther away from the only confrontation which matters and which the author is determined to evade.

In this confrontation the regents and regentesses stare at Hals, a destitute old painter who has lost his reputation and lives off public charity; he examines them through the eyes of a pauper who must nevertheless try to be objective, i.e., must try to surmount the way he sees as a pauper. This is the drama of these paintings. A drama of an "unforgettable contrast."

Mystification has little to do with the vocabulary used. Mystification is   25
the process of explaining away what might otherwise be evident. Hals was the first portraitist to paint the new characters and expressions created by capitalism. He did in pictorial terms what Balzac did two centuries later in literature. Yet the author of the authoritative work on these paintings sums up the artist's achievement by referring to

> Hals's unwavering commitment to his personal vision, which en-
> riches our consciousness of our fellow men and heightens our awe
> for the ever-increasing power of the mighty impulses that enabled
> him to give us a close view of life's vital forces.

That is mystification.

In order to avoid mystifying the past (which can equally well suffer pseudo-Marxist mystification) let us now examine the particular relation which now exists, so far as pictorial images are concerned, between the present and the past. If we can see the present clearly enough, we shall ask the right questions of the past.

Today we see the art of the past as nobody saw it before. We actually perceive it in a different way.

This difference can be illustrated in terms of what was thought of as perspective. The convention of perspective, which is unique to European art

Still from *Man with a Movie Camera* by
Vertov.

and which was first established in the early Renaissance, centres everything
on the eye of the beholder. It is like a beam from a lighthouse — only instead
of light travelling outwards, appearances travel in. The conventions called
those appearances *reality*. Perspective makes the single eye the centre of the
visible world. Everything converges on to the eye as to the vanishing point
of infinity. The visible world is arranged for the spectator as the universe
was once thought to be arranged for God.

According to the convention of perspective there is no visual reciprocity. There is no need for God to situate himself in relation to others: he is
himself the situation. The inherent contradiction in perspective was that it
structured all images of reality to address a single spectator who, unlike
God, could only be in one place at a time.

After the invention of the camera this contradiction gradually became
apparent.

> I'm an eye. A mechanical eye. I, the machine, show you a world
> the way only I can see it. I free myself for today and forever from
> human immobility. I'm in constant movement. I approach and
> pull away from objects. I creep under them. I move alongside a

30

Still Life with Wicker Chair by Picasso,
1881–1973.

running horse's mouth. I fall and rise with the falling and rising
bodies. This is I, the machine, manoeuvring in the chaotic movements, recording one movement after another in the most
complex combinations.

Freed from the boundaries of time and space, I co-ordinate any
and all points of the universe, wherever I want them to be. My way
leads towards the creation of a fresh perception of the world. Thus
I explain in a new way the world unknown to you.[1]

The camera isolated momentary appearances and in so doing destroyed
the idea that images were timeless. Or, to put it another way, the camera
showed that the notion of time passing was inseparable from the experience
of the visual (except in paintings). What you saw depended upon where you
were when. What you saw was relative to your position in time and space.
It was no longer possible to imagine everything converging on the human
eye as on the vanishing point of infinity.

This is not to say that before the invention of the camera men believed
that everyone could see everything. But perspective organized the visual field
as though that were indeed the ideal. Every drawing or painting that used
perspective proposed to the spectator that he was the unique centre of the
world. The camera — and more particularly the movie camera — demonstrated that there was no centre.

The invention of the camera changed the way men saw. The visible
came to mean something different to them. This was immediately reflected
in painting.

For the Impressionists the visible no longer presented itself to man in   35
order to be seen. On the contrary, the visible, in continual flux, became fugitive.
For the Cubists, the visible was no longer what confronted the single eye,

---

[1]This quotation is from an article written in 1923 by Dziga Vertov, the revolutionary Soviet film director.

Church of St. Francis at Assisi.

but the totality of possible views taken from points all round the object (or person) being depicted.

The invention of the camera also changed the way in which men saw paintings painted long before the camera was invented. Originally paintings were an integral part of the building for which they were designed. Sometimes in an early Renaissance church or chapel one has the feeling that the images on the wall are records of the building's interior life, that together they make up the building's memory — so much are they part of the particularity of the building.

The uniqueness of every painting was once part of the uniqueness of the place where it resided. Sometimes the painting was transportable. But it could never be seen in two places at the same time. When the camera reproduces a painting, it destroys the uniqueness of its image. As a result its meaning changes. Or, more exactly, its meaning multiplies and fragments into many meanings.

This is vividly illustrated by what happens when a painting is shown on a television screen. The painting enters each viewer's house. There it is surrounded by his wallpaper, his furniture, his mementoes. It enters the atmosphere of his family. It becomes their talking point. It lends its meaning

Virgin of the Rocks by Leonardo da Vinci,
1452–1519, National Gallery.

to their meaning. At the same time it enters a million other houses and, in each of them, is seen in a different context. Because of the camera, the painting now travels to the spectator rather than the spectator to the painting. In its travels, its meaning is diversified.

One might argue that all reproductions more or less distort, and that therefore the original painting is still in a sense unique. Here is a reproduction of the *Virgin of the Rocks* by Leonardo da Vinci.

Having seen this reproduction, one can go to the National Gallery to   40
look at the original and there discover what the reproduction lacks. Alternatively one can forget about the quality of the reproduction and simply be reminded, when one sees the original, that it is a famous painting of which somewhere one has already seen a reproduction. But in either case the uniqueness of the original now lies in it being *the original of a reproduction*. It is no longer what its image shows that strikes one as unique; its first meaning is no longer to be found in what it says, but in what it is.

This new status of the original work is the perfectly rational consequence of the new means of reproduction. But it is at this point that a process of mystification again enters. The meaning of the original work no longer lies in what it uniquely says but in what it uniquely is. How is its unique existence evaluated and defined in our present culture? It is defined as an object whose value depends upon its rarity. This value is affirmed and gauged by the price it fetches on the market. But because it is nevertheless "a work of art" — and art is thought to be greater than commerce — its market price is said to be a reflection of its spiritual value. Yet the spiritual value of an object, as distinct from a message or an example, can only be explained in terms of magic or religion. And since in modern society neither of these is a living force, the art object, the "work of art," is enveloped in an atmosphere of entirely bogus religiosity. Works of art are discussed and presented as though they were holy relics: relics which are first and foremost evidence of their own survival. The past in which they originated is studied in order to prove their survival genuine. They are declared art when their line of descent can be certified.

Before the *Virgin of the Rocks* the visitor to the National Gallery would be encouraged by nearly everything he might have heard and read about the painting to feel something like this: "I am in front of it. I can see it. This painting by Leonardo is unlike any other in the world. The National Gallery has the real one. If I look at this painting hard enough, I should somehow be able to feel its authenticity. The *Virgin of the Rocks* by Leonardo da Vinci: it is authentic and therefore it is beautiful."

To dismiss such feelings as naive would be quite wrong. They accord perfectly with the sophisticated culture of art experts for whom the National

National Gallery.

Virgin of the Rocks by Leonardo da Vinci, 1452–1519, Louvre.

The Virgin and Child with St. Anne and St. John the Baptist
by Leonardo da Vinci, 1452–1519.

Gallery catalogue is written. The entry on the *Virgin of the Rocks* is one of the longest entries. It consists of fourteen closely printed pages. They do not deal with the meaning of the image. They deal with who commissioned the painting, legal squabbles, who owned it, its likely date, the families of its owners. Behind this information lie years of research. The aim of the research is to prove beyond any shadow of doubt that the painting is a genuine Leonardo. The secondary aim is to prove that an almost identical painting in the Louvre is a replica of the National Gallery version [see p. 721].

French art historians try to prove the opposite.

The National Gallery sells more reproductions of Leonardo's cartoon of 45 *The Virgin and Child with St. Anne and St. John the Baptist* than any other picture in their collection. A few years ago it was known only to scholars. It became famous because an American wanted to buy it for two and a half million pounds.

Now it hangs in a room by itself. The room is like a chapel. The drawing is behind bullet-proof perspex. It has acquired a new kind of impressiveness. Not because of what it shows — not because of the meaning of its image. It has become impressive, mysterious, because of its market value.

The bogus religiosity which now surrounds original works of art, and which is ultimately dependent upon their market value, has become the

**National proportion of art museum visitors according to level of education:
Percentage of each educational category who visit art museums**

	Greece	Poland	France	Holland		Greece	Poland	France	Holland
With no educational qualification	0.02	0.12	0.15	—	Only secondary education	10.5	10.4	10	20
Only primary education	0.30	1.50	0.45	0.50	Further and higher education	11.5	11.7	12.5	17.3

Source: Pierre Bourdieu and Alain Darbel, *L'Amour de l'Art*, Editions de Minuit, Paris 1969, Appendix 5, table 4.

substitute for what paintings lost when the camera made them reproducible. Its function is nostalgic. It is the final empty claim for the continuing values of an oligarchic, undemocratic culture. If the image is no longer unique and exclusive, the art object, the thing, must be made mysteriously so.

The majority of the population do not visit art museums. The . . . table [on p. 722] shows how closely an interest in art is related to privileged education.

The majority take it as axiomatic that the museums are full of holy relics which refer to a mystery which excludes them: the mystery of unaccountable wealth. Or, to put this another way, they believe that original masterpieces belong to the preserve (both materially and spiritually) of the rich. Another table indicates what the idea of an art gallery suggests to each social class.

Of the places listed below, which does a museum remind you of most?

	Manual workers	Skilled and white-collar workers	Professional and upper managerial
	%	%	%
Church	66	45	30.5
Library	9	34	28
Lecture hall	–	4	4.6
Department store or entrance hall in public building	–	7	2
Church and library	9	2	4.5
Church and lecture hall	4	2	–
Library and lecture hall	–	–	2
None of these	4	2	19.5
No reply	8	4	9
	100 (*n* = 53)	100 (*n* = 98)	100 (*n* = 99)

Source: As above, appendix 4, table 8.

In the age of pictorial reproduction the meaning of paintings is no longer attached to them; their meaning becomes transmittable: that is to say it becomes information of a sort, and, like all information, it is either put to use or ignored; information carries no special authority within itself. When a painting is put to use, its meaning is either modified or totally changed. One should be quite clear about what this involves. It is not a question of reproduction failing to reproduce certain aspects of an image faithfully; it is a question of reproduction making it possible, even inevitable, that an image will be used for many different purposes and that the reproduced image, unlike an original work, can lend itself to them all. Let us examine some of the ways in which the reproduced image lends itself to such usage.

Venus and Mars by Botticelli, 1445–1510.

Reproduction isolates a detail of a painting from the whole. The detail is transformed. An allegorical figure becomes a portrait of a girl.

When a painting is reproduced by a film camera, it inevitably becomes material for the film-maker's argument.

A film which reproduces images of a painting leads the spectator, through the painting, to the film-maker's own conclusions. The painting lends authority to the film-maker.

This is because a film unfolds in time and a painting does not.

In a film the way one image follows another, their succession, constructs   55
an argument which becomes irreversible.

In a painting all its elements are there to be seen simultaneously. The spectator may need time to examine each element of the painting but whenever he reaches a conclusion, the simultaneity of the whole painting is there to reverse or qualify his conclusion. The painting maintains its own authority.

Procession to Calvary by Brueghel, 1525–1569.

Paintings are often reproduced with words around them.

This is a landscape of a cornfield with birds flying out of it. Look at it for a moment. Then [look at the top of p. 727].

Wheatfield with Crows by Vincent van Gogh, 1853–1890.

This is the last picture that Van Gogh painted before he killed himself.

Wheatfield with Crows by Vincent van Gogh, 1853–1890.

It is hard to define exactly how the words have changed the image but undoubtedly they have. The image now illustrates the sentence.

In this essay each image reproduced has become part of an argument 60 which has little or nothing to do with the painting's original independent meaning. The words have quoted the paintings to confirm their own verbal authority. (The essays without words in this book may make that distinction clearer.)

Reproduced paintings, like all information, have to hold their own against all the other information being continually transmitted.

Consequently a reproduction, as well as making its own references to the image of its original, becomes itself the reference point for other images. The meaning of an image is changed according to what one sees immediately beside it or what comes immediately after it. Such authority as it retains, is distributed over the whole context in which it appears.

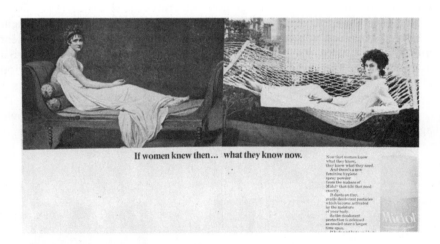

If women knew then... what they know now.

Because works of art are reproducible, they can, theoretically, be used by anybody. Yet mostly — in art books, magazines, films or within gilt frames in living-rooms — reproductions are still used to bolster the illusion that nothing has changed, that art, with its unique undiminished authority, justifies most other forms of authority, that art makes inequality seem noble and hierarchies seem thrilling. For example, the whole concept of the National

Cultural Heritage exploits the authority of art to glorify the present social system and its priorities.

The means of reproduction are used politically and commercially to disguise or deny what their existence makes possible. But sometimes individuals use them differently.

Adults and children sometimes have boards in their bedrooms or living-rooms on which they pin pieces of paper: letters, snapshots, reproductions of paintings, newspaper cuttings, original drawings, postcards. On each board all the images belong to the same language and all are more or less equal within it, because they have been chosen in a highly personal way to match and express the experience of the room's inhabitant. Logically, these boards should replace museums.

65

What are we saying by that? Let us first be sure about what we are not saying.

We are not saying that there is nothing left to experience before original works of art except a sense of awe because they have survived. The way original works of art are usually approached—through museum catalogues, guides, hired cassettes, etc. — is not the only way they might be approached. When the art of the past ceases to be viewed nostalgically, the works will cease to be holy relics — although they will never re-become what they were before the age of reproduction. We are not saying original works of art are now useless.

Woman Pouring Milk by Vermeer, 1632–1675.

Original paintings are silent and still in a sense that information never is. Even a reproduction hung on a wall is not comparable in this respect for in the original the silence and stillness permeate the actual material, the paint, in which one follows the traces of the painter's immediate gestures. This has the effect of closing the distance in time between the painting of the picture and one's own act of looking at it. In this special sense all paintings are contemporary. Hence the immediacy of their testimony. Their historical moment is literally there before our eyes. Cézanne made a similar observation from the painter's point of view. "A minute in the world's life passes! To paint it in its reality, and forget everything for that! To become that minute, to be the sensitive plate . . . give the image of what we see, forgetting everything that has appeared before our time. . . ." What we make of that painted moment when it is before our eyes depends upon what we expect of art, and that in turn depends today upon how we have already experienced the meaning of paintings through reproductions.

Nor are we saying that all art can be understood spontaneously. We are not claiming that to cut out a magazine reproduction of an archaic Greek head, because it is reminiscent of some personal experience, and to pin it on to a board beside other disparate images, is to come to terms with the full meaning of that head.

*   *   *

The idea of innocence faces two ways. By refusing to enter a conspiracy, 70
one remains innocent of that conspiracy. But to remain innocent may also
be to remain ignorant. The issue is not between innocence and knowledge
(or between the natural and the cultural) but between a total approach to
art, which attempts to relate it to every aspect of experience, and the esoteric
approach of a few specialized experts who are the clerks of the nostalgia of
a ruling class in decline. (In decline, not before the proletariat, but before the
new power of the corporation and the state.) The real question is: To whom
does the meaning of the art of the past properly belong? To those who can
apply it to their own lives, or to a cultural hierarchy of relic specialists?

The visual arts have always existed within a certain preserve; originally
this preserve was magical or sacred. But it was also physical: it was the
place, the cave, the building, in which, or for which, the work was made.
The experience of art, which at first was the experience of ritual, was set
apart from the rest of life — precisely in order to be able to exercise power
over it. Later the preserve of art became a social one. It entered the culture
of the ruling class, whilst physically it was set apart and isolated in their
palaces and houses. During all this history the authority of art was inseparable from the particular authority of the preserve.

What the modern means of reproduction have done is to destroy the authority of art and to remove it — or, rather, to remove its images, which they
reproduce — from any preserve. For the first time ever, images of art have
become ephemeral, ubiquitous, insubstantial, available, valueless, free.
They surround us in the same way as a language surrounds us. They have
entered the mainstream of life over which they no longer, in themselves,
have power.

Yet very few people are aware of what has happened because the means
of reproduction are used nearly all the time to promote the illusion that
nothing has changed except that the masses, thanks to reproductions, can
now begin to appreciate art as the cultured minority once did. Understandably, the masses remain uninterested and sceptical.

If the new language of images were used differently, it would, through
its use, confer a new kind of power. Within it we could begin to define our
experiences more precisely in areas where words are inadequate. (Seeing
comes before words.) Not only personal experience, but also the essential
historical experience of our relation to the past: that is to say the experience
of seeking to give meaning to our lives, of trying to understand the history
of which we can become the active agents.

The art of the past no longer exists as it once did. Its authority is lost. In 75
its place there is a language of images. What matters now is who uses that
language for what purpose. This touches upon questions of copyright for
reproduction, the ownership of art presses and publishers, the total policy of
public art galleries and museums. As usually presented, these are narrow
professional matters. One of the aims of this essay has been to show that
what is really at stake is much larger. A people or a class which is cut off

from its own past is far less free to choose and to act as a people or class than one that has been able to situate itself in history. This is why — and this is the only reason why — the entire art of the past has now become a political issue.

QUESTIONS

Reading

1. According to Berger, what has replaced the art of the past?
2. This essay is excerpted from the book *Ways of Seeing*. Four of the book's essays use both words and images, and the other three use only images. How do the images in this essay support and illustrate Berger's argument? What might you understand about the argument from looking at the images alone, without Berger's text?
3. What changes does Berger attribute to the invention of the camera?

Exploratory Writing

1. Do you agree with Berger that perceiving original works of art as imbued with a special mystery or power that reproductions lack is evidence of a "bogus religiosity," and that a viewer's sense of the work's importance is actually based on its market value (paragraph 41)? Find an example of an original artwork or artifact, and discuss why, in your view, it supports or refutes Berger's points.
2. Tell about a time when you were misled by a picture — when you thought you were "seeing" one thing but in fact you were "seeing" something else entirely. How did this change the way you respond to images?
3. In pairs, choose any image from this essay and, without thinking too much, jot down all of your responses to the image. What do you think it means? What does it tell you about the artist who created it? What do you really see when you look at the image? When you are done, compare and contrast your ideas and perceptions with those of your partner. Did the two of you "see" different things in the same image?

Making Connections

1. What does Berger mean when he writes that the art of the past has been displaced by a *language of images*? Choose any other essayist in this casebook, and summarize how the idea of a *language of images* fits in with his or her discussion. How is a language of images different from a language of words?
2. McCloud (p. 693) and Berger both trace histories of visual art, but for different purposes. Make a list of each writer's claims about the

history of visual art. Do any of their claims overlap? How do each author's claims correspond to the purpose or motive driving his historical account?

McCloud's claims	Berger's claims

Essay Writing

1. Each essay in this casebook deals, in some way, with *illusions* or *misperceptions*. Using examples from any or all of them, write your own essay explaining what *illusion* means. You can also use outside case studies or examples from your own life.

Gray Matter: The Brain and the Self

In the past twenty years, neurobiologists and cognitive scientists have made rapid advances in the area of brain research — in large part because of new technologies that allow them to scan and observe the brain (including electroencephalography [EEG], functional magnetic resonance imaging [fMRI], and positron-emission tomography [PET]. These advances have helped countless people with brain injuries or disorders. In addition, they have begun to shed new light on perception, emotion, consciousness, and cognition. As a result, advances in brain research are also advances in the understanding of the self.

The six essays collected in this casebook examine the relationship between the brain and the self from a variety of perspectives. They include a portrait of cognitive neuroscientist Dr. John Gabrieli, who uses fMRI to study memory (Shannon Moffett, "Watching the Brain"); a brain researcher's reflection on her own experience of having a stroke (Jill Bolte Taylor, "Morning of the Stroke"); an evolutionary biologist's discussion of the faulty history of the study of women's brains (Stephen Jay Gould, "Women's Brains"); a case study about a pathological case of laughter that speculates about the brain physiology of humor (V. S. Ramachandran, "The Woman Who Died Laughing"); a writer's reflections on the relationship between memory and imagination (Patricia Hampl, "Memory and Imagination"); and a memory researcher's explanation of the impulse to tell autobiographical stories (Daniel Schacter, "Of Time and Autobiography").

The brain is, to say the least, a complex organ. Even neuroscientists don't understand it fully. You won't be an expert on all things neurological after reading these six essays, but you will have learned quite a bit about how brain research is illuminating questions about how we become who we are. With that foundation, you might write in response to particular essays included here, you might compare two of these texts, or you might write about the implications raised by several of them. Reading these essays may also lead to new questions best explored through further research. The questions that follow each reading are intended to give you the opportunity to write in response to these texts and, when appropriate, to use them as a foundation for research into the questions they address.

Watching the Brain

Shannon Moffett

Shannon Moffett, a one-time struggling actress, wrote The Three-Pound Enigma: The Human Brain and the Quest to Unlock Its Mysteries *while a medical student at Stanford University School of Medicine. Although a number of other popular theories also explicate consciousness and the mind-brain-body connection, Moffett's book adds a humanizing perspective by looking at the pioneering doctors and scientists who research these issues and what makes them tick. Moffett completed her MD in 2006 and is now a practicing doctor. This piece is an excerpt from* The Three-Pound Enigma *(2006).*

In the summer of 1998, Dr. John Gabrieli was in Boston, staying with his parents while helping his brother campaign for a Democratic congressional seat. The other members of the campaign were college students, at least twenty years younger than Gabrieli. "I think they viewed me as kind of pathetic," he later told me. "You know, doesn't have a job and he's working on the campaign and he's living with his parents," he said. "I don't really know, but I had this vague sense that they were all looking at me as this sort of sad person, just lucky to get a job for the summer."

That impression is, if inaccurate, maybe understandable. At well over six feet tall, Gabrieli has a slight stoop and a tight-jawed manner of speaking that, combined with his invariably self-deprecating sense of humor, keep him from ever appearing at ease. He dresses exclusively in khakis, button-downs, and either loafers or Hush Puppies. He wears brown tortoiseshell spectacles and combs his auburn hair smoothly from a side part. Comparisons to Clark Kent are made the more inevitable by his tendency to sprinkle his speech with exclamations worthy of Smallville (as in "Gee, I will say this, I feel like I had a happy childhood"), so it's not hard to picture his young co-workers quickly consigning him to their "loser" lists.

Imagine their surprise, then, when they turned on the radio at campaign headquarters and heard the host of the National Public Radio program *All Things Considered* announce his guest, a professor of psychology and neuroscience and an authority on memory: John Gabrieli of Stanford University.

Gabrieli had been invited to discuss the strange case of a man recently picked up by police in Jacksonville, Florida. Found wandering along the highway amid the smoke from a brush fire, the man had given his name as Terry Dibert, said he was twenty-three years old, and told the officers he needed to get back to Fort Bragg, North Carolina, where his army unit was stationed and his wife, Julie, was soon to give birth to their first child. Yet when the police called Fort Bragg, they learned that Dibert's unit had been gone for years.

Dibert was subsequently identified as a thirty-four-year-old accountant who'd been missing from his home — not in North Carolina but in central Pennsylvania — for over a week. He was, in fact, married to a woman named Julie, but she had borne the first of their three children eleven years earlier, while they were living at Fort Bragg. Dibert appeared to have lost the memories created during more than a decade of life, including those of his move to Pennsylvania, the birth of his children, and his new job as a business manager for a central Pennsylvania school district.

Such a phenomenon makes good headlines: a Webzine called *Paranormal Pages* came out with "Time Traveler Goes Back to 1987," as if that would, naturally, be the year anyone who could turn back the clock would visit. It soon became clear that Dibert wasn't claiming to have been abducted by space aliens, but that his condition had natural causes. At that point the legitimate press rushed to cover the story as well, which was why Gabrieli was featured on NPR.

In the course of the interview, Gabrieli explained that memories take years to "consolidate," a still poorly understood process of cementing them in the brain, and that if an injury occurs in the right spot at any point during those years, the memories still consolidating can be lost or temporarily inaccessible. He also touched on the theory of multiple memory systems, which explains why Dibert — whose injury was then still a mystery — could lose all memories of experiences from the previous eleven years yet still drive his car as proficiently as ever.

There was tension in Gabrieli's voice during the interview (he is, by his own account, extremely shy), and the segment lasted only a couple of minutes. Yet even this quick glimpse into his world gave his cocampaigners an image of him as an expert in a cutting-edge science, scouting ahead into the unknown territory of the mind.

Or at least, as employable. "Yeah," he told me, "later they all said, 'Were you on NPR? You have a job and everything?!'"

What Gabrieli has is more than a job. It is a quest that eats up the bulk of his waking hours ("Gee whiz, so let's see, most days I get in about seven a.m. and I leave about seven or eight p.m. Five days times twelve hours equals sixty, and most Saturdays and Sundays I'm in about half a day") and keeps him too busy for hobbies or even a lunch break. What Gabrieli has is a lab.

The Gab Lab, as it's called internally, is devoted to cognitive neuroscience, a field that scarcely existed thirty years ago but is today the subject of numerous international scientific meetings and dozens of journals. Cognitive neuroscience has been called the expensive branch of philosophy. It could also be called empiric philosophy: its practitioners try to figure out how and where we perform mental tasks or experience mental states.

When I first arrived at the lab, a catacomb of offices, conference rooms, and library space in one of the red-roofed sandstone buildings surrounding Stanford's mission-style quad, Gabrieli interrupted a meeting to introduce me around. As I followed him down the hall, I noticed an old *Peanuts* cartoon posted on the wall, a rueful nod to cognitive neuroscience's theoretical nature:

> LINUS: When I grow up, I'd like to study about people. People interest me. I'd like to go to some big university and study all about people.
> CHARLIE BROWN: I see . . . You want to learn about people so that with your knowledge you will be equipped to help them.
> LINUS: No. I'm just nosy.

We reached a room in which two beautiful young women were seated side by side at computer monitors; one of them was Gabrieli's lab manager. She offered to find me a work space with a computer and then insisted when I told her not to bother, cheerfully installing me in an unused office. Everyone in the lab seemed young, happy, and eager; the bulletin boards were covered with postcards and photos of lab members on vacation in exotic places, and when I later spoke with some of them, it seemed none could praise Gabrieli enough, a fact he modestly brushes off. When I told him I had heard the word "flexible" over and over from colleagues when they described him, he said, "Well, if it means you don't know what you're doing and you have no particular mission and you just muddle through, then I think I'm flexible, sure."

While the scores of scientific papers Gabrieli has authored and the various national and international advisory boards on which he sits reveal that he clearly does know what he's doing, it would be hard to say Gabrieli has any one particular mission, as his interests are unusually eclectic. Cognitive neuroscience encompasses processes as varied as visual perception, mathematical calculations, and falling in love, so most cognitive neuroscientists specialize. Although Gabrieli's stated specialty is memory, he takes frequent side trips. His lab also investigates olfaction (the study of how we smell and what happens to our brain when we do), learning disorders (dyslexia, attention-deficit/hyperactivity disorder), face recognition, and, in a dabbling kind of way, the controversial question of how people of different races perceive one another visually.

But a common theme to most of the Gab Lab's work is a technique called functional magnetic resonance imaging, or fMRI. Functional MRI is one of the newest imaging tools used to study the brain. For decades, magnetic resonance imaging (MRI) has made possible high-definition images of soft-tissue structures that X-rays don't resolve well, like muscles, ligaments, and the brain. MRI was originally used to create static images, revolutionizing our ability to detect early cancers of organs like the liver or the kidney, as well as other soft-tissue abnormalities, such as torn ligaments, which are generally undetectable by X-ray. But in the early 1990s, scientists like Gabrieli began using magnetic resonance scanners to both show the architecture of the brain and watch it as it works — that is, as we think.

The basis of fMRI is a concept so simple most fifth-graders can rattle it off: blood provides working cells with oxygen and other nutrients and removes waste products like carbon dioxide. Because harder-working cells need more oxygen and nutrients and give off more waste, they need more blood. So if you could find some way to measure blood flow within the brain, you could theoretically determine when the brain — or a given part of it — is working hardest and when it is relatively quiescent.

This idea is not new. In his book *The Principles of Psychology*, William James, the nineteenth-century philosopher of mind, wrote of a contemporary, an Italian physician named Mosso. According to James, Mosso hypothesized that when we think, we must require increased blood flow to the brain. To prove his theory, he had human subjects lie on a table, which he then carefully balanced on a fulcrum. After instructing the subjects to remain absolutely motionless, he gave them various mental tasks. According to Mosso, as his subjects started thinking harder, the end of the table supporting their heads invariably sank slightly — a phenomenon he attributed to increased blood perfusing the brain tissue. While his apparatus was crude to the point of being ridiculous, Mosso's concept was sound and today is the basis of cutting-edge neuroimaging. FMRI measures the flow of blood to structures and areas within the brain when they're active, or functional.

Functional MRI is easy to fall in love with. I was enchanted with my first sight of an fMRI scan: a gray-scale picture of a cross-section of a human brain, like a slice of the head taken parallel with the floor. The brain's anatomy was clearly visible in black and white, but patches in the occipital lobe at the back of the brain glowed brilliant yellow and orange to show activation of that area in response to a visual stimulus.

It was vertiginous, like looking in two mirrors reflecting each other: this picture allowed me to use my eyes to tell my brain what happens inside someone else's brain when they use their eyes to look at the world. I was only observing someone else's work, but it seemed like a miracle, a glimpse into the previously unknown. I felt the way Galileo must have when he looked through his telescope, or Armstrong when his foot hit the moon.

FMRI may be easy to love, but not to explain. When I asked Gabrieli   20
how it works, he declined to answer, claiming a lack of expertise in the physics involved. Instead, he sent me to see his longtime collaborator, Dr. Gary Glover. Glover is a physicist and, before coming to Stanford, was a

member of the team at General Electric that developed magnetic resonance imaging in the seventies. "You'll like him," Gabrieli told me. "He'll be wearing shorts."

Glover did greet me at the door of the seventeen-thousand-square-foot Lucas Center, Stanford's state-of-the-art MRI facility, of which he is the director, wearing khaki shorts and Birkenstock sandals. Right away he took me down to the basement of the center to see an fMRI scanner, which looked like a six-foot sugar cube with a hole bored through the center at waist height. The white cube is a refrigerator, which keeps the magnet inside it from overheating. That magnet is a metal coil, like a gigantic electrified — and thus magnetized — Slinky. The refrigerator and the coil surround a narrow platform that slides in and out of the hole in the center of the cube. A subject lies on the platform, with her head on a pillow made of Styrofoam beads. Once the subject's head is in place, a vacuum pump sucks all the air out from between the beads, making a rigid mold of the head and holding it completely still, as subjects must be absolutely motionless within the coffin-like center of the device, often for over an hour at a time, repeatedly performing mental tasks while their brains are scanned. That fact and the earsplitting racket the scanner makes as it works mean subjects must be carefully screened for claustrophobia.

While I was there, one of Gabrieli's students was working at a flat-panel monitor in the control room, separated from the scanner by a solid wall of glass. She was programming a series of pictures for that day's experiment; later those pictures would appear simultaneously on her display and on a similar display suspended within the scanner above the subject's head.

After the tour, Glover led me to his office and headed immediately for a whiteboard, covered from top to bottom with equations scribbled in red marker. He took an eraser, rubbed out a pie-size clearing in the middle of the board, and stood there, marker poised. "The basic idea," he told me, "is that people are weakly magnetic." And then the marker hit the board and he was off into spin.

It isn't possible to explain magnetic resonance imaging without first talking about an atomic quality physicists call spin, a feature of an atom's nucleus imparted to it by the electrons orbiting around it. For this reason it's hard to describe, as those electrons have both particle-like and wavelike properties. But it's easiest to get your mind around the concept if you imagine each atom as a spinning top. There is an axis around which the top spins, and that axis points in a particular direction. Not all atoms have nuclear spin — helium, for instance, as one of the noble gases, does not — but those that do have spin act as minuscule magnets in essentially the same way an electromagnet does: spinning electrical charges create a magnetic field that lies along the axis around which the charges spin.

Normally, the tiny spins of the atoms in your body have no net effect — your watch still works, compasses don't go haywire when you   25 walk by — because the spin axes are all lying around randomly and so tend to cancel one another out. But if a person is placed in a strong magnetic field such as the one created by the coil of a magnetic resonance scanner, some of the spins move into alignment with that larger magnetic field, whose axis runs along the length of the platform on which the subject lies.

There are two ways in which an atom can align with the magnetic field: either parallel or antiparallel to it. The antiparallel configuration is slightly higher energy, meaning that it's more likely to change position; the difference between the two alignments is something like the difference between a quarter resting on its edge and one resting flat. A few atoms, just a couple per million, line up with their spins antiparallel to the magnetic field created by the scanner.

Once the atoms are lined up, either parallel or antiparallel to the larger magnetic field, you "perturb the system," as Glover put it, by hitting it with a radio-frequency pulse, a brief burst of a rotating magnetic field. The pulse provides enough energy to flip a few more of the atoms from the parallel toward the higher-energy antiparallel alignment. When the pulse ends, these flipped atoms relax back into the lower-energy state. The effect is as if many small magnets were tracing a path from one alignment to the other. MRI works by placing a sensor beside that path, so that it picks up the magnetic signal from the flipped atoms as they relax back down to the lower-energy state.

The scanner is set to detect one specific atom — usually hydrogen, as there's a lot of it in the human body in the form of water — and uses additional magnetic fields to tag the specific location of each hydrogen atom as it traces its path from the high- to the low-energy alignment. The scanner can then create an image based on the locations of those hydrogen atoms and the fact that they behave differently depending on the kind of tissue they're in — fat, bone, or muscle, for example.

With all this talk of atoms and alignments, it's easy to get lost in the theory and forget that what you're dealing with in an MRI scanner is a magnet with the same properties as the little doodads we stick on our refrigerators — albeit three hundred times stronger. Anyone who works with MRI quickly learns to leave her wallet outside the scanning room to avoid losing the information encoded in the magnetic strips of her credit cards. Neither researchers nor subjects can wear jewelry or metal hair clips, as they may be sucked right up into the magnet or simply get so hot from all the moving atoms that they burn their wearer. And the reason the Lucas Center had only flat-panel monitors long before they were widely used was not cosmetic. Traditional cathode-ray-tube screens "go all wonky," says Glover, because of the strong magnetic field.

Some people in particular shouldn't be exposed to the magnet. Glover   30
gave the example of a patient who had worked in a machine shop prior to being scanned. It is not uncommon, he told me, for people who've worked

in machine shops to have metal fragments lodged in their eyes, even without their knowing it. In this case, when the patient was put in the scanner and the magnet turned on, a splinter of metal he didn't know was in his eye moved into alignment with the scanner's magnetic field, nicking a blood vessel in the back of his eye on its way. No one knew this had happened, and the buildup of blood eventually compressed the retinal cells as they entered the optic nerve, resulting in blindness in that eye. "So," Glover told me, "every screening from then on has that kind of question in it: 'Have you ever worked in a machine shop?'"

Glover's explanation so far only brings us to magnetic resonance imaging, the sort of garden-variety MRI. . . . But for Glover and the "psychos" — as he calls Gabrieli and those more interested in the brain than in the science that allows them to look at it — the real fascination is with functional MRI. In fMRI, the basic image is created through MRI, and then thought processes are tracked via changes in that image caused by fluctuations in blood flow, with increased blood flow to a particular area of the brain reflecting increased activity in that spot.

In earlier functional brain-imaging techniques, such as positron-emission tomography (PET) scans, and even early fMRI, a patient or subject was injected with a contrast agent — a substance that would give off a traceable signal as it traveled around the body in the blood. But those agents are, for the most part, radioactive, meaning an increased risk of cancer with each injection. Repeat studies were virtually impossible, and studies in children rarely done. In the early 1990s, however, scientists at AT&T's Bell Laboratories came up with a way to measure blood flow based on properties of the blood itself. Hemoglobin, the molecule in the blood that carries oxygen, has significant magnetization only when it is not carrying oxygen. Deoxygenated blood is therefore highly magnetized and so interferes with the magnetic signal from the hydrogen in surrounding tissue, paradoxically causing a *reduction* in magnetic signal. Conversely, an influx of fresh, oxygenated (and thus less magnetized) blood to an area of the brain interferes less and *raises* the magnetic signal detectable from hydrogen in the surrounding tissue.

In other words, when Gabrieli's students put a subject in the scanner and show her pictures to learn what happens in her brain when she recognizes an image, the scanner records an increase in magnetic signal from the brain areas doing the recognizing. It is this difference in signal dependent on blood-oxygen level (the technique is called BOLD, for blood-oxygen-level dependent) that allows scientists to explore how and where we think.

Cognitive neuroscience is, as Glover said once he'd finished his explanation, "a big field," and since its development, fMRI — which because it is apparently harmless allows for study of children's brains and repeated adult experiments — has been used to study questions as varied as where in our brains we experience emotion, how arachnophobes' brains react to spiders, and how damaged brains . . . reorganize to function normally. The tools

Glover uses to aid scholars in that big field are also big: As he walked me out of the Lucas Center, which he helped design, Glover said, "See that hatch?" pointing through a wall of glass to a ten-foot-square steel lid set in the ground. He told me parts of the center's fMRI scanner had been lowered by crane through the hatch to reach its basement resting place. One of those parts was the magnet itself, which, he said, weighs about thirteen and a half tons.

Glover and his enormous magnet arrived at Stanford at almost the same time Gabrieli's circuitous career path landed him there. Although he was an English literature major at Yale in the 1970s, Gabrieli told me he had nevertheless planned to be a doctor like his father, who was a surgeon and clinical pathologist. "As long as I can remember, that was the thing I planned on being," he told me. "I think because my father was a physician and that was well spoken of."   35

It certainly must have been. Sometime during the days I spent with Gabrieli, I spoke with his mother on the phone from Boston. She couldn't say enough about doctors and doctoring. Upon learning that I was in medical school, she said, "Oh, there is nothing more beautiful, believe me, nothing. We thought John would be a doctor, but he was so decided to go into research. We weren't delighted with it, believe me. It was very unexpected. But he just got carried away."

What carried Gabrieli away was the study of human memory. After graduating from Yale, he got a job in Dr. Suzanne Corkin's lab at MIT. Around the time Gabrieli joined her, Corkin was performing a series of groundbreaking experiments on memory that followed in the footsteps of the pioneering Canadian scientist Dr. Brenda Milner. Many of those experiments focused on one person, a man Gabrieli refers to as "the noted patient HM."

HM is famous among those who study the brain and the mind, although he himself doesn't know it. As a teenager and well into his twenties, HM suffered from debilitating epilepsy, experiencing dozens of seizures a day. In 1953, when he was twenty-seven, HM decided to undergo surgery to remove the area of his brain where the seizures began. For the operation, he was referred to Dr. William Scoville, a man alternately lauded and reviled in the mountains of literature about HM's case but who, through his treatment of HM and subsequent decision to make public the grievous results of that treatment, has probably contributed more to the understanding of memory than any other scholar.

When Scoville prepared to operate on HM, he was, in a sense, flying in the dark. Surgery for epilepsy was not new: the first such operation (which was successful) had been performed almost seventy years earlier. But Scoville had been unable to localize where in HM's brain the seizures started, so he didn't really know which part of the brain he ought to remove. A common place for seizures to begin in epileptics, however, is the hippocampus, an area within the temporal lobe.

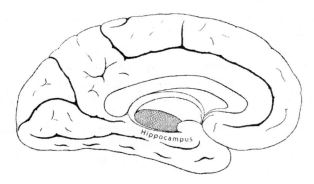

This is a sagittal section, a slice taken parallel to a line drawn from the nose to the back of the head along the midline.

The hippocampus, like almost all structures in the brain, is really two 40 structures, one in each hemisphere. In the absence of other information, Scoville chose to remove HM's hippocampus, considering it the most likely focus of his seizures. Because he didn't even know on which side of HM's brain the seizures were beginning, Scoville chose to remove the hippocampus bilaterally. He also took out portions of the brain near the hippocampus on both sides; the entire area from which Scoville removed tissue is known collectively as the medial temporal lobe and comprises the hippocampus and structures known as the amygdala and the uncus.

HM is still alive today, and in a sense Scoville's operation was a success: HM's epilepsy, most agree, is better. But as Gabrieli says, there was "this tremendous side effect" of the surgery, "which has gotten him into every psychology textbook and medical textbook that's published, which is: For all practical purposes, from that day forward to the present, he has not been able to remember a new event or a new fact for more than a few seconds."

HM can no longer make any new conscious memories. Because of his case and research sparked by it, we now know that the hippocampus is vital to our capacity to create and store memories, although science is just beginning to study how exactly it performs those functions.

At the same time that HM's horrible outcome made clear the importance of the hippocampus to memory, it also made it clear that the hippocampus isn't the only part of the brain that allows us to remember who we are and what has happened to us. HM can easily tell you stories from his childhood, can tell you who the president was when he started high school, can recognize celebrities famous when he was growing up and sing songs from that time — in short, he has a full set of memories of his life until a few years before his surgery.

That he is missing memories even from years before the surgery gives credence to one theory of the hippocampus's role in memory consolidation, which is that the record your brain keeps of experiences stays in the hippocampus for years before being transferred — maybe gradually, maybe all at once — to other parts of the brain. Terry Dibert's case also supports that theory. After the police identified him, Dibert was taken to a hospital in Pennsylvania, where he was diagnosed with a benign fluid-filled cyst that had been pressing on a part of his brain called the fornix. The fornix serves as a pathway from the hippocampus to other parts of the brain, and it may be that the cyst blocked the flow of information along it. Such a blockage would prevent Dibert from accessing more recent memories stored in the hippocampus, yet would still allow him to retrieve older memories consolidated and stored elsewhere.

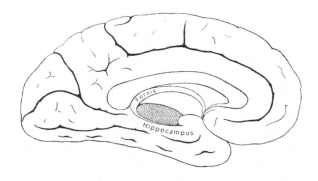

Once the cyst was drained, most of Dibert's newer memories returned, but HM was not so lucky. He is now in his seventies, yet he cannot remember where he has lived during the last sixty years or so. He cannot remember anyone he has met since years before his surgery, or even what he had for lunch half an hour ago. "He doesn't know that men have gone to the moon," Gabrieli says. "His parents have passed away, and he doesn't know. No matter how dramatic an event's personal consequences, no matter how publicly discussed, they are all a blank to him."[1]

45

---

[1]HM's particular brand of amnesia has inspired any number of books and movies, some of them more scientifically accurate than others. In *50 First Dates*, for example, the conceit is that Drew Barrymore's character has a similar amnesia following brain damage incurred during a car accident. Conveniently for the plot, she is able to retain memories over the course of a day, allowing her to have some kind of meaningful relationship with her swain, played by Adam Sandler. In reality, of course, even in the unlikely event that a car accident had caused bilateral medial temporal lobe damage, her disability would be more like that of HM and of Ten Second Tom, another character in the movie. Ten Second Tom is played only for laughs and can't carry on even a simple conversation because by the time he's finished introducing himself, he's already forgotten that he's done so.

What he can do is talk, push buttons, and report his sensations and memories — or lack thereof — as any human can and no mouse or monkey, no matter how well trained, is able to. Thus HM, a quiet Catholic boy from Connecticut with an eighth-grade education, revolutionized the study of memory. "Before HM," Gabrieli told me, "most research on amnesics was just documenting how really *bad* their memory was. For years and years that was it." But now science had a patient with an unusually "pure" amnesia — HM showed no signs of dementia or other brain damage — and what's more, the exact location of his brain lesion was known. And "he's an excellent subject for experiments," Gabrieli says. "Most subjects we run, three minutes into the experiment they're checking their watch — the fun's over, now come trials three through nine thousand. But he's awesome because he has no idea that he's been doing something for a while. Boredom is meaningless to him; he only knows the last five seconds of his life." Which means that researchers — who sometimes seem to share this boredom deficit — are able to sit with HM for hours, showing him pictures, numbers, or words and testing his memory for those pictures, numbers, or words five seconds, ten seconds, thirty seconds, minutes, hours, days, or years later.

It may seem inhumane to use HM in this way. It's a conundrum: His intelligence is completely intact, so he can understand and sign an informed consent, and he does for each experiment. But he has no way of knowing that it's the twentieth, thirtieth, or hundredth such form he's been presented with. However, besides the fact that there is a clear and enormous benefit to science gained by studying HM, Gabrieli points out that it's senseless to think of him as you would another, normal subject. "You could be mean, if you wanted, and explain to him, 'Your memory is like the worst anybody's had. You're in all the textbooks as a horrible memory person,' right? But by the time you're on your third or fourth sentence, he's already fading on the first sentence, and moments later he won't remember it anyway."

Because Gabrieli worked directly with HM, his lectures are often reduced for long stretches to impromptu discussions of HM's predicament. He never seems to tire of the topic, however, answering all questions with the same sense of raw wonder in which they are invariably posed. At one lecture I attended, during which easily twenty minutes were spent with hands waving in the air, Gabrieli fielded a query about HM's feelings on his own appearance, given that he can't remember all the years he's lived to bring him to his current age. "Excellent question," Gabrieli said. "Does he look into the mirror every day and shriek?" It turns out he doesn't: somehow, despite the fact that when asked, HM will guess his age to be somewhere in his twenties or early thirties, some part of his brain has gotten used to the face of an old man gazing out from his reflection. Asked about HM's personal growth, Gabrieli said, "As far as one can tell, he's had no change in personality or emotional growth or anything.

Now" — with a smile — "many people are identified as being childish in their forties, fifties, and seventies, so it's hard to actually prove that."[2]

In that lecture, Gabrieli used HM to illustrate the theory of multiple memory systems, as his case provided some of the basis for the model. The significance of the experiments that did so was not immediately recognized, however. In the early 1960s, long before Gabrieli was to work with her, Brenda Milner put HM through a standard battery of tests of brain and memory function and noticed that on certain kinds of tasks he didn't do any worse than people with normal memories. One of those tasks was mirror drawing: subjects were taught to trace between two lines on a piece of paper while watching their hands only in a mirror. A person with a normal brain will be terrible at mirror drawing initially, then gradually improve as her brain correlates messages from the eyes with the signals it must send the muscles in order to achieve the required hand movements. Normal subjects will also, of course, consciously remember having practiced the skill.

HM, on the other hand, does not remember ever having performed it   50
before, though he's probably done it scores of times by now. Each time he has to have the rules explained to him all over again. But in what must have been one of the eerier moments in science, Milner and her team noticed that HM nonetheless got better at staying within the lines. He got better at the same rate, in fact, as normal subjects.

When Milner's results were published, the neuroscience community's reaction to this news about HM was equivocal. Not much was concluded about memory as a whole. It wasn't until 1980 — when, among other developments, Dr. Neal Cohen and Dr. Larry Squire, at the University of California at San Diego, published a paper with the precise if unwieldy title "Preserved Learning and Retention of Pattern-Analyzing Skill in Amnesia: Dissociation of Knowing How and Knowing That" in the journal *Science* — that there was a paradigm shift in how scientists think about human memory. Cohen and Squire stated clearly and courageously their belief, based on Milner's data and their own experiments showing normal improvement in reading of mirror-image words by people with amnesia, that "amnesia seems to spare information that is based on rules or procedures, as contrasted with information that is data-based or declarative."

In other words, they believed there to be at least two memory systems, of which our conscious memory — the memory we use to recall past experiences, traditionally considered the whole of memory — is only one. Squire

---

[2]Gabrieli is known for his dry sense of humor. At a conference I attended, one speaker introduced her talk by describing how she'd run into him the day before and had mentioned the subject of her talk, which was Alzheimer's disease. "Are you going to be very controversial," he asked her, "and come out against it?"

wrote years later that "this finding broadened the scope of what amnesic patients could do, and suggested a major distinction between declarative forms of memory, which are impaired in amnesia, and non-declarative forms of memory, which are preserved in amnesia."

And that, to this day, is the basic distinction between what scientists refer to as declarative memory and nondeclarative memory: If amnesics can do it, it relies on nondeclarative memory systems. If they can't, it's a function of declarative processes. Gabrieli admits that such a definition is problematic. No one knows where in the brain nondeclarative memories are produced or stored, and there's no independent definition of either declarative or nondeclarative memory, although in general, declarative memory is defined as conscious recollections of events or information, and nondeclarative memory refers to physical or cognitive skills. What definitions do exist are still under debate, in a field so riddled with overlapping terminology that Endel Tulving, a kind of patriarch of modern memory research, once wrote a paper in which he felt it necessary to include a table correlating the terms used by different investigators for different types of memory (for example, declarative memory is sometimes called episodic, semantic, or explicit, and nondeclarative memory is also known as procedural or implicit).

One of the nondeclarative forms of memory Gabrieli studied in HM and in normal control subjects, and continues to study today with the help of fMRI, is a phenomenon called priming. To understand priming, imagine taking two groups of subjects and showing a list of words to group A. The list might include, among others, the words *stamp, landmark, speak,* and *clock.* Group B doesn't get a list. Later, you give everyone in both groups a list of word stems, like this: *sta——, tem——, lan——, sen——,* and ask them to complete the stems with any word they'd like, telling group A that the stems have no relation to the list they were previously given. However, most of the subjects in group A, having seen the list, will add *mp* to the first stem to make *stamp,* and the third they'll complete as *landmark.* There will be normal variation in responses completing the other stems. The subjects in group B, who didn't see a previous word list, will also have normal variation in completing the *sta* and *lan* stems.

This finding demonstrates that recent sight of the words *landmark* and *stamp* had somehow made those words more accessible in the minds of those in group A. That discovery isn't remarkable in normal subjects, as you might assume they're consciously remembering having seen those words recently. But as Gabrieli says, "You'll tell HM that the word stems have no relation to the first word list, and he'll say, 'What first list?'" Yet HM and other amnesics will still tend to fill in the previously seen words when presented with the appropriate stems, despite having no conscious recollection of seeing the words. This phenomenon, which can be demonstrated in other ways, is known as priming and refers to, as Gabrieli has written, "a change in the processing of a stimulus, usually words or pictures, due to prior exposure to the same or related stimulus."

Priming and amnesics' ability to acquire skills without consciously re-membering their acquisition were discovered before the development of fMRI, but since then Gabrieli and others have tried to use the technology to learn where such memories are stored. While such work is still under way, both priming and improvement at skilled tasks appear to be accompanied by activation changes in brain areas related to the sense used in the study task. For instance, Gabrieli's group did an fMRI experiment with auditory priming in which they asked subjects to determine whether a recorded sound (of a dog barking or a door slamming, for example) had been made by an animal or not. Subjects demonstrated priming by responding more quickly to sounds they had heard before than to sounds they hadn't. In those cases, their auditory cortices showed a *decrease* in activation, a find-ing that has been interpreted to mean that the repetition of the sound had somehow made the auditory cortex more efficient at processing it, even when the subject herself was unaware of having previously heard the sound.

There are other instances in which our brains appear to be processing stimuli without our awareness. Gabrieli's research has expanded beyond memory in part because he makes it a policy to let his students explore areas they find interesting. It was one such student who convinced Gabrieli to let him use fMRI to explore olfaction and who then demonstrated that inhaled chemicals can affect the brain without consciously being smelled. In those experiments, a compound called oestra-1,3,5(10),16-tetraen-3yl acetate was spritzed into a "sniff halter," a contraption that fit over subjects' noses and allowed them to inhale the pure compound. The subjects claimed to de-tect no odor whatsoever. Yet on fMRI, their brains showed significant acti-vation in certain precise areas — the same areas in all subjects tested — when the substance was introduced. How does this happen? What allows a compound to be consciously recognized as a smell? What effect do the un-consciously neuroactive substances have? It is this kind of mystery that Gabrieli loves and that fMRI helps him to unlock.

The discovery of priming, the work showing that amnesics have intact skill learning, and subsequent research hinting at even more types of uncon-scious learning and detection are leading to a new understanding of both memory and consciousness, one Gabrieli compares to a symphony orchestra. "All of the brain is a learning machine," he says, "but each part is learning in its own way and for its own domain of knowledge." What those ways are and where that learning happens are still under investigation. Nevertheless, such findings have made a big splash among those interested in the mind, since some interpret them to be scientific evidence for Freud's cognitive un-conscious. Although it is generally spurned by modern scientists as supersti-tion, there are those who believe Freud's theory is showing new merit in light of these developments. It now appears, Gabrieli said, that just as Freud thought, "we might be moving around daily, driven by these kinds of mem-ories all the time, but we don't even realize it's a memory that's driving us to do something or believe something or say something." It's possible, he suggests, that "we're operating on a system that doesn't even know where we learned something, just like HM."

QUESTIONS

Reading

1. You might think of Moffett's essay as a portrait in words. Dr. John Gabrieli is a real human being, a physician, a brain researcher, and a public intellectual. He is also a *character* in Moffett's portrait. Moffett chooses her words carefully to create Gabrieli as a certain kind of character — for example, "What Gabrieli has is more than a job. It is a quest that eats up the bulk of his waking hours" (paragraph 10). What does a statement such as this one suggest about Gabrieli as a character? What are his traits and idiosyncrasies? What's unique about him, according to Moffett? Be sure to use other examples of Moffett's language in your response.

2. What does Moffett mean when she refers to cognitive neuroscience as "the expensive branch of philosophy" or "empiric philosophy" (paragraph 11)? In what ways is the work of Gabrieli's Gab Lab scientific? In what ways is it philosophical?

3. What is fMRI? How does it work? Why has it been so important in the recent explosion of brain research?

Exploratory Writing

1. The caption accompanying Moffett's diagram showing the location of the hippocampus in the brain reads: "This is a sagittal section, a slice taken parallel to a line drawn from the nose to the back of the head along the midline." Use a dictionary or do an Internet search to find out what *sagittal* and *midline* mean. Then, imagine you're explaining the diagram to a group of high school students. In your own words, explain what view of the brain this shows us. Why is it important to understand the diagram in order to follow Moffett's line of thinking?

2. In Moffett's words, "declarative memory is defined as conscious recollections of events or information, and nondeclarative memory refers to physical or cognitive skills" (paragraph 53). Write two paragraphs — the first describing one of your *declarative memories* and the second describing one of your *nondeclarative memories*. Be prepared to read your paragraphs out loud.

3. Pretend you are an intern in Gabrieli's lab, with the assigned task of imagining what life is like for HM. In Moffett's words, "HM is famous among those who study the brain and the mind, although he himself doesn't know it" (paragraph 38). Write a brief, intended for Gabrieli and his colleagues, explaining what life is like for HM and making

suggestions about his case with regard to ethical considerations. Should HM continue to be the subject of scientific research even though such research, in the wrong hands at the wrong time, harmed him so severely? How does such research affect his quality of life? What would be lost if his case were no longer studied?

Making Connections

1. What is the relationship between memory and identity? Many of the readings in this casebook explore the question — especially Daniel Schacter's "Of Time and Autobiography" (p. 793), Patricia Hampl's "Memory and Imagination" (p. 782), and Jill Bolte Taylor's "Morning of the Stroke" (p. 752). What do you learn about the relationship between memory and identity from reading these pieces? What unique perspectives does each author bring to the question? How does the perspective of each writer — Moffett the medical student, Schacter the psychiatrist, Hampl the memoirist, Taylor the neuroanatomist and stroke survivor — shape his or her approach to the question? What do you learn by reading their essays side by side that you wouldn't learn by reading any one of them on its own?

Essay Writing

1. Moffett's essay portrays John Gabrieli's profound personal investment in his work, an investment shared in various forms by all the writers whose essays are included in this casebook. Choose one of the other writers and find out everything you can about his or her life and work, then write a profile representing his or her personal and professional commitments. When conducting your research, start with the headnote to the essay (and the essay itself). Does the writer have a Web site? What can you learn from it? What books has he or she written, and in what journals has he or she been published? Does the writer teach or work in a laboratory? Be sure to choose a writer about whom you can find enough information to write a compelling profile.

Morning of the Stroke

Jill Bolte Taylor

Neuroanatomist Jill Bolte Taylor is in a unique position to reflect on the massive stroke she experienced one morning in 1996. After Taylor told the story of her stroke to an invited audience at the 2008 TED (Technology, Entertainment, Design) conference, she found a worldwide audience on YouTube. Time *magazine named Taylor one of the 100 most influential people of 2008. "Morning of the Stroke" is an excerpt from Taylor's book,* My Stroke of Insight *(2008). As in her TED talk, Taylor narrates the experience of recognizing her symptoms — including euphoria and dissociation — as the stroke gripped her. She narrates the account from two perspectives, that of the woman in the throes of a severe brain hemorrhage and that of the brain researcher with the rare opportunity to analyze her symptoms from the inside out. In the book, she also describes her career before and after the stroke, her eight-year recovery, and the spiritual and intellectual insights she gained from the experience.*

It was 7:00 a.m. on December 10, 1996. I awoke to the familiar tick-tick-tick of my compact disc player as it began winding up to play. Sleepily, I hit the snooze button just in time to catch the next mental wave back into dreamland. Here, in this magic land I call "Thetaville" — a surreal place of altered consciousness somewhere between dreams and stark reality — my spirit beamed beautiful, fluid, and free from the confines of normal reality.

Six minutes later, as the tick-tick-tick of the CD alerted my memory that I was a land mammal, I sluggishly awoke to a sharp pain piercing my brain directly behind my left eye. Squinting into the early morning light, I clicked off the impending alarm with my right hand and instinctively pressed the palm of my left hand firmly against the side of my face. Rarely ill, I thought how queer it was for me to awaken to such a striking pain. As my left eye pulsed with a slow and deliberate rhythm, I felt bewildered and irritated. The throbbing pain behind my eye was sharp, like the caustic sensation that sometimes accompanies biting into ice cream.

As I rolled out of my warm waterbed, I stumbled into the world with the ambivalence of a wounded soldier. I closed the bedroom window blind to block the incoming stream of light from stinging my eyes. I decided that exercise might get my blood flowing and perhaps help dissipate the pain. Within moments, I hopped on to my "cardio-glider" (a full body exercise machine) and began jamming away to Shania Twain singing the lyrics, "Whose bed have your boots been under?" Immediately, I felt a powerful and unusual sense of dissociation roll over me. I felt so peculiar that I questioned my well-being. Even though my thoughts seemed lucid, my body felt irregular. As I watched my hands and arms rocking forward and back, forward and back, in opposing synchrony with my torso, I felt strangely detached from my normal cognitive functions. It was as if the integrity of my mind/body connection had somehow become compromised.

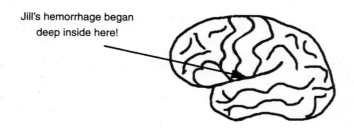

Jill's hemorrhage began
deep inside here!

Feeling detached from normal reality, I seemed to be witnessing my activity as opposed to feeling like the active participant performing the action. I felt as though I was observing myself in motion, as in the playback of a memory. My fingers, as they grasped onto the handrail, looked like primitive claws. For a few seconds I rocked and watched, with riveting wonder, as my body oscillated rhythmically and mechanically. My torso moved up and down in perfect cadence with the music and my head continued to ache.

I felt bizarre, as if my conscious mind was suspended somewhere between my normal reality and some esoteric space. Although this experience was somewhat reminiscent of my morning time in Thetaville, I was sure that this time I was awake. Yet, I felt as if I was trapped inside the perception of a meditation that I could neither stop nor escape. Dazed, I felt the frequency of shooting pangs escalate inside my brain, and I realized that this exercise regime was probably not a good idea.

Feeling a little nervous about my physical condition, I climbed off the machine and bumbled through my living room on the way to the bath. As I walked, I noticed that my movements were no longer fluid. Instead they felt deliberate and almost jerky. In the absence of my normal muscular coordination, there was no grace to my pace and my balance was so impaired that my mind seemed completely preoccupied with just keeping me upright.

As I lifted my leg to step into the tub, I held on to the wall for support. It seemed odd that I could sense the inner activities of my brain as it adjusted and readjusted all of the opposing muscle groups in my lower extremities to prevent me from falling over. My perception of these automatic body responses was no longer an exercise in intellectual conceptualization. Instead, I was momentarily privy to a precise and experiential understanding of how hard the fifty trillion cells in my brain and body were working in perfect unison to maintain the flexibility and integrity of my physical form. Through the eyes of an avid enthusiast of the magnificence of the human design, I witnessed with awe the autonomic functioning of my nervous system as it calculated and recalculated every joint angle.

Ignorant to the degree of danger my body was in, I balanced my weight against the shower wall. As I leaned forward to turn on the faucet, I was startled by an abrupt and exaggerated clamor as water surged into the tub. This unexpected amplification of sound was both enlightening and disturbing. It brought me to the realization that, in addition to having problems with coordination and equilibrium, my ability to process incoming sound (auditory information) was erratic.

I understood neuroanatomically that coordination, equilibrium, audition and the action of inspirational breathing were processed through the pons of my brainstem. For the first time, I considered the possibility that I was perhaps having a major neurological malfunction that was life threatening.

Fibers Passing Through the Pons of the Brainstem

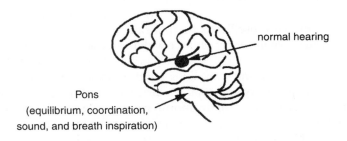

normal hearing

Pons
(equilibrium, coordination,
sound, and breath inspiration)

As my cognitive mind searched for an explanation about what was happening anatomically inside my brain, I reeled backward in response to the augmented roar of the water as the unexpected noise pierced my delicate and aching brain. In that instant, I suddenly felt vulnerable, and I noticed that the constant brain chatter that routinely familiarized me with my surroundings was no longer a predictable and constant flow of conversation. Instead, my verbal thoughts were now inconsistent, fragmented, and interrupted by an intermittent silence.

10

Language Centers

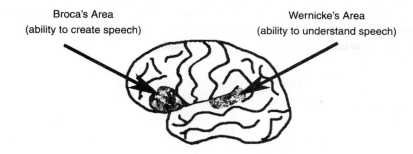

Broca's Area
(ability to create speech)

Wernicke's Area
(ability to understand speech)

When I realized that the sensations outside of me, including the remote sounds of a bustling city beyond my apartment window, had faded away, I could tell that the broad range of my natural observation had become constricted. As my brain chatter began to disintegrate, I felt an odd sense of isolation. My blood pressure must have been dropping as a result of the bleeding in my brain because I felt as if all of my systems, including my mind's ability to instigate movement, were moving into a slow mode of operation. Yet, even though my thoughts were no longer a constant stream of chatter about the external world and my relationship to it, I was conscious and constantly present within my mind.

Confused, I searched the memory banks of both my body and brain, questioning and analyzing anything I could remember having experienced in the past that was remotely similar to this situation. *What is going on?* I wondered. *Have I ever experienced anything like this before? Have I ever felt like this before? This feels like a migraine. What is happening in my brain?*

The harder I tried to concentrate, the more fleeting my ideas seemed to be. Instead of finding answers and information, I met a growing sense of peace. In place of that constant chatter that had attached me to the details of my life, I felt enfolded by a blanket of tranquil euphoria. How fortunate I was that the portion of my brain that registered fear, my amygdala, had not reacted with alarm to these unusual circumstances and shifted me into a state of panic. As the language centers in my left hemisphere grew increasingly silent and I became detached from the memories of my life, I was comforted by an expanding sense of grace. In this void of higher cognition and details pertaining to my normal life, my consciousness soared into an all-knowingness, a "being at *one*" with the universe, if you will. In a compelling sort of way, it felt like the good road home and I liked it.

By this point I had lost touch with much of the physical three-dimensional reality that surrounded me. My body was propped up against the shower wall and I found it odd that I was aware that I could no longer clearly discern the physical boundaries of where I began and where I ended. I sensed the composition of my being as that of a fluid rather than that of a solid. I no longer perceived myself as a whole object separate from everything. Instead, I now blended in with the space and flow around me. Beholding a growing sense of detachment between my cognitive mind and my ability to control and finely manipulate my fingers, the mass of my body felt heavy and my energy waned.

Orientation Association Area
(physical boundaries, space, and time)

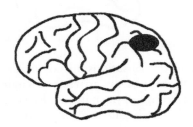

When the shower droplets beat into my chest like little bullets, I was   15
harshly startled back into this reality. As I held my hands up in front of my face and wiggled my fingers, I was simultaneously perplexed and intrigued. *Wow, what a strange and amazing thing I am. What a bizarre living being I am. Life! I am life! I am a sea of water bound inside this membranous pouch. Here, in this form, I am a conscious mind and this body is the vehicle through which I am ALIVE! I am trillions of cells sharing a common mind. I am here, now, thriving as life. Wow! What an unfathomable concept! I am cellular life, no — I am molecular life with manual dexterity and a cognitive mind!*

In this altered state of being, my mind was no longer preoccupied with the billions of details that my brain routinely used to define and conduct my life in the external world. Those little voices, that brain chatter that customarily kept me abreast of myself in relation to the world outside of me, were delightfully silent. And in their absence, my memories of the past and my dreams of the future evaporated. I was alone. In the moment, I was alone with nothing but the rhythmic pulse of my beating heart.

I must admit that the growing void in my traumatized brain was entirely seductive. I welcomed the reprieve that the silence brought from the constant chatter that related me to what I now perceived as the insignificant affairs of society. I eagerly turned my focus inward to the steadfast drumming of the trillions of brilliant cells that worked diligently and synchronously to maintain my body's steady state of homeostasis. As the blood poured in over my brain, my consciousness slowed to a soothing and satisfying awareness that embraced the vast and wondrous world within. I was both fascinated and humbled by how hard my little cells worked, moment by moment, just to maintain the integrity of my existence in this physical form.

For the first time, I felt truly at one with my body as a complex construction of living, thriving organisms. I was proud to see that I was this swarming conglomeration of cellular life that had stemmed from the intelligence of a single molecular genius! I welcomed the opportunity to pass beyond my normal perceptions, away from the persevering pain that relentlessly pulsed in my head. As my consciousness slipped into a state of peaceful grace, I felt ethereal. Although the pulse of pain in my brain was inescapable, it was not debilitating.

Standing there with the water pounding onto my breasts, a tingling sensation surged through my chest and forcefully radiated upward into my throat. Startled, I became instantly aware that I was in grave danger. Shocked back into this external reality, I immediately reassessed the abnormalities of my physical systems. Determined to understand what was going on, I actively scanned my reservoir of education in demand of a self-diagnosis. *What is going on with my body? What is wrong with my brain?*

Although the sporadically discontinuous flow of normal cognition was virtually incapacitating, somehow I managed to keep my body on task. Stepping out of the shower, my brain felt inebriated. My body was unsteady, felt heavy, and exerted itself in very slow motion. *What is it I'm trying to do? Dress, dress for work. I'm dressing for work.* I labored mechanically to choose my clothes and by 8:15 a.m., I was ready for my commute. Pacing my apartment, I thought, *Okay, I'm going to work. I'm going to work. Do I know how to get to work? Can I drive?* As I visualized the road to McLean Hospital, I was literally thrown off balance when my right arm dropped completely paralyzed against my side. In that moment I knew. *Oh my gosh, I'm having a stroke! I'm having a stroke!* And in the next instant, the thought flashed through my mind, *Wow, this is so cool!* 20

I felt as though I was suspended in a peculiar euphoric stupor, and I was strangely elated when I understood that this unexpected pilgrimage into the intricate functions of my brain actually had a physiological basis and explanation. I kept thinking, *Wow, how many scientists have the opportunity to study their own brain function and mental deterioration from the inside out?* My entire life had been dedicated to my own understanding of how the human brain creates our perception of reality. And now I was experiencing this most remarkable stroke of insight!

When my right arm became paralyzed, I felt the life force inside the limb explode. When it dropped dead against my body, it clubbed my torso. It was the strangest sensation. I felt as if my arm had been guillotined off!

I understood neuroanatomically that my motor cortex had been affected and I was fortunate that within a few minutes, the deadness of my right arm subtly abated. As the limb began to reclaim its life, it throbbed with a formidable tingling pain. I felt weak and wounded. My arm felt completely depleted of its intrinsic strength, yet I could wield it like a stub. I wondered if it would ever be normal again. Catching sight of my warm and cradling waterbed, I seemed to be beckoned by it on this cold winter morning in New England. *Oh, I am so tired. I feel so tired. I just want to*

Movement and Sensory Perception

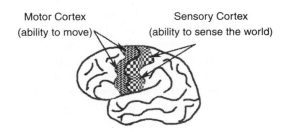

Motor Cortex
(ability to move)

Sensory Cortex
(ability to sense the world)

rest. I just want to lie down and relax for a little while. But resounding like thunder from deep within my being, a commanding voice spoke clearly to me: *If you lie down now you will never get up!*

Startled by this ominous illumination, I fathomed the gravity of my immediate situation. Although I was compelled by a sense of urgency to orchestrate my rescue, another part of me delighted in the euphoria of my irrationality. I stepped across the threshold of my bedroom, and as I gazed into the eyes of my reflected image, I paused for a moment, in search of some guidance or profound insight. In the wisdom of my dementia, I understood that my body was, by the magnificence of its biological design, a precious and fragile gift. It was clear to me that this body functioned like a portal through which the energy of who I am can be beamed into a three-dimensional external space.

This cellular mass of my body had provided me with a marvelous temporary home. This amazing brain had been capable of integrating literally billions of trillions of bits of data, in every instant, to create for me a three-dimensional perception of this environment that actually appeared to be not only seamless and real, but also safe. Here in this delusion, I was mesmerized by the efficiency of this biological matrix as it created my form, and I was awed by the simplicity of its design. I saw myself as a complex composite of dynamic systems, a collection of interlacing cells capable of integrating a medley of sensory modalities streaming in from the external world. And when the systems functioned properly, they naturally manifested a consciousness capable of perceiving a normal reality. I wondered how I could have spent so many years in this body, in this form of life, and never really understood that I was just visiting here.

Even in this condition, the egotistical mind of my left hemisphere arrogantly retained the belief that although I was experiencing a dramatic mental incapacity, my life was invincible. Optimistically, I believed that I would recover completely from this morning's events. Feeling a little irritated by this impromptu disruption of my work schedule, I bantered, *Okay, well, I'm having a stroke. Yep, I'm having a stroke . . . but I'm a very busy woman! All right, since I can't stop this stroke from happening, then, okay, I'll do this for a week! I'll learn what I need to know about how my brain creates*

25

Territory of Jill's Hemorrhage
(shaded oval area)

Motor Cortex
(ability to move)

Sensory Cortex
(ability to sense the world)

Orientation
Association
Cortex
(physical boundaries,
time, and space)

Broca's Area
(ability to create speech)

Wernicke's Area
(ability to understand speech)

my perception of reality and then I'll meet my schedule, next week. Now, what am I doing? Getting help. I must stay focused and get help.

To my counterpart in the looking glass I pleaded, *Remember, please remember everything you are experiencing! Let this be my stroke of insight into the disintegration of my own cognitive mind.*

QUESTIONS

Reading

1. Taylor uses a memoir form as a means of *reflecting* on scientific research. Doing so allows her to express a sense of awe at what her stroke reveals about the relationship between the brain and her sense of self. In your own words, explain how Taylor understands that relationship. How would her account be different if she were writing in more conventionally scientific terms?

2. *Voice* is the personality of a piece of writing. A writer will adopt different voices for different purposes in different contexts. With this in mind, reread the italicized sections of Taylor's account. How would you describe the voice in the italicized passages? How is this voice different from the primary voice of the account? Why do you think Taylor uses more than one voice to tell her story?

3. Taylor often uses the language of neurobiology — especially terms for regions of the brain and physiological functions — to explain the symptoms of her stroke. Brain regions she discusses and illustrates include *pons*, *Broca's area*, *Wernicke's area*, *motor cortex*, and *orientation association cortex*. Physiological functions she discusses include *coordination*, *equilibrium*, *orientation*, *audition*, *inspirational breathing*, and *sensory modalities*. Choose two terms that you think are particularly important, and write a paragraph in which you define these terms and explain how and why they're crucial to understanding Taylor's account. To come up with your definitions, start

with Taylor's text. If you need more information, consult a dictionary or an online reference work.

Exploratory Writing

1. Taylor begins her account of her stroke with a description of dozing in dreamland. Using a double-entry format, make a list of phrases Taylor uses to describe dreamland and her stroke symptoms. Once you've completed your lists, write a paragraph comparing Taylor's descriptions of dreamland and her stroke symptoms.

Dreamland	Stroke symptoms

2. Taylor incorporates simple diagrams of the human brain to help readers visualize the regions she describes. Her intention is to help readers understand where in the brain her particular symptoms originated. Choose a symptom that you find interesting or puzzling. Then, find the diagram that represents the origin of that symptom. Using Taylor's descriptions and diagrams, prepare a brief presentation for the class, explaining the origin of the symptom.

Making Connections

1. Use a search engine to find several online accounts written by people who have survived strokes. Drawing on "Morning of the Stroke" and any relevant reading in this casebook, write an essay that makes an argument about how these accounts represent the effects of stroke on the identities of survivors. For this project, you might also want to look for Taylor's book, *My Stroke of Insight*, in the library, to give you a more detailed sense of her views on the relationship between her stroke and her identity.

Essay Writing

1. Watch the video of Taylor's account of her stroke on the TED Web site: **http://www.ted.com/index.php/talks/jill_bolte_taylor_s_powerful_stroke_ of_insight.html**. What do you learn from the video that you didn't learn from Taylor's written account? What did you learn from the written account that you didn't learn from the video? How did your impression of Taylor change after watching the video?

Women's Brains

Stephen Jay Gould

Stephen Jay Gould (1941–2002) was a professor of biology, geology, and the history of science at Harvard University for more than thirty years. He was also a baseball fan and a prolific essayist. In 1974 he began writing "This View of Life," a monthly column for Natural History, *where he not only explained and defended Darwinian ideas of evolution but also exposed abuses and misunderstandings of scientific concepts and methods. Some of the most recent of his more than twenty books are* Crossing Over: Where Art and Science Meet *(2000),* The Structure of Evolutionary Theory *(2002),* Triumph and Tragedy in Mudville: A Lifelong Passion for Baseball *(2003), and* The Hedgehog, the Fox, and the Magister's Pox *(2003). The following essay appeared in* Natural History *in 1992.*

In the prelude to *Middlemarch*, George Eliot[1] lamented the unfulfilled lives of talented women:

> Some have felt that these blundering lives are due to the inconvenient indefiniteness with which the Supreme Power has fashioned the natures of women: if there were one level of feminine incompetence as strict as the ability to count three and no more, the social lot of women might be treated with scientific certitude.

Eliot goes on to discount the idea of innate limitation, but while she wrote in 1872, the leaders of European anthropometry were trying to measure "with scientific certitude" the inferiority of women. Anthropometry, or measurement of the human body, is not so fashionable a field these days, but it dominated the human sciences for much of the nineteenth century and remained popular until intelligence testing replaced skull measurement as a favored device for making invidious comparisons among races, classes, and sexes. Craniometry, or measurement of the skull, commanded the most attention and respect. Its unquestioned leader, Paul Broca (1824–1880),

---

[1]*George Eliot*: The pen name of Marianne Evans (1819–1880), British novelist. *Middlemarch* (1871–1872) is considered her greatest work. [Eds.]

professor of clinical surgery at the Faculty of Medicine in Paris, gathered a school of disciples and imitators around himself. Their work, so meticulous and apparently irrefutable, exerted great influence and won high esteem as a jewel of nineteenth-century science.

Broca's work seemed particularly invulnerable to refutation. Had he not measured with the most scrupulous care and accuracy? (Indeed, he had. I have the greatest respect for Broca's meticulous procedure. His numbers are sound. But science is an inferential exercise, not a catalog of facts. Numbers, by themselves, specify nothing. All depends upon what you do with them.) Broca depicted himself as an apostle of objectivity, a man who bowed before facts and cast aside superstition and sentimentality. He declared that "there is no faith, however respectable, no interest, however legitimate, which must not accommodate itself to the progress of human knowledge and bend before truth." Women, like it or not, had smaller brains than men and, therefore, could not equal them in intelligence. This fact, Broca argued, may reinforce a common prejudice in male society, but it is also a scientific truth. L. Manouvrier, a black sheep in Broca's fold, rejected the inferiority of women and wrote with feeling about the burden imposed upon them by Broca's numbers:

> Women displayed their talents and their diplomas. They also invoked philosophical authorities. But they were opposed by *numbers* unknown to Condorcet[2] or to John Stuart Mill.[3] These numbers fell upon poor women like a sledge hammer, and they were accompanied by commentaries and sarcasms more ferocious than the most misogynist imprecations of certain church fathers. The theologians had asked if women had a soul. Several centuries later, some scientists were ready to refuse them a human intelligence.

Broca's argument rested upon two sets of data: the larger brains of men in modern societies, and a supposed increase in male superiority through time. His most extensive data came from autopsies performed personally in four Parisian hospitals. For 292 male brains, he calculated an average weight of 1,325 grams; 140 female brains averaged 1,144 grams for a difference of 181 grams, or 14 percent of the male weight. Broca understood, of course, that part of this difference could be attributed to the greater height of males. Yet he made no attempt to measure the effect of size alone and actually stated that it cannot account for the entire difference because

---

    [2]*Marquis de Condorcet* (1743–1794): A French mathematician and revolutionary. [Eds.]

    [3]*John Stuart Mill* (1806–1873): A British economist and philosopher. [Eds.]

we know, a priori, that women are not as intelligent as men (a premise that the data were supposed to test, not rest upon):

> We might ask if the small size of the female brain depends exclusively upon the small size of her body. Tiedemann has proposed this explanation. But we must not forget that women are, on the average, a little less intelligent than men, a difference which we should not exaggerate but which is, nonetheless, real. We are therefore permitted to suppose that the relatively small size of the female brain depends in part upon her physical inferiority and in part upon her intellectual inferiority.

In 1873, the year after Eliot published *Middlemarch,* Broca measured the 5 cranial capacities of prehistoric skulls from L'Homme Mort cave. Here he found a difference of only 99.5 cubic centimeters between males and females, while modern populations range from 129.5 to 220.7. Topinard, Broca's chief disciple, explained the increasing discrepancy through time as a result of differing evolutionary pressures upon dominant men and passive women:

> The man who fights for two or more in the struggle for existence, who has all the responsibility and the cares of tomorrow, who is constantly active in combating the environment and human rivals, needs more brain than the woman whom he must protect and nourish, the sedentary woman, lacking any interior occupations, whose role is to raise children, love, and be passive.

In 1879, Gustave Le Bon, chief misogynist of Broca's school, used these data to publish what must be the most vicious attack upon women in modern scientific literature (no one can top Aristotle). I do not claim his views were representative of Broca's school, but they were published in France's most respected anthropological journal. Le Bon concluded:

> In the most intelligent races, as among the Parisians, there are a large number of women whose brains are closer in size to those of gorillas than to the most developed male brains. This inferiority is so obvious that no one can contest it for a moment; only its degree is worth discussion. All psychologists who have studied the intelligence of women, as well as poets and novelists, recognize today that they represent the most inferior forms of human evolution and that they are closer to children and savages than to an adult, civilized man. They excel in fickleness, inconstancy, absence of thought and logic, and incapacity to reason. Without doubt there exist some distinguished women, very superior to the average man, but they are as exceptional as the birth of any monstrosity, as, for example, of a gorilla with two heads; consequently, we may neglect them entirely.

Nor did Le Bon shrink from the social implications of his views. He was horrified by the proposal of some American reformers to grant women higher education on the same basis as men:

> A desire to give them the same education, and, as a consequence, to propose the same goals for them, is a dangerous chimera. . . . The day when, misunderstanding the inferior occupations which nature has given her, women leave the home and take part in our battles; on this day a social revolution will begin, and everything that maintains the sacred ties of the family will disappear.

Sound familiar?[4]

I have reexamined Broca's data, the basis for all this derivative pronouncement, and I find his numbers sound but his interpretation ill-founded, to say the least. The data supporting his claim for increased difference through time can be easily dismissed. Broca based his contention on the samples from L'Homme Mort alone — only seven male and six female skulls in all. Never have so little data yielded such far-ranging conclusions.

In 1988, Topinard published Broca's more extensive data on the Parisian hospitals. Since Broca recorded height and age as well as brain size, we may use modern statistics to remove their effect. Brain weight decreases with age, and Broca's women were, on average, considerably older than his men. Brain weight increases with height, and his average man was almost half a foot taller than his average woman. I used multiple regression, a technique that allowed me to assess simultaneously the influence of height and age upon brain size. In an analysis of the data for women, I found that, at average male height and age, a woman's brain would weigh 1,212 grams. Correction for height and age reduces Broca's measured difference of 181 grams by more than a third, to 113 grams.

I don't know what to make of this remaining difference because I cannot   10 assess other factors known to influence brain size in a major way. Cause of death has an important effect: degenerative disease often entails a substantial diminution of brain size. (This effect is separate from the decrease attributed to age alone.) Eugene Schreider, also working with Broca's data, found that men killed in accidents had brains weighing, on average, 60 grams more than men dying of infectious diseases. The best modern data I can find (from American hospitals) records a full 100-gram difference between death by degenerative arteriosclerosis and by violence or accident. Since so many of Broca's subjects were elderly women, we may assume that lengthy degenerative disease was more common among them than among the men.

---

[4]When I wrote this essay, I assumed that Le Bon was a marginal, if colorful, figure. I have since learned that he was a leading scientist, one of the founders of social psychology, and best known for a seminal study on crowd behavior, still cited today (*La psychologie des foules*, 1895), and for his work on unconscious motivation.

More importantly, modern students of brain size still have not agreed on a proper measure for eliminating the powerful effect of body size. Height is partly adequate, but men and women of the same height do not share the same body build. Weight is even worse than height, because most of its variation reflects nutrition rather than intrinsic size — fat versus skinny exerts little influence upon the brain. Manouvrier took up this subject in the 1880s and argued that muscular mass and force should be used. He tried to measure this elusive property in various ways and found a marked difference in favor of men, even in men and women of the same height. When he corrected for what he called "sexual mass," women actually came out slightly ahead in brain size.

Thus, the corrected 113-gram difference is surely too large; the true figure is probably close to zero and may as well favor women as men. And 113 grams, by the way, is exactly the average difference between a 5 foot 4 inch and a 6 foot 4 inch male in Broca's data. We would not (especially us short folks) want to ascribe greater intelligence to tall men. In short, who knows what to do with Broca's data? They certainly don't permit any confident claim that men have bigger brains than women.

To appreciate the social role of Broca and his school, we must recogize that his statements about the brains of women do not reflect an isolated prejudice toward a single disadvantaged group. They must be weighed in the context of a general theory that supported contemporary social distinctions as biologically ordained. Women, blacks, and poor people suffered the same disparagement, but women bore the brunt of Broca's argument because he had easier access to data on women's brains. Women were singularly denigrated but they also stood as surrogates for other disenfranchised groups. As one of Broca's disciples wrote in 1881: "Men of the black races have a brain scarcely heavier than that of white women." This juxtaposition extended into many other realms of anthropological argument, particularly to claims that, anatomically and emotionally, both women and blacks were like white children — and that white children, by the theory of recapitulation, represented an ancestral (primitive) adult stage of human evolution. I do not regard as empty rhetoric the claim that women's battles are for all of us.

Maria Montessori did not confine her activities to educational reform for young children. She lectured on anthropology for several years at the University of Rome, and wrote an influential book entitled *Pedagogical Anthropology* (English edition, 1913). Montessori was no egalitarian. She supported most of Broca's work and the theory of innate criminality proposed by her compatriot Cesare Lombroso. She measured the circumference of children's heads in her schools and inferred that the best prospects had bigger brains. But she had no use for Broca's conclusions about women. She discussed Manouvrier's work at length and made much of his tentative claim that women, after proper correction of the data, had slightly larger brains than men. Women, she concluded, were intellectually superior, but men had prevailed heretofore by dint of physical force. Since technology has abolished force as an instrument of power, the era of women may soon be upon us: "In such an epoch there will really be superior human beings, there will really be men strong in morality and in sentiment. Perhaps in this way the reign of women is approaching, when the enigma of her anthropological superiority will be deciphered. Woman was always the custodian of human sentiment, morality and honor."

This represents one possible antidote to "scientific" claims for the con-   15
stitutional inferiority of certain groups. One may affirm the validity of bio-
logical distinctions but argue that the data have been misinterpreted by prejudiced men with a stake in the outcome, and that disadvantaged groups are truly superior. In recent years, Elaine Morgan has followed this strategy in her *Descent of Woman*, a speculative reconstruction of human prehistory from the woman's point of view — and as farcical as more famous tall tales by and for men.

I prefer another strategy. Montessori and Morgan followed Broca's philosophy to reach a more congenial conclusion. I would rather label the whole enterprise of setting a biological value upon groups for what it is: irrelevant and highly injurious. George Eliot well appreciated the special tragedy that biological labeling imposed upon members of disadvantaged groups. She expressed it for people like herself — women of extraordinary talent. I would apply it more widely — not only to those whose dreams are flouted but also to those who never realize that they may dream — but I cannot match her prose. In conclusion, then, the rest of Eliot's prelude to *Middlemarch*:

> The limits of variation are really much wider than anyone would imagine from the sameness of women's coiffure and the favorite love stories in prose and verse. Here and there a cygnet is reared uneasily among the ducklings in the brown pond, and never finds the living stream in fellowship with its own oary-footed kind. Here and there is born a Saint Theresa, foundress of nothing, whose loving heartbeats and sobs after an unattained goodness tremble off and are dispersed among hindrances instead of centering in some long-recognizable deed.

QUESTIONS

Reading

1. In paragraph 3, Gould claims, "Numbers, by themselves, specify nothing. All depends upon what you do with them." What exactly does Gould do with numbers?
2. How does Gould's use of numbers differ from what Broca and his followers did with numbers? Specifically, what distinguishes Gould's and Broca's methods of calculating and interpreting the facts about women's brains?

3. It might also be said, "Quotations, by themselves, specify nothing. All depends upon what you do with them." What does Gould do with quotations in this essay?
4. Why does Gould quote so extensively from Broca and his followers, particularly from Le Bon? What purpose do all of these quotations serve in connection with the points that Gould is trying to make about women's brains and "biological labeling"?

Exploratory Writing

1. Gould begins and ends his essay with passages from George Eliot's *Middlemarch*. Rewrite these passages in modern English. Do your best to translate them into language a novelist of today might use while capturing Eliot's original meaning.
2. Imagine a world in which "biological labeling" were widely accepted, shaping social and educational policy. Write a detailed description of the schools in such a world.

Making Connections

1. Gould reexamines influential moments in the history of brain science, evaluating the data and conclusions of previous researchers with the benefit of today's growing body of knowledge about the brain. In fact, this is the process through which science develops — new researchers building on and revising yesterday's knowledge. From the other readings in this casebook, find two or three instances in which the writers discuss how previous theories about the brain have been reevaluated. What were these theories? Why were they reevaluated? What new theories are replacing them?

Essay Writing

1. Brain research is often highly theoretical and specialized, but the knowledge it generates has many practical and social implications. Choose two of the essays in this casebook, and compare and contrast the practical or social implications of the research they discuss.

The Woman Who Died Laughing

V. S. Ramachandran

V. S. Ramachandran, a prominent neurologist, is the director of the Center for Brain and Cognition and a professor in the Psychology Department and Neurosciences Program at the University of California, San Diego. Born in Tamil Nadu, India, Ramachandran received his MD in Madras, India, before pursuing a PhD from Trinity College at the University of Cambridge, England. His early interest in visual perception evolved into groundbreaking research in behavioral neurology — work that has shaped our contemporary understanding of the brain. British ethologist Richard Dawkins calls him "the Marco Polo of neuroscience." In addition to authoring the acclaimed book Phantoms of the Brain *(1999), Ramachandran has published more than 180 papers in scientific journals; is editor in chief of the* Encyclopedia of Human Behaviour; *and, as of 2005, holds a lifetime honorary fellowship at the Royal Institution of Great Britain. His work has frequently been featured in the international media, such as PBS and BBC, and in 1997 he was named "one of the hundred most prominent people to watch in the next century" by* Newsweek *magazine.*

God is a comedian performing before an audience that is afraid to laugh.
— FRIEDRICH NIETZSCHE

God is a hacker.

— FRANCIS CRICK

On the morning of his mother's funeral in 1931, Willy Anderson — a twenty-five-year-old plumber from London — donned a new black suit, clean white shirt and nice shoes borrowed from his brother. He had loved his mother very much and his grief was palpable. The family gathered amid tearful hugs and sat silently through an hour-long funeral service in a church that was much too hot and stuffy. Willy was relieved finally to get outdoors into the chilly open air of the cemetery and bow his head with the rest of the family and friends. But just as the gravediggers began lowering his mother's roped casket into the earth, Willy began to laugh. It started as a muffled snorting sound that evolved into a prolonged giggle. Willy bowed his head farther down, dug his chin into his shirt collar and drew his right hand up to his mouth, trying to stifle the unbidden mirth. It was no use. Against his will and to his profound embarrassment, he began to laugh out loud, the sounds exploding rhythmically until he doubled over. Everyone at the funeral stared, mouth agape, as the young man staggered backward, desperately looking for retreat. He walked bent at the waist, as if in supplication for forgiveness for the laughter that would not subside. The mourners could hear him at the far end of the cemetery, his laughter echoing amid the gravestones.

That evening, Willy's cousin took him to the hospital. The laughter had subsided after some hours, but it was so inexplicable, so stunning in its inappropriateness, that everyone in the family felt it should be treated as a medical emergency. Dr. Astley Clark, the physician on duty, examined Willy's pupils and checked his vital signs. Two days later, a nurse found Willy lying unconscious in his bed, having suffered a severe sub-arachnoid hemorrhage, and he died without regaining consciousness. The postmortem showed a large ruptured aneurysm in an artery at the base of his brain that had compressed part of his hypothalamus, mammillary bodies and other structures on the floor of his brain.

And then there was Ruth Greenough, a fifty-eight-year-old librarian from Philadelphia. Although she had suffered a mild stroke, she was able to keep her small branch library running smoothly. But one morning in 1936, Ruth had a sudden violent headache, and within seconds her eyes turned up and she was seized with a laughing fit. She began shaking with laughter and couldn't stop. Short expirations followed each other in such rapid succession that Ruth's brain grew oxygen-starved and she broke into a sweat, at times holding her hand to her throat as if she were choking. Nothing she did would stop the convulsions of laughter, and even an injection of morphine given by the doctor had no effect. The laughter went on for an hour and a half. All the while, Ruth's eyes remained turned upward and wide open. She was conscious and could follow her doctor's instructions but was not able to utter a single word. At the end of an hour and a half, Ruth lay down completely exhausted. The laughter persisted but was noiseless — little more than a grimace. Suddenly she collapsed and became comatose, and after twenty-four hours Ruth died. I can say that she literally died laughing. The post-mortem revealed that a cavity in the middle of her brain (called the third ventricle) was filled with blood. A hemorrhage had occurred, involving the floor of her thalamus and compressing several adjacent structures. The English neurologist Dr. Purdon Martin, who described Ruth's case, said, "The laughter is a mock or sham and it mocks the laugher at the time, but this is the greatest mockery of all, that the patient should be forced to laugh as a portent of his own doom."[1]

More recently, the British journal *Nature* reported a modern case of laughter elicited by direct electrical stimulation of the brain during surgery. The patient was a fifteen-year-old girl named Susan who was being treated for intractable epilepsy. Doctors hoped to excise the tissue at the focal point of her seizures and were exploring nearby areas to make sure they did not remove any critically important functions. When the surgeon stimulated Susan's supplementary motor cortex (close to a region in the frontal lobes that receives input from the brain's emotional centers), he got an unexpected response. Susan started laughing uncontrollably, right on the operating table (she was awake for the procedure). Oddly enough, she ascribed her merriment to everything she saw around her, including a picture of a horse, and added that the people standing near her looked incredibly funny. To the doctors, she said: "You guys are just so *funny* standing around."[2]

The kind of pathological laughter seen in Willy and Ruth is rare; only a   5
couple of dozen such cases have been described in the medical literature. But when you gather them together, a striking fact jumps out at you. The abnormal activity or damage that sets people giggling is almost always located in portions of the limbic system, a set of structures including the hypothalamus, mammillary bodies and cingulate gyrus that are involved in emotions. . . . Given the complexity of laughter and its infinite cultural overtones, I find it intriguing that a relatively small cluster of brain structures is behind the phenomenon — a sort of "laughter circuit."

But identifying the location of such a circuit doesn't tell us why laughter exists or what its biological function might be. (You can't say it evolved because it feels good. That would be a circular argument, like saying sex exists because it feels good instead of saying it feels good because it motivates you to spread your genes.) Asking why a given trait evolved (be it yawning, laughing, crying or dancing) is absolutely vital for understanding its biological function, and yet this question is rarely raised by neurologists who study patients with brain lesions. This is astonishing given that the brain was shaped by natural selection just as any other organ in the body, such as the kidney, liver or pancreas, was.

Fortunately, the picture is changing, thanks in part to "evolutionary psychology." . . . [3] The central tenet of this controversial field is that many salient aspects of human behavior are mediated by specialized modules (mental organs) that were specifically shaped by natural selection. As our Pleistocene ancestors romped across ancient savannas in small probands, their brains evolved solutions to their everyday problems—things like recognizing kin, seeking healthy sexual partners or eschewing foul-smelling food.

For example, evolutionary psychologists would argue that your disgust for feces — far from being taught to you by your parents—is probably hard-wired in your brain. Since feces might contain infectious bacteria, eggs and parasites, those ancestral hominids who had "disgust for feces" genes survived and passed on those genes, whereas those who didn't were wiped out (unlike dung beetles, who probably find the bouquet of feces irresistible). This idea may even explain why feces infected with cholera, salmonellosis or shigella are especially foul smelling.

Evolutionary psychology is one of those disciplines that tend to polarize scientists. You are either for it or vehemently against it with much arm waving and trading of raspberries behind backs, much as people are nativists (genes specify everything) or empiricists (the brain is a blank slate whose wiring is subsequently specified by the environment, including culture). The real brain, it turns out, is far messier than what's implied by these simpleminded dichotomies. For some traits — and I'm going to argue that laughter is one of them — the evolutionary perspective is essential and helps explain why a specialized laughter circuit exists. For other traits this way of thinking is a waste of time (. . . the notion that there might be genes or mental organs for cooking is silly, even though cooking is a universal human trait).

The distinction between fact and fiction gets more easily blurred in   10
evolutionary psychology than in any other discipline, a problem that is exacerbated by the fact that most "ev-psych" explanations are completely untestable: You can't run experiments to prove or disprove them. Some of the proposed theories — that we have genetically specified mechanisms to help us detect fertile mates or that women suffer from morning sickness to protect the fetus from poisons in foods — are ingenious. Others are ridiculously far-fetched. One afternoon, in a whimsical mood, I sat down and wrote a spoof of evolutionary psychology just to annoy my colleagues in that field. I wanted to see how far one could go in conjuring up completely arbitrary, ad hoc, untestable evolutionary explanations for aspects of human behavior that most people would regard as "cultural" in origin. The result was a satire titled "Why Do Gentlemen Prefer Blondes?" To my amazement, when I submitted my tongue-in-cheek essay to a medical journal, it was promptly accepted. And to my even greater surprise, many of my colleagues did not find it amusing; to them it was a perfectly plausible argument, not a spoof.[4] (I describe it in the endnotes in case you are curious.)

What about laughter? Can we come up with a reasonable evolutionary explanation, or will the true meaning of laughter remain forever elusive?

If an alien ethologist were to land on earth and watch us humans, he would be mystified by many aspects of our behavior, but I'll wager that laughter would be very near the top of the list. As he watches people interacting, he notices that every now and then we suddenly stop what we're doing, grimace and make a loud repetitive sound in response to a wide variety of situations. What function could this mysterious behavior possibly serve? Cultural factors undoubtedly influence humor and what people find funny — the English are thought to have a sophisticated sense of humor, whereas Germans or Swiss, it is said, rarely find anything amusing. But even if this is true, might there still be some sort of "deep structure" underlying all humor? The details of the phenomenon vary from culture to culture and are influenced by the way people are raised, but this doesn't mean there's no genetically specified mechanism for laughter — a common denominator underlying all types of humor. Indeed, many people have suggested that such a mechanism does exist, and theories on the biological origins of humor and laughter have a long history, going all the way to Schopenhauer and Kant, two singularly humorless German philosophers.

Consider the following two jokes. (Not surprisingly, it was difficult to find examples that are not racist, sexist or ethnic. After a diligent search I found one that was and one that wasn't.)

A fellow is sitting in a truck stop café in California, having lunch, when suddenly a giant panda bear walks in and orders a burger with fries and a chocolate milkshake. The bear sits down, eats the food, then stands up, shoots several of the other customers and runs out the door. The fellow is astonished, but the waiter seems completely undisturbed. "What the hell is going on?" the customer asks. "Oh, well, there's nothing surprising about that," says the waiter. "Just go look in the dictionary under 'panda.'" So the guy goes to the library, takes out a dictionary and looks up "panda" — a big furry, black and white animal that lives in the rain forest of China. It eats shoots and leaves.

A guy carrying a brown paper bag goes into a bar and orders a drink.   15 The bartender smiles, pours the drink and then, unable to contain his curiosity, says, "So, what's in the bag?" The man gives a little laugh and says, "You wanna see? Sure, you can see what's in the bag," and he reaches in and pulls out a tiny piano, no more than six inches tall. "What's that?" asks the bartender. The man doesn't say anything; he just reaches into the bag a second time and pulls out a tiny man, about a foot tall, and sits him down next to the piano. "Wow," says the bartender, absolutely astonished. "I've never in my life seen anything like that." The little man begins to play Chopin. "Holy cow," says the bartender, "where did you ever get him?" The man sighs and says, "Well, you see, I found this magic lamp and it has a genie in it. He can grant you anything you want but only gives one wish." The bartender scowls, "Oh, yeah, sure you do. Who are you trying to kid?" "You don't believe me?" says the man, somewhat offended. He reaches into his coat pocket and pulls out a silver lamp with an ornate curved handle. "Here it is. Here's the lamp with the genie in it. Go ahead and rub it if you don't believe me." So the bartender pulls the lamp over to his side of the counter and, looking at the man skeptically, rubs the lamp. And then POOF, a genie appears over the bar, bows to the bartender and says, "Sire, your wish is my command. I shall grant thee one wish and one wish only." The bartender gasps but quickly gains his composure and says, "Okay, okay, give me a million bucks!" The genie waves his wand and all of a sudden the room is filled with tens of thousands of quacking ducks. They're all over the place, making a terrible noise: Quack, quack, quack! The bartender turns to the man and says, "Hey! What's the matter with this genie? I asked for a million bucks and I get a million ducks. Is he deaf or something?" The man looks at him and replies, "Well, do you really think I asked for a twelve-inch pianist?"

Why are these stories funny? And what do they have in common with other jokes? Despite all their surface diversity, most jokes and funny incidents have the following logical structure: Typically you lead the listener along a garden path of expectation, slowly building up tension. At the very end, you introduce an unexpected twist that entails a complete reinterpretation of all the preceding data, and moreover, it's critical that the new interpretation, though wholly unexpected, makes as much "sense" of the entire set of facts as did the originally "expected" interpretation. In this regard, jokes have much in common with scientific creativity, with what Thomas Kuhn calls a "paradigm shift" in response to a single "anomaly." (It's probably not coincidence that many of the most creative scientists have a great sense of humor.) Of course, the anomaly in the joke is the traditional punch line and the joke is "funny" only if the listener gets the punch line by seeing in a flash of insight how a completely new interpretation of the same set of facts can incorporate the anomalous ending. The longer and more tortuous the garden path of expectation, the "funnier" the punch line when finally delivered. Good comedians make use of this principle by taking their time to build up the tension of the story line, for nothing kills humor more surely than a premature punch line.

But although the introduction of a sudden twist at the end is necessary for the genesis of humor, it is certainly not sufficient. Suppose my plane is about to land in San Diego and I fasten my seat belt and get ready for touchdown. The pilot suddenly announces that the "bumps" that he (and I) had earlier dismissed as air turbulence are really due to engine failure and that we need to empty fuel before landing. A paradigm shift has occurred in my mind, but this certainly does not make me laugh. Rather, it makes me orient toward the anomaly and prepare for action to cope with the anomaly. Or consider the time I was staying at some friends' house in Iowa City. They were away and I was alone in unfamiliar surroundings. It was late at night and just as I was about to doze off, I heard a thump downstairs. "Probably the wind," I thought. After a few minutes there was another thud, louder than the one before. Again I "rationalized" it away and went back to sleep. Twenty minutes later I heard an extremely loud, resounding "bang" and leapt out of bed. What was happening? A burglar perhaps? Naturally, with my limbic system activated, I "oriented," grabbed a flashlight and ran down the stairs. Nothing funny so far. Then, suddenly I noticed a large flower vase in pieces on the floor and a large tabby cat right next to it—the obvious culprit! In contrast to the airplane incident, this time I started laughing because I realized that the "anomaly" I had detected and the subsequent paradigm shift were of trivial consequence. All of the facts could now be explained in terms of the cat theory rather than the ominous burglar theory.

On the basis of this example, we can sharpen our definition of humor and laughter. When a person strolls along a garden path of expectation and there is a sudden twist at the end that entails a complete reinterpretation of the same facts *and* the new interpretation has trivial rather than terrifying implications, laughter ensues.

But why laughter? Why this explosive, repetitive sound? Freud's view that laughter discharges pent-up internal tension does not make much sense without recourse to an elaborate and far-fetched hydraulic metaphor. He argued that water building up in a system of pipes will find its way out of the path of least resistance (the way a safety valve opens when too much pressure builds up in a system), and laughter might provide a similar safety valve to allow the escape of psychic energy (whatever that might mean). This "explanation" really doesn't work for me; it belongs to a class of explanations that Peter Medawar has called "analgesics" that "dull the ache of incomprehension without removing the cause."

To an ethologist, on the other hand, any stereotyped vocalization   20
almost always implies that the organism is trying to *communicate* something to others in the social group. Now what might this be in the case of laughter? I suggest that the main purpose of laughter might be to allow the individual to alert others in the social group (usually kin) that the detected anomaly is trivial, nothing to worry about. The laughing person in effect announces her discovery that there has been a false alarm; that the rest of you chaps need not waste your precious energy and resources responding to a spurious threat.[5] This also explains why laughter is so notoriously contagious, for the value of any such signal would be amplified as it spread through the social group.

This "false alarm theory" of humor may also explain slapstick. You watch a man — preferably one who is portly and self-important — walk down the street when suddenly he slips on a banana peel and falls down. If his head hit the pavement and his skull split open, you would not laugh as you saw blood spill out; you would rush to his aid or to the nearest telephone to call an ambulance. But if he got up casually, wiped the remains of the fruit from his face and continued walking, you would probably burst out laughing, thereby letting others standing nearby know that they need not rush to his aid. Of course, when watching Laurel and Hardy or Mr. Bean, we are more willing to tolerate "real" harm or injury to the hapless victim because we are fully aware that it's only a movie.

Although this model accounts for the evolutionary origin of laughter, it by no means explains all the functions of humor among modern humans. Once the mechanism was in place, however, it could easily be exploited for other purposes. (This is common in evolution. Feathers evolved in birds originally to provide insulation but were later adapted for flying.) The ability to reinterpret events in the light of new information may have been refined through the generations to help people playfully juxtapose larger ideas or concepts — that is, to be creative. This capacity for seeing familiar ideas from novel vantage points (an essential element of humor) could be an anti-dote to conservative thinking and a catalyst to creativity. Laughter and humor may be a dress rehearsal for creativity, and if so, perhaps jokes, puns and other forms of humor should be introduced very early into our elementary schools as part of the formal curriculum.

Although these suggestions may help explain the logical structure of humor, they do not explain why humor itself is sometimes used as a psychological defense mechanism. Is it a coincidence, for example, that a disproportionate number of jokes deal with potentially disturbing topics, such as death or sex? One possibility is that jokes are an attempt to trivialize genuinely disturbing anomalies by pretending they are of no consequence; you distract yourself from your anxiety by setting off your own false alarm mechanism. Thus a trait that evolved to appease others in a social group now becomes internalized to deal with truly stressful situations and may emerge as so-called nervous laughter. Thus even as mysterious a phenomenon as "nervous laughter" begins to make sense in the light of some of the evolutionary ideas discussed here.

The smile, too, may have similar evolutionary origins, as a "weaker" form of laughter. When one of your ancestral primates encountered another individual coming toward him from a distance, he may have initially bared his canines in a threatening grimace on the fair assumption that most strangers are potential enemies. Upon recognizing the individual as "friend" or "kin," however, he might abort the grimace halfway, thereby producing a smile, which in turn may have evolved into a ritualized human greeting: "I know you pose no threat and I reciprocate." Thus in my scheme, a smile is an *aborted* orienting response in the same way that laughter is.

The ideas we have explored so far help explain the biological functions 25 and possible evolutionary origin of humor, laughter and smiling, but they still leave open the question of what the underlying neural mechanisms of laughter might be. What about Willy, who started giggling at his mother's funeral, and Ruth, who literally died laughing? Their strange behavior implies the existence of a laughter circuit found mainly in portions of the limbic system and its targets in the frontal lobes. Given the well-known role of the limbic system in producing an orienting response to a potential threat or *alarm,* it is not altogether surprising, perhaps, that it is also involved in the aborted orienting reaction in response to a *false alarm* — laughter. Some parts of this circuit handle emotions — the feeling of merriment that accompanies laughter — whereas other parts are involved in the physical act itself, but at present we do not know which parts are doing what.

There is, however, another curious neurological disorder, called pain asymbolia, which offers additional hints about the neurological structures underlying laughter. Patients with this condition do not register pain when they are deliberately jabbed in the finger with a sharp needle. Instead of saying, "Ouch!" they say, "Doctor, I can feel the pain but it doesn't hurt."

Apparently they do not experience the aversive emotional impact of pain. And, mysteriously, I have noticed that many of them actually start giggling, as if they were being tickled and not stabbed. For instance, in a hospital in Madras, India, I recently examined a schoolteacher who told me that a pin-prick I administered as part of a routine neurology workup felt incredibly funny — although she couldn't explain why.

I became interested in pain asymbolia mainly because it provides additional support for the evolutionary theory of laughter that I've proposed [here]. . . . The syndrome is often seen when there is damage to a structure called the insular cortex — buried in the fold between the parietal and temporal lobes (and closely linked to the structures that were damaged in Willy and Ruth). This structure receives sensory input, including pain from the skin and internal organs, and sends its output to parts of the limbic system (such as the cingulate gyrus) so that one begins to experience the strong aversive reaction — the agony — of pain. Now imagine what would happen if the damage were to disconnect the insular cortex from the cingulate gyrus. One part of the person's brain (the insular cortex) tells him, "Here is something painful, a potential threat," while another part (the cingulate gyrus of the limbic system) says a fraction of a second later, "Oh, don't worry; this is no threat after all." Thus the two key ingredients — threat followed by deflation — are present, and the only way for the patient to resolve the paradox is to laugh, just as my theory would predict.

The same line of reasoning may help explain why people laugh when tickled. You approach a child, hand stretched out menacingly. The child wonders, "Will he hurt me or shake me or poke me?" But no, your fingers make light, intermittent contact with her belly. Again, the recipe — threat followed by deflation — is present and the child laughs, as if to inform other children, "He doesn't mean harm. He's only playing!" This, by the way, may help children practice the kind of mental play required for adult humor. In other words, what we call "sophisticated cognitive" humor has the same logical form as tickling and therefore piggybacks on the same neural circuits — the "threatening but harmless" detector that involves the insular cortex, cingulate gyrus and other parts of the limbic system. Such co-opting of mechanisms is the rule rather than the exception in the evolution of mental and physical traits (although in this case, the co-opting occurs for a related, higher-level function rather than for a completely different function).

These ideas have some bearing on a heated debate that has been going on among evolutionary biologists in general and evolutionary psychologists in particular during the last ten years. I get the impression that there are two warring camps. One camp implies (with disclaimers) that every one of our mental traits — or at least 99 percent of them — is specifically selected for by natural selection. The other camp, represented by Stephen Jay Gould, calls members of the first camp "ultra-Darwinists" and argues that other factors must be kept in mind. (Some of the factors pertain to the actual selection process itself and others to the raw material that natural selection can act on. They complement rather than contradict the idea of natural selection.) Every biologist I know has strong views on what these factors might be. Here are some of my favorite examples:

- What you now observe may be a bonus or useful by-product of something else that was selected for a completely different purpose. For example, a nose evolved for smelling and warming and moistening air but can also be used for wearing spectacles. Hands evolved for grasping branches but can now be used for counting as well.

- A trait may represent a further refinement (through natural selection) of another trait that was originally selected for a completely different purpose. Feathers evolved from reptilian scales to keep birds warm but have since been co-opted and transformed into wing feathers for flying; this is called preadaptation.

- Natural selection can only select from what is available, and what is available is often a very limited repertoire, constrained by the organism's previous evolutionary history as well as certain developmental pathways that either are permanently closed or remain open.

I'd be very surprised if these three statements were not true to some extent   30
regarding the many mental traits that constitute human nature. Indeed, there are many other principles of this sort (including plain old Lady Luck or contingency) that are not covered by the phrase "natural selection." Yet ultra-Darwinists steadfastly adhere to the view that almost all traits, other than those obviously learned, are specific products of natural selection. For them, preadaptation, contingency and the like play only a minor role in evolution; they are "exceptions that prove the rule." Moreover, they believe that you can in principle reverse engineer various human mental traits by looking at environmental and social constraints. ("Reverse engineering" is the idea that you can best understand how something works by asking what environmental challenge it evolved *for*. And then, working backward, you consider plausible solutions to that challenge. It is an idea that is popular, not surprisingly, with engineers and computer programmers.) As a biologist, I am inclined to go with Gould; I believe that natural selection is certainly the single most important driving force of evolution, but I also believe that each case needs to be examined individually. In other words, it is an empirical question whether some mental or physical trait that you observe in an animal or person was selected for by natural selection. Furthermore, there are dozens of ways to solve an environmental problem, and unless you know the evolutionary history, taxonomy, and paleontology of the animal you are looking at, you cannot figure out the exact route taken by a particular trait (like feathers, laughter or hearing) as it evolved into its present form. This is technically referred to as the "trajectory" taken by the trait "through the fitness landscape."

My favorite example of this phenomenon involves the three little bones in our middle ear — the malleus, incus and stapes. Now used for hearing, two of these bones (the malleus and incus) were originally part of the lower jaw of our reptilian ancestors, who used them for chewing. Reptiles needed flexible, multielement, multihinged jaws so they could swallow giant prey, whereas mammals preferred a single strong bone (the dentary) for cracking nuts and chewing tough substances like grains. So as reptiles evolved into mammals, two of the jawbones were co-opted into the middle ear and used for amplifying sounds (partly because early mammals were nocturnal and relied largely on hearing for survival). This is such an ad hoc, bizarre solution that unless you know your comparative anatomy well or discovered fossil intermediates, you never could have deduced it from simply considering the functional needs of the organism. Contrary to the ultra-Darwinist view, reverse engineering doesn't always work in biology for the simple reason that God is not an engineer; he's a hacker.

What has all this got to do with human traits like smiling? Everything. If my argument concerning the smile is correct, then even though it evolved through natural selection, not *every* feature of a smile is adaptive for its current demand. That is, the smile takes the particular form that it does not because of natural selection alone but because it evolved from *the very opposite* — the threat grimace! There is no way you could deduce this through reverse engineering (or figure out its particular trajectory through the fitness landscape) unless you also knew about the existence of canine teeth, knew that nonhuman primates bare their canines as a mock threat or knew that mock threats in turn evolved from real threat displays. (Big canines are genuinely dangerous.)

I find great irony in the fact that every time someone smiles at you she is in fact producing a half threat by flashing her canines. When Darwin published *On the Origin of Species* he delicately hinted in his last chapter that we too may have evolved from apelike ancestors. The English statesman Benjamin Disraeli was outraged by this and at a meeting held in Oxford he asked a famous rhetorical question: "Is man a beast or an angel?" To answer this, he need only have looked at his wife's canines as she smiled at him, and he'd have realized that in this simple universal human gesture of friendliness lies concealed a grim reminder of our savage past.

As Darwin himself concluded in *The Descent of Man:*

> But we are not here concerned with hopes and fears, only with truth. We must acknowledge, as it seems to me, that man with all his noble qualities, with sympathy which he feels for the most debased, with benevolence which extends not only to other men but to the humblest creature, with his God-like intellect which has penetrated into the movements and constitution of the solar system — with all these exalted powers — man still bears in his bodily frame the indelible stamp of his lowly origin.

Notes

1. Ruth and Willy (pseudonyms) are reconstructions of patients originally described in an article by Ironside (1955). The clinical details and autopsy reports, however, have not been altered.

2. Fried, Wilson, MacDonald and Behnke, 1998.

3. The discipline of evolutionary psychology was foreshadowed by the early writings of Hamilton (1964), Wilson (1978) and Williams (1966). The modern manifesto of this discipline is by Barkow, Cosmides and Tooby (1992), who are regarded as founders of the field. (Also see Daly and Wilson, 1983, and Symons, 1979.)

The clearest exposition of these ideas can be found in Pinker's book *How the Mind Works*, which contains many stimulating ideas. My disagreement with him on specific details of evolutionary theory doesn't detract from the value of his contributions.

4. V. S. Ramachandran, 1997.

5. Ramachandran, 1998.

Bibliography

Barkow, J. H., Cosmides, L., & Tooby, J. (1992). *The adapted mind*. New York: Oxford University Press.

Daly, M., & Wilson, M. (1983). *Sex, evolution, and behavior*. Boston: Willard Grant.

Fried, I., Wilson, C., MacDonald, K., & Behnke, E. (1998). Electric current stimulates laughter. *Nature, 391*, 850.

Hamilton, W. D. (1964). The genetic evolution of social behavior. *J Thor Biol, 7*, 1–52.

Ironside, R. (1955). Disorder of laughter due to brain lesions. Presidential address, Neurological section, Royal Society of Medicine, London.

Pinker, S. (1997). *How the mind works*. New York: W. W. Norton.

Ramachandran, V. S. (1997). Why do gentlemen prefer blondes? *Med Hypotheses, 48*, 19–20.

Ramachandran, V. S. (1998). Evolution and neurology of laughter and humor. *Med Hypotheses*. In press.

Symons, D. (1979). *The evolution of human sexuality*. New York: Oxford University Press.

Williams, G. (1966). *Adaptation and natural selection*. Princeton, NJ: Princeton University Press.

Wilson, E. O. (1978). *On human nature*. Cambridge, MA: Harvard University Press.

QUESTIONS

Reading

1. With his "false alarm theory," Ramachandran suggests that laughter's evolutionary purpose may be "to alert others in the social group . . . that the detected anomaly is trivial, nothing to worry about" (paragraph 20). However, he also states that laughter, like any human trait, serves social

and cultural purposes beyond its evolutionary origins. What are some of these purposes? Which of them seems most compelling or persuasive to you?

2. Ramachandran is *reporting* on history and research in neurobiology that may help explain the origins and functions of laughter. In doing so, he cites a wide variety of sources — historical case studies, recently published research, anecdotes, and firsthand observation of patients. Choose two of these sources, and write about how each contributes to Ramachandran's discussion of laughter. Why has Ramachandran included these sources? What information or ideas does each source allow him to explore?

3. Ramachandran discusses two jokes on pages 772–73. Why does he choose the jokes he does? What ideas about humor and laughter does each of them illustrate? Do you find the jokes funny? Why or why not?

Exploratory Writing

1. Think of a time when you laughed out loud unexpectedly. What made you laugh? After reading Ramachandran's essay, how might you interpret your own laughter? Which of his theories seem to illuminate your experience?

2. In a small group, prepare a presentation in which you first tell a joke to the rest of the class and then draw on Ramachandran's essay to explain how the joke works, why it's funny, and what social functions it and similar jokes might serve.

Making Connections

1. Ramachandran suggests that humor and "scientific creativity" are closely related. In her essay "Memory and Imagination" (p. 782), Patricia Hampl discusses artistic creativity. Compare Ramachandran's and Hampl's explanations of creativity. How does each define creativity? What elements do scientific and artistic creativity share? What's different about them?

2. Ramachandran's discussion of laughter focuses on its origins in the brain and its social functions. Most of the readings in this casebook emphasize the relationship between the brain and individual identity. Most of them also suggest that understanding the brain has social implications as well. Drawing on the readings in this casebook, write an essay that explores two or three related social implications of brain research. Be sure to identify and name particular social implications, and explain how they are (or are not) related.

Essay Writing

1. In his exploration of the meaning of laughter and humor, Ramachandran summarizes several case histories. He tells the stories of individuals who have experienced laughter in unusual or interesting ways in order to draw conclusions about where laughter comes from and how humor works. Write your own case history — about yourself or about someone you've observed or interviewed — exploring a particular experience with laughter that might shed light on its meaning or functions. Notice that Ramachandran quotes outside sources in order to make sense of the cases he describes. You might do the same, quoting Ramachandran or another source. (For another example of a case history, see Jill Bolte Taylor's "Morning of the Stroke" [p. 752].)

Memory and Imagination

Patricia Hampl

Patricia Hampl (b. 1946) is an acclaimed memoirist from St. Paul, Minnesota. After earning her MFA from the University of Iowa in 1970, she worked as an editor and later became English Regents Professor at the University of Minnesota. Her first memoir, A Romantic Education *(1981), concerns Hampl's Czech heritage; and her second,* Virgin Time: In Search of the Contemplative Life *(1993), explores her Catholic upbringing.* The Florist's Daughter — *a novelistic memoir — examines the opposing worldviews of her Irish American mother and her Czech American father and their "ordinary" lives in the city of St. Paul. Published in 2007, this work garnered high praise from critics and was ranked by the* New York Times *as one of the "100 Notable Books of the Year." Hampl has also published collections of stories, poems, and non-fiction. Her writing has been recognized by a Guggenheim Fellowship, two fellowships from the National Endowment for the Arts, and a MacArthur Fellowship. This piece originally appeared in* I Could Tell You Stories: Sojourns in the Land of Memory *(2000).*

When I was seven, my father, who played the violin on Sundays with a nicely tortured flair which we considered artistic, led me by the hand down a long, unlit corridor in St. Luke's School basement, a sort of tunnel that ended in a room full of pianos. There, many little girls and a single sad boy were playing truly tortured scales and arpeggios in a mash of troubled sound. My father gave me over to Sister Olive Marie, who did look remarkably like an olive.

Her oily face gleamed as if it had just been rolled out of a can and laid on the white plate of her broad, spotless wimple. She was a small, plump woman; her body and the small window of her face seemed to interpret the entire alphabet of olive: her face was a sallow green olive placed upon the jumbo ripe olive of her habit. I trusted her instantly and smiled, glad to have my hand placed in the hand of a woman who made sense, who provided the satisfaction of being what she was: an Olive who looked like an olive.

My father left me to discover the piano with Sister Olive Marie so that one day I would join him in mutually tortured piano-violin duets for the edification of my mother and brother who sat at the table spooning in the last of their pineapple sherbet until their part was called for: they put down their spoons and clapped while we bowed, while the sweet ice in their bowls melted, while the music melted, and we all melted a little into one another for a moment.

But first Sister Olive must do her work. I was shown middle C, which Sister seemed to think terribly important. I stared at middle C, and then glanced away for a second. When my eye returned, middle C was gone, its slim finger lost in the complicated grasp of the keyboard. Sister Olive struck it again, finding it with laughable ease. She emphasized the importance of middle C, its central position, a sort of North Star of sound. I remember thinking, middle C is the belly button of the piano, an insight whose originality and accuracy stunned me with pride. For the first time in my life I was astonished by metaphor. I hesitated to tell the kindly Olive for some reason; apparently I understood a true metaphor is a risky business, revealing of the self. In fact, I have never, until this moment of writing it down, told my first metaphor to anyone.

Sunlight flooded the room; the pianos, all black, gleamed. Sister Olive,   5
dressed in the colors of the keyboard, gleamed; middle C shimmered with meaning, and I resolved never — never — to forget its location: it was the center of the world.

Then Sister Olive, who had had to show me middle C twice but who seemed to have drawn no bad conclusions about me anyway, got up and went to the windows on the opposite wall. She pulled the shades down, one after the other. The sun was too bright, she said. She sneezed as she stood at the windows with the sun shedding its glare over her. She sneezed and sneezed, crazy little convulsive sneezes, one after another, as helpless as if she had the hiccups.

"The sun makes me sneeze," she said when the fit was over and she was back at the piano. This was odd, too odd to grasp in the mind. I associated sneezing with colds, and colds with rain, fog, snow, and bad weather. The sun, however, had caused Sister Olive to sneeze in this wild way, Sister Olive who gleamed benignly and who was so certain of the location of the center of the world. The universe wobbled a bit and became unreliable. Things were not, after all, necessarily what they seemed. Appearance deceived: here was the sun acting totally out of character, hurling this woman into sneezes, a woman so mild that she was named, so it seemed, for a bland object on a relish tray.

I was given a red book, the first Thompson book, and told to play the first piece over and over at one of the black pianos where the other children were crashing away. This, I was told, was called practicing. It sounded alluringly adult, practicing. The piece itself consisted mainly of middle C, and I excelled, thrilled by my savvy at being able to locate that central note amidst the cunning camouflage of all the other white keys before me. Thrilled too by the shiny red book that gleamed, as the pianos did, as Sister Olive did, as my eager eyes probably did. I sat at the formidable machine of the piano and got to know middle C intimately, preparing to be as tortured as I could manage one day soon with my father's violin at my side.

But at the moment Mary Katherine Reilly was at my side, playing something at least two or three lessons more sophisticated than my piece. I believe she even struck a chord. I glanced at her from the peasantry of single notes, shy, ready to pay homage. She turned toward me, stopped playing, and sized me up.

Sized me up and found a person ready to be dominated. Without introduction she said, "My grandfather invented the collapsible opera hat."   10

I nodded, I acquiesced, I was hers. With that little stroke it was decided between us — that she should be the leader and I the sidekick. My job was admiration. Even when she added, "But he didn't make a penny from it. He didn't have a patent" — even then, I knew and she knew that this was not an admission of powerlessness, but the easy candor of a master, of one who can afford a weakness or two. With the clairvoyance of all fated relationships based on dominance and submission, it was decided in advance: That when the time came for us to play duets, I should always play second piano, that I should spend my allowance to buy her the Twinkies she craved but was not allowed to have, that finally, I should let her copy from my test paper, and when confronted by our teacher, confess with convincing hysteria that it was I, I who had cheated, who had reached above myself to steal what clearly belonged to the rightful heir of the inventor of the collapsible opera hat. . . .

There must be a reason I remember that little story about my first piano lesson. In fact, it isn't a story, just a moment, the beginning of what could perhaps become a story. For the memoirist, more than for the fiction writer, the story seems already *there*, already accomplished and fully achieved in history ("in reality," as we naively say). For the memoirist, the writing of the story is a matter of transcription.

That, anyway, is the myth. But no memoirist writes for long without experiencing an unsettling disbelief about the reliability of memory, a hunch that memory is not, after all, *just* memory. I don't know why I remembered this fragment about my first piano lesson. I don't, for instance, have a single recollection of my first arithmetic lesson, the first time I studied Latin, the first time my grandmother tried to teach me to knit. Yet these things occurred too and must have their stories.

It is the piano lesson that has trudged forward, clearing the haze of forgetfulness, showing itself bright with detail decades after the event. I did not choose to remember the piano lesson. The experience was simply there, like a book that has always been on the shelf, whether I ever read it or not, the binding and title showing as I skim across the contents of my life. On the day I wrote this fragment I happened to take that memory, not some other, from the shelf and paged through it. I found more detail, more event, perhaps a little more entertainment than I had expected, but the memory itself was there from the start. Waiting for me.

Wasn't it? When I reread the piano lesson vignette just after I finished it, 15
I realized that I had told a number of lies. I *think* it was my father who took
me the first time for my piano lesson, but maybe he only took me to meet
my teacher and there was no actual lesson that day. And did I even know
then that he played the violin — didn't he take up his violin again much
later as a result of my piano playing and not the reverse? And is it even remotely accurate to describe as "tortured" the musicianship of a man who
began every day by belting out "Oh What a Beautiful Morning" as he
shaved? More: Sister Olive Marie did sneeze in the sun, but was her name
Olive? As for her skin tone — I would have sworn it was olivelike. I would
have been willing to spend the better part of a morning trying to write the
exact description of an imported Italian or Greek olive her face suggested: I
wanted to get it right.

But now, were I to write that passage over, it is her intense black eyebrows I would see, for suddenly they seem the central fact of that face, some
indicative mark of her serious and patient nature. But the truth is, I don't
remember the woman at all. She's a sneeze in the sun and a finger touching
middle C.

Worse: I didn't have the Thompson book as my piano text. I'm sure of
that because I remember envying children who did have this wonderful book
with its pictures of children and animals printed on the pages for music.

As for Mary Katherine Reilly. She didn't even go to grade school with me
(and her name isn't Mary Katherine Reilly — but I made that change on purpose). I met her in Girl Scouts and only went to school with her later, in high
school. Our relationship was not really one of leader and follower; I played
first piano most of the time in duets. She certainly never copied anything
from a test paper of mine: she was a better student, and cheating just wasn't
a possibility for her. Though her grandfather (or someone in her family) did
invent the collapsible opera hat and I remember that she was proud of this
fact, she didn't tell me this news as a deft move in a childish power play.

So, what was I doing in this brief memoir? Is it simply an example of the
curious relation a fiction writer has to the material of her own life? Maybe.
But to tell the truth (if anyone still believes me capable of the truth), I
wasn't writing fiction. I was writing memoir — or was trying to. My desire
was to be accurate. I wished to embody the myth of memoir: to write as an
act of dutiful transcription.

Yet clearly the work of writing a personal narrative caused me to do 20
something very different from transcription. I am forced to admit that memory is not a warehouse of finished stories, not a gallery of framed pictures.
I must admit that I invented. But why?

Two whys: Why did I invent and, then, if memory inevitably leads to
invention, why do I — why should anybody — write memoir at all?

I must respond to these impertinent questions because they, like the
bumper sticker I saw the other day commanding all who read it to QUESTION
AUTHORITY, challenge my authority as a memoirist and as a witness.

It still comes as a shock to realize that I don't write about what I know, but in order to find out what I know. Is it possible to convey the enormous degree of blankness, confusion, hunch, and uncertainty lurking in the act of writing? When I am the reader, not the writer, I too fall into the lovely illusion that the words before me, which read so inevitably, must also have been written exactly as they appear, rhythm and cadence, language and syntax, the powerful waves of the sentences laying themselves on the smooth beach of the page one after another faultlessly.

But here I sit before a yellow legal pad, and the long page of the preceding two paragraphs is a jumble of crossed-out lines, false starts, confused order. A mess. The mess of my mind trying to find out what it wants to say. This is a writer's frantic, grabby mind, not the poised mind of a reader waiting to be edified or entertained.

I think of the reader as a cat, endlessly fastidious, capable by turns of   25 mordant indifference and riveted attention, luxurious, recumbent, ever poised. Whereas the writer is absolutely a dog, panting and moping, too eager for an affectionate scratch behind the ears, lunging frantically after any old stick thrown in the distance.

The blankness of a new page never fails to intrigue and terrify me. Sometimes, in fact, I think my habit of writing on long yellow sheets comes from an atavistic fear of the writer's stereotypic "blank white page." At least when I begin writing, my page has a wash of color on it, even if the absence of words must finally be faced on a yellow sheet as much as on a blank white one. We all have our ways of whistling in the dark.

If I approach writing from memory with the assumption that I know what I wish to say, I assume that intentionality is running the show. Things are not that simple. Or perhaps writing is even more profoundly simple, more telegraphic and immediate in its choices than the grating wheels and chugging engine of logic and rational intention suppose. The heart, the guardian of intuition with its secret, often fearful intentions, is the boss. Its commands are what a writer obeys — often without knowing it.

This is the beauty of the first draft. And why it's worth pausing a moment to consider what a first draft really is. By my lights, the piano lesson memoir is a first draft. That doesn't mean it exists here exactly as I first wrote it. I like to think I've cleaned it up from the first time I put it down on paper. I've cut some adjectives here, toned down the hyperbole there (though not enough), smoothed a transition, cut a repetition — that sort of housekeeperly tidying up.

But the piece remains a first draft because I haven't yet gotten to know it, haven't given it a chance to tell me anything. For me, writing a first draft is a little like meeting someone for the first time. I come away with a wary acquaintanceship, but the real friendship (if any) is down the road. Intimacy with a piece of writing, as with a person, comes from paying attention to the revelations it is capable of giving, not by imposing my own notions and agenda, no matter how well intentioned they might be.

I try to let pretty much anything happen in a first draft. A careful first 30 draft is a failed first draft. That may be why there are so many inaccuracies in the piano lesson memoir: I didn't censor; I didn't judge. I just kept moving. But I would not publish this piece as a memoir on its own in its present state. It isn't the "lies" in the piece that give me pause, though a reader has a right to expect a memoir to be as accurate as the writer's memory can make it.

The real trouble: the piece hasn't yet found its subject; it isn't yet about what it wants to be about. Note: What *it* wants, not what I want. The difference has to do with the relation a memoirist — any writer — has to unconscious or half-known intentions and impulses in composition.

Now that I have the fragment down on paper, I can read this little piece as a mystery which drops clues to the riddle of my feelings, like a culprit who wishes to be apprehended. My narrative self (the culprit who invented) wishes to be discovered by my reflective self, the self who wants to understand and make sense of a half-remembered moment about a nun sneezing in the sun.

We store in memory only images of value. The value may be lost over the passage of time (I was baffled about why I remembered my sneezing nun), but that's the implacable judgment of feeling: *This*, we say somewhere within us, is something I'm hanging on to. And, of course, often we cleave to things because they possess heavy negative charges. Pain has strong arms.

Over time, the value (the feeling) and the stored memory (the image) may become estranged. Memoir seeks a permanent home for feeling and image, a habitation where they can live together. Naturally, I've had a lot of experiences since I packed away that one from the basement of St. Luke's School; that piano lesson has been effaced by waves of feeling for other moments and episodes. I persist in believing the event has value — after all, I remember it — but in writing the memoir I did not simply relive the experience. Rather, I explored the mysterious relationship between all the images I could round up and the even more impacted feelings that caused me to store the images safely away in memory. Stalking the relationship, seeking the congruence between stored image and hidden emotion — that's the real job of memoir.

By writing about that first piano lesson, I've come to know things I 35 could not know otherwise. But I only know these things as a result of reading this first draft. While I was writing, I was following the images, letting the details fill the room of the page and use the furniture as they wished. I was their dutiful servant — or thought I was. In fact, I was the faithful retainer of my hidden feelings which were giving the commands.

I really did feel, for instance, that Mary Katherine Reilly was far superior to me. She was smarter, funnier, more wonderful in every way — that's how I saw it. Out friendship (or she herself) did not require that I become her vassal, yet perhaps in my heart that was something I sought. I wanted a way to express my admiration. I suppose I waited until this memoir to begin to find the way.

Just as, in the memoir, I finally possess that red Thompson book with the barking dogs and bleating lambs and winsome children. I couldn't (and still can't) remember what my own music book was, so I grabbed the name and image of the one book I could remember. It was only in reviewing the piece after writing it that I saw my inaccuracy. In pondering this "lie," I came to see what I was up to: I was getting what I wanted. Finally.

The truth of many circumstances and episodes in the past emerges for the memoirist through details (the red music book, the fascination with a nun's name and gleaming face), but these details are not merely information, not flat facts. Such details are not allowed to lounge. They must work. Their labor is the creation of symbol. But it's more accurate to call it the *recognition* of symbol. For meaning is not "attached" to the detail by the memoirist; meaning is revealed. That's why a first draft is important. Just as the first meeting (good or bad) with someone who later becomes the beloved is important and is often reviewed for signals, meanings, omens, and indications.

Now I can look at that music book and see it not only as "a detail" but for what it is, how it acts. See it as the small red door leading straight into the dark room of my childhood longing and disappointment. That red book *becomes* the palpable evidence of that longing. In other words, it becomes symbol. There is no symbol, no life-of-the-spirit in the general or the abstract. Yet a writer wishes — certainly we all wish — to speak about profound matters that are, like it or not, general and abstract. We wish to talk to each other about life and death, about love, despair, loss, and innocence. We sense that in order to live together we must learn to speak of peace, of history, of meaning and values. The big words.

We seek a means of exchange, a language which will renew these ancient concerns and make them wholly, pulsingly ours. Instinctively, we go to our store of private associations for our authority to speak of these weighty issues. We find, in our details and broken, obscured images, the language of symbol. Here memory impulsively reaches out and embraces imagination. That is the resort to invention. It isn't a lie, but an act of necessity, as the innate urge to locate truth always is.   40

All right. Invention is inevitable. But why write memoir? Why not call it fiction and be done with it? And if memoir seeks to talk about "the big issues," of history and peace, death and love — why not leave these reflections to those with expert or scholarly knowledge? Why let the common or garden variety memoirist into the club? I'm thinking again of that bumper sticker: Question Authority. Why?

My answer, naturally, is a memoirist's answer. Memoir must be written because each of us must possess a created version of the past. Created: that is, real in the sense of tangible, made of the stuff of a life lived in place and in history. And the downside of any created thing as well: We must live with a version that attaches us to our limitations, to the inevitable subjectivity of our points of view. We must acquiesce to our experience and our gift to transform experience into meaning. You tell me your story, I'll tell you mine.

If we refuse to do the work of creating this personal version of the past, someone else will do it for us. That is the scary political fact. "The struggle of man against power," Milan Kundera's hero in *The Book of Laughter and Forgetting* says, "is the struggle of memory against forgetting." He refers to willful political forgetting, the habit of nations and those in power (Question Authority!) to deny the truth of memory in order to disarm moral and ethical power.

It is an efficient way of controlling masses of people. It doesn't even require much bloodshed, as long as people are entirely willing to give over their personal memories. Whole histories can be rewritten. The books which now seek to deny the existence of the Nazi death camps now fill a room.

What is remembered is what becomes reality. If we "forget" Auschwitz,   45
if we "forget" My Lai, what then do we remember? And what is the purpose of our remembering? If we think of memory naively, as a simple story, logged like a documentary in the archive of the mind, we miss its beauty but also its function.

The beauty of memory rests in its talent for rendering detail, for paying homage to the senses, its capacity to love the particles of life, the richness and idiosyncrasy of our existence. The function of memory, while experienced as intensely personal, is surprisingly political.

Our capacity to move forward as developing beings rests on a healthy relation with the past. Psychotherapy, that widespread method for promoting mental health, relies heavily on memory and on the ability to retrieve and organize images and events from the personal past. We carry our wounds and, perhaps even worse, our capacity to wound, forward with us. If we learn not only to tell our stories but to listen to what our stories tell us — to write the first draft and then return for the second draft — we are doing the work of memory.

Memoir is the intersection of narration and reflection, of storytelling and essay writing. It can present its story *and* consider the meaning of the story. The first commandment of fiction — Show, Don't Tell — is not part of the memoirist's faith. Memoirists must show *and* tell. Memoir is a peculiarly open form, inviting broken and incomplete images, half-recollected fragments, all the mass (and mess) of detail. It offers to shape this confusion — and, in shaping, of course, it necessarily creates a work of art, not a legal document. But then, even legal documents are only valiant attempts to consign the truth, the whole truth, and nothing but the truth to paper. Even they remain versions.

Locating touchstones — the red music book, the olive Olive, my father's violin playing — is satisfying. Who knows why? Perhaps we all sense that we can't grasp the whole truth and nothing but the truth of our experience. Just can't be done.

What can be achieved, however, is a version of its swirling, changing   50
wholeness. A memoirist must acquiesce to selectivity, like any artist. The version we dare to write is the only truth, the only relationship we can have with the past. Refuse to write your life and you have no life. That is the stern view of the memoirist.

Personal history, logged in memory, is a sort of slide projector flashing images on the wall of the mind. And there's precious little order to the slides in the rotating carousel. Beyond that confusion, who knows who is running the projector? A memoirist steps into this darkened room of flashing, unorganized images and stands blinking for a while. Maybe for a long while. But eventually, as with any attempt to tell a story, it is necessary to put something first, then something else. And so on, to the end. That's a first draft. Not necessarily the truth, not even *a* truth sometimes, but the first attempt to create a shape.

The first thing I usually notice at this stage of composition is the appalling inaccuracy of the piece. Witness my first piano lesson draft. Invention is screamingly evident in what I intended to be transcription. But here's the further truth: I feel no shame. In fact, it's only now that my interest in the piece quickens. For I can see what isn't there, what is shyly hugging the walls, hoping not to be seen. I see the filmy shape of the next draft. I see a more acute version of the episode or — this is more likely — an entirely new piece rising from the ashes of the first attempt.

The next draft of the piece would have to be true re-vision, a new seeing of the materials of the first draft. Nothing merely cosmetic will do — no rouge buffing up the opening sentence, no glossy adjective to lift a sagging line, nothing to attempt covering a patch of gray writing.

I can't say for sure, but my hunch is the revision would lead me to more writing about my father (Why was I so impressed by that ancestral inventor of the collapsible opera hat? Did I feel I had nothing as remarkable in my own background?). I begin to think perhaps Sister Olive is less central to this business than she appears to be. She is meant to be a moment, not a character. I'm probably wasting my time on her, writing and writing around her in tight descriptive circles, waiting for the real subject to reveal itself. My father!

So I might proceed, if I were to undertake a new draft of the memoir.   55
I begin to feel a relationship developing between a former self and me.

And even more important, a relationship between an old world and me. Some people think of autobiographical writing as the precious occupation of the unusually self-absorbed. Couldn't the same accusation be hurled at a lyric poet, at a novelist — at anyone with the audacity to present a personal point of view? True memoir is written, like all literature, in an attempt to find not only a self but a world.

The self-absorption that seems to be the impetus and embarrassment of autobiography turns into (or perhaps always was) a hunger for the world. Actually, it begins as hunger for *a* world, one gone or lost, effaced by time or a more sudden brutality. But in the act of remembering, the personal environment expands, resonates beyond itself, beyond its "subject," into the endless and tragic recollection that is history. We look at old family photographs in which we stand next to black, boxy Fords, and are wearing period costumes, and we do not gaze fascinated because there we are young again, or there we are standing, as we never will again in life, next to our mother. We stare and drift because there we are historical. It is the dress, the black car, that dazzle us now and draw us beyond our mother's bright arms which once caught us. We reach into the attractive impersonality of something more significant than ourselves. We write memoir, in other words. We accept the humble position of writing a versio   the consolation prize for our acknowledgment we cannot win "the whol truth and nothing but."

I suppose I write memoir because of the radiance of the past — it draws me back and back to it. Not that the past is beautiful. In our communal memoir, in history, the darkness we sense is not only the dark of forgetfulness. The darkness is history's tunnel of horrors with its tableaux vivants of devastation. The blasted villages, the hunted innocents, the casual acquiescence to the death camps and tiger cages are back there in the fetid holes of history.

But still, the past is radiant. It sheds the light of lived life. One who writes memoir wishes to step into that light, not to see one's own face — that is not possible — but to feel the length of shadow cast by the light. No one owns the past, though typically the first act of new political regimes, whether of the left or the right, is an attempt to rewrite history, to grab the past and make it over so the end comes out right. So their power looks inevitable.

No one owns the past, but it is a grave error (another age would have   60 said a grave sin) not to inhabit memory. Sometimes I think it is all we really have. But that may be melodrama, the bad habit of the memoirist, coming out. At any rate, memory possesses authority for the fearful self in a world where it is necessary to claim authority in order to Question Authority.

There may be no more pressing intellectual need in our culture than for people to become sophisticated about the function of memory. The political implications of the loss of memory are obvious. The authority of memory is a personal confirmation of selfhood, and therefore the first step toward ethical development. To write one's life is to live it twice, and the second living is both spiritual and historical, for a memoir reaches deep within the personality as it seeks its narrative form and it also grasps the life-of-the-times as no political analysis can.

Our most ancient metaphor says life is a journey. Memoir is travel writing, then, notes taken along the way, telling how things looked and what thoughts occurred. Show *and* tell. But I cannot think of the memoirist as a tourist. The memoir is no guide book. This traveler lives the journey idiosyncratically, taking on mountains, enduring deserts, marveling at the lush green places. Moving through it all faithfully, not so much a survivor with a harrowing tale to tell as that older sort of traveler, the pilgrim, seeking, wondering.

QUESTIONS

Reading

1. Hampl tells her opening story in precise detail, as though her memory of the scene is both vivid and complete. Make a list of striking images from this story.
2. In Hampl's words, "no memoirist writes for long without experiencing an unsettling disbelief about the reliability of memory" (paragraph 13).

What does this statement suggest about the origins of the images in your list? If Hampl didn't actually remember them all, how did she generate them? How does this make you feel about what you've read?

3. Explain the irony in the following statement: "Memoir must be written because each of us must possess a created version of the past" (paragraph 42).

Exploratory Writing

1. Think of a formative experience of your own and then write a first draft that tells the story of this experience in great detail (as in Hampl's story about learning to play the piano). After you finish, read the story with a colored pen or highlighter in hand. Mark anything that strikes you as an invention, an exaggeration, or a distortion.

2. Hampl claims, "A careful first draft is a failed first draft" (paragraph 30). What does she mean? How does her claim relate to your own writing?

Making Connections

1. Hampl, a memoirist, explains what it feels like for a writer to "create" memory, and makes arguments about the value of memoir. In "Of Time and Autobiography" (p. 793), psychiatrist and memory researcher Daniel Schacter explains *how* memories are created. Drawing on Schacter's essay, write about a detail from Hampl's opening memoir as if it were an *engram*. How does Schacter's explanation of memory shed new light on Hampl's memory — or memory in general?

Essay Writing

1. Hampl's essay focuses on the role of memory in the ongoing creation of self and identity. In many of the readings in this casebook, the self is re-created when brain function is disrupted. Drawing on at least three of these readings, write an essay about how the brain "creates" the self. How does a healthy brain enable us to create our sense of self? How can a damaged brain re-create this sense of self?

2. Revise the draft of the memoir you wrote for question 1 under "Exploratory Writing." If Hampl is right, no memoir will ever be fully accurate, but the value of a memoir lies in "creating" the past in ways that will help others understand it. With this in mind, your goal should be to "create" a memory in writing that strikes a productive balance between accuracy and effectiveness.

Of Time and Autobiography

Daniel Schacter

Daniel Schacter (b. 1952) is a professor of psychology at Harvard University, where he has taught since 1991. After earning his PhD from the University of Toronto in 1981, he has focused his research on psychological and biological aspects of human memory and amnesia, illuminating the distinctions between conscious and nonconscious memory, the brain mechanisms of memory distortion, and the effects of aging on memory. In addition to serving on numerous advisory boards, including the American Journal of Psychology, *Schacter has written three books, edited seven volumes, and published more than two hundred scientific articles and chapters. His books include* Searching for Memory: The Brain, the Mind, and the Past *(1996);* Forgotten Ideas, Neglected Pioneers *(2001); and* The Seven Sins of Memory: How the Mind Forgets and Remembers *(2001). Among other honors, he was awarded the John Simon Guggenheim Memorial Fellowship in 1998. The following is an excerpt from* Searching for Memory.

The artist Mildred Howard likes to relate visual stories about her family. Her parents moved their growing family from Texas to California at the beginning of World War II. Mildred, the youngest of ten children, was the only one born in California. Growing up, she listened intently to the stories of her parents, brothers, sisters, aunts, and uncles about their trials and adventures in the Texas countryside. She was especially moved by the tales of her elderly Aunt Mildred, a repository of family lore who mesmerized her young niece with colorful renditions of past events. In *Rose (Roosevelt)* (figure 1) the artist invites us to imagine one of Aunt Mildred's stories by reprinting a photograph from her family album on an old window frame and providing us with hints of the underlying narrative. Mildred Howard was enthralled by the oral history of her family but sometimes felt a twinge of jealousy that she had not been there herself to witness the escapades that she heard about. Perhaps this is one reason she has worked for years to capture in pictures the faded yet vital recollections of family stories that date back to before her birth. "The sepia-toned images of handsome men and women in their Sunday best," notes one observer about Howard's work, "speak of family pride dimmed through the passage of time and diminished

FIGURE 1 Mildred Howard, *Rose (Roosevelt)*, 1992. 28 × 18 × 2". Mixed media on window frame. Gallery Paule Anglim, San Francisco.

Two well-dressed young men surround a miniature window-within-a-window containing a photo of the artist's Aunt Mildred in her younger days. Are these two young suitors who vied for Aunt Mildred's affections? Relatives who participated with Aunt Mildred in some important or mysterious bit of family history? We don't know the particulars, but we can guess that it is an absorbing tale.

memory."[1] The distant, almost translucent quality that characterizes some of the old memories is communicated effectively in *Caney Creek* (figure 2). Time and memory are inextricably interwoven; memories always refer to the past and often shape the future. Mildred Howard acknowledges this relationship by commemorating distant events with aged objects. She appreciates that our understanding of who we are and who we will become depends on memories that may fade, change, or even strengthen as time inexorably passes. And it is from this ongoing dynamic between time and memory that our autobiographies — the stories we tell about our lives — are born. We

FIGURE 2 Mildred Howard, *Caney Creek*, 1991. 21 × 24 × 6". Mixed media on window frame. Nielsen Gallery, Boston.

Three faint figures — members of the artist's family in rural Texas — fade like blurs into a receding background. A window frame scarred by peeling paint and cracked surfaces surrounds their image, further heightening the sense of an old memory ravaged by time. Six empty bottles of cream soda stand in front of the figures. For Howard, these empty vessels evoke images of a rousing family get-together or of conversations with brothers and sisters on a hot afternoon.

cannot hope to understand memory's fragile power without examining what happens to memory as time passes, and considering how we translate the residues of experience that persist across time into tales of who we are.

The Receding Past

In the first experimental analysis of remembering and forgetting ever reported, an epoch-making study by the German psychologist Hermann Ebbinghaus in 1885, lengthening the delay between encoding and retrieval produced dramatic increases in forgetting. Ebbinghaus, who served as his own and only subject, set about memorizing long lists of nonsense syllables. He then carefully tested himself at different times after learning. Ebbinghaus remembered progressively less at each of the six delays that he used, ranging from one hour to one month. The rate of forgetting was relatively rapid at the early delays and slowed down at later ones. Ebbinghaus forgot a great deal between a one-hour delay and a nine-hour delay, whereas he lost relatively little between a one-day delay and a two-day delay. Many later researchers have also found that the rate of forgetting is slowed down by the passage of time.[2]

Psychologists have more recently investigated how memory for everyday personal experiences is influenced by the passage of time. In the early 1970s the psychologist Herbert Crovitz rediscovered and refined a method for studying memories of real-life experiences that had been described by the nineteenth-century British scientist Sir Francis Galton. The method, now commonly referred to as the Crovitz procedure, is simple. Think of a specific memory from anytime in your life that comes to mind first when you are given the word *table*. Once you have retrieved a memory, do your best to assign a date to it. Now try the same procedure using the cue word *hurt*, and then do it one more time with the cue word *run*.

In Crovitz's experiments, people retrieved memories from many different points in their lives, ranging from a few minutes prior to the experiment to the early years of childhood. He found that the more recent time periods yielded the most memories, the more distant time periods the fewest. (When I tried the experiment myself, I remembered leaving some papers on a table for a colleague a week earlier; dislocating my finger playing baseball as a child; and running to catch a taxi in New York City several months earlier.) The drop-off in reported memories was steepest in the recent time periods and more gradual in the remote time periods.[3]

Despite a few deviations, the general rule that memories become gradually less accessible with the passage of time holds in many situations. It is sometimes surprising how much we may forget when a sufficient amount of time has passed. For example, survey researchers interviewed 590 people who were known to have been injured in an automobile accident during the preceding year. Almost everyone who was interviewed within three months of the accident remembered this disturbing event (fewer than 4 percent did not report it). But 27 percent of people interviewed between nine and twelve months after the accident failed to report it. "The obvious reason for this trend," the authors of the study comment, "is a decreased ability to recall the occurrence of a motor vehicle accident as the time between the date of the accident and the date of interview increases."[4]

Why is the passage of time associated with decreasing memory? As time passes, we encode and store new experiences that interfere with our ability to recall previous ones. I can remember what I had for breakfast today, but not what I had for breakfast on this day a year ago, because I have had many breakfasts since then that interfere with my ability to pick out any single one from the crowd. Interfering events of this kind may give rise to an increasingly fuzzy or blurred engram as time passes.[5] Many researchers would agree that blurring or even loss of information from the engram plays a role in the pervasive forgetting that afflicts us all. But some have contended that no information is ever lost from memory — that all experienced events exist somewhere in the mind, pretty much in their original form, simply awaiting the right cue to elicit them.

The memory researchers Elizabeth and Geoffrey Loftus asked psychologists to choose between two theories of forgetting. One theory holds that everything that happens is permanently stored in the mind, so that details we cannot remember at a particular time could eventually be recovered with the right technique. The other theory holds that some experiences may be permanently lost from memory, and would never be able to be recovered by special techniques. Eighty-four percent of psychologists chose the first option. This conclusion might appear to be justified by evidence I considered earlier concerning the importance of retrieval cues in remembering. It is likely, for instance, that many people who forgot about their motor vehicle accidents after a year could be induced to remember the event if given a specific retrieval cue, such as a detailed description of the circumstances surrounding the accident. But . . . there are problems with the idea that all experiences are kept forever in some dark corner of the brain.[6]

The idea received seemingly strong support from the oft-described brain-stimulation studies conducted by the Canadian neurosurgeon Wilder Penfield during the 1950s. In the Loftus and Loftus survey, psychologists frequently pointed to Penfield's work as crucial evidence favoring the idea that all experiences are permanently stored in the mind. Penfield's observations were certainly dramatic. Prior to operating on patients who required brain surgery, Penfield carefully placed an electrode on the surface of the exposed temporal lobe. The patient was fully conscious as Penfield turned on an electrical current. Sometimes he elicited surprising memories of seemingly long-forgotten events. "Yes, sir, I think I heard a mother calling her little boy somewhere," reported one patient. "It seemed to be something that happened years ago." Another patient exclaimed, "Yes, Doctor, yes, Doctor! Now I hear people laughing — my friends in South Africa." When asked if he could recognize them, the patient replied, "Yes, they are two cousins, Bessie and Ann Wheliaw."[7]

To Penfield, such examples revealed a lasting record of experiences in the brain: "It is clear that the neuronal action that accompanies each succeeding state of consciousness leaves its permanent imprint on the brain."[8] If we could just figure out a way to find the unchanging neural imprints that our brains preserve forever, Penfield thought, we could remember or even relive everything we have ever experienced. Maybe the passing of time does not, after all, erode or erase the brain's recordings of past events; it might merely wreak havoc with our ability to replay our dusty old records.

Although the idea has an undeniable appeal — it leaves open the possibility that we could all achieve Proust's and Magnani's dreams of recapturing the past fully — many psychologists and neuroscientists now concur that Penfield's results provide little support for this rather romantic proposition. Only 40 of the 520 patients who received temporal lobe stimulations reported any mental experiences that could be interpreted as memories. Even more important, Penfield failed to document whether his patients'

10

experiences were memories of actual past incidents or mere fantasies or hallucinations.

In a more recent investigation, French researchers described similar mental experiences in patients with temporal lobe epilepsy. What the researchers called the "dreamy state" was either evoked by electrical stimulation in the vicinity of the temporal lobes or occurred spontaneously during the aura that precedes a seizure. Patients sometimes reported the experience of remembering, but they tended to recall generic scenes rather than specific events. "I saw before my eyes the house of a friend in my grandmother's village," said one patient, "then it disappeared and I saw the house in Brittany where I spend my summer vacations." "I was in my kitchen, in front of the sink, dressed as usual," reported another. Still other patients described strange feelings of déjà vu, such as one who related "[t]he impression of having already done what I am in the process of doing; it seems to me that I have already lived through the entire situation; with a feeling of strangeness and often of fear."[9] It is important that these subjective feelings of remembering result from electrical activity in temporal lobe structures because this region of the brain plays a paramount role in memory. But, just as in Penfield's studies, the patients' reports provide no indication of a permanent record of specific memories that is impervious to the passage of time.

The idea that all experiences are recorded forever, requiring only a Proustian taste, sight, or smell to come dancing into consciousness, can never be disproved on purely psychological grounds. Even if we show that a person cannot remember an experience in response to a wide variety of retrieval cues, it is always possible that some other cue would result in sudden recall. And there is no question that providing cues, or reinstating the physical or mental context that prevailed during an experience, sometimes does lead to recall of seemingly lost experiences. However, neurobiological research with invertebrate organisms has shown that the neural changes that underlie some simple forms of memory can weaken and even disappear over time. Nobody has yet demonstrated that the same thing happens in mammals. But this kind of finding suggests that as time passes, there may be a diminution in the strength of connections among neurons that represent particular experiences. At a biological level, some engrams might literally fade away over time.[10]

The two extreme positions about the causes of forgetting — that it occurs either because an engram has disappeared from storage or because a fully intact engram* is merely inaccessible at the moment owing to retrieval failure — are too simplistic. Rather than arguing about whether or not all

---

*In an earlier chapter from the book *Searching for Memory: The Brain, the Mind, and the Past,* Schacter defines the term *engram* as "the enduring change in the nervous system (the 'memory trace') that conserves the effects of experience across time" (57). [Eds.]

experiences are preserved forever, we need to refine our ideas about why forgetting occurs. It seems likely that as time passes, interference from new experiences makes it progressively more difficult to find a retrieval cue that elicits an increasingly blurred engram. The cognitive psychologist Marigold Linton conducted a well-known study of her own memory that confirms this point. She wrote brief descriptions, every day, concerning at least two specific events in her life; she then tested her memory for random samples of these events at several points in time. The study had been under way for fourteen years when Linton reported on it in 1986. She notes that for about a year after the occurrence of an episode, it "can be accessed readily — with virtually any cue."[11] However, as more time elapses, and the engram becomes more blurry, the range of cues that elicits a specific episode progressively narrows. This means that when we suddenly and unexpectedly recover a seemingly forgotten memory, it may be because we have luckily stumbled upon a retrieval cue that matches up perfectly with a faded or blurred engram.

When I visited a summer camp where I worked as a waiter twenty-five years earlier, I drove by a spot on the lake that offers a lovely view back toward the camp. As I was looking out from my car, I suddenly remembered when several friends and I visited that exact spot — the only other time I had ever been to that part of the lake. I hadn't thought about the incident for a quarter-century, and I could not recall exactly what we had been doing or who else was there. But I am pretty certain there are few if any cues other than the sight of the camp across the lake that would have led me to recall this hazy memory.

These considerations also lead to another important implication for the relationship between the retrieval cue and the engram. All things being equal, when memory is probed soon after an event, the engram is a rich source of information and may even be the dominant contributor to recollective experience. Relatively little retrieval information is needed to elicit the appropriate engram, and the retrieval cue will play a more or less minor role in shaping the subjective experience of remembering. If I ask you to remember what you did just before you picked up this book, you probably will not have a problem recalling the incident. I need not provide you with extensive cues to elicit the memory, and your recollection of the event would probably be similar regardless of how I cue you. The same is often true of favorite past episodes that we have recounted frequently: we tell the same story over and over again, regardless of which particular cues elicit it.

However, the nature of the cue-engram relationship is likely to be quite different for episodes from the distant past that we have not recounted many times. Now that the engram of the event is a more impoverished source of information, considerable cueing may be needed to elicit memory for the episode, and the properties of the retrieval cue itself may figure quite prominently in shaping the rememberer's recollective experience. If, for

15

example, I ask you to recollect events that transpired at your Thanksgiving dinner of six years ago, you will need a variety of retrieval cues in order to remember explicitly much of what happened. Now the quality of your recollective experience may indeed depend significantly on precisely which cues are used to trigger recollection. Suppose, for instance, you recall that six Thanksgivings ago, your old friend George flew in for the holiday; you attempt to cue additional recollections by thinking about him. Suppose further that in the intervening years, you and George had a serious disagreement and you no longer feel as warm toward him as you once did. These properties are now incorporated into your permanent knowledge of George, and they may play a role in shaping your memories of what happened at that Thanksgiving dinner. You may be inclined to recollect that he made a disparaging remark or that he behaved inappropriately, even though the engram of the event contains only vague information about what occurred. Because the engram is so impoverished, recollective experience may be determined more heavily by salient properties of the cue, which itself has stored associations and meanings in memory.

Weakening and blurring of engrams over time is, on the face of it, an unpleasant reality of memory. It is frustrating, even disturbing, to realize that past experiences are constantly slipping away from us, some rapidly and others imperceptibly. But we would be far worse off if we did not forget. In Jorge Luis Borges's jarring story "Funes, the Memorious," a young man remembers the tiniest details of all that has happened to him. He remembers every leaf of every tree he has ever seen and every separate occasion on which he has seen them: "I have more memories in myself alone than all men have had since the world was a world." But the price of perfect retention is high: Funes's mind is so cluttered with precise memories that he is incapable of generalizing from one experience to another. He has difficulty fathoming why a dog he encounters has the same name at one moment as it has a minute later. "To think is to forget a difference, to abstract," Borges reminds us. Years after Borges wrote this story, the Russian neuropsychologist Alexander Luria described a much-celebrated mnemonist, Shereshevskii, who was plagued by Funes's fictional problem: he was overwhelmed by detailed but useless recollections of trivial information and events. He could recount without error long lists of names, numbers, and just about anything else that Luria presented to him. This served him well in his job as a newspaper reporter, because he didn't have to write things down. Yet when he read a story or listened to other people, he recalled endless details without understanding much of what he read or heard. And like Funes, he had great difficulty grasping abstract concepts.[12]

Forgetting, though often frustrating, is an adaptive feature of our memories. We don't need to remember everything that has ever happened to us; engrams that we never use are probably best forgotten. The cognitive psychologist John Anderson has argued convincingly that forgetting memories over time is an economical response to the demands placed on memory by the environment in which we live. We are better off forgetting trivial experiences than clogging our minds with each and every ongoing event, just in case we might want to remember one of those incidents someday.[13] But we do need to form an accurate picture of the general features of our world, and it turns out that we are reasonably adept at doing so. Our recollections of the general contours of our pasts are often reasonably accurate. Perhaps paradoxically, if we, like Funes or Shereshevskii, were constantly overwhelmed by detailed memories of every page from our pasts, we would be left without a coherent story to tell.

Notes

1. The quote is from David Bonetti's review of Mildred Howard's exhibition at the Paule Anglim Gallery, San Francisco, *Art News,* November 1991, p. 154. My discussion of Howard's family background is based on personal conversations with the artist and on two exhibition catalogs: Mildred Howard, *1991 Adaline Kent Award Exhibition,* San Francisco Art Institute, and Mildred Howard, *TAP: Investigation of Memory,* Intar Gallery, New York, 1992.

2. For an English translation of Ebbinghaus's classic monograph, see Ebbinghaus (1885/1964).

3. Crovitz and Schiffman (1974). For the work of Galton that Crovitz rediscovered and modified, see Galton (1879).

4. The study on recall of accidents is by Cash and Moss (1972) and is cited in Loftus (1981). The quote is from Cash and Moss (1972), p. 5, as cited by Loftus (1982), p. 127.

5. The interference theory of forgetting has a long and distinguished history in the experimental study of memory. See, for example, Postman and Underwood (1973).

6. The idea that all experiences are stored permanently in memory is reviewed critically by Loftus and Loftus (1980).

7. Penfield's experiments are reported in Penfield and Perot (1963) and are reviewed carefully by Loftus and Loftus (1980) and Squire (1987). The quotes from the patients are from Penfield and Perot (1963), pp. 653 and 650, respectively.

8. Penfield (1969), p. 165.

9. Quotes are from Bancaud, Brunet-Bourgin, Chauvel, and Halgren (1994), pp. 78–79.

10. Neurobiological evidence for the loss of synaptic connectivity is provided by Bailey and Chen (1989).

11. Linton (1986), p. 63.

12. For Funes, see Borges (1962); the quote is from p. 112. The story of Shereshevskii is told by Luria (1968).

13. For forgetting as an adaptive response to the structure of the environment, see Anderson and Schooler (1991).

Bibliography

Anderson, J. R., & Schooler, L. J. (1991). Reflections of the environment in memory. *Psychological Science, 2,* 396–408.

Bailey, C. H., & Chen, M. (1989). Time course of structural changes at identified sensory neuron synapses during long-term sensitization in aplysia. *Journal of Neuroscience, 9,* 1774–1781.

Bancaud, J., Brunet-Bourgin, F., Chauvel, P., & Halgren, E. (1994). Anatomical origin of déjà vu and vivid 'memories' in human temporal lobe epilepsy. *Brain, 117,* 71–90.

Borges, J. L. (1962). *Ficciones.* New York: Grove.

Cash, W. S., & Moss, A. J. (1972). Optimum recall period for reporting persons injured in motor vehicle accidents (DHEW-HRA No. 72-1050). Washington, DC: U.S. Public Health Service.

Crovitz, H. F., & Schiffman, H. (1974). Frequency of episodic memories as a function of their age. *Bulletin of the Psychonomic Society, 4,* 417–418.

Ebbinghaus, H. (1885/1964). *Memory: A contribution to experimental psychology.* New York: Dover.

Linton, M. (1986). Ways of searching and the contents of memory. In D. C. Rubin (Ed.), *Autobiographical memory* (pp. 50–67). Cambridge: Cambridge University Press.

Loftus, E. F. (1981). Memory and its distortions. In A. G. Kraut (Ed.), *The G. Stanley Hall lecture series* (pp. 123–154). Washington, DC: American Psychological Association.

Loftus, E. F., & Loftus, G. R. (1980). On the permanence of stored information in the human brain. *American Psychologist, 48,* 518–537.

Penfield, W. (1969). Consciousness, memory, and man's conditioned reflexes. In K. Pribram (Ed.), *On the biology of learning.* New York: Harcourt, Brace, and World.

Penfield, W., & Perot, P. (1963). The brain's record of auditory and visual experience. *Brain, 86,* 595–696.

Postman, L. B., & Underwood, J. (1973). Critical issues in interference theory. *Memory and cognition, 1,* 19–40.

Squire, L. R. (1987). *Memory and brain.* New York: Oxford University Press.

QUESTIONS

Reading

1. What do you think Schacter means when he refers to "memory's fragile power" (paragraph 1)?
2. What is an *engram*? (See the note on p. 798 and Schacter's discussion in paragraph 13.) What is the relationship between an *engram* and a *retrieval cue*?
3. Schacter argues that "forgetting . . . is an adaptive feature of our memories" (paragraph 18). What does he mean? Do you agree?

Exploratory Writing

1. Schacter, a scientist, turns to the arts to illustrate his explanation of how memory works. Why does he discuss Mildred Howard's photographic artwork? What do these pieces illustrate that words alone could not?
2. Create a visual diagram of a memory, thinking of it as an *engram*. What are the elements of this memory? What are its sensory elements? What are its emotional and intellectual elements? What retrieval cues help you create this memory? Be creative and find a way to draw the relationship between these elements.

Making Connections

1. The selections in this casebook tend to translate specialized brain research into language, stories, and arguments that will draw the attention and interest of nonspecialists. How successful are they? Which readings are most effective at helping you understand specialized research? Which readings do you find confusing? Why? What techniques are most effective when it comes to helping nonspecialists understand scientific research?

Essay Writing

1. You are the curator of a museum exhibition entitled "Images of Memory." Choose an image (or a series of images) that represent memory, and write the copy that would appear on the wall near the image(s). Explain how the image represents memory. Does the image make an argument about memory? How does it make use of its medium or materials? What tone or mood does it convey? (You may choose an image you already know about, find one online, or use one of Mildred Howard's pieces.)

Appendix: The Research Process

Research can take a variety of forms: browsing through a bookstore or the Internet, interviewing people, scrolling through notes, or using research databases — just to name a few. How much and what kind of research is needed will be determined by the question at the heart of a writer's inquiry and his or her goals for the writing project.

Many of the readings contained in this book — especially the paired readings and casebooks — will provoke you to ask questions whose answers will require some research. In this chapter, we will offer you resources and advice for making the research process — no matter what the project — manageable and productive. You will learn to develop a research question, use the Internet (including search engines, library databases, and newspapers and magazines) effectively, evaluate sources, and organize your ideas and materials.

We will also offer strategies for writing as well as guidelines for documenting your work, such as how to incorporate quotations, paraphrase sources, document sources, and format a Works Cited list.

Developing a Research Question

A strong research question is one that can't be answered off the top of your head, or with a quick look at an encyclopedia or a dictionary. It can be adequately answered in a single assignment or semester. For example, the question, "Where was Thomas Jefferson educated?" is probably too narrow, whereas "What were the many accomplishments of Jefferson's presidency?" is probably too ambitious. A more productive and manageable question lies somewhere in the middle — for example, "How did Thomas Jefferson's education influence some of his most important decisions as president?"

A question such as this contains a blueprint for the kinds of research you'll conduct to answer it. You'll need to know where Jefferson went to school and something about what he learned there. You'll also need to know something about the major decisions Jefferson had to make during his presidency. Biographies can help with both questions, but they may not be enough. You may need to find books and articles by historians about the period when Jefferson was president and some of the major political issues of that time. Then you'll need to choose two or three decisions and learn more about these, again probably from books and articles by historians.

Throughout the process, you'll need to evaluate your topic. Is it too narrow? Is it too broad? You might decide that it makes the most sense to narrow the topic to a single decision Jefferson had to make — perhaps a particularly tough decision. This would make it easier to answer your question, and it would ensure that the question is a significant one, since tough decisions are generally more interesting and important than easy ones. In short, be open to letting your topic and your question evolve as you learn more about it.

Using the Internet Effectively

Whatever your topic or question, a Web search is probably going to be your first step. Of course, the Web contains vast collections of information and data on a multitude of topics. Although some of this information is useful and reliable, some of it is misleading or downright false. While the Internet itself is not organized to help you sort out what's useful and what's misleading, some of the tools you'll use to navigate it are. It's a good idea to be aware of the various tools available and to understand how they'll help you find different kinds of sources.

Research Tools

- **Search engines** like Google or Yahoo! organize information based on how frequently sites on a given subject are visited. So, a search for *"Thomas Jefferson"* will bring up Web sites containing Jefferson's name. Most of these won't help you much if you're researching how Jefferson's education might have influenced an important decision he had to make. If you add a search term and try *"Thomas Jefferson"* + *education,* you'll get closer. (Note that quotation marks around a multiword search term will look for Web sites on which those words appear in the exact order you've indicated.) You might also try *"Thomas Jefferson"* + *presidency* or *"Thomas Jefferson"* + *decisions.* You will get a lot of "hits" with any of these searches, but it will be up to you to sort out what's reliable or valuable and what's not. (See "Evaluating Sources" below.)

- **Google Scholar** is a specialized search engine that searches academic publications. Your hits will most likely be written by professional historians or writers associated with a college or university. You will still get more information than you need, and most of it won't address your research question directly. Therefore, you'll have to use your judgment in choosing sources that will help you understand — and write about — your topic.

- **Library databases** are even more specialized, since most academic disciplines have developed particular databases to serve their needs. Your school's library most likely has subscriptions to several of them. There are also databases, such as Lexis/Nexis, that search articles from newspapers and magazines. Consult your instructor or a librarian about which databases might help you find what you're looking for.

- **Newspapers and magazines** very often have their own Web archive, and it's often a good idea to go straight to it. You can find the publication's title through a conventional search engine — for example, by typing "The Washington Post" or "The Economist" into Google. If the publication has its own Web site, it will usually be one of the first few hits you get. Most of these archives are searchable.

Evaluating Sources

A good source is both useful and reliable. If you're looking for information on Thomas Jefferson's education, an article from an academic journal discussing his ideas on architecture may be reliable but probably not useful. A Web site with a bias — for example, one that uses his educational theories to promote home schooling or, worse, one that cites his ownership of slaves to defend the institution of slavery — is probably not reliable. However, the Web site of Jefferson's alma mater, the College of William and Mary, is likely to contain some interesting information about his time there. Of course, the college is probably using Jefferson's time there to promote itself, so while its Web site may be a valuable source, it won't be enough. A thorough research project would need to compare the information from this type of source against accounts offered in other sources that offer different perspectives.

There are some questions you can ask yourself about any given source that will help you evaluate it:

- What questions is the source asking? How do these questions overlap with my own questions?

- Is the source affiliated with an organization? If so, is the organization reliable? Is it likely to have a bias?

- Is the source authored by an individual? If so, who is it? What is the author's background? What are the author's credentials? Is it likely that the author has a bias?

- If the source is a Web site, what is the suffix? Is it .com, .org, .net, or .edu? What does that suffix tell you about the source?
- What role might the source play in the essay you're developing? Would you quote it directly, to consult it for background information, or to incorporate facts or data that it offers?

These questions will help you form judgments about the sources you find. Ask them — and keep asking them — throughout the process. It's a good idea to keep notes on these questions for each source, either on index cards or in a file on your computer. As your research develops, it's likely that your own interest and point of view regarding certain sources will evolve. The important thing is to ask the questions and use your judgment. If you're not sure about your own judgment, ask someone you trust — a friend or classmate, an instructor, a librarian — to take a look at your source, and discuss some of the questions above.

Organizing Your Ideas and Materials

Once you are confident your research question is right and you've gathered most of your evidence, you might want to sketch your essay. An essay sketch is looser and more flexible than an outline, but it also represents your ideas in more detail. It's a good idea to do this before you write a draft, as it will help you sort out your ideas and serve as a blueprint for writing. You might use the format below to sketch your essay, or modify it to suit your own needs.

The essay sketch that follows is designed to represent the thinking and organizing for the student essay featured at the end of this chapter, "All the News That's Fit to Print?" by Margaret Donaldson (p. 818).

Essay Sketch

What is your topic?

Coverage of environmental issues in the *New York Times*.

What is your research question?

How thorough is the *New York Times*'s coverage of environmental issues during a single week? How representative is this of press coverage of the environment more generally?

What's your best guess about how you'll answer your research question? (The answer will be your preliminary thesis, or hypothesis.)

I propose that examining every page of the *New York Times* for a single week and looking for articles on environmental issues will reveal that the paper pays lip service to environmental issues but does not address the crisis with enough thoroughness or substance. This lack of thoroughness and substance is representative of mainstream press coverage of the environment.

List several pieces of evidence you may use in your essay, including the *names of your sources, relevant citation information (or page numbers)*, and, where appropriate, *notes on the role those sources might play in your essay.* (You may want to include the actual quotations.)

- Four front-page articles printed during the week in question: 1. March 28, 2008: "Harlem to Antarctica for Science, and for Pupils," by Sara Rimer; 2. March 29, 2008: "High Rice Cost Creating Fears of Asia Unrest," by Keith Bradsher; 3. March 31, 2008: "As Jobs Vanish and Prices Rise, Food Stamp Use Nears Record," by Erik Eckholm; 4. April 8, 2008: "$8 Traffic Fee for Manhattan Gets Nowhere," by Nicholas Confessore.
- Felicity Barringer, "Group Seeks E.P.A. Rules on Emissions from Vehicles." Note: This will be helpful in a discussion of articles on state-level responses to environmental problems.
- Diane Cardwell, "Faster, Maybe. Cheaper, No. But Driving Has Its Fans": "Despite the threat of traffic jams, honking horns, and the urban version of road rage, these New Yorkers choose to drive, whether to shave time off their commutes, run their errands with less hassle, or have a few moments to themselves inside mobile oases." Note: This article will be helpful in showing the paper's strengths in covering environmental issues, because it is critical of the choice to commute by car in a city with plenty of mass transit.
- Jennifer Conlin, "Going Green in the Blue Mountains." Note: This article is typical of much of the paper's coverage. Ironically, it encourages extravagance while paying lip service to environmentalism.

Write a draft of your introduction.

For two weeks, I followed the *New York Times,* keeping a record of all the stories either directly or indirectly related to the environment. I had my doubts about finding many articles, since despite its great importance, environmental health frequently does not receive the attention it deserves. As I began collecting stories, I did find articles related to environmental issues, although in most, the environment was not the primary focus. I continued to follow the *Times* after I stopped collecting articles, and noticed that as Earth Day approached, more pieces were published about environmental issues. This trend culminated in the *New York Times Magazine* "Green Issue," released on Earth Day.

The bulk of the magazine focused on innovative green technologies (virtually all of which have yet to break into the mainstream) and possible strategies for reducing human impact on the planet. The magazine was informative and interesting, but it is unfortunate that the environment receives that kind of in-depth news coverage only once a year.

Incorporating Quotations

For most research essays, you will want to quote many of your sources directly. Choose your quotations carefully. Be sure they help you advance your discussion of your research question and that they say something you could not say more effectively in your own words. Also, be sure to integrate the quotations. You want to make sure it's clear why you've included them. Following a few simple guidelines will help you do that:

1. Always introduce quotations with a signal phrase or sentence that gives readers the information they need to understand what the source is.

2. Always include a citation, formatted according to the guidelines of the citation style you're using for the essay. (In this chapter, we use MLA style. See "Documenting Sources" below.)

3. Always follow up a quotation with some discussion or analysis that makes it clear to readers how the quotation relates to the discussion at hand.

Paraphrasing Sources

It sometimes makes more sense to paraphrase a source rather than to quote it directly. In fact, in some academic fields, this is very common. In the social sciences, for example, presenting a piece of information or data from a source is often more important than quoting direct language (whereas in the humanities, it's often crucial to quote the language of a source). Paraphrasing can also help you make a complex or difficult source more accessible to readers.

When you paraphrase, it's important that you represent your source accurately.

- Be sure you read and reread it until you are confident of its meaning.

- Convey that meaning in your own words. Be sure to cite the source, just as you would if you were quoting it.

- Introduce your source and offer some discussion or analysis that links it to the general project of your essay — again, just as you would do when quoting a source directly.

Documenting Sources

Writers document their sources to let readers know where they found their information. This not only reassures readers that the source is trustworthy but also gives them the opportunity to find that source for themselves if it sparks their interest. You will almost surely be asked to use a variety of citation "styles" in the various courses that you take in college. The most common styles include those promoted by the Modern Language Association (MLA), the American Psychological Association (APA), and *The Chicago Manual of Style* (Chicago). The guidelines we offer here are all based on MLA style. Be sure to check with your professors about what style they prefer. (It's a good idea to own a good writing manual or handbook that includes detailed information about all three of the major documentation styles.)

Parenthetical Citations

A *parenthetical citation* is just what it sounds like: a citation, in parentheses, that tells readers a little about your source. If you introduce your source with a signal phrase that includes the author's name, then in most cases all you need in parentheses is a page number. For example:

> Pollan writes, "For us to wait for legislation or technology to solve the problem of how we're living our lives suggests we're not really serious about changing — something our politicians can't fail to notice. They will not move until we do" (19).

If the example above did not include the author's name in the signal phrase, then it would require his name in the citation. For example:

> An argument can be made that "for us to wait for legislation or technology to solve the problem of how we're living our lives suggests we're not really serious about changing — something our politicians can't fail to notice. They will not move until we do" (Pollan 19).

In short, most parenthetical citations include either just a page number or an author's last name and a page number. That's because a parenthetical citation will lead readers to your Works Cited list, at the end of your essay. The goal is to provide the information readers will need to locate the source there, with as little fuss as possible. With that in mind, keep your parenthetical citations simple, so that they don't interrupt the flow of your writing. No commas or other punctuation is necessary within the parentheses.

Other Common Citations

You're likely to use some of the following common forms of citation in writing research papers.

Citing a Work by Two Authors

If we hope to understand the economy, "we must pay attention to the thought patterns that animate people's ideas and feelings" (Akerlof and Shiller 1).

Citing a Work with an Unknown Author

A recent opinion article in the *New York Times* makes the argument that wealthy nations of the world must work together to solve the current economic crisis ("The Economic Summit" A28).

Citing an Indirect Source   If you draw on a statement made by one author that is quoted in the work of another author, be sure to indicate this by including the abbreviation *qtd. in* (for "quoted in"). For example:

According to psychoanalyst and Holocaust researcher Dori Laub, "Bearing witness to a trauma is . . . a process that includes the listener" (qtd. in Hornstein 167).

Citing an Electronic Source   In many cases, online sources don't include page numbers of any kind. In this case, just include the name(s) of the author(s). For example:

According to one critic, "The more that the earth's sinks are stressed, the harder it is to find ways of disposing of pollution" (Buell).

Readers will see that this is an online source when they go to your Works Cited list.

Sometimes online sources will include paragraph, section, or screen numbers. In cases such as this, use the abbreviation *par.*, the abbreviation *sec.*, or the full word *screen*, followed by the appropriate number. If the citation includes the name of the author, include a comma after it (and before the abbreviation). For example:

One author makes the point that "As a child, Blake viewed the world in the light of what Wordsworth, in his 'Ode: Intimations of Immortality,' would later call a 'visionary gleam'" (Vulte, sec. 1).

Citing a Long Quotation from a Source   There are some special formatting details to keep in mind when you quote more than three lines from a source. A quotation of four or more lines should be "blocked" — meaning it should start on a new line and be indented ten spaces. The parenthetical citation for a blocked quotation should come after the end punctuation. For example:

> Literary critic James Wood ends his recent and influential book *How Fiction Works* with the following claim:
>
> > Realism, seen broadly as truthfulness to the way things are, cannot be mere verisimilitude, cannot be mere lifelikeness, or lifesameness, but what I must call lifeness: life on the page, life brought to different life by the highest artistry. And it cannot be a genre; instead, it makes other forms of fictions feel like genres. For realism of this kind — lifeness — is the origin. (247)

Formatting a Works Cited List

Your Works Cited list will include all the works you cite in your essay. Use the following guidelines to be sure you format your list accurately:

- Begin on a new page, after the last page of your essay; number the Works Cited page as the next page of your essay.
- Do not number the entries in your Works Cited list.
- Center your heading, **Works Cited**, one inch from the top of the page; you may use bold type for the heading, but don't underline it or use quotation marks.
- Double-space the list.
- List entries alphabetically, according to author's last name. If a source does not list an author, alphabetize it according to the first major word of the title.

The following Works Cited entries give examples of most sources you will need to cite. Follow their formats exactly, according to the kind of source you are citing.

Books

Books by One Author

List the author, last name first. Italicize the title. Include the city of publication, the publisher's name, and the date of publication. (Use the abbreviation "UP" for "University Press," as in *Princeton UP* or *U. California P.*)

> Wood, Michael. *How Fiction Works*. New York: Farrar, Straus and Giroux, 2008. Print.

Books by Two or Three Authors

List authors in the order on which they appear on the title page of the book. List second and third authors with first names first.

> Akerlof, George, and Robert J. Shiller. *Animal Spirits: How Human Psychology Drives the Economy, and Why It Matters for Global Capitalism*. Princeton: Princeton UP, 2009. Print.

Books by More Than Three Authors

List only the first author, followed by a comma and the abbreviation *et al.* (meaning "and others").

> Adritti, Rita, et al. *Test Tube Women*. London: Pandora, 1984. Print.

Two or More Books by the Same Author

List two or more books by the same author in alphabetical order, according to title. For each entry after the first, use three hyphens, followed by a period, instead of the author's name.

> Pollan, Michael. *The Botany of Desire: A Plant's-Eye View of the World*. New York: Random House, 2002. Print.
>
> ---. *In Defense of Food: An Eater's Manifesto*. New York: Penguin, 2008. Print.
>
> ---. *The Omnivore's Dilemma: A Natural History of Four Meals*. New York: Penguin, 2006. Print.

Edited Book

> Fleck, Ludwig. *Genesis and Development of a Scientific Fact*. Ed. Thaddeus J. Trenn and Robert K. Merton. Chicago: U. Chicago Press, 1979. Print.

Revised Edition

> Comley, Nancy, et al. *Fields of Reading: Motives for Writing*. 9th ed. New York and Boston: Bedford/St. Martin's, 2010. Print.

Anthology

> Andrew Carroll, ed. *Operation Homecoming: Iraq, Afghanistan, and the Home Front, in the Words of U.S. Troops and Their Families*. New York: Random House, 2006. Print.

Work in an Anthology

> McIntyre, Vestal. "Mom-Voice." *Boys to Men: Gay Men Write about Growing Up.* Ed. Ted Gideonse and Rob Williams. New York: Da Capo Press, 2006. 223-242. Print.

More Than One Work in the Same Anthology

List each essay separately with a cross-reference to the entire anthology.

> Gideonse, Ted, and Rob Williams. *Boys to Men: Gay Men Write about Growing Up.* New York: Da Capo Press, 2006. Print.

> McIntyre, Vestal. "Mom-Voice." Gideonse and Williams 223-242. Print.

> Bahr, David. "No Matter What Happens." Gideonse and Williams 69-88. Print.

Periodicals

JOURNALS

A journal is a periodical aimed at a very specific audience (often experts in a field — for example, literary history, artificial intelligence, or cattle farming). Because of this, journals often contain specialized language that can be difficult to read, but since they represent the latest research in a particular field, they're important for many research projects.

Article in a Journal with Continuous Pagination throughout an Annual Volume

> Olutayo, A. O., and O. Akanle. "Fast Food in Ibadan: An Emerging Consumption Pattern." *Africa: The Journal of the International African Institute* 79 (2009): 207-227. Print.

Article in a Journal with Separate Pagination in Each Issue

> Beldecos, A., et al. "The Importance of Feminist Critique for Contemporary Cell Biology." *Hypatia* 3 (Spring 1988): 61-76. Print.

MAGAZINES

Because magazines are usually designed for a general audience, they are generally easier to read than journals. When it comes to a magazine article, it's a good idea to evaluate your source by finding out what you can about the magazine's reputation and the background of the article's author.

Article in a Monthly or Bimonthly Magazine

A magazine article will often not appear in consecutive pages, but may begin on page 48, skip to page 73, and continue on page 75. In cases like this, include the number of the first page, followed by a plus sign.

> Ruch, Sarah. "The Power of Greens." *Organic Gardening* Feb./Mar. 2009: 64+. Print.

Article in a Weekly Magazine (Signed or Unsigned)

> Max, D. T. "The Unfinished: David Foster Wallace's Project." *New Yorker* 9 Mar.
> 2009: 48+. Print.
>
> "Obama Abroad." *The Nation* 2 Apr. 2009: 3. Print.

Article in a Newspaper

> Gumbrecht, Jamie. "Global Peace Walk Ends with a Bang." *Atlanta Journal-
> Constitution* 6 Apr. 2009: 1B. Print.

Internet Sources

Complete source information is sometimes tricky to find online. When citing Internet sources, include whatever information you can find: the title of the Web site (italicized), the date of publication (if available), the date you accessed the source, the author (if there is one), the Web site's host organization, and so on. Note that some of the following examples include only date of access; in these cases, publication dates were not available. Also, the MLA considers articles from print periodicals made available online (often on the publication's own Web site) to be nonperiodical publications cited only on the Web. (See the below example from the *Atlantic*.)

Nonperiodical Publication Cited Only on the Web

> Shenk, Joshua Wolf. "What Makes Us Happy?" *The Atlantic.com*. Atlantic Monthly
> Group, June 2009. Web. 20 July 2009.

Nonperiodical Publication on the Web Cited with a Print Publication Date

> James, William. *The Varieties of Religious Experience: A Study in Human Nature*.
> New York: Longman, Green, and Co., 1911. *Google Book Search*. Web. 20 May
> 2009.

A Work on the Web with Publication Data for Another Medium Besides Print

> *What to Do on a Date*. Dir. Ted Pesha. Coronet Instructional Films, 1950. *Internet
> Archive*. Web. 20 May 2009.

Scholarly Journal

> Baptiste, Ian E. "Wages of Niceness: The Folly and Futility of Educators Who
> Strive to *Not* Impose." *New Horizons in Adult Education and Human Resource*
> *Development* 22.2 (2008): 6-28. Web. 20 May 2009.

A Periodical Publication in an Online Database

> Velleman, J. David. "The Genesis of Shame." *Philosophy and Public Affairs* 30
> (2001): 27-52. *JSTOR*. Web. 20 May 2009.

Material Accessed on a CD-ROM, DVD, Diskette, or Tape

> "Consciousness." *The Oxford English Dictionary*. 2nd ed. New York: Oxford UP,
> 2005. CD-ROM.

E-mail

> Hann, Joelle. "Re: Copyediting." Message to Jason Tougaw. 24 Mar. 2009. E-mail.

Other Nonprint Sources

Television or Radio Program

> "DIY Universe." *Radiolab*. WNYC. 26 March 2009. Radio.

Videotape, Movie, Record, or Slide Program

> *Persepolis*. Dir. Marjane Satrapi and Vincent Paronnaud. Sony Pictures, 2007. DVD.

Sample Student Research Paper (in MLA Style)

The following student essay, by Margaret Donaldson, responds to an assignment that asked students to track the publication of articles in a single newspaper (in this case, the *New York Times*) on a single issue and report on their findings. Because of the requirements of the assignment, Donaldson's sources are almost all articles from the newspaper (with the exception of the one book she cites). Many research essays will focus on a greater variety of sources, but that will depend on the questions at hand and what kinds of sources help answer these questions. In addition, while Donaldson's instructor allowed her to use personal opinion in her essay, other instructors do not. Check with your instructor — and read the assignment carefully — if you're not sure.

Donaldson 1

Margaret Donaldson
English 101
Professor Greene
May 2008

All the News That's Fit to Print?

The writer begins with a hook and then establishes a motive: to explain that "environmental health" is often at the root of media stories about environmental catastrophe. She then presents the research required to demonstrate this.

The media, more often than not, bear bad news about the environment. Headlines like, "Hermaphrodite Frogs Found in Suburban Ponds" or "High Rice Cost Creating Fears of Asia Unrest" are commonplace in today's press. Tragic, discouraging reports have become so standard that most readers simply brush them off as just another catastrophic headline. It is not always mentioned, but environmental health is usually at the root of these disastrous stories. For two weeks, I followed the *New York Times,* keeping a record of all the stories either directly or indirectly related to the environment. At first, I had my doubts about finding many articles, since despite its great importance, environmental health frequently does not receive the attention it deserves. As I began collecting stories, I did find articles related to environmental issues, although in most, the environment was not the primary focus. I continued to follow the *Times* after I stopped collecting articles, and noticed that as Earth Day approached, more pieces were about environmental issues. This trend culminated in the *New York Times Magazine* "Green Issue," released on Earth Day. The bulk of the magazine focused on innovative green technologies (virtually all of which have yet to break into the mainstream) and possible strategies for reducing human impact on the planet. The magazine was informative and interesting, but it is unfortunate that the environment receives that kind of in-depth news coverage only once a year.

The writer describes her research process. This is not always necessary — or pertinent — but here it clarifies how and why she found the sources under discussion.

Thesis statement.

Environmental issues received minimal front-page coverage: the four stories I found there were connected to environmental matters, but none spotlighted the environment as the main issue. The National and Business sections had the

Donaldson 2

most reports linked to the environment, with nineteen articles
and three briefings each. Most of these articles were concerned
with oil, which is not surprising considering the major role oil
plays in the formulation of American policy. The oil reports
highlighted rising costs, oil spills, and the search for new oil
reserves, but there were none about alternative fuels or efforts
made to alleviate our national addiction to oil. At the same
time, these reports all had to do with the negative aspects of
oil addiction. Many might criticize the *Times* for its lack of
alternative fuels coverage, focusing more on issues related to
oil. Nevertheless, I do not think it is a bad thing to give
considerable attention to all the problems created by our
reliance on oil; hopefully, it will lead readers to the conclusion
that we must reduce overall fuel consumption.

The writer introduces a quotation with a signal phrase, including the author and title of the article she quotes.

For example, in a Business section article titled, "Fuel
Costs Just Part of Airlines' List of Woes," Jeff Bailey wrote,
"Record-high fuel prices and the industry's fragile finances
have led to a new round of bankruptcies among smaller
carriers" (C1). Bailey went on to explain that as airlines

The writer uses a parenthetical citation, announcing the author's name in the signal phrase. She includes the page number in parentheses.

shrink, demand stays high, and "flights are growing more
crowded and unpleasant" (C1). In my opinion, articles like this
one imply to readers that their lifestyles cannot be maintained
without a cheap oil supply. It leads me to the conclusion that
we must decide whether to continue relying on oil—the

*The writer offers a three-part analysis:
1. The newspaper offers adequate coverage of "environmental degradation";
2. However, that coverage doesn't focus enough on the root of the problems; and
3. Focusing on the root of the problems might motivate people to help solve them.*

availability of which causes so many problems and promises to
create more—or transition to alternative fuels. Moreover,
because our current lifestyles cannot be sustained without
cheap oil, a change of lifestyle is in order. I think the *Times*,
particularly in the National and Business sections, gave
adequate coverage to the effects of environmental
degradation, like high prices and resource shortages.
Unfortunately, it rarely made it clear that our inattentiveness
to the environment is one of the root causes of those
problems. More attention might create more motivation to
preserve the few resources that are left.

The writer uses transitional language to move from a discussion of one type of source to another.

While most of the reports I found were related to environmental degradation, a few were about steps being taken to restore environmental health. For example, William Yardley wrote an article titled, "For Seattle Shoppers, Paper or Plastic Could Come with a 'Green Fee.'" Seattle Mayor Greg Nickels is hoping this proposal would "reduce waste, reduce production of paper and plastic, and encourage still more people here to be faithful to their bumper-sticker gospel: 'Think Globally, Act Locally'" (A10). Another environmental effort was reported in Felicity Barringer's "Group Seeks E.P.A. Rules on Emissions from Vehicles." Barringer wrote of "a coalition of states, cities, and environmental groups . . . seeking to force the Environmental Protection Agency to regulate emissions of heat-trapping gases from new cars and trucks or show that such regulation is unnecessary" (A16). Both these articles were printed in the National section. I think it is excellent that states are taking environmental matters into their own hands, given the

The writer analyzes her source by comparing it to other articles that focus on similar problems and issues.

lethargic attitude of the federal government. Most of the articles that focused on oil were either about corporations or the federal government. Reports on efforts to protect the environment were more concerned with the roles played by individual states. States feel the effects of environmental degradation more quickly than the federal government and are therefore more apt to make changes that benefit their communities. That states are willing to bypass the federal government to attempt environmental protection reform is a clear indicator that the national government is not fulfilling its duties.

The writer uses transitional language.

In addition to providing commentary on the degradation of the environment and efforts to conserve, the *Times* also did stories about excessive consumption by Americans. Each week, a special Section called "Escapes" includes a column titled, "Your Second Home." These weekly stories range in topic from tips on buying a second home to forgoing the vacation home

Donaldson 4

and purchasing a recreational vehicle. The article "A New View Every Day" by Steve Bailey claims, "If you can live with the price of fuel, a well-maintained RV can keep you comfortable, whether you're in Death Valley, the Everglades, or a Wal-Mart parking lot" (F2). Personally, I think it is ridiculous to promote the use of an RV or the purchase of a second home when articles just pages earlier detail the social and economic turmoil created by industry's addiction to oil. The headline news, geared more toward the international community, regularly describes food crises and natural disasters around the world. Features like "Your Second Home" provide Americans with opportunities to escape the hardships of the real world, supporting the disproportionate standard of living between global regions.

The writer draws attention to her own point of view — and even her bias. Depending on the assignment, this can be an effective strategy. Some college assignments, however, may discourage writers from doing this. Check with your instructor.

"Faster, Maybe. Cheaper, No. But Driving Has Its Fans" by Diane Cardwell also features excess consumption. The story was on the first page of the New York Report section, next to three large photographs of New Yorkers and their comfortable sedans. I liked this article, as opposed to "Your Second Home," because while it emphasized the popularity of automobiles, Cardwell drew more attention to the utter ridiculousness of commuting in a car while living in New York City, a place with ample access to mass transit. Cardwell writes, "Despite the threat of traffic jams, honking horns, and the urban version of road rage, these New Yorkers choose to drive, whether to shave time off their commutes, run their errands with less hassle, or have a few moments to themselves inside mobile oases" (B1). The story was quite critical of the automobile culture, citing the hassles of driving in New York, especially high parking fees and congestion. Nevertheless, all the interviewees refused to consider life without their cars. Eugene Yates of the Bronx, who lives two blocks away from a train station, says, "I hate standing up when I get in the train station. Then you got to wait on the train, then the train is late, then it's this, then it's

The writer refers to the photos that accompanied the newspaper article she discusses.

Donaldson 5

The writer makes a strong and emotional claim — almost in the style of an editorial. The strategy is effective because she has established her essay as an opinion piece substantiated by evidence, and the claim is clearly linked to that evidence.

that. I can't stand the hassle" (B1). I am ashamed to hear these words from a fellow American. The real hassle will come when Manhattan begins flooding as a direct result of climate change.

The writer presents a contrasting point.

In contrast, efforts by New York to limit automobile congestion in the city received significant attention during the two weeks I collected articles. This issue was covered on the front page, but the headline was disappointing: "$8 Traffic Fee for Manhattan Gets Nowhere" (Confessore A1). I found the best reports about the shot-down traffic fee proposal in the editorial section of the newspaper. I particularly enjoyed reading this section because it is the area of the paper where journalists are allowed to not only express opinions, but also offer ideas for solutions. For example, after the congestion pricing proposal lost, contributor Gene Russianoff suggested conducting a "detailed environmental review of all options for reducing traffic" (A25), including driving-day restrictions and mandated car pooling. The same day, contributor Owen D. Gutfreund proposed "adjusting tolls to take into account the vehicle's cost and fuel efficiency and the wear and tear on roads that different cars cause" (A25). Throughout the paper, the *Times*

The writer notes how one type of source — articles from the Opinion section — is different from the others. It focuses more intently on environmental problems.

did not give the environment much space. But in the Opinion section, it came up repeatedly, in editorials, op-eds, and letters; there was even a cartoon about nuclear power. People are concerned about the environment, and the *Times* Opinion contributors are writing about it. Unfortunately, calls for change do not seem to be getting anywhere. I hope the time comes soon when we can stop talking about change and actually start working toward it. Nevertheless, discussion is obviously necessary, and I felt the Opinion section did a decent job of including commentary on environmental issues.

The writer considers a new source — the weekly features sections.

Articles pertaining to "green culture," which probably appealed more to the average reader than the usual depressing headlines, could be found in the various weekly features

Donaldson 6

sections. One such article, titled, "Latest College Reading Lists: Menus with Pho and Lobster," by Michael S. Sanders, discussed the trend of serving higher-quality, healthier, more sustainably grown food in college dining halls. In a related story called "Good News About Rising Food Prices," journalist Kim Severson wrote, "[i]f American staples like soda, fast-food hamburgers, and frozen dinners don't seem like such a bargain anymore, the American eating public might turn its attention to ingredients like local fruits and vegetables, and milk and meat from animals that eat grass" (F1) as the price of cash crops like corn and soy rises. Both these stories were published in the Dining In special insert.

Similarly, the special Travel section insert featured the article "Going Green in the Blue Mountains" by Jennifer Conlin. Conlin writes, "Lying under a thick patchwork quilt, breathing in the fresh mountain air, I felt like a true eco-traveler as I listened reverently to a morning medley of nature streaming through my window: the chirping of a cockatoo, the scuffle of a passing lizard, the rustling of leaves . . ." (1). Articles like this one, as well as the two food features mentioned above, appeal to the indulgent desires of many upper-middle and upper-class citizens. They advocate extravagance, but only as long as it is "green." On the other hand, I do not find anything inherently wrong with these articles; at least they are trying to provoke some sort of environmental consciousness in even the most self-indulgent readers.

Special inserts also made room for advances in environmental technology. A Tech Innovation insert boasted four environmental articles, all explaining new green technologies. I found "A Cleaner, Leaner Jet Age Has Arrived" by Matthew L. Wald to be the most interesting. According to Wald, "the industry is scrambling to build greener airplanes — to save weight and improve engine efficiency, with an eye toward reducing operating costs and emissions" (2). It is

Donaldson 7

comforting to know that efforts are being made to design technologies that will enable people to live in a more sustainable way, and it is also encouraging to see people get credit in reputable publications like the *New York Times* for working toward a more sustainable future.

After discussing several pieces of research, the writer draws a conclusion.

Nonetheless, I was somewhat unimpressed with the overall coverage given to the environment. The National and Business sections did contain reports related to environmental issues, but few discussed environmental issues like global warming or sustainable options in great detail. Granted, there were quite a few editorials written by contributors in the Opinion section, and feature stories were periodically published in special inserts. But the environment is crucial to our future, and perhaps we should pay regular — not periodical — attention to it. Moreover, excepting the one-time Tech Innovation insert, few articles explored options for reducing environmental degradation.

That is where the *New York Times Magazine* "Green Issue" stepped in. Its pages had many examples of ways we could reduce our carbon footprint. Its brief articles covered topics that ranged from green-jobs programs to the slow food movement to skyscrapers that double as gardens. These short articles were extremely interesting and provided hope for the future. However, it eventually becomes monotonous to keep discussing the future, when we face real climate change issues now. The short articles focused primarily on new technologies, while the "Not-So-Free Ride" piece by Stephen J. Dubner and Steven D. Levitt proposed regulation in the form of taxes at the tolls and the pump, as well as insurance programs that offer discounts for driving less. This article reminded me of George Monbiot's book *Heat: How to Stop the Planet Burning*. Monbiot writes, "Manmade global warming cannot be restrained unless we persuade the government to force us to change the way we

The writer paraphrases a source.

The writer brings in a new kind of source — a book — to contextualize her discussion of the newspaper's coverage of environmental problems.

Donaldson 8

live" (xv). I think Monbiot makes a valid point, but I also believe we will have a very hard time persuading the government to force us to change our lifestyles when we show no serious desire to change.

The writer offers an evaluation of her source when she introduces it.

If no one else is changing, why should I? Michael Pollan does an excellent job in his "Why Bother?" article answering this question, which everyone seems to be asking these days. Pollan writes, "For us to wait for legislation or technology to solve the problem of how we're living our lives suggests we're not really serious about changing—something our politicians can't fail to notice. They will not move until we do" (19). If everyone waits for everyone else to take action, nothing will get done. In his article, Pollan brings up the significance of individual action, a heavily debated issue. Throughout this past semester, I have said in my reaction papers that government legislation is the key to reversing climate change and establishing a more sustainable world; that we must do much more than change our lightbulbs, as Al Gore suggested in his film, *An Inconvenient Truth*. But now I have come to the realization that there is no key to reversing climate change, which Pollan makes clear in his article. It is going to take more than regulation, and it is going to take more than technology. That is why working toward a more sustainable world is so daunting, and why virtually no one, including governments, corporations, and individuals, has truly taken significant steps toward solving this problem. We must stop speculating about global warming while putting off taking significant action against it. There are no instant solutions, but we can make great strides by increasing governmental environmental regulation and putting more sustainable technologies that we already have into practice. That said, individual action is essential, because without individual action, there is no way legislative or technological advances can be made.

The writer contextualizes her discussion within the course for which she writes the essay. This may not always be appropriate, but in this case it is consistent with her assignment.

Donaldson 9

At first, I was irritated that very few articles in the *New York Times* exclusively focused on environmental issues. The motto of the *Times* is "all the news that's fit to print." One would assume that environmental news should not only be fit to print, but receive considerable attention, as a healthy planet is crucial to human existence. The *Times* does a good job reporting the devastating effects of environmental degradation, like food shortages and natural disasters. But the bad news is already incorporated into our daily lives, while the good news is still just a feature, fit for a special insert or a weekly magazine, but not for the front page. The media may bear bad news, but if we want positive coverage, we need to create some positive news. There will not be environmental change until we actually implement the changes suggested in special features. If living "green" were a common lifestyle, there would be no need for a "Green Issue." When we make sustainable living and environmental preservation a priority, then it will cease to be a special feature, becoming a front-page headline and a way of life.

Donaldson 10

Works Cited

Bailey, Jeff. "Fuel Costs Just Part of Airlines' List of Woes." *New York Times* 10 Apr. 2008, late ed.: C1+. Print.

Bailey, Steve. "A New View Every Day." *New York Times* 11 Apr. 2008, late ed.: F2. Print.

Barringer, Felicity. "Group Seeks E.P.A. Rules on Emissions from Vehicles." *New York Times* 3 Apr. 2008, late ed.: A16. Print.

- - -. "Hermaphrodite Frogs Found in Suburban Ponds." *New York Times* 8 Apr. 2008, late ed.: F2+. Print.

Bradsher, Keith. "High Rice Cost Creating Fears of Asia Unrest." *New York Times* 29 Mar. 2008, late ed.: A1+. Print.

Cardwell, Diane. "Faster, Maybe. Cheaper, No. But Driving Has Its Fans." *New York Times* 31 Mar. 2008, late ed.: B1+. Print.

Confessore, Nicholas. "$8 Traffic Fee for Manhattan Gets Nowhere." *New York Times* 8 Apr. 2008, late ed.: A1+. Print.

Conlin, Jennifer. "Going Green in the Blue Mountains." *New York Times* 6 Apr. 2008, late ed., Travel sec.: 1+. Print.

Dubner, Stephen J., and Steven D. Levitt. "Not-So-Free Ride." *New York Times Magazine* 20 Apr. 2008, late ed.: 40+. Print.

Gore, Al, narrator. *An Inconvenient Truth*. Dir. Davis Guggenheim. Lawrence Bender Productions, 2006. Film.

Gutfreund, Owen D. "Pick on the Big Guys." Editorial. *New York Times* 9 Apr. 2008, late ed.: A25. Print.

Monbiot, George. *Heat: How to Stop the Planet Burning*. Cambridge: South End Press, 2007. Print.

Pollan, Michael. "Why Bother?" *New York Times Magazine* 20 Apr. 2008, late ed.: 19+. Print.

Redniss, Laura. Cartoon. *New York Times* 28 Mar. 2008, late ed.: A23. Print.

Russianoff, Gene. "Take Alternate Route." Editorial. *New York Times* 9 Apr. 2008, late ed.: A25. Print.

Sanders, Michael S. "Latest College Reading Lists: Menus with
    Pho and Lobster." *New York Times* 9 Apr. 2008, late ed.:
    F1+. Print.

Severson, Kim. "Good News about Rising Food Prices." *New York
    Times* 2 Apr. 2008, late ed.: F1+. Print.

Wald, Matthew L. "A Cleaner, Leaner Jet Age Has Arrived." *New
    York Times* 9 Apr. 2008, late ed.: Technology sec.: 2. Print.

Yardley, William. "For Seattle Shoppers, Paper or Plastic Could
    Come with a 'Green Fee.'" *New York Times* 5 Apr. 2008,
    late ed.: A10. Print.

Acknowledgments

Diane Ackerman. "Why Leaves Turn Color in the Fall." From *A Natural History of the Senses.* Copyright © 1990 by Diane Ackerman. Reprinted with permission of Random House, Inc.

Gloria Anzaldúa. "How to Tame a Wild Tongue." From *Borderlands/La Frontera: The New Mestiza.* Copyright © 1987, 1999 by Gloria Anzaldúa. Reprinted with permission of Aunt Lute Books.

James Baldwin. "If Black English Isn't a Language, Then Tell Me, What Is?" Originally published in *The New York Times*, July 29, 1979. Collected in *The Price of the Ticket*, published by St. Martin's Press. Copyright © 1979 by James Baldwin. Reprinted by arrangement with the James Baldwin Estate.

Emily Bazelon. "The Next Kind of Integration." From *The New York Times Magazine*, July 20, 2008. Copyright © 2008 The New York Times. All rights reserved. Used by permission and protected by the Copyright Laws of the United States. The printing, copying, redistribution, or retransmission of the Material without express written permission is prohibited.

John Berger. "Hiroshima." From *The Sense of Sight.* Copyright © 1985 by John Berger. Reprinted with the permission of Pantheon Books, a division of Random House, Inc. "Ways of Seeing." From *Ways of Seeing*, by John Berger. Copyright © 1972 by John Berger. Used by permission of Viking Penguin, a division of Penguin Books Group.

Bruno Bettelheim. "Joey: A 'Mechanical Boy.'" From *Scientific American* 200 (1959). Copyright © 1979 by Scientific American. All rights reserved.

Paul Bloom. "Is God an Accident?" From *The Atlantic Online*, December 2005. Reprinted with permission of *The Atlantic.*

Christina Boufis. "Teaching Literature at the County Jail." From *The Common Review* 1, no. 1. Copyright © 2001 by Christina Boufis. Used with permission of the author.

Jan Harold Brunvand. "Urban Legends: 'The Boyfriend's Death.'" From *The Vanishing Hitchhiker: American Urban Legends and Their Meanings.* Copyright © 1981 by Jan Harold Brunvand. Reprinted with permission from W.W. Norton & Company, Inc.

Nicholas Carr. "Is Google Making Us Stupid?" From *The Atlantic*, July/August 2008. Copyright © 2008 by Nicholas Carr. Used with permission of the author.

Rita Carter. "A Stream of Illusion." From *Exploring Consciousness.* Copyright © 2002 by Rita Carter. Used with permission of the University of California Press.

Amanda Coyne. "The Long Good-bye: Mother's Day in Federal Prison." From *Harper's Magazine*, May 1997. Copyright © 1997 by Amanda Coyne. Reprinted with permission of the author.

Junot Díaz. "Homecoming, with Turtle." Originally published in *The New Yorker*, June 14 & 21, 2004. Used with permission of Junot Díaz and Aragi, Inc.

Joan Didion. "On Keeping a Notebook." From *Slouching Toward Bethlehem.* Copyright © 1966, 1968 by Joan Didion. Used with permission of Farrar, Straus & Giroux, LLC.

Barbara Ehrenreich. "Nickel and Dimed: On (Not) Getting By in America." Excerpt from *Nickel and Dimed: On (Not) Getting By in America.* Copyright © 1999 by Barbara Ehrenreich. Used with permission of Henry Holt and Company, LLC.

Atul Gawande. "The Checklist." Originally published in *The New Yorker*, December 10, 2007. Used with permission of the author.

Guillermo Gómez-Peña. "The Virtual Barrio @ the Other Frontier." From *Clicking In: Hot Links to a Digital Culture*, edited by Lynn Hershman Leeson. Copyright © 1996. Reprinted with permission of Guillermo Gómez-Peña (www.pochanostra.com).

Anthony Grafton. "Future Reading: Digitization and Its Discontents." From *The New Yorker*, November 5, 2007. Reprinted with permission of the author.

Temple Grandin. "Thinking in Pictures: Autism and Visual Thought." From *Thinking in Pictures.* Copyright © 1995, 2006 by Temple Grandin. Used with permission of Doubleday, a division of Random House, Inc.

Art Credits

Page 317: Painting by Kazuhiro Ishizu. From *Unforgettable Fire: Pictures Drawn by Atomic Bomb Survivors*. Hiroshima Peace Memorial Museum. General Research Division, The New York Public Library, Astor, Lenox and Tilden Foundations.

Page 318: Painting by Sawami Katagiri. From *Unforgettable Fire: Pictures Drawn by Atomic Bomb Survivors*. Hiroshima Peace Memorial Museum. General Research Division, The New York Public Library, Astor, Lenox and Tilden Foundations.

Pages 376, 379, 380, 381: Eight "Joey" drawings from *The Empty Fortress*, by Bruno Bettelheim. Used by permission of Raines & Raines, author's representatives.

Page 388: Asteroid 243 Ida (NASA/NSSDC).

Pages 509, 512: Courtesy Wikipedia Foundation.

Page 637: "Map of the United States: Per Pupil Spending in Public Elementary and Secondary Schools by County": U.S. Census Bureau, National Center for Educational Statistics. Ryan Morris/*The Atlantic.*

Page 667: From *The Great Dialogues of Plato*, by Plato, translated by W. H. D. Rouse, copyright © 1956, renewed © 1984 by J. C. G. Rouse. Used by permission of Dutton Signet, a division of Penguin Group (USA), Inc.

Page 673: Courtesy Derby University Enterprises, Derby, UK.

Page 674: Figure illustrating inattentional blindness provided by Daniel Simons. Simons, D. J., & Chabris, C. F. (1999). "Gorillas in Our Midst: Sustained Inattentional Blindness for Dynamic Events." *Perception*, 28, 1059–74.

Page 675: Courtesy Ron Rensink, Departments of Psychology and Computer Science, University of British Columbia.

Page 711: René Magritte, *The Key of Dreams* © 2010 C. Herscovici, London/Artists Rights Society (ARS), New York.

Pages 712, 715, 716, 717, 719, 720 (top), 727 (bottom), 728, 729: From *Ways of Seeing*, by John Berger, copyright © 1972 by John Berger. Photos and illustrations © BBC Publications 2010. All Rights Reserved.

Page 714: Frans Hals, "Regents of the Old Men's Alms House" and "Regentesses of the Old Men's Alms House." Reprinted by permission of Frans Halsmuseum.

Page 718: Pablo Picasso, *Still Life with Wicker Chair* © 2010 Estate of Pablo Picasso/Artists Rights Society (ARS), New York.

Pages 720, 721: Leonardo da Vinci, *Virgin of the Rocks*. Reproduced by courtesy of the Trustees, The National Gallery, London/Art Resource, NY.

Page 721: Leonardo da Vinci, *Virgin of the Rocks*, c. 1483. Louvre Museum, Paris. Photo credit: Scala/Art Resource, NY.

Page 722: Leonardo da Vinci, *The Virgin and Child with St. Anne and St. John the Baptist.* Reproduced by courtesy of the Trustees, The National Gallery, London/Art Resource, NY.

Page 724: Sandro Botticelli, *Venus and Mars*, c. 1485. © National Gallery, London/Art Resource, NY.

Pages 725, 726: Pieter Brueghel the Elder, *Jesus Carrying the Cross, or Procession to Calvary*, 1564. Photo Credit: Erich Lessing/Art Resource, NY.

Pages 726, 727: Vincent van Gogh, *Wheatfield with Crows*. Van Gogh Museum Foundation, Amsterdam, The Netherlands, Art Resource, NY.

Page 730: Jan Vermeer, *The Kitchenmaid* (or *Woman Poring Milk*). Rijkmuseum, Amsterdam, The Netherlands, Art Resource, NY.

Pages 744, 745: From *The Three-Pound Enigma: The Human Brain and the Quest to Unlock Its Mysteries* © 2006 Shannon Moffett. Used by permission of the author. All rights reserved.

Pages 753, 754, 755, 756, 758, 759: From *My Stroke of Insight: A Brain Scientist's Personal Journey.* Copyright © 2006 by Jill Bolte Taylor. Used with permission of Viking, a division of Penguin Group (USA).

Page 794: *Rose (Roosevelt)*. Courtesy of the artist, Mildred Howard. Used by permission.

Page 795: *Caney Creek*. Courtesy of the artist, Mildred Howard. Used by permission.

Rhetorical Index

Author and Title Index